D0931587

Handbook of
Survey Research

QUANTITATIVE STUDIES IN SOCIAL RELATIONS

Consulting Editor: Peter H. Rossi

UNIVERSITY OF MASSACHUSETTS
AMHERST, MASSACHUSETTS

In Preparation

Derek Hum and A. Basilevsky, **THE ESTIMATION OF LABOR SUPPLY USING EXPERIMENTAL DATA:** *The U. S. Guaranteed Income Experiments*

Ronald S. Burt, **CORPORATE PROFITS AND COOPTATION:** *Networks of Market Contraints and Directorate Ties in the American Economy*

Peter Schmidt and Ann D. Witte, **THE ECONOMICS OF CRIME:** *Theory, Methods, and Applications*

Published

Peter H. Rossi, James D. Wright, and Andy B. Anderson (Eds.), **HANDBOOK OF SURVEY RESEARCH**

Joan Huber and Glenna Spitze, **SEX STRATIFICATION:** *Children, Housework, and Jobs*

Toby L. Parcel and Charles W. Mueller, **ASCRIPTION AND LABOR MARKETS:** *Race and Sex Differences in Earnings*

Paul G. Schervish, **THE STRUCTURAL DETERMINANTS OF UNEMPLOYMENT:** *Vulnerability and Power in Market Relations*

Irving Tallman, Ramona Marotz-Baden, and Pablo Pindas, **ADOLESCENT SOCIALIZATION IN CROSS-CULTURAL PERSPECTIVE:** *Planning for Social Change*

Robert F. Boruch and Joe S. Cecil (Eds.), **SOLUTIONS TO ETHICAL AND LEGAL PROBLEMS IN SOCIAL RESEARCH**

J. Ronald Milavsky, Ronald C. Kessler, Horst H. Stipp, and William S. Rubens, **TELEVISION AND AGGRESSION:** *A Panel Study*

Ronald S. Burt, **TOWARD A STRUCTURAL THEORY OF ACTION:** *Network Models of Social Structure, Perception, and Action*

Peter H. Rossi, James D. Wright, and Eleanor Weber-Burdin, **NATURAL HAZARDS AND PUBLIC CHOICE:** *The Indifferent State and Local Politics of Hazard Mitigation*

The list of titles in this series continues on the last page of this volume

Handbook of
Survey Research

Edited by

Peter H. Rossi
James D. Wright
Andy B. Anderson

Social and Demographic Research Institute
Department of Sociology
University of Massachusetts
Amherst, Massachusetts

ACADEMIC PRESS

A Subsidiary of Harcourt Brace Jovanovich, Publishers

New York   London
Paris   San Diego   San Francisco   São Paulo   Sydney   Tokyo   Toronto

ACADEMIC PRESS, INC.
111 Fifth Avenue, New York, New York 10003

United Kingdom Edition published by
ACADEMIC PRESS, INC. (LONDON) LTD.
24/28 Oval Road, London NW1 7DX

Library of Congress Cataloging in Publication Data
Main entry under title:

Handbook of survey research.

(Quantitative studies in social relations)
Includes index.
1. Social surveys--Addresses, essays, lectures.
2. Sampling (Statistics)--Addresses, essays, lectures.
3. Sociology--Research--Methodology--Addresses, essays,
lectures. I. Rossi, Peter Henry, Date.
II. Wright, James D. III. Anderson, Andy B. IV. Series.
HN29.H294 1983   301'.072   83–3869
ISBN 0–12–598226–7

PRINTED IN THE UNITED STATES OF AMERICA

83 84 85 86   9 8 7 6 5 4 3 2 1

To the Memory of

Paul F. Lazarsfeld, Samuel A. Stouffer, and Angus Campbell

*Innovative pioneers in the development of
social science applications of sample surveys*

Contents

CONTRIBUTORS   xiii
PREFACE   xv

Chapter 1

Sample Surveys: History, Current Practice, and Future Prospects
Peter H. Rossi, James D. Wright, and Andy B. Anderson

    1.1. Introduction   1
    1.2. A Short History of Sample Surveys   2
    1.3. Survey Research in the 1980s   9
    1.4. Current Developments and Issues in Survey Research   15
    1.5. The Handbook of Survey Research   18
    References   19

Chapter 2

Sampling Theory
Martin Frankel

    2.1. Introduction   21
    2.2. Stratified Sampling   37
    2.3. Cluster Sampling   47
    2.4. Advanced Topics   57
    2.5. Further Reading and Other Topics   65
    Bibliography   66

Chapter 3

Measurement
George W. Bohrnstedt

    3.1. Measurement   70
    3.2. Platonic and Classical True Scores   70

3.3. Reliability and Validity Defined   73
3.4. The Effect of Unreliability on Statistical Estimates   74
3.5. Reliability as a Function of the Number of Independent Measures   77
3.6. Types of Reliability   79
3.7. Factor Analysis and Internal Consistency   89
3.8. Validity   97
3.9. Conclusion   114
References   115

Chapter 4

Management of Survey Organizations
Kenneth Prewitt

4.1. Introduction   123
4.2. The Goals of a Survey Research Organization   125
4.3. The Management Issue   133
4.4. A Personal Postscript   143
References   144

Chapter 5

Applied Sampling
Seymour Sudman

5.1. Introduction   145
5.2. How Good Does the Sample Need to Be?   146
5.3. Inappropriate Sample Designs   149
5.4. The Use of Biased Samples for Screening   150
5.5. Defining the Population   150
5.6. Problems with Overdefining the Population   152
5.7. Operational Definitions of the Population   153
5.8. Small-Scale Sampling with Limited Resources   153
5.9. A Credibility Scale   154
5.10. Examples   158
5.11. Simple Random Sampling   163
5.12. Random Numbers   164
5.13. Systematic Sampling   166
5.14. Are Systematic Samples Simple Random Samples?   169
5.15. The Uses and Limitations of Lists   170
5.16. Blanks and Ineligibles on Lists   172
5.17. Duplications   173
5.18. Omissions from Lists   175
5.19. The Use of Telephone Directories and Random Digit Dialing   177
5.20. Screening for Special Populations   179
5.21. How Big Should the Sample Be?   180
5.22. Current Sample Sizes Used   180
5.23. The Reasons for Stratified Sampling   182
5.24. Appropriate and Inappropriate Uses of Stratification   182
5.25. The Strata Are of Primary Interest   185
5.26. Variances Differ between Strata   186

5.27. Costs Differ by Strata 190
5.28. Additional Reading 191
References 192

Chapter 6

Questionnaire Construction and Item Writing
Paul B. Sheatsley

6.1. Introduction 195
6.2. Standardized Questionnaires 196
6.3. Mode of Administration 198
6.4. Type of Sample to Be Interviewed 199
6.5. Qualities of a Good Questionnaire 200
6.6. Deciding on Content 202
6.7. Writing the Questions 205
6.8. Question Order and Format 219
6.9. Pretesting 225
6.10. Back to the Drawing Board 227
6.11. Data-Base Considerations 228
6.12. Other Types of Instruments and Materials 229
6.13. Summary 230
References 230

Chapter 7

Measurement: Theory and Techniques
Andy B. Anderson, Alexander Basilevsky, and Derek P. J. Hum

7.1. Introduction 231
7.2. Measurement Theory 236
7.3. Scaling Techniques 246
7.4. Concluding Remarks 281
Bibliography 281

Chapter 8

Response Effects
Norman M. Bradburn

8.1. Introduction 289
8.2. Model for Conceptualizing Factors That Affect Responses 291
8.3. Empirical Studies of Response Effects 293
8.4. Conclusions 318
References 318

Chapter 9

Data Collection: Planning and Management
Eve Weinberg

9.1. Objectives of the Survey Interview 329
9.2. Tasks to Accomplish the Objectives 330

9.3. Summary   357
References   357

Chapter 10

Mail and Other Self-Administered Questionnaires
Don A. Dillman

10.1. Introduction   359
10.2. The Total Design Method   360
10.3. Limitations of Mail Surveys   368
10.4. Costs   370
10.5. Other Self-Administered Questionnaires   373
10.6. Conclusion   376
References   376

Chapter 11

Computers in Survey Research
Nancy Karweit and Edmund D. Meyers, Jr.

11.1.   Introduction   379
11.2.   Instrument Design   379
11.3.   Sampling   382
11.4.   Field Monitoring   384
11.5.   Coding and Editing   386
11.6.   Data Capture   387
11.7.   Data Cleaning   392
11.8.   Scale-Index Construction   397
11.9.   Data Base Organization   398
11.10. Data Retrieval   404
11.11. Statistical Analysis   408
11.12. Documentation   409
11.13. Report Writing   411
11.14. Concluding Remarks   412
References   413

Chapter 12

Missing Data
Andy B. Anderson, Alexander Basilevsky, and Derek P. J. Hum

12.1. Introduction   415
12.2. The Analysis of Experimental Design Models Using
       Incomplete Data   420
12.3. Missing Data in Survey Samples   434
12.4. Regression Analysis with Incomplete Observations   449
12.5. Other Multivariate Models   469
12.6. Summary   479
References   481

Chapter 13

Applications of the General Linear Model to Survey Data
Richard A. Berk

13.1. Introduction	495
13.2. The Two-Variable Regression Model	496
13.3. The Multivariate Model	522
13.4. Some Common Problems with the Multivariate Model	534
13.5. Some Concluding Observations	542
References	543

Chapter 14

Analyzing Qualitative Data
D. Garth Taylor

14.1. Introduction	547
14.2. Modeling the Distribution of Cases in a Contingency Table	549
14.3. Latent Structure Analysis	564
14.4. Linear Models for Qualitative Data	574
14.5. Conclusion	601
References	606

Chapter 15

Causal Modeling and Survey Research
Ross M. Stolzenberg and Kenneth C. Land

15.1. Introduction	613
15.2. Some Basic Principles of Nonexperimental Causal Inference	615
15.3. Some Types of Recursive Causal Models and Their Representation	631
15.4. Some Uses of Nonrecursive Causal Models	658
15.5. Conclusion	671
References	672

Chapter 16

Surveys as Social Indicators: Problems in Monitoring Trends
Elizabeth Martin

16.1. Introduction	677
16.2. Two Puzzles: Assessing Trends in Criminal Victimization and Confidence in American Institutions	679
16.3. Sources of Survey Noncomparability	681
16.4. Conclusions and Recommendations	729
References	737

INDEX	745

Contributors

Numbers in parentheses indicate the pages on which the authors' contributions begin.

Andy D. Anderson (*1, 231, 415*), Social and Demographic Research Institute, University of Massachusetts, Amherst, Massachusetts 01003

Alexander Basilevsky (*231, 415*), Department of Mathematics and Statistics, University of Winnipeg, Winnipeg, Manitoba, Canada R3B 2E9

Richard A. Berk (*495*), Department of Sociology, University of California, Santa Barbara, Santa Barbara, California 93106

George W. Bohrnstedt (*69*), Program in Measurement, Indiana University, Bloomington, Indiana 47401

Norman M. Bradburn (*289*), National Opinion Research Center, University of Chicago, Chicago, Illinois 60637

Don A. Dillman (*359*), Department of Sociology, Washington State University, Pullman, Washington 99164

Martin Frankel (*21*), Department of Statistics, Baruch College, City University of New York, New York, New York 10010

Derek P. J. Hum (*231, 415*), Department of Economics, University of Manitoba, Winnipeg, Manitoba, Canada R3T 2N5

Nancy Karweit (*379*), Center for Social Organization of Schools, Johns Hopkins University, Baltimore, Maryland 21218

Kenneth C. Land (*613*), Department of Sociology, University of Illinois, Urbana, Illinois 61801

Elizabeth Martin (*677*), Bureau of Social Science Research, 1990 M Street, N.W., Washington, D.C. 20036

Edmund D. Meyers, Jr. (*379*), Boys Town Center, 14100 Crawford Street, Boys Town, Nebraska 68010

Kenneth Prewitt (*123*), Social Science Research Council, 605 Third Avenue, New York, New York 10017

Peter H. Rossi (*1*), Social and Demographic Research Institute, University of Massachusetts, Amherst, Massachusetts 01003

Paul B. Sheatsley (*195*), National Opinion Research Center, University of Chicago, Chicago, Illinois 60637

Ross M. Stolzenberg (*613*), Rand Corporation, Santa Monica, California 90406

Seymour Sudman (*145*), Survey Research Laboratory, University of Illinois, Urbana, Illinois 61801

D. Garth Taylor (*547*), Department of Political Science, University of Chicago, Chicago, Illinois 60637

Eve Weinberg (*329*), Policy Research Corporation, 307 N. Michigan Avenue, Chicago, Illinois 60601

James D. Wright (*1*), Department of Sociology, University of Massachusetts, Amherst, Massachusetts 01003

Preface

Sample surveys have become the major mode of empirical research in a wide variety of social science disciplines and their associated applied fields. Sample surveys provide much of the data that monitor trends in our society, test our theoretical understanding of social and social psychological processes, provide intelligence to market researchers, guide the campaign strategies of hopeful candidates for public office, and in general give us much of our current knowledge about our society.

Knowledge about how properly to conduct sample surveys has developed out of the efforts of a wide variety of disciplines. Contributions to the development of sample surveys have come from statistics, psychology, sociology, demography, political science, marketing, education, and so on through the entire list of the basic social sciences and associated applied fields. Correspondingly, the work to be consulted by someone interested in developing sample survey skills or by a practicing survey researcher is scattered throughout the social science literature in more than a score of professional treatises and monographs.

The decision to undertake the editing of this *Handbook* arose out of the frustration of trying to organize a graduate course in survey design and analysis and finding that there were no suitable comprehensive treatments of the major topics in that area. To be sure, there were several good introductory level texts suitable for upper division undergraduate courses and there were also several excellent extended treatments of each of the major topics. But, there was no single source that covered the major issues in survey design and analysis at a relatively advanced level and that could serve as a graduate-level text.

The editors are also practicing researchers, using sample survey approaches in their scholarly work and in applied social researches. All of the separate skills involved in the design and analysis of sample surveys have grown into specialties that are difficult for generalist survey researchers to master in detail. Over the past decade we each have often experienced the dread fear that our practices in some particular respect were falling behind the current state of the art in that area. We have often felt the need for some central reference work that could guide one to the appropriate specialized literature. This was a second source of motivation for the editing of this handbook.

It is our highest hope that the *Handbook of Survey Research* will prove valuable both to advanced students and to practicing survey researchers who seek a detailed guide to the major issues in the design and analysis of sample surveys and to current state of the art practices in sample surveys. To that end, we have invited contributions from persons who we knew were knowledgeable and skilled in the topics in question. All have made important contributions to the development of sample survey methods and all are persons who use sample surveys in their own research. Current state of the art survey research practices are explained and described in this book by persons whose own work best exemplifies those practices.

The *Handbook* has been long in the making: The practitioners of the best are busy persons for whom the preparation of these chapters was often a diversion from heavy commitments to their ongoing research. We are grateful to the authors for managing to find the time to write their chapters and patiently to see them through several revisions.

We have been aided throughout by many persons whose help must be acknowledged. The outline was commented upon by the authors, out of which came many useful suggestions about revisions in organization. Various versions of chapters and commentaries on them were typed and retyped by the cheerful and highly skilled team of Jeanne Reinle and Cynthia Coffman, whose work is gratefully acknowledged.

Chapter 1

Sample Surveys: History, Current Practice, and Future Prospects

Peter H. Rossi, James D. Wright, and
Andy B. Anderson

1.1. INTRODUCTION

This handbook is an introduction to current theory and practice of sample survey research. It addresses both the student who desires to master these topics and the practicing survey researcher who needs a source that codifies, rationalizes, and presents existing theory and practice. Although the topical coverage is not encyclopedic, we believe that most of the important issues are covered.

Sample surveys are currently one of the more important basic research methods of the social sciences and an important tool for applied purposes in both the public and private sectors. Like the social sciences with which it is associated, the sample survey is a relatively new device for learning about society and social processes, coming into prominence as a research technique only in the last 50 years.

Sample surveys consist of relatively systematic, standardized approaches to the collection of information on individuals, households, or larger organized entities through the questioning of systematically identified samples of individuals. Three basic technical developments come together to constitute the core of the sample survey method:

1. *Sampling noninstitutionalized human populations:* Techniques have been developed that enable the drawing of unbiased samples of the noninstitutionalized population.
2. *The art of asking questions:* Enough experience has accrued to make it possible to write questionnaires and interview schedules that will elicit valid and reliable answers on a wide variety of topics.

HANDBOOK OF SURVEY RESEARCH

3. *Multivariate data analysis:* Technical developments in data processing along with developments in statistics make it possible to calculate the net relationships between variables embedded in complex relationships with other variables.

Although the development of the sample survey method necessarily depended on progress in each of these areas, these developments were given considerable impetus by the growing complexity of our society in the last half century. It has become increasingly apparent that the management of large-scale economic enterprises and large government agencies requires data that can only be obtained directly from the persons involved in the topic in question. Data on the preferences held by the American population for one consumer product or another, for one or another public policy or political candidate, aspirations for occupational success or family solidarity, and the like, simply cannot be obtained without asking individuals directly. In addition, there are many kinds of data that turn out to be easier to obtain through sample surveys than by alternative methods, for example, household expenditures on medical care.

Accordingly, the three technical underpinnings listed here are the central topics of the chapters in the handbook. We also show how survey data are used for basic and applied purposes.

1.2. A SHORT HISTORY OF SAMPLE SURVEYS

Surveys are conducted for the purpose of collecting data from individuals about themselves, about their households, or about other larger social units. In this broad sense, surveys of some sort have been conducted ever since people began needing information on the distribution and size of human communities and their social characteristics. We can only speculate that primitive surveys consisted of global characterizations and very rough approximations. It is clear that the populations of ancient settlements and national states, such as Rome or classical Athens, were known by their rulers and chroniclers only in fairly vague terms (Benevelo, 1980). Occasional censuses (e.g., the Domesday Book) that have survived provide somewhat better estimates, at least on simple head counts; however, until the rise of the modern bureaucratic state and popular elections, the need for precision and for periodic updating was slight.

Censuses and surveys were born out of the needs of the modern state bureaucracies, as the term *statistics* implies. Our census in the United States, mandated in the Constitution, derives from the need to apportion territory into constituencies of electorates roughly equal in size. The addition to the census of topics other than simple head counts was a matter of a developing consciousness that the running of the state required more and more information about the status of the population and about organized entities such as farms, factories, and business enterprises.

Nineteenth-century surveys tended to resemble censuses in being attempts to cover the total populations of communities. For example, Booth's late-nineteenth-century survey of the poor of London was a block-by-block, house-hold-by-household survey, more or less systematic in its coverage of topics (Fried & Elman, 1968). Dubois's 1892 survey (1967) of the Philadelphia Negro community was a household-by-household canvass using schedules that resembled closely the forms used by the 1890 census covering basic demographic and employment data.

The social surveys that were at the heart of the early twentieth-century "survey movement" were also total censuses of the cities studied, merging census data with special surveys of topics—such as housing conditions—that were not covered in the decennial censuses. The work of the early human ecologists of the Chicago School was also based on the same model: Thrasher (1927) attempted to map the location of all the juvenile gangs in Chicago; Reckless (1933) surveyed all the houses of ill fame for his spotmaps showing the locations of bordellos in Chicago (and thereby spawning a plethora of satirical aphorisms on why sociologists need foundation grants to find things any other citizen would know "naturally").

Similarly, preelection surveys conducted by newspapers to forecast election results were based on the notion that the bigger the sample, the better the forecast. The Literary Digest straw polls of telephone subscribers were based on returns of millions of ballots mailed to all telephone subscribers in the United States. Newspapers sent reporters and hired canvassers, with paper ballots and ballot boxes, to busy intersections to intercept voters to conduct straw votes. Those who conducted the straw votes based their claim for forecasting accuracy on the numbers of persons polled. Note that the rationale for forecasting accuracy was not a sampling one, it was based on the notion that the larger the N, the greater the accuracy, a notion that is only true if N is quite close to the universe size.

The consumer marketing research that started after World War I initially operated on a different model that was not imitative of censuses. Rather, the model was that of the psychophysical laboratory in which a small number of subjects are brought to a location for standardized testing. In the laboratory model, the processes being investigated were pan-human and hence any assemblage of subjects was as valid as any other assemblage. Early product testing asked assemblages of consumers to express their comparative preferences for an array of packages or asked consumers to try out a new brand. Consumers were located through stores or social clubs, or they were simply asked to volunteer through ads in newspapers.

Modern surveys evolved out of these roots. From the psychologists dabbling in market research came the techniques of questioning persons on preferences through carefully administered standardized inquiries. From the journalists came the notion that people could be questioned about preferences among candidates, and from this it was an easy step to the idea of studying preferences among policies. From the social surveys came the idea that social conditions could be measured and then counted. All that remained was to add the ideas of probability sampling.

Although some of the basic ideas of sampling had been around for a long time, the sampling of noninstitutionalized human populations required the development of special procedures that went beyond thoroughly mixing black and white balls in an urn or picking slips of paper out of a thoroughly shaken up wire basket. Population registries did not exist, nor were any serial numbers widely assigned to elements of the American population. Random or systematic sampling of civilian, noninstitutionalized populations simply could not be accomplished.

The early political polls that began to appear in the 1930s managed to solve the sampling problem by approaching it in a quite different fashion. The polltakers were more concerned that the samples interviewed "mirrored" the American voting population in important respects. Quotas were set for interviewers that would produce an age and sex distribution among respondents that corresponded to that of the U.S. voting population. Quotas were fulfilled initially by interviewers approaching prospective respondents in any locale they chose. In some respects, this procedure was a modification of the earlier newspaper straw votes. The age and sex quotas enabled street interviewers to identify by sight whether any individual encountered fulfilled the quotas given. (Age quotas were given with wide ranges: e.g., 21–35, 36–55, 55 or over.) Today we can only speculate about how much of the early survey interviewing took place on busy street corners, and bus and trolley stops, as opposed to being the result of house-to-house canvassing. Implicit quotas were also set by regions of the country as interviewer assignments were set by the national pollsters proportional to each voting population. Incidentally, this restriction to polling voters explains why the early polls had few, if any, blacks among respondents; few blacks were enfranchised in the South and majority of that group resided there at the time.

Interviewing techniques and item writing were correspondingly primitive. Interviews were short, lasting 5–10 minutes; no topic was explored in any depth, and little background information (e.g., socioeconomic status or household size or composition) was obtained about respondents. Reading items from the early polls, one is struck by the cliches used in the questions. Apparently, the stock phrases used by the newspapers and magazines to characterize public issues were viewed as "colloquial speech" and were incorporated into items to enhance their intelligibility.

Analytical techniques were also primitive. Marginal distributions were calculated and occasionally cross tabulations by region, sex, and age were published. To be sure, even if an analyst wanted to do more complicated analyses, the paucity of data in any one survey precluded this in any event.

Although viewed from the perspective of contemporary practice in sample surveys, the early polls were very primitive indeed, they were a considerable forward step. "Representative" sampling of the quota variety is certainly inadequate, but it is undoubtedly better than reliance on college freshmen or social clubs, or on mailed questionnaires that achieved response rates around 15%. Responses to one or two primitively worded items are a better measure of public sentiment on a policy issue than counting pro and con letters received by people in Congress. Marginal distributions were better estimates of the contours of public opinion than the impressions of journalists. Certainly, these primitive sample surveys were more efficient than conducting total censuses.

The polls of such early pollsters as the Gallup Organization and the Crossley Polls, published as syndicated columns in the newspapers in the early 1930s, were not the only sample surveys undertaken. These and other sample survey organizations were busy most of the time on consumer research, establishing the readership of magazines, the listenership of radio networks and programs, and the market shares of consumer goods. Strangely, academic research in the social sciences did not adopt this method, at least in its initial development. For example, early texts in social research methods used in sociology (Lundberg, 1929; Young, 1949) had sections devoted to surveys but virtually no space was given to sample surveys and no mention was made of polls. However, some sample surveys were undertaken: For example, Elin Anderson (1937) undertook a sample survey of interethnic relations in Burlington, Vermont, in 1933, drawing his sample from schedules filled out in a total household census of that city.[1] More typical were the nonuse of sample surveys by the two prominent community studies of the period (Lynd & Lynd, 1937; Warner and associates, 1942) whose data collection methods are only fuzzily described in the resulting volumes. More typically, Thurstone (1929), in developing his attitude scaling methods, used college students as subjects. Murphy, Murphy, and Newcomb's (1937) compendium of published works in "experimental" (i.e., empirical) social psychology cited almost exclusively studies that used college students or other captive groups as subjects.

The polls (and sample surveys by derivation) apparently received a considerable boost on the road to respectability by their superior performance in predicting the outcome of the 1936 Roosevelt–Landon presidential election, especially in comparison to the failure of *Literary Digest* mail straw ballot. This David and Goliath contest pitted the seemingly enormous *Literary Digest* mail poll of millions of telephone subscribers against the seemingly weak and puny 1500 interviews conducted each by Gallup and Crossley. The superiority of sex- and age-quota interviewing in comparison to the low return (15%) from a mailed questionnaire sent to better-off American households made a convincing case that small but carefully drawn samples could do better than huge numbers picked from a partial sample frame with little or no effort to achieve reasonable response rates.

Toward the end of the 1930s, survey research began to infiltrate the universities. At Princeton, Hadley Cantril established the Office of Public Opinion

---

[1] Exact sampling methods used by Anderson are not described in the monograph.

Research and at Newark University, Paul F. Lazarsfeld established the Office of Radio Research that was later to move to Columbia and metamorphose into the Bureau of Applied Social Research.

Demographers at the Bureau of the Census, in collaboration with applied statisticians, began to develop sampling methods for meeting demands for timely measures of unemployment levels. A later 1930s attempt to measure unemployment used short questionnaires delivered by letter carriers, requesting a response by return mail if there were any unemployed persons in the household. Needless to say, this survey's findings quickly went into the wastebaskets of all antagonists, who denounced its obvious faults. There was also concern for measuring the health status of the American population, with the first National Health Survey being conducted using clustered sampling, with clusters apparently chosen judgmentally.

One outcome of the Census Bureau's sampling efforts was to produce the series of techniques that are the foundation of today's most highly regarded population sampling method, area probability sampling. Sampling was also introduced into the Census itself with a subsample of the households reached in the 1940 Census receiving detailed questions on housing, employment, and occupations.

Public opinion polling was first systematically used for policy purposes after World War II began in Europe and as the President sought to obtain more timely assessments of public sentiment toward such pro-Allied measures as the Lend–Lease Act. Hadley Cantril, of the Office of Public Opinion Research at Princeton University, was called upon to advise the President and the Secretary of State.

Election polling moved into the academy as well with Lazarsfeld's (1944) small-scale Sandusky, Ohio panel study of the 1940 election. This was a landmark study in several respects. First, it represents the entry of academic social science into the empirical study of voting behavior through sample surveys. Second, in the Sandusky study interviews were longer and they treated topics in greater depth than was typical in political polls. Finally, and most important, analysis methods were multivariate, although they were still cast in the multiway cross-tabulation mode. It should be noted that Lazarsfeld and his colleagues made no use of statistical inference models; the sampling is described as "visiting every fourth house" and no tests of significance or confidence intervals appear in the entire monograph. This landmark study did not come out of political science or out of sociology. Lazarsfeld was extending his interest in studying the social psychology of decision making from consumer buying decisions to voter decision making.

The use of surveys by the U.S. government during World War II provided additional credibility to the sample survey. Within the Department of Agriculture, the Division of Program Surveys provided information on a variety of topics ranging from consumer acceptance of food rationing to estimates of farm productivity. The Office of Price Administration contracted with the newly founded National Opinion Research Center (NORC), then at the University of

Denver, to gauge the public acceptability of price controls on consumer goods. The State Department also contracted with NORC to assess how new turns in foreign policy were being met by the public. But the most extensive use of sample surveys was through the Department of the Army's Information and Education Branch, headed by Samuel A. Stouffer and staffed by young men and women many of whom were later to become members of the new survey oriented faculty in social science departments throughout the country.[2] Of course, taking sample surveys of soldiers, using mainly self-administered questionnaires, presented no special hurdles as a sampling problem. What was of interest in the four-volume monograph series that was published (Stouffer and associates, 1947 through 1950) is that the research was conducted for policy reasons and was given attention by army commands. In addition, the analysis methods used served as a model for survey researchers in the postwar period.

With the end of the war, the social scientists who ran sample surveys for the government filtered back into academia. The Department of Agriculture's Division of Program Surveys was abolished by congressional legislation specifically prohibiting that department from conducting surveys of any sort, seeming retribution on the part of conservative southern legislators for a number of community surveys that showed the oppressed condition of Southern blacks. The staff of the division (including Rensis Likert, Angus Campbell, and Leslie Kish) moved en masse to the University of Michigan to found the Survey Research Center (SRC). Stouffer moved to Harvard's newly founded Department of Social Relations. Seeking a stronger university connection, the National Opinion Research Center affiliated with the University of Chicago and moved to Chicago. Lazarsfeld's Office of Radio Research at Columbia changed its name to the Bureau of Applied Social Research and moved closer to the academic departments.

The 1948 presidential elections brought additional attention to the political polls when the major public polls failed to predict the reelection of Harry Truman. By this time the ideas of polling had been sufficiently entrenched so that the major impact of this event was to strengthen sample survey procedures. The area probability methods that had been developed at the Bureau of the Census and used successfully in the development of Monthly Labor Force Survey became the sampling method of choice. Major commercial polls and survey organizations modified their methods to restrict interviewer discretion in choosing respondents, often designating specific tracts or blocks within which interviewing was to take place. Area probability sampling with random selection of respondents within households became the standard procedure specified in federal contracts.

If there was ever any skepticism concerning the candor with which Americans would answer survey inquiries, it was badly shaken by the publication of the so-called Kinsey Report (Kinsey and associates, 1948). Kinsey's inter-

[2] Members included sociologists Louis Guttman, Robin Williams, Edward A. Suchman, Shirley Star, John Clausen, as well as psychologists Carl Hovland, Arthur Lumsdaine, and William Bennet.

views with haphazard samples of males about their sexual experiences brought to light completely unexpected levels of "deviant" sexual practices, and that at least proved that it was possible to interview about seemingly very private affairs and to ask "threatening" questions. It is now accepted that there are probably no topics about which it is impossible to interview, assuming a sensitive and intelligent questionnaire.

By the end of the 1950s the sample survey was a firmly established research tool in academic social science and was used heavily by the public and private sectors as a device to gather information. Two major national survey organizations, SRC and NORC, were closely affiliated with major social science departments in major universities. A score of locally oriented survey centers had been founded, affiliated with many universities, including Wisconsin, Berkeley, Indiana, and others. The small private firms of the 1940s oriented primarily to market research had grown into large firms, including Audits and Surveys, Market Facts, the Nielson Company, Opinion Research Corporation, and others. Political polling also took hold with many smaller firms operating to test the trends in voter preferences for political candidates (and to provide campaign consultation). Within the federal government, sample surveys conducted by the Bureau of the Census provided monthly measures of the labor force and annual assessments of demographic and socioeconomic trends on the household level.

In the 1960s there were three extremely important developments. First, electronic computers evolved to the point such that survey organizations began to substitute tapes for card oriented equipment, allowing faster processing of survey data and more complicated analyses. By the end of the 1960s, statistical packages were available, some of them (such as OSIRIS and SPSS) being developed by the survey centers themselves.

Second, the federal government considerably increased its use of sample surveys and its general support for social science research. Federal funds for the training of social scientists and for the support of "basic" social science research increased by many magnitudes. With the start of new social programs under the War Against Poverty, sample surveys were increasingly called on to provide information on the distribution and extent of social problems as well as to evaluate the effectiveness of programs put into place. New firms arose in the private sector to meet the demand for social science research of an evaluative sort, including Abt Associates, Mathematica, and Westat. Older organizations, including the Rand Corporation, Stanford Research Institute (SRI), Systems Development Corporation, added social science divisions. Although national survey research centers affiliated with universities did not multiply, new sample survey firms, including some that arose out of splits within older firms, appeared in the commercial sector.

The third major development was the melding of sample surveys with other methods. The randomized field experiments undertaken in connection with the poverty program joined experimental design with sample surveys. Economists, who had not been prominent among sample survey users, began to apply econometric modeling to survey data and to participate in the design and fielding of sample surveys.

The 1970s continued the trends of the 1960s, with a trailing off of support toward the end of the decade. Perhaps the major developments during this decade were growing concerns with the drastic rise in survey costs and a decline in response rates. Since survey interviewing is a labor intensive activity, the costs of conducting face-to-face interviews rose with increasing wage rates. In addition, the pool of married women seeking part-time employment, a large source of interviewers, declined as more and more of this group sought full-time (and better paying) employment in other jobs. For a variety of reasons including rising urban crime rates and fewer and fewer persons being at home during daylight hours, response rates appeared to decline along with a rise in the number of attempts needed to complete interviews. Soaring costs and declining response rates were probably the impetus to reexamine methods that had been earlier discarded as ineffective. The use of mail surveys was reexamined along with telephone interviewing. Procedures were developed that raised response rates in mailed surveys to acceptable levels, at least under some circumstances (see Chapter 10, pp. 359–377). Random digit dialing methods make it possible to do simple random sampling of telephone households at apparently no significant loss of quality in data collected through telephone interviews (Groves & Kahn, 1979). The use of telephone interviewing also facilitated the use of computer assisted interviewing (CATI) in which interview questions are flashed in appropriate order on a cathode ray screen with the interviewer keying in the response directly. Not only does CATI produce a data tape, but most systems will also screen responses for inconsistencies with previous responses, thereby lowering the time and costs devoted to "cleaning" interviews.

Taking fuller advantage of the computing capacities of modern electronic computers, more sophisticated analysis methods have been applied to survey data. Multivariate log linear models that more closely accommodate to the categorical character of survey responses were made possible because the computer can run quickly and inexpensively through the iterative calculations involved.

1.3. SURVEY RESEARCH IN THE 1980s

Accurate measures of the current total size of survey research activities are simply nonexistent. The fragmentary data that do exist suggest an industry composed of five subsectors that only partially overlap in activity, and who together each year contact 32 million households, conducting 100 million interviews (National Research Council, 1981).[3] Assuming that each interview is

---

[3] Estimates are based on a sample survey in which respondents were asked whether anyone in their households had been contacted for interviews, yielding the finding that 46% had been contacted over a period of 4 years with an average number of 3.3 contacts.

priced on the average at $25, the total income of the industry is about $2.5 billion. Assuming a higher per interview price, closer to $50, doubles the estimated gross income of the industry to about $5 billion. Since survey interviewing varies widely in cost depending on sampling design, length of interview, method (face-to-face or by telephone or mail), the total gross of the survey research industry is probably between these two estimates.

How many persons are employed in survey research activities is even less well known. A compilation of the 16 largest private and academic units engaged in "subjective" surveys (National Research Council, 1981) with a total gross of $400 million in 1979, counted 5900 employees, over half of whom were field workers (i.e., interviewers and supervisors). Assuming that same income-to-employee ratio applies to the rest of the industry, we estimate somewhere between 40,000 and 60,000 employees in the survey research industry, about half of whom are field workers. Of course, the total number of persons who receive some employment from the industry during any one year is likely to be much larger since fieldwork forces are notoriously transient, with interviewers frequently moving in and out of what is largely part-time employment.

Professional employees engaged in the design and analysis of surveys and who have some professional training and/or extensive experience at a professional level are probably some small fraction of the total employment. Assuming a ratio of 1 in 10, we estimate between 4000 and 6000 professional survey researchers. How many of these have received professional social science training is, of course, unknown. Many of the first generation to obtain employment as professionals in survey research in the post World War II period were not specially trained in university departments for that activity, largely because such training was not given in most graduate social science departments. Even in the current period, entry into survey research on a professional level is often enough not predicated on specific training. This can occur because many aspects of survey research are still largely art and craftlore, activities in which experience and practice may be as important as formal training. The design of survey instruments and the management of survey operations depend more on having had relevant experience than on formal training. Of course, no one can become a skilled sampling expert without formal training nor are analysts likely to pick up the necessary skills on the job for complex multivariate analyses, but for many positions and for conducting simple surveys, formal training is not a strict prerequisite.

Main Sectors of the Survey Industry

The organizations that conduct sample surveys of individuals, households, and other social units can be conveniently divided into four sectors with a fifth residual category of rather mixed character. Each of the sectors more or less specializes in certain types of surveys, although in many instances they compete with each other on specific survey tasks.

THE FEDERAL GOVERNMENT SECTOR

Although many of the surveys conducted for policy purposes are contracted out to other sectors, as will be described, the federal government maintains a very large survey establishment, mainly for the purpose of conducting periodic surveys that form important series. The Bureau of the Census conducts the Monthly Labor Force Survey, using a revolving panel of 60,000 households who are contacted once a month for reports on the labor force participation of household members. This quasi-panel survey is also used for the annual Current Population Survey conducted as of April 1 each year in which the demographic characteristics of the households are obtained in detail. Periodically, households in the sample are asked special questions designed to provide one time information on specific topics: for example, participation in the 1976 presidential election or on occupational mobility across generations (Blau & Duncan, 1967).

The Bureau of the Census also conducts for the Department of Justice, the National Crime Survey, a periodic household survey of crime victimizations. For the Department of Housing and Urban Development, the Census conducts the Annual Housing Survey, using a dwelling unit sample, that keeps track of housing conditions in the United States.

Special ad hoc, one-time surveys are also undertaken by the Bureau of the Census for other government departments. For the Department of Health, Education and Welfare, the Census conducted a Survey of Income and Education, in which more than 100,000 households were questioned in detail about educational attainment and household income. A preretirement survey of persons 55–60 was conducted for the Social Security Administration.

In addition, some of the best methodological research on the technical aspects of sampling and survey administration is conducted by the Bureau of the Census.

Other government agencies also directly undertake sample surveys. The National Center for Health Statistics conducts the National Health Survey. The Federal Bureau of Investigation collects crimes reported to the police through annual surveys of police departments.[4]

Sample surveys directly undertaken by the federal government tend to be periodic studies designed to monitor changes in the socioeconomic aspects of households, or very large scale surveys with sample sizes in the 100,000 range. The Bureau of the Census has traditionally shied away from sample surveys involving "subjective" issues such as opinions on political issues or relatively private matters such as contraception. These and other subjective topics along with smaller surveys are left to the academic and private, profit making sectors to perform under grants and contracts.[5]

---

[4] The resulting Uniform Crime Reports published annually are not based on samples, strictly speaking, but constitute ideally total universe censuses.

[5] It should also be noted that in Census Bureau's surveys a long time tends to elapse from initiation to delivery of resulting computer tapes, a factor causing at least one agency to shift from the Census to the academic sector for one of its surveys.

THE ACADEMIC SECTOR

There are only three university-connected national sample survey organizations, the National Opinion Research Center, affiliated with the University of Chicago, the Institute for Social Research (Survey Research Center) at the University of Michigan, and the Institute for Survey Research at Temple University. All three were established in the 1940s.[6] In addition, the Research Triangle Institute, a nonprofit research organization loosely affiliated with the three major universities in the Raleigh–Durham area might be viewed as at least partially academic. In 1979–1980, the three academically affiliated survey organizations had budgets totaling $26 million,[7] between .5% and 1% of the total industry gross.

In addition, there are many universities that maintain survey organizations that have only local, state, or regional sampling or data-collection capabilities, including Wisconsin, Illinois, Universities of California at Berkeley and Los Angeles, Massachusetts, Washington State, and Indiana universities. These range widely in budget and activity.

These academically affiliated organizations do not account for all of the survey activity taking place within academia, nor do they even come close. Many academics contract with the larger centers or with private sector survey organizations for their survey work. Others conduct their own small-scale surveys, putting together an ad hoc organization for the occasion. Finally, the holdings of the several survey data archives (mainly, the Inter-University Consortium for Political and Social Research at Michigan, The Roper Center at the University of Connecticut and Yale, and the Louis Harris Data Center at North Carolina) are used extensively by academic social scientists for secondary analyses.

The extensiveness of the use of surveys in the social science disciplines is best indexed by the proportion of articles in the major social science journals reporting survey data: public opinion, 87%; sociology, 53%; political science, 33%; economics, 28%; and social psychology, 12% (National Research Council, 1981). Only demographic Census data in sociology, economic data (generated largely from universe surveys), and small scale experiments and classroom surveys in social psychology compete with surveys as the source for basic data in scholarly social science work.

THE PRIVATE SECTOR

The largest private sector firms engaged in surveys dwarf the academic organizations. A. C. Nielson, whose major activities consist of estimating television program audiences, grossed $321 million in 1979–1980. Other very large private sector organizations include IMS International ($88.8 million), special-

[6] The Institute for Survey Research at Temple was instituted in 1957. The "founders" were the major research personnel of National Analysts, Inc., a then private Philadelphia research firm, who left en masse for Temple University when National Analysts was sold to Booz, Allen, and Hamilton.

[7] Parceled out (1979–1980) as follows: NORC, $16.4 million; ISR (Michigan), $14.1 million; and ISR (Temple), $5.0 million.

izing in the measurement of sales and inventories of pharmaceuticals; SAMI ($54.4 million), specializing in estimating the movement in and out of inventory of consumer goods; Arbitron ($47.1 million), providing competition to Nielson in the measurement of television program coverages; and Burke International Corporation ($42.6 million), specializing in advertising surveys. Each of these very large firms has at its core some repetitive estimation task for which there are many clients. Custom tailored surveys on special topics are not their usual business. Indeed, some would not even consider bidding for contracts that would require intensive interviewing, say, on political issues or the private worries of individuals.

In contrast, in 1979–1980 the private firms that compete with the academic survey centers tend to all be about the same gross sales size: Market Facts, $19.3 million; Westat, Inc., $14.4 million; Audits and Surveys, $14 million; Chilton Research Service, $12 million; and National Analysts, $8 million.[8] The private firms whose polls receive attention in the mass media tend to be smaller: Yankelovich, Skelly and White ($11.8 million); Louis Harris and Associates ($9.3 million); Opinion Research Corporation ($8.2 million); and the Gallup Organization (no gross sales available). In addition there are scores of smaller firms and subsidiaries of larger enterprises who engage in sample survey work.

These firms do not represent the full extent of the private sector participation in survey work. Several organizations contract out their survey work to either academic survey centers or private firms. Abt Associates, subsisting largely on government contracts for applied social research, until recently contracted out survey work to NORC, Westat, and the Research Triangle Institute. The Rand Corporation and SRI International ordinarily contract out their survey business. Often consortia composed of pairs and triplets of research firms jointly enter bids for survey work with the firms agreeing on a division of labor that leaves the survey fieldwork in the hands of one of the partners. At least one research firm, Mathematica, specializes in setting up special survey operations for its own research contracts and will take on subcontracts for others.[9]

THE MASS MEDIA SECTOR

Television networks and newspapers, sometimes jointly, have also entered the sample survey field, mainly to provide findings for their broadcasting or publishing needs. The CBS–*New York Times* poll began operating in 1976, questioning sample respondents on their reactions to public issues and on their candidate preferences in national elections. The NBC Network, in collaboration with AP news services, set up a similar organization at about the same

---

[8] Westat, Inc., was founded and owned by former Bureau of the Census employees and engaged mainly in contract work for the federal government.

[9] Mathematica specializes in the longitudinal survey work that is involved in large scale field experiments, for example, the Seattle and Denver Income Maintenance Experiments, the Supported Work Experiments.

time. More recently, the ABC Network and the *Washington Post* have jointly entered the opinion polling scene. Many major newspapers (e.g., *The Chicago Tribune, The Boston Globe*) have in-house survey capabilities. Clearly, poll findings make news sufficiently attractive to viewers and readers for the media to enter the industry, apparently subsidizing the costs.

Of course, the Gallup Organization and Lou Harris and Associates also release findings to the press and the other media. All told, there are an estimated 174 national, regional, or state polls sponsored or entirely run by national and local media (Bailar & Lanphier, 1978).

The end results of this survey activity are literally hundreds of news items reporting the results of surveys. Polling is as much a feature of the media as the comics and horoscope!

AD HOC AND IN-HOUSE SURVEYS

The final sector of the sample survey industry is a mixed collection of ad hoc survey organizations and in-house survey operations. Many surveys are conducted by putting together an organization specially for that purpose. Academics may conduct a survey in a nearby city or county; a planning office may conduct a housing preference survey among residents of a particular community, and so on. Some of the ad hoc surveys so conducted may be of the highest quality and some may be fairly amateurish.

In-house surveys are conducted by an organization that is ordinarily not engaged in surveys. For example, AT&T conducts scores of sample surveys of its employees and customers; or a university may conduct a sample survey of its alumni, students, or of its faculty or other employees. As in the case of ad hoc surveys, quality levels of in-house surveys vary widely.

The size of the fifth sector of the sample survey industry is also largely unknown. Presser (in National Research Council, 1981) states that about 30% of the surveys reported in sociological journals were conducted by the author (and presumably not by an ongoing survey organization). How many ad hoc surveys and in-house surveys are conducted by the many possible organizations that could do so is of course completely open to speculation.

An Overview of the Survey Industry

In the 1980s, the sample survey industry is very much alive and active, still growing and finding for itself more and more applications. Whether the gross income of the industry is $2 or 5 billion is not clear, but it is fairly obvious that from a very small beginning in the period immediately after World War II, the total enterprise has grown enormously. The entry of the federal government into the funding of surveys has been especially critical, accounting possibly for as much as a third of the funds expended.

The topics covered by sample surveys now run the gamut from the very private concerns of citizens to their experiences with consumer products. There appears to be no limit to what sorts of questions may be asked in surveys just as there appears to be considerable willingness on the part of individuals to spend 2 or 3 hours answering the questions of surveyors.

1.4. CURRENT DEVELOPMENTS AND ISSUES IN SURVEY RESEARCH

The procedures and methods of sample surveys are by no means fixed. New procedures are continually being developed and old ones improved. Several procedures that were abandoned in the past have been revived in new and improved forms, as, for example, telephone interviewing and mail surveys. We can expect that this current decade will see additional developments and changes in the theory and practice of sample surveys. Some of these changes will arise out of structural and economic exigencies; the funding available for social science research generally, especially from the federal government, shows signs of declining, and at the same time the costs of conducting surveys have risen. Some changes will arise out of autochthonous processes, representing the "natural" evolutionary changes of technology.

Rising Survey Costs and Lowered Federal Support

As noted earlier, the costs of conducting sample surveys along the traditional lines of face-to-face interviews conducted in respondents' homes have risen sharply. There is no reason to believe that such trends will change in the latter 1980s. Respondents will remain difficult to locate at home and labor costs seem likely to continue rising. These trends will continue to provide strong incentives to improve cost savings innovations started in the 1970s and to develop new approaches. Telephone and mail survey techniques will continue to be refined to the point where acceptable return rates and high quality data are obtained. Although there is considerable speculation about the potentialities of interactive cable television (in which viewers can register reactions that can be recorded in a central studio), the coverage of cable systems is still low and biased against large urban places. Serious response biases are likely to appear. We can expect that proposals will be advanced that are addressed to these two issues and which may make interactive cable systems useful for at least some purposes.

Computer-assisted telephone interviewing coupled with random digit dialing methods show considerable promise for considerable reductions in the costs of collecting survey data, at least for surveys in which visual displays of questionnaire items are not needed. Bringing computer assisted interviewing into homes by using small portable terminals appears to be a development that might be useful for some types of detailed interviewing in which visual displays for respondents can be used. Whether the appropriate hardware can be developed and whether initial capital investment costs can also be lowered appears problematic.

Other avenues to cost reduction may lie in the further development of mail surveys. Especially important is the development of appropriate respondent-motivating tactics that can raise response rates to reasonable levels.

The reduction of federal support for human services and for large scale transfer payment programs, coupled with a profoundly held conservative distrust of social science, appear to mean a reduction in federal support for all sorts of social science research efforts. The Reagan administration has tried to cut federal research funds severely in at least two of the federal agencies—the National Science Foundation and the National Institute of Mental Health—that have provided heavy support for sample survey work. Cutbacks in such programs as food stamps, school lunches, and grants to local educational authorities have also affected cutbacks in the survey work that was used to monitor and evaluate those programs. Whether or not the current trends presage continued decline in support is not clear. However, it seems unlikely that growth trends will resume again for some years. These current trends may mean that many of the small sample survey enterprises in some of the sectors will disappear, leading to a still greater concentration of survey work in the hands of the larger enterprises. Smaller research centers in academia may disappear along with the smaller private firms.

For social scientists this reduction in support will mean greater reliance on the existing data archives and more intensive exploitation of archive holdings. Of course, decreased support for the social sciences may also mean that the data archives will not be as well supported as they have been in the past, with corresponding implications for growth in archive holdings and services to users.

Reductions in funding also fuel motivation for cost reduction innovations. For academics, this may mean greater reliance on self-administered surveys with captive college student populations, a retrograde step for many substantive areas. For larger survey organizations this may mean strong incentives to shift to telephone interviewing and mail surveys.

Issues in Measurement

Despite the strong influence of the psychometric tradition in the early years of sample survey development, the short survey questionnaires and the reliance on single-item measures of attitudes have meant a neglect of measurement error issues in sample survey work. As analytical methods became more complex in the 1970s and as econometricians turned their attention to survey data that were disaggregated, more attention was shown to measurement issues. Here the problem is the impact of unreliability and invalidity on survey results. For example, it became increasingly clear (and alarming) that unreliability in single item measures was a major factor in producing results that were simply uninterpretable when using structural equation models. In the evaluation of social programs it became apparent that effects of unreliability can often obscure real effects when they are present, thereby enhancing the chances of Type II error.

Advances in dealing with such measurement errors appear likely to take two directions. In the first place, there will be some attention to the appropriate phrasing of survey items in order to reduce unreliability. Recent technical work (Schuman & Presser, 1977; Sudman & Bradburn, 1974) has considerably advanced our understanding of how the formal characteristics of questionnaire items affect responses (see Chapter 8). Although we are far from a theory of response effects, these pioneer studies have advanced our understanding considerably. The second path to improved measurement lies in the use of mathematical models to uncover the underlying unobserved processes that generate responses (Goodman, 1972a, 1972b; Jöreskog, 1973). This development rests essentially on combining responses to items to form proxies for such unobserved variables.

These two directions are not mutually exclusive or contradictory. If successful, each will contribute to enhancing the utility of sample survey data.

Issues in the Analysis of Survey Data

Earlier methods of survey data analysis were severely handicapped by the inability of existing card-based tabulating equipment to make calculations that were more complicated than simple counts and cross-tabulations. Widespread access to electronic computers in the 1960s and 1970s considerably expanded the capacity of survey analysts to use more sophisticated data analysis procedures. The development of log linear methods in the 1970s that were specially designed for use with the kinds of data typically generated by sample surveys also took advantage of the new computer capacities to make thousands of tedious computations.

As more sophisticated analytical techniques became available and alternative ways of analyzing survey data came into common use, it became increasingly clear that data analysis could not consist simply of the products of routine application of automatic procedures. The role of a priori knowledge and theory building became more and more obvious. Not only does the analysis need to be sensitive to the formal characteristics of the data themselves, but statistical results are often dependent on the implicit or explicit modeling of the phenomenon in question, such models lying implicitly behind the use of one or another mode of analysis. Hence, a regression equation cannot be sensibly built by throwing in anything that correlates with the dependent variable. It has to be built on some understanding of the process itself. Routines that systematically maximized the amount of variance "explained," as in stepwise regression procedures or Automatic Interaction Detection, were increasingly regarded as violating the prescription that analyses of data should be based on a priori modeling of the phenomenon being studied.

1.5. THE HANDBOOK OF SURVEY RESEARCH

As late as 1961, Gerhard Lenski, in his classic book, *The Religious Factor,* referred to the sample survey as "a new research technique [1961, p. 12]." In the ensuing 20 years, the arts and sciences of sample surveys have developed considerably and the activity as a whole is now a multi-billion-dollar industry. Our purpose in compiling this handbook was to record the contemporary state of the art in selected aspects of survey design and analysis. To be sure, not every important topic has been covered, but most of them have been. Extensive bibliographies have been provided by most of the authors, to which readers may turn for additional information on all the topics covered.

The *Handbook of Survey Research* divides, roughly, into three major parts. Part 1, consisting of the first four chapters, sets forth the basic theoretical issues involved in sampling, measurement, and the management of survey organizations. Part 2, Chapters 5 through 12, is more applied in focus, dealing mainly with "hands-on," how-to-do-it issues: how to draw theoretically acceptable samples, how to write questionnaires, how to combine responses into appropriate scales and indices, how to avoid response effects and measurement errors, how actually to go about gathering survey data, how to avoid missing data (and what to do when you cannot), and other topics of a similar nature. Finally, Part 3, the last four chapters, considers the analysis of survey data, with separate chapters for each of the three major multivariate analysis modes currently in use, and one chapter on the uses of surveys in monitoring overtime trends.

Entire books can be, and have been, written on each of the chapter topics, and so it would be presumptuous indeed to suppose that the coverage provided here is even approximately complete. Survey specialists will find these treatments at times cryptic, whereas novices will often find the same treatments to be hopelessly abstract and detailed. In contracting for the various chapters that appear here, the editors specified topical areas to be covered, but let each author decide on the depth and level of the treatment. We have not tried to impose any consensus on the individual authors as to "correct" survey theory or practice, since there are wide and legitimate differences of opinion on many such matters. That these differences of opinion can be found in the following pages is not the result of editorial sloth or indolence, rather it is a reflection of the substantive complexities involved in many of the topics.

The business of survey research, to be sure, has its detractors: Some argue against the method on philosophical or even metaphysical grounds; others on the apparently atheoretical nature of the enterprise; still others on the dehumanization that is seen to be inherent in assigning numbers to human phenomena. Once unpacked and demystified, most of the arguments against doing surveys turn out to be arguments against doing surveys poorly, and on this point we readily agree. Bad surveys give all surveys a bad name. We are not so foolish as to suppose that the publication of this handbook will put an end to bad surveys, but we do hope that it will lessen their frequency, and it is to this end that the *Handbook of Survey Research* is dedicated.

REFERENCES

Anderson, E.
  1937 *We Americans: A Study of Cleavage in an American City*. Cambridge: Harvard University Press.
Bailar, B. A., and C. M. Lanphier
  1978 *Development of Survey Methods to Assess Survey Practices*. Washington, D.C.: American Statistical Association.
Benevelo, L.
  1980 *The History of the City*. Cambridge: MIT Press.
Blau, P. M., and O. D. Duncan
  1967 *The American Occupational Structure*. New York: Wiley.
Dubois, W. E. B.
  1967 *The Philadelphia Negro*. New York: Schocken.
Fried, A., and R. Elman, Eds.
  1968 *Charles Booth's London*. New York: Pantheon.
Goodman, L. A.
  1972a "A general model for the analysis of surveys." *American Journal of Sociology,* 77, 1035–1086.
  1972b "A modified multiple regression approach to the analysis of dichotomous variables." *American Sociological Review, 37*, 28–46.
Groves, R., and R. Kahn
  1979 *Surveys by Telephone*. New York: Academic Press.
Jöreskog, K. G.
  1973 "A general method for estimating a linear structural equation system." In A. S. Goldgerger and O. D. Duncan (eds.), *Structural Equation Models in the Social Sciences*. New York: Seminar Press.
Kinsey, A., and Associates
  1948 *Sexual Behavior in the Human Male*. Philadelphia: Saunders.
Lazarsfeld, P., H. Gaudet, and B. Berelson
  1944 *The People's Choice*. New York: Columbia University Press.
Lenski, G.
  1961 *The Religious Factor*. Garden City, N.Y.: Doubleday.
Lundberg, G.
  1929 *Social Research*. New York: Dryden.
Lynd, R., and H. S. Lynd
  1937 *Middletown in Transition*. New York: Harcourt Brace.
Murphy, G., L. M. Murphy, and T. Newcomb
  1937 *Experimental Social Psychology*. New York: Harper and Bros.
National Research Council
  1981 *Survey Measurement of Subjective Phenomena*, Vols. 1 and 2. Washington, D.C.: National Academy Press.
Reckless, W. C.
  1933 *Vice in Chicago*. Chicago: The University of Chicago Press.
Schuman, H., and S. Presser
  1977 "Question wording as an independent variable in survey analysis." *Sociological Methods and Research* 6 (November): 151–176.

Stouffer, S. A., and Associates
  1947–1950   *Studies in Social Psychology in World War II* (4 vols). Princeton: Princeton University Press.
Sudman, S., and N. M. Bradburn
  1974   *Response Effects in Surveys: A Review and Synthesis.* Chicago: Aldine.
Thrasher, F. M.
  1927   *The Gang.* Chicago: The University of Chicago Press.
Thurstone, L. L., and E. L. Chave
  1929   *The Measurement of Attitude.* Chicago: The University of Chicago Press.
Warner, W. L., and Associates
  1942–1959   *The Yankee City Series,* Vols. 1–4. New Haven: Yale University Press.
Young, P. V.
  1949   *Scientific Social Surveys and Research.* New York: Prentice–Hall.

Chapter 2

Sampling Theory

Martin Frankel

2.1. INTRODUCTION

Survey sampling theory is a branch of statistics concerned with the methods and techniques of selecting samples whose results may be projected to larger populations. The process of selecting samples and projecting from these samples to larger populations has gone on for centuries. Not until the development of probability sampling, however, has the process become more a science than an art.

When probability sampling was first introduced into survey research, many practitioners felt that although the method was scientifically sound, it was too costly and restrictive. Many researchers predicted that after a short period of time it would be discarded in favor of traditional quota or purposive (nonprobability) methods. Much of this early skepticism was based on a misunderstanding of the nature of probability sampling methods. Many researchers mistakenly believed that the only type of probability sampling was simple random (element) sampling.

In selecting a probability sample, it is necessary to adhere to one basic principle. Within this limitation, it is possible to select samples that are compatible with a wide variety of survey research designs. The basic principle that distinguishes probability sampling from other types of sampling is the condition that each element in the population is given a known nonzero probability of being selected into the sample. By adhering to this condition, the research assures that various techniques of statistical inference may be validly applied in the projection of sample results to larger populations. Nonadherence to this condition (i.e., the use of nonprobability sampling) does not necessarily guaran-

HANDBOOK OF SURVEY RESEARCH

tee that the use of the techniques of statistical inference will produce invalid conclusions. The fundamental problem associated with the use of nonprobability samples is the fact that validity of the inferences drawn from such samples is neither assured nor testable.

In order to understand the various methods and techniques of probability sampling, it is first necessary to examine briefly the basic concepts of statistical inference. One of the difficulties associated with this task stems from the fact that drawing inferences from samples has become so much a part of our everyday experience that it is difficult to back away and examine the basic process.

Consider, for example, the medical researcher who administers a certain dosage of a drug to a group of 500 test rats and similar quantities of plain water to a control group of 500 rats. After a certain amount of time, it is observed that 350 of the 500 test rats have developed a certain disease, whereas none of the control rats have developed the disease. Without making any inference, the researcher is entitled to say that 70% of the rats tested developed a certain disease when a certain drug was administered. Of course, the usefulness of this statement itself is very limited unless some inference is made from the specific group of 500 rats used in the experiment to some larger population. Most likely, the researcher and the researcher's audience will automatically take the first step in the inference process by assuming either implicitly or explicitly that among the particular breed or strain of rat tested, approximately 70% will develop the same disease under the same test conditions. Although this first step of extrapolation or "inference" may appear to be quite reasonable we must ask whether or not this is the case. Is it reasonable to assume that the results of an experiment based on 500 rats would be repeated if it were tried on a group of 10,000 rats?

Now suppose that a social researcher stopped 500 people at a particular street corner and asked them whether or not they favored the use of capital punishment in the case of first degree murder. If 350 of these 500 people favored capital punishment, is it reasonable for the researcher to say that approximately 70% of all people living in the United States would have similar opinions?

Suppose that a second social researcher interviewed a national probability sample of 500 persons 18 years of age and older. Of the 500 persons interviewed, 350 indicated that they were in favor of a specific form of federal assistance to nonpublic schools. Is it reasonable to infer that approximately 70% of all persons 18 years and older living in the United States would respond favorably to the same question?

If we consider the samples used by the two social researchers, most people would probably accept the inferences drawn from the national probability sample as being reasonably valid. Most people would also agree that it is inadvisable to make similar national inferences from the street corner sample used by the first social researcher. The sample of rats used by the medical researcher poses a more complex statistical problem, however. Clearly, this sample was not selected in such a way that it would qualify as a "probability sample." Yet, our past experience might tell us that inferences drawn from samples of this type have a good chance of being correct. The feature that differentiates this nonprobability sample of rats from the nonprobability sample used by the first social researcher is our "subjective" evaluation of its ability to produce reasonably accurate inferences. Our assessment of the sample used by the second social researcher does not require this subjective evaluation. It qualifies as a probability sample and thus it may be used in a valid fashion as input to statistical inference.

Statistical Inference

Statisticians have developed several mathematical theories that may serve as the basis for inferences from a sample to a larger population. One of these theories, and probably the best known, is often referred to as the "classical theory of inference." Another, which has been used increasingly in recent years, is most commonly known as the "Bayesian theory of inference."

Both of these theories make use of mathematical functions that describe the relationship between samples and populations. The classical theory focuses on one side of this relationship, the various samples that might result, given a certain population. Bayesian theory looks at the inverse of this relationship, the various populations that might exist given a certain sample. If we are to make use of either the classical or Bayesian techniques of statistical inference, it is necessary to make assumptions concerning the form of the functional relationship between sample and population. In certain instances, it may be reasonable to assume that this relationship is known even if the process used in sample selection was not explicitly random (i.e., did not involve the use of random number tables, etc.). In other situations it will be necessary for the researcher to employ explicit randomization techniques (probability sampling) to assure that the relationship between population and sample will follow a known functional form. In order to describe these functions and the way that they are used in developing the framework for statistical inference it is first necessary to become familiar with several concepts and definitions.

POPULATION AND ELEMENT

The concepts of population and element are jointly defined. The *population* is defined as a set of elements; an *element* is defined as the basic unit that comprises the population. Some examples of populations are (*a*) all persons, 18 years or older, living in dwelling units within the 48 continental United States on January 1, 1978; (*b*) all business establishments, with public retail outlets, employing more than 100 persons, in the Los Angeles Standard Metropolitan Statistical Area as of June 30, 1976; (*c*) all admissions to nonfederal hospitals, in the state of New Jersey, during the time period August 1, 1976 to July 31, 1977.

In addition to the general term *population,* the more specific terms *target population* and *survey population* are often used. The target population is that collection of elements that the researcher would like to study. The survey population is the population that is actually sampled and for which data may be obtained. Most often, the survey population will differ from the target population because of noncoverage and nonresponse. For example, if telephone sampling were used to select a sample of U.S. adults, persons living in households without telephones would be systematically excluded from the survey population, although they would be in the target population. Furthermore, those adults with phones who refuse to participate in the survey represent a corresponding group of persons that are in the target population, but not in the survey population.[1]

SAMPLE, SAMPLE DESIGN, PROBABILITY SAMPLES, NONPROBABILITY SAMPLES

A *sample* is defined as a subset of the population. A *sample design* is a set of rules or procedures that specify how a sample (subset of the population) is to be selected. Certain sample designs will produce *probability samples*. Probability samples are selected when the sample design explicitly gives each element in the population a known (calculable) nonzero probability of inclusion in the sample. This process of explicitly giving each population element a nonzero chance of selection is usually accomplished through the use of a table of random numbers. All samples that do not qualify as probability samples are classified as nonprobability samples. The *sample design* is the set of rules that specifies how the table of random numbers is used in conjunction with the population elements to produce the sample.

A very important feature of probability sample designs is that these designs produce a sample space. The sample space, which shall be discussed in more detail later, is the set of all possible samples that might be selected under the selection rules specified by the sample design.

Simple random samples are the most basic type of probability samples. Although their practical usefulness is somewhat limited in large-scale survey research, their theoretical simplicity makes them useful as a baseline for comparison with other sample designs. This theoretical simplicity also makes the simple random sample a useful device in the explanation of a number of basic sampling concepts. Chapter 5 by Sudman explains the standard method of selecting a simple random sample.

Using the simple random sample as an example of a probability sample, it is possible to develop many of the concepts used in statistical inference. We assume a population of N elements. Each of these population elements has associated with it a particular value for variable y. If we are dealing with a

---

[1] The term *frame population* is sometimes used to describe the population covered by the sampling frame. In the example discussed, the frame population would be composed of all U.S. adults who live in households with telephone numbers that had a chance of being selected into the sample. The frame population is usually larger than the survey population because the former includes elements for which data was not obtained.

human population, the variable might be age to nearest year, number of years of completed schooling, or last year's income. The symbol Y_j is used to denote the value of variable y associated with the jth population element, where j may take on values from 1 to N. Thus, Y_4 would be the value of variable y for the fourth element in the population. Population *parameters* are summary values computed over the entire population. The population mean

$$\bar{Y} = \frac{1}{N} \sum_j Y_j, \qquad (2.1)$$

is one example of a population parameter. The population variance

$$\sigma^2 = \frac{1}{N} \sum_j (Y_j - \bar{Y})^2 \qquad (2.2)$$

is another example.

Just as Y_j is used as a symbol for a variable value associated with a "generic" element in the population, the symbol y_i is used to denote the observed or recorded value associated with a single generic element in the sample. Thus y_4 would be the observed or recorded value of the variable y associated with the fourth element in the sample. It is important to note that the numbering of elements in a particular sample is independent and distinct from the numbering used for elements in the population. Thus the thirty-fourth element in the population may be the third element in a particular sample. For simplicity, we will assume that whenever a population element is selected into a sample, the variable value Y_j will be observed or recorded without error.

Summaries of the values associated with sample elements are usually called sample estimators. The sample mean

$$\bar{y} = \frac{1}{n} \sum_i y_i \qquad (2.3)$$

is an example of a sample estimator. The sample variance

$$s^2 = \frac{1}{n-1} \sum_i (y_i - \bar{y})^2 \qquad (2.4)$$

is another example of a sample estimator.

Under the theory of classical inference, one of the most crucial but complex concepts is that of the sampling distribution of an estimator. For a particular population, and a specific sample design, the sampling distribution of a certain sample estimator is the set of all possible results that might be observed from the estimator along with the frequency or probability of each result. This concept is best illustrated by the following example. Suppose that we have a population of $N = 6$ households (elements). The variable value of interest is the average weekly expenditure for food.

Household j	Average weekly expenditure for food (\$) Y_j
1	20
2	40
3	70
4	30
5	60
6	50

Two parameters from this population are the population mean

$$\bar{Y} = \frac{1}{N} \sum_{j=1}^{N} Y_j = \frac{1}{6} (20 + 40 + 70 + 30 + 60 + 50) = 45,$$

and the population variance

$$\sigma^2 = \frac{1}{N} \sum_{j=1}^{N} (Y_j - \bar{Y})^2 = \frac{1}{6} [(20 - 45)^2 + (40 - 45)^2 + (70 - 45)^2$$

$$+ (30 - 45)^2 + (60 - 45)^2 + (50 - 45)^2] = 291\tfrac{2}{3}$$

Now, suppose we draw a simple random sample of size $n = 2$ from this population. Referring to a table of random numbers we select the numbers 2 and 5, which in turn select population elements with values 40 and 60. Thus $y_1 = 40$ and $y_2 = 60$. From this particular sample, the value of the sample mean (2.3) is $\bar{y} = (40 + 60)/2 = 50$. And the sample variance (2.4) is $s^2 = [(40 - 50)^2 + (60 - 50)^2]/1 = 200$.

Now, suppose instead of considering a single sample drawn from this population we actually select all of the possible samples that might have been drawn. In this particular case, there are a total of 15 distinct samples that might have been the sample selected by using the table of random numbers.[2]

Table 2.1 lists the 15 possible simple random samples of size $n = 2$ that might have been selected from the population of $N = 6$ elements. This table also shows the values associated with the two sample elements, and the sample mean $\bar{y}$ that would result. For example, for sample number 8 we find the sample that includes population elements 2 and 5. The values for these elements are 60 and 40. Thus, the sample mean $\bar{y}$ is 50.

This set of 15 possible means constitutes the sample distribution of $\bar{y}$ for a simple random sample design of size $n = 2$ from the population of size $N = 6$ specified in Table 2.1. In Table 2.2, this distribution of $\bar{y}$'s is tabulated in frequency distribution form.

Several features of this sampling distribution should be noted. First the average of the 15 possible sample means is equal to 45. The value 45 also

[2] This assumes that we do not make a distinction among different orderings of the sample elements. Thus, the sample in which population element 2 is selected first and population element 5 is selected second is considered the same as the sample in which element 5 is selected first and element 2 is selected second.

TABLE 2.1
Fifteen Possible Samples of Size $n = 2$ from Population Size $N = 6$

Sample number	Population elements in the sample	Variable values for the sample elements	Sample mean $\bar{y}$
1	1 and 2	40, 20	30
2	1 and 3	70, 20	45
3	1 and 4	30, 20	25
4	1 and 5	60, 20	40
5	1 and 6	50, 20	35
6	2 and 3	70, 40	55
7	2 and 4	30, 40	35
8	2 and 5	60, 40	50
9	2 and 6	50, 40	45
10	3 and 4	30, 70	50
11	3 and 5	60, 70	65
12	3 and 6	50, 70	60
13	4 and 5	60, 30	45
14	4 and 6	50, 30	40
15	5 and 6	50, 60	55

happens to be the mean of the six element values in the population. This is no accident. The average of the possible sample means is called the expected value of the estimator $\bar{y}$ and is usually denoted as $E(\bar{y})$. For any simple random sample design of n elements from a population of N elements it can be proven that the expected value of the estimator $\bar{y}$ will be equal to the mean of the population values [i.e., $E(\bar{y}) = \bar{Y}$]. This property is not always true for all sample designs and all sample estimators.

In those situations where the expected value of an estimator is equal to a population parameter, the estimator is termed an unbiased estimator of that parameter. To the extent that the expected value of an estimator differs from a population parameter, the estimator is said to be biased and the amount of the

TABLE 2.2
Sampling Distribution of Sample Mean $\bar{y}$

Value of $\bar{y}$	Frequency
25	1
30	1
35	2
40	2
45	3
50	2
55	2
60	1
65	1

difference is termed the bias. In certain situations this bias will be known, and may be corrected. In other situations the degree of bias may be only approximated.

The shape of the sampling distribution of $\bar{y}$'s is not the same as the shape of the distribution of the element values in the population. Values in the population have a range 20–70. The set of possible sample means has a range 25–65, 10 units less. More importantly, the original population values are uniformly distributed throughout their range, whereas the set of sample means is more concentrated toward the mean of 45. The sampling distribution of the estimator $\bar{y}$ from simple random samples of size $n = 3$ is even less dispersed around the population mean.

In developing inferences from samples we make use of the theoretical result called the "central limit theorem," which states that for reasonably large sample sizes (say $n = 30$ or more), the distribution of the possible sample means $\bar{y}$ will tend toward a normal distribution.

At first, it may seem somewhat illogical that the process by which a researcher can make inference from a single sample should be based on a property that applies to the set of all of the possible samples that might have been selected under a particular sample design. Under the classical method of inference, the linkage between the single sample actually selected and the set of all possible samples that might have been selected is based on the notion that the sample actually selected by the researcher is in fact a sample of *one* from the set of all possible samples in the sampling distribution. Suppose, for example, we know that for a particular sample design (e.g., simple random selection of $n = 100$ cases) the sampling distribution of possible sample means will be normally distributed with mean equal to the population mean and standard deviation equal to 5. We may use tables of the normal distribution to determine that the probability is 95% that the mean obtained from a particular sample will differ by no more than 10 from the mean of the entire population. This determination relies on the fact that approximately 95% of the area under a normal distribution falls between plus and minus two standard deviations from the mean. Since the process of selecting the simple random sample of 100 observations may be thought of as selecting one mean from the sampling distribution of $\bar{y}$, and since the distribution of the possible sample means is normal with mean equal to the population mean and standard deviation equal to 5, 95% of the samples that might be selected under this design will have sample means that differ from the population mean by no more than 10 units.

The confidence interval is the mechanism employed in classical statistical theory to make the actual statement of inference. It involves a probability level (often chosen as either 95 or 99%) and a set of limits. For example, suppose that in a simple random sample of 150 out of the 15,000 students attending a certain university, the average weekly expenditure for room and board was found to be $35.75 with a standard deviation of $18.50. The 95% confidence limits for the average weekly room and board expenditures for all students attending the university would be approximately $32.75 to 38.75 (or 35.75 ± 3.00). These limits were set using a statistic called the *standard error*. Calculation of the standard error is shown later in this section. Under classical inference theory, this set of bounds is interpreted as follows: The sampling procedure used had a 95% chance of producing a set of limits that encloses the average weekly expenditures of *all* students attending the college. It should be noted that this statement is not the same as a statement that the chances are 95% that the average weekly expenditures for all students at the university falls between $32.75 and 38.75. Under classical theory we are not permitted to assign a probability value to whether or not the entire population mean falls between the limits $32.75 and 38.75. The reason for this prohibition is that the unknown, average weekly expenditures for *all* students is a fixed value and not a random variable: Either it is between the limits or it is not. Thus, according to classical theory, making a probability statement about whether or not the population mean is contained within a specified set of bounds would be as inappropriate as making probabilistic statements about whether or not it rained yesterday.

The inferential probability statement that may be made under classical theory is based on the entire set of possible samples that might have been selected under the sample design. Each of these possible samples will yield a set of 95% confidence limit bounds. For 95% of these samples and associated confidence limit bounds, the average weekly expenditure value for the population (i.e., the population value, or parameter) will fall within these bounds. Thus, although we do not know whether or not the population mean actually falls within the bounds computed for the particular sample selected (i.e., $32.75–38.75), we may state that there was a 95% chance that the sample selected is one whose bounds will cover the true population mean.

One of the major reasons for the increased popularity of the Bayesian method of statistical inference is the rather indirect method of reasoning associated with the classical procedure. From the standpoint of the applied user of statistics, the Bayesian approach permits the use of inferential statements that are much more direct and more easily understood.

The actual form of Bayesian inferential statements about population parameters is identical to the form used in classical confidence statements. Specifically a Bayesian credible interval (the term *credible* is used rather than the term *confidence*) consists of a probability level and a set of limits. Although the numbers associated with a Bayesian credible interval may be the same as the numbers associated with a classical confidence interval, the interpretation is quite different. Suppose, for example, that based on data from a certain probability sample, a 95% credible interval on the average weekly expenditures for students at a certain university was $32.75–38.75. The interpretation of this Bayesian inferential statement would be that the probability is 95% that the average weekly expenditures for all students falls between $32.75 and 38.75. In this case, we are treating a population parameter as an unknown random variable.

In addition to the fact that Bayesian inferential statements are directly interpretable without resort to the notion of repeated sampling, the statistical theory of inference that may be used to produce such statements provides a formal way of combining prior information obtained from previous studies into the inference process.

In summary, both the classical and Bayesian methods of making statistical inferences from sample results require that we be able to specify the mathematical form of either the sampling distribution (classical) or the likelihood function (Bayesian). If probability sampling techniques are used in the selection of the sample and if the sample is of reasonable size (usually taken as meaning more than 30 independent selections), we may make use of the central limit theorem to assume that the required distribution relating sample and population is normal. In those instances where the sample is selected by nonprobability sampling methods, the researcher may assume normality of either the sampling distribution or the likelihood function, on a strictly ad hoc basis, or by assuming that there existed randomization in the entire population.[3] As previously noted, however, this assumption is untestable within the context of the sample results.

Given the assumption of normality, it is possible to produce confidence or credible limits if we can specify the first two moments of the normal distribution (i.e., if we can specify the mean and variance or standard deviation). If the sample estimator has expectation equal to the population parameter, the mean of the appropriate sampling distribution will be equal to the population parameter we wish to estimate. Thus, the only remaining task is to obtain an estimate of the standard error.

Before discussing the formulas used in estimating standard errors for simple random samples, we take note of the fact that the variance and standard deviation may be used as measures of variability at different levels. They may be used to describe variability among the values of variable y for all elements in the population or all elements in the sample. In addition variance and standard deviation may be used as measures of variability among the possible sample estimates in the sampling distribution (e.g., the sampling distribution of the sample mean $\bar{y}$. In an attempt to diminish the possibility of confusion among these levels, the term *standard error* is used to describe the *standard deviation* for a sampling distribution of a statistic. Thus, rather than referring to the standard deviation of the sample mean, we will use the term *standard error of the sample mean*. In both cases we are describing the variation among the possible sample means that could result for a given sample design.

For simple random samples of n elements the standard error of the sample mean $\bar{y}$ is given by

$$S.E.(\bar{y}) = \left[\left(1 - \frac{n}{N}\right)\frac{S^2}{n}\right]^{1/2}, \tag{2.5}$$

where n is the sample size, N is the population size, and S^2 is a modified form of the element variance in the population[4]

---

[3] Under this assumption, any arbitrary selection from the population would yield a simple random sample.

[4] In most sampling texts, the parameter S^2 is used rather than σ^2 in order to simplify the derivation of various theorems and proofs. Note: $S^2 = [N/(N-1)]\sigma^2$.

$$S^2 = \frac{1}{N-1} \sum_{j=1}^{N} (Y_j - \bar{Y})^2. \qquad (2.6)$$

The term $[1 - (n/N)]$ that appears in (2.5) is known as the *finite population correction factor*. This factor represents the decrease in the standard error that results from the nonduplication constraint imposed in the sample selection process. The letter f is sometimes substituted for n/N in formulas applied to simple random samples. In the general case, the letter f may be used in any instance where the sample design is *epsem* (i.e., all elements in the population have equal selection probabilities). Simple random samples have the added property that $f = n/N$.

This formula for the standard error of $\bar{y}$ involves a population parameter S^2. Since it is very unlikely that we would know the value of this parameter (we are sampling in order to estimate $\bar{Y}$), it must be estimated from the sample in conjunction with $\bar{y}$.

For simple random samples the sample variance

$$s^2 = \frac{1}{n-1} \sum_{i=1}^{n} (y_i - \bar{y})^2 \qquad (2.7)$$

is an unbiased estimator of S^2. This estimate s^2 is substituted for S^2 in Eq. (2.5) to give a sample derived estimate of the standard error of $\bar{y}$. Thus

$$\text{S.E.}(\bar{y}) = \left[\left(1 - \frac{n}{N} \right) \frac{s^2}{n} \right]^{1/2}. \qquad (2.8)$$

For samples of size 30 or more, the $(1 - \alpha) \times 100\%$ confidence, or credible limits, on the population mean $\bar{Y}$ would be computed as

$$\bar{y} \pm Z_{\alpha/2} \text{ S.E.}(\bar{y}), \qquad (2.9)$$

where $Z_{\alpha/2}$ is the standard normal deviate value which corresponds to an area of $(1 - \alpha)$.

Proportions are special cases of means in which the variable value associated with an element may be 1 if the element is in the defined group, and 0 otherwise.

If we let P denote the population proportion and p denote the sample proportion, the standard error of the estimate p from a simple random sample of n elements is given by

$$\text{S.E.}(p) = \left[\left(1 - \frac{n}{N} \right) \frac{S_p^2}{n} \right]^{1/2}, \qquad (2.10)$$

where

$$S_p^2 = \left(\frac{N}{N-1} \right) P(1 - P). \qquad (2.11)$$

The corresponding sample estimate of S.E.(p) is given by

$$\text{S.E.}(p) = \left[\left(1 - \frac{n}{N} \right) \frac{s_p^2}{n} \right]^{1/2}, \qquad (2.12)$$

where

$$s_p^2 = \frac{N}{N-1} p(1-p) \doteq p(1-p). \tag{2.13}$$

For samples of size $n = 50$ and p not close to 0 or 1, $(1 - \alpha) \times 100\%$ confidence or credible limits for the population proportion P are given by $p \pm Z_{\alpha/2}$ S.E.(p).

The reader should take note of the fact that with the formula just given we are using data obtained from the sample in two ways. First, the sample is used to produce an estimate of a population parameter (i.e., a mean or proportion). Second, the sample data is being used as input to the construction of a confidence or credible interval—a statistical evaluation of how close the sample estimate comes to the parameter being estimated. Thus the sample is being used to produce both the estimate itself and an evaluation of the estimate.

Samples that can provide this "self-evaluation" are called *measurable samples*. The satisfaction of the probability sampling conditions are necessary but not sufficient conditions for measurability. That is, measurable samples must be probability samples, but not all probability samples are measurable. Further, it must be stressed that the formulas just described are only valid for simple random sample designs. In later sections, I describe the formulas appropriate for the estimation of standard errors from other measurable probability sampling designs that are not simple random samples (SRS).

Development of the Sample Design

The development of a sample design for any survey research study must be considered an integral part of the overall study design. Although a number of texts and articles have viewed the development of a sampling plan as a discrete step to be undertaken once the overall survey design plan has been well formulated, practical researchers have learned that these two steps cannot be divorced. More often than not, the study design will involve more than one basic objective. Within the context of these basic objectives, the two most important factors affecting the final sample design are the availability of funds and the availability of population frames. Both of these factors define a possible set of sample design alternatives. Once this set of limits has been determined, evolution of the final sample design is carried out by examining the tradeoffs among various sample design alternatives with respect to the overall, but typically multiple, study design objectives. Experience has shown that in this process it is necessary to develop and refine further the various overall study design objectives, since it is usually the case that no single sample design will be optimal for all of them. The researcher must then attempt to develop a priority ordering and range of tolerable sampling errors among the multiple objectives of the research.

The following simplified example is indicative of this process. Suppose a researcher is interested in assessing certain attitudes among adults living within a major metropolitan area. For various reasons, it is felt that this interviewing must be conducted on a face-to-face basis. In addition to the determination of attitudes for the area as a whole, it is felt that there will be major differences in attitudes among persons living in the central city and the suburbs. The researcher is interested in examining these differences. The adult population of the entire metropolitan area is 500,000. Approximately 100,000 of these adults live in the central city and 400,000 live in the suburbs.

Since there is no reasonably complete listing of adults or housing units within the area, a multistage area sample will be used. The sample will be selected in three stages. In stage one, blocks will be selected with probabilities proportional to the estimated number of dwelling units. In stage two, selected blocks will be listed and subsampled with probabilities inversely proportional to the probability used in stage one. Finally, within each dwelling unit selected in stage two, all adults will be enumerated (listed) and a single adult will be selected at random for interviewing. Based on data from other studies and anticipated costs of listing, travel, and interviewing, it is determined that the optimal cluster size is 10 interviews per selected block. It is determined, on the basis of available funds, that the sample size will be approximately 1000 interviews.

Within these overall sample design limits, the researcher must now examine the tradeoffs associated with various allocations or distributions of 1000 sample cases among the central city and suburban portions of the metropolitan area. From the standpoint of estimating overall attitudes for the entire metropolitan area, the lowest standard error of estimation is often achieved when the sample is distributed in proportion to the distribution of the population. In this case, 20% of the sample (200 cases) would be assigned to the central city and 80% of the sample (800 cases) would be assigned to the suburbs. For the estimation of differences in attitudes between central city and suburbs, however, the lowest standard error of estimation for central city versus suburb differences often occurs when the sample is allocated equally to the two portions of the metropolitan area. In this latter situation, 50% of the sample (500 cases) would be allocated to the central city and 50% of the sample (500 cases) would be allocated to the suburbs.

By working with each of the design objectives separately, we find the optimal sample allocation for one of the basic design objectives is not the same as the optimal sample allocation for the other basic objective. Faced with this dilemma, we must examine the "tradeoffs" (i.e., anticipated standard errors of estimation) associated with these two allocation schemes with respect to both of the design objectives. In addition, we must examine the anticipated standard errors of estimation associated with various "compromise" designs. An example of these anticipated standard errors is shown in Table 2.3.

As this table indicates, there is no single allocation that simultaneously minimizes the anticipated standard error for estimates of the entire metropolitan area and estimates of differences between the central city and suburbs. As a result, the decision as to which allocation is best depends on the relative importance of the two basic study objectives. If both study objectives are viewed as

TABLE 2.3
Standard Errors of Estimates for Alternate Central City-Suburbs Allocations

Sample cases allocated to		Standard error for estimates of	
			Differences between
		Entire metropolitan	central city and
Central city	Suburbs	area	suburbs
200	800	.0223	.0559
250	750	.0225	.0516
300	700	.0229	.0488
350	650	.0234	.0468
400	600	.0241	.0456
450	550	.0250	.0449
500	500	.0261	.0447

important, the allocation of 350 cases in the central city and 650 in the suburbs might be a reasonable compromise in terms of "relative closeness" to the minimum obtainable standard errors. This reasoning does not take into account the absolute magnitude of the errors themselves. Given that the standard errors for difference are almost twice those associated with the overall proportion, one might choose the allocation 500 : 500.

Although this example is somewhat oversimplified, it does illustrate the general problem associated with the development of a sampling design. It is usually the case that a survey will have a number of basic objectives. From the standpoint of sampling theory, these multiple objectives may call for different, and sometimes conflicting, sampling strategies.

The availability of funds and the availability of sampling frames will usually impose limits on the set of possible sample designs. By making use of the various design techniques to be discussed in the next sections, sampling plans may be developed that will be optimal (i.e., will minimize the sampling error) with respect to a single design objective. Typically, it will not be possible to find a single design that is optimal with regard to all of the major study objectives. The final step in the development of a sample design will consist of either selecting one of the designs initially considered or developing some sort of compromise among two or more of the initial designs.

In rare situations it may be possible to approach the question of sample design without initial budget constraints. Specifically, it may be possible to develop study objectives that specify desired precision levels for various sample estimators. If there are multiple study objectives (i.e., multiple parameters for which sample estimates are sought), the process of developing a sample design will be quite similar. In this case, however, the process of selecting the ultimate sample design will involve a choice among alternatives that will satisfy all of the stated study objectives at lowest overall cost.

Design Effect and Related Concepts

Before beginning a more complete discussion of specific types of nonsimple random sampling, we briefly discuss the concept of design effect, design (cost) efficiency, and effective sample size. These concepts will allow us to assess alternative nonsimple random sample designs from the standpoint of a statistical and cost efficiency. When simple random sampling was first described, it was noted that this type of sampling has only limited application in large-scale survey research investigations. However, it provides a theoretically simple design from which concepts may be illustrated and a relatively simple benchmark by which more practical sample designs may be assessed.

The assessment of sample design efficiency is accomplished through the use of three related measures: the design effect, the design cost efficiency, and the effective sample size. The design effect is the ratio of the sampling variance (squared standard error) of a particular sample estimate using a specified (nonsimple random) sample design to the sampling variance for the same estimate based on a simple random sample with the same number of cases. For example, if for a certain estimate derived from a specified nonsimple random sample the design effect was 3.5, this would mean that the variance of the estimate was 3.5 times larger than it would have been with a simple random sample of the same number of cases. Although this comparison tells us about the statistical efficiency of a sample design, it neglects the fact that the cost per case may be different for the sample design specified and an equal sized simple random sample. This cost difference is taken into account by the design cost efficiency factor. The design cost efficiency factor is the design effect multiplied by the ratio of the cost per case for the design under consideration to the cost per case for simple random sampling. If this coefficient is equal to unity, the design under consideration has the same cost efficiency as simple random sampling. If this coefficient is less than one, our design is more cost efficient than simple random sampling. If the coefficient is greater than one, our design is less cost efficient than simple random sampling. In the example we just considered, suppose that the cost per case for the design under consideration was $10 and the cost per case if we were to use simple random sampling was $40. The design cost efficiency factor would be $3.5 \times (10/40) = .875$. This would indicate that the design under consideration was more cost efficient than a simple random sample, although unless costs are considered, the simple random sample would appear superior.

Finally, the effective sample size is defined as the actual sample size (number of cases) divided by the design effect. In our example, if the total sample size was 1000 cases and the design effect was equal to 3.5 then the effective sample size would be $1000/3.5 = 287$. This would mean that for the particular population parameter being estimated the sample design actually used produces the same standard error as would a simple random sample of 287 cases. It should be recognized however, that the $1000 \times \$10 = \$10,000$ cost for our design of 1000 cases with an effective sample size equal to 287 would only cover the cost of a simple random sample of $10,000/$40 = 250 cases. Thus, although there is a large drop-off from actual sample size to effective sample size for the design under consideration, it is still superior to a simple random sample of "equal cost."

Remainder of the Chapter

In the introduction to this chapter, the assertion was made that the researcher has extensive flexibility in developing cost effective and practical probability samples. Three of the basic techniques that allow for this flexibility are (*a*) stratification; (*b*) clustering; and (*c*) multistage selection. These techniques may be used separately or in combination with each other.

Stratification, which is covered in Section 2.2, permits the researcher to subdivide the population into mutually exclusive and exhaustive subpopulations, or strata. Within these strata, separate samples are selected and sample estimates of stratum specific parameters are calculated. Finally, these separate sample estimates are combined, in an appropriate fashion, to produce parameter estimates for the entire population.

Clustering, covered in Section 2.3, allows for the selection of sample cases in groups or clusters, rather than on an individual basis. This technique may significantly reduce field costs while permitting the use of population frames that are not explicit element-by-element lists of the population. Without the technique of clustering, most national personal interview samples of persons would be completely impractical. Without the ability to group elements into clusters we would require a complete and explicit listing of all individuals in order to select the sample. Assuming that this list could be constructed and that the sample was selected, our inability to cluster sample cases would lead to uncontrolled geographic dispersion that might require a separate interviewer for each sample case.

Multistage selection permits the selection of samples when explicit listings of sampling units (elements or clusters) are not available. Without this technique, only populations for which these explicit lists were available could be sampled. The imposition of this explicit list restriction alone would eliminate the use of probability sampling methods in most large-scale survey research investigations. Multistage sample selection is almost always accomplished within the context of a clustered sample design. These designs typically use stratification as well. Multistage selection techniques are discussed in the first part of Section 2.4 (Advanced Topics).

Section 2.4 also considers various sample design issues and techniques that facilitate the computation of standard errors for both complex and simple statistics for complex sample designs.

Sources for further reading and a brief discussion of sampling topics which were not covered in this chapter are found in Section 2.5.

2.2. STRATIFIED SAMPLING

Introduction

The basic notion of stratified sampling has a great deal of intuitive appeal. First, the entire population to be sampled is divided into separate and distinct subpopulations or strata. Next, a separate and independent sample is selected within each strata. Data collected for each of these samples are used to develop separate within-stratum estimates. Finally, these separate stratum estimates are combined (weighted) to form an overall estimate for the entire population. In general, whenever stratified sampling procedures are used, each of these steps must be followed. In some cases, however, certain mathematical conditions will allow one or more of these steps to be carried out implicitly.

There are three basic reasons why stratification is used in probability sampling.

1. The use of appropriate stratification may greatly increase sample efficiency (i.e., lower sampling variance).
2. By creating explicit strata, we may assure that certain key subgroups will have sufficient sample size for separate analysis.
3. The creation of strata permits the use of different sample designs for different portions of the population.

Increased efficiency is probably the most common reason why stratification is used in the design of probability samples. When stratification is not used, the sampling variability of sample estimators is related to the variability that exists among the basic units in the population. For a given variable, this variability is measured about the overall population mean. By dividing the population into strata, sampling error becomes a function of within-stratum variability. If the within-stratum variation is less than the overall variation, stratified sampling procedures will result in decreased sampling errors.

Assurance of sufficient sample size for separate subgroup analysis is another important reason for using stratified sampling. A nonstratified equal probability sample will yield sample cases from various subgroups in proportion to their distribution in the general population. Thus, with a nonstratified, equal probability design, we expect that if a particular subgroup represents 5% of the total population, it will constitute approximately 5% of the total sample. By creating separate strata consisting of particular subgroups of interest, we are free to increase or decrease the relative distribution of these subgroups in the sample.

Stratified sampling procedures also may be employed because of problems in obtaining adequate population frames. It is sometimes impossible to obtain a single frame that covers the entire population in a uniform manner. Stratified design gives us the ability to make use of separate frames in different forms, which may be pieced together to cover the entire population. Stratified techniques also provide a mechanism for dealing with partial population frames that may overlap one another.

Basic Formulas

We assume a population of N elements, divided into H strata. These strata are assumed to be mutually exclusive and mutually exhaustive. The symbol $N_h(h = 1, \ldots, H)$ denotes the number of population elements in the hth stratum. Thus $N = \Sigma_{h=1}^{H} N_h$. The symbol Y_{hi} is used to represent the value for variable y associated with the ith element in the hth stratum $(i = 1, \ldots, N_h)$.

Using this notation, the population mean for variable y is expressed as

$$\bar{Y} = \frac{1}{N} \sum_{h=1}^{H} \sum_{i=1}^{N_h} Y_{hi}. \qquad (2.14)$$

If we define the mean for the hth stratum as

$$\bar{Y}_h = \frac{1}{N_h} \sum_{i=1}^{N_h} Y_{hi}, \qquad (2.15)$$

the expression for the population mean $\bar{Y}$ may be rewritten as

$$\bar{Y} = \frac{1}{N} \sum_{h=1}^{H} \sum_{i=1}^{N_h} Y_{hi} = \sum_{h=1}^{H} \frac{N_h}{N} \bar{Y}_h = \sum_{h=1}^{H} W_h \bar{Y}_h, \qquad (2.16)$$

where

$$W_h = \frac{N_h}{N}. \qquad (2.17)$$

The symbol W_h, which is often called the "stratum weight," denotes the proportion of the population contained within the hth stratum.

The fact that the overall population mean may be expressed as the weighted sum of the individual stratum means provides the key to population estimation. The sample within each stratum is used to estimate the population mean $\bar{Y}_h$ for that stratum. These estimated stratum means are then combined, using the weights W_h to estimate the overall population mean. Letting $\bar{y}_h$ denote the sample mean from the hth stratum, the overall population mean $\bar{Y}$ is estimated by

$$\bar{y}_w = \sum_{h=1}^{H} W_h \bar{y}_h. \qquad (2.18)$$

The term *allocation* is used to describe the distribution of sample cases among the various strata. In designing a stratified sample, the only basic requirement with respect to sample allocation is that there be a minimum of one sample selection within each of the strata.[5] Having a sample of at least one element within a stratum assures that we may produce the required estimate $\bar{y}_h$ for use in Formula (2.18).

If the sample design used within each of the strata allows for the estimation of the sampling variance of $\bar{y}_h$, these stratum specific variance estimates $\text{var}(\bar{y}_h)$ may be combined to produce an estimate of the sampling variance for $\bar{y}_w$, the overall weighted estimate as follows:

$$\text{var}(\bar{y}_w) = \sum_{h=1}^{H} W_h^2 \, \text{var}(\bar{y}_h). \tag{2.19}$$

In the remainder of this section we will assume that simple random element sampling is used within all strata. Formulas for other types of within-stratum sampling will appear in subsequent sections. It should be remembered, however, that when stratified sampling is employed, the selection of elements within stratum may make use of any probability sampling method. The sample designs do not have to be identical across strata, and in fact, a different sampling procedure may be used within each of the strata that comprise the total population.

If a simple random sample of n_h elements is selected within each of the H strata, the overall weighted estimate of the population mean may be written as

$$\bar{y}_w = \sum_{h=1}^{H} W_h \bar{y}_h = \sum_{h=1}^{H} \frac{1}{n_h} W_h \sum_{i=1}^{n_h} y_{hi}, \tag{2.20}$$

where y_{hi} denotes the value for variable y of the ith sample element in the hth stratum, and $\bar{y}_h$, the sample mean from the hth stratum,

$$\bar{y}_h = \frac{1}{n_h} \sum_{i=1}^{n_h} y_{hi}. \tag{2.21}$$

Under the condition that at least two elements are selected from each of the strata (i.e., $n_h \geq 2$, for all $h = 1, \ldots, H$) the sampling variance of the estimate $\bar{y}$ is computed as

$$\text{var}(\bar{y}_w) = \sum_{h=1}^{H} W_h^2 (1 - f_h) \frac{s_h^2}{n_h}, \tag{2.22}$$

where s_h^2, the within component of variance for the hth stratum, is defined as

$$s_h^2 = \frac{1}{n_h - 1} \sum_{i=1}^{n_h} (y_{hi} - \bar{y}_h)^2, \tag{2.23}$$

and $f_h = n_h/N_h$, the uniform probability of selection within the hth stratum.

---

[5] This minimum of one element per stratum assures only that we may estimate the sample mean for that stratum. To calculate a within-stratum variance, two independent primary units are necessary. In this section we have assumed that the primary units are elements. As will be discussed later, these primary units may be clusters of elements.

Formulas (2.22) and (2.23) provide the mathematical explanation of potential reduction in sampling variance when stratification is employed. These formulas depend on the within-stratum component of the basic element variance and the stratum allocations. In simple random sampling without stratification, the variance of the sample mean is dependent on both the within and between components of total variance and the sample size.

Proportionate Stratified Sampling

In proportionate stratified sampling, allocation of the sample among the various strata is made proportionate to the number of population elements that comprise the strata. This may be expressed as

$$n_h = n(N_h/N) = nW_h, \qquad \text{for all } h = 1, \ldots, H. \qquad (2.24)$$

Proportionate allocation results in an overall equal probability of selection sample design (*epsem*). As such $f_h = n_h/N_h$, the uniform probability of selection within the hth stratum is equal to $n/N = f$, for all $h = 1, \ldots, H$. Within the limitations that arise due to the fact that the values $n_h = W_h n$ may not be integers, the use of proportionate allocation leads to simplification in the estimation of the overall population mean. By application of condition (2.24) to formula (2.20) the weighted sample mean may be expressed as

$$\bar{y}_{w(\text{prop})} = \frac{1}{n} \sum_{h=1}^{H} \sum_{i=1}^{n_h} y_{hi}. \qquad (2.25)$$

This mathematical simplification that allows us to bypass the separate calculation of within-stratum means has led to the term *self-weighting* as a description of proportionate stratified sampling.

It should be noted that although computation of the estimated population mean involves the same formula that is used in the case of nonstratified sampling, the same identity does not hold with respect to the estimated sampling variance of $\bar{y}_{w(\text{prop})}$. Estimation of the sampling variance of $\bar{y}_{w(\text{prop})}$ may be based on the general formulas given by (2.22) and (2.23) or by

$$\text{var}(\bar{y}_{w(\text{prop})}) = \frac{1-f}{n} \sum_{h=1}^{H} W_h s_h^2, \qquad (2.26)$$

where s_h^2 is the previously defined within-stratum variance for the hth stratum and f is the uniform overall probability of selection $f = n/N = f_h = n_h/N_h$, for all h.

Proportionate stratified sampling is robust in the sense that it will always have sampling variance that is less than or equal to the sampling variance from a nonstratified simple random sample. Recalling that the design effect (DEFF) expresses the ratio of the sampling variance for the design under consideration to the variance of a simple random sample of the same size, DEFF for proportionate allocation is given by

$$\text{DEFF}(\bar{y}_{w(\text{prop})}) \doteq 1 - \frac{\sum_{h=1}^{H} W_h (\bar{Y}_h - \bar{Y})^2}{S^2}, \qquad (2.27)$$

where

$$S^2 = \frac{1}{N-1} \sum_{h=1}^{H} \sum_{i=1}^{N_h} (Y_{hi} - \bar{Y})^2. \qquad (2.28)$$

The second term in (2.27) may never be less than zero. Thus, the design effect for a proportionate stratified design will never be greater than unity. To the extent that the stratum means $\bar{Y}_h$ differ from each other, the second term in expression (2.27) will increase with a corresponding decrease in design effect. This situation, often described as within-strata homogeneity, may produce significant decreases in sampling variance relative to equal size simple random samples.

Optimal Allocation

In certain instances, the use of allocations that are not proportionate to stratum sizes may result in even more dramatic decreases in sampling variance than are possible with proportionate allocation. In general, these situations occur when the basic element variances S_h^2 are quite different in at least two of the population strata and we know the general magnitude of these differences. Disproportionate allocation may be a two-edge sword, however. Unlike the situation that exists when proportionate allocation is employed, disproportionate allocation may result in sampling variances that are larger than those that would have been attained had simple random sampling been used. Thus, disproportionate stratified sample designs should be approached with caution.

Under the assumption that the costs associated with all phases of the survey are the same across the various strata, the minimum possible design effect (minimum possible variance) will occur when the sample allocation in each stratum is made proportionate to the population size for the stratum times the element standard deviation within the stratum.[6] This condition may be written as

$$n_h = k N_h S_h, \qquad \text{for all } h = 1, \ldots, H, \qquad (2.29)$$

---

[6] The formula for optimal allocation is often ascribed to Neyman and the method is sometimes called "Neyman allocation." (Neyman, J. "On the two different aspects of the representative method: The method of stratified sampling and the method of purposive selection," *Journal of the Royal Statistical Society, 97* (1934), 558–625.) In fact, the basic idea for this type of allocation may be found in Tschuprow, A. "On the mathematical expectation of the moments of frequency distributions in the case of correlated observations," *Metron, 2* (1923), 646–680.

where N_h is the population size within the hth stratum, S_h is the element standard deviation within the hth stratum,

$$S_h = \left[\frac{1}{N_h - 1} \sum_{i=1}^{N_h} (Y_{hi} - \bar{Y}_h)^2 \right]^{1/2} \tag{2.30}$$

and k is a positive constant.

For a given total sample size n, allocation $(n_1, n_2, n_3, \ldots , n_H)$ may be determined by using (2.29).[7]

$$k = \frac{n}{N \Sigma_{h=1}^{H} W_h S_h} \tag{2.31}$$

To the extent that the allocation of a stratified sample satisfies condition (2.29), its design effect (ratio to simple random variance) will be

$$\text{DEFF}(\bar{y}_{w(\text{opt})}) \doteq 1 - \frac{\Sigma_{h=1}^{H} W_h (\bar{Y}_h - \bar{Y})^2}{S^2} - \frac{\Sigma_{h=1}^{H} W_h (S_h - \bar{S})^2}{S^2}, \tag{2.32}$$

where

$$\bar{S} = \sum_{h=1}^{H} W_h S_h. \tag{2.33}$$

Remembering that decreases in the design effect indicate increases in efficiency, the following points should be noted. The second and third terms in (2.32) must always be nonnegative. As a result, an allocation that satisfies condition (2.29) will never be less efficient than a nonstratified simple random sample. The first two terms in (2.32) are the same two terms that express the design effect for proportionate allocation (2.27). Thus, the degree to which optimal allocation represents an improvement over proportionate allocation depends on the magnitude of the third term, $\Sigma_{h=1}^{H} W_h (S_h - \bar{S})^2/S^2$. To the extent that the stratum specific element standard deviations S_h differ from each other and their weighted mean $\bar{S}$, optimal allocation will produce significant gains in efficiency over proportionate allocation.

Lest the reader be left with the impression that gains in sample efficiency will always result from designs that attempt to use optimal allocation, the following cautions should be kept in mind. The formulas that express the conditions for optimal allocation do so in terms of population parameters. To the extent that the stratum specific standard deviations S_h must be estimated or guessed, the resulting allocations may be far from optimal. If estimates of these parameters are too far off, the resulting allocation may produce sampling variances that are larger than either simple proportionate allocation or even simple random sampling.

The second point to be remembered is that most surveys are not designed

---

[7] This formula may lead to sample sizes n_h that exceed the corresponding population sizes N_h. For strata where $n_h > N_h$, the sample size should be set equal to the population size, and the formula should be reapplied to the remaining strata.

to provide estimates for a single variable. Even if the relevant stratum specific standard deviations S_h are known for each of the variables of interest, an allocation that is optimal for one may be quite inefficient for another. In general, optimal allocation techniques resulting in disproportionate allocation have application in samples of organizations or establishments where the basic variables measured are correlated with the size of the organization; the formation of strata can be based on this size. Optimal allocation may also be appropriate in situations where the costs of data collection are very different among the various strata. When the per unit costs of the survey are different among the strata, the maximum efficiency per dollar will be achieved when the sampling rates in the strata are made proportional to the stratum specific standard deviation divided by the square root of the stratum specific per element cost. This may be expressed as

$$f_h = K \frac{S_h}{\sqrt{J_h}}, \tag{2.34}$$

or

$$n_h = KN_h \frac{S_h}{\sqrt{J_h}}, \tag{2.35}$$

where S_h is the per element standard deviation within the hth stratum, J_h is the per element cost of the survey within the hth stratum, and K is a positive constant.

Using the cost units J_h, a sample will have total cost $C = \Sigma_{h=1}^H J_h n_h$. For a fixed budget C_0, minimum variance for the estimate $\bar{y}_w$ will be achieved when

$$K = C_0/N \sum_{h=1}^H W_h S_h \sqrt{J_h}. \tag{2.36}$$

The formulation given by (2.34), (2.35), and (2.36), which explicitly recognizes the possibility that survey costs may vary among strata, may produce sample allocations that seem to contradict basic statistical principles. In particular, for a fixed budget, optimal allocation procedures will most likely not produce the sample design with the maximum number of cases. For example, suppose we have two strata, of equal size, $N_1 = N_2$, and with equal unit variances, $S_1^2 = S_2^2$. Further, suppose that the per unit costs of data collection are $J_1 = 1$ and $J_2 = 4$, and the total budget for the survey is $C_0 = 3000$. If, for purposes of measurability, we impose a minimum sample size of two on each of the strata, this budget will support a sample of 2994 cases, ($n_1 = 2992$ and $n_2 = 2$). For these conditions, however, the most efficient sample design [lowest var($\bar{y}_w$)] will result with a total sample size of 1500 cases ($n_1 = 1000$ and $n_2 = 500$).

Allocation Considerations for Rates and Proportions

When the major purpose of the survey is the estimation of percentages and proportions, we may take advantage of certain simplifications that occur in the formulas for stratified sampling. Letting p_h denote the sample proportion from the hth stratum, the weighted estimate of the population proportion p from any stratified sample is given by

$$p_w = \sum_{h=1}^{H} W_h p_h. \tag{2.37}$$

Assuming that simple random sampling is used within all strata, the variance of p_w is given by

$$\text{var}(p_w) = \sum_{h=1}^{H} W_h^2 (1 - f_h) \frac{p_h(1 - p_h)}{n_h - 1}. \tag{2.38}$$

For proportionate allocation, the general variance formula may be approximated as

$$\text{var}(p_{w(\text{prop})}) \doteq \frac{(1 - f)}{n} \sum_{h=1}^{H} W_h p_h (1 - p_h). \tag{2.39}$$

The design effect for a proportionate allocation within simple random sampling within strata becomes

$$\text{DEFF}(p_{w(\text{prop})}) \doteq 1 - \frac{\sum_{h=1}^{H} W_h (P_h - P)^2}{P(1 - P)}, \tag{2.40}$$

where P, the proportion over the entire population, is simply

$$P = \sum_{h=1}^{H} W_h P_h \tag{2.41}$$

If the allocation among strata satisfies the optimality conditions stated by (2.29) to (2.31), the design effect for the estimated proportion $p_{w(\text{opt})}$ is given by

$$\text{DEFF}(p_{w(\text{opt})}) = \text{DEFF}(p_{w(\text{prop})}) - \frac{\sum_{h=1}^{H} W_h (S_h - \bar{S})^2}{S^2}, \tag{2.42}$$

where $\bar{S} = \sum_{h=1}^{H} W_h S_h$; $S_h = [P_h(1 - P_h)]^{1/2}$; and $S^2 = P(1 - P)$.

Assuming that per stratum costs are fairly constant, and the major purpose of the survey is the estimation of percentages or proportions, it is unlikely that optimal allocation will significantly depart from proportional allocation. This result follows from the fact that over a wide range of possible proportions, the corresponding unit standard deviation is fairly constant. The only exception to this occurs when it is possible to divide the population into strata that differ greatly with respect to the attributes under study.

Poststratification

The term *poststratification* is applied to procedures for which the sizes of the various strata are known, but it is impossible to apply stratified selection procedures. In this case, we may apply stratification weights to subpopulation means that are defined on a post hoc basis (i.e., after the data collection is accomplished). In the poststratification process, information obtained in the data-collection phase may serve completely or partially to define inclusion within weighting strata.

In its simplest form, poststratification can be applied to a simple random element sample. Using the previous notation, with the addition of "ps" to denote poststratum, the poststratified mean $\bar{y}_{wps}$, would be computed as

$$\bar{y}_{wps} = \sum_{h=1}^{H} W_{hps}\bar{y}_{hps} \tag{2.43}$$

where $\bar{y}_{hps}$ denotes the per element mean from the hth poststratum, and W_{hps} denotes the weight for the hth poststratum (the proportion of the total population associated with the hth poststratum). The variance of this estimate may be approximated by

$$\text{var}(\bar{y}_{wps}) \doteq \frac{1-f}{n} \sum_{h=1}^{H} W_{hps}s_{hps}^2 + \frac{1-f}{n} \sum_{h=1}^{H} W_{hps}(1-W_{hps})\frac{s_{hps}^2}{n_{hps}} \tag{2.44}$$

where s_{hps}^2 and n_{hps} are the element variance and sample size within the hth poststratum and f is the uniform sampling rate used in the initial simple random sample.

The first term of the variance expression is identical to the variance associated with a proportionate stratified sample with simple random samples within strata. The second term reflects an increase in variance that occurs when the poststratified weighting of the sample must take the place of the implicit weighting in proportionate allocation.

It should be noted that in certain instances where it is impossible to classify the entire population prior to sample selection, it is not always necessary to resort to poststratification. If the population sizes are known, we may determine a sample allocation and apply simple random sampling to the entire population until the allocation is satisfied. In this process, once we have selected a sufficient number of cases within a stratum, all subsequent selections within that stratum are discarded. Although this may appear like a form of "quota sampling," it may be demonstrated that this procedure is identical in probability structure to a procedure in which selection is carried out independently, by simple random sampling within each stratum.

Stratified Sampling Formulas for "Case Weights"

One of the byproducts of the increased availability of computer programs for processing survey data has been the practice of assigning a weight to each sample case when nonepsem designs are used.[8] This weight will be different from the stratum weights W_h used in the previous sections and in standard sampling texts. In the case of stratified sampling, with simple random element selection within each stratum, the "case weight" assigned to ith sample element within the hth stratum should be

$$WT_{hi} = N_h/n_h.[9] \tag{2.45}$$

If we let

$$y'_{hi} = WT_{hi}y_{hi}, \tag{2.46}$$

the formula for the estimate of the population mean given by (2.18) may be written as

$$\bar{y}_w = \frac{\sum_{h=1}^{H}\sum_{i=1}^{n_h} y'_{hi}}{\sum_{h=1}^{H}\sum_{i=1}^{n_h} WT_{hi}}. \tag{2.47}$$

By similar manipulation, the formula for the estimated variance of $\bar{y}_w$ given by (2.22) and (2.23) may be expressed as

$$\text{var}(\bar{y}_w) = \left(\sum_{h=1}^{H}\sum_{i=1}^{n_h} WT_{hi}\right)^{-2} \sum_{h=1}^{H} (1 - f_h)n_h s_h'^2, \tag{2.48}$$

where

$$s_h'^2 = \left[\sum_{i=1}^{n_h} y_{hi}'^2 - \frac{(\sum_{i=1}^{n_h} y'_{hi})^2}{n_h}\right]\Big/(n_h - 1). \tag{2.49}$$

Although these formulas may appear more complex than their counterparts introduced earlier, they are well suited for computers. By making use of the case weights WT_{hi} it is not necessary to separately enter values for the stratum mean weights ($W_1, W_2, \ldots, W_H$). If the sampling fractions f_h are

[8] This weight may be normed so that the sum of all weights will equal the total number elements in the population. Alternatively, it may be normed to sum to the total sample size or the effective sample size. In this latter situation, an average design effect may be determined over a large set of variables, and the effective sample size set equal to the actual sample size divided by the average design effect. Use of effective sample size in this context has been suggested as a method for obtaining approximately correct test levels in program packages where srs formulas are applied and n is taken as the sum of the weights.

[9] Formula (2.45) assumes that data are available for all initially selected sample cases. In actual surveys where nonresponse is present, this formula will often be changed so that the sum of the weights within the stratum will equal the population stratum size. A very simple adjustment would set $WT_{hi} = N_h/m_h$, where m_h denotes the number of completed cases within the hth stratum. A similar approach of assigning case weights is often used when poststratification adjustments are applied. Although the formulas given in the remainder of this chapter ignore the extra variance contribution associated with poststratification (see 2.44), this neglected term is often small. Thus, as an approximation, the more general formulas (using case weights) given in later sections of this chapter may be used in the case of prestratification, poststratification, or some combination of these methods.

such that the finite population correction factors $(1 - f_h)$ should not be assumed to be 1, they may be computed from the case weights as

$$f_h = n_h \bigg/ \sum_{i=1}^{n_h} WT_{hi}. \tag{2.50}$$

2.3. CLUSTER SAMPLING

Introduction

Up to this point, we have focused on sample designs that resulted in the selection of individual elements. These elements might have been selected by simple random or **systematic** selection, either from an entire population or separately from two or more strata. In all cases, however, the final and ultimate unit selected has been the individual population element. Using the techniques we have discussed so far, suppose we wish to select a national sample of 1500 persons age 18 and over, living in households, in order to obtain personal interview data about general attitudes, labor force participation, and utilization of health care services. Let us further suppose that we were able to obtain a complete name and address list of all persons in our population. Using address information we might first stratify our sample on the basis of the 9 basic census divisions. Next we might subdivide each of these 9 strata into two or three groupings on the basis of urbanization (e.g., central cities of metropolitan areas, noncentral cities of metropolitan areas, and nonmetropolitan areas). We might then select a proportionate stratified sample from 27 strata using either simple random selection or systematic selection within each stratum.

This sample should permit sound statistical estimates. The cost would be extremely high, however, perhaps prohibitively high, because of logistical problems associated with interviewing a dispersed sample. Respondents would live in close proximity only in a few large metropolitan areas and in the United States less than 50% of the sample would be found in such centers. Outside the major population centers, sample points would be widely dispersed. A great deal of effort and money would be required to interview each respondent.

Fortunately the problems usually can be avoided. By making use of the techniques of cluster sampling, we select respondents in groups (e.g., five or so in the same block or neighborhood) and still maintain a probability sample. Information collected by the cluster sampling approach will not, on a per case basis, possess the same degree of reliability as an element sample. But, by appropriate choice of a cluster size, the corresponding decrease in cost will more than make up for this loss.[10] In addition, cluster sampling provides a way

[10] The choice of an optimal cluster size is discussed in a later section. The situation described here is very common. Specifically we may have certain design options that will produce highly efficient samples when viewed on a per case basis (i.e., when examined in terms of design effect). These highly efficient designs must be compared in terms of total cost with designs that have lower per case efficiencies. Thus, rather than examining design effects we must examine effective sample sizes per unit cost.

to select probability samples when a complete element specific frame is not available. In the example just presented, we assumed that a complete listing of all persons 18 years of age and older was actually available for the United States. In fact, such lists, if they exist at all, are not generally available. Cluster sampling, however, requires only that we list clusters. Such lists (e.g., a list of all blocks or blocklike units within the United States) do exist and are accessible to the public.

The Theory of Cluster Sampling

Following the lead of most sampling texts, this chapter presents the theory of cluster sampling in two parts. The first part assumes the rather unrealistic situation in which we have access to sampling frames of naturally formed clusters that have equal numbers of elements. In this case, the mathematical theory associated with sampling and sample estimation is exact and relatively straightforward. Then we consider the realistic situation in which clusters contain unequal numbers of elements. In this case, the theory and many of the formulas become significantly more complex.

Cluster Sampling Theory—Equal Size Clusters

We assume a population of N elements, partitioned into A clusters each consisting of B elements ($A \times B = N$). We use $Y_{\alpha\beta}$ to denote the value for variable y associated with the βth element ($\beta = 1, \ldots , B$) in the αth cluster ($\alpha = 1, \ldots , A$). The population mean $\bar{Y}$ may be expressed as the simple mean of the element values in the population

$$\bar{Y} = \frac{1}{A \times B} \sum_{\alpha=1}^{A} \sum_{\beta=1}^{B} Y_{\alpha\beta}. \qquad (2.51)$$

Defining the mean for the αth cluster as

$$\bar{Y}_\alpha = \frac{1}{B} \sum_{\beta=1}^{B} Y_{\alpha\beta}, \qquad (2.52)$$

the population mean may also be expressed as the mean of the A individual cluster means

$$\bar{Y} = \frac{1}{A} \sum_{\alpha=1}^{A} \bar{Y}_\alpha. \qquad (2.53)$$

If we select a simple random sample of size a out of A clusters, and include in our sample all B elements that comprise each of the selected clusters, our total sample size will be $n = a \times B$. Our sample will qualify as epsem since each element in the population will have an equal probability of entering the sample. The uniform probability of selection is $f = a/A$. For this sample design, an unbiased estimator of the population mean is given by the simple mean of all sample element values

$$\bar{y}_{cl} = \frac{1}{a \times B} \sum_{\alpha=1}^{a} \sum_{\beta=1}^{B} y_{\alpha\beta}, \tag{2.54}$$

where $y_{\alpha\beta}$ denotes the value for variable y associated with the βth element in the αth sample cluster.

Alternatively, if we define the element mean of the αth sample cluster as

$$\bar{y}_{\alpha} = \frac{1}{B} \sum_{\beta=1}^{B} y_{\alpha\beta}, \tag{2.55}$$

we may express the per element sample mean $\bar{y}_{cl}$ as

$$\bar{y}_{cl} = \frac{1}{a} \sum_{\alpha=1}^{a} \bar{y}_{\alpha}. \tag{2.56}$$

The estimator of the sampling variance of $\bar{y}_{cl}$ is given by

$$\text{var}(\bar{y}_{cl}) = (1 - f) \frac{s_a^2}{a} \tag{2.57}$$

where

$$s_a^2 = \frac{1}{(a-1)} \sum_{\alpha=1}^{a} (\bar{y}_{\alpha} - \bar{y}_{cl})^2. \tag{2.58}$$

The symbol s_a^2 denotes a variance of cluster means about the estimated population mean. This formula (2.57) makes it clear that we are treating the cluster sample of n elements as a simple random sample where the basic units are cluster means, $\bar{y}_{\alpha}$. Since the overall estimate of the population mean (2.56) is the per unit mean of the cluster means, expression (2.57) follows from simple random sampling theory.

Within Cluster Subsampling

It is not necessary to gather data from all units within a selected cluster. We may sample within each of the selected clusters. We will assume a first stage of sampling that consists of a simple random (with replacement) selection of a out of A first-stage units (clusters) each of size B. For those units selected, we follow with a second stage of sampling (without replacement) of b out of B units. By this two-stage process we select a sample of size $n = a \times b$ elements. The resulting sample is epsem and the uniform probability of selection is $f = (a/A) \times (b/B)$. If b out of B elements are selected within the cluster, the cluster mean can be defined as

$$\bar{y}_{\alpha} = \frac{1}{b} \sum_{\beta=1}^{b} y_{\alpha\beta}. \tag{2.59}$$

The estimated population mean, then, is

$$\bar{y}_{cl} = \frac{1}{a} \sum_{\alpha=1}^{a} \bar{y}_{\alpha}. \tag{2.60}$$

This formula is equivalent to the one used in the case where no cluster subsampling takes place.

Whenever cluster sampling makes use of within-cluster subselection, there are two basic approaches that may be used in the development of sample variance estimators. One approach is based on components of variance models in analysis of variance (ANOVA). These formulas give sampling variance of an estimator of the population mean, as well as a within cluster and between cluster components of variance. The second approach makes use of the concept of "ultimate clusters."[11] The multistage sample design that results in the selection of a set of a ultimate clusters of elements is treated as if all elements were partitioned into ultimate clusters and a single stage sample were drawn. In this section, we will cover both of these approaches to variance estimation. In the remainder of this chapter, however, we will make use of the ultimate cluster approach to variance estimation.[12]

If selection is carried out without replacement at both the first stage and the second stage of sampling, the variance of $\bar{y}_{cl}$ is estimated, in an unbiased fashion by

$$\text{var}(\bar{y}_{cl}) = \left(1 - \frac{a}{A}\right)\frac{s_a^2}{a} + \left(1 - \frac{b}{B}\right)\frac{a}{A}\frac{s_b^2}{ab}, \tag{2.61}$$

where

$$s_a^2 = \frac{1}{(a-1)}\sum_{\alpha=1}^{a}(\bar{y}_\alpha - \bar{y}_{cl})^2 \tag{2.62}$$

and

$$s_b^2 = \frac{1}{a(b-1)}\sum_{\alpha=1}^{a}\sum_{\beta=1}^{b}(y_{\alpha\beta} - \bar{y}_\alpha)^2. \tag{2.63}$$

In this formulation, the sampling variance given in (2.61) is broken into a between cluster component and a within cluster component by the first and second terms, respectively.

The ultimate cluster approach to variance estimation is designed to simplify computations in those cases where the number of primary (first-stage) selections is small relative to the total number of primary units (i.e., $a/A \doteq 0$).

---

[11] The term "*ultimate*" *cluster* was introduced by Hansen, Hurowitz, and Madow in 1953, "The term 'ultimate cluster' is used to denote the aggregate of units included in the sample from a primary unit [p. 242]." The term is sometimes misunderstood to mean the final segments used in national multistage samples. Used correctly, all final segments that are derived from a single primary selection make a single ultimate cluster.

[12] The ultimate cluster approach is used because of its simplicity and generality. The component method of variance estimation may be carried out for most measurable designs. However, this approach must be altered to fit each individual design.

In this case the variance of the cluster mean $\bar{y}_{cl}$ may be reasonably approximated:[13]

$$\text{var}(\bar{y}_{cl}) = (1 - f)s_a^2/a \qquad (2.64)$$

where $f = ab/AB$ and s_a^2 is defined by (2.62).

Intraclass Correlation and Design Effect

If subsampling is done from equal-size clusters, the design effect $\text{DEFF}(\bar{y}_{cl})$ is approximately

$$\text{DEFF} = [1 + (b - 1)\text{roh}] \qquad (2.65)$$

where b denotes the size of the ultimate cluster used in the design and roh is a measure of the intraclass correlation for variable y.[14] The intraclass correlation roh is a measure of the degree to which element values within the same cluster are similar to one another. If all elements within the same cluster have exactly the same value, the intraclass correlation measure roh is equal to $+1$. If element values are assigned to clusters at random, roh is equal to zero. The lowest possible value for roh is $-1/(b - 1)$. This occurs if there are b different values for variable y and if each of these possible values appears once in each cluster. In most applications, the value of roh will be positive. If roh can be estimated from a pretest or from prior studies, its value may be used in conjunction with cost models to determine the optimal cluster size.

---

[13] The ultimate cluster approach assumes that the first stage sampling rate is sufficiently small so that the effect of the finite population correction at that stage will be negligible. Expressed in a different way, it assumes that the set of all possible samples that might be selected if all ultimate units were first created and then sampled is the same as the set of samples that might be selected with the sample design actually used.

[14] The intraclass correlation coefficient described by *roh* differs slightly from its usual definition. The intraclass correlation is usually defined as

$$\text{RHO} = 1 - \left(\frac{S_b^2}{S^2}\right)\left(\frac{N}{N - 1}\right)$$

where

$$S^2 = \frac{1}{N - 1}\sum_{\alpha=1}^{A}\sum_{\beta=1}^{B}(Y_{\alpha\beta} - \bar{Y})^2,$$

and

$$S_b^2 = \frac{1}{A(B - 1)}\sum_{\alpha=1}^{A}\sum_{\beta=1}^{B}(Y_{\alpha\beta} - \bar{Y}_\alpha)^2.$$

The measure of intraclass correlation used in (2.65) is defined as $\text{ROH} = 1 - (S_b^2/S^{*2})$, where $S^{*2} = S_a^2 + (B - 1/B)S_b^2$. Using the same components, the value S^2 may be expressed as $(N - 1/N)S^2 = (A - 1/A)S_a^2 + (B - 1/B)S_b^2$, thus, the difference between RHO and ROH is quite small.

For example, let the cost of sampling and data collection be expressed as:

$$C = nc + aC_a \qquad (2.66)$$

where

C = total cost,
n = total sample size,
c = cost per element that does not depend on the number of clusters used in the design,
a = the number of distinct clusters,
C_a = costs that are dependent on the number of clusters, expressed on a per cluster basis.

Under this model, the optimum cluster size b is

$$\text{optimum } b = \left[\frac{C_a(1 - \text{roh})}{c \text{ roh}}\right]^{1/2} \qquad (2.67)$$

These same ideas can be extended to cluster samples having three or more stages. An initial selection of a clusters is made from a population of A clusters. Each selected cluster is subsampled at the rate b/B. The resulting subsampled units may be further subsampled. If the selection probabilities are kept constant across relevant units at each stage of selection, the final sample will be epsem. In situations where subsampling involves more than a single stage, component of variance estimators are available but usually are cumbersome. The ultimate cluster approach to variance estimation (2.64) may be used, as given, by letting $\bar{y}_\alpha$ denote the mean of the αth ultimate cluster and f the overall selection probability through all stages of sampling (i.e., $f = f_1 \times f_2 \times f_3 \times \cdots$).

Cluster Sampling Theory—Unequal Size Clusters

In most situations, the nonelement level frames available for sampling consist of clusters of unequal size. Some examples of these frames are lists of schools (as a nonelement level frame of students), lists or maps of blocks or blocklike units (as a nonelement level frame for households or persons), and lists of departments (as a nonelement level frame of employees). By making use of single or multistage selection, we may use frames of this sort to produce probability samples. At each stage of the sampling process, we need to obtain frames only for the units that have not fallen out of the selection process at prior stages. For example, suppose we wish to select a sample of adults in a city and are unable to obtain a complete and up-to-date list of this population on an element level basis (i.e., individual names and addresses for all adults). We might begin by obtaining a complete list of block or blocklike units that completely covers all areas in the city. In the first stage of sampling, we select an epsem sample of these blocks with probability f_1. Prior to the second stage of sampling we obtain a listing of dwelling units for those blocks that were selected into the sample at the first stage. Thus, we develop our second stage frame only for the units that were not dropped out in the prior (first) stage of sampling. This list of dwelling units is then subsampled at a constant rate. That is, within each primary selection (each block selected at stage one) we sample dwelling units at a fixed sampling rate f_2. All adults within the dwelling units selected at the second stage of sampling constitute our final epsem sample.

In this situation each ultimate cluster consists of the adults selected within each block chosen at the first stage of sampling. Assuming that we applied equal probability sampling at both the first and second stages, our final sample would be epsem ($f_1 \times f_2 = f$, for all adults). Of special interest to us is the fact that the resulting ultimate clusters of adults are not of equal size. In fact, given the rather inefficient sample design we have hypothesized, there would be extensive variability in the sizes of the ultimate sample clusters. This variability in cluster size does not, in general, invalidate our survey estimates. It does make the statistical theory associated with these estimates significantly more complex, however. Most standard statistical theory views the sample mean as a sum of random variables divided by a fixed constant sample size. Whenever we deal with a probability sample of clusters that are unequal in size, however, the ultimate sample size that results is also a random variable. Expressed another way, if we apply an equal probability selection procedure to a frame of unequal size clusters, the expected sample size will be $E(n) = fN$, where f is the overall equal probability of selection and N is the total population size (possibly unknown). Depending on the particular first-stage units selected, the particular sample size may be quite different from $E(n)$. From a statistical standpoint, the fact that the sample size is no longer constant, forces us to view the sample per element mean as a ratio of random variables.

Using the ultimate cluster approach, our population is viewed as consisting of A ultimate clusters each of size X_α elements. Individual population element values for variable Y are denoted by $Y_{\alpha\beta}$, where $\alpha = 1, \ldots, A$ and $\beta = 1, \ldots, X_\alpha$. The mean for the total population may be expressed as

$$\bar{Y} = R = \frac{\sum_{\alpha=1}^{A} \sum_{\beta=1}^{X_\alpha} Y_{\alpha\beta}}{\sum_{\alpha=1}^{A} X_\alpha} \tag{2.68}$$

We have used the symbol R in place of $\bar{Y}$ to indicate that when these clusters are sampled, the estimator formed by the sample mean will be a ratio of two random variables.

If we define Y_α as the total for variable y from the αth cluster

$$Y_\alpha = \sum_{\beta=1}^{X_\alpha} Y_{\alpha\beta}, \tag{2.69}$$

we may also express the population mean R as the ratio of the sum of the cluster totals Y_α divided by the sum of the cluster sizes X_α:

$$R = \sum_{\alpha=1}^{A} Y_\alpha \bigg/ \sum_{\alpha=1}^{A} X_\alpha \tag{2.70}$$

If we select a simple random sample of a ultimate clusters out of the population of A ultimate clusters, the per element population mean is estimated by

$$r = \sum_{\alpha=1}^{a} y_\alpha \bigg/ \sum_{\alpha=1}^{a} x_\alpha \qquad (2.71)$$

where the symbol y_α denotes the total for variable y for the αth ultimate cluster selected into the sample, and the symbol x_α denotes the number of elements in the αth ultimate cluster selected into the sample. The symbol r is used instead of $\bar{y}$ to indicate that the estimator, although computed as a mean, is statistically a ratio estimator.

Because the sample mean is a ratio, it is subject to some degree of statistical bias [i.e., $E(r) \neq R$].[15] For the moment, however, we shall assume that this bias is trivial. For estimators of this type, the sampling variance is only partially determined by the number of selected units and the basic variability among the ultimate cluster totals y_α. Estimation of the sampling variance of r also involves the variability among the cluster sizes x_α and the covariance (correlation) between the cluster totals and the cluster sizes (x_α, y_β pairs).

The sample estimator of the variance of r is given by

$$\text{var}(r) = \frac{1-f}{x^2} a(s_y^2 + r^2 s_x^2 - 2rs_{xy}), \qquad (2.72)$$

where

$$s_y^2 = \frac{1}{a-1} \left(\sum_{\alpha=1}^{a} y_\alpha^2 - \frac{y^2}{a} \right), \qquad (2.73)$$

$$s_x^2 = \frac{1}{a-1} \left(\sum_{\alpha=1}^{a} x_\alpha^2 - \frac{x^2}{a} \right), \qquad (2.74)$$

$$s_{xy} = \frac{1}{a-1} \left(\sum_{\alpha=1}^{a} x_\alpha y_\alpha - \frac{xy}{a} \right), \qquad (2.75)$$

$$y = \sum_{\alpha=1}^{a} y_\alpha, \qquad (2.76)$$

$$x = \sum_{\alpha=1}^{a} x_\alpha. \qquad (2.77)$$

The units of expression for s_y^2, s_x^2, and s_{xy} are cluster totals. It should be noted that in the case of the ratio estimator r, the expression for $\text{var}(r)$ is an approximation developed from the first order terms of the Taylor series expansion of y/x.

The coefficient of variation associated with final element sample size provides an upper limit on the degree of bias associated with the ratio estimator r.

[15] An upper limit for bias(r) is given by (2.79).

The coefficient of variation of the element sample size may be estimated as

$$cv(x) = \frac{[(1 - f)as_x^2]^{1/2}}{x} \tag{2.78}$$

An approximate upper limit on the absolute bias of r divided by the standard error of r is given as

$$\frac{|bias(r)|}{var(r)^{1/2}} \leq cv(x) \tag{2.79}$$

In general, $cv(x)$ should be less than .10 (10%). Various empirical studies have shown that for values of $cv(x)$ that are less than .20 (20%), the estimator given by (2.72) provides a reasonably good approximation for the variance, and in fact, the mean square error of the ratio estimator r.

Sample Estimators of the Population Total

For the sample designs discussed prior to the section on unequal size clusters, all sample means could be changed into estimators of the population totals by use of the factor N, the total number of elements in the population. In a similar fashion, the variance of the estimator $N\bar{y}$ is given by $var(N\bar{y}) = N^2 var(\bar{y})$. In the case of ratio means, the situation is somewhat different.

First, in situations where the sample design involves the selection of unequal size clusters, the total number of elements N in the population may be unknown. It is not necessary to know the total population size because the frame for a sample involving unequal size clusters need not be an element level list of the entire population.

Second, in those instances where the population size N is known, its use may not provide the best (lowest variance) estimate of the population total.

Under the assumption that the overall probability of selection for elements is equal, the population total for variable y may be estimated as

$$Fy = F \sum_{\alpha=1}^{a} y_\alpha \tag{2.80}$$

where $F = 1/f$, the inverse of the uniform probability of selection, and $y = $ the sample total for variable y.

The estimate of the sampling variance of Fy is given by

$$var(Fy) = F^2(1 - f)as_y^2 \tag{2.81}$$

If the number of elements in the population is known, we have a second option with respect to estimation of the population total Y. Recalling that in the case of unequal size clusters, we have used the symbol X to denote the number of elements in the population; our alternate estimate of Y is given as

$$Xr = X \sum_{\alpha=1}^{a} y_\alpha \bigg/ \sum_{\alpha=1}^{a} x_\alpha. \tag{2.82}$$

The estimated sampling variance of Xr is computed as

$$\text{var}(Xr) = X^2 \text{ var}(r). \tag{2.83}$$

If X is known, the determination of an appropriate estimator should be based on the relative magnitude of the corresponding variances for Xr and Fy. It is possible that different estimators may be preferred for different variables. Depending on the computer programs available, this determination of estimators may be based on the following expression:

$$\frac{\text{var}(Xr)}{\text{var}(Fy)} = 1 + \left[\frac{\text{cv}(x)^2}{\text{cv}(y)^2} - 2\rho_{xy} \frac{\text{cv}(x)}{\text{cv}(y)} \right], \tag{2.84}$$

where

$$\text{cv}(y) = [(1 - f)as_y^2]^{1/2}/y, \tag{2.85}$$

$$\rho_{xy} = \frac{s_{xy}}{(s_x^2 s_y^2)^{1/2}}, \tag{2.86}$$

and $\text{cv}(x)$ is given by (2.78).

Cluster Sampling with Unequal Probabilities of Selection

The formulas presented in the preceding sections on unequal cluster sampling assume a uniform probability of selection for all elements. This restriction was applied for simplicity of presentation and is not necessary when using such designs. We may, within the context of single or multistage cluster sampling, apply different probabilities of selection to sampling units at any stage of selection. In a later section we discuss how varying the probabilities may be used to control ultimate cluster size. In the present section, we assume that each element selected into the sample may carry a different probability.

A simple example of this type of unequal probability comes from an extension of the hypothetical unequal cluster size sample involving blocks in a city at stage one and all adults within selected households at stage two. Initially, we assume that interviews would be conducted with all adults residing within selected households. Since blocks as well as households within blocks are selected with equal probabilities, the probability of selection for individuals is also equal. Suppose that we modify this design by selecting a single adult from each selected household. In this case, the probability of selection associated with a particular adult would be inversely proportional to the number of adults in the household containing the adult. As a result, the elements that comprise each ultimate cluster (block) will have different selection probabilities.

In order to describe the appropriate formulas for such situations we will require a slightly more extensive notation system.

Let $y_{\alpha\beta}$ = the value for variable y associated with the βth sample element of the αth ultimate cluster.

$x_{\alpha\beta} \equiv 1$ (a counter variable) for the βth sample element within the αth ultimate cluster.

$f_{\alpha\beta}$ = the probability of selection associated with the βth sample element within the αth ultimate cluster.

Weighted values of $y_{\alpha\beta}$ and $x_{\alpha\beta}$ are defined as

$$y'_{\alpha\beta} = y_{\alpha\beta}/f_{\alpha\beta}, \tag{2.87}$$

and

$$x'_{\alpha\beta} = x_{\alpha\beta}/f_{\alpha\beta}, \tag{2.88}$$

Ultimate cluster totals y'_α and x'_α are formed as

$$y'_\alpha = \sum_{\beta=1}^{x_\alpha} y'_{\alpha\beta}, \tag{2.89}$$

and

$$x'_\alpha = \sum_{\beta=1}^{x_\alpha} x'_{\alpha\beta}, \tag{2.90}$$

where both sums are taken over the x_α elements that comprise the αth ultimate cluster.

The weighted per element ratio mean r is estimated as

$$r = \sum_{\alpha=1}^{a} y'_\alpha \Big/ \sum_{\alpha=1}^{a} x'_\alpha \tag{2.91}$$

This is exactly the same estimation form used with equal probabilities of selection with y'_α and x'_α substituted for y_α and x_α, respectively.

The variance of r is computed as

$$\text{var}(r) = \frac{a}{(x')^2} (s_{y'}^2 + r^2 s_{x'}^2 - 2rs_{x'y'}), \tag{2.92}$$

with terms $(x')^2$, $s_{y'}^2$, $s_{x'}^2$, and $s_{x'y'}$ as defined by (2.73) to (2.77), substituting x'_α for x_α and y'_α for y_α.

This variance estimator does not include terms corresponding to the equal probability finite population correction factor. In most situations the finite population correction will be very close to unity, and thus may be ignored. For further discussion the reader is directed to Kish (1965).

2.4. ADVANCED TOPICS

Unequal Size Cluster Sampling with Stratification

Unequal size cluster sampling, with one or more stages, is often used within the framework of a stratified design. As noted in our discussion of stratification, different selection techniques may be applied within each of the strata that comprise the total population. Thus, a design might make use of simple random element sampling within strata where element level lists are available, and unequal size cluster sampling in strata where a frame does not exist at the individual element level.

When cluster sampling is used with stratification, there are two basic approaches that may be followed in the estimation of the overall population mean. The *separate ratio estimator* approach, which is analogous to the approach taken with simple random element sampling within strata, involves the separate estimation of a per element mean for each stratum. These separate mean estimates are then combined with population weights W_h to produce the estimate of the mean for the entire population. This approach requires known stratum weights.

A second approach, called the *combined ratio method,* uses the inverse of the probabilities of selection to produce an estimate of Y_h and X_h (i.e., the population totals for the variable y and the number of elements) within each stratum. Rather than estimating the ratio mean for each stratum, the estimates of Y_h are added across strata to produce an estimate of the population total for variable y. In a similar fashion, the estimates of X_h are added across strata to produce an estimate of X for the entire population. The ratio of these two estimates yields the final mean—per element—estimate for the entire population.

Formulas for the combined and separate ratio estimators of the population mean $\bar{Y}$ and their corresponding estimators of variance require the following definitions. We assume an ultimate cluster model with H stratum and a_h ultimate clusters per stratum. The symbol $x_{h\alpha}$ denotes the number of elements selected in the αth ultimate cluster in stratum h.

Let

$y_{h\alpha\beta}$ = the value for variable y from the βth element within the αth ultimate cluster of the hth stratum.

$x_{h\alpha\beta} \equiv 1$, a counting variable defined for the βth element within the αth ultimate cluster of the hth stratum.

$f_{h\alpha\beta}$ = the probability of selection associated with the βth element within the αth ultimate cluster of the hth stratum.

The "weighted" values of $y_{h\alpha\beta}$ and $x_{n\alpha\beta}$ are defined as

$$y'_{h\alpha\beta} = y_{h\alpha\beta}/f_{h\alpha\beta} \tag{2.93}$$

and

$$x'_{h\alpha\beta} = x_{h\alpha\beta}/f_{h\alpha\beta}. \tag{2.94}$$

The "weighted" ultimate cluster total for y and x are defined as

$$y'_{h\alpha} = \sum_{\alpha=1}^{x_{h\alpha}} y'_{h\alpha\beta} \tag{2.95}$$

and

$$x'_{h\alpha} = \sum_{\alpha=1}^{x_{h\alpha}} x'_{h\alpha\beta}, \tag{2.96}$$

where both sums are taken over the $x_{h\alpha}$ elements within the $h\alpha$th ultimate cluster.

The weighted stratum totals y'_h and x'_h, which are the sample estimators of the corresponding stratum totals in the population, are defined as

$$y'_h = \sum_{\alpha=1}^{a_h} y'_{h\alpha} \tag{2.97}$$

and

$$x'_h = \sum_{\alpha=1}^{a_h} x'_{h\alpha}. \tag{2.98}$$

In both cases these sums are formed across the a_h ultimate clusters within the hth stratum.

The "combined" ratio estimator of the per element mean $\bar{Y}$ is defined as:

$$r = \sum_{h=1}^{H} y'_h \bigg/ \sum_{h=1}^{H} x'_h \tag{2.99}$$

Alternatively, if we define the symbols y' and x', the weighted sample estimators of population totals Y and X, by

$$y' = \sum_{h=1}^{H} y'_h \tag{2.100}$$

and

$$x' = \sum_{h=1}^{H} x'_h, \tag{2.101}$$

we may also express the "combined" ratio estimator r as

$$r = y'/x'. \tag{2.102}$$

If the number of elements in each of the hth strata is known outside the context of the survey, we may alternatively estimate the per element population mean by the separate ratio estimator r_s. Letting W_h denote the proportion of the population elements in stratum h, the separate ratio estimator is formed as

$$r^* = \sum_{h=1}^{H} W_h r_h, \tag{2.103}$$

where r_h, the sample estimator of the per element mean in the hth stratum is defined as

$$r_h = y'_h/x'_h. \tag{2.104}$$

The variance of the combined ratio estimator r and the separate ratio estimator r^* is expressed in terms of unit variances and covariances for stratum totals, y_h' and x_h'. Let

$$\text{var}(y_h') = \frac{a_h}{a_h - 1} \left[\sum_{\alpha=1}^{a_h} y_{h\alpha}'^2 - \frac{y_h'^2}{a_h} \right], \tag{2.105}$$

$$\text{var}(x_h') = \frac{a_h}{a_h - 1} \left[\sum_{\alpha=1}^{a_h} x_{h\alpha}'^2 - \frac{x_h'^2}{a_h} \right] \tag{2.106}$$

and

$$\text{cov}(x_h', y_h') = \frac{a_h}{(a_h - 1)} \left(\sum_{\alpha=1}^{a_h} x_{h\alpha}' y_{h\alpha}' - \frac{x_h' y_h'}{a_h} \right) \tag{2.107}$$

The estimator of the variance of the combined ratio estimator r is given by

$$\text{var}(r) = \frac{1}{(x')^2} \sum_{h=1}^{H} [\text{var}(y_h') + r^2 \, \text{var}(x_h') - 2r \, \text{cov}(x_h', y_h')]. \tag{2.108}$$

The estimator of the variance of the separate ratio estimator r^* is given by

$$\text{var}(r^*) = \sum_{h=1}^{H} \frac{W_h^2}{(x_h')^2} [\text{var}(y_h') + r_h^2 \, \text{var}(x_h') - 2r_h \, \text{cov}(x_h', y_h')]. \tag{2.109}$$

It should be noted that neither of these formulas includes the finite population correction factor. In the case where the value of these factors is not small, and the probability of selection within the hth stratum is uniformly f_h, the term $(1 - f_h)$ may be added to the estimators of the variance and covariance given by (2.105) through (2.107).[16]

Sample Selection of Cluster Samples with Probabilities
Proportional to Some Estimated Measure of Size

Although ratio estimators are designed to cope with cluster units that are unequal in size, extreme cluster size variability is usually not desirable. From a statistical standpoint, extreme variation in cluster size may lead to nontrivial bias in the ratio estimator itself. A large coefficient of variation in cluster size may weaken the applicability of the Taylor series approximation used in developing an estimator of the sampling variance for r. Moreover, large variability in cluster size lessens our ability to control the total number of units selected in the total sample. It makes the estimation of interviewer load for particular clusters very difficult to anticipate prior to the final stage of sample selection. If the final stage of sample selection involves the listing of housing units by the interviewer, such a situation may be intolerable.

[16] An excellent discussion of finite population correction terms when varying probabilities are used within strata may be found in Section 11.7 of Kish (1965).

   Assuming that an overall equal probability sample is desired, the variability in ultimate cluster size will be related to the sizes of the primary sampling units and the selection probabilities applied to these units in the various stages of sampling. If, as was the case in our example of blocks in a city, the probability of selection is uniform in the first stage, we are "locked-in" to the natural variability that exists in the blocks. If we want an epsem sample we must subsample within blocks at a constant rate. If we try to equalize the cluster size in each sample block (by varying the probabilities of selection), the inequality in cluster size will reappear when we apply appropriate weights.

   When faced with first-stage selection units of highly variable size, two techniques may be employed to control variability in ultimate cluster size. Both techniques maintain equal overall probabilities of selection and require estimates of the number of elements within the primary units. These estimates need not be precise or even objective. In general, any degree of positive correlation between estimated size and actual size may be used to induce some degree of size control over variability in ultimate clusters.

   One of these techniques involves the formation of strata on the basis of *estimated primary unit size*. Within each stratum, uniform probabilities of selection are applied to all units at each stage of sampling. Across strata, however, selection probabilities at each stage are set so as to result in equal average size of ultimate clusters.

   The second technique, called *PPS sampling*, involves the use of unit specific variable probabilities at two or more of the stages of selection.[17] In a two-stage sample, this would involve a first-stage selection of primary units with probabilities proportional to the estimated size of the units. Within selected first-stage units, the probability of selection would be determined in order to produce an equal probability of selection across all elements, in all units. This type of selection process may be described by the following formula.

$$f = \left(\frac{a\ \text{MOS}_\alpha}{\sum_{\alpha=1}^A \text{MOS}_\alpha}\right)\left(\frac{b}{\text{MOS}_\alpha}\right), \tag{2.110}$$

where

   MOS_α = the estimated number of elements within the αth primary
         unit in the sampling frame (Measure Of Size),

   a = the desired number of primary selections,

   $b = f \sum_{\alpha=1}^A \text{MOS}_\alpha/a.$

The summation of size measures is taken over all units in the sampling frame from which the selection is to be made. Thus, it is a constant.

---

[17] The letters PPS stand for probability proportional to size. In actual applications, the actual cluster sizes are not known, and must be estimated. The term *measure of size* is often used to describe the estimates, which may be subjective as well as objective, of the cluster sizes in the population.

62 **Martin Frankel**

As a simple illustration, suppose we have a city that contains approximately 200,000 households distributed among 2000 blocks of unequal, but known size. Further, suppose we wish to select an epsem sample of households with overall probability 1/200 in order to yield a sample size of 1000 households. Finally, assume that the sample is to be distributed among 100 primary selections (blocks).

If we select our sample with equal probabilities for all units at each stage, we must use a selection rate of 1/20 at stage one and 1/10 at stage two. If we use the PPS approach, the first-stage probability of selection for the αth block would be set at

$$\frac{a \; \mathrm{MOS}_\alpha}{\Sigma_{\alpha=1}^{A} \; \mathrm{MOS}_\alpha} = \frac{100 \; \mathrm{MOS}_\alpha}{200,000} = \frac{\mathrm{MOS}_\alpha}{2000}.$$

The second-stage selection probability for the αth block would be b/MOS_α, where from (2.110) $b = 200,000/(200)(100) = 10$.

Now, let us consider what would happen to two different size blocks in the population. Suppose block A contains 50 households. If it is selected in the first stage of the first design, it will be subsampled at the rate 1/10 and thus contribute 5 households to the sample. This same block, if selected by the PPS design, will be subsampled at the rate $b/\mathrm{MOS}_\alpha = 10/50$, and will contribute 10 households to the sample. Block B, on the other hand, contains 200 households. If selected by the first design it will be subsampled at the rate 1/10 and contribute 20 households to the sample. If this same block were selected by the PPS design it would only contribute 10 households to the total sample since it would be subsampled at the rate $b/\mathrm{MOS}_\alpha = 10/200$. Thus, under the first design, blocks A and B would have ultimate cluster sizes of 5 and 20, respectively. Using the PPS design, the same blocks would yield ultimate clusters of 10 households.

The complete control of cluster size shown in our example will only occur when the estimated sizes (MOS_α) used in the first stage of selection are in perfect accord with the actual sizes found at the time of second-stage selection. In order to maintain equal probability, subsampling must occur with a rate b/MOS_α, even when the estimated measure of size and the actual size are not the same. As long as there is some degree of positive association between the measures of size used in selecting the first-stage sample and the actual sizes found at the time of subsampling, we will decrease variation in cluster size.

Simple Replicated (Interpenetrating) Subsampling

In order to provide for the estimation of sampling variance, a sample design must provide some degree of internal replication. Normally, this condition for measurability requires a minimum of two independent primary selections from each of the strata that define the total population. However, this requirement does not guarantee the availability of a simple formula for the estimation of variance. In general, as the sample design, or the weighting procedure, or the survey estimate becomes more complex, so does the appropriate formula for estimation of variance. The replicated subsampling approach provides a method that assures the availability of an unbiased and easy to compute estimate of sampling variance.

The basic strategy of replicated subsamples may be divided into four basic steps:

1. Assuming that the total sample is to consist of primary selections (which will produce the desired sample size of n elements), a sample design is developed that will involve the selection of a/k primary units. The value of k must be some integer greater than one and less than a (Deming, 1960, advocates the use of $k = 10$). As long as the conditions required for probability sampling are satisfied, there exists complete flexibility in the design of the sampling plan to select the a/k primary units. The sample design may be as simple as simple random or systematic selection of a/k elements with no stratification. It may be quite complex and involve stratification, unequal size clusters, unequal probabilities, and multiple stages of sampling.

2. Once the sample design is specified, the actual selection process is carried out separately and independently k times, producing k replications.[18]

3. Once data collection is complete, each subsample is processed separately and independently to produce the required estimates of population parameters. For any particular survey estimate there will be k independent "replications" of this estimate. Let e_i denote the survey estimate produced from the ith replicated subsample.

4. The overall survey estimate of the population parameter is developed as

$$\bar{e} = \frac{1}{k} \sum_{i=1}^{k} e_i. \tag{2.111}$$

The sampling variance of $\bar{e}$ is estimated as

$$\text{var}(\bar{e}) = \frac{1}{k(k-1)} \sum_{i=1}^{k} (e_i - \bar{e})^2. \tag{2.112}$$

The method of replicated subsampling provides a flexible method for selecting probability samples that is both simple to implement and has a great deal of intuitive appeal to both statisticians and nonstatisticians. As a result, it is often used when evidence, based on a probability sample, is introduced in the courtroom or in administrative proceedings. Its simplicity does, however, lead to certain limitations. First, since each replicated subsample is of size a/k rather than a, the maximum number of possible strata is reduced. Second, unbiased variance estimation is available for the estimate $\bar{e}$, but this "mean of the replicates" estimator may have larger variance and bias than an estimator developed from individual data values that are pooled across all subsample

---

[18] When multistage sampling is used, all stages except the last should involve selection with replacement. If selection with replacement is used at all stages, the finite population correction factor should not be used. If selection is epsem within each replicate at the rate f/k, the factor $(1 - f)$ should be added to (2.112).

replicates. Finally, the "degrees of freedom" associated with the estimated variance of $\bar{e}$ is equal to $k - 1$. For example, if we use $k = 10$ replicated subsamples each of size 200 elements, 95% confidence interval estimates would involve the factor $t_9 = 2.262$ rather than $z = 1.96$.

Despite these limitations, the method of replicated subsamples provides a very flexible framework for sample design in a great number of survey situations.

Paired Selection Designs for BRR and JRR Variance Estimation

For producing complex estimates there are design alternatives that allow the estimation of sampling errors and remove some of the restrictions imposed by the method of simple replicated subsampling. The paired selection model assumes that the population is partitioned into $a/2$ strata. Within each of these strata, it is assumed that there will be two independent primary selections (ultimate clusters). Following the first stage of sampling there may be any number of subsequent stages and selection may involve equal or unequal final probabilities for elements.

Jackknife repeated replication (JRR) estimates of sampling variance are constructed as follows: We assume $H = a/2$ strata each consisting of two ultimate clusters.

1. Let S denote the entire sample along with any case specific weights that may be required to compensate for unequal probability of selection or poststratification weighting.
2. Let J_h denote the hth jackknife replicate formed by including all cases not in the hth stratum, removing all cases associated with one of the ultimate clusters in the hth stratum and including, twice, the elements associated with the other ultimate cluster in the hth stratum.
3. Let CJ_h denote the hth complement jackknife replicate formed in the same way as the hth jackknife replicate with the eliminated and doubled ultimate clusters interchanged.

We will assume that the function that describes the survey estimate developed from the entire sample is $g(S)$.

The jackknife repeated replication estimator for the variance of $g(S)$ is given by

$$\text{var}_{\text{JRR}}\,[g(S)] = \frac{1}{2}\sum_{h=1}^{H}\{[g(J_h) - g(S)]^2 + [g(CJ_h) - g(S)]^2\} \qquad (2.113)$$

where $g(J_h)$ and $g(CJ_h)$ denote the estimate formed from the individual data values (with optional case weights) from the J_h and CJ_h jackknife and complement samples, respectively.

Balanced repeated replication (BRR) estimates of variance are computed by a slightly different procedure: (a) let H_i denote the ith half-sample formed by including one of the two ultimate clusters in each of the H strata; (b) let C_i denote the ith complement half-sample formed by the ultimate clusters not included in H_i. The process of dividing the sample into half and complement half is repeated K times, where K is the smallest multiple of 4 that exceeds H. The patterns of half and complement half samples are determined so that they satisfy an orthogonal design with each stratum represented by a column, each half-sample by a row, the selection being made of a prespecified ultimate cluster by +1 and the other by −1. The balanced repeated replication estimate of the variance of $g(S)$ is given by

$$\text{var}_{\text{BRR}}\,[g(S)] = \frac{1}{2K}\sum_{i=1}^{K}\{[g(H_i) - g(S)]^2 + [g(C_i) - g(S)]^2\}, \quad (2.114)$$

where $g(H_i)$ and $g(C_i)$ denote the estimate corresponding to $g(S)$ which is derived from the ith half and complement half-sample, respectively. If the estimate is dependent upon the absolute magnitude of the case weights, H_i and C_i should be reweighted, using the same procedures applied to S, to reflect their smaller size.

Confidence limits and tests based upon JRR or BRR variances should assume H degrees of freedom. A more complete description of both methods may be found in Frankel (1971), and Cochran (1977).

2.5. FURTHER READING AND OTHER TOPICS

This chapter has given the reader some of the flavor (without proofs) of the basic theory of survey sampling. Its scope of coverage is far from complete. Notable exclusions include: sampling theory for telephone frame sampling, sample estimation methods involving regression and difference estimators, sampling in time, sample designs for panel studies, multiphase sampling, systematic sampling, methods of controlled selection, development of master sampling frames, and recent developments in the area of finite sampling theory.

Despite efforts by a number of mathematical statisticians, basic theory for complex sample designs in use today has not been unified. Dissemination of new developments in sample design (selection and estimation) occurs on an informal basis and via proceedings and journals. There is still a great time lag between development and appearance in textbooks. Indeed many of the ad hoc principles used by those who design samples do not appear in any textbook. This situation is not due to the lack of excellent texts and textbook authors, but is more the result of the diversity and complexity of the field. The bibliography that follows is divided into three sections: elementary topics, mathematical theory, and practical applications. This classification is simply a subjective guide. Many of the books that are classified as applied, also contain mathematical theory; whereas some of the books classified as elementary, occasionally require a nonelementary knowledge of statistical theory.

BIBLIOGRAPHY

Elementary

Arkin, H.
   1974   *Handbook of Sampling for Auditing and Accounting* (2nd ed.). New York: McGraw–Hill.
Scheaffer, R. L., W. Mendenhall, and L. Ott
   1979   *Elementary Sampling Theory* (2nd ed.). North Scituate, Mass.: Duxbury Press.
Slonim, M. J.
   1967   *Sampling*. New York: Simon and Schuster.
Stuart, A.
   1962   *Basic Ideas of Scientific Sampling*. New York: Hafner.
Sudman, S.
   1976   *Applied Sampling*. New York: Academic Press.
Williams, W. H.
   1978   *A Sampler on Sampling*. New York: Wiley.
Yamane, T.
   1967   *Elementary Sampling Theory*. Englewood Cliffs, N.J.: Prentice–Hall.

Applied

Deming, W. E.
   1960   *Sample Design for Business Research*. New York: Wiley.
Frankel, M. R.
   1971   *Inference from Complex Samples*. Ann Arbor: Institute for Social Research.
Hansen, M. H., W. N. Hurwitz, and W. G. Madow
   1953   *Sample Survey Methods and Theory*. Vol. 1. New York: Wiley.
Jessen, R. L.
   1978   *Statistical Survey Techniques*. New York: Wiley.
Kish, L.
   1965   *Survey Sampling*. New York: Wiley.
Murthy, M. N.
   1967   *Sampling Theory and Methods*. Calcutta, India: Statistical Publishing Society.
Raj, Des.
   1972   *The Design of Sample Surveys*. New York: McGraw–Hill.
Rosander, A. C.
   1977   *Case Studies in Sample Design*. New York: Marcel Decker.
Sukhatme, P. V., and B. V. Sukhatme
   1970   *Sampling Theory of Surveys and Applications*. Ames, Iowa: Iowa State University Press.
Yates, F.
   1960   *Sampling Methods for Censuses and Surveys* (3rd ed.). New York: Hafner.

Mathematical Theory

Cassel, C. M., C. E. Sarndal, and J. H. Wretman
   1977   *Foundations of Inference in Survey Sampling*. New York: Wiley.
Cochran, W. G.
   1977   *Sampling Techniques* (3rd ed). New York: Wiley
Deming, W. E.
   1950   *Some Theory of Sampling*. New York: Wiley (available in Dover edition, 1966).

Hansen, M. H., W. N. Hurwitz, and W. G. Madow
    1953   *Sample Survey Methods and Theory*. Vol. 2. New York: Wiley.
Johnson, N. L., and H. Smith, Eds.
    1969   *New Developments in Survey Sampling*. New York: Wiley.
Konijn, H. S.
    1973   *Statistical Theory of Sample Survey Design and Analysis*. New York: American Elsevier.
Namboodiri, N. K.
    1978   *Survey Sampling and Measurement*. New York: Academic Press.
Raj, Des.
    1968   *Sampling Theory*. New York: McGraw–Hill.

Chapter 3

Measurement[1]

George W. Bohrnstedt

Measurement is a sine qua non of any science. It is therefore somewhat surprising that historically survey researchers have paid scant attention to examining the reliability and validity of their measurements. Of current texts on survey research methods, only Moser and Kalton (1972) present a mathematical treatment of ways for assessing reliability and validity. And even then only six pages are given to the topic. Babbie (1973) refers to the logic of reliability theory in his treatment of index construction, but he bypasses the rather extensive literature that would have provided the student of survey research methods with a more rigorous approach to the topic. Although Warwick and Lininger (1975) introduce the terms *reliability* and *validity* when discussing questionnaire design, they in fact never define them. Yet few if any survey researchers would deny the importance of knowing whether or not one's items measure what they are intended to measure (i.e., whether they are *valid*) and knowing the degree to which items on remeasurement would order individuals responding to them in the same way (i.e., whether they are *reliable*). For this reason we present a more formal treatment of error theory than is ordinarily found in survey research methods textbooks.

[1] Partial support for writing this chapter came from NIMH Training Grant PHS T32 MH 15789-02. The author appreciates useful comments from Robert Somers, Velma Kameoka, Michael Sobel, and his seminars in measurement in 1980 and 1981. Finally, the programming help of Fred Jones is greatly appreciated.

HANDBOOK OF SURVEY RESEARCH

3.1. MEASUREMENT

Measurement is the assignment of numbers to observed phenomena according to certain rules. Thus one might assign the number 1 to all males and 0 to all females; a 0 to those who report they have never attended church or temple in the past month, a 1 to those who reported going one to three times, and a 2 to those who indicated weekly attendance. It is the *rules of correspondence* between the manifest observations and the numbers assigned that define measurement in a given instance. In the latter example, measurement is relatively crude. In designing rules of correspondence one should use the most refined measures available, since the better the measure the more accurately the underlying relationships between variables can be assessed. Thus, in the church attendance example it would have been better to have recorded directly the number of times church or temple attendance occurred.

Since Anderson *et al.* discuss types of measurement in detail in Chapter 12, I will say no more about it here. Instead, I will discuss measurement *error*. When a researcher assigns a number, it is always to an *observable response*. But an important question is what the relationship is between the observed response and the underlying *unobserved* variable that served to generate the response. The difference between the observable and the unobservable variables is defined as *measurement error*.

In the simplest situation we can think of a person's p response x_p as being a linear function of some unobserved "true" variable τ_p and measurement error ε_p, that is, $x_p = \tau_p + \varepsilon_p$ and measurement error is defined as $\varepsilon_p = x_p - \tau_p$.

For a variable x *measured across persons* the assumed relationship between the observed and true scores is

$$x = \tau + \varepsilon. \tag{3.1}$$

3.2. PLATONIC AND CLASSICAL TRUE SCORES

The nature of the true score is problematic. Psychologists, who have been very influential in the development of measurement theory rarely think of τ as an "actual" true score. The variables they examine are primarily cognitive or affective; hence it makes little sense to think of someone's true attitude or emotion in the same sense that it makes sense to think of someone's true 1983 after-tax income, or someone's true vote in the 1980 presidential election. Therefore they often define someone's true score on variable x as the expected value if someone were remeasured an infinite number of times on that variable, that is, $E_p(x) = \tau_p$ where $E_p(\cdot)$ refers to an expected value across a single person.[2]

Survey researchers have tended to think of τ in a second way as well. Sudman and Bradburn (1974) distinguish between two types of responses: be-

---

[2] In general, an expected value is defined as $E(\cdot) = \Sigma x p(x)$. In other words, it is best thought of as a mean.

havioral and psychological states. Behavioral responses are at least in theory verifiable; hence the notion of a real true score, or what psychometricians call a *Platonic true score* (Sutcliffe, 1965), makes sense. True psychological states can only be inferred indirectly, and for this reason the notion of a Platonic true score makes little sense in their measurement. But for behavioral states Platonic scores may be reasonable. In this case the assumed relationships between the true score (Platonic) and the observed x is

$$x = \tau^* + \varepsilon, \tag{3.2}$$

where τ^* refers to a Platonic true score. The assumption of the two different models—(3.1) and (3.2)—makes them substantially different.

For example, given the definition of non-Platonic or *classical true scores* and errors, it follows directly that

$$E(\varepsilon) = 0, \tag{3.3}$$

where $E(\cdot)$ is across persons. That is, the mean (or expected value) of the errors of measurement is zero. Furthermore, classical true scores are assumed to be uncorrelated with the errors of measurement, that is,

$$C(\tau, \varepsilon) = 0. \tag{3.4}$$

The errors of measurement ε_i for a classical true score τ_i associated with an observed x_i, where i refers to the ith item, are assumed to be uncorrelated with other true scores τ_j and their errors of measurement ε_j as well, that is

$$C(\tau_i, \varepsilon_j) = C(\tau_j, \varepsilon_j) = 0. \tag{3.5}$$

From these assumptions it also follows that

$$\sigma_x^2 = \sigma_\tau^2 + \sigma_\varepsilon^2, \tag{3.6}$$

the observed variance is the sum of the true score and error variances.

By contrast, when one assumes Platonic true scores, the mean of the errors of measurement may or may not equal zero. In any given situation τ_i^* might be measured with error. If on an infinite number of remeasurements on person p $E_p(x)$ does not equal τ_p^*, then x_p is said to be a *biased* measure of τ_p^*, which means that $E(\varepsilon_p) \neq 0$. In survey research (Cochran, 1968; Hansen, Hurwitz, & Bershad, 1961) *response bias* β is defined as

$$\beta = E(\varepsilon) = E(\tau^*) - E(x), \tag{3.7}$$

where the expected value is taken across persons.

And when one assumes Platonic true scores, it is possible to test whether the true scores are independent of their errors by computing the covariance of τ^* and ε across persons, that is

$$C(\tau^*, \varepsilon) = C(\tau^*, \tau^* - x) = \sigma_{\tau^*}^2 - C(\tau^*, x). \tag{3.8}$$

If (3.8) is nonzero, then the true scores and errors are not independent. Furthermore, if the two are not independent, it follows that

$$\sigma_x^2 = \sigma_{\tau^*}^2 + \sigma_\varepsilon^2 + 2C(\tau^*, \varepsilon). \tag{3.9}$$

That is, the variance of the observed responses is not only the sum of the true score and error variances, but of twice the covariance between the true score and its error as well.

When one can assume one's true scores are Platonic one has the advantage of being able to test what are definitions and assumptions in classical test theory. However, even for behavioral variables it is relatively rare for one to have independently verifiable measures of a true score. (And when one does it is often difficult to assess the validity of the "true" scores themselves!) That is, it seems clear that all behavioral measures cannot be assumed to be Platonic measures as well. For a useful philosophical discussion of the status of Platonic measures in the behavioral sciences, see Burke (1963).

In studies that have utilized verifiable criteria to examine bias, two broad conclusions can be drawn. First, there is a tendency for persons to overreport socially desirable behaviors and to underreport negative ones. That is, it is unlikely that the mean of errors of measurement equals zero. Examples include (*a*) a study by Parry and Crossley (1950) which found that persons overreport donations to Community Chest, voting in city and congressional elections, having a library card and driver's license; and (*b*) the Lansing, Ginsburg, and Braaten (1961) report that persons underreport having borrowed cash from the bank. Second, the more socially undesirable one's true standing, the more underreporting occurs; that is, true scores and errors of measurement are nonzero. Thus studies by Wyner (1976, 1980) show that the greater the number of times criminals have actually been arrested, the greater the underreporting of arrests.

When the mean of the errors of measurement is nonzero, the estimate of the mean of the variable to be estimated will be biased, as (3.7) implies. But most other statistics such as correlations and regression coefficients are unaffected as long as the assumption that the errors of measurement are uncorrelated with the true scores holds. Unfortunately, when the mean of the measurement errors is not zero for reasons of social desirability, it is also likely that the true scores and the errors of measurement are *not* independent. In this case estimates of all statistics of general interest will be biased. If one has estimates of correlations between true scores and measurement errors and estimates of the correlation between measurement errors of the variables under study, one can compute unbiased estimates of relations among variables. However, even in the case of two variable relations, these estimates can be cumbersome to compute. The reader interested in how to obtain such estimates should see Wyner (1976) for details. Space limitations do not allow us to go into the complex details here despite the importance of the issue.

3.3. RELIABILITY AND VALIDITY DEFINED

Reliability refers to the extent to which the variance of an observed x is due to random sources or to "noise." Therefore, reliability is defined as the ratio of variance in x due to nonrandom sources to the total variance.

The reliability of x, labeled ρ_x, is simply the ratio of true score variance to the observed variance,

$$\rho_x = \sigma_\tau^2 / \sigma_x^2. \tag{3.10}$$

While perhaps not obvious from casual inspection, the square root of (3.10) equals the correlation between the true and observed score. To see this, note that

$$\rho_{\tau x} = C(\tau, x)/\sigma_\tau\sigma_x \tag{3.11a}$$

$$= \frac{C(\tau, \tau + \varepsilon)}{(\sigma_x\sqrt{\rho_x})\sigma_x} \quad \text{[from (3.1) and (3.10)]} \tag{3.11b}$$

$$= \frac{\sigma_\tau^2}{\sigma_x^2 \sqrt{\rho_x}} \quad \text{[from (3.5) and the fact that } C(\tau, \tau) = \sigma_\tau^2] \tag{3.11c}$$

$$= \sqrt{\rho_x} \quad \text{[from (3.10)]}. \tag{3.11d}$$

From (3.10) and (3.6) it immediately follows that

$$\rho_x = 1 - (\sigma_\varepsilon^2 / \sigma_x^2) \tag{3.12}$$

as well. Hence (3.12) is an alternative expression for the reliability of a measure. Since a variance is a nonnegative quantity, it is clear from (3.12) that the reliability of a measure is between 0 and 1. The greater the error variance, relative to the observed variance, the closer the reliability is to zero. And when the error approaches zero, the closer the reliability is to unity.

Note that if one knows ρ_x it follows immediately from (10) that

$$\sigma_\tau^2 = \sigma_x^2\rho_x. \tag{3.13}$$

That is, *the true score variance of x equals the observed variance multiplied by the reliability of the measure.*

The correlation between τ and x, $\rho_{\tau x}$, is called the *theoretical validity* of a measure x because it is a measure of how well an observed item correlates with some latent, theoretical construct of interest. Following Lord and Novick (1968, p. 261), we differentiate theoretical validity from *empirical validity*, where the latter is the correlation between x and a second *observed* variable y. That is, *empirical validity can only be assessed in relation to an observed measure.* Hence, it makes no sense to speak of the empirical validity of x in the singular. Given these definitions and the assumptions of true score theory,

Lord and Novick (1968, p. 72) link the concepts of reliability and validity by proving that

$$\rho_{xy} \leq \rho_{\tau x} = \sqrt{\rho_x},\qquad(3.14)$$

that is, *the empirical validity of a measure x in relation to a second measure y cannot exceed the theoretical validity or the square root of its reliability.* This means that the square root of the reliability of a measure is an upper bound to its validity with respect to any criterion measure. It also makes clear what is intuitively obvious: *No measure can be valid without also being reliable, but a reliable measure is not necessarily a valid one.*

Although it may not seem intuitively obvious, a biased measure can be a perfectly reliable one. Think of a scale that weighs everything 5 pounds heavier than it really is. Despite this problem, the scale's reliability is unaffected. To see this we simply note that the variance of $x + 5$ is equal to the variance of x. And since the reliability coefficient is the ratio of σ_τ^2 to σ_x^2, it is clear that constant biases do not affect the reliability of measurement.

3.4. THE EFFECT OF UNRELIABILITY ON STATISTICAL ESTIMATES

Until this point we have not made explicit how one's estimates of statistics such as means, standard deviations, and correlation coefficients are affected by unreliability of measurement. Assuming that measurement errors in the long run equal zero [i.e., the assumption made in (3.3)], it follows immediately from (3.1), that

$$\mu_x = E(x) = E(\tau) = \mu_\tau.\qquad(3.15)$$

In the long run for both Platonic and classical true scores, the mean of the observed scores equals the mean of the true scores as long as the observed measures are unbiased. If one has Platonic true scores which are measured with bias, that is, $\beta \neq 0$ in (3.7), then it is obvious that (3.15) does not hold.

Instead, when $\beta \neq 0$,

$$\mu_x = E(x) = \beta + \mu_\tau,\qquad(3.16)$$

which is just another way of saying that instruments resulting in measures that are systematically biased at the individual level will also yield biased estimates in the aggregate.

Since bias is a meaningless concept when one has classical measures, it is clear that (3.15) always holds for them.

Although not mentioned when (3.13) (that is, $\sigma_\tau^2 = \sigma_x^2 \rho_x$) was presented, it follows that, in a sample, *the variance of the true scores can be estimated by multiplying the variance of an observed score by its reliability estimate.* Assuming measurement error is random, the true score variance is less than or equal to the observed score variance. [This point is obvious from (3.6) as well.] Note that (3.13) makes it clear that the reliability of one's measures approaches zero as the observed true score variance approaches zero.

Interestingly, *the covariance between two variables x and y is unaffected by errors of measurement in the two variables*. This is proven by expressing $C(\tau_x, \tau_y)$ in terms of observables and measurement errors:

$$
\begin{aligned}
C(\tau_x, \tau_y) &= C(x - \varepsilon_x, y - \varepsilon_y) \\
&= C(x, y) - C(x, \varepsilon_y) - C(\varepsilon_x, y) + C(\varepsilon_x, \varepsilon_y) \\
&= C(x, y) - C(\tau_x + \varepsilon_x, \varepsilon_y) - C(\varepsilon_x, \tau_y + \varepsilon_y) + C(\varepsilon_x, \varepsilon_y) \\
&= C(x, y) - C(\tau_x, \varepsilon_y) - C(\varepsilon_x, \varepsilon_y) - C(\varepsilon_x, \tau_y) \\
&\qquad - C(\varepsilon_x, \varepsilon_y) + C(\varepsilon_x, \varepsilon_y) \\
&= C(x, y),
\end{aligned}
\tag{3.17}
$$

since by (3.4) and (3.5), $C(\varepsilon_x, \tau_y) = C(\varepsilon_y, \tau_x) = C(\varepsilon_x, \varepsilon_y) = 0$.

Although the covariance is not affected by measurement error, the correlation coefficient is. Since $\rho_{\tau_x\tau_y} = C(\tau_x, \tau_y)/\sigma_{\tau_x}\sigma_{\tau_y}$, it follows from (3.13) and (3.17) after some algebra that

$$
\rho_{\tau_x\tau_y} = \rho_{xy}/\sqrt{\rho_x\rho_y}.
\tag{3.18}
$$

Notice that the correlation between x and y approaches $\rho_{\tau_x\tau_y}$ as ρ_x and ρ_y approach unity. Equation (3.18) is the best known of the *attenuation formulas*. It expresses the fact that *the true correlation between x and y is attenuated by measurement error* (Lord & Novick, 1968, pp. 69–74).

While errors in both x and y affect the correlation between the two variables, *the regression coefficient with y dependent on x is affected only by errors in x*—the independent variable. In general, $\beta_{\tau_y\tau_x} = C(\tau_y, \tau_x)/V(\tau_x)$. It follows from (3.13) and (3.17) after some algebra that

$$
\beta_{\tau_y\tau_x} = \beta_{yx}/\rho_x.
\tag{3.19}
$$

Since the intercept $\alpha_{\tau_y\tau_x} = \mu_{\tau_y} - \beta_{\tau_y\tau_x}\mu_{\tau_x}$, it follows from (3.15) and (3.19) that

$$
\alpha_{\tau_y\tau_x} = \mu_y - (\beta_{yx}/\rho_x)\mu_x.
\tag{3.20}
$$

that is, *the intercept is also only affected by measurement error in the independent variable, x*.[3]

In the three-variable case, the effects of measurement error are more complicated. The true partial correlation coefficient $\rho_{\tau_x\tau_y \cdot \tau_z}$ is given by

$$
\rho_{\tau_x\tau_y \cdot \tau_z} = \frac{\rho_z\rho_{xy} - \rho_{xz}\rho_{yz}}{\sqrt{\rho_x\rho_z - \rho_{xz}^2}\sqrt{\rho_y\rho_z - \rho_{yz}^2}}
\tag{3.21}
$$

---

[3] One exception is the intercept in the regression equation, which is dependent on accurate estimates of the means.

(A proof can be found in Bohrnstedt, 1969.) To show the effects of measurement error on the partial correlation coefficient, assume that the three disattenuated (observed) coefficients ρ_{xy}, ρ_{xz}, and ρ_{yz} all equal .5. Assume further that the reliability of x, y, and z is .8 in each case. Then the observed partial correlation, $\rho_{xy \cdot z}$, equals .333. Since $\rho_{xy \cdot z}$ does not take measurement error into account, one might expect the coefficient corrected for measurement error— using (3.21)—to be larger. And indeed this is the case since $\rho_{\tau_x \tau_y \cdot \tau_z}$ equals .385. But now consider the case where ρ_{xy}, ρ_{xz}, and ρ_{yz} again all equal .5, but where ρ_x and ρ_y equal .8 and ρ_z equals .6. In this case it would again seem likely that $\rho_{\tau_x \tau_y \cdot \tau_z}$ should be larger than .333, the observed $\rho_{xy \cdot z}$. But it is not. Simple calculation using (3.21) shows that it equals .217. *Thus although errors in measurement usually attenuate higher order partial correlations, they do not always do so,* as the last example illustrates. It would be nice to be able to provide the reader with some guidelines indicating when partial correlations will and will not be attenuated, but frankly I know of none.

The true regression coefficient in the three-variable case for the regression of τ_y and τ_x controlling for τ_z is given by

$$\beta_{\tau_y \tau_x \cdot \tau_z} = \left(\frac{\sigma_y}{\sigma_x} \right) \frac{\rho_z \rho_{xy} - \rho_{yz} \rho_{xz}}{\rho_x \rho_z - \rho_{xz}^2}. \tag{3.22}$$

This result has similarities to those discussed in connection with both (3.19) and (3.21). It is similar to (3.19) in that careful inspection of (3.22) makes clear that errors of measurement in the dependent variable y do not affect the true regression coefficient. This result generalizes to the k-variable case as well: *Errors in the dependent variable do not affect the true regression coefficient.* Equation (3.22) is also similar to (3.21) in that errors in measurement generally attenuate the estimate of the true regression coefficient; but it is possible to find examples in which the observed coefficient is actually larger than the true one.

The reader interested in more technical treatments of regression estimation in the multivariate case in which measurement error is taken into account should read Warren, White, and Fuller (1974) and Fuller and Hidiroglou (1978).

To summarize, assume the assumptions of classical measurement theory hold and measurement error exists:

1. The observed mean equals the true mean.
2. The variance of the observed scores is larger than that of the true scores.
3. In two-variable cases, the observed correlation and regression coefficient are smaller than the true coefficients.
4. In the k-variable case the observed partial correlation coefficients and regression coefficients are usually, but not always, smaller than the true coefficients.
5. Errors of measurement in the dependent variable do not affect the estimate of the true regression coefficient.

Parallel Measures

Although we have defined reliability and examined the effects of unreliability on estimates of common statistics, we have not yet described how one can estimate the reliability of a measure. In this section we describe one way—by correlating parallel measures.

Two measures, x and x', are defined as parallel if $x = \tau + \varepsilon$, $x' = \tau + \varepsilon'$ and $\sigma_\varepsilon^2 = \sigma_{\varepsilon'}^2$. Note that both x and x' are assumed to reflect the same underlying true score τ. And the definition of parallel measures guarantees that the means and variances of x and x' are equal, that is, $\mu_x = \mu_{x'}$ and $\sigma_x^2 = \sigma_{x'}^2$. These facts follow from (3.15) and (3.16), respectively. Furthermore, if z is another variable and $x_1, x_2, x_3, \ldots$ are parallel measures, then $\rho_{x_1 x_2} = \rho_{x_2 x_3} = \rho_{x_3 x_4} = \cdots$ and $\rho_{x_1 z} = \rho_{x_2 z} = \rho_{x_3 z} = \cdots$. That is, the *intercorrelations among parallel measures are all equal and the intercorrelations of all parallel measures with some other criterion variable are all equal to one another.*

Obviously it is very difficult to construct parallel measures in practice. But if one does so and correlates them, the result is an estimate of the reliability of x. This is easy to show:

$$
\begin{aligned}
\rho_{xx'} &= C(x, x')/\sigma_x \sigma_{x'} \\
&= C(\tau + \varepsilon, \tau + \varepsilon')/\sigma_x^2 && \text{[from (3.1)]} \\
&- C(\tau, \tau)/\sigma_x^2 && \text{[from (3.4) and (3.5)]} \\
&= \sigma_\tau^2/\sigma_x^2 \\
&= \rho_x && \text{[from (3.10)]}. \quad (3.23)
\end{aligned}
$$

The parallel measure approach to the estimate of reliability is largely of historical interest in view of the restrictive definition of parallel measures. More useful approaches are discussed in the following sections.

3.5. RELIABILITY AS A FUNCTION OF THE NUMBER OF INDEPENDENT MEASURES

It makes intuitive sense that one's confidence in the actual or true value of a particular phenomenon should increase as the number of independent measurements of a phenomenon increase for a given level of reliability of measurement. One would be more confident with a pair of independent measures of political liberalism each with a reliability of .6 than with a single scale measure. And we would be even more confident if we had four such independent measures, and so on. It is this intuitive reasoning that forms the rationale for using multiple items rather than a single one to measure a construct (Bohrnstedt, 1969; Curtis & Jackson, 1962). The assumption is that errors in measurement will be random, that is, will cancel each other out, and the average of all the measurements is a better estimate of the true value than any single one.

It is also clear that one needs fewer independent measures to achieve a given level of confidence when the reliability of each individual measurement is high. If one knows a measure has a reliability of .9, one might accept a single measurement, whereas one might need eight or nine independent assessments for a measure with a reliability of .5 to have the same degree of confidence in what the true value is.

The relationship between the reliability of a composite x_n (where $x_n = \sum_{i=1}^{n} x_i$) and n parallel measures of known reliability was derived independently by Spearman (1910) and Brown (1910). They showed that the reliability of a measure that is n times longer than the original is

$$\rho_{x_n} = \frac{n\rho_x}{1 + (n-1)\rho_x} \tag{3.24}$$

where ρ_{x_n} is the reliability of the composite.

Figure 3.1 shows increase in reliability as a function of the number of independent measures for various initial reliabilities. The implication for survey research is obvious. When one has relatively good items, only a few are needed to achieve a relatively high degree of reliability; more are needed the lower the reliability of each individual measurement. Thus if one demands a reliability of .8 for x_n it can be achieved with two items with individual reliabilities of .7, four of .5 or ten of .3.

Equation (3.24) and Figure 3.1 demonstrate that the *reliability of a measure composed of parallel items is a joint function of* (a) *the number of items comprising it, and* (b) *the reliability of the individual items comprising it.* The

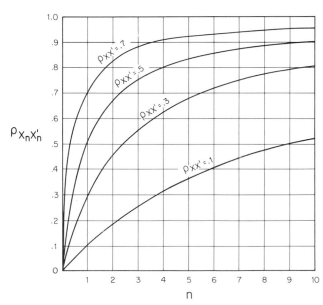

FIGURE 3.1 Diagram for showing increase in reliability as a function of increase in the length of scale (*n*) for different initial reliabilities.

higher the reliability of the items the fewer needed to achieve a given level of reliability. Or the lower the reliability of the items, the more needed to achieve the same degree of reliability.

3.6. TYPES OF RELIABILITY

To this point, our discussion of reliability has been largely theoretical and historical. We now discuss specific ways to assess reliability. Generally, reliability measures can be divided into two major classes: measures of *stability* and measures of *equivalence*.

Measures of Stability

A person's response to a particular item or set of items may vary from occasion to occasion. The respondents may not be certain how they feel about an issue or person, may be distracted by other matters, may be tired or ill, and so on. All of these will contribute to errors of measurement and therefore depress the reliability of the items. Given that error exists, the problem is how to assess it in a way that satisfies the definition of reliability given in (3.10). Historically the most popular way to evaluate it has been to correlate respondents' responses at one point in time with their responses at some later point in time. Reliability evaluated by correlating a measure across time is called a *measure of stability* or, more commonly, *test–retest* reliability. The assumption being made is that shown in Figure 3.2. The item or scale is assumed to correlate with itself across time because of an underlying unobserved true variable τ. The equations linking the observed responses at Time 1 and Time 2 to τ are

$$x_1 = \tau + \varepsilon_1 \quad \text{and} \quad x_2 = \tau + \varepsilon_2. \tag{3.25}$$

But it is clear to see that if it is assumed that $\sigma^2_{\varepsilon_1} = \sigma^2_{\varepsilon_2}$ and that $C(\varepsilon_1, \varepsilon_2) = 0$, it follows that

$$\rho_{x_1 x_2} = \rho_x. \tag{3.26}$$

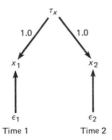

FIGURE 3.2 A schematic representation of the test–retest correlation as an estimate of reliability.

That is, *if these assumptions hold, the test–retest correlation is the reliability of the measure.*

There are some problems with test–retest reliability estimates, however. One is likely to obtain different estimates depending on the amount of time between measurement and remeasurement. Generally it is found that the shorter the time interval the higher the estimate of reliability. Why should this be true?

First, there is the problem of memory. If the interval between measurement and remeasurement is short the respondents may remember their earlier responses, making them appear more consistent with respect to the true content than they in fact are. To handle this problem some researchers employ a *parallel forms test–retest* procedure. A different but presumably parallel form of the measure is used at the second administration. For example, one may begin with 20 items presumed to measure, say, anomie. Ten of the items are administered at Time 1 and summed into a composite measure and the other ten are administered and scored in parallel fashion at Time 2. Recall from our earlier discussion that truly parallel items have the same error variance, correlate identically with each other, and correlate identically with criterion variables. Obviously, these are difficult if not impossible conditions to meet, and it should be clear that few "parallel forms" of measures are actually in fact parallel. However, if one can be satisfied that two forms are reasonably parallel, their employment across time reduces the degree to which respondents' memory can inflate the reliability estimate.

A second problem with the test–retest approach has to do with the assumption that the errors of measurement ε_1 and ε_2 are uncorrelated. If the errors of measurement are in some sense systematic and not random, *one would expect that the same sources of bias might operate each time measurement occurs, thereby making the assumption of uncorrelatedness of errors in measurement highly suspect.* But in the simple test–retest model, there is no way to estimate correlated measurement error. However, Blalock (1970), Hannan, Rubinson, and Warren (1974), and Jöreskog and Sörbom (1977) have shown how the use of multiple indicators to measure the underlying variable can yield enough information in some cases to allow for the estimation of correlated measurement error. We shall examine this approach in a later section.

A third problem is that *true change cannot be distinguished from unreliability* in a simple test–retest reliability design, and obviously the longer the time interval between measurement and remeasurement, the greater the probability that respondents will have in fact changed on the underlying unobserved variable. It should be clear that if individuals have in fact changed, a low test–retest correlation does not necessarily mean that the reliability of one's measure is poor. Several attempts to deal with the true change versus unreliability problem by using multiple remeasurements have appeared in the last 10 years. Building on the pioneering work of Heise (1969), papers by D. E. Wiley and

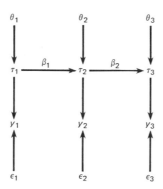

FIGURE 3.3 A three-wave model.

J. E. Wiley (1970), Werts, Jöreskog, and Linn (1971), D. E. Wiley and J. E. Wiley (1974), and Hargens, Reskin, and Allison (1976) have extended this approach. All assume that errors of measurement are uncorrelated across time, that one has measures on an item at three points in time, and that the unobserved latent variables are uncorrelated with the errors in measurement. This situation is represented schematically in Figure 3.3. The structural equations linking the underlying unobserved variable to itself across time are

$$\tau_1 = \theta_1, \tag{3.27a}$$

$$\tau_2 = \beta_1 \tau_1 + \theta_2, \tag{3.27b}$$

$$\tau_3 = \beta_2 \tau_2 + \theta_3. \tag{3.27c}$$

The three measurement equations linking the observed items to the underlying unobserved variable τ_i are

$$y_1 = \tau_1 + \varepsilon_1, \tag{3.28a}$$

$$y_2 = \tau_2 + \varepsilon_2, \tag{3.28b}$$

$$y_3 = \tau_3 + \varepsilon_3. \tag{3.28c}$$

Notice that the model assumes that the underlying latent variable is causally related to itself across time with lag-1 effects only, that is, it is assumed that τ_1 has only an *in*direct effect on τ_3 through τ_2. D. E. Wiley and J. A. Wiley (1970) make the additional assumption that the variance of the measurement errors is a constant across time. That is, they assume that $V(\varepsilon_i) = V(\varepsilon)$ for $i = 1, 2$, and 3. Using this specification, Wiley and Wiley show that the six parameters of the model can be estimated as well as three separate reliability coefficients—one for each of the three time points. After some algebraic manipulations Wiley and Wiley show that the six parameters of the model can be estimated by the following quantities:

Parameter	Estimator
β_2	$\hat{C}(y_1, y_3)/\hat{C}(y_1, y_2)$
$V(\varepsilon)$	$\hat{V}(y_2) - [\hat{C}(y_2, y_3)/\hat{\beta}_2]$
$V(\theta_1)$	$\hat{V}(y_1) - \hat{V}(\varepsilon)$
β_1	$\hat{C}(y_1, y_2)/\hat{V}(\theta_1)$
$V(\theta_2)$	$\hat{V}(y_2) - [\hat{\beta}_1\hat{C}(y_1, y_2) + \hat{V}(\varepsilon)]$
$V(\theta_3)$	$\hat{V}(y_3) - [\hat{\beta}_2\hat{C}(y_2, y_3) + \hat{V}(\varepsilon)]$,

$$(3.29)$$

where the caret refers to sample estimators of population parameters. Obviously the estimates of *greatest* interest are for β_1 and β_2—the two stability coefficients.

Obtaining the estimates of the three reliability coefficients is only somewhat less tedious. One begins by substituting (3.27a) in (3.28a), (3.27b) into (3.28b), and (3.27c) into (3.28c). Then the measurement equations can be expressed in terms of the structural parameters.

$$y_1 = \theta_1 + \varepsilon_1, \tag{3.30a}$$

$$y_2 = \beta_1\theta_1 + \theta_2 + \varepsilon_2, \tag{3.30b}$$

$$y_3 = \beta_2(\beta_1\theta_1 + \theta_2) + \theta_3 + \varepsilon_3. \tag{3.30c}$$

Now taking variances of (3.30a–c), recalling (3.5), and assuming $C(\theta_i, \varepsilon_i) = C(\theta_i, \theta_j) = 0$ for $i \neq j$ we have

$$V(y_1) = V(\theta_1) + V(\varepsilon), \tag{3.31a}$$

$$V(y_2) = \beta_1^2 V(\theta_1) + V(\theta_2) + V(\varepsilon), \tag{3.31b}$$

$$V(y_3) = \beta_2^2[\beta_1^2 V(\theta_1) + V(\theta_2)] + V(\theta_3) + V(\varepsilon). \tag{3.31c}$$

Taking variances of (3.27a), (3.27b), and (3.27c), it follows that the variances of the underlying unobserved variables are simply

$$V(\tau_1) = V(\theta_1), \tag{3.32a}$$

$$V(\tau_2) = \beta_1^2 V(\theta_1) + V(\theta_2), \tag{3.32b}$$

$$V(\tau_3) = \beta_2^2[\beta_1^2 V(\theta_1) + V(\theta_2)] + V(\theta_3). \tag{3.32c}$$

Now using the definition of reliability given in (3.10), it follows that

$$\hat{\rho}_1 = \hat{V}(\theta_1)/\hat{\sigma}_{y_1}^2, \tag{3.33a}$$

$$\hat{\rho}_2 = [\hat{\beta}_1^2 \hat{V}(\theta_1) + \hat{V}(\theta_2)]/\hat{\sigma}_{y_2}^2, \tag{3.33b}$$

$$\hat{\rho}_3 = \{\hat{\beta}_2^2[\hat{\beta}_1^2 \hat{V}(\theta_1)] + \hat{V}(\theta_2)] + \hat{V}(\theta_3)\}/\hat{\sigma}_{y_3}^2. \tag{3.33c}$$

We now have estimates for β_1 and β_2, the two stability (or change) parameters, as well as estimates of the reliability of the variable at all three points in time under the assumption of equal measurement error variance across time. Data from Wheaton, Muthen, Alwin, and Summers (1977) provide an example of how to use the Wiley and Wiley model. They present data that were collected at three points in time (1966, 1967, and 1971) from 932 respondents in two rural regions of Illinois.[4] The data used here are from the Srole (1956) *anomia* scale.

$$\hat{V}(y_1) = 12.96, \qquad \hat{C}(y_1, y_2) = 8.30, \qquad \hat{C}(y_1, y_3) = 6.75,$$

$$\hat{V}(y_2) = 11.83, \qquad \hat{C}(y_2, y_3) = 6.82, \qquad\qquad\qquad (3.34)$$

$$\hat{V}(y_3) = 12.53$$

Inserting these data in (3.29) yields the following parameter estimates:

$$\hat{\beta}_2 = .813, \qquad \hat{V}(\varepsilon) = 3.441, \qquad \hat{V}(\theta_1) = 9.519,$$

$$\hat{\beta}_1 = .872, \qquad \hat{V}(\theta_2) = 1.151, \qquad \hat{V}(\theta_3) = 3.544 \qquad (3.35)$$

These estimates can in turn be inserted in (3.33a), (3.33b), and (3.33c) to provide reliability estimates of the anomia measure for 1966, 1967, and 1971:

$$\hat{\rho}_1 = .734, \qquad \hat{\rho}_2 = .709, \qquad \text{and} \qquad \hat{\rho}_3 = .725. \qquad (3.36)$$

Several points are worth noting. First, $\hat{\beta}_1$ is greater than $\hat{\beta}_2$ as one might expect since $\hat{\beta}_1$ is an estimate of stability for measures separated by a single year, whereas $\hat{\beta}_2$ estimates stability for measures separated 4 years. Second, the three estimates of reliability are relatively stable; that is, they are very close to each other in size. Third, it can be easily calculated from (3.34) that $r_{12} = .67$ and $r_{23} = .56$. Note that both these test–retest correlations are smaller than the three reliability estimates obtained using the Wiley and Wiley technique. This difference undoubtedly results from the fact that *simple test–retest correlations confound change (or stability) with unreliability.* My own experience suggests that simple test–retest correlations usually underestimate the reliability of a measure.

Werts *et al.* (1971) demonstrate that if one has measured a variable at k points in time, one can obtain estimates of reliability and stability for all measurement waves except for the first and last without making the assumption of constant measurement error variance made by D. E. Wiley and J. A. Wiley (1970). The technique used for estimation is due to Jöreskog (1970, 1973), and it has the flexibility that allows one to *test* the assumption of equal reliabilities and equal stabilities across time. Assuming one has data at four or more points in time on a variable, the Werts *et al.* (1971) approach has obvious advantages over that of D. E. Wiley and J. A. Wiley (1970). The reader is encouraged to explore this approach since the assumptions of the Wiley and Wiley model can actually be tested. Its limitation is the number of time points required.

Both the D. E. Wiley and J. A. Wiley (1970) and Werts *et al.* (1971) approaches to the estimation of reliability do not allow for correlated measurement error across time. As indicated earlier, the assumption of uncorrelated

[4] See Summers, Hauglo, Scott, and Folse (1969) for further description of the research design.

measurement error across time may be an unrealistic one in most circumstances. J. A. Wiley and M. G. Wiley (1974) present a model for estimating
reliability and stability allowing for correlated measurement error when one has
measures taken at three *equally* spaced points in time but under the assumption
that (*a*) the regression of the true score at time *t* on that at time $t - 1$ is a
constant β, and (*b*) that the regression of the errors of measurement at time *t* on
those at time $t - 1$ is also a constant π. Furthermore, it is assumed that
measurement error is constant across time. They then show that:

$$V(y_1) = V(\theta_1) + V(\varepsilon), \tag{3.37a}$$

$$V(y_2) = \beta^2 V(\theta_1) + V(\theta_2) + V(\varepsilon), \tag{3.37b}$$

$$V(y_3) = \beta^2[\beta^2 V(\theta_1) + V(\theta_2)] + V(\theta_3) + V(\varepsilon). \tag{3.37c}$$

They also prove that the parameters of the model can be estimated as follows:

Parameters	Estimates
β	$[(\hat{C}(y_1, y_2) - \hat{C}(y_2, y_3)]/[\hat{V}(y_1) - \hat{V}(y_2)]$
π	$\{[\hat{C}(y_1, y_3) - \hat{\beta}^2\hat{V}(y_1)]/[\hat{C}(y_1, y_2) - \hat{\beta}\hat{V}(y_1)]\} - \hat{\beta}$
$V(\varepsilon)$	$[\hat{C}(y_1, y_2) - \hat{\beta}\hat{V}(y_1)]/(\hat{\pi} - \hat{\beta})$
$V(\theta_1)$	$\hat{V}(y_1) - \hat{V}(\varepsilon)$
$V(\theta_2)$	$\hat{V}(y_2) - \hat{\beta}^2\hat{V}(\theta_1) - \hat{V}(\varepsilon)$
$V(\theta_3)$	$\hat{V}(y_3) - \hat{\beta}^2[\hat{V}(y_2) - \hat{V}(\varepsilon)] - \hat{V}(\varepsilon).$ (3.38)

For the Summers data used in the previous example, we obtain the following
estimates for the J. A. Wiley and M. G. Wiley (1974) correlated measurement
model:

$$\begin{aligned}
\hat{\beta} &= \quad 1.1310, \\
\hat{\pi} &= \quad .475, \\
\hat{V}(\varepsilon) &= \quad 10.392, \\
\hat{V}(\theta_1) &= \quad 2.568, \\
\hat{V}(\theta_2) &= \quad -2.969, \\
\hat{V}(\theta_3) &= \quad -0.329.
\end{aligned} \tag{3.39}$$

Notice that both the estimates for $V(\theta_2)$ and $V(\theta_3)$ are *negative*, unacceptable
values since variances by definition are nonnegative quantities. These results
suggest that one or more of the assumptions underlying the model are being
violated. Since we know that these data were collected at *un*equally spaced
intervals in time, the assumptions that β and π are constants seem almost
certain to be violated, which may account for the unacceptable estimates.

　　Hargens *et al.* (1976) argue that the assumption that true scores are causally related across time may be an unrealistic one in some circumstances and

posit some alternative models that allow for latent variables that are causally related to the true scores. And Wheaton *et al.* (1977) argue that the single-variable multiple-wave models may be unrealistic in that they ignore that other variables besides the true scores at time $t - 1$ may be causally related to the true score at time t. They also argue for examining multivariate–multiwave models with *multiple* as opposed to single indicators—models that allow for correlated measurement error across time as well. I agree with the multiple indicator approach taken by Wheaton *et al.* (1977) and will return to it later in this chapter.

Measures of Equivalence

Whereas historically reliability has more often been assessed using measures of stability, in recent decades an alternative approach has gained in popularity—the use of measures of equivalence. Parallel items administered at the same point in time and correlated to estimate reliability is an example of a measure of equivalence. The assumption is made that the two items have the same underlying true score and as such are equivalent, and hence equally good measures of the true score. In a sense the two items can be thought of as an instant test–retest. As noted earlier in the chapter, one need not be limited to a pair of parallel items. Indeed, since reliability is partially a function of the number of items used, it makes good sense to build composites or scores which are sums of items so long as one can assume the items in a given score have the same underlying true score.

One of the earliest varieties of equivalence measures to appear were the *split-half* methods. In the split-half approach to reliability the total number of items in a composite is divided into two halves and the half-scores are then correlated. Since the actual measure is twice as long as the half-score being correlated, the correlation is usually inserted in the Spearman–Brown prophecy formula with $n = 2$ [see Eq. (3.24)] to get an estimate of the reliability of the total composite. Some researchers used the odd-numbered items for one half-test and the even-numbered for the other. Another approach was to use the first $n/2$ items for one half-test and the last $n/2$ items for the other where n refers to the total number of items. Yet another version of the split-half approach was to use randomly selected items (without replacement) to build the half-tests. Obviously each of these methods could yield conflicting estimates of the reliability of the half-tests. Indeed, for a composite $2n$ items long, the total number of splits is $(2n!)/2(n!)(n!)$. For example, for a 10-item score there are 126 different possible splits. It is small wonder then that split-half techniques began to fall into disuse as more precise methods for estimating reliability were developed.

It should be mentioned in passing that split-half methods have also often been used in a test–retest format where one version is used at Time 1 and a second version is used at Time 2. In this case the splits are assumed to be parallel composites. This procedure is followed as a possible way to deal with memory effects which might confound test–retest reliability estimates using the same composite across time. In this case the simple zero-order correlation between the two halves is taken as the reliability estimate—that is, it is not inserted into the Spearman–Brown formula since the total composite is never employed, only the half-score.

The split-half techniques have gradually been replaced by *internal consistency* methods for the estimate of reliability with cross-sectional data. Internal consistency reliability estimates utilize the covariances among all the items simultaneously rather than concentrating on a single correlation between two arbitrary splits.

Kuder and Richardson (1937) were the first to devise a measure of equivalence that utilized all the covariances among the items. However, their formulas KR20 and KR21 could only be used with dichotomous items. Hoyt (1941) and Guttman (1945) presented generalizations of the KR formulas for polychotomous items. But by far the most popular generalization has been coefficient α developed by Cronbach (1951), where

$$\alpha = \frac{n}{n-1}\left[1 - \frac{\sum_{i=1}^{n} V(y_i)}{\sum_{i=1}^{n} V(y_i) + 2\sum_{i<j}^{n}\sum^{n} C(y_i, y_j)}\right] \qquad (3.40a)$$

$$= \frac{n}{n-1}\left[1 - \frac{\sum_{i=1}^{n} V(y_i)}{\sigma_x^2}\right] \qquad (3.40b)$$

where $x = \sum_{i=1}^{n} y_i$. Importantly, α in general is a *lower bound* to the reliability of an unweighted composite of n items. That is, $\rho_x \geq \alpha$. This important relationship was shown by Novick and Lewis (1967). However, as Lord and Novick (1968, p. 90) point out, α equals the reliability of the composite if the n measures are either parallel or tau-equivalent. (Tau-equivalent measures are defined as measures with the same true scores but not necessarily with equal measurement error variances, whereas parallel measures are also defined as having equal error variances. Hence the assumption of tau-equivalence is less restrictive than that of parallelism.) Indeed, if one's n measures are tau-equivalent or parallel, α is exactly equal to the Spearman–Brown prophecy formula, that is, to (3.24). In practice it is rare for one's items to be tau-equivalent and therefore α will give a lower bound estimate to reliability. However, unless one's items deviate substantially from being at least tau-equivalent (something one can get a quick-and-dirty estimate of by examining the interitem covariances for rough equality) α will give quite good estimates of reliability.

Two points deserve brief mention. First, if one's items are dichotomous it is easy to prove that α is exactly equal to the formula for KR20. Second, Cronbach (1951) proved that α is equal to the average of all possible split half correlations among the n items. Although any particular split-half might be closer than α to the true reliability there obviously is no a priori way to know this. This demonstrates why it is better to estimate the reliability of an n-item composite using α instead of an arbitrary split-half estimate.

TABLE 3.1
Covariance and Correlation Matrices for Items in Competitiveness Desirability
Score (N = 869 Males)[a]

	1	2	3	4	5	6	7	8	9
1	**.534**	.115	.168	.085	.118	.090	.167	.144	.129
2	.245	**.411**	.114	.062	.140	.080	.104	.065	.148
3	.255	.197	**.814**	.061	.118	.117	.177	.093	.272
4	.197	.164	.115	**.348**	.087	.012	.103	.084	.054
5	.255	.345	.207	.233	**.401**	.072	.140	.123	.125
6	.181	.183	.189	.030	.167	**.465**	.093	.052	.105
7	.285	.202	.244	.217	.275	.170	**.645**	.078	.127
8	.318	.164	.167	.230	.314	.123	.157	**.383**	.093
9	.214	.280	.366	.111	.240	.187	.192	.182	**.679**

[a] The covariances are above the main diagonal; correlations below. The main diagonal
contains the item variances.

An example of how to use alpha presented in Bohrnstedt (1970) and drawn
from a study by Ford, Borgatta, and Bohrnstedt (1969) is reproduced here. A
series of items were designed to measure the amount of competitiveness desired in a job by new college-level personnel hired by a large company. The
following nine items were added into a single measure called *competitiveness
desirability:*

1. Salary increases would be strictly a matter of how much you accomplished for the company.
2. The company is known to be involved in heavy competition.
3. Persons are supposed to "get the boot" if they don't make good and
   keep making good.
4. There are opportunities to earn bonuses.
5. Competition would be open and encouraged.
6. The supervisor might be highly critical.
7. There is emphasis on the actual production record.
8. Salary increases would be a matter of how much effort you put in.
9. The rewards could be great, but many people are known to fail or quit.

Based on a sample of 869 males hired, the covariance matrix shown in Table 3.1
was obtained. To compute α, we need $\sum_{i=1}^n V(y_i)$ which is simply the sum of the
elements in the diagonal, that is,

$$\sum_{i=1}^9 V(y_i) = (.534 + .411 + \cdots + .679) = 4.680.$$

In addition, we need to compute $V(y_i)$, the variance of the total scale. The
reader can verify that this variance is equal to the sum of the elements in the
main diagonal plus twice the sum of the off-diagonal elements above the main
diagonal. We already have computed the sum of the diagonal. Now the sum of

the off-diagonals is

$$\sum_{\substack{i=1 \\ i<j}}^{9} \sum_{j=1}^{9} C(y_i, y_j) = (.115 + .168 + \cdots + .093) = 3.915$$

and twice this sum is 7.830. Add to this the sum of the diagonal and one obtains $\sigma_x^2 = 12.510$. Hence, $\alpha = \frac{9}{8}(1 - 4.68/12.510) = .704$. That is, the internal consistency reliability estimate for the *competitiveness desirability* score is .704.

If one can assume that all one's items have equal variances, the formula for alpha simplifies to

$$\alpha = \frac{n\bar{\rho}_{ij}}{1 + (n - 1)\bar{\rho}_{ij}}, \qquad (3.41)$$

where $\bar{\rho}_{ij}$ refers to the average correlation among the n items. Even if the item variances are only approximately equal, Eq. (3.41) provides an excellent quick-and-not-too-dirty estimate of alpha. As a guide, if all one's items in a composite use the same response format, the use of Eq. (3.41) will usually not differ from alpha, using (3.40) by more than .01. For example, using the correlations instead of the covariances in Table 3.1, and using (3.41) instead of (3.40b) yields a value of .707 compared to .704, even though the item variances appear to vary somewhat. Since most researchers routinely compute item intercorrelations, (3.41) can be used very quickly to compute an estimate of alpha when item variances are even roughly equal. The reader interested in more details about the computation of alpha might consult Nunnally (1967) or Bohrnstedt (1969).

When discussing the D. E. Wiley and J. E. Wiley (1970) and Werts *et al.* (1971) approaches to reliability estimation, it was implicit that there may be more than one reliability estimate. To this point we have discussed internal consistency measures as though there is some true reliability "out there" known only to the Almighty. In fact, however, it makes sense to think of multiple reliabilities in the case of internal consistency measures as well. One can compute as many coefficients as one has subgroups to which one wants to generalize. For example, if one intends to do separate analyses by sex, race, and age of the respondent, then separate reliability estimates for each break-down of these three variables should be computed. And if sex-by-race analyses are to be done, reliability estimates for each sex-by-race category should be computed. In general the reliability estimates computed within subgroups will be smaller than that for the entire population of respondents (Lord & Novick, 1968, pp. 129–131). This is easily demonstrated. Let P' be a randomly drawn subpopulation of respondents with true scores restricted to a *specified* set of τ values. Assume that errors of measurement are homoscedastic, that is, that $E(\varepsilon|\tau) = \sigma_\varepsilon^2$ for all τ. The reliability of the observed measure x' on the subpopulation ρ' is given by

$$\rho_{x'} = 1 - (\sigma_\varepsilon^2/\sigma_{x'}^2). \qquad (3.42)$$

But it follows from solving (3.12) for σ_ε^2 that $\sigma_\varepsilon^2 = \sigma_x^2(1 - \rho_x)$. Substituting this result into (3.42) yields

$$\rho_{x'} = 1 - (\sigma_x^2/\sigma_{x'}^2)\,(1 - \rho_x). \tag{3.43}$$

It is clear that ρ_x equals $\rho_{x'}$ when $\sigma_x^2 = \sigma_{x'}^2$. Otherwise $\rho_{x'}$ is a strictly decreasing function of the ratio of σ_x^2 to $\sigma_{x'}^2$. Thus when we restrict the population to P' and reduce the variance of x', $\rho_{x'}$ will be smaller than ρ_x. For example, if $\rho_x = .8$ and $\sigma_x^2/\sigma_{x'}^2 = 1.1$, then $\rho_{x'} = .78$. As Lord and Novick point out, this result depends heavily on the assumption that the errors of measurement are homoscedastic. If they are not, the reliability of the restricted subpopulation may actually exceed that of the unrestricted population. Given that reliability estimates vary across subpopulation, researchers should routinely report the observed variance on which a given reliability estimate is calculated.

We have merely touched on an important issue in these last few paragraphs. We have not treated the question of whether or not there might be an interaction between persons and conditions of measurement administration (e.g., questionnaire versus interview, race of the respondent and race of the interviewer) which in the procedures discussed thus far is lumped with measurement error. Although procedures for examining these questions are still being developed, survey researchers interested in what are commonly called response effects in survey research (Sudman & Bradburn, 1974) might benefit from reading Cronbach, Gleser, Nanda, and Rajaratnam (1972) on the theory of generalizability and Lord and Novick's (1968, Chapter 8) treatment of generic true scores.

3.7. FACTOR ANALYSIS AND INTERNAL CONSISTENCY

Since one of the explicit purposes of factor analysis (Harmon, 1967) is to reduce a set of measures to some smaller number of latent, unobserved variables, it is not surprising that several writers have been interested in the relationship between factor analysis and the reliability of measurement (Cattell & Radcliffe, 1962; Bentler, 1968; Heise & Bohrnstedt, 1970; Jöreskog, 1971; Allen, 1974; Smith, 1974a, 1974b). There are various models for factor analysis (Harmon, 1967) all of which can be broadly classified as either exploratory or confirmatory.

In *exploratory factor analysis* one is primarily interested in data reduction, that is, the representation of n manifest variables by m unobserved latent variables ($m < n$). Unfortunately it turns out that for any set of manifest indicators there are an infinite number of solutions that can account for the observed covariances among the observed variables equally well. To be able to obtain a unique solution some constraints need to be placed on the solutions. In exploratory factor analysis the usual one is to "rotate" the initial solution to the most "simple structure." Although there are various analytic techniques for achieving simple structure (e.g., varimax and promax), they all have roughly the same goal in mind. In the ideal solution each item would be strongly related to one and only latent factor. In this ideal situation one would have located the most "pure" indicators of the underlying factors. Since this ideal is rarely (if ever) achieved with real data, one instead settles for solutions which minimize the complexity of the items, where complexity refers to the number of significant nonzero coefficients linking an item to the factors.

The general factor model is given by

$$z_i = \lambda_{i1}F_1 + \lambda_{i2}F_2 + \cdots + \lambda_{im}F_m + b_iS_i + c_iE_i, \qquad (3.44)$$

where z_i is an observed item i (in standardized form, that is, transformed to a mean of zero and standard deviation of unity); $F_1, F_2, \ldots, F_m$ are the latent "common" factors; S_i is a "specific" factor; E_i is a random measurement component; and λ_{ij}, b_i, and c_i are coefficients associated with the parameters. A common factor is one with at least two items with significant coefficients linked to it. A specific factor is a source of variation from a latent variable associated specifically with item i. It is assumed that the specific factor and measurement error are mutually uncorrelated. Furthermore, it is assumed that the common factors are uncorrelated with the specific factors and measurement errors. To summarize, each item is seen to be a function of three independent sources of variance—m common factors, one specific factor and measurement error. In fact, however, in cross-sectional studies, such as the usual survey, there is no way to uniquely estimate the variance associated with the specific factor and measurement error. Hence, the factor models, which are in fact measured, are of the form:

$$z_i = \sum_{j=1}^{m} \lambda_{ij}F_j + d_iU_i \qquad (3.45)$$

where $U_i = S_i + E_i$ and is called the "uniqueness" of an item.

The details of how the λ_{ij} are estimated is far too complex and detailed to present here. The interested reader can pursue the topic in Harman (1967).

Consider the model with a *single* common factor:

$$z_i = \lambda_iF + d_iU_i. \qquad (3.46)$$

This model is quite similar to the usual formula for decomposing an item into "true" and "error" components [see Eq. (3.1)]. It is this similarity which undoubtedly has lead to the attempts to link factor analysis to reliability theory. There are two important differences between Eq. (3.46) and Eq. (3.1). First, the factor model assumes that each item may be differentially related to the underlying unobserved variable, whereas the true score model assumes that each item is linked to the underlying true score with a coefficient of unity. Second, although not a necessity, most of the programmed factor analysis methods standardize the variables, whereas the observed variables in the true score model normally are assumed to be in their natural metric.

The fact that the factor analysis model allows for differentially "good" items can be seen as an advantage over the classical true score approach where all items must be equally good to estimate the reliability of a composite.[5] Applying Heise and Bohrnstedt's (1970) model, in which they adopt Lord and Novick's definition of *reliability* as the ratio of true score to observed variance, to (3.46) yields their estimate of reliability, called Ω. Specifically

$$\Omega = 1 - \frac{\sum_{i=1}^{n} V(y_i) - \sum_{i=1}^{n} V(y_i) h_i^2}{\sum_{i=1}^{n} \sum_{j=1}^{n} C(y_i, y_j)} \tag{3.47}$$

where h_i^2 is the communality[6] of item i. Although it is easy to demonstrate that Ω is a better estimate of reliability than Cronbach's (1951) α (Greene & Carmines, 1980), there are several problems with the Heise–Bohrnstedt approach. First, there are several exploratory factor analytic models that can be used to estimate (3.45), all of which give slightly different estimates of the λ_{ij} and hence the h_i^2. Second, one may find that a single-factor model does not fit the observed covariances very well; hence additional factors may be needed to account for the factors. Third, when more than a single factor is needed to account for the data, one is faced with the problem that an infinite number of rotations will fit the data equally well.[7] To deal with the case of multiple factors, Heise and Bohrnstedt introduce the concepts of validity and invalidity. In their model, validity refers to what was earlier called *theoretical* validity—the correlation between one's measure and the construct it is presumed to measure. Invalidity refers to variance in a measure that is reliable due to factors other than those one intends to measure with a set of items. Heise and Bohrnstedt demonstrate that the reliable variance can be decomposed into the sum of valid and invalid variances when the factors are constrained to be uncorrelated.

Bentler (1968) independently developed a measure similar to that of Heise and Bohrnstedt, which he called α_0. Armor (1974), Allen (1974), and Smith (1974b) have developed measures similar to Ω or have refined the original Heise–Bohrnstedt measure. Most of these measures are compared and contrasted in an excellent review article by Greene and Carmines (1980).

Despite the limitations just outlined, the estimation of reliability using exploratory factor-analytic methods continues to be useful and popular. A computer program is now available (Levine & Bohrnstedt, 1982) that computes six different reliability coefficients, item-to-total correlations, and the results of a canonical factor analysis. As useful as exploratory factor analysis has been for the estimation of the reliability of composites, confirmatory factor analytic methods may hold even more promise.

In *confirmatory factor analysis* (Jöreskog, 1969), one specifies a priori that certain elements have specified values. For example, if one believes that item i

---

[5] Recall that Cronbach's α is a lower bound to reliability unless one has items which are tau-equivalent or parallel.

[6] The communality of an item is the amount of variance in the item which can be explained by the common factors (see Harman, 1967). In the case of a single factor the communality of item i is simply λ_{ij}^2.

[7] Heise–Bohrnstedt suggest that the unrotated factors appear to make the most substantive sense for most problems.

is a function of only one factor, the λ_{ij} for all factors but one are constrained to be zero. To see how the exploratory and confirmatory models differ, we formalize the factor-analysis model further. In matrix notation the basic factor analysis model is

$$\mathbf{y} = \mathbf{\Lambda f} + \mathbf{u} \tag{3.48}$$

where $\mathbf{y}$ is a vector of n observed values, $\mathbf{f}$ is a vector of order $m < n$ latent common factors, $\mathbf{u}$ is a vector of uniquenesses and $\mathbf{\Lambda}$ is an $n \times m$ matrix of factor coefficients or loadings. It is assumed that $E(\mathbf{f}) = E(\mathbf{u}) = \mathbf{0}$. It is further assumed that $E(\mathbf{uu'}) = \mathbf{\Psi}$ is a diagonal matrix, that is, that the uniquenesses are uncorrelated with each other. Finally, we define $E(\mathbf{ff'}) = \mathbf{\Phi}$ as the matrix of intercorrelations among the m factors. Jöreskog (1969) shows that to obtain unique maximum likelihood estimates of the elements of $\mathbf{\Lambda}$ and $\mathbf{\Phi}$, one must impose n^2 restrictions on them. In exploratory factor analysis, where there are no formal hypotheses about the factors, it is convenient to do this by choosing these restrictions such that $\mathbf{\Phi} = \mathbf{I}$ and $\mathbf{\Lambda' \Psi^{-1} \Lambda}$ is diagonal. In a confirmatory factor analysis, however, where one has hypotheses about which items load on which factors and about the relationship of the factors to one another, it makes sense to choose these restrictions by requiring that some elements of $\mathbf{\Lambda}$ and/or $\mathbf{\Phi}$ be zero. Again, this is done on the basis of a priori notions of which factors are being measured by which items and whether or not the factors are correlated.

   Importantly, the maximum likelihood characteristics of confirmatory factor analysis yield a χ^2 goodness-of-fit test to evaluate the likelihood that an observed covariance matrix could have been generated by the restricted model. Furthermore, the χ^2 test can be fruitfully used to see whether models which have more restrictions (and hence are more parsimonious) fit as well as models with fewer restrictions. Examples of how this test can be used will be provided later in the chapter.

Congeneric Measures

   We will now show how confirmatory factor analysis has been fruitfully wed to reliability theory by Jöreskog in his classic paper on congeneric measurement (Jöreskog, 1971). A set of measures $x_1, x_2, \ldots, x_n$ are defined as congeneric if their true scores, $\tau_1, \tau_2, \ldots, \tau_n$, correlated unity with each other, implying that a random variable τ exists such that all the τ_i are linearly related to it. That is, congeneric measurement implies that

$$\tau_i = \mu_i + \beta_i \tau \tag{3.49}$$

and since $x_i = \tau_i + \varepsilon_i$, it follows on substitution that

$$x_i = \mu_i + \beta_i \tau + \varepsilon_i. \tag{3.50}$$

It is assumed that $E(\varepsilon_i) = 0$, $C(\tau, \varepsilon_i) = 0$, and $C(\varepsilon_i, \varepsilon_j) = 0$. If one's measures are non-Platonic, the metric of τ is unknown and arbitrary so some constraint is necessary. Hence we assume that $V(\tau) = 1.0$. Furthermore note that

$$V(x_i) = \beta_i^2 + \theta_i^2 \tag{3.51}$$

where θ_i^2 is defined as the variance of ε_i. It now follows from (3.10) that the reliability of item i is given by

$$\rho_i = \beta_i^2/(\beta_i^2 + \theta_i^2). \tag{3.52}$$

Now let $\mathbf{x}$, $\boldsymbol{\mu}$, $\boldsymbol{\beta}$, and $\mathbf{e}$ be column vectors of order n with elements x_i, μ_i, β_i, and e_i, respectively. Then (3.50) can be rewritten in vector form as

$$\mathbf{x} = \boldsymbol{\mu} + \boldsymbol{\beta}\tau + \mathbf{e}. \tag{3.53}$$

If $\boldsymbol{\Sigma}$ is the covariance matrix of $\mathbf{x}$ and $\boldsymbol{\theta}^2$ is a diagonal matrix of error variances, then $E(\mathbf{x}\mathbf{x}') = \boldsymbol{\Sigma}$ and

$$\boldsymbol{\Sigma} = \boldsymbol{\beta}\boldsymbol{\beta}' + \boldsymbol{\theta}^2. \tag{3.54}$$

Eq. (3.6) is the basic equation of the factor model with one common factor. If one can assume that the x_i follow a multivariate normal distribution, the parameters of the model can be efficiently estimated by Jöreskog's (1969) maximum likelihood method. The method yields large sample standard errors for all of the parameter estimates as well as the overall chi-square goodness-of-fit statistic referred to previously, which allows one to *test* the assumption that one's measures are congeneric.

While the definition of congeneric measures comes much closer to the assumption most survey researchers make, compared to those of parallel measurement and tau-equivalence, it is still unlikely that the model adequately describes the measurement characteristics of most of the items used. As Alwin and Jackson (1980) show, it is difficult to imagine items so "pure" that their variation is due to a single construct. As they point out, a set of items that can be fit by a single factor and hence may appear to be congeneric will often prove not to be when factored with items from other content domains.

One of the reasons that it is difficult to find measures which are congeneric is related to the sensitivity of the χ^2 goodness-of-fit test to sample size. If one's N is large, as it is in most survey research, it will be rare to find any set of n items ($n > 3$) that can be fit by the congeneric model. To deal with this problem, Tucker and Lewis (1973) propose a "reliability" coefficient that is designed to measure the variance in the observed covariances that is due to the common factors. The coefficient is given by

$$\hat{\rho} = (M_k - M_{(k+1)})/(M_k - 1) \tag{3.55}$$

where $M_k = \chi_k^2/df_k$ and $M_{(k+1)} = \chi_{(k+1)}^2/df_{(k+1)}$. The χ^2 and degrees of freedom are those associated with maximum likelihood factor analytic solutions where k and $k + 1$ common factors have been extracted. Equation (3.55) makes it clear that if the ratio of the chi-square to the degrees of freedom approaches unity for $k + 1$ factors, the Tucker–Lewis coefficient also approaches unity. Indeed, a quick method of determining how good a fit is involves computing the ratio of the obtained χ^2 value to its degrees of freedom. If it is close to unity the fit is quite excellent. In practice, however, it is rare to find such good fits except in the trivial cases where the degrees of freedom are few.

I will go through an example using the Tucker–Lewis coefficient shortly. But before examining the coefficient's use, it must be pointed out that there are no hard-and-fast rules for what a large Tucker–Lewis coefficient is. My own experience suggests that .90 is not bad, but I am still gaining experience with it, so little faith should be put in this criterion at this time.

Despite the fact that it is rare to find items that are congeneric, the congeneric model provides an ideal to be sought in choosing items. The best items are those that are "pure" with respect to a single underlying construct. If one attempts to choose items with the congeneric model in mind, then the theoretical validity of a composite score based on them should be high.

If one's items are congeneric, they can be combined into a linear composite:

$$y = \mathbf{w'x} \tag{3.56}$$

where $\mathbf{w'}$ is a $1 \times n$ vector of weights applied to the $n \times 1$-item vector, $\mathbf{x}$. Now substitution of (3.53) into (3.56) yields

$$y = \mathbf{w'\mu} + (\mathbf{w'\beta})\tau + \mathbf{w'\varepsilon} \tag{3.57}$$

Taking the variance of (3.57) applying the definition of reliability given in (3.10), Jörkeskog (1971) shows that the reliability of y is given by

$$\rho = \mathbf{w'\beta\beta w}/\mathbf{w'sw} \tag{3.58}$$

He further shows that ρ is a maximum when the w_i are chosen to be proportional to β_i/θ_i^2.

As an example, we can examine whether the items in Table 3.1 are congeneric. The data were analyzed using COFAMM.[8] The results are shown in Table 3.2. Notice first that $\chi^2_{27} = 119.3$, and $\chi^2/df = 4.42$, meaning that the items do not fit the congeneric model particularly well. We have nevertheless computed reliability estimates for the congeneric model in order to see how they compare to that from alpha. For the unit-weighted composite the estimate is .707; for the weighted composite .720. Obviously, the values do not differ appreciably from one another. It should be stressed that if one has congeneric measures, (3.58) will, in the population, provide an exact estimate of the reliability of a weighted composite. But when the items do not fit a congeneric model, (3.57) provides a lower bound to the reliability of the composite—just as α does, albeit a different one in most cases.

Since a single factor model does not fit the data well, how many factors are needed to fit the data? The most expeditious way to answer this question is to factor the items using a maximum likelihood exploratory factor analysis com-

---

[8] The program COFAMM was written by Dag Sörbom and Karl G. Jöreskog and is available from National Educational Services, P.O. Box A3650, Chicago, Illinois 60690.

TABLE 3.2
Fitting the Competitiveness Desirability Items to a
Congeneric Model

Item number	β_i	θ_i^2	ρ_i	w_i
1	.388*	.383*	.282	1.01
2	.316*	.311*	.243	1.02
3	.424*	.634*	.221	.67
4	.208*	.305*	.124	.68
5	.357*	.273*	.318	1.31
6	.224*	.415*	.108	.54
7	.378*	.502*	.222	.75
8	.281*	.304*	.206	.92
9	.397*	.522*	.232	.76

$$\chi_{27}^2 = 119.3, \, p < .000,$$

$$\rho = .707, \, \rho_w = .720, \, \alpha = .704$$

* Significant at .05 level.

puting the Tucker–Lewis reliability coefficients for analyses extracting one, two, three, four, and five factors.[9] This strategy was followed for the nine competitiveness desirability items in Table 3.1 using EFAP.[10] The results from these analyses are shown in Table 3.3. As indicated earlier, no hard and fast criterion exists for determining when factorization is complete. For this example a conservative decision suggests four factors are needed, since it requires a four-factor solution to obtain a p-value of .05 or greater. A four-factor solution results in a Tucker–Lewis p-value of .98, which is very acceptable. A less conservative decision would accept a two-factor decision given that it results in a Tucker–Lewis p-value of .92. The three-factor solution is not different enough from the two-factor solution to merit serious consideration. My decision would be to accept the two-factor solution, although, as indicated earlier, there is a certain amount of arbitrariness to the decision.

As indicated earlier, the Heise–Bohrnstedt (1971) procedure allows one to estimate the theoretical validity and invalidity of a composite. In this example, the validity of the weighted composite is .859 and the invalidity .0001. This strongly suggests that it is the first factor which is contributing virtually all of the variance to the composite. Although the second factor is statistically significant, its contribution to the variance of the composite is virtually nil. The comparable figures for the unweighted composite are .853 and .0001.

What general conclusion can be drawn about the congeneric model? First, while the assumptions of the model are obviously more compatible with the characteristics we associate with "good" items in survey research than the

[9] No more than five factors can be extracted for nine items since the degrees of freedom are exhausted. The formula for degrees of freedom is given by $df = [(n - m)^2 - (n + m)]/2$.

[10] The program EFAP was written by Karl G. Jöreskog and Dag Sörbom and is available from National Educational Services, P.O. Box A3650, Chicago, Illinois 60690.

TABLE 3.3
Maximum Likelihood Factoring of Competitiveness
Desirability Items (N = 869)

Number of factors	χ^2	df	χ^2/df	p	Tucker–Lewis ρ
0	954.5	36	26.5	***	—
1	119.3	27	4.4	***	.87
2	59.2	19	3.1	***	.92
3	32.8	12	2.7	***	.93
4	8.6	6	1.4	.20	.98
5	1.6	1	1.6	.21	.98

*** Significant at or beyond the .001 level.

assumptions of either tau-equivalent or parallel measures, it is clear as we gain experience with actual data sets that we rarely have measures which fit a single-factor congeneric model. This suggests, as Alwin and Jackson (1980) argue, that the multiple-factor model may be more appropriate than the congeneric model in describing a set of items. Second, our limited, but ever growing experience suggests that one should try to develop congeneric items. Results with what might be called "near-congeneric" items suggest one can construct items where nearly all of the common factor variance can be explained by the first unrotated factor.[11] Relatively little of the variance is due to other reliable, but unwanted common factors. Thus while the items may not perfectly fit a congeneric model, in fact items which are built with that model in mind often behave quite similar to congeneric items. It is for this reason, we suspect, that estimates of the internal consistency reliability, whether Cronbach's alpha, Heise–Bohrnstedt's omega, Armor's theta or Jöreskog's congeneric approach is employed, yield estimates which are very similar to one another.

The moral seems clear; while the tools for assessing internal consistency reliability have become powerfully refined and useful, what counts much more in the final analysis is care and thoughtfulness in *developing* items in the first place.

This completed our discussion of methods for estimating reliability. We now move to a discussion of validity.

[11] Again, Heise and Bohrnstedt (1970) take the position that the unrotated solution makes the most sense since the first unrotated factor explains the greatest amount of variance in the items. While Heise and Bohrnstedt are mute on the question of whether additionally extracted factors should be orthogonal to the first factor or not, it is this author's contention that they should be *unless* one has good theoretical reasons to allow them to be correlated. By constraining them to be uncorrelated, one is able to estimate how much reliable variance is due to the first factor compared to the others. If allowed to correlate, there is no way to decompose the variance in the items into that due to (*a*) the first factor, (*b*) all other common factors, and (*c*) uniqueness. However, it needs to be stressed that this formulation assumes that the items are from a single domain, that is, do not measure more than one substantive construct.

3.8. VALIDITY

Validity has different meanings. However, a very general definition can be given. *Validity indicates the degree to which an instrument measures the construct under investigation.* Thus a valid measure of sex role identity is one which measures that construct and not some other one. Or, a valid measure of anomie measures that construct only and not naysaying as well.

As indicated earlier, a useful conceptual distinction is between *theoretical* and *empirical* validity. The former refers to the correlation between the underlying, latent construct and the observed measure, whereas the latter refers to a correlation between the observed measure and some other observed criterion.

The American Psychological Association (1974) distinguishes between three types of validity—(*a*) *criterion-related,* (*b*) *content,* and (*c*) *construct.* Criterion-related validity is the same as what we have labeled empirical validity. Construct validity is a general concept that subsumes what we called theoretical validity. We do not think that content validity is a measure of validity per se, but rather is a procedure which results in theoretical validity. We now explore the types of validity in more depth.

Criterion-Related Validity (Empirical Validity)

Criterion-related validity is defined as the correlation between a measure and some criterion variable of interest. Since the criterion variable might be one which exists in the present or one which one might want to predict in the future, criterion-related validity is broken into two types: predictive and concurrent.

Predictive validity is an assessment of an individual's future standing on a criterion variable and can be predicted from present standing on a measure. For example, if one constructs a measure of work orientation its predictive validity for job performance might be ascertained by administering it to a group of new hirees and correlating it with some measure of success (e.g., supervisors' ratings, advances within the organization) at some later point in time. Importantly, no measure has a single predictive validity coefficient; it has varying validities depending upon the criterion of interest as the example just provided should make clear. Furthermore, confidence in the predictive validity of a measure with respect to a single criterion should reflect the quality of the sample taken, whether and how often the result has been replicated and the amount of time between assessments.

Concurrent validity is assessed by correlating a measure and a criterion of interest at the *same* point in time. A measure of the concurrent validity of an attitude measure of religiosity with respect to church attendance could be assessed in a single interview, for example. Just as for predictive validity, there are as many concurrent validities as there are criteria one may want to explain—there is no single concurrent validity for a given measure.

Since survey researchers rarely predict behavior, validity assessed with concurrent measurement is a more feasible alternative. One can rather easily

assess the concurrent validity of a measure of political conservatism by correlating it with reported voting behavior. And the concurrent validity of a measure of religious orthodoxy can be checked by correlating it with reported
attendance at religious services.

A type of concurrent validity uses the *known group technique*. If one
knows that certain groups vary on a variable of interest, they can be used to
validate a new measure of it. For example, one would expect that those who
report they are of no religious identification to score substantially lower on a
measure of religious orthodoxy than those who belong to established religious
groups.

Concurrent validation can also be evaluated by correlating a measure of X
with extant measures of X. However, this procedure assumes that the extant
measures of X are themselves valid. And if they are, then unless one has a more
efficient way to measure X, one can ask why a new measure is being constructed! We find this form of concurrent validation of limited value given that
survey research measurement is not a well advanced art.

A measure which has concurrent validity with respect to a criterion may or
may not be predictively valid. A set of items which measures attitudes toward
political issues may correlate highly in August as to which political party a
certain man *believes* he will vote for in November, but may correlate rather
poorly with the *actual* vote in November.

Many of the constructs of interest to survey researchers do not have
criteria against which the validity of a measure can be easily ascertained. When
they do, the criteria may themselves be so poorly measured that the validity
coefficients are badly attenuated due to measurement error. For these reasons,
survey researchers have found the criterion-related validities to be of limited
use.

Content Validity

One can imagine a *domain of meaning* that a particular construct is intended to measure. *Content validity* refers to the degree that one has represen-
tatively sampled from that domain of meaning. One can think of a given domain
as having various facets (Guttman, 1959) and just as one can use stratification
to obtain a sample of persons, one can use stratification principles to improve
the content validity of one's measure.

While content validity has received close attention in the construction of
achievement and proficiency measures with psychology and educational psychology, it has usually been ignored among political scientists and sociologists
using survey methods. Many researchers have instead been satisfied to construct a few items on an ad hoc, one-shot basis in the apparent belief that they
are measuring what they intended to measure. In fact, the construction of good
measures is a tedious, arduous, and time-consuming task.

Although it may sound like a good idea to sample the facets of a domain of
meaning for a given construct, the fact that the domain can not be enumerated

in the same way that a population of persons or objects might be makes the task less rigorous than one would like. While the educational psychologist can sample four-, five-, six-, etc., letter words in constructing a spelling test, no such clear criteria exist for the survey researcher who wanders into the muddy waters of social measurement. But some guidelines can be provided. First, the researcher should search the literature carefully to determine how various authors have used the concept which is to be measured. The survey researcher has several excellent handbooks which summarize social measures in use, including Robinson and Shaver's (1973) *Measures of Social Psychological Attitudes;* Robinson, Rusk, and Head's (1968) *Measures of Political Attitudes;* Robinson, Athanasiou and Head's *Measures of Occupational Attitudes and Occupational Characteristics;* Shaw and Wright's (1967) *Scales for the Measurement of Attitudes;* and Miller's (1977) *Handbook of Research Design and Social Measurement.* These volumes not only contain lists of the measures but provide existing data on the reliability and validity of the measures as well (usually scant!). But since these books are out of date as soon as they are shipped off to press, researchers developing their own methods must do additional literature searches as well. Second, researchers should rely on their own observations and insights and ask whether they yield additional facets to the construct under consideration. This is especially important should researchers have particular hunches as to how the concept relates to a (set of) dependent variable(s).

Using these two approaches one develops *sets* of items, one each to capture the various facets or strata within the domain of meaning. There is no simple criterion by which one can judge whether or not a particular domain of meaning has been properly sampled. However there are a couple of precautions which can be taken to help ensure the representation of the various facets within the domain.

First, the domain can be stratified into its major facets. One first notes the most central meanings of the construct, making certain that the stratification is exhaustive, that is, all major meaning facets are represented. If a particular facet appears itself to involve a complex of meanings, it should be subdivided further into substrata. A concept such as "feelings of powerlessness" could be subdivided into political, economic, occupational, and familial powerlessness, for example. *The more one refines the strata and substrata the easier it is to construct the items later, and the more complete the coverage of meanings associated with the construct.*

Second, one should write several items to reflect the meanings associated with each stratum and substratum. How "several" translates into numbers will depend on the ingenuity and diligence of the researcher. But several should mean at least 7–10 items for each (sub)stratum. One can always exclude items from the instrument that do not perform well, but an item excluded at this early step is lost forever. Importantly, items almost never perform in the way we think they will. This is another reason for building a large item pool at this stage of the research. If one builds only 4 items for a given measure and only 2 of them are internally consistent, one is stuck with a 2-item measure—almost certain to have no more than moderate internal consistency reliability since we saw earlier that reliability is partially a function of the number of items in a score. On analyzing a set of items, one may find a stratum thought to be unidimensional is in fact not. If one has a large item pool, there still may be a sufficient number of items to establish measures with decent internal consistency; if not, one is stuck with two- or three-item composite scores.

After developing the items one should pretest them on a sample of persons similar to those with whom one intends to use them more generally. The pretest sample should be large enough to use powerful multivariate tools such as the maximum likelihood techniques discussed earlier in this chapter. The evaluation of the items is a matter of determining their construct validity, in my opinion, and for that reason the discussion of how one evaluates the goodness or badness of an item is presented in the next section. Furthermore, as already mentioned, it is my opinion that what the American Psychological Association calls content validity is not a type of validity at all but rather is a set of procedures for sampling content domains[12] which if followed help to ensure construct validity. Although I enthusiastically endorse the procedures, I reject the concept of content validity on the grounds that there is no rigorous way to assess it except by using the methods of construct validation.

Construct Validity

"A construct is . . . a theoretical idea developed to explain and to organize some aspects of existing knowledge. . . . It is a dimension understood or inferred from its network of interrelationships [American Psychological Association, 1974, p. 29]." The *Standards* further indicate that in establishing construct validity

> the investigator begins by formulating hypotheses about the characteristics of those who have high scores on the [measure][13] in contrast to those who have low scores. Taken together, such hypotheses form at least a tentative theory about the nature of the construct the [measure] is believed to be measuring.
> Such hypotheses or theoretical formulations lead to certain predictions about how people . . . will behave . . . in certain defined situations. If the investigator's theory . . . is correct, most of his predictions should be confirmed. If they are not, he may revise his definition of the construct, or he may revise the [measure] to make it a better measure of the construct he had in mind [p. 30].

The notion of a construct implies hypotheses of two types. First, it implies that items from one stratum within the domain of meaning correlate together because they all reflect the same underlying construct or "true" score. Second,

---

[12] Other authors who also stress the domain sampling concept are Tryon (1957) and Nunnally (1967).

[13] When the word "measure" appears in brackets it has been substituted for "test" in the original.

whereas items from one domain may correlate with items from another domain, the implication is that they do so only because the constructs themselves are correlated. Furthermore, it is assumed that there are *hypotheses* about how measures of different domains correlate with one another. To repeat, construct validation involves two types of validation. The first is what we have been calling *theoretical validity*—an assessment of the relationship between the items and an underlying, latent unobserved construct. The second involves confirming that the latent variables themselves correlate as hypothesized. If either or both sets of hypotheses fail, then construct validation is absent. If one can show theoretical validity but hypotheses about the interrelations among these constructs fail, either it suggests that one is not measuring the intended construct, or that the theory is wrong or inadequate. The more unconfirmed hypotheses one has involving the constructs the more one is likely to assume the former rather than the latter. One may have a construct which has good theoretical validity, but it may not be the construct one thought was being measured!

If one verifies hypothesized interrelations among constructs, it still may be that theoretical validity is poor. Suppose one has aggregated a set of items together which represent several substrata of a domain, or perhaps even represent several domains. If some or all of these domains are related to a criterion construct of interest, the hypothesized correlation will obtain. But a much better procedure would be to purify the measures by building subscores, or separate domain scores in order to determine which of them best correlate with the criterion construct.

The hypotheses implied by the notion of construct validity can be represented by a diagram as shown in Figure 3.4. If items had perfect construct validity, they would reflect one and only one construct, and the construct

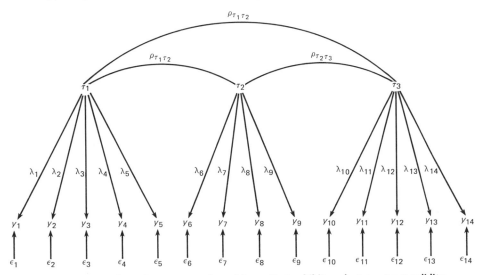

FIGURE 3.4 A schematic representation of items that exhibit perfect construct validity.

would correlate as hypothesized. Although two items reflecting different constructs might intercorrelate, it would be because of the covariation between the constructs. To see this note that

$$x_1 = \lambda_1 \tau_1 + \varepsilon_1, \tag{3.59a}$$

and

$$x_5 = \lambda_5 \tau_2 + \varepsilon_5. \tag{3.59b}$$

It follows straightforwardly that

$$C(x_1, x_5) = \lambda_1 \lambda_5 C(\tau_1, \tau_2) \tag{3.60}$$

assuming that the τs are uncorrelated with the errors and the errors are uncorrelated with one another.

Note further that all of the items shown in Figure 3.4 fit the congeneric model. This fact may suggest to the reader that the most appropriate way to evaluate and screen items from various content domains (or from the substrata of a single domain) is with confirmatory factor analysis. In fact, experience suggests that this is *not* the case. First, as pointed out earlier, it is rare for a set of items to fit a congeneric model perfectly; second, when items fail to fit the model, it is not always easy to tell what structure best explains the covariation among the items. For these reasons, unless one has a compelling reason for believing that a single factor model is the correct one, an exploratory factor analysis done with a maximum likelihood procedure such as EFAP or the Rao option of SPSS seems most appropriate. The following set of steps is recommended:

1. Do an exploratory factor analysis.
2. Decide how many factors are needed to explain the covariation among the items using both the χ^2 and Tucker–Lewis statistics as guides.
3. Examine both the rotated and unrotated solutions when $m > 1$ in order to determine whether the factors beyond the first are substantively meaningful or merely unwanted "nuisance" factors.
4. Remove those items which are poorly related to no factors or which clearly represent more than a single domain.
5. Refactor the remaining items but this time use a confirmatory analysis in order to verify that the items are congeneric or near congeneric.

As an example, consider the items in Table 3.4 drawn from the *NORC General Social Survey* (National Opinion Research Center, 1974). The seven items taken together appear to represent a construct which might be labeled "current life satisfaction" since the items tap the areas of job, finances, hobbies, family, friends, health, and the community. The data used to evaluate the items are from 375 employed, married males who participated in the 1974 national survey. The correlations among the seven items along with their means and standard deviations are also shown in Table 3.4. The covariances among the items were computed, and, following Step 1, were analyzed with EFAP. The pertinent results from an analysis of the covariance matrix are

TABLE 3.4
Means, Standard Deviations, Correlations and Covariances for Seven Satisfaction Items
(N = 375)[a]

Item	1	2	3	4	5	6	7
City	1.000	.708	.348	.637	.394	.250	.251
Hobbies	.299	1.000	.525	.616	.406	.103	.115
Family life	.249	.360	1.000	.540	.341	.091	.042
Friendships	.364	.338	.500	1.000	.428	.184	.100
Health	.214	.211	.300	.301	1.000	.145	.072
Financial situation	.214	.085	.127	.204	.153	1.000	.134
Job	.227	.100	.062	.118	.080	.234	1.000
Means	5.101	5.363	6.255	5.828	5.872	3.382	2.101
SD	1.505	1.570	.929	1.162	1.224	.776	.735

[a] Covariances are above main diagonal and correlations below. See *General Social Survey Codebook* for exact wording of items.

shown in Table 3.5. Both the two- and three-factor solutions fit the observed covariance matrix quite well. But the Tucker–Lewis coefficient of 1.00 associated with the two-factor solution argues strongly for it instead of the three-factor solution. The rotated two-factor oblique solution is shown in Panel B of

TABLE 3.5
Maximum Likelihood Exploratory Factor Analysis of Seven Satisfaction Items (N = 375)

A. Fit of different models

Number of factors	χ^2	df	χ^2/df	p	Tucker–Lewis ρ
0	356.36	21	16.97	.000	—
1	39.84	14	2.85	.000	.88
2	8.00	8	1.00	.434	1.00
3	.30	3	.10	.960	1.06

B. Promax rotated two-factor solution

Items	Factor I	II	Uniqueness
1	.40	.62	1.52
2	.72	.15	1.84
3	.69	−.07	.42
4	.76	.15	.66
5	.46	.13	1.22
6	.03	.33	.48
7	−.07	.39	.41

Correlation between factors = .39

TABLE 3.6
Fitting Six Satisfaction Items to a Two-Factor
Congeneric Model

Item	Factor		θ_i^2
	I	II	
2	.77*	.00^a	1.87
3	.65*	.00^a	.44
4	.83*	.00^a	.66
5	.53*	.00^a	1.22
6	.00^a	.49*	.37
7	.00^a	.28*	.47

$r_{1,II} = .00$, $\chi_8^2 = 5.89$, $\chi^2/df = .74$, $p \geq .66$

^{a} Parameter constrained to be zero.
* Significant at the .05 level.

Table 3.5. It strongly suggests the presence of two substantive factors—one clearly identified with what appears to be job-related satisfaction and the other general satisfaction. The first item—satisfaction with city—is related to both factors. While it is logical that satisfaction with city is related to both general and job-related satisfaction, this item is clearly not a pure indicator of either type and, hence, following Step 4, is eliminated.

Following Step 5, the remaining six items were then refactored using COFAMM where items 2, 3, 4, and 5 were constrained to load only on the first factor and items 6, 7 only on the second. The two factors were allowed to correlate freely, however. The results are shown in Table 3.6.[14] Notice that the items in this case fit a congeneric model very closely, since $\chi_8^2 = 5.89$. It must be pointed out, however, that good fits are much harder to achieve when one begins with a larger item pool. (Recall, only seven items were "sampled" from the satisfaction domain.) It is interesting to note that although allowed to correlate freely, the estimated correlation between the two constructs is 0. This strongly suggests that simply adding up all the items a priori into a single overall current satisfaction index would have been a gross error.

Since the two measures fit the congeneric model, (3.58) can be used to compute the reliability of the two composites. Assuming the items are unit weighted (rather than differentially weighted), the reliability of the general satisfaction construct is .637 and that of the job-related construct .411. The fact that the congeneric model nearly fits the data perfectly offers some (although only limited) evidence that all of the reliable variance is also valid (see Heise & Bohrnstedt, 1970). That is, the theoretical validity of the two measures is just the square root of the reliabilities or .799 and .641, respectively. These are not particularly impressive figures. They point out the importance of beginning

[14] The results have been rescaled or standardized such that the variance of the items equals unity in each case. For the details of how this is done, see Jöreskog and Sörbom (1977) or Alwin and Jackson (1980).

with a larger item pool. If we had six or eight measures, the reliability and theoretical validity coefficients might well have been considerably more impressive.

Another critical step in examining the validity of these two constructs would be to demonstrate that they correlate as hypothesized with other constructs, that is, to examine the construct's empirical validity. For example, we might expect that someone who is dissatisfied might also feel anomic. Therefore, one shred of evidence for the validity of the measures might come from showing them to be correlated to a measure of anomie. Since the Srole (1956) anomie scale was included in the 1974 *General Social Survey,* we correlated it with the two satisfaction measures. It correlated $-.17$ with general satisfaction and $-.19$ with job-related satisfaction.

We might also expect job-related satisfaction to be related to income. This correlation is .23. We might also expect those on welfare to be less satisfied with both general and job-related satisfaction. These two correlations are $-.16$ and $-.17$, respectively. While small, this *pattern* of correlations suggests a modest amount of empirical validity for the two measures. Taken together, the indices for both theoretical and empirical validity suggest that additional developmental work (i.e., developing additional items evaluated in new samples) is needed before one should feel comfortable with these two measures of satisfaction.

The Multitrait–Multimethod Matrix and Construct Validity

Campbell (1953, 1956) has been a prominent advocate of the use of *multiple methods* in the measurement of social variables. In particular, he has argued that some of the variance in measures may be a function of how they are measured. Whether one uses projective or nonprojective, direct observational or participant observational, physiological or cognitive measures may contribute heavily to the observed responses. Survey researchers have long worried whether one obtains differential responses as a function of using the interview rather than the questionnaire, same-race interviewers rather than interviewers of a different race, and so on. More recently there has been a concern with whether responses obtained from telephone interviews differ from those obtained face-to-face.

To the degree that different methods provide the same or very similar results, the construct demonstrates what Campbell calls *convergent validity* (1954) or *triangulation* (1953, 1956). Campbell and Fiske (1959) argue that to justify a new construct measure, one must establish *discriminant validity* in addition. That is, a new measure must not correlate too highly with measures of other constructs or it is not distinguishable from them. Quite clearly Campbell and Fiske's concepts of convergent and discriminant validity taken together can contribute evidence for a measure's construct validity.

Campbell and Fiske suggest that convergent and discriminate validity can be investigated within the *multitrait–multimethod matrix.* An example of such

TABLE 3.7
A Synthetic Multitrait–Multimethod Matrix for Validating Measures of Anomie (A), Misanthropy (M), and Prejudice (P) Using Face-to-Face Interviews, Telephone Interviews, and Questionnaires[a]

Constructs	Variable	Face-to-face interview			Telephone interview			Questionnaire		
		A	M	P	A	M	P	A	M	P
Face-to-face interview										
A	y_1	—								
M	y_2	.36	—							
P	y_3	.26	.35	—						
Telephone interview										
A	y_4	.65	.22	.31	—					
M	y_5	.19	.61	.12	.40	—				
P	y_6	.14	.15	.54	.32	.45	—			
Questionnaire										
A	y_7	.50	.37	.42	.51	.33	.40	—		
M	y_8	.32	.47	.39	.27	.42	.41	.51	—	
P	y_9	.38	.35	.47	.35	.37	.44	.49	.57	—

[a] The three validity diagonals are boldface. Each heterotrait–monomethod triangle is enclosed by solid lines and each heterotrait–heteromethod triangle is enclosed by broken lines.

a matrix is shown in Table 3.7. The correlations in this table are fictitious but are chosen to illustrate how one might show construct validity for measures of anomie, misanthropy and prejudice using three methods of measurement— face-to-face interviews, telephone interviews and a questionnaire completed by the respondent. Campbell and Fiske label the correlations between constructs measured by a single method the *heterotrait–monomethod triangles*. There are three of them enclosed by solid lines in Table 3.7. And a *heteromethod block* is made up of a *validity diagonal* (italicized values in the table) and two *hetero-trait–heteromethod triangles* (enclosed by dashed lines in the table). Conver-gent validity is ascertained by an examination of the validity diagonals—they obviously should be high. Discriminant validity is established when the values in the heterotrait–heteromethod triangles are not as high as those in the validity diagonal, and the values in the heterotrait–monomethod triangles are not as high as the reliabilities of the measures.[15] While Campbell and Fiske provide these very general criteria for evaluating the convergent and discriminant valid-ity of constructs, they do not provide any statistical criteria for evaluating it. For this reason several such criteria have been suggested (Althauser & Heber-lein, 1970; Althauser, Heberlein, & Scott, 1971; Boruch, Larkins, Wolins, & Mackinney, 1970; Conger, 1971; 1974; Hubert & Baker, 1978; Jackson, 1969,

[15] As Eq. (18) shows, when the two reliabilities and the observed correlation between two measures are equal, the true score correlation between the measures is unity.

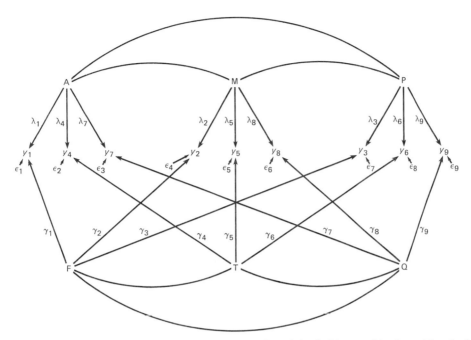

FIGURE 3.5 A confirmatory factor analytic representation of the fictitious multitrait–multimethod data shown in Table 3.8 for three constructs—Anomie (A), Misanthropy (M), and Prejudice (P)—and three methods—Face-to-face interview (F), Telephone interview (T), and Questionnaire (Q).

1975; Jöreskog, 1971; Werts, Jöreskog, & Linn, 1972; Werts & Linn, 1970b). In reviewing these criteria, both Alwin (1974) and Schmitt, Coyle, and Saari (1977) argue that the most appropriate way to evaluate the matrix is with confirmatory factor-analytic methods (Jöreskog, 1971; Werts & Linn, 1970b; Werts, Jöreskog, & Linn, 1972). I share in that evaluation. A confirmatory factor analytic representation of the data shown in Table 3.7 is shown in Figure 3.5.[16] Note that each of the nine variables is expressed as a function of a construct and the method used to assess it. For example, $y_1 = \lambda_1 A + \gamma_1 F + \varepsilon_1$, that is, the first item is a function of the construct anomie being assessed by a face-to-face interview. The next item, y_4, is a function of the construct anomie as assessed by a telephone interview, and so on. Note further that estimates of the correlations among the three constructs are obtained as well as correlations among the three methods. That is, it is possible to ascertain whether the methods are independent of each other or whether they, too, are correlated. In this example, it is also possible to estimate the correlations among methods and constructs. It may be, for example, that the methods operate differently across constructs. One might find a positive correlation

[16] The example discussed required at least three traits and three methods to estimate all the possibly relevant coefficients. More details about the relationship between the number of methods and constructs needed in order to meet the identification requirement of confirmatory factor analytic methods with multitrait–multimethod data can be found in Alwin (1974).

between using a questionnaire and prejudice, but not between prejudice and the other two methods. That is, those showing prejudice are more likely to do so when responding to a questionnaire than when interviewed either face-to-face or on the telephone.

To test whether the methods are correlated with the constructs, two separate analyses would be done. In the first, one would allow the methods and construct factors to be freely correlated; in the second these factors would be fixed a priori to equal zero. One could then compare the χ^2 values obtained from the two analyses and determine whether the fit is significantly better when the methods are allowed to correlate with the constructs. If the fit does improve significantly, one interprets the correlations. If not, one has the advantage of being able to estimate the variance in each y_i due to the construct and that due to the various methods (see Jöreskog, 1971, for an example). However, to be able to estimate further the amount of variance *each* method uniquely contributes to the variance of an item, evidence must be garnered that the methods themselves are uncorrelated. In particular, one must be able to show that the fit of the covariance (or correlation) matrix implied by a model in which the methods factors are fixed to be uncorrelated with the content factors *and* in which the correlations between methods factors are also fixed to be zero, is not worse than a model in which the only constraints are that the methods factors are uncorrelated with the content factors. I suspect that it will be relatively rare to find these conditions met in actual survey data, but it is important to note that the method does allow one to test for the possibility.

Assuming a confirmatory analytic model of the sort just described does adequately account for the observed covariances (or correlations) among the variables, one is still faced with how to evaluate whether Campbell and Fiske's (1959) criteria for convergent and discriminant validity are met. Alwin (1974) describes a set of procedures for doing so, and the interested reader is encouraged to examine this excellent article for details.

I have provided only one fictitious example, but I hope that survey researchers see that the multitrait–multimethod matrix might be used fruitfully to examine response effects within the larger context of establishing the construct validity of measures. The obvious disadvantage to the approach is the need to fully cross methods and constructs—a task that is not only expensive but may evoke respondent resistance. But the approach would seem to at least be worth exploring with subsets of respondents in the development of new survey measures or in validating existing ones.[17]

Structural Equation Models with Unobserved Variables

In the final section of this chapter I briefly introduce the reader to some recent developments in statistical modeling that provide the researcher using

[17] We know of only one attempt to apply this method in survey research to this point. It is a study by Andrews and Crandall (1976) in which six aspects of well-being are measured by six methods.

multiple measures with a set of highly sophisticated tools for estimating causal relations with survey data.[18] The technique is a generalization of Jöreskog's confirmatory factor analysis. In particular, assuming one has a theory linking the unobserved, latent variables or factors together, and assuming one can meet identification requirements along with a standard set of assumptions of regression and true score models, this technique (Jöreskog, 1970, 1973; Long, 1976) allows one simultaneously (a) to estimate the parameters linking the indicators or items to the underlying, latent factors (the *measurement equations*) and (b) to estimate the parameters linking the unobserved variables to each other as well (the *structural equations*). Just as is true for confirmatory factor analysis, the technique allows one to constrain parameters to equal one another or to equal any fixed value (usually 0 or 1). In addition, again assuming a given model is identified, the technique allows for reciprocal causation or feedback among the dependent or endogenous variables and for correlated measurement error. The allowance for correlated measurement error is especially useful when one has longitudinal data where it seems likely that the errors of measurement associated with a given item will be correlated across time (Wheaton *et al.*, 1977). If one can assume that the items follow a multivariate normal distribution, a χ^2 statistic can be used to evaluate the overall goodness of fit of the covariance matrix implied by the model and that actually observed.[19]

Importantly, the estimated structural coefficients linking the latent variables of the model together are automatically corrected for attenuation due to measurement error. Therefore, the rather cumbersome procedures discussed in the section on the effect of unreliability of measures do not have to be employed. Furthermore, when one has multiple indicators, the estimates of the structural parameters are more exactly and efficiently estimated than they are by using the correction for attenuation formulas—Eqs. (3.18)–(3.22). Therefore, these methods should have wide appeal to survey researchers employing multiple-item measures of constructs.

An example of a structural equation model with multiple indicators is shown in Figure 3.6. The problem is to estimate the effect of deviant behavior (marijuana use and premarital sex) on change in religious values during the years of student protest, 1964–1968. Following Lord (1963), Bohrnstedt (1969), Cronbach and Furby (1970), Heise (1970), Werts and Linn (1970), and Jöreskog and Sörbom (1977), change is measured as the effect of a variable at Time 2 controlling for itself at Time 1. Here, the effect of drug use on change is

---

[18] The technique can also be used to estimate structural models where one has a single indicator of each variable and the indicator is assumed to be measured perfectly. That is, the technique can be used to estimate standard path analytic models (Land, 1969; Duncan, 1966, 1975) as well.

[19] For the sake of brevity and so as not to burden the reader with some rather complex mathematics, the details of the model as well as a rigorous statement of assumptions is not provided here. However, the would-be user of the technique is strongly encouraged to examine the primary sources and/or to seek expert advice before attempting to use the techniques. In particular, the researcher using these techniques needs to be especially careful to pay attention to the identification problem. The issue is too complex to discuss here, but approaches to the identification problem in structural models with unobserved variables can be found in Wiley (1973).

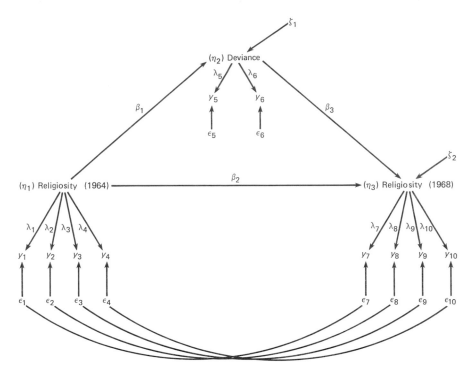

FIGURE 3.6 A structural equation model with multiple indicators estimating the effects of deviant behavior use on religious values.

equal to the coefficient linking it to religiosity at Time 2 controlling for religiosity at Time 1. Notice that the model assumes that all of the items are congeneric—that is, that each item is a reflector of one and only one construct. We have also assumed that the coefficient associated with an item in 1964 is the same in 1968. That is, we are assuming the meaning of the items is temporally invariant. Furthermore, it is assumed that the errors of measurement for an item at Time 1 may be correlated with the errors of measurement for that same item at Time 2, but that all other errors in measurement are mutually uncorrelated. This assumption follows from the fact that it is probably unreasonable to assume that all of the reliable variance in the items is due to the underlying common factors. If some of what is being called random measurement error is in fact reliable, specific variance,[20] then one should expect the errors of measurement to be correlated across time.[21] The model also assumes that the latent factors are uncorrelated with their errors of measurement and

[20] The reader is referred back to our earlier discussion of sources of variance in factor models. Potential sources of variance in an item are due to common factors, a reliable specific factor and random measurement error.

[21] Obviously if one allows for specific reliable factors, strictly speaking the items are not congeneric. However, one might argue they are congeneric with respect to the common factors.

that the disturbances of the drug use and Time 2 religiosity variable are uncorrelated with each other and with the religiosity variable at Time 1.

There are three sets of measurement equations implied by Figure 3.6. The first links y_1 through y_4 with the single independent or endogenous variable, religiosity (1964). These equations are

$$y_1 = \eta_1 + \varepsilon_1 \quad \text{and} \quad y_i = \lambda_i\eta_1 + \varepsilon_i \quad \text{for} \quad i = 2, 3, 4, \quad (3.61)$$

where the λ_i are the coefficients or weights linking the y_i to η_1—the latent variable religiosity (1964). We have fixed λ_1 to 1.0 in order to fix the metric of η_1. The second set of measurement equations links the two indicators of the latent variable, deviance (η_2)

$$y_5 = \eta_2 + \varepsilon_5 \quad \text{and} \quad y_6 = \lambda_6\eta_2 + \varepsilon_5, \quad (3.62)$$

and the third set links the same items as in (3.61), measured this time 4 years later to the latent variable religiosity (1968) (η_3).

$$y_i = \lambda_{i-6}\eta_3 + \varepsilon_i \quad \text{for} \quad i = 7, 8, 9, 10. \quad (3.63)$$

The two structural equations linking the latent, unobserved variables together are

$$\eta_2 = \beta_1\eta_1 + \zeta_2 \quad \text{and} \quad \eta_3 = \beta_2\eta_1 + \beta_3\eta_2 + \zeta_3. \quad (3.64)$$

The data were collected from men and women who entered the University of Wisconsin as freshmen in 1964 and who completed followup questionnaires, including a supplementary "personal form," which inquired about their drug use and sexual behavior. Details of the data analyzed here can be found in Schultz, Bohrnstedt, Borgatta, and Evans (1977). The four religiosity items inquired about the importance of religious belief, the importance of religion to foster the moral development of civilization, the need for stricter observance of the Sabbath, and the belief in life after death. The items were coded 0 for "definitely disagree" to 3 for "definitely agree." The two deviance items are measures of premarital sex and marijuana use.[22] Premarital sex was a simple yes–no variable coded 0 or 1; and marijuana use was coded 0 for never used, 1 for used only once or twice, and 2 for regular use. The correlations and standard deviations for the item are displayed in Table 3.8. The covariances were used to analyze two different models. In the first, the errors in measurement were assumed to be uncorrelated with each other. In the second, the errors of measurement for an item measured in 1964 were allowed to correlate with that same item's errors of measurement in 1968. Both models were estimated using LISREL.[23] The model estimated with uncorrelated measurement errors had an associated χ^2 value of 277.6 with 35 df—not a particularly good fit. When items' errors of measurement were allowed to correlate freely from 1964 to 1968, the

[22] All students who reported having sex before reaching 17.5 years of age were removed from the analysis, as were students who were married by 1968.

[23] The LISREL program was written by Karl G. Jöreskog and Dag Sörbom (1981).

TABLE 3.8
Correlations and Standard Deviations for the Ten Religiosity and Deviance Items in Figure 3.6[a]

	Items									
	1	2	3	4	5	6	7	8	9	10
1	1.00									
2	.50	1.00								
3	.49	.45	1.00							
4	.52	.44	.46	1.00						
5	−.25	−.26	−.23	−.25	1.00					
6	−.12	−.09	−.13	−.16	.26	1.00				
7	.40	.27	.33	.32	−.29	−.14	1.00			
8	.37	.38	.32	.33	−.28	−.15	.55	1.00		
9	.36	.33	.46	.36	−.28	−.16	.60	.52	1.00	
10	.43	.33	.36	.58	−.32	−.20	.55	.50	.56	1.00
SD	.98	.86	.88	1.00	.77	.49	1.01	.87	.86	1.04

[a] The item wordings are: y_1 and y_7: "Everyone should believe in and practice some religion"; y_2 and y_8: "The best way to foster the moral development of civilization is through organized religion"; y_3 and y_9: "There should be stricter observance of the Sabbath, the religious day of rest"; and y_4 and y_{10}: "There is a life after death." Items 5 and 6 measured marijuana use and premarital sexual behavior, respectively. See text for how the items were coded.

estimated model had an associated χ^2 of 51.3 with 31 df. The improvement in fit can be assessed by a χ^2 test with 4 df. The χ^2 equals 226.3, indicating an improvement in fit statistically significant far beyond the .05 level. Furthermore, the overall fit of the data to the model is also significant beyond the .01 level.

Bentler and Bonett (1980) have generalized the Tucker–Lewis (1963) coefficient to apply to more general structural equation models with latent variables. One computes a χ^2 goodness-of-fit test for a null model in which all free structural parameters are estimated to be zero and then compares this fit to that obtained for the substantive model of interest. The coefficient is given by

$$\hat{\rho} = \frac{(\chi_0^2/df_0) - (\chi_1^2/df_1)}{(\chi_0^2/df_0) - 1} \tag{3.65}$$

where (χ_0^2/df_0) is the χ^2 of the null model divided by the degrees of freedom and (χ_1^2/df_1) is the chi-square associated with the substantive model of interest divided by its degrees of freedom. The null model for the data in Table 3.8 yields $\chi_{45}^2 = 3523.05$. Using this result $\hat{\rho} = .99$, suggesting a very good fit indeed.[24] All of this suggests that the covariances in Table 3.8 can be accounted

[24] While the Tucker and Lewis (1963) and Bentler and Bonett (1980) coefficients are useful given the sensitivity of the chi-square test associated with the estimation of covariance models to sample size, they are not without their own problems. First, the criterion of .90 or greater as indication of an adequate fit may lead to underfitting the data on some occasions. For example, in the example just presented, the same model as that shown in Figure 3.6 but without correlated

TABLE 3.9
Parameter Estimates for the Correlated Measurement Model in Figure 3.6[a]

	1			2	
Parameter	Unrescaled	Rescaled		Parameter	Estimate
λ_1	1.00^c	.72		$V(\varepsilon_1)$	$.43^b$ (.03)
λ_2	$.78^b$ (.03)	.56		$V(\varepsilon_2)$	$.42^b$ (.02)
λ_3	$.83^b$ (.03)	.60		$V(\varepsilon_3)$	$.43^b$ (.02)
λ_4	$.95^*$ (.04)	.68		$V(\varepsilon_4)$	$.53^b$ (.03)
λ_5	1.00^c	.54		$V(\varepsilon_5)$	$.30^b$ (.05)
λ_6	$.34^b$ (.05)	.18		$V(\varepsilon_6)$	$.21^b$ (.01)
λ_7	1.00^d	.79		$V(\varepsilon_7)$	$.42^b$ (.03)
λ_8	$.78^d$	.61		$V(\varepsilon_8)$	$.39^b$ (.02)
λ_9	$.83^d$	.65		$V(\varepsilon_9)$	$.31^b$ (.02)
λ_{10}	$.95^d$	.75		$V(\varepsilon_{10})$	$.50^b$ (.03)
β_1	$-.38^b$ (.04)	$-.50$		$r\varepsilon_1\varepsilon_7$	$.03^b$ (.02)
β_2	$.58^b$ (.05)	.53		$r\varepsilon_2\varepsilon_8$	$.06^b$ (.02)
β_3	$-.44^b$ (.10)	$-.30$		$r\varepsilon_3\varepsilon_9$	$.09^b$ (.02)
$V(\zeta_1)$	$.516^b$ (.04)			$r\varepsilon_4\varepsilon_{10}$	$.23^b$ (.02)
$V(\zeta_2)$	$.217^b$ (.05)			$\chi^2_{31} = 51.3, p \geq .01$	
$V(\zeta_3)$	$.295^b$ (.03)			$N = 1034$	

[a] Standard errors are in parentheses. The scaled and unrescaled results are identical for the estimates in column (2) of the table.
[b] The coefficient is at least twice the size of its standard estimated.
[c] The value was fixed rather than estimated.
[d] The coefficient was constrained to equal that item's coefficient for 1964.

for adequately by the correlated measurement with constrained lambdas model in Figure 3.6.

The parameter estimates for the model are displayed in Table 3.9. Although the analysis was done on the covariance matrix, the results have also been rescaled such that both the latent variables and the items have unit variance, since standardized solutions allow one to compare the relative size of coefficients. Therefore, both the unrescaled and the rescaled results are shown in Table 3.9.

All of the indicators are significantly related to the constructs they are presumed to measure, although the coefficient associated with premarital sexual behavior is not very large ($\lambda_6 = .34$). This suggests that marijuana use and premarital sex may not be indicators from the same domain. One would want to consider seriously alternative indicators of deviance in respecifying the model.

measurement errors yields $\hat{\rho} = .91$. Yet as we saw the chi-square test indicates that the model with correlated measurement fits the data much better. And as the results in Table 3.9 show the correlation between ε_4 and ε_5 is non-trivial. Second, the null models these methods employ assume one knows nothing about the measurement or structural models under study. To the degree that one does have some previous knowledge, e.g., about the structure of the items in the measurement model, the Tucker–Lewis and Bentler–Bonett models may lead one to underfit one's data. Michael Sobel and I are examining this issue as this chapter goes to press.

But for the purpose of illustration, assume that the deviance domain is adequately measured by the two items. The estimates of the structural parameters suggest that those who engaged in deviance as college students in the 1960s were not random with respect to religiosity as freshmen. In particular, the net effect (standardized) of religiosity in 1964 on deviance by 1968 was −.50. Furthermore, having engaged in deviant behaviors had a significant impact on change in religiosity between 1964 and 1968 ($\beta_3 = -.30$).

The correlations between measurement errors are all statistically significant, even though relatively small in size. The exception is the correlation of .23 between the measurement errors for the item "There is a life after death." An examination of $r_{4,10}$ in Table 3.8 indicates that this particular item has a higher across-time correlation than the others, probably because it specifies a more fundamental religious belief than the other three items.

I hope that this brief introduction to structural equation models with unobserved variables illustrates their potential utility for survey researchers. Those interested in applications similar to that presented here are encouraged to examine examples using Current Population Study data to estimate response errors in earning function for nonblack males (Bielby & Hauser, 1977) and in models of status inheritance and mobility (Bielby, Hauser, & Featherman, 1977a,b).

Three limitations of these methods must be noted. First, the χ^2 statistics are highly sensitive to sample size. Therefore any model estimated on a large sample is unlikely to ever fit the data really well. Therefore the χ^2 statistic is best used to compare the relative fit of competing models utilizing the same variables as was done in the example above. Second, the models cannot at present incorporate nonlinearity in the variables. This means that where interaction effects are anticipated separate analyses need to be done for the relevant subgroups. Third, the models are limited in the number of variables which can be included in a given analysis, although the capability of the program has been expanded with more recent versions of it.

Despite these limitations, these methods are very useful in obtaining unbiased, efficient estimates of relationships among latent variables.[25] The reader interested in Jöreskog's work will find a recent compendium of his writings useful (Jöreskog & Sörbom, 1979).

3.9. CONCLUSION

We have covered much ground in a few pages, perhaps more than can reasonably be done in this much space. The first goal has been to make a plea to survey researchers to pay more attention to questions of measurement error, reliability, and validity than they have in the past. A second goal has been to

---

[25] A generalization of Jöreskog's methodology for the analysis of covariance structures is available in Bentler and Weeks (1980). Another useful variation of this methodology is Lee (1980).

introduce a set of techniques for estimating reliability and validity. As must be clear to even the casual reader, the area has become an increasingly complex and technical one. It simply does not make sense to discuss *the* reliability and *the* validity of a measure. It is hoped that it is also clear that the development of measures is not a task that can be done casually. Careful thought is needed in writing the items. Then extensive analyses need to be done in order to refine and validate the items. The process can literally take *years* if done well. In retrospect, perhaps we have overemphasized the importance of techniques and underemphasized the role of good theory and reflective thinking in the measurement process. Without the techniques one would probably never know how good or poor one's items were. But the fact remains that too often far too little time goes into the writing of the items, and once written and employed in the field, no technique, no matter how "fancy" or sophisticated, can salvage a set of lousy items.

Finally, we have stressed the use of measurement models that grew out of classical measurement theory because they have proved to be very useful in our own work. Other approaches are available and may prove to be as useful as the one taken here. Two of them are magnitude estimation and latent trait techniques. The former grows out of S. S. Stevens's (1951) work in psychophysics. The interested reader might consult Wegener (1982) for recent applications. Latent trait techniques were developed by Rasch (1960) and Birnbaum (1968). The models are also very similar to Lazarsfeld's (1950) latent structure analysis. A recent application of this technique to the analysis of attitude data can be found in Reiser (1981).

REFERENCES

Allen, Michael P.
   1974   "Construction of composite measures by the canonical factor regression method." Pp. 51–78 in H. L. Costner (ed.), *Sociological Methodology: 1973–74*. San Francisco: Jossey–Bass.
Althauser, Robert P.
   1974   "Inferring validity from the multitrait–multimethod matrix: another assessment." Pp. 105–127 in H. L. Costner (ed.), *Sociological Methodology: 1973–74*. San Francisco: Jossey–Bass.
Althauser, Robert P. and Thomas A. Heberlein
   1970   "A causal assessment of validity and the multitrait–multimethod matrix." Pp. 151–169 in Edger F. Borgatta and George W. Bohrnstedt (eds.), *Sociological Methodology: 1970*. San Franciso: Jossey–Bass.
Althauser, Robert P., Thomas A. Heberlein, and R. A. Scott
   1971   "A causal assessment of validitity: The augmented multitrait–multimethod matrix." Pp. 374–399 in H. M. Blalock, Jr. (ed.), *Causal Models in the Social Sciences*. Chicago: Aldine–Atherton.
Alwin, Duane F.
   1974   "Approaches to the interpretation of relationships in the multitrait–multimethod matrix." Pp. 79–105 in Herbert L. Costner (ed.), *Sociological Methodology: 1973–74*. San Francisco: Jossey–Bass.

1977   "Making errors in surveys: An overview." *Sociological Methods and Research* 6 (November):131–150.
Alwin, Duane F. and David J. Jackson
   1980   "Measurement models for response errors in surveys: Issues and applications," Pp. 68–119 in Karl F. Schuessler (ed.), *Sociological Methodology: 1980*. San Francisco: Jossey–Bass.
American Psychological Association
   1974   *Standards for Educational and Psychological Tests*. Washington: American Psychological Association.
Andrews, Frank M. and R. Crandall
   1976   "The validity of measures of self-reported well-being." *Social Indicators Research* 3:1–19.
Armor, David J.
   1974   "Theta reliability and factor scaling." Pp. 17–50 in Herbert L. Costner (ed.), *Sociological Methodology: 1973–74*. San Francisco: Jossey–Bass.
Babbie, Earl R.
   1973   *Survey Research Methods*. Belmont, California: Wadsworth.
Bentler, Peter M.
   1968   "Alpha-maximized factor analysis (Alphamax): Its relation to alpha and canonical factor analysis." *Psychometrica* 33:335–346.
Bentler, P. M. and D. G. Bonett
   1980   "Significance tests and goodness of fit in the analysis of covariance structures." *Psychological Bulletin* 88:588–606.
Bentler, P. M. and D. G. Weeks
   1980   "Linear structural equations with latent variables." *Psychometrika* 45:289–308.
Bielby, W. T. and R. M. Hauser
   1977   "Response error in earnings functions for nonblack males." *Sociological Methods and Research* 6 (November):241–280.
Bielby, W. T., R. M. Hauser and D. L. Featherman
   1977a "Response errors of nonblack males in models of the stratification process." *American Journal of Sociology* 82 (May):1242–1288.
   1977b "Response errors of black and nonblack males in models of status inheritance and mobility." *Journal of the American Statistical Association* 72 (December):723–735.
Birnbaum, A.
   1968   "Some latent trait models and their use in influencing an examinee's ability." In F. M. Lord and M. R. Noviclz (eds.), *Statistical Theories of Mental Test Scores*. Reading, Massachusetts: Addison-Wesley.
Blalock, Hubert M.
   1970   "Estimating measurement error using multiple indicators and several points in time." *American Sociological Review* 35 (Feb.):101–111.
Bohrnstedt, George W.
   1969   "A quick method for determining the reliability and validity of multiple item scales." *American Sociological Review* 34 (August):542–548.
   1969   "Observations in the measurement of change." Pp. 113–136 in E. F. Borgatta (ed.), *Sociological Methodology: 1969*. San Francisco: Jossey–Bass.
   1970   "Reliability and validity assessment in attitude measurement." Pp. 80–99 in G. Summers (ed.), *Attitude Measurement*. Chicago: Rand-McNally.
Boruch, R. F., J. D. Larkin, L. Wolins and A. C. MacKinney
   1970   "Alternative methods of analysis: Multitrait–multimethod data." *Educational and Psychological Measurement* 30:833–853.
Brown, W.
   1910   "Some experimental results in the correlation of mental abilities." *British Journal of Psychology* 3:296–322.

Burke, Cletus J.
  1963 "Measurement scales and statistical models." In M. H. Marx (ed.), *Theories in Contemporary Psychology*. New York: Macmillan.
Campbell, D. T.
  1953 *A Study of Leadership among Submarine Officers*. Columbus: Ohio State University Research Foundation.
  1954 "Operational delineation of 'what is learned' via the transposition experiment." *Psychological Review* 61:167–174.
  1956 *Leadership and Its Effects upon the Group*. Monograph No. 83. Columbus: Ohio State University Bureau of Business Research.
Campbell, D. T. and D. W. Fiske
  1959 "Convergent and discriminant validation by the multitrait–multimethod matrix." *Psychological Bulletin* 56:81–105.
Cattell, R. B. and J. Radcliffe
  1962 "Reliability and validity of simple and extended weighted and buffered unifactor scales." *British Journal of Statistical Psychology* 15:113–128.
Cochran, W. G.
  1968 "Errors of measurement in statistics." *Technometrics* 10:637–666.
Conger, A. J.
  1971 "Evaluation of multimethod factor analyses." *Psychological Bulletin* 75 (June):416–420.
Cronbach, L. J.
  1951 "Coefficient alpha and the internal structure of tests." *Psychometrika* 16:297–334.
Cronbach, L. J. and L. Furby
  1970 "How we should measure 'change'—or should we?" *Psychological Bulletin* 74 (July):68–80.
Cronbach, L. J., G. C. Gleser, H. Nanda, and N. Rajaratnam
  1972 *The Dependability of Behavioral Measurements*. New York: Wiley.
Curtis, Richard F. and Elton F. Jackson
  1962 "Multiple indicators in survey research." *American Journal of Sociology* 68 (Sept.):195–204.
Duncan, Otis D.
  1966 "Path analysis: Sociological examples." *American Journal of Sociology* 72:1–16.
  1975 *Introduction to Structural Equation Models*. New York: Academic Press.
Ford, R. N., E. F. Borgatta, and G. W. Bohrnstedt
  1969 "Uses of the work components study (WCS) with new college level employees." *Journal of Applied Psychology* 53:367–376.
Fuller, Wayne A. and Michael A. Hidiroglou
  1978 "Regression estimates after correction for attenuation." *Journal of the American Statistical Association* 73 (March):99–104.
Golding, S. L. and E. Seidman
  1974 "Analysis of multitrait–multimethod matrices: A two step principal components procedure." *Multivariate Behavioral Research* 9 (October):479–496.
Greene, Vernon L. and Edward G. Carmines
  1980 "Assessing the reliability of linear composites." Pp. 160–175 in Karl Schuessler (ed.), *Sociological Methodology: 1980*. San Francisco: Jossey–Bass.
Groves, Robert and Robert L. Kahn
  1979 *Surveys by Telephone*. New York: Academic Press.
Guttman, Louis
  1945 "A basis for analyzing test–retest reliability." *Psychometrika* 10:255–282.
  1959 "A structural theory for intergroup beliefs and action." *American Sociological Review* 24:318–328.
Hanna, M. T., R. Rubinson, and J. T. Warren
  1974 "The causal approach to the measurement error in panel analysis: Some further contin-

gencies.'' Pp. 293–323 in H. M. Blalock, Jr., *Measurement in the Social Sciences*. Chicago: Aldine.

Hansen, M. H., W. N. Hurwitz, and M. A. Bershad
1961   "Measurement errors in census and surveys." *Bulletin of the International Statistical Institute* 38(2):359–374.

Hargens, L. L., B. F. Reskin, and Paul D. Allison
1976   "Problems in estimating error from panel data: An example involving the measurement of scientific productivity." *Sociological Methods and Research* 4 (May):439–458.

Harmon, H. H.
1967   *Modern Factor Analysis* (2nd edition). Chicago: University of Chicago Press.

Heise, David R.
1969   "Separating reliability and stability in test–retest correlation." *American Sociological Review* 34 (February):93–101.
1970   "Causal inference from panel data." Pp. 3–27 in Edgar F. Borgatta and G. W. Bohrnstedt (ed.), *Sociological Methodology: 1970*. San Francisco: Jossey–Bass.

Heise, David R. and George W. Bohrnstedt
1971   "Validity, invalidity and reliability." Pp. 104–129 in Edgar F. Borgatta and George W. Bohrnstedt (eds.), *Sociological Methodology: 1971*. San Francisco: Jossey–Bass.

Hoyt, C.
1941   "Test reliability estimated by analysis of variance." *Psychometrika* 6:153–160.

Hubert, L. J. and F. B. Baker
1978   "Analyzing the multitrait–multimethod matrix." *Multivariate Behavioral Research* 13 (April):163–180.

Jackson, D. N.
1969   "Multimethod factor analysis in the evaluation of convergent and discriminant validity." *Psychological Bulletin* 72:30–49.
1975   "Multimethod factor analysis: A reformulation." *Multivariate Behavioral Research* 10:259–275.

Jöreskog, Karl G.
1969   "A general approach to confirmatory maximum likelihood factor analysis." *Psychometrika* 34:183–202.
1970   "A general method for analysis for covariance structures." *Biometrika* 57:239–251.
1971   "Statistical analysis of sets of congeneric tests." *Psychometrika* 36:109–134.
1973   "A general method for estimating a linear structural equation system." In A. S. Goldberger and O. D. Duncan (eds.), *Structural Equation Models in the Social Sciences*. New York: Seminar Press.

Jöreskog, Karl G. and Dag Sörbom
1977   "Statistical models and methods for analysis of longitudinal data." In D. J. Aigner and A. S. Goldberger (eds.), *Latent Variables in Socioeconomic Models*. Amsterdam: North-Holland.

Jöreskog, K. G. and D. Sörbom
1979   *Advances in Factor Analysis and Structural Equation Models*. Cambridge, Massachusetts: Abt Books.

Jöreskog, K. G. and D. Sörbom
1981   *LISREL. Analysis of Linear Structural Relationships by the Method of Maximum Likelihood*. Chicago: International Educational Services.

Kuder, G. F. and M. W. Richardson
1973   "The theory of the estimation of test reliability." *Psychometrika* 2:135–138.

Land, K. C.
1969   "Principles of path analysis." Pp. 3–37 in E. F. Borgatta (ed.), *Sociological Methodology: 1969*. San Francisco: Jossey–Bass.

Lansing, J. B., G. P. Ginsburg and K. Braaten
1961   *An Investigation of Response Error*. Studies in Consumer Savings, No. 2 Urbana: Bureau of Economic and Business Research, University of Illinois.

Lazarsfeld, P. F.
1950 "A conceptual introduction to latent structure analysis." In P. F. Lazarsfeld (ed.), *Mathematical Thinking in the Social Sciences*. New York: Free Press.

Lee, Sik-Yum
1980 "The penalty function method in constrained estimation of covariance structure models." *Psychometrika* 45:309–324.

Levine, Lawrence M. and George W. Bohrnstedt
1982 "New developments in the assessment of reliability: The LINREL programs." *Educational and Psychological Measurement* 42:195–199.

Long, J. Scott
1976 "Estimation and hypothesis testing in linear models containing measurement error: A review of Jöreskog's model for the analysis of covariance structures." *Sociological Methods and Research* 5:157–206.

Lord, F. M.
1963 "Elementary models for measuring change." Pp. 21–38 in C. W. Harris (ed.), *Problems in Measuring Change*. Madison: University of Wisconsin Press.

Lord, F. M. and M. R. Novick
1968 *Statistical Theories of Mental Test Scores*. Reading, Massachusetts: Addison-Wesley.

Miller, D.
1977 *Handbook of Research Design and Social Measurement* (3rd edition). New York: David McKay.

Moser, C. A. and G. Kalton
1972 *Survey Methods in Social Investigation* (2nd edition). New York: Basic Books.

National Opinion Research Center
1974 *National Data Program for the Social Sciences: General Social Survey*. Chicago: National Opinion Research Center, University of Chicago.

Novick, Melvin R. and Charles Lewis
1967 "Coefficient alpha and the reliability of composite measurements." *Psychometrika* 32:1–13.

Nunnally, Jum C.
1967 *Psychometric Theory*. New York: McGraw-Hill.

Parry, H. J. and H. M. Crossley
1950 "Validity of responses to survey questions." *Public Opinion Quarterly* 14:61–80.

Rasch, G.
1960 *Probabilistic Models for Some Intelligence and Attainment Tests*. Copenhagen: Danish Institute of Educational Research.

Reiser, Mark
1980 "Latent trait modeling of attitude items." In G. W. Bohrnstedt and E. F. Borgatta (eds.), *Social Measurement: Current Issues*. Beverly Hills: Sage.

Robinson, J. P., R. Athanasiou and K. B. Head
1969 *Measures of Occupational Attitudes and Occupational Characteristics*. Ann Arbor: Institute for Social Research.

Robinson, J. P., J. G. Rusk and K. B. Head
1968 *Measures of Political Attitudes*. Ann Arbor: Institute for Social Research.

Robinson, J. P. and P. R. Shaver
1973 *Measures of Social Psychological Attitudes*. Ann Arbor: Institute for Social Research.

Schmitt, N., B. W. Coyle and B. B. Saari
1977 "A review and critique of analysis of multitrait–multimethod matrices." *Multivariate Behavioral Research* 12 (October):447–478.

Schulz, B., G. W. Bohrnstedt, E. F. Borgatta, and R. R. Evans
1977 "Explaining premarital sexual intercourse among college students: A causal model." *Social Forces* (September):148–165.

Shaw, M. and J. Wright
1967 Scales for the Measurement of Attitudes. New York: McGraw-Hill.

Smith, Kent W.
  1974 "On estimating the reliability of composite indexes through factor analysis." *Sociological Methods Research* 2 (May):485–510.
  1974 "Forming composite scales and estimating their validity through factor analysis." *Social Forces* 53 (Dec.):168–180.
Spearman, Charles
  1910 "Correlation calculated with faulty data." *British Journal of Psychology* 3:271–295.
Srole, L.
  1956 "Social integration and certain corollaries: An exploratory study." *American Sociological Review* 21:709–716.
Sudman, Seymour and Norman M. Bradburn
  1974 *Response Effects in Surveys.* Chicago: Aldine.
Summers, G. F., R. L. Houglo, J. T. Scott, and C. L. Folse
       Before Industrialization. A Rural Social System Base Study. Bulletin No. 736. Urbana: Agricultural Experiment Station, University of Illinois.
Sutcliffe, J. P.
  1965 "A probability model for errors of classification I. General considerations." *Psychometrika* 30:73–96.
Tryon, R. D.
  1957 "Reliability and behavior domain validity: Reformulation and historical critique." *Psychological Bulletin* 54:229–249.
Tucker, Ledyard R. and Charles Lewis.
  1973 "A reliability coefficient for maximum likelihood factor analysis." *Psychometrika* 38:1–10.
Warren, Richard D., J. K. White and W. A. Fuller
  1974 "Are errors in variables analysis of managerial role performance." *Journal of the American Statistical Association* 69:886–893.
Warwick, Donald P. and Charles A. Lininger
  1975 *The Sample Survey: Theory and Practice.* New York: McGraw-Hill.
Wegener, B.
  1982 *Social Attitudes and Psychophysical Measurements.* Hillsdale, New Jersey: Lawrence Erlbaum Associates.
Werts, Charles E., Karl G. Jöreskog and Robert L. Linn
  1971 "Comment on 'the estimation of measurement error in panel data.' " *American Sociological Review* 36 (February):110–112.
  1972 "A multitrait–multimethod model for studying growth." *Educational and Psychological Measurement* 32:655–678.
Werts, Charles E. and Robert L. Linn
  1970 "A general linear model for studying growth." *Psychological Bulletin* 73:17–72.
  1970 "Path analysis: Psychological examples." *Psychological Bulletin* 74:193–212.
Wheaton, B., B. Muthen, D. F. Alwin, and G. F. Summers
  1977 "Assessing reliability and stability in panel models." Pp. 84–136 in D. R. Heise (ed.), *Sociological Methodology: 1977.* San Francisco: Jossey–Bass.
Wiley, David E.
  1973 "The identification problem for structural equation models with unmeasured variables." Pp. 69–84 in A. S. Goldberger and O. D. Duncan (eds.), *Structural Equation Models in the Social Sciences.* New York: Seminar Press.
Wiley, David E. and James A. Wiley
  1970 "The estimation of measurement error in panel data." *American Sociological Review* (February):112–117. [Also see David R. Heise "Comment," p. 117.]
Wiley, James A. and Mary G. Wiley
  1974 "A note on correlated errors in repeated measurements." *Sociological Methods and Research* (November):172–188.

Wyner, Gordon A.

1976   Sources of Response Errors in Self-Reports of Behavior. Unpublished Ph.D. dissertation. University of Pennsylvania.

1980   "Response Errors in Self-Reported Number of Arrests." *Sociological Methods and Research* 9 (November):161–177.

Chapter 4

Management of Survey Organizations[1]

Kenneth Prewitt

4.1. INTRODUCTION

In the early 1960s Paul Lazarsfeld, with colleagues at the Bureau of Applied Social Research, mounted a survey of "the types of arrangements by which American colleges and universities have tried to make room for empirical social research [Lazarsfeld, 1961, p. 1]." They discovered a pluralistic set of arrangements. There were bureaus, institutes, centers, and laboratories. There were differences among the units in patterns of funding, in research specialization, in professional staffing, in teaching and training programs, and in how the units were linked to the parent institutions that spawned them. Cutting across these differences in organization and function was the shared goal of establishing an institutional home for empirical work in the social sciences. Lazarsfeld was to describe this development "as one of the outstanding features of the twentieth century," an innovation in higher education comparable in scope and importance to the integration of humanistic studies in the sixteenth century and the establishment of the prototype modern university in Germany in the nineteenth century.

[1] From 1976 through September, 1979, I directed the National Opinion Research Center, a moderately sized, nonprofit survey research organization affiliated with, though legally independent from, the University of Chicago. NORC was founded in 1941 and became affiliated with the University of Chicago in 1947, continuing to maintain a permanent office in New York. NORC performs a mixture of government contract and academic grant research, providing survey services for resident scholars and also for colleagues in universities and research organizations throughout the country. Although I have attempted to generalize about management questions, there has been no attempt to conduct a serious investigation of other survey organizations. My observations are undoubtedly parochial and primarily reflect management experiences at NORC.

HANDBOOK OF SURVEY RESEARCH

In the over two decades since the Lazarsfeld survey there has been a steady expansion in the scope of operation and number of empirical social science organizations not only in universities but increasingly in government and in the private sector. The proliferation has been caused by changes in the complexity of empirical research and in the funding and utilization of social science research.

As empirical social science becomes more complex, there is the obvious need for an intricate division of labor and coordination of diverse skills. The standard academic department of sociology or political science was and remains ill-equipped to manage complicated research projects. Special centers or institutes have been established to take on the management task and to maintain a technical support staff. These research units have had an important multiplier effect, not only greatly increasing the research productivity of the social scientists, but also justifying the research centers and furthering their proliferation and expansion.

Simultaneous with the growing complexity of empirical social science, and in part causing it, have been significant changes in the funding and utilization of social science. This story has been told many times and need not be detailed here. The shift from grant research to contract research, the growing emphasis on applied social science, and the consequent transformed relationship between the federal government and the suppliers of social science knowledge have created a market for the kind of research product much more likely to emerge from a multidisciplinary research organization than the typical university department (Biderman & Sharp, 1972).

It has not been easy to integrate the research centers into the university. The problems of integration and management with which deans struggled several decades ago have not lessened with the spread of the research organization across the academic setting. The inability of universities to work out suitable arrangements may in part explain why so much empirical social science, especially large-scale survey research, has drifted away from the university to find its home in both nonprofit and commercial consulting and research firms (although it would take some sophisticated research to determine the soundness of this hypothesis).

Insofar as large-scale empirical research leaves the university it will ease those management problems associated with the uneasy integration of the research institute into the academic program of the university. (It will also do harm to the empirical social sciences, but that is a topic for another essay.) Escaping the university, however, will not resolve all or even the most critical management problems facing the social research organization. This is especially apparent in survey research. Critical organizational issues persist whether large-scale survey research projects are managed wholly within the university, in university-associated research institute, or in firms set up outside the university.

We review management problems in survey organizations along two dimensions. First, there is the familiar dimension of simultaneously serving purposive goals and survival goals. Can the survey organization do what it wants to do and still survive? Conversely, in trying to survive does the survey organization subvert its reason for being? This first problem is standard in any organization, and the task is simply to see how the tension manifests itself and is handled in survey organization.

The second problem is more specific to survey organizations. It has to do with managing the two somewhat conflicting functions of scientific direction and project management, and seeing to it that they are as integrated as possible. We must remember that survey organizations are production shops. A sizable nonprofessional staff is employed to produce the many documents without which there is no survey: sampling maps and lists, training materials, completed questionnaires, code sheets, edited tapes, computer runs, typed drafts of reports, and published papers. Production as extensive as that implied by large-scale social surveys requires project management, indeed, but also, and especially, management is called upon to serve the demanding goals of scientific research and researchers. This states in brief form a major management challenge for the survey organization—simultaneously promoting science, which does not necessarily prosper under tight management, and ensuring that production of survey data occurs in a reasonably cost-efficient manner, which does require tight management.

4.2. THE GOALS OF A SURVEY RESEARCH ORGANIZATION[2]

The goals announced by a survey organization differ depending on whether the organization is in the profit or nonprofit sector; whether it primarily conducts academic grant research, government contract research, or commercial research; whether it is affiliated with a university or is an independent organization; whether it is large or small; and, not insignificantly, whether it likes being the size it is. But if we move to a sufficiently high level of abstraction, there are at least two goals all survey organizations share: *prestige* and *survival*. A third goal, *growth*, cuts in complicated ways across prestige and survival depending on the setting of the organization.

Prestige

Prestige is sought in and for itself. Prestige is also instrumental in achieving other goals by enhancing an organization's market position in an increasingly competitive industry. The most familiar form of prestige is intellectual or substantive—the prestige earned by the well-received scholarly monograph, the sound and influential policy recommendation, the methodological innovation in

---

[2] My comments are largely restricted to survey research organizations that emphasize empirical social science and policy research. They are not intended to cover market research firms, syndicated public polling organizations, or firms that conduct polls for political candidates.

statistical analysis or data collection, and the like. To achieve such prestige the survey organization must attract and retain quality researchers and provide the institutional setting within which they can do their work. Though not easily accomplished, *how* an organization increases its stock of intellectual prestige is straightforward. It requires an agenda that integrates institutional goals with scholarly biographies of good researchers. However, it is an error to conclude that the prestige of a survey organization is solely measured by the quality of its scholarly writings or its policy recommendations. Although less commonly recognized, there are two other important forms of prestige: reputation for successful project management and the ability to win contracts.

Successful project management reduces itself to producing quality survey data on schedule and within budget. Increasingly, the prestige of a survey organization is linked to its record of successful management so defined. In the contract world of fixed schedules, deliverables, audits, and technical officers, with their required standards for response rates, field procedures, analysis, and the like, we should not be surprised that poor management erodes institutional prestige just as good management augments it. Similar requirements and standards are beginning to creep into the grant research world and thus cannot be escaped by avoiding contract research even if that were economically feasible.

If the reputation of an organization among clients turns on its management record, the prestige of individuals within the organization and across the survey industry is similarly affected. Prestige is earned by persons who successfully manage large-scale surveys. The curricula vitae of these senior project managers reflect their career in survey management, and are not dissimilar from the vitae of academics, which reflect careers of scholarly achievement. Similarities do not end with vitae. Just as the survey organization must recruit and retain quality social scientists, so it must recruit and retain quality survey managers. Just as it must provide an institutional setting for the former function, it must for the latter function. To acknowledge the similarities between these two forms of prestige, successful scholarship and successful management, glosses over the unhappy fact that nurturing prestige for one function may require arrangements at cross purposes with nurturing prestige for the other. We return to this problem later.

As sources of prestige, scholarly work and successful project management result from the growing importance and complexity of surveys in disciplinary and policy research. The third source of prestige, winning contracts, is more a result of changes in the funding environment. Competitive bidding for government contract research forces survey research firms to measure themselves against each other. When most studies were grant-supported and the supply of research funds was diffused, the competition between organizations was much more muted. The flow of large-scale survey support into government contracts has changed this picture. There is direct competition between technical designs, operational strengths, and analysis plans. That competition is based on rules (RFP specifications) that are clear to all competitors and, for the most part, appear to be equitably applied by the referees (review panels). As in athletic contests, cumulative victories—sometimes even a single dramatic victory—gain prestige for the winning team.

This is not the standard way to think about prestige in survey organizations. Nevertheless, because direct competition is a natural outcome of government procurement procedures and because an ever larger share of support for social science survey research is won or lost as a result of these procedures, the survey world has accomodated itself to winning as a source of prestige. There are various management implications of contract bidding—few of them welcomed. There is, for instance, the need to develop a marketing strategy, although most university-based organizations would prefer a different label. ("Marketing strategies" do not fit well with the academic culture.) There is also the complication of sorting out one's relationships with other organizations that are, on the one hand, adversaries in a sometimes fiercely competitive milieu and, on the other hand, colleagues and fellow researchers with whom one instinctively and appropriately shares information.

Survival

Survival is a standard goal of all organizations. The interesting management issues emerge when survival or maintenance needs are in conflict with purposive goals of the organization such as client services, intellectual contribution, or profits. Pressures to survive can easily distort programs designed to achieve more basic or fundamental goals. In this regard, survey organizations are like any other type of organization, constantly trying to manage into existence a cluster of programs and policies that will ensure organizational survival and promote the purposive goals that justify the organization's existence in the first place.

At the simplest, and as we shall see, somewhat misleading, level, survival is being able to pay the bills. This involves a complex of accounting procedures and fiscal considerations: overhead rates, cash flow, salary structures, rates of return on project development funds, productivity, and (for many organizations) profit margins. Each of these clearly involves specific management strategies, but in this chapter we keep the discussion on the more general level.

As in other businesses that sell a product or a service, survey organizations live in an uncertain fiscal environment. The survey organization customarily seeks more work than it could comfortably perform. Should these efforts lead to an unexpectedly high success rate on grant proposals or contract bids, there would be an imbalance between the organization's resources and its responsibilities: too little of the former to deal with too much of the latter. If the success rate is unusually low, the imbalance works in the opposite direction, leaving underutilized resources. There are upside as well as downside risks in trying to coordinate the match between staff resources and project volume.

Other factors contribute to the uncertain fiscal environment. Firms that do a high proportion of their work under government contracts find that changes in scope of work can alter the magnitude of a given project by as much as 100%. If the project is a very large one and if the changes in scope have not been anticipated, the plans that carefully orchestrate the flow of projects through the organization can become quickly fouled. Organizational budgets are affected by schedule changes that involve unexpected cash-flow problems, different staff allocations, and even adjustments in overhead rates (if a major staff effort is required in a fiscal year other than the one budgeted).

Survival, if viewed only as paying the bills, involves, then, two interrelated problems: (a) *volume*—maintaining a reasonable balance between resources and responsibilities; and (b) *distribution*—reasonable spread of work throughout each fiscal year and across several years. Up to a point, maldistribution of work can cause more problems than too little work (an issue we return to later).

Achieving the appropriate volume and distribution of project work is particularly difficult because survey centers—most of which are "soft money" research organizations—manage themselves without the benefit of a fixed budget. They differ in this regard from universities and government bureaus, which generally enter the fiscal year with a reasonably firm idea of their budgets. Sometimes those budgets are tight, as has been true of universities in recent years, but give or take 5%, they are known in advance. Their task is to accomplish goals within the constraints of the budget. This is not so with survey organizations. Being dependent on sales, many survey organizations will not know their volume and, therefore, the budget, until well into the fiscal year. It is against this uncertainty that goals must be formulated, programs sustained, and personnel commitments negotiated. Management is more the art of fine tuning than of achieving predetermined goals with fixed resources.

The paying of bills taken alone gives a somewhat misleading perspective on survival because it leaves unspecified the kind of bills that must be paid. We should back up a moment and remind ourselves what a survey organization is: It is primarily people who possess an identifiable array of skills, competencies, and experiences. Stated differently, the inventory of a survey organization is the knowledge and capabilities of its staff. Only incidentally does inventory include physical plant and equipment. Paying the bills, therefore, largely reduces to meeting the payroll. Worries about the cost of housing the staff and maintaining the equipment are at the periphery of a survey organization's concerns. The central survival issue is maintaining staff quality.

Consider first the interviewing staff. For the handful of research organizations that recruit and train their own interviewers rather than relying on service bureaus, maintaining a quality interviewing staff is particularly vexing.[3] If the field staff is not kept busy, interviewers are apt to grow stale, forget their training, suffer decay of their skills, and drift away in search of more dependable employment. If organizational survival means protecting the inventory of

---

[3] NORC recruits and trains its own interviewing staff. Every interviewer is given general training in interview techniques before being assigned to a particular project. To my knowledge only two or three other organizations have a similar practice, including the Census Bureau and the Survey Research Center at the Institute for Social Research.

staff talent, then keeping the field staff working looms large as a management problem.

The distinction between survival as paying the bills and survival as maintaining staff quality can now be sharpened. Because interviewers are part-time employees who are on the payroll only when they work, they represent no major bill-paying problems. But the very fact that they are not working presents the organization with staff-maintenance problems. If we interpret survival only as meeting the payroll, therefore, then intermittent or even no work for the interviewing staff has no negative effect on survival. But we have argued that this interpretation is far too limited. An organization concerned with surviving as a quality organization must keep its interviewers busy and up to standards.

The same principle applies to permanent staff, though the application here is more complicated. Permanent staff members must be paid whether there are active projects which employ their skills or not. Of course, such people could be laid off and rehired as projects wane and wax, but such a policy would soon strip the organization of its best staff members—not to mention the destructive effect it would have on overall employee morale.

Organizational survival is reduced, then, to two principles in the context of two fiscal realities, unpredictable business volume and uneven flow of projects: (a) to find enough work for the interviewing staff to avoid decay in the level of quality in the field operation; (b) to perform a balancing act that will provide enough projects to keep the permanent staff employed. It is not money per se that determines organizational survival; it is the allocation of money across tasks and through time that determines survival.

There are various interesting twists to the management problems that accompany this interpretation of survival. Quality staff will be retained not just because their salaries are paid, though this is necessary, but also because their morale is high and they like their work. Certainly at the professional level the challenge of the job is as important as the salary attached to it. Here survey organizations share features of law firms, universities, hospitals, and other institutions that employ large professional staffs.

From the perspective of paying salaries regularly, what the survey organization needs is predictable work spread across several years. Translated, this means having a few major projects that will involve repeated surveys on an annual or a semiannual basis for several years. The advent of large-scale, multiyear, standard surveys and panel studies has helped enormously to stabilize those survey organizations able to secure such contracts.

From the standpoint of staff morale and job challenge, however, this highly useful financial base can become a source of problems. There is no challenge involved in doing the same tasks year after year; repeated work is often boring work. Survey organizations—at least those in the academic and nonprofit sector—thrive on solving new and ever more complicated design and implementation problems. An assembly line organization that repeats the same basic tasks every 6 or 12 months will find it difficult to keep its best professional staff intact no matter how well it pays them.

Any survey organization, therefore, needs a project mix that not only smooths out the financial base but that is also in a healthy state of change. Unfortunately, predictability and change often do not come in the same package. It is necessary to take the risks involved with sacrificing the security of regular and predictable projects to gain the rewards of new and different projects.

Obviously, money is a means to survival, the necessary but hardly sufficient condition. To presume that survival is simply a money problem is to miss the point. Survival is maintaining the organization's inventory of talent. This implies management strategies that are far more complex than just being able to pay the bills or being able to pay staff salaries. At a minimum, the organization must secure a project that intellectually rewards and challenges the staff. Whether this project mix should cohere around a planned research agenda is a difficult question for the management of a survey organization to resolve. The organization can plan for survival in the narrow sense of fiscal planning, project development expenditures, overhead management, and personnel projections, but we have argued that survival is an intellectual as well as fiscal matter.

To what extent can the survey organization plan for its intellectual survival? Writing over 3 decades ago, Angus Campbell (1953) listed planning as one of the chief responsibilities of the research administrator. Though difficult, it is possible to "plot a general course which a research group will seek to follow, with rather clear definition of boundaries and some anticipated rate of progress." Campbell, however, immediately qualified his advice with the observation that "planning also requires an adaptability to changes in external circumstances [p. 228]." It is likely that in retrospect Campbell would attribute his own legendary success as a research administrator less to his plans than to his adaptability.

Only in a limited way could or should the research process be planned. Experience, as well as an extensive sociology of science literature, informs us that the best research proceeds on its twisting and turning course as investigations reject hypotheses, give birth to new ones, and turn up wholly unexpected findings. Unfortunately, in the contemporary survey research organization the need for maximum flexibility in intellectual planning is contrary to the requirements of contracts and clients as they impose themselves on the organization at large. The management task is to provide the research program with appropriate flexibility while introducing sufficient planning to achieve project obligations and to secure long-range fiscal stability. This is a task more easily written down than accomplished.

Growth

The two goals already reviewed—prestige and survival—are shared by many types of survey organizations, although, of course, the manner in which these goals are understood and achieved may vary. As we turn to the third goal, that of organizational growth, the variability in whys and wherefors is so great that it renders summary review practically impossible. There is in the first instance the distinction between profit and nonprofit firms. Whereas growth is mandated for the former by the need to increase profits for owners and stockholders, the latter do not feel this pressure.

Nonprofit firms also differ from each other. A survey organization that is affiliated with a university must consider its role within that institution. This role may suggest growth to secure the service function within the university or to satisfy imperialistic impulses. Or the role may suggest nongrowth in order to maintain a low profile or to coordinate comfortably with other research units and departments of the university. It is not unusual for nonprofit organizations to operate under a no-growth policy.

The question of whether the survey organization should grow cannot be separated from its cousin, what the optimum size of a survey organization is? Charles Glock (1951) observed over 30 years ago that, "We know very little about the optimum size of research organizations [p. 133]," which is a state of ignorance not reduced in the intervening years. It is not even clear how to investigate the size issue. There is a certain minimum size necessary if the organization is to sustain the capacity to carry out surveys at all. Certain levels of technical skills (sampling, questionnaire construction, field operations, programming) and support services (data processing, office management) must be maintained for there to be serious surveys. But beyond the minimum capability we quickly move into a gray area. The small organization can engage in trade-offs, perhaps buying the consulting services of a sampling statistician so that it can invest in an automated telephone capability, or using a service bureau for interviewers rather than training its own. Each trade-off will limit both the survey methodologies that can be effectively used and the kind of substantive research that will be conducted.

If we could specify the minimum necessary size to have a survey capability (and it is larger than many research organizations starting to dabble in surveys initially believe it to be),[4] there remains the question of "how large to get." Part of what drives an organization to reach a certain size are decisions about how many substantive research programs to staff. Each substantive program needs the critical mass that will sustain scholarly discourse and cooperation. Social scientists who gravitate to large research organizations receive intellectual satisfaction from collective efforts and group research. (The solitary type of researcher is likely to avoid the institute or center.) Thus there are important intellectual and motivational reasons for growth.

Changing survey technology also urges growth on the survey organization. To fail to keep pace with new research technologies is to risk decay. To try to keep pace without at least modest growth would tax managerial skills. Growth

---

[4] While I was director of NORC, I received several delegations from other universities seeking advice on how to establish a survey research center on their campuses. They were invariably shocked when I listed the minimum capital investment required. They almost always underestimated initial staff requirements, space demands, and the problems of fiscal uncertainties associated with contract and grant support.

provides the resources that can be invested for the future when surveys will be conducted differently from the way they are today.

Survey researchers need only read this book to become convinced of the existence of rapid changes in survey technology. Some of these are in computer hardware and software: key to disk entry, automated data management systems, computer-driven interviewing systems, interactive editing and cleaning, conversational data analysis. But technological advance is not limited to computer-linked systems; there are well-known advances in sampling theory and, therefore, in design possibilities. Sampling statistics is not the only area of survey research continually transformed by rigorous scientific analysis. The concept of survey error rather than just sampling error is making its way into the field; research into the art of asking questions, coupled with psychometrics and measurement theory, is having far-reaching effects on the what and how of measurement. The list of technological improvements could go on: new techniques for locating hard to find respondents, studies of the nonrespondent and the reluctant respondent, models of error structures, new analytic techniques for longitudinal and panel data, field experiments, and so forth.

The point is clear. Whether we call it an art, a craft, or a science, survey methodology is in an expansion phase. All survey organizations want to keep up with new developments. Many organizations, especially those housed in academic settings, want to contribute to these developments. Neither keeping pace nor contributing can be accomplished without some surplus resources, meaning resources over and above those necessary to manage the present mix of projects and to analyze the current store of data. An organization that is shrinking in size and volume, or even one in a steady-state position, will seldom find the resources necessary to invest in new technologies. Growth, then, becomes the means to the goal of technological advancement.

For every benefit of growth, however, we can also list a cost—indeed, probably list more costs than benefits. Consider the managerial culture of survey organizations. Many survey centers wish to manage themselves with a minimum of hierarchy and bureaucratic routines. Face-to-face informal management is preferred and retained as long as possible. But informal arrangements begin to break down with increase in dollar volume and number of projects, until at a certain point the congenial, personal, collegial atmosphere is replaced by the businesslike, impersonal, hierarchical atmosphere. Old employees find this uncomfortable. It is hard to draw a line and say that on one side is the collegium and the other side is the bureaucracy, but informal arrangements are hard to sustain when the annual project volume gets much above $5 or $6 million. Growth, then, imposes organizational practices that are often unanticipated and even less often welcomed.

There are also diseconomies of scale. Growth strains the ability of the survey organization to maintain quality of operations. In the absence of professional schools for training survey researchers, operations skills are learned through job experience. Apprenticeship training requires time and patience on the part of the trainer and the trainee. Organizational growth, if at all rapid, requires staff expansion at exactly those times in the organization's history when its senior and most experienced staff are too busy to nurture the skills of new employees. New staff combined with overworked supervisors is a mixture hardly conducive to maintaining quality standards. Planned growth can avoid most deterioration of quality, but only if the organization reminds itself that experience and performance covary more highly in survey research than in many other professions.

A final comment about the optimum size of the survey organization recalls our earlier discussion of the uncertain fiscal environment. A survey organization will frequently have a mixture of projects, ranging from the quite small to the very large. To use NORC as an example, in a typical year NORC will have as many as a dozen projects at less than $100,000, some of which will be no larger than a summer salary for a principal investigator and some computer money. Then there will be a half-dozen or so projects in the $200,000–500,000 range, a few projects in the $750,000 range, and one or two that in a given year might exceed $2 million. What is clear in the financial history of NORC is that surges and declines in volume are not at all driven by how many small or modestly sized projects it has but by whether it has one, two, or three of the very largest projects. Large percentage swings in volume, then, turn on a small number of events that in the nature of the funding world are not under the control of the organization. Insofar as NORC is typical there are clear implications for the optimum size of survey organizations. The larger the organization, the more vulnerable it is to unpredictable and substantial fluctuations in size. Unless there are ways to cushion these fluctuations, the survey organization is well advised to stay on the conservative side in choosing its optimum size.

4.3. THE MANAGEMENT ISSUE

The preceding discussion of the three goals of prestige, survival, and growth, especially as they pertain to survey organizations, sets the context for the key management issue. Those survey organizations that aspire to stature as centers for the empirical social sciences must manage the tensions between two partially incompatible functions. There is the function of scientific direction, which recognizes the survey organization as an important extension of the social sciences, and there is the function of project management, which recognizes that the survey organization is linked to the contractual world of government and, often, to the competitive world of business. The tension between scientific directions and project management is reviewed at some length in the following, but first we touch briefly on several other management problems and principles.

The Managerial Task

Though a product of the social sciences, the survey organization is different from particular disciplines in an important way. Social science academic departments are methodologically pluralistic but substantively focused. The survey research center is pluralistic with respect to substantive research interests, usually having a multidisciplinary program, but its research shares a common methodology. Survey methodology calls for a complex division of labor and task specialization in areas of design, instrumentation and measurement, sampling, field procedures, data entry, data processing, analysis, report writing. Survey methodology is the most labor intensive of all social-science methodologies, indeed more labor intensive than most natural science methodologies. The staff required to conduct a single major social science field experiment can easily reach 2000. The management of survey research, therefore, is mostly the management of people.

There are, of course, parts of the survey process where machines rather than persons are the production units, especially in the area of automated data entry and data processing. There are indications that data collection itself might gradually become more automated. Some firms have automated features of telephone interviewing, and others have made modest attempts to use portable terminals to partially automate the face-to-face interview. These areas of automation notwithstanding, survey research remains a very labor intensive industry.

Not only people have to be managed. There are also the tasks of managing schedules, deliverables, final products, and, of course, budgets. But much of what is interesting about the management of schedules, products, and budgets concerns people management. For example, because surveys are labor intensive, schedules generally can be accelerated only by adding more staff labor. Budgets, as we have already observed, are based mostly on project payrolls. To monitor the budget is largely to attend to how much labor is going into different tasks. Seldom will cost overruns be the result of faulty estimates of nonlabor costs; they frequently will result from underestimates of the staff effort required to administer a complex questionnaire or trace respondents or code open-ended answers. Poor management of staff labor will directly affect schedules and budgets more than anywhere else in the survey process. Of course, deliverables and products, whether scholarly monographs, policy evaluations, or simply clean data tapes, depend upon assigning the right people to the correct task with the appropriate resources and creating the incentives that motivate performance.

The staff of the survey organization can be classified according to four levels: (a) the field staff, interviewers, and their field supervisors: (b) technical support staff; (c) senior professional staff; and (d) research administration or senior management. This classification leaves out the nontechnical support services, such as business management, personnel, administrative data processing, and the like. Management in these areas does not present problems unique to survey organizations, except as these areas are affected by the management of surveys themselves. We restrict the discussion to staff whose primary responsibilities are directly associated with surveys.

Field Staff

Management of a field staff presents challenges very different from those involved in managing the office staff. The nature of a large survey precludes face-to-face supervision of the interviewers in the field. For these employees, the home serves as office, and they go to work in the residences and businesses of thousands and thousands of individual respondents. Although the interviewing work is validated by supervisors, validation is really a fail-safe device rather than a direct management tool. To be effective with its field staff, the survey organization must create a remote control supervisory system.

It may be said that this is a challenge faced by other industries as well. Any firm that uses a national sales force to make house calls has to establish such a remote control system. But the insurance industry or the cosmetic firm has advantages denied the survey organization. They can pay commissions on actual sales rather than paying by the hour. The survey organization, by contrast, runs a risk if it pays by the completed questionnaire rather than on an hourly basis. From the point of view of data quality, piece rates create a perverse incentive. Cases that involve the least amount of travel time or that are easiest to complete will receive the interviewers' attention, whereas the more difficult cases are neglected—and new forms of bias will be introduced into the data.

A more fundamental difference between the insurance firm and the survey organization is that there can be as many ways to sell insurance as there are brokers, but there can be only one way in which to ask a survey question. The survey organization must standardize the way in which all interviewers behave toward all respondents. The management problem is not simply to create incentives to work; this can be accomplished with wage rates and review systems. Rather, the problem, much more difficult, is one of ensuring that distant interviewers are accurately, systematically, and completely following a definite set of instructions. The remote control management system must reduce variability in behavior across an entire field staff working essentially on its own.

Training is the most critical part of this remote control system. Training, of course, is supported with several auxiliary methods: question-by-question specifications, field edit procedures, validation checks, central office edits that search for interviewer weaknesses, periodic reviews of interviewer quality, and the like. But all these are auxiliary to the training process.

It is training that teaches the interviewer the norms associated with the interviewing task. It is these norms internalized by the interviewer that become the remote control management system. It is the norm of persistence, for instance, that maintains high response rates, the norm of neutrality that reduces bias associated with interviewer effects. Training is not only the source of generalized norms, it also teaches project-specific tasks: how to interpret a particular question, to administer a given form, to follow up on nonrespondents, and so forth. With respect to the field staff, therefore, the major management challenge is to establish a remote control system that will motivate effort and ensure timely and accurate performance.

Technical Staff

I will not attempt to specify categories that clearly distinguish professional from technical staff. We can make do with the loose distinction between those who delegate a series of different tasks and those who complete delegated tasks. The senior professional staff have responsibility for a series of tasks that must be performed in any survey. They delegate those tasks and then assemble the product as it passes from one task group to the next. Technical people stay close to an actual task itself. Whatever the assignment, they burrow deeper and deeper into it: writing a software routine, training interviewers, formatting questionnaires, preparing cleaning and editing specifications. Obviously, there are times when some parts of these tasks will be subdivided and further delegated. But in a loose sense the distinction between the professional and technical staffs turns on the number and variety of tasks that are delegated and therefore coordinated.

There are two major management principles that govern the way in which technical staffs should be organized. First, only up to a point will adding more personnel accelerate the completion of a task. Because survey organizations are labor intensive, it is always tempting to solve schedule difficulties by expanding the staff. But if, for example, two programmers are to develop a receipt control system and they fall behind schedule, to add another programmer may help, however, to add another three or four may actually slow down the schedule, because of new coordination and supervision responsibilities. This well-known feature of software development applies to many technical tasks in a survey. If the person drafting a medical history questionnaire is behind schedule, putting three more persons on that task will not necessarily produce a completed questionnaire in one-fourth as much time. Without excessive coordination and meetings it may be impossible for a staff of three or four to prepare an integrated questionnaire.

Managing the technical tasks in survey preparation and implementation therefore requires a close sense of the limits of delegation of tasks and division of labor. No general rule can be specified, but there is a point at which the costs of supervision and coordination will outweigh the seeming advantages of further subdivision. Realistic project scheduling keeps this point in mind.

The second general management principle has to do with assembling the whole. It is easy to compartmentalize the typical survey into study design, sampling, instrument development, interviewer training, field work, editing, data entry and cleaning, data processing, analysis, report writing. Each component benefits from technical specialization. In a large survey organization, some of these components will become identifiable departments: sampling department, field department, data processing department. But even where size does not require formal departments, there will be a division of labor organized around the several components of the survey.

Given specialization, it is easy to forget that the survey is an integrated product. Each component is connected to all other components. Data processing, for instance, should be integrated with questionnaire design in order to achieve efficiency at the data-entry and data-cleaning stages. Survey organizations can have separate sampling departments and field departments, but there is no tidy separation in the work itself.

The management issue is clear. On the one hand, there is much to be gained by specialization, departmentalization, and division of labor among the technical staff. On the other hand, the survey is not a series of discrete parts to be assembled when each part is completed. Rather, it is an integrated whole. The successful design and implementation of each part depends on successful completion of all other parts. Management of the technical staff must take advantage of specialization while ensuring that the movement of the survey from department to department integrates the final product. There are many concrete ways to work this out, but the principle remains the same. For any given survey, there must be project management responsible for producing the integrated product. It will not do to presume that one group of technical specialists (e.g., sampling statisticians) will complete the survey to a point and then simply pass it to the next department (e.g., instrument developers), who in turn will hand it over to the next stage (data collection in the field). Specialization works in a survey organization only if a management system is sensitive to the integrated nature of the final product.

Senior Professional Staff

Two kinds of functions must be present in the senior professional staff: (*a*) scientific direction, which could go under such headings as design and analysis, principal investigator skills, or study direction; and (*b*) project management, which could also be called survey operations management. Scientific direction depends heavily on the ability to conceptualize and design studies as well as to analyze and interpret the data collected. Project management is necessary if quality data are to be collected on time and within budget with due regard to design considerations and analysis possibilities.

Scientific direction skills are generally found in persons with advanced training in the social sciences and statistical disciplines—and, increasingly, in schools or programs of public policy. Project management skills have generally been acquired through experience. Professionals in survey management have worked their way up through a survey organization. (Although in principle these skills could be taught in academic programs or professional schools, Lazarsfeld's hopes for a professional degree in survey research have yet to be realized in an American university.)

The tough question is how to organize the two different sets of senior professional skills required by a survey organization. People who combine both skills can be trained or recruited to serve in roles that merge scientific direction and project management. In practice, however, survey management skills are acquired by someone who already has a Ph.D. in statistics or one of the social sciences. Another possibility is for the survey organization to construct separate career lines, recruiting and promoting one set of people with principal investigator skills and another with operations management skills. The first organizational strategy combines two somewhat different skills in the same people, whereas the second locates different skills in separate categories of people.

We can describe advantages and disadvantages of each strategy by comparing the strategies in terms of three organizational needs: (*a*) recruitment and retention of senior staff; (*b*) utilizing their talents, which beyond the obvious need to sell their time involves having research projects underway that are an effective match with the interests and skills of the professional staff; and (*c*) getting highest quality research accomplished on budget and on schedule—that is, successfully managing projects.

By way of preface to our more detailed review, let us note at the outset that the most severe disadvantage of separating scientific direction from project management is that it leads to overlapping lines of authority, untidy project management charts, and similar organizational messiness. On these grounds it might be rejected out of hand (and has been by several survey organizations). What keeps it around is its comparative advantages in areas of recruitment and utilization.

The major disadvantage of the alternative strategy is that it is hard, very hard, to recruit persons who combine analytic abilities in the social sciences and the ability to manage complex surveys. The pool of people who rank among the best substantive social scientists or statisticians and also stand high among the best survey managers is indeed small. To depend upon this pool limits the recruitment choices of the survey organization. Choices expand considerably, however, when recruiting from two separate pools, that of the best social scientists or policy researchers, on the one hand, and that of the best survey managers, on the other. To insist that the same person possess both kinds of skills risks lowering standards on both counts.

Survey operations is full-time work; so, too, is scientific direction. The design and analysis requirements of the social experiment, the policy evaluation, or the panel study should be assigned to the best social-science minds the society has available. Further, as the aspects of surveys become increasingly complex—tracing hard-to-locate respondents; designing and then administering complex and detailed questionnaires; meeting contractually agreed upon response rates; tracking multiyear panels; monitoring million dollar survey budgets; cleaning, editing, and processing huge data files—skills not customarily attained by persons whose reference group remains their academic colleagues are imperative.

I do not mean to exaggerate the recruitment difficulties visited upon the organization that combines skills of scientific direction and survey management. For some projects and under some conditions, one project director can perform successfully at every phase, from design through operations and implementation to analysis. To build an organization on this principle, however, is to ignore advantages of specialization and division of labor. It is true that some talented survey-operations professionals will want to keep their hands in design and analysis; and there are principal investigators who, from time to time, will enjoy running an entire study. No doubt there are a few people who excel at both tasks, but probably only a few. The organization that tries to combine skills in the same person and hold standards constant will necessarily find the recruitment task more difficult.

Matters get more complex as we turn from recruitment to utilization. Successful utilization is the ability to fund projects that make suitable use of the particular mix of scientific and operations skills in a given survey organization. We immediately recognize that scientific skills are not interchangeable across projects. A study of labor mobility requires design and analysis skills that differ from those required for a project to evaluate delivery of community health services. It is equally true, though less well understood, that survey direction skills are not necessarily interchangeable across data-collection methodologies. The survey director who excels at managing telephone interviewers may be less practiced in managing several site offices, although it is the case that survey managers are more likely to be generalists with respect to different operations methodologies than senior social scientists are with respect to different substantive problems.

We can also consider the relative marketing advantages of the different ways to organize the senior professional staff. When this staff is composed of two sets of persons, a set specializing in design and analysis and another set specializing in survey management, a greater range of projects can be undertaken. The organization that has separated the analytic and management skills has greater flexibility in staffing projects. It is easier to find research projects that appeal to and take advantage of the special talents of principal investigators when their substantive interests can be attached to any of several complex data-collection methodologies. It is easier to make effective use of survey management skills when they can be attached to any of several different substantive research problems. It is difficult to find projects that effectively use the skills of the person trained in a certain substantive discipline *and* experienced in a certain operations methodology.

We should guard against overstating the argument. Just as it is possible to recruit persons talented in both scientific direction and survey management, it is possible to find projects that take advantage of particular combination of talents. There are survey organizations that successfully practice this strategy. However, in survey organizations, as in so much of the world, specialization does provide flexibility.

Alas, there is a trade-off. What is gained in recruitment and utilization of skilled managers must be balanced against what is lost in rationalizing the management structure. The problem: how to construct a management system that links not two sets of skills but two sets of skilled people? The source of the problem: Both sets of people are senior professionals and thus cannot be lodged in a hierarchical structure in which either design and analysis is subordinate to survey operations or survey operations is subordinate to design and analysis. Such a hierarchy would smuggle the strategy of combination back into the organization by presuming that whichever skill was assigned the subordinate position could somehow be managed by the other.

To allow specialization, therefore, is to establish two spheres of expertise located in two sets of people. If the organization takes seriously the professional expertise of each set of persons (as it should), then it has, in effect, established two spheres of influence. The management task is straightforward: Get the two spheres of influence to work harmoniously and cooperatively toward the shared goals of the organization. Although it may be straightforward, the task is not simple.

There are two layers of problems associated with having dual spheres of influence, those that are project specific and those related to overall management of the organization. The problems are easily illustrated. At the project level, for example, the scientific director wants to squeeze an additional research assistant out of the budget in order to track an interesting analytic issue that had not been anticipated and therefore was not budgeted. The project manager feels that an extra training session for the field editors is necessary because the questionnaire turned out to be more complex than had been anticipated when the budget was prepared. When the project director is a single person this trade-off between analysis and data quality is very much easier to decide than when project direction includes both a principal investigator and a separate operations manager.

Project-specific problems are exacerbated when the study is a government contract rather than a grant. Now there is a third party, the technical project monitor in the government agency. This person will simultaneously be talking with the principal investigator about design and analysis issues and with the operations manager about field procedures and scheduling–budget matters. Different interpretations can be placed on what the project monitor is saying, if indeed the same things are being said in every conversation. Care can be taken to establish a single line of communication from the client agency to the survey organization; in the middle of a complex and fast-moving study, however, informal channels are almost always established. These channels can be opened at several levels of responsibility: sampling director, site manager, field coordinator, data processor, budget monitor, contract officer. Establishing some control over the instructions and information flowing between the project and the client is difficult under the best of management structures. It is certainly more difficult when the management structure is based upon two separate spheres of influence.

The difficulties that beset a particular project have analogues at the level of the organization itself. In creating two areas of expertise and two spheres of

influence, the organization must then establish an overall management structure that recognizes the separate and indispensable contributions of each
sphere. Trade-offs have to be made. Should limited project-development resources be invested in search of a study that fully utilizes the field staff and
thereby maintains its quality? Or should these resources be used to develop a
project that will provide training for a cadre of research assistants?

To adopt a policy of specialization among the senior professional staff is to
invite the managerial problems associated with dual spheres of influence. There
are no simple solutions. Certain institutional arrangements can facilitate effective work relationships, such as mutually agreed upon schedules and budgets,
clear specification of responsibilities, open lines of communication, and a court
of appeal when differences of judgment do occur. But these institutional arrangements have to be accompanied by such organizational intangibles as mutual respect for different forms of knowledge, a conscious agreement upon the
broader goals of the organization, sensitivity to the constraints and demands
associated with different tasks, and, of course, simple human trust.

Whether an organization can bring about these institutional and interpersonal arrangements depends on factors that go beyond the scope of this chapter. It is obvious that there is a trade-off involved in the two different ways of
constructing the senior staff. The survey organization that tends toward a
strategy of specialization pays a price in managerial rationalization for the
benefits of greater flexibility in staff recruitment and staff utilization. The survey organization that seeks to combine different project skills in the same
persons complicates its recruitment and utilization problems but benefits from
more streamlined, less cumbersome management structures.

Senior Management

Perhaps the most important administrative responsibility of persons who
actually direct survey organizations is to establish the major principles of management. Two principles are in conflict. On the one hand, there are principles
borrowed from the academy that stress professional autonomy and provide for
a laissez-faire organization. On the other hand, there are standard principles of
centralization and hierarchy normally invoked in organizations with staff specialization and the need to coordinate effort toward an integrated product.

Because survey organizations have roots in the university, that which
characterizes academic management influences survey management. The typical academic department is a collection of near-equal professionals administered by one of their own who is temporarily assigned the duties of chairing. An
organization chart, if one could be found, would be virtually flat. Although
more complicated structures govern divisions and professional schools, even
deans and academic vice-presidents are uncomfortable with (or unwilling to
risk) a chain of command that would establish multiple layers of authority
between administration and faculty. To be sure, there is variability. Large
public universities differ from small private colleges; but compared to the cor-

porate sector or the government agency, even the most bureaucratized universities persist in granting a large measure of autonomy to departments, and within departments, to individual faculty. Decentralization is the major principle of organization for the university, and is presumed to serve the knowledge-seeking and knowledge-transmitting purposes of the academy.

In research institutions there is an uneasiness, if not resistance, to staff hierarchies, chain-of-command control systems, steep organizational charts, and managerial directives. Part of the uneasiness flows from the top down, for many senior administrators are persons initially trained in research. Angus Campbell (1953) noted many years ago that the role of the researcher-turned-administrator is an ambiguous one. "As a product of an academic background, he will almost certainly be influenced by the individualistic values which characterize the faculty culture [p. 225]." It is not unusual to find survey organizations directed by individuals reluctant to be directing (Hunt, 1977).

In tension with the decentralized principles of management borrowed from the university are the pressing needs for coordination, centralization, and direction. In the research organization, writes Peter Rossi (1964), "decisions have to be made continually, responsibilities for particular activities have to be allocated to different persons, men have to pace their work to the paces of others. There are strong strains to produce a bureaucratic organization for research activities in which there is a much more clear line of authority than is necessary for the teaching activities of a department [p. 1146]." The pressures to bureaucratize have, if anything, become stronger in the years that have elapsed since Rossi wrote. Surveys have become more complex, and contract research has added many scheduling, reporting, and monitoring requirements.

The ongoing task of senior management is to accommodate the conflicting principles of centralization and decentralization, coordination and autonomy. The middle ground is often management through participation. Research administrators do something more than chair but something less than direct. They encourage staff participation in decisions that importantly affect the operation and direction of the organization (Seashore, 1962, p. 3).

In the survey organization, like many organizations composed of professionals, expertise is prized over status. A given problem is more likely to be handed over to who knows the most than to who has the formal authority. To manage by expertise requires more organizational flexibility than what is usually found in chain-of-command hierarchies. But some hierarchy must be preserved. The successful survey is, finally, the result of coordinated effort by staff with different skills and statuses in the organization. The coordinated effort and the integrated product have to be administered into being, not left to emerge from the autonomous activity of a collection of individual researchers and technical staff.

There is no final resolution of the conflicting principles of decentralization characteristic of most research and professional organizations and centralization imposed by the requirements of conducting surveys. Senior management in survey organizations learn to live with the persistence of both principles and attempt to extract the mixture that allows researchers and research to flourish.

4.4. A PERSONAL POSTSCRIPT

Social scientists prefer to write material that transcends time-bound descriptions of current practices. Such an effort has not guided the preparation of this chapter. At least three major factors affecting the management of survey organizations are in great flux: (a) the institutionalization of survey research, especially the proliferation of policy research and consulting firms; (b) the funding environment, especially the relationship between suppliers of social-science knowledge and the procurement policies of the federal government; and (c) the response of survey technology to the complex analytic demands placed on it.

Of these three factors, the third, I believe, is the most critical. The heavy use of survey research by the mission agencies of the federal government has imposed severe demands both on survey technology and on the organizations that have conducted the large-scale evaluation studies and social experiments. There have been complex design requirements, illustrated in the effort of the early Income Maintenance Experiments to develop a model for the selection of program participants that would take into account anticipated labor-market response. There have been difficult issues in the relationship between sampling and field work, illustrated in the requirement of the Labor Department's NLS that a panel be established of 12,000 youths, ages 14–21, with oversamples of economically disadvantaged white, black, and Hispanic youth, and a specially coordinated survey of military youth. There have been equally complex issues in coordinating field work with data processing, illustrated in the National Medical Care Expenditure Survey with its requirement that seven personal and telephone interviews be conducted in 15,000 households within a 14-month period, and that the results of early interviews in the sequence inform the asking of questions in subsequent interviews. There have also been designs that require merging several different data files, illustrated in the National Center for Educational Statistics' NLS which involves a self-administered questionnaire to a sample of 72,000 high school sophomores and seniors, as well as a coordinated aptitude test and the collection of school records, interviews with parents and with school administrators.

State-of-the-art survey technology has been strained by demanding design, sampling, field, processing, and analysis requirements. If state-of-the-art survey technology has been taxed, so also, and perhaps even more so, have state-of-the-art organizational arrangements.

There is no reason to anticipate a slackening in the demand for increasingly complex survey designs. A corollary will be the need for new management techniques. Although I believe that many of the principles noted in this chapter will survive into the future, I also acknowledge a time-boundedness to what I have attempted to describe as current problems and practices. Just as the literature of the early 1950s (Cambell, 1953; Glock, 1951) or of the early 1960s (Lazarsfeld, 1961, 1962; Rossi, 1964) are only partial guides to what we experience today, a publication in the 1980s is only a partial guide for the next several decades. Management will be transformed in response to increasing complexity of empirical social science and the changing role that survey data play in the social sciences and in the society.

ACKNOWLEDGMENT

In addition to colleagues at NORC, especially Norman Bradburn, Celia Homans, and Bob Mcdonald, exdirectors of NORC, Peter Rossi and Jim Davis, have helped shape the arguments in this chapter. Jean Converse and Al Biderman were also very helpful in supplying ideas and bibliographic suggestions.

REFERENCES

Biderman, A. D., and L. M. Sharp
  1972   "Evaluation research: Procurement and method." *Social Science Information* 11(June–
         August): 141–170.
Campbell, A.
  1953   "Administering research organizations." *American Psychologist* 8(June): 225–230.
Glock, C. Y.
  1951   "Some implications of organization for social research." *Social Forces* 39(December):
         129–140.
Hunt, R. G.
  1977   "Social science in social decisions: The role of the university social research center."
         Unpublished paper, March 29.
Lazarsfeld, P. F.
  1961   "Observations on the organization of empirical social research in the United States."
         With the collaboration of Sidney S. Spivack. pp. 1–35n *"Information" Bulletin of the
         International Social Science Council.* No. 22 (December).
  1962   "The sociology of empirical social research." *American Sociological Review* 27(Decem-
         ber): 757–767.
Rossi, P. H.
  1964   "Researchers, scholars and policy makers: The politics of large scale research." *Daeda-
         lus* 93(Fall): 1142–1161.
Seashore, S. E.
  1962   "The Institute for Social Research: A description and analysis of an institutional context
         for social research." American Sociological Association, Washington D.C., August.

Chapter 5

Applied Sampling

Seymour Sudman

5.1. INTRODUCTION

This chapter introduces some basic ideas on how to select and evaluate survey research samples. Much of the material has been taken from the book *Applied Sampling* (Sudman, 1976). Readers who need additional information on sampling should consult chapter 3 that book as well as the list of additional readings given at the end of that chapter.

This chapter starts with examples of appropriate and inappropriate sample designs and the use of biased samples in the early stages of a research study. This is followed by a discussion of how to define the population being studied, both theoretically and operationally. The next sections discuss the evaluation of small-scale samples. A series of studies with varying levels of credibility are given as examples and are critiqued.

The discussion then turns to simple random samples and includes sections on random numbers and their use, systematic samples, and short-cut procedures for sampling, including examples. Next there is a discussion of the use of lists, as well as problems caused by blanks, duplications, and omissions. There is a discussion of the use of telephone directories and random digit dialing methods for telephone surveys.

The next section deals with the question of how big the sample should be and gives some examples of current sample sizes for different types of studies. The last major topic discussed is stratified sampling. After some examples of situations where stratification is inappropriate, the use of stratification is discussed when the strata are of primary importance, when variances differ between strata, and when costs differ. The chapter ends with some suggested additional reading.

5.2. HOW GOOD DOES THE SAMPLE NEED TO BE?

It should be made clear immediately that there is no uniform standard of quality that must always be reached by every sample. The quality of the sample depends entirely on the stage of the research and how the information will be used. At one extreme there is exploratory data gathering, used in the process of generating hypotheses for later study. At the other extreme are large-scale continuing studies used to supply the input for major policy decisions of the federal government. Obviously, the levels of accuracy required differ in these two extreme cases. Thus, one of the earliest decisions that must be made in planning a study is how good must the sample be.

A series of examples ranging from high to low levels of accuracy, where the quality of the sample seems to be appropriate to the requirements, illustrate the different levels of accuracy required. In contrast, several other examples of samples where the quality is either too high or too low are cited.

EXAMPLE 5.1 THE CURRENT POPULATION SURVEY

The largest continuing personal sample of households in the United States is the Current Population Survey (CPS), conducted monthly and continually published by the Bureau of the Census. The sample is located in 449 sample areas comprising 863 counties and independent cities. Some 60,000 housing units are designated for the sample each month; about 52,500 of them, containing about 105,000 persons 16 years of age and older, are occupied by households. The remainder are vacant or converted to nonresidential use.

That the sample be very large and carefully controlled is necessary because the data from the Current Population Survey are the only source of monthly estimates of total employment and unemployment as well as the only comprehensive source of information on the personal characteristics of the total population between the decennial censuses (U.S. Bureau of the Census, 1954–present, 1966).

Major government economic and welfare programs are influenced by changes of a few tenths of a percent in CPS data from month to month. For this reason, the sample is large enough so that the sampling errors of the total estimates of unemployment are only about .1%.

The sample has grown from 25,000 total units a month in 1943, to 40,000 units in 1957, to 60,000 units in 1967 because of the increased concern about local area economic and social problems. There is some probability that even larger samples will be taken in the future.

It is interesting to note that in addition to being cheaper and more timely, the data from the Current Population Survey are generally considered to be more accurate for many purposes than the decennial census. This is because continuing attention is given to the hiring and training of an experienced staff of interviewers and to the careful design of detailed questionnaires so that responses obtained are less subject to error. It is not possible, of course, to provide the same detail about small geographic areas from any sample, no matter how large, as from a complete census.

EXAMPLE 5.2 THE GALLUP POLL (GALLUP, 1972; PERRY, 1960)

Probably the best known of all continuing U.S. polls, the Gallup Poll reports not only on presidential elections but also on all major public issues as they arise. The poll is syndicated and appears in major newspapers, each of which pays a small fee for the publication rights. The syndication fees support the service and determine the size and quality of the sample.

The sample for each survey consists of 1500 adults selected from 320 locations using area sampling methods. At each location, the interviewer is given a map with an indicated starting point and is required to follow the map, going in a specified direction. At each occupied dwelling unit, the interviewer must attempt to meet sex quotas. Although this block quota sampling procedure is not completely unbiased since it misses people who are less likely to be home, it appears to provide results that are near enough to true values to give politicians and the public a sense of public attitudes about an issue. The election predictions when compared to the results indicate the general accuracy of the sample.

EXAMPLE 5.3 THE DETROIT AREA STUDY

A rapidly growing trend in social science departments of major universities is the use of practical experience to teach research methods. The oldest and best known of these programs is the Detroit Area Study (DAS) operated by the Survey Research Center, University of Michigan. Each year a different project is conducted with the topic decided from among competing proposals submitted by faculty members. The project is executed in the field by a combination of professional interviewers and beginning graduate students. The students also process the data and analyze some portion of it by mutual agreement with the project director. Frequently, papers prepared to fulfill class requirements are later published in professional journals.

Although the University of Michigan provides some of the operating funds for the DAS, additional funds are usually obtained from outside granting agencies. The size of the sample and the complexity of the design thus vary from year to year, depending on the aims of the study and the resources available, but generally a probablity sample of around 500 interviews is obtained. Because of the limited time available to students, restricting the study to the Detroit Standard Metropolitan Statistical Area makes it possible for each student to do some interviewing under careful supervision of the Survey Research Center. Obviously, this geographic restriction determines the kinds of projects that are possible to do and limits the generalizability of the findings.

EXAMPLE 5.4 UNFUNDED DOCTORAL DISSERTATION RESEARCH

This is best described using as an example a composite of the kinds of research samples that are possible assuming only the effort of the doctoral candidate and out-of-pocket expenditures of less than $1000, usually paid by the candidate with some help from his or her department. If a general population sample and face-to-face interviewing are required, the samples are typically in a single place and the number of respondents usually ranges from 200 to 300. The interviewing is all done by the candidate or by the candidate with a few helpers, either paid or unpaid. The selected place is chosen to be easily reached by the candidate to avoid travel costs. There is usually a city directory available to reduce sampling costs.

If the questionnaire lends itself to telephone interviewing, the sample can be spread over a larger area, particularly if a WATS line is available. The sample is selected either from telephone directories or by the use of random digit dialing. Since no travel time or costs are incurred, a larger sample ranging up to 500 cases is possible. The actual sample size depends on the complexity and length of the questionnaire as well as phone charges, if any.

Frequently, special populations such as professionals (lawyers, dentists, teachers) or organizations (schools, hospitals, business establishments) are chosen for analysis. This generally reduces the attainable sample size since much more effort must be expended to locate the special population and to obtain cooperation. Thus, with face-to-face interviewing, samples of as few as 50–100 cases are frequently all that can be reached. With phone interviewing, samples of 200–300 are possible if WATS lines are available.

With some professional groups, mail surveys are possible, particularly if the survey has the endorsement of national or local leadership. Depending on the availability of lists, the sample can be national, regional, or local. Sample sizes of 500–1000 are used since the major cost is postage and printing. To obtain a reasonable cooperation rate, at least one and usually two or three follow-up mailings are necessary. Finally, if cooperation is still low, additional phone calls are made to a subsample of about one-third of nonrespondents.

EXAMPLE 5.5 PILOT TESTS, EXPLORATORY RESEARCH, MOTIVATIONAL RESEARCH

The lowest quality samples generally consist of 20–50 respondents usually chosen at the convenience of the researcher. If household respondents are used, the interviewer is free to select the household from anywhere in a broad geographic area, although sometimes a block or census tract are specified. Sometimes a church or other voluntary group will be used for either a self-administered questionnaire or a group interview. If the researcher is connected with a university or school, the respondents may be the students in a classroom.

These types of samples are appropriate at the earliest stages of a research design when one is first attempting to develop hypotheses and procedures for measuring them. Then, along with reading the literature and discussing ideas with colleagues, friends, and relatives, exploratory data gathering is worthwhile. Any sort of a sample may be useful when very little is known. Just a few interviews can pinpoint major problems with questions and dimensions of the topic that the researcher may have ignored.

5.3. INAPPROPRIATE SAMPLE DESIGNS

Whether a sample design is appropriate or not depends on how it is to be used and what resources are available. In some cases it may be fair to say that the sample design is appropriate for the available resources, but that the analysis and generalizations made from the sample go too far.

Consider the student who is doing unfunded research. It would be inappropriate for that student to attempt or be advised to attempt a large national study. The resources available are just not adequate for the task. Any such study attempted is very likely to be badly executed with very low cooperation rates from respondents. Almost all researchers will agree that a small study well-designed and executed is superior to a large study that has been messed-up. On the other hand, it is generally possible for a student writing a doctoral dissertation to do more than the lowest quality exploratory research discussed in Example 5.5. Frequently research is labeled as "exploratory" merely to protect it from criticism against a poorly designed or executed sample.

At the opposite extreme are federal government research and evaluation projects; but here, too, inappropriate samples are sometimes seen. For example, during the funding of model cities programs by the Office of Economic Opportunity, an evaluation of the effectiveness of the programs was required. As a standard procedure, OEO required a population sample of 1% of the households in a model city. Although there may have been some political reasons for this decision that were never made clear, there was no statistical rationale for the procedure. This rule resulted in samples that were probably too large in the largest cities in the United States and too small in smaller metropolitan areas. In all these places, sampling variability depends not on the percentage of the population, *but almost entirely on the sample size alone.* If one wanted the same level of reliability in each model city then identical sample sizes should have been taken. Even assuming that the larger cities were more important than the smaller ones, sample-size decisions should have been made on the basis of the accuracy required to evaluate the effectiveness of various programs and not on the size of the population.

The greatest use of inappropriate samples, however, is by professors in the social sciences. Given the availability of a large sample of *captive* respondents in beginning classes, many academics never consider the use of broader and more representative samples, even if resources are available. For these professors, a high quality study is one where the sample consists of students at several schools selected because the study director has friends there. In many cases, the task required of students is completely inappropriate to their current status, such as asking the student to assume a leadership role in a business organization or to make a household buying decision.

Even where the task is appropriate, the subordinate relationship of the student to the instructor leads to exaggerated responses that cannot be duplicated in real-world samples. For example, the well-known Rosenthal (1966) studies that have been conducted to indicate experimenter effects have used students as experimenters and subjects. Most of the observed effects would probably vanish if a general population sample were used.

5.4. THE USE OF BIASED SAMPLES FOR SCREENING

In some cases the use of very small and poorly chosen samples may be justified as the first stage of a screening process if the directions of the biases are known. Consider the research process for discovering new drugs to treat various forms of cancer. Hundreds of such drugs have been proposed and it is impossible to test each drug on a large, carefully drawn sample of patients. Instead, the drugs that appear most promising on the basis of experiments with animals are tried on very small samples of patients at hospitals near the researcher. If the new drug were ineffective on this sample it would usually be discarded since there are so many other drugs to try and there is little reason to believe that the drug would work on some other group.

If, on the other hand, the drug is effective with some of the patients, it would then receive more careful testing on larger samples with careful controls for placebo effects and the selection of patients. In other words, the sample biases in this case are expected to be in the direction of overstating the effectiveness of the drug.

A more cheerful example of the same procedure is the use of employees of a company to test new products that are produced in research and development. If the employees dislike the new product, or even if they express some reservations, the product is in serious trouble and will probably fail to reach the marketplace. The sample biases are such that one would generally expect employees to be more interested and enthusiastic about a company's new product than would be the general public. If the employees are enthusiastic the product is then tested further on real-world populations.

5.5. DEFINING THE POPULATION

A sample is most generally defined as a subset from a larger population. This would suggest that before thinking about samples one would already have a clear picture of the universe or population (the terms are used interchangeably) from which the sample is to be selected. Unfortunately, researchers frequently forget to make explicit the universe they wish to study or assume that the universe corresponds to the sample selected. This leads to strange definitions of universes such as the universe of all college freshmen in beginning psychology classes, or the universe of readers of a specific magazine or newspaper, when in fact the real universe under study is the total adult population of the United States. It is better to have a clear sensible definition of the target universe and to then carefully describe the sample than to have a misshapen universe definition to fit a strange sample.

The first step in defining a population is to decide whether it is a population of individuals, households, institutions, transactions, or whatever. The source from which the data are to be collected need not be identical to the population definition. If a mail questionnaire is sent to college presidents asking for information about riots on the campus, the population is of colleges and not of college presidents. Similarly, one household member may report on household income or savings if the universe is household spending units or may report on employment of individual members of the household if the universe is individuals. Although most of the time the choice between a universe of individuals or households will be clear, there is a fuzzy area in the middle. Should studies of consumer behavior, media usage, and leisure time activities use populations of individuals or households? The decision is a difficult one and will depend on the specific purposes of the study, but the important thing is that the issue be considered carefully and decided as the study is being planned.

Once the unit of analysis has been determined, the next decisions involve what units to exclude. The following criteria need to be considered:

1. *Geography:* Unless the study relates to a policy question for a local area such as a state, city, or other political unit, the geographic definition of the universe is usually the entire United States, although even this limits the generalizability to other countries.

2. *Age of individuals:* Generally some minimum age is established. For attitudes on public issues the minimum age is usually 18; for studies of employment the minimum age is usually 16; for media readership the minimum age is either 10 or 12. Ordinarily there is no maximum age, but there can be if the study deals with women of childbearing age or newly married couples.

3. *Other demographic variables:* Sex, race, marital status, and education are other variables sometimes used to define a population. Whereas sex is seldom ambiguous, almost all other variables need to be defined carefully. For example, if the sample is limited to white respondents, are Puerto Ricans, Indians, Filipinos, and other orientals to be included or excluded? If the study is of black respondents, should African and Latin American blacks be included?

4. *Other individual variables:* Citizenship, voter registration, and intent to vote are crucial variables to define in any studies of election behavior, but may or may not be important for other studies of public opinion.

5. *Household variables:* If the unit of analysis is the household, one must first define a household. The census definition that is usually used defines a household as everyone living in a housing unit, a housing unit being occupied by tenants who do not live and eat with any other persons in the structure and being where there is (*a*) either direct access from the outside of the building or through a common hall and (*b*) complete kitchen facilities for the use of the occupants.

Even this very precise definition needs further explanation. Mobile homes, trailers, tents, boats, or railroad cars are excluded if vacant (as are vacant housing units), if used only for business, or if used only for vacations. Occupied rooms in hotels and motels are included if the residents have no usual place of residence elsewhere.

The characteristics of the household must also be defined carefully. If the population is limited to households of a single race then a decision must be made about mixed households. Sometimes the race of the household is defined as that of the head of the household, whereas other times the households are excluded. If the requirement is that the household be intact, that is with both a husband and wife, then decisions must be made on how to treat couples who are separated, either legally or otherwise. For example, how one would treat a household where the husband is a sailor on a nuclear submarine and is not home now, but who lives at home when his ship is in port.

The most difficult family characteristic to define is income, particularly in poverty areas where it is hard to determine who is and who is not a permanent household member. Since a definition of poverty depends on both income and size of family, whatever definition is used to determine whether an individual is included in the family should also be used in determining if that individual's income should or should not be included in household income.

Even if the sampling unit is institutions, decisions must be made as with households and individuals. With organizations there is often a minimum size limit, such as excluding from the universe business firms with fewer than five employees. In sampling a population of colleges and universities one would need to decide whether or not to include 2-year colleges, religious seminaries, military universities, postgraduate institutions, unaccredited schools, business colleges, and the like. The decision would depend, of course, on the aims of the study.

5.6. PROBLEMS WITH OVERDEFINING
   THE POPULATION

One should avoid overdefining a population if it is not critically necessary to do so. Beginners sometimes think that setting narrow age and income limits makes the study easier to do and reduces variability in the results. Although doing this may reduce variance in the sample data, it also rules out the possibility of generalizing to a broader universe. Operationally, narrow definitions of the universe greatly increase the cost and difficulty of finding respondents. There are no published lists and no easy ways of finding men between the ages of 20 and 40 with incomes $8000–$12,000. This requires the screening of a very large sample of the general population and asking of questions that are difficult to ask at the beginning of an interview and are always subject to response errors. The simpler the universe definition, the easier and less costly to find the sample.

5.7. OPERATIONAL DEFINITIONS OF THE POPULATION

Although a population should not be defined to mirror a convenient sample, the definition should be possible to implement in the field. Thus, rather than defining a population as consisting of all women still capable of bearing children, it is preferable to define the population of women between the ages of 12 and 50. Although this definition by age may exclude a few women who are capable of childbearing and include some who are not, the more general definition is not operational. Similarly, in a study of the effects of noise on residents near an airport, it is better to define the population as all those living within 1 mile of the airport rather than defining the population as all those affected by airplane noises. It should be recognized that statistical inferences from the sample can only be made about the sample population. To the extent that the sample population differs from the target population, inferences about the target population must be subjective.

Although it is useful to have census information about a defined population, this is not always possible or necessary. Studies of religious groups, criminals, and homosexuals may have well-defined populations although no census material is available. Samples selected from these populations are not usually representative of the total special population. Most studies of criminals are done in prisons, which biases the sample toward those criminals who are more likely to be arrested and convicted. Studies of homosexuals have usually been conducted in bars or with members of organized groups such as the Mattachines, and are biased toward those members of the population who are most active socially. The careful studies done with these groups point out the sample deficiencies rather than attempt to revise the definition of the population.

5.8. SMALL-SCALE SAMPLING WITH
LIMITED RESOURCES

Most social scientists without any training in sampling get their ideas on what to do from reading other people's research in scientific journals. The reviewers of journal articles, however, are themselves not always experts in sampling and are primarily concerned with the substance of the article and the analytic procedures used. Thus, the quality of sampling in published studies varies enormously. Many of the studies reported are based on small-scale samples that have serious limitations, which are sometimes recognized and often ignored.

This section reviews a selection of studies taken from some issues of the *American Sociological Review*, the *American Journal of Sociology*, and *Public Opinion Quarterly* and comments on the quality of sampling used in these studies. This is by no means a random sample of studies. Very large national and cross-national studies have been omitted. Of studies using the same sampling methods, only one or two were chosen for illustration. Although some of the studies reviewed here have inappropriate sample designs, the editorial screening process has prevented most of the studies with really bad samples from ever seeing the light of day. The purpose of this discussion is to alert researchers with limited resources to procedures for improving the quality of their samples as well as to suggest criteria for reader evaluation of sample credibility of published research.

In criticizing some of these studies, we are not concerned with their theoretical or analytical procedures. A poor sample design should not lead the reader to believe that the findings of a study are necessarily invalid or that contrary results are indeed correct. Rather, concern about sampling methods should lead to reduced credibility of the findings and an increase in the uncertainty about their generalizability. The refutation of study findings must come from other studies with greater credibility.

5.9. A CREDIBILITY SCALE

To formalize the notion of credibility and organize the discussion, a credibility scale has been developed for judging small-scale samples. The credibility scale includes the factors that samplers would generally consider in looking at a sample: the generalizability of the findings, sample size, the execution of the sample design, and the use of the available resources. The items included in the scale and the weights assigned are given in Table 5.1.

The weights assigned and the scoring of individual studies are personal judgments, so different samplers might assign different weights and might rank samples somewhat differently than they are listed here. These weights should not be used uncritically to distinguish between samples with similar levels of quality. Nevertheless, readers should be able to detect the differences between the best and worst sample designs and be able to apply them in their critical reading as well as in their planning and write-ups of their own sample designs. It should also be noted that even the best of the designs discussed in this chapter have serious flaws and do not compare to larger standard samples.

GEOGRAPHY

Before turning to a discussion of the specific studies, a brief discussion of the factors in the scale may be helpful. Greatest emphasis is placed on how well the data may be generalized. Unless one is dealing with a small special population located in a single location, a limited sample does not usually represent the total universe. If one observes the same results in several locations with widely different populations, however, one has a great deal more confidence in their generality than if the sample is only of a single location. The greatest relative increase in quality is achieved by increasing the number of locations from one

TABLE 5.1
Credibility Scale for Small Samples

Characteristics	Score
A. Generalizability	
1. *Geographic spread*	
Single location	0
Several locations combined	
Several locations compared	
Limited geography	4
Widespread geography	6
Total universe	10
2. *Discussion of limitations*	
No discussion	0
Brief discussion	3
Detailed discussion	5
3. *Use of special populations*	
Obvious biases in sample that could affect results	−5
Used for convenience, no obvious bias	0
Necessary to test theory	5
General population	5
B. Sample size	
Too small even in total for meaningful analysis	0
Adequate for some, but not all major analyses	3
Adequate for purpose of study	5
C. Sample execution	
Poor response rate, haphazard sample	0
Some evidence of careless field work	3
Reasonable response rate, controlled field operations	5
D. Use of resources	
Poor use of resources	0
Fair use of resources	3
Optimum use of resources	5
Maximum total points possible	35

to two, and comparing the results from the different sites. Combining the results of several locations could conceal important site effects and should be done only after a careful analysis has indicated no significant site differences.

The researcher with limited funds may feel that control of the field work and quality of data collection will be improved by limiting the sample to a single location, but this assumption should be examined very carefully. Frequently, it will be found that tighter control can be maintained over small crews in several locations than over a larger interviewing group in one location, although it may require more effort by the field supervisor or project director.

Another alternative, observed in Example 5.6, is for two researchers in widely scattered locations to collaborate. The results obtained by combining resources are substantially better than the sum of two separate studies. Still another helpful method for increasing sample credibility is to compare the results of a study to those of earlier studies. If the results of the study replicate those of earlier studies, both the old and new studies gain in credibility, even if the methodologies and questionnaires differ. If, however, the results of a study contradict the results of earlier studies, one is faced with serious problems of deciding whether the differences are caused by sample differences, different measurement procedures, or something else.

DISCUSSION OF LIMITATIONS

A careful discussion of the sample limitations of the study is useful, especially for readers with limited sampling backgrounds. Thus, a study that carefully states and explores its possible sample biases gains rather than loses credibility.

As an example consider the following excerpts from Lenski's, *The Religious Factor* (1963):

> The study was carried out in the Midwestern metropolis of Detroit, fifth largest community in America today, and probably eleventh largest in the world. Here, by means of personal interviews with a carefully selected cross-section of the population of the *total* community (i.e., suburbs as well as central city), we sought to discover the impact of religion on secular institutions. Strictly speaking, the findings set forth in this volume apply only to Detroit. However, in view of the steady decline of localism and regionalism in America during the last century, it seems likely that most of these findings could be duplicated by similar studies in other communities. This is a matter to which we shall return later in this chapter. . . [p. 1].
>
> In its economics, politics, ethnicity, and religion, Detroit most closely resembles Cleveland, Pittsburgh, Buffalo, and Chicago. In common with these communities, Detroit is noted for heavy industry, high wages, a large industrial population, a large proportion of eastern European immigrants of peasant background, and a rapidly growing Negro minority recently arrived from the rural South. Among the major metropolitan centers it bears least resemblance to New York and Washington, both of which differ markedly in terms of economics, ethnicity, and religion, and, in the case of voteless Washington, in terms of politics as well.
>
> Despite these local peculiarities it seems probable that most of our findings in Detroit can be generalized and applied to other major metropolitan centers throughout the country, with the possible exception of the South. This appears likely for two reasons. In the first place, the issues we investigated are basically national in character, and not local. Advances in transportation and mass communication mean that people all over the country are nowadays subject to similar pressures and influences. Local and even regional peculiarities have been progressively eroded. More and more the nation is becoming a political, economic, religious, and social unit. Secondly, Americans are becoming more and more mobile. *Of those now living in greater Detroit, nearly two thirds were born elsewhere.* More than half were born outside of Michigan, and therefore outside the sphere of Detroit's direct influence, and within the orbit of some other metropolitan center. This constant movement of population also hampers the development of regional peculiarities, and promotes the homogeneity of the national population.
>
> In the last analysis, however, the only sure test of the generalizability of the findings of a study based on a single community can come from similar studies conducted elsewhere. For this reason, throughout this book references will be made (usually in footnotes) to earlier studies which have dealt with similar problems elsewhere. In

this way the reader will be better able to judge to what degree the findings of this study are unique to Detroit, and to what degree they may apply to other communities [pp. 33–34].

Although the extended discussion of sample limitations possible in a book or monograph must be condensed in a journal article (if not by the author then by the editors) some discussion of the critical differences between the sample and universe should be included.

USE OF SPECIAL POPULATIONS

The use of special populations may sometimes be a powerful tool for testing a theory. In a study of the socialization of children, samples of school children are highly appropriate. For testing organizational effects on managers or workers, the firm is the logical place to start. In one of our examples, cadets at a military academy are used to study professional socialization.

In some cases the use of a special population may lead to obvious or potential biases. Thus, the use of college students to represent the total population leads to major education and social-class biases. In addition, the authority relation between the students and the researcher may be such that response effects are greatly magnified.

A common use of special populations is in secondary analyses when data initially collected for one purpose are reanalyzed for a different purpose. If the initial data were from a general population sample, then, of course, there are no problems. Potential biases arise when a special population is treated as a regular population sample in the reanalysis. This procedure is sometimes justified because it makes very efficient use of limited resources. In this case, it is especially important that the sample be critically examined by the researcher for all possible biases.

SAMPLE SIZE

The adequacy of the sample depends on the details of the analysis. Few studies seen in the literature have samples that are too small when only the total sample is used. For most analyses, however, breakdowns of the sample are required; for many breakdowns, the observed samples are inadequate. A general rule is that the sample should be large enough so that there are 100 or more units in each category of the major breakdowns and a minimum of 20–50 in the minor breakdowns.

SAMPLE EXECUTION

The quality of a sample depends not only on its design, but also on its execution. Low cooperation rates may indicate sloppy fieldwork and lack of follow-up procedures. A frequent example of this is seen in mail surveys that use a single mailing and obtain low cooperation rates, when additional mailings could increase cooperation to the generally accepted level of about 80%. The biases in mail samples are toward respondents with more education and who are most interested in the topic.

Even worse are personal samples where the interviewer is allowed to select the respondents or households to be interviewed. Here no measure of cooperation is possible and the biases are likely to be toward the most accessible respondents. These are more likely to be female, unemployed, middle-aged or older, and middle class.

USE OF RESOURCES

Although independent of judgments about the absolute quality of a sample, it seems appropriate to consider how well the sample was designed and executed with the resources that were available. Several of the following examples report studies that were conducted in response to a specific news event. In these cases, the researchers rushed into the field with very limited resources. If they had waited to obtain funds and select a careful sample, the timeliness of the research would have vanished. Even here, however, some sampling methods are far better than others. A quick phone sample, for example, is far superior to street-corner interviewing since it is far less biased and no more costly.

The use of natural clusters such as classrooms when the study deals with children or college students is also an efficient use of limited resources. On the other hand, if the study is to be conducted by mail, then heavy clustering is an inefficient use of resources since it reduces the generalizability of the results without reducing costs.

5.10. EXAMPLES

The following examples are listed in decreasing order of credibility, based on the credibility scale of Table 5.1 and on my judgment. A brief discussion of the aim of the study and the sampling method used is given as well as the scores on the individual components of the scale. For additional information about the studies, readers are urged to consult the original articles which should be readily accessible.

EXAMPLE 5.6 "EFFECTS OF VERTICAL MOBILITY AND STATUS INCONSISTENCY:
A BODY OF NEGATIVE EVIDENCE" (JACKSON & CURTIS, 1972) AND
"COMMUNITY RANK STRATIFICATION: A FACTOR ANALYSIS" (ARTZ, CURTIS,
FAIRBANK, & JACKSON, 1971)

Both these studies are based on the same sample of six communities: three in Indiana and three in Arizona. Male heads of households were drawn randomly from the street address sections of city and suburban directories. The sample size was 686 males in Phoenix and between 300 and 400 in the other cities. In Indianapolis, the interviewing was part of the Indianapolis Area Project, a training program similar to the Detroit Area Study. In the other cities, interviewing was done by Elmo Roper Associates, a well-known research firm.

The first study attempted to determine whether dimensions of social rank combine additively or whether interactions appear to support the notions of status inconsistency or vertical mobility. The results favored the additive models. The second study, a factor analysis of rank measures, suggested that stratification systems vary by community context.

Credibility score 31/35 = .89.

Generalizability 6: The use of six locations widely separated and of different sizes is very useful. As Jackson and Curtis (1972) put it:

> Analyzing our problem in several rather different communities allows us to estimate whether mobility and/or inconsistency effects are more or less general, or whether they appear only in certain social settings. It also allows us to see which effects do not replicate across cities in any fashion and hence should possibly be labeled chance fluctuations.

The results reported in this first study are used to disconfirm a theory. As is well recognized, the requirements to confirm a theory are substantially stronger than to disprove one. Here the absence in six different communities of positive evidence of status inconsistency and vertical mobility would lead most readers to accept the research and reject the theory.

Discussion of limitations 5: A careful discussion of the selected communities.

Use of special populations 5: The universe is limited to male household heads, which seems appropriate given the aims of the study. Households are selected at random from city directories.

Sample size 5: It is clear that the sample sizes here are ample for the analysis.

Sample execution 5: Although the completion rates are not given, and it would have been useful to have them, all evidence is that the study was done very carefully.

Use of resources 5: This sample has two excellent examples of the careful use of resources. First it combines research with training of students. Second, it combines the resources of researchers in Indiana and Arizona.

Although this is not a national study, some readers may feel that the sample size is too large for this study to be considered small scale. The quality of this study would not suffer very much, however, if the samples were considerably smaller, or if only four instead of six communities had been used. Thus, many of the techniques seen here could be used by researchers with more limited funds.

EXAMPLE 5.7 "SOCIAL POSITION AND SELF-EVALUATION: THE RELATIVE IMPORTANCE OF RACE" (YANCY, RIGSBY, & MCCARTHY, 1972)

This study evaluates the effects of race, sex, city, age, education, marital status, and employment on self-esteem and stress. Race has minimal effects when other variables are controlled. The study was conducted with 362 blacks and 350 whites in Nashville, Tennessee, and 215 blacks and 252 whites in Philadelphia, Pennsylvania.

Employing 1960 census information and any information available on subsequent neighborhood change, in both cities residential areas that were thought to hold lower-, working-, and middle-class blacks and whites were selected. Within each residential area, blocks were randomly chosen. Specific dwellings were selected by systematically interviewing in every fifth dwelling unit. Within each dwelling unit, the interviewer attempted to interview the head of the household, but interviewed a second adult when it became clear that the household head was unavailable. The nonresponse rate, given three call-backs, was under 5% in each city. An effort was made to match race of interviewer with race of respondent, but approximately 35% of black respondents were interviewed by white interviewers. An analysis indicated no effects of the race of the interviewer on the results related to stress.

Credibility score 30/35 = .86.

Generalizability 5: Here is another example of researchers, one in Philadelphia, the others in Nashville, combining their resources to give the results in two locations. Although slightly less convincing than the results in six locations, these results are far better than if only one city had been used. Note also that this research was intended to disconfirm a theory so that fewer locations are needed.

Discussion of limitations 5: There is a discussion of the differences between the two sites and the general effects of city and region.

Use of special populations 5: This is a general population sample with the head of the household interviewed.

Sample size 5: Clearly adequate.

Sample execution 5: Carefully done with a very low noncooperation rate.

Use of resources 5: The resources for this study were obviously less than for the previous example, but they were well utilized by combining researchers from two locations.

EXAMPLE 5.8 "THE DEVELOPMENT OF POLITICAL ORIENTATION AMONG
BLACK AND WHITE CHILDREN" (ORUM & COHEN, 1973)

Black and white school children in grades 4–12 were studied in four urban areas in Illinois. Self-administered questionnaires were obtained from 2365 students, split equally between black and white and male and female. Fifty percent of the sample was from an inner-city, lower-class, black public school system; 10% from an inner-city, middle- to upper-class integrated school. The other two areas each contributed 20% of the sample, with one constituting a lower-middle to working class public school system and the other a middle-class public school system, both being principally composed of white students.

Credibility score 29/35 = .83.

Generalizability 5: The sample benefits from four quite different areas, but the generalizability is limited because all students are from Illinois. Particularly in studying attitudes of black children, comparisons between the North and South could be important.

Discussion of limitations 5: There is a careful comparison of the results of this study with the results of other studies indicating some similarities, but also some disparities.

Use of special populations 5: The use of school children here is necessary for the analysis.

Sample size 4: Although in total this sample is very large, most of the analyses are carried out controlling for race, occupation of chief wage-earner (blue collar, white collar), and grade in school (4–6, 7–8, 9–10, 11–12). Some of the analyses of differences are based on rather small samples.

Sample execution 5: Except for children absent on the day the form was administered, there was no noncooperation once the school agreed to cooperate.

Use of resources 5: A very efficient use of limited resources using self-administered forms in a classroom and using graduate students in the Survey Research Practicum at the University of Illinois, Urbana, to collect the data.

EXAMPLE 5.9 "POWER AND IDEOLOGICAL CONFORMITY: A CASE STUDY"
(GARNIER, 1973)

This is a study of professional socialization at Britain's Sandhurst Military Academy indicating that conformity to the staff's goals is achieved. The sample size of 883 comprised 92% of the cadets at the academy during 1967.

Credibility score 26/35 = .74.

Generalizability 1: Although this is only at a single location, some effort is made to generalize by a discussion of other studies. If resources were available one could attempt to extend this study to other military academies in the United States or to officer candidate schools and other military training programs.

Discussion of limitations 5: Given the limited nature of this study, the discussion of limitations is excellent. In addition to calling it a case study, the author concludes the paper with the following remark:

> It must be noted that these findings stem from a case study. While the findings presented here seem reasonable, they are nevertheless based on limited evidence. If the study of socialization, and particularly socialization taking place within organizations, is going to proceed further, the time may have come to manipulate the variables isolated here in the laboratory. If the laboratory is too artificial a setting, then future researchers should make sure that the variables described in the literature are systematically manipulated. Only then can reasonable findings become scientific [p. 362].

Use of special populations 5: Military academies are appropriate settings for studies of power.

Sample size 5: Since all cadets were included, the sample size is clearly sufficient for this case study. For broader generalization, the sample could be increased by using more sites.

Sample execution 5: The 92% cooperation rate is very good and indicates careful fieldwork and follow-up procedures.

Use of resources 5: The use of self-administered forms to all cadets indicates a careful use of resources.

EXAMPLE 5.10 "HOW FAST DOES NEWS TRAVEL?" (SCHWARTZ, 1973–1974)

The shooting of Governor George Wallace on 15 May 1972 provided an opportunity to measure how fast nationally significant news travels. Interviews were conducted by phone in New York City between 5:00 and 10:00 P.M. on the day of the shooting. Six interviewers completed 312 three-question interviews.

Credibility score 23/35 = .66.

Generalizability 0: A single location, with no discussion of other studies of the spreading of news.

Discussion of limitations 3: There is a discussion of the limitations of the study due to the fact that it was done in New York City, that only persons home between 5:00 and 10:00 P.M. were interviewed, and that households with unlisted numbers were omitted. It would have been useful to know the completion rate, the number of refusals, the number not at home, and the number of men and of women in the sample. Comparisons to other studies such as the Kennedy assassination would also have been valuable in interpreting these results.

Use of special populations 5: The use of a phone sample of the general population is appropriate here because of the need for speed. Random-digit dialing might have been possible.

Sample size 5: About 60 interviews per hour were obtained. For the purposes of this study this seems sufficient since the key question merely asked "Have you heard the news. . . ."

Sample execution 5: Although the details are sketchy, the shortness of the questionnaire suggests that very few of the persons who were reached refused to answer the three questions. Obtaining more than 300 interviews in an evening is an accomplishment.

Use of resources 5: Although this is obviously not a perfect sample, it is a very good example of the optimum use of limited resources to collect timely data when a significant event has occurred.

EXAMPLE 5.11 "RACE, SEX, AND VIOLENCE: A LABORATORY TEST OF THE
SEXUAL THREAT OF THE BLACK MALE HYPOTHESIS" (SCHULMAN, 1974)

Data from a laboratory experiment with 84 white male students at the University of California at Santa Barbara is used to support the psychoanalytic view of racism, that it is a function of the sexual threat of the black male.

Credibility score 7/35 = .20.

Generalizability 0: Data were gathered for students at only one school and there was no discussion of similar findings elsewhere.

Discussion of limitations 2: The characteristics of the students participating in the experiment are given, but no comparison is made to the population of all college students or to the general population.

Use of special populations −5: Clearly, the college students are selected here for convenience, not to support a theory. Although the author believes that the theory is supported because the students are generally liberal and educated, my judgment is that this is just the sort of situation in which students will respond to the authority of the experimenter and give the expected results. Thus, I find these results totally unconvincing. The same results on a general population sample, even if limited geographically, would make a substantial difference in credibility for this kind of study.

Sample size 2: The sample is split into four treatment groups for analysis, and because of an error in operation one group has only 14 subjects whereas the other three groups have 27, 23, and 20 subjects.

Sample execution 5: There is no evidence of bias in the class that was selected for this experiment. Twenty subjects were eliminated because they indicated an awareness of other similar experiments or because of an error in conducting the experiment.

Use of resources 3: The ready availability of college students makes them the subjects for most experiments conducted by university researchers. Yet as this example indicates, this procedure may seriously affect the credibility of results. The use of noncollege populations instead of, or in addition to, college students can greatly improve the quality of a sample.

It should be obvious to readers that there are very substantial differences in the quality of the samples presented in these examples. The examples given first are clearly better than those described later. There seems to be no value in arbitrarily assigning words like *good* and *poor* to the studies at the top and bottom of the list, since the changes in quality are continuous rather than discrete. As anyone who has ever graded examinations knows, it is far easier to recognize high quality than to decide how much poor quality should be penalized.

It should also be evident from the examples that limited resources need not necessarily lead to low quality samples. The imaginative use of special populations when applicable, collaboration with other researchers, and comparisons with other studies all help to improve the quality of a sample. The appropriate use of mail and phone methods should always be considered. Some careful thinking early is always better than later regrets and apologies.

5.11. SIMPLE RANDOM SAMPLING

Researchers with limited resources are indeed fortunate if the population they are studying and their data collection methods allow them to use simple random sampling procedures. These procedures are easy and inexpensive for sample selection, data analysis, and sampling variance computation.

It is important to recognize, however, that in many cases simple random sampling is not appropriate. We shall first discuss the general conditions when simple random sampling is optimum and consider some illustrations. In contrast, we shall then consider examples of problems where simple random samples are not appropriate, either because there is no way to select a simple random sample or because other more complex methods are also much more efficient. When other methods are preferable, it would be a serious mistake to use simple random-sampling procedures merely because they are easy.

Probability samples are defined as those samples where every element in the population has a known, nonzero probability of selection. These samples are sometimes called *random* samples, but since the term *random* is used in different ways by statisticians and samplers the term *probability sample* is less likely to cause confusion. Note that it is not necessary that the probabilities of selection be equal for all elements, and this will not be the case for the more complex samples discussed later. *Simple random* samples, however, are defined as those for which (*a*) the probabilities of selection are equal for all elements, and (*b*) sampling is done in one stage with elements of the sample selected independently of one another in contrast to more complex samples where the selection is done in two or more stages and where clusters rather than individual elements are chosen.

5.12. RANDOM NUMBERS

The word *random* as used in sampling does not mean haphazard or catch-as-catch-can, but rather that some well-designed probability mechanism is used in the sample selection. It is the use of this probability mechanism at each point in the selection that distinguishes probability samples from judgment samples.

When one first thinks of ways of obtaining a random process one might consider the use of playing cards, dice, spinners or roulette wheels, or drawing names or numbers out of a hat or a fishbowl. The problem with all of these procedures is that they are slow and there are major difficulties in maintaining randomness in the long run. Thus, playing cards must be shuffled and imperfections in the shuffling lead to the repetition of sequences already observed. Expert card players make use of nonrandomness in shuffling by remembering how cards were played in the previous deal.

A classic example of the difficulty of obtaining randomness using numbers in a fishbowl was the initial use of this procedure for determining the order of selection of men for the draft during the war in Vietnam using birthdates. The dates of the year were poured into a bowl with January going in first and December last. Although the bowl was then stirred vigorously to obtain randomness, a much higher number of December dates were chosen early whereas January dates were chosen later. Subsequently, the procedure was revised so that there were two bowls. A date of the year was selected from the first bowl and an order rank from 1 to 365 was selected from the second. Much greater care was also taken in the way both bowls were filled and mixed, and the new process appeared to be essentially random.

Even dice and roulette wheels are subject to uneven wear after hundreds of thousands of uses and become nonrandom. The most convenient and accurate procedure for obtaining a random process is through the use of tables of random numbers. The largest printed table is *A Million Random Digits* by The Rand Corporation (1955). The table is also available on IBM cards for use in computer programs.

The Rand random digits were generated by an electronic roulette wheel. A random-frequency pulse source passed through a five-place binary counter and was then converted to a decimal number. The process continued for 2 months and even with careful tuning of the equipment the numbers produced at the end of the period began to show signs of nonrandomness indicating that the machine was running down. This nonrandomness was eliminated by adding pairs of digits together. This illustrates the difficulties in attempting to generate random numbers by virtually any process.

To know if the numbers in a table of random numbers are indeed random, several statistical tests can be performed. The primary test is to observe the distribution of the digits 0 through 9 for the total table and parts of it. One expects that each digit will occur 10% of the time. Overall in the Rand Table the frequencies vary from 9.93% for the digit 9, to 10.06% for the digit 2, indicating no significant deviation from randomness. Other tests include "poker" tests of five digits to count the duplication of digits in blocks of five and run tests to look for evidence of serial correlation between numbers.

How does one use a table of random numbers for sampling? One of the first questions that worries a new user is where to start. The simple answer is that it does not matter. One may start anywhere in the table and move in any direction. An easy procedure is to start at the beginning and read down. The only error to avoid is starting at a given place because one knows the distribution of numbers at that place. An even worse sin is to reject a sample because somehow it does not look right and to continue using random numbers until a likely looking sample is selected. Obviously this destroys the probability character of the sample and makes it a judgment sample. (In some cases, however, the initial sample selection may uncover serious problems with the use of simple random sampling and suggest that a more complex procedure is required. A new sample draw using optimum procedures would not be cheating on probability methods.)

Once a starting point is selected, the number of columns of digits read must be sufficient to give each element in the population a chance of selection. If there are 70,000 elements in the population one would need to use five columns of digits, if 900 elements in the population only three columns would be needed. The groupings in the table itself are only for ease in reading.

To make the random selections, the elements of the universe are numbered and the selection of random numbers continues until the desired sample size is reached. Some of the random numbers chosen will be larger than the size of the universe and these numbers are discarded, as are any duplicate numbers. Thus in sampling the population with 70,000 elements, any number starting with 7, 8, or 9 would be ignored except for the number 70,000 itself.

If one is selecting from a population where the size of the first digit is small such as sizes of 250, 3400, and 11,000, there will be many more random numbers discarded than are used. Some statisticians have suggested procedures for using a higher fraction of these numbers, but the arithmetic although extremely simple becomes time-consuming if large samples are required. The easiest thing to do is to have a large table and to use only eligible numbers.

If the same random number is selected more than once, the second and subsequent selections are discarded. This means that the procedure is simple random sampling without replacement. The effect of this is to reduce the sampling error of the estimate; the reduction is largest when the sample chosen is a substantial fraction of the total population. This is most easily seen when the total population is studied. Then there is, of course, *no* sampling error.

EXAMPLE 5.12 SAMPLING FROM THE UNIVERSITY OF ILLINOIS STUDENT DIRECTORY

The University of Illinois at Urbana–Champaign Student Directory for a recent year consisted of a total of 33,271 names. The names are not numbered, but since the book is set from an IBM printout there are exactly 97 names on each of the pages. This fact is useful since it eliminates the need to count some pages and provides a check for manual counting. Alternatively, it would be possible to obtain a new printout already numbered.

Suppose one wishes to select a sample of 20 students for a pilot test of a new questionnaire. Using the following abbreviated table of random numbers one would read the numbers in groups of five to give each student a chance of selection. Reading first down and then across, the first five numbers are ignored because they are too large. The next four numbers are chosen, and then three numbers are skipped, and so on. The process continues until the twentieth number is selected and then the sampling stops.

Table of Random Digits

78986	45691	79922	40294	52672	46262	58177	55586
83230	59025	72573	(10) 18282	45513	82933	(17) 27817	47485
58846	(5) 01946	(7) 00367	38926	58508	36119	(18) 20874	35592
51999	(6) 19130	90645	68287	33553	38330	(19) 13265	99744
61096	59042	57643	(11) 00032	79958	(14) 08614	71178	23270
(1) 30226	69093	63119	84323	(13) 28281	49514	(20) 26440	24786
(2) 02073	65554	56777	79666	40379	(15) 12544	24225	63822
(3) 05250	86448	68145	82707	79180	95248	74151	48197
(4) 08014	95229	(8) 03319	(12) 30045	59371	95039	13334	14496
76489	52722	(9) 25901	44752	99943	(16) 08909	16161	92356

5.13. SYSTEMATIC SAMPLING

The use of simple random samping may be a long and tedious process if the sample and population are both large and manual procedures are used. Suppose, for example, that one has a list of 1 million inhabitants or voters in a large city and wishes to choose a sample of 1000. Intuitively, most people when asked how to sample would reply "take every thousandth case." This procedure of taking every ith case is widely used by professional samplers and is called *systematic sampling*. Because of its simplicity and usefulness in complex sampling situations, systematic sampling is probably used far more frequently than simple random sampling.

To do systematic sampling, one needs just two things—the *sampling interval* and a *random start*. The sampling interval if one has a list and wishes to approximate simple random sampling is merely the ratio $i = N/n$ of the number of elements in the population N to the desired sample size n.

A table of random numbers is used to select the initial number between 1 and i, called the random start. This ensures that every element in the population has an equal chance of selection and guards against the possible small bias that might occur if the first or last member in the interval were always selected. In the sample of 1000 from the list of 1 million residents, suppose the random start selected is 243. Then, the selected elements in the population would be 243, 1243, 2243, 3243, . . . , 999,243.

Use of Length Measures

Although systematic sampling eliminates the extensive use of a table of random numbers it still would appear to require complete counting of the universe. If the sampling is done manually, the use of some shortcuts can reduce this counting procedure considerably. Consider a city directory that has two columns per page, 100 names per column, and 500 pages, or a total of 100,000 names, all unnumbered. If a sample of 1000 names is required, it is easy to see that this can be obtained by selecting one name per column. Once a random start is selected and counted in one column, the distance of the random start from the top of the page may be measured on a strip of cardboard and this strip of cardboard placed on subsequent columns to locate the sample members.

Usually, however, the column length will not be identical to the required interval. If the column length is shorter than the interval this would mean that selecting one unit per column would give a sample larger than required. In this case, it might be easier to choose the larger sample and then to delete systematically until the proper sample size is obtained. *A useful property of simple random samples is that a simple random subsample of a simple random sample is also a simple random sample.*

If, as is often the case, the sampling interval i is not a whole number, the easiest solution is to use as the interval the whole number just below or above i. Usually, this will result in a selected sample that is only slightly larger or smaller than the initial sample required and this new sample size will have no noticeable effect on either the accuracy of the results or the budget. For samples where the interval i is small (generally for i less than 10), so that rounding has too great an effect on the sample size, it is possible to add or delete the extra cases. As suggested previously, it is usually easier to round down in computing i so that the sample is larger and then to delete systematically.

EXAMPLE 5.13 SYSTEMATIC SAMPLE FROM THE UNIVERSITY OF ILLINOIS STUDENT DIRECTORY

Using the same student directory as in Example 5.12 let us select a systematic sample of 300 students. The sampling interval is 33,271/300 = 110.90 or 111. Since there are 343 complete pages of 97 names and 1 partial page, a systematic sample of one name per page will yield a sample of either 343 or 344 names depending on the random start selected. Then to obtain a sample of 300, note that 300/344 = .87 or just about 7/8. Thus, deleting every eighth name after a random start yields a sample of 300 or 301. This procedure may seem more complicated, but in practice it is far faster than having to count intervals of 111 cases. An equivalent procedure would be to first randomly delete one-eighth of the pages in the directory and then to select one name per page from the remaining pages.

Another method to use if the interval is longer than the column length is to measure the length of the interval on a cardboard strip, being careful to omit margins and then to measure off intervals on the cardboard strip. This is subject to possible errors in placing the strip, but if done carefully it should have no noticeable bias on the results. If the sampling interval is smaller than the number of units per page then several selections per page may be made at random, and the cardboard strip marked to indicate each of the selections.

The use of measurement methods may be very helpful if the population is not printed on a list, but is arranged on cards or in file drawers. For the sample to be unbiased however, it is necessary that all files be of the same thickness since otherwise a fatter file has a higher probability of being selected. It is also necessary to ensure by some spot checking that the density of files per unit of length is reasonably identical throughout the files.

Suppose one needed to select a systematic sample of 1000 students. The sampling interval is now 33,271/1000 or 33.3. Although it would be possible to take every thirty-third or every thirty-fourth student, this would require counting and numbering all students in the directory. Noting that there are 97 names per page, if one divides 97 by either 33 or 34 one would get slightly less than 3 names per page (2.9). Rather than counting, it is far easier to make 3 selections per page and then to use a cardboard strip to locate sample members. Making 3 selections per page yields a sample of 1029–1032 names depending on how many are selected from the partial final page. Randomly deleting 10 pages with 3 names each or every thirty-fifth name would yield the approximate desired sample, or one might decide to keep the larger sample.

All of these procedures may be programmed and executed on a computer. If the population is already on tape or IBM cards, the computer run will be far more efficient than these manual methods suggest. In this case, fractional sampling intervals need not be rounded to whole numbers since the computer can handle fractions with no loss of efficiency. If the data are in printed form or in files and a complete computer tape is not required except for sampling, it will usually not pay to use the computer since the manual sampling will be faster than the data preparation and punching for the computer.

5.14. ARE SYSTEMATIC SAMPLES SIMPLE RANDOM SAMPLES?

The reader may wonder if systematic and simple random samples are the same. The theoretical answer is that systematic samples are really complex samples with unknown properties and that they may be substantially different, sometimes better, sometimes worse, than simple random samples. A very careful discussion of theoretical possibilities is given in Cochran (1963). The practical answer is that for those cases where simple random sampling is appropriate, simple random samples and systematic samples will be about the same except in very unusual situations of periodicities. It is important in using systematic sampling to inspect the lists before starting to ensure that there are no obvious periodicities. Nevertheless, in more than 20 years of experience I found only one case in which a systematic sample produced very strange results, and this was evident as soon as the sample was selected.

EXAMPLE 5.14 PERIODICITY IN A SYSTEMATIC SAMPLE

Residents in several communities were interviewed about their attitudes toward the neighborhood and their satisfaction with neighborhood services. The sampling for this study was a complex multistage sample. Three years later a follow up study was done with a subsample of one-eighth of the initial sample to study changes in attitudes. This sample was selected using systematic sampling with a sampling interval of eight and a random start of four. Surprisingly, although the initial sample had been about half male and half female, this systematic sample was all female.

An investigation revealed that the initial respondents had not been numbered sequentially as the questionnaires were returned, as is usually done. Instead, the final digit of the respondent number was used to indicate sex of respondent with even numbers used for women and odd numbers for men. This numbering scheme was not known until the sample was selected, but since both the random start and sampling interval were even, the sample consisted entirely of women. Once this was discovered, the sample was discarded, and another selected after first sorting out the sexes.

This example illustrates one of the possibilities that could make a systematic sample worse than a simple random sample-periodicities in the list. Other periodicities are conceivable, such as in lists of military personnel arranged by platoons, factory workers arranged by work units, or elementary school students in classes. However, in the real world it is very unlikely that there would be exact periodicities corresponding to the sampling interval when dealing with lists of people.

One case where one should avoid systematic sampling is the sampling of time periods. Suppose one were going to sample traffic on a street or shoppers at a store that was open 24 hours a day. With any sampling interval it is difficult to avoid some time periodicities. For example, if the decision is made to sample 12 quarter hours during the week, the sampling interval would be 56 since there are 672 quarter hours per week. In this case, the sample would consist entirely of all odd or all even hours, and the same quarter-hour segment for every hour selected. (The reader should verify this by choosing a random start and listing the selected times.)

In sampling of nonhuman populations such as businesses, financial accounts, temperature or climate, or lumber or crop yields there may not only be periodicities in the data but also some linear trends. Thus, savings deposits measured over time may show substantial increases due to inflation. For these cases neither simple random sampling nor systematic sampling is appropriate. The optimum sampling procedures involve stratified sampling (see Section 5.22).

The claim has sometimes been made for systematic sampling that it is more efficient than simple random sampling because it eliminates autocorrelation in the sample, that is, the similarity of adjacent elements. On a voter list, a systematic sample would not select members from the same household, whereas this could occur in a simple random sample. In practice, this improvement is so small that it can be ignored. If autocorrelation is an important issue as in economic time series then it is again better to use explicit stratification.

There is an important exception in which systematic sampling may substantially improve sample efficiency by being a form of implicit stratification. This is the case when the sampling is of large geographic areas such as counties or other clusters rather than of individuals. The detailed discussion of this situation is beyond the scope of this chapter but is discussed in Sudman (1976, Chap. 7).

To summarize, systematic samples are not really simple random samples, but they behave as simple random samples and have the same precision in almost all cases of interest involving human populations. They are used instead of simple random samples not because they produce better data but because they are easier to use. Systematic samples are often described by samplers as pseudosimple random samples.

5.15. THE USES AND LIMITATIONS OF LISTS

Probably the most difficult task in sampling from lists is finding the appropriate list. It may be helpful to mention the kinds of populations for which no lists exist. There is no list of the entire population or all the households in the United States. One might consider using the Census of Population and Housing, but this information is closely guarded by the Census Bureau to protect confidentiality and is never released for sampling purposes. The Census Bureau will consider requests to select samples but all the sampling is done by Census Bureau personnel and no confidential information is released. However, most readers of this book who needed a national population sample would be better off using one of the existing field organizations with a national sample.

From the preceding discussion it follows that there are no population lists of men or women, young people, old people, blacks or whites, or by income. A researcher sometimes hears of mailing lists that provide this sort of information, but although mailing lists may be useful for people trying to sell something, they are usually worthless for sampling. Mailing lists are derived primarily from membership and subscription lists and it is not possible to specify the population they represent. Thus a sample selected from a mailing list of boys under age 16 would probably be based on membership in the Boy Scouts or subscription to *Boy's Life* magazine, and would obviously not be a sample of all boys.

At the local level, however, population and household lists are available for most medium sized cities in the range of about 50,000–800,000 people. About 1400 of these directories are published by R. L. Polk and Company, 6400 Monroe Boulevard, Taylor, Michigan 48180. The directories are usually available for free use at the local public library or Chamber of Commerce Office as well as for sale by Polk. For sampling purposes, most directories contain both an alphabetical list of names of residents and businesses and a street address directory of households. Since the directories are revised every 2 or 3 years, the street address directory is reasonably accurate. It misses only new construction that occurs after the directory is published. The alphabetical list is subject to greater error over time since many families and individuals will move in or out of the area or to some new address. Although the directories are subject to listing errors, these are usually corrected in subsequent directories. Overall, the quality of the lists is usually as good or better than the lists that could be obtained by a careful researcher starting from scratch using new listers. Of course, the use of existing lists is far cheaper.

If the population consists of members of some professional organization there will probably be a membership directory published. Some organizations such as the American Medical Association and the American Dental Association have put their directories on tape for mailing and sampling purposes. If one does not know the complete name and address of the organization the easiest place to find this information is in the *Encyclopedia of Associations* published by the Gale Publishing Company of Detroit.

Lists of business establishments grouped by SIC (Standard Industrial Classification) codes may be purchased from Dun and Bradstreet, New York City. These lists are revised relatively infrequently so that they contain names of establishments that are no longer in business. Lists of schools and colleges are available from publications of the U.S. Office of Education and from state and local superintendents of education. Ordinarily, lists of teachers and students are not available for elementary and high schools, but are available in published directories for individual universities. National mailing lists of college students and teachers have been prepared, but they should be used cautiously since in the past schools have been omitted and the lists quickly become outdated.

5.16. BLANKS AND INELIGIBLES ON LISTS

There are three common problems in the use of lists. The treatment of these problems is discussed in this and the next two sections. The first problem is that the list may contain blank or ineligible units. Suppose one uses the systematic sampling procedure discussed previously, in which the selected unit on a page is obtained by measuring down from the top of the page. For explicitness, assume the sample is to be selected from a city directory in which the names are in alphabetical order. The population to be studied may consist either of households or of individuals. The selected line on the page, however, instead of containing a name of an individual may list the name of a business firm or professional office, or in some listings a school, park, or government office. These are ineligible listings. Blanks are obtained if there is no listing at all on the line, due to spacing between letters of the alphabet, or because the column ends in the middle of a page, or if a name is on the line, but the address given is incorrect because the unit has been demolished or is vacant. One might first consider going through the list and removing all ineligible listings, but in a large list such as a city directory this is clearly impractical.

Two intuitive procedures for solving the problem of blanks and ineligibles usually occur to the naive sampler. Unfortunately, both of these naive procedures introduce serious biases into the sampling. The first *incorrect* procedure is to take the next name on the list. The other *incorrect* procedure is to count down a fixed number of eligible names from the top of the page. Both of these methods give a higher probability of selection to people or households whose names follow ineligible listings. In some cases it is hard to know what kind of bias this introduces into the results, but in directory listings it is likely that the name after a business or professional listing will be the home address of the same person. Thus, using the incorrect procedures yields a sample with too many doctors and butchers and too few college professors and other working types.

The correct solution to the problem of blanks or ineligibles is really straightforward. They should be ignored and not included in the sample. This requires, however, that the sampling interval be adjusted to account for the expected number of exclusions. If one knows that $p\%$ of some list is eligible where $1 - p\%$ consists of ineligibles or blanks, the sampling interval is $i = Np/n$ where, as before, N is the total size of the list and Np is the number eligible and is the desired sample size.

Estimation of the proportion of the list that is unusable can be done either based on prior experience with the list or by counting the proportion ineligible on a sample of 5–10 pages. If this estimate is either too high or too low, additional sampling may be required to obtain the desired sample size or there may need to be some random deletion of the selected sample.

While considering the problem caused by ineligible or blank listings, samplers generally make an estimate of the cooperation rate that is likely to be obtained from the selected sample. In national samples, experience indicates that most field organizations obtain about 75–80% cooperation from the designated sample. Interviewers from the Bureau of the Census obtain higher cooperation, about 95%, on the monthly Current Population Survey, and very high cooperation rates of 95–100% are obtained by many organizations in small towns and on farms. The cooperation rate drops as city size increases to as low as 70% in the largest metropolitan areas. Based on past experience with similar populations, one should make a realistic estimate of the cooperation rate c and oversample to obtain the desired sample size. The sampling interval i is then computed by $i = Npc/n$.

EXAMPLE 5.15 COMPUTING THE SAMPLING INTERVAL i FOR A CITY DIRECTORY

Suppose one wishes to select a sample of 1000 completed cases from the city directory for Peoria, Illinois. The directory has 367 pages with three columns per page and 84 lines per column, or a total of 92,484 lines. Note that it is not necessary to assume, nor is it the case, that each column has the same number of households. Some columns will have more businesses or blank lines. If one of these lines is selected, the line is not used. A systematic sample of 10 pages indicates that 63.1% of the lines contain a household listing, 9.0% contain a business listing, 17.2% contain a street name or ZIP code, 7.4% are blank, and 3.3% contain advertising. Assuming that the cooperation rate is expected to be 80%, the sampling interval would be 92,484(.631)(.80)/1000 or 46.7.

The easiest procedure would be to note that selecting two lines at random from each column would be a sampling interval of 84/2 or 42 which is smaller than 46.7 and would yield a larger sample. The expected sample based on the previous estimates is about 1389, although this is only an estimate. An actual sample was selected using this interval and two random lines per column, numbers 5 and 27. The number of households selected was 1441. Since only 1250 are needed assuming a cooperation rate of 80%, one computes the ratio of 1250/1441 and notes that .867 is approximately equal to the fraction 7/8 which is .875. Thus, randomly deleting every eighth element in the sample of 1441 after a random start yields a sample of 1260. Usually at this stage the sampling would end, since given the uncertainty about the final cooperation rate, the deletion of 10 additional cases to reach exactly 1250 would not be very important.

5.17. DUPLICATIONS

In simple random sampling, each element of the population must have an equal probability of selection. If some individuals or households appear on the list more than once, some possible biases are introduced. Although often these biases will be very small, they may sometimes be serious.

EXAMPLE 5.16 DUPLICATE ENTRIES IN A CONTEST

A candy company once ran a contest and received several hundred thousand entries. The company was interested in estimating the average number of entries submitted by persons who had entered the contest. A sample of entries was selected and a count was made of the number of times entries had been submitted by the persons submitting the sample entries. The company was upset to learn that, based on their sample, the average person submitted more than 50 entries. An outside researcher informed of these results pointed out, however, that the sample was heavily biased toward persons making multiple entries. The probabilities of selection for the sample were not equal, but were proportional to the number of entries. The correct estimate was actually much smaller, only about 7 entries per person.

To make the discussion more explicit suppose there is a contest in which 330,000 entries are received from 100,000 different persons. The distribution of number of entries is given in Table 5.2. It is obvious that the actual mean number of entries is 3.3 per person. If a 1 in 1000 sample of entries is selected this sample will heavily overrepresent persons with a large number of entries as may be seen in the last column of Table 5.2. If, mistakenly, a mean is computed from this sample of entries, the observed value will be 9.5 or about three times the actual mean.

EXAMPLE 5.17 DUPLICATIONS USING MULTIPLE LISTS

The American Public Health Association (APHA) wanted to select a sample of persons engaged in public health activities. No single list of such persons

TABLE 5.2
Persons and Entries for Hypothetical Contest Example

Number of entries	Number of persons	Total entries	Sample of 1 in 1000 entries
1	50,000	50,000	50
2	20,000	40,000	40
3	10,000	30,000	30
5	8,000	40,000	40
10	7,000	70,000	70
20	5,000	100,000	100
	100,000	330,000	330

$$\text{Actual mean} = \frac{330,000}{100,000} = 3.3$$

$$\text{Computed mean} = \frac{50 + 2(40) + 3(30) + 5(40) + 10(70) + 20(100)}{330}$$

$$= \frac{3120}{330} = 9.5$$

existed, but the combined membership lists of five organizations were thought to include virtually everyone in the field. It was recognized, however, that some persons might belong to two, three, four, or even all five organizations. Unless these duplicates were removed, persons more active in organizational activities as indicated by multiple memberships would have higher probability of selection. In this case, since the APHA wanted an unduplicated mailing list for purposes other than the sample survey, the 50,000 total names were cross-checked and a net list of 37,000 names was obtained. The cross-checking of names is a costly task and need not be done for the entire list unless an unduplicated list is required for other purposes.

EXAMPLE 5.18 A SAMPLE OF STUDENTS AND STAFF AT
THE UNIVERSITY OF ILLINOIS

A survey of housing needs of both students and staff at the University of Illinois was conducted using both the student and the staff directories. Duplications arise because some students (particularly graduate students) were listed in both directories. A total sample of 1000 was wanted. Using an interval of every forty-fourth name in both directories, a sample of 1049 were selected of which 96 were found in both lists. Half of these 96, or 48, were randomly omitted leaving a sample of 1001 individuals who all had an equal probability of selection.

Some lists are arranged in ways that make it very difficult or impossible to determine duplications in advance. Thus, a register of manufacturing firms arranged by types of product might well list the same firm several times; discovering the duplication would be difficult because there might be hundreds of product categories. Similarly, one could not determine multiple car ownership of a sample of car owners chosen from a list of current license numbers, if the numbers were arranged in numerical rather than alphabetical sequence. In this case it is possible to determine the duplication by asking a question during the survey interview to determine the number of times the person or firm was listed ("How many cars do you own?" or "How many different products does this firm make?").

To keep the sample unbiased one would then need to discard some completed interviews so that all respondents would have equal probabilities of selection. It is wasteful to discard interviews that have already been collected. The better alternative would be to weight the results by the inverses of the probabilities of selection. Thus, sample elements that were discovered to have been listed k times would be weighted by $1/k$. No longer a simple random sample, this process is really a stratified sample.

5.18. OMISSIONS FROM LISTS

The most serious problem in using lists is the omission of an important fraction of the total population. Small listing errors can usually be ignored, such as typographical and clerical errors in a city directory, but some lists, by their coverage, exclude important segments of the total population. A telephone directory for a city excludes persons without telephones or with unlisted numbers. A list of registered voters excludes people who have recently moved, noncitizens, as well as those have chosen not to register. A list of the largest firms in an industry excludes all firms below the cutoff.

Three alternatives are possible for handling omissions in lists: (*a*) discarding the list; (*b*) using the list and ignoring omissions; (*c*) using the list with supplementation. Each of these strategies is appropriate under different conditions. Before deciding on the strategy one should use, the purposes of the study and the quality of the list should be considered. The quality of a list may be estimated by comparison to census data if available, or by comparison to other lists or new listings. Thus, if in a small town a voter registration list contained 2210 names and the 1970 census of population indicated a population of 2290 persons 18 and over, then the voter list would be adequate and the few omissions could be ignored. If, on the other hand, a voter list for a large city contained only 60% of the population when compared to census figures, it would probably be discarded.

If one were uncertain about the quality of a city directory, one could send listers out to relist a sample of 20 blocks. If the new listing showed that less than 2 or 3% of the old list was wrong, it could be used with confidence for even a careful study. Any new list that a researcher developed would probably have at least 5% errors, according to some careful experiments conducted by Kish and Hess (Kish, 1965, p. 531). For preliminary studies or for when precise estimates are not needed, lists containing 80–90% of the total population are often used with omissions ignored.

Frequently the best way to obtain a careful sample while keeping costs of sampling low is to use an available list and supplement it with other procedures. For many of the largest metropolitan areas, telephone directories list 70–90% of all households. However, careful studies cannot ignore households without phones or unlisted phones. To supplement the directory lists, listers are sent out to a sample of blocks to list households without telephones. The lister is provided with a list of households who have listed phones obtained from a street address phone directory. Such a directory is published for the 35 largest standard metropolitan statistical areas and lists phone households in geographic rather than alphabetical order. The lister then lists all households in the sample areas that are not already on the list.

There is a simple criterion for determining if combined lists are preferable to a totally new listing—the cost of the combined lists should be lower than the cost of the new listing. If there are no savings, the incomplete list is discarded. Generally, for studies of the general population, the difficulties in obtaining current voting lists and supplementing them with new listings make this method more costly than totally new listings, so voting lists are only valuable when one wishes to study voting behavior. Similarly, in studying low-income households, the combined use of welfare records and new listings is usually so difficult to integrate that new listings are commonly used.

5.19. THE USE OF TELEPHONE DIRECTORIES AND RANDOM DIGIT DIALING

Since so many researchers with limited budgets are using phone interviews, a brief discussion of methods for improving the quality of telephone directory listings may be helpful. Obviously, no method can affect those households without phones. If this bias is important, some face-to-face interviewing is necessary. It is possible, however, to obtain interviews from households with unlisted phones by the use of random digit dialing methods.

In their simplest form, random digit dialing procedures ignore telephone directories entirely and select numbers to be called using tables of random numbers. Every working telephone number in the population has an equal probability of selection using this method. The problem with the procedures is that it also produces a very large majority of numbers that are not in use at all or that are used by businesses or institutions. It is possible to obtain the central office exchanges that are in operation—that is, the first three digits of the telephone number after the area code. It is not usually possible to get the numbers within a central office that are being used. Glasser and Metzger (1972) estimated from a sample of 30,000 numbers that only one in five was usable.

A simple combination of directory sampling and random digit dialing is far more efficient than pure random digit dialing. One first selects a random (or systematic) sample of household listings from the directory and ignores the last three digits. A table of random numbers is then used to select these digits. It can be shown that this procedure greatly increases the probability of obtaining a working household number. Using this procedure about one-half of all selected numbers are usable.

There is some arbitrariness in the decision to ignore the last three digits. It is possible to ignore only the last digit or the last two digits of the selected number from the directory. This is most efficient in eliminating nonworking and nonhousehold numbers, but increases the possibility of bias due to missing new series of numbers being activated. Using all but the last three digits does not eliminate this bias entirely but ensures that it will not be very large.

It is possible to get almost completely unbiased samples of households with telephones and to avoid most nonworking numbers. One procedure developed by Waksburg (1978) samples 100 consecutive telephone numbers from a working exchange. From this cluster of 100 numbers, one is selected and called. If it is not a working number, no additional numbers are chosen from that cluster. If it is a working number, calls are made until the required number of households per cluster is reached. The major savings from this procedure is that clusters of 100 with no working numbers are very quickly eliminated.

Another procedure using directories is to select one number from the directory as the start of a cluster (Sudman, 1973). Additional numbers are called in sequence until a given fixed number of households with *listed* numbers are contacted. In this method, additional households with unlisted numbers are picked up in the cluster.

Both of these methods give each household with a telephone equal ultimate probabilities of selection, although they are not really simple random samples, since they involve selection in several stages. Both methods have some defects. Using directories involves obtaining them and eliminating communities listed in more than one directory. This is not difficult at a state or local level, but is much more costly for a national study unless an available computerized list is used. Also directory sampling misses completely the few new exchanges that are opened after the directory is printed. The Waksburg procedure has problems when the initial number called cannot be identified as working or nonworking. This occurs in rare cases when the number rings, although it is not working.

Before using random digit dialing one should first estimate the proportion of unlisted phones in the population. Outside of the very largest cities the proportion of unlisted phones is under 5%, and the additional cost of two calls for one working number using the most efficient procedures is probably not worth the small reduction in bias, remembering that households without phones are still excluded. In the largest cities and some of their suburbs as many as 40% of all phones may be unlisted. It is in these places that random digit dialing is most appropriate.

If information on the percentage of unlisted phones cannot be obtained from the local phone company, an estimate can be made by comparing the number of household listings in the directory to the estimate given in the census of housing for the same place.

EXAMPLE 5.19 SELECTING A SAMPLE FROM THE CHICAGO PHONE DIRECTORY
USING RANDOM DIGIT DIALING

The initial step in the process is the selection of listings from the directory using the systematic sampling methods discussed earlier in this chapter. Table 5.3 gives a small sample of five listings and the random numbers chosen from these listings. Note that if the initial listing is not a household phone no random substitution is made. This eliminates calls to exchanges that are entirely used for commercial purposes.

TABLE 5.3
Chicago Phone Directory Listings and Random Digit Replacements

Initial listing	Type of unit	Random digits selected	Listing actually contacted
FI6-5656	Commercial	—	—
276-7915	Residential	064	276-7064
287-6871	Commercial	—	—
HE4-3501	Residential	392	HE4-3392
729-1224	Residential	898	729-1898

5.20. SCREENING FOR SPECIAL POPULATIONS

Although general population samples are still of great importance, there has been an increasing trend toward studies of special populations. In some cases, a satisfactory list may be available, but in many cases it is necessary to start with a general population sample and then to screen households or individuals for the desired characteristic.

In the simplest case, suppose one wished to select only respondents in a restricted age group. An estimate of the proportion p of the total population in this age group is available from current census data. One would simply select a sample $1/p$ times larger than would have been required if all respondents were eligible, taking into account all the other reasons for increasing the initial sample size discussed in Section 5.16.

In reality, the situation is more complex since it may not be possible to obtain the screening information required or some of the screening information may be incorrect. This will typically require a larger sample initially, but the exact sampling rate can only be determined in a pilot test.

Screening can become very expensive if the proportion p of the special population is small. In some cases, however, the population may cluster geographically. (Examples would be racial, ethnic, or religious groups or either high- or low-income households.) Sampling procedures have been developed for reducing screening costs in this situation. In face-to-face interviewing, these methods involve using very large clusters and sequential procedures to determine whether any members of the special population can be found in the cluster. See Sudman (1976, section 9.6).

For telephone interviewing, variations of the Waksberg procedure described in the last section have been used. Instead of merely requiring that the initial number called be a working number, the additional requirement is imposed that the initial number household contain a member of the special population. Just as before, if the number called does not yield a member of the special population no additional calls are made in that cluster. If the initial number does yield a member of the special population, screening calls are made until the required number of members of the special population in the cluster are reached. This procedure is only efficient when the special population is geographically clustered.

If the special population is rare, not geographically clustered, and no list is available, screening will be difficult and costly. A procedure currently being developed and tested is called network sampling. Under this procedure, the person responding to a screening interview reports not only about members in the household, but also about close relatives (typically sons and daughters, parents and siblings) who live in other households. This remains a strict probability sample since it is possible to compute the probability of an individual being selected. This probability is proportional to the number of persons who could have named the individual in a screening interview. Network procedures can reduce the amount of screening required by more than one-half.

5.21. HOW BIG SHOULD THE SAMPLE BE?

One of the first questions that confronts the designer of a new study is how big the sample should be. Although it appears to be a simple straightforward question, it is one of the most difficult to answer precisely.

There are several ways of approaching this problem. The easiest is an empirical approach that seeks what sample sizes have been used by others with similar problems. It is useful, especially for an inexperienced researcher, to be able to check his or her judgment about appropriate sample sizes against those of other social scientists. The next section of this chapter presents actual sample sizes used in a large number of studies.

There is a more formal approach not developed here, that emphasizes the need to balance the value of increased information with the costs of gathering the data. The problem may be considered from the viewpoints of both the designer of a study and the funding organization. The designer of a study must recognize that if the study is to be funded by someone else, then the organization funding the study will ultimately make the decision on sample size. Although the precise benefits of most basic social science research cannot be well specified, an optimum sample size can be determined in business and policy applications if gains and losses of alternative decisions are known.

One important question that is frequently overlooked entirely is whether or not new sample information should be gathered *at all*. The decision depends on both the cost and the value of the new information. If the fixed costs of the study exceed the value then no new sampling is justified. The value of information depends on what is already known and is, thus, best described using Bayesian statistics rather than the classical statistics with which most readers are familiar. For additional discussion of the formal Bayesian approach see Schlaifer (1959) and Sudman (1976, chap. 5).

5.22. CURRENT SAMPLE SIZES USED

This section summarizes the sample sizes of several hundred studies used in a literature review of response effects in surveys (Sudman & Bradburn, 1974). Whereas in some cases the sample sizes used appeared inappropriate for the purposes, the modal sample sizes reflect current practices and are a useful guide for planning. Table 5.4 is not intended to replace formal procedures for sample-size determination, but to give the inexperienced researcher some way of checking judgments against others in the same field. Since Table 5.4 is split into broad subject matter areas, a researcher in a specialized field can replicate these results by noting the sample sizes reported in the specialized journals for the field. In addition to the modes, the seventy-fifth and twenty-fifth percentiles are also given to indicate the range of sample sizes.

It may be seen that national studies, regardless of subject matter, typically have samples of 1000 or more. Regional studies vary considerably depending

TABLE 5.4
Most Common Sample Sizes Used for National and Regional Studies by Subject Matter

Subject matter	National			Regional		
	Mode	Q_3	Q_1	Mode	Q_3	Q_1
Financial	1000+	—	—	100	400	50
Medical	1000+	1000+	500	1000+	1000+	250
Other behavior	1000+	—	—	700	1000	300
Attitudes	1000+	1000+	500	700	1000	400
Laboratory experiments	—	—	—	100	200	50

on the topic, but, as expected, they usually have smaller samples. The topic of the study is not really the basic factor that determines sample size. As indicated earlier, sample size depends on how many subgroups of the population one wishes to study. Table 5.5 gives some typical sample sizes in which few or no subgroups are to be analyzed and where many subgroups are of interest. There are also some sample sizes given when the population consists of institutions or firms, rather than people or households. These sample sizes assume that the optimum stratified sampling procedures to be discussed in the following are used. The sample sizes for institutions are generally smaller because of these optimum procedures and because the sample is frequently a large fraction of the total population. As with Table 5.4, Table 5.5 should be used as an initial aid, rather than a substitute for formal judgment.

PILOT OR PRETESTS

Pilot tests are an important step in developing survey instruments. It is extremely difficult even for experienced social scientists to write a questionnaire with no confusing or ambiguous questions. A pilot test of 20–50 cases is usually sufficient to discover the major flaws in a questionnaire before they damage the main study. The larger sample is required if there is some concern that some subgroups in the population, such as those who are retired or who have less education, will have difficulties.

TABLE 5.5
Typical Sample Sizes for Studies of Human and Institutional Populations

Number of subgroup analyses	People or households		Institutions	
	National	Regional or special	National	Regional or special
None or few	1000–1500	200–500	200–500	50–200
Average	1500–2500	500–1000	500–1000	200–500
Many	2500+	1000+	1000+	500+

5.23. THE REASONS FOR STRATIFIED SAMPLING

It is frequently useful to divide the total population into subgroups, called strata, for purposes of making the sample more efficient. We shall now discuss when stratified sampling is and is not appropriate and how to determine optimum strata sample sizes.

We assume that the amount of money to be spent on data collection as well as how the data are to be collected has already been determined, and that the costs of the data collection methods are known. Given these constraints, the efficiency of a sample is measured by the size of its sampling error relative to other samples that cost the same. Stratified sampling is intended to provide the smallest sampling error and hence the most information for the available resources.

It will soon be clear to the reader that there is no optimum all-purpose stratified sample. Different designs are optimal depending on the topics studied and how the data are to be analyzed. The most troublesome problem is deciding on a sampling strategy when a single study is used for multiple purposes. Then, it is seldom possible to find a sample that is optimum for all purposes. Instead, some compromise sample must be found. This is discussed next.

The principal situations for the use of optimum stratified sampling are:

1. The strata are themselves of primary interest.
2. Variances differ between the strata.
3. Costs differ by strata.

5.24. APPROPRIATE AND INAPPROPRIATE USES OF STRATIFICATION

Stratified sampling is frequently considered by researchers who basically have no belief that probability sampling methods work. Used with probability sampling, these procedures can sometimes greatly increase field costs without improving the sample. Used instead of probability sampling, these procedures may yield a sample that is actually far worse than a probability sample. Before turning to appropriate uses of stratification, it may be worthwhile to warn readers of inappropriate uses.

EXAMPLE 5.20 INAPPROPRIATE USE OF STRATIFICATION
TO ENSURE RANDOMNESS

Naive researchers with high anxiety levels will often be concerned that a sample using probability methods will yield very strange results, a large oversampling of men, an undersampling of middle-aged persons, distorted income distributions, or other catastrophes. To ensure against this, they insist that the sample be stratified so that age, race, sex, occupation, income, education, household size, and other variables are guaranteed to be perfectly represented. (Lest any readers think that I am setting up a straw horse to be demolished, this example is based on numerous requests for just such sampling.) If one takes the request literally, there is just no way to comply with it. The census data that would be needed for strata controls would not be available in such detail to preserve the privacy of individual households. Even if one could estimate strata totals, the cost of matching these perfectly in the field would be prohibitive since hundreds of additional screening interviews would be required to match strata controls exactly. Finally, the effects on the data of this tortuous process would probably be undetectable.

EXAMPLE 5.21 INAPPROPRIATE USE OF STRATIFICATION
WITH NONPROBABILITY SAMPLES

Before area probability sampling methods were developed, a frequent procedure used was to establish quotas for the interviewer. The interviewer was requested to get five men and five women; one woman with high income, two with middle incomes and two with low incomes, and do the same for the men. Such instructions or those specifying other demographic controls never specified exactly where or how the sampling was to be done, so that the interviewer typically found respondents in the most convenient locations, generally close to home. Not only did these procedures introduce serious biases, but the idea of a known sampling variability became almost meaningless. Estimates of sampling errors depend on the assumption that it is possible to draw repeated samples using the same procedures. When each interviewer can do as he or she chooses, and changes the procedures from one study to another, no real replication is possible. The use of strata quotas did not correct for these defects but merely concealed them for the most obvious variables.

Today, little geographically uncontrolled sampling is done, except for pilot testing and for preliminary studies in shopping centers. Here the use of strata controls can be helpful in pinpointing subgroups who may have special difficulty with the questionnaire. (Many survey organizations use a form of quota sampling instead of repeated callbacks to account for respondents who are not at home. This form of quota sampling has well-specified characteristics and can be replicated.)

EXAMPLE 5.22 INAPPROPRIATE USE OF STRATIFICATION
TO ADJUST FOR NONCOOPERATION

Another spurious use of stratification is to correct for major problems in sample cooperation. Even if the sample design is excellent, little trust can be put in a sample in which only 5 or 10% of the population cooperates. (Such low cooperation is often found in poorly designed mail surveys of the general population.) Then, the hapless data collector will often attempt to demonstrate that the sample is adequate by comparing the sample distribution to known census data for several demographic characteristics. Even if there are no large biases in these comparisons there is still no assurance of the quality of the data for unmeasured variables. Usually, with very low cooperation, there will also be some noticeable biases in the demographic characteristics. Then, in an effort to salvage something from the wreck, the data are weighted on one or more demographic variables to correct for the sample biases. The weighting is likely to correct only for the variables included, and not for the major variables for which information is being collected.

The use of weights to correct for sample biases due to noncooperation is called poststratification, since it is done after the sampling. It is a legitimate procedure to correct for minor differences between the sample and the universe due to sampling error and differential cooperation. Thus, in national surveys, poststratification is sometimes used to adjust for the lower cooperation in central cities than in rural areas. Except for very large studies such as in the next example where very precise national estimates are required, poststratification is usually not worth the added complexity in data handling and analysis.

The reader may wonder after the last several examples whether it is ever appropriate to stratify a sample if the strata are to be sampled proportionately. Under some circumstances, stratification will be inexpensive and some gains can be expected. This occurs when the stratification is of primary sampling areas (PSUs) for a national survey and not by households. Stratification of PSUs is done during the normal sample selection process and need not require any additional field costs. Usually a systematic sample of PSUs is selected using multistage sampling procedures. In this case, the stratification involves arranging the PSUs by variables that are expected to be related to the variables to be studied, rather than having the PSUs arranged in alphabetical order or in haphazard fashion. The variables usually used are region of the country, degree of urbanization, proportion nonwhite, and some socioeconomic measure such as income or education.

The effects of such stratification are moderate. Sampling errors are generally less than 10% smaller than they would have been without stratification, but unless much time and expense has been devoted to agonizing over how to stratify, there is no reason not to do so.

EXAMPLE 5.23 THE CURRENT POPULATION SURVEY

This very large and careful sample has already been discussed in Example 5.1. The PSU stratification involves the following variables: (*a*) standard metropolitan statistical area or not; (*b*) rate of population change; (*c*) percentage of population living in urban areas; (*d*) percentage of population in manufacturing; (*e*) principal industries; (*f*) average value of retail trade; (*g*) proportion of nonwhite population.

A trenchant comment on the stratification efforts is found in a Technical Paper prepared by the Census Bureau on the methodology of the CPS (1963):

> A great many professional man-hours were spent in the stratification process. However, it is questionable whether the amount of time devoted to reviews and refinements paid off in appreciable reductions in sampling variances. Intuitive notions about the gains from stratification can be misleading. Methods of stratification that appear to be very different often lead to about the same variances . . . [p. 6].

5.25. THE STRATA ARE OF PRIMARY INTEREST

Social scientists almost never look only at the total population. Even media articles such as results from the Gallup Poll report on attitudes by race, sex, education, region of the country, and other demographic variables. For most Gallup Polls, however, it is evident that reports about the total population are more important than information about subgroups.

Suppose, on the other hand, one is concerned about the effects of discrimination on wages paid to women and minority groups such as blacks. Here, total population figures are of little interest. What one wishes to do is to compare the incomes of blacks and whites, men and women, the minority and majority groups.

The optimal sampling designs for these two cases can be quite different. In the case in which estimates of the total population are of primary importance, one needs a proportionate or self-weighting sample of the entire population. *For comparison of subgroups, the optimum sample is one in which the sample sizes are equal in the subgroups, since this minimizes the standard error of the difference.*

If one wishes to compare men and women on any variable as well as make estimates of the total population then there is no problem since the two groups are almost evenly split in the population. If, however, one wants to compare blacks and whites, a proportional sample would be very inefficient since nine-tenths of the sample would be white, whereas one would want a sample with equal numbers of whites and blacks. For this case, one would sample the black population at about nine times the rate of the white population to get equal samples. In general, for comparing two groups, the less common group would be sampled at the rate p/q relative to the more common group where p is the proportion of the more common group and q of the less common group. For three or more groups, the sampling rates for any two of the groups are inversely proportional to their proportions in the populations. Thus, if group A is 60% of the total population, group B is 30% and group C is 10%, then the sampling rate for group C is six times the sampling rate for group A, and three times the sampling rate for group B, whereas the sampling rate for group B is twice that for group A.

Unfortunately, when one optimizes the sample for group comparisons, the sample is no longer optimal for estimating the total population. This may not be of concern if one is uninterested in totals, but the most common situation is to be interested in both. Three strategies are used in this case, all compromises between the different needs.

1. *Split the difference:* Suppose one were equally concerned about total unemployment in a community and the unemployment rates of blacks and whites. A sample of 30% black and 70% white, or one-third black and two-thirds white could be a reasonable compromise between the extremes of proportional and equal-sized samples.

2. *Determine a minimum acceptable total sample size, if sampling is proportional, and then use remaining resources to augment the smaller subgroups.*

3. *Determine minimum subgroup sample sizes if equal-sized samples are selected for each subgroup, and then use remaining resources to improve estimates of the total.*

The "split the difference" procedure is probably the most widely used. If disproportionate sampling is used, it will normally require screening the population before the main data-gathering interview. That is, an initial probability sample must be selected that is large enough to include the required number of respondents for the final sample. All elements in the initial sample receive a classifying interview. The respondents in the most oversampled stratum identified in this first interview all receive the main interview, whereas respondents in the other strata are subsampled.

5.26. VARIANCES DIFFER BETWEEN STRATA

The earliest use of optimum stratified sampling was by Neyman (1934), who in a classic paper demonstrated that if strata variances differ, the optimum sample allocation among strata is given by

$$n_h^* = \frac{N_h \sigma_h}{\Sigma_h N_h \sigma_h} n \quad \text{or} \quad n_h^* = \frac{\Pi_h \sigma_h}{\Sigma_h \Pi_h \sigma_h} n \tag{5.1}$$

where

N_h = total elements in the population in stratum H;

Π_h = proportion of total population in stratum H;

σ_h = standard deviation in stratum H;

n = the total sample size;

n_h^* = optimum sample size in stratum H.

The principal use of formula (5.1) is *not* with human populations, but with institutional populations such as universities, schools systems, and hospitals and with business firms. The differences in variances between large and small firms and institutions are far larger than between persons for most variables. Optimum sampling procedures for human populations are sometimes used on expenditure studies but this requires an initial screening.

It is a general (although not universal) rule that as elements become larger and more complex, the variability between them increases. Thus, the difference in the number of patients served or in total annual budgets is far greater between the 10 largest hospitals than between 10 small hospitals. This suggests that institutions and firms be stratified by size and that larger samples be taken from the strata consisting of the larger sized institutions. If the variances for each stratum are known from past experience, then formula (5.1) is used directly.

If the variances are not known, then a measure of size for the strata may be used to approximate the variances, as in Example 5.24. Size measures may be based on number of employees, number of clients, annual budget, total sales, amount of equipment, square feet of space occupied, or other size variables. If more than one size measure is available, the one most closely related to the critical variables in the study should be used. In a study of personnel policies, number of employees would be a better size measure than sales or clients served. This measure of size will not usually be perfectly correlated with the variances so that the sample rates chosen will not be quite optimum, but will still be far more efficient than a proportionate self-weighting sample.

EXAMPLE 5.24 OPTIMUM SAMPLING FOR A
STUDY OF HOSPITALS
Suppose one is interested in the employment practices of hospitals: wage rates, employee benefits, treatment of minority employees, recruitment procedures, and the like. The complete listing of hospitals is found in the *Guide* issue of *Hospitals* published by the American Hospital Association. Table 5.6 gives data on payroll and number of employees for hospitals broken down by size into six groups. (The data are based on a sample of the 1971 list.)

Table 5.7 gives the sample allocations under five different procedures for a total sample of 1000 hospitals. Estimates of the total sampling variance are also given for payroll and number of employees.

1. The proportional sample allocates the sample based on the number of hospitals per stratum or by Π_h.

2. The optimum payroll sample allocates on the basis of

$$n_h = \frac{\Pi_h \sigma_h \text{ (payroll)}}{\Sigma_h \Pi_h \sigma_h \text{ (payroll)}} \, n.$$

TABLE 5.6
Characteristics of U.S. Hospitals by Number of Beds

Number of beds	Number of hospitals	Π_h	Average payroll ($thousands)	Payroll σ_h ($thousands)	Average number of employees	Employees σ_h
Under 50	1614	.246	266	183	54	25
50–99	1566	.238	384	316	123	51
100–199	1419	.216	1,484	641	262	95
200–299	683	.104	3,110	1347	538	152
300–499	679	.103	5,758	2463	912	384
500 and over	609	.093	10,964	7227	1548	826
Total	6570	1.000				

TABLE 5.7
U.S. Hospital Study Sample Sizes Using Various Procedures and Total σ^2 for $n = 1000$

		Optimum		Using total beds as measure of size	
Number of beds	Proportional	Payroll	Employees	(1)	(2)
Under 50	246	34	36	28	19
50–99	238	57	71	83	56
100–199	216	104	120	150	103
200–299	104	106	93	120	82
300–499	103	192	231	191	131
500 and over	93	507	449	428	609
Total	1000	1000	1000	1000	1000
σ^2 employees	71.0	17.1	16.5	17.2	20.6
σ^2 payroll (thousands)	4908	871	908	941	982

3. The optimum employees sample allocates on the basis of

$$n_h = \frac{\Pi_h \sigma_h \text{ (employees)}}{\Sigma_h \Pi_h \sigma_h \text{ (employees)}} \, n.$$

4. Estimates (1) and (2) in Table 5.7 using total beds assume that only the data on number of hospitals in each stratum are available. It is still possible to estimate size by taking the midpoint of the interval and multiplying by the number of hospitals. Thus, the number of beds in hospitals with under 50 beds is estimated by multiplying the midpoint 25 by 1614 for an estimate of 40,350. Similarly, in the stratum for hospitals with 300–499 beds, the estimated number of beds is 400×679 or 271,600. It is often the case, as in Table 5.6, that one has no way of determining the midpoint for the largest stratum. Estimate (1) assumes that the midpoint is twice as large as the lower bound, that is, 1000 beds. Estimate (2) avoids the issue by taking all the hospitals in the largest stratum and allocating the remaining sample of 391 hospitals among the remaining strata. The allocation is simply on the basis of size and requires no previous estimate of σ. (In many real world applications we would have size measures but no estimates of σ.)

$$n_h = s_h / \Sigma s_h,$$

where s_h is the estimated number of beds in the stratum.

The important feature of Table 5.7 is that all the size allocations are similar and all result in variances only one-fourth or one-fifth as large as those from proportional sampling. To put it another way, a proportional sample would need to be four or five times larger to have the same variance as the sample using size measures.

Which of the samples using size measures is the optimum? The table indicates that no sample is optimum for all purposes. Obviously, if one were only interested in payroll data for various types of workers the optimum payroll sample would be best. If one were interested in recruitment procedures, the optimum employee sample would be best. But the differences between these two samples are slight and even using number of beds would increase the variance only a little for these variables and might be optimum for others. If multiple measures of size are available, one should choose the one that is most current and that appears to be most highly correlated with the most important variables in the study. As the example illustrates, however, it is not necessary to agonize over the choice or to search for a perfect measure to achieve major improvements in sample efficiency.

SAMPLING ALL ELEMENTS IN LARGEST STRATUM

In many populations the number of institutions in the largest stratum will be small, but the variance in this stratum will be very large. This will be especially true for business firms that have multiple plants or retail establishments. The variance in the largest stratum will be much larger than for hospitals which are limited to a single geographic location. For these populations it will be the case that any optimum allocation using a size measure would indicate a sample size in the largest stratum that is larger than the number of elements in that stratum. The simple solution is to take *all* the elements in the largest stratum. If this is done, there is then *no* sampling variance in that stratum. This alone usually reduces the total sampling error substantially. The total sample remaining is then allocated among the remaining strata as in the previous example.

LARGER SAMPLE SIZE

Suppose instead of a sample of 1000 hospitals that the sample size is 1500. Then Table 5.8 gives the optimum allocations. Note that in all cases, the largest stratum is completely sampled, there is only one estimate using total beds as a measure of size, and all three procedures give very similar optimum samples.

TABLE 5.8
U.S. Hospital Study Sample Sizes for *n* = 1500

Number of beds	Optimum		Using total beds as measure of size
	Payroll	Employees	
Under 50	61	58	44
50–99	103	115	129
100–199	189	194	233
200–299	191	150	187
300–499	347	374	298
500 and over	609	609	609
Total	1500	1500	1500

5.27. COSTS DIFFER BY STRATA

In Section 5.18 we discussed the use of combined methods for improving sample efficiency. The major feature of these combined methods is that the costs vary depending on the procedure used. Thus, using a phone interview combined with personal interviews for those without phones, the costs are much higher in the nonphone stratum than in the phone stratum. Similarly, if the procedure involves a mail questionnaire followed by telephone calls to nonrespondents, the costs will be higher for the phone stratum than for the mail stratum.

An optimum procedure in this case is shown by Neyman (1934) and Hansen *et al.* (1953), is to sample strata inversely proportional to the square roots of per interview costs c_h in the different strata. Combining this result with the one in the previous section, the optimum sample allocation by strata is:

$$n_h^* = \frac{\Pi_h \sigma_h / \sqrt{c_h}}{\Sigma_h \Pi_h \sigma_h / \sqrt{c_h}} n \tag{5.2}$$

Unlike the examples in the last section, most applications where costs differ deal with human populations so that usually the variances are equal in the strata and the formula simplifies to:

$$n_h^* = \frac{\Pi_h / \sqrt{c_h}}{\Sigma \Pi_h / \sqrt{c_h}} n \tag{5.3}$$

Since the sampling rates depend on square roots of costs, small differences such as those observed in different regions or city sizes can be ignored, but major differences in cost by type of procedure can substantially influence sample allocations.

EXAMPLE 5.25 COMBINED USE OF MAIL PROCEDURE
AND PERSONAL FOLLOW-UP

A study was conducted to determine the current attitudes of physicians toward smoking and their own smoking behavior. The results were used by the Public Health Service in anticigarette smoking campaigns. A budget of $50,000 was allocated for data collection. It was estimated that about 40% of the physicians would respond to a mail survey with two follow-ups at a cost of about $1 per completed case. The other 60% would require either a long-distance phone interview or a face-to-face interview at a cost of about $25 per completed case. Table 5.9 gives the optimum sampling design and compares it to less desirable alternatives. Here the variance for the optimum design is 25% lower than for proportional sampling, illustrating that the advantages of optimum allocation increase as the cost differences become larger.

The initial mailing to physicians required a mail sample of 14,762 since only 40% of this mail sample would respond to give the optimum sample size of 5905. The cost of $1 per completed case includes the cost of the total mailing.

TABLE 5.9
Sample Sizes for Study of Physicians' Smoking Habits

Stratum	Π_h	All personal c_h	Proportional	Combined methods c_h	Proportional	Optimum
Mail responders	.4	25	800	1	1299	5905
Personal responders	.6	25	1200	25	1948	1764
Total			2000		3247	7669
σ^2			σ^2		$.6\sigma^2$	$.46\sigma^2$

From formula (5.3) the sample of 1764 doctors to be contacted personally is one-fifth of the initial sample who did not cooperate, since $\sqrt{\$1/\$25} = \frac{1}{5}$. The least desirable alternative is not shown in Table 5.9 although it is common among naive researchers—the use of mail only. Unless one expects mail response as high as can be achieved by personal methods, funds must be left in the budget for the personal follow-ups.

5.28. ADDITIONAL READING

I strongly suggest that some of the examples given in this chapter be read in their original versions, with particular attention to the technical appendices that discuss the sample design. In addition, there are many other studies that will include discussions of the sampling designs used. You may wish to consult the following bibliographies:

Bureau of the Census Catalog (published annually)
NORC Bibliography of Publications (1961 and supplements)
Institute for Social Research *List of Publications* (9)
Bureau of Applied Social Research *Bibliography* (1967 and updates)
Survey Research Center, *Publications List*
U.S. National Center for Health Statistics, *Programs and Collection Procedures* (1963–present)

In addition to the technical journals in their own fields, readers will find useful examples of sample designs in:

Public Opinion Quarterly
Journal of the American Statistical Association
Journal of the Royal Statistical Society, Series A

Sampling Texts

Cochran, W., *Sampling Techniques* (1963)
Deming, W. E., *Sample Design in Business Research* (1960)
Hansen, M., W. Hurwitz, and W. Madow, *Sample Survey Methods and Theory*, 2 vols., (1953)

Kish, L., *Survey Sampling* (1965)
Stephan, F., and P. McCarthy, *Sampling Opinions* (1958)
Sudman, S., *Applied Sampling* (1976)

These books are all useful and are all aimed at slightly different audiences. My book *Applied Sampling* is written at a simple level in the same style as this chapter with many examples. The Cochran text is the most mathematically sophisticated, but is still very clear and readable for those with good mathematical foundations. The other books combine practical applications and mathematical derivations. The Kish book deals mainly with the kinds of problems seen at a large survey organization like the Survey Research Center, University of Michigan. The Hansen, Hurwitz, and Madow examples are primarily those taken from their U.S. Census Bureau experience whereas Deming, as indicated in his title, uses business examples. Finally, Stephan and McCarthy deal with field problems of respondent availability, cooperation, and the general topic of sample biases.

Special Topics

Random numbers: For readers interested in knowing more about how random numbers are generated and tested, the introduction to the Rand Corporation's *A Million Random Digits* (1955) is probably the best brief source.

Systematic sampling: The discussions of the theory of systematic sampling found in Kish (1965) and Hansen, Hurwitz, and Madow (1953) are useful, but the most careful and complete discussion is in Cochran (1963, chap. 8).

Lists: The discussion in Kish (1965, section 2.7) parallels the discussion in this chapter and provides some additional illustrations.

Use of telephone directories and random digit dialing: Additional details may be found in papers by Glasser and Metzger (1972); Sudman (1973) in the *Journal of Marketing Research;* and Waksberg (1978) in the *Journal of the American Statistical Association.*

REFERENCES

Artz, R., R. Curtis, D. Fairbank, and E. Jackson
  1971 "Community rank stratification: A factor analysis." *American Sociological Review* 36(December): 985–1001.
Bureau of Applied Social Research
  1967 and updates *Bibliography, from Its Founding to the Present.* New York: BASR, Columbia University.
Cochran, W. G.
  1963 *Sampling Techniques* (2nd ed.). New York: Wiley.
Deming, W. E.
  1960 *Sample Design in Business Research.* New York: Wiley.

Gallup, G. H., Ed.
  1972   *The Gallup Poll: Public Opinion, 1935–1971*. 3 vols. New York: Random House. (Preface and introductory chapter.)
Garnier, M.
  1973   "Power and ideological conformity: A case study." *American Journal of Sociology* 79(September): 343–363.
Glasser, G. J., and G. D. Metzger
  1972   "Random-digit dialing as a method of telephone sampling." *Journal of Marketing Research* 9: 59–64.
Hansen, M. H., W. N. Hurwitz, and W. G. Madow
  1953   *Sample Survey Methods and Theory*. 2 vols. New York: Wiley.
Institute for Social Research
         List of publications. Ann Arbor: ISR, University of Michigan.
Jackson, E. F., and R. F. Curtis
  1972   "Effects of vertical mobility and status inconsistency: A body of negative evidence." *American Sociological Review* 37(December): 701–713.
Kish, L.
  1965   *Survey Sampling*. New York: Wiley.
Lenski, G.
  1963   *The Religious Factor*. Garden City, N.Y.: Doubleday.
National Opinion Research Center
  1961 and supplements   *Bibliography of Publications, 1941–1960*. Chicago: NORC.
  1964   *NORC Social Research, 1941–1964: An Inventory of Studies and Publications in Social Research*. Chicago: NORC.
Neyman, J.
  1934   "On the two different aspects of the representative method: The method of stratified sampling and the method of purposive selection." *Journal of the Royal Statistical Society* 97: 558–606.
Orum, A. M., and R. S. Cohen
  1973   "The development of political orientation among black and white children." *American Sociological Review* 38(February): 62–74.
Perry, P.
  1960   "Election survey procedures on the Gallup Poll." *Public Opinion Quarterly* 24: 531–542.
Rand Corporation
  1955   *A Million Random Digits with 100,000 Normal Deviates*. Glencoe, Ill.: Free Press.
Rosenthal, R.
  1966   *Experimenter Effects in Behavioral Research*. New York: Appleton.
Schlaifer, R.
  1959   *Probability and Statistics for Business Decisions*. New York: McGraw–Hill.
Schulman, G. I.
  1974   "Race, sex, and violence: A laboratory test of the sexual threat of the black male hypothesis." *American Journal of Sociology* 79(March): 1260–1277.
Schwartz, D. A.
  1973–1974   "How fast does news travel?" *Public Opinion Quarterly* 37(Winter): 625–627.
Stephan, F. F., and P. McCarthy
  1958   *Sampling Opinions*. New York: Wiley.
Sudman, S.
  1973   "The uses of telephone directories for survey sampling." *Journal of Marketing Research* 10: 204–207.
  1976   *Applied Sampling*, New York: Academic Press.
Sudman, S., and N. M. Bradburn
  1974   *Response Effects in Surveys: A Review and Synthesis*. Chicago: Aldine.
Survey Research Center
         Publications List. Berkeley: SRC, University of California.

U.S. Bureau of Labor Statistics
  1954–present   *Employment and Earnings*. (Continuing series.)
  1966   *The Consumer Price Index: History and Techniques*. Bulletin 1517. Washington, D.C.:
         U.S. Government Printing Office.
  1959–1966   *Monthly Report on the Labor Force, 1959–1966*.
  1963   *The Current Population Survey—A Report on Methodology*. Technical Paper No. 7.
         Washington, D.C.: U.S. Government Printing Office.
  1967   *Concepts and Methods Used in Manpower Statistics from the Current Population Survey*.
         Current Population Reports, Series P-23, No. 22. Washington, D.C.: U.S. Government
         Printing Office.
  1971   *Handbook of Methods for Surveys and Studies*. Bulletin 1711. Washington, D.C.: U.S.
         Government Printing Office.
         Bureau of the Census Catalog. Washington, D.C.: U.S. Government Printing Office.
         Current Population Reports. Series P-20, P-23, P-25, P-26, P-27, P-28, P-60, and P-65.
         Washington, D.C.: U.S. Government Printing Office.
U.S. National Center for Health Statistics
  1963–present   *Programs and Collection Procedures*. Vital and Health Statistics, Series 1.
         Washington, D.C.: U.S. Government Printing Office.
Waksberg, J.
  1978   "Sampling Methods for Random Digit Dialing." *Journal of the American Statistical
         Association*. 73(March): 40–46.
Yancey, W. L., L. Rigsby, and J. D. McCarthy
  1972   "Social position and self-evaluation: The relative importance of race." *American Journal
         of Sociology* 78(September): 338–370.

Chapter 6

Questionnaire Construction and Item Writing

Paul B. Sheatsley

6.1. INTRODUCTION

Although survey research implies almost by definition some sort of questionnaire to be administered to a sample of individuals, it is important to realize that the questionnaire is simply an instrument, a tool, to be employed in the study of a research problem. As such, it may or may not be the most suitable instrument for the task.

Some or much of the information to be sought may already be available in, for example, statistics compiled by federal government agencies or other sources, or in the files of such survey research archives as the Roper Public Opinion Research Center or the Interuniversity Consortium for Political and Social Research. For some studies, direct observation or measurement, such as counting traffic or the Nielsen television ratings based on actual operation of the television set, may be superior to retrospective questioning of individual respondents. Field experiments, in which the investigator devises a scenario and then records people's responses to the contrived situation, have a long history in social research. Content analysis of newspaper or magazine articles and advertisements may provide a better record of changes over time than asking people today about their recollections of the past. All of these methods have their own weaknesses, of course, as does using questionnaires; the point is that we should not automatically assume that a brand new questionnaire is the only means to provide the answer to every research problem.

If it appears that a questionnaire is the most suitable instrument for the research task, one must still ask whether it can do the job. It may be, for example, that people simply do not have the information: They cannot recall it,

HANDBOOK OF SURVEY RESEARCH

cannot predict it, or are ignorant of the matter under investigation. The problem of ignorance can be controlled, of course, by careful sample selection. Obviously, one would not ask the general public about the editorial policy or content of the *American Sociological Review*. Such a survey should be restricted to readers of the journal or to a similar professional audience. Yet most of us have been exposed at one time or another to interviews or questionnaires that have sought our opinions about subjects far removed from our ken. We may also have been asked to provide information on our job experience or salary levels over a long period of time, our childhood medical history, our expectations or motivations in some long ago period, or other details of the past that are either beyond our recall or subject to wild error. Similarly, questions that ask us what we would do if we inherited $1 million or what we expect to be the biggest problems facing us 10 years from now, or even what our plans are for the next year or two, can elicit little more than "best guesses" with a wide margin of error. A questionnaire can bring out only what is in the mind of the respondent, and this is task enough. To probe for what is not in the respondent's mind is a disservice to the respondent and is also unlikely to produce data of any validity and utility.

One other consideration before deciding to use a questionnaire is the willingness or readiness of the respondent to reply. Certainly the best questionnaire writers today, aided by changes in the social climate, have pushed back the frontiers from the recent past when it was generally assumed that one could not ask questions about drinking, drugs, sexual behavior, income, cancer, and a host of other taboo items in a household interview situation. But even today valid answers to such topics require careful introduction, proper survey auspices, and a well-planned line of questioning that does not depend on one or two blunt items. Even today, one may well question whether the questionnaire is the most suitable means of collecting data on such phenomena as the incidence of child abuse or the proportion of people who indulge in various forms of cheating, or even of measuring the extent of such socially disapproved behavior as gambling, "deviant" sex practices, or excessive use of alcohol or drugs. Obviously, any questionnaire, even if it consists of only a single question on the topic, can produce some data. In general, the more questions one asks on the topic, the more money one is prepared to spend on the survey, and the more proficient the line of questioning, the better the data will be. But there is always a point at which further investment will fail to produce equivalent returns—and sometimes this point is reached very early. Sometimes a little thought will show that a questionnaire is simply not worth the available time and budget, because people either do not have or will not easily reveal the information that the researcher seeks.

6.2. STANDARDIZED QUESTIONNAIRES

Once researchers decide that questioning people is the best way to obtain the necessary information, they are then faced with the task of designing a suitable instrument. If researchers themselves or a small team of colleagues are collecting the data, and if the data are not to be handled statistically, it may be that no formal questionnaire is required. In interviewing community leaders, for example, about some topic of local concern, a standardized questionnaire may inappropriately narrow the discussion and prevent a full exploration of each respondent's views. Instead, one might prepare a brief interviewer guide, listing perhaps a dozen major questions, with appropriate probes listed under each. This will ensure that all obvious items are covered, but will allow ample room for the researchers to probe the unexpected response or to follow up on unforeseen factors they may have overlooked. Such interviews can be tape recorded, classified crudely by a number of dimensions, and analyzed qualitatively rather than statistically.

But if the researcher requires a large sample, numbering in the hundreds or the thousands, if the services of many interviewers will be employed; and if the data will be subject to statistical analysis, the task of designing a standardized instrument cannot be avoided. There must be a prescribed wording for each question, so that each respondent receives the same stimulus. One cannot have different interviewers asking the various items the way it seems best to them or improvising variations on the wording for different respondents. There is abundant evidence that even slight variations in question wording can significantly affect response (Payne, 1951). There must also be a prescribed order for asking the questions, and for the same reasons. Again, there is evidence that responses to certain kinds of questions vary significantly depending on the items that precede and follow them (Bradburn & Mason, 1964). Finally, there must be prescribed definitions or explanations to ensure that the questions are handled consistently. If one asks, for example, *Do you read a newspaper regularly?* the word *regularly* (and perhaps the words *read* and *newspaper* as well) must be defined for the interviewers, so they can answer respondents' requests for clarification if they occur, and so they will know how to probe such replies as *Regularly every Sunday* or *I read it more often than not*.

There are obvious disadvantages in using a standardized questionnaire, and one hears them often from critics of survey research: People understand the questions differently; respondents are forced into what may seem to them an unnatural reply; they have no opportunity to qualify their answers or to explain their opinions more precisely; they may feel they have already answered the question when the interviewer asks other prescribed questions on the same topic; and so on. But there is really no alternative to the use of standardized questionnaires in large-scale surveys. Without standardized question wordings and sequence, and standardized instructions to interviewers, researchers would be unable to measure or control response effects; they would receive an unacceptable number of uncodable responses; and they would be completely overwhelmed by the sheer mass of idiosyncratic material. Thus arises the challenge to the researcher—to design and develop a standardized instrument that will meet the data needs, but is also crafted well enough that every respondent will grasp the intent of each item and will be willing and able to respond to it.

An important consequence of the use of a standardized questionnaire is that, once it is printed, the researcher is committed to it and can do little or nothing to improve it. In informal interviewing, one can adapt questions, shift tactics, change procedures as the data collection proceeds. With a standardized questionnaire, administered by dozens of interviewers working simultaneously in many different locations, the researchers may not even be aware of any problem with the instrument until the field work is largely completed. If they suddenly have some great new thought and now see that an important question has been omitted, they cannot suddenly stop 50 or 100 interviewers and tell them to add the item. These considerations emphasize the importance of careful design and pretesting of the survey instrument. The most ingenious sample design, skilled interviewing, and sophisticated analytical techniques cannot redeem a survey that asked the wrong questions or asked them poorly. For this reason alone, it is clear that questionnaire design is a crucial element in survey research.

6.3. MODE OF ADMINISTRATION

Many issues of questionnaire design hinge upon the mode of its administration. The two basic modes are self-administration by the respondent and administration by an interviewer who asks the questions. Each of these can be subdivided or combined in various ways.

In the most frequent type of self-administered questionnaire, no interviewer is present. The most common example is the mail survey (see Chapter 10 by Dillman). Respondents receive the questionnaire in the mail, read the accompanying letter or instructions, and fill it out at home or elsewhere at their leisure. The major advantage of this mode of administration is its low cost, since there are no interviewer time commitments or travel charges. Mail surveys may sometimes produce more valid responses to certain types of questions where the presence of an interviewer might be inhibiting (see Chapter 9 by Weinberg). They are often a good means of collecting data from very specialized and highly motivated groups, such as opera-goers or members of a professional organization. The disadvantages of mail surveys are many, and they often outweigh the advantages. Response rates are generally low, with resultant large biases. Less-educated persons may have trouble following the instructions. Inadequate answers cannot be probed for a more specific or relevant response. If respondents are puzzled by an item, there is no interviewer to explain it to them. Question order biases may also occur because the respondent can study the whole questionnaire before answering the first question. One is not always sure that the person to whom the questionnaire is addressed is the one who fills it out. If respondents are ignorant, they can look up the answer or ask someone.

Another type of self-administered questionnaire is frequently given to groups of respondents, with an interviewer present, such as students in a classroom or a group of shoppers invited to a meeting room. Here the presence of the interviewer can ensure a high completion rate and can be used to reassure respondents, to answer their questions, and even to edit their completed questionnaires. Costs, of course, are higher when the group must be specially assembled and one or more interviewers are sent to the meetings. There is also potential bias if school children fill out questionnaires in the classroom, factory employees perform the task on company time, or shoppers are paid to come to the researcher's office. Furthermore, such samples are usually inefficient for large-scale research because members of the groups are not independently selected. One would have to sample a large number of high school classrooms, for example, to generalize about high school students as a group.

Personal interviews, in which an interviewer asks the questions and fills out the questionnaire, can similarly be subdivided into face-to-face interviews, usually in the respondent's home or office, and telephone interviews. Finally, the two major modes may themselves be combined, as in a personal interview which includes a self-administered component, or a self-administered group interview that has the interviewer later asking a series of questions.

The mode of administration is relevant to questionnaire design because a questionnaire designed for one mode may not be applicable to the other. An obvious distinction is that when the questionnaire is designed for personal interview, the interviewer who uses it will be a trained individual who is already able to or who can be taught to use it proficiently under all circumstances (see Chapter 10 by Dillman). The self-administered questionnaire, on the other hand, will be filled out by untrained respondents who never saw the instrument before, will never see it again, and have no particular incentive to try to do a good job. It follows that self-administered questionnaires should generally be kept as simple, short, and self-explanatory as possible. Instructions should be brief and clear, answer categories unambiguous, and the line of questioning should avoid complicated skip patterns. In contrast, questionnaires designed for personal interview need be limited in their length and complexity only by time and cost factors. Although not to be recommended to amateur or journeyman researchers operating with less than million dollar budgets, there are examples of surveys that have employed 150-page questionnaires of devilish complexity and detail and have achieved very high response rates.

6.4. TYPE OF SAMPLE TO BE INTERVIEWED

Besides the mode of administration—personal interview or self-administered—a second major variable affecting questionnaire design is the type of sample from whom data are to be sought. One can imagine, for example, various extreme types: on the one hand, elementary school children, high school dropouts, people with little understanding of the subjects being asked about; and on the other, professionals, graduate students, corporate officers, community officials. It is clear, whether the questionnaire is to be self-administered or the questions asked by an interviewer, that the instrument design task will be quite different, depending on the sophistication of the group. In the first case, one would be dealing for the most part with subjects who have a limited attention span, perhaps little interest in the subject matter, and a low-level capability in handling abstract ideas and subtle differences. In the other case, researchers need not hesitate to probe their subjects in considerable detail, to introduce fine distinctions, and to ask the respondents to perform fairly complex tasks.

Since the general public consists by definition of *all* types of individuals—all ages, education levels, types of neighborhood, and life experiences—the researcher who wishes to study a population sample, rather than some specialized group of people, is faced with a difficult task. It is a test of the researcher's skill to design a questionnaire that is simple enough for universal comprehension but not so childish or elementary that it will serve to alienate the interested and well informed. The researcher must pay due heed to the complexity of the topic and show an understanding of all the relevant variables, but keep the language and sequence of the questions within the reach and comprehension of the least-educated member of the sample.

It might be noted that because questionnaires are usually written by educated persons who have a special interest in and understanding of the topic of their inquiry, and because these people usually consult with other educated and concerned persons, it is much more common for questionnaires to be overwritten, overcomplicated, and too demanding of the respondent than they are to be simpleminded, superficial, and not demanding enough.

6.5. QUALITIES OF A GOOD QUESTIONNAIRE

Unlike sampling and data processing, questionnaire design is not a science or technology but remains an art. Given the same research task and the same hypotheses, six qualified questionnaire writers will be likely to come up with six instruments that differ widely in their choice of items, line of questioning, use of open-ended questions, and length of time the interview takes. Frequently, a good a priori case can be made for any of them. Furthermore, all researchers know that when they start analyzing their data, they are sure to find that some of the questions are useless to the task, whereas others that are sorely needed were somehow omitted from the design. There are no pat or simple rules for questionnaire writing. Most texts and articles on the subject are pitched on a vague general level, such as "Decide what information you need," or they consist of highly specific admonitions, such as "Be sure alternatives are mutually exclusive." The authors of these instructions are experienced researchers who know their field, but it is very hard to tell someone how to design a useful questionnaire.

One might start by looking at the general purposes that any questionnaire is designed to serve. These seem in most cases to be three in number. A well-designed questionnaire should: (*a*) meet the objectives of the research; (*b*) obtain the most complete and accurate information possible; and (*c*) do this within the limits of available time and resources.

To observe that a questionnaire should meet the research objectives may seem obvious, but it certainly does not happen every time, often because the questionnaire was poorly designed. Researchers become seduced by their own particular prejudices or interests into elaborating some less important variable while devoting less attention to a more important one. For lack of hard thought, consultation, pretesting, or familiarity with the literature, one may completely omit from the questionnaire some important aspect of the subject. Much of this is inevitable; none of us is omniscient. Indeed, the very fact that we are studying something means we do not know it all and thus cannot conceive of all possibilities. Every survey is bound to leave some questions unanswered and to provide a need for further research. But the purpose of a good questionnaire is to minimize these problems by trying to forestall them.

It is perhaps equally obvious that a good questionnaire should provide the most complete and accurate information possible. Even when the questionnaire is carefully crafted to meet the research objectives, the accuracy and completeness of the data it produces are far from guaranteed. This is because the people who provide the information—the respondents—intervene in the process. Respondents may misunderstand the questions, they may reject the premises on which the questions are based, or they simply may refuse to answer. Worse, they may lie to the interviewer or attempt to conceal their actual behavior or attitudes. The questions may be so far above their understanding and experience that they answer at random rather than confess their ignorance. When these things occur, the questionnaire is a poor one, no matter how well it seemed to meet the survey's objectives when it was designed. The good questionnaire must be organized and worded to encourage respondents to provide the most accurate and complete information they can.

The third property of a good questionnaire—to provide the required information within existing cost and time constraints—may not seem quite as obvious, but is nevertheless very real. A questionnaire that provides data too late to be of real use or which causes researchers to run out of money before they can complete the analysis is a bad questionnaire, no matter how well it seemed to serve the objectives of the inquiry. Clearly, if one had unlimited time and unlimited funds, and could spend hours and hours with the respondents, one could devise more informative questionnaires—although not necessarily more efficient ones.

But in the real world, time and cost constraints are always present. Of all the surveys conducted today, only a very few start with researchers figuring out what they want to do and applying for what they consider to be the necessary funds. Even in these cases, budgets are usually reduced before a researcher gets the grant. The typical case is that of a client or sponsoring agency who has a problem, who has a specified (and usually, to the researcher, inadequate) budget to support the research, and who asks the researcher to design a study that will fit that budget and can be completed by a particular deadline. There is nothing wrong with limited surveys conducted on modest budgets. Indeed, it would be hard to argue that the most expensive surveys and those that have taken the longest time to complete have produced the largest body of useful information or have contributed the most to the advancement of survey methodology. "Quickie" surveys conducted at limited cost often provide the most effective policy guidance.

Time and cost affect all aspects of survey research, of course, but they have special importance to questionnaire design because they impose a limit on the number of questions the researcher can ask. A crucial element in budgeting a survey is the average length of the interview because this affects the number of calls an interviewer can make in a day, the number of interviewers to be employed and trained, the amount of data that must be processed and analyzed, and so on. The length of the interview is usually predetermined—20 min, 40 min, 1 hr, or whatever—and the task of the questionnaire designer is to fashion the most useful instrument possible within that constraint.

6.6. DECIDING ON CONTENT

All questionnaire writers have their own approach to instrument design, and the various approaches will also be modified according to the objectives and circumstances of the research—whether writers craft their own studies or do a job for a client; whether they work alone, with colleagues, or as part of an organization; whether they seek descriptive data about some phenomenon or are testing research hypotheses; and whether they have much or little time and money available. The following five steps, however, are generally applicable.

1. Decide what information is required.
2. Draft some questions to elicit that information.
3. Put them into a meaningful order and format.
4. Pretest the result.
5. Go back to 1.

Note that one does not start by writing down questions. It is not difficult to think up a hundred questions about any problem worthy of study, and talking to other people will suggest hundreds more. But unless researchers have some conceptual or analytical framework to guide them, there is no particular reason for choosing any one question over another. Actual drafting of the questions can usually be done fairly quickly and there is no hurry about it. The first task, and the hardest, is to figure out which factors are relevant to the problem. What are the things one needs to know from the respondent in order to meet the survey's objectives? This is the first question that needs to be answered.

Most research begins with at least a vague notion of the kinds of information required, if only because someone must have been sufficiently impressed to budget money for the inquiry. If researchers themselves have submitted a successful proposal, they have made a good start on the questionnaire design. If they are doing a job for a client, the client will have defined the problem and will have specified or suggested the necessary information. Researchers should know, however, that clients are very often vague or biased about their needs and it is the researcher's task to clarify the goals, try to establish operational measurements, and probe for other relevant variables that the client may have overlooked.

Additional help is available from many sources, of which one of the most obvious is the literature search. Researchers should know what work has been done on the same or similar problems in the past, what factors have not yet been investigated, and how the present survey can build on what has already been discovered. Another source of help is discussion of the problem with friends and colleagues. Conversations with them may suggest new ideas, alter one's assumptions, or help in clarifying doubtful points. Consultation with experts, people with firsthand knowledge of the problem or who have spent time studying it, are almost always helpful. These need not be paid consultants. Most scholars, businesspeople, government officials, and the like will be glad to spend half an hour or more discussing with a researcher their own ideas and experience about a topic that concerns them.

A final source of ideas in selecting the content of the questionnaire lies not in experts or in the literature, but among the population one intends to survey. A half-dozen exploratory conversations with representatives of the group, perhaps roughly stratified by age, sex, education, or other presumably significant variables, will often provide researchers with a glimpse of reality that may sharply alter some of their preconceptions. Researchers may find that some consideration thought to be important seems to be quite irrelevant to the people they are talking to, or that they have deep concerns that were not previously realized. Out of one or more of these kinds of efforts, researchers can usually develop a fairly good outline of the kinds of information they need to obtain from the survey instrument.

A Checklist of Variables

Researchers have long sought to codify the various dimensions of public opinion that should normally be covered in survey research. One of the earliest of these was Gallup's "quintamensional" technique, which he recommended as necessary for a full understanding of a person's opinion (Gallup, 1947).

First, he said, is the respondent's *knowledge* or awareness of the issue. Almost always, researchers should include some measure of knowledge, so they can distinguish among the well informed, the poorly informed, and the unaware. Knowledge is usually highly correlated with education, but not always. Knowledge can be measured by asking a single question or by asking a whole battery of questions. Second is the respondent's *interest* in the problem or concern about it. Some people are apathetic about the issue, others highly concerned. The researcher should be able to specify the general level of interest or concern and identify the various types of people along this continuum. Third are respondents' *attitudes* toward the issue, the direction of their opinions. Are they for or against, satisfied or dissatisfied—do they approve or disapprove? Fourth, *why* do respondents feel the way they do? What are the reasons? This is not always easy to get at—respondents themselves may not know or be able to explain their reasons—but researchers should try to find out, if they are to understand the responses they receive. Fifth, how *strongly* is the opinion held? What is the intensity of the attitude? This is not the same as interest or concern. Concerned respondents may feel a lot of conflict in their opinions; the unconcerned may be very dogmatic.

These five dimensions may seem most applicable to Gallup-type inquiries, such as preferences between presidential candidates or opinions about proposed legislation, but they should not be ignored in any serious research. If one is studying, let us say, smoking behavior, one would certainly want to include questions about respondents' knowledge and experience with smoking, their interest or concern about smoking, their attitudes and opinions about smoking, their reasons for holding these opinions, and how strongly they feel.

Most experts have agreed on the five dimensions of opinion just enumerated, but have suggested various others that may also be important in particular cases: for example the *saliency* of the issue in respondents' minds. Is the problem one that is "on the top of their heads," one that they are likely to mention spontaneously? Or is it something they do not ordinarily think about unless an interviewer or someone else brings up the matter? Respondents' *expectations* for the future may strongly affect their present attitudes. If they perceive that things are getting better, their opinions will probably differ from those they would hold if they thought things were getting worse.

Because there are sometimes large differences between attitudes and behavior, respondents' *readiness to act* is often an important dimension. One cannot predict any individual's behavior, but one can come much closer if attitudes are tested by posing "what if" situations to see if respondents maintain their opinions under all circumstances or qualify or change them depending on conditions.

Perception of others' beliefs is often an important dimension. The phrase *pluralistic ignorance* describes the situation in which most individuals believe *X* but are convinced that the large majority of people believe *Y*. Sizable proportions of a neighborhood sample, for example, have been found to say that they themselves would not object to a black family moving next door but that other people in the area would not stand for it.

People's attitudes and behavior are affected by such *demographic* factors as their sex, age, race, level of education, and place of residence, and almost all surveys routinely include these items. The respondent's occupation and marital status are also recorded on most surveys, and frequently the researcher may want to classify the sample by religious affiliation, political preference, ethnicity, number of children, or other demographic variables.

Beyond these rather obvious variables that may intervene to affect the respondent's opinions and behavior lie an infinity of others that may or may not be relevant to the particular survey at hand. The following will serve only as examples: (*a*) exposure to television, newspapers, radio; (*b*) leisure time activities; (*c*) stage in life cycle; (*d*) personality or values, as measured by a scale of items; (*e*) group memberships; (*f*) social relations: visiting, talking with friends, neighbors; (*g*) length of time in community, plans to stay; and (*h*) satisfaction with job, family, housing, neighborhood, and the like. The list is limited only by the researcher's creativity, except that one must keep in mind the cost and time restraints. In the end, since one cannot ask everything, the choice of the content of the questionnaire must be narrowed to those items that are expected to be most productive in terms of their contribution to what one needs to know from the completed interviews.

6.7. WRITING THE QUESTIONS

Once researchers have decided on what is to be included in the questionnaire, they can start drafting question items that will elicit the needed information. It is interesting that survey research is perhaps the only profession to try to deal seriously with the problems of question asking. There is good reason for this—of course—the accuracy and validity of our data depend entirely on the questions we ask and the ways in which our respondents perceive and respond to them.

In ordinary conversation, the questions people ask are seldom to the point (*How's it going? What's new? What do you want to do?*) and are often biased toward a particular response (*Everything okay? A little more coffee?*). Answers are equally unsatisfactory for research purposes (*Pretty good. Not much. I guess. Why not?*). One does not expect professional rigor in everyday conversation, but one might think that physicians, lawyers, loan officials, personnel officers, and other professionals would have studied the art of questioning. Although law students may study the art of cross-examination and medical students may receive some general rules for eliciting a medical history from the patient, most researchers would not give high marks to these professionals and others who, like us, rely on questioning for their information.

They read poorly worded items from forms, or they improvise questions that are hard to understand, impossible to answer in the terms requested, or are seriously biased or leading. Doctors, for example, often proceed quickly down a checklist (*Any trouble urinating? Any pain in chest? Any trouble with joints?*), then unconsciously start leading the patient (*No trouble sleeping? No trouble with vision, hearing?*), without giving the patient a chance to reflect or to mention some concern.[1] Any of us who have faced cross-examination by an adversary lawyer or seen these enacted on television know how unfair a ques-

---

[1] Chapter 10 of Kahn and Cannell (1957) reproduces the transcript of a diagnostic interview conducted by a physician. The authors' comments are instructive.

tion can be and how yes–no responses to such questions can mislead those who must interpret the reply.

Even in survey research, the literature on question writing is relatively sparse. A certain 1500-page handbook of marketing research, for example, includes articles on almost every phase of survey procedures, but there is no specific chapter and only scattered advice on how to write survey questions. Therefore a small book written by Stanley Payne, *The Art of Asking Questions* (1951), is remarkable in several respects: It was written more than 30 years ago and is now in its tenth printing; it was written not by an academic but by a practicing researcher in opinion and market research; it is the only book Payne ever wrote and it remains the best on the subject—brief, highly readable, with many amusing and instructive examples.

A formidable difficulty in bringing order to the subject of question writing, like that of questionnaire design in general, is the overwhelming variety of surveys. Just as the design of the survey instrument depends upon the research objectives, the mode of administration, and the type of sample to be surveyed, so the specific questions must be pointed precisely at the research objectives, must be suitable for the method of administration (self-administration or personal interview), and must be phrased at the respondents' level of understanding. This means that questions that work in one situation may be unproductive in another and that few general rules can be found to apply in all circumstances.

Open versus Closed Questions

Survey questions can be classified broadly into two forms: open and closed. Open questions (sometimes called open ended) ask for a reply in the respondent's own words: *What do you like most about . . . ? Why do you feel that way? What are your favorite TV programs?* No answers are suggested; respondents must improvise their own. Closed questions (sometimes called multiple choice) ask respondents to choose one of two or more categories that have been suggested to them: *Do you expect to vote for X or Y? Do you approve or disapprove of . . . ? Here are three statements. Please tell me which one comes closest to your opinion.* Closed questions can have 2 alternatives (as *approve* or *disapprove*), 3, 4, 5, or even 100—as when respondents are shown a thermometer with 100 degrees and asked to rate the degree of their liking, disliking, or other feeling.

The main advantage of open questions is that they allow respondents to answer in their own frames of reference, entirely uninfluenced by any specific alternatives suggested by the interviewer. They also reveal what is most salient to respondents, what things are foremost in their minds. Closed questions do not permit this. For example, one could ask (open) *What do you like least about living in this neighborhood?* or one could ask (closed) *Here are five things people have told us they do not like about this neighborhood. Which one do you like least?* In response to the open question, many respondents may mention something not on the list of five; had one asked the closed question instead, one would never have known their actual opinions. Another group might give one answer on the open question but a different one on the closed, because the list of five reminded them of something they had not thought of when they answered the open question. This may be acceptable, but the researcher should be aware that some of the closed responses were selected only because respondents were reminded of them.

Compared to open questions, closed questions therefore have a number of disadvantages. They suggest answers that respondents may not have thought of before; they force respondents into what may be an unnatural frame of reference; and they do not permit them to express the exact shade of their meaning. In answering an open question, respondents can attach qualifications to their answers or emphasize the strength of their opinions.

But open questions have disadvantages as well. They inevitably elicit a great deal of repetitious, irrelevant material. Respondents will often miss the point of the question, pour out a great many words that bear on the issue only marginally, or engage in long awkward pauses while they try to organize or articulate their thoughts. The interviewer must then do some sensitive probing to bring respondents back to the subject, to clarify their answers, or to encourage them to elaborate. Individuals also differ a great deal in their ability to articulate, with the result that differences in responses may reflect differences in ability to express opinions as much as real differences in shades of opinion.

The researcher should know too that there is great interviewer variability in the handling of open questions. This variability occurs first in eliciting the response; some interviewers are alert to recognize irrelevant, incomplete, or ambiguous responses whereas others will accept what is given and go on to the next question. There is interviewer variability also in the recording of the response. Though interviewers are customarily trained to record verbatim, they differ in their ability to do so and some editing is usually necessary, in any case. Unfortunately, the editing, whether due to inability to keep up with the flow of words or to the discarding of material deemed repetitious or irrelevant, is selective, so that what is actually recorded may not accurately reflect the respondent's full meaning. With closed questions, specified alternatives, and answer categories to code, there is much less variability in interviewer performance. It should also be mentioned that respondents tend to answer open questions in different dimensions, and these must be probed unless the researcher is to be confronted with responses that cannot be combined. If asked when they moved into their present home, for example, answers may come in such terms as: *Seven years ago. When my wife died. A short while ago. When the kids were little.*

Finally, all the verbatim material has to be coded and reduced to manageable categories anyway, and opportunities for clerical and judgmental errors are infinite, so why not let the respondents code themselves from a list of categories? Open questions certainly take more time and cost more money. Interviewers must be trained on what constitutes an acceptable answer; they must spend more interviewing time in probing and recording. The researcher must examine a sample of responses and build codes; coders must be trained and supervised, and their work checked. Closed questions avoid all of this.

Efforts are sometimes made to combine the open and closed forms of question, but these are rarely successful. One example is to ask a closed question but allow for an "other" answer: *Did you vote for* X *because of his personality, his stand on the issues, or for some other reason?* This type of question gives the respondent a chance to mention something else, but many who would have chosen a different reason if it had been suggested to them will simply choose between personality and issues without troubling themselves to think of anything else. Others may take advantage of the open alternative and confuse matters for the researcher by saying something like, He *does have a good personality but I also like his sincerity.*

Another means of combining open and closed questions is to ask the question open, provide code categories on the questionnaire, and instruct the interviewer to code the response. This works well enough when the categories are limited and clear cut [e.g., *How did you first hear about* (news event)? Code: *TV, radio, newspaper, talking with someone*], but few codes are that simple. If the responses refer to attitudes or sentiments, the variations will be enormous, and interviewers will be hard put to classify them. A response that touches on two categories may be coded in either, or both, or it may be written in as "other," depending upon the interviewer and the situation. The interviewer has too much else to do and cannot be relied on to consider these fine distinctions.

For all these reasons, then—time, cost, interviewer variability, respondent variability, coding and analytical problems—the researcher is generally well advised, on any large-scale survey, to close up as many questions as possible. Open questions are usually employed only: (*a*) when there are too many categories to be listed or foreseen (*What are some of the things you like about this neighborhood?*); (*b*) when one wants the respondent's spontaneous, uninfluenced reply (*What do you think is the biggest problem facing the country?*); (*c*) to build rapport during the interview, following a long series of closed questions that may make respondents feel they have no chance to express themselves (*Now here's another question. Tell me how you feel about this*); or (*d*) in exploratory interviewing and pretesting, when the researcher wants to get some idea of the parameters of an issue, with a view to closing up the questions later.

Response Categories

Open questions permit respondents to frame their own unique replies. Closed questions permit researchers to specify the answer categories most suitable to their purposes. Many questions form natural dichotomies (*Do you own an automobile? Are you registered to vote?*) and often the researcher will just want to sort the sample into two groups: those who approve versus those who disapprove, or those who have knowledge of a particular issue versus those who are ignorant of it. But quite often the natural dichotomy provides a poor response distribution. For example, if one asks the question, *Are you satisfied or dissatisfied with the medical care you receive?* only about 20% of a national sample will express dissatisfaction; the great majority will say they are satisfied. This is not unreasonable, because people are often reluctant to criticize doctors and other experts; they are probably getting care as good as they know how to get or can afford, and if they were very unhappy they would probably switch to another source of care. But if one asks **How** *satisfied are you with the medical care you receive—very satisfied, somewhat satisfied, or not satisfied?* the marginal distribution will look more like 50% very satisfied, 35% somewhat satisfied, and 15% not satisfied. The first two groups, which became combined in the dichotomous version, may well turn out to be quite different in terms of their characteristics, behavior, and other attitudes.

As this example illustrates, it is frequently useful to sort people into more than two response categories, and this accounts for the popularity of five-point scales such as: strongly agree (or approve), probably agree, undecided, probably disagree (or disapprove), and strongly disagree. A five-point scale provides flexibility, too, in that the researcher can look at all five groups in the total sample, but can easily combine the two agree positions and/or the two disagree positions when wanting to look at subgroups of smaller size.

Theoretically, it might seem that one could gain constantly increasing refinement by using seven, nine, eleven, or even more scale points, but when one gets above five, serious problems arise. Beyond five categories, it becomes almost impossible to describe the positions in English and one must resort to some sort of scale or thermometer that forces respondents to answer in terms of numbers rather than give their opinions, a task that some people find difficult. Many people, too, have trouble coping with more than five positions on a scale and may pick a position that only roughly approximates their attitude. Especially if they have not thought much about the issue, they will resent being asked to make such fine distinctions. Finally, it is difficult to deal with a large number of categories in the analysis of the data and the researcher usually aggregates them back into a small number of groups anyway.

It is worth noting some common response categories that appear on professional surveys, for they have a number of advantages. First, they are well tested. Most of them have been used on a wide variety of questions, over and over again, and they have been found to work well, both in terms of respondent understanding and of the reliability of the distinctions they provide. Second, they have wide applicability because they can fit almost any subject matter. Some of these are:

1. *Excellent–good–fair–poor:* Useful for any kind of rating: your own state of health; the job the President is doing; housing, schools, transportation, etc. in this community.

2. *Approve–disapprove; favor–oppose; are you for or against; good idea–bad idea:* These can be used for almost anything you want a respondent's opinion on. They can easily be probed with *How strongly do you feel?* to provide additional categories.

3. *Agree–disagree:* Can be used with a wide variety of statements or propositions and can also be easily supplemented by asking *How strongly?*

4. *Too many–not enough–about right; too much–too little–about right amount:* Useful for measuring people's satisfaction with amounts: attention paid by the media; goods or services of one kind or another; amount spent by government in various areas, etc.

5. *Better–worse–about the same:* Useful for comparisons with past or expectations for future. Can be expanded to five points by asking *Very much better–slightly better–*etc.

6. *Very–fairly–not at all:* As in *How important is each of these* (subjects), *How interested are you in* (subject)? *How satisfied are you with* (subject)?

7. *Regularly–often–seldom–never:* Frequency of many kinds of activity.

8. *Always–most of the time–some of the time–rarely or never:* Another measure of frequency.

9. *More likely–less likely–no difference:* A measure of probability of the respondent's action, given some hypothetical circumstance: *If your party nominated a woman for president, would you be more likely to vote for the candidate, less likely, or wouldn't it make any difference in how you voted?*

A further advantage of these standard formulations, in addition to their wide applicability and easy understandability by most respondents, is their adaptability to *lists* of items. For example, the interviewer can say: *I'm going to read you some events in the news lately and you tell me for each one whether you're very interested in that, fairly interested, or not interested at all.* or *Now I want to read you some statements and you tell me whether you agree or disagree with each one.* In this way, one can very quickly get respondent opinions on a great many items. One should be warned, however, that when the number of items exceeds 8 or 10, many respondents will get bored and answer aimlessly, without real thought, simply to get through the list as quickly as possible. With a large number of such items, it is best to ask them in groups and to alternate them with other types of questions.

A problem frequently faced by the questionnaire writer is whether to include the middle, or neutral, alternative in the wording of the question or whether to reserve this category for only those occasions when the respondent volunteers it. Examples are such categories as *about the same, about right,* and *no difference.* Decisions are usually based on the researcher's expectations of the frequency distributions. On some issues, suggestion of the neutral alternative may lead the majority of respondents to select that answer just because it seems a safe and easy escape from a difficult or distasteful choice. In such cases it may be wise to suggest only the extreme categories and reserve the middle alternative for those respondents who spontaneously answer in those terms. Guidance on such matters can often be obtained from a study of past surveys about the issue or from trying out various forms of the question on pretest respondents.

Common research practice is to omit the don't know, can't decide, or no opinion category from the wording of the question and to use this category only if the respondent volunteers such a response—indeed, in many cases, only if the respondent continues to hold to this answer in the face of the interviewer's best efforts to force a choice. As in most matters of question wording, however, there can be no standard rule. The rationale for omitting the DK (don't know) response from the wording of the question rests ultimately on the belief that *I don't know* is the easy, lazy answer that respondents will tend to choose if they realize it is available as an option. Many people, for example, customarily preface their response with *Well, I don't know* but then go on to give their opinion. One can argue further that nobody really *knows*, when the issue is a matter of preference or values, and that to suggest such a response is tantamount to inviting respondents to refuse to express their opinions. Consequently, interviewers are normally instructed to probe the DK response with some such phrase as *Just your own opinion* or *Of course, nobody really knows, but how do you feel about it?* Assuming that the researcher has built into the questionnaire the proper measures of the structure of the opinion, this procedure enables one to sort the sample into approve–disapprove or agree–disagree and then to analyze the two groups in terms of their respective knowledge of the issue, its salience to them, their interest in it, and the other dimensions that we have noted.

Too often, however, such protective analytical measures are not included, with the result that uninformed or uninterested respondents are forced into stating an opinion that they never thought of before and may never think of again. Although poll results rarely report more than 10 or 15% answering DK on opinion issues, the "true" DK proportion might be as high as 80% on some items if respondents were permitted or encouraged to say, *I have no idea about that.* Consequently, questionnaire writers are perfectly free to break with common practice and ask, *Do you approve or disapprove, or haven't you thought enough about it to say?*—provided that in their judgment such a wording will better serve the research objectives.

In general, questionnaire writers will do well to avoid using such answer categories as "depends" or "other" when asking closed questions. Almost any opinion depends on something, is contingent upon certain circumstances, and some people are more conscious of this than others. To accept a reply of *It depends* means that certain respondents have avoided the implicit or explicit premises of the question, which are often stated by the interviewer in the form of probes: *Well, in general, what would you say?* or *All things considered.* If respondents continue to maintain that *It all depends,* they should then be coded as DK on the grounds that they cannot decide among the stated options.

Questions that encourage or permit the respondent to give an "other" answer are subject to the same argument. If the question is a good one, there should be no legitimate "other" answer; only one issue should be addressed and the stated alternatives should be all-inclusive and mutually exclusive. Any response of *other,* therefore, must either be irrelevant (outside the terms of the question) or comprise some qualification attached to one of the stated alternatives. If the response is outside the terms of the question, the interviewer should ask it again or use an appropriate probe. If it is a qualified response, it should be handled the same way as *Depends: In general, all things considered.*

It should also be noted that "depends" and "other" answers simply confound the analysis if they are accepted as legitimate responses. One cannot tell whether they are from respondents who would have expressed positive or negative opinions had they been properly probed, or whether they are truly DKs. In consequence, they either have to be discarded from the analysis entirely or lumped with the DK group as a residual category.

Questions that ask for numerical data (*How many children have you ever had? How far do you travel to work? What is your annual family income before taxes?*) are usually asked in open form, but response categories may be either precoded or written in by the interviewer. If researchers have no idea what kind of distribution to expect or if they are interested in calculating means or other statistical properties of the distribution, they can instruct the interviewer to write in the number as given and then keypunch it directly. On the other hand, if one wishes only to classify respondents into predetermined groups, one can precode these groups on the questionnaire and ask the interviewer to code one of them. Thus, one might provide 10 income levels ranging from $2000 or less to $50,000 or more, or 6 distance-from-job groups ranging from less than 1 mile to 40 miles or more.

Some Principles of Question Writing

Again, because questions should be written to produce the most complete and valid information from each respondent, and because their wording and content will be affected by both the mode of administration of the questionnaire and the type of sample questioned, there can be no all-purpose rules that, if duly followed, will automatically result in a well-written questionnaire. The following paragraphs can only suggest a few basic principles that, when violated, usually (but not always) result in respondent confusion, misunderstanding, lack of comprehension, or response bias.

A first rule pertains to the sort of words, the vocabulary, one uses in writing survey questions; and the rule is: Keep it simple. Journalists are taught this same rule, but close attention to any daily newspaper or news telecast will provide many examples of words and phrases that are probably understandable to most people, but that would cause a great deal of confusion if used in a survey of the general population.[2] Since questionnaires are usually written by educated people who consult with other educated people, it is only natural for researchers to assume that words and concepts familiar to them are familiar to everyone else. But this is far from the case. Even among educated people, there will be many who have no particular knowledge of the subject being investigated and, among the less advantaged such as welfare clients, minority groups or those with limited English, the use of long words, technical words, or complex phrases can defeat the entire purpose of the survey.

This is true because a question that is asked in a difficult or complex manner will produce many DK or "no opinion" responses from people who could readily have expressed their opinion if the question had been put to them more simply and clearly. Perhaps even more important, those who do not understand the question will nevertheless come up with an answer because the researcher has obligingly provided them with answer categories. It is only human to attempt to conceal ignorance and confused respondents are much more likely to answer "approve" or "disapprove" than they are to confess that they do not understand what the question is about. It is true, of course, that complex notions cannot easily be stated in words of one syllable, but with appropriate thought, effort, and pretesting, it is always possible to simplify the language that first comes to mind. Payne, in the book previously cited, has an instructive last chapter in which he provides an example of how one can take a difficult question that most people have never considered before and turn it into something understandable to all. But it takes him 41 consecutive revisions of the original question to achieve a wording that he thinks will be workable for his final pretest.

Closely related to keeping the vocabulary simple is avoiding lengthy questions. Payne thinks that good questions can be held to 25 words or less and he presents some empirical evidence that short questions produce better data than long ones. (See also Chapter 8.) One need not insist on a particular number of words, but certainly the fewer the better. Although we may be accustomed to reading lengthy sentences and paragraphs, this is quite different from listening to them. Ordinary conversation consists mostly of short exchanges and few of us enjoy listening to lengthy presentations. Our memories and spans of attention are limited. In listening to something we may not have much interest in, our minds are likely to wander, we hear certain words and not others, we remember some parts of what is said but not all.

The following question, for example, was asked of a national sample by a well-known survey organization:

> *In Spain, Italy and France, the communist parties in those countries now say they are independent of Moscow and other communist countries. They have*

---

[2] Examples include *decontrol of natural-gas prices, nuclear technology, moratorium on debt, discriminatory intent, sub-Cabinet posts, buffer zone.*

even been critical of the Russians on violating human rights. Some people think this is a major change in the outlook of communist parties in Europe and a major split in the communist world. Others are still suspicious that the communists are all the same and are only talking about differences with Russia to get votes for themselves in European countries, so they can attain power. Do you feel communists in Europe are really different now from other communists or do you think there is no real difference between communists of any country?

This is an exaggerated but very real example of the *Some people say. . . . Other people say. . . . What do you think?* school of question writing, and it has quite obvious dangers. One might first question the patience and ability of each of 100 interviewers or more to read the entire question, word for word, in a manner that will hold the respondent's interest. Even given unusually skilled and sensitive interviewers, a great many respondents must tune out after a sentence or two and catch only a few key words here and there. If the respondent does misinterpret, misunderstand, or fail to attend to the question's wording, the researcher will never know, because the respondent will probably answer in terms of one or the other category provided. The seemingly even-handed summary of opposing arguments may still be unknowingly loaded in one direction or the other, additional arguments are not stated, and some respondents will even disagree with the premises of the question. Finally, the opinions expressed by the persons exposed to this particular presentation of the issue will probably not reflect the opinions of the general public who have not been asked to face the question in just this way. It would seem far better to try to craft a simpler question to get at the issue, and to supplement this with measures of knowledge, strength of opinion or interest in the matter, or to ask a series of briefer questions on various aspects of the issue.

In wording questions, it is almost always important to specify alternatives, rather than to present one side of an issue and ask respondents for their reactions. This is because people tend to agree with any plausible proposition unless the alternatives are presented to them or they have very firm opinions. For example, *Do you think the President is doing a good job of handling foreign policy?* will elicit more approval than the question that asks for a rating in terms of excellent–good–fair–poor. Similarly, *It has been suggested that. . . . Does this seem like a good idea to you?* (Yes or No), will draw more approval than the more even-handed *Does this seem like a good idea or a bad idea?* It is important to make the respondent aware that any position is acceptable and that the interviewer is not just seeking agreement to propositions handed down by the researcher.[3]

---

[3] This paragraph may seem inconsistent with earlier remarks about the virtues of agree–disagree questions. The inconsistency will be resolved if it is understood that the usual purpose of agree–disagree items is to place the respondent at some point on a scale based on those items. The famous *Prison is too good for sex criminals; they should be publicly whipped or worse* is a useful component of the F-scale of Authoritarianism, but one would not recommend it as the best measure of attitudes toward the treatment of sex criminals.

In a sense, specifying only one alternative is a form of loaded question, since it suggests a particular response and puts the burden on the respondent to disagree. But even when alternatives are specified, it is easy to load one alternative. A not uncommon form of loading is to present an argument for one side of the question but not for the other; for example, *Would you approve of spending more for defense in order to keep up with Russia, or would you disapprove? Would you favor hiring more policemen to cut down on crime in the streets, or would you oppose hiring more policemen?* Another common loading effect occurs when one alternative is associated with some symbol that is generally respected (or scorned): *The President has urged all Americans. . . . Do you approve or disapprove? Many experts believe . . . but other people disagree. What is your opinion?*

Although we are all familiar with loaded questions designed to show that the public supports a particular political candidate or cause or commercial product, the reputable research professional will make every effort to avoid influencing respondents and to allow for the equal expression of all points of view. This is not always easy, however, since all of us operate on the basis of unconscious assumptions and biases that we may share with our acquaintances but which are quite unacceptable to other segments of the public. One way of overcoming such a blindness is to discuss your questionnaire and the wording of the individual items with a "devil's advocate"—someone known to have radical or extreme opposing views on the issue. Thus, if a white racist and a black militant, or a male chauvinist and a radical feminist, both agree that your questions are fair, you can proceed with some assurance.

Like most rules of question wording, however, the injunction to avoid loaded questions should sometimes be disregarded. Respondents sometimes feel threatened by a question because they think that their opinions or behavior may mark them as deviant or inferior. In such a case, to load the question will often produce a more truthful answer. Kinsey, in his pioneering sex studies, was one of the first to employ this technique. When he started asking respondents about their masturbatory behavior, he found that few would even admit to the practice, so he changed his opening question in this area to *How old were you the first time you masturbated?* The question is loaded because it assumes respondents have had the experience and places the burden on them to deny it, but Kinsey found that hardly anyone denied it and most people were able to answer quite easily. By asking the question in that manner, the researcher indirectly informed respondents that the experience was a common one and they need feel no shame in answering truthfully. This technique is still used today in such questions as, *Many people were not able to get all the education they would have liked. What was the last grade you completed in school?* This deliberately loaded wording helps dissuade respondents from exaggerating the amount of their education by making it easier for them to admit that they left school at an early age.

Similarly, depending upon the survey's purposes, the researcher can deliberately (and legitimately) load the wording of the alternatives presented in the question. Because people are often reluctant to criticize the medical care they receive, it was suggested earlier that instead of asking if people were satisfied or dissatisfied with medical care, it would probably be better to ask if they were very satisfied, fairly satisfied, not satisfied. If one were interested in picking up all of the dissatisfaction that may exist, one could load the alternatives even further: *Are you **entirely** satisfied with the medical care you receive, or are there some things you're not entirely satisfied with?* This version will produce a biased estimate of overall satisfaction but will do a better job than the unloaded question in providing examples of dissatisfaction.

Some Common Errors in Question Writing

DOUBLE-BARRELED QUESTIONS

These are single questions that ask for opinions about two different things. If respondents like one thing but not the other, they are unable to answer. For example: *How satisfied are you with your wages and hours at the place where you work?* If the respondents are satisfied with their hours but not with their wages, they cannot reply in terms of very satisfied–fairly satisfied–not at all. The researcher should ask two questions, not one.

THE FALSE PREMISE

In order to build the B-1 bomber, should the government raise taxes or cut back on other expenses? If respondents do not want the government to build the B-1 bomber, they cannot answer.

VAGUE, AMBIGUOUS WORDS

If a space is set aside for "income" on a self-administered questionnaire or if respondents are asked *What is your income?* answers will come in all sorts of terms: hourly pay, weekly salary, monthly or annual earnings (sometimes before taxes, sometimes in take-home pay), respondent's own earnings, family income, sometimes including nonsalary income and sometimes not. Income is a complex subject and to get it fully and exactly requires a large number of questions. But even if researchers just want to classify respondents into broad income groups, they must still specify what they mean: for example, total family income, before taxes, during the last year, including income from all sources.

One can cite many examples of questions that fail to specify the terms within which the respondent is to answer: for example, *Do you read a Sunday newspaper?* or *Do you attend the opera?* Does this mean have respondents ever done it, do they do it regularly, have they done it within the last year, or what? Researchers should specify what they mean: *Do you do it regularly, occasionally, or never?* or *How many times have you done it within the last month or year?* The question, *How long have you lived here?* is subject to similar difficulties. Does the researcher mean at this address, in this neighborhood, in this city, state, region, or what?

The best way to detect and improve vague, ambiguous words is through pretesting, because at least one respondent is likely to ask, *What do you mean?*

OVERLAPPING ALTERNATIVES

One cardinal rule for question writing is to make the alternatives mutually exclusive. Even though the respondent may have trouble choosing between them, it should not be possible to agree with more than one. Examples of overlapping alternatives: *Are you generally satisfied with your job, or are there some things about it you don't like? Do you usually take the bus to work, or do you sometimes drive your car?* These questions need "tightening," so that respondents cannot truthfully answer *Yes* or *No* to both alternatives.

DOUBLE NEGATIVES

A regularly published national survey asked: *All in all, would you favor or oppose Congress passing a law not allowing any employer to force an employee to retire at any age?* Forty-nine percent voted in favor, 39% were opposed, and 12% were not sure, but it is not at all clear that all respondents were voting on the same thing. Any question that asks respondents whether they approve or disapprove of prohibiting something or not doing something is a potential source of confusion. Respondents often answer, *No* or *I don't think so* with the intent of their response quite ambiguous. Common examples are found on batteries of agree–disagree items. Because there is a tendency to agree more often than to disagree, researchers are usually careful not to point all their statements in the same direction, but to phrase half the items so that a favorable attitude must be expressed by disagreement. This often means that the respondent's answer must say, "I *disagree* that the statement is false"—an awkward statement and a potential source of considerable error.

INTENTIONS TO ACT

Early market researchers quickly learned that simplistic questions such as *Would you buy this product if it were available?* were useless for the prediction of purchase behavior. It will be noted that the Gallup Poll does not ask people to predict their behavior on election day, but rather asks, *If the election were held today, would you probably vote for Candidate A or Candidate B?* Yet we still find many survey questions that ask, *Would you be willing to pay X number of dollars for this form of health insurance?* or *Suppose a new movie theater opened in this neighborhood. About how often would you attend?* Such questions may be of interest and even of possible use in the researcher's analysis, but they are generally worthless as predictors of sales of insurance policies or movie tickets.

People are generally poor predictors of their own behavior because of changing circumstances and because so many situational variables intervene. Researchers are much better off if they attempt to get a valid picture of respondents' *past* behavior and their *present* circumstances, attitudes, needs, and values. The researcher is then in a position to make wiser forecasts of group or mass behavior than individuals are to predict their own behavior.

Demographic Questions

Every survey will contain some background items about the respondent's personal characteristics. Certain items such as age, sex, race, occupation, and education are asked almost automatically. Others such as political preference, religion, ethnicity, military service, labor union affiliation, ages of children, and the like, are asked as the needs of the survey dictate. In a personal interview, sex and race are usually recorded by observation rather than asking the respondent. Age is asked in terms of date and year of birth or age at last birthday.

Occupation is more complicated and, depending upon the amount of detail required, can evolve into a page or two of questions. The mere fact of employment is sometimes ambiguous because of seasonal work, part-time work, layoffs, strikes, and illness. People sometimes hold two or more jobs. They tend to exaggerate their job titles and to describe their duties in vague terms. If exact information is required, it is better to ask two questions, each with a probe: *What is your occupation? (What is your job title? What do you do on the job?)* and *What kind of business or industry is that? (What do they do or make?)* Interviewers must be trained to obtain clear answers to these questions. Occupation and industry can then be coded into U.S. Census categories.

If only a crude measure of occupational status is needed, respondents can be shown a card showing the nine major Census categories, with suitable examples of each, and asked to code themselves; or interviewers can ask the respondent's occupation and then code it themselves. In the latter case, interviewers will require a large amount of training in the distinctions among the categories, and, in either case, there will be little or no check on the accuracy of the coding.

The main difficulty with classifying respondents according to education is the propensity of respondents to exaggerate the amount of schooling they obtained. There are often problems, too, in disentangling informal education, such as adult or vocational courses that are not for academic credit.

Making Use of Census and Other Surveys

In drafting demographic questions, researchers will be wise to make their definitions, question wordings, and answer categories the same as those employed by the Census. Not only will they be interested in checking the characteristics of their own samples with those shown by the Census, but the findings will be easier to interpret and to communicate to others if they use standard definitions of such concepts as *employment* or *dwelling unit* rather than idiosyncratic definitions. The Census, for example, usually breaks down age by decade at 25–34, 35–44, and so forth. Researchers who have coded their age groups at 21–29 or 26–35 will be hard put to make accurate comparisons.

The same point applies to other types of questions and other survey sources. If a question similar to one the researcher is trying to write has been usefully employed on some other survey in the past, there is usually an advantage in using it. Not only does it save effort, but it permits comparison with another body of data. Gallup, Roper, Harris, NORC, Michigan are all sources of national survey data and a review of the literature will usually inform researchers of other more specialized surveys from which they may be able to draw relevant items.

It is true that old questions are often deficient in their wording or are no longer suitable because of changing times. Obviously, there is no use repeating an irrelevant question or one that did not work before. But even though an old question may be something less than perfect, it may still pay to use it as is, rather than to tinker with it and destroy comparability. One can always ask an additional question or two to clarify or supplement the old one, and one should realize that any brand new question is quite likely to have its own defects.

6.8. QUESTION ORDER AND FORMAT

After deciding on the content of the questionnaire—the variables to be measured—and after drafting specific items designed to elicit that content, the researcher's next task is to group these questions into some reasonable order and put them into questionnaire format. Implicit in the task of ordering the questions is the preparation of some sort of standardized survey introduction to be given the respondent. Although the introduction is usually printed on the questionnaire, it may not appear there at all. The introduction may be in the form of an advance letter addressed to the prospective respondent, or a telephone call explaining the purpose of the survey and requesting an appointment for an interview.

Whatever its mode, the introduction is crucial. If the survey task sounds overly demanding, if its purpose seems trivial or threatening, or if respondents suspect the survey to be only some kind of cover-up for a subsequent sales attempt, they will probably refuse to participate. Once individuals refuse the interview, the odds are heavily against converting them to cooperation. If the introduction prepared by the researcher leads 30 or 40% of the respondents to refuse, it is a bad survey, no matter how well designed the questionnaire is. How to approach respondents and persuade them to be interviewed is properly a part of interviewer training and has no place here, but since a standardized questionnaire must have a standardized introduction, what the researcher asks interviewers to say in that introduction impinges upon questionnaire design.

Fortunately, the words *I'm doing a survey* still retain their magic for most people. Almost everyone understands the interviewer's intention—to ask them some questions—and most people will be pleased to participate. They will, however, have certain reservations and a standardized introduction should usually reveal two more important facts: (*a*) who the survey is for; and (*b*) what it is about. This information should be given as briefly as possible. Long explanations usually tell respondents more than they want to know, and provide them with an opportunity to ask questions and to think of objections. Most people are anxious to know what the first question is, and the researcher is well advised to get to it as soon as possible. Once respondents answer the first question, they are usually committed and will seldom break off the interview.

In terms of who is doing the survey, it is always preferable to answer truthfully: *I'm a graduate student and doing this survey for my dissertation, I'm with* (name of the research agency). *We do many surveys all over the country,* or *The Department of Transportation is interested in people's opinions on a number of things.* Sometimes, however, the name of the sponsor will bias responses or encourage refusals. It would obviously be poor research practice, for example, to say, *I'm making a survey for Crest toothpaste. What kind of toothpaste do you use?* Naming a magazine or a life insurance company as a survey sponsor may suggest to the respondent some kind of sales attempt.

Again, on the subject of the survey, it is best to be honest with the respondent unless this would bias answers or encourage refusals. One would not describe the survey as being about local transportation and then ask, *What do you think are the biggest problems in this neighborhood?* because one has already suggested transportation as a problem and answers to the question will clearly be influenced. One would probably not explain that the questions are "about rape" because many people would find this topic upsetting or unpleasant, or that they are about "nuclear energy" because few people feel qualified to be interviewed on that subject. Usually, it is best to describe the purpose and content of the survey in general terms: *It's about community problems* or *current issues,* or *family life.* And then say, *The first question is. . . .*

In general, the introduction should not include any additional information beyond the survey's general purpose and content. In most cases, it is not necessary to explain how long the interview will take, that answers are confidential, that the results will be published or will serve various needs. Interviewers, of course, should be provided with answers to such common questions as *How long will it take?* and *How did you pick me?* but there is no need to volunteer such information if the respondent does not request it.[4]

Ordering the Questions

Most of the rules for questionnaire design and question writing can be freely disregarded from time to time if the researcher can justify the exception, but there is one general rule for the ordering of questions that routinely applies to every survey: Make the opening question an easy, nonthreatening one. The first question is crucial because it is the respondent's first exposure to the interview and sets the tone for the nature of the task to be performed. If respondents find the first question difficult to understand, or beyond their knowledge and experience, or embarrassing or threatening in some way, they are likely to break off immediately. If, on the other hand, they find the opening

---

[4] But note that many federal agencies now require survey contractors to read respondents a preliminary statement explaining that they are not compelled to answer and that the content of their answers will not be made available to any third party except as required by law.

question easy and pleasant to answer, they are encouraged to continue. Researchers sometimes use throwaway questions as openers, simply to warm up respondents and accustom them to their role before proceeding to the more difficult or sensitive items.

The corollary to the preceding rule, of course, is to approach the difficult or sensitive questions only when the respondent is well into the interview. It is possible to obtain accurate answers from respondents about such subjects as alcohol consumption, illegal drug usage, gun ownership and sexual behavior, but only after the interviewer has had time to build up confidence and trust. If such questions are asked early on, the respondent is likely to become suspicious or defensive, thus risking either a breakoff or a false or evasive response. It is for these reasons that demographic items such as age, income, occupation, and education are usually placed at the end of the interview. Some respondents feel these matters are personal; others may feel defensive or apologetic about them.

In general, the questions should flow in some kind of psychological order, so that one question leads easily and naturally into the next. Questions on one subject, or one particular area of a subject, should be grouped together and asked consecutively before proceeding to the next subject or the next area. Respondents may find it disconcerting to keep shifting from one topic to another or to be asked to return to some subject they thought they gave their opinions about earlier. If the questionnaire is concerned with some aspect of the respondent's behavior over time—occupational history, or episodes of family illness during the past 6 months—one naturally proceeds chronologically. One can either start with the most recent job or episode and work back, or one can start with the beginning of the time period (*when you left high school* or *starting last January*) and work up to the present.

When the questionnaire does include a number of different topics, it is helpful to prepare the respondent for a shift in attention by saying something like, *Now I have some different questions* or *Now some questions about the neighborhood you live in,* or whatever. Respondents normally enjoy a change of pace or a different kind of task in the course of an interview. They quickly become bored and restless when asked, for instance, the same group of 12 questions about each of 5 different things, or when they are asked a long consecutive battery of items all in the same format, such as "agree or disagree." It usually improves response, therefore, to vary the respondent's task from time to time. An open-ended question here and there, even if it is not coded and tabulated, may provide much-needed relief from a long series of questions in which respondents have been forced to limit their replies to precoded categories. A question in which respondents are handed a card to look at or are asked to perform some small task like sorting cards or marking positions on a scale helps to vary the pace and provide diversion from the long litany of precoded responses.

Ordinarily, one starts with a broad question about a topic or issue and then asks more specific questions. For example, *What are some of the things you like about this neighborhood? What are some of the things you don't like so much?* then, *How would you rate each of the following services in this neighborhood?—transportation, safety, schools, job opportunities, amusements,* and the like, and finally the most specific questions: *Would you approve or disapprove of adding an express bus service, putting more police on the streets?* and so forth. There are two reasons for this general rule. If one asks the specific questions first, the attention given to them will probably influence opinions on the general questions asked later; and it is felt that respondents can usually give more thoughtful answers to the specific questions when they have been given an opportunity to consider them in broader context.

Sometimes, however, opposite considerations prevail and researchers may follow the reverse procedure. Thus, one might ask a battery of questions about particular aspects of the neighborhood and then ask, *All in all, how would you rate this as a place to live?* This procedure is particularly appropriate if the issue is a complex one or one that the respondent has not thought about much. For example, instead of asking respondents to choose among six different plans for a national health insurance program, it is probably better to start with more specific questions about various aspects of the problem of financing health care. This gives them more time to organize their thoughts and more background on which to base their replies when they are later asked to make overall choices among the six different plans.

Length of the Questionnaire

Aside from the abundance of data that a long questionnaire can provide and the expanded opportunities for analysis and understanding of the respondent's opinions and behavior, one can make two other arguments in its favor. First, a large part of any survey's efforts and cost are devoted to finding the designated respondents, making contact with them, and persuading them to agree to the interview. On the most difficult cases, as much as 10 hours of tracing the respondent, interviewer travel on repeated callbacks, and attempts to convert a refusal may be expended in an effort to obtain a 30-min interview. It follows that, once the interview is begun, an extra 5 or 10 min of questioning, in the course of which one might cover another 20 items, is not likely by itself to break the budget.

It is also true that the preparation of respondents for the interview and its psychological length for them are much more important than the actual number of minutes it requires, in determining the respondent's cooperation. Thus, a 20-min interview can seem insufferable if the content of the questionnaire is difficult or boring or makes the respondent feel uneasy. On the other hand, a 2-hour interview may be quite a pleasurable experience if respondents perceive the survey to be of value, recognize their own importance to it, and have been prepared for the length of time it actually requires.

On the other hand, long questionnaires have many disadvantages. Aside from the additional interviewer time they require, they have the effect of raising costs at every stage of the survey process: They consume more paper and supplies, more typing time, more time spent writing instructions and training interviewers, more supervisor time, more editing time, more coding, more data processing, and more computer time. Also, long interviews are more likely to be interrupted by other demands on the respondent's time. This will result either in a breakoff, hurried answers given without consideration, or a return trip by the interviewer to finish the job—all of which are undesirable. Finally, if an interview takes 2 hours, the interviewer can probably complete only one per evening instead of two or three shorter ones, thus increasing travel time and mileage.

In general, it may be said that most questionnaires are too long, rather than too short, in that many of the items are found to contribute little or nothing to the analysis. To a certain extent, this is inevitable, since the researcher never knows in advance how it will all come out. Certain items with seemingly high potential may turn out to be useless, others may unexpectedly suggest important findings. At the end of every survey, the researcher is prepared to write a better questionnaire than the one sent into the field, but of course by then it is too late. But this common result simply emphasizes the importance of taking the necessary time in the first place to think through the exact information required, to write the most efficient questions to elicit those data, and to try out the questionnaire through pretesting. The researcher must be prepared to justify every item in the instrument by some explicit statement of its purpose. One must resist the temptation to add items just because they might be "interesting."

Questionnaire Format

Most companies that employ their own interviewers to work on several different surveys a year have developed their own conventions of questionnaire format and try to follow those consistently from one survey to another. This is desirable in that interviewers, once having learned to follow the conventions, can record responses more accurately and quickly, and coders, keypunchers, or other personnel who prepare the questionnaires for data entry can also proceed more efficiently. The conventions themselves may differ widely. Some companies or research institutes print the wording of the questions in capital letters; some print the answer categories in boldface; some place answer categories to the left, others to the right; some ask interviewers to check boxes, others prefer them to circle code numbers; some use printed arrows or different colors to emphasize skip directions; and so on.

Any of these conventions is acceptable, depending on the researcher's own preference, that of the interviewers and data-processing people, and the budget. Boldface type and printing in two or more colors are more expensive, for example, and underlining can serve the same purposes. Interviewers, coders, and keypunchers generally seem to prefer each answer category to appear on a separate line with the response codes or boxes on the right. The majority of agencies seem to use capital letters only for instructions to the interviewer: for example, ASK ONLY IF CURRENTLY MARRIED.

Most single precoded questions will have the answer categories and codes placed vertically, as in example 6.1 here:

Example 6.1

During the next 6 months, do you expect that the prices of most things you buy will go up, go down, or stay about the same?

Go up 1
Go down..................... 2
Stay about the same 3
Don't know 4

But when one asks a series of items that employ the same answer categories, a horizontal format, in which the answer categories are listed side by side, will save a great deal of space (example 6.2):

Example 6.2

I'm going to read you a list of statements and you tell me for each one of them whether you agree with it or disagree. The first statement is . . .

	Agree	Disagree	Don't know
Statement A	1	2	3
Statement B	1	2	3

For verbatim responses to open questions, it is recommended that one leave white space below the questions rather than providing lines for the interviewer or respondent to write in. Since people's handwriting varies considerably in size, the open space provides more flexibility. The amount of space provided will naturally vary with the length of the expected response. If a brief categorical answer is all that is required, a line or two of space is sufficient. If multiple answers are solicited, or the responses will probably need some probing on the part of the interviewer, more space should be allotted. One should be aware that the amount of material recorded tends to expand with the amount of space provided; thus, in order to discourage abbreviation, paraphrasing, and a natural inclination of the interviewer to accept the first response given, it is better to leave too much space than not enough.

Although it might seem that one could save money and also influence respondents to believe that their task will be a brief one through the use of a short questionnaire in crowded format, such a procedure is usually shortsighted. A cluttered format makes the interviewer's task more difficult and generally leads to more interviewer error, whereas the effect on respondents may be quite unexpected. If they have already spent 10 min on the interview and note the interviewer just turning to Page 2 of what looks like an eight-page questionnaire, they are likely to become very restless. On the other hand, if the questionnaire contains ample white space and each item is properly set off by itself with its own instructions and answer categories, the interviewer will make fewer mistakes and respondents will feel they are making progress as the interviewer flips from one page to another every few minutes.

Items which are to be asked of only a subgroup of respondents should be grouped together if possible and disposed of in a single section of the questionnaire, rather than interspersed throughout the instrument. Thus: ASK Qs. 24–30 ONLY IF CURRENTLY MARRIED. ALL OTHERS SKIP TO Q. 31. The line of questioning will often depend upon the respondent's reply to an earlier question. For example, if respondents have never heard of a subject, one will probably not want to ask them a battery of follow-up questions about it; if they have just moved into a neighborhood, one would not ask them to compare conditions there now with the way they were 5 years ago. Such cases are easily handled by instructions such as: IF NO, SKIP TO Q. 25; IF YES, ASK A–B–C.

To be avoided if possible are more complicated skips within skips, and especially skip directions that require the interviewer to refer to other pages of the questionnaire. An example of the latter would be: ASK Q. 49 ONLY IF RESPONDENT CURRENTLY EMPLOYED FULL-TIME (Q. 34) AND ALSO MARRIED WITH CHILDREN (Qs. 19 & 23). Such a direction slows up the interview while interviewers find the proper references and may lead to error if interviewers instead rely on their own memories of what respondents previously said. If the problem cannot be solved by other means, it is useful to have interviewers, when they ask Qs. 19, 23, and 34, flip ahead to Q. 49 and again enter the response into space provided there. This will unerringly guide their procedure when they come to the question.

Unless the questionnaire consists of only one or two pages, a booklet format is recommended, with questions printed on both sides of the page, rather than a group of pages stapled in the upper left corner. Care must be taken to reserve ample margin on both sides of each page. It is shortsighted to attempt to save money by accepting an inferior job of duplication. Smudgy or lightly printed type, lopsided margins, typographical errors, or a poor quality of photocopying can result in errors far more costly than the small amount of money saved.

6.9. PRETESTING

The fourth stage of questionnaire design, it will be recalled—following specification of the information required, the construction of question items to obtain that information, and the ordering and formatting of the items into a draft of the instrument—is to try out the questionnaire on a pretest sample.

It is recommended that researchers themselves conduct two or more pretest interviews, and not with their colleagues or family, but with strangers in their homes. The reason for this precept is that one of the best ways to learn how to write a good questionnaire is to try to interview with a poor one. When respondents just sit there dumbly saying *Don't know,* or when they keep asking *What do you mean?* or when they are asked to rate 16 different things on a 6-point scale and say *Just put me down for fair on all of them,* or when one stumbles awkwardly through a clumsily worded question—when such things occur, the principles of good questionnaire design become very real.

Pretests can range anywhere from half a dozen interviews done locally to pilot studies of 100 cases or more conducted in several different localities and then tabulated to see how various items behave statistically. It usually takes no more than 12–25 cases to reveal the major difficulties and weaknesses in a pretest questionnaire. It is usually wise to assign three or more different interviewers to a pretest, to gain the benefit of a variety of interviewer reactions; and each interviewer should do at least three interviews in order to become accustomed to the questionnaire.

Although pretest samples need not be drawn with probability, they should be more than "convenience" samples. Using respondents drawn from around the office or from acquaintances is not very helpful and can be misleading. They know you, and this knowledge will affect their behavior and their responses. They are also likely to be people much like yourself in many ways. Respondents who are interviewed on pretests should be strangers who are interviewed under field conditions, usually in their homes.

One should also attempt to obtain a reasonably representative sample of pretest interviews. Thus, if one is surveying the general public, it would not be wise to pretest only in white middle-class neighborhoods. It is usually advisable to set quotas for the pretest and this can be made a part of the pretesters' assignments. Thus, each might be instructed to get half men and half women, and then assigned to particular blocks or neighborhoods, for example, a black neighborhood, a working-class area, a suburban community. Since men under 30 years of age and working women are often missed in pretest interviewing, interviewers might be instructed to be sure to include at least one person with one of these characteristics.

An essential part of any pretest is the debriefing of the interviewers after they have completed their task. If the pretest has been done locally, bring them together for a morning or afternoon or for a full day. The interaction within the group and their joint reporting is usually far more instructive than what can be learned from talking to them one by one. If the interviewers are widely scattered and unable to come to the office for debriefing, they should be personally debriefed by telephone. Written report forms that simply ask them to describe any problems or recommendations they have are generally less satisfactory. Debriefings usually start with general comments on the length of the interview and any problems gaining respondents' consent or holding their interest, and then proceed to an item-by-item review of the instrument. Obviously, researchers will also want to read the pretest interviews and tabulate the response frequencies to get an idea of the marginal distributions they may expect and the number of vague or DK answers.

Since an important consideration in most pretests is the length of the questionnaire, it is important to provide places for interviewers to record the time at the beginning and end of the interview and to tabulate this information. It may also be desirable to spot similar time boxes at various places within the questionnaire, to gain knowledge of the average number of minutes spent on particular sections of the instrument. It is perfectly permissible to pretest a questionnaire that is clearly too long, for the purpose of trying out a variety of items and then deleting those that are not productive or that respondents have trouble answering. But if the interview has been budgeted for 30 minutes' duration and the median time required on the pretest interviews is 40 minutes, substantial cuts clearly must be made. Though it may be tempting to believe that other interviewers will be more efficient or that the first three or four interviews always take longer than later ones, the researcher must be strongly advised not to rely on such hopes. As often as not, the actual interviews will turn out to take even more time than those obtained in the pretest, and the odds are heavy that the time will not be significantly shorter.

6.10. BACK TO THE DRAWING BOARD

After the pretest the researcher can return to Stage 1 of the questionnaire-design process and think through again the kind of information necessary to answer the problem that the survey is intended to illuminate. Sometimes it is clear after just 10 or 12 interviews that certain content areas that were originally considered to be important are quite irrelevant to respondents and hardly worth pursuing. Other areas to which only a question or two had been allotted in the first draft may now seem deserving of more extended questioning. A reading of the interviews or the remarks of particular respondents may suggest entirely new variables that had previously been overlooked.

The researcher can then look at the wording, order, and format of the questions used on the pretest. Is each item producing the kind of information needed? What role will the item play in the proposed analysis? Is the question meaningful to respondents? Are they able to understand it? Can they answer it in the terms in which it is asked? Did the pretest interviewers feel they were getting valid and reliable information? Newly invented questions are almost always open to improvement by rewording them slightly to make them clearer, simpler, more readily understandable. Was the order of the questions logical, so that the interview flowed smoothly and the respondent's train of thought was not interrupted? Did some parts of the questionnaire arouse suspicion; did other parts seem repetitious or boring? Were interviewers able to read the questions naturally without stumbling over the words? Were they able to follow the skip instructions and other directions on the questionnaire without error? Timely consideration of matters of this kind will enable the researcher to sharpen and refine the instrument to make it ever more efficient in fulfilling its task.

If the survey is of a routine nature, similar to others that have been performed in the past, or if the questionnaire makes large use of questions that have been well tested on earlier studies, a few changes here and there may be sufficient to ready it for the field without further pretesting. But if the survey is breaking new ground and using many new questions or techniques invented solely for this purpose, a second pretest is strongly recommended. Indeed, some surveys have gone through four or five successive pretests, with each new draft representing an improvement over the old. A common error is to write entirely new questions, change the wording of many others, or assume that one has cut 10 min of interviewing time by making certain deletions—and then to send the revised version into the field without trying it out. Major changes must always be pretested to be sure they have the desired effect. Once the instrument has been placed in the hands of interviewers and the data collection gets under way, there is no opportunity to make revisions.

6.11. DATA-BASE CONSIDERATIONS

After several iterations of drafting and pretesting the instrument, the researcher will finally decide on the final form and contents of the questionnaire. At this point, it is essential that one give some attention to the management of the data base that the questionnaire will produce. A set of completed interview schedules is, after all, not the end-product of the survey; those completed schedules have to be coded, keypunched, and rendered into computer-analyzable form.

Processing the data into machine-readable format can be greatly facilitated through proper questionnaire design. Given identical contents, one format for the questionnaire may make the data difficult or tedious to code and keypunch, whereas a different format may make the coding and keypunching easy and straightforward. The ease with which completed questionnaires can be processed once they are returned to the office is therefore the last major criterion that determines the questionnaire design.

The most important data-base consideration of this type is that the questionnaire itself indicate just where in the data base the information from each question is to be located—in particular, which card (or card–image equivalent) of the data base, and which specific column on the card. Often, a survey will contain in the left or right margin next to each question a notation such as *3 : 21*. This means that the data from that specific question are to be coded into the twenty-first column of the third card. A questionnaire format in this fashion is called "precolumning" the instrument, and it is a major determinant of the ease with which the data can be processed once the interviews are completed. Precolumning has the further advantage that it makes the researcher think in advance about the structure and size of the data file being created. This information is useful when planning out the analysis or trying to budget computer costs.

In order to precolumn, one has to anticipate how many columns of the computer card each item will take up. One column is adequate for anything up to 9 response categories, but two columns are necessary when the number of responses is 10 to 99, and so on. The general rule is, err on the long side. It is much easier simply to leave an unneeded column blank than to try and squeeze in an additional necessary but unforeseen column. For example, some people have more than 9 children, so unless the researcher is willing to settle for "9 or more children" as an analytic category, two columns must be allowed for in recording the response. (Furthermore, since no one will have more than 99 children, two columns will be sufficient.)

In general, data-base management costs tend to be underestimated in preparing initial research budgets and so are a major source of cost overrun on the overall survey. Often, the data-base management costs are increased needlessly simply because the questionnaire was not designed with the ensuing management of the data base in mind. The final format of the questionnaire—its ultimate design, in other words—should therefore facilitate to the maximum extent possible the subsequent coding, keypunching, and processing of the information. For additional discussion of the role of questionnaire design in data-base management, see Chapter 12 by Anderson, Basilevsky, and Hum.

6.12. OTHER TYPES OF INSTRUMENTS AND MATERIALS

Much of the material in this chapter has been in the context of questionnaires designed for personal interviews, but with certain modifications the general principles apply equally to telephone interviews or self-administered questionnaires. One should note, however, that data collection instruments do not necessarily take the form of questionnaires. Sometimes they are report forms, record sheets, or rating forms that may not ask any specific questions but that provide categories for either the interviewer or the respondent to fill by entering a code, a number, or a written response. Examples might be: miles traveled, purpose of trip, expenses (parking, tolls, gasoline, etc.); or number of full-time employees, number of part-time employees, average hours worked last week. Even on personal interviews, there are usually other data collection instruments or aids besides the questionnaire. These might include showcards or other material that the respondent is asked to examine; various rating tasks to be performed by the interviewer, such as the respondent's attitude toward being interviewed or the condition of the home or neighborhood; household enumeration folders, call record sheets, and so on. All such forms and materials require the same careful design as the questionnaire: consideration of the kind of information needed, clarity and brevity in the wording of the various categories or items and in the instructions for their use, logical ordering of the items, an easy format to follow, and actual testing before they are put into final use.

6.13. SUMMARY

It should be clear that there are no simple, rigorous rules for questionnaire design and question writing. Each survey presents a new challenge. The reason is that each instrument is part of an overall research design, with its own type of sample, its own mode of data collection, its own research objectives, and its own time and budget constraints. If essentially the same survey is fielded several times a year, year after year, a collection of rules can gradually be compiled. But because the instrument is designed to serve the overall purpose of the survey, and not to control it, the infinite variety of survey purposes dictates that the rules must necessarily be flexible.

This chapter has summarized some of the general principles that normally apply and to indicate the kinds of decisions and choices that researchers must make when they write questionnaires. In the end, a good survey instrument is the product of hard intellectual effort over a sustained period, and of simple trial and error. Experience also helps, but no one of these can substitute for the others.

REFERENCES

Babbie, E. R.
  1973 *Survey Research Methods*. Belmont, Cal.: Wadsworth.
Bradburn. N. M., and W. Mason
  1964 "The effect of question order on responses." *Journal of Marketing Research* 1(November): 4.
Bradburn, N. M. *et al.*
  1979 *Improving Interview Method and Questionnaire Design*. San Francisco: Jossey–Bass.
Gallup, G. H.
  1947 *Public Opinion Quarterly* 11: 385–393.
Kahn, R. L., and C. F. Cannell
  1957 *The Dynamics of Interviewing*. New York: Wiley.
Oppenheim, A. N.
  1946 *Questionnaire Design and Attitude Measurement*. New York: Basic Books.
Payne, S. L.
  1951 *The Art of Asking Questions*. Princeton: Princeton University Press.
Sudman, S., and N. M. Bradburn
  1974 *Response Effects in Surveys*. Chicago: Aldine.

Chapter 7

Measurement: Theory and Techniques

Andy B. Anderson, Alexander Basilevsky, and
Derek P. J. Hum

7.1. INTRODUCTION

Measurement is one of the most important topics in social science and it receives a considerable amount of attention in our literature. Indeed, some would say we are preoccupied with measurement. One of the reasons for the preoccupation is that many of our concepts are subjective and illusive. This is not the case for all social variables, although even such seemingly straightforward notions as sex, income, and race prove troublesome as one gets closer to the task of measurement. Certainly, for many of the key concepts in social science, measurement is difficult: attitudes, opinions, beliefs, knowledge, fears, abilities, ambitions, perceptions, psychological traits, interests, preferences, and others. This chapter is concerned with the measurement of these more perplexing concepts, and in particular with attitudes, opinions, and related matters, though very little of what we say is necessarily restricted to that domain. The literature on these techniques frequently is labeled "attitude scaling." This is a bit of a misnomer; the general logic of these techniques is often applicable to a much wider range of social and psychological concepts.

By any reasonable standard, measurement has been and continues to be a principle concern in the social sciences and, in our view, the attention is warranted. Four types of issues are especially important. First, there are philosophical concerns, issues belonging to epistemology and the philosophy of science. What is the nature of measurement and what is its role in the scientific process? Second, classical measurement theory, coming mainly from the psychometric literature, has concentrated on reliability and validity. A third area, the theory of measurement, is a relatively recent field of endeavor aimed at developing formal models of measurement. This work has been centered in mathematical psychology. Fourth, social scientists have devoted a considerable amount of attention to specific techniques for constructing measurements, that is, methods for obtaining measurements of unobserved variables from responses to questions.

This is not the only reasonable division of the literature on measurement nor is it exhaustive, but it provides a convenient way to organize the chapter. First, we consider briefly in this introduction some of the issues in the first area, the nature of measurement and its role in science. The second area is the topic of Chapter 3 by George Bohrnstedt. The theory of measurement is discussed in our Section 7.2. Finally, we review scaling methods in Section 7.3 with particular attention to factor analysis.

Measurement has been defined in a variety of ways. For our purposes, the definition proposed by S. S. Stevens works well: "measurement is the assignment of numerals to objects or events according to rules [1951, p. 22]." Any rule, other than a randomization rule, will do. The nature of the rule is crucial because it determines what kinds of mathematical operations we can legitimately perform on the measurements.[1] At the lowest level, the rule may result in numbers that serve only as markers, symbols used to label mutually exclusive and exhaustive categories. At higher levels, the rule may produce numbers that can be treated as real numbers, real in the mathematical sense, on which we may perform all the mathematics appropriate to the reals. The various levels of measurement found in the social sciences are discussed further in Section 7.2. Regardless of level, measurement is crucial to science. To emphasize the role of measurement in science, and at the risk of oversimplification, one may say that science is, among other things, a search for relationships among variables. At its most primitive level, a relationship requires at least two variables each having at least two values. A simple 2 × 2 table illustrates. In a survey, respondents may be grouped by gender (male–female) and by virtue of agreement or disagreement to an attitude statement.

	Female	Male
Agree		
Disagree		

Response

FIGURE 7.1 A relationship requires at least two variables each having at least two values, as in this 2 × 2 table of survey responses.

Examination and perhaps statistical manipulation of the frequencies falling in the four cells will establish the relationship between the two variables. Of

[1] We are not here concerned to draw some of the distinctions traditionally made: intensive and extensive measurements, or fundamental and derived measurements. Nor are we drawing a distinction between the notions of numeral and number; Stevens used the two interchangeably (see Stevens, 1959, p. 19).

course, one need not be restricted to two levels; a variable may have many levels. The levels may be only categorical (e.g., types of psychosis) or they may have stronger properties like the quantitative scales used to measure intelligence or attitude toward members of a minority group. Nor are we restricted to two-variable relations; in fact, few bivariate relationships in social science prove to be interesting for more than a short period of time. But, regardless of the nature and number of the categories and regardless of the number of variables, we first must measure the variables.

There are groups within the social sciences who believe we cannot validly quantify and, indeed, that we cannot have a social science. It should be clear that we are not in accord with this position. More to the point, we are not here joining the debate. We state initially our assumption that we can study social and psychological phenomena scientifically and that to do so it is necessary to measure. One need not buy the extreme position of classical operationism, which argued that the *only* meaning of a concept is its operational definition; to appreciate that we have to measure in order to evaluate our hypothesized relationships, to verify or falsify them. Measurement is necessary. It is also useful. By turning abstract concepts into measurements, we have available a rich repertoire of mathematical techniques that introduces precision, economy of thought, and powerful tools of analysis. A simple thought experiment demonstrates the gains in precision and economy. Attempt to describe verbally the relationship represented by the simple curve $f(x) = e^x$. A lengthy, well-crafted paragraph begins to capture the nature of the relationship. The power of reasoning that comes from having mathematical machinery at our disposal is known to every school child. Even elementary logical problems are more easily solved by following the rules of set theory or formal logic. The complicated conceptual problem of finding the minimum path through a set of points is made tractable by the elementary concepts of graph theory. The problem of establishing functional relationships involving many variables probably cannot even be stated clearly, much less solved, without the tools of traditional mathematical analysis.

It would be an error, however, to leap straight from the recognition of the need to measure to a position that simply sets about generating numbers as if all procedures were equally acceptable. Measurement remains problematic in the social sciences. The existence of readily available computer programs for doing even the more complex types of scaling has made it possible to produce indices of this or that concept without ever giving a thought to the violence one may be doing to the concept. One occasionally gets the impression that the choice of a scaling model is largely a matter of convenience: program availability, time requirements, and the ease with which the program can be run. The brief against this practice comes from work in the theory of measurement. Measurement involves a theoretical domain, our area of substantive concern reflected as an empirical relational system, and a domain represented by a particular selected numerical relational system. Further, there is a mapping function that carries us from the empirical system into the numerical system. We manipulate the numerical system and observe results in order to better understand the empirical system. If the fit is good, that is, if we have an isomorphic or homomorphic mapping (as discussed in the next section) then, indeed, we gain insight into our substantive problem. But, if our map is bad, so will be our intellectual travel. By leaping immediately from the understanding of the importance of measurement to the techniques, we run the risk of misrepresenting the empirical domain. In short, our numbers do not reflect what we want them to reflect. How can this be avoided? The usual answer is that one needs sound theory and an understanding of the mathematics of the relevant sort.

Yet this position can also be overstated. The most straightforward argument against it is that this approach can be sterile. If we insist on having measurements *before* we do science and sound theory *before* we measure, then where are we to get the theory? If it can be found in vacuo and apart from scientific inquiry, then why do science? Of course, it cannot be. Part of the difficulty is that we often treat measurement as something logically and temporally prior to data analysis. First we measure. Then we use the resulting variables in mathematical models to test hypotheses. If confirmed, the hypotheses become relationships enmeshed in a growing web of theory. There is a sense in which this is correct but in a more important way, this view profoundly misstates the place of measurement in science. There is no measurement without theory. Theory precedes measurement or, more properly, every measurement implies theory. Coombs reminds us that "our conclusions, even at the level of measurement and scaling [which seems such a firm foundation for theory building], are already a consequence of theory. A measurement or scaling model is actually a theory about behavior, admittedly on a miniature level, but nevertheless theory; so while building theory about more complex behavior it behooves us not to neglect the foundations on which the more complex theory rests [1964, p. 5]." Probably most social scientists would accept the argument that all good measurement has a theoretical foundation.

We tend to think of the physical sciences as having no comparable problems. After all, as we are rhetorically reminded, how difficult can the measurement of temperature be, for example, compared with some of the subjective states we must address? In fact, the history of attempts to measure temperature indicates quite nicely the way in which measurement, theory, and observation go hand in hand and often do so in the best iterative fashion, with successive revision and improvement. A full review of the history is not useful here but, if one can accept a greatly oversimplified recounting, the point is worth consideration. Even before scientific attempts to deal with temperature, people observed subjective states corresponding loosely to temperature. Objects touched gave different sensations of amount of heat. As the need to treat temperature more precisely and rigorously arose, attempts were made to find other more reliable (and safer) ways to measure temperature. Probably for the same reasons that the measurements were needed in the first place (the observation that other things happen as temperature changes), the focus was on the correlates of temperature. Noticing that increases in temperature result in the expansion of some compounds, scientists attempted to investigate the properties of such materials and their rate of expansion.[2] The choice was not simple. Putting a material in a glass tube and observing its expansion is not a satisfactory solution. First, there is the problem of choice of materials. All materials do not have desirable properties. Water, for example, expands when it freezes, contracts above freezing, and expands again as a gaseous state is approached. Moreover, the desirable exchange properties are absent. One would expect by analogy to observable heat transactions that of two bodies in contact with one another, the one with the higher thermometer reading would produce an increase in the volume of the other at the expense of its own volume. The rule holds in general, but for water it breaks down. In *Die Principien der Warmelahre*, Mach observes: "Two masses of water at 3 and 5°C both diminish in volume when in contact. Two masses of water at 10 and 15°C represent the normal case, but two masses of water at 1 and 3°C behave in a way exactly opposite to the analogy [Ellis, 1966, p. 183]."[3] Moreover, the exchange between the water or any other liquid and the glass tube must be taken into account, and the rates of expansion are not uniform. That is, substances do not expand proportionately to one another with equal changes of heat state. The measurement of temperature, then, involves a considerable amount of theory *and* observation. We must develop principles that hold for the expansion of different substances and for the exchange of heat, and we must test these principles empirically with various substances. Eventually, the result is a reasonably accurate thermometer with an arbitrary starting point and an arbitrary, but uniform, unit of measurement or scale. The purpose of this digression is to make clear two points. Measurement does involve theory. But it is also empirical and iterative in the best scientific sense. In fact, it makes little sense to talk of measurement as anything other than science proper. All the steps are there: observation, conjecture, testing, revision, the development of more inclusive principles to account for the evidence and to guide the subsequent conjectures and test. Measurement is science and to pull the process out as a separate component in the scientific process distorts the concept and the process.

The most defensible position seems to lie somewhere between the extremes. On the one hand, social science would be brought to a screeching halt if we were to insist that all analysis wait until we have a fully axiomatic theoretical measurement model. On the other hand, it makes little sense to run about asking haphazard questions under the misbegotten impression that some statistical routine will make sense of our nonsense. Between the two extremes, there is a defensible position that argues that some thought go into measurement prior to asking questions, that assumptions about the properties of the underlying conceptual variable be examined, that a choice of measurement technique for turning responses into numerals or numbers be made, however tentatively,

[2] Volume of a material, of course, is not the only correlate of temperature.
[3] The quotation is taken from the appendix to *Basic Concepts of Measurement* by Ellis. The translation is by M. J. Scott–Taggart and Ellis (Ellis, 1966, p. 183).

but that we be prepared to abandon or alter our measurement models if the evidence warrants it. Inherent in this position is the view that measurement is an iterative process, as is science in general, and that we progressively improve our techniques. Further, to consider measurement apart from either theory or analysis is an error. The stronger the theory, other things equal, the better the measurement. Better measurement permits, but does not guarantee, better analysis, which in turn assists in building stronger theory. The more we know going into the survey research, other things equal, the better the answers we get. At whatever level we go in, we should use the analysis to inform us about, among other things, the measurement properties of our variables. Although all of this has the smack of a pedantic platitude, it is important enough to have warranted this restatement. The concern explains the structure of the rest of this chapter. We next review the literature on the theory of measurement. We do not argue that this level of formalization must be achieved before any research is done, but the foundations are sufficiently important to justify a review. Then we examine the basic techniques that form the traditional methods of measurement and scaling.

7.2. MEASUREMENT THEORY

Basic Concepts and Definitions

A *set* S is a collection of objects or abstract entities of any kind. For example, the collection of all returned responses to a mail-out questionnaire is a set. The collection of all individuals who are candidates for a specific political office is a set. If an element x is a member of the set S, we denote it by $x \in S$. If x is not a member of the set, it is denoted by $x \notin S$. A set may be described either by listing all of its elements, where possible, or by specifying the rule or properties by which membership in the set can be determined. A set may contain either a finite or an infinite number of elements. The set of all countries in the world is finite. On the other hand, the set of all positive integers has an infinite number of members.

Given two sets, A and B, consider an *ordered pair* (a, b) where $a \in A$ and $b \in B$. The collection of all such ordered pairs is referred to as the *Cartesian product* of A and B and is denoted by $A \times B$. For example, if $\mathbb{R}$ is the set of all real numbers, the familiar two-dimensional plane can be written as the Cartesian product $\mathbb{R} \times \mathbb{R}$ or $\mathbb{R}^2$. The concept of a Cartesian product is readily extended to any number of sets. Consequently, the Cartesian product of n sets, each set being the real line $\mathbb{R}$ will define the n-dimensional real space $\mathbb{R}^n$, whose elements are the ordered n-tuples or vectors $(x_1, x_2, \ldots, x_n)$. The ith element of x_i or $x \in \mathbb{R}^n$ is commonly called the ith coordinate of x.

The Cartesian product of a set with itself conveniently leads to the notion of a *binary relation*. In most general language a binary relation is any statement about two objects that is meaningful in the sense that it can be classified as true or not true. For example, the comparisons of any two objects with respect to size, weight, and the like, are special instances of binary relations. Indicating which of two objects, commodities, or situations one prefers is a binary relation statement. More formally, a binary relation on the set A is a subset P of the Cartesian product A^2. If the ordered pair (a, b) is an element of P, we write aPb to denote that a is related to b by P or alternatively, a is P-related to b. A common relation in economics and other social sciences is the "preference relation" in which aPb means that an individual indicates a preference for a over b when comparing the two elements. The elements a and b may represent consumptions items in the context of economics, political candidates in the context of an electoral decision, or social situations in the context of a socio-logical inquiry.

Having introduced the concept of a binary relation in general terms, we may now proceed to establish the essential properties or attributes of a relation by applying it to any single element of a set, any pair of elements in the set, and finally to any trio of elements in the set. These results will then determine whether or not a relation possesses the attributes of *reflexivity, symmetry,* and *transitivity.* Often, in some developments of the logical nature of relations—particularly in establishing preference structures—these attributes of a relation are referred to as axioms. Specifically, for any a, b, and c that are elements of the set A and the binary relation P:

A1: P is *reflexive* if aPa for all $a \in A$.
A2: P is *symmetric* if aPb implies bPa for all a and $b \in A$.
A3: P is transitive, if aPb and bPc implies aPc for all a, b, $c \in A$.

A relation that has the above attributes (or satisfies the above axioms) of reflexivity, symmetry, and transitivity is rather special and is called an *equivalence relation.* The prototypal example of an equivalence relation is $=$, is equal to, but many other equivalence relations also exist. Other examples include the relations "is in the same class as" and "lives in the same block as." The special nature of an equivalence relation E deserves some comment. The importance of the equivalence relation for the subsequent development of measurement theory is that it enables the elements of a given set to be partitioned into nonoverlapping equivalence classes. This partitioning is equivalent to the formation of mutually exclusive and exhaustive categories, an operation sufficient, as we later show, to constitute measurement at the nominal level. The equivalence class of any element $a \in A$ is simply the set of all elements for which aEa holds.

Consider another binary relation R. Let R have the properties of $<$ ($a < b$ read as a is less than b); this is an example of the R relationship. Other examples of R relationships are "is taller than" and "has higher status than." These relationships are nonreflexive, nonsymmetric, and transitive. The transitivity axiom is especially significant because it allows all elements of the set to be compared and ranked. For example without the transitivity attribute, even if aPb and bPc, the element a cannot be directly compared to c and no ranking is possible. Hence transitivity is essential to establishing an *ordering* (quasi-ordering, preordering, etc.) of the elements of a set. Accordingly, this relation permits an ordering of the equivalence classes. Orderings are termed *strong* (strict) if ties are not permitted in pairwise comparisons; *weak* if ties are permitted. A binary relation that is reflexive and transitive but permits ties between distinct members of a set is sometimes termed *preordering* or *quasi-ordering*.

Consider again two sets, A and B, and suppose it is possible to associate an element a_i from A with an element b_j from B. This correspondence between elements of the two sets is termed a *mapping* of A to the set B. The element of B associated with an element of A is called the *image* of the element of A under the mapping. If each element of A has one and only one image in B, the mapping is said to be from the set A **onto** B. Similarly, if there exist elements of B that are not images of A, then the mapping is said to be from A **into** B. We may now see that the common notion of a *function* in mathematics is simply a special type of mapping. A function is simply a mapping of a set A (domain) into a set B (range). The most familiar type of function in mathematics is probably the real-values function; that is, a subset of $\mathbb{R} \times \mathbb{R}$ in which both elements in the ordered pairs are real numbers. In other words, a function maps the real line into the real line.

Recall that a binary relation may be viewed as a mapping from a set A to some subset of P of the Cartesian product of the set with itself, $A \times A = A^2$. We now introduce the concept of a *binary operation* on a set whereby two elements of a set A may be combined to produce a third element in the set. Specifically, a binary operation O on a set A is a mapping from $A \times A$ into A. That is, for each ordered pair (a_1, a_2) in A^2, the binary operation O will determine a unique element $a_1 O a_2 \in A$. If $a_1 O a_2 \notin A$, then O is not a binary operation. Let I be the set of all integers. Then the familiar + (addition) is a binary operation since the sum of any two integers is still an integer and therefore a member of the set I. On the other hand ÷ (division) is not a binary operation on I since one integer divided by another need not be an integer and hence need not be a member of the set I.

We now have only one more concept to consider, namely, that of a *morphism* or *homomorphism*. This is a significant concept for any development of measurement theory in the social sciences. Let A be a set on which the binary operation O is defined and let B be another set on which the binary operation Q is defined. Then a morphism μ is simply a mapping from the set A to the set B such that $\mu(a_1 O a_2) = \mu a_1 Q \mu a_2$. The mapping μ must preserve operations in order to be a morphism. If $a_1 O a_2 = a_3 \in A$, then μa_3 must also equal $\mu a_1 Q \mu a_2$. In other words, the image of a_3 must also equal the combination of images of a_1 and a_2 under the binary operation defined on the image set. If the mapping μ is a *one-to-one* mapping from A onto B, then the mapping is said to be *isomorphic*.

The concept of a homomorphism or isomorphism is especially significant and important for our purposes. Algebraic systems may be viewed as sets on which operations are defined and modern algebra in mathematics is concerned with characterizing different algebraic systems and the relationships between different systems. Therefore, given a specific algebraic system whose properties are known, any other system that is isomorphic to it will have the same properties. This means that we can replace any system with one that is isomorphic to it since both have identical properties. The significance of isomorphisms for measurement in the social sciences is clear. Most social scientists (even physical and natural scientists) are familiar with and comfortable with the real number system whose properties are readily understood and accepted. Also, the set of permissible operations customarily performed with the real number system is well established. Accordingly, if the substantive content of various social science disciplines can be shown to be homomorphic or isomorphic with the set of real numbers, then the subject matter or entities can be "quantified," or "measured," and further analyzed by means of standard allowable mathematical techniques and statistical procedures. Mathematics and statistics constitute a set of rigid, precise, and explicit rules for structuring statements. Consequently, a mathematical representation of a problem, where possible, allows a characterization of the real world that is efficient and useful. However, establishing the nature of a homomorphism between the subject matter and the real line, and exploring its implications, is no trivial matter in the quantitative social sciences.

Relational Systems and the Representation Problem

We have seen how objects of sets may be classified into equivalence classes and ordered. The next basic problem of measurement theory concerns the rationale for assigning numbers to an ordered set and the extent to which these numbers are meaningful and unique. We seek to establish, therefore, a homomorphism between some set A and the set of real numbers $\mathbb{R}$, since, if our conceptualization of the empirical phenomena can be shown to have the same structure as $\mathbb{R}$, then operations permitted on $\mathbb{R}$ can be employed to derive conclusions about the phenomena. The representation problem of measurement theory, then, is to define a mapping or functional representation from a set A to a set of real numbers.

Researchers in the social sciences often construct theories of segments of reality and certain essential features are often embodied in a formal system or model. Admittedly, the characterization of a field of study as an empirical system is itself a process of immense difficulty and abstraction calling upon human experience and the conceptualization of data, objects, and relations. This process, however, is logically antecedent to measurement and the representation problem, as we define the terms.

Define a *relational system* $(A, T_1, \ldots, T_m)$, where A is a nonempty set and $T_1, \ldots, T_m$ are m specified relations on the set A. An *empirical relational system* is one in which the elements of the set A are identifiable entities of an empirical nature, such as commodities, political candidates, weights, attitude statements, social situations. A relational system is *numerical* if A is the set of real numbers. Accordingly, we may view the relation between the world and its model representation as a correspondence between an empirical and a numerical relational system.

Let us define a *congruence relation* for the relational system $(A, T_1, \ldots, T_m)$ as an equivalence relation E on the set A if and only if, for each T_i, and the set $A = [a_{hj}]$, $a_{hj}Ea_{gj}$ for all $j = 1, \ldots, k$ implies that $T_i(a_{h1}, \ldots, a_{hk}) = T_i(a_{g1}, \ldots, a_{gk})$. This definition is not very intuitive. Essentially, a congruence relation establishes that a certain *substitution* property holds. For example, in the measurement of weight, the equivalence relation a_1 is equal in weight to a_j is a congruence relation and any body of the same weight as a_1 could be substituted for a_1 regardless of shape, color, and the like, and the relation would still hold. Finally, a relational system is said to be *irreducible* if and only if the equivalence relation E is the only congruence relation for the system. (See Pfanzagl, 1968, pp. 20–21, for further details regarding congruence relations and irreducible systems.)

We are now in a position to define the concept of a scale in terms of a homomorphism between relational systems (Suppes and Zinnes, 1963; also Pfanzagl, 1968). An *n-dimensional scale* is a homomorphism m of an irreducible empirical relation system $(A, T_1, \ldots, T_m)$ into an n-dimensional numerical relation system $(\mathbb{R}^n, S_1, \ldots, S_m)$ where, as before, $\mathbb{R}^n$ is the nth Cartesian product of the set of real numbers. T_i and S_i are sets of specified relations defined on A and $\mathbb{R}^n$, respectively. A *one-dimensional scale* is the special case $n = 1$; that is, a mapping from an empirical set to the real number system $\mathbb{R}$. It is common to refer to any representation of an ordering established by measuring preferences or judgment statements of an individual as a *utility scale* or *utility function*. (See Coombs, Dawes, and Tversky, 1970, for an elementary treatment of the representation problem in terms of functions. In the context of representing preference orderings by utility functions, the seminal work is by Debreu, 1954, 1959. See also Rader, 1963.)

Scales (or functions) are not in general unique. A whole class of scales exists that will map a given irreducible empirical relational system homomorphically into a given numerical relational system. Where no criterion exists to select a given scale from members of its equivalence class, we are left with having to attempt to characterize the properties and relationships among various numerical scales resulting from the representation. In fact, scale types may be fruitfully classified and labeled depending upon the relative uniqueness of the set of permissible mappings.

To summarize the discussion to this point, *measurement* is viewed as the representation of an empirical relational system by a numerical relational system.[4] The representation should be such that relations among the objects of study are preserved by the number assignment process.

---

[4] Strictly speaking, the mathematical relational system need not be numerical in the narrow sense. "Assignment of vectors, sets, intervals, geometric objects, etc. is a perfectly legitimate form of measurement if a representation theorem stating a homomorphism from an empirical relational system to a mathematical relational system can be proved [Roberts, 1979, p. 254]."

Admissible Transforms and Classifications of Scales

Since a given scale may not be unique, the question naturally arises as to the freedom one has in specifying or constructing a particular scale. For a given representation characterizing the relationship of an empirical relational system, the scale may be required to preserve the ordering of elements, or to preserve the ordering of differences between values assigned to elements, and so forth. Intuitively, for a given scale that adequately represents the empirical relational system (i.e., is a measurement), any other scale will also be permitted (and referred to as an *admissible transformation*) if it preserves the representation relation between the empirical and numerical relations. Formally, let $\alpha = (A, T_1, \ldots, T_m)$ be an empirical relational system, $\beta = (\mathbb{R}, S_1, \ldots, S_m)$ be a numerical relational system, and $\mathbb{R}$ is the set of real numbers. A transformation Γ from $\mathbb{R}$ into itself is said to be *admissible* with respect to a representation f if the mapping $g(x) = \Gamma[f(x)]$ for all $x \in A$, is also a representation of α by β. The set of all admissible transformations consequently determines the scale type and the degree of uniqueness of a measurement.

We may therefore combine the definition of a scale with its set of admissible transformations to create a taxonomy of scale types. Without loss of generality let f be a one-dimensional scale of the irreducible relational system $(A, T_1, \ldots, T_m)$ into $(\mathbb{R}, S_1, \ldots, S_m)$ and let $\Gamma_\mathbb{R}$ be the set of admissible transformations of f. Extension to n-dimensional scales involves merely replacing $\mathbb{R}$ with $\mathbb{R}^n$. The different scale types may be commonly classified as follows.

1. *Nominal:* f is a nominal scale if $\Gamma_\mathbb{R}$ is the set of all one-to-one mappings from $\mathbb{R}$ to $\mathbb{R}$.
2. *Ordinal:* f is an ordinal scale if $\Gamma_\mathbb{R}$ is the set of all monotonically increasing, continuous mappings from $\mathbb{R}$ to $\mathbb{R}$.
3. *Interval:* f is an interval scale if $\Gamma_\mathbb{R}$ is the set of all positive linear transformations of f.
4. *Difference:* f is a difference scale if $\Gamma_\mathbb{R}$ is the set of mappings differing from f by a constant.
5. *Ratio:* f is a ratio scale if $\Gamma_\mathbb{R}$ is the set of mappings differing from f by a positive multiple.
6. *Absolute:* f is an absolute scale if the only permissible transformation of f is the identity transformation.

The above taxonomy of scales is neither exhaustive nor universally accepted yet, we feel, it represents a useful set of distinctions. For example Stevens (1946, 1951), who is generally credited with originating the study of scale types, distinguished four categories—ratio, interval, ordinal, and log interval, the latter being a scale type where $\Gamma_\mathbb{R}$ is a set of power transformations thereby enabling a logarithmic transformation of f to result in an interval scale. Economists, in their particular concern with utility scales or functions, distinguish principally between ordinal and cardinal measures, interpreting cardinality to mean a scale or function unique up to a group of linear transformations.

Economists, too, have the bad habit of treating *measurability* to mean representable by a cardinal scale; hence they speak of ordinal utility as nonmeasurable (see, for example, Takayama, 1974, p. 201). However, in passing, this issue little troubles economic research since the important major empirical and theoretical consequences of economics need only assume an ordinal utility function to derive most of the properties and restrictions of demand functions. The economists' concern and interest in demand functions are obvious since these include as arguments primarily observable empirical entities such as price, quantities, and income. Economists also concern themselves with the interesting questions of inferring an ordering from "revealed preference" observations (Arrow, 1959; Houthakker, 1950; Samuelson, 1947) and whether or not a given demand function could have resulted from a given utility scale; the so-called integrability problem (Houthakker, 1950; Hurwicz, 1971; Samuelson, 1950). Finally, to illustrate that no universally accepted set of categories exists, Pfanzagl (1968, pp. 29–30) in his important *Theory of Measurement* refused to use the term *cardinal scales* at all—preferring to include interval, difference, and ratio scales together as simply one-dimensional scales that are unique up to a group of linear transformations. Scales are termed *interval, difference,* or *ratio* if they are unique up to a positive linear transformation, shift transformation, or dilation transformation, respectively.

The definition and classification of various scale types in terms of admissible transformations is formal rather than intuitive. For this reason, a further discussion and examples might prove useful. *Nominal scales* are those that merely classify the elements of an empirical set such as the numbers assigned to members of an athletic team. Because the numbers themselves have no significance aside from the classification, nominal scales give only a minimum of information.

An *ordinal scale* preserves a ranking of the elements of an empirical set. This is an important case of practical relevance since the ordinal properties of the real number system can be usefully employed. Nonetheless, the choice of $\mathbb{R}$ or $\mathbb{R}^n$ as a numerical relational structure is a convention, albeit a convention strongly dictated by familiarity and computational convenience. Binary relations of preference (or utility), indifference, and the like, result in ranking relations and therefore ordinal scales. (See Debreu, 1954, for necessary and sufficient conditions with respect to ordinal scales representable by a real-valued function.) A well-known example of a preference ordering *not* representable by a real-valued function is the famous lexicographic ordering (see Debreu, 1959, for proof; see Coombs, 1964, for illustrations).

Interval scales are scales so named because the intervals between scale values can be meaningfully compared. The intervals are known and equal. Because the set of admissible transformations for interval scales is the set of positive linear transformations, the scale values are determined uniquely except for choice of origin and unit of measurement. Interval scales obviously give more information than do ordinal scales since they preserve a *metrical operation* rather than a mere ranking. For a development of interval scales based upon metrical operations, see Pfanzagl, 1968. Familiar examples of interval scales are the Fahrenheit and centigrade measures of temperature, or the famous Von Neumann–Morgenstern (1947) system of utility presented in their *Theory of Games and Economic Behaviour.*

Difference scales and *ratio scales* require even stronger constraints on the numerical measures. A difference scale must have a unique unit of measure but may have an arbitrary origin. Difference scales are not common. An example of a difference scale is the relation difference in number of feet on the set of all animals. In contrast, *ratio scales* have a unique origin but an arbitrary unit of measure. Scales of weight are exemplary examples since the choice of either *pounds* or *kilograms* is arbitrary whereas zero weight is meaningful as a unique origin.

Finally, an *absolute scale* is the extreme of a nominal scale. No transformation, excepting the identity transformation, is permitted. Counting is an example of an absolute scale.

We may summarize our entire discussion of the foundations of measurement as involving:

> for any particular empirical relational structure, the formation of a set of axioms that is sufficient to establish two types of theorems: a representation theorem, which asserts the existence of a homomorphism ϕ into a particular numerical relational structure, and a uniqueness theorem, which sets forth the permissible transformations $\phi \rightarrow \phi'$ that also yield homomorphisms into the same numerical relational structure. A measurement procedure corresponds to the construction of a ϕ in the representation theorem [Krantz, Luce, Suppes, and Tversky 1971, p. 12].

Meaningful Statements and Meaningful Statistics[5]

It is clear that since scale types are classified in terms of their sets of admissible transformations, one must know the scale type before one can interpret the numbers assigned. Logical inferences based upon measurement must be invariant with respect to the set of admissible transformations. Similarly, interpretation of statistics depends upon knowledge of the scale type. In sum, the meaningfulness of statements depends upon the uniqueness of the scale being used to state something about the empirical system.

We define a statement S as formally *meaningful* only if its truth or falsity is invariant under all admissible transformation of its scale values (Suppes and Zinnes, 1963). The significance of this definition is that meaningfulness depends upon particular measurement models through which numerical values are assigned.

Consider the familiar issue of relating money magnitudes or other empirical entities to utility. The statement that an extra $100 or 10 apples will increase an individual's utility by 10% is not a meaningful statement for economists whose measurement model asserts that utility is measured only on an ordinal

---

[5] This section draws heavily from the treatment of meaningfulness by Pfanzagl (1968, chap. 18) and Roberts and Schulze (1973).

scale. The statement is not meaningful since its truth value may be changed by any admissible monotonic transformation. On the other hand, if a similar statement were made based upon the Von Neuman–Morgenstern system of utility, such a statement would be meaningful since it is based upon an interval scale, which economists regard as cardinal utility. Similarly, a statement such as *the difference in utility between x and y is greater than the difference between w and z* is meaningful because such a statement implies an interval scale or cardinal utility.

Cases of meaningful and meaningless statistics are also possible. For example, the simple *arithmetic mean* of n values is meaningless for ordinal scales since the mean value statistic is destroyed by arbitrary monotone transformations. However, for ordinal data, the *median* is a meaningful statistic.

The sum of two values $x_1 + x_2$ is meaningful if both values are from the same interval scale, but is not if x_1 and x_2 are measured in different ratio scales. As another example, the familiar standard deviation S,

$$S(x_1, \ldots, x_n) = \left[\sum_{i}^{n} (x_i - \bar{x})^2/(n - 1) \right]^{1/2}$$

is a meaningful statistic for interval scales. Finally, although both the mean $\bar{x}$ and standard deviation S are meaningful for interval scales, the statistic coefficient of variation $S/\bar{x}$ is not. However, the coefficient of variation is a meaningful statistic for ratio scales.

The concept of *meaningful* is sufficiently important to warrant another example in more detail. Temperature is frequently measured on either a centigrade or Fahrenheit scale. Both are interval levels of measurement with arbitrary zero points. The two are related by a linear transformation. The following statement is based on a meaningless index: Yesterday the temperature was 25°C and today it is 50°C, *twice as hot*. The implied ratio 50/25 = 2 is meaningless for interval level measurements. To see this, we convert the two measurements into their Fahrenheit equivalents and observe that 25°C = 77°F and 50°C = 122°F, but 122/77 ≠ 50/25. The temperatures in the two ratios are equivalent, however, our statement using the ratio 50/25 is not invariant under linear transformation of the scale values. It is a meaningless statement.

The concept of meaningfulness that depends upon the uniqueness of a particular scale is quite restrictive and has led to the notion of *meaningful parametrization* (see Pfanzagl, 1968, for a formal definition). Meaningful parametrization permits numerical statements to depend upon the parameters of an admissible transformation. We illustrate the notion of meaningful parametrization with our continuing example of the relation between utility and income.

Frisch (1936) proposed the empirical relation between utility U and money income M as

$$U = \frac{\alpha}{\ln M - \ln \beta}$$

where ln is the natural logarithm, and α and β are constants. If the mappings U and M are unique up to positive multiples, then all admissible mappings to U and M are specified as $U^* = SU$ and $M^* = tM$, respectively. Accordingly, we say Frisch's relation is meaningfully parametrized if

$$U^* = \frac{\alpha^*}{\ln M^* - \ln \beta^*}$$

where α^* and β^*, the constants (or dimensionless constants), depend upon the parameters of the admissible transformation. Letting $\alpha^* = S\alpha$ and $\beta^* = t\beta$, we see that

$$\frac{\alpha}{\ln M - \ln \beta} = U = \frac{1}{S} U^* = \frac{1}{S} \frac{S\alpha}{\ln tM - \ln t\beta} = \frac{\alpha}{\ln M - \ln \beta},$$

hence Frisch's relation is meaningfully parametrized. On the other hand, Waugh (1935) proposed, as an empirical law relating utility to money income, that

$$U = \frac{\alpha}{\ln \ln M - \ln \ln \beta},$$

which is *not* a meaningful parametric relationship. Suppes and Zinnes (1963) provide the example: $m_1(a) = \alpha \log m_2(a)$, which is meaningfully parametrized only if m_1 is a ratio scale and m_2 is unique up to a power transformation.

To restate the notion of meaningful parametrization, we note that the concept of a meaningful relation dependent upon unique scales is highly restrictive. Consequently, to paraphrase Pfanzagl (1968, p. 50), consider the practical situation in which all values obtained by measuring with a fixed scale m satisfies a k-ary relation T on the set B. Although T may not be a meaningful relation in the sense of invariance under all admissible transformations of its scale value, that fact that the scale values satisfy T does say something about the real world. The measured objects satisfy the relationship T with scale m. If we change the scale, we must also change the relationship to a new one, say T^*, so that for every admissible scale m we have a specific k-ary relation T_m describing the relation. This family of relations together with its parametrization then yields statements about the empirical relational system. Consequently we can characterize the meaningfulness of parametrization by the admissible transformations.

Concluding Remarks

This section on measurement theory may seem a bit formal, even pedantic, to a researcher with a box full of interviews, needing some way to turn the responses into indices of social class or attitude toward the feminist movement. There is, though, a point to be made. What we can do to our numbers depends on the way the measurements were constructed. Measurement is not just any arbitrary arithmetic manipulation of responses; it is a theory of the phenomenon being measured. The theory may be relatively strong or weak in the assumptions it makes, but theoretical assumptions are being made, implicitly or explicitly. If the theory is wrong, or if our numerical relational system is not related homomorphically to our empirical relational system, then the arithmetic we perform on our numbers will not answer questions about the empirical relational system—or worse, it will answer them incorrectly. In a time that permits the facile use of various computer algorithms to turn responses into numbers, this point is important. *All measurement is theory* in some sense and we ignore the theory at our peril.

This is not to argue that we should not undertake measurement until we have a formal measurement theory. The process, as we argued in the introduction, ought to be iterative. Measurements ought to reflect the theoretical structure of the phenomena they purport to represent and the results of analysis using these measurements ought to be used to refine the theory, which in turn will affect the measuring process, and so on through the business of science. But, at the present, it seems to be the theoretical side of measurement that gets the slight. Choosing a scaling technique often is a matter of finding which computer programs are available, easy to use, etc. It is this inattention to the theoretical aspects of the measurement process that led us to undertake the formal presentation. We can turn now to the major techniques used to produce measurements from responses.

7.3. SCALING TECHNIQUES

Introduction

This section reviews the principal scaling techniques used in social research. These are the methods most often used to turn responses obtained in surveys into numerical indices for use in analysis. Our objective is to provide an overview of the major techniques with some attention to their logic and to the major advantages and shortcomings. It is not possible within the scope of this chapter to treat all techniques used nor to treat the selected techniques in detail. We have attempted to provide enough information so that a reader will be able to evaluate the applicability of a technique to a particular data set, and we have provided references that cover the techniques in the detail needed for a thorough understanding.

We avoid presenting a taxonomy of scaling techniques. A variety of such categorical schemes is available (see Coombs, 1964; Torgerson, 1958). These are useful, particularly if one has a theoretical interest in measurement and scaling and not just in selecting a method for a particular problem. However, in a review of the principal methods it seems not worthwhile to use the scarce supply of pages to develop and present a taxonomical scheme.

The product of most of the methods we present is measurement at the ordinal level or above, the major exception being latent class analysis that produces nominal level measures. Whether the other techniques produce ordinal or interval measures is a matter of debate. It is probably fair to say that ordinality is all that can be assumed if one rigorously employs the principles presented in the theoretical section of this chapter. However, there is a well-known and continuing debate in the social sciences over the issue.

The debate is not so much over the matter of whether or not the measures are really interval or not, but rather over the advantages and shortcomings of assuming an interval level even if the data may be only ordinal. The debate is well documented and, consequently, will not be reviewed here.[6] It is sufficient for our purposes to summarize the two positions. The conservative position argues that if the data cannot be assumed to be above ordinal in the measurement scheme, then one should use only those statistical techniques appropriate for ordinal level measurement for the reasons discussed in the theory section. The other view argues that more powerful statistical techniques assume interval level and that the consequences of assuming data are interval when in fact they are ordinal are so small in most cases that the gain in statistical elegance and power justifies any distortion produced by the more pretentious measurement assumption (for a recent statement, see Bohrnstedt and Borgatta, 1981). We do not take a position on each technique presented in this chapter. Unless otherwise stated, one may assume that the techniques produce ordinal level measurements that are routinely treated in the social sciences as if they were interval level measures.

Single Item Measurement

The simplest form of attitude measurement is based on a single item that elicits a single response. For example, attitude toward a particular political figure may be operationally defined by a response indicated on a scale:

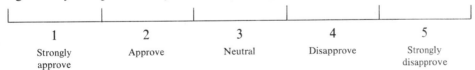

1	2	3	4	5
Strongly approve	Approve	Neutral	Disapprove	Strongly disapprove

The scale may be only nominal categories. Or, we may treat the categories as ordered, as we do in the example, or even as interval level or above, although this may be presumptuous. Whenever the attitude toward a single object is measured on the basis of a single response, the scale is called single item measurement. For some types of measurement in survey research, single item measures are adequate. There is no obvious reason why age or education should require a set of 12 scaled items to elicit the needed information. However, if the information cannot be assessed as directly, the difficulties increase.

[6] See, for example, Labovitz (1970, 1971); Mayer (1970, 1971); O'Brien (1979a, 1979b); Vargo (1971); Wilson (1971).

For variables such as attitudes, beliefs, values, personality characteristics, and so on, a single item measuring device is a risky venture.

The problem exists regardless of whether the item being assessed is an attitude object (Richard Nixon, the United Nations, Proposition 2½) having many characteristics or a statement about the relevant attitude object (the United Nations is an effective agent for peace) to which the respondent indicates degree of agreement or disagreement. The problem resides in our inability to get a response that measures only the relevant attitude. The response is usually a composite of various things such as item specific components, a general attitude component, and error of various sorts. Presumably, we are interested in the general attitude. If we have information only from one response per object per respondent, it is not possible to estimate or separate the components. Treating the response as a good measure (reliable and valid) is risky.

It is well known that slight variations in question wording and format can produce large variations in response percentages. Any single wording may produce responses due primarily to some idiosyncrasy of the particular statement and not to the underlying attitude one wants to measure. McNemar (1946) reviewed the literature on the issue and forcefully recommended that we discard single item measurement in the area of attitude and opinion research and use instead measurement by attitude scales. Others have repeated the warnings. S. Schuman and Duncan (1974) go further and show that in addition to distorting response distributions, variation in item wording and format can affect conclusions about basic background correlates of an attitude. Also see H. Schuman and Presser (1977).

McKennel (1977) succinctly summarizes by saying that research on the issue has "established beyond doubt the serious deficiencies of single items and the superiority of multi-item scales in respect of such matters as reliability, unidimensionality and freedom from specific wording bias [p. 182]." It is because of these problems that attitude scaling came into prominence. The techniques that follow represent attempts to avoid the pitfalls of single item measurement.

Thurstone Scales

Thurstone scales are produced by one of several related techniques, the more important of which are the method of paired comparisons, the method of equal appearing intervals, and the method of successive intervals. These are among the earliest attempts to scale attitudes (Thurstone, 1928a, 1928b; Thurstone and Chave, 1929). All three methods begin by having a group of "judges" make judgments on a set of statements about the attitude object. These judgments are used to assign scale scores to each statement reflecting the degree to which the statement is favorable or unfavorable. Subsequently, each respondent is presented with the set of statements and is asked to indicate the ones he or she accepts or agrees with. The sum of the scale scores assigned to the indicated items becomes the respondent's attitude score. These methods of

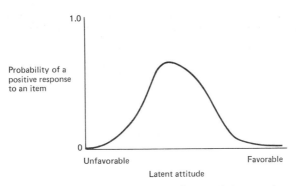

FIGURE 7.2 Each item or statement has a characteristic operating curve.

scale construction are relatively laborious in comparison to most other methods, and they are not often seen in contemporary attitude research. However, during the 1930s and 1940s, they were widely used and highly regarded ways to measure attitudes and opinions. Because they are rarely used today, we cover them only briefly.

All three methods are adapted from ideas Thurstone took from the psychophysics laboratory. The technique is based on the Law of Comparative Judgment which provides a rationale for ranking psychological stimuli along a continuum that has no known physical counterpart to which the psychological continuum might be related. As Edwards (1957) points out, this "made possible the quantitative investigation of all kinds of values and subjective experiences [p. 20]." Items (statements) are assumed to be dichotomous (agree–disagree). The operating characteristics are assumed to be unimodal and, usually, normally distributed. The operating characteristic of an item is a quantitative statement of the expected effect given the items location along the latent attitude continuum. The ordinate typically is the probability of a positive response and the abscissa is the location on the attitude dimension. Thurstone scaling generally assumes operating characteristics like the one shown in Figure 7.2. The technique assumes that attitude statements can be placed along an underlying continuum (running from extremely unfavorable to extremely favorable). Judges are used to establish the placement.

The *method of paired comparisons* presents each judge with every possible pair of statements and asks for every pair: Which statement is more favorable toward the attitude object? Over the set of judges,[7] we find for each pair of statements the proportion of times one statement is judged as preferable to another. If half of the judges say statement i is more favorable and half say j is more favorable, then the locations of these two statements on the underlying attitude continuum should be near each other. If, however, the proportion saying i is more favorable greatly exceeds the proportion saying j is more

---

[7] Thurstone at one time recommended using 100 or more judges. More recent recommendations cut this to 25–50.

favorable, then the two statements must be different with respect to "degree of favorableness" and, hence, they should be located at different points on the attitude continuum. The differences in the statement locations is assumed to be some function of the proportion of times i is judged more favorable.

The construction of the scale, that is, the placement of the statements, is accomplished by assuming the discriminal process (for attitudes, the reaction to an attitude statement) is normally distributed. The process may be thought of as the distribution of responses one would obtain if a subject reacted to an attitude item many times. The fluctuation is assumed to be due to random error, which increases the tenability of the normality assumption, around the mean response which is assumed to be the best estimate of the true scale value of the item. In practice, one usually uses the responses of many people rather than many responses of one person to establish the distribution. The distributions usually overlap. For example, responses to two items, normally distributed around their respective means, will overlap if their means are close enough. The area of overlap represents a "confusion" area. Sometimes one item would be judged higher (more favorable) and sometimes the other. Because the discriminal processes are assumed to be normal, the distribution of *differences* in the discriminal processes also will be normal. The mean of these differences is the best estimate of the scale separation of the items on the underlying attitude continuum. However, this cannot be estimated directly. But, estimates can be obtained by calculating $P_{i>j}$, the proportion of times item i was judged greater than item j. If the two items are located at the same point, then the mean difference ought to be zero. If one item is more frequently chosen over the other, the mean difference will depart from zero. Under the assumption that the differences are normally distributed with a standard deviation of 1.0, the zero point can be expressed as a Z score that reflects the number of standard deviations it, the zero point, is above or below the mean difference. From a standard normal curve table, the proportion $P_{i<j}$ can be entered to find the corresponding normal deviate. For example, if i is judged greater than j 90% of the time, then Z_{ij} is approximately 1.28. This locates the item relative to the zero point. One must translate the difference in mean responses $(\bar{r}_i - \bar{r}_j) = \bar{r}_d$ (now expressed as a Z score) back into the σ of the obtained differences.

It is well known that

$$\sigma_{x_1-x_2} = (\sigma_{x_1}^2 + \sigma_{x_2}^2 - 2r_{12}\sigma_{x_1}\sigma_{x_2})^{1/2} \tag{7.1}$$

Since $\bar{r}_d$ is simply a difference in means, the interval separating i and j can be expressed as $\bar{r}_d = Z_{ij}\sigma_d$ where σ_d is calculated exactly as shown in (7.1). That is

$$\bar{r}_d = (\bar{r}_i - \bar{r}_j) = Z_{ij}(\sigma_i^2 + \sigma_j^2 - 2r_{ij}\sigma_i\sigma_j)^{1/2} \tag{7.2}$$

Equation (7.2) is the general form of the law of comparative judgment. In actual practice, one usually makes simplifying assumptions such as equal variance or zero correlation between discriminal distributions.[8] The method of paired com-

---

[8] The mechanical procedures for accomplishing the scaling are given in Edwards (1957). Details on the underlying logic are presented by Nunnally (1967, pp. 50–54), on whom our discussion has depended heavily.

parison quickly becomes unmanageable as the number of items increases because the number of separate judgments required of each judge is equal to the number of possible pairs of items. For *n* items, there are $n(n - 1)/2$ pairs.

The method of equal appearing intervals is much simpler to use, particularly with a large number of items, because only one judgment is required for each item. Judges are asked to sort statements into a fixed number of categories. Typically 7, 9, or 11 categories are arranged in order of favorableness. Judges are instructed to sort the items so that the intervals between categories are "subjectively equal." A statement is given the median value of the category scores assigned to it by the judges.

The method of successive intervals also only calls for each judge to make one judgment per statement, but it does not assume the intervals are of equal size. Judges again place the statements into 7, 9, or 11 ordered categories. The judgments on each item are then examined and the proportions of judges who place the item in each category are calculated and expressed as cumulative distributions. The model assumes the cumulative distributions are normal ogives. The interval widths are estimated from the cumulative distributions and each item is given the median judgment. Again, Edwards (1957) is a good source for procedural details.

For all three types of Thurstone scales, the methods described here are simply the first step: the scaling of the attitude items. All three procedures assign scale scores to attitude statements. Some statements may be rejected because they do not work well. Judges may be discarded. In the end, a set of scaled statements is produced. These are then given to the respondents whose attitudes are to be measured. Respondents indicate the statements with which they agree. For each respondent, the attitude score is equal to the sum of the scale values of the statements they endorsed.

SUMMARY

Thurstone scaling represents one of the first attempts to quantify attitudes using rigorous methods. It is this historical contribution more than current practice that recommends its inclusion in a discussion of scaling methods. Criticisms of the technique focus on four problems. First, item selection is a problem. How one chooses a set of items so as to represent an underlying attitude dimension is a lingering question in all attitude research. Thurstone was aware of the problem and he and his associates did discuss ways to weed out undesirable items.[9] Second, the setting of the statement scale values by the use of judges assumes that the judges and the respondents share the same attitude. More specifically, it is assumed that the scores assigned by the judges to the statements is a valid placement of the statements on the attitude continuum for the respondents.[10] This is open to question. Third, it happens that very

[9] No single technique exists even now for answering this question. However, characteristics of good statements are found in many sources. See, for example, Edwards (1957) or McIver and Carmines (1981).

[10] This issue was debated in the scaling literature. Green (1954) summarized the empirical results by saying that "we can expect the bias to be small or negligible in most cases [p. 351]."

few items have the assumed operating characteristic. The operating characteristic implies that each item receives agreement in only one segment of the
attitude continuum and that the probability of agreement decreases as one
moves in either direction from the mean of that segment. Nunnally points out
that this assumption—and it is a problem with all nonmonotonic models—is
like assuming spelling words can be placed along a difficulty continuum such
that each is spelled correctly only by people in a narrow band of ability. A word
(or item) at the lower end would be spelled correctly only by poor spellers.
Moving from ability measurement to attitude measurement only compounds
the problem (see Nunnally, 1967, pp. 69 and 529–531). Finally the technique is
laborious and produces scales that are not demonstrably superior to other
commonly used methods.

Likert Scales

Likert scales, also called summated rating scales, are among the most
commonly used scaling methods in social research. The procedure is relatively
easy to use and has intuitive appeal. A set of statements is selected each of
which reflects favorably or unfavorably on the attitude object. After each statement there is an agreement scale. Respondents are asked to indicate on the
scale the degree to which they agree or disagree with each statement. The
agreement scale may have only two choices (agree–disagree) or it may have
more choices permitting an indication of the degree of agreement–disagreement. Five categories are commonly used (strongly agree, agree, neutral, disagree, and strongly disagree), although some applications omit the neutral category and some add even more categories to permit finer distinctions to be
drawn.

It is usually recommended that an equal number of positive and negative
statements be used. For positive statements the categories are scored (in the
five category case) 1, 2, 3, 4, 5, with 1 indicating strongly disagree and 5
indicating strongly agree. If the statement is unfavorable toward the subject,
the scoring is reversed. The respondent's attitude score is the sum of the scores
on the separate items.

For example, assume that we want to measure attitude toward the United
Nations. A set of evaluative statements about the United Nations is selected.
For example, we may select the following:

The United Nations helps reduce the chances
of a major war occurring.

Strongly disagree	Disagree	Neutral	Agree	Strongly agree
1	2	3	4	5

The United Nations has become a propo-
ganda podium for Communist countries.

Strongly disagree	Disagree	Neutral	Agree	Strongly agree
1	2	3	4	5

After the respondent has indicated his or her response to each statement, the scores are summed and the respondent's attitude is assumed to be represented by the sum. High total scores represent favorable attitudes toward the object and low scores represent unfavorable attitudes, although this can easily be reversed in any particular application.

The basic assumptions of Likert scales are straightforward. First, we assume there is a continuous underlying attitude dimension and that each item is monotonically related to that continuum. The operating characteristic is of the form shown in Figure 7.3. The exact form of the relationship is not important but a more favorable attitude should produce a higher expected score on any particular item. Second, it is assumed that the sum of the item scores is monotonically related to the attitude. That is, a higher total score indicates a more favorable attitude. Usually we assume that the sum is a linear function of the individual items equally weighted, although this is not a necessary assumption. Third, we assume a single common factor. In general, this is equivalent to the assumption that we are measuring only one underlying common attitude. More formally, each item score is assumed to be the weighted combination of two independent factors, one of which is the attitude we are attempting to measure, the other factor being some specific component belonging to the individual item.

Other additional assumptions might be made for specific applications. Lord (1952) used dichotomous items and assumed the item operating characteristics were normal ogives. Lazarsfeld's latent distance model also has been used (see McIver and Carmines, 1981, p. 24 and the discussion of latent structure analysis in later sections of this chapter).

The first stage of constructing a Likert scale is the selection of the items. The theoretical universe of potential attitude statements is always an unwieldy notion. Restricting attention to statements commonly encountered helps but it suggests that a content analysis of media and/or everyday conversations should be done, a step rarely taken. The selection of good statements remains one of the unresolved problems in attitude measurement. Although no definitive set of procedures exists, it is possible to offer two general suggestions. First, a good theoretical understanding of the attitude to be measured is needed. This truism, vacuous as it seems, means at the very least that we be able to write a few paragraphs about the attitude, why we think it is related to other variables in

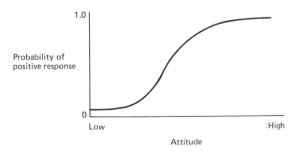

FIGURE 7.3 Operating characteristic of Likert scales.

the research and distinguishing it from similar attitudes. Good definitions do not imply measurement but good measurement always implies good definition. Conceptual work at this level helps the choice of reasonable items and usually saves work at the later stage of item analysis. Second, much of what can be said about writing good questions can be used to construct good attitude statements. Standard references provide suggestions for avoiding such problems as confusing vocabulary and the mixing of two or more issues in a single statement (see Oppenheim, 1966; Payne, 1951; and Sheatsley, Chapter 6 of this book).

Once statements have been selected, they should be pretested.[11] Results from the pretest can be used to discard problematic items. Pretesting has several components. First, discard any item that has little or no variation across respondents. If almost everyone answers the same way then the item simply adds a constant to all respondent's scores. A second step requires that one examine the relationship of each item to the total score. In particular, it is recommended that the correlation between each item and the total score be examined. In general, one wants items that correlate highly with the total score.[12] If an item fails this test, it is dropped from the statement set. For more information about item analysis, see Davis (1951, 1952), Nunnally (1967), or any standard reference in the field of ability testing.

Once a set of items has been selected, scale scores can be computed for each respondent by summing over the scores on each item. However, it is worthwhile to subject the final score to further scrutiny by computing scale reliability. A variety of methods are available. Split-half reliability is a technique that splits the scale (randomly usually) into halves, computes the correlation between the two, and adjusts this correlation so as to compensate for the fact that the total scale has more items than either half. A high correlation suggests the scale is reliable. If the items were to be split in a different way, a different correlation could result. An approach that most researchers feel is preferable (see McIver & Carmines, 1981, p. 29) is based on the interitem correlation matrix. Cronbach's alpha is defined as $\alpha = N\bar{\rho}/[1 + \bar{\rho}(N - 1)]$, where N is the total number of items and $\bar{\rho}$ is the mean correlation among the N items. If the intercorrelations are high, the items are assumed to be measuring the same thing. Other things equal, high interitem correlation will produce a high alpha. Several other measures are variations on alpha.

---

[11] It is possible, of course, to skip the pretest. One then analyzes items from the main sample and discards useless items before calculating the final scale score. This is never recommended. Much useless information will have been collected and there is no guarantee that there will be a sufficient number of good items to form a scale.

[12] Likert originally used a different criterion of internal inconsistency. Based on total scores, two groups were formed using the highest and lowest scorers, usually the bottom and top quartiles. Then, for each item, a t-test for the difference between group item means was performed. The t-ratio was used as an indicator of differentiability; that is, low ratios indicate that the item failed to discriminate between people with high and low total scores. If an item failed this test, it would be dropped. This procedure has the same goal as the item-to-total correlation analysis but it is computationally simpler. In an age when digital computers were not yet available, that advantage was large. Now, the correlation method is preferable because it uses information on all respondents, not just the extremes (see McIver & Carmines, 1981, p. 25).

Standard computer packages such as the newest versions of SPSS greatly facilitate item analysis. For example, program RELIABILITY in SPSS provides the correlation of each item with the total score (less that item), the scale reliability with each item deleted, and other useful information.

The items in a Likert scale need not be weighted equally. One may a priori assign different weights to different items. Or, empirical results can be used to differentially weight the items. For example, items may be weighted to maximize the correlation of total score to some criterion variable. Factor analysis can be used to obtain weights. In ability testing, items are sometimes weighted to maximize reliability. Although weighting is possible, in practice most Likert scales treat items equally. One reason for equal weighting is that the resulting scale usually correlates quite highly with scores from weighted scales. Although primarily concerned with test construction and not attitude measurement, Nunnally (1967) reports that "there is overwhelming evidence that the use of differential weights seldom makes an important difference [p. 278]."

Researchers often accept a high reliability coefficient as evidence that a single underlying dimension is being assessed. This does not necessarily follow; two or more factors of equal strength could underlie the items (Green, 1954, p. 352). A better test of the dimensionality of the scale is provided by the various factor analytic techniques discussed in the last section of this chapter. Factor analysis has an additional advantage: If the scale is composed of items measuring two (or more) attitude dimensions, the analysis will reveal the dimensions and will indicate which items belong to which dimensions and how they should be weighted to compose the scales.

SUMMARY

The success of Likert scales, like other attitude measurement techniques, depends heavily on the original set of statements used. If these are bad items, it is unlikely that any mathematical mastication will produce good measurements. Even if good items are chosen and even if high reliability is attained, undimensionality is not guaranteed. Other work, factor analysis, usually is needed. Another criticism of Likert scales is their lack of reproducibility, a concept discussed in the section on Guttman scales. In brief, the point is that the same total score can be obtained in a variety of ways. In the extreme case, it is possible for two respondents, both having scores of 5 to have disagreed with each other on every item on a 10 item scale. Of course, if this occurred over many pairs of respondents, the items would be found to be bad and would be discarded.

The main advantages of Likert scaling are:

1. It is easily accomplished.
2. It makes only a few assumptions (the assumed operating curve, for example) that generally are plausible.
3. The success of the scaling can be evaluated through standard techniques of item analysis, reliability analysis and factor analysis.

Guttman Scaling

Guttman developed a scaling technique for measuring attitudes that have an accumulative property (Guttman, 1944, 1947, 1950a, 1950b). Guttman scaling, also called scalogram analysis and cumulative scaling, is based on a relatively straightforward notion of unidimensionality. Think of a variable along which a set of items can be ordered. That is, it is possible to determine for any pair of items which one has more of property X. In the case of a measurement of length, this would involve the simple comparison of two objects, say boards of uniform dimension varying only in length. For each pair of boards, it can be determined if they differ in length and, if so, which is the longer. The result of comparing the boards is an ordering of boards by length. In this example the property, length, is clearly unidimensional. However, when the underlying property is an abstract social or psychological dimension, one can be less sure about such matters. Still, perhaps we are convinced that such a dimension does exist. For example, assume an ability called geometric reasoning. Assume that people vary with respect this variable; that is, two people can be ordered with respect to the variable. But how? Measurements of some sort are needed, responses that presumably reflect to some degree the property about which we are concerned. Suppose respondents are asked to work a single problem. Each person answers correctly or incorrectly. The result would put people into two classes. That may not be sufficient; more degrees of graduation may be needed. Consequently, they are given, say, three problems: A, B, and C. Suppose that the problems themselves can be assumed to be ordered by degree of difficulty. If the assumption about degree of difficulty being a unidimensional phenomenon is correct, apart from carelessness, distractions, and the like, one would expect those people getting the most difficult problem, say, Problem A, also to get the next most difficult (Problem B) and the easiest problem (Problem C) as well. In fact, for three problems a particular pattern should emerge. Letting "+" indicate that the person got the problem correct and "0" indicate that they missed it, the patterns in Figure 7.4 should occur. Row 1 shows the response pattern for those people getting all three correct. Row 2 shows the response pattern for those getting two correct and one wrong, row 3 shows the response pattern for those people getting only one correct, and the fourth row indicates the pattern for people missing all three problems. The most important property of this table, for our purposes, is that each score, where score is equal

	Problem		
	A	B	C
Response types	+	+	+
	0	+	+
	0	0	+
	0	0	0

FIGURE 7.4 Response pattern for three problems of increasing difficulty, assuming degree of difficulty is unidimensional.

A	B	C
0	+	+
+	0	+
+	+	0

FIGURE 7.5 Three ways to get two out of three problems correct.

to the number of correct problems, occurs in only one way. In principle, it is possible for people getting two of the three correct to do it in a variety of ways (see Figure 7.5). For all three of these response types, two problems were answered correctly. However, under the assumption that the items are ordered with respect to difficulty, we do not expect two of the three patterns to obtain. If we assume A is the most difficult, B next, and C the simplest, then there should be only one way to get two of the three correct and that is shown in the second row of the first table. Anyone missing one problem should miss the most difficult. The other two should be answered correctly. The same sort of reasoning can be applied to row three. If the problems are ordered with respect to difficulty, then a person getting one and only one of them correct should get the easiest one correct and miss the two harder problems. Whenever a pattern such as is exhibited in the first table occurs, the items or problems are said to be "scalable." Getting such a pattern is taken to be evidence in support of the assumption that the phenomenon can be thought of as a unidimensional scale and that the items can be placed along the scale.

Notice that attempting to place the items in such a pattern is a test of scalability. If it is successful—and we have not yet discussed the amount of deviation from pattern that is acceptable—then two things have been accomplished. First, the property (ability, attitude, value) has been found to be unidimensional. Second, people have been ordered with respect to that property. This occurs because people are in one of the four types of pattern and the patterns are ordered with respect to ability. Specifically, ordinal values can be assigned to the patterns in the table (see Figure 7.6). Nothing is known about the size of intervals between the scores nor about the zero point. But, the score does reflect the relative position (rank) along the underlying dimension. That is, the score is a monotonic function of ability to reason geometrically. The operating characteristic of a Guttman scale is shown next.

Guttman scaling was designed to measure attitudes. The underlying assumption is that attitude is a unidimensional phenomenon and that statements

A	B	C	Assigned score
+	+	+	3
0	+	+	2
0	0	+	1
0	0	0	0

FIGURE 7.6 Ordinal values can be assigned to the patterns in the table.

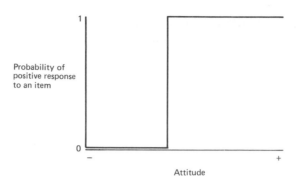

FIGURE 7.7 Operating characteristic of a Guttman scale.

favorable or unfavorable about the attitude object can be ordered. Some statements (items) may reflect a less favorable attitude and some may reflect a more
favorable attitude. For example, assume we are interested in measuring attitude toward a particular political candidate. We have a theoretical universe of
statements about the candidate. The number of grammatically correct English
statements is obviously infinite. Statements may be sampled from media
sources, say, or they may be made up. Presumably, the statements are delim-
ited in such a way that the basic evaluative component is attended to; that is,
we would not include statements such as *Candidate X is 58 years old*. Items are
selected and given to a group of respondents. Each respondent agrees or disagrees with each item. The heart of the analysis is the attempt to scale the
responses. It may be the case that only some of the items are found to form a
scale. If so, the others may be discarded. Once the scale is formed, the assignment of ordinal measurements is automatic. The created variable can then be
used in other analysis.

Although the idea is simple, the practice of scalogram analysis is more
complicated. Modern procedures used to form a Guttman scale begin with a
matrix with items as columns and respondents as rows. The respondent *x* item
matrix contains ones and zeroes indicating each individual's response (agree =
1; disagree = 0) to each item. The problem is to permute the rows and columns
of the matrix in such a way that a scalable response pattern is obtained. Of
course, data will not always be scalable. But, if they are, the correct ordering
can be found by counting the number of agree responses for each respondent
and the number of agree responses for each item. The columns are then permuted so that items are ranked from highest to lowest with respect to the
number of agree responses received and the rows are permuted so that respondents are ranked from highest to lowest with respect to the number of items to
which the respondents agreed.[13] If the data are perfectly scalable in the Guttman sense, the matrix will be in a triangular pattern as discussed earlier. The
matrix will not look exactly like the pattern in Figure 7.7 for the obvious reason

[13] See McIver and Carmines (1981) for an example of this procedure using a small data set.

that there are more respondents than response patterns and, consequently, each pattern may appear more than once. Nevertheless, they should be grouped together and should exhibit the triangular property.[14]

In practice, a perfect scale rarely is obtained. To get the "best" scale possible, it is necessary to have some error criterion. Guttman proposed that one count the total number of changes in response required to obtain perfect scalability. That is, how many agrees must be changed to disagrees and vice versa in order to get a perfect pattern? That number represents "errors" and a measure of the success of the scaling endeavor, called the coefficient of reproducibility, was defined as

$$R = 1 - (\text{errors/total responses})$$

A value of 1 indicates perfect reproducibility; from every respondent's scale score we can exactly reproduce his or her response pattern. The lower R, the greater the departure from scalability. Guttman recommended that an R of .90 or greater be taken as acceptable evidence that the items are scalable.

Edwards (1957, p. 184) credits Goodenough with the suggestion leading to a more sensitive definition of error. For each respondent a predicted response pattern is generated from his or her total score and this pattern is compared to the observed pattern. Every discrepancy is counted as an error. In general, the Edwards–Goodenough method will give a lower coefficient of reproducibility.[15]

Edwards points out that the revised measure is sensitive to marginal distributions; items with extreme marginals inflate the coefficient. He proposed (1957) the calculation of an index called MMR, the minimum marginal reproducibility, as a way to protect against marginal inflation. Standard programs now routinely report both figures. Edwards discusses a strategy for comparing the two figures to evaluate a scale. Also see McIver and Carmines (1981, p. 49).

A variety of other issues attend the use of Guttman scales but fall beyond the scope of this chapter. Readers interested in pursuing these matters may wish to obtain additional information on the following matters:

1. *Nonscale types* are response patterns that represent errors, or nonscalable response patterns, that occur with some regularity. If a particular nonscale type is observed, it may serve to identify an interesting group of respondents. Guttman argued that the existence of nonscale types usually indicated the presence of more than one dimension.
2. *Statistical tests* of various types have been proposed for Guttman scales. This literature is not reviewed here. See Chilton (1966, 1969); Sagi (1959); Schuessler (1961).

[14] Prior to the availability of electronic computers, the permutations sometimes were accomplished by using a board with holes representing the cells of the matrix and marbles (present or absent) representing the responses (agree–disagree). See Suchman (1950) for a description of the device and its use.

[15] The two methods of error counting are related to the procedures used to obtain the scale. The original procedure has come to be called the Cornell technique and the latter the Goodenough–Edwards technique. For procedural detail, see Edwards (1957) or McIver and Carmines (1981).

3. If the deterministic assumption implied by the step function operating curve of Guttman scales is dropped, and an alternative monotonic operating characteristic is assumed, Guttman scaling can be considered as a special case of the latent distance models discussed later in this section. An alternative probabilistic version of Guttman scaling is presented in van der Venn (1980).
4. There are multidimensional versions of Guttman scaling. See Lingoes (1968).

SUMMARY

Guttman scaling is one of the most commonly used methods for scaling attitude and opinion items. It may be appropriate whenever items are thought to fall along a continuum in a cumulative manner such that a positive response to any one item implies a positive response to all items falling below it. The procedure scales the items, evaluates scalability (in the Guttman sense) and, if an acceptable scale can be obtained, respondents are automatically assigned an attitude score from their response patterns.

Guttman scaling can be criticized on several grounds. First, there is the ubiquitous issue of selection of the items. What is the theoretical population from which a set of statements is a sample? How are the items to be selected?

Second, trace lines like those assumed in Guttman scales (Figure 7.6) are not realistic. This implies a perfect correlation between the item and the underlying dimension and this almost never happens. According to Nunnally, an individual item's correlation with the total score typically is .40 or lower. Moreover, Nunnally (1967) argues that even in areas where the underlying attribute might be thought to be scalable, such as spelling ability, the trace lines are usually relatively flat and linear (p. 64).

The complaint that Guttman scales are deterministic rather than probabilistic is often heard and, in our judgment, the point is often overstated. Guttman was well aware of the problem. Indeed, he discussed data sets that failed to scale due to random errors. He called them quasi-scales. As Stouffer pointed out in the overview to the classic *Measurement and Prediction* (Stouffer, Guttman, Suchman, Lazarsfeld, Star, and Claus, 1950, p. 7), Guttman's quasi-scale can be derived as a special case of Lazarsfeld's latent structure analysis.

A third criticism is that scalability does not guarantee a step function trace line. Nunnally points out that if items are spaced far enough apart in difficulty, the triangular pattern may be obtained even though the trace lines are quite flat.[16] He gives an example of a few items that prima facie are not from a simple dimension which would, nonetheless, scale well if administered to a diverse population. He argues (1967), "To take an extreme case, if there are three items that respectively are passed by 10 percent, 50 percent and 90 percent of the people, the triangular pattern will be obtained almost perfectly regardless of what the items concern [p. 65]."

---

[16] He is arguing primarily from the standpoint of psychological measurement and, in particular, ability testing.

Latent Structure Analysis

Latent Structure Analysis was developed by Paul Lazarsfeld. The most comprehensive presentation of the method is in *Latent Structure Analysis* by Lazarsfeld and Henry (1968) although papers developing the technique appeared throughout the 1950s and 1960s.[17] To see the logic of the general latent structure model, it is useful to note Green's observation (1954) that attitudes may be operationally defined as "syndromes of response consistency [p. 359]." Responses used to measure the attitude should be intercorrelated. Indeed, for many techniques (e.g., Likert scales, and factor scaling) the interitem correlations are crucial data in constructing and evaluating the attitude scale. Latent structure analysis assumes that the interitem correlations are due only to the underlying attitude variable (the latent variable). That is, the latent variable accounts for all the observed interitem relations. It follows then that if the latent variable could be held constant, or "partialed out," the items would be mutually independent. For respondents at any set level of the latent variable, the items should be independent. Each item is considered to have an operating characteristic giving the probability of a positive response (in the case of a latent distance model using dichotomous items) as a function of the item's location on the latent variable. Notice that although the function has a step form like Guttman scaling's operating characteristic, the probability is not zero before the change and not 1 after it.

Letting x be the latent variable, $f_i(x)$ is the operating characteristic of item i. The distribution of *scores* on x is represented as $\phi(x)$, a probability density function. Any arbitrary interval about a point x $(x, x + dx)$ will contain $[\phi(x) dx]$, the proportion of respondents having attitude scores in that interval. The proportion of the respondents who (*a*) are in the specified interval and (*b*) respond positively to item 1 is simply $f_i(x)\phi(x) dx$. The integral of this expression yields total proportion who respond positively to item i on p_i, or $\int_{-\infty}^{+\infty} f_i(x)\phi(x) dx$.

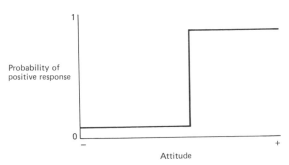

FIGURE 7.8 In Latent Structure Analysis, each item is considered to have an operating characteristic giving the probability of a positive response as a function of the item's location on the latent variable.

[17] See, for example, Lazarsfeld (1950, 1954, 1959, and 1965).

The proportion who agree to both items i and j, for any x, is the product of the separate probabilities (or proportions), $f_i(x)f_j(x)$, because we assume the items are independent if x is constant. The proportion of people who respond positively to i and j and are in any fixed interval about x is the three term product $f_i(x)f_j(x)\phi(x)\ dx$. The value of p_{ij}, to the total proportion responding positively to i and j, is again the integral of this expression p_{ij}, or $\int_{-\infty}^{+\infty} f_i(x)f_j(x)\phi(x)\ dx$. We can construct the same sort of expression for any pair of items and we can extend the representation to involve all triples of items, all sets of four, and so on. In general, for any number of items

$$p_{ijkm. \ . \ .} = \int_{-\infty}^{+\infty} f_i(x)f_j(x)f_k(x)f_m(x) \cdot \cdot \cdot \phi(x)\ dx \qquad (7.3)$$

The full set of equations, called the accounting equations by Lazarsfeld, completely describes the interitem relationships.

All of the left-hand terms, the p_i, the p_{ij}, the p_{ijk}, and so forth are observable. The right-hand side contains the unknown latent parameters and the j unknown respondent distributions. To make this general model solvable, it is necessary to make assumptions about the operating characteristics and/or the attitude distribution. Depending on the assumptions made, several different specific models can be derived.

Latent class analysis is a model based on the assumption that the observed interrelations among the items are due to respondents falling into two or more distinct subgroups. The result is an attitude measured at the nominal level. That is, respondents are put into attitude types. If the $f_i(x)$ operating characteristics, which Lazarsfeld called trace lines, are specified to be of some known form with x continuous, then the model is called a *latent distance model*. The latent distance model is usually considered to be a probability analog of the Guttman scale (Torgerson, 1958, p. 374). The characteristic step-function form of Guttman scale trace lines is not the only form suitable. Any model with monotonic trace lines, provided the items have acceptable discrimination, could be used. Indeed, Torgerson points out that the field of test theory since 1931 has used the normal ogive in conjunction with the assumptions of local independence. Additional information on the use of the latent structure type model in the area of test theory can be found in Bach and Wood (1971), Birnbaum (1968), Lazarsfeld (1960), Lord (1953), Rasch (1960) and Samejima (1969). An application of the type of the latent trait model used in ability testing to attitude measurement can be found in Reiser (1981).

Latent structure analysis has not yet been widely used in survey research. Early on, this may have been due to the complexity of the technique relative to the other methods described here. At the present, there appears to be a growing interest in the technique. It is only in recent years that the needed numerical algorithms have become available. An excellent review of the new methods including a maximum likelihood version of latent structure analysis can be found in Clogg (1981). From his review of recent developments, particularly contributions by Goodman (1974a, 1974b, 1974c, 1975, 1978) and Haberman (1974, 1976, 1977, 1979), Clogg (1981) argues that the "tremendous potential of the latent structure technique as a general language for the expression of social theory [p. 217]'' may now be realized.

Unfolding Analysis

Coombs developed a scaling method for analyzing preference data (1950, 1964). The respondent is usually asked to rank items in order of preference.[18] It is assumed that the items fall along a single underlying continuum. For example, suppose our items are political figures and that preference is a result of location of the political figures along a liberal–conservative continuum. Each political figure has an unknown location on the continuum. We assume each respondent also has a location on the continuum. Unfolding analysis considers that a respondent prefers items, here political figures, that are closer to his or her own position. The respondent's position, called the ideal point, determines the preference ordering: The closest political figure will be the most preferred, the next closest will be second, and so on. For example, let us suppose that we are concerned with four political figures (A, B, C, D) and three respondents (I, II, III). Assume that the political figure and respondent locations are as shown in Figure 7.9 (adapted from Green, 1954). Person I would have the preference order BCAD because B is closest to I's ideal point, C is next, A next, and D farthest away. If the scale were "folded" at I, we would get a single line with the point ordered BCAD. Similarly, we can fold at II and get respondent II's ordering BCDA, and fold at III to get CBDA. The "folding" is a useful metaphor because we are assuming that distance alone and not direction is the determining factor.

The data came to us (folded) in the form of the various rank orders. The task of unfolding analysis is to "unfold" the continuum, that is, to construct it, placing the items and the respondents so as to be consistent with the observed preference rankings. It is possible to get more information. Specifically, if the unfolding is successful, we can get information about the relative magnitudes of the intervals between items. If a respondent is located halfway between two items, he or she will prefer the two equally. But, if a respondent is not on the midpoint between two items, the items will be ordered with the closer item being preferred. In Figure 7.9, respondent I prefers A to D because I is on the A side of the AD midpoint.[19] The midpoints can be ordered as well. The AD midpoint can be located left of BC, for example. It follows, then, that the A to B distance must be greater than the C to D distance. To see this, suppose II had given the preference ranking CBAD. In this case, we would have to place the

---

[18] The technique is more general than this statement suggests. First, it is not necessary that the data be preference data. A respondent could rank items in terms of the degree to which they agree or disagree with them or do some other ordering task. That task, though, should be thought to involve judgments having the same logical structure as preference data. Second, data need not be completed orderings. Under certain conditions, paired comparisons data will suffice or data generated by the task of picking K of N objects and ordering them.

[19] Midpoints are shown in the diagram by the arrows.

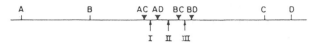

FIGURE 7.9 Political figure (A, B, C, D) and respondent (I, II, III) location.

AD midpoint to the right of BC and this would make the A to B distance smaller than the C to D interval.

In summary, unfolding analysis attempts to construct a single latent variable (called the J scale for joint scale) with items and respondents placed along it in ways that can account for the respondents' preference orderings. If the attempt is not successful, it may mean that multiple criteria are being used or that individuals do not share a common criterion in making judgments. The technique has not been widely used in survey research. Early on, this was probably due to the lack of a general algorithm for obtaining the solution. Even with the advent of programs for doing unidimensional and multidimensional unfolding, the technique has been used relatively infrequently. Marketing research appears to have made more use of the method than other areas of social research (Green & Carmone, 1969). McIver and Carmines (1981) argue that the lack of use is misleading and that its potential "in the social sciences is substantial and that it has been only partially realized at the present time [p. 71]."

A multidimensional version of unfolding analysis was formulated by Bennet and Hays (1960) and Hays and Bennet (1961). However, solutions were difficult to achieve with realistic data sets and involved a certain amount of trial and error. Efficient algorithms for the multidimensional case are now available as programs in the wider family of multidimensional scaling programs.

The Semantic Differential

The semantic differential is sometimes used as a method of measuring attitudes. In the principle source (Osgood, Suci, & Tannenbaum, 1954) the technique is presented as a method for assessing the connotative meaning of concepts. The format is a familiar one. A concept is presented at the top of the page. Underneath appears a set of bipolar adjectival scales, usually with seven points. The respondent is instructed to rate the concept on the scales according to what the concept means to him or her. For example, the concept "United Nations" might be rated on scales such as:

UNITED NATIONS

Good	___	___	___	___	___	___	___	Bad
	1	2	3	4	5	6	7	
Weak	___	___	___	___	___	___	___	Strong
	1	2	3	4	5	6	7	
Active	___	___	___	___	___	___	___	Passive
	1	2	3	4	5	6	7	

The instructions usually explain that if the concept at the top of the page is very closely related to the adjective at one end of the scale, the category next to that adjective should be marked. If the concept is quite close, the second from the end category is appropriate and the third category indicates the concept is only slightly related to one side as opposed to the other. The neutral category is in the center. Respondents are urged to work quickly using their immediate impressions of the meaning of the concepts to them.

Factor analytic studies over many concepts and many pairs of bipolar adjectives and using subjects from several countries have shown the scales rather consistently reflect three major underlying dimensions. The evaluative dimension depends heavily on scales such as good–bad, clean–dirty. The activity dimension is represented by scales like fast–slow, active–passive, and potency is composed of scales such as strong–weak and hard–soft. The rated concept is assigned a connotative meaning equal to its location in the three dimensional semantic space. Dimensional coordinates may be calculated using the original factor loadings on the various scales or with factor loadings from the particular research on which the data were gathered. Some applications use unweighted combinations of scales previously shown to be relatively pure on the three factors.

Osgood and Tannenbaum (1955) have argued that the evaluative dimension can be used as an attitude measurement. Their theory of attitude change, the theory of cognitive congruity, is based on attitudes measured using bipolar adjectival scales heavily loaded or the evaluative dimension.

One occasionally encounters attitude measures using the format of the semantic differential but with other bipolar adjectival scales employed. The seven-point bipolar scales thus employed probably should be thought of as special cases of summated ratings and the term *semantic differential* should be reserved for applications using the Osgood *et al.* instrument, scales and theory. Strictly speaking, *semantic differential* refers to a particular way to measure meaning and not to any set of bipolar adjectival scales.

The semantic differential, or its evaluative component, has been widely used in social research. Its advantages are obvious. The technique is easily used and a respondent can rate a number of concepts on a number of scales quite quickly. Applications have ranged from psychological diagnostics to marketing research, from attitude measurement to cross-cultural research (see Snider & Osgood, 1969). Moreover, because of the extensive and rigorous theoretical and methodological work done by Osgood, Suci, Tannenbaum and others, we know a considerable amount about the technique and the properties of the resulting measures.

Disadvantages in general have more to do with specific applications than with the technique per se. For example, when applied to political figures, the activity and potency dimensions may coalesce. Or, there are instances in which particular adjectives seem to change meaning when used to rate particular concepts (scale–concept interactions).

Magnitude Scaling

Magnitude estimation is a technique used in psychophysics to measure subjective variables such as loudness, brightness, warmth, and various other sensations. These sensations are the psychological counterpart to some objectively measured physical dimension. The goal is to establish the relationship between the psychological variable and the physical variable. Psychophysicists have developed various procedures that require subjects to indicate a magnitude corresponding to a subjective sensation. For example, a subject may be given a reference stimulus (e.g., a particular light having a particular intensity) and a number (say, 50) that corresponds to the subjective brightness of the light. Using the reference stimulus and its value of 50, subjects assign numbers to subsequent lights to reflect how much stronger or weaker each is compared to the reference light.

Over a wide variety of types of physical variables and using various methods to express the estimated magnitude, a remarkable regularity has emerged. The magnitude estimates reflecting the subjective evaluation are related to the stimulus values by a power function. Specifically, $\psi = kP^\beta$, where ψ is the perceived magnitude, P is the physical value of the stimulus, β is a power to which P is raised, and k is a constant that depends on the units used. Different modalities of sensation appear to have characteristic exponents, but the general form of the relationship holds well. This general form implies that equal stimulus ratios produce equal subjective ratios.

The basic strategy developed for measuring subjective sensations to physical stimuli has been used more recently to scale such variables as aesthetic value of works of art, preference, the value of money, crime seriousness, social standing, attitudes, and others (see Lodge, 1981, and Stevens, 1968, for more examples). In these applications as well, the basic power law has gained support. As a result, magnitude estimation has been proposed as a means for measuring attitudes (Hamblin, 1974; Lodge, 1981; Stevens, 1968).

The technique is thought to be superior to the scales of the Likert type which use a set of ordered categories (e.g., strongly agree, agree, neutral, disagree, strongly disagree) on several grounds. First, for category scales, precision is limited by the number of categories employed. Humans are often capable of making finer distinctions and therefore, category scales lose information. Magnitude estimation permits much finer gradations to be expressed. Second, social scientists who take the measurement injunctions seriously are unwilling to treat the ordered category scales as anything beyond ordinal measurement. Magnitude scaling produces quantitative measures. Finally, category scales limit respondents' ability to indicate extreme agreement or extreme disagreement. The most extreme response that can be given is to check one of the two terminal categories; magnitude estimation imposes no such limitation.

Two general types of magnitude estimation have been used in survey research. The first approach scales a set of stimulus items (e.g., evaluative adjectives like *so–so, excellent, bad, disgusting, perfect*). Respondents are first given instructions and practice using metric stimuli. The most commonly used estimation modalities are line drawing and numeric estimation.[20] In line drawing, the respondent draws a line, choosing the length to represent the favorableness, degree of approval, and the like of each stimulus, after having been given a reference line and a reference stimulus (e.g., an adjective such as *fair*). Numeric estimation is similar, except the magnitude attached to the reference stimulus is a number and the judgments about the other stimuli are numbers. Following the magnitude estimation of the stimuli, the technique proceeds in a fashion similar to traditional category scales. An attitude object is presented and an evaluative adjective is selected as the most appropriate for that object. A political figure, for example, may be judged to be "terrific." Subsequent analysis establishes the coefficient and exponent for the power law and this then permits the scaling of the adjectives. The respondents' adjective–attitude object pairings, then, constitute measurement of attitude toward the object.

A second approach asks the respondent to express the evaluation of each attitude object directly, using a magnitude estimation modality such as line drawing or numeric estimation. Again, a reference line is established. Usually, subjects are given instructions to draw a line (or give a number) representing some sort of midpoint on a traditional category scale. Following the establishment of the reference magnitude, respondents are presented with the attitude objects and are asked to draw a line (or give a number) representing their opinion of the stimulus object relative to the opinion represented by the reference line or number.

The direct scaling has an advantage over the stimulus scaling approach in that respondents do not have to first give the judgments needed to scale the stimuli. The primary disadvantage of magnitude scaling appears to be the time required to use the technique. A lengthy interview is required to put a respondent through the instruction warm-up session and then the estimation task. In surveys where many issues other than the measurement of a single attitude must be attended to, the expense may be prohibitive. Lodge (1981), however, gives suggestions about compromises that are reported to cut the time required to about 5 min for instruction and practice and 5–12 sec for each magnitude estimate (pp. 74–76). Examples of instructions used, questions formed, and other procedural details also are found in Lodge.

Other Techniques

There are other techniques important in the measurement literature that so far have failed to find their way into survey research. *Additive conjoint measurement* and *polynomial conjoint measurement* are relatively sophisticated methods that simultaneously (conjointly) measure the dependent and independent variables. The resulting measurements constitute an axiomatic measurement structure in the rigorous sense discussed in Section 7.2 of this chapter.

[20] A study reported by Lodge (1981) uses both and averages results.

Additive models in which the independent variables contribute to the dependent variable noninteractively have been of interest to economists for some time. Early work in utility theory, for example, sometimes assumed utility functions to be additive over the components of commodity bundles. For the most part, the additivity was simply assumed and, furthermore, the assumption was often demonstrably false. Some axiomatic work was done by Frisch (1947), Von Neumann and Morgenstern (1947), Debreu (1960), and others. Recent work has been centered in mathematical psychology. See Krantz *et al.* (1971, pp. 245–366) for a thorough discussion and review of work in this area. Most work by psychologists has used laboratory data with repeated measures on a subject in a fully crossed factorial design. The data requirements make these techniques difficult to use in the typical survey research application. Moreover, there are rather special technical requirements to be met if the conjoint measurement structure is to be realized, including certain cancellation axioms, solvability conditions, and others. These are difficult to meet with survey data. Nonetheless, work continues at a rapid pace and it is likely that in the future, measurement in survey research will be influenced by these rigorous developments.

Nonmetric multidimensional scaling methods, and the related Guttman–Lingoes smallest space analysis series, have been widely used in survey research but almost exclusively as general data analytic schemes rather than as measurement techniques. These methods permit us to represent N objects as points in a space of any specified dimensionality. The configuration of points is determined to correspond to a matrix of measures of proximity, similarity, resemblance, and the like. The distances between points in the solution configuration are monotonic transformations of the proximities, or the "best fitting" monotonic transformations that can be found. A measure of "badness of fit" is used to indicate the success of the solution in the space of each dimensionality tested. The goal is to obtain a space of the minimum dimensionality that preserves the monotonic relationship satisfactorily.[21] A successful solution will have the objects represented as points such that the interpoint distances are ordered approximately the same as the proximities: Objects perceived to be quite similar will be close in the space whereas objects judged to be quite different will be far apart, and so on. In the original applications, the proximities were judgments of perceived similarity. As a way of representing perceptions of the objects, the techniques are quite powerful and have become a major tool in perceptual psychology. Applications have been found in market research by letting the objects be products and by interpreting the solution configurations as representing consumer perceptions of the products. Beyond applications in "cognitive mapping," these methods have been used to analyze measures of taxonomic resemblance by numerical taxonomists; and, if correla-

---

[21] An excellent introduction to the techniques can be found in Kruskal and Wish (1978). A more detailed treatment of the various types of multidimensional scaling, along with practical instructions for using the standard programs, is given in Schiffman, Reynolds, and Young (1981). The most widely cited standard reference is still Shepard, Romnay, and Nerlove (1972).

tions or other measures of association between variables are substituted for the proximities, the techniques become nonmetric, rough analogs to factor analysis.

The cognitive and perceptual mapping applications would seem to offer a new set of measuring devices for survey research. However, several factors have kept this from happening. First, again the data gathering requirements are high. Although complete data are not necessary, the most stable solutions result when judgments are obtained on all $\binom{n}{2}$ pairs of the n objects and that is difficult in the context of the typical survey aimed at measuring a variety of variables on individuals in the sample. Second, the dimensions of the solution space are purely mathematical constructions, geometric degrees of freedom used to get a satisfactory solution; the empirical meanings of the dimensions cannot be established without additional information. This may be accomplished in several ways. For example, supplementary rating scales may be used to rate the objects and the obtained ratings may be compared to the objects' ordering on the dimensions or on dimensions achieved through rotation. This, too, adds to the data collection problems. Moreover, it is not clear that the resulting dimensions, once interpreted, are superior to using the scales alone or using dimensions obtained by factoring the scales. Third, there is a problem related to the decision about whether the analysis is to be done at an individual level or at an aggregate level. If data are analyzed at the individual level, the resulting configurations often are not comparable. That is, they are not necessarily of the same dimensionality nor do the individual dimensions correspond. Consequently, finding a common dimension to provide measures of perception and evaluations of the objects—which is, after all, the primary goal of the techniques considered in this chapter—is problematic. If data are aggregated and a single solution is obtained for the entire sample, one loses the ability to obtain individual measures of attitude, perception, evaluation, and the like. Even the individual difference models such as INDSCAL (Carroll & Chang, 1970) only permit individuals to vary with respect to the weights attached to the same common dimensions presumed to underlie the groups' perceptions.

In short, these techniques are extremely important tools in the repertoire of social scientists, but they have not so far led to important measurement applications in survey research. As an exploratory method to be used to assist in the development of measurement scales, they are quite impressive. As general analytic approaches to the analysis of structure, they seem especially important.

Factor Analysis

Factor analysis can be viewed as consisting of a broad set of techniques (models) that encompass several related procedures such as principal components, principal factor analysis, image factor analysis, and maximum-likelihood factor methods. The immediate objective of factor analysis is to reduce a set of intercorrelated responses (the variables), or alternatively, a set of respondents (the individuals), to a smaller set of unobserved "factors" or latent variables which presumably give rise to the observed data and correlation (covariance) matrix.

For example, in the area of "intelligence" (ability) testing, we may have many questions or problems for respondents to solve and we may be interested in knowing if the pattern of responses and their intercorrelations can be accounted for by placing respondents on a few underlying dimensions such as verbal ability, reading comprehension, mathematical ability, and the like. In fact, much of factor analysis was first developed in response to problems in the area of intelligence and ability testing. In survey research, we are more likely to have a series of attitude or opinion statements to which subjects indicate the degree to which they agree or disagree, as discussed in the section on summated ratings. Each item can be considered a variable, and the matrix of intercorrelations among these variables can be obtained. The survey researcher may be interested in knowing if the responses to the attitude statements can be accounted for by placing respondents on a few underlying attitude dimensions. If so, and if we obtain these dimensions and each respondent's location (score) on each dimension, we will have constructed measurements, fewer in number, that can be used in data analysis.

In this way factor analysis provides the researcher with summary, empirical, multidimensional indices or measurements that are not observed directly but that may be used as variables in statistical analysis. For example, we are frequently interested in quantifying notions such as political identification, socioeconomic class, general intelligence and aptitude, economic price indices, and general attitudes people may have toward particular events, institutions, or issues. The central concept is that due to the complexity of the unobserved latent variables, their measurement is probably multidimensional, that is, defined in a vector space of dimensionality greater than one. This is because it may not be possible to measure a given set of objects on a single scale. A political party, for example, can be left in terms of, say, factors such as institutional attitudes and social philosophy, but perhaps relatively central or right with respect to other variables such as monetary policy, full employment, and social security.

Many of the difficulties concerning the measurement of latent variables can be solved by factor-analytic techniques, which on a mathematical–statistical level share a common dependence on the properties of latent roots and latent vectors of symmetric, positive semidefinite (Gramian) matrices. Factor analysis has played an important role in shaping much of contemporary measurement theory and practice in the social sciences. Although initially developed within the context of "quantitative" or continuous psychological tests, factor analysis has also been successfully adapted to "qualitative" or discrete, categorical data.[22] For further detail concerning the general properties of factor analysis models the reader is referred to the bibliography.

---

[22] The first mathematical treatment of the factor model is due to the statistician Karl Pearson, 1901.

The Role of the Unit of Measure

Certain factor analytic models, such as principal components and principal factor analysis, are not invariant with respect to the statistical metric used. Thus, *post*standardizing the variables and factors does not yield the same loadings and scores as when the variables (and thus the factors–components) are *pre*standardized to unit variance. The same applies to the role of the mean vector $\bar{x}$, since expressing the observed measurements as deviations about the means yields a different factor structure than when the observations are measured in terms of the natural origin. Four distinct analyses are therefore possible when the model is not invariant, and this in turn gives rise to four possible types of Gramian matrices which can be used (Table 7.1). The choice of metric will usually depend on whether the observed variables are expressed in equivalent (i.e., convertible) units of measure, and whether the influence of the mean vector $\bar{x}$ is to be taken into account.

Convertible Units of Measure. When all variables are measured in comparative units so that they can all be expressed in terms of a single measurement unit, either the covariance or the inner product matrix becomes appropriate for analysis. The choice of covariances or inner products will then depend on whether general levels (mean values) are thought to be important. Usually when dealing with ratio or interval scale data, a measure of association is specified to be independent of any addition of a constant number k. In this case the covariance matrix becomes the natural choice since the covariance between any two variables x and y does not depend on the addition of constant terms; that is, $\mathrm{cov}(x + s), (y + t) = \mathrm{cov}(x, y)$ where s and t are arbitrary constants. Note, however, that the importance of the mean values is largely dependent on the particular application of factor analysis. For example, when estimating growth curves it may turn out to be more useful not to express the variables in terms of deviations about their respective means (see Sheth, 1969).

Diverse (Nonconvertible) Units of Measure. In practice, much of social survey data is expressed in diverse units of measure. In this case, the measured

TABLE 7.1
Four Types of Positive Semidefinite Matrices
Which Can Be Used in Factor Analysis

Data standardized to unit variance	Data expressed as deviations about means	
	Yes	No
Yes	Correlation matrix	Cosine matrix
No	Covariance matrix	Inner product matrix

variables usually are converted to unit length (unit standard deviation) and a factor analysis is performed on the correlation matrix. Again, if the general level or scale of measurement is thought to be important (as in some contingency table analyses—see Maxwell, 1961) then cosines can be employed instead of correlations.

Many factor analysis models such as maximum-likelihood and other scaled models (see Mulaik, 1972) are invariant with respect to unit of measurement, that is, to constant multiplication, and will yield the same standardized loadings and scores whether the covariance or correlation matrix is used or not. Since scaled models take into account errors of measurement, they are probably more appropriate for social survey data where error is common. Maximum-likelihood factor analysis is now widely available in standard packages such as SPSS and BMD and no longer presents computational difficulties.

Statistical Significance Testing

When the response variables consist of observations for the entire population, the only source of randomness is due to error of measurement (unreliability) and to unique factors (individual effects). However, the purpose of conducting sample surveys generally is to obtain accurate estimates of population parameters, since it is usually expensive to conduct population censuses. Factor analysis models are therefore more often computed from random samples rather than populations, and this introduces a second source of randomness—that due to sampling. Since random sampling effects are of no substantive interest, the factor parameters (loadings, scores, and latent roots) must be subjected to statistical tests to decide which are insignificant in the population. The nature of the test will depend on the type of factor model used. Normally significance testing is conducted for two models—principal components and ML factor analysis.

The Principal Components Model. Let n be the sample size and let $L =$ $\text{diag}(l_1, l_2, \ldots, l_k)$ and $P = (p_{ij})$ be the latent roots and vectors of a sample covariance matrix $\mathbf{S} = [1/(n-1)]\,(\mathbf{X}^T\mathbf{X})$ where $\mathbf{X}$ denotes the $n \times k$ data matrix of n observations on k variables adjusted for their means. The p_{ij} and l_i are now random variables that possess the following distributional properties (Anderson, 1963; Girshick, 1939).

1. The variance–covariance matrix of the latent vector elements p_{ij} is given by

$$\mathbf{E}(p_{ig} - \pi_{ig})(p_{jh} - \pi_{jh}) = \frac{\lambda_i}{n} \sum_{m \neq i}^{k} \frac{\lambda_m}{(\lambda_m - \lambda_i)^2} \pi_{mg}\pi_{mh}$$

$$- \frac{\lambda_j \lambda_i}{n(\lambda_j - \lambda_i)^2} \pi_{jg}\pi_{ih} \qquad (7.4)$$

where λ_i and π_{ij} are the true (population) values. Since these are unknown they must be replaced by l_i and p_{ij} on the right-hand side of (7.4). The first expression yields variances and covariances in a single vector, whereas the second applies to covariances between p_{ij} in different latent vectors. Thus we have the important result that although the latent vectors of a sample are orthogonal (uncorrelated), their elements need not be independent. For further discussion and illustration see Jackson and Hearne (1973). When **X** represents a $(n \times k)$ multivariate normal sample matrix, drawn from a normal population, the p_{ij} are normally distributed and we can test whether the latent vector elements (and the loadings) are insignificantly different from zero.

2. For a random sample drawn from an $N(\mu, \Sigma)$ population, $\sqrt{n}(l_i - \lambda_i)$ is distributed as the $N(0, 2\lambda_i^2)$ normal distribution, $i = 1, 2, \ldots, k,$ and is independently distributed of the other $(k = 1)$ sample latent roots. This enables us to construct confidence intervals for the population roots λ_i, given the observed values l (see Morrison, 1967, pp. 248–249).

3. Tests for the equality of the last $(k - m)$ latent roots have been given by Bartlett (see Lawley and Maxwell, 1971), for both the covariance and the correlations matrices, although difficulties are encountered for the latter case. More recently Anderson (1963) has given the χ^2 test

$$\chi^2 = -(n - 1) \sum_{j=1}^{r} \ln l_i + (n - 1) \left(\frac{1}{rk} \sum_{j=1}^{r} l_j \right) \tag{7.5}$$

with $(1/2)r(r + 1) - 1$ degrees of freedom to test equality of r intermediate terms, where the remaining large and small roots are unrestricted as to magnitude and multiplicity (for testing the significance of the largest root, given the remaining $k - 1$ are equal, see Kshirsagar, 1961).

Although the joint distribution of the sample roots l_i $(i = 1, 2, \ldots, p)$ is known for any sample size n (see Narasimham, 1968), no distributional results are available for individual roots, except for large samples. The results quoted here therefore only hold for large n.

Maximum Likelihood Factor Analysis. An equivalent methodology applies to the maximum likelihood factor model outlined for principal components. It is important to keep in mind that factor analysis differs from the principal component model in that factor analysis is covariance (rather than variance) oriented; that is, factor analysis embodies a definite hypothesis that the observed k variables have been generated by precisely $m \leq k$ common factors. It is this hypothesis that is tested in the maximum likelihood factor model, where it is assumed that $x \sim N(\mu, \Sigma)$. Since an examination of the testing procedures requires familiarity with more advanced statistics and matrix algebra, we will not go into the actual testing procedures. The interested reader is referred to Jöreskog (1963), Morrison (1967), Lawley and Maxwell (1971), and Mulaik (1972, pp. 168–169). Most computer programmes that contain maximum likelihood factor analysis also have facilities for testing the common factors, where we proceed to test for the existence of 1, 2, . . . , m common factors until the appropriate number has been determined. These tests are usually based on the χ^2 distribution and depend on the proportion of residual (unexplained) variance to indicate whether m common factors have generated the observed covariances (correlations) between the observed variables. Statistical significance, however, need not have anything to do with substantive interpretation of the factors, since a statistically significant factor may not always be identified correctly in terms of empirical phenomena.[23] This is because the assumption of multivariate normality of the data matrix X is not always satisfied, and a statistically significant factor need not necessarily have high explanatory power in terms of the amount of variance explained.

The χ^2 tests of significance therefore test the null hypothesis of the presence of precisely m common factors against the alternative hypothesis of more than m common factors. Since in social surveys m is usually never known, the χ^2 test is in fact used to test the null hypothesis of m common factors *and* to determine the value of m. Because of this simultaneity it is sometimes suggested that the sample be divided into two equal parts, that m be determined from the first half, and then the null hypothesis of m common factors tested with the second half. Usually, however, one first tests $m = 1$ (at some appropriate level of significance) against $m > 1$ and if $m = 1$ is rejected we test for $m = 2$ against $m > 2$ and so on. This process is continued until we obtain a value $m = m_0$ for which the test does not show significance whereas for any smaller value of m the null hypothesis is rejected.

Factor Identification and Rotation of Factors. Once factor loadings and scores are computed and tests carried out, the next logical step is to relate the common factors to the originally observed responses. Since both the loadings and the scores are computed, factor analysis is basically an internal process of generating measurements or variables (unlike, for example, the regression model where both the dependent as well as the explanatory variables are observed), so that any substantive identification of the factors ultimately resides in the degree to which the common factors are correlated with the observed variables. Since the correlations are given directly by the factor loadings, the first step in identifying the common factors lies in examining the pattern and magnitudes of the loadings.

Orthogonal Rotations. Consider the common factor loadings given in Table 7.2. Here we have six observed variables $x_1, x_2, . . . , x_6$ and two common factors ϕ_1 and ϕ_2. As Table 7.2 stands, however, it is not a very useful guide to the identification of ϕ_1 and ϕ_2 since both possess uniformly high loadings for the six response variables. Either ϕ_1 or ϕ_2 can therefore serve equally well as a characterization of the x_i, although both are required to account for the communalities h_i^2. The distribution of the loadings is deceptive because their magni-

---

[23] A statistically insignificant factor, however, will be usually substantively unidentifiable in a large sample.

TABLE 7.2
Common Factor Loadings a_{ij} and Their
Communalities h_i^2 (Sums of Squares) for Six
Response Variables, where $h_i^2 = a_{i1}^2 + a_{i2}^2$

| | Common factors | | |
Response variables	ϕ_1	ϕ_2	h_i^2
x_1	.50	.70	.74
x_2	.40	.50	.41
x_3	.60	.60	.72
x_4	.70	−.60	.85
x_5	.60	−.70	.85
x_6	.50	−.80	.89

tudes (and signs) are influenced by the particular location of the axes ϕ_1 and ϕ_2, which are arbitrary. To provide a more effective visual aid, the loadings can be plotted on a two-dimensional graph, as in Figure 7.10. Here two things can be noticed. First, the response variables form two distinct clusters in the common

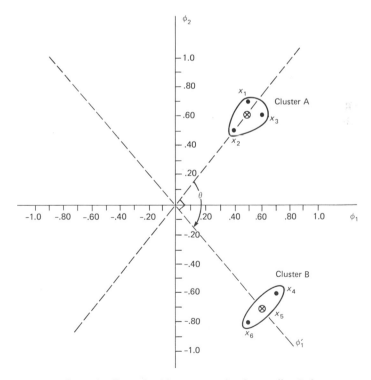

FIGURE 7.10 Common factor loadings of Table 7.2 rotated orthogonally: ⊗ denotes a mean point of a cluster.

factor space, and second, ϕ_1 and ϕ_2 can be made to coincide with the clusters by rotating clockwise the two common factor axes through an angle ϕ, to a new position ϕ_1' and ϕ_2'. If the new position of the orthogonal axes is accepted as a reference point, new loadings can be computed, which should simplify identification of the two common factors.

Thus from Table 7.3 we see that the first common factor can be identified from x_4, x_5, and x_6, whereas the second is associated with x_1, x_2, and x_3. Depending on the nature of the x_i the two factors can be named accordingly. Since rotation of the factors (axes) is always possible, their location possesses no intrinsic meaning, and the loadings are therefore chosen with respect to that location of the axes which possesses maximal interpretability of the initial response variables x_i. Theoretically therefore, there are an infinite number of factor solutions possible, but only a small number will have any useful interpretation. In terms of the rotated axes the response variables can be expressed as

$$x_1 = .86 \; \phi_2' + e_1$$
$$x_2 = .64 \; \phi_2' + e_2$$
$$x_3 = .84 \; \phi_2' + e_3$$
$$x_4 = .92 \; \phi_1' + e_4$$
$$x_5 = .92 \; \phi_1' + e_5$$
$$x_6 = .94 \; \phi_1' + e_6$$

if the remaining loadings are insignificantly different from zero. Note that the total communality h_i^2 of the two common factors remains unchanged (Table 7.3) so that the statistical explanatory power of the original and new factor locations is constant.

Since the factors ϕ_1' and ϕ_2' are orthogonal, rotation of ϕ_1 and ϕ_2 to new positions ϕ_1' and ϕ_2' is known as orthogonal rotation. In our present example with only two common factors, it is relatively straightforward to measure off the new loading values from the axes ϕ_1' and ϕ_2'. In practice, however, when

TABLE 7.3
Rotated Orthogonal Factors ϕ_1' and ϕ_2'

Response variables	Rotated factors		
	d_1'	d_2'	h_i^2
x_1	−.05	.86	.74
x_2	0	.64	.41
x_3	.10	.84	.72
x_4	.92	.15	.85
x_5	.92	0	.85
x_6	.94	−.10	.89

dealing with large-scale surveys we can frequently expect 5, 10, or more common factors to emerge. In this case rotation can no longer be achieved by simple graphical techniques, and new optimum locations of the common factors must be determined through maximization of some algebraic criterion. Several criteria exist, and choice depends upon the particular feature of the loadings we wish to concentrate attention on (see Mulaik, 1972). In order to provide a concrete example, we briefly describe a criterion frequently employed in practice—the "varimax" method which, as its name suggests, seeks to maximize variances of the loadings in a certain predetermined fashion.

Originally due to Kaiser (1958), several versions of the varimax procedure are available (see Horst, 1965, chap. 18; Lawley & Maxwell, 1971). The common factors may be rotated in pairs or simultaneously. Let B denote the final loading matrix with elements b_{ij}, after the rotation is completed, as in Table 7.3. Comparing Tables 7.2 and 7.3, we note that identification or interpretability of the two factors is achieved by the fact that the loadings have moved to two opposite poles, namely toward 1 (or -1) and zero, for each factor. Since this can be characterized by an increase in the variance of the loadings (per factor), Kaiser (1958) defines the simplicity (interpretability) of a given common factor ϕ_j as

$$V_j = \frac{1}{k} \sum_{i=1}^{p} (b_{ij}^2)^2 - \frac{1}{k^2} \left(\sum_{i=1}^{k} b_{ij}^2 \right)^2, \tag{7.6}$$

which represents the variance of the squared loadings of ϕ_j. Squared loadings are used because a loading can be either negative or positive, and because b_{ij}^2 is the contribution to the communality h_i^2 of response x_i of the jth common factor of ϕ_j. It is easy to see that (7.6) achieves high values as some b_{ij}^2 approach 1, whereas the remaining b_{ij}^2 approach 0. Values of 1 and 0 for the b_{ij}^2 are rare in practice, and the rotated loadings b_{ij} are chosen such that

$$V^* = \sum_{j=1}^{m} V_j^* \tag{7.7}$$

is maximized. Since the b_{ij} are not initially known actual computations are iterative.

Criterion (7.7) gives a greater weight to those variables with high communalities since each contributes as the square of the loading. Variables with less residual variance therefore play a larger role in determining the new position of the common factor axes. Kaiser (1958) also defines the "normal" criterion

$$V_j = \frac{1}{k} \sum_{i=1}^{k} \left(\frac{b_{ij}^2}{h_i^2} \right)^2 - \frac{1}{k^2} \left(\sum_{i=1}^{k} \frac{b_{ij}^2}{h_i^2} \right)^2 \tag{7.8}$$

where $V = \sum_{j=1}^{m} V_j$ is maximized. Formula (7.8) gives equal weight to low and high communality, since the squared loadings are normed by the communality h_i^2. Kaiser prefers criterion (7.8), although it should be kept in mind that (7.8) gives equal preference, to both reliable as well as unreliable variables when deciding on the angle of rotation.

The varimax criterion is widely available in software computer programs; it can be used to rotate factors from any factor model. All that is required as input are the initial factor loadings a_{ij}. Other criteria also exist, such as the "quantimax," "transvarimax," "equamax," and "passimax," and the reader is referred to Mulaik (1972) for more detail.

Oblique Rotation. It is clear from Figure 7.10 that it is possible to rotate the axes and still maintain orthogonality only because the two clusters of A and B are *in fact* orthogonal to each other. Very often the response variables will not form orthogonal clusters (Figure 7.11) and a more general system of axes is required, the so-called oblique axes system. There is no hard and fast rule for deciding a priori which system is more appropriate. Usually an orthogonal rotation is first attempted, and if the new loadings b_{ij} are still not identifiable, an oblique rotation is then carried out. It is clear, however, that orthogonal axes are a special case of the oblique case since the only difference between the two systems is that oblique factors are correlated whereas orthogonal factors are not. The degree of correlation depends on the relative positions of the clusters. Since the oblique common factors are no longer orthogonal the new loadings (coordinates) are measured obliquely, that is, parallel to the new axes rather than to the original orthogonal axes. Again alternative criteria are available and are discussed in Harman (1967).

Another issue when identifying factors concerns the signs of the loadings. Consider a three-factor equation of some response variable x_i, $x_i = .13F_1 -$

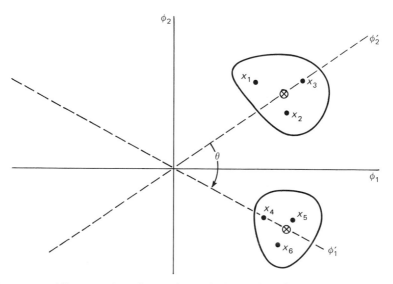

FIGURE 7.11 An oblique rotation of ϕ_1 and ϕ_2, clockwise through an angle θ. $\otimes$ denotes the centroid of the cluster.

.91F_2 + .24F_3 say, where F_2 has been identified as a factor which picks up low socioeconomic status. The equation can also be written as

$$X_i = 13F_1 - .91G_2 + .24F_3$$

where $G_2 = -F_2$, so that the second factor must now be identified in terms of high socioeconomic status. Changes in signs of large loadings are frequently carried out to facilitate or simplify the labeling of factors.

Constructing Factor Scales

One important part of the output of factor analysis contains two sets of numbers: the factor loadings, which measure correlation between the observed measurements and the factors; and the factor scores, which indicate the relative position of each individual on that factor. As pointed out earlier, the first step in any factor analysis consists in identifying the factors by means of rotations. Due to the nature of most social data, optimal identification of factors in terms of observed measurements (variables) is usually achieved in terms of oblique (correlated) factors. Once the factors have been identified in terms of substantive behavior (attributes), the factor scores can be considered as measuring the relative locations of the individuals on the factors. The factors, in effect, become latent variables on which the individuals are scaled or measured.

Suppose, for example, a set of n respondents is requested to answer a questionnaire consisting of 10 items (questions), each one of which represents a Likert scale where 5 = strongly agree; 4 = agree; 3 = neutral; 2 = disagree; 1 = strongly disagree. We wish to (a) uncover, if possible, a relatively small number of continuous factors which result in the attitudes; and (b) scale each individual along each one of the continuous but unobserved factors. It is assumed that although the response is measured by discrete numbers, the latent attitudes are in fact continuous. It is these latent attitudes which we wish to measure using the questionnaire.

Suppose the 10 questions pertain to a country's immigration policy and general economic conditions, such that x_1, x_2, x_3, x_4, and x_5 are intended to measure attitudes toward immigration (both white and nonwhite), whereas x_6, x_7, x_8, x_9, and x_{10} measure the degree of economic insecurity of the respondents. Assume the factor loadings are given by Table 7.4, where Factor 1 has been identified (interpreted) as a measure of latent racial prejudice and Factor 2 measures the extent of economic insecurity. To scale (measure) each of the n individuals along the racial prejudice and insecurity scales we proceed as follows. Consider an individual who responded in the manner of Table 7.5. To compute this individual's total score for Factor 1 we first reverse the negative signs for the large loadings. Thus for question x_2 the respondent can be taken as "not disagreeing," or as "agreeing." He therefore received a score of (6 − 2) = 4, which is the "agreed" score. Similarly, x_3 obtains a score of (6 − 4) = 2. Then this total score for Factor 1 (racial prejudice) is .703(5) + .741(4) +

TABLE 7.4
Factor Analysis of the Correlation Matrix of $x_1, x_2, \ldots, x_{10}$ after Suitable Rotation

		Factor 1	Factor 2	Communality
More white immigration:	x_1	+.703	+.301	.5848
More boat people immigration:	x_2	−.741	−.267	.6204
Nonwhites are good citizens:	x_3	−.750	+.184	.5964
Whites are good citizens:	x_4	+.682	+.371	.6027
Whites are more hard working:	x_5	+.837	−.173	.7306
Economic depression imminent:	x_6	−.271	+.871	.8320
Dollar is very unstable:	x_7	+.103	+.787	.6300
Situation is improving:	x_8	+.080	−.880	.7808
Government is doing good job:	x_9	−.371	+.784	.7523
Jobs are plentiful:	x_{10}	−.219	−.850	.7705

.750(2) + .682(3) + .837(4) = 13.375/5 = 2.675, indicating an almost neutral attitude toward nonwhites (and whites). Similarly the same individual's total score on Factor 2 is .871(4) + .787(5) + .880(4) + .784(4) + .850(5) = 18.325/5 = 3.665 indicating a higher score for economic insecurity, Factor 2.

The principal recommendation for factor scaling is that it provides a method of measuring dimensions that cannot be observed with accuracy. Since only common factors are scaled, the resultant measurements are largely free of measurement error and other individual differences among the respondents. Note, however, that factor scales are only uncorrelated when the variables indicate that an orthogonal structure is relevant. Lack of orthogonality between the factors, though, need not present major difficulties since latent attitudes, it can be argued, may in reality be correlated. Thus racial prejudice (Factor 1) may very well be positively correlated with economic insecurity (Factor 2). Finally, the factors depend on the variables included (and excluded) from the factor analysis, and to this extent cannot be theory free. The predictive (or

TABLE 7.5
Observed Response Score for Individual i, on the 10 Questions

Question	Observed response
x_1	5
x_2	2
x_3	4
x_4	3
x_5	4
x_6	4
x_7	5
x_8	2
x_9	4
x_{10}	1

explanatory) ability of the factor scales will therefore depend on the relevance of the questionnaire design.

A distinctive feature of factor scaling is that is does not assume each item (question) to be of equal value when determining the individual's scores. Thus items with low loadings are given small weight, and those with very small magnitudes are omitted from the calculations altogether. What constitutes a small loading is more-or-less arbitrary—however, if a sample of individuals is taken it becomes more relevant to exclude statistically insignificant loadings rather than loadings which are deemed to be small.

7.4. CONCLUDING REMARKS

In this chapter, we attempted to do a number of things. First, we argued for the importance of measurement in survey research and in science in general. Survey research is frequently confronted with the problem of measuring abstract and subjective states including attitudes, beliefs, opinions, personality traits, and so on through a long list of concepts for which measurement is particularly difficult. Solving the measurement problem should involve work at two levels: theory and method. We argued that all measurement involves theory and that any measurement technique must contend with the correspondence between the theoretical notion being measured and the technique used to produce the measures. The basic concepts of measurement theory were presented. We then turned to the principal techniques used in survey research to produce measures. Major techniques were reviewed briefly and references for detailed information were presented. Factor analysis was given particular attention because of its importance in contemporary measurement work.

BIBLIOGRAPHY

Anderson, T. W.
    1963   "Asymptotic theory for principal components analysis." *Annuals of Mathematical Statistics* 34: 127–148.
Armor, D. J. and A. S. Couch
    1972   *Data-Text Primer*. New York: The Free Press.
Arrow, K.
    1959   "Rational choice functions and orderings." *Economica* 26: 121–127
Bennet, J. F., and W. L. Hays
    1960   "Multidimensional unfolding: Determining the dimensionality of ranked preference data." *Psychometrika* 25: 27–43.
Birnbaum, A.
    1968   "Some latent trait models and their use in inferring an examinee's ability." In F. M. Lord and M. R. Novick (eds.), *Statistical Theories of Mental Test Scores*. Reading, Mass.: Addison–Wesley.

Bock, R. D., and R. Wood
1971 "Test theory." *Annual Review of Psychology* 22: 193–244.
Bohrnstedt, G., and E. F. Borgatta
1981 "Level of measurement: Once again." In G. Bohrnstedt and E. F. Borgatta (eds.), *Social Measurement: Current Issues*. Beverly Hills: Sage.
Carmines, E. G., and R. A. Zeller
1980 *Reliability and Validity Assessment*. Sage University Paper Series on Quantitative Applications in the Social Sciences, G7-017. Beverly Hills: Sage Publications.
Carroll, J. D., and J. J. Chang
1970 "Analysis of individual differences in multidimensional scaling via an *N*-way generalization of 'Eckart–Young decomposition'." *Psychometrika* 35: 283–319.
Chilton, R. J.
1966 "Computer generated data and the statistical significance of scalograms." *Sociometry* 29: 175–181.
1969 "A review and comparison of simple statistical tests for scalogram analysis." *American Sociological Review* 34: 237–244.
Cliff, N.
1973 "Scaling." *Annual Review of Psychology* 24: 473–506.
Clogg, C. C.
1981 "New developments in latent structure analysis." In David J. Jackson and Edgar F. Borgatta (eds.), *Factor Analysis and Measurement in Sociological Research*. Beverly Hills: Sage.
Coombs, C. H.
1950 "Psychological scaling without a unit of measurement." *Psychological Review* 57: 145–158.
1964 *A Theory of Data*. New York: Wiley.
Coombs, C. H., R. M. Dawes, and A. Tversky
1970 *Mathematical Psychology: An Elementary Introduction*. Englewood Cliffs, N.J.: Prentice–Hall.
Davis, F. B.
1951 "Item selection techniques." Pp. 266–328 in E. F. Lindquist (ed.), *Educational Measurement*. Washington, D.C.: American Council on Education.
1952 "Item analysis in relation to education and psychological testing." *Psychology Bulletin* 49: 97–119.
Debreu, G.
1954 "Representations of preference ordering by a numerical process." In R. M. Thrall, C. H. Coombs, and R. L. Davis (eds.), *Decision Processes*. New York: Wiley.
1959 *Theory of Value*. New York: Wiley.
1960 "Topological methods in cardinal utility theory." Pp. 16–20 in K. J. Arrow, S. Karlin, and D. S. Suppes (eds.), *Mathematical Methods in the Social Sciences*. Stanford, Cal: Stanford University Press.
Edwards, A. L.
1957 *Techniques of Attitude Scale Construction*. New York: Appleton–Century–Crofts.
Ellis, B.
1966 *Basic Concepts of Measurement*. London: Cambridge University Press.
Ekman, G.
1962 "Measurement of moral judgment: A comparison of scaling methods." *Perceptual and Motor Skills,* 15: 3–9.
Frisch, R.
1936 "The problem of index number five." *Econometrica* 4: 38.
1947 "General choice field theory." Pp. 64–67 in *Report of Third Annual Research Conference on Economics and Statistics*. Cowles Commission for Research in Economics.
Girschick, M. A.
1939 "On the sampling theory of roots of determinantal equations." *Annals of Mathematical Statistics* 10: 203–224.

Goodenough, W. H.
1944 "A technique for scale analysis." *Educational and Psychological Measurement* 4: 179–190.

Goodman, L. A.
1974a "Exploratory latent structure analysis using both identifiable and unidentifiable models." *Biometrika*, 61: 215–231.
1974b "The analysis of systems of qualitative variables when some of the variables are unobservable. Part 1: A modified latent structure approach." *American Journal of Sociology*, 79: 1179–1259.
1974c "The analysis of systems of qualitative variables when some of the variables are unobservable. Part 2: The use of modified latent distance models." Unpublished manuscript.
1975 "A new model for scaling response patterns: An application of the quasi-independence concept." *Journal of the American Statistical Association* 70: 755–768.
1978 "A note on the estimation of parameters in latent structure analysis." Technical Report No. 59. Department of Statistics, University of Chicago. (Forthcoming in *Psychometrika*.)

Gorsuch, R. L.
1974 *Factor Analysis*. Philadelphia: W. B. Saunders.

Green, B. F.
1954 "Attitude measurement." In G. Lindzey *et al.* (eds.), *Handbook of Social Psychology*. Vol. 1. Reading, Mass: Addison–Wesley.

Guttman, L.
1944 "A basis for scaling qualitative data." *American Sociological Review* 9: 139–150.
1947 "The cornell technique for scale and intensity analysis." *Educational and Psychological Measurement* 7: 247–279.
1950a "Basis for scalogram analysis." In Stouffer *et al.* (eds.), *Measurement and Prediction*. Princeton: Princeton University Press. (Wiley Science Edition, 1966).
1950b "The problem of attitude and opinion measurement." In Stouffer *et al.* (eds.), *Measurement and Prediction*. Princeton: Princeton University Press. (Wiley Science Edition, 1966.)

Haberman, S. K.
1974 "Log-linear models for frequency tables derived by indirect observation: Maximum likelihood equations." *Annals of Statistics* 2: 911–924.
1976 "Iterative scaling procedures for log-linear models for frequency tables derived by indirect observation." *Proceedings of the American Statistical Association* 45–50. (1975 Statistical Computing Section.)
1977 "Product models for frequency tables involving indirect observation." *Annals of Statistics* 5: 1124–1147.
1979 *The Analysis of Qualitative Data: Vol. 2. New Development*. New York: Academic Press.

Hamblin, R. L.
1974 "Social attitudes: Magnitude measurement and theory." In. H. M. Blalock, Jr. (ed.), *Measurement in the Social Sciences*. Chicago: Aldine.

Harman, M. M.
1967 *Modern Factor Analysis*. Chicago: University of Chicago Press.

Hays, W. L., and J. F. Bennet
1961 "Multidimensional unfolding: Determining configuration from complete rank order preference data." *Psychometrika*, 26: 221–238.

Horst, P.
1965 *Factor Analysis of Data Matrices*. New York: Holt, Rinehart and Winston.

Houthakker, H. S.
1950 "Revealed preference and the utility function." *Economica*, 17: 159–174.

Hurwicz, L.
1971 "On the problem of integrability of demand functions." *Preferences, Utility and Demand*. New York: Harcourt Brace Jovanovich.

Jackson, J. E., and G. T. Hearne
  1973 "Relationship among coefficients of vectors used in principal components." *Technometrics* 15: 601–610.
Jöreskog, K. G.
  1963 *Statistical Estimation in Factor Analysis: A New Technique and Its Foundation.* Stockholm: Almquist and Wiksell.
Kaiser, H. F.
  1958 "The varimax criterion for analytic rotation in factor analysis." *Psychometrika* 23: 187.
Kim, Jae-On, and C. W. Mueller
  1978 *Factor Analysis: Statistical Methods and Practical Issues.* Beverly Hills: Sage Publications.
Krantz, D. H., R. D. Luce, P. Suppes, and A. Tversky
  1971 *Foundations of Measurement.* Vol. 1. New York: Academic Press.
Kruskal, J. B. and M. Wish
  1978 *Multidimensional Scaling.* Vol. 2. in *Qualitative Applications in the Social Sciences.* Beverly Hills: Sage Publications.
Kshirsagar, A. M.
  1961 "The goodness of fit of a single hypothetical principal component." *Biometrika* 48: 397–407.
Labovitz, S.
  1970 "The assignment of numbers to rank order categories." *American Sociological Review* 36: 515–524.
  1971 "In defense of assigning numbers to ranks." *American Sociological Review* 26: 521–522.
Lawley, P. N., and A. E. Maxwell
  1971 *Factor Analysis as a Statistical Method.* London: Butterworths.
Lazarsfeld, Paul F.
  1950 Chapters 10 and 11 in S. A. Stouffer *et al.* (eds.), *Measurement and Prediction.* Princeton: Princeton University Press.
  1954 "A conceptual introduction to latent structure analysis." Chapter 7 in Paul F. Lazarsfeld (Ed.), *Mathematical Thinking in the Social Sciences.* New York: The Free Press.
  1959 "Latent structure analysis." Pp. 476–535 in S. Koch (Ed.), *Psychology: A Study of a Science.* Vol. 3. New York: McGraw–Hill.
  1960 "Latent structure analysis and test theory." In H. Gulliksen and S. Messick, *Psychological Scaling.* New York: John Wiley.
  1965 "Latent structure analysis." Pp. 37–54 in S. Sternberg *et al.* (eds.), *Mathematics and Social Sciences.* The Hague: Mouton.
Lazarsfeld, Paul F., and Neil W. Henry
  1968 *Latent Structure Analysis.* Boston: Houghton Mifflin.
Lingoes, James C.
  1968 "The multivariate analysis of qualitative data." *Multivariate Behavioral Research* 3(January): 61–94.
Lodge, M.
  1981 *Magnitude Scaling.* Beverly Hills: Sage.
Lodge, M., D. Cross, B. Tursky, M. A. Foley, and H. Foley
  1976 "The calibration and cross-model validation of ratio scales of political opinion in survey research." *Social Science Research* 5: 325–347.
Lodge, M., and B. Tursky
  1981 "The social–psychological scaling of political opinion." In B. Wegener (ed.), *Social Attitudes and Psychophysical Measurement.* Hillsdale, N.J.: Erlbaum.
Lord, F. M.
  1952 *A Theory of Test Scores.* Psychometric Monograph No. 7. Richmond: The William Byrd Press.
  1953 "The relation of test score to the trait underlying the test." *Educational and Psychological Measurement* 13, 517–548.

Marks, L. E.
  1974 *Sensory Processes: The New Psychophysics.* New York: Academic Press.
Maxwell, A. E.
  1961 *Analyzing Qualitative Data.* London: Methuen.
Mayer, L. S.
  1970 "Comments on 'The assigment of numbers to rank order categories'." *American Sociological Review* 25: 916–917.
  1971 "A note on treating ordinal data as interval data." *American Sociological Review* 36: 519–520.
McIver, John P., and E. G. Carmines
  1981 *Unidimensional Scaling.* No. 24 in Quantitative Applications in the Social Sciences. Beverly Hills: Sage Publications.
McKennell, A. C.
  1977 "Attitude scale construction." In C. A. O'Muircheartaigh and C. Payne (eds.), *The Analysis of Survey Data.* Vol. 1. New York: Wiley.
McNemar, Q.
  1946 "Opinion–Attitude methodology." *Psychological Bulletin* 3: 289–374.
Morrison, D. F.
  1967 *Multivariate Statistical Methods.* New York: McGraw–Hill.
Mulaik, S. A.
  1972 *The Foundations of Factor Analysis.* New York: McGraw–Hill.
Narasimham, G. V. L.
  1968 "The asymptotic theory of certain characteristics roots of econometric equation systems." *Econometrica* 36: 95–97. (Supplement).
Nunnally, J. C.
  1967 *Psychometric Theory.* New York: McGraw Hill.
O'Brien, R. M.
  1979a "On Kim's multivariate analysis of ordinal variables." *American Journal of Sociology* 85: 668–669.
  1979b "The use of Pearson's r with ordinal data." *American Sociological Review* 44: 851–857.
Oppenheim, A. N.
  1966 *Questionnaire Design and Attitude Measurement.* New York: Basic Books.
Osgood, C. E., G. J. Suci, and P. H. Tannenbaum
  1957 *The Measurement of Meaning.* Urbana, Il.: University of Illinois Press.
Osgood, C. E., and P. H. Tannenbaum
  1955 "The principal of congruity in the prediction of attitude change." *Psychological Review* 62: 42–55.
Payne, S. L.
  1951 *The Art of Asking Questions.* Princeton: Princeton University Press.
Pearson, K.
  1901 "On lines and planes of closest fit to systems of points in space." *Philosophical Magazine* 2: 559–572. (Sixth revision.)
Pfanzagl, J.
  1968 *Theory of Measurement.* New York: Wiley.
Rader, T.
  1963 "Existence of a utility function to represent preference." *Review of Economic Studies* 30: 229–232.
Rasch, G.
  1960 *Probabilistic Models for Some Intelligence and Attainment Tests.* Copenhagen: Danish Institute of Educational Research.
Reiser, M.
  1981 "Latent train modelling of attitude items." In George W. Bohrnstedt and Edgar F. Borgatta (eds.), *Social Measurement: Current Issues.* Beverly Hills: Sage Publications.

Roberts, S.
   1979   *Measurement Theory*. Vol. 7 in *Encyclopedia of Mathematics*. Reading, Mass: Addison–Wesley.
Roberts, B. and Schulze, D.
   1973   *Modern Mathematics and Economic Analysis*. New York: Norton.
Sagi, P. C.
   1959   "A statistical test for the significance of a coefficient of reproducibility." *Psychometrika* 24: 19–27.
Samejima, F.
   1969   "Estimation of latent ability using a response pattern of graded scores." *Psychometric Monograph 17*.
Samuelson, P.A.
   1947   *Foundations of Economic Analysis*. Cambridge, Mass: Harvard University Press.
   1950   "Problem of integrability and utility theory." *Economica* N.S. 17.
Schiffman, S. S., M. L. Reynolds, and F. W. Young
   1981   *Introduction to Multidimensional Scaling*. New York: Academic Press.
Schuessler, K. F.
   1961   "A note on statistical significance of scalograms." *Sociometry*, 24: 491–499.
Schuman, H., and S. Presser
   1977   "Question wording as an independent variable in survey analysis." *Sociological Methods and Research*, 6.
Schuman, S., and O. D. Duncan
   1974   "Questions about attitude survey questions." In H. L. Costner (ed.), *Sociological Methodology, 1973–1974*. San Francisco: Jossey–Bass.
Shepard, R. N., A. K. Romney, and S. Nerlove
   1972   *Multidimensional Scaling and Applications in Behavioral Science*. Vol. 1 and 2. New York: Seminar Press.
Sheth, J. N.
   1969   "Using factor analysis to estimate parameters." *Journal of the American Statistical Association*. 64: 808–822.
Shinn, A., Jr.
   1969   "An application of psychophysical scaling techniques to the measurement of national power." *Journal of Politics*, 31: 932–951.
   1974   "Relations between scales." In H. M. Blalock (ed.), *Measurement in the Social Sciences: Theories and Strategies*. Chicago: Aldine.
Snider, J. G., and C. E. Osgood, Eds.
   1969   *Semantic Differential Technique*. Chicago: Aldine.
Stevens, S. S.
   1946   "On the theory of scales and measurement." *Science* 103: 667–680.
   1951   "Mathematics, measurement and psychophysics." In S. S. Stevens (ed.), *Handbook of Experimental Psychology*. New York: Wiley.
   1959   "Measurement, psychophysics and utility." In C. W. Churchman and P. Ratoosh (eds.), *Measurement Definitions and Theories*. New York: Wiley.
   1966   "A metric for the social consensus." *Science*, 151: 530–541.
   1968   "Measurement statistics and the schemapiric view." *Science*, 161: 849–856.
   1969   "On predicting exponents for cross-modality matches." *Perception and Psychophysics*, 6: 251–256.
   1972   *Psychophysics and Social Scaling*. Morristown, N.J.: General Learning Press.
   1975   *Psychophysics: Introduction to Its Perceptual, Neural, and Social Prospects*. New York: Wiley.
Stouffer, S. A., L. Guttman, E. A. Suchman, P. F. Lazarsfeld, S. A. Star, and J. A. Clause
   1950   *Measurement and Prediction*. Princeton: Princeton University Press. (Wiley Science Edition, 1966.)

Suchman, E. A.
   1950   "The scalogram board technique." Pp. 91–121 in S. A. Stouffer *et al.* (eds.), *Measurement and Prediction*. Princeton: Princeton University Press.
Suppes, P., and J. Zinnes
   1963   "Basic measurement theory." In R. D. Luce, R. R. Bush, and E. Galanter (eds.), *Handbook of Mathematical Psychology*, Vol. 1. New York: Wiley.
Takayama, A.
   1974   *Mathematical Economics*. Dryden Press
Thurstone, L. L.
   1928a   "Attitudes can be measured." *American Journal of Sociology*, 33: 529–554.
   1928b   "The measurement of opinion." *Journal of Abnormal and Social Psychology*. 22: 415–430.
Thurstone, L. L., and E. J. Chave
   1929   *The Measurement of Attitude*. Chicago: University of Chicago Press.
Torgerson, W. S.
   1958   *Theory and Methods of Scaling*. New York: Wiley.
van der Ven, A. H. G. S.
   1980   *Introduction of Scaling*. New York: Wiley.
Vargo, L. G.
   1971   "Comment on 'The assignment of numbers to rank order categories'." *American Sociological Review*, 36: 517–518.
Von Neumann, S. and O. Morgenstern
   1947   *The Theory of Games and Economic Behavior*. Princeton: Princeton University Press.
Waugh, F. W.
   1935   "Marginal utility of money in the United States, 1917–1921 and from 1922–1932." *Econometrica* 3: 376–399.
Wilson, T. P.
   1971   "Critique of ordinal variables." *Social Forces*, 49: 432–444.

Chapter 8

Response Effects[1]

Norman M. Bradburn

8.1. INTRODUCTION

Errors in surveys can be conveniently divided into sampling and nonsampling errors. The discussion of nonsampling errors themselves can be further divided into: (*a*) errors arising from difficulties in the execution of the sample, for example, by failure to get interviews with all members of the selected sample or by item nonresponse; and (*b*) errors caused by other factors, for example, respondents misinterpreting a question or deliberately lying. This chapter is concerned with this second type of nonsampling error; errors arising from nonresponse are treated in Chapter 5 on applied sampling and Chapter 12 on missing data.

We prefer to call the types of nonsampling errors dealt with in this chapter response effects because it is not always clear that they are to be thought of as errors in the usual sense of the term. To some extent the topics covered overlap those treated at a theoretical level in Chapter 7 on the theory of measurement and measurement error. However, we will be concerned here mainly with the empirical evidence for the nature and size of response effects arising from different parts of the questioning process that is central to data collection in sample surveys.

In social research using survey methods, we are usually concerned with two distinct types of data. One type describes actual or anticipated behavior of

[1] The preparation of this chapter was partially supported by NSF grant GS-43245 and the National Opinion Research Center. The author wishes to thank Carol Stocking, Carrie Miles, and the Survey Methodology Information System, Statistical Research Division, Bureau of the Census, for their help in preparing the references.

individuals or groups. The other type describes psychological states such as thoughts, feelings, beliefs, and opinions that are not directly accessible to anyone but the respondent. In the first case, that of behavior, we can conceive that there is, in principle, a "true" value even though it may be unobserved. Thus it is possible to think about bias in the responses, that is, systematic errors leading to estimates of behavior that are either higher or lower than the true value. In practice, of course, we typically do not have perfect measures of behavior even from nonsurvey methods, and rely on surveys to make our estimates. Hence our interest in understanding the source of measurement errors arising from survey operations.

For the second type of data, that which we shall call generically attitudinal data, it is not as clear that there is, even in principle, any true value. Whether or not one conceives of a true value as existing depends on one's theoretical conception of the particular variables. Our measurements of attitudinal variables are actually measures of behaviors that are conceptualized as indicators of some underlying construct. These measurements may be direct observations of actual behavior, responses to questions about behavior or of attitudes, or occasionally physiological measures (e.g., galvanic skin response, polygraph) taken in conjunction with verbal reports or in response to stimuli such as pictures and videotapes (Clark & Tifft, 1966). Since the measurement here is never of the phenomena directly, it is perhaps better to eschew the concept of response error altogether and merely consider the extent to which different ways of measuring the variable affect the type of response one gets. Differing investigators might disagree as to which measurement is more nearly true, but they can at least agree on the amount of response effects that different methods produce.

Before reviewing the literature on response effects, let us consider an example that shows some of the common factors affecting their size and direction. Consider the problem of asking about family income during the past year. Several different things spring readily to mind that might make us suspect we are not getting an accurate measurement of income. First, respondents might deliberately omit some types of income that they do not want anyone to know about, such as income from illegal sources or income not reported on their income tax forms. They may forget about some income (e.g., dividends or interest on a savings account) or report faulty estimates of income for which good records are not readily available. A third problem may arise from their misunderstanding the question or not defining the concept of income the same way the investigator does. For example, should gifts, inheritances, or insurance payments be reported as income? The question may not make it clear what the investigator has in mind when asking about income. Respondents may also include income from the wrong time period. This type of memory error is called telescoping. The error is in remembering when something happened, rather than whether it happened or not. Finally, some respondents may deliberately inflate their income reports to impress the interviewer or to make themselves look better off than they in fact are.

Readers should note that we are not treating refusals to be interviewed or to answer single questions as response effects. To some extent this is an arbitrary decision, but we feel that the omission of data entirely is a subject sufficiently distinct that it is best treated separately as part of the problems involved with failing to carry out the sampling plan fully. These problems are treated in Chapter 12.

We can summarize these types of errors by noting that they fall into three classes: (a) deliberate or motivated errors in which the respondent adds or omits information in order to make a good impression on the interviewer or to prevent the interviewer from finding out something; (b) memory errors that may be about whether something happened or when it happened; and (c) communication errors, that is, errors caused by the investigator not making clear to the respondent what is being asked, or respondents failing to make clear their responses to the interviewer so that a wrong answer is recorded. To minimize response effects, investigators must be sensitive to the factors in research design that affect all three types.

8.2. MODEL FOR CONCEPTUALIZING FACTORS THAT AFFECT RESPONSES

In order to organize the discussion of response effects, we first sketch briefly a conceptual model of the data collection process. This model, which has been developed more fully elsewhere (Sudman & Bradburn, 1974), conceives of the research interview as a microsocial system. The system consists of two roles linked by the task of transmitting information from the respondent to the interviewer (and ultimately to the investigator). In the most general sense, we judge how effectively the task has been carried out by the quality of the data that result.

We distinguish three sources of variation in the quality of the data: from the characteristics of the task itself; from the interviewer's performance; and from the respondent. Much of the research on response effects has focused on interviewer and respondent characteristics. This concentration of effort is probably misplaced because it is the task itself that gives rise to what Orne (1969) has called the "demand characteristics of the situation." The demand characteristics, in turn, play the predominant role in determining the behavior of the actors in the situation. Thus variables affecting the characteristics of the task are at the heart of a model of response effects. Indeed, the empirical literature suggests that *the characteristics of the task are the major source of response effects and are, in general, much larger than effects due to interviewer or respondent characteristics.*

The task in survey research is to obtain information from a sample of respondents about their (or someone else's) behavior and/or attitudes. The respondent's role is to provide that information; the interviewer's, to obtain the information in the manner prescribed by the researcher (who defines the task by drawing the sample, designing the questionnaire, and specifying the observations to be employed in the research). If respondents are to be "good" respondents, they must provide accurate and complete information. Careful attention must be given to motivating respondents to play such a role and to defining the situation for them so that they know accurately what it is that they are to do. Similarly, through training, supervision, and careful specification of the questionnaire and its mode of administration, the investigator sets the standards by which interviewers will be judged on how well they have performed their role.

Within this general framework, we can see that there are three sources of variance in response that we might consider as response effects. The first source is the respondents themselves. Although we expect that most of the variance in responses among respondents is due to real differences, it is possible that there are personality differences among respondents that systematically affect their willingness to give accurate responses, particularly to certain kinds of questions, such a those that might affect their self-esteem. In addition, other factors, such as the presence of other people during the interview, events that happened to the respondent before the interview began, or social pressures not to cooperate with strangers, may undermine the willingness of respondents to take the time or make the effort to be good respondents. Although many of these factors are outside the control of the investigator, they must be recognized as potential sources of response effects. If the potential size of these effects is known, subsequent adjustments to the data may be made to take their effect into account during analysis.

The interviewer's role may be more or less prescribed. In some surveys, interviewers are given considerable freedom in defining the task for themselves and for respondents, particularly with regard to the formulation of questions or the follow-up of answers to previous questions. Today, however, most large-scale surveys use heavily structured questionnaires that leave little room for independent judgment about what questions to ask, what order to ask them in, or what to do when respondents answer one way rather than another. Interviewers, of course, do not always carry out their instructions exactly, nor is it possible to anticipate every contingency; some things must be left to the interviewer's common sense. Thus, the potential for response effects due to differences in interviewer behavior is still real, even in the most tightly structured survey.

In addition, and perhaps more importantly, some interviewer effects may arise from extrarole characteristics of the interviewer that do not reflect interviewer behavior at all. It is inevitable that respondents will perceive interviewers not only as someone performing a particular role, but also in terms of other role characteristics such as sex, race, age, and perhaps ethnic, political, or other affiliations. The perception of these other characteristics does not necessarily mean they will cause respondents to behave differently, but the potential is there and must be recognized. We review some of the literature on interviewer characteristics as a source of response effects later in this chapter.

The task is defined by the investigator. How the task is constituted determines to a considerable extent whether or not there will be communication errors, memory errors, and even whether there will be deliberate distortion of information. Task definition is primarily a matter of what questions are asked, how they are asked—that is, their form and wording—the order in which they are asked, and the mode of administration of the questionnaire. It is also the source of the largest response effects (Sudman & Bradburn, 1974). Unfortunately it is also the part of the research process to which the least serious attention is typically given. Why this should be is not entirely clear, but it is partly because the research on questionnaire construction is not highly developed and there is no theory of instrument design analogous to the theory of sampling. Although the art of asking questions has long been recognized and craftlore has developed among experienced survey researchers, there has been little systematic research until recently on the effects of different types of questions. Where research has been done, it has rarely been in a consistent framework that would allow findings from one study to inform those of another; the findings have been plagued with inconsistencies. A science of question formulation is still in its infancy.

In this chapter review of the empirical literature is organized according to the three major kinds of response effects: task, interviewer, and respondent. Somewhat arbitrarily, task variables are divided into five types: (*a*) method of administration; (*b*) open versus closed questions; (*c*) question order; (*d*) length and wording of questions; and (*e*) memory. The topics are not completely independent and many studies deal with interactions between variables that are treated under different headings and may appear in different places. Similarly, although we can discuss some research that deals with response effects and associated interviewer and respondent characteristics independently, much of the research concerns the interactions between interviewer and respondent characteristics and, in some instances, between task variables and interviewer or respondent characteristics. Readers who are looking for information about some particular topic are advised to look in several different sections rather than relying entirely on the section headings.

8.3. EMPIRICAL STUDIES OF RESPONSE EFFECTS

Task Variables

METHOD OF ADMINISTRATION

The principal methods of administration of questions are personal or face-to-face interviews, telephone interviews, and self-administered questionnaires. Self-administered questionnaires may be delivered in person to respondents or mailed. Of course, combinations of methods are often desirable from a practical standpoint, and one frequently wants to compare results from studies using different methods. It is thus particularly important to know the extent to which the method of administration itself may alter responses.

Contrary to the common belief favoring face-to-face interviews, there is no clearly superior method that yields better results for all types of questions. Sudman and Bradburn (1974) analyzed the results of a large number of studies that presented data for several thousand questions and found no consistent or large effects. Similar results were found by Dillman (1978) and Groves and Kahn (1979). Over all the studies compared, face-to-face interviews produced slight overreporting; telephone and self-administered questionnaires slight underreporting for behavioral items. Variance in results was high and not consistent in direction. The superiority of one method over another appears to depend on other factors such as the degree of sensitivity of the questions.

Jonsson (1957) conducted a well-controlled experiment with well-motivated subjects to test the difference between self-administered questionnaires and personal interviews. His respondents were 207 students in Swedish day-continuation schools (*folkhögskolor*). He inquired about a large range of subjects all of which could be validated against existing records or by physical measurements. He found few statistically significant differences between the two methods, although the validity coefficients tended to be slightly higher in the personal interviews.

He speculated that this slight difference might result from respondents in the personal interview being more motivated to respond with care to questions that they considered unimportant than they would be with the self-administered form. On the other hand, the self-administered form appeared to be slightly superior for items that required very definite information from the respondent and questions that were so easy that the respondent did not need any help from the interviewer in interpreting them. Jonsson interpreted his findings as being consistent with an earlier study by Marks and Mauldin (1950) that indicated that self-administered questionnaires were better for items that might suffer from rounding errors (e.g., age, education), but that personal interviews were better for items that required a more complex definition (e.g., months worked, income, days absent from work).

Because self-administered questionnaires are more private and do not require the respondent to reveal possibly embarrassing information directly to another person, self-administered questionnaires are often used with items that are thought to be threatening or sensitive. In a careful study of self-administered, personal, and telephone interviews, Hochstim (1962, 1967) found a greater tendency for respondents to report negative information about themselves with self-administered questionnaires or telephone interviews than with face-to-face interviews. Thorndike, Hagen, and Kemper (1952) compared responses to self-administered and personal interviews about psychosomatic symptoms during a household survey. On average, respondents in the self-administered form reported about 15% more symptoms than did respondents who were personally interviewed, although for one item about constipation, the incidence was twice as high for the self-administered as for the personal interview.

In another well-known study, Kahn (1952) compared the responses of 162 male employees who were asked a series of questions about working conditions, as well as demographic data, using both face-to-face interviews and self-administered questionnaires. Small differences were found on items relating to the work group or to factual information such as length of time on present job. The greatest differences between methods were found on items related to the respondents' perceptions of the company. On the personal interviews, 73% stated that the company was well run and 64% stated that it was a good place to work, as compared with only 40% and 43%, respectively, on the self-administered questionnaires.

Similar differences between methods appear to obtain for items with socially desirable answers. Knudsen, Pope, and Irish (1967) reported differences by method of administration for items dealing with sex norms. Women were asked whether premarital sex relations were all right with a man a woman plans to marry, with a man she loves, with a man she likes a lot, and with a man she is friendly with. Less than 20% of the respondents who were personally interviewed reported that it was all right to have premarital sex, compared with 31% who so reported on the self-administered form. These results may also have been influenced by the threat of self-disclosure since the respondents in this study had all been premaritally pregnant.

Sudman, Greeley, and Pinto (1965) conducted a survey of Catholic households. For a set of items related to religious and ethical issues, one member of the household was interviewed face to face and another member of the household was given the same items in a self-administered form. The results did not show consistent differences between the two methods. Out of a total of 44 items, respondents gave more socially acceptable answers to the face-to-face interviews to 10 of the items, less socially acceptable answers to 3 items, and there were no differences between the methods on 31 of the items. This study indicates that although a socially desirable answer may be likely, one cannot conclude a priori that there will definitely be differences between self-administered surveys and personal interviews. Social desirability responses depend more on the substance of the question than on the form of administration.

Telephone interviews lie somewhere between self-administered questionnaires and face-to-face interviews in their degree of impersonality. Because of the cost advantages and their suitability for many types of studies, they are becoming increasingly popular as a mode of administration. Therefore, there is mounting interest in potential response effects that might be associated with telephone interviews.

There is a general consensus that telephone interviewing yields results as valid as face-to-face interviews and that for most items one can move freely from face-to-face to telephone interviewing and back again if one wishes (Dillman, 1978; Groves & Kahn, 1979; National Center for Health Services

Research, 1977). The Current Population Survey conducted monthly by the Census Bureau employs telephone interviews for respondents except for households in the first and fifth weeks of their participation. The Census Bureau is reported to have evaluated carefully the use of the telephone in both its CPS and Medicare panel (National Center for Health Services Research, 1977). Comparison of response rates, the reliability of answers across waves, and the distribution of responses reveal no statistically significant differences between telephone reinterviews and personal reinterviews. Data on birthdates when checked against birth certificates were found to be equally valid when collected by telephone interviews or by face-to-face interviews (Institute for Survey Research, 1975). Reliability data on items previously reported in personal interviews have been found in several studies to be the same whether the reinterview is conducted in person or by telephone (Bradburn, 1969, chap. 5; Institute for Survey Research, 1975).

Hochstim (1967) and Thornberry and Scott (1973) compared data on standard health items collected by telephone and personal interviews and found no significant differences, although Hochstim did find some differences on items that reflected negatively on the respondent, as mentioned previously.

Data on sensitive topics apparently can be obtained in telephone interviews as validly as with face-to-face interviews. Coombs and Freedman (1964) have used telephone procedures as follow-ups to personal interviews asking questions on pregnancies, family planning, and related topics. They report telephone interviews are as satisfactory as personal interviews. Mooney, Pollack, and Corsa (1968) report similar success with sensitive topics such as menstruation. A somewhat more complicated result was reported by Henson, Roth, and Cannell (1974). For items from standard mental health scales they found no differences between telephone and personal interviews for those items that were extremely threatening or only mildly threatening, but for moderately threatening items, respondents described themselves more positively in the telephone interviews.

Some questions cannot be asked the same way over the telephone as they can in personal interviews either because they require visual displays or because the interviewer needs to be able to respond to visual cues from the respondent. There is some suggestion that telephone interviewing might be more sensitive to question-wording changes than personal interviews. For example, Colombotos (1969) reports that when physicians were asked how many journals they read, they gave a lower number on the telephone than in person. When the question was changed to ask them to list the journals they read regularly, the difference between telephone and personal interviews disappeared. Face-to-face interview questions about income as well as those about reading different magazines typically use cards or visual aids to aid accurate recall. Special care should be taken when such questions are used in telephone interviews. Some experimentation must be conducted to determine the proper way to ask those questions on the telephone.

If questionnaires are particularly complex or visual aids are absolutely necessary, these materials can be mailed out in advance to the respondent to be used when the telephone interview is conducted. This technique has been used with success in surveys of physicians conducted by the National Opinion Research Center.

A specialized method that can be incorporated into personal interviews in order to reduce response distortion for particularly threatening questions is the random response technique (Warner, 1965). The name of the technique is somewhat misleading since it is the question rather than the answers that are randomized. The basic idea behind the technique is to have the respondent use some probability mechanism with a known probability distribution, such as flipping a coin or throwing a die to select the question to be answered. For example, the respondent is given a coin and asked to answer one or two questions either *yes* or *no*. The questions might be: *I have had an abortion,* and *I was born in the month of January.* The respondent tosses the coin but does not show the results of the toss to the interviewer. If the coin comes up heads, the respondent is instructed to answer the question about abortions; if it comes up tails, the question about the birthdate is answered. Since the response categories for both questions are the same, the respondent can answer simply yes or no without the interviewer knowing what question is actually being answered. The true proportion of the sample that answered *yes* to the threatening question (e.g., about abortions) can be estimated by knowing the probability that respondents answered the threatening question (50% in the case of tossing a coin), the total sample size, the true proportion of yes answers to the alternative question (approximately 1/12 in the case of being born in any particular month), and the total number of yes answers given by respondents. Formulas for computation of the estimates of answers to the threatening question and the standard errors of the estimates are given in Greenberg, Abdul–Ela, Simmons, and Horwitz (1969).

The method has shown promise of giving higher (more valid) estimates for behaviors about which one expects severe underreporting. Brown and Harding (1973) studied drug usage among military personal. In all cases of drug usage except marijuana, the reported use was greater by randomized response than by an anonymous self-administered questionnaire. The increase in reported use was greater among officers than among enlisted men. Randomized response techniques have been used among the general population in Taiwan in a study of induced abortion (I-Cheng, Chow, & Rider, 1972). The rates estimated by randomized response were higher than those obtained by other methods and more in line with what the true rate was expected to be. Similar results have been found for abortion in urban North Carolina (Abernathy, Greenberg, & Horwitz, 1970), for earned family income (Greenberg, Kuebler, Abernathy, & Horwitz, 1971), and degree of fault in auto accidents (Greenberg et al., 1969).

Whereas methods may differ in the degree to which they obtain valid data from threatening questions, no method seems to eliminate underreporting entirely. Locander, Sudman, and Bradburn (1976) conducted an experiment to test the joint effects of question threat and method of administration on re-

sponse distortion. Using personal interview, telephone interview, self-administered questionnaires, and the randomized response technique, four levels of
threatening questions were posed, ranging from reports of having a library card
to questions about arrest for drunken driving. For each of the questions, validation data from record checks were obtained. The results indicated that response distortion increased sharply as threat increased. None of the data-
collection methods was clearly superior to all other methods for all types of
threatening questions. Randomized response gave the lowest distortion on
questions about socially undesirable acts, but even this procedure resulted in a
35% underreporting of drunken driving.

The random response technique has also been used to study attitudes.
Wiseman, Moriarty, and Schafer (1975–1976) investigated the use of personal
interviews, self-administered questionnaires, and the random response technique in eliciting attitudes on race–prejudice, political, and moral issues that
they thought might be sensitive to methods differences. They selected five
issues that they had previously determined were answered differently when
given in a personal interview and in a self-administered questionnaire. When
they repeated the items with a new sample using the random response technique, they found, contrary to their hypothesis, that responses to the random
response technique did not differ from those obtained by the personal interview, but were significantly different from those obtained by the self-administered questionnaire. The explanation for this finding is not clear, but the study
suggests that use of the random response technique for attitudinal questions
may pose some unsuspected hazards.

Although no method is clearly superior, there are a few generalizations
that we can tentatively derive from the literature. For factual questions that are
not threatening to the respondent or do not have highly socially desirable
answers, all methods work well. When asking questions that have been developed for face-to-face interviews in telephone or self-administered questionnaires, special care must be taken to ensure that they can be appropriately used
with these methods of administration. The form of the questions may have to
be adapted to different data-collection methods.

With sensitive questions or those associated with a high degree of social
desirability, the more anonymous methods of administration appear to work
somewhat better; that is, they lower the degree of under- or overreporting. The
data here are not entirely consistent and more work needs to be done to define
precisely those conditions under which the more anonymous methods do in
fact produce better data. Offsetting the potential benefits of anonymity, however, is the increased motivation that may come from the interviewer being
with the respondents in person and encouraging them to take the time to consider the questions carefully.

OPEN VERSUS CLOSED QUESTIONS

For many years one of the most hotly debated topics in survey research
concerned the relative merits of open versus closed questions (B. S.

Dohrenwend & Richardson, 1963). The view of most experienced investigators is that closed questions produce more relevant and comparable responses, but that open questions produce fuller and "deeper" replies that more accurately reflect nuances of meaning that are lost by forcing the respondent into a fairly tightly controlled set of alternative answers.

Although all investigators do not agree on the exact meaning of *open* and *closed* as applied to questions and questionnaires, there is general agreement that the term *closed* refers to those questions that can be answered by a short response selected from a limited number of options. B. S. Dohrenwend and Richardson (1963) note that there are in fact three types of closed questions: questions in which respondents select a particular choice (e.g., *often, sometimes, never*); questions to which respondents answer *yes* or *no*; and questions in which the respondents identify some specific person, place, time, or quantity (e.g., *Where were you born?*).

Another ambiguity in terminology concerns the form of the interview schedule or questionnaire. Questions may be open in form, but still specified so that the interviewer must ask certain questions in specified ways and in a particular order. Alternately, the investigator may simply specify a set of topics about which information is to be obtained and leave it up to the interviewer to formulate the exact questions and establish the order as seems best with the flow of conversation. Although there is probably a tendency for open questions to go with an open interview schedule, the two need not go together. However, even if the order and wording of open questions are specified, interviewers are trained to probe respondents' answers to make sure that they are understandable, cover the topic as completely as possible, and can be coded at some later date. Interviewers require more training when using open questions and particularly when using open interview schedules.

In their review of methodological studies, Sudman and Bradburn (1974) failed to find any overall superiority for *either* open or closed questions. For behavioral items, the only sizable effect was for closed questions in self-administered questionnaires to produce substantial underreporting (e.g., amount of drinking, frequency of drug use). Further analysis suggested that there is an interaction between question form and the threat of the questions. For non-threatening questions, the form of the question did not make a difference. For threatening behavioral questions, there are lower levels of reporting with closed questions than with open questions. For attitudinal items, the response effects were slightly larger for closed than for open questions. Although the differences were small, the authors hypothesized that the closed-question format may increase the threat of the question because it forces the respondent to choose one from a number of options. Similar findings were reported for both behavioral and attitudinal items that had socially desirable answers.

The most careful experimental study of the effects of open versus closed questions has been done by B. S. Dohrenwend (1965). She conducted a controlled laboratory study that maximized the standardization of the pattern of questioning in the interviews, the experience of the interviewers, and the experience about which the respondents were interviewed. The experimental conditions varied both the form of the questions (open versus closed) and the subject matter of the interview (behavior versus attitudes). The interviews were divided into two parts so that each interview contained open and closed questions and covered both behavior and attitudes in a carefully counterbalanced design. Each of four highly experienced female interviewers conducted 2 interviews in each of the four experimental conditions, yielding 32 interviews in all. The respondents were female undergraduates at Cornell who were interviewed about their experiences in a controlled pseudo-experiment that preceded the experimental interviews. The activities in the psuedo-experiment had been recorded so that behavioral reports of what went on during that period could be validated.

The results generally indicated that closed questions were not inferior to open questions, although the data were not unequivocal. With regard to efficiency, there was relatively little difference between question forms, although there were some interactions with interviewers suggesting that some interviewers work better with one form of question than with the other. There was also an interaction with subject matter such that responses to open questions contained more self-revelation than responses to closed questions when the subject matter was about behavior, but not when it was about subjective evaluations. Responses to open questions about attitudes were also significantly shorter than those to open questions about behavior, whereas length of responses to closed questions did not vary with subject matter. Dohrenwend suggests that closed questions exert a tighter control over respondents' answers and thus do better when reluctance to respond may make respondents restrict their answers on open questions.

There was no evidence in the data that open questions were superior in obtaining responses of either greater depth or greater validity. There were no main effects on the validity of the responses, but there was a higher order interaction involving form, subject matter, and interviewer. This effect was due to the inability of one interviewer to elicit valid behavioral reports when using open questions. This result raises the possibility that open questions are more susceptible to interviewer effects. Depth of responses (as measured by the proportion of statements that were judged as self-revealing) was no different *in general* between the two forms of questions, but again there was an interaction such that the highest number of self-revealing statements came in closed questions about attitudes. Dohrenwend argues that this interaction contradicts the notion that closed questions are ineffective as a technique for in-depth interviewing. Data reported by Ellis (1947, 1948) also support the view that closed questions can elicit more self-revealing data than open questions, although his study confounds mode of administration (face-to-face interview versus self-administered questionnaire) with question form.

Experiments by Schuman and Presser (1978) indicate that open- and closed-ended questions about attitudes can produce different ordering of responses even when the closed-ended responses have been carefully devised from responses to the open-ended form. The experiments used split ballots to investigate form effects on questions about work values and about "the most important problem facing this country." The data show clearly that the form in which questions are asked affects the marginal distributions and the rankings between open and closed forms. They conclude that any substantive use of univariate distributions for attitudinal items where both open- and closed-question forms are possible is hazardous.

The somewhat conflicting nature of data concerning effects of question form and threatening behavioral reports led to a field experiment in which open and closed questions were systematically varied, along with other variables, to test their effects on reports of threatening behavior such as alcohol and drug use and sexual behavior (Blair, Sudman, Bradburn, & Stocking, 1977). The experiment consisted of a nationwide sample survey of leisure activities in which eight different questionnaires were used. The eight questionnaires were formed by varying two levels of question structure (open versus closed), two levels of question length (questions with introductions of 30 words or more versus those with less than 30 words) and two levels of wording familiarity (a standard wording verus a form that allowed respondents to supply their own words for critical activities). It should be noted that although the two types of question structure were called open and closed, they both would have been classified as closed by B. S. Dohrenwend and Richardson (1963). The questions were the type they called identification questions; for example, *How many times did you do* X *in the past year* (month, 24 hours, etc.). The variable manipulated was not the question wording itself, but whether or not there were explicit answer categories given to respondents that they had to use in giving their responses. In both cases the responses were numerical in form, and thus were selected either from an explicit list, in the case of the closed questions, or from an implicit list, as in the open form.

The results of this experiment strongly supported the hypothesis that using open-ended response categories reduced underreporting of the frequency or intensity of threatening behaviors, but not whether the respondent had ever engaged in the activity. Effects ranged from 14% greater reporting of frequency of sexual intercourse during the past month to 108% greater reporting of frequency of masturbation. Over a large number of items dealing with frequency or quantity of alcohol consumption, drug use, and sexual behavior, the average increase in frequency or amount reported was 52% for the open as compared with the closed version of the questions.

The results of this experiment do not contradict Dohrenwend's findings, but they do add an important specification for questions dealing with threatening topics: namely, that not all forms of closed questions (in her sense) are equally good. There is good evidence that precoding questions (forcing respondents to select from explicit predetermined response categories) will lead to substantial underreporting of the frequency and amount of threatening behaviors. It should be noted, however, that the question form affected only the frequency or amount of behavior reported, not reports of whether or not the behavior had ever had engaged in. The latter is affected by characteristics of the respondent and not of the way in which questions are asked (Bradburn *et al.*, 1978).

Although there is little consistent evidence that open questions are superior to closed questions, except in the special case of not providing precoded categories, B. S. Dohrenwend (1965) does mention two instances in which investigators may still want to rely on open questions. First, when investigators want a measure of the salience of topics to the respondents, a spontaneous response to an open question is often and appropriately used. For example, open questions about personal worries or the biggest problem facing the nation will continue to be used when a measure of the salience of particular topics is desired. The second, and perhaps most important, use of open questions is in pretesting questions when the investigator wants to explore many dimensions of a topic and is unsure exactly what questions to ask. Extensive use of open questions with small samples may allow the investigator to develop better closed questions which, when used on larger samples, will yield the best results. Premature use of new and untested closed questions may, in the long run, cause more damage than moderate use of open quetions.

QUESTION ORDER

No topic in questionnaire construction is more vexing or resistant to easy generalization than that of question order. That question order can affect the distribution of responses to items has been amply demonstrated. For example, Sayre (1939) reported that asking about willingness to pay a license fee in order to have radio programs without advertising before rather than after asking for estimates of time taken up by radio advertising produces lower estimates of time given to advertising. She also reported that asking about the license fee first increases the favorableness of attitudes toward radio advertising. A manual prepared by the American Marketing Association (1937) reported a study of women's attitudes toward advertising which suggested that attitudes were more favorable when elicited *after* questions about dresses than before. In a famous study, Cantril and Research Associates (1944) showed that the order in which substantially related questions are presented will affect the responses to the questions. Respondents were more willing to allow Americans to enlist in the German army when the question came after a question about willingness to allow enlistments in the British army than when the question came before. Similar results were found in an unpublished NORC study (1946) and in a study by Hyman and Sheatsley (1950), where there was a strong order effect for questions regarding reciprocity between the USSR and the United States in the free exchange of news.

On the other hand, a number of studies have failed to find order effects. In the NORC study of occupational prestige ranking (1947), four separate forms listing occupations in different orders were used to obtain prestige rankings. No significant differences among the rankings were found on any of the four forms. Metzner and Mann (1953) showed that grouping of related questions had relatively little effect of the intercorrelation of items, but did not give any data on possible effects on response means. Trussel and Elinson (1959) failed to find any significant differences in the number of conditions reported per person between presenting a list of chronic diseases before or after a list of symptoms. Bradburn and Mason (1964) failed to find any effect on questions concerning self-reports of mental health symptoms and self-evaluations when blocks of questions were systematically rotated through the questionnaire.

In their review of methodological studies, Sudman and Bradburn (1974) also failed to find any sizable or consistent response effects associated with placement of questions after related questions. The largest average effect was a negative one that occurred for behavioral items appearing early in the interview, but placed after questions with related content.

The evidence suggests that under some conditions the order of presentation of questions can have important effects on responses, but that under other conditions it makes little or no difference. We cannot at present say with certainty what conditions make question order an important source of response effects. There is enough fragmentary evidence, however, to make a beginning.

There are five ways in which changing the order of questions might produce effects. First, the order in which questions are presented may affect the saliency of particular topics, or at least aspects of topics, by providing differential contexts within which responses are elicited. Segall (1959) has shown such order effects on judgments of controversial statements, and Landon (1971) has demonstrated "contextual contamination" of ratings of teachers due to order effects. Noelle–Neumann (1976) has shown similar contextual effects on attitudes in Germany. Hayes (1964) has demonstrated experimentally that the context provided by item order cannot only influence attitude items individually, but can also affect the distribution of Guttman scale types in a sample. We expect that attitudes about topics that have generally low salience would be more susceptible to order effects than would those that are highly salient to the respondent. This type of effect might be called a saliency effect.

A second type of effect results from the overlap in content between sections. Thus, for example, a few general questions relating to work, marriage, and family adjustment might appear together with questions about overall life satisfaction. If further, more detailed, questions about specific areas of life come later in the questionnaire in sections devoted to those topics, respondents might feel that they are repeating themselves if they mentioned a problem again. An effect such as this one, which in some respects is the opposite of a saliency effect, might be called a redundancy effect. The average negative effect cited earlier for behavioral items that came after related questions might be due to redundancy effects.

A third type of effect related to the influence of earlier judgments on later ones. As in the Cantril and Research Associates study (1944), having committed oneself to the more popular view that it is all right for Americans to fight in the British army, respondents appear inconsistent if they oppose Americans fighting in the German army. This type of effect might be called a consistency effect. It appears to be the principal type of effect that has been demonstrated in the literature.

A fourth type of effect that might occur, particularly if the interview is a long one, results from the overall position of questions in the questionnaire, rather than from their relation to one another. Questions appearing in the latter part of the interview might be answered in a more perfunctory manner. Such an effect might be called a fatigue effect.

Finally, it is possible that there is an opposite to the fatigue effect. In general we expect that respondents are somewhat more nervous or hesitant in the beginning of interviews and that rapport builds as the interview proceeds. Experienced survey researchers usually put their more sensitive questions further along in the questionnaire so that the interviewer will have time to establish a good relationship with the respondent and prevent their breaking off early. This type of effect might be called a rapport effect.

Relatively little research has been done on fatigue or rapport effects. Sudman and Bradburn (1974) found that threatening questions about behavior that came in the early past of questionnaires tended to have lower levels of reporting than those coming late in the questionnaires. For nonthreatening questions about behavior the effects were small, but tended to be in the opposite direction (positive in the early portions, negative in the later ones). There appears to be some empirical evidence to support the general practice of putting more sensitive questions in the latter parts of the interview.

We have identified several different types of potential order effects. There is no general theory that will tell investigators when they will find such effects or how to avoid them, although our discussion should alert investigators to those types of situations that are most likely to produce important effects. Where possible, one should try to carry out experiments to determine empirically the size and direction of actual effects in any specific data-collection effort.

QUESTION LENGTH AND WORDING

Question length has only recently been recognized as a variable that might cause important response effects. Professional practice has tended to emphasize parsimony—the shorter and simpler the better. Extra words are ruthlessly eliminated in an effort to keep the interview flowing. Until recently it was simply assumed that shorter is better, but recent studies have called this assumption into question.

The change in thinking was sparked by the experimental work of Marquis and Cannell (1971), but it is also supported by findings from psychological experiments (Cieutat, 1964; Greenspoon, 1955; Hildum & Brown, 1956; Krasner, 1958; Ogawa & Oakes, 1965; Salzinger, 1959; Shaffer, 1955). These studies applied verbal reinforcement principles in interviewing situations and found that verbal reinforcement of responses increases the amount of response given by respondents. Since questions act as stimuli for respondents, it is plausible that longer stimuli will in fact elicit longer replies and that longer replies may, at least for some types of questions, be better replies.

The basic experiments conducted by Marquis and Cannell (1971); Marquis, Cannell, and Laurent (1972); and Laurent (1972) consisted in three modifications of the standard Health Interview Survey, a household survey conducted regularly by the Census Bureau for the National Center for Health Statistics in order to estimate a number of health related problems, illnesses, and use of medical care facilities. The three experimental treatments consisted of: (a) a *reinforcement condition* in which the interviewer reinforced respondents every time they reported a symptom, condition, or illness by using one of several reinforcing statements, by using extra words both in introducing new sections of the interview, and when asking certain questions, by looking at the respondent, smiling and using appropriate hand and arm gestures, and by including a list of symptoms to sensitize respondents to health reporting; (b) a *sensitization condition* in which the sensitizing list of symptoms was given at the beginning of the interview, but none of the reinforcing techniques were used; and (c) a *control condition* in which the sensitization list was placed near the end of the interview (where it could have no effect on reporting of other health information) and no reinforcing techniques were used. The dependent variables were the average frequencies of reported health information such as the average number of reported chronic and acute conditions per person, the number of symptoms reported, and the number of physician visits reported.

Interviewers were trained for 1 week. Much of the time was spent in practice interviewing with emphasis on close adherence to the different interviewing techniques. The sample was restricted to women living within the Detroit city limits and was selected from census tracts with low to middle average income, a high proportion of white inhabitants, and less than 18% of its female population aged 65 and over.

The reinforcement condition produced more reports of symptoms, conditions, and illnesses than did the sensitization condition. On average, the effect of reinforcement was to produce about 29% more reports of symptoms; the biggest increases were for symptom classified as highly embarrassing (e.g., bladder trouble, hemorrhoids). The reinforcement technique also resulted in 25% more chronic and acute conditions reported by respondents for themselves and 24% more conditions reported by proxy for a designated other member of the household. There was an interaction between the embarrassment level of the condition reported and the person about whom questions were asked. Reinforced respondents reported a larger number of less embarrassing conditions for themselves but a larger number of more embarrassing conditions for the proxy person. Marquis and Cannell suggest that this interaction may in fact involve an order effect in that these types of conditions were asked about later in the interview when the opportunity to report for the proxy was present.

No significant differences were found between reinforcement and sensitization conditions in the number of physician visits reported either for the respondent or for the proxy. Also, there were few differences between the sensitization and the control conditions, suggesting that the warm-up effect, which was basically an attempt to increase the saliency of health reporting, was not very strong.

Building on the rather striking findings of this experiment, the experiment, described previously, by Blair *et al.* (1977) included length of question as one of the experimental variables in the different questionnaire forms. In the long condition an introduction greater than 30 words prefaced the sections dealing with each of the threatening questions about behaviors; in the short version, a much shorter introduction was used. The basic questions remained the same in both versions. As in the Marquis and Cannell experiment, the longer version produced higher reports of behaviors. On average the long version yielded about 24% higher reports of frequency and amount of behavior, the same order of magnitude increase that Marquis and Cannell found for reports of symptoms. The effects of length and open format appear to be additive so that for some items reports of frequency or amount of behavior may be two to three times greater on the long–open form than on the short–closed form.

Increasing the length of questions or their introduction, of course, does not increase reporting for all questions. Averaging across a large number of studies with varied content, Sudman and Bradburn (1974) found no general effects related to length of the question in face-to-face interviews. They did, however, find a sizable underreporting for short questions (12 words or less) for group administered questionnaires. This finding is a warning that the general procedure of keeping questions on self-administered questionnaires as short as possible may have some hazards attached to it, at least for items asking for reports of behavior.

It should be noted that in the Marquis and Cannell experiment, not only were the introductions and questions longer, but interviewers also gave more reinforcement to respondents for reports of symptoms, illnesses, and physician visits. The reason that length and reinforcement are believed to have this facilitating effect on behavioral reports is that respondents have more time to focus their attention on the topic about which they are being asked. The longer introduction to sections of questions gives respondents time to begin thinking about their behavior in that area and to remember what they have done. The reinforcement rewards them for their reports and increases their motivation to give accurate information—that is, to perform the respondent role well. We would expect these effects to show up particularly on questions that require some real effort on the part of respondents to recall what they have done, particularly when these things may not be too salient or when the questions are threatening or embarrassing and respondents are reluctant to admit to them. For behaviors that are extremely infrequent and/or very salient, and for attitudinal questions, we would not necessarily expect the same effect.

Studies of question wording defy any simple summary. It has been known for many years (Rugg, 1941) that changes in the wording of questions, such as asking whether something should be allowed or forbidden to do something, can have large effects on the univariate distributions. Although many single studies have been conducted (see Payne 1951; Schuman & Presser, 1977), the results have not fallen into neat patterns that allow us to formulate general rules to inform investigators when their questions will be particularly sensitive to wording changes and when they will not. The general tenor of the empirical data, however, has made investigators skeptical of interpreting the absolute frequencies of responses to attitudinal questions, and made it very difficult to compare distributions of responses over time unless the wording of the questions remains constant. Typically investigators do not establish the sensitivity of questions to wording changes.

Until recently it has been assumed that changes in wording only affected the univariate distributions and that bivariate distributions were not affected. Thus even though the marginal distributions of responses to attitude questions might change as wording changed, relationships between variables would remain fairly stable. A research program on question wording conducted by Schuman and Presser (1977, 1978) has demonstrated that bivariate distributions are also affected by the wording of the question, although we still do not know exactly the conditions under which such effects occur.

To give one example of the type of research in this program, Schuman and Presser (1979) investigated the effects of giving, as contrasted with not giving, respondents an explicit *no-opinion* alternative to questions about attitudes toward the leaders of different countries. The questions asked about the perceived peaceful intentions of the leaders of Russia, Middle East countries, and Portugal—a range of presumed salience for most respondents. Using a split-ballot technique, the investigators looked at the effects of explicitly offering a *no-opinion* response category versus recording *no opinion* only when respondents volunteered the response. As expected, the proportion of *no-opinion* responses was much higher (about 20%) when *no opinion* was an explicitly offered response category. It should be noted that even when respondents had to volunteer *no opinion,* the proportion of *no opinions* was substantial, particularly for the low-salience item about Portugal.

The most important finding was that the intercorrelation among the items was affected by the question wording. When respondents were encouraged to give an opinion by the omission of the explicit *no opinion* category, the responses to the items were positively intercorrelated, omitting those who spontaneously gave a *no-opinion* response. When respondents were discouraged from giving an opinion unless they had a formulated one by offering an explicit *no-opinion* category, not only were the proportion of *no opinions* much higher to all questions, the intercorrelation among the responses to the items disappeared. Apparently among those who held an opinion about the leader of the different countries, there was no generalized favorable or unfavorable opinion. Only when the investigators "forced" respondents to have an opinion, did the positive correlations appear. Replications of this type of experiment indicate that the effect does not necessarily appear with other questions.

Obviously the relationship among attitudes is a very complex problem and is affected by question wording. At this point we do not have a good understanding of the factors that influence these relationships nor of the conditions under which question wording will have a significant impact. Investigators should be warned, however, that the conclusions about attitude clusters or ideology based on particular question wording may be of limited generality if they are based on data exclusively from one set of questions of the same wording. Some substantive findings may be the product of methodological artifacts.

MEMORY

Sample surveys are frequently employed to estimate the frequency or amount of certain kinds of behaviors when records for the relevant population are either nonexistent or difficult to obtain. Questions in these surveys ask respondents to remember past behavior and to report it as accurately as possible. Although much of the research on response effects has dealt with variables that may affect the willingness of respondents to answer questions (i.e., to avoid deliberately omitting things) and that may improve the communication process so that respondents understand the questions in the way the investigator intends, it is clear that memory plays a very large role in determining the accuracy of respondent reporting.

Two kinds of memory errors are distinguished in the literature. These two types tend to operate in opposite directions, one tending toward underreporting bias and the other toward overreporting bias. The first is forgetting an event entirely, whether it is a visit to a physician, the purchase of a product, the use of a drug, a visit to a friend, or whatever. The second kind of error involves the compression of time, such that an event is remembered as having occurred more recently than it actually did. Thus, a respondent who reports a trip to the doctor during the past month when the doctor's records show that the visit took place 6 weeks ago has made a compression-of-time error. This type of error is called telescoping.

We can speak of memory *errors* rather than effects with regard to behavioral events because such events can, at least in principle, be verified by checking other records. It is possible to ask about present or past attitudes, but since there is no external criterion against which to validate attitudes, it is difficult to disentangle attitude change from memory errors, unless, of course, one is doing repeated measures over time and has a prior record of the respondent's attitude reports. In this section, we shall be concerned with memory factors in relation to behavioral reporting.

Memory errors in surveys can be reduced by the use of supplementary devices used with questionnaires. We have already noted that the length of questions or introductions to sections of the questionnaire can substantially increase behavioral reports. This effect is thought to result from the added stimulus and time that respondents are given to think about the topic and to formulate their thoughts on it. In addition, for studies in which accurate recall of documented events is necessary (such as consumer expenditures or hospital visits), respondents may be asked to consult records such as bills or tax returns. Another method widely used to increase recall accuracy is called aided recall. This method consists of explicitly presenting the possible answers to respondents and asking whether they had done any of a series of things. Aided recall is used extensively in readership or audience surveys where the investigators want accurate recall of magazine readership or media exposure.

These two methods—use of records and aided recall—unfortunately tend to have opposite effects on memory errors. Use of records generally controls overreporting due to telescoping, but has practically no effect on errors of omission. Aided recall, on the other hand, reduces the number of omitted events, but does not necessarily reduce (and may even increase) telescoping effects (Sudman & Bradburn, 1974). Judicious use of both methods is necessary to ensure accurate responses.

Even though use of records may not affect errors of omission, there is evidence to support the common-sense belief that using records will increase the accuracy and detail of the information that is actually reported, such as the price of particular goods and services or the place where they were purchased. Horn (1960) reports that 47% of the respondents who consulted records gave the correct balance in their savings account; but only 31% of the respondents who did not check their records gave the correct balance. The large amount of error that persists even when records are used also shows that although records improve reporting, they are not a panacea and do not totally eliminate error. Unfortunately, Horn was not able to discover the factors accounting for the remainder of the error in respondents' reporting.

The best studies of telescoping effects on memory are those conducted by Neter and Waksberg (1964). They not only measured telescoping but also proposed a procedure, called bounded recall, for eliminating this type of error. Bounded-recall procedures can only be used in panel studies where respondents are interviewed several times. At the beginning of the second or later interviews (bounded interviews), respondents are reminded what they said about their behavior (typically expenditures) during the previous interview, and then are asked about additional behavior since that time. The new behavior is also checked against previous reports to make sure that no duplication has occurred. The bounded-recall procedure requires a considerable amount of control over the data in order to provide interviewers with the correct information from the previous interview and thus has been used less widely than it deserves. New computer-oriented data-base management systems, however, are making bounded recall a more feasible method. We would expect its use to increase in the near future, at least for studies in which accuracy of behavior reports over a period of time is of prime importance.

In the Neter and Waksberg study both bounded and unbounded recall procedures were studied for periods ranging from 1 to 6 months, with different household members designated as respondents: head, spouse of head, joint interview with head and spouse, or any knowledgeable adult. No significant differences were found in the reports of different respondents in a given house-hold for expenditures on alterations and repairs, the subject of their study. For larger jobs (in terms of dollars spent), there was no evidence of omissions, and the telescoping effects decreased over the 6-month period. For small repairs the omissions rate increases over time so that the 1-month bounded recall reports of expenditures are higher than the 6-month unbounded recall.

It should be emphasized that although bounded-recall procedures correct for telescoping effects, they do not eliminate errors due to omissions. When one is concerned with many small or relatively inconsequential behaviors, such as small purchases or short trips, bounded recall may not help except for short recall periods since errors due to omission become larger over longer periods of time.

The time period involved in recall substantially affects the size of memory errors. As one would expect, the longer the time period being asked about, the greater the errors. Because total response error resulting from faulty memory is the product of both omissions and overreporting due to telescoping, the effects are not a simple linear function of time.

Sudman and Bradburn (1973) have developed a model of the effect of time on memory in the survey interview. This model specifies formally the relation-ship between estimates of errors of omission and errors due to telescoping. Errors of omission are seen as a simple exponential function of time multiplied by a constant. The constant is determined by factors such as the social desir-ability or undesirability of an event or the likelihood that the respondent is aware of the event (e.g., a purchase). Telescoping errors are viewed as a logarithmic function of subjective time, where the value that translates calen-dar time into subjective time is determined by the frequency of the events being recalled.

Two interesting generalizations follow from the model. First, the model implies that for long time periods there will be very substantial omission of events, regardless of telescoping. For most events the omission rate simply overpowers the overreporting due to telescoping. Second, the model implies that there is a time other than zero when omission and telescoping errors balance to produce the best level of reporting. If the investigator is interested only in the net level of reporting, it would pay to spend some resources to estimate the size of the relevant parameters of the model in order to find out the optimum time period to use for a recall period. Readers interested in the details of the model and data on the relevant parameters for some commonly studied events (e.g., consumer expenditures), should consult the original article (Sud-man & Bradburn, 1973).

Interviewer Variables

Because most data-collection procedures operate through the agency of interviewers, the interviewer has long been seen as a potential source of error. One can easily imagine characteristics or behaviors of interviewers that, either by themselves or in interaction with characteristics of respondents, might bias the resulting data. Early work by Katz (1942) and the classic work of Hyman and his associates at NORC (Hyman, 1954) demonstrated empirically that such effects exist. The assumption has continued that such effects exist and that they are pervasive and substantial in size.

In their review of the literature, however, Sudman and Bradburn (1974) found the situation much less clear. In many instances, characteristics of respondents and interviewers had no apparent effect on response; in other studies, whether or not there was an effect depended on the subject matter of the study. Even when response effects due to interviewer and respondent characteristics could be demonstrated, the evidence suggested that they were small compared to the size of effects from the task variables previously discussed. To some extent, then, the belief in pervasive and substantial interviewer effects is a consequence of the intuitive appeal of the idea and the ready availability of data on these variables rather than on empirical demonstrations of the comparative size of response effects arising from different sources.

Since interviewers are not a random sample of the population, studies of interviewer characteristics are limited to the range of age, education, and social class most commonly found among interviewers. Thus there is little information about interviewers over 45 years of age or those with less than a high school education. Males and poorly educated interviewers have been used in special situations where there was a desire to match characteristics with those of the respondents or to test the effect of differences in respondent–interviewer matching.

One important finding is that college students used as interviewers produce much larger response effects than other interviewers. The average response effect for interviewers under the age of 25 (mainly college students) was nearly three times larger than that for all other interviewers. It is not entirely clear why this large an effect should occur. The most likely hypothesis is that the younger interviewers were inexperienced or not very well trained or both. Since many studies using students as interviewers are products of methods classes in which students are learning interviewing for the first time, such an interpretation is plausible. Other data reported by Sudman and Bradburn indicate that experience is important in reducing response effects; response effects are twice as high for inexperienced as for experienced interviewers. Investigators who must rely on students as interviewers should be warned that training and supervision is perhaps even more important for this group of interviewers than for others. One must resist the temptation to believe that because students are highly motivated and bright, they will be able to cope with the interviewing task without the same training and supervision that is necessary with the more typical interviewer.

On average, higher status interviewers produce larger response effects for attitudinal questions than do lower status interviewers. In order for interviewer's social status to affect responses, respondents must be aware of the interviewer's status. Such awareness is probably impossible to avoid in classroom situation or in situations where the interviewer is known to the respondent, but good experienced interviewers of the general public know how to adapt their dress and behavior to the probable social status of the respondents.

The classic study of social class differences in interviewing is that of Katz (1942). He measured the effect of the social status of Gallup interviewers by comparing a group of 9 male, middle-class interviewers to a group of 11 working-class male interviewers. The procedure involved quota sampling so that some of the reported differences may be associated with sample execution rather than the joint characteristics of interviewers and respondents. Middle-class interviewers of the type employed by Gallup may have had a greater tendency to select middle-class respondents whereas working-class interviewers may have interviewed more working-class respondents. In addition it is likely that the middle-class interviewers were more experienced than the working-class interviewers. Half of the interviewers were under 25. Thus the results of the study should be interpreted with some caution.

Substantial differences were found in reports of attitudes on some issues. On questions relating to labor issues, Katz found that the working-class interviewers obtained more prolabor responses, particularly from union members, than did the middle-class interviewers. There was an average difference of 12 percentage points between the middle-class and working-class interviewers when interviewing union respondents on labor questions; the difference was 7 percentage points for nonunion respondents. On other issues, however, the differences were not as dramatic or were nonexistent. For example, on war issues (the study was conducted in March 1941), the middle-class interviewers obtained slightly more interventionist responses than did working-class interviewers, a difference that corresponds with the known relation between social class and interventionist attitudes prior to World War II. On questions relating to government ownership of electric companies, steel mills, and banks, however, the differences between the two groups of interviewers were slight.

In a more recent study, Weiss (1968) found that lower status interviewers did *not* obtain more valid reports of behavior from welfare mothers than did higher status interviewers. Again, however, differential experience may have influenced results even though attention was given to training the lower status interviewers. The study did not investigate the effects of interviewer differences on attitude measurement.

It is regretable that there has been no really definitive study in which all relevant variables affecting responses except interviewer social status have been controlled and both behavior and attitudes are measured. I suspect that if such a study were done, the differences between interviewers would be minimal.

Perhaps most attention has been given to the question of sex and race matching between interviewers and respondents. The effects of the sex of interviewers has been studied mostly in connection with studies of sexually related topics or other sensitive issues. Although the data are limited, the largest response effects were found when both respondents and interviewers were male, and only small differences were found between females interviewed by male and female interviewers. Other studies such as Johnson and Delameter (1976) and Robins (1974) failed to show any sex differences between male and female interviewers on surveys involving sex and drug usage, respectively.

The results of racial matching of interviewer and respondent have been more consistent, at least for questions involving racial attitudes. Williams (1964), in a study of black residents in North Carolina, showed no differences between black and white interviewers for attitudinal questions with low threat, but found differences of about 10 percentage points in response to higher threat items such as approval or disapproval of sit ins. NORC conducted an early similar study in Memphis in which 1000 black adults were interviewed, half by white and half by black interviewers (Hyman, 1954). Differences averaged about 15 percentage points on those items dealing with race such as *Is the army fair to Negroes now?* In a more recent study Schuman and Converse (1971) used professional black interviewers and white students from the Detroit Area Study in interviews with about 500 black households. Of the 40 questions on racial opinions examined, the race of the interviewer explained 2% or more of the variance for 32% of the questions; for the 29 nonracial opinion questions, race of interviewer explained 2% or more of the variance on only 3% of the questions. Hatchett and Schuman (1975–1976) found a race-of-interviewer effect among white respondents for items involving race relations content.

Respondent effects due to respondent and interviewer race depend very heavily on the content of the question. For questions dealing directly with racial attitudes, race of interviewer appears to make a difference; for other items, it does not.

Interviewer expectations about the difficulties in obtaining sensitive information have been studied by Sudman, Bradburn, Blair, and Stocking (1977). At the beginning of the training period for a survey involving many questions of a highly personal nature, for example, on drug use and sexual behavior, interviewers filled out a questionnaire about their expectations of what would be easy or difficult about the study. The authors hypothesized that there would be a relationship between expectations of difficulties in interviewing and actual difficulties encountered. This hypothesis was supported by the data, but the effects were not very large. Depending on the question, those interviewers who did not expect difficulties or underreporting obtained 5–30% higher reports of behavior in response to sensitive questions. However, when a number of possible confounding variables were controlled, interviewer variance accounted for 2–7% of the total variance.

For surveys involving sensitive topics, it is a good idea to obtain a pretraining measure of the interviewer's expectations about difficulties with threatening questions. Then either those interviewers who expect considerable difficulties should not be assigned to that study or time should be spend in training sessions to change their expectations and teach them how to handle problems that might arise.

Blair (1978) has investigated interviewer performance during interviews.

His study involved direct measures of interviewer performance derived from an analysis of tape recordings of the interviews. From these tapes he found that interviewers do in fact frequently alter the wording of the questions as printed in the questionnaire and add words or phrases of their own. Over one-third of the questions were not read exactly as written and, somewhat surprisingly, more experienced interviewers made more reading errors.

Further analysis of interviewer behavior, however, indicated that the occurrence of considerable amounts of nonprogrammed speech on the part of the interviewers may not necessarily be a bad thing. For example, there was a relationship between the characteristics of the respondent and the amount of nonprogrammed interviewer speech. More nonprogrammed speech occurred with older respondents. Older respondents give more inappropriate answers and more often ask for clarification. In addition, interviewers tend to probe more with older respondents to make sure that they understand their responses. That more experienced interviewers tend to use nonprogrammed speech more often also reflects that they are more likely to probe and to give feedback that tends to promote greater rapport with the respondent and make the interview flow more freely.

There was no evidence in the Blair study that the occurrence of nonprogrammed speech affected the quality of the responses as measured by under- or overreporting. It was not related to tension in the interview nor did it appear to be more frequent in those sections of the questionnaire dealing with the threatening questions. It would appear that interviewers use their own judgment in speaking to respondents and depart from the written questionnaire when it seems appropriate in a particular interview situation.

It seems clear from the Blair data that trained interviewers are capable of using good judgment in adjusting their speech behavior (and almost certainly other behaviors which were not observed) to fit the circumstances of specific interviews in order to complete the interviews successfully. Since one cannot completely standardize every aspect of the interview situation as long as there is considerable variance among respondents, we should not expect interviewers to be completely programmed. Indeed one of the virtues of good interviewers is that they are flexible and can adjust their behavior and speech appropriately to the situations they find themselves in. Such flexibility is a real asset in carrying out surveys of the general population. Efforts to standardize questions should not lead to a rigidity that requires interviewers to abandon their common sense.

The principal conclusion one draws from the available studies of interviewer–respondent characteristics is that interviewer characteristics which are clearly perceivable by respondents, such as sex and race, may make a substantial difference for attitudinal questions related to these characteristics. The evidence is most clear with regard to racial differences, but effects may possibly occur for sex or age of interviewer too, at least for some items. Interviewer expectations about difficulties in asking threatening questions may have some negative impact on interviewer behavior, but such problems can be substantially controlled by selection and training. Popular notions notwithstanding, there is no evidence that interviewer characteristics other than those associated with training and experience have consistent effects across a large variety of subject matters.

Readers may be surprised at the conclusion that interviewer effects are such a small source of response effects, particularly when compared with effects associated with questionnaire wording. The fact that so much of survey research is conducted through the agency of interviewers makes the interviewer as a potential source of error a subject of obvious interest. But the considerable body of literature on interviewer effects built up over the years fails to confirm our intuition that interviewers will be a major source of response effects. Why should this be? I believe it is due primarily to the fact that most interviewing by survey organizations is done by professional interviewers who are trained to be sensitive to and avoid the kinds of biases that interviewers might inject into the interviewing situation. The major effects found are related precisely to those characteristics that are visible and about which the interviewers themselves can do nothing.

The fact that interviewers contribute little to the observed variance in responses should not be taken as a license to forget about the interviewers as a potential source of response effects. Instead it should reinforce the idea that interviewer training and supervision are extremely important in making it possible to obtain data from interviews without the interviewers introducing unwanted variance. Neglect of interviewer training and supervision may negate the generalization about minimal interviewer effects for any particular study that fails to take the evidence seriously.

Respondent Variables

In most studies respondent differences are thought of as *true* variance, that is, the subject of interest to the study. In the social sciences, most surveys are conducted to investigate the relationship between behavior and attitudes, on the one hand, and respondent characteristics on the other. There is, however, one class of respondent variables that is frequently discussed as being part of error variance, namely, certain personality dispositions that are believed to distort responses systematically and thus conceal true relationships. This class is variously studied under the rubric of response set, response style, social desirability, acquiescence, and so forth. The existence of a response bias associated with respondents may act to alter observed relations between an independent and a dependent variable in ways that either produce relationships when none really exist or cause systematic under- or overestimation of relationships.

The literature on response sets is large and cannot be reviewed thoroughly here. Several reviews exist (Jackson & Messick, 1958; McGee, 1967; Phillips,

1971) to which the reader can refer for a comprehensive review. In this section we shall consider a more limited set of studies that pertain more specifically to surveys.

The notion of response set, although not invented by them, was rather spectacularly launched by Couch and Keniston (1960) who attempted to show that many of the findings of the famous authoritarian personality study (Adorno *et al.*, 1952) could be accounted for by positing a personality disposition to agree with statements regardless of their content—a so-alled yea-saying bias. The publication of their paper set off a rash of studies trying to develop positive and negative statements with which to measure attitudinal dimensions. By using balanced items, survey researchers tried to minimize the impact of any such response sets or styles.

The Couch and Keniston hypothesis has not gone unchallenged. Rorer (1965) found no evidence to suggest a response set existed outside of a guessing situation. He interpreted the Couch and Keniston findings as a function of item content, not of personal style. Other researchers (e.g., Bradburn, Sudman, Blair, & Stocking, 1978; Orne, 1969) have interpreted the yea-saying phenomenon as reflecting the norms governing communication situations, such as interviews, rather than as reflecting personality characteristics. Lenski and Leggett (1960) embedded a pair of mutually contradictory statements in an interview. They found that the greater the social distance between the interviewer and the respondent, the more likely respondents were to agree with both statements. Carr (1971), in a discussion of the Srole anomia scale, suggests that acquiescence is not only a psychological phenomenon and measurement problem, but a behavioral fact resulting from the class and racial structure of society.

One of the most widely used instruments to study response styles is the Marlowe–Crowne Social Desirability Scale (Crowne & Marlowe, 1964), Crowne and Marlowe conceptualized a need for social approval and hypothesized that individuals vary in the degree to which they possess this need. Those with a stronger need for approval will be more likely to select socially desirable answers on a questionnaire. Thus questionnaires that enquire about socially desirable or undesirable behavior or attitudes (which includes a very large proportion of surveys in social science research) will be subjected to response biases due to the differential strength of this need among respondents. Crowne and Marlowe developed a set of items that were culturally approved but untrue for nearly everyone (e.g., *I never resent being asked to return a favor*) or culturally disapproved but true for nearly everyone (e.g., *I sometimes try to get even, rather than forgive and forget*). They suggest that scores on their scale indicate the strength of the respondent's need for social approval and likely bias toward socially desirable responses. Although Crowne and Marlowe's research moved from a response bias to a personality trait interpretation of this scale, other researchers have used Marlowe–Crowne scores as statistical correction factors, to estimate the true relationships between variables affected by this type of response bias.

The Marlowe–Crowne scale (or some subset of items from it) is becoming a popular method of investigating and controlling for social desirability bias in surveys. It has already been included in a number of surveys (Bachman, 1970; Campbell, Converse, & Rodgers, 1976; Clancy & Gove, 1974; Gove & Geerken, 1977; Klassen, Hornstra, & Anderson, 1975; McCready & Greeley, 1976; Phillips & Clancy, 1970, 1972; Smith, 1967; Stocking, 1978). It has had a particularly contentious career in surveys of mental health symptoms and life satisfaction, two topics of surveys that are closest to the types of variables that originally gave rise to the development of the scale.

The controversy over response bias has been most intense in the context of studies relating social class to mental illness. Phillips and Clancy tested the hypothesis that the frequently found inverse relationship between social class and mental health symptoms was a function of the greater sophistication of middle- and upper-class respondents about the undesirability of certain symptoms. In a pilot study Phillips and Clancy (1970) found no systematic effect of yea-saying on scores on the Langer inventory of mental health symptoms, but they did find that more of the variance in scores was accounted for by social desirability than by socioeconomic status. In subsequent research (Phillips & Clancy, 1972) they found that respondents with higher Marlowe–Crowne scores reported more socially desirable attitudes and behavior such as being very happy, being very religious, having many friends, and visiting a doctor. Although the differences were generally small, they concluded that high Marlowe–Crowne scores affect people's responses and may account for the correlation between socioeconomic status and attitudinal and behavioral variables. They would interpret these correlations as spurious, since they believe that respondents with high Marlowe–Crowne scores are dissimulating in order to present a more desirable self.

These conclusions have not gone unchallenged (Clancy & Gove, 1974; Harvey, 1971; Seiler, 1973, 1976). A study by Gove and Geerken (1977) provides data from a nationwide survey that strongly challenges the response bias interpretation of the standard correlates of mental health ratings. In this study, the authors test three different types of response style indicators—yea-saying, the perception of the desirability of a given trait, and the need for social approval, as measured by a modified version of the Marlowe–Crowne scale, for their impact on the correlations between seven demographic variables (sex, race, education, income, age, marital status, and occupation) and three different indicators of mental health (psychiatric symptoms, self-esteem, and feelings of positive affect). They conclude that the response variables have very little impact on the relationships between mental health indicators and demographic variables.

In another study, also based on data from a nationwide study, Stocking (1978) tested two different interpretations of the social approval variable as measured by the Marlow–Crowne scale. One interpretation, similar to that of Phillips and Clancy, is that need for social approval is a response bias variable that distorts the relations. The other interpretation is that it reflects real differences in the norms and self-image of respondents and that it should be treated as part of the true variance. Stocking concludes that the data support the latter interpretation, and that investigators should treat scores on the Marlowe–Crowne scale as indicators of real differences among individuals and not as a sign that respondents are consciously lying about their attitudes or behavior. Although the debate will probably continue for some time, the evidence appears to favor interpreting the "social desirability response set" as a part of the real differences among respondents and not as some sort of response bias to be eliminated as a measurement artifact.

8.4. CONCLUSIONS

This chapter has presented a conceptual framework for viewing response effects and has reviewed briefly the literature on the principal sources of these effects. I have distinguished three sources of variation: that coming from the characteristics of the survey task itself; that coming from the interviewer and the interviewer–respondent interaction; and that which might be thought of as coming from characteristics of the respondent. Although the data are rarely unequivocal, I have tried to assess the state of the art today and to give some summations for what I believe to be the principal sources of response effects, both for behavior and for attitudinal variables. In general, it appears that the characteristics of the task itself, for example, the mode of administration of the interview; the order of the questions; open versus closed questions; the length and wording of the questions; and memory factors play the major role in producing response effects. To a lesser extent, characteristics of the interviewer and the respondent may be important as a source of response bias, but the literature is far from clear whether such variables are to be considered part of response effects or not.

It is clear from the literature that response effects from whatever sources can make substantial contributions of the variance in responses to surveys and serious investigators need to give at least as much, if not more, attention to them as they do to problems of sampling error and nonresponse bias. As the literature begins to develop in a more systematic form and some of the uncertainties that now exist are resolved, we will be in a better position to develop a systematic theory of response effects. For now, we must be content to be on guard against them and to test out their possible effects wherever possible before we conduct our research.

REFERENCES

Abernathy, J., B. Greenberg, and D. Horvitz
    1970   "Estimates of induced abortion in urban North Carolina." *Demography* 7: 19–29.
Adorno, T. W., E. Frenkel-Brunswick, D. J. Levinson, and R. N. Sanford
    1950   *The Authoritarian Personality*. New York: Harper and Bros.
American Marketing Association
    1937   *The Technique of Marketing Research*. New York: McGraw–Hill.

Arndt, J., and E. Crane
   1975   "Response bias, yea-saying and the double negative." *Journal of Marketing Research* 12(May): 218–220.
Atteslander, P., and H. U. Kneubühler
   1975   *Verzerrungen im interview: Zu einer fehlertheorie der Befragung.* Studien zur Sozialwissenschaft. Band 32. Opladen: Westdeutscher Verlag.
Bachman, J. G.
   1970   *Youth in Transition, Vol. II, The Impact of Family Background and Intelligence on Tenth-Grade Boys.* Ann Arbor: Institute for Social Research.
Bailar, B., L. Bailey, and J. Stevens
   1977   "Measures of interviewer bias and variance." *Journal of Marketing Research* 14(August): 337–343.
Bailey, M. B., P. W. Haberman, and J. Sheinberg
   1966   "Identifying alcoholics in population surveys: A report on reliability." *Quarterly Journal of Studies on Alcohol* 27: 300–315.
Barath, A., and C. F. Cannell
   1976   "Effect of interviewer's voice intonation." *Public Opinion Quarterly* 40(Fall): 370–373.
Barr, A.
   1957   "Differences between experienced interviewers." *Applied Statistics* 6(November): 180–188.
Belson, W. A.
   1966   "The effects of reversing the presentation order of verbal rating scales." *Journal of Advertising Research* 6(4): 1–11.
Berg, I. A., (ed.)
   1967   *Response Set in Personality Assessment.* Chicago: Aldine.
Berg, I. A., and G. M. Rapaport
   1954   "Response bias in an unstructured questionnaire." *Journal of Psychology* 38(October): 475–481.
Blair, E., S. Sudman, N. M. Bradburn, and C. B. Stocking
   1977   "How to ask questions about drinking and sex: Response effects in measuring consumer behavior." *Journal of Marketing Research.* 14(August): 316–321.
Bowers, W. J., and R. B. Stearns
   1972   *Questioning Sequencing Effects on Response to Sensitive Questions in the Self-Administered Questionnaire.* Final Report under Contract No. 1035084, U.S. Department of Commerce. Boston: Northeastern University.
Boyd, H. W., and R. Westfall
   1965   "Interviewer bias revisited." *Journal of Marketing Research* 2(February): 58–63.
Bradburn, N. M.
   1969   *The Structure of Psychological Well-Being.* Chicago: Aldine.
Bradburn, N. M., and W. M. Mason
   1964   "The effect of question order on responses." *Journal of Marketing Research* 1(1964): 57–61.
Bradburn, N. M., S. Sudman, E. Blair, and C. B. Stocking
   1978   "Question threat and response bias." *Public Opinion Quarterly* 42(Summer): 221–234.
Brannon, R., G. Cyphers, S. Hess, S. Hesselbart, R. Keane, H. Schuman, T. Viccaro, and D. Wright
   1973   "Attitude and action: A field experiment joined to a general population survey." *American Sociological Review* 38: 625–636.
Brown, G. H.
   1974   "Drug usage rates as related to method of data acquisition." Technical Report 74-20. Arlington, Va.: Human Resources Research Organization. August.
Brown, G. H., and F. Harding
   1973   "A comparison of methods of studying illicit drug usage." Technical Report 73-9. Arlington, Va.: Human Resources Research Organization. April.

Cahalan, D.
  1960 "Measuring newspaper readership by telephone—Two comparisons with face-to-face interviews." *Journal of Advertising Research* 2(December): 1–6.
  1968 "Correlates of respondent accuracy in the Denver validity study." *Public Opinion Quarterly* 32(Winter): 607–621.
Campbell, D. T., and P. J. Mohr
  1950 "The effect of ordinal position upon responses to items in a check list." *Journal of Applied Psychology* 34: 62–67.
Cannell, C. F., G. Fisher, and T. Bakker
  1965 "Reporting of hospitalization in the health interview survey." *Vital and Health Statistics.* National Center for Health Statistics. DHEW Publication No. 1000, Series 2, No. 6. Washington, D.C.: U.S. Government Printing Office.
Cannell, C. F., and F. J. Fowler
  1963 "A comparison of a self-enumerative procedure and a personal interview: A validity study." *Public Opinion Quarterly* 27(Summer): 250–264.
  1965 "Comparison of hospitalization reporting in three survey procedures." *Vital and Health Statistics.* National Center for Health Statistics. DHEW Publication No. 1000, Series 2, No. 8. Washington, D.C.: U.S. Government Printing Office.
Cannell, C. F., F. J. Fowler, Jr., and K. H. Marquis
  1968 "The influence of interview and respondent psychological and behavioral variables on the reporting in household interviews." *Vital and Health Statistics.* National Center for Health Statistics. DHEW Publication No. 1000, Series 2, No. 26. Washington, D.C.: U.S. Government Printing Office.
Cannell, C. F., and R. Henson
  1974 "Incentives, motives and response bias." *Annals of Economic and Social Measurement* 3: 307–314.
Cannell, C. F., and R. L. Kahn
  1968 "Interviewing." Pp. 526–595 in G. Lindzey and E. Aronson (eds.) *The Handbook of Social Psychology* (2nd ed.), Vol. 2. Reading, Mass.: Addison–Wesley.
Cannell, C. F., Lois Oksenberg, and Jean M. Converse
  1977a "Striving for response accuracy: Experiments in new interviewing techniques." *Journal of Marketing Research* 14(August): 306–315.
  1977b *Experiments in Interviewing Techniques: Field Experiments in Health Reporting, 1971–77.* Washington, D.C.: National Center for Health Services Research, Office of Scientific and Technical Information (HRA) 78-3204.
Cantril, H., and Research Associates
  1944 *Gauging Public Opinion.* Princeton: Princeton University Press.
Carr, L. G.
  1971 "The Srole items and acquiescence." *American Sociological Review* 36(April): 287–293.
Cieutat, V. J.
  1964 "Sex differences in verbal operant conditioning." *Psychological Reports* 15: 259–275.
Clancy, K., and W. Gove
  1974 "Sex differences in respondents' reports of psychiatric symptoms: An analysis of response bias." *American Journal of Sociology* 80(July): 205–216.
Clark, J. P., and L. L. Tifft
  1966 "Polygraph and interview validation of self-reported deviant behavior." *American Sociological Review* 31(August): 516–523.
Colombotos, J.
  1969 "Personal versus telephone interviews—Effect on responses." *Public Health Report* 84(September): 773–782.
Converse, J. M.
  1976–1977 "Predicting no opinion in the polls." *Public Opinion Quarterly* 40(Winter): 515–530.

Coombs, L. C., and R. Freedman
  1964 "Use of telephone interviews in a longitudinal fertility study." *Public Opinion Quarterly* 28(Spring): 112–117.
Couch, A., and K. Keniston
  1960 "Yeasayer and naysayers: Agreeing response set as a personality variable." *Journal of Abnormal and Social Psychology* 60(March): 151–174.
Crowne, D. P., and D. Marlowe
  1964 *The Approval Motive: Studies in Evaluative Dependence.* New York: Wiley.
DeLamater, J., and P. MacCorquodale
  1975 "The effects of interview schedule variations on reported sexual behavior." *Sociological Methods and Research* 4(November): 215–236.
Dillman, D. A.
  1978 *Mail and Telephone Surveys: The Total Design Method.* New York: Wiley Interscience.
Dohrenwend, B. S.
  1965 "Some effects of open and closed questions on respondents' answers." *Human Organization* 24(Summer): 175–184.
Dohrenwend, B. S., J. Colombotos, and B. P. Dohrenwend
  1968 "Social distance and interview effects." *Public Opinion Quarterly* 32(Fall): 121–129.
Dohrenwend, B. S., and S. A. Richardson
  1963 "Directiveness and nondirectiveness in research interviewing: A reformulation of the problem." *Psychological Bulletin* 60: 475–485.
Dohrenwend, B., J. A. Williams, and C. P. Weiss
  1969 "Interview bias effect: Toward a reconciliation of findings." *Public Opinion Quarterly* 33(Spring): 121–129.
Dohrenwend, B. P.
  1966 "Social status and psychological disorder: An issue of substance and an issue of method." *American Sociological Review* 31(February): 14–34.
Dohrenwend, B. P., and D. Crandell
  1970 "Psychiatric symptoms in community, clinic and mental hospital groups." *American Journal of Psychiatry* 126(May): 1611–1621.
Dohrenwend, B. P., and B. S. Dohrenwend
  1969 *Social Status and Psychological Disorder: A Causal Inquiry.* New York: Wiley–Interscience.
Dowling, T. A., and R. H. Shachtman
  1975 "On the relative efficiency of randomized response models." *Journal of the American Statistical Association* 70(March): 84–87.
Ellis, A.
  1947 "Questionnaire versus interview methods in the study of human love relationships, I." *American Sociological Review* 12: 541–553.
  1948 "Questionnaire versus interview methods in the study of human love relationships, II." *American Sociological Review* 13: 61–65.
Ferber, R.
  1966 *The Reliability of Consumer Reports of Financial Assets and Debts.* Urbana, Ill.: Bureau of Economic and Business Research, University of Illinois.
Ferber, R., J. Forsythe, E. S. Mayne, and H. Guthrie
  1969 "Validation of a national survey of consumer financial characteristics: Savings accounts." *Review of Economic and Statistics* 51(November): 436–444.
Goodstadt, M. S., and V. Gruson
  1975 "The randomized response technique: A test on drug use." *Journal of the American Statistical Association* 70(December): 814–817.
Gove, W., and M. R. Geerken
  1977 "Response bias in surveys of mental health: An empirical investigation." *American Journal of Sociology* 82(May): 1289–1318.

Greenberg, B., A.-L. Abdul–Ela, W. Simmons, and D. Horvitz
  1969 "The unrelated question randomized response model, theoretical framework." *Journal of the American Statistical Association* 64: 520–539.
Greenberg, B., R. Kuebler, J. Abernathy, and D. Horvitz
  1971 "Application of randomized response technique in obtaining quantitative data." *Journal of the American Statistical Association*. 66: 243–250.
Greenspoon, J.
  1955 "The reinforcing effect of two spoken sounds on the frequency of two responses." *American Journal of Psychology* 68: 409–416.
Greenwald, H. J., and J. D. Clausen
  1970 "Test of relationship between yeasaying and social desirability." *Psychological Reports* 27: 139–141.
Groves, R. M., and R. Kahn
  1979 *Comparing Telephone and Personal Interview Surveys*. New York: Academic Press.
Groves, R. M., and J. C. Scott
  1976 *An Attempt to Measure the Relative Efficiency of Telephone Surveys for Social Science Data Collection* (Presented at the annual meeting of the American Association for Public Opinion Research, Ashville, North Carolina, May 13–16).
Hare, A. P.
  1960 "Interview responses: Personality or conformity?" *Public Opinion Quarterly* 24(Winter): 679–688.
Harvey, T.
  1971 "Comment on response bias in field studies of mental illness." *American Sociological Review* 36(June): 510–512.
Hatchett, S., and H. Schuman
  1975–1976 "White respondents and race-of-interviewer effects." *Public Opinion Quarterly* 39(Winter): 523–528.
Hauck, M.
  1974 *Use of the Telephone for Technical Surveys*. Urbana, Ill.: University of Illinois, Survey Research Laboratory.
Hayes, D. P.
  1964 "Item order and Guttman scales." *American Journal of Sociology* 70(July): 51–58.
Heberlein, T. A., and R. Baumgartner
  1978 "Factors affecting response rates to mailed questionnaires." *American Sociological Review* 43(August): 447–462.
Henson, R., A. Roth, and C. F. Cannell
  1974 *Personal vs. Telephone Interviews on Reporting of Psychiatric Symptomology*. Ann Arbor: University of Michigan.
Henson, R., C. F. Cannell, and S. Lawson
  1976 "Effects of interviewer style on quality of reporting in a survey interview." *The Journal of Psychology* 93: 221–227.
Herriot, R. A.
  1977 "Collecting income data on sample surveys: Evidence from split-panel studies." *Journal of Marketing Research* 14(August): 322–329.
Hildum, D. C., and R. W. Brown
  1956 "Verbal reinforcement and interviewer bias." *Journal of Abnormal and Social Psychology* 53: 108–111.
Hitlin, R.
  1976 "A research note on question wording and stability of response." *Social Science Research* 5(March): 39–41.
Hochstim, J. R.
  1962 "Comparison of three information-gathering strate   in a population study of sociomedical variables." In *Proceedings of the American Statistical Association,* Social Statistics Section. pp. 154–159.

1967   "A critical comparison of three strategies of collecting data from households." *Journal of the American Statistical Association* 62(September): 976–989.

Horn, W.
    1960   "Reliability survey: A survey on the reliability of response to an interview survey." *Der Haag: Het PTT-bedriff 10* (October): 105–156.

Hyman, H. A.
    1954   *Interviewing in Social Research.* Chicago: University of Chicago Press.

Hyman, H. H., and P. B. Sheatsley
    1950   "The current status of American public opinion." In J. C. Payne (ed.), *The Teaching of Contemporary Affairs: Twenty-first Yearbook of the National Council for the Social Studies.* Washington: National Council for the Social Studies.

Ibsen, C. A., and J. A. Ballweg
    1974   "Telephone interviews in social research: Some methodological considerations." *Quality and Quantity* 8: 181–192.

I-Cheng, C., L. P. Chow, and R. V. Rider
    1972   "The randomized response techniques as used in the Taiwan outcome of pregnancy study." New York: A Publication of the Population Council 33, No. 11: 265–269.

Institute for Survey Research
    1975   "Final report of a study of supplementary security income redetermination." Submitted to the Social Security Administration by the Institute for Survey Research, Philadelphia: Temple University.

Jackson, D. N., and S. J. Messick
    1958   "Content and style in personality assessment." *Psychological Bulletin* 55: 243–252.

Johnson, W. R., N. A. Sieveking, and E. S. Clanton III
    1974   "Effects of alternative positioning of open-ended questoins in multiple-choice questionnaires." *Journal of Applied Psychology* 59(December): 776–778.

Johnson, W. T., and J. D. Delamater
    1976   "Response effects in sex surveys." *Public Opinion Quarterly* 40(Summer): 165–181.

Jones, R. A., J. Sensing, and J. V. Haley
    1974   "Self-descriptions: Configurations of content and order effects." *Journal of Personality and Social Psychology* 30(July): 36–45.

Jonsson, C.-O.
    1957   *Questionnaires and Interviews: Experimental Studies Concerning Concurrent Validity on Well-Motivated Subjects.* Stockholm: The Swedish Council for Personnel Administration.

Kahn, R. L.
    1952   "A comparison of two methods of collecting data for social research: The fixed-alternative questionnaire and the open-ended interview." Unpublished doctoral dissertation. University of Michigan.

Kahn, R. L., and C. F. Cannell
    1957   *The Dynamics of Interviewing.* New York: Wiley.

Katz, D.
    1942   "Do interviewers bias poll results?" *Public Opinion Quarterly* 6: 248–268.

Keating, E., D. G. Paterson, and C. H. Stone
    1950   "Validity of work histories obtained by interview." *Journal of Applied Psychology* 34: 6–11.

Kjøller, M.
    1975   *Interaktionen Mellem Interviewer og Respondent* (Interviewer–Respondent Interaction). Copenhagan: The Danish National Institute of Social Research. Studie 32 (contains English summary.)

Klassen, D., R. K. Hornstra, and P. B. Anderson
    1975   "Influence of social desirability of symptom and mood reporting in a community survey." *Journal of Consulting and Clinical Psychology* 43(4): 448–452.

Knudsen, D. D., H. Pope, and D. P. Irish
1967 "Response differences to questions on sexual standards: An interview–questionnaire comparison. *Public Opinion Quarterly* 31: 290–297.

Kofron, J. H., J. A. Bayton, and B. Z. Bortner
1969 *Guidelines for Choosing between Long-Distance Telephone and Personal Interviewing.* Philadelphia: Chilton Research Services. (Presented to the Advertising Research Foundation 15th Annual Conference, New York, 15 October.

Krasner, L.
1958 "Studies of the conditioning of verbal behavior." *Psychological Bulletin* 55: 148–170.

Kraut, A. I., A. D. Wolfson, and A. Rothenberg
1975 "Some effects of position on opinion survey items." *Journal of Applied Psychology* 60(December): 774–776.

Landon, E. L., Jr.
1971 "Order bias, the ideal ratings and the semantic differential." *Journal of Marketing Research* 8(August): 375–378.

Lansing, J. B., Gerald P. Ginsburg, and Kaisa Braaten
1961 *An Investigation of Response Error. Studies in Consumer Savings, No. 2.* Urbana, Ill.: University of Illinois, Bureau of Economic and Business Research.

Larsen, O. N.
1952 "The comparative validity of telephone and face-to-face interviews in the measurement of message diffusion from leaflets." *American Sociological Review* 17: 471–476.

Laurent, A.
1972 "Effects of question length on reporting behavior in the survey interview." *Journal of the American Statistical Association* 67(338): 298–305.

Laurent, A., C. F. Cannell, and K. H. Marquis
1972 "Reporting health events in household interviews—Effects of an extensive questionnaire and a diary procedure." *Vital and Health Statistics*. National Center for Health Statistics. DHEW Publication No. 1000, Series 2, No. 49. Washington, D.C.: U.S. Government Printing Office.

Lenski, G. E., and J. C. Leggett
1960 "Caste, class and deference in the research interview." *American Journal of Sociology* 65: 463–467.

Levine, D. D., and H. P. Miller
1957 "Response variation encountered with different questionnaire forms: An experimental study of selected techniques in agriculture." Washington, D.C.: Bureau of the Census. U.S. Government Printing Office. April.

Locander, W., and J. P. Burton
1976 "The effect of question form on gathering income data by telephone." *Journal of Marketing Research* 13(May): 189–192.

Locander, W., S. Sudman, and N. M. Bradburn
1976 "An investigation of interview method, threat and response distortion." *Journal of the American Statistical Association* 71(354): 269–275.

Marks, E. S., and W. P. Mauldin
1950 "Response errors in census research." *Journal of the American Statistical Association* 45: 424–438.

Marquis, K. H.
1970 "Effects of social reinforcement on health reporting in the household interview." *Sociometry* 33(June): 203–215.

Marquis, K. H., and C. F. Cannell
1971 "Effect of Some Experimental Techniques on Reporting in the Health Interview." *Vital and Health Statistics*. National Center for Health Statistics. DHEW Publication No. 1000, Series 2, No. 41. Washington, D.C.: U.S. Government Printing Office.

Marquis, K. H., C. F. Cannell, and A. Laurent
1972 "Reporting for health events in household interviews: Effects of reinforcement, question

length and reinterviews." *Vital and Health Statistics*. National Center for Health Statistics. DHEW Publication No. 1000, Series 2, No. 45. Washington: U.S. Government Printing Office.

Marquis, K. H., J. Marshall, and S. Oskamp

1972   "Testimony validity as a function of question form, atmosphere and item difficulty." *Journal of Applied Social Psychology* 2: 167–186.

Martin, D.

1962   "The validity of income reported by a sample of families who received welfare assistance during 1959." *Journal of the American Statistical Association* 57(September): 680–685.

McCready, W. C., and A. M. Greeley

1976   *The Ultimate Values of the American Population*. Beverly Hills: Sage.

McGee, R. K.

1967   "Response set in relation to personality orientatin." In Irwin A. Berg (ed.). *Response Set in Personality Assessment*. Chicago: Aldine.

McKenzie, J. R.

1977   "An investigation into interview effects in market research." *Journal of Marketing Research* 14(August): 330–336.

Metzner, H., and F. Mann

1952   "A limited comparison of two methods of data collection: The fixed alternative questionnaire and the open-ended interview." *American Sociological Review* 17: 486–491.

1953   "Effects of grouping related questions in questionnaires." *Public Opinion Quarterly* 17(Spring): 136–141.

Mooney, W. H., B. R. Pollack, and L. Corsa, Jr.

1968   "Use of telephone interviewing to study human reproduction." *Public Health Reports* 83(December): 1049–1060.

Nakamura, C. Y.

1959   "Salience of norms and order of questionnaire items: Their effect on responses to the items." *Journal of Abnormal and Social Psychology* 59(July): 139–142.

National Center for Health Services Research

1977   *Advances in Health Survey Research Methods*. Proceedings of a National Invitational Conference. Washington, D.C.: DHEW Publication No. (HRA) 77-3154.

National Opinion Research Center

1946   "Placement of questions on the ballot." Unpublished Memorandum, Denver: University of Denver.

1947   "Nation-wide attitudes on occupations: Preliminary report, the social status of ninety occupations." Mimeographed. Denver: University of Denver.

Neter, J., and J. Waksberg

1964   "A study of response errors in expenditures data from household interviews." *Journal of the American Statistical Association* 59(305): 18–55.

Noelle–Neumann, E.

1962   *Über den Methodischen Fortschritt in der Umfrageforschung."* Allenbacher Schriften No. 7. Allensbach und Bonn: Verlag fur Demoskopie. (With English translation.)

1976   "Die Empfindlichkeit Demoskopischer Messinstrumente Frageformulierungen and Fragebogenaufbau." In Elizabeth Noelle-Neumann (ed.) *Allensbacher Jahrbuch der Demoskopie, 1976*. Wien: Verlag Fritz Molden.

Northrop, R. M., and O. L. Deniston

1967   "Comparison of mail and telephone methods to collect program evaluation data." *Public Health Reports*. 8(August): 739–745.

Ogawa, J., and W. F. Oakes

1965   "Sex of experimenter and manifest anxiety as related to verbal conditioning." *Journal of Personality* 33: 553–569.

Oksenberg, L., and C. F. Cannell

1977   "Some factors underlying the validity of response in self report." *International Statistical Bulletin* 48(3): 324–346.

Orne, M. T.
    1969   "Demand characteristics and the concept of quasi-controls." Pp. 143–179 in R. Rosenthal
           and R. L. Rosnow (eds.), *Artifact in Behavioral Research*.New York: Academic Press.
Parry, H. J., and H. M. Crossley
    1950   "Validity of responses to survey question." *Public Opinion Quarterly* 14: 61–80.
Payne, S. L.
    1951   *The Art of Asking Questions.* Princeton: Princeton University Press.
    1974   "Data collection methods: Telephone surveys." In R. Ferber (ed.), *Handbook of Market-
           ing Research.* New York: McGraw–Hill.
Perreault, W. D., Jr.
    1975   "Controlling order–effect bias." *Public Opinion Quarterly* 39(Winter): 544–551.
Phillips, D. L.
    1971   *Knowledge from What?* Chicago: Rand McNally.
    1973   *Abandoning Method: Sociological Studies in Methodology.* San Francisco: Jossey–Bass.
Phillips, D. L., and K. Clancy
    1970   "Response biases in field studies of mental illness." *American Sociological Review* 35:
           503–515.
    1972   " 'Modeling effects' in survey research." *Public Opinion Quarterly* 36(Summer): 246–
           253.
Presser, S.
    1977   "Survey question wording and attitudes in the general public." Unpublished Doctoral
           Dissertation, Department of Sociology, University of Michigan.
Presser, S., and H. Schuman
    1978   "The measurement of a middle position in attitude surveys." In *Proceedings of the
           Survey Methods Section.* Washington, D.C.: American Statistical Association.
Quinn, S., and W. A. Belson
    1969   *The Effects of Reversing the Order of Presentation of Verbal Rating Scales in Survey
           Interviews.* London: London School of Eocnomics and Political Science, Survey Re-
           search Centre.
Robins, L. N.
    1974   *The Vietman Drug User Returns.* Executive Office of the President, Special Action Office
           for Drug Abuse Prevention. Special Action Office Monograph, Series A, No. 2. May.
           Washington D.C.: U.S. Government Printing Office.
Rogers, T. R.
    1976   "Interviewing by telephone and in person: Quality of responses and field performance."
           Public Opinion Quarterly 40(Spring): 51–65.
Rorer, L.
    1965   "The great response bias myth." *Psychological Bulletin.* 63(March): 129–156.
Rugg, D.
    1941   "Experiments in wording questions: II." *Public Opinion Quarterly* 5: 91–92.
Salzinger, K.
    1959   "Experimental manipulation of verbal behavior: A review." *Journal of General Psychol-
           ogy* 61: 65–94.
Sayre, J.
    1939   "A comparison of three indices of attitude toward radio advertising." *Journal of Applied
           Psychology* 23: 23–33.
Schuman, H., and J. M. Converse
    1971   "Effects of black and white interviewers on black response in 1968." *Public Opinion
           Quarterly* 35(Spring): 44–68.
Schuman, H., and O. D. Duncan
    1974   "Questions about attitude survey questions." Pp. 232–251 in H. L. Costner (ed.), *Socio-
           logical Methodology 1973–1974.* San Francisco: Jossey–Bass.
Schuman, H., and S. Presser
    1977   "Question wording as an independent variable in survey analysis." *Sociological Methods
           and Research* 6(November): 151–176.

1977–1978   "Attitude measurement and the gun control paradox." *Public Opinion Quarterly* 41(Winter): 427–439.
   1978   "Open versus closed questions in attitude surveys." (Paper delivered at the annual meetings of the American Association for Public Opinion Research, Roanoke, Va., June.)
   1979   "The assessment of 'no opinion' in attitude surveys." In K. Schuessler (ed.), *Sociological Methodology*. San Francisco: Jossey–Bass.

Segall, M.
   1959   "The effects of attitude and experience on judgment of controversial statements." *Journal of Abnormal and Social Psychology* 58: 61–68.

Seiler, L.
   1973   "The 22-item scale used in field studies on mental illness: A question of method, a question of substance and a question of theory." *Journal of Health and Social Behavior* 14(September): 252–264.
   1976   "Sex differences in mental illness: Comment on Clancy and Gove's interpretations." *American Journal of Sociology* 81(May): 1458–1463.

Shaffer, J. D.
   1955   "The reporting period for a consumer purchase panel." *Journal of Marketing* 19: 252–257.

Smith, D. H.
   1967   "Correcting for social desirability response sets in opinion-attitude survey research." *Public Opinion Quarterly* 31(Spring): 87–94.

Smith, L. L., W. T. Federer, and D. Raghavarao
   1974   "A comparison of three techniques for eliciting answers to sensitive questions." *Proceedings of the Social Statistics Section*. Washington, D.C.: American Statistical Association.

Stember, H.
   1951   "Which respondents are reliable?" *International Journal of Opinion and Attitude Research* 5: 475–479.

Stocking, C. B.
   1978   "The Marlowe–Crowne scale in survey data." Unpublished doctoral dissertation, Department of Sociology, University of Chicago.

Sudman, S.
   1964   "On the accuracy of recording of consumer panels." Parts 1 and 2. *Journal of Marketing Research* 1(March): 14–29; (August): 69–83.
   1966   "New uses of telephone methods in survey research." *Journal of Marketing Research* 3(May): 163–167.

Sudman, S., and N. M. Bradburn
   1973   "Effects of time and memory factors on response in surveys." *Journal of the American Statistical Association* 68(344): 805–815.
   1974   *Response Effects in Surveys: A Review and Synthesis*. Chicago: Aldine.

Sudman, S., N. M. Bradburn, E. Blair, and C. Stocking
   1977   "Modest expectations: The effects of interviewers' prior expectations on responses." *Sociological Methods and Research* 6(November): 177–182.

Sudman, S., and R. Ferber
   1974   "A comparison of alternative procedures for collecting expenditure data for frequently purchased products." *Journal of Marketing Research* 11(May): 128–135.

Sudman, S., A. Greeley, and L. Pinto
   1965   "The effectiveness of self-administered questionnaires." *Journal of Marketing Research* 2: 293–297.

Summers, G. F., and A. D. Hammonds
   1966   "Effect of racial characteristics of investigator on self-enumerated responses to a Negro prejudice scale." *Social Forces* 44:515–518.
   1969   "Toward a paradigm for respondent bias in survey research." *The Sociological Quarterly* 10(Winter): 113–121.

Thornberry, O., and H. D. Scott
    1973   "Methodology of a health interview survey for a population of one million." Paper presented at the 101st Annual Meeting of the APHA, San Francisco, November.
Thorndike, R. L., E. H. Hagen, and R. A. Kemper
    1952   "Normative data obtained in the house-to-house administration of a psychosomatic inventory." *Journal of Consulting Psychology* 16: 257–260.
Tousingnant, M., G. Denis, and R. Lachapelle
    1974   "Some considerations concerning the validity and use of the Health Opinion Survey." *Journal of Health and Social Behavior* 15(September): 241–252.
Trussell, R. E., and J. Elinson
    1959   *Chronic Illness in a Rural Area: The Hunterdon Study.* Cambridge, Mass.: Harvard University Press.
Tuchfarber, A. J., W. R. Klecka, B. A. Bardes, and R. W. Oldendick
    1976   "Reducing the Cost of Victim Surveys." In G. Skogen (ed.), *Sample Surveys of the Victims of Crime.* Cambridge, Mass.: Ballinger Books.
Warner, S. L.
    1965   "Randomized response: A survey technique for eliminating evasive answer bias." *Journal of the American Statistical Association* 60(March): 63–69.
Wedell, C., and K. U. Smith
    1951   "Consistency of interview methods in appraisal of attitudes." *Journal of Applied Psychology* 35: 392–396.
Weiss, C. H.
    1968   "Validity of welfare mothers' interview responses." *Public Opinion Quarterly* 32(Winter): 622–633.
Williams, J. A., Jr.
    1964   "Interviewer–respondent interaction." *Sociometry* 27: 338–352.
Willick, D. H., and R. K. Ashley
    1971   "Survey question order and the political party preferences of college students and their parents." *Public Opinion Quarterly* 35(Summer): 189–199.
Wiseman, F., M. Moriarty, and M. Shaffer
    1975–1976   "Estimating public opinion with the randomized response model." *Public Opinion Quarterly* 39(Winter): 507–513.
Withey, S. B.
    1954   "Reliability of recall of income." *Public Opinion Quarterly* 18: 197–204.

Chapter 9

Data Collection: Planning and Management

Eve Weinberg

9.1. OBJECTIVES OF THE SURVEY INTERVIEW

Preceding chapters have discussed issues of survey design, sampling (both theoretical and applied), measurement, costs, management, questionnaire construction, item analysis and scaling, and response bias. All of these issues affect and are affected by the data that are collected. Later chapters—on data processing, analysis, and special applications—also discuss issues that affect and are affected by the data that have been or are to be collected. No wonder the data collection chapter lies at the center of the book.

Survey researchers tend to pay a good deal of attention to survey design and analysis, sometimes forgetting that the quality of the research can be no better than the quality of the data collected. Whether one decides to conduct all the interviews, hire a few research assistants to do the job, contract with an interviewing service (there are many in the market research area), hire an interviewing supervisor who in turn will hire and train the interviewers, or contract with a survey organization to carry out all survey operations and deliver clean data, the objectives of the survey interview remain the same—to facilitate the collection of information about the population under study in a uniform and reliable way. This objective holds for any type of data: factual, attitudinal, or opinion; and for any form of question: open- or closed-ended. The objective remains the same whether the data are collected by face-to-face personal interview, by telephone interview, or by self-administered questionnaire.

Data collection should accomplish the objectives of uniformity and reliability using the funds and time available. Data collection tends to be the most

labor intensive aspect of a survey and, therefore, often accounts for the greatest single expenditure of funds. The research design defines the *population to
be studied* but at the operational level of data collection, interviewers and their
supervisors are concerned with the *people to be interviewed*. The time allocated for data collection should be related to the availability of these people.
Their availability and cooperativeness can affect costs and time. Reliability will
be achieved if a high proportion of them participate in the survey and give the
interviewer accurate and reliable information about themselves. Uniformity
will be achieved if the interviewers are properly trained, use well-designed
survey instruments that are administered consistently, and follow instructions
specified by the survey director. The goal of doing this within both the time and
monetary budgets will be reached if planning is realistic and predictions about
the population are correct. The remainder of this chapter delineates the tasks to
be done to accomplish the objectives.

9.2. TASKS TO ACCOMPLISH THE OBJECTIVES

Planning

DATA-COLLECTION BUDGET

With the high cost of survey research, most surveys require initial planning
at the time the grant application or proposal is being written and funds are being
requested. Proposals to government agencies often require a specific task
schedule. Even when this is not required, it is wise to lay out a time and task
schedule for the entire project. This may have to be revised once the amount of
available funds is known. However, having gone through the process first, it
will be easy to identify those costs that are relatively fixed and those that lend
themselves to manipulation.

For example, assume the plan calls for a survey of 2000 persons to be
interviewed face to face on a 1.5-hour questionnaire with a data-collection
period of 12 weeks. Assume further that the funding agency is able to fund the
survey for only 75% of the total requested, so that the scope of the survey must
be reduced by 25%. Should the researcher cut the sample size, change the
sample design, decrease the interview length, increase the length of the field
period (in order to use fewer interviewers and therefore less supervision),
reduce the analysis plans, or what? If the assumptions made in the initial
budget were explicit by task and length of time, the reduction in the scope of
work can be accomplished rationally so as to minimize cuts in areas of highest
priority to the research.

It is important for the researcher to know, for example, that a half-hour
reduction in the length of interview (i.e., from 1.5 to 1 hour, on the average) can
effect a change of as much as two interviewer-hours per completed case. At,
say, $4 per hour, that could result in a raw decrease (excluding the effect on
overhead) of $6000. Actual interviewing time accounts for only about 20% of

total interviewer time, but the more efficient use of trips to the field with a 1-hour interview plus the $\frac{1}{2}$ hour reduction in the questionnaire can make the difference just shown. Interviewers can plan to conduct their first interview in an evening from 6:30 to 7:30 PM. Even if it should run a bit late, the next interview can begin between 8:30 and 9:00 PM. But, if a 1.5-hour interview runs a little longer or starts a little late, a second 1.5-hour interview is not possible in the same evening. Not only is it difficult to schedule, but a 1.5-hour interview is more taxing for the interviewer and requires a comparably longer rest period before conducting the next one.

Suppose, however, that the interview is as short as the researcher can make it without sacrificing crucial data. Then it may be necessary to get along with fewer cases. Again, it is important to know the number of interviewer hours per case. If, based on sample distribution and other survey requirements, the 1.5-hour interview was budgeted at, say, 7 hours per case, then a reduction in sample size from 2000 to 1500 would result in a saving of $14,000 in direct interviewing costs alone. A reduction of 3500 interviewer hours could also mean a reduction of as much as 300–350 supervision hours, depending on the ratio of supervision time to interviewing time in the original budget.

In our hypothetical budget we assumed that, at 7 interviewer hours per case, an interviewer working 20–25 hours a week could be expected to complete an average of 3.5 interviews per week. Since we budgeted for a survey of 2000 1.5 hour interviews to be collected in a 12-week period, it is easy to see that about 50 interviewers have to be recruited. We also assumed that they would require 20 hours of training.

If the sample size were cut from 2000 to 1500, either the number of interviewers could be reduced from about 50 to about 37 or 38, or the field period could be reduced from 12 to 9 weeks. If the survey is national in scope, requiring at least one interviewer in each of 50 or so primary sampling units, shortening the field period is the preferable option. But, if the survey is in one location, it would be more economical to reduce the size of the interviewing staff, thereby reducing the recruiting and training tasks as well. These examples illustrate the importance of understanding the task, time, and cost components of the data collection plan and budget.

TASK SCHEDULE

The time required to implement a survey, from the time the basic design issues are settled to the time the last interview is ready to be processed, is just as important as the data collection plan and budget. A field pretest should be among the first tasks scheduled.

Pretests. Pretests serve a variety of functions, but they should be conducted on people very much like those to be sampled. If the survey population is a low-income group in a central city in the Northeast, it would be unwise to pretest the instrument on a college class in the Midwest. If nurses are the target population, then some nurses should be identified to be pretest respondents.

Pretests may be useful in developing new items. Researchers often use open-ended questions on pretests in developing more structured questions with closed-ended response categories for use in the main survey. Pretests conducted on reasonably large (100 or more) properly selected samples may be useful in deciding which items to keep and which to discard. If items fail to discriminate on important variables, for example, they may be dropped.

Pretests also provide estimates of the length of the interview. Pretesters should be asked to note the time in slots provided at the end of each section of the questionnaire or every 8–10 pages if there are no special sections of the questionnaire. Timing questionnaire sections not only indicates if it is necessary to cut, but, in addition, it points out where to cut. Unless more than one pretest is planned, it is best to pretest the questionnaire when it is not more than 15% too long. If as much as 25% of the time has to be cut, another pretest is required to determine whether the interview flows smoothly and to determine what effect the regrouping of questions has on the total interview. Perhaps some questions that were deleted helped to provide the context for those that are left.

Even items that have been used in other surveys should be pretested in the new context, both for length of total interview and to learn whether the items are understood by respondents in the way the researcher intended.

Pretests help to identify places where an interviewer instruction is needed or questions for which a show card would be helpful to respondents. In telephone interviews, the pretest can help to identify questions that are too long or too complicated.

Recruitment and Training. Recruitment and training of the interviewers are tasks that must be scheduled. Even if the survey is to be carried out by an organization that has a staff of interviewers, it is still necessary to select and contact the interviewers appropriate for a particular survey. A good rule of thumb is that, in most places, one supervisor can recruit, select, and prepare for training 10–20 interviewers in about 4–6 weeks. This allows for attrition of applicants who drop out and for those who are deemed unsuitable by the supervisor. If a large staff is needed, more supervisory staff and/or more time are required.

Once the staff of interviewers is chosen, training can begin. New interviewers require from 5 to 15 hours of training in general interviewing skills and techniques, depending on the number of interviewers assigned to the training group and the complexity of the study. Some additional time should be allowed for interviewers to apply those skills to the particular survey questionnaire with which they will work. Questionnaires, interviewing procedures, and last-stage sample selection often carried out by the interviewer vary so greatly in complexity and volume that it is not possible to say what the appropriate amount of training time should be. The detailed discussion of training later in this chapter includes the elements of training that should be covered before interviewers are given an assignment. It should be noted that recruitment, selection, and training of interviewers can be carried out simultaneously with sample selection, final questionnaire revision, and printing of survey materials.

Data Collection Period. The data collection period should be scheduled to begin only when all survey materials are ready so that interviewers are not hampered by lack of questionnaires, forms, or other tools. If the sampled population is to receive letters in advance of the interviewer's call, time should be allowed for these to be mailed either by the office or by the interviewers themselves. Length of the data collection period will vary with a number of factors: the sample size, geographic distribution of the population, accessibility of the sample respondents (e.g., a sample of employed persons would have to be interviewed primarily during evenings and weekends; a sample of former drug addicts, some of whom are still addicted, will make themselves as inaccessible as they can; elderly persons may not wish to open the door to a stranger), location of the interviewers (where do they live in relation to the respondents?), length of the interview, any last-stage sampling procedures (e.g., a sample of dwelling units must be enumerated and screened for women between 15 and 45 years of age; or a sample of households must be enumerated, a random respondent selected for interview, and an appointment made to return if that person is not at home).

If a *random digit dial* sample is to be used for telephone interviews, the distance between interviewers' and respondents' homes is important only if the interviews are to be conducted from interviewers' homes and/or toll or long distance calls are involved. For RDD telephone samples, the main considerations should be the proportion of nonworking numbers and business numbers. Once the sample is selected, someone can be assigned to "clean" it to minimize the number of these unproductive numbers included in interviewer assignments. There are reverse directories in most cities that can be used for this purpose.

Interviewer Supervision. Interviewer supervision is often the key to good quality and good production on the part of the interviewing staff. A ratio of about 1:8 or 1:10 is adequate for most surveys. Since interviewers are often part-time workers, this means that one 30 hour-a-week supervisor can supervise 10 interviewers working an average of 20–25 hours a week. With this ratio, however, it is necessary at the beginning to have some additional help with the review of completed interviews so that interviewers can get quick feedback on the quality of their work.

Select the Appropriate Data Collection Method

The research design in many instances dictates a particular data-collection method. As we have seen in the previous section, however, design decisions have considerable cost impact, and it is wise to review the various data collection options with someone experienced in survey operations.

Data can be collected by face-to-face interviews, telephone interviews, self-administered questionnaires, group administration, or group discussions (often called focus groups). Any given survey may use one or several of these methods. For the purposes of this discussion we assume that interviewers are equally carefully selected and well trained for all methods required of them.

GROUP DISCUSSION

In the early stages of questionnaire development it may be useful to bring together for a *group discussion* 8–10 persons who are representative of the population to be studied with a leader to direct the discussion. The purpose of such a group is to learn *how* people think about the topic of the survey and what sorts of language they use to describe their thoughts and feelings. The discussion can help in the formulation of questionnaire items by suggesting lines of questioning that were not obvious to the researcher. The discussion can be recorded on sound or video recorders, and can take place in rooms equipped with observation decks behind one-way glass. The group discussion method is particularly useful as an exploratory device.

GROUP ADMINISTRATION

Administering the questionnaire to a group of individuals affords the researcher the opportunity to control the setting and the conditions under which data are collected. Uniformity, one of the major data collection objectives, can be achieved since one administrator can collect data from a number of groups. This method requires that the group is either already an existing group that gathers together regularly for other purposes, or that the individuals are willing to come to a given location for the purpose of the survey. An example of a preexisting group would be students who are already gathered in a classroom. With the permission of the school, even young students have been asked to fill out answer sheets or questionnaires with the teacher or other administrator providing the stimuli in the form of instructions, task clarification, and reading of the questions. Another example is workers in a factory who are compensated for their time by being allowed to participate in the survey during working hours. This method requires that participants be able to follow instructions and fill in an answer sheet. If questionnaires are provided, the questions must be phrased so that they can be easily understood. The administrator's role should be limited to helping clarify the questions—not dealing with aspects of answers. An advantage of this method is cost. The same instrument can be administered simultaneously to 30 people as inexpensively as to one. But a disadvantage is that the questions must be limited to what can be asked and answered in a self-administered form.

Group administration of a questionnaire can be used as a screening device for later personal interviews. For example, suppose a researcher were interested in interviewing parents of sixth-grade children with certain characteristics in a certain school district. All sixth-graders could be given the questionnaire in their classrooms and the parents could be selected based on responses to these questionnaires.

SELF-ADMINISTERED QUESTIONNAIRES

Chapter 10 is devoted entirely to the topic of self-administered question-naires and mail surveys. I mention self-administered questionnaires here only as one of several methods of data collection that a researcher may employ in combination with other methods. One very effective way to employ self-admin-istered questionnaires is in combination with face-to-face interviews. For ex-ample, one might conduct a survey using primarily face-to-face personal inter-views and include a short self-administered questionnaire to be given to the respondent at the end of the personal interview. One reason to do this would be to provide some additional privacy if the subject matter of the study concerns a sensitive issue. For example, the interview could include questions concerning the respondent's attitudes about and general experience with a subject such as sex, drugs, or alcohol consumption. The self-administered questionnaire could ask more specific questions about respondent's personal experience. The re-spondent should be informed both by the interviewer and in the introduction on the questionnaire that in order to provide even more privacy for the respon-dent, the interviewer will provide a stamped envelope in which the completed questionnaire can be sealed and mailed directly to the research office.

Another way to use self-administered forms as part of a personal inter-view, one that varies the pace during the interview, is to have some fairly simple questions printed on a sheet to be handed to respondents to fill out themselves. Verbal ability tests, sometimes included in interviews, can be ad-ministered in this way.

Another example is the leave-and-mail-back or leave-and-pick-up ques-tionnaire. The survey could require that in addition to interviewing personally the specified adult in a household, self-administered questionnaires should be left for high school students, if any, to fill out and mail back, or the question-naires could be left at the time the adult is personally interviewed and picked up later by the interviewer.

As these examples show, the self-administered questionnaire can be used in combination with a personal interview to provide special kinds of additional data at relatively little additional cost.

TELEPHONE INTERVIEWS

Two factors have been primarily responsible for the increased and more effective use of telephone interviews in recent years—the advent of ran-dom-digit-dial sampling, and the increasing crime rate which has affected costs and response rates of face-to-face interviews. A number of different methods now exist for specifying area codes and selecting telephone numbers randomly by computer or other random process. By specifying area codes and the first three digits one can limit the sample geographically. In addition to the random-digit-dial method, telephone interviews can also be conducted with persons selected by characteristics other than their telephone number. For example, some years ago a sample of journalists, having been systematically selected from several levels within their employing news media organizations, were successfully interviewed by telephone. Similarly, a sample of physicians or many other specific population groups can often be easily interviewed by telephone.

Several studies have provided fairly conclusive evidence that personal interviews done by telephone are in most ways equivalent to personal face-to-face interviews and in some ways they are better (Colombotos, 1965; Groves & Kahn, 1979; Koons, 1974; Rogers, 1976). People who are unwilling to open the door to let a stranger (no matter how properly identified) into their home, for example, are often willing to talk over the telephone. It should be mentioned, however, that some resistance is being found to the "intrusion" of the telephone. In some of these instances people have indicated their willingness to give the interview in person but not over the phone, but more often they remain suspicious of the nature of the call.

Advantages of telephone interviews include the opportunity for closer supervision of the work. Telephone interviews can be conducted from a central location to which interviewers come. Supervisors with an extension phone can "observe" the interview, thereby allowing for closer supervision than in the field, making possible more consistently high quality work. With closer supervision and control of interview quality, the objectives of both uniformity and reliability have a greater probability of being met.

Telephone interviews have an advantage over self-administered questionnaires in that they are interactive. If the respondents indicate by their answer that they have misunderstood the question, the interviewer is in a position to probe or to repeat the question until it has been properly understood. The answer to the self-administered questionnaire is reviewed only long after the respondent has given it. If the topic is "sensitive," the telephone may offer the distance necessary for respondents to express themselves more honestly, since they do not have to face the interviewer. Evidence on this is not conclusive, however.

A disadvantage of telephone compared to face-to-face interviews is the inability to use visual aids such as flash cards to help respondents select the appropriate answers. (However, it is sometimes possible to mail respondents visual-aid materials in advance of the phone interview.) Techniques have been developed in which some kinds of items are administered in two stages over the phone as a substitute for handing the respondent a flash card. For example, imagine a set of items to which respondents are asked to indicate their agreement or disagreement first, and the degree of agreement or disagreement next. In a face-to-face interview the interviewer could simply hand the respondent a card with four response categories—agree strongly, agree somewhat, disagree somewhat, disagree strongly—and ask the respondent to pick one. Although the two-stage technique works, it clearly takes longer. Most researchers decide to settle for a dichotomy rather than a four-point scale, and use a single question on the telephone asking for agreement or disagreement.

FACE-TO-FACE INTERVIEWS

Often called the personal interview, the face-to-face interview has traditionally been considered the most reliable method for collecting attitudinal, opinion, and some kinds of factual data from the general population and from some special population groups. It also tends to be the most expensive form of data collection if the sample is drawn probabilistically. Why is it more costly? After all, an hour interview should take no longer in person than on the phone. Actually, it usually does take slightly longer in person since the respondent and the interviewer spend a few minutes getting comfortable and settled before the interview is begun. For the telephone interview, at least one of the two is already settled and ready to begin. But, what is much more time consuming is traveling between the interviewer's home and the respondent's, locating the exact address, establishing that it is the correct household or correct person, and coming back to interview respondents if they are not at home on the first visit. It has been established (Sudman, 1967) that a 1-hour face-to-face interview can take between 4 and 5 hours of interviewer time. (Of course, the telephone interview also requires more than 1 hour on the phone. In order to find the right person at home with time to do the interview, the interviewer may have to try the number several times to get an answer and several more before completing the interview.)

The face-to-face interview has some definite advantages over all other forms of survey data collection. The interviewer can see the respondents and their surroundings. If the research requires some observation of these surroundings, surely it is worthwhile to conduct the interview in person. Even if the observation of surroundings is not required, the in-person interview provides an opportunity to observe the nonverbal behavior of the respondent which may be highly relevant to the research. For particularly long interviews, those lasting 1.5 hours or more, it is easier to keep the respondent's attention in a face-to-face interview. A good interviewer can put the respondent at ease and, by friendly but businesslike questioning, be able to obtain open and frank responses. *She looks like the kind of person you just want to tell things,* and *She looked like she knew what she was doing,* are statements respondents often make about interviewers when the office calls back to verify the interview or to retrieve some crucial but missing piece of information.

Are there particular types of respondents who are best interviewed in person? Certainly those with no phones, who tend to be the older, more rural, and poorer segments of the population, have to be interviewed in person. Face-to-face interviewing is also preferable whenever the questionnaire requires the use of scales, the sorting of pictures or word cards, showing of flash cards containing response categories, or other exchanges of material between interviewer and respondent. Face-to-face interviewing is a necessity if the research design requires that both heads of the household be interviewed together. This type of design is often used to promote better recall about facts and figures, the assumption being that "two heads are better than one."

Ideally, the research design should specify the data collection method, which in turn should inform the budgeting process. Often, however, limited funds are available and the researcher must accommodate the data collection method to the size of the budget. The data collection methods described in this section can be used individually (e.g., telephone interviewing only), or in combination with other methods (e.g., in-person interviews combined with self-administered forms). For all methods requiring interviewers, it is of utmost importance to consider carefully how the interviewers will be recruited, trained, and supervised. The following sections deal with those issues.

Recruitment and Selection of Interviewers

Hiring interviewers is basically the same as hiring for any job. Applicants must be attracted, then screened, and then selected. As with other professions, the nature and requirements of the job dictate the way in which applicants can be located, the process through which they are screened, and the basis on which they are selected.

RECRUITMENT SOURCES

Newspapers are probably the most efficient means of recruiting applicants for interviewing jobs. Daily papers with wide circulation provide maximum exposure for an advertisement. However, in some cases, a smaller recruitment area may be more desirable. In large urban areas, neighborhood weekly newspapers may be the best means of locating applicants for a specific part of the city. Individuals interested in part-time employment or employment within their own neighborhood are likely to use the Help Wanted ads in neighborhood papers to find work.

In nonurban locations or within urban neighborhoods, contacts with local officials and organizations can yield interviewer applicants. Church groups, the League of Women Voters, and the Parent–Teacher's Association may be able to provide assistance by publicizing the recruitment among its membership, providing names of individuals who might be interested or suggesting other recruitment points. In small or isolated areas, conversations with shopkeepers or the local police may produce the same results. Notices on bulletin boards in stores, churches, and hospitals can also be effective.

The information provided in a newspaper ad or bulletin board notice should enable potential applicants to determine if they are in fact eligible for the job. The number of hours required per week, the duration of the job, the pay rate, and the nature of the work (e.g., interviewing for a social research project) should be clearly stated. Any specific requirements, such as use of a car or fluency in a second language, should also be spelled out. If no experience in interviewing is needed, this should be stated. Individuals or organizations used to recruit applicants should be provided with the same kind of information. A clear, simple description of the job will be helpful to a local contact person in searching for appropriate applicants.

GROUP RECRUITMENT

A group recruitment session is an efficient way to provide the next level of information to those who respond to ads or local contacts. In such a session, requirements for the job are explained. The nature of the study, the type of work involved, and the application process are also described. Interested persons are asked to complete a written application and arrange for a personal interview. If a sufficient number of recruiter–trainers are available, the group session can be bypassed and personal interviews arranged directly for each applicant.

The written application should include information about education, work history, and references. Applicants should also be asked to indicate any limitations on their availability (including small children, other jobs, or school) and what days and/or hours are affected by these situations. Any physical condition that limits the applicant's activity should also be noted. Finally, if questions such as: *What skills do you think would be most important in a good interviewer?* are included on the application, the answers can be explored further during the personal interview.

TRYOUT QUESTIONNAIRES

Some survey research organizations use a tryout questionnaire as part of the application process. This is usually a brief questionnaire containing a sample of various types of questions used in data collection instruments. A short manual or "specifications" for the tryout questionnaire is also provided. Applicants are asked to complete these questionnaires (perhaps one with a friend and one with someone the applicant does not know) and to bring the questionnaires to the personal interview. This procedure gives applicants the opportunity to work with interviewing materials and to experience the interviewing situation. Tryout questionnaires should not be used exclusively to predict an applicant's success or failure as an interviewer, since such a questionnaire is administered without the benefit of complete training on interviewing techniques. But applicants' use of the tryout questionnaire can demonstrate their ability to work with written materials, follow directions, absorb the kind of information provided in the specifications, and it can be a self-selection device. Applicants who find that they do not like the experience drop out and no longer require the time of the recruiter or trainer.

TESTS

Simple testing is another method of screening applicants for interviewing jobs. For example, if a survey involves a great many calculations, a test of basic arithmetic skills might be in order for all applicants. There are varying opinions on the value of tests for clerical aptitude of interviewers. Results of such tests may be used to reinforce hiring decisions that are based on other, less quantitative criteria.

PERSONAL INTERVIEW

The personal interview provides the opportunity to meet applicants one-to-one, seeing them at the range a respondent would. A personal interview allows the recruiter to obtain additional information about the applicant and to clarify information already provided on the application. If tryout questionnaires were used, these interviews should be reviewed. Applicants should be encouraged during the interview to ask questions. A businesslike but friendly atmosphere can help applicants provide the kind of information needed to assess their potential as interviewers.

Finally, when the application process is complete, hiring decisions must be made, using the body of information collected about each applicant. The following paragraphs list, with short descriptions, some criteria that can be used to evaluate this information. The list is not in order of importance.

Age. In general, individuals under age 18 often have time commitments and responsibilities that conflict with the duties of the professional interviewer. Aside from this, there is no ideal age for an interviewer. The best interviewers possess a level of maturity that enables them to bridge generation gaps, rather than cause them.

Sex. The subject matter of the interview or the type of respondent who will be interviewed may dictate the sex of the interviewer. It should be noted that although interviewing tends to attract women because it is usually part-time work requiring somewhat flexible hours, a growing number of men are becoming interested in this kind of work arrangement.

Physical Condition. Interviewing is hard work. It may require a great deal of walking and stair climbing to locate respondents. The interviewing situation requires concentrated attention, which can be extremely tiring. Although an interviewer need not be a perfect physical specimen, general good health is important. It should be noted that the more limited activity involved in telephone interviewing has opened up interviewing to physically handicapped individuals.

Physical Appearance. A pleasant, neat appearance is essential for any work involving personal contact with the public.

Education. A high school diploma or general equivalency degree is usually the minimum standard. However, depending on the location or the group from which applicants are recruited, this may not be a relevent criterion. When it is not, the standard should simply be the ability to read and write with ease. In general, some college work is desirable, if only because college usually requires work with written materials of some complexity. Higher education also may provide some exposure to the research process, an understanding which is helpful if the interviewers are to grasp their role. However, an applicant who feels that a college education automatically produces an expert in the field may, in fact, be unable to understand and comply with the specific role of the interviewer.

Work History. Previous jobs and the reasons for leaving them should be considered. Sometimes experience that seems related to interviewing may in fact pose a conflict. The former salesperson or retired missionary must be able to understand that many "people" skills and techniques are not appropriate to the interviewing task. Because many women use interviewing to reenter the job market after a long absence, it is a good idea to ask about any volunteer or nonpaying work the applicant might have done in the interim. The application should provide a place to list both types of work references. The most recent employer should be contacted to verify the applicant's reason for leaving and to obtain the employer's assessment. It should be noted that previous interviewing experience does not guarantee that an individual is suitable for other interviewing work. Interviewers with other experience must be willing to accept the standards and techniques of the survey for which they are being considered.

Intelligence. Interviewing requires the ability to grasp concepts of survey work, work with written materials, read with ease and understanding, and make sound decisions based on concepts and skills learned in training. The ability to express oneself easily and accurately is also a valuable tool.

Personality and Attitude. A generalized interest in people and in talking and listening to them is desirable in an interviewer. Extreme forms of this, including missionary zeal, condescension, or a self-proclaimed ability to get along with anybody can have a disastrous effect on respondents and the data they provide. A clear understanding of personal prejudices is often a better sign than a professed open mind. Squeamishness about various types of people, their homes, neighborhood, or lifestyles, may limit an interviewer's ability to work in a variety of situations. Applicants who can speak freely about their concerns about the job frequently possess the stability and security that are the basis for an open mind. An applicant who is overly aggressive will probably react to a respondent in the same way. Although timidity is not likely to aid the completion of an interview, neither will an excessive interest in selling oneself.

Motivation. The peculiarities of interviewing work are such that some applicants may view it as a way to earn easy money. In fact, the independence with which interviewers work creates its own special set of demands. Since they are essentially unsupervised during the course of a working day, self-discipline and the ability to plan and use time efficiently are important. For instance, although working hours are flexible to a degree, interviewers are frequently faced with the problem of arranging hours for a respondent's convenience rather than their own. In order to produce a certain amount of work in a specified amount of time, interviewers must be able to understand the task, the time involved, and their own capabilities, and then work accordingly.

Availability and Mobility. The most well-qualified interviewers are of little use if they are not available to produce the amount of work planned. In addition, interviewers must also be available to work at appropriate times. For example, a sample of business executives will usually be interviewed during business hours; whereas a general population selected from an area probability sample of dwelling units requires calls on evenings and weekends. An applicant who cannot provide the necessary number of hours appropriately distributed will not provide sufficient return on the investment of training and supervision time. An applicant should have whatever degree of mobility is needed to reach respondents. In large cities, this may be the ability to use public transportation efficiently. In rural or isolated areas, a car in good working condition is a necessity.

ASSESSMENT AND SELECTION

In selecting interviewers, it is not uncommon to find oneself in the position of having to choose between two equally well-qualified applicants. It is less frequent, though not uncommon, that the researcher or supervisor, after exhaustive recruiting, is faced with having to select interviewers from a group who are all below some ideal level of qualification. An applicant's suitability for a particular survey should be judged on the basis of the subject matter of the survey, the complexity of the questionnaire, the kind of sample and types of respondents, the demands of the training program, and the overall level of effort required to complete an assignment. It should be remembered that interviewers are made, not born. A comprehensive training program and careful supervision are major factors in the building of a competent interviewing staff.

Ordinary good business practices should be used throughout the application process. If interested persons are asked to telephone for information, the number should be staffed during business hours. Likewise, all written enquiries should receive a response. Applicants who attend group recruitment sessions or come in for personal interviews should be told when to expect notification of hiring decisions, and in what form they will be notified. If possible, they should be provided with a number to call to obtain additional information. Finally, the persons hiring should keep orderly records of each applicant, including the application form, a written assessment of the personal interview, and the final hiring decision.

Training of Interviewers

Interviewer training can be divided into two categories: general or basic training on interviewing skills and techniques and briefing on specific survey questionnaires and procedures. The first supplies the interviewer with a core of basic skills, the second applies those skills to a particular situation. Both require learning a set of identifiable skills. In both situations, the trainer must present the material, make evaluations of the trainees' understanding, and positively reinforce desired skills and behaviors (and negatively reinforce undesired behaviors) exhibited by the trainees.

Interviewer recruitment and training are usually geared toward a specific survey, even by survey organizations who employ interviewers on an ongoing basis. Once that survey is completed, the researcher has no further tasks for the interviewers, and the survey organization may not have another survey ready for field work in the particular locality or for particular interviewers. In practice, therefore, the basic and specific aspects of interviewer training are often combined in one training period. Survey-specific materials (e.g., questionnaire or sampling requirements) are used to illustrate basic interviewing techniques and to teach certain skills. The advantage of this combined approach is that the more general and basic skills that interviewers must learn are taught in an atmosphere of immediate and practical application.

CHOOSING THE APPROPRIATE TRAINING METHOD

The objective of interviewer training is to have a cadre of interviewers who possess the necessary skills to accomplish the interviewing task for which they were hired. It is easy to discard some methods as unsuitable for interviewer training. Rote learning, for example, simply asks the trainee to absorb rather than integrate information. Although this can be a successful technique for teaching more limited kinds and amounts of information, it is not appropriate to the dynamics of interviewing. The trial-and-error method of learning, implying a one-to-one combination of interviewer and trainer in the field, is for most surveys too costly in relation to the benefits and too unwieldy.

The best method for teaching the interviewing role and interviewing skills may be called the inductive method. By this method, learners (in groups) are asked to move, step by step from item to item, using what they have already mastered to help them learn the next level of information. Participation is encouraged as trainees are asked to apply their general knowledge to new and specific situations and concepts. New learning reinforces old, as interviewers build the set of skills they will need.

Interviewers who have been recruited to work on a telephone survey from their own homes can be briefed on the survey-specific materials in small groups on telephone conference calls. This technique of training reinforces the use of the telephone and is the only alternative when interviewers (due to handicaps or other limitations) accept telephone assignments because their mobility is limited.

When working with interviewers who have had previous survey interviewing experience, it is important to find out to what extent they understand the general and basic interviewing skills and techniques necessary to carry out a specific interviewing job. If this issue is satisfactorily resolved, home study of a clear and complete interviewer manual may be sufficient preparation for a survey. This can be supplemented by completion of a quiz that is corrected by a supervisor and returned to the interviewer, with or without discussion.

LEARNING TO THINK AS AN INTERVIEWER

Interviewer training, particularly for novices, serves two main purposes. It helps trainees learn their role in the survey process and teaches them the particular tasks that comprise the interviewer's job. Interviewers need to learn to **think** as interviewers, to assume their new roles by discarding inappropriate behaviors and by learning to use the tools and techniques of the interviewing profession.

Thus, training begins with the identification of the interviewer's role. A brief discussion of the total survey process provides a context for spotlighting the interviewer's role. Interviewers should gain a general understanding and appreciation of the steps that precede data collection—the identification of the research problem, the study design, the sample design, and the questionnaire development process. They should be aware of the requirements of the processes that follow data collection—coding, data reduction, data processing, data analysis, and report writing. With that foundation in the scientific endeavor of survey research, training can turn to specific interviewing skills, reinforcing with explanations and illustrations the survey process as a whole and the interviewer's role.

Trainees will learn to think as interviewers as they proceed through the training program. To claim professional interviewer status, a person must become skilled in performing interviewing tasks by learning how to use the tools of the trade. Experience shows that the novice interviewer expresses most anxiety about "people refusing to be interviewed" or about how to "explain the survey to people." The best way to allay those fears is to help interviewers feel comfortable with survey instruments and competent about being able to carry out the important job of collecting the data. Having mastered the task of doing the interview, interviewers can then think more professionally about the task of getting the interview. Once they acquire familiarity and competence in working with questionnaires and other survey instruments, they will feel more secure about asking people for an interview. They will have learned to **think** as interviewers and will be ready to spend constructive time on the techniques of location and contacting the sample population.

A TYPICAL TRAINING AGENDA

The following agenda is appropriate for basic training of new interviewers (or for a review session for experienced interviewers) to prepare them to work on a survey.

1. Presentation of the nature, purpose, and sponsorship of the survey
2. Discussion of the total survey process
3. Role of the professional survey interviewer (including a discussion of ethics of interviewing—confidentiality, anonymity, and bias issues)
4. Role of the respondent (helping respondent learn how to be a respondent)
5. Profile of the questionnaire (identification of types of questions and instructions, answer codes, precolumning numbers for data processing, etc.)
6. Importance and advantages of following instructions (examples of disadvantages to interviewer when instructions are not followed)
7. How to read questions (including correct pacing, reading exactly as printed and in order, conversational tone)
8. How to record answers (for each type of question)

9. How and when to probe (definition and uses of probes for each type of question)
10. Working in the field or on the phone (preparing materials, scheduling work, introduction at the door or on the phone, answering respondent's questions, setting the stage for the interview)
11. Sampling (overview of types of samples, detailed discussion of interviewer's responsibilities for implementation of last stage of sampling on specific survey)
12. Editing (reviewing completed interviews for legibility, missed questions, etc.)
13. Reporting to supervisor (frequency and types of reports required)

Depending on the complexity of the specific survey, the educational level of the trainees, and the availability of funds, this training program can be conducted in 5 hours or less (for experienced interviewers, a moderately complex instrument, and straightforward interviewing procedures) and may take 50 hours or more for new interviewers with little education on a survey of some complexity.

TEACHING SPECIFIC SKILLS

Teaching each skill involves the same general pattern.

1. The skill is introduced with a discussion of its importance and the task to be accomplished.
2. The skill is practiced by role playing, paper and pencil exercises, group discussion, or other methods.
3. The use of the skill is reinforced throughout the rest of training.

At the beginning, interviewers are asked to draw on their own general experience to think about how having the skill will help them do the task. As each new skill is introduced, interviewers will be asked to draw on what they have learned already to deal with the task at hand (i.e., the new skill to be learned). The learning process and the importance of interviewers participating fully in its rewards should be emphasized. Trainees must be constantly made aware of how much they already know, how much they are learning, and how each skill helps to deal with the next task. For example, correct pacing in reading the questions to the respondents is a specific skill to be learned. It is introduced with a review of how to read the questions in the questionnaire (a skill already covered). The task to be accomplished is that of having the respondent hear and understand the question, best accomplished by a slow, even pace (at a rate of approximately two words per second). In the long run, the slow pace saves time because respondents tend to understand the questions at first reading, requiring less repetition. The slow pace makes the interviewer's job easier because respondents take questions more seriously and consider their answers more carefully. Respondents tend also to speak more slowly in response to open-ended questions that require the interviewer to record responses verbatim (a skill to be covered later). Even pacing does not imply a monotonous or mechanical reading of the question. Interviewers should be asked to read questions while the trainer and the other trainees listen. If tape recorders are available, trainees can listen to their own pace and improve on it. The skill of correct pacing should be reinforced throughout training whenever an interviewer exhibits it particularly well by complimenting that person, or when someone reads too fast by pointing out that an already learned skill is not being practiced. The group should be encouraged to engage in this type of reinforcement, and not leave it entirely to the trainer. Positive reinforcement of proper use of a skill and negative reinforcement of improper or nonuse is as important as the initial teaching of the skill.

TRAINING TECHNIQUES

A variety of techniques and practices can be used to teach and reinforce interviewing skills and to prepare interviewers for work on a specific survey. If the training group consists of all new interviewers, the training period will probably require more than one day. It is best to provide the general basic training first and concentrate on the specific survey materials later. Some techniques and practices that can be used include home study, written exercises, role playing in pairs or trios, "round-robin" interviewing, self-interviewing, practice interviewing with uninformed respondents, and, when necessary for a particular survey, a presentation of technical material.

Home Study. Home study should be assigned after basic training and should pertain to the specific survey materials. A packet of materials can be distributed containing the questionnaire, an interviewer manual (sometimes called interviewer specifications), and any other materials relevant to understanding the survey. Home study requirements can range from reading the questionnaire and interviewer manual to completing exercises based on the material in the manual, to administering a practice interview or "interviewing" oneself. Reconvening in group sessions should reinforce for the interviewer the material in the home study packet, provide the opportunity for extended discussion and illustration of material, and provide for the trainer an opportunity for personal evaluation of the interviewers' understanding the material.

Written Exercises. Written exercises can be used in many ways, as part of home study or during the group training session, as diagnostic or evaluative tools. Exercises can ask interviewers simply to repeat material already covered or found in the manual (e.g., *Define* _____) or to illustrate points (*Give three examples of* _____). Exercises can provide experience with using skills to solve problems (*What would you do if* . . . or *Which of the following is considered to be* _____). Finally, an exercise can test the interviewer's understanding of the concepts of the questionnaire (e.g., *Why is a certain kind of respondent asked a special set of questions?*).

In developing exercises, it is important to specify for the trainer exactly what is being tested. Each item in an exercise should help the trainer answer one or more of these questions: Have the interviewers learned the skill or read the materials? Do they understand how to use what they have learned or read? Can they apply it to a variety of situations? Interviewers will benefit from a group discussion of a completed exercise in which the trainer can clarify points and help interviewers understand their mistakes.

Round-Robin Interviewing. Round-robin interviewing is one form of role playing in which the trainer, using a script, takes the role of respondent. Each interviewer takes a turn administering some questions, as the rest of the group follows along and also records the responses. This technique gives interviewers a chance to read and hear questions read aloud. The script can be designed to test both knowledge of the questionnaire and interviewing technique. Reinforcement is important. As interviewers read and record, the trainer and other interviewers reinforce proper pacing of the interview and the use of probing techniques. The trainer or members of the group may also use this opportunity to give negative reinforcment to improper use of previously discussed interviewing techniques. The trainer should require each interviewer to say aloud what is being recorded and what instructions are being followed. In addition to providing the answers from the script, the trainer may wish to step out of role to ask how a question might be handled in other kinds of situations.

In preparing scripts for role playing, there is a temptation to develop elaborate or uncommon situations to test the interviewer's grasp of the material. Do not give in to temptation. Keep it simple. An interviewer who has a good command of interviewing skills and understands the basic content and logic of a questionnaire is usually able to adapt to a wide range of situations and respondents.

Because one purpose of round-robin interviewing is to illustrate how the questionnaire works in various situations, it is sometimes desirable to prepare more than one script for the more difficult or complex sections of a questionnaire. In using such excerpts, it is important to provide all role information needed that would have been answered earlier in the interview.

Interviewers may **administer the interview** to themselves as a way of getting acquainted with the subject matter and structure of the questionnaire. This provides a chance to illustrate the use of alternate skip patterns on the questionnaire, and can be particularly enlightening if the instrument collects historical data on, for example, jobs or health, experiences that all trainees will have had but to varying degrees, thereby illustrating alternate skip patterns.

Interviewing in Pairs. Practice interviewing in pairs, with one interviewer acting as the respondent and the other as interviewer, provides experience with the flow of the complete interview. The respondent can be asked to play a fictional person, using a fact sheet containing data pertinent to the questionnaire. Although this technique does not afford the trainer the same degree of control as the round-robin technique, it does provide valuable experience with the questionnaire and comes closer to a real interview situation. The trainer can circulate, observing pairs and making notes for later discussion.

Interviewers in Trios. Interviewers can also be grouped into trios, with the third person acting as an observer, reporting back to a group discussion with problems and questions. Practice in pairs or trios is particularly valuable as preparation for the first real interview in the field when a practice interview with a noninformed respondent is not feasible.

Interviews with Noninformed Respondents. Practice interviews with non-informed respondents are excellent training tools because they provide an experience that is essentially the same as conducting an interview on the real survey. Interviewers can usually arrange to interview a friend, although prior knowledge about the individual can detract from the authenticity of the experience. If time allows, an alternative is to ask each interviewer to provide the name of a friend who has agreed to be interviewed. The friend is then assigned to another interviewer in the group. In this way, cooperation is assured, but the interviewer does not know the respondent.

Interviews with Prearranged Respondents. A practice interview with a pre-arranged, paid respondent is also a valuable technique, especially for unique samples. Respondents can be recruited and screened so that a variety of persons possessing the unique characteristic can be interviewed.

Practice interviews are a good way to culminate training for a survey. As a final follow-up, interviewers can discuss their experiences and propose solutions to problems they encountered. The completed questionnaires can be collected for editing by the trainer or supervisor, or interviewers can exchange instruments and edit each other's work before handing them in. Either procedure is then followed by an item-by-item review of problems and errors.

At an appropriate time during the training there should be a discussion of the nature, purpose, and sponsorship of the survey along with any *technical information* about the subject that is necessary or could aid an interviewer in carrying out the survey tasks. A survey of drug use, for example, should include a presentation regarding types of drugs, drug abuse, and the jargon of drug users. For a study of home energy use, an explanation of commonly used heating systems could be useful. These kinds of presentations can help interviewers do a better job in data collection because they gain a better understanding of the subject matter of the research.

Interviewer Manuals

FUNCTION

Interviewer manuals may be general enough to be used as reference books and guides, such as those used by the University of Michigan's Survey Research Center; or, they can be survey specific. Our focus here is on the survey-specific manual (also referred to as interviewer specifications). One function of interviewer manuals, whether general or survey specific, is to reinforce the basic interviewing skills and techniques previously learned.

An interviewer manual should be thought of as a tool, both for the researcher and the interviewer. It is the researcher's tool to communicate with interviewers, and therefore should provide all information necessary to enable the interviewer (after studying it) to feel prepared to embark on the survey with confidence and self-assurance. The interviewer should be able to use the manual as a document of orientation to the survey and as a reference throughout the survey period. When deciding what to include in such a manual, researchers or interviewing supervisors need only ask themselves: Will it help the interviewer do a better job in carrying out the tasks of this survey? If the answer is yes, include it; if no, leave it out. Following that adage will prevent manual writers from writing unnecessarily long manuals and will encourage them to provide sufficient information and review of basic techniques most relevant to the specific survey.

CONTENT

Manuals should begin with a short description of the background, purpose, and sponsorship of the survey. This section should provide interviewers with information they can pass on to respondents. If, on a particular survey, any portion of this should not be transmitted to respondents because of its biasing effects, it is best not to make the information available to interviewers. It is perfectly acceptable to interviewers to be told, for example, that the purpose of the survey is to "get people's ideas on a number of topics," even though the researcher may be focusing on one specific subject area. Interviewers can even be told that the sponsor of the study does not wish to be known, and that they must therefore tell respondents who ask: "I do not know who is paying for the project but the survey is being conducted at such and such university or by so and so survey company." Interviewers will communicate this most credibly and efficaciously if they really do not know.

The "background, purpose, and so forth" section of the manual should include a statement of who and what is to be studied; that is, the population to be sampled and the general subject matter of the interview. In general, interviewers should be informed of the scope of the survey. They should be told whether it is a general population study of the U.S. population or a community survey of the people living in specified census tracts of a given city, or a random sample of all U.S. physicians, or a sample of in-patients in a specified week in selected hospitals, or the like. They should be told the total sample size—10,000 households, 2000 physicians, 300 hospital patients, 1500 viewers of a TV series. Knowing the scope of the survey helps interviewers appreciate the importance of their own role in it. Interviewers can also use this information to convince respondents of the importance of their participation.

Having described the nature, background, and purpose of the study, the manual should then proceed to discuss the interviewer's job on the survey.

This is an excellent place to carry out another function of the manual—that is, to set expectations for interviewers. For example, suppose the survey concerns attitudes of the general public about the Internal Revenue Service (IRS) and is supported by U.S. Treasury Department funds. It would be extremely important to tell the interviewers that although the survey is sponsored by the Treasury Department, the IRS will receive only summary statistics and will never know who was interviewed. There should be a discussion of the kinds of objections respondents are likely to raise with specific suggestions to interviewers about how to respond to each type of objection. When the researcher fails to set expectations at the outset, interviewers will set their own, and they will respond to those expectations in ad hoc, unpredictable, and perhaps undesirable ways. A statement such as *We know that some people will refuse to be interviewed on this topic, however we expect that you will be able to interview successfully at least seven or eight out of every ten persons assigned to you*, is a very effective way to communicate to interviewers what you expect their performance to be.

The manual should discuss procedures specific to the survey. On some surveys, for example, letters are sent to respondents prior to the interviewer's call. The manual should discuss these kinds of procedures and the interviewer's role in them. It should also delineate clearly what the interviewer's tasks are prior to and immediately after the actual interview. Interviewers should be told in the manual how to handle various field problems: for example, refusals, not-at-homes, non-English-speaking respondents, or the number of calls interviewers are expected to make before notifying the supervisor. There should be a section that discusses reporting to the supervisor, interviewer payment policies, and so forth. Finally, the interviewer manual should contain a section devoted entirely to the interview and question-by-question instructions or specifications for the questionnaire.

Management of Data Collection

The task of managing data collection can be the responsibility of the researcher; it can be done by the interviewer supervisor; or it may be assigned to someone in between, all depending on the size of the project and the availability of funds and staff. No matter who has the specific responsibility, the tasks are essentially the same—supervision of interviewers, including progress and flow of work, quality and cost control, monitoring survey progress and response rates.

Supervision of Interviewers. The task of supervising interviewers requires a supervisor–staff ratio of about 1 : 10. If interviewers are working an average of 20–30 hours a week, the supervisor will probably need to work about that many hours or perhaps a little more. This ratio allows the supervisor to review the interviewers' work, be available for questions and advice, have a scheduled weekly conference with each interviewer, have telephone contact between weekly conferences, transfer cases among interviewers if necessary, keep on top of production of the required number of interviews, and review and approve weekly time and expense reports from the interviewers. Depending on the demands, complexities, and goals of particular projects, one or more of these activities may be handled in other ways. For example, on very large projects an entire cadre of editors may be hired to review the completed questionnaires for interview quality and recording error and to fill out edit sheets reporting these errors. These editors may have their own supervisor whose position is parallel to the interviewer supervisor's in the organization. In the case of large and complex surveys, feedback to the interviewer should still be left to the interviewer supervisor, who is considered the link between the interviewers and the rest of the survey personnel, even though the supervisor may use edit sheets to help. Surveys large enough to require their own editing departments are rare. More likely, the interviewer supervisor will need some part-time assistance at the beginning of the survey to provide the necessary quick feedback to all interviewers on the quality of their work. Toward the end of the data collection period, however, the supervisor will be able to reduce the number of interviewer supervision hours because the size of the interviewing staff will have been reduced.

Having summarized the tasks entailed in interviewer supervision, we turn now to the importance of the style or tone of supervision. The interpersonal interaction between supervisor and interviewer can affect survey production, data quality, and costs, in positive or negative directions and is, therefore, an important aspect of supervision. Interviewers who work in the field are on their own while they are performing the major part of their job—data collection. They need to know that they can call their supervisor to get answers to questions, to report their successes as well as their failures, to have a sympathetic ear for the problems that have confronted them, to get encouragement when they are depressed about survey progress, and to be spurred on to work harder or more in order to complete more interviews sooner. Someone has described the supervisor's role as being one of alternately holding and slapping the hands of interviewers. The supervisor represents the researcher to the interviewer and must therefore communicate and reinforce the need for precision and accuracy in interviewing. The supervisor must be alert to slippage in interviewers' skills and must provide the necessary on-the-job training and reinforcement where and when needed. The supervisor must stimulate the interviewers to think through and try to solve at least some of the problems that they face.

A good supervisor will listen to a problem and then ask the interviewer for suggestions. Interviewers often will arrive at creative and effective solutions by themselves in conversations with the supervisor. The creative supervisor will remember these solutions and pass them on (giving credit to their originator) to other interviewers with similar problems. Supervisors can, at the same time, make clear which kinds of solutions are not acceptable and why. Supervisors should reinforce the expectations stated in the interviewer manual. This can be done simply and informally. A supervisor can say to an interviewer "That was excellent. You exceeded our expectations for _____. I hope that you will make progress and meet the expectations we have for you on _____."

Supervisors must watch each interviewer's progress. It is better to terminate an interviewer than to listen to constant excuses about why nothing was done. The supervisor must know his or her interviewing staff well enough to be able to distinguish between valid reasons and trivial excuses for not completing work as promised.

The supervisor is in the best position to approve interviewers' time and expense forms. The supervisor knows how much completed work accompanies each time report and can evaluate the appropriateness of the time charged. Interviewers whose time is excessive can be taught to work more efficiently if such practices are caught early.

QUALITY CONTROL

Controlling the quality of the survey is important. Careful interviewer selection and training are recommended with survey quality in mind. Interviewer manuals are written with the intent of affecting positively the quality of the survey. Supervision of interviewers, as discussed, constitutes ongoing training of interviewers in group as well as individual conferences; face-to-face as well as on the phone. All these activities are an integral part of quality control. However, there are some specific activities usually referred to as quality control that relate to controlling the quality of the interviewer's work and thereby the quality of the data. These activities are field editing, validation, observation of interviews, and retrieval of missing data.

Field Editing. Field editing takes two forms—that which interviewers do to review their own work, and that done by the supervisor, office editor, or coder. The purpose of self-editing is for interviewers to correct any errors they can spot in reviewing the completed questionnaire, to clarify any illegible handwriting or abbreviations, and to learn from mistakes so as not to repeat them on future interviews. The purpose of office editing is to review interviewers' work and to give them quick feedback. Office editors or supervisors often find that interviewers do not detect their own errors and appreciate quick feedback that sharpens their skills. We recommend a complete edit of the first two interviews completed by each interviewer as quickly as possible so that interviewers know where they need improvement. After that, a sample of each interviewer's work should be reviewed and feedback should be provided through the supervisor.

Interview Validation. Validation that the interview was conducted as claimed and that the data are valid can be done in a number of ways. The researcher should specify the objectives of validation on a particular survey and then select the best means to meet those objectives. A formal reinterview (i.e., reasking some portion of the interview) is the most precise, and the most costly, form of validation even when done for only a relatively small subsample. A thank-you letter to respondents (usually all of them) can have a form enclosed for respondents to fill out and return as a validation that the interview was conducted. This is probably the least costly but also least reliable form of validation. It is least reliable because people who were not interviewed may also not take the trouble to return the form stating that fact. The form of validation most often used is a telephone call to respondents, thanking them for participating in the survey and asking a few survey questions again as indicators of the validity of the data. If it is made clear to respondents that the call is part of a routine quality control procedure, rather than checking on the interviewer, they are usually most cooperative and often volunteer comments about the interviewer's behavior that can be passed on to the interviewer as compliments or as criticisms.

Depending on the objectives, either a sample of each interviewer's work or a sample of all completed interviews can be drawn. If the latter is done, then specific case numbers can be designated for validation, and as soon as they arrive in the office, validation can be attempted. When this method is chosen, the designation should be done prior to the interviews. If the plan is to validate 10% of the completed interviews, irrespective of which interviewer completed the case, then it is wise to select every seventh case number rather than every tenth since some will never result in completed interviews. If the decision is to sample some percentage of each interviewer's work, then it is best to select every nth completed interview turned in by each interviewer, and validate those.

Validation can be done either by the supervisor or a senior interviewer, preferably not one who is assigned to the particular survey as an interviewer. It can be done either blind or with the completed interview in front of the validator. The former has the advantage of enabling the validator to compare the two responses on the spot and informally probe any seeming inconsistency. The decision as to which method is best should be made in light of the objectives for a particular study.

If routine validation results in serious inconsistency on a single interview, several more interviews completed by that interviewer should be validated. If it becomes clear that some interviews have been falsified, the responsible interviewers should be terminated immediately, all of their work should be validated and any interviews showing inconsistencies should be reassigned.

Interview Observation. Observation of interviews can be done in at least three ways—(a) by accompanying the interviewer to the field and observing in person; (b) by listening to a tape recording of the interview; or (c) by listening on an extension to a telephone interview. The observation of the interview in the field is the most costly. It is the only way, however, that the supervisor can see what actually occurs before and during a face-to-face interview. Editing a completed questionnaire can only control the quality of what is actually recorded on the questionnaire. It does not allow the supervisor to judge the quality of the interviewer's questioning or probing ability and does not even indicate whether the recording is true to the respondent's answer. Observation does facilitate this type of evaluation. Supervisors who accompany interviewers to the field usually ask the interviewer to introduce them to the respondent as "someone who is learning to interview," so as to put both the respondent and the interviewer more at ease. The supervisor should only observe, making no comments whatsoever during the interview. The appropriate time for comments is afterward in the interviewer's car or at a nearby coffee shop. Supervisors may want to make notes on their own copy of the questionnaire as the interview proceeds. The introduction at the door, how the interviewer gets from there to the first question, nonverbal behavior throughout the interview, and how the interviewer ends the interview and departs are all areas for observation and later discussion.

If the survey requires face-to-face interviewing but field observations are not feasible, interviewers should take turns tape recording a sample of their interviews. Most respondents do not object to a tape of the interview, particularly if interviewers explain the routine nature of it and that the supervisor wants to listen in order to "help me do a better job." Assurance must be given to respondents that no identifying information will be on the tape. Taped interviews can be "observed" in sections, and any problems can later be played back and reviewed with the interviewer.

Telephone interviews conducted from a central location are the easiest to monitor because special monitoring phones are available that allow the supervisor to listen in to any of several interviewer stations without being detected by either the interviewer or the respondent. Immediate feedback can be given to the interviewer after the observed interview. If several interviewers are observed making the same type of error, immediate retraining of the group can be instituted.

Missing Data Retrieval. Retrieval of missing data can be accomplished on an ad hoc basis if considerable amounts are found to be missing from a few interviews. However, it is best to consider this activity in advance and to plan for systematic retrieval if the survey objectives can be met only by obtaining all data for certain questions. At the beginning of the survey the researcher should identify items critical to the analysis. Questionnaires should be checked for missing information on those items and a plan for calling respondents should be developed to retrieve missing information. If the items considered critical are factual in nature, there should be no problem with calling respondents and asking them those questions out of context. If the items are attitudinal or opinion questions, serious consideration should be given to the effect of asking them out of the context of the rest of the questionnaire. It might be best to settle for some missing data rather than collect data for a few individuals under vastly different conditions.

COST CONTROL

In order to control costs, one must be thoroughly familiar with the cost components. Data collection has many cost components not immediately obvious to the uninitiated. As mentioned early in this chapter, each interview requiring approximately 1 hour to administer can cost the project up to 4 or 5 hours of interviewer time. (Twice that much time may be needed if the population to be interviewed is widely dispersed, highly mobile, or not interested in being located.) The cost components of a data collection operation requiring face-to-face interviewing of a household population include interviewer time and expenses for the following tasks: (*a*) clerical preparation to go to the field; (*b*) traveling to the area; (*c*) locating specific addresses; (*d*) contacting the sampled households, and when required, enumerating the household in order to determine the randomly selected individual to be interviewed; (*e*) interviewing the selected individual (sometimes requiring a second trip); (*f*) traveling back home (or to the next respondent); (*g*) editing the interview; (*h*) reporting to the supervisor. Assignments should be made so as to minimize travel. If an interviewer can drive to the area, locate all the assigned addresses, enumerate most of the sampled households, and do an interview on the first trip, then two or three interviews should be scheduled for the second trip. The per-case travel cost will be considerably less than if a separate trip is required for each household. The supervisor should be able to control interviewer costs by helping the interviewers use their time efficiently. For example, if it is clear that most respondents in certain areas work during the day, then interviewers should be told to limit their contacting and interviewing time to after 6 P.M. and weekends. In reviewing each interviewer's work, the supervisor should check to see if editing time charged appears to be well spent. If not, this should be discussed with the interviewer. In general, supervisors should approve each time and expense report turned in by interviewers before payment. The interviewer's supervisor knows whether or not the charges are reasonable and can question any that are not substantiated.

The cost components for telephone surveys are similar to those requiring face-to-face interviewing minus the travel. If the calls are long distance, the telephone charges must be taken into account.

MONITORING PROGRESS AND RESPONSE RATES

The researcher or survey manager must keep in close touch with the progress of the survey. The interviewer supervisor should be asked to provide weekly reports of progress. Response rates can then be computed by dividing the number of completed interviews by the number eligible for interview. At the beginning of a data collection period, it is prudent to subtract the "no contact yet" category from the total eligible so that the rate reflects the percentage of completions of those contacted. This serves as an early indicator of problems. If, for example, a high refusal rate appears to be developing, the researcher can begin to develop strategies for overcoming the problem. It may be that some interviewers are getting more refusals than others. The supervisor should try to deal with this problem, either by giving additional training to specific interviewers or by transferring the "problem" interviewers to other geographic areas where they may not encounter the same kind of resistance.

Perhaps a large-scale effort must be mounted to convert refusals later in the survey.

Weekly progress reports serve the additional purpose of forcing the supervisor to look at the "forrest" as well as the "trees," and to provide the researcher with a picture of how things are going. If progress is considerably slower than expected, the problem (or problems) must be identified and necessary action taken. Perhaps too many interviewers have dropped out, and new ones need to be recruited. Perhaps interviewers are not working the number of hours they indicated they would. Perhaps the supervisor is not keeping on top of the interviewers in an effective manner. Perhaps the eligibility rate is lower than expected and a supplementary sample must be drawn. Perhaps the task is more complex than anticipated and will take longer to complete. If the latter is the case, this should send up a red flag on the budget as well, and some drastic decisions may have to be made before it is too late. At any rate, the weekly progress report is an excellent tool if properly used. Although I refer here to weekly progress reports, some surveys are of fairly short duration and daily or semiweekly reports are more appropriate.

The researcher or survey manager should request quality control reports from the interviewer supervisor. Such reports should give the manager an idea of the overall performance of the interviewing staff, and thus an opportunity to supervise the supervisor. Once coding begins, the manager must devise a system of data flow from the interviewer supervisor to the coding supervisor. The next step of quality control can then begin, and the interviewer supervisor should get additional feedback from the coding operation about the quality of the data and about specific problems that could be solved by interviewers. Effective communication between coding and interviewing is not easy to achieve but is well worth the effort.

Ongoing review of progress and response rate will prove its worth toward the end of the data collection period when the ultimate decisions must be made. It is at this point that the researcher–manager must look at progress, response rate, and costs and set priorities. If a certain number of interviews collected is the most important issue, then, by definition, response rate and cost are secondary. The researcher has decided to settle for whatever the response rate is when the "magic" number is reached, and either there is enough money or they must find money somewhere. It may be that response rate is the most important issue. (Most researchers feel that 70% is a minimum response rate.) In that case, number of cases and cost become secondary. If costs are the main issue, then ways should be found to reach a satisfactory response rate within the available funds. The earlier it is determined that no additional funds can be made available for data collection, the easier it is to intervene in a constructive way to achieve a satisfactory conclusion to the survey without a loss in quality. For example, one can subsample nonrespondents and make an all out attempt to convert some refusals. It may even be that time is most important—that the deadline cannot be extended because the analysis must be complete by a certain date. If that is so, every effort should be made in advance to have enough resources to complete the data collection task within the time allotted. Whatever the priorities of a particular survey are, they should be clearly stated by the midpoint of the data collection period, at the latest, so that appropriate action can be taken to achieve satisfactory results.

9.3. SUMMARY

The objectives of the survey interview, as discussed at the beginning of this chapter, are to collect reliable and uniform data within the time and cost constraints of the survey. Data collection, because of its labor intensive nature, often accounts for the single biggest item in the budget. All aspects of the data collection effort must be carefully planned—allocating sufficient time and appropriate staff to each task.

Prior survey activities constrain or facilitate quality data collection. The method of data collection (e.g., telephone, face to face) has an effect on the resources of time and money. The function of the planning phase is to identify the problems that are likely to occur and develop strategies to deal with them.

Recruitment and selection of interviewers should be carried out with a view toward the overall objectives of the research. Guidelines for these processes have been presented. Interviewers must be trained to perform the data collection task. They must acquire specific skills and learn to think as interviewers. These skills, the techniques for teaching them, and the techniques for identifying trainees who should have been rejected have been discussed.

Interviewer manuals should serve the function of informing, setting expectations, anticipating problems, and offering alternative solutions. The best interviewer manuals include only information that will help the interviewer do a better job of data collection.

The management of data collection should include the setting of priorities, monitoring of both quality and quantity of the work, and continually asking the question *Are the objectives of the survey being met within the available resources?*

ACKNOWLEDGMENT

The author acknowledges with thanks the contribution to the sections on recruiting and training by Jane Morse, formerly of the National Opinion Research Center, now at Horizon House Institute of Philadelphia.

REFERENCES

Colombotos, J.
   1965   "The effects of personal versus telephone interviews on socially acceptable responses."
   Public Opinion Quarterly 30: (Fall, 1965), 457–458.

Groves, R. M., and R. L. Kahn
  1979   *Surveys by Telephone: A National Comparison with Personal Interviews*. New York: Academic Press.
Koons, D.
  1974   "Current Medicare survey: Telephone interviewing compared with personal interviews." Response Research Staff Report No. 74-4, U.S. Bureau of the Census, Statistical Research Division. Washington, D.C.
Rogers, T.
  1976   "Interviews by telephone and in person: Quality of responses and field performance." *Public Opinion Quarterly* 40: 51–65.
Sudman, S.
  1967   *Reducing the Cost of Surveys*. Chicago: Aldine. P. 76.

Chapter 10

Mail and Other Self-Administered Questionnaires[1]

Don A. Dillman

10.1. INTRODUCTION

Mail questionnaires, the first of two topics that will be covered in this chapter, have an obvious appeal. What could be easier and more efficient than conducting surveys through the mail? The researcher simply has to write the questionnaire and then prepare it for mailing. The otherwise time-consuming legwork of locating respondents is done by the U.S. Postal Service; respondents interview themselves at their own convenience. Interviewer salaries and travel costs, the major expenditures incurred in face-to-face interviews, are thereby eliminated making it feasible to survey thousands of people for the same cost as a few hundred interviews. Further, since postage rates do not increase with geographical dispersion, the data collection costs for national surveys may approximate those for city and county surveys.

Indeed, if mail surveys reached their potential in practice, it is doubtful that many researchers would employ either face-to-face or telephone interviews. However, for understandable reasons, mail surveys have often performed poorly. Users have usually been plagued by low response rates, even to short questionnaires. Current and complete listings of the general public do not exist, and samples drawn from telephone directories, utility lists, or other sources are invariably incomplete and are therefore inherently inferior to those established by area-probability sampling methods. Further, the absence of an interviewer often means questions are misread and misinterpreted by respondents. As a result, researchers have considered the mail survey inherently inferior to other methods, to be used only when there is no other choice.

[1] Work on this chapter was supported under Project 0377 of the Washington State University Agricultural Research Center, Pullman, Washington 99164.

10.2. THE TOTAL DESIGN METHOD

Although the mail questionnaire has certain limitations that cannot be overcome (which we shall discuss later), its capabilities greatly exceed those that tradition has ascribed to it. Attainment of high response rates to mail questionnaires of a length sufficient for social science research is now possible. Recent research reveals that good response to lengthy questionnaires (8–12 pages) can be obtained from a variety of populations including the heterogeneous and difficult to survey general public (Dillman, 1972, 1978). For example, response rates of over 90% have been obtained from university alumni, citizens on statewide task forces, chief justices of state supreme courts, and sociologists employed in land-grant universities. Response rates in excess of 80% have been achieved in surveys of university students, high school home economics teachers, and state employees. Finally, response rates in excess of 70% have been regularly attained in general public surveys conducted in North Carolina, Washington, Kentucky, Texas, and other states. These surveys were about a variety of topics ranging from crime victimization to attitudes about community growth.

The response rates just cited were not obtained by merely capitalizing on some unique feature of each population; rather, they were achieved through the application of a standard set of mail procedures, described elsewhere (Dillman, 1978) as the Total Design Method (TDM). Thus the potential now exists for surveying any population with a standard set of productive, tested mail procedures. Such a possibility holds substantial promise, as researchers no longer need to be concerned with finding or developing group-specific gimmicks (e.g., raffle tickets, letters from supervisors, and delivery by company instead of regular mail) as aids to achieve high response rates. Released from such concerns, researchers' energies can be concentrated on learning standard procedures that can be used time after time with a high likelihood of success. Supporting this statement, the 28 studies that have thus far used the TDM in its entirety have produced an average response rate of 77%. Another 22 studies that have used the TDM to a considerable degree, but not completely, have averaged a 67% response rate. No study using the complete TDM has achieved a response rate below 60%. These studies have used questionnaires containing from 1 to 26 pages of questions, with the most common (as well as average) size being 10 pages (Dillman, 1978).

The Total Design Method (TDM) consists of two parts (a) identifying and designing each aspect of the survey process that may affect response in a way that maximizes response rates; and (b) organizing the survey effort in a way that assures that the design intentions are carried out in complete detail. The TDM thus overcomes two of the most nagging problems that typically inhibit response rates. One problem results from the tendency of past research to limit response inducing efforts in a single survey to only a few stimuli (e.g., followups or personalization) while ignoring other factors that might influence respondent behavior (e.g., higher postage rates and questionnaire format). A maximum effort to obtain respondent cooperation has not been made if stimuli known to encourage response (e.g., multiple mailings and highly personalized communication) are used in conjunction with questionnaires in which personal items precede questions that directly relate to the purposes of the questionnaire. Yet, a reading of the mail questionnaire literature suggests that such partial approaches are typical. The second inhibitor of response can be described as unrealized good design intentions (e.g., failure to print enough questionnaires which prevents intended follow-up mailings from being completed). A prime example of this error occurs when researchers take a "wait-and-see" attitude on follow-up mailings, so that the advantages of a precisely scheduled follow-up sequence simply cannot be realized. To prevent these problems an administrative plan is developed. The TDM can be viewed as the completed architectural plan and building schedule showing how a successful mail survey project is to be completed.

Manipulation of all aspects of a survey project requires consistency among the parts. The necessary consistency is obtained through the application of exchange theory as developed by Blau (1964), Thibaut and Kelly (1959), and Homans (1968). Our basic assumption is that a person is most likely to respond to a questionnaire when the perceived costs of doing so are minimized, the perceived rewards are maximized, and the respondent trusts that the expected rewards will be delivered. Respondent costs can be reduced in many ways, such as transforming a bulky questionnaire that looks difficult to fill out into one that appears trim and easy, avoiding condescending statements such as *this survey is being done to help you solve your problems,* and including prepaid return envelopes. Social rewards can also be provided in many ways: explaining how a study will be useful to the respondent (or to a group with which he or she identifies); saying thanks; according individual attention to respondents through personalized letters; and offering tangible rewards ranging from copies of results to cash. Establishment of trust, perhaps the most difficult of the concepts to implement, is established through official sponsorship by "trusted" authorities, use of letterhead stationery from a legitimate sponsor, and incentives provided in advance.

Interactions between the implementation procedures of the three concepts must be carefully considered. Exchange theory suggests, for example, that any gain that we might expect to accrue from making a questionnaire easy to complete (decreasing the cost) could be offset by failing to explain in a cover letter why filling out the questionnaire is useful in a way valued by the respondent (offering a reward). All the efforts directed toward potential respondents are aimed at stimulating the return of accurately completed questionnaires. According to our perspective, whether people actually do respond is based on the overall evaluation they make of the survey rather than an isolated reaction to specific aspects of that survey. This, plus the fact that most surveys request a fairly high cost activity (giving personal opinions and information) from respondents and most researchers have few rewards to offer, means that the researcher cannot ignore any of the elements we have discussed and hope to get high response.

The TDM survey procedure can conveniently be divided into two parts:

(*a*) questionnaire construction; and (*b*) survey implementation. Each aspect consists of a number of precise steps, the details for which have been published elsewhere (Dillman, 1978). Adherence to the step-by-step procedures should produce an attractive, easy to complete questionnaire that respondents will, it is hoped, find interesting to do. Each step contributes to the whole much as individual pieces of a jigsaw puzzle contribute to the creation of an attractive picture. Pieces left undone, besides being noticeable, detract from the completed parts.

The general principles followed in constructing TDM questionnaires are as follows:

1. The questionnaire is designed as a booklet, the normal dimensions being $6\frac{1}{2} \times 8\frac{1}{4}$ in.

2. The questionnaire is typed on regular sized ($8\frac{1}{2} \times 11$ in.) pages and these are photo-reduced to fit into the booklet, thus providing a less imposing image.

3. Resemblance to advertising brochures is strenuously avoided; thus, the booklets are printed on white paper. Slightly lighter than normal paper (16 versus 20 lb.) is preferred to ensure low mailing costs.

4. No questions are printed on the first page (cover page); it is used for an interest-getting title, a neutral but eye-catching illustration, and any necessary instructions to the respondent.

5. Similarly, no questions are allowed on the last page (back cover); it is used to invite additional comments and express appreciation to the respondent.

6. Questions are ordered so that the most interesting and topic-related questions (as explained in the accompanying cover letter) come first; potentially objectionable questions are placed later and those requesting demographic information last.

7. Special attention is given to the first question; it should apply to everyone, be interesting, and be easy to answer.

8. Each page is formulated with great care in accordance with principles such as these: lowercase letters are used for questions and uppercase letters for answers; to prevent skipping items each page is designed so that whenever possible respondents can answer in a straight vertical line instead of moving back and forth across the page; overlap of individual questions from one page to the next is avoided, especially on back to back pages; transitions are used to guide the respondent much as a face-to-face interviewer would warn of changes in topic to prevent disconcerting surprises; only one question is asked at a time; and visual cues (arrows, indentations, spacing) are used to provide directions.

Application of the Principles: An Example

Brief as these principles might seem, the implications for what a researcher must do when constructing a questionnaire are anything but simple. For example, consider the case of a recent TDM survey measuring housing satisfactions, needs, and preferences of the general public. The original list of questions began with sex, marital status, age, and other personal characteristics; moved next to housing attributes and cost; then to satisfaction; and finally to future needs and preferences. In accordance with the principles just outlined the questions were rearranged so that those on housing attributes and satisfactions (the purpose of the survey as explained to respondents) were placed at the beginning of the questionnaire, and the demographic questions were placed on the last two pages with the inevitably sensitive family-income question being the final item.

To add interest to the first pages of the questionnaire, line illustrations of alternative housing-structure types were drawn. The illustrations were for respondents to use in describing their present home. Drafting of the remaining pages required minor reordering of some questions to prevent individual questions from spreading over more than one page and to prevent blank spaces or excessive crowding on others. When it became apparent that the questions would not fit onto 11 pages an important decision was made: to eliminate one page by condensing space on the other 10 pages and eliminating the questions that were most marginal to the study's purpose. When faced with choosing between 12-page booklets (10 pages of questions and the remaining 2 for cover pages) and 16, the next higher unit of 4, I normally strive for the smaller inasmuch as my research has shown that larger size reduces response (from the general public) by about 10 percentage points (Dillman, 1978). The questions eliminated were not crucial to the study; therefore, their omission was judged more acceptable than the probably lower response rate. Individual pages were completed by adding appropriate transitions to simulate the conversation flow generated by a well-trained interviewer wherever topic changes occurred. The results of the questionnaire construction for the final two pages of the questionnaire are shown in Figure 10.1. These pages, which contain several commonly asked demographic questions, illustrate several additional features of the questionnaire construction process: alignment of questions and differential use of capital and small letters.

The front cover illustration presented special problems for people living in different types of dwellings. The selection of any one (e.g., single-family dwelling) could have a negative impact on those who live in other housing types, perhaps discouraging them from completing the questionnaire. Our solution was to ask an artist to prepare five somewhat abstract cubicles of varying heights each of which enclosed one or more human figures. The illustration was judged adequate when pretests showed that it clearly conveyed the notion of different kinds of homes. A study title, *Your Home: Does it Meet Your Needs?* was then added to the cover. To further communicate the nature of the study a descriptive subtitle was added, *A Statewide Study of Washington Residents: Problems with Present Housing and Hopes for the Future.* The cover page, shown in Figure 10.2, was completed with instructions for who was to complete the questionnaire and a special insert for households with two adult members.

Finally we would like to ask some questions about yourself for the statistical analysis.

Q-29 In what Washington county is your home located?
_____ COUNTY

Q-30 What town or city do you depend on most for goods and services?
_____ TOWN OR CITY

Q-31 In general how satisfied are you with the community in which you live?
1 EXTREMELY DISSATISFIED
2 QUITE DISSATISFIED
3 SOMEWHAT DISSATISFIED
4 NEITHER SATISFIED OR DISSATISFIED
5 SOMEWHAT SATISFIED
6 QUITE SATISFIED
7 EXTREMELY SATISFIED

Q-32 Are you:
1 MARRIED
2 DIVORCED
3 WIDOWED
4 SEPARATED
5 SINGLE

Q-33 Since a big part of this study concerns your feelings about the home in which you presently live, it is very important for us to know who lives in your household. Please list everyone, starting with yourself.

Who? (e.g., wife, husband, son, daughter, parent, friend)   Age (in years)   Sex (M=male F=female)

1 Yourself
2
3
4
5
6
7

Q-34 Do you (or your spouse) have any children in addition to any mentioned above?
1 NO
2 YES   (if yes) How many under 18? _____
How many over 18? _____

Q-35 Within the next five years do you expect the number of people living in your home to most likely increase, decrease, or stay the same?
1 TO INCREASE
2 STAY THE SAME
3 TO DECREASE

Please answer these questions for yourself and your spouse or LIVING PARTNER if you have one.

YOURSELF | YOUR SPOUSE or LIVING PARTNER

Q-36 Are you: (Circle number of answer)   Is this person: (Circle number of answer)
1 EMPLOYED FULL TIME
2 EMPLOYED PART TIME
3 UNEMPLOYED
4 FULL TIME HOMEMAKER
5 RETIRED

Q-37 Your usual occupation: Their usual occupation:
_____ TITLE   _____ TITLE
_____ KIND OF WORK   _____ KIND OF WORK
_____ COMPANY OR BUSINESS   _____ COMPANY OR BUSINESS

Q-38 The highest level of education you have completed: Their highest level of education completed:
1 NO FORMAL EDUCATION
2 GRADE SCHOOL
3 SOME HIGH SCHOOL
4 HIGH SCHOOL GRADUATE
5 SOME COLLEGE
6 COLLEGE GRADUATE
7 SOME GRADUATE WORK
8 A GRADUATE DEGREE

Q-39 Where you lived most of your life before adulthood: Where they lived most of their life before adulthood:
1 SMALL TOWN LESS THAN 2,500
2 TOWN 2,500 TO 9,999
3 CITY 10,000 TO 49,999
4 CITY 50,000 TO 149,999
5 CITY 150,000 OR MORE

Q-40 Before adulthood did you live mostly: Before adulthood did they live mostly:
1 ON A FARM
2 IN COUNTRYSIDE
3 IN TOWN OR CITY

Q-41 Finally, which of these broad categories describes your total family income before taxes, in 1976.
1 LESS THAN $5,000
2 $5,000 TO $9,999
3 $10,000 TO $14,999
4 $15,000 TO $19,999
5 $20,000 TO $24,999
6 $25,000 TO $34,999
7 $35,000 TO $49,999
8 $50,000 OR MORE

FIGURE 10.1 Example of page construction for TDM questionnaire.

YOUR HOME

Does It Meet

Your Needs?

Apartment?   Townhouse?   Duplex?   Single family house?   Mobile Home?   Other?

A   STATEWIDE   SURVEY   OF   WASHINGTON

RESIDENTS: PROBLEMS   WITH   PRESENT

HOUSING   AND   HOPES   FOR   THE   FUTURE

If you are married or share your home with another adult, then either of you may
complete the questionnaire. But, we would like for the one who does not complete
the questionnaire to give us their opinions on the unattached "extra page" which
is enclosed.

If you are the only adult in your home, then please fill out the questionnaire and
leave the "extra page" blank.

This is the first statewide study of its kind ever done, and we really appreciate
your help! Many thanks!

The Home Economics Research Center and the Department of Rural Sociology
Washington State University, Pullman, Washington 99164

FIGURE 10.2 Example front cover for TDM questionnaire.

The back cover page began with the statement, *Is there anything else you would like to tell us about your present home or the kind of home in which you would like most to live?* Using this page to invite additional comments suggests to respondents that they should first answer all the questions contained within the questionnaire. The back cover is *not* a spillover space for questions that could not be fit onto the preceding pages. If located here, these questions would be seen first by many respondents; and, if the ordering principles have been followed in complete detail, the most sensitive questions (e.g., politics, religion, and income) would be the ones seen first. The intent of the covers is to stimulate interest in the contents of the questionnaires while encouraging additional unstructured feedback from respondents.

I have used this example in an attempt to convey the most important point about constructing mail questionnaires—namely, actual questionnaire construction is a difficult and time-consuming task. Producing a satisfactory instrument cannot be considered a simple afterthought to be accomplished once one has decided what questions are important to a study. Nor is it a half-hour editing job on an inventory list of questions. Unorganized, boring questionnaires containing vague and confusing directions are one of the most important factors giving mail questionnaires a bad name. The mail questionnaire has no interviewer to stimulate interest in it or to compensate for any of its inadequacies. It is for these reasons that one usually finds it necessary to go through six, eight, or sometimes a dozen drafts and intermittent pretests before deciding that a questionnaire is adequate. Even some people who attempt to use the TDM have not paid attention to producing an attractive, interesting questionnaire that will stand alone when the respondent pulls it from the envelope. This represents a significant barrier to high response.

TDM Implementation Procedures

The TDM implementation procedures are as detailed as those regarding questionnaire construction, and consist of the following:

1. A one-page cover letter (on $10\frac{3}{8} \times 7\frac{1}{8}$ in stationery) is prepared. It explains (a) that a socially useful study is being conducted; (b) why each respondent is important; and (c) who should complete the questionnaire. It also promises confidentiality in conjunction with an identification system used to facilitate follow-up mailings.
2. The exact mailing date is added onto the letter, which is then printed on the sponsoring agency's letterhead stationery.
3. Individual names and addresses are typed onto the printed letters in matching type and the researcher's name is individually signed with a blue ballpoint pen using sufficient pressure to produce slight indentations.
4. Questionnaires are stamped with an identification number, the presence of which is explained in the cover letter.
5. The mailout packet, consisting of a cover letter, questionnaire, and business reply envelope ($6\frac{3}{8} \times 3\frac{1}{2}$ in.) is placed into a monarch-size envelope ($7\frac{3}{8} \times 3\frac{3}{4}$ in.) on which the recipient's name and address have been individually typed (address labels are *never* used) and first-class postage is affixed.
6. Exactly 1 week after the first mailout, a postcard follow-up reminder is sent to all recipients of the questionnaire.
7. Three weeks after the first mailout, a second cover letter and questionnaire is sent to everyone who has not responded.

8. Seven weeks after the first mailout, a second cover letter complete with another cover letter and replacement questionnaire is sent by certified mail.

Questionnaire Construction and Survey

The TDM implementation procedures constitute a carefully integrated system. Restricting the size of our questionnaire booklet to somewhat unusual dimensions ($6\frac{1}{8} \times 8\frac{1}{4}$ in.) means that one can use smaller mailout and return envelopes, thus allowing the total packet to be mailed for the cost of one first-class postage stamp. However, it is not only the extra cost that one seeks to avoid. The mailout should present the least imposing image that is possible. The questionnaire's arrival in a small envelope helps project a desired brief and easy-to-do image. The mailout procedures also rely on a heavy dose of personalization applied in a variety of ways, including individually typed addressed and real signatures that convey to respondents that they are important to the study's success. First-class postage further conveys their importance, as does printing of the actual mailing date on the questionnaire and the precisely timed follow-up sequence.

When details of the TDM are presented to would-be users, some respond with disappointment that we do not offer an easy to apply gimmick that will assure good response, regardless of what other details are left undone. Such a hope is futile, making as little sense as it does for an artist to paint a portion of his or her canvas in very bright colors in hopes that a bare spot will go unnoticed. Mail questionnaire recipients tend to make holistic evaluations of the questionnaire packet they receive through the mail just as art viewers make overall judgments of a particular work of art. Further, elements left undone that are highly inconsistent with other elements tend to elicit a negative (or no) response. Other researchers, who accept the importance of the holistic approach to mail questionnaires, have sought to avoid some of the effort necessary for properly executing the TDM by evaluating each detail in hopes of deleting some while having a minimum effect on response rate. Among the most often mentioned suggestions for change are form letters with the general salutation (*Dear Friend* or *Dear Citizen*) and signature printed in place, address labels on envelopes, omitting mailing dates, not adhering to precisely scheduled mailout dates, and substituting bulk-rate for first-class postage.

It is difficult to assess the impact that the omission of particular details might have on response rate. The TDM's recent development means that the experimentation necessary to test the effects of each of the many elements that comprise it has not yet been done. Thus, although we know the overall effects of the elements that intertwine to form the TDM, we cannot attribute a certain percentage of effect to each element individually or in interaction with others. An exception to this lack of knowledge concerns personalization procedures. An experiment conducted in a TDM survey of university alumni compared completely personalized letters with form letters. It showed that the personalized procedures increased response rates from 85 to 92% (Dillman & Frey, 1974). Another experiment, this one in a TDM survey of the general public in Arizona, showed that personalized procedures increased response rates from 64 to 72% (Carpenter, 1975). When interpreting these results, however, it should be realized that neither experiment used the possible extremes in personalization. For example, the alumni survey did not use address labels (a certain early warning signal that the letter is part of a mass mailing) on the nonpersonalized mailing. Similarly, the general public survey used one of the most significant aspects of personalization—individually applied, pressed, blue ballpoint pen signatures—on the nonpersonalized treatment.

Research is currently being conducted on the effects of the variations in follow-ups. A study by House, Gerber, and McMichael (1977) showed that certification of the third follow-up mailing is more effective than regular first-class postage; completed questionnaires were returned by 43% who received the third follow-up certified mail compared to 20% that received it by first-class mail. Another experiment, conducted by Nevin and Ford (1976) suggests that the content of the second TDM follow-up (which informs people that their questionnaire has not yet been received) is more effective than a follow-up letter that sets a deadline date for the return of their questionnaire; the returns to this mailing were 38 and 23%, respectively.

These studies have only scratched the surface of the need to evaluate the importance of each element comprising the TDM. Although few in number, they provide strong evidence that response rates achieved by the TDM are the result of more than an intensive follow-up effort. It remains for future research to determine the importance of each element.

10.3. LIMITATIONS OF MAIL SURVEYS

The substantial improvements that have been made in the response rate and quality capabilities of the mail questionnaire do not mean that they will perform adequately in all situations. There are some very substantial limitations that have not been overcome, and stand as barriers to greater use of mail questionnaires.

One problem is the difficulty of accessing a representative sample of a particular population. The TDM mail questionnaire procedures I have outlined depend upon having a name and address to which the questionnaire can be mailed. Although accurate up-to-date listings of specialized populations (e.g., clergy and union leaders) can often be obtained, there are no such listings for the general public. The sources often used for drawing such samples include telephone directories, city directories, driver's license files, and utility lists. All of these sampling frames exhibit shortcomings (see Dillman, 1978; Dillman, Christenson, Carpenter, & Brooks, 1974; Sudman, 1976).

Telephone directories, the most readily available and therefore the most commonly used sample source for general public surveys, suffer from two inherent shortcomings: some people do not have telephones, and among those who do there are many who request that their number and address not be listed in the published directory. Although the percentage of households with telephones has steadily increased over the years and now stands at about 95% (U.S. Bureau of the Census, 1976, p. 533), the percentage of unlisted numbers, especially in large cities, has also increased (Rich, 1977). Another difficulty with telephone directories is that they are inevitably somewhat out of date, so that any survey that samples from telephone directories will omit newer residents. The effects of these shortcomings vary greatly from one place to another; whereas some communities have very few households without telephones and virtually no unlisted numbers, others have large numbers of both. Thus the adequacy of the telephone directory as a sample source varies greatly from one location to another. Since a full discussion of the deficiencies of sample sources is beyond the scope of this chapter, suffice it to say that all have problems and none can match the ability of area probability sampling methods used for face-to-face interviews.

For some survey purposes, such as accurately predicting the percentage voting for candidates in an impending election or establishing the incidence of poverty among various geographic segments of the population, the shortcomings of such lists can be fatal. For other purposes, such as examining relationships among such variables as the influence of voter characteristics on candidate preferences, where one is not concerned about making precise parameter estimates, the deficiencies of sampling from telephone directories or some other list may sometimes be tolerated. Nonetheless, the difficulty of obtaining a representative sample remains a very significant disadvantage of the mail questionnaire compared to face-to-face interviews.

A second disadvantage of mail questionnaires is that among those who do refuse to be surveyed there is likely to be a greater portion of people with lower education (Goudy, 1976). Filling out surveys requires literacy skills not needed for responding verbally to an interview. Although the effect is not always serious, it is an important shortcoming for many surveys.

A third major disadvantage of the mail questionnaire is the difficulty of adequately handling certain kinds of questions—namely, open-ended items, tedious and boring questions, screen formats, and items that must be asked in a particular sequence. For example, in order to obtain adequate responses to open-ended questions neutral probing efforts to clarify unclear answers are essential; this requires the presence of an interviewer. Responses to open-ended questions in mail questionnaires are likely to be short, difficult to interpret, and more likely, as contrasted with close-ended questions, to be skipped. A survey that must rely heavily on open-ended questions should be done by some means other than the mail questionnaire.

Questions that are tedious and boring (e.g., several pages of redundant and abstract attitude items or perhaps a complete medical history on all family members) also present problems for mail questionnaires. Although most questionnaire topics can be made more interesting to respondents than they appear initially, there are limits to how much improvement can be made without for-feiting the collection of vital information. Further, some topics and kinds of questions are far more difficult to work with than others.

Another type of question that sometimes presents problems to users of the mail questionnaire is the use of many screen questions. It is not difficult to instruct respondents to skip a few questions if they answer a (screen) question in a particular way; however, when large numbers of questions are screened from respondents and the eligibility to answer certain ones depends upon an-swers to more than one of the preceding questions there is substantial risk that respondents will become confused.

Still another kind of question format that presents special problems in mail surveys is a series of questions that must be asked in a particular sequence. For example, people may be asked how a particular concern such as water pollu-tion ranks among several other concerns such as inflation and crime. This question is then followed by a detailed series of items about water pollution. It is important that the questions be answered in the order they are asked to prevent answers to later ones from influencing those to the former. Not all questionnaires need to contain questions of the types we have just discussed, but when a study's objectives require their extensive use, the results obtained on mail questionnaires are not likely to be satisfactory.

A fourth general disadvantage of mail questionnaires, especially in relation to telephone interviews, is the length of time required for the implementation. The TDM procedures we have discussed require nearly 2 months for imple-mentation, even after a final questionnaire is in hand, more time than can be allowed for some types of studies (e.g., election surveys). And, the time cannot be shortened as in interview studies by simply hiring more interviewers.

The limitations discussed here may prohibit the use of mail questionnaires in certain survey situations; in other situations none of them may be relevant. Most common, however, is likely to be the situation in which one must weigh these disadvantages against those of other survey methods, one of which, relative costs, is discussed next.

10.4. COSTS

How much does it cost to do a TDM mail survey? This question can be answered no more easily than that of how much it costs to go on a vacation. I can perhaps suggest averages, but the variation is likely to be substantial. Frequently when the cost question is asked, researchers want to know all costs for every single aspect of planning and conducting a survey, analyzing the data, and writing up a final report. In other instances they assume that typewriters, clerical staff, and even a graphics illustrator are fixed costs of the sponsoring organization; thus, they are interested in only the additional out-of-pocket costs that will be incurred for data collection. Therefore, it is not surprising that the costs reported by one researcher are likely to be double or even triple those reported by another.

The purpose of this section is to enable various researchers working under different assumptions to make cost estimates that apply to their own survey situation. In Table 10.1 itemized costs are shown for doing TDM statewide general public surveys of Washington residents based on ones conducted in 1977 (Dillman, *et al.,* 1978; Tremblay, *et al.,* 1977) with the costs updated to July 1982. Twelve-page questionnaires (containing 10 pages of questions) that could be mailed for the minimum first-class postage were used. Costs are

TABLE 10.1
Sample Budgets for TDM Mail Surveys

	Large statewide survey of general public $N = 4500$	Small statewide survey of general public $N = 450$	Your survey?
General costs			
Draw systematic sample from telephone directories or other sample source	$ 1350	$ 150	_____
Purchase mailout envelopes	210	40	_____
Purchase business reply envelopes	160	30	_____
Print questionnaires	775	275	_____
Graphics design for cover	125	125	_____
Telephone (toll charges)	200	20	_____
Supplies (miscellaneous)	400	60	_____
Type, proof, and store names in automatic typewriters	1500[a]	190[a]	_____
Subtotal	$ 4720	$ 890	_____
First mailout			
Print cover letter	$ 150	$ 30	_____
Address letters and envelopes	1500[a]	165[a]	_____
Postage for mailout	910	95	_____
Prepare mailout packets	825[a]	115[a]	_____
Postage for returned questionnaires (business reply envelopes)	250	25	_____
Process, precode returns	375[a]	55[a]	_____
Subtotal	$ 4010	$ 485	_____
Postcard follow-up			
Purchase postcards	$ 585	$ 60	_____
Print postcards	220	30	_____
Address postcards	675[a]	75[a]	_____
Prepare mailout	225[a]	30[a]	_____
Process, precode returns	375[a]	55[a]	_____
Postage for returned questionnaires (business reply envelopes)	250	25	_____
Subtotal	$ 2330	$ 275	_____

(*continued*)

TABLE 10.1 (*continued*)

	Large statewide survey of general public $N = 4500$	Small statewide survey of general public $N = 450$	Your survey?
Third mail out			
Print coverletter	$ 125	$ 125	_____
Address letters and envelopes	1425[a]	150[a]	_____
Prepare mail out packets	600[a]	75[a]	_____
Postage for mail out	500	50	_____
Process, precode returns	375[a]	50[a]	_____
Postage for returned questionnaires	170	17	_____
Subtotal	$ 3195	$ 367	_____
Fourth mail out			
Print cover letter	$ 75	$ 20	_____
Address letters and envelopes	375[a]	40[a]	_____
Prepare mail out packets	450[a]	50[a]	_____
Postage for mail out (certified)	1700	170	_____
Process, precode returns	225[a]	25[a]	_____
Postage for returned questionnaires	170	17	_____
Subtotal	$ 2995	$ 322	_____
Professional supervision of Clerical Staff	$ 2250	$ 750	_____
Grand total	$19,500	$3089	_____
Mean cost per potential respondent	$ 4.33	$ 6.86	_____
Mean cost, omitting professional supervision	$ 3.83	$ 5.75	_____
Mean cost assuming free access to existing clerical staff	$ 1.85	$ 2.81	_____

[a] Costs calculated on basis of clerical labor at $4.50 per hour and first-class postage at 20¢ per ounce. All operations involving typing of names and addresses onto letters, envelopes, and postcards included additional charge for use of memory typewriters.

reported by expenditure area and are further separated by phase of the study. No keypunching or computer processing costs are included. Labor costs are calculated at the then prevailing local rate for part-time clerical help, the type of labor normally used in our studies. Professional supervision costs are based upon the number of hours actually spent by the principal investigator providing direct supervision of data collection activities.

These data show that smaller surveys are relatively more expensive to conduct, with the potential respondent cost being $2.53 higher than for large-scale surveys ($6.86 versus $4.33). Elimination of the cost for professional supervision (often considered a fixed cost) brings the two surveys to within about $2 of each other ($5.75 versus $3.83). The reason for these differences is simply the economies of scale that accrue to large-scale surveys. Nearly all aspects of surveying, from buying envelopes to typing names onto postcards, are subject to varying degrees of economies of scale as the number of potential respondents increases.

If a researcher is in the fortunate position of having a clerical staff, the costs for which need not be charged against the survey budget, then costs can be dramatically lowered, in this case to less than $3 per respondent in the small-scale survey. For the sake of comparison I show the even lower cost of $1.85 for doing a large-scale survey in this manner, but hasten to add that it is seldom realistic to absorb the clerical operations for surveys of this magnitude into the ongoing operations of most organizations.

A final caveat. The costs shown here should be viewed only as rough guidelines; because they are designed to describe all surveys they may end up accurately describing no one specific survey. I have seen instances of TDM surveys reported as costing $20–25 per potential respondent because the researcher felt that such things as consultant fees, expensive computer equipment, and professional time spent drafting and redrafting the questionnaire should be charged to the survey budget. It is not unusual for the computer costs of data analysis to far exceed those reported here for data collection. The last column of Table 10.1 labeled "Your survey," is placed here both to emphasize potential variation as well as a convenience for those who might like to think through the possible costs of doing their own survey.

Even with such variations included, the inevitable conclusion is that data collection by mail is relatively inexpensive; in general, the costs will be substantially lower than those encountered for either face-to-face or telephone interview surveys.

10.5. OTHER SELF-ADMINISTERED QUESTIONNAIRES

The mail questionnaire represents only one type of self-administered questionnaire. There are numerous other situations in which respondents are asked to administer a questionnaire to themselves and the delivery and/or retrieval method does not involve use of the mail. Each of these other uses of the self-administered questionnaire has certain advantages and disadvantages that distinguish it from the mail survey, as will be discussed.

One use of self-administered questionnaires is to simultaneously survey two or more family members or some other small group. If a single interviewer conducts face-to-face interviews with each person of a small group in sequence, there is a risk that answers given by the first respondent may be overheard by persons interviewed later, and conceivably influence their responses. An alternative to the self-administered questionnaire, in this situation, might be to have several interviewers come to a family's home so that more than one interview could be conducted at a time. However, the logistics of accomplishing simultaneous interviews often make this a less than adequate solution. For example, houses are sometimes too small to separate respondents so that interviews do not interfere with one another. To achieve adequate separation may even require moving into the nonpublic areas of a home (e.g., a bedroom or rumpus room), creating some discomfort for respondents and interviewers alike.

A second, but closely related, use of the self-administered questionnaire is to obtain honest answers which might embarrass respondents to sensitive questions. The case for using self-administered questionnaires in this way has been appropriately summarized by Sudman and Bradburn (1974), based on findings from their own research as well as that done by others: "If the topic is threatening, more complete reporting may be obtained from self-administered rather than personal interviews . . . where a socially desirable answer is possible on attitudinal questions there is greater tendency to conform on personal interviews than on self-administered questionnaires [p. 66]."

There are two reasons why respondents often offer socially desirable answers in a face-to-face interview. One is the belief that to answer honestly would be to disclose behavior or opinions that run counter to those the respondent "thinks the interviewer sees as desirable." The second reason is similar disclosure to other family members or co-workers who may be listening to the interview. A self-administered questionnaire that the respondent is asked to complete even while the interviewer sits and waits can overcome both problems. This use of self-administered questionnaires must be considered one of the most important.

Third, self-administered questionnaires can be utilized to supplement the information obtained via face-to-face interviews. The questionnaire is left with the respondent at the close of the interview to be picked up, or mailed back, at a later time. This is commonly done when respondents are asked to keep diary-like information over a period of time following the initial interview. In other cases it is used to obtain information from another member of the household, not at home during the time of the original interview. Still another reason for employing a supplemental self-administered questionnaire is to obtain additional information from the respondent while keeping the interview to a reasonable length, primarily as a simple courtesy aimed at preventing the respondent from becoming tired. However, such use has to be weighed against the probability that the respondent will not complete and return it at a later time.

A fourth use of self-administered questionnaires may be simply described as a drop-off and pickup procedure. The questionnaire is delivered to the respondent's home or office and a date set for returning to pick up the completed questionnaire. This procedure is most commonly used when there is limited geographical dispersion among potential respondents and when the elimination of interviewing time will allow large numbers to be contacted in a short period of time. The success of the procedure depends on the quality of original contacts and persistence of follow-ups. Unfortunately, it is sometimes used to avoid having to hire good interviewers, or because interviewers are not available. Then both the delivery and pickup procedure can be so haphazard they produce poor results. This perhaps has led to it being viewed as a quick and dirty procedure producing results that are seldom any better.

Finally, the self-administered questionnaire can be used to survey large groups of people simultaneously (e.g., students or employees of a particular organization). The intrinsic appeal in this case is that a survey requiring weeks to complete by either mail questionnaires or face-to-face interviews can sometimes be done in a matter of hours. The self-administered questionnaire has the further appeal of possibly producing a higher response rate than could otherwise be obtained. It prohibits exchange of information between early and late respondents. Such intermediate contacts between those already surveyed and those waiting to be surveyed might influence how, or even whether, later ones will participate. The use of this technique is not necessarily limited to groups that regularly meet. For example, in one survey a state organization called together the agency directors from every county of the state for the sole purpose of completing a self-administered questionnaire (Klonglan, Beal, Bohlen, & Mulford, 1966).

The various types of self-administered questionnaires discussed can generally be viewed as occupying a middle ground between mail questionnaires and face-to-face interviews, retaining some of the advantages while overcoming some of the disadvantages of each. In general, various self-administered procedures make it possible to lower costs below those incurred by expensive face-to-face interviews. Indeed, the cost efficiencies achieved are often the major motivation for considering switching to self-administered procedures. At the same time, a degree of interviewer control over the survey process is maintained, so that sampling procedures are rigidly adhered to and the unanticipated problems of respondent eligibility and objections to being surveyed can be overcome.

The privacy of the response situation that is possible with mail questionnaires can also be maintained, thus minimizing the likelihood of social desirability bias. At the same time, the inherent weakness of mail questionnaires (e.g., implementation or rigid sampling procedures) stemming primarily from lack of personal contact are avoided. The researcher is no longer dependent on motivating a respondent to respond only through the written word. Of particular importance is that the implementation time required for both mail and face-to-face surveys can be reduced considerably. In situations where potential respondents are geographically located in clusters (or can be brought together in one geographic location) and sensitive issues are being surveyed, the self-administered questionnaire is more than simply a feasible alternative; it may be the most desirable alternative.

Perhaps the biggest barrier to the increased use of self-administered questionnaires is that face-to-face interview schedules are poorly suited for self-administration. Complicated skip directions and lengthy parenthetic interviewer instructions are confusing to the uninitiated and may even be threatening. The TDM questionnaire construction procedures discussed earlier in this chapter offer considerable help in overcoming these problems. A questionnaire that is designed to stand entirely on its own in a mail survey, with no help from direct personal contact, should certainly do no less well when deliv-

ered in person to potential respondents. Therefore, the future of self-administered questionnaires seems very bright.

10.6. CONCLUSION

The mail and other types of self-administered questionnaires discussed in
this chapter hold a great potential for social research. But, that potential is not
yet realized. Nor is it likely to be realized until all aspects of the survey
process, particularly questionnaire construction, are viewed with the same
attention to detail that researchers are accustomed to giving other research
procedures (e.g., sample design and statistical analysis).

A commonality of the mail and all other forms of self-administered questionnaires is that they must stand alone during some or all of the survey process. The absence of an interviewer means there is no one to persuade respondents to complete boring lists of questions or to clarify confusing instructions.
Constructing self-administered questionnaires that respondents find interesting
and easy to do and will therefore complete requires skills that are not normally
part of the repertoire of most social scientists: turning unorganized lists of
questions into a carefully ordered set; providing a convincing explanation of
why it is important for a respondent to complete the questionnaire; and making
questionnaires visually attractive rather than leaving them wordy and dull.

It is for these reasons that we have placed substantial emphasis in this
chapter on questionnaire construction procedures. These matters, often seen
as optional by users of face-to-face interviews, must now be seen as mandatory. The future success of self-administered questionnaires hinges on convincing people to take the time to complete a questionnaire and to do it well.

In sum, the successful use of mail and other self-administered questionnaires requires "extra effort." But, for those willing to make that effort the
benefits, for example, lower survey costs and data from populations that would
not normally be surveyed, are substantial.

REFERENCES

Blau, P. M.
    1964   *Exchange and Power in Social Life*. New York: Wiley.
Carpenter, E. H.
    1975   "Personalizing mail surveys: A replication and reassessment." *Public Opinion Quarterly*
           38: 614–620.
Dillman, D. A.
    1972   "Increasing mail questionnaire response in large samples of the general public." *Public
           Opinion Quarterly* 36: 254–257.
    1978   *Mail and Telephone Surveys: The Total Design Method*. New York: Wiley–Interscience.
Dillman, D. A., J. A. Christenson, E. H. Carpenter, and R. M. Brooks
    1974   "Increasing mail questionnaire response: A four state comparison." *American Sociologi-
           cal Review* 39: 744–756.

Dillman, D. A., J. E. Carlson, and W. R. Lassey
  1978   "Absentee landowners and soil erosion control on palouse farms." College of Agriculture
         Research Center Circular No. 607. Pullman, Washington: Washington State University.
Dillman, D. A., and J. H. Frey
  1974   "Contribution of personalization to mail questionnaire response as an element of a previ-
         ously tested method." *Journal of Applied Psychology* 59: 296–301.
Goudy, W. J.
  1976   "Interim nonresponse to a mail questionnaire: Impacts on variable relationships." *Public
         Opinion Quarterly* 40: 360–369.
Homans, G. C.
  1961   *Social Behavior. Its Elementary Forms*. New York: Harcourt, Brace and World.
House, J. S., W. Gerber, and A. J. McMichael
  1977   "Increasing mail questionnaire response: A controlled replication and extension." *Public
         Opinion Quarterly* 41: 95–99.
Klonglan, G. E., G. M. Beal, J. M. Bohlen, and C. L. Mulford
  1966   "Prediction of local civil defense directors' role performance: Minnesota, Georgia, and
         Massachusetts." Rural Sociology Report No. 52. Ames, Iowa: Department of Sociology
         and Anthropology, Iowa State University.
Nevin, J. R., and N. M. Ford
  1976   "Effects of a deadline and a veiled threat on mail survey responses." *Journal of Applied
         Psychology* 61: 116–118.
Rich, C. L.
  1977   "Is random digit dialing really necessary." *Journal of Marketing Research* 14: 300–305.
Sudman, S.
  1976   *Applied Sampling*. New York: Academic Press.
Sudman, S., and N. M. Bradburn
  1974   *Response Effects in Surveys: A Review and Synthesis*. Chicago: Aldine.
Thibaut, J. W., and H. H. Kelly
  1959   "The social psychology of groups." New York: Wiley.
Tremblay, K. R. Jr., D. A. Dillman, and J. J. Dillman
  1977   "Housing satisfactions and preferences of Washington residents: A 1977 statewide sur-
         vey." College of Agriculture Research Center Circular No. 605. Pullman, Washington:
         Washington State University.
U.S. Bureau of the Census
  1976   *Statistical Abstract of the United States: 1976*. 97th ed. Washington, D.C.: U.S. Govern-
         ment Printing Office.

Chapter 11

Computers in Survey Research

Nancy Karweit and Edmund D. Meyers, Jr.

11.1. INTRODUCTION

This chapter discusses the uses of computers in survey research. Typically, discussions of computing in survey research have focused exclusively on the statistical processing of data. Although not denying the importance of this topic, this chapter takes a broader view, focusing on the involvement of the computer in all phases of the survey research process. In discussing these numerous uses, the chronological order of the life of a typical survey is followed. That is, topics are taken up in the order they would ordinarily be encountered in the execution of a survey research project from instrument design to report writing, namely: (*a*) instrument design; (*b*) sampling; (*c*) field monitoring; (*d*) coding and editing; (*e*) data capture; (*f*) data cleaning; (*g*) scale–index construction; (*h*) data base organization; (*i*) data base retrieval; (*j*) statistical analysis; (*k*) documentation; (*l*) report writing.

Several steps may be combined, or the sequence may be rearranged for a particular survey. For example, surveys using telephone interviewing procedures combine sampling, field monitoring, and cleaning phases. The sequence of steps, however, serves as a convenient organizing scheme.

11.2. INSTRUMENT DESIGN

Instrument Development

Like writing a paper, developing a questionnaire or other survey instrument typically involves numerous drafts. Usually, this recycling is carried out

HANDBOOK OF SURVEY RESEARCH

by repeatedly cutting and pasting a typed version of the questionnaire. An obvious, albeit seldom used, alternative to this tedious process is to use the word-processing capability of a computer. Although a variety of word-processing systems exist, the basic ingredients include a keyboard for entering text (sometimes connected to a display screen and sometimes to a typewriterlike printer), some sort of magnetic storage medium (i.e., a mag card, a floppy disk, or a "hard" disk), a source of intelligence (i.e., a microprocessor or a minicomputer), and a letter-quality printing mechanism. Using the memory of the magnetic medium and the processing capabilities of the computer, one can easily move through numerous drafts of the instrument being designed; along the way, one need be concerned only with the changes made in the questionnaire between the previous and the current draft.

Instrument Format

Once the content and wording of the survey have been decided, an important design consideration still remains—namely, how to unobtrusively place the information required for computer processing on the instrument. The placement of card and column locations for data on the 1980 General Social Survey (see Figure 11.1) is one example of how computer needed information can be unobtrusively incorporated. The deck number appears at the top of the page; the card column number appears in the right-hand margin.

Another feature of the format of this questionnaire is that numeric codes have been assigned to each response, including the don't know category. Although nonnumeric codes can be processed by most statistical packages (e.g., SPSS, BMDP), coding values as strictly numeric in the first place seems simplest, since recoding to numeric values is required for most statistical applications anyway. Also, it is convenient and efficient to have the same missing data value throughout, if possible.

There is a distinction among the various word processors between those able and those not able to transmit text in machine-readable form to the computer doing the statistical processing (see Section 11.11 and 11.12 for a discussion of this important communications capability). The point is to retain in machine-readable form whatever has been keyed so that it can be utilized in another step of the survey research process *without* the labor and the errors of reentering the text of the questionnaire. Computer-based word processing and telecommunications exist in a rather stable form. It is our experience that the fiscal efficiencies introduced by such resources pay for the hardware and software within a reasonable period of time; so these things are more basic tools than luxuries.

There is yet another mechanism whereby computing resources might aid with the instrument development process: a question bank. Although we are not aware of the existence of this application, we can find no serious impediment to implementing what we propose. Previously used questionnaire items

ASK EVERYONE:
47. When you rated the importance of various qualities for children, were you thinking mostly about boys, mostly about girls, or about both boys and girls equally?

Mostly about boys	1	65/
Mostly about girls	2	
About both boys and girls equally	3	
Don't know	8	

48. Here are two statements. Will you tell me which one you agree with <u>more</u>?

    A. First, the younger generation should be taught by their elders to do what is right.
    B. Second, the younger generation should be taught to think for themselves even though they may do something their elders disapprove of.

Taught by their elders	1	66/
Taught to think for themselves	2	

49. Would you say your own health, in general, is excellent, good, fair, or poor?

Excellent	1	67/
Good	2	
Fair	3	
Poor	4	
Don't know	8	

Now to change the subject . . .
50. Do you think the use of marijuana should be made legal, or not?

Should	1	68/
Should not	2	
No opinion	8	

51. Do you favor or oppose the death penalty for persons convicted of murder?

Favor	1	69/
Oppose	2	
Don't know	8	

52. Would you favor or oppose a law which would require a person to obtain a police permit before he or she could buy a gun?

Favor	1	70/
Oppose	2	
Don't know	8	

FIGURE 11.1 Subset (Page 32) of 1980 General Social Survey

including the question, the precoded response choices, frequency distributions, the study and sample with which this item was previously used, could be stored in the question bank. The most obvious advantage of this proposal is the ability to construct a new questionnaire by merely indicating which items one would like to include. Of greater importance, however, is the ease of replicating the instrumentation of earlier research and, thus, encourage the continuity that is beneficial to all types of research. One could examine how an item was used previously (e.g., with low-ability adolescents) in light of one's current proposed sample; although the wording might have worked well in a previous use, the current sample might suggest either rewording or continuing the search for appropriate instrumentation. In like manner, the univariate distribution might encourage or discourage replication of an item; if the previous use did not distribute respondents well, then verbatim repetition would be inadvisable. Combining this proposal with word-processing technology makes it possible (*a*) to modify previous question wordings to suit current needs (e.g., modifying income ranges to reflect current inflation); and (*b*) to add the newly devised instrument back into the question bank.[1] Much of the question-bank proposal is currently being attempted manually; it is our contention that automation of the process would materially enhance the instrument design phase of the survey research process.

Computing and Instrument Design

In designing the survey instrument using word-processing capabilities, the business of revising the wording and the ordering and format of the survey can be made substantially easier. An added advantage is that the question content and response codes can be retained in machine readable form for repeated use throughout the computer life of the survey.

In closing this section on instrument design, we underscore the importance of involving computing staff in the instrument design process. Decisions made about the format of the survey instrument without benefit of their computer knowledge may create quite serious problems in later phases of computer processing of the survey. So, involvement of computer staff at the earliest stages of design has decided benefits later on.

11.3. SAMPLING

Drawing a Sample for a New Survey

Although we lack precise data on the relative frequency of the fielding of new surveys and secondary analyses of existing surveys, the recent trend appears to be toward secondary analyses whenever possible. Part of the interest in secondary analyses is no doubt motivated by the rising costs of fielding, conducting, and completing a survey.

Reliance on existing data sets may be cost efficient, but archived data often do not ask the question exactly as the secondary analyst would want or survey precisely the population of interest. There are several procedures that appear to offer significant cost savings over traditional survey sampling and fielding techniques. With the advent and acceptance of these procedures, significant enough savings may be realized so that fielding new surveys will witness a revival. The use of telephone interviewing and the companion use of random digit dialing for selection of the sample are two such specific examples. Telephone interview techniques are described elsewhere—here we focus on random digit dialing (RDD).

---

[1] If univariate frequency distributions are to be included, one would have to wait until the completion of the data gathering phase. By retaining as much as possible in machine-readable form, this is not a burdensome task.

RANDOM DIGIT DIALING (RDD)

Random digit dialing is a sampling procedure used in telephone surveys that gives all working numbers an equal chance of selection whether they are or are not listed in the telephone directory. Cummings (1979) explains the procedure. The sampling procedure begins with the list of active area code–central office code combinations and adds to that a 4-digit random number. These generated numbers comprise the sampling frame. To avoid the problem of generating numerous nonworking or nonresidential phone numbers, a multi-stage sampling procedure has been developed (Waksberg, 1977). Clusters of 100 consecutive numbers comprise the primary sampling frame. Because the telephone company typically assigns new numbers consecutively, finding a working number in one cluster means that it is likely that other working numbers will also appear in that cluster. Thus, if a cluster yields a working number, it is sampled further; if it does not, it is not sampled further.

Several studies have compared the population characteristics of those reached by random digit dialing (telephone survey) to those reached by standard interview, sampling techniques (Klecka & Tuchfarber, 1978). After comparing the response patterns and population characteristics obtained using random digit dialing and personal interview procedures, Klecka and Tuchfarber conclude that: "overall, the data provide strong empirical evidence that random digit dialing telephone surveys can replicate the results of surveys which use a complex sampling design and personal interviewing [p. 113]."

The potential bias introduced to the sample by exclusion of households without telephones (over 13%) was examined by Tull and Albaum (1977) who used the 1970 Census data to carry out a simulated RDD survey. They cross-tabulated values for selected characteristics of houses, demographic variables, and access to telephone. They found that households with telephones available were more likely to have "white, male heads of a higher average age, income and education level and to have the spouse present than those household heads with no telephone available [p. 394]." However, these differences were not large and, as Tull and Albaum suggest, may be well within the accuracy requirements of the survey.

Drawing a Sample from an Existing Survey for Exploratory Analyses or for Replication Studies

Appreciable computer expense can be saved by carrying out exploratory analyses on a systematic sample of the data. Unless the population of interest is extremely small, sampling of the data set for carrying out preliminary runs can be a highly efficient procedure. The sample might also be split (randomly) into two halves and exploratory analyses conducted on one and replication on the other. This procedure would seem to have obvious advantages if the size of the sample were large enough.

11.4. FIELD MONITORING

Once the instrument has been designed and the sample identified, the next step is to field the survey. Here we describe four ways in which computing resources can be used profitably.

Materials Delivery

There are several ways in which the computing resource can make the delivery of materials to the field a more manageable task. Consider a file of names and addresses of potential respondents. This can be used to generate mailing labels.[2] Also, by utilizing word-processing resources, one can include a personalized cover letter explaining the goals of the research project, thus encouraging cooperation. In addition, envelopes may be printed as well. With a minor growth in file size, it is then reasonable to keep track of completed instruments. That, in turn, facilitates follow-up mailings to nonrespondents. Then, with some minor additional programming, one can easily obtain progress reports (e.g., completion rate at any point in time), listings of reluctant respondents, and the like.

Follow-Up Probes

When a project is gathering data from a sample of respondents over two or more points in time, data gathered at one wave can be used to enhance the data gathering at a subsequent wave. The respondent's name, address, and identification number are often affixed to the instrument by means of a self-adhesive label; when the label includes information from a previous data gathering, then the interviewer might say something like "Let's see. The last time we were here, the household consisted of. . . . Has anyone moved out? Moved in?" Thus, the approach reduces the time of the interview, builds rapport with the respondent, and increases the overall accuracy of the data.

It is possible to think of a follow-up instrument being completely machine generated; however, we are not aware of anyone who has implemented the notion. Skip patterns could be diminished or perhaps eliminated by utilizing information from earlier waves of data, and the entire questionnaire could be individually tailored to what is already known about a specific respondent. Line printer costs are going down whereas speeds are going up; so the technology is less of an impediment than most people recognize.[3] It will be interesting to see

[2] It is helpful to know that the U.S. Postal Service requires large mailings to be presented in ZIP code order; this is much more easily accomplished by machine prior to printing labels than it is by hand after printing.
[3] The newer off-line page printing systems are capable of printing two 8.5 × 11 in. pages per second with extremely high print quality. Although the cost of the gadgetry is quite high, the cost per page printed is extremely low; such circumstances often give rise to service bureaus investing in the machinery and then making it available at reasonable cost.

whether this approach is adopted in future years as computer line printing costs decrease.

Automated Monitoring

Computing technology can be highly beneficial in monitoring a survey. An automated monitoring system helps prevent interviews and instruments from falling into proverbial cracks, and it can significantly improve the efficiency of a field operation. Keeping tabs on refusals, not-at-homes, completions, and the like, permits field management to implement corrective measures when necessary. Interviewers are given information on their expected completion rates over time as well as their actual completion rates to date, since the mere existence of such information can improve their performance.[4] Thus, the management then becomes aware of which staff members need help, closer supervision, or special rewards.

An automated monitoring system often includes a mechanism for constructing a frequency tabulation at any point in time; so it is reasonable to generate such tables on a systematic basis in order to monitor all aspects of a field effort. Then, using what is called exception reporting in data processing circles, the system can readily identify specific sampling regions, interviewers, or respondents that merit attention. Finally, for those survey organizations concerned with managing a large field staff, automated monitoring offers an objective assessment of interviewer performance.[5]

Tracking Software

Finally, we provide a specific example of effective computer utilization in the tracking of respondents who were initially interviewed in 1966 and who were studied again in 1979–1980.[6]

The "base year" data were gathered in 1966 as a simple cross-sectional sample with no thought given to subsequent longitudinal research (Slocum & Bowles, 1966). At that time, the respondents were juniors and seniors enrolled in public high schools in the State of Washington. Thus, the more recent follow-up research started with their names, addresses, class (junior or senior), and parental marital statuses in 1966. In order to carry out the next research effort, the critical task proved to be locating individuals so that they could be reinterviewed.

---

[4] A graphic representation of expected and actual completion rates has been found to be especially effective.

[5] One example of such software is the NORC Automated Survey System (NASS); for further information and documentation, contact the National Opinion Research Center, 6060 S. Ellis Avenue, Chicago, Il. 60637.

[6] David A. Chapin, at the Boys Town Center for the Study of Youth Development, developed and implemented this software, and shared his experiences and observations with us.

The tracking effort is similar to automated monitoring in numerous ways, yet the tracking software focused on individuals rather than on instruments. The 1966 information was used to initiate numerous tracking treatments including: writing a letter to the parents–respondent (addressed as: *Mr. & Mrs. Smith* or *John Smith*) with up to three follow-up letters; utilizing reunion mailing lists from large schools and writing a letter to the individual respondents with up to three follow-up letters; and attempting through diverse means to contact the respondent, ranging from calling neighbors (city directories from 1966 and 1978 were used to locate individuals who stayed in the neighborhood) to contacting persons sociometrically identified as friends in the 1966 data (see Call, Otto, & Spenner, 1982, for a full description of the tracking effort).

The computer-based tracking proved to be quite effective. Compared to its manual counterpart, the machine tracking significantly reduced manpower requirements and thus cost. Numerous reports were generated easily and whenever needed; like automated monitoring, the reports were both tabular summaries and exception reports (i.e., individuals not yet located). Many letters were generated quickly by using a combination of data and word processing, and the correspondence was extensively personalized by references in the body of the letter being based on information accumulated in 1966. The ultimate file was a comprehensive collection of respondent information which visibly eased the ultimate data-gathering effort in 1979–1980.[7] The tracking provided a daily status report—by treatment—of the progress in locating the 1966 respondents for the current research (Otto, Vaughn, Call, & Spenner, 1979). Starting with a 1966 sample in excess of 6500 individuals, the tracking activity located 98.6% of the sample in 24 months.

11.5. CODING AND EDITING

Once completed instruments are returned from the field, the next step typically involves coding and editing of the data. The term *coding* usually refers to the translation of responses to open-ended questions into numeric codes. For example, consider the following interview items:

A. What kind of work do (did you normally) do? That is, what (is/was) your job called?
   OCCUPATION: _____

B. IF NOT ALREADY ANSWERED, ASK:
   What (do/did) you actually do in that job? Tell me, what (are/were) some of your main duties?

   _____

---

[7] More accurately, the tracking activity continued through both a telephone interview (predominately life history data) and a self-administered mailed questionnaire.

C. What kind of place (do/did) you work for?

INDUSTRY: _____

D. IF NOT ALREADY ANSWERED, ASK:
    What (do/did) they (make/do)?

_____

Using the *Dictionary of Occupational Titles,* the coder translates occupation into one of approximately 20,000 numeric codes. Occupation and industry codes are good models of intricate coding structures that are mutually exclusive and exhaustive. It is usually the case that complex coding is done by specialists in particular areas; when resident experts are not available, it is advisable to subcontract the coding to an organization that does have such specialists.[8] Other, less complex coding of open-ended responses is carried out by any trained coder.

Editing refers to checking for compliance with the instructions included within the instrument. For example, on a self-administered questionnaire, an editor would scan the completed instrument to ensure that the "check only one" directions had indeed been followed; this is necessary if a single code is to be entered into a specific field. On any questionnaire, the skip patterns are edited for compliance with instructions; the correctness of the branching should eventually be tested in the data-cleaning phase, and it is preferable to eliminate error at the editing phase rather than correct it at the cleaning phase. Editing can also refer to checking the internal consistency of responses; such testing should be repeated at the cleaning step.

In order to obtain consistency of coding and editing, it is advisable to provide written directions covering every detail of the process. Those doing such tasks on a regular basis usually have general coding–editing documentation plus detailed documentation unique to each research project. Coding and editing specifications serve the coding staff, the data analyst, and—should the data be archived eventually—the secondary analyst.

When coding and editing are meticulously carried out, then data capture can proceed without hesitation. In the data capture step (see next section), attention is focused upon speed and accuracy of keying; therefore, the coding–editing step must prepare for that by locating obvious errors and by calling attention to the substance of the respondent's answers to the instrument.

11.6. DATA CAPTURE

By *data capture,* we mean the process by which information is generated in a form suitable for processing by a computer. It has been estimated that 20–

_____

[8] For instance, a social-science survey research organization might need medical science coding expertise (to classify ailments, diseases, procedures, etc.) occasionally but not often enough to justify retaining such staff.

40% of the total computing costs of conducting a survey is attributed to these data entry activities (Ferrara & Nolan, 1974, p. 27). Consequently, the execution of this activity greatly affects the project finances.

We distinguish two types of data entry techniques—*source data entry,* in which data are prepared at its source in machine-readable form, and *transcriptive data entry,* in which data are prepared on documents at the source and then later transcribed to either a machine-readable medium or directly into the computer. The difference between the two techniques is that transcriptive data entry requires a keying operation of some sort whereas source data entry does not. Examples of transcriptive data entry devices include card punches, paper tape punches, and key to disk devices. Examples of source data entry devices include optical character readers and mark sense readers. Some survey research instruments may be a combination of the two types.

Transcriptive Data Entry

Transcriptive data entry techniques consist of procedures in which the source data are first coded and then transcribed by some special entry device into machine-readable form. Coding data on questionnaires and then keypunching them onto computer cards is one commonly used transcriptive data entry procedure in survey research.

The survey instrument is frequently designed so that an operator may transcribe the data directly from the instrument itself. An average key operator can key about 8000 strokes per hour of which about 2–4% will be in error (Schwab & Sitter, 1974, p. 13). These errors may be detected at the time they are made or later by a separate process of rekeying (verifying) the data on a special key machine (a verifier).

Buffered key to device machines increase productivity 10–25% over conventional machines and verifiers (Ferrara & Nolan, 1974, p. 28). With these devices the data are not actually translated to a physical device until after verification. With such a system, the operator can key *and* verify up to 8000 strokes per hour, thus representing an appreciable time savings.

In many instances, the survey item can be keyed directly into the computer, using a terminal as the entry device. The desirability of this type of arrangement depends in large part on how charges for computer time and terminal connect time are made and whether this step can be efficiently combined with an editing procedure. This method is particularly attractive when a whole screen of information can be keyed and then edited and entered into the computer. Because one is entering a screen (e.g., 22 lines of information) at a time, the overhead for using the computer terminal as an input device is appreciably reduced.

The disadvantages of transcriptive techniques are that they require an extra step that can introduce two types of errors: (*a*) misreading; and (*b*) mistranscription. Detection and correction of these errors, then, becomes a major activity; for more discussion see the section on data quality.

Source Data Entry

The distinguishing feature of this mode of data preparation is the recording of data directly in machine-readable form so that transcription of the data is unnecessary. Examples of source data entry devices include Optical Character Readers (OCRs), on-line terminals, and magnetic character readers. Because source data entry procedures do not require the transcription of data, errors are not generated by incorrect copying. In addition, because source data techniques frequently do not require additional personnel to enter the data, they may be less costly than transcriptive procedures. However, the additional cost of renting special equipment or the cost of special forms may make source data techniques impractical for small surveys. Moreover, the possibility that the device may interfere with the interview or survey must be carefully considered.

OPTICAL CHARACTER READERS AND OPTICAL MARK READERS

Optical character readers (OCR) and optical mark readers (OMR) differ by the type of input they can read and translate. OCR equipment can read printed, typed, or handwritten data, whereas OMR equipment can read only marks on predesignated portions of the page. Although OCRs potentially offer the advantage of being extremely flexible because the data can be read by either humans or computers, the demanding and exacting handprinting requirements make these readers less useful for survey researchers.[9]

Of the two optical reading procedures, mark sense reading has had the most widespread use in surveys. Earlier uses of this procedure (e.g., the Equality of Opportunity Survey, Coleman, Campbell, Hobson, McPartland, Mood, Weinfield, & Yok, 1966) required a separate answer sheet on which the marks were placed. This procedure no doubt introduces errors as the respondent strives to match up his or her answer sheet with the questionnaire. An improvement in the procedure permits the response to be marked right beside the question. This procedure, then, can be used to capture the data conveniently and accurately. An interesting additional feature has been incorporated in the most recent "High School and Beyond" survey (see Figure 11.2). Key questions contain a bubble beside the question number. Upon collecting the tests, the test administrator determines if these key items were answered or not. If not answered the administrator asks the student whether he or she intentionally left the item out or just forgot it. The bubble beside the question is used to indicate this question condition.

Optical mark readers may be connected directly to a computer or to an off-line device. Under program control, the data editing can take place as data are read, and any sheets containing unreadable or inconsistent codes can be rejected into a separate stacker. Because the only special equipment required is a soft lead pencil and preprinted forms, this technique is not expensive; moreover, the training necessary to accurately use the technique is minimal, and most respondents could be expected to be able to use this technique.

[9] One estimate of the reject rate with *trained* personnel suggests that nearly 10% of handwritten input is unreadable by OCR techniques (House, 1974, p. 33).

15. Approximately what is the average amount of time you spend on homework a week? (MARK ONE)

    No homework is ever assigned .... ☐
    I have homework, but I don't do it .... ☐
    Less than 1 hour a week .... ☐
    Between 1 and 3 hours a week .... ☐
    More than 3 hours, less than 5 hours a week ...... ☐
    Between 5 and 10 hours a week .... ☐
    More than 10 hours a week .... ☐

16. Between the beginning of school last fall and Christmas vacation, about how many days were you absent from school for any reason, not counting illness? (MARK ONE)

    None .... ☐
    1 or 2 days .... ☐
    3 or 4 days .... ☐
    5 to 10 days .... ☐
    11 to 15 days .... ☐
    16 to 20 days .... ☐
    21 or more .... ☐

17. Between the beginning of school last fall and Christmas vacation, about how many days were you late to school? (MARK ONE)

    None .... ☐
    1 or 2 days .... ☐
    3 or 4 days .... ☐
    5 to 10 days .... ☐
    11 to 15 days .... ☐
    16 to 20 days .... ☐
    21 or more .... ☐

18. How old were you when you first worked for pay, not counting work around the house? (MARK ONE)

    11 or younger .... ☐
    12 .... ☐
    13 .... ☐
    14 .... ☐
    15 .... ☐
    16 .... ☐
    17 .... ☐
    18 .... ☐
    19 .... ☐
    20 or older .... ☐
    Never have worked for pay .... ☐

FIGURE 11.2 Subset (Page 5) of High School and Beyond Senior Questionnaire

DIRECT ENTRY TERMINAL DEVICES[10]

Checks for validity can be made by the computer, and appropriate messages displayed so that the data can be corrected at the point of entry. This capability of editing data as they are being entered offers the possibility of reducing the time and effort necessary to obtain an edited data base.

An especially appealing symbiosis combines the use of an on-line terminal and telephone interviewing. In this application, the computer can be used to generate the appropriate questions to be asked, dependent on response patterns given. The questions might be displayed on a cathode ray tube and the

[10] The terminal devices here could be either "stupid" (no program function) or possess varying degrees of "intelligence" (programability), varying from modest microprocessors to complete minicomputers (e.g., Digital Equipment Corporation's VT78 contains a PDP-8 processer and up to 32 K bytes of memory).

responses then keyed in. As the data are entered, checks for consistency and "wild" values can be made. If clarification is needed, the program then directs the interviewer to the appropriate question. Such a computer–telephone interview combination nicely integrates data collection, entry, and editing into a single operation. However, the cost of renting specialized data entry devices (e.g., typewriter terminals, cathode ray tubes, or intelligent terminals), as well as the computer cost for carrying out the on-line editing must be considered.

SPECIALIZED SOURCE DATA ENTRY DEVICES

There are some specially designed source data entry devices that may be useful for survey researchers. One example is a device utilized to collect data in a study of animal behavior. This particular instrument consists of a keyboard contained on an $8\frac{1}{2} \times 11$ in. pad and a battery chargeable memory device. The entire device fits easily into a standard briefcase. Observers who watch monkey behavior record it by keying a predesignated code into the memory (e.g., 01 for monkey eating a banana). As the code is entered, a time of day is automatically recorded. At the end of a data collection period, the memory is "dumped" onto disk storage on the computer. For data capture that involves only a few codes and that needs to be synchronized with a clock, this type of instrument may be of considerable value.

AUTOMATED INTERVIEWING

Now, we turn to a specialized use of technology that combines a number of steps in the survey research process into a comprehensive system: Computer Assisted Telephone Interviewing, CATI (Shure & Meeker, 1978). An interviewer dials a sampled telephone number and then carries out the interview from questions appearing on a video terminal in a fashion not dissimilar to computer assisted instruction. There are options for switching to a different language instrument, usually from English to Spanish. All skip patterns are automated; so the interview is thus simplified. Open-ended responses are keyed into the computer for storage and subsequent processing, allowing the interview to be interrupted and then continued at a later point in time.

It is worth emphasizing that this is a functioning system, and it is one which has migrated successfully from the computer on which it was created to other PDP-11 minicomputers (Shure, C. M. Rogers, M. S. Rogers, & Seward, 1979).[11] Indeed, it is known to be operating in at least one market research firm, recognized as being a highly competitive business.

CATI can be described utilizing the same step-by-step process we are using here to discuss computers in survey research. To start, CATI assumes a fully designed instrument; however, the instrument is ingested in machine-readable form into CATI. More importantly, the structure of the instrument is also entered into the computer; that is, both skip patterns and interviewer instructions are included within the CATI system. In support of sampling via

---

[11] Text editors and word processing capabilities exist in abundance on PDP-11 minicomputers; however, these resources are not incorporated into CATI, since they do not need to be.

random digit dialing, CATI includes an implementation of the Waksberg sampling algorithm.[12]

Various monitoring capabilities are incorporated into CATI; using the telephone number as the entity sampled, the system keeps track of completions, retries, refusals, and the like; and it schedules call-backs of various types. Associated with these features, CATI is capable of generating status reports on the entire study, interviewer performance reports, and reports on the disposition of each call. The traditional steps of coding and editing are mostly unnecessary, since all skip patterns are executed automatically and since only legal codes are accepted. However, with respect to open-ended items, some form of text-scanning must be carried out in order to convert keyed responses into desired numeric codes; doing this by machine (instead of via the customary manual process) is less prone to error and inconsistency, and it again leaves a machine-readable documentation trail. Data capture, obviously, is accomplished by CATI, since the interviewer types or keys responses at the terminal as the interview progresses. Finally, the data cleaning process (see Section 11.7) is effectively unnecessary, since the cleaning process is carried out while the interview is in progress; in other words, most inconsistencies are caught by CATI while the respondent is still on the telephone, and the interview can be backed up if necessary to create a clean, consistent data record.

CATI makes excellent use of computing resources within the confines of a telephone interview by integrating so many of the steps of the survey research process into a single, comprehensive system. The only frustrating aspect of this constructive exploitation of technology is that it does not generalize to a face-to-face interview.[13]

11.7. DATA CLEANING

Perhaps the most unpleasant aspect of data processing for the survey researcher is the detection and resolution of errors in the survey data. Although the introduction of errors into the data is almost a certain occurrence, most researchers tend to view discovery of errors with surprise, deal with them with frustration, and blame them for unexpected delays in carrying out their analyses. Some of the frustration in dealing with errors should be expected and consequently planned for in the budget and in the time schedule. In order to "plan" for errors in the research project, some rough idea of the types of errors, the procedures for their correction, and their relative frequency of occurrence are needed. Such estimates are, unfortunately, difficult to obtain.

[12] A primary sample consists of a 10-digit telephone number where the two least significant digits are selected at random (e.g., 402/498-1500 through 402/498-1599). If that number reaches a residence, then a secondary sample is drawn consisting of additional random numbers drawn in the same range without replacement.

[13] Most experiments with portable terminals have failed because of the bias introduced into the interview by the terminal.

Researchers, understandably viewing errors as a nuisance, typically have not kept track of what kind of error occurred, how it was detected, and how it was corrected or resolved. That is, although there is considerable need for it, there appears to be little systematic evidence on the subject of error occurrence and detection in survey research.

We are concerned here with the detection and correction of errors in the data that are generated in the process of preparing the data for computer processing. That is, we are not concerned with response errors or the misapplication of statistical procedures. We take as correct the responses given to the survey and discuss situations in which these responses are subject to error.

Detection of Errors

The first step in data processing usually entails transcribing data from the original document to some machine-readable form. In this process, about 2–4% of the data can be conservatively expected to be mistranscribed (Schwab & Sitter, 1974, p. 13). The errors arise from two situations: (a) the transcriber (e.g., keypunch operator, coder) misreads the source document but correctly transcribes the misinterpreted data; and (b) the transcriber reads the source document correctly but mistranscribes the data. In a study of the relative occurrence of these types of errors, Beckley (1967; cited in Judd, 1973) found that in 100,000 numbers, 86% of the errors were due to misreading of the document (situation a). The remaining errors arose from omission, insertion, shift errors, or from transposition of digits (e.g., 2327 becoming 2372). Judging from the results of Beckley's study, independent verification of any transcription involving reading and interpreting of handwritten responses is advisable.[14]

Along this line, it is important to note that the usual key verification procedure is *not* an independent verification technique. Because verification operators have access to what the original keypunchers punched, in cases of ambiguity (i.e., misreading the data), they are likely to be influenced by the original keypunchers' interpretation. In particular, if in doubt, they will probably read the response the same as the first operators did. Several studies (reported by Minton, 1969) of the rate at which verifiers (in this nonindependent technique) failed to detect error suggest that, on average, about 4% of the keypunch errors will go undetected.

An independent verification technique would have two operators independently entering the data and then compare the two batches of work. However, even under the best of circumstances (i.e., independent verification), a certain small percentage of errors may be expected to pass through undetected.

Some of the transcription errors may be caught at the time of transcription by features of the transcribing device. Quite extensive editing may be carried out under program control on an "intelligent" terminal, including checking for

---

[14] Some survey research organizations find 10% verification to be adequate *if* a very thorough cleaning procedure is repeatedly used.

outliers and checking for internal consistency of the data. That is, these terminals can be programmed to test for univariate range checks ($a \leqq x \leqq b$) and multivariate, contingency tests, (if $x_1 \leqq a$ then $x_2 \leqq b$). For example, if specific columns contain the month of the year, then legitimate values would be specified to be 1–12 and any value outside that range would be in error. Multivariate contingency tests are used to check for the internal consistency of variables for the respondent. The program specifies the nature of the interrelationship among the variables by a set of if–then conditions. More than two variables could be involved in these specifications.

A general cleaning procedure is part of most social statistics packages. The researcher specifies the rules for the data edit that are checked by the computer program. The program may simply print out the offending case and variable or in some cases it may assign (impute) a value for the variable dependent on complex imputation algorithms. For one example, see the discussion of the interactive cleaning software later in this chapter.

The error detection procedures discussed thus far involve *deterministic* checks of the data. That is, the computer program checks whether variables contain specific codes and/or combinations of codes. For large data sets containing a high number of variables, the number of logical or contingency checks may be quite large. When an error is detected, the usual data editing procedure simply informs the user that there is an inconsistency somewhere in a specific relationship without isolating which variable is causing the problem. Naus, Johnson, and Montalvo (1972) describe a probabilistic technique for identifying which *particular* variable is in error, given the violation of specified logical relations. Incorporation of similar probabilistic procedures into computer editing programs should not be difficult; however, such an approach is not yet available in typical data checking programs.

The Naus *et al.* procedure detects when logical constraints are violated. Another potential error situation occurs as an unlikely response pattern, although logical constraints may not have been violated. Determination of a likely response pattern may refer to the interrelationship among variables (their joint distribution) or to the univariate distribution of traits across the sample. For example, if in a sample of women of childbearing age, the average number of children ever born was, say, .6 then one would be alerted to difficulties either in the sample or in the responses (and their coding) of the childbearing question. In this case, the computer program could be used to compute the sample average and compare it to a prior specified value. In the case of the interrelationship of variables, the computer might have stored the likelihood of the cooccurrence of two values of two variables and compare the observed distribution to the expected one. Again, using the fertility questionnaire as an example, if it is known that the likelihood of childbirth before age 14 is say .01, then when the number of cases began to deviate from this expected proportion by some amount (e.g., ±.005) the program would make note of this suspicious pattern.

When an if–then error is corrected, it is customary to reclean all data for that observation; since a change in one datum might invalidate other if–then relationships or even single-field specifications.

Regardless of the sophistication of the error detection procedure, the researcher is still faced with the task of resolving the error, the subject of the next section.

Resolution of Errors

We describe five options that singly or in combination might be used to resolve detected errors.

1. Consult the original interview or questionnaire to determine if the error is due to mistranscription.
2. Contact the respondent again to clarify the response or to obtain missing data.
3. Estimate or impute a response to resolve the error by various imputation techniques.
4. Discard the response or designating it as bad or missing data.
5. Discard the entire case.

Of course, if telephone interview–editing are combined, correction can be made on the spot. In more traditional ways of delivering surveys, options 1, 4, and 5 are most often utilized. Option 2—recontacting the respondent—may be uneconomical because it may introduce a different kind of bias into the responses. A few computer procedures for imputation of values are briefly described in the following. The use of option 4 versus option 5 may produce samples and variables with quite different statistical properties. For estimating parameters in regression type procedures, the choice of option 4 or 5 consists of choosing pairwise or listwise procedures. More details on this problem may be found in Chapter 12 in this volume. In this chapter, we are concerned only with computer techniques for the allocation of missing data.

HOT-DECK PROCEDURE

In this technique, the response of the last "similar" respondent is used to supply an estimate of the missing or erroneous data. It is called a hot-deck procedure because the substitute responses are continually updated or kept hot as the data set is read into the computer. Rockwell (1975) describes the use of this hot-deck procedure for the allocation of children ever born to women with this item missing in the 1970 Census 5% sample. A 156-cell matrix was used to classify the population by race (2 cells), family relationships (16 cells), and years since first marriage (13 cells). The last-processed female for whom number of children was reported had that value stored in the appropriate cell of this matrix. Then, this last-processed value would be used for the next woman with missing data having those racial, family relationship, and years since marriage values.

LEAST-SQUARES TECHNIQUES

Again, the idea is to use good data to estimate bad or missing data. There are several variants of this technique, all of which assume that the missing datum assigned is one that satisfies specific consistency equations or relationships in the data. A *consistency relationship* might be a specific logical (e.g., if–then) set of conditions, *or* an algebraic relationship (e.g., $x = y + 2z$). Freund and Hartley (1967) present a procedure in which weighting factors may be attached to the consistency equations, indicating the priority with which they are to be satisfied. Similarly, some variables are assumed to be more reliable than others and so should be permitted to be changed less than others. To satisfy these two conditions, they minimize the weighted sum of squared differences between the original and corrected data plus the weighted sum of squares of the discrepancies of the consistency equations. This technique was evaluated by a simulated error experiment in which "errors" were randomly introduced into a survey. The results of the experiment were then compared with the "true" results, which were in this case known. Two correction procedures (of the many) are of interest in this comparison. The first detected gross errors and corrected them by a hot-deck sort of procedure. The second and following procedures detected the error and then reconciled it by applying the least-squares procedure to the consistency equations. The application of the least-squares procedure produced a definite improvement over the hot-deck technique alone.

GENERAL IMPUTATION PROCEDURES

However, as Fellegi and Holt (1976) discuss, this least-squares procedure is appropriate only in situations in which the data are quantitative. In the event of categoric data, that is, for data in which there is no basis for assuming an underlying metric, this least-squares approach is inappropriate. Fellegi and Holt present a flexible procedure for automatic data editing and imputation that is applicable to qualitative and quantitative data and that can handle logical and/or arithmetic constraints in the editing specification. Their procedure consists of identifying the smallest set of variables whose values could be changed so that the resulting record will satisfy all edits and then imputing values for those fields that will maintain the distribution of data as represented by the records that passed the edits.

Interactive Edit, Error Detection, and Resolution

In most survey research applications, the data processing involved with data editing, error detection, and resolution is carried out in a batch mode.[15] In

---

[15] *Batch mode* or *batch processing* is defined by Sonquist and Dunkelberg (1977) p. 418 as follows:

> In a batch-oriented computing system the unit of work done by the computer is the *job*. Jobs may have one or several *steps*. Each step involves the execution of a program and acceptance of input and the

a typical application, the surveys would be edited, open-ended items coded, and the data would then be keyed and verified. Next, the data–edit program would be run and wild and inconsistent codes found. From the information in the edit run, corrections would be made and then the edit run carried out again. Because correcting one error may introduce another, the entire process is repeated numerous times.

The recycling of errors and the efficiency of the batch mode of cleaning data, has led to the reasonable suggestion that *interactive* editing may be a time-saving procedure. Under such a system, the revision of the file would be checked for accuracy before it is applied, thus eliminating some of the passes across the data. If the revision were found to be incorrect, then clarification would be required at that time.

11.8. SCALE–INDEX CONSTRUCTION

At this point in the life of the survey, the data have been coded, entered, edited, and cleaned. A typical next step in the preparation of data for statistical analysis is the construction of various scales or indices. We use the term *scale* or *index* loosely, to mean any new variable formed by manipulation of original variables or by addition of variables from an external source.

This phase of variable construction can involve quite trivial and/or quite complex sets of computer operations. A simple recode of a variable to reverse the order of the responses is one example of new variable construction. Another example is the summation of distinct items to form subscales and total scales according to some predefined inventory.

Other types of variable construction may follow a much more open-ended route. Iterative procedures may be used to add–delete items from a scale to maximize reliability. Aggregation of individual level responses to some group level may also produce variables for contextual analyses. A different type of variable construction involves merging data from another source with the existing data. A common example is merging information about the county of residence from the city–county data book with an individual's record. The usefulness of assigning standard codes to variables, such as cities and counties, is suggested by this last example.

Given the variety of tasks involved in creating new variables and the range of complexity, general statements are not easily made—except for one: the need for documentation! Adequate notes of what took place are imperative to

production of output. Steps can be set up to *execute* one after the other without physical intervention. This is sometimes called *chaining*. A step in a multistep job generally either accepts input and control information and leaves files in the computer for subsequent steps, or it accepts files from tapes, disks, or other storage media and prints output. Sometimes both will be produced. Frequently, if an early step aborts or *abends* (*ab*normal *end*ing) the files required by subsequent steps are not prepared and those steps fail, too. In the case of either failure or success, all the output from all steps is collected and delivered in one piece to the *user* who submitted the job. He generally has no access to his control information or his data after the job has been *submitted* (either by turning a deck of cards in to an operator at the computer center, or loading the coded computer instructions directly into a reading device) [p. 418].

provide information several months later concerning the details of the variable construction. One suggestion is to keep a special notebook just for this purpose. The entries need not be elaborate, but should contain the date, some unique identification code for the computer print out (e.g., the run number, spool file number), and some comment of explanation about the run. These notes are indispensible for secondary researchers, whether another person or the original survey researcher several months after the variable construction.

11.9. DATA BASE ORGANIZATION

This section is concerned with the organization of the survey data into a data base. Its purpose is to familiarize the survey researcher with some basic ideas in data base storage and management. This section discusses data base storage, and the next section discusses data base retrieval.

Several responses motivated our inclusion of these sections. One reason is our belief that the data gathered by survey researchers is becoming increasingly more complicated structurally. A terminology to describe these structures is conceptually useful. A second reason for understanding more about data base management is simply to be in a better position to evaluate the various available software packages. Without knowledge of the basic concepts, the researcher is not in a position to know whether package A or B is better or if neither will work.

We start with an example of a complex data structure. Consider data relating to census tracts, households, families, and individuals. These data could be viewed as four distinct and separate files; however, given that relationships exist among the four files, it may be more useful to organize the data into a single data base. Because individuals are family members who comprise households that are located in census tracts, the structure of these data is a hierarchy. To efficiently use these data in their full complexity, we need to be able to represent the linkages among the components as well as the elements of the data base.

In thinking about the organization of the data base, it is conceptually useful to distinguish between *logical* and *physical* representations. By *logical representation* we mean the scheme for perceiving the data structure. By *physical representation* we mean the procedure for actually linking up the elements of the data base. The logical framework is the way we think about the data; the physical framework is the way the data are actually linked. Essentially, we are concerned here with alternative logical arrangements of complex data structures.

Conceptual Data Models

The terms *data model* and *conceptual data model* are often used to refer to the user's view of the organization of data. To repeat, the data model is an abstract concept and may have little to do with how the data are physically stored (Date, 1977). In fact, one primary objective for implementing data base management systems is to free the user from the concern over physical representation of the data base.

The various approaches to organizing a data base involve different ways of representing the *linkages* among the *elements* of the data base. An element here may be thought of as a record, whereas a link may be understood as the relationship of this record to other record(s) in the data base. Although numerous approaches are possible, there are three basic data base organizing schemes: (*a*) the relational approach; (*b*) the hierarchical approach; (*c*) the network approach.

RELATIONAL

The distinguishing characteristic of the relational approach is that elements and linkages among elements are represented in a uniform manner. For example, consider a contextual data file containing both school level data and student level data; see part A of Figure 11.3. The links are contained within the records, that is, the link is understood because the data are contained in the same physical record (Kroenke, 1977, p. 195). Because there is a one-to-one correspondence between the records, the relational approach is also referred to as a one-to-one linking.

HIERARCHICAL

In hierarchical data, a record takes its full meaning only the context of other records. For example, consider a household–individual data file; see part B of Figure 11.3). There are two types of records: household records and individual records.[16] An individual is a member of one household, thus establishing a one-to-many linking between households and individuals. In more general terms, the household record is often referred to as the parent record.

NETWORK

A network is a more general structure than a hierarchy in the sense that a network record can have any number of parents. For example, consider a data file of teachers, classes, and students where team teaching is being done; see part C of Figure 11.3. This example illustrates the fundamental nature of this type of structure—the linkage of many elements to many other elements or a many-to-many linking. Another substantive example well suited to a network structure would be interlocking directorates, in which the boards of major industrials and major banks are linked—directly and indirectly—through memberships on those boards.

Some combination of these three conceptual models can be used to describe most survey research data. Next we provide some specific examples.

---

[16] The household record at the top of the tree is called the *root;* other descriptive terminology includes *nodes, branches, parents, children,* and *siblings*.

A — Relational: school-level and student-level

school Ol	student OOOl
school Ol	student OOO2
school Ol	student OOO3
⋮	
school mm	student nnnn

B — Hierarchical: household / individual

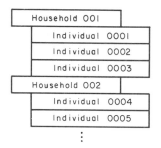

C — Network: teachers, classes (team taught), and students

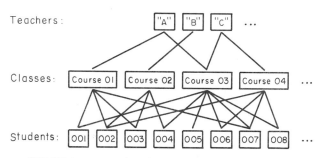

FIGURE 11.3 Examples of conceptual data models.

Sociometric Data. Sociometric data is, by definition, information about linkages. When one adolescent names another as his best friend, there is a link (pointer) from the data record of the first to the data record of the second adolescent. Given the possibility of mutual choice, a many-to-many linkage among the records exists. The collectivity of such links is clearly a network model.

Other forms of data—which are not thought of as being sociometric by survey researchers—are in fact consistent with the sociometric model. For example, the linkages among classes, students, and teachers can be seen as a network. Classes contain many students, students attend multiple classes, and teachers are responsible for several classes (this was used as an example of a network data model in Figure 11.3). Whenever linkages are perceived as a many-to-many phenomenon, a network model is appropriate.

Strict Hierarchies. Some social phenomena occur as natural hierarchies. An example is the High School and Beyond project where the data model consists of state, school district, high school, and student. This is referenced as a "strict" hierarchy because a unit at any level points to no more than one unit at the next higher level; a student is affiliated with one high school, and a school district is linked to but one state.[17]

General Hierarchies. Some social relationships are not dense enough to be actually considered network structures (many-to-many linkages), but neither are they strict hierarchies. These structures are called "general" hierarchies and we take another example from High School and Beyond as illustrative. In addition to student data, parents were also surveyed. Each student may be thought of as "owning" some array of parents, and this fits the strict hierarchy concept. However, when brothers and sisters become the unit of analysis and attributes of their parents are linked to them, the structure becomes not a one-to-many mapping but a few-to-many mapping. Thus, the data do not easily fit relational, hierarchical, or network approaches. One could perceive of it as a network structure, yet the sparseness of the sibling links makes this approach seem not worthwhile. On the other hand, one would not want to ignore the sibling links and treat the data as a strict hierarchy.

Life Histories. We provide another example of a complex data set whose structure does not precisely match the three typical approaches of data-base systems. The Retrospective Life History Study, conducted at the Johns Hopkins University, obtained data from 1589 respondents who documented chronologically various major life events (e.g., education, marital status, occupation). For each respondent, there was a matrix such that rows represented time in months and columns represented variables; thus, the complete data file contains 1589 such matrices. Conceptually, this is a three-dimensional matrix of individuals by time by variables. The total conceptual matrix contains more than 1.7 billion cells, but the proportion of meaningful data in that matrix is .0003.

From the standpoint of representing the complexity of the data using one of the three approaches, the life history data do not conform exactly to any of the three approaches. A stand alone data base storage and retrieval system had to be developed for this data (Karweit, 1973). An additional consideration in the storage of these data is the need to flexibly retrieve information to conform to differing units of analysis (e.g., the individual, events, transitions) and to

---

[17] Invariably there is at least one exception to everything. The Dresden School District represents the collaboration of Norwich, Vermont, and Hanover, New Hampshire.

differing definitions of variables (e.g., the state of a variable defined in terms of calendar time, age, or occurrence of another event).

The preponderance of commercial Data Base Management Systems (DBMS) leads us to wonder if developing special software to handle complex social survey data will be a thing of the past. In the next section, we discuss some of the prospects for extensive application of these systems in survey research.

Prospects for Data Base Management Systems

Given the varieties of data bases, what computer software exists to define and store the schema and data? Here, we discuss data storage in the sense of schema definition; data retrieval and processing is discussed in the following section. Commercial DBMSs exist in abundance, are exceptionally well documented, thoroughly debugged, and tend to be more expensive than survey researchers can afford. The commercial market initiated the interest in conceptual data structures, and the commercial data base management systems have implemented the three models (repeatedly) and some variants of those models. One could use a commercial DBMS to define the schema of a network structure and eventually to carry out retrievals; however, we see some limitations relevant to the interests of survey researchers, and some of the qualifications merit discussion.

A commercial DBMS was designed for various applications of business administration. But, what is ideal for a personnel data base or for an inventory control system is not necessarily functional for sociometric data. In order to define a schema, the survey researcher would be using systems and documentation couched in an alien set of terminology. Looking ahead a bit, the DBMS is designed to retrieve a small subset of the data base efficiently, but the DBMS is not as practical for returning all observations. These systems are designed for extensive daily transactions; by contrast, the survey researcher is geared toward occasional data entry and considerable retrieval activity. The commercial DBMS is designed so that fields, records, and files can be added to a data base in midstream without interfering with existing applications software; the survey applications have no need for this sort of capability. In general, we believe that these DBMSs address their software development energy to problems that are mostly irrelevant to survey research. On the other hand, the implementation of certain software structures saves time and expense, thus allowing the researcher to implement more appropriate software.

With respect to hierarchical structures, there are a few software resources that meet the needs of survey researchers in the area of schema definition and storage, but we limit our discussion to the example of Scientific Information Retrieval (SIR).[18] Although the SIR documentation (Robinson, Anderson, Cohen, Gadzik, Karpel, Miller, & Stein, 1980) discusses the resource in the tradi-

---

[18] In addition, OSIRIS IV and RAMIS II can process hierarchical data files.

tional DBMS terminology, we find this to be misleading. SIR is more accurately recognized as a storage and retrieval system. In particular, SIR can produce rectangular files, SPSS system files, or BMDP system files. Additionally, it has its own modest control language (patterned after SPSS) for computation–aggregation, imputation–distribution, and numerous other functional tasks. Returning to schema definition and storage as the primary point of this section, SIR is designed in a manner that is totally compatible with the needs of survey researchers. Data files can be ingested one file at a time (typically the way data are obtained), since it is just as reasonable to input one part of one file now and another part later. The schema definition is used to define various record types (e.g., the format and content of individual-level data records) and to define the hierarchical links between them. One's thinking about logical data structures, if hierarchical, is matched by SIR's capacity to process such records. Therefore, the physical data storage tends not to matter so much any more (as long as it works and does so efficiently).

As will be observed in the next section, there are retrieval software resources not discussed here due to a lack of data model definition capability. Ideally, one should try to start with a data base facility that does have this definition resource; a second choice would be something with retrieval-only facilities; and the last choice becomes do-it-yourself software. It is that bottom line last choice that was needed in order to process the Retrospective Life History data base. It is our expectation that future years will see more activity in this general area of system development and possibly less in statistical analysis systems.

Gathering versus Using

Thinking more abstractly about conceptual data models, there is a tendency to think about the data in the form or structure in which it is gathered in the field. This may or may not be appropriate, and we offer a specific example of a data file and how it might be related to the overall data base.

The High School and Beyond project gathered data from high school teachers using a Teacher's Comment Form instrument. This questionnaire asked about one page's worth of questions concerning the teachers' attitudes toward their school. Additionally, the balance of the instrument contained lists of student names to elicit comments from the teacher about each individual student.[19] The instrument was a particularly efficient mechanism for gathering the desired data. But one wonders whether the format of the instrument should dictate one's thinking about the use of the data. As gathered, the data would have the teacher as the unit of analysis; on the other hand, with some rearrang-

---

[19] It has been suggested that Scientific Information Retrieval (SIR) is able to process hierarchies well. Actually, if a data base is mostly hierarchical and partly network, SIR can still— although with some awkwardness—process the data base. Therefore, software restrictions do not dictate the perception of the data structure. As a general rule, such restrictions should never—but often do—govern one's thinking about structure.

ing of information, the comment (of a teacher about one student) could be the unit of analysis. Which makes sense? Actually, both do. In terms of conceptual data models, the other High School and Beyond data fit a strict hierarchy quite well. As gathered, the Teacher Comment Form would require a network approach. In these terms, how does one see the data?

One use of the teacher data is to report on the schools in which they work. In practical terms, one would want the one page's worth of teacher reports on the institution, ignoring their comments about students. With the data in this form, there would be as many observations as there are individual teachers. Returning to conceptual data models, the strict hierarchy could be preserved by linking these data records to the high schools. Then, for example, teacher reports about the proportion of time spent maintaining discipline could be aggregated to the school level to form a systemic or contextual variable.

Another use of the data would be to capture the comments about individual students within the high schools. With this approach, it might be necessary to rewrite the data file such that there would be as many records as there are comments, possibly repeating the teacher attitudes toward school with each comment about a student.[20] Returning to conceptual data models, this rearranged form of the data would have each student "owning" a set of teacher comments about that specific adolescent. We see a strict hierarchy again. With this structure, the comments of teachers about a given student could be aggregated up to the student level in the form of a mean teacher perception of that student. This reasonably simple rewriting of the gathered data is consistent with one's substantive thinking about the complete data base, and it permits easier use of the natural hierarchy than would be true with a network model.

The point of this tangent discussion of the Teacher Comment Form is to encourage thinking about data structures in a somewhat abstract sense—certainly in a storage-free context as well as a software-independent context—in order to determine how the data might be used. That sort of modeling, obviously enough, is what schema definition is.

11.10. DATA RETRIEVAL

The preceding discussion—particularly that of the Student Record Form and that of the Retrospective Life History Study—suggests that the approach to storing data is often significantly different from what is desired for data analysis. One may want to work with a specific level of analysis (e.g., student versus school); to define contingent variables (i.e., first job after leaving military service); or to examine the effects of links on individual attitudes (i.e., the

---

[20] As the data were gathered and initially keyed, there were a small number of fields containing teacher attitudes toward their school and then up to 92 sets of comments about students. Combining the attitudes with one set of comments and writing a record, repeated as many times as comments about students were encountered, would effectively restructure the file.

effect of friends' and of friends' friends' attitudes on the individual's perceptions). The present section is devoted to such considerations.

The logic of statistical analysis (see the following section) imposes some constraints on data retrieval. These are so obvious that they may be overlooked, yet it is valuable to observe explicitly that one cannot cross-tabulate tracts by households any more than one can correlate schools and students. It is, of course, mandatory that the variables in any specific analysis represent common units; and this simplifies the *goal* of the data retrieval process, although not necessarily the process itself.

The output of retrieval may be perceived to be a logical work file. Whether it physically is a work file or something totally different matters little to the data analyst as long as the intended analysis can be accomplished. The retrieved data might actually be a simple rectangular raw data file; it might be an SPSS system file; or it could be a set of inverted lists inside a computer. Whatever, it is worthwhile to think about logical work files. To this end, we discuss the steps that are employed in the retrieval process; then, we describe software available to perform those steps.

Retrieval Steps

As was true with data storage, our discussion of data retrieval steps focuses upon individual possibilities, yet actual practice is often a combination of these. For didactic purposes, we describe these steps individually.

STRAIGHTFORWARD FETCH

The simplest procedural step is a straightforward fetching or retrieving of records. In the case of a simple cross-section, one merely wants to transmit the data from the storage system to the analysis system. Even in highly complex files, when the focus of attention is on data gathered at a given unit level, this remains an extremely common operation.

SUBSETTING

The straightforward fetch may be complicated by imposing some logic on which records are to be retrieved. Subsetting on the variables dimension could be done by a list (i.e., specifying a list of health related or other variables), by asking for wave-3 variables only, or by definition (i.e., all demographic variables). Subsetting on the observations dimension could be as simple as seeking the subset of respondents in the Cumulative GSS from a specific year, or as difficult as a sampling operation such that one obtains a 10% random sample of observations in a large data base for exploratory data analysis. Further, it is common to employ Boolean logic in defining a subset; for example, one might want to retrieve data records for observations representing hearing-impaired Hispanic students attending school in the Southwest. In hierarchical files, one might want to retrieve records of individuals who are living in large households; here, one must follow links from individual records to household records to determine whether specific individual records are to be retrieved. Again, combinations of subsetting procedures are frequently necessary.

LINKAGES

Sociometric data may be exploited by comparing one record with the record pointed to and then moving some data from the target record to the pointing record. For example, if student A identifies B as best friend or as the individual most desirable to emulate, then B's educational aspirations could be added to A's data record in a retrieval run so that they can be compared in a subsequent analysis run. A slightly more complicated operation would involve determining whether A's selection of B was reciprocated such that symmetric and asymmetric selections could be compared in terms of their effect on the influencing of educational aspirations. Further, when the choice is not reciprocated, the secondary linkages can be pursued in order to determine the indirect effects of the attitudes and behaviors of friends of friends to determine whether such has any explanatory power over and above the primary sociometric choice.

AGGREGATION

With respect to hierarchical data, it is often useful to chase links among records in order to aggregate information from one level to a higher level. For instance, if teachers report their perceptions of general disciplinary problems in their schools, then the average of teacher reports can be added to the school record to serve as an indicator of level of law and order within the institution. In some circumstances, it is also valuable to be able to include the standard deviation about that mean as a separate school-level measure. In these cases, one is chasing all links from units at one level to a record at a higher level. Other aggregate measures include counts, sums, minima, and maxima.

DISTRIBUTION

Contextual effects—also called climate, systemic, and environmental effects—require distributing a value at one level of a hierarchy to all linked records at a lower level. Imputing a value down the hierarchy means merely repeating it in the appropriate records at the lower level. In aggregation, we considered the example of computing teacher data up the hierarchy to the school level; so an example of distribution would be imputing that school-level value to all student records associated with that school. Then, one might analyze, for example, school-level law-and-order effects on individual student academic achievement.

Most other retrieval steps are combinations of the simpler ones discussed here. Once a researcher moves from the constrained thinking of how data were gathered into the more general perception of how they might be analyzed, the only limit is one's imagination. Of course, availability of appropriate software may prove to be a hindrance; so we move on to a consideration of how to implement some of the retrieval steps already discussed.

Retrieval Software

Three general levels of retrieval software are considered here. We start with a retrieval system that takes advantage of the schema definition of Section 11.9 of this chapter; then, we suggest how to finesse some of these operations in a packaged statistical system; and we conclude with do-it-yourself software.

As of this writing, Scientific Information Retrieval (SIR) offers the best example of a software package combining schema definition and data retrieval. The interest in SIR is its ability to produce SPSS system files, BMDP system files, and traditional BCD rectangular files; so SIR output can be readily input to statistical analysis packages familiar to survey researchers. The user communicates to the system with a set of commands. The following example combines aggregation and distribution (Robinson *et al.*, 1980, p. 6–26):

```
RETRIEVAL
PROCESS CASES
. PROCESS REC      2
.   MOVE VARS      DISTNUM, ENROLL, NTEACH
.   PROCESS REC    3,WITH(DISTNUM)
.     MOVE VARS    SCHOOLNO, TEACHERS, STUDENTS
.     PROCESS REC  4,WITH(DISTNUM,SCHOOLNO)
.       COMPUTE    NCLASS=CNTR(CLASSID)
.       COMPUTE    CLSIZE=MEANR(SIZE)
.       COMPUTE    CLCAP=MEANR(CAPACITY)
.     END PROCESS REC
.     PERFORM PROCS
.   END PROCESS REC
. END PROCESS REC
END PROCESS CASES
SPSS SAVE FILE FILENAME=ANALYZ2
END RETRIEVAL
```

Our intent is not to teach SIR retrieval conventions; rather, this set of commands is displayed in order to provide the reader some notion of the level of simplicity–complexity required in order to carry out a combined aggregation and distribution retrieval. As suggested elsewhere, we anticipate an expansion of the number of such packages over the coming years, and we hope that the power and ease of use will improve over time.

Another possibility for coping with complex data structures relies on finessing things through a powerful statistical analysis package (SAS Institute, 1979). The most promising candidate for this currently is the Statistical Analysis System (SAS). Here, one could create several SAS data sets and then utilize the SET, MERGE, and UPDATE facilities to exploit linkages among files. This hits us as an interesting compromise between using a DBMS and becoming a programmer; it is somewhere between the black-box and the do-it-yourself approaches, since it requires the user to comprehend what is to be linked and how, without requiring software development expertise. One advantage of SAS is that it executes efficiently on IBM hardware; for some, a disadvantage is that it functions on no other hardware. Increasingly, survey researchers are perceiving SAS's data analysis resources to be superior to those of SPSS. SAS's intermediate-level data-handling resources offer one mechanism for processing complex files.

Finally, one can attempt to deal with complex data by means of user-written programs. When one encounters a data file as complex as the Retrospective Life History Study (a highly sparse three-dimensional matrix of individuals by time by variables), then there is little choice but to develop software that will permit efficient storage along with powerful retrieval; in this example, a viable solution would involve producing a rectangular work file that could be input to a standard analysis package. Under other circumstances, one might be forced to exercise this bottom line option; however, we strongly recommend exploring existing data retrieval software before considering writing one's own, since this is a particularly difficult, time consuming, and error prone method of programming.

Survey research has been steadily migrating from simple, rectangular data files to complex, hierarchical ones. Yet software development is lagging behind to a significant degree. The current software tools are often inadequate for the needs of survey researchers, yet we project that these circumstances will improve significantly during the coming years. Thus, in time, one will be able to move more quickly to issues of data analysis, precisely where this chapter is now headed.

11.11. STATISTICAL ANALYSIS

By far the largest use of the computer in survey research has been for statistical analyses of the data. By far the most common approach is the use of standard statistical packages. Given this emphasis, it is somewhat curious that attempts to evaluate, document, and disseminate information about various computing packages is a rather recent phenomenon. There is beginning to appear, however, a wealth of information for the consumer of comprehensive statistical packages. Provided in this information is descriptive information (what the package does), evaluations (how users rank the package), commentary (advise to look out for an inaccuracy in procedure x), and contact information (authorship, location, types of computers). The volume edited by Ivor Francis (1979) provides a good sampling of the capabilities of the most commonly used packages and should be a part of every computing center library where survey data analysis is done.

In this section, then, we will not attempt to focus on specifics of packages. Instead, we suggest that the survey analyst refer to the Francis volume and to works listed in the bibliography of this chapter. We focus on some constraints facing the survey researcher in selecting a data analysis package.

Inertia and Disinterest

Regardless of improvements in efficiency, convenience, and statistical accuracy, most survey researchers probably continue to use the first package they ever used. Frequently, the language of the package becomes so internalized that analysis plans are described in package procedure terms, not statistical terms. This incorporation of the procedures as part of the vocabulary of doing research is often coupled with a genuine disinterest in learning any more about computing software than is minimally necessary to get the job done. The inertia and disinterest, then, serve as considerable constraints to using new or other packages.

Quality of Implementation

Another point that bears discussion is the differences in quality of implementation of a package on different computing systems. Not all implementations of SPSS or BMDP, for example, are equally efficient, so that the evaluation of a specific package also depends on how it operates on the particular hardware available. There are good and bad renditions of the software, largely dependent on whether there was a successful marriage of the particular hardware advantages to the software requirements. Another computer center with the same hardware may provide valuable information about the quality of the software on that system.

Data Exchange

Another factor that is of growing concern to the survey researcher is the ability to exchange data between packages. Survey researchers will probably not be able to do everything they want to do within a single comprehensive statistical package. They may perform editing with a stand-alone package, preliminary and descriptive analyses with a comprehensive package, but use other stand alone computational programs (e.g., LISREL or ECTA) for additional statistical analyses. Consequently, both the comprehensiveness of the package and the exportability of data from the package are of concern. Some packages will quite readily allow crossover from other foreign packages (e.g., SAS will read BMDP and SPSS system files). The data exchange problem is not just between large packages and their system files, however, as researchers will probably always need some procedure not yet included, or impractical to include, in a comprehensive package. Part of the package selection procedure, then, should entail determining how easy it will be to export data to other software.

11.12. DOCUMENTATION

The usefulness of adequate documentation is hard to argue about, but like most things that are "good" for you, documentation is difficult to carry out on a sustained basis. In this section, we direct attention to some benefits of documentation, and provide some suggestions that may make documentation more of a habit.

Most survey researchers think of computer documentation solely in terms of the codebook for the data tape. Yet, there are persuasive arguments for adequate documentation all along the way. We discuss some benefits in the following paragraphs.

Disaster Recovery

A routine part of any survey data analysis is the discovery of a major problem, be it misspecification of a variable in a series of regression, an error in formation of a variable, or use of the wrong version of the data set. There are several ways to attempt to recover. One is to start all over again, basically from a cleaned data set. Another is to trace back to where the error was introduced and simply begin recovery from that point. Recovery is made significantly easier if every transaction made against the file is written down. This documentation can be in the form of a computer diary that contains, minimally, the date, the source file, the transaction, the output file, and cross-reference to the computer print out. An example might be:

Date	Source → Output		Transaction
4–16–80	OBS.RAW	OBS.SORT	sort position 1–5, classroom id. Listing is spool file #1589.
4–16–80	OBS.SORT OBS.TOTAL	OBS.FINAL	MERGE.SPSS gives procedure for merge of SORT and TOTAL to produce FINAL. Positions 1–5 SORT 1–5 TOTAL. Spool file #1592.
4–16–80	OBS.FINAL	OBS.LISTING	OBS.SPSS contains regression control specification. Output file was printed as job #1595.

Estimation of Computing Expenses

In planning the budget for a new survey, the estimation of expenses for computing is usually far from a fine science. Guesses multiplied by 2 provide the basis for most budget plans. The documentation of the daily activities provides a good data base for estimating not only how much computer time was used but how it was used. It can isolate in retrospect where the most time consuming and computer consuming parts of the project are located. Documentation of these actual expenditures would provide important information for planning future studies.

Codebook Documentation

There are packages that permit automatic generation of a data codebook as part of the data generation procedure (see Francis, 1979). This generation process greatly simplifies the creation of the codebook and, in combination with word processing capability, seems to offer an ideal use of the computer for accomplishing a tedious task. In addition to documenting how each variable was created, the codebook should contain marginals on each variable, and even cross-tabulations with major variables, such as race and sex, if appropriate.

11.13. REPORT WRITING

Will a computer write that definitive journal article? No, of course not, but the technology can help an author go through numerous revisions more readily; and it could impact the quality of the final version. There are some ways to improve the readability and accuracy of the written report, and the mechanisms may cut costs along the way.

Word processing has been discussed in other sections of this chapter, but it merits reiterating at this step in the survey research process. In using word processing, text is keyed onto a magnetic medium (e.g., disk) and played back on paper on command. In addition, using a small processor, the text can easily be edited and corrected. One can cut and paste electronically so that words, paragraphs, or large sections can be moved about with a few operator keystrokes. Word changes, typographical errors, and major modifications can be carried out quickly and efficiently. Whatever was considered correct can be left untouched and then played back on paper, along with changes, at will. It is a near classic use of machinery to relieve drudgery and improve the quality of product.

First, considerable tedium is saved, since it is not necessary to proofread an entire draft; only changes need be checked. Second, word processing reduces the wear and tear on the typist, since the printing is predominantly machine driven. Third, as a result of the first two points, there is no need to hesitate about making one more round of changes and improvements, perhaps transforming a very good piece of writing into an excellent one, since the process will not introduce more errors than are being rectified. Fourth, word processing speeds the cycle of drafts so that papers can be completed in a more timely fashion. Fifth, by reducing the time required of a typist, word processing has been demonstrated to save enough in staff costs to more than cover machinery costs.

Everything just argued is valid for a stand-alone word processing configuration; however, we have been arguing throughout this chapter for word processing with a direct communications link to the statistical processor. With such a link, one can capture segments of statistical output for direct insertion into papers and reports. Of course, format changes may be required, but those are the tasks for which word processing is particularly well designed. Just the increase in accuracy of the final paper makes it worth considering this approach. It is a bit ridiculous to have one machine produce statistical output and then require a staff member to reenter the same thing into another machine.[21]

Surely, some readers are agreeing in principle but will argue that the finances of their institution prevent the acquisition of word processors. One is reminded of the observation that it takes two full professors working overtime to accomplish the work of one competent secretary. Look again. Word-processing technology indeed can be cost effective in most instances.

11.14. CONCLUDING REMARKS

In concluding this chapter on computer usage, we reemphasize four themes. First, there is a division of labor between investigators and computing staff which we believe should be demarcated in every survey research effort. In short, the investigator has the responsibility for carrying out the entire project, and the proper role of computing staff is to facilitate that effort. The analogy that comes to mind is the division of labor between an author and a publishing house; even if the publisher has skilled proofreaders, the author is responsible for the typographical errors that appear in the final product. Some researchers, inadvertently or otherwise, have permitted this distinction to become blurred, and one drifts into circumstances where the computing staff is consulting on statistical methodology, sampling procedures, and other such topics with which they may be familiar but are not, by definition, experts. The computing staff should be authorities on the use of specific programs, but the investigator is responsible for selecting the procedures appropriate to the data as well as the interpretation of the resulting statistics.

Second, we have observed examples—admittedly rare—of survey researchers who plan their work in writing in considerable detail; various tasks are clearly articulated, and deadline dates are explicitly noted. Assisting such researchers with computing tasks is enjoyable, since (a) the obvious work is already articulated; and (b) it is possible, seeing an entire plan of work, to suggest other uses of computers in survey research. Those who plan very carefully in advance tend to have much smaller computer expenditures then "random walk" researchers. More important, by consulting with computing staff early and systematically throughout the survey research, these investigators avoid both redundant and corrective steps. Data processing plays such a large role in survey research that it is imperative to involve computing staff from the outset of a project and to keep them involved throughout. The cost of doing otherwise can be staggering.

[21] In fact, the same observation holds for moving a paper from the word processor to the publisher. It is indeed ridiculous to rekey what already exists in machine-readable form. Unhappily, the conventions and standards are not up to a level that would permit widespread implementation of what is seen as desirable. Some publishers are accomplishing this currently, and many more will be in coming years.

Third, we stress the importance of good documentation. In addition to the obvious documentation consisting of a codebook, there is a need to document in writing all major and many minor decisions, steps, and processes along the way. These include sampling, coding, variable (index) construction, and the like. Documentation pays off in terms of continuity of work, reduced staff and machine costs, and increased productivity. Software documentation is typically done so that another programmer can readily maintain the program at some subsequent date; just as typically, the next programmer turns out to be oneself, but—due to elapsed time—it does not matter. In like manner, survey researchers need to learn to document their work comprehensively, since even if another does not need the information—they will eventually be faced with struggling to remember what was done and how.

Fourth, we encourage survey researchers to broaden their view of the role of the computer in survey research. Typically, survey researchers involve the computer only in the statistical analyses of the data. Yet, there are numerous tasks that can be accomplished with computers independent of standard analysis packages. Once one overcomes this myopia, there are no serious limitations to what can be carried out readily and successfully utilizing some computing resource.

REFERENCES

Call, V. R. A., L. B. Otto, and K. I. Spenner
    1982   "Entry into careers." *Tracking Respondents: A Multi-Method Approach*. Vol. 2. Lexington, Mass.: Lexington-Heath.
Coleman, J. S., E. Q. Campbell, C. J. Hobson, J. McPartland, A. M. Mood, F. D. Weinfield, and R. L. York
    1966   *Equality of Educational Opportunity*. Washington, D.C.: U.S. Office of Education.
Cummings, K. M.
    1979   "Random digit dialing: A sampling technique for telephone surveys." *Public Opinion Quarterly* 43: 233–244.
Date, C. J.
    1977   *An Introduction to Database Systems*. (2nd Ed.). Reading, Mass.: Addison–Wesley.
Felligi, I. P., and D. Holt
    1976   "A systematic approach to automatic edit and imputation." *Journal of the American Statistical Association* 71(March): 17–35.
Ferrara, R., and R. L. Nolan
    1974   "New look at computer data entry." In. W. C. House (ed.), *Data Base Management*. New York: Petrocelli Books.
Francis, I., Ed.
    1979   *A Comparative Review of Statistical Software*. Netherlands: International Association for Statistical Computing.
Freund, R. J., and H. O. Hartley
    1967   "A procedure for automatic data editing." *Journal of the American Statistical Association* 62(June): 341–352.
House, W., Ed.
    1974   *Data Base Management*. New York: Petrocelli Books.
Judd, D. R.
    1973   *Use of Files*. New York: Elsevier.

Karweit, N.
  1973 "Storage and retrieval of life history data." *Social Science Research* 2(March): 41–50.
Klecka, W. R., and A. J. Tuchfarber
  1978 "Random digit dialing: A comparison to personal surveys." *Public Opinion Quarterly* 42: 105–114.
Kroenke, D.
  1977 *Database Processing*. Chicago: Science Research Associates.
Levine, J. H.
  1972 "The sphere of influence." *American Sociological Review* 37: 14–27.
Martin, J.
  1975 *Computer Data-Base Organization*. Englewood Cliffs, N.J.: Prentice–Hall.
Minton, G.
  1969 "Inspection and correction of errors in data processing." *Journal of the American Statistical Association* 64(December): 1256–1275.
Naus, J., T. G. Johnson, and R. Montalvo
  1972 "A probabalistic model for identifying errors in data editing." *Journal of the American Statistical Association* 67(December): 943–950.
Otto, L. B., V. R. A. Call, and K. I. Spenner
  1979 *Design for a Study of Entry into Careers*. Boys Town, NE: Boys Town Center for the Study of Youth Development.
Robinson, B. N., G. D. Anderson, E. Cohen, W. F. Gazdzik, L. C. Karpel, A. H. Miller, and J. R. Stein
  1980 *SIR User's Manual* (2nd ed.). Evanston, Ill: SIR.
Rockwell, R. C.
  1975 "An investigation of the imputation and differential quality of data in the 1970 census." *Journal of the American Statistical Association* 70(March): 39–42.
SAS Institute, Inc.
  1979 *SAS User's Guide*. 1979 ed. Raleigh, N.C.: SAS Institute.
Schuessler, K. F., Ed.
  1977 *Sociological Methodology 1978*. San Francisco: Jossey–Bass.
Schwab, B., and R. Sitter
  1974 "Economic aspects of computer input–output equipment." In William C. House (ed.), *Data Base Management*. New York: Petrocelli Books.
Shure, G. H., and R. J. Meeker
  1978 "A minicomputer system for multiperson computer-assisted telephone interviewing." *Behavior Research Methods and Instrumentation* 10: 196–202.
Shure, G. H., C. M. Rogers, M. S. Rogers, and L. Seward
  1979 *CATI User Documentation—Version II*. Los Angeles: Center for Computer-Based Behavioral Studies, University of California at Los Angeles.
Slocum, W. L., and R. T. Bowles
  1966 "Educational and occupational aspirations and expectations of high school juniors and seniors in the state of Washington." Final report to the Office of Education, U.S. Department of Health, Education, and Welfare. Project No. ERD-257-65. Pullman, Wash.: Washington State University.
Sonquist, J. A., and W. C. Dunkelberg
  1977 *Survey and Opinion Research*. Englewood Cliffs, N.J.: Prentice–Hall.
Tull, D. S., and G. S. Albaum
  1977 "Bias in random digit dialed surveys." *Public Opinion Quarterly* 41: 389–395.
Waksberg, J.
  1977 "Sampling methods for random digit dialing." *Journal of the American Statistical Association* 73: 40–46.

Chapter 12

Missing Data: A Review of the Literature

Andy B. Anderson, Alexander Basilevsky, and
Derek P. J. Hum

12.1. INTRODUCTION

When statistical models and procedures are used to analyze a random sample, it is usually assumed that no sample data are missing. In practice, however, this is rarely the case for survey data. The literature on missing data deals chiefly with two types of problems. First, we note in passing that samples are at times intentionally designed so that certain prespecified values, rather than sample points, are omitted. These are called censored or truncated samples. For example, let P denote the poverty line in terms of money income per year per family. Then a survey of low-income families might yield a sample truncated to include only those families whose annual income is smaller than or equal to P, those with income greater than P being "censored." Since the probability of deletion of a given observation is dependent on the value of that observation, a random sample is only taken from a restricted subpopulation whose income distribution is generally different from that of the entire population. Samples drawn from truncated distributions often pose special statistical problems and such systematic a priori exclusions are usually motivated by very particular needs or circumstances. For a more complete treatment of censored samples see Nelson and Hahn (1972).

The second type of problem posed by missing data—and the type that will be our main concern—is one in which observations are missing randomly from the sample. Assume that sample data are collected in a case (respondent) by variable (response) matrix $\mathbf{X}$ with rows denoting individuals and columns denoting the variables. It makes little difference whether data are omitted intentionally (usually in a preassigned pattern) or by accident if each sample point

HANDBOOK OF SURVEY RESEARCH

(individual) is drawn independently from all other sample points. This is because in a large random sample a nonrandom pattern of missing data will still contain essentially the same distribution of values as that found in the intact sample. Consequently the cases are formally similar. In what follows it is assumed that *missing data* refers to randomly (and unintentionally) missing data unless otherwise specified. This general class of missing data problems will concern us most. In practice it is frequently the case that nonrandomness of missing data is imposed by some systematic causal factors that depend on the structure of the sample. Although this is common in social surveys (for example when high income groups refuse to report their incomes more frequently than do people with low incomes), we do not propose to treat at length this type of nonrandomly missing data. Very little is known concerning this type of nonrandomness since a priori information is usually required in its treatment. In addition, the literature is not consistent even in the case of randomly missing data. It is therefore more fruitful to provide the reader with an account of the types of problems and their solutions that have been proposed in the literature in the case of the more straightforward random case. We touch on Bayesian methods, however, which require a priori knowledge of the distribution of missing values in a multivariate sample; and, we return briefly to the issue of nonrandomly missing data in the last section.

Data may be said to be missing randomly in a number of ways. There are four principal definitions of *randomly missing data* employed in the literature, which we distinguish for future reference.

1. *Type I:* Let $\mathbf{X} = (x_{ij})$ be a $(n \times r)$ data matrix with n individuals observed over r variables. Then data are said to be missing randomly if the *pattern* of missing elements x_{ij} is distributed randomly within $\mathbf{X}$. For example, data missing entirely from an upper left-hand portion of $\mathbf{X}$ would not be said to be missing randomly in this sense. Nonrandomly missing data of Type I usually result from intentional omissions, in order to economize data collection costs.

2. *Type II:* (Glasser, 1964). Let $\mathbf{W} = (w_{ij})$ be an indicator matrix with elements defined as

$$w_{ij} = \begin{cases} 1 & \text{if } x_{ij} \text{ observed} \\ 0 & \text{if } x_{ij} \text{ missing,} \end{cases}$$

and let the expectation $E(w_{ij}) = \Pi_j$ for $i = 1, 2, \ldots, n$, where Π_j refers to the probability of data being observed for the jth variable. Then data are said to be missing randomly if the joint distribution of any set of the w_{ij} is equal to the product of the probabilities of the individual w_{ij}, that is, $E(w_{i1} w_{i2} \cdots w_{ir}) = E(w_{i1})E(w_{i2}) \cdots E(w_{ir})$. Randomness in this sense implies that for a given individual the occurrence of missing elements on a particular variable, irrespective of magnitude, is not associated with the occurrence of missing data on other variables.

3. *Type III:* Let $\mathbf{X} = (y_1, y_2, \ldots, y_n)^{\mathrm{T}}$ be a $(n \times 1)$ random data vector. Then the values $y_1, y_2, \ldots, y_m$ $(m < n)$ are said to be missing randomly if the

population distribution of the missing data $y_1, y_2, \ldots, y_m$ is identical to the population distribution of the entire vector $\mathbf{Y}$. In this case, randomness refers to the *magnitudes* of the missing values, and when satisfied ensures that no particular range of magnitudes is missing disproportionately.

4. *Type IV:* Let $\mathbf{Y}$ and $\mathbf{X}$ be any two vectors. Then data are said to be missing randomly for $\mathbf{Y}$ and/or $\mathbf{X}$ if and only if the missing $\mathbf{X}$ values (say) are not systematically related to the missing $\mathbf{Y}$ values. This type of randomness is of particular importance in regression analysis where one (or more) of the data vectors are treated as observations on independent variables since it ensures that regression coefficients and the coefficient of multiple determination are not biased (or inconsistent).

The four types of randomness are logically independent of each other in the sense that the presence (or absence) of any one type of randomness need not necessarily imply the presence (or absence) of another type. We will refer to these types in the remainder of the chapter except where context makes it obvious which type is being assumed.

Data may be missing randomly in one or more of the preceding senses for a variety of reasons, the most common being sample frame omissions, errors in the execution of a sample, interviewer errors (skip logic errors in the survey instrument, omitted questions, illegible recording of the response, etc.), instruments (or parts of instruments) being lost, refusal of individuals to answer particular questions or to be interviewed, respondents never found, incapacitated respondents, and attrition in the case of a panel-design sample. Also, we may at times wish to delete logically impossible (or implausible) values rather than keep them in the sample. A panel design is particularly important in the social sciences that deal with nonstationary or evolutionary time processes as well as cross-sectional static differentiations. In such a design, where cross-sections are usually observed over a period of time, subjects may decide to drop out for various reasons during the course of the surveys. Thus all succeeding interviews will be lost and the subject is said to have attrited from the sample. One important example of attrition is geographic mobility—people move, and it becomes costly to find and keep them within the survey panel over long distances.

Although attrition is always a major concern in causing data to be missing, occasionally the missing data can be estimated or reconstructed due to redundancies in the data set itself; for example, unavailable income may be reconstructed or estimated from a knowledge of the wage rate and total number of hours worked. The principle that prevention is the most effective cure certainly holds for missing data problems, and according to an old maxim attributed to Snedecor, the only true solution to the missing data problem is to not have any. The important considerations here involve rigorous quality control procedures, editing, coding, keypunching, and careful handling of the data. Attention also should be paid to methods for increasing participation rates, such as effective advertising, good credentials for interviewers, guarantees of anonymity for the respondent, motivating and interesting introductions, well-designed question-naires, payment for participation, and adequate call-back procedures including following up refusals. Thus care (and money) invested in prophylactic activities will be by far the most effective way to deal with the missing data problem. Other methods that may be effective in minimizing missing data include reduc-tion of the length of a questionnaire and the intentional omission of certain questions for a randomly predetermined part of the sample, for example, the matrix sampling methods (Shoemaker, 1973).

Despite all efforts, however, data will usually be missing. Two broad strat-egies often adopted when data are randomly missing (Types II, III, and IV) are (a) deletion; and (b) estimation. The deletion strategy usually involves deleting those individual cases that have missing data and then calculating estimates from the complete sample. When data are missing randomly the estimates resulting from the deletion strategy are generally unbiased (but may have to be adjusted by correction terms) but less efficient than when no data are missing. An equivalent procedure is that by Yates (1933), Tocher (1952), and others, by which so-called neutral values are substituted for missing data. A linear model (analysis of variance, regression analysis) is fitted to available data such that the missing values are estimated ("predicted") by the linear hyperplane.

The second broad strategy first estimates the missing observations in some way, and then proceeds with the statistical analysis of the data set as if it had been complete. This is usually done in one of two ways, by (a) comparing individuals; or (b) comparing variables. When partial information is available concerning an individual who failed to respond to a particular question (i.e., no rows of matrix X are entirely missing) it is frequently possible to estimate the missing responses by comparing that individual with others in the sample who most resemble the person. Alternatively, we may assume that a missing obser-vation for some individual on a given variable is best estimated by the mean (expected value) for the nonmissing observations for that variable, or by infor-mation available from other variables. Note that in a random sample the indi-viduals represent independent sample points, so that it makes no sense to estimate missing values by correlating rows of the data matrix X. In this case missing data are estimated by first grouping (clustering) individuals and then assigning group-specific means to the missing data. The most common proce-dure for estimating randomly missing values in socioeconomic data, however, is by a regression, principal components, or factor analysis performed on the variables. Since each of the models requires different assumptions the missing value estimates will generally differ, and the methodology by which missing data are estimated is therefore of some importance. For example, most regres-sion analysis models assume that the independent variables are error free, and if such a regression model is used an estimate of a missing observation will be biased and inconsistent. Thus if the explanatory variables contain substantial error, it may prove pointless to estimate the missing values.

So far we have only mentioned the situation in which data are missing unintentionally from the sample. However some surveys may, for reasons of efficiency, intentionally omit data from a sample in a predetermined pattern (Type I randomness). If the individuals are sampled at random as shown in Table 12.1 the eight intentionally missing observations can still be regarded as missing randomly according to Types II, III, and IV, since the probability that a given observation is absent is not dependent on the value of that observation— both low as well as high values are equally likely to have been omitted. We shall consider, therefore, both unplanned as well as planned data omissions provided randomness is not disturbed.

The problem of missing data presents itself most generally when, following a sample survey or an experiment, the responses are to be structured into a coherent data base to serve the user at large. At times, when redundancies exist among the variables, it is possible to construct intervals (or exact values) within which the missing observations must lie, and missing data can then be imputed within the general data cleaning and editing process before it is entered into the data base. This may be desirable if the tentative nature of such estimates is made explicit or if special advantages exist at the editing step (e.g., interviewer recall). As a general rule, however, it is probably best to denote missing observations by blanks or special codes and permit the specialized user to supply his or her own estimates in the context of the particular statistical model being used.

The procedures for dealing with missing data vary depending in part on the type of statistical model being used to analyze data. We consider the following types of models with emphasis on the first three.

1. Estimation of parameters in experimental design models (ANOVA and MANOVA), where missing data result in empty cells and unequal cell frequencies
2. Estimation of parameters of the multivariate normal distribution when data are missing both intentionally and unintentionally
3. Least-squares regression procedures (for the normal distribution or otherwise) for estimating regression parameters, the missing observations, and other statistics associated with least-squares regression (intentional and unintentional data omissions)

TABLE 12.1

x_1	x_2	x_3
x_{11}	x_{12}	—
x_{21}	x_{22}	—
x_{31}	x_{32}	—
x_{41}	x_{42}	—
x_{51}	—	x_{53}
x_{61}	—	x_{63}
x_{71}	—	x_{73}
x_{81}	—	x_{83}

4. Missing data problems in factor analysis, principal components analysis, and discriminant analysis
5. Missing data problems in contingency table analysis

12.2. THE ANALYSIS OF EXPERIMENTAL DESIGN MODELS USING INCOMPLETE DATA

The first statistical model that we consider is the linear least-squares model used to analyze various experimental designs, both univariate analysis of variance (ANOVA) as well as multivariate (MANOVA) analysis of variance. Data randomly missing on the dependent variable were important in experimental research because missing data wasted information and threatened validity. The classical solutions to missing data in experimental designs later were adapted to the more general regression case, and extended to the case where data were missing on both dependent and independent variables. The solutions considered here, therefore, serve as a useful introductory point for a review of the missing data problem. We consider them in detail even though true experimental designs are not common in survey research.

Problems Resulting from Disproportionality

Missing data commonly produce disproportionalities in the cells of experimental designs. Classical analysis of variance techniques are greatly facilitated when cells contain equal numbers of subjects. When the cells not only are unequal but disproportional as well, substantial adjustment is required. Technically, an orthogonal experimental design is made nonorthogonal by disproportional cell frequencies, the addition theorem for sums of squares does not hold, and the sum of squares of partitioned components ordinarily will not be equal to the total sum of squares. Because covariances between independent variables do not vanish as in orthogonal designs, it is possible to find in a two-way factorial design, for example, that the sum of squares between cells actually is less than the total of its constituent row and column sums of squares.

Tests of significance and parameter estimates generally are biased when standard ANOVA computations are done on data made nonorthogonal by disproportionality. To avoid the entanglement, laborious computational adjustments may be required. In fact, before electronic digital computers and the more sophisticated desk calculators were widely available, it was commonly recommended that experimenters assign an excess of subjects to cells so that if attrition produced disproportionality, cases could be randomly discarded in order to put the design back in balance. Analytically and economically, discarding continues to be the simplest solution for some types of research. But in social research, the shortcoming is obvious: Data are wasted. In an income maintenance experiment, for example, a subject may represent an investment of thousands of dollars and data at that price are not lightly discarded. We

review, in turn, four alternative computational techniques to adjust for disproportionality: (*a*) the unweighted means method; (*b*) the expected frequencies
method; (*c*) the weighted means approach; and (*d*) least-squares or regression
approaches.

THE UNWEIGHTED MEANS METHOD

The *method of unweighted means* is one of the most commonly encountered solutions to the disproportionality problem in analysis of variance designs.[1] The technique, originally suggested by Yates (1933), is one of the more
easily used procedures and has become a standard item in major textbooks on
statistical analysis and experimental design (Cochran & Cox, 1957; Scheffe,
1959; Schuessler, 1971; Searle, 1971a, Winer, 1971). In a two-way factorial
analysis of variance, approximate estimates are produced for main effects with
the approximation becoming poorer as cell frequencies become increasingly
disproportional. The sum of squares within groups is found as usual, but each
cell is treated as a single entry having a value equal to the cell mean. An
analysis of variance is done as though the design were a two-way ANOVA with
one case per cell, with the exception that the sums of squares due to main
effects and interaction must be weighted by the harmonic mean of the cell
frequencies.[2] The mean squares produced by the unweighted means procedure
tend not to be distributed as a chi-squared distribution and the F ratios also
become affected by the degeneracy. A correction factor for the numerator's
degrees of freedom apparently encourages better behavior, and Gosslee and
Lucas (1965) conclude that the adjusted test statistics are acceptable. Searle
(1971a, p. 367), however, adds the additional caution that the ratio for any two
cells of $1/\sqrt{n_{ij}}$ to $1/\sqrt{n_{ij}}$, where the n_{ij} are the two respective cell sizes, should
be close to 1.0. In the analysis, cell means are treated as though they were
measurements having uniform sampling error, the sampling errors being approximately equal. The sampling error of a cell mean is proportional to $1/\sqrt{n_{ij}}$,
and therefore the two values of $1/\sqrt{n_{ij}}$ should be approximately equal. Searle
suggests that a ratio of $2:1$ is tolerable but that a ratio of $4:1$ should not be
accepted. If any cells are empty, the method of unweighted means is appropriate.

THE EXPECTED FREQUENCIES METHOD

Snedecor and Cox (1935) developed a technique appropriate whenever cell
disproportionality results from sampling a disproportional population. For in-

---

[1] For a concise review of the disproportionality problem and an applied comparison of some of
the techniques mentioned in this section, see J. D. Williams (1972). Earlier comprehensive reviews
are given in Snedecor and Cox (1935) and Tsao (1946). Bancroft (1968) places heavy emphasis on
techniques appropriate for unequal and disproportionate data. Finally, Searle's *Linear Models*
(1971a) presents a thorough treatment of linear statistical models applied to unbalanced or disproportionate data.

[2] Some references do not adjust main effects and interactions, choosing instead to correct the
error sum of squares by multiplying it by the reciprocal of the harmonic mean of the cell frequencies, which is an algebraically equivalent adjustment (Walker & Lev, 1953; J. D. Williams, 1972).

stance, a random sample of a population measured and then grouped on race and income would not be expected to fall into cells proportionally. Nonetheless, an *expected frequency* can be generated for each cell using marginal totals in exactly the same manner that one obtains expected frequencies in a contingency table chi-squared test of independence. These frequencies are proportional. Using the elementary identity $\Sigma X = n\bar{X}$ the cell means are multiplied by the appropriate expected frequencies to produce adjusted cell sums that are entered into the standard ANOVA formulas for proportional data. This method of expected cell frequencies is a comparatively undemanding route to an approximate solution (Myers, 1966). Again, no empty cells are permitted.

THE WEIGHTED MEANS APPROACH

The *weighted means approach,* also due to Yates (1934), offers a third approximation which is appropriate if all cells contain at least one case. The logic of the weighted means adjustment is more easily discussed if prefaced by Schuessler's (1971) observation that when frequencies are disproportional, marginal means may vary because of row effects, column effects, and row–column interaction effects (p. 159). To correct the condition, unweighted row means are found, for example, and a weighted mean of these unweighted row means can be constructed. Variation of the unweighted row means around that weighted mean will then reflect either row effect or error variation. A sum of the weighted squared deviations of the unweighted means about the weighted mean permits construction of an unbiased estimate of the population variance, σ^2, under the assumption of a true null hypothesis of no row effects. An independent error term is available for the denominator of a test statistic. The sum of squares for the interaction term is the straightforward sum $\Sigma\Sigma(\bar{X}_{ij} - \bar{X}_{i.} - \bar{X}_{.j} + \bar{X}_{..})^2$, where the $\bar{X}_{i.}$, $\bar{X}_{.j}$, and $\bar{X}_{..}$ are accordingly the unweighted row, column, and grand means, and $\bar{X}_{ij}$ is the cell mean. According to some sources, only two factors are permitted, one of which must have only two levels (Steinhorst & Miller, 1969; J. D. Williams, 1972), but disagreement attends the restriction. Both Bancroft (1968) and Schuessler (1971) discuss applications beyond two-way tables. Both authors state that the technique can be particularly helpful when interaction effects are present, and furthermore the method of fitting constants, discussed in the following, can be used in conjunction with weighted means analysis to find main effects by fitting constants and interactions by weighted means. An additional advantage of the weighted means procedure can be seen in the distributional behavior of the mean squares; specifically, the mean squares are chi-square distributed and can be used to construct F ratios for hypothesis testing. Some sources refer to the technique as the method of weighted squares of means (Anderson & Bancroft, 1952; Schuessler, 1971).

THE REGRESSION APPROACH, WITH A DIGRESSION

Data analysis based on the least-squares or *regression approach* represents a generally applicable technical solution to the disproportionality problem. The computational complexity of the regression approach had made it impractical previously and approximate solutions had to be used. However, the necessary computer programs are now widely available. Actually, there is not one but several least-squares techniques. The most straightforward manner of presenting the analytic logic of the various methods requires a slight digression in the form of a series of comparisons between alternative forms of a simple linear model. For comparative purposes, we recall that the fixed effects version of a two-way factorial ANOVA design expresses an individual Y_{ijk} value on the dependent variable as the sum $Y_{ijk} = \mu + \alpha_i + \beta_j + \alpha\beta_{ij} + \varepsilon_{ijk}$ where standard notation holds: μ is the grand mean; α_i and β_j represent, respectively, the unique parametric contributions of the ith row and jth column, or simply the main effects due to the two independent variables; $\alpha\beta_{ij}$ is the two-way interaction; and ε_{ijk} is the residual error. The usual constraints hold: ε_{ijk} is $N(0, \sigma_\varepsilon)$, and $\Sigma_i\alpha_i = \Sigma_j\beta_j = \Sigma_j(\alpha\beta)_{ij} = \Sigma_i(\alpha\beta)_{ij} = 0$. Disproportional data typically will prevent the last assumption from being met, but the problem may be recast as a series of regression models.

Assuming for purposes of illustration two levels of A and three of B, then the A effect is examined in the context of conventional dummy variable regression. Letting U be the unit vector, b_0 the intercept, X_1 the row dummy variable, b_1 the regression coefficient of Y on X_1, and ε the residual error in fitting the model, the following form obtains: $Y = b_0U + b_1X_1 + \varepsilon$. Following Williams, the model will be labeled Model I (J. D. Williams, 1972, p. 74). Williams's Model II states the conventional dummy variable form for the B effect, requiring two dummy variables because of the three levels of B. $Y = b_4U + b_2X_2 + b_3X_3 + \varepsilon$. Putting the combined main effects of A and B into Model III, the model becomes $Y = b_5U + b_6X_1 + b_7X_2 + b_8X_3 + \varepsilon$. Model IV adds the interactions in dummy variable form to produce $Y = b_9U + b_{10}X_1 + b_{11}X_2 + b_{12}X_3 + b_{13}X_4 + b_{14}X_5 + \varepsilon$, the dummy variable equivalent of the two-way factorial model previously expressed in traditional form. Fitting each of the models to a single data set will produce various pieces of information, including the following: the sums of squares attributable to the different models; the sum of squares due to deviation from prediction; the total sum of squares (SS_T); and the R^2 for each model.

The multiple coefficient of determination R^2 has the conventional but highly useful property of being interpretable as the proportion of the variance in Y accounted for by a particular model. The proportion of the variation in Y, due to regression on A and B combined (but with no interaction term), can be expressed as $R^2[\alpha_i, \beta_j]$; $R^2[\alpha_i]$ is the proportion of Y's variation accounted for by the regression of Y on A alone, and so on. The rationales of the various least-squares techniques are easily and intuitively reflected using the R^2 components in the framework of an ANOVA summary table. The method of fitting constants, the first of the least-squares procedures to be discussed, provides a case in point. The technique uses a least-squares criterion to fit alternative forms of the general linear model, proceeding by adjusting one main effect for the other main effect, adjusting the second for the first, then adjusting interaction for the two main effects (Graybill, 1961; Schuessler, 1971; Williams, 1972). Therefore the sums of squares reflect only that portion of an effect independent of the other effects.

In terms of an ANOVA summary table,[3] the method of fitting constants has the following sources of variation:

Source of variation	df	SS
A	$a - 1$	$SS_T[R^2(\alpha_i, \beta_j) - R^2(\beta_j)]$
B	$b - 1$	$SS_T[R^2(\alpha_i, \beta_j) - R^2(\alpha_j)]$
AB	$(a - 1)(b - 1)$	$SS_T[R^2(\alpha_i, \beta_j, \alpha\beta_{ij}) - R^2(\alpha_i, \beta_j)]$
Error	$N - ab$	$SS_T[1 - R^2(\alpha_i, \beta_j, \alpha\beta_{ij})]$
Total	$N - 1$	SS_T

The component sums of squares demonstrate how the A effect, for example, reflects the sum of squares due to A, eliminating the effects of B. Model III is used to get a regression on A and B combined, then this effect is adjusted by subtracting R^2 due to regression on B as given in Model II. The result is to produce an A effect that is independent of the B effect, and the same adjustment procedure is used to get the B effect. Effectively, the fitted constants procedure obtains estimates of main effects through an additive model, using interaction terms to account for deviations from additivity. An ordering of main effects and interactions is implied in that each effect is adjusted only for effects at an equal or lower level but not for higher order effects. The method of fitting constants is formally equivalent to dummy variable regression and corresponds to the second model of Overall and Spiegel (1969) that they call the experimental design method.

A second variation of the regression approach, the unadjusted main effects method, finds main effects directly, but the interaction term is found as in the case of fitted constants. The following summary table demonstrates specifically the way main effects are tapped directly.

Source	df	SS
A	$a - 1$	$SS_T[R^2(\alpha_i)]$
B	$b - 1$	$SS_T[R^2(\beta_j)]$
AB	$(a - 1)(b - 1)$	$SS_T[R^2(\alpha_i, \beta_j, \alpha\beta_{ij}) - R^2(\alpha_i, \beta_j)]$
Error	$N - ab$	$SS_T[1 - R^2(\alpha_i, \beta_j, \alpha\beta_{ij})]$
Total	$N - 1$	SS_T

The main effects represent the separate regressions of $\mathbf{Y}$ on A and of $\mathbf{Y}$ on B, each independent variable being allowed to "claim" the sum of squares due to regression from Models I and II, respectively. The two effects no longer are

[3] The arithmetic simply involves multiplying the total sum of squares (SS_T) in $\mathbf{Y}$ times the relevant R^2. Since R^2 can be expressed as $R^2 = (1 - [SS_E/SS_T]) = SS_R/SS_T$, where SS_E is the error sum of squares, and SS_R is the sum of squares due to regression, then it follows that by multiplying both sides by SS_T we get $SS_T(R^2) = SS_R$, and it is these separate components that go into the summary table.

unentangled as was the case in the previous model where the contribution was of the form $SS_T[R^2(\alpha_i, \beta_j) - R^2(\beta_j)]$, a decomposition that corrected each main effect for the other. Of three major least squares methods, the unadjusted main effects model resembles most closely the usual ANOVA calculations and hypothesis testing (J. D. Williams, 1972). The unadjusted main effects method is formally equivalent to the model used in a procedure proposed by Jennings, 1967.

Finally, a hierarchical model developed by Cohen (1968) adjusts each effect only for those effects that are put above it in order of scientific or policy importance to the researcher. Of the three, only the hierarchical analysis will yield partitioned sums of squares that sum to the total sum of squares. This summary table clarifies the adjustment sequence:

Source	df	SS
A	$a - 1$	$SS_T[R^2(\alpha_i)]$
B	$b - 1$	$SS_T[R^2(\alpha_i, \beta_j) - R^2(\alpha_i)]$
AB	$(a - 1)(b - 1)$	$SS_T[R^2(\alpha_i, \beta_j, \alpha\beta_{ij}) - R^2(\alpha_i, \beta_j)]$
Error	$N - ab$	$SS_T[1 - R^2(\alpha_i, \beta_j, \alpha\beta_{ij})]$
Total	$N - 1$	SS_1

Clearly, the magnitude of the effects may be altered by changing the order of importance, but that may be a small price to pay for a decrease in the probability that significant effects will mutually cancel out. Cohen discusses a variety of applications that capitalize on the hierarchical models' unique features (Cohen, 1968). The hierarchical analysis is equivalent to the two-way linear model analyses presented by Searle (1971, p. 286). Searle's presentation consistently maintains intuitive appeal, but goes beyond discursive generalization to demonstrate the mathematical principles (and matrix manipulations) that permit solution to the normal equations in the face of highly disproportional data that may well include empty cells.

Overall and Spiegel (1969) have reported on an additional procedure, their Method I, or *complete linear model analysis,* which Williams only mentions in his closing paragraph. Every effect in the model now undergoes adjustment for the other terms, as shown in this summary table:[4]

Source	df	SS
A	$a - 1$	$SS_T[R^2(\alpha_i, \beta_j, \alpha\beta_{ij}) - R^2(\beta_j, \alpha\beta_{ij})]$
B	$b - 1$	$SS_T[R^2(\alpha_i, \beta_j, \alpha\beta_{ij}) - R^2(\alpha_i, \alpha\beta_{ij})]$
AB	$(a - 1)(b - 1)$	$SS_T[R^2(\alpha_i, \beta_j, \alpha\beta_{ij}) - R^2(\alpha_i, \beta_j)]$
Error	$N - ab$	$SS_T[1 - R^2(\alpha_i, \beta_j, \alpha\beta_{ij})]$
Total	$N - 1$	SS_T

[4] The formula for the error term appears in the Overall and Spiegel article as "$SS_T[R(1 - R(\ _i, \ _j, \ _{ij})]$," which is presumed to be a typographical error and is corrected as shown above.

The approach was presented as a single consistent model incorporating main effects and interactions and having useful similarity to general linear model analysis. However, the adjustment of a main effect for an interaction effect was assessed by the authors as being informative and useful only in particular circumstances, for instance, in a search for pervasive main effects that cannot be accounted for entirely by more specific cell (interaction) effects (Overall & Spiegel, 1969, p. 319). Reportedly, the model is particularly bothered by collinearities among the classification variables. Discussions of the various features that might make one technique more appropriate than others for specific problems are given by J. D. Williams (1972) and Overall and Spiegel (1969). For a discussion of techniques for estimating variance components in mixed or random designs with disproportional data, see Henderson (1953) and Searle (1971a). Disproportionality, for all practical purposes, ceases to be a major problem with the advent of the computer implemented least-squares models. Attrition and missing data, nevertheless, create mischief of other sorts.

Data Loss

As previously noted, attrition of respondents from a survey based on an experimental design will result in data loss, by definition. Beyond that truism, attrition can also cause additional data waste, particularly in research designs having nonmanipulated variables. Even a standard experimental design may employ one or more "control" covariables that are observed but not manipulated. Designs may also have more than one dependent variable, and the possibility therefore arises of missing one or more variables. Additionally, a subject may drop out of a panel design experiment after the t replication, or a respondent may answer all but one or two questions in a survey. A subject may fail to attend a scheduled experimental session after having filled out a form giving age, sex, and other information. In a social experiment such as the guaranteed annual income experiments, for example, a subject may respond to the initial census but refuse to participate when approached for enrollment into the randomly assigned experimental (treatment) group, or the subject may enroll and participate for some portion but not all of the entire time.

These examples raise the question of what to do with cases having partial data. A substantial amount of background and preexperimental information may be available, and indeed several prior measures on the dependent variables may have already been completed. These data cannot be discarded since complete data loss is unacceptable from both a scientific and monetary point of view. The partial data may be of intrinsic value in determining bias, threats to internal validity, sample representativeness, and the like.

THE YATES PROCEDURE

The first published treatments of the problem of missing data (Allen & Wishart, 1930; Bartlett, 1937; Tocher, 1952; Yates, 1933, 1934, 1936a, 1936b;

Yates & Cochran, 1938; Yates & Hale, 1939) appear in the context of the experimental design (ANOVA) linear regression model

$$\mathbf{Y} = \mathbf{X}\boldsymbol{\beta} + \boldsymbol{\varepsilon} \tag{12.1}$$

where $\mathbf{Y}$ is an $(n \times 1)$ column vector of measurements (observations) produced by n experimental units, $\mathbf{X}$ is a $(n \times r)$ matrix of $r < n$ treatments and interactions (the design matrix), $\boldsymbol{\beta}$ is the $(r \times 1)$ vector of coefficients (effects) to be estimated, and $\boldsymbol{\varepsilon}$ is the random error vector. The linear hypothesis (12.1) is usually estimated by ordinary least squares (OLS) with the following assumptions: (a) the elements of $\boldsymbol{\varepsilon}$ are uncorrelated, with zero mean and constant variance σ^2, and usually assumed to be normally distributed; (b) $\mathbf{X}$, which denotes random and/or nonrandom effects, contains no error components, so that $E(y) = \mathbf{X}\boldsymbol{\beta}$. It is well-known that the OLS estimator of $\boldsymbol{\beta}$ is given by

$$\hat{\boldsymbol{\beta}} = (\mathbf{X}^T\mathbf{X})^{-1}\mathbf{X}^T\mathbf{Y} \tag{12.2}$$

which is unbiased and possesses least variance.[5] Under the normality assumption of $\boldsymbol{\varepsilon}$ (or $\mathbf{Y}$), $\hat{\boldsymbol{\beta}}$ is the maximum likelihood estimator.

When one or more elements of $\mathbf{Y}$ are missing, the experiment becomes unbalanced, and Yates's solution consists of reintroducing plausible fictitious values (the so-called neutral values) in such a way that the balance of the experiment is restored. Allen and Wishart (1930), who first considered the problem, provided formulas appropriate in the case of a single missing observation in a randomized block and in a Latin square design, and Yates (1933) suggested an iterative computational procedure when more than one observation is missing. Yates also presents formulas for the missing values and variances of treatment means with missing values, and in what follows we refer to the Allen–Wishart and Yates solutions as the *Yates method*.

$r = $ the number of treatments;

$t = $ the number of blocks;

$B = $ the total yield of the remaining units in the block where the missing unit appears;

$T = $ the total of the yields of the treatment;

$G = $ the grand total.

Then, for a single missing observation y_i in a randomized block experiment we have

$$\hat{y}_i = \frac{tB + rT - G}{(t - 1)(r - 1)} \tag{12.3}$$

as an estimate of y_i. The difference between the mean of a treatment with a missing yield estimated by Yates's method and one with no missing units has

---

[5] When $\boldsymbol{\varepsilon}$ is not distributed normally, $\hat{\boldsymbol{\beta}}$ need not be the least variance estimator, as for example in the case when $\boldsymbol{\varepsilon}$ is a double exponential (Laplacian) or a Cauchy random variate.

variance

$$\frac{\sigma^2}{r}\left[2 + \frac{r}{(r-1)(t-1)}\right] \tag{12.4}$$

and,

$$\text{var}(\hat{y}_i) = \frac{(r+t-1)\sigma^2}{(r-1)(t-1)} \tag{12.5}$$

(Norton, 1955). For the Latin square design we have

$$\hat{y}_i = \frac{t(r + C + T) - 2G}{(t-1)(t-2)} \tag{12.6}$$

and,

$$\frac{\sigma^2}{r}\left[2 + \frac{t}{(r-1)(r-2)}\right] \tag{12.7}$$

for the variance of the treatment mean (Yates, 1933). The variance of the estimated missing value is given by

$$\text{var}(\hat{y}_i) = \frac{3t - 2}{(t-1)(t-2)}\sigma^2 \tag{12.8}$$

(Nelder, 1954), where

$t =$ the number of rows, columns, and treatment

$R, C =$ the total yields of the remaining unit in the row and column, respectively, in which the missing unit appears.

In practice T^2 is not known and must be replaced by its estimated value $\hat{T}^2$.

Reviews of Yates's method are available in R. L. Anderson (1946), Cochran and Cox (1957), Shearer (1973). For a derivation of (12.3) and (12.6) see Jaech (1966), together with an example of its use in Youden squares designs. The problem of missing y observations however becomes more complex when various other incomplete block designs are considered—see Cornish (1940a, 1940b, 1940c, 1941a, 1941b, 1943, 1944) for an extension of Yates's method to incomplete randomized blocks, quasi-factorial designs (incomplete randomized blocks, lattice squares and square, triple and cubic lattices), as well as to the problem of recovering interblock information in quasi-factorial designs (see also R. L. Anderson, 1946).

The basic idea behind Yates's method is straightforward. Suppose that m of the total n observations on $\mathbf{Y}$ are missing, and assume for convenience that the m missing values of $\mathbf{Y}$ and the corresponding rows of $\mathbf{X}$ are rearranged and partitioned so that model (12.1) can be written as

$$E(\mathbf{Y}) = \begin{bmatrix} Y_{n-m} \\ \cdots \\ Y_m \end{bmatrix} = \begin{bmatrix} X_{n-m} \\ \cdots \\ X_m \end{bmatrix} \beta = \mathbf{X}\beta \qquad (12.9)$$

where $(n - m)$ elements of $\mathbf{Y}$ are observed. Yates's procedure (apparently due to a suggestion from Fisher) is to insert "fictitious" or "neutral" values $\gamma^{\mathrm{T}} = (\gamma_1, \gamma_2, \ldots, \gamma_m)$ in place of the m missing observations, in such a way so as to minimize the residual sum of squares, $\varepsilon^{\mathrm{T}}\varepsilon$. When the missing data have been "filled in," the analysis of variance proceeds in the usual way with the number of missing observations subtracted from the total and residual degrees of freedom. Substituting the symbols $\gamma^{\mathrm{T}} = (\gamma_1, \gamma_2, \ldots, \gamma_m)$ for the m missing values we have

$$E \begin{bmatrix} Y_{n-m} \\ \cdots \\ \gamma \end{bmatrix} = \begin{bmatrix} X_{n-m} \\ \cdots \\ X_m \end{bmatrix} \beta, \qquad (12.10)$$

where the phrase *estimation of missing observations* in this context refers to the estimation of $E(\gamma) = X_m\beta$. From the general theory of vector spaces we know this is possible if and only if the rows of $\mathbf{X}_m$ belong to the same row space as $\mathbf{X}_{n-m}$. Assuming $E(\gamma)$ is estimable, we then select values $\hat{\gamma}^{\mathrm{T}} = (\gamma_1, \gamma_2, \ldots, \gamma_m)$ such that

$$(Y_{n-m} \vdots \gamma)[\mathbf{I}_n - \mathbf{X}(\mathbf{X}^{\mathrm{T}}\mathbf{X})^{-1}\mathbf{X}^{\mathrm{T}}] \begin{bmatrix} Y_{n-m} \\ \cdots \\ \gamma \end{bmatrix} \qquad (12.11)$$

is minimized where $\mathbf{P} = \mathbf{X}(\mathbf{X}^{\mathrm{T}}\mathbf{X})^{-1}\mathbf{X}^{\mathrm{T}}$ and $(\mathbf{I}_n - \mathbf{P})$ are symmetric projection matrices. Expression (12.11) can be minimized using Yates's iterative procedure. Wilkinson (1958a) uses De Lury's (1946) suggestion that Yates's computational method can be simplified by equating each unknown with its estimated value as derived from the formally completed data. Wilkinson's method uses matrices and is easily programmable. Other alternative techniques that have been used in the past are given by Healy and Westmacott (1956). Shearer (1973) provides an algorithm that can be used in certain fractional designs as well as in designs replicated in any manner. For a matrix treatment see also Wilkinson (1960).

The method of "neutral values" has the following properties:

1. Estimates of error variance and treatment means are unbiased but the treatment sum of squares, as calculated from the augmented data, is biased upward. Although this bias can be readily estimated, its magni-

tude is small enough in practice to be ignored (R. L. Anderson, 1946; Yates, 1933).

2. The procedure is equivalent to choosing the missing values in such a way as to make the model fit perfectly at these points; that is, the residuals that correspond to the missing observations are set to zero (Jaech, 1966; Sclove, 1972). It is from this property that the term *neutral values* is derived.

3. In view of (2), the bias correction in (1) must be conditional on the correctness of the model specification (see Nelder, 1954). For example, when interaction terms are ignored, estimates of the missing values are systematically biased.

Yates's method can be viewed as a procedure of "predicting" the m missing values given that model (12.1) holds, which itself is estimated from the $(n - m)$ observed data points. The missing value estimates are then simply the values predicted by model (12.1) such that $\hat{\mathbf{Y}}_m = \hat{\boldsymbol{\gamma}}$. Two opposing interpretations are at times given to such estimates. One, given by Snedecor, Cox, and Williamson (1952, pp. 383–384; 1953, p. 427) is that the values of $\hat{\boldsymbol{\gamma}}$ are not intended as estimates of the missing data, but rather are merely numerical fictions to be inserted into the empty spaces of $\mathbf{Y}$, so that loss of information is reduced. The linear model (12.1) can be estimated and tested, so the argument goes, without the calculation of the missing values, since if the model is appropriate (and if the experiment is properly performed), Yates's procedure leads to unbiased estimates of the treatment means. The opposing view (see Nelder, 1954, p. 400) is that even though the "fictitious" values are perhaps not *explicitly* meant to be estimates, this does not alter the fact that they are *implicitly* estimates of the missing observations. Therefore, unbiasedness must be conditional on the correct specification of the linear model. Although the distinction between a fictitious number and a sample estimate may appear somewhat academic, it is nevertheless of some conceptual importance since Yates's procedure can yield logically impossible values such as negative yields. Our own view of the matter is that Nelder is probably closer to the truth, since in view of property (2), the nonmissing data are first used to estimate the linear model, which is in turn employed to estimate the missing values. The estimated missing values are therefore OLS estimates of the expected values of the missing observations, and therefore must be conditional on the correct specification of (12.1) since otherwise the missing value estimates are biased.

THE TOCHER PROCEDURE

Tocher (1952, pp. 49–50) considers the problem and Yates's solution from a somewhat different point of view, and derives an exact formula for Yates's regression estimator and for adjusting the variances of comparisons affected by the missing values. Tocher's procedure is in fact an analysis of covariance that is first mentioned explicitly by Bartlett (1937, pp. 150–151; see also R. L. Anderson, 1946) for the case where a single observation is missing. Following Kruskal's (1961) noncoordinate methods, Seber (1966, pp. 73–74) gives a covariance analysis derivation of Tocher's result, and Coons (1957) provides a use of covariance analysis and shows the applicability of the covariance model to missing data involving experiments of any design. Our discussion is based on Draper (1961).

Consider the linear model (12.1) with the usual OLS assumptions 1–3 where $\mathbf{Y}$ and $\mathbf{X}$ are partitioned as

$$
\mathbf{Y} = \begin{bmatrix} \mathbf{Y}_1 \\ \cdots \\ \mathbf{Y}_2 \end{bmatrix}, \qquad \mathbf{X} = \begin{bmatrix} \mathbf{X}_1 \\ \cdots \\ \mathbf{X}_2 \end{bmatrix} \tag{12.12}
$$

where m of the $\mathbf{Y}$ values ($\mathbf{Y}_2$) are missing, $(n - m)$ $\mathbf{Y}$ values ($\mathbf{Y}_1$) are present, and $\mathbf{X}$ is partitioned accordingly. Then

$$
E(y) = E \begin{bmatrix} \mathbf{Y}_1 \\ \cdots \\ \mathbf{Y}_2 \end{bmatrix} = \begin{bmatrix} \mathbf{X}_1 \\ \cdots \\ \mathbf{X}_2 \end{bmatrix} \beta \tag{12.13}
$$

as before. The OLS estimator of β is based on only the observed $\mathbf{Y}$ values and corresponding rows of $\mathbf{X}$, so that

$$
\begin{aligned}
b &= (\mathbf{X}_1^\mathsf{T} \mathbf{X}_1)^{-1} \mathbf{X}_1^\mathsf{T} \mathbf{Y}_1 \\
&= (\mathbf{X}^\mathsf{T} \mathbf{X} - \mathbf{X}_2^\mathsf{T} \mathbf{X}_2)^{-1} \mathbf{X}_1^\mathsf{T} \mathbf{Y}_1 \\
&= [\mathbf{X}^\mathsf{T} \mathbf{X} - \mathbf{X}_2^\mathsf{T} \mathbf{X}_2 (\mathbf{X}^\mathsf{T} \mathbf{X})^{-1} (\mathbf{X}^\mathsf{T} \mathbf{X})]^{-1} \mathbf{X}_1^\mathsf{T} \mathbf{Y}_1 \\
&= (\mathbf{X}^\mathsf{T} \mathbf{X})^{-1} [\mathbf{I} - \mathbf{X}_2^\mathsf{T} \mathbf{X}_2 (\mathbf{X}^\mathsf{T} \mathbf{X})^{-1}]^{-1} \mathbf{X}_1^\mathsf{T} \mathbf{Y}_1 .
\end{aligned} \tag{12.14}
$$

Using the identity

$$
(\mathbf{I} + \mathbf{A} \mathbf{B})^{-1} = \mathbf{I} - \mathbf{A} (\mathbf{I} + \mathbf{B} \mathbf{A})^{-1} \mathbf{B} \tag{12.15}
$$

on the term in square brackets of (12.14), where we let $\mathbf{A} = -\mathbf{X}_2^\mathsf{T}$, $\mathbf{B} = \mathbf{X}_2 (\mathbf{X}^\mathsf{T} \mathbf{X})^{-1}$, we have

$$
b = (\mathbf{X}^\mathsf{T} \mathbf{X})^{-1} [\mathbf{I} + \mathbf{X}_2^\mathsf{T} \mathbf{M} \mathbf{X}_2 (\mathbf{X}^\mathsf{T} \mathbf{X})^{-1}] \mathbf{X}_1^\mathsf{T} \mathbf{Y}_1 \tag{12.16}
$$

where

$$
\mathbf{M} = [\mathbf{I} - \mathbf{X}_2 (\mathbf{X}^\mathsf{T} \mathbf{X})^{-1} \mathbf{X}_2^\mathsf{T}]^{-1} . \tag{12.17}
$$

Since observations are only missing for $\mathbf{Y}_2$, b can be readily computed from (12.16). It can be shown that the estimated (predicted) values of the missing observations are given by

$$
\begin{aligned}
\hat{\mathbf{Y}}_2 &= \mathbf{X}_2 b \\
&= \mathbf{M} \mathbf{X}_2 (\mathbf{X}^\mathsf{T} \mathbf{X})^{-1} \mathbf{X}_1^\mathsf{T} \mathbf{Y}_1 \\
&= \mathbf{M} \mathbf{X}_2 b_0
\end{aligned} \tag{12.18}
$$

where

$$b_0 = (\mathbf{X}^T\mathbf{X})^{-1}[\mathbf{X}_1^T \vdots \mathbf{X}_2^T] \begin{bmatrix} \mathbf{Y}_1 \\ \cdots \\ 0 \end{bmatrix}$$

$$= (\mathbf{X}^T\mathbf{X})^{-1}\mathbf{X}_1^T\mathbf{Y}_1 \tag{12.19}$$

is the OLS estimator obtained by inserting zeroes for the m missing observations in $\mathbf{Y}_2$. Replacing the m zeroes by the estimated values $\hat{\mathbf{Y}}_2$ and carrying out the regression calculations again yields

$$(\mathbf{X}^T\mathbf{X})^{-1}\mathbf{X}^T\mathbf{Z} = (\mathbf{X}^T\mathbf{X})^{-1}(\mathbf{X}_1^T\mathbf{Y}_1 + \mathbf{Y}_2^T\hat{\mathbf{Y}}_2)$$

$$= (\mathbf{X}^T\mathbf{X})^{-1}[\mathbf{X}_1^T\mathbf{Y}_1 + \mathbf{X}_2^T\mathbf{M}\mathbf{X}_2(\mathbf{X}^T\mathbf{X})^{-1}\mathbf{X}_1^T\mathbf{Y}_1]$$

$$= (\mathbf{X}^T\mathbf{X})^{-1}[\mathbf{I} + \mathbf{X}_2^T\mathbf{M}\mathbf{X}_2(\mathbf{X}^T\mathbf{X})^{-1}]\mathbf{X}_1^T\mathbf{Y}_1$$

$$= \mathbf{b}. \tag{12.20}$$

where we use (12.18) and (12.16), and

$$\mathbf{Z} = \begin{bmatrix} \mathbf{Y}_1 \\ \cdots \\ \hat{\mathbf{Y}}_2 \end{bmatrix}.$$

Tocher's procedure can be summarized in the following three steps:

1. Let $\mathbf{Y}_2 = 0$ for the missing observations and calculate b_0 as in (12.19). This yields the first stage regression estimate.
2. Calculate $\hat{\mathbf{Y}}_2$ from (12.18), using also the correction factor $\mathbf{M}$ as in (12.17). $\mathbf{M}$ is a $(m \times m)$ matrix, which reduces to a scalar for the case of one missing observation. Note also that although $\mathbf{Y}_2 = 0$, in general $\hat{\mathbf{Y}}_2 \neq 0$.
3. Replace the m zeroes $\mathbf{Y}_2$ by $\hat{\mathbf{Y}}_2$, and using (12.20) compute the final OLS estimator $\mathbf{b}$.

The covariance matrix of $\mathbf{b}$ is given by

$$\hat{\sigma}^2 = (\mathbf{X}_1^T\mathbf{X}_1)^{-1} = (\mathbf{X}^T\mathbf{X})^{-1} + (\mathbf{X}^T\mathbf{X})^{-1}\mathbf{X}_2^T\mathbf{M}\mathbf{X}_2(\mathbf{X}^T\mathbf{X})^{-1} \tag{12.21}$$

where only $n - m - r$ degrees of freedom are used to compute $\hat{\sigma}^2$, the residual variance. In view of (12.19) and (12.20) Tocher's procedure also minimizes the residual sum of squares (for a method that does not, see Draper and Stoneman, 1964). Draper (1961) also shows that the missing values $\mathbf{Y}_2$ are estimated by the covariance analysis method in such a way that the sum of squares is minimized. Tocher's procedure is therefore equivalent to that of Yates but obviates iterative calculations when $m > 1$. It is probably also easier to incorporate into a standard regression digital computer package. Seber (1966, p. 74) shows that the estimator $\mathbf{b}$ is numerically equivalent to the least-squares estimator obtained by using only the reduced data $\mathbf{Y}_1$ and $\mathbf{X}_1$, that is, the "list-wise" deletion estimator.

$$\mathbf{b} = (\mathbf{X}_1^T\mathbf{X}_1)^{-1}\mathbf{X}_1^T\mathbf{Y}_1, \tag{12.22}$$

so there would seem to be little advantage in using Yates's and Tocher's methods as opposed to the more straightforward formula (12.22). For this reason the classical missing value(s) problem in experimental design is more properly referred to as a problem of balance and cell disproportionality rather than that of "estimating" missing values.

OTHER APPROACHES

Many other techniques are equivalent or closely related to the classical "neutral value" approach developed by Yates. Huitson (1966, p. 21) suggests an equivalent method (unless 20% or more of the data are missing) that also minimizes the error sum of squares; missing observations do not contribute to degrees of freedom. Other variations are common. One or more relevant concomitant variables can be introduced, thus breaking the design into subgroups. Missing data are then estimated by the means of the subgroups, although empty cells may be encountered. Whenever cells are empty, estimation of cell means must be based on data in other cells. None of the available methods are completely satisfactory unless the form of the response surface is known, a condition rarely met. Winer (1962, p. 281) presents a simple procedure that is useful if it can be assumed that no interaction is present. Bennet and Franklin (1954, pp. 382–384) present an estimation procedure that minimizes interaction effects. Federer (1955, pp. 124–134) also reviews several additional compromise techniques. An approach used by Kelly, Boggs, and McNeil (1969, p. 250) assigns the missing datum that value of a score that is selected randomly from the appropriate experimental group, which is seen to be preferable to Huitson's method because it does not result in the artificial reduction of within-group variance. The technique is comparatively common in practice, as is a related method which assigns scores by the formula $x = \bar{X} + \varepsilon$, where $\bar{X}$ is the group mean and ε is a random normal $N(0, \sigma^2)$ variate.

Estimation techniques can become more detailed or complicated in a variety of ways. Simply by increasing the number of variables used in composing the groups a more precise estimate may be obtained. However, empty cells quickly appear. Assorted alternative precision matching techniques have been employed that attempt to match missing data cases to complete data cases, assigning the missing datum the value of the case matching it most closely on a set of specified variables. Here, the nonmatched case is analogous to the empty cell problem. Bisco (1970, p. 174) suggests that cases be matched as best they can, replacing missing data with the corresponding value for the case matching on the largest number of nonmissing independent variables. Many of these procedures discussed are based on one fashion or another on the assumption that cases similar on the independent and concomitant variables will be similar on the dependent variable. That logic carried to conclusion suggests a variety of more sophisticated estimation models, some of which are to be examined in the next sections.

A more general model than (12.1) has been considered by Box, Draper, and Hunter (1970), McDonald (1971a,b), and Box (1971)—multivariate analysis of variance (MANOVA) where more than one dependent variables are considered. The $(n \times 1)$ vector $\mathbf{Y}$ is now a $(n \times k)$ data matrix of measurements on n experimental units, where k responses (characters) are under study. The linear model now becomes $E(\mathbf{Y}) = \mathbf{X}\boldsymbol{\beta}$ where $\boldsymbol{\beta}$ is a $(r \times k)$ matrix of coefficients. When testing hypotheses or obtaining confidence intervals it is also assumed that the rows of $\mathbf{Y}$ (the experimental units) are sampled from a k-variate normal distribution with a $(k \times k)$ covariance matrix $\boldsymbol{\Sigma}$. As in the single response (ANOVA) experiments, the original structure of the experiment is lost when response data are missing. Two situations can occur—complete rows of $\mathbf{Y}$ may be missing, or else missing values can be scattered throughout the matrix. Where one or more of the nk elements of $\mathbf{Y}$ are missing in an arbitrary pattern, the design will in all likelihood be the general incomplete multiresponse model, considered by Strivastava (1966). In many of such experiments however an appropriate analysis is not known, either for testing the linear hypothesis or for the estimation of linear combinations of the coefficients β. An additional problem is that Wilks's (1932) likelihood ratio criterion for testing hypotheses on all the multiple responses simultaneously cannot be applied—Rao (1956), however, provides a modified version of the likelihood ratio test when observations are missing on one response only.

Hartley and Rao (1968) and Hartley and Hocking (1971) have also considered a variant of the missing observation problem, the analysis of variance with missing classifications. Here model (12.1) still holds, but in addition to the n-vector $\mathbf{Y}$ of responses from completely classified units we have a set of m responses y_j^* $(j = 1, 2, \ldots, m)$ recorded for incompletely classified units in the sense that each of the m additional rows of the design matrix may be any of k alternatives $\mathbf{X}_i^T$ $(i = 1, 2, \ldots, k)$. This means that $E(y_j^*)$ may be one of k alternatives $\mathbf{X}_i^T \boldsymbol{\beta}$. Hartley and Rao (1968) derive a combined likelihood equation to solve the combined estimation–classification problem, the maximization of which requires nonlinear integer programming.

From the preceding discussions, it may be seen that the missing data problem does not assume its full dimensions in the case of experimental design models, since the main problems here are associated with the balance of the experiment and disproportionalities of cells. For these reasons the analysis of variance models form a special case of more general problems encountered in multivariate analysis when data are missing.

12.3. MISSING DATA IN SURVEY SAMPLES

Although data from experimental designs form a useful starting point, for historical and logical reasons, a more common situation involves nonexperimental multidimensional sample surveys. As previously noted, despite all careful effort of quality control, missing data will occur because of field procedure errors, illegible responses, skipped questions, lost documents, refusals to answer, and the like. The general problem under these circumstances is the estimation of mean vectors and covariance (correlation) matrices (or their functions), using multidimensional samples with missing data. Two cases can be distinguished: the case of fixed variables and the case of multivariate random variates. In the case of fixed variables, missing data points are usually approximated by curve-fitting (least-squares) techniques, and the relevant parameters can then be calculated from the completed data (Buck, 1960; Dear, 1959; Walsh, 1961), with corrections applied when needed. The second case of random variables involves procedures that require distributional assumptions (multivariate normality) to obtain maximum-likelihood (ML) estimates, either in exact analytical (*closed*) form or as limit points of numerical (*open form*) iterative processes (T. W. Anderson, 1957; Beale & Little, 1975; Dempster, Laird, & Rubin, 1977; Edgett, 1956; Lord, 1955a; Martley & Hocking, 1971; Matthai, 1951; Morrison, 1971, 1973; Orchard & Woodbury, 1972; Wilks, 1932). The two cases are not mutually exclusive and techniques employed in the one frequently resemble those in the other. The guiding principle here is that parameter estimates that include sample points for which data are missing randomly (Type III and Type IV) for some variables are generally more precise than estimates based on the sample where individuals with missing data are deleted completely. Since data are assumed to be missing randomly, the question of bias does not usually arise.

Since the focus of this section is upon the issue of estimating mean vectors and covariance matrices, the problem of estimating OLS regression curves and other multivariate models with incomplete data is deferred. However, since regression analysis as well as other multivariate methods (both random and nonrandom variables) can themselves be used to estimate parameters and missing values, these procedures also are considered here, because their main purpose is to estimate missing values rather than regression parameters. At the same time, a discussion of some of the more naive and traditional methods for estimating missing data, such as replacing missing values with zero values or the means of the relevant variables, is postponed until the next section when we consider regression analysis. However, it is clear that due to the unavoidable overlap between the two topics, the methods of regression analysis considered in the next section are also relevant for the maximum-likelihood procedures discussed in the following, and vice versa.

Techniques for computing parameter estimates and missing data points have been developed for two situations—when data are missing in specific patterns, and when data are missing in random patterns. For a general ML algorithm which is applicable to many situations see Dempster *et al.* (1977). We continue to assume, as before, that the missing values are random.

Data Missing in Specific Patterns (Type I Nonrandomness)

The first published treatment concerning the estimation of parameters (moments) and their sampling properties when data are missing is by Wilks (1932), who considered the bivariate normal distribution. The data are missing in a pattern such that m observations are available for x, n observations for y, and s observations are available for both. For instance, Table 12.2A illustrates a situation for a sample size of $N = 10$, where we have $m = 4$, $n = 3$, and $s = 3$. Note that even though data are missing in a nonrandom pattern, Type III and Type IV randomness is assumed to hold. Wilks provides maximum likelihood (ML) estimates of the population means μ_x, μ_y, the standard deviations σ_x and σ_y, and the correlation coefficient ρ for the following three cases.

1. Estimation of μ_x and μ_y, for given estimates of σ_x, σ_y, and ρ
2. Estimation of σ_x and σ_y, for given estimates of μ_x, μ_y, and ρ
3. Estimation of σ_x, σ_y, and ρ for given values of μ_x and μ_y

The expressions prove to be rather complex and Wilks additionally considers more simple estimators and their sampling properties. He shows that his estimates for μ_x, μ_y, σ_x, σ_y, and ρ are more efficient than the alternate "naive" estimates: the sample mean $\bar{x}$ based on $m + s$ values for μ_x, $\bar{y}$ based on $n + s$ values for μ_y, and so on. Thus when two variables have a sample correlation $\hat{\rho}$, information on one variable can be used to improve estimates of the mean and standard deviation of the other. Matthai (1951) compares the relative efficiencies of Wilks's estimators to that of the naive estimators that do not use $\hat{\rho}$. As expected, the relative efficiency of the Wilks estimators increase as $\hat{\rho}$ increases, that is, as more extraneous information is brought to bear on the sample moments of a normal variate. The procedure is not entirely free of difficulties, however, since with missing data $\hat{\rho}$ may prove to be unreliable and inconsistent in the sense that it exceeds unity. Matthai (1951) attempts to extend Wilks's methodology by considering the ML estimation procedure with more than two variables, but obtains explicit solutions only for the trivariate case. An inherent difficulty of the ML approach to estimating parameters from incomplete normal data—and one that the Wilks–Matthai approach does not resolve—is that it is not possible generally to obtain analytically explicit (closed form) solutions to the ML equations unless data are missing in certain specific patterns—patterns that Hartley and Hocking (1971) refer to as "nested" and Bhargava (1962) terms "monotonic." In general the ML equations must be solved by numerical iterative techniques (see Beale & Little, 1975; Dempster et al., 1977; Hartley & Hocking, 1971). Monotonic patterns, which frequently occur in panel type survey data, form a triangular array of

TABLE 12.2A

| x | x_1 | x_2 | — | x_4 | — | x_6 | x_7 | x_8 | x_9 | x_{10} |
| y | — | y_2 | y_3 | y_4 | y_5 | — | y_7 | y_8 | y_9 | y_{10} |

TABLE 12.2B

x	x_1	x_2	$\cdots$	x_n	x_{n+1}	$\cdots$	x_n
y	y_1	y_2	$\cdots$	y_n	—	$\cdots$	—
z	—	—	$\cdots$	—	z_{n+1}	$\cdots$	z_n

complete submatrices (see also Morrison, 1972). For a ML treatment of missing data from panel surveys (the so-called attrition problem) see Marini, Olsen, and Rubin (1977).

Investigating special cases of monotonic missing data patterns, Lord (1955b) and Edgett (1956) provide explicit solutions for the trivariate case. Lord considers the case of three random variables where data are complete on one and missing for the other two, as illustrated in Table 12.2B. Here x and y are assumed to have a bivariate normal distribution, as well as x and z (the correlation between y and z is not estimable). Lord derives explicit ML estimators for the bivariate normal parameters (including the regression coefficients) as well as their sample variances, and considers their relative efficiencies. As can be expected, the estimates of some parameters improve when all data are used, but an interesting—and perhaps not intuitively obvious—result is that estimators of some parameters are not more efficient than those obtained when data are deleted.

Edgett (1956) deals with three jointly distributed normal variates (Table 12.2C) but assumes that data are missing only from one variable. The ML procedure for the trivariate normal density yields nine equations that provide explicit solutions for the nine parameters (three means and six variances and covariances). Edgett also obtains the ML estimators of the regression equation

$$x = \beta_0 + \beta_1 y + \beta_2 z \tag{12.23}$$

in terms of the estimated moments of the trivariate normal.

Although both Lord and Edgett provide explicit solutions, it is not apparent how the two procedures can be extended to the general multivariate case. T. W. Anderson (1957) provides a general nested ML procedure capable of extension to the multivariate normal distribution, which subsumes both Lord's and Edgett's procedures as special cases. Anderson's method expresses the normal density as the product of marginal densities and conditional densities, and uses ML regression coefficients to estimate means and second moments. The latter can be given explicitly as solutions to the likelihood equations for certain nested data patterns.

TABLE 12.2C

x	x_1	x_2	$\cdots$	x_n	x_{n+1}	$\cdots$	x_n
y	y_1	y_2	$\cdots$	y_n	y_{n+1}	$\cdots$	y_n
z	z_1	z_2	$\cdots$	z_n	—	$\cdots$	—

Consider an r-dimensional normal distribution $N(\mu, \Sigma)$ consisting of r variables $v_1, v_2, \ldots, v_r$ (observed without error). Only n_1 observations are available on the entire set of r variables and a second sample of size n_2 is observed for a subset, say $v_1, v_2, \ldots, v_s$. Thus no observations are available in the second sample for the variables $v_{s+1}, v_{s+2}, \ldots, v_r$ and the submatrix in the bottom right-hand corner is empty (Table 12.3). Clearly there is no problem in estimating the $(1 \times s)$ mean vector nor the $s \times s$ covariance matrix for $v_1, v_2, \ldots, v_s$ for which the sample is complete. The mean vector and the $(r - s) \times (r - s)$ covariance matrix for $v_{s+1}, v_{s+2}, \ldots, v_r$ also can be estimated from the first sample size n_1. Assuming that the missing values are representative (Type III and Type IV randomness), the estimated normal parameters of $v_{s+1}, v_{s+2}, \ldots, v_r$ based on the partial sample will be unbiased. However, since only a part of the sample is used, the estimates will not be as efficient as they could be and the question again arises as to whether or not data on $v_1, v_2, \ldots, v_s$ can be used to improve the parameter estimates of $v_{s+1}, v_{s+2}, \ldots, v_r$ when the two sets of variables are jointly distributed, that is, correlated. In general, the question can be answered affirmatively since covariance adjustments of this type often improve the raw estimates based on the subsample.

As an illustration of this point, as well as an example of how monotonically missing data facilitate estimation, consider Dempster's method (1969, pp. 260–264). Let $\bar{\mathbf{X}}$ denote the $(n \times s)$ sample mean vector of $v_1, v_2, \ldots, v_s$ based on the complete sample of size $n - n_1 + n_2$, and let $\bar{X}_1^{(1)}, \bar{X}_1^{(2)}$, and $\bar{X}_2^{(1)}$ be the means of the submatrices of the partitioned data matrix as in Table 12.3. Also let

$$\mathbf{K} = \begin{bmatrix} \mathbf{K}_{11} & \vdots & 0 \\ \cdots\cdots & \vdots & \cdots\cdots \\ \mathbf{K}_{21} & \vdots & \mathbf{K}_{22} \end{bmatrix}$$

TABLE 12.3

	V_1			V_2			
v_1	v_2	$\cdots$	v_s	v_{s+1}	v_{s+2}	$\cdots$	v_r	
$X_1^{(1)}$				$X_2^{(1)}$				n_1
$(n_1 \times s)$			Σ_{11}	$(n_1 \times r - s)$			Σ_{12}	
$X_1^{(2)}$				$X_2^{(2)}$				n_2
$(n_2 \times s)$			Σ_{21}	(missing)				
X_1				X_2				

be any matrix that is partitioned conformably with Table 12.3, and define a transformation

$$\begin{bmatrix} \mathbf{U}_1 \\ \cdots \\ \mathbf{U}_2 \end{bmatrix} = \begin{bmatrix} \mathbf{K}_{11} & \vdots & 0 \\ \cdots & & \cdots \\ \mathbf{K}_{21} & \vdots & \mathbf{K}_{22} \end{bmatrix} \begin{bmatrix} \mathbf{V}_1 \\ \cdots \\ \mathbf{V}_2 \end{bmatrix}. \tag{12.24}$$

Then

$$\begin{aligned}
\begin{bmatrix} \mathbf{V}_1 \\ \cdots \\ \mathbf{V}_2 \end{bmatrix} &= \begin{bmatrix} \mathbf{K}_{11} & \vdots & 0 \\ \cdots & & \cdots \\ \mathbf{K}_{21} & \vdots & \mathbf{K}_{22} \end{bmatrix}^{-1} \begin{bmatrix} \mathbf{U}_1 \\ \cdots \\ \mathbf{U}_2 \end{bmatrix} \\
&= \begin{bmatrix} \mathbf{K}_{11}^{-1} & \vdots & 0 \\ \cdots & & \cdots \\ -\mathbf{K}_{22}^{-1}\mathbf{K}_{21}\mathbf{K}_{11}^{-1} & \vdots & \mathbf{K}_{22}^{-1} \end{bmatrix} \begin{bmatrix} \mathbf{U}_1 \\ \cdots \\ \mathbf{U}_2 \end{bmatrix} \\
&= \begin{bmatrix} \mathbf{H}_{11} & \vdots & \mathbf{H}_{12} \\ \cdots & & \cdots \\ \mathbf{H}_{21} & \vdots & \mathbf{H}_{22} \end{bmatrix} \begin{bmatrix} \mathbf{U}_1 \\ \cdots \\ \mathbf{U}_2 \end{bmatrix},
\end{aligned} \tag{12.25}$$

say, where $\mathbf{K}_{11}$ and $\mathbf{K}_{22}$ are square and nonsingular. The inverse of the partitioned matrix $\mathbf{K}$ is obtained in the usual way (e.g., see Morrison, 1967, p. 66). Then equating components of (12.25) and the preceding partitioned matrix we obtain the two relations

$$\mathbf{H}_{21}\mathbf{K}_{11} + \mathbf{H}_{22}\mathbf{K}_{21} = 0$$

$$\mathbf{H}_{21}\mathbf{K}_{11} = -\mathbf{H}_{22}\mathbf{K}_{21} = \mathbf{L}^{\mathrm{T}} \tag{12.26}$$

where $\mathbf{L}^{\mathrm{T}}$ is an arbitrary $(r - s) \times s$ matrix defined by (12.26). In view of the linear transformation (12.24) the sample information contained in U_1 and U_2 is the same as the original sample information V_1 and V_2. Let the means $\bar{Y}_1$ and $\bar{Y}_2^{(1)}$ correspond to means $\bar{X}_1$ and $\bar{X}_2^{(1)}$, respectively, for the transformed sample U_1 and U_2. Then, in terms of row vectors the sample means are related by

$$[\bar{Y}_1\mathbf{H}_{11}^{\mathrm{T}} \vdots \bar{Y}_1\mathbf{H}_{21}^{\mathrm{T}} + \bar{Y}_2^{(1)}\mathbf{H}_{22}^{\mathrm{T}}] = [\bar{X}_1 \vdots \bar{X}_2^{(1)} - (\bar{X}_1^{(1)} - X_1)\mathbf{L}] \tag{12.27}$$

where the $(1 \times (r - s))$ mean vector of the set V_2 is given by

$$\begin{aligned}
\bar{X}_2 &= \bar{X}_2^{(1)} - (\bar{X}_1^{(1)} - \bar{X}_1)\mathbf{L} \\
&= \bar{X}_2^{(1)} + \bar{X}_1^{(2)}\mathbf{L}.
\end{aligned} \tag{12.28}$$

Equivalent expressions for the covariance matrix of the r variables involving $\mathbf{L}$ can be derived and are also given in Dempster (1969, p. 262).

Since the estimates depend on the arbitrary $s \times (r - s)$ matrix $\mathbf{L}$, the first question that comes to mind is how to determine $\mathbf{L}$ from the sample. Rather than view Table 12.3 as a missing data matrix, we may consider Table 12.3 as a data matrix of n_1 observations on r variables, where *extra* data are available on a subset of the variables. In this case we wish to predict (estimate) the "missing" data from $X_1^{(2)}$, given the best linear predictor of the set V_2 in terms of V_1 that determines matrix $\mathbf{L}$. Computationally this may be carried out as follows.

1. Define

$$\bar{X}_2^{(1)} = X_1^{(1)}\mathbf{B} + \mathbf{E} \tag{12.29}$$

where $\mathbf{B}$ is an $s \times (r - s)$ matrix of coefficients and $\mathbf{E}$ is an $n_1 \times r$ matrix of residuals. Assuming V_1 and V_2 are not independent, the least (regression) squares ML estimate of $\mathbf{B}$ is

$$\hat{\mathbf{B}} = \Sigma_{11}^{-1}\Sigma^{(1)} \tag{12.30}$$

where $\Sigma^{(1)}$ is the $s \times r$ covariance matrix between V_1 and V_2, obtained from sample n_1.

2. The predicted (estimated) missing values are then

$$\hat{X}_2^{(2)} = X_2^{(2)}\hat{\mathbf{B}}. \tag{12.31}$$

Thus a possible choice is $\hat{\mathbf{B}} = \mathbf{L}$, and using the property

$$\bar{\hat{X}}_2^{(2)} = \bar{X}_2^{(2)} = \bar{X}_1^{(1)}\mathbf{L} \tag{12.32}$$

we arrive at (12.28), that is, the sample means of V_2 are obtained by summing the observed means $\bar{X}_2^{(1)}$ and the means of the predicted values $\bar{X}_1^{(1)}\mathbf{L}$.

3. To obtain the ML estimates of the mean vector and covariance matrix (and perhaps the regression coefficients), we may either use the standard formulations (see Dempster, 1969, pp. 261–262), or else fill in the missing values by their estimates given by (12.31). We can then proceed to calculate parameters in the usual way using both observed and estimated (predicted) values.

Note that matrix $\mathbf{L}$ is not unique since it depends on the linear model specification of the type (12.29), as well as the estimation method. For example, generalized (weighted) least squares could have been used if one suspected individuals in sample n_2 have different variance than in n_1. For all practical intents, this method can be considered as a special case of Buck's procedure when $\hat{\mathbf{B}} = \mathbf{L}$.

Nicholson (1957) considers block triangular data for the special and most simple case when data are missing only on one variable (Table 12.2c). He also assumes that the missing observations are confined to the dependent variable in a multivariate normal regression model. In Nicholson's case ML (least-squares) prediction is used to estimate the missing observations on the dependent variable, and in this sense his procedure can be seen as analogous to the classic ANOVA procedures considered in Section 12.2. Consequently incomplete samples cannot be used when interest lies in prediction, since the regression coefficients are the same whether the entire or only the incomplete part of the sample is used. More recently Morrison (1971) has considered the case of missing data (on one variable) in a multivariate normal distribution, and obtains the exact expectations and variances of the ML estimates of the mean vector and the covariance matrix. He also investigates the bias and relative efficiency of the estimates in small samples (see also Morrison, 1972; Morrison & Bhoj, 1973; Ratkowsky, 1974). Earlier Bhargava (1962) had considered testing repeated measurement (panel sample) hypotheses by likelihood ratio statistics, and Bhoj (1971) had tabulated percentage points for one- and two-sample tests on normal mean vectors. Other estimation problems have also been considered in the more specialized normal bivariate case, where observations are missing on one variate only. Thus Mehta and Gurland (1969, 1973) derive a statistic for testing a hypothesis concerning the correlation coefficient when the variances of the two marginal distributions are equal, and use the statistic to estimate the difference of the means (see also Morrison, 1973; Rao, 1952, pp. 161–163). Lin (1971) reports a statistic that utilizes the ML estimate and derives an estimate of the difference of the two means. The methods proposed here employ iterative computation, and Lin and Stivers (1974) develop a noniterative procedure for testing the difference between two means in normal samples (for significance testing of means see Lin, 1973).

Gathering data is expensive, in certain cases, for example the Guaranteed Annual Income (GAI) experiments wherein experimental respondents are also recipients of monthly payments over a period of years. In such circumstances considerable economy could be achieved by designing the sample so that data are missing, for example as in Table 12.3, while specifying that certain precision requirements be satisfied. Hocking and Smith (1972) consider such a minimum cost sample allocation procedure for block triangular (monotonic) data and derive ML estimates of the normal parameters, their sampling variances, and standard deviations of the regression coefficients. Optimal sample sizes are then determined in the usual way by a constrained minimization of cost subject to variance inequality constraints on the estimated parameters.

Although triangular or monotonic patterns of missing data are fairly straightforward to use and yield explicit solutions of the ML equations, other more involved patterns can be encountered in practice. Trawinski and Bargmann (1964), for example, consider a pattern that can be employed in experimental testing in educational research. In order to avoid respondent fatigue, recall error, and the like, a subset of size u of r variables under study is observed in each of the K groups of n experimental units (the respondents) so that the ith group ($i = 1, 2, \ldots, k$) is represented by an $n \times u$ matrix of observations. For example, in Table 12.4 we have $k = 3$ groups of respondents each observed for $u = 2$ variables, where there are $n = 4$ respondents in each group. The ML equations must be solved iteratively to obtain estimates of the $r \times r$ covariance matrix of the variables, and the regression parameters. The iterative calculations are involved and the authors propose an approximate iterative procedure that appears to be more straightforward to use. A systematic simulation evaluation of Trawinski and Bargmann's ML procedure has not been made despite the apparent usefulness of the method in reducing data requirements. For more detail on partial "matrix sampling" see Shoemaker (1973).

TABLE 12.4

X_1	X_2	X_3
X	X	
X	X	
X	X	
X	X	
X		X
X		X
X		X
X		X
	X	X
	X	X
	X	X
	X	X

With the exception of Wilks's (and Matthai's) method, all the procedures considered so far share the common property that data are assumed missing in certain specific patterns. This will usually arise only by design, except in revolving panel surveys. Also the estimation of the missing values is not always considered explicitly. The more common situation is one whereby a given cross-sectional data matrix is designed to be complete, but due to factors beyond the researcher's control, observations are missing, both randomly and in a random pattern. The choice now faced by the researcher is similar to the preceding one—either delete respondents for whom data are missing on some variables (and thus lose efficiency), or employ suitable estimation techniques for data missing in random patterns. It was seen before that when data are missing in certain patterns, some (but not all) ML techniques rely implicitly on regression type prediction to estimate the missing values and then calculate moments for both the observed and predicted portions of the sample. The idea of predicting (estimating) missing values can be extended to cases in which data are not necessarily normal, or in which data are missing in haphazard patterns. We next consider the nonnormal case and then describe other ML methods.

Data Missing in Random Patterns (Types II, III, and IV Randomness)

THE PRINCIPAL COMPONENTS METHOD

The first procedure that explicitly estimates random patterns of missing data without distributional assumptions appears to be that of Dear (1959) who uses a linear principal components model to estimate the missing values. Dear decomposes a data matrix into known (observed) elements and unknown (unobserved) elements. Let $\mathbf{X} = (x_{ij})$ be an $n \times r$ data matrix of n observations (respondents) on r variables (characteristics), and let $\mathbf{I}_x = (w_{ij})$ denote the $n \times r$ "indicator" matrix, where w_{ij} is defined

$$w_{ij} = \begin{cases} 0 & \text{if } x_{ij} \text{ is observed} \\ 1 & \text{if } x_{ij} \text{ otherwise} \end{cases}$$

Also let $\mathbf{I}$ be an $n \times r$ matrix whose elements are 1's and let $\otimes$ denote the direct element by element product of two matrices. Then matrix $\mathbf{X}$ can be expressed as

$$\mathbf{X} = (\mathbf{I} - \mathbf{I}_x) \otimes \mathbf{X} + \mathbf{I}_x \otimes \mathbf{X} \tag{12.33}$$

where it is easy to verify that

$$\mathbf{X}^{(k)} = (\mathbf{I} - \mathbf{I}_x) \otimes \mathbf{X}$$

and

$$\mathbf{X}^{(u)} = \mathbf{I}_x \otimes \mathbf{X} \tag{12.34}$$

represent the known and unknown elements, respectively. For example when $n = 3$ and $r = 2$ we have

$$\mathbf{X}^{(k)} = \begin{bmatrix} x_{11} & x_{12} \\ x_{21} & 0 \\ 0 & x_{13} \end{bmatrix}, \quad \mathbf{X}^{(u)} = \begin{bmatrix} 0 & 0 \\ 0 & b \\ a & 0 \end{bmatrix} \tag{12.35}$$

where $x_{31} = a$ and $x_{22} = b$ are the missing elements and therefore are not known. Dear assumes that $\mathbf{X}^{(k)}$ can be decomposed (see Timm, 1970) as

$$\mathbf{X}^{(k)} = \mathbf{m}\mathbf{w}^T + R \tag{12.36}$$

where $\mathbf{m}$ is a $(n \times 1)$ vector, $\mathbf{w}^T$ is a $(1 \times r)$ vector, and R is an $n \times r$ matrix of residuals. Thus Dear's method is equivalent to replacing the missing observations by zeroes[6] when forming matrix $\mathbf{X}^{(k)}$, which in turn is then decomposed into an estimated part $\mathbf{m}\mathbf{w}^T$ and a residual "error" part R. The elements of $\mathbf{m}$ and $\mathbf{w}^T$ are estimated by the principle of least squares, which suggests the minimization of

$$\text{tr}(\mathbf{R}^T\mathbf{R}) = \text{tr}[\mathbf{X}^{(k)T}\mathbf{X}^{(k)} - 2\mathbf{X}^{(k)T}\mathbf{m}\mathbf{w}^T + \mathbf{w}\mathbf{m}^T\mathbf{m}\mathbf{w}^T] \tag{12.37}$$

where "tr" denotes the trace of a square matrix. Differentiating partially with respect to $\mathbf{m}$ and $\mathbf{w}$ yields the usual least squares estimates

$$\mathbf{m} = \frac{\mathbf{X}^{(k)}\hat{\mathbf{w}}}{\hat{\mathbf{w}}^T\hat{\mathbf{w}}} \quad \text{and} \quad \mathbf{w} = \frac{\mathbf{X}^{(k)T}\hat{\mathbf{m}}}{\hat{\mathbf{m}}^T\hat{\mathbf{m}}}, \tag{12.38}$$

which must be solved simultaneously, unlike the usual regression problem where either $\hat{\mathbf{m}}$ or $\hat{\mathbf{w}}$ is given. Substitution and rearrangement of terms yields

$$(\mathbf{X}^{(k)T}\mathbf{X}^{(k)}) - \lambda\mathbf{I}\hat{\mathbf{w}} = 0 \tag{12.39}$$

---

[6] Or mean values if deviations about means are considered.

where

$$\hat{\lambda} = \frac{\hat{w}^T X^{(k)} \hat{w}}{\hat{w}^T \hat{w}} \tag{12.40}$$

are the latent roots and w are latent vectors of the symmetric covariance (correlation) matrix of the known elements $X^{(k)T} X^{(k)}$. The expression $tr(R^T R)$ is then maximized by selecting that latent vector $\hat{w}$ that corresponds to the largest latent value $\hat{\lambda}$. Let

$$\hat{M} = \begin{bmatrix} \hat{m}_1 & \hat{m}_1 & \cdots & \hat{m}_1 \\ \hat{m}_2 & \hat{m}_2 & \cdots & \hat{m}_2 \\ \vdots & \vdots & \cdots & \vdots \\ \hat{m}_n & \hat{m}_n & \cdots & \hat{m}_n \end{bmatrix} \qquad \hat{W} = \begin{bmatrix} \hat{w}_1 & & & \\ & \hat{w}_2 & & 0 \\ 0 & & \ddots & \\ & & & \hat{w}_r \end{bmatrix} \tag{12.41}$$

be $n \times r$ and $r \times r$ matrices that contain the estimated elements of the vectors $\hat{m}$ and $\hat{w}$, respectively. Then the estimate of the unknown elements $X^{(u)}$ is constructed as

$$X^{(u)} = (I_x \otimes \hat{M}) \hat{W}. \tag{12.42}$$

For example, in the case of the 3×2 matrix in 12.35 we have

$$\begin{bmatrix} 0 & 0 \\ 0 & 1 \\ 1 & 0 \end{bmatrix} \otimes \begin{bmatrix} \hat{m}_1 & \hat{m}_1 \\ \hat{m}_2 & \hat{m}_2 \\ \hat{m}_3 & \hat{m}_3 \end{bmatrix} \begin{bmatrix} \hat{w}_1 & 0 \\ 0 & \hat{w}_2 \end{bmatrix} = \begin{bmatrix} 0 & 0 \\ 0 & \hat{m}_2\hat{w}_2 \\ \hat{m}_3\hat{w}_1 & 0 \end{bmatrix} \tag{12.43}$$

where estimates of a and b are given by $\hat{a} = \hat{m}_3\hat{w}_1$ and $\hat{b} = \hat{m}_2\hat{w}_2$. Once the missing values are filled in by their estimates, the means, covariances, and the like can be obtained in the usual way. In summary, Dear's procedure involves first estimating the principal components loadings and scores from the observed sample, where missing entries are zero-filled, and then using these to estimate the missing observations.

Various extensions of Dear's method suggest themselves. One possibility is to replace missing observations by the observed mean values of the variables $\bar{X}_j (j = 1, \ldots, r)$, where for each observation x_{ij} we have $x_{ij} = \bar{X}_j + \delta_{ij}$ $(i = 1, \ldots, n)$, calculate the leading principal components and obtain estimates for the missing values, replace the means by the new estimates, and continue to recycle estimates through the components model until stable values are obtained. Also the variables can be weighted in order to reflect differential accuracy due to unequal number of missing observations, for each variable.

REGRESSION METHODS

A second general procedure for estimating missing observations uses regression methods, a technique created by Buck (1960) and Walsh (1961). Rather than decompose a data matrix into known and unknown parts, Buck

TABLE 12.5

X_1	X_2	$\cdots$	X_4	
x_{11}	x_{12}	$\cdots$	x_{1r}	
x_{21}	x_{22}	$\cdots$	x_{2r}	complete data
.	.		.	
.	.		.	
.	.		.	
x_{m1}	x_{m2}	$\cdots$	x_{mr}	
$x_{m+1,1}$	.	$\cdots$	$x_{m+1,r}$	
$x_{m+2,2}$	.	$\cdots$	$x_{m+2,r}$	some data missing
.			.	
.			.	
$x_{n,1}$		$\cdots$	$x_{n,r}$	

estimates the missing data directly by least-squares regression, and distinguishes between situations in which individuals have only one observation missing per variable and situations where individuals have more than one observation missing. Generally, for a given data matrix not all individuals will have missing data. Assume that m individuals have complete records that are arranged as the first m rows, and $(n - m)$ individuals have missing data points (Table 12.5). Under circumstances in which at most one observation per variable is missing, Buck's procedure can be summarized as follows:

1. For those m individuals for whom data are complete, estimate r linear regression equations using each variable in turn as the dependent variable. This yields, for any kth observation on the jth variable,

$$E(\hat{x}_{kj}) = \hat{\beta}_0 + \hat{\beta}_1 x_{k1} + \hat{\beta}_2 x_{k2} + \cdots + \hat{\beta}_{j-1} x_{k,j-1}$$
$$+ \hat{\beta}_{j+1} x_{k,j+1} + \cdots + \hat{\beta}_r x_{k,r} \qquad (12.44)$$

where $(j = 1, 2, \ldots, k)$.

2. Without loss of generality, assume that the ith individual has a missing observation on the jth variable. The dependent variable in this case is x_j, and from the regression equation (12.44) we have the estimate

$$E(\hat{x}_{ij}) = \hat{\beta}_0 + \hat{\beta}_1 x_{i1} + \cdots + \hat{\beta}_{j-1} x_{i,j-1}$$
$$+ \hat{\beta}_{j+1} x_{i,j+1} + \cdots + \hat{\beta}_k x_{ik} \qquad (12.45)$$

as the estimate for the missing observation x_{ij}.

When each of the $(n - m)$ individuals have more than one value missing, the preceding procedure is repeated for each missing observation. If v variates are missing for a given individual then from the first m complete rows of the data matrix we compute the multiple regression for each missing variate on x −

v other variates. Buck also shows that if missing values are replaced by estimated values and the covariance matrix is calculated, the variances (but not the
covariances) are biased. However, a straightforward correction term is provided by Buck and further investigated by Beale and Little (1975), who also
consider an iterative version of Buck's estimator. It should be kept in mind,
however, that when variables are observed with error, extra information is
needed concerning the error terms when correcting for bias.

Buck's method does not utilize all of the sample information since the
initial regression equation (12.44) that is used to estimate the missing values is
itself estimated only on the complete part of the sample. A more general approach is developed by Walsh (1961), apparently independently of Buck's
work, utilizing the entire sample information to estimate the missing data. The
advantages of Buck's method are the relative simplicity of use and the straightforward manner in which the covariance matrix calculated from the filled-in
sample can be corrected for bias (which results when missing observations are
estimated). The method also has fairly high relative efficiency. No degrees of
freedom, however, should be attributed to the estimated missing data when
computing mean values, variances, and covariances [an error that is committed
by Kosobud (1963), for example] since this results in a specious improvement
in efficiency.

Evaluation of Rival Procedures

The success of any method for estimating missing data will be dependent
on the extent of correlation among the variables in the multivariate sample, on
the percentage of data missing, and the correct specification of the particular
linear model used to estimate the missing values. For the most general case
where multivariate data are missing in random patterns, no sampling properties
of the estimates are available. Consequently, this frequently leaves research
workers with little basis for choosing from a large array of techniques, or for
comparing published techniques with variants that they may wish to employ.
The most common method of evaluating rival procedures in these circumstances is by Monte Carlo methods. These are usually expensive and time
consuming, and they do not always yield definitive answers. However, at
present they constitute the main guide as to the accuracy of missing data
estimation. Four commonly used techniques to estimate covariance and correlation matrices from incomplete data are (a) discarding individuals with incomplete data; (b) Wilks's (1932) method; (c) Dear's (1959) method, and (d) Buck's
(1960) procedure. An evaluation of them was carried out by Timm (1970), who
attempted to establish the relative superiority of a given technique for different
proportions of randomly missing data, sample size, number of variables, and
the "average intercorrelations" of the variables as measured by Kaiser's measure of average intercorrelation $0 \le \gamma \le 1$, where

$$\gamma = \frac{\lambda_1 - 1}{r - 1} \qquad (12.46)$$

and λ_1 is the dominant (largest) eigenvalue of a given correlation matrix $\mathbf{R}$. Employing correlation matrices published in previous studies (for $r = 2, 5$, and 10) Timm used the Kaiser and Dickman method to generate complete data matrices of size $h = 50, 100$, and 200 such that $\mathbf{\Sigma} = \mathbf{R}$, where $\mathbf{\Sigma}$ is the covariance matrix. From these data matrices two incomplete data matrices are obtained, each with 1, 10, and 20% of the data deleted at random. Using these data with two replicates, the effect of sample size ($N = 50, 100, 200$), number of variables ($r = 2, 5, 10$), percentage missing data (1%, 10%, 20%), and average intercorrelations of variables ($\gamma = .2, .5, .8$) are examined for the four estimation techniques, both for the estimated covariance matrix $\hat{\mathbf{\Sigma}}$ and the estimated correlation matrix $\hat{\mathbf{R}}$. Timm (1970) draws the following conclusions from his comparative study.

1. No clear preference can be shown for estimating either $\mathbf{\Sigma}$ or $\mathbf{R}$ by a given method when data are missing.

2. When 1% of the data are missing no uniformly best technique exists to estimate $\mathbf{\Sigma}$ or $\mathbf{R}$. However, in all but a few cases the Dear and Buck techniques are superior to the Wilks or the listwise deletion techniques for both $\mathbf{\Sigma}$ and $\mathbf{R}$. For $\mathbf{\Sigma}$, the Dear method is better when intermediate or high correlations exist among the variables, whereas Buck's method is preferable when correlation is low. For $\mathbf{R}$, Buck's method is also marginally better. For both matrices, however, Buck's procedure is superior in terms of relative efficiency.

3. When 10% of the data are missing, again no uniformly best technique exists, but preference should be given to the Buck technique for estimating $\mathbf{\Sigma}$ when high or intermediate correlations exist between the variables (except for $r = 2$), whereas for low correlations no technique is dominant. For $\mathbf{R}$, Buck's method functions best for $r > 5$. Again, in the case of both matrices, Buck's method is best as far as average efficiency is concerned, especially in the case of estimating $\mathbf{\Sigma}$.

4. When 20% of the data are missing, again no uniformly best procedure exists for both $\mathbf{\Sigma}$ and $\mathbf{R}$. For $\mathbf{\Sigma}$, Buck's method is better when variables are highly correlated. Dear's procedure works best for intermediate correlations, although both are effective when correlation is low (except for $r = 2$, in which case the complete data technique is most effective). As far as average relative efficiency is concerned, however, Buck's method is superior. For $\mathbf{R}$, the picture is less clear. Wilks's method is better for low intercorrelation of variables; Dear's procedure is best for high intercorrelation, whereas the Buck technique is to be preferred for intermediate correlation. Again, Buck's method seems to be marginally better as far as the average relative efficiency is concerned.

To summarize, Wilks's method and the complete data procedure appear to perform poorly when compared to Buck's or Dear's methods, irrespective of the size of n, r, or the percentage of data missing. Buck's procedure appears marginally better. The reason for this last result perhaps is that Dear's method requires the initial replacement of missing values by zeroes, and that only the first principal component, which may bias the final estimates, be used. However, since Dear's procedure uses the first principal component to estimate the missing values, it is not clear why Dear's method performs relatively better for low correlation rather than high correlation. Perhaps this may be corrected if more components are retained when using Dear's method. It should be kept in mind, however, that both procedures depend on the existence of intercorrelations among the variables, and in the limit when all variables have correlations of zero both methods break down. Both Buck's and Dear's methods make no distributional assumptions for the data, although insofar as both methods make use of linear least-squares estimates, they would be expected to perform better in the case of a multivariate normal sample.

Maximum Likelihood Estimates and Algorithms

When the data matrix $\mathbf{X}$ represents a sample from a multivariate normal distribution $N(\mu, \Sigma)$, the principle of maximum likelihood can be used to derive estimates of μ and Σ. This provides an explicit statistical rationale and methodology for estimating the normal parameters, as well as regression coefficients in the case of a conditional normal distribution. Thus Orchard and Woodbury (1972) develop a ML estimation algorithm based on what they term the *missing information principle,* which they feel can provide a general, unifying method for ML estimation where some data are missing. Since ML procedures are generally iterative there has been much recent interest in developing efficient estimation algorithms.

The methodological principle behind Orchard and Woodbury's approach is that the unknown missing values are random variables and thus are estimated along with the parameters of the distribution. It follows that estimates of the missing values are also random variables even in the case when the "true" unobserved missing data are fixed. Although certain authors disagree (Hartley & Hocking, 1971, pp. 818–819), this view seems consistent with ML estimation theory that regards sample estimates of fixed parameters as random variables. The variation ascribed to missing value estimates is then added to the usual sampling variation so that error variances of parameters are increased when data are missing.

The procedure is to partition the likelihood equation of the data as

$$L(\mathbf{X}|\theta) = L_1(\mathbf{X}|\mathbf{Z}, \theta)L_2(\mathbf{Z}|\theta)$$

where $\mathbf{X}$ is the complete data matrix, $\mathbf{Z}$ the observed (incomplete) data matrix, and θ are the parameters to be estimated. The method then proceeds by finding the so-called score matrices. The interested reader is referred to Orchard and Woodbury (1972, p. 705) for estimators of the missing data, mean vector, and the covariance matrix obtained by this method. Let Z_i represent observations for the ith individual. Then $\hat{Z}_i = Z_{i,0} + \hat{Z}_{i,m}$ where $Z_{i,0}$ is the observed portion, with missing observations replaced by zeroes, and $\hat{Z}_{i,m}$ is the estimated missing portion, with again zeroes in the positions corresponding to an observed component. The method is similar to that of Hartley and Hocking (1971) who obtain the marginal distribution of the missing values and then integrate out the missing values over a suitable range. The ML estimates of the parameters are then obtained directly from the marginal distribution of the observed data. Orchard and Woodbury's method, however, makes use of the regression of the missing data $Z_{i,m}$ on the observed data $Z_{i,0}$, as well as the conditional covariance matrix of the missing data given the observed data.

Orchard and Woodbury's work appears to represent one of the first systematic attempts to develop a general, unifying methodology for treating missing data in the case of multivariate normal data. The procedure can, in principle, be applied to estimate parameters of the multivariate normal, linear regression (ANOVA), and other multivariate models assumed to be normal. In a different sense, of course, ML methods may themselves be considered specialized approaches of, say, Buck's (1960) method that makes no distributional assumptions.

Other iterative estimation methods for missing data similar to ML techniques are also used. An iterative version of Buck's (1960) method provides estimates that are very similar to the Orchard and Woodbury procedure. A description of the iterated Buck method and its comparison with the Orchard and Woodbury method is provided by Beale and Little (1975). Additionally, a simulation comparison by Beale and Little—considered in a later section—indicates that the iterated Buck method is marginally better than the Orchard and Woodbury ML estimator, within the parameters selected by the authors.

12.4. REGRESSION ANALYSIS WITH INCOMPLETE OBSERVATIONS

The previous two sections considered the problem of estimating mean vectors and covariance (correlation) matrices when observations are missing randomly from the data matrix $\mathbf{X}$, either in prespecified or arbitrary patterns. It was observed that for both block-triangular (monotonic) and arbitrary patterns, multivariate linear models (particularly the OLS regression model) can be used to estimate missing observations and means, covariances, and correlations can then be calculated in the usual way from the filled-in data matrix. In this section we consider the closely associated problem of specifically estimating the linear OLS regression model

$$\mathbf{Y} = \mathbf{X}\boldsymbol{\beta} + \boldsymbol{\varepsilon} \qquad (12.47)$$

when some data are missing. Here, rather than serving as a convenient tool to estimate parameters, the regression plane is itself of interest. The OLS regression equation (12.47) can be considered as an extension of the ANOVA model considered in section 12.2 (see, for example, Cohen, 1968) where the explanatory variables X can be either discrete or continuous (or both), fixed or stochastic. In what follows, unless otherwise stated, we assume X to consist of random variables observed jointly with Y rather than predetermined before sampling so that both Y and X generally vary in repeated samples. Also, we initially assume that all variables are continuous, that is, quantitative scales. As a result, unlike the ANOVA model, data can now be missing on both the dependent and independent variables.

The situation is as follows. A random sample of n individuals is selected, and for each of these individuals $r + 1$ observations on the variables $Y, X_1, X_2,$ . . . , X_r are desired. However for some (or all) individuals one or more (but not all) of the Xs and Y are missing. Again the question naturally arises: Is it better to ignore individuals with partially missing data or is it possible to utilize the partial data in order to improve the regression estimates. With the exception of randomness and continuity of the explanatory variable X, all remaining OLS assumptions of (12.1) are assumed to hold for (12.47). For most nonexperimental data these assumptions are unrealistic. However, the OLS model is widely used even with nonexperimental data and provides a convenient starting point for further analysis. We first consider the so-called zero-order methods (see Afifi & Elashoff, 1966).

Zero-Order Methods

Earlier methods employed to correct for missing data in regression analysis tended to follow those used for the ANOVA model and were rather *ad hoc*. It was only after more systematic study of the problem that shortcomings and better alternatives were realized. However in many cases the relatively naive methods can be fruitfully applied. Since they are simple to use and generally do not result in complex formulas they are still frequently employed. Before considering more involved methods we therefore first consider three well-known zero-order methods for handling missing data:

1. Complete deletion of all individuals from whom at least one variable is missing (listwise deletion method)
2. Pairwise deletion of individuals for covariance calculations for whom one variable in the pair is missing
3. Replacing missing values by mean values of the variables

The most straightforward method of handling missing data in regression analysis is to discard observations from the sample for which data are not complete. This can be accomplished in two ways—either by discarding all individuals with incomplete observations and applying OLS to the complete observations only (method 1), or alternatively by computing covariances between all pairs of variables using only those observations having values for both variables (method 2). One then uses these covariances to compute regression coefficients. Generally, not all variables contain the same number of observations so that covariances (variances) rather than the usual sums of cross-products (sums of squares) are used. Note that in general deletion of variables (as opposed to individuals) is not a very attractive option, even when the variables dropped do not account for very significant variance of Y, since this can result in biased regression coefficients when the explanatory variables are not orthogonal. Note that pairwise and listwise deletion methods are not equivalent to replacing the missing observations by appropriate mean values. This will become more clear when we discuss inconsistencies that can arise when using the pairwise deletion method.

DELETION AND THE YATES–TOCHER PROCEDURE

The method of discarding all individuals with missing observations is formally equivalent to the classic ANOVA methods of Yates (1933) and Tocher (1952) described in Section 12.2, except that in the general nonexperimental regression situation observations can be missing on both the dependent and independent variables. The procedure here is again to minimize the sum of squares of residuals

$$\sum_{i=1}^{n} [y_i - \bar{y}^c - \beta_1(x_{i1} - \bar{x}_1^c) - \cdots - \beta_r(x_{ir} - \bar{x}_r^c)]^2 \tag{12.48}$$

with respect to the x_{ij}, y_i, and the βs; where $\bar{y}^c$ and $\bar{x}_j^c$ are means based on the nonmissing observations (Afifi & Elashoff, 1966). Haitovsky (1967, appendix) presents a proof of the equivalence of discarding all missing data in (12.47) and the classical method (Yates–Tocher) of assigning "neutral" values or zero residuals to (12.47). When values are missing randomly the coefficients $\hat{\beta} = (\mathbf{X}^T\mathbf{X})^{-1} \mathbf{X}^T\mathbf{Y}$ estimated from the complete sample (listwise deletion) are still unbiased (and, of course, consistent), and their variance–covariance matrix is of the usual form

$$\hat{\sigma}^2(\mathbf{X}^T\mathbf{X})^{-1} \tag{12.49}$$

where the sample residual variance $\hat{\sigma}^2$ is now estimated as

$$\hat{\sigma}^2 = \frac{n - 1}{n - r - 1} (\mathbf{Y}^T\mathbf{Y} - \mathbf{Y}^T\mathbf{P}_x\mathbf{Y}) \tag{12.50}$$

where $\mathbf{P}_x = \mathbf{X}(\mathbf{X}^T\mathbf{X})^{-1} \mathbf{X}^T$ is the symmetric projection (idempotent) matrix based on the complete part of the sample of size n. The coefficient of multiple determination R^2 is therefore also restricted to the complete part of the sample since all incomplete observations are automatically assigned zero residuals. In view of (12.50), the sole effect of missing data is therefore a decrease in the efficiency of $\hat{\beta}$ due to the reduced sample size. Clearly, the method of discarding data can be employed when data are missing on the dependent variable, the independent variables, or both. Note also that the independent variables can be considered either fixed or stochastic, although Kmenta (1971, p. 337) states that the nonstochastic case is only of interest when all data are available for Y but are missing on some independent variables X. However, in the ANOVA model considered in Section 12.2, the independent variables are fixed (nonstochastic) and data are precisely missing on the dependent variable, so that Kmenta's restriction for the more general regression model seems unnecessary. Further, when data are missing only on the dependent variable, we obtain Nicholson's (1957) situation that deals with the problem of triangularly missing data in the regression case (see Section 12.2).

PAIRWISE DELETION

When a small proportion of individuals have missing data (say 5–10%) then dropping them entirely from the sample is often the simplest, if not optimal, solution. The listwise procedure, however, has the drawback of being wasteful of data. The amount of data wasted is particularly high when the number of missing observations per individual is small (relatively to the number of variables) but many individuals have some data missing. For example in the extreme case, when all individuals in the sample have only one (not necessarily the same) variable missing the listwise deletion method would discard all cases. In similar and less extreme situations, the pairwise deletion method is frequently employed, where covariances (correlations) between any pair of variables are computed using only those observations that have nonmissing values on both, and the means and variances are obtained by using all available observations for that particular variable. Although some data are still discarded, the waste is clearly much smaller than for the listwise deletion method. A problem with pairwise deletion methods, however, is that the resulting covariance matrix of the independent variable is no longer necessarily Grammian. The resulting correlation matrix may be inconsistent (i.e., it will contain some impossible values).

In pairwise deletions, the normal equations

$$\Sigma_{xx}\hat{\beta} = \Sigma_{xy} \tag{12.51}$$

are solved for the $(r \times 1)$ vector of coefficients $\hat{\beta}$ where the (i, j)th element of the $(r \times r)$ sample covariance matrix Σ_{xx} of the independent variables, $\text{cov}(X_i, X_j)$ $(i \neq j; i, j = 1, 2, \ldots, r)$, is computed only from those observations that are common to both X_i and X_j. The same procedure is used to compute $\text{cov}(Y, X_i)$ $(i = 1, 2, \ldots, r)$, the elements of Σ_{xx}. Similarly, variances $(i = j; i, j = 1, 2, \ldots, r)$ are computed from all available observations on the X_i. The normal Eq. (12.51) are then written in terms of sample covariance matrices rather than the sums of squares and cross-products, X^TX and X^TY, since in general the degrees of freedom are not equal for all elements of Σ_{xx} and Σ_{xy}.

Let n_{ij} and n_{iy} be the number of observations common to X_i and X_j (number of individuals for whom both X_i and X_j are observed, and X_i and Y are observed, respectively), and let N_{ij} be the $(r \times r)$ degrees of freedom matrix and N_{iy} the $(r \times 1)$ degrees of freedom vector, with typical elements $(n_{ij} - 1)$ and $(n_{iy} - 1)$, respectively. Then

$$N_{ij} \otimes \Sigma_{xx} = X^TX, \qquad N_{iy} \otimes \Sigma_{xy} = X^TY \tag{12.52}$$

where $\otimes$ denotes the direct element by element matrix product, and X^TX and X^TY are computed from the n_{ij} and n_{iy} complete pairs. From (12.51) and (12.52) we have (see Haitovsky, 1967)

$$\mathbf{\Sigma}_{xx}\hat{\boldsymbol{\beta}} = \frac{1}{\mathbf{N}_{iy}} \otimes \mathbf{X}^{\mathsf{T}}\mathbf{Y}$$

$$= \frac{1}{\mathbf{N}_{iy}} \otimes [\mathbf{X}^{\mathsf{T}}(\mathbf{X}\boldsymbol{\beta} + \boldsymbol{\varepsilon})]$$

$$= \frac{\mathbf{N}_{ij}}{\mathbf{N}_{iy}} \otimes \left[\frac{1}{\mathbf{N}_{ij}} \otimes \mathbf{X}^{\mathsf{T}}\mathbf{X}\boldsymbol{\beta}\right] + \mathbf{\Sigma}_{x\varepsilon}$$

$$= \mathbf{N} \otimes \mathbf{\Sigma}_{xx}\boldsymbol{\beta} + \mathbf{\Sigma}_{x\varepsilon} \qquad (12.53)$$

where, notationally, $1/\mathbf{N}_{ij}$ and $1/\mathbf{N}_{iy}$ denote matrices with elements $1/(n_{ij} - 1)$ and $1/(n_{iy} - 1)$, respectively, and $\mathbf{N} = (\mathbf{N}_{iy}/\mathbf{N}_{ij})$ is the matrix that contains ratios of degrees of freedom of the form $(n_{iy} - 1)/(n_{ij} - 1)$. Note that n_{iy} and n_{ij} are also random variables since their values will generally vary from sample to sample. Taking expectations yields

$$E(\hat{\boldsymbol{\beta}}) = \mathbf{\Sigma}_{xx}^{-1}[\mathbf{N} \otimes \mathbf{\Sigma}_{xx}] \neq \boldsymbol{\beta} \qquad (12.54)$$

where $E(\mathbf{\Sigma}_{x\varepsilon}) = 0$, no errors are present in $\mathbf{X}$, and $\mathbf{\Sigma}_{xx}$ is of full rank. If $\mathbf{\Sigma}_{xx}$ were singular, the normal Eqs. (12.51) could still be solved by the use of a suitable generalized matrix inverse.

It is evident from (12.54) that the least-squares solution is generally biased unless all n_{ii}s and n_{iy}s are equal, since only in this case does $\mathbf{N} = (\mathbf{N}_{iy}/\mathbf{N}_{ii}) = \mathbf{I}_r$, the $(r \times r)$ unit matrix. Also, $\hat{\boldsymbol{\beta}}$ is an inconsistent estimator when $n_{ij} \to \infty$, $n_{iy} \to \infty$ unless n_{ij}/n_{iy} approaches unity. The intercept term $\hat{\beta}_0$ is computed in the usual way as

$$\hat{\beta}_0 = \bar{Y} - \sum_{i=1}^{r} \bar{X}_i\hat{\beta}_i, \qquad (12.55)$$

by one of two alternative methods. If not too much data are missing on the independent variables the means $\bar{X}_i$ are calculated in the usual way. If a large number of observations on the X_i are missing, Haitovsky (1967) suggests that Lord's (1955) ML estimator be used. Using (12.53) the covariance matrix of $\hat{\boldsymbol{\beta}}$ is given by

$$\mathbf{\Sigma}_{\hat{\boldsymbol{\beta}}} = E[(\hat{\boldsymbol{\beta}} - \boldsymbol{\beta})(\hat{\boldsymbol{\beta}} - \boldsymbol{\beta})^{\mathsf{T}}]$$

$$= E\{[\mathbf{\Sigma}_{xx}^{-1}(\mathbf{N} \otimes \mathbf{\Sigma}_{xx}) - \mathbf{I}]\,\boldsymbol{\beta} + \mathbf{\Sigma}_{xx}^{-1}\mathbf{\Sigma}_{x\varepsilon}\}$$

$$\times \{[\mathbf{\Sigma}_{xx}^{-1}(\mathbf{N} \otimes \mathbf{\Sigma}_{xx}) - \mathbf{I}]\boldsymbol{\beta} + \mathbf{\Sigma}_{xx}^{-1}\mathbf{\Sigma}_{x\varepsilon}\}^{\mathsf{T}}$$

Multiplying the right-hand side yields

$$\mathbf{\Sigma}_{\hat{\boldsymbol{\beta}}} = [\mathbf{\Sigma}_{xx}^{-1}(\mathbf{N} \otimes \mathbf{\Sigma}_{xx}) - \mathbf{I}]\boldsymbol{\beta}\boldsymbol{\beta}^{\mathsf{T}}[\mathbf{N}^{\mathsf{T}} \otimes \mathbf{\Sigma}_{xx} - \mathbf{I}] + E[\mathbf{\Sigma}_{xx}^{-1}\mathbf{\Sigma}_{x\varepsilon}\mathbf{\Sigma}_{x\varepsilon}^{\mathsf{T}}\,\mathbf{\Sigma}_{xx}^{-1}]$$

$$= [\mathbf{\Sigma}_{xx}^{-1}(\mathbf{N} \otimes \mathbf{\Sigma}_{xx}) - \mathbf{I}]\boldsymbol{\beta}\boldsymbol{\beta}^{\mathsf{T}}[\mathbf{N}^{\mathsf{T}} \otimes \mathbf{\Sigma}_{xx} - \mathbf{I}]$$

$$= + \sigma^2\left[\mathbf{\Sigma}_{xx}^{-1}\left(\frac{\mathbf{N}_{ij}}{\mathbf{N}_{iy}\mathbf{N}_{jy}} \otimes \mathbf{\Sigma}_{xx}\right)\mathbf{\Sigma}_{xx}^{-1}\right], \qquad (12.56)$$

since

$$E[\Sigma_{x\varepsilon}\Sigma_{x\varepsilon}^{\mathrm{T}}] = E\left[\frac{1}{\mathbf{N}_{iy}} \otimes \mathbf{X}^{\mathrm{T}}\varepsilon\right]\left[\frac{1}{\mathbf{N}_{jy}} \otimes \varepsilon^{\mathrm{T}}\mathbf{X}\right]$$

$$= \frac{1}{\mathbf{N}_{iy}\mathbf{N}_{jy}} \otimes [\mathbf{X}^{\mathrm{T}}E(\varepsilon\varepsilon^{\mathrm{T}})\mathbf{X}]$$

$$= \sigma^2 \frac{\mathbf{N}_{ij}}{\mathbf{N}_{iy}\mathbf{N}_{jy}} \otimes \Sigma_{xx} \tag{12.57}$$

where $\mathbf{N}^{\mathrm{T}} = (n_{ji}/n_{jy})$. When $n_{ij} = n_{iy} = n_{jy}$ we obtain the usual expression $\Sigma_{\hat{\beta}} = \sigma^2\Sigma_{xx}^{-1}$. Since σ^2 is unknown it is estimated from the sample residuals as

$$\hat{\sigma}^2 = \frac{\mathrm{SSE}}{n_y - r} = \left[\mathrm{Var}(y) - \sum_{i=1}^{r} \hat{\beta}_i\Sigma_{xy}\right]\frac{n_y}{n_y - r} \tag{12.58}$$

where $\mathrm{Var}(y)$ is computed from all existing observations on $\mathbf{Y}$. Finally, the adjusted multiple correlation coefficient is given by Haitovsky (1967) as

$$\bar{R}^2 = 1 - \frac{\hat{\sigma}^2}{\mathrm{Var}(y)} \tag{12.59}$$

For a more general form of the coefficient of multiple correlation see Rubin (1976a).

A well-known special case of the pairwise deletion model is that of Glasser (1964), who considers the case where data are missing only on the independent variables. Earlier, Federspiels, Monroe, and Greenberg (1959) considered an equivalent method to construct correlation matrices. Glasser defines the usual indicator matrix $\mathbf{W}$ (see Section 12.1), and two types of mean values,

$$\bar{X}_{j(j)} = \sum_{i=1}^{n} \frac{w_{ij}X_{ij}}{n_{ij}}, \qquad \bar{X}_{j(jk)} = \sum_{i=1}^{n} \frac{w_{ij}w_{ik}X_{ij}}{n_{jk}} \tag{12.60}$$

where $n_j = \sum_{i=1}^{n}w_{ij}$, the number of individuals for whom X_j is observed; $n_{jk} = \sum_{i=1}^{n}w_{ij}w_{ik}$, the number of individuals for whom both X_j and X_k are observed. Thus $\bar{X}_{j(j)}$ is the mean of X_j based on observed values of X_j, and $\bar{X}_{j(jk)}$ denotes the mean of X_j based on those observed values of X_j for which X_k is also observed. When all data are observed both means revert to the usual sample means $\bar{X}_j$. Similarly, the mean of $\mathbf{Y}$ is defined as

$$\bar{Y}_{(j)} = \sum_{i=1}^{n} \frac{w_{ij}Y_i}{n_j} \tag{12.61}$$

so that $\bar{Y}_{(j)}$ is the mean for individuals on whom X_j is observed. Note that means $\bar{X}_{j(jk)}$ and $\bar{Y}_{(j)}$ depend also on missing values on variables other than X_j and Y. The (j, k)th element of the sample covariance Σ_{xx} is then defined as

$$\sigma_{jk} = \sum_{i=1}^{n} \frac{w_{ij}(X_{ij} - \bar{X}_{j(jk)})w_{ik}(X_{ik} - \bar{X}_{k(jk)}]}{n_{jk} - 1} \tag{12.62}$$

so that only complete pairs of observations for both variables X_j and X_k are used to compute their covariance σ_{jk}. Thus when Σ_{xx} is computed the missing values of **X**—which are initially replaced by zeroes when the $\bar{X}_{j(jk)}$ are compared—are replaced by one of $\binom{r}{2}$ means $\bar{X}_{j(jk)}$, depending on the pair of variables X_j, X_k whose covariance σ_{jk} is being computed, that is, each mean is specific to a particular covariance. Also, note that the sum of deviations about means $\bar{X}_{j(jk)}$, $\bar{X}_{k(jk)}$ is no longer zero since

$$\sum_{i=1}^{n} w_{ij}X_{ij} = \sum_{i=1}^{n} w_{ij}(X_{ij} - \bar{X}_{j(jk)})$$

$$= N_j\bar{X}_{j(j)} - N_j\bar{X}_{j(jk)}$$

$$\neq 0.$$

For reasons that are unclear, Glasser uses the $\bar{X}_{j(jk)}$ rather than the $\bar{X}_{j(j)}$ to compute covariances. This procedure usually results in greater data loss than would normally be expected, since observations are deleted pairwise even when mean values are calculated.

The covariance vector Σ_{xy} is computed in a similar fashion, where

$$\sigma_{jy} = \sum_{i=1}^{n} \frac{w_{ij}(X_{ij} - \bar{X}_{j(j)})(Y_i - \bar{Y}_{(j)})}{n_j - 1} \qquad (j = 1, 2, \ldots, r) \quad (12.63)$$

Regression coefficients are then given by

$$\hat{\boldsymbol{\beta}} = \boldsymbol{\Sigma}_{xx}^{-1}\boldsymbol{\Sigma}_{xy} \qquad (12.64)$$

and the constant term by

$$\hat{\beta}_0 = \bar{Y} - \bar{X}_{j(j)}\hat{\boldsymbol{\beta}}$$

$$= Y - \sum_{j=1}^{n} \hat{\beta}_j\bar{X}_{j(j)} \qquad (12.65)$$

since no data are assumed to be missing on Y. The estimated regression plane is then

$$\hat{\mathbf{Y}} = \hat{\beta}_0 + \sum_{j=1}^{r} \hat{\beta}_j X_j$$

$$= \bar{Y} + \sum_{j=1}^{r} \hat{\beta}_j(\mathbf{X}_j - \bar{X}_{j(j)}). \qquad (12.66)$$

Note that in (12.64), the deviations about means now sum to zero since $\sum_{j=1}^{n}(\mathbf{X}_{ij} - \bar{X}_{j(j)})w_{ij} = 0$, for $j = 1, 2, \ldots, r$. The estimator (12.64) is biased (see 12.54) in general, but Glasser argues that when Type IV randomness holds, $\hat{\beta}$ is a consistent estimator as $n_{jk} \to \infty$. A property of Glasser's estimator is that efficiency declines as correlation between the independent variables increases.

OTHER ZERO-ORDER METHODS

Variants of the zero-order method are considered by Afifi and Elashoff (1966, 1967) and Cohen (1968, 1975). When data are missing only for the independent variables Cohen (1975) considers a model of the type

$$\mathbf{Y} = \beta_0 + \beta_1 X_1 + \beta_2 X_2 + \alpha_1 D_1 + \alpha_2 D_2 + \varepsilon \qquad (12.67)$$

$$\begin{bmatrix} y_1 \\ y_2 \\ y_3 \\ y_4 \\ y_5 \end{bmatrix} = \beta_0 + \beta_1 \begin{bmatrix} - \\ x_{21} \\ x_{31} \\ x_{41} \\ - \end{bmatrix} + \beta_2 \begin{bmatrix} x_{12} \\ - \\ x_{32} \\ - \\ x_{52} \end{bmatrix} + \alpha_1 \begin{bmatrix} 1 \\ 0 \\ 0 \\ 0 \\ 1 \end{bmatrix} + \alpha_2 \begin{bmatrix} 0 \\ 1 \\ 0 \\ 1 \\ 0 \end{bmatrix} + \varepsilon$$

where the D_i ($i = 1, 2$) are 0–1 dummy variables that assume the value of 1 when the corresponding observation on X_i ($i = 1, 2$) is missing and zero otherwise, missing values being replaced by zeroes. Note that (12.67) can also be interpreted as involving substitutions of "arbitrary" constants α_1 and α_2 in place of the missing observations, which is analogous to the Yates–Tocher "neutral values" method. Model (12.67) provides a useful method for testing whether the *pattern* of missing observations is random (Type I) with respect to **Y** and the independent variables. Thus a significant correlation between D_1 and D_2 indicate that individuals for whom data are missing on X_1 also tend to have data missing for X_2 (and vice versa), and significant α_i ($i = 1, 2$) imply that group means of the Ys for individuals with missing data on X_i and those with complete data on X_i are different. For a numerical example the reader is referred to Cohen (1975, pp. 275–279), where the so-called hierarchical version of model (12.67) is considered.

A closely related technique, described by Rummel (1970, p. 266) for use in factor analysis can be easily adapted for the multiple regression model by defining a new "missing data variable" whose ith entry consists of the total number of observations missing, across the independent variables, for individual i.[7] Again, this technique takes into account only nonrandomness of occurrence of missing data.

Rummel states that when the missing data variable is statistically independent of the explanatory variables, the influence of the missing observations can be ignored, which is not necessarily the case since either Type II or Type IV randomness can still be violated, and the resultant regression coefficients will be biased.

Finally, a frequently used straightforward zero-order technique fills in the missing values (dependent or independent variables) by the sample means of the observed variables, computed from the nonmissing values. The rationale behind this procedure is that, in the case of the normal distribution, the sample mean provides an optimal estimate of the most probable value; that is, the value that we would expect to occur on the average before an observation is made. Of course, if we suspect that each variable is not distributed normally, but for

---

[7] However, significance of the $\hat{\alpha}_i$ does not necessarily imply that the missing data are missing nonrandomly, in the sense of Type III or Type IV.

example as the double exponential (Laplacian) distribution, the sample median is usually a better choice. Although the mean value replacement method is very similar to pairwise deletion, since deviations about means for the missing values result in zeroes, the two methods are not equivalent and usually result in different regression estimates. Although mean value replacement obviates the problem of non-Grammian covariance matrices it does have its drawbacks: (*a*) replacing missing values by means (or zeroes when variables are expressed as deviations about means) artificially reduces sample variances, and can introduce the problem of heteroscedastic error terms in the OLS regression model; (*b*) replacing missing independent variable values by their means introduces errors in the explanatory variables. The regression slopes will therefore tend to be biased. The effects of heteroscedasticity and error in the independent variables may very well be to render the OLS regression coefficients so inefficient and biased as to cancel potential gains due to the substitution.

To reduce the artificial drop in the sample variances, a modified zero-order method is at times used, the so-called hot deck method (e.g., see Ford, 1976; Pregibon, 1975). The procedure consists of first sorting (clustering) all individuals in the sample into subgroups, by any method thought to be appropriate, and then filling in the missing values by the group-specific means rather than by the overall means of the variables. The method is particularly appropriate when distinct clusters do in fact exist, which is frequently the case for survey data.

First-Order Methods

Zero-order methods attempt to use univariate or bivariate information, such as sample means or covariance, to provide estimates of the missing values. Generally in a multivariate sample, information additional to that contained in the mean values is available to estimate missing observations usually in the form of other simultaneously observed (or predetermined) correlated variables. In an attempt to improve missing data estimates various researchers (T. W. Anderson, 1957; Buck, 1960; Dear, 1959; Edgett, 1956; Lord, 1955b; Matthai, 1951; Nicholson, 1957; Walsh, 1961; Wilks, 1932) have turned their attention to multivariate correlational methods, such as regression and principal components analysis, in order to estimate the missing values first, and then compute regression estimates from the completed sample. At this point statistical procedures used to estimate missing data need not be necessarily the same as the final model to be estimated. Consequently all the methods outlined in Section 12.3 can be used to estimate missing values in the regression context, and no new points arise, although properties of the regression parameters are generally dependent on the particular technique used. Two-stage methods for estimating statistical models with missing data that employ information other than sample means and missing–nonmissing dichotomous variables are usually referred to as first-order methods (see Afifi & Elashoff, 1966).

When multivariate normality is assumed, the maximum likelihood results of Wilks (1932), Matthai (1951), Lord (1955a,b), Edgett (1956), Nicholson (1957), and T. W. Anderson (1957) can be used to obtain regression estimators in closed form, for monotonically missing data. As seen, ML methods generally result in iterative solutions when data are missing in a random pattern; this is also the case when estimating a multivariate regression plane. Iterative estimates provide a natural higher order extension of first-order methods since evidence now exists that they are generally superior to the first-order procedures. The first authors to describe an iterative least-squares regression estimator are Federspiel *et al.* (1959). They insert mean values as initial estimates of the missing data, obtain OLS regression coefficients, and use these to compute new estimates of the missing values. The process is continued until the estimates do not differ significantly. More recently Jackson (1968) has provided an evaluation of the method in a discriminant analysis context (to be considered in the following) and indicates that iteration appears to improve the OLS estimates. Although no work appears to have been done on the topic, it seems probable that iteration can also provide a useful extension of Dear's principal components method.

Finally, Bayesian variants of the first-order method have been developed by Dagenais (1974) and Press and Scott (1975, 1976). Dagenais considers the model

$$\mathbf{Y} = \beta_0 + \sum_{j=1}^{r} \beta_j X_j + \varepsilon \qquad (12.68)$$

where Y or one or more of the X_js are missing. It is assumed that other variables not included in (12.68) are also available such that we have the side relations

$$\begin{bmatrix} X_1 \\ X_2 \end{bmatrix} = \begin{bmatrix} Z_1 & 0 \\ 0 & Z_2 \end{bmatrix} \begin{bmatrix} \theta_1 \\ \theta_2 \end{bmatrix} + \begin{bmatrix} V_1 \\ V_2 \end{bmatrix} \qquad (12.69)$$

where Z_1 and Z_2 are two sets of extra available variables and the residuals ε and V are normally distributed. Data can be missing for any variable(s) of (12.68) and (12.69), and under assumptions of "vague" prior knowledge Dagenais (1974) considers seven combinations of missing data cases for the variables in systems (12.68) and (12.69), some of which are mutually exclusive. The basic idea is to obtain the posterior probability density function of the parameters to be estimated [regression slopes of (12.68), (12.69), and second moments of ε and V], for the various cases, where the prior density of the unknown parameters expresses so-called prior ignorance and is made proportional to

$$(\sigma^2)^{-1}|S|^{-3/2} \qquad (12.70)$$

where σ^2 is the common variance of the ε and $|S|$ is the determinant of the covariance matrix of V_1 and V_2. The marginal posterior probability density function of the relevant parameters is then obtained by numerical integration.

Press and Scott (1975, 1976) employ a somewhat similar procedure to that of Dagenais (1974), where data are missing on the dependent and/or independent variables. A vague invariant prior distribution of the regression parameters is also assumed and missing values are estimated from the other variables in the set. However, it appears to be difficult to obtain a simple expression for the marginal density of the regression slopes except for very special patterns of missing data; solutions are generally obtained iteratively. There is thus a certain formal similarity between ML and Bayesian techniques in this respect. It must be kept in mind, however, that Bayesian methods are dependent on prior knowledge (theoretical or empirically established), which if based on incorrect assumptions can have a biasing effect on the regression coefficients.

Comparison of Missing Data Estimators

Having described and commented on the various estimators available for estimating regression equations, we now present a relative evaluation of the sampling properties of missing data estimators, based on the published literature. Due to the complex analytical properties of missing multivariate data estimators, very few exact results are known concerning their relative efficiencies; comparative advantages of various procedures are usually evaluated by means of numerical simulation techniques.

Because of its relatively more restricted nature, the bivariate regression model is usually amenable to a more wide selection of missing data estimates. Thus Afifi and Elashoff (1967, 1969a) consider the bivariate regression model

$$y = \beta_0 + \beta_1 x + \varepsilon \qquad (12.71)$$

for the following missing data procedures:

1. Listwise deletion on the complete part of the sample only or
2. A zero-order method, where sample means are substituted for the m_x missing x values and m_y missing y values, respectively, and unweighted least squares applied. The resulting OLS estimator β_0 is biased but an unbiased version defined as $\hat{\beta}_u^0 = (n_x/n_c) \hat{\beta}_0$ is used, where n_x values of x are complete and the total bivariate sample contains no complete observations
3. A modified zero-order procedure. "Arbitrary" constants α_1 and α_2 are substituted for each missing y and x, respectively, and the least squares regression line is estimated from the completed sample. This procedure evidently corresponds to the dummy variable method (12.65).
4. Mixed methods combining (1) and (2)
5. First-order estimator where the regressions of y on x and x on y are computed from the complete part of the sample consisting of n_c observations. The missing y values are then estimated from the first regression and the missing x values from the second regression, and OLS then used on the completed sample. Again both a biased and an unbiased version are presented.
6. Two-stage method. First, estimate the regression of x on y from n_c complete observations by OLS. Second, estimate the m_x missing x val-

ues from this regression, and then estimate the regression of y on x from the n_y completed observations. The method evidently discards those xs for which y is not observed. Again, a biased and an unbiased version of the estimator are given.

7. Wilks's (1932) ML estimators of the means, variance, covariance, and regression parameters.

Afifi and Elashoff (1967, 1969a) provide asymptotic sampling properties of the preceding estimators for the bivariate case, as well as numerical evaluations of relative efficiencies. The authors conclude the following:

1. The efficiencies of the zero-order and modified zero-order estimators decrease as total sample size n increases, with ρ_{xy}, m_x/n, and m_y/n kept fixed. Also keeping m_x and m_y constant, efficiency decreases as ρ_{xy} increases.
2. The zero-order and modified zero-order methods are generally superior to listwise deletion OLS when $|\rho_{xy}| \leq .30$ and $n \leq 70$. Also the superiority of the zero-order methods seems to increase when m_x/n and m_y/n are greater than $\frac{1}{4}$.
3. For n and m_x/n (or m_y/n) fixed, the efficiency of the zero-order and modified zero-order methods estimators increases, for those values of ρ_{xy} where those estimators have good efficiency [see (2) above].
4. For fixed n, $(m_x + m_y)$ and $|m_x - m_y|$, the zero-order and modified zero-order estimators have highest efficiency when $m_x < m_y$ for small values of $|\rho_{xy}|$.
5. The two-stage estimator and Wilks's (1932) ML estimator generally outperform other estimators described in (1)–(7). The relative success of Wilks's ML estmiator probably indicates the normal nature of the author's simulation data, rather than an inherent advantage of ML methods.

Since the estimators considered by Afifi and Elashoff (1967, 1969a) are consistent, their numerical evaluation is carried out for large samples, and the chief sampling property of interest is therefore efficiency. In a further small sample study, Afifi and Elashoff (1969b) show by numerical simulation that both the first-order and two-stage estimators (unbiased versions) have little bias and good efficiency in samples as small as $n = 20$. The biased versions that do not correct for available sample size tend to largely overestimate β, however. The authors conclude that estimators with good asymptotic efficiencies generally have small bias and good small sample efficiency, particularly when as much as 40% of both x and y values are missing (and $n = 20$). The two-stage (unbiased version) estimator is singled out by the authors as being of potential usefulness for both large and small samples, and it can also be used in place of Wilks's ML estimators. It must be kept in mind, however, that the preceding results pertain, strictly speaking, to the bivariate model (12.71) and need not necessarily carry over by analogy to the more general multivariate case.

Based partially on intuitive reasoning and on Afifi and Elashoff's (1967, 1969a, 1969b) results, it may appear that first-order methods can be expected to outperform zero-order estimators, particularly the listwise deletion (Yates To-cher) OLS. That this is not necessarily the case in small samples is shown by H. A. Thomas (1958) and Fiering (1962) for the bivariate and trivariate regression equations. Let

$$I = \left[1 - \frac{(n - n_y)}{n}\left[\frac{(n_y - 2)\rho_{xy}^2 - 1}{n_y - 3}\right]\right]^{-1}$$
(12.72)

for the bivariate case where n complete observations are available for x, and n_y for y ($n_y < n$) and I is the relative information index defined as the ratio of the variance of $\hat{\beta}$ when computed from the sample of size n_y (Yates–Tocher OLS) divided by the variance of $\hat{\beta}$ when computed from all data by a first-order procedure. When I exceeds unity the first-order procedure is therefore prefera-ble to the Yates–Tocher method. From (12.72) it can be seen that $I \geq 1.0$ only when $\rho_{xy}^2 \geq (n_y - 2)^{-1}$ and therefore the first-order method is only guaranteed to be more efficient for large values of n_y, given some fixed value of ρ_{xy}^2. Fiering (1962) extends Thomas's result (12.72) to the trivariate case with data missing for the dependent variable only and provides convenient tables for I.

Glasser (1964) carries out a large sample evaluation of the zero-order pairwise deletion method with the listwise deletion OLS. After establishing the consistency of his proposed pairwise deletion estimator Glasser (1964) con-cludes the following from a numerical evaluation of the trivariate regression equation.

1. Maximum efficiency of the pairwise deletion estimator is achieved when the correlation ρ_{12} between the two independent variables X_1 and X_2 is identically zero, and efficiency decreases as ρ_{12} increases, all else held con-stant.

2. When percentages of missing observations for X_1 and X_2 are equal, X_1 and X_2 being incomplete to any degree, the relative efficiency of $\hat{\beta}_1$ and $\hat{\beta}_2$ computed by pairwise deletion is higher than the listwise OLS estimator, when-ever $|\rho_{12}| \leq \sqrt{\frac{1}{3}}$. Also ρ_{12} may be greater than this value and still yield greater efficiency of the pairwise deletion procedure, depending on the degree of in-completeness of the data.

3. When $|\rho_{12}| > \sqrt{\frac{1}{3}}$ the pairwise deletion estimator is less efficient than the listwise OLS estimator, all else held constant.

An improvement over Glasser's (1964) pairwise deletion estimator (large samples) is provided by Dagenais (1971), also for the trivariate case. Although Dagenais's (1971) estimator is also consistent, it is generally more efficient than that of Glasser, with efficiency *increasing as* ρ_{12} increases. This is evidently a useful property for multivariate social data, which tends to be correlated. Dage-nais's (1971) estimator also has smaller asymptotic variance than listwise dele-tion OLS, but a subsequent study by Dagenais (1972) indicates that his original estimator is not very efficient in small samples, and is much poorer in terms of mean square error—even in large samples. An alternative consistent estimator is suggested by the author; it has smaller asymptotic variance than that of the listwise deletion zero-order method. A correction for bias is also provided, which makes the estimator suitable for small samples. A simulation comparison is carried out by Dagenais (1972) between his two estimators and that of Glasser (1974) and listwise deletion OLS, from which the following conclusions emerge.

1. The Glasser (1964) pairwise deletion method and Dagenais's (1971) estimator perform poorly in terms of means square error, even in large samples.
2. The performance of the Dagenais (1972) estimator is better than listwise deletion, its relative superiority increasing as the sample size decreases.
3. Dagenais's (1972) estimator improves, relatively, as the coefficient of multiple determination (R^2) decreases—thus when $R^2 \geq .95$, for example, the listwise procedure yields better results. Also, ρ_{xy} seems to have little effect on the mean square error of the estimator.
4. As the percentage of complete observations decreases the superiority of Dagenais's (1972) estimator also decreases.

This research effort, which attempts to shed light on the relative merits of missing data estimators and conditions under which they appear to be optimum, is confined to the bivariate and trivariate regression models. Haitovsky (1967), however, carries out a series of simulation experiments for the general multivariate model and evaluates the pairwise deletion and listwise deletion zero-order methods, for two, four, and five independent regression variables. Eight sets of regression data are generated, which differ with respect to the distribution of the independent variables (normal and uniform distributions), the correlations between them, the R^2 value, the relative weights in the regression of highly correlated independent variables, and their variability as compared to that of the residual error term. Varying proportions of artificially created missing values are then used in order to evaluate the two methods. Haitovsky's findings are as follows.

1. The listwise deletion OLS estimator is markedly superior to the pairwise deletion method, both with respect to efficiency and bias. The bias in the pairwise deletion estimator is ascribed to inconsistency of the covariance matrix (non-positive-definiteness), whereas inefficiency is largely seen to be due to the so-called nuisance parameters encountered when variances of the partial regression coefficients are computed.

2. Glasser's (1964) first conclusion is confirmed, but not the second (p. 461). Indeed, Haitovsky finds that even when $\rho_{12} = 0$ the pairwise deletion estimator is still less efficient than the listwise deletion method.

In addition, it appears from Haitovsky's (1967) numerical tables that the number of independent variables plays an insignificant role in determining efficiency and bias of the two zero-order estimators, although the independent role of this effect cannot be easily or conveniently determined from Haitovsky's experimental set-up and tables. It is not clear what role, if any, is played by the R^2 statistic, either the corrected or the uncorrected version.

A more recent study (Kim & Curry, 1977) indicates that for multivariate normal samples with randomly missing data the pairwise deletion method is superior to listwise deletion for OLS models and for path analysis when 1, 2, 5, and 10% of the data are missing. The authors compare the two procedures in terms of the deviations between the true and the pairwise and listwise deletion regression coefficients. They do not examine standard errors of the coefficients or standard errors of estimate.

Kelejian (1969) provides exact sampling properties of the listwise deletion method and a first-order estimator that, to the present authors' best knowledge, represents the only successful attempt to establish relative efficiency measures for the multivariate regression equation by analytic means. Let

$$\mathbf{Y} = \mathbf{X}\alpha + \mathbf{Z}\beta + \varepsilon \tag{12.73}$$

by the usual multivariate OLS model where $\mathbf{X}$ is a $(n_1 \times 1)$ vector, $\mathbf{Z}$ a $(n \times r)$ matrix of additional independent variables and $\mathbf{Y}$ is a $(n \times 1)$ vector of observations on the dependent variable. The problem considered by Kelejian (1969) is to compare relative efficiencies of the listwise deletion and a first-order regression method for the case where no data are missing for $\mathbf{Y}$ and for the set $\mathbf{Z}$, but only $n > n_1 < r + 1$ observations on $\mathbf{X}$ are available. Although the $n_2 = n - n_1$ missing values for $\mathbf{X}$ can occur in any pattern, Kelejian assumes Type III randomness that ensures consistency. The sample is then partitioned as

$$\mathbf{Y}_1 = \mathbf{X}_1\alpha + \mathbf{Z}_1\beta + \varepsilon_1 \tag{12.74}$$

$$\mathbf{Y}_2 = \mathbf{X}_2\alpha + \mathbf{Z}_2\beta + \varepsilon_2 \tag{12.75}$$

where the equations correspond to the two parts of the sample of size n_1 and n_2, respectively. All vectors in (12.75) are therefore complete but $\mathbf{X}_2$ is an empty vector. Also assume the regression relation

$$\mathbf{X}_2 = \mathbf{Z}_2\gamma + U_2 \tag{12.76}$$

from which the missing values $\mathbf{X}_2$ are estimated. Eliminating the unknown missing values $\mathbf{X}_2$ by substituting (12.76) into (12.75) yields

$$\mathbf{Y}_2 = \mathbf{Z}_2\Pi + V \tag{12.77}$$

where

$$\Pi = \gamma\alpha + \beta. \tag{12.78}$$

Equation (12.74) can also be written in the more compact form

$$\mathbf{Y}_1 = [\mathbf{X}_1 \vdots \mathbf{Z}_1] \begin{bmatrix} \alpha \\ \cdots \\ \beta \end{bmatrix} + \varepsilon_1$$

$$= \mathbf{P}_1\mathbf{C} + \varepsilon_1 \tag{12.79}$$

say. Let $\hat{\mathbf{C}}_{LS}$ denote the zero-order listwise deletion OLS estimator, $\hat{\mathbf{C}}$ the first-order estimator, and $\mathbf{C}^*$ the minimum variance linear unbiased estimator of $\mathbf{C}$ as $n_2 \to \infty$, when γ is known. Kelejian (1969) then shows that

$$\mathbf{C}^* = \hat{\mathbf{C}}_{LS} + [(\mathbf{P}_1^T\mathbf{P}_1)^{-1}\mathbf{R}^T][\mathbf{R}(\mathbf{P}_1^T\mathbf{P}_1)^{-1}\mathbf{R}^T]^{-1}[\hat{\Pi} - \mathbf{R}\mathbf{C}_{LS}] \quad (12.80)$$

and

$$\hat{\mathbf{C}} = \hat{\mathbf{C}}_{LS} + \mathbf{H}_1^{-1}[I_r + \hat{R}^T Z_2^T Z_2 \hat{R} \mathbf{H}_1^{-1}]^{-1}\hat{R}^T Z_2^T Z_2 [\hat{\Pi} - \hat{R}\hat{\mathbf{C}}_{LS}] \quad (12.81)$$

where $R = [\gamma \vdots I_r]$, I_r is the $(r \times r)$ unit matrix, $H_1 = \mathbf{P}_1^T\mathbf{P}_1$, $H_2 = \mathbf{P}_2^T\mathbf{P}_2$, and $P_2 = [X_2 \vdots Z_2]$. It is clear from (12.80) and (12.81) that both C^* and $\hat{C}$ are restricted OLS estimators so that $\hat{C}$ and C^* differ from $\hat{\mathbf{C}}_{LS}$ to the extent to which the restriction

$$\hat{\Pi} = \hat{R}\hat{\mathbf{C}}_{LS}$$

$$= \gamma\hat{\alpha} + \hat{\beta} \quad (12.82)$$

are not satisfied. Since in practice γ is not known it must be estimated from (12.82) by OLS.

To examine the large sample properties of $\hat{C}$ and $\hat{\mathbf{C}}_{LS}$ we must consider the following three cases, where $\lambda = n_1/n_2$ and (1) $\lambda \to \infty$, (2) $\lambda \to 0$, and (3) $\lambda \to 1$.

1. $\lambda \to \infty$: In this case, $\hat{C}$ and $\hat{\mathbf{C}}_{LS}$ both have equal asymptotic covariance matrices since $(\hat{C} - \hat{\mathbf{C}}_{LS})$ is of smaller order (in probability) than $n_1^{-1/2}$. Also, let $\hat{\gamma}^T = (\bar{X}_1, 0, \ldots, 0)^T$ where the mean value $\bar{X}_1$ is also a zero-order estimator of the n_2 missing $\mathbf{X}$ values. Let $\hat{C}_0$ be the zero-order estimator of $\mathbf{C}$ obtained by applying OLS to the completed sample. The estimator $\hat{C}_0$ also has the same asymptotic covariance matrix as $\hat{\mathbf{C}}_{LS}$. Both zero-order estimators are therefore equally efficient and as efficient as the first-order estimator in large samples when the proportion of missing data is small, which accords well with intuitive reasoning. Zero-order estimators, however, are easier to compute.

2. $\lambda \to 0$: Asymptotic variances of the regression parameters $\hat{C}$ are larger than corresponding elements of $\mathbf{C}^*$, and the asymptotic variance of the first-order estimator of α is equal to that of the listwise deletion estimator. Kelejian derives a general expression for the relative efficiencies of $\hat{\beta}$ and $\hat{\beta}_{LS}$, which for the trivariate regression case reduces to

$$\frac{\sigma_{\hat{\beta}}^2}{\sigma_{\hat{\beta}LS}^2} = 1 + \frac{\alpha^2\sigma_x^2(1 - R_{xz}^2) - \sigma_\varepsilon^2(1 - R_{xy}^2)}{\sigma_\varepsilon^2\sigma_x^2}$$

$$= 1 + F \quad (12.83)$$

where $\sigma_{\hat{\beta}}^2$ and $\sigma_{\hat{\beta}LS}^2$ are asymptotic variances of the first-order and the zero-order listwise deletion estimators of $\boldsymbol{\beta}$, respectively; σ_x^2 and σ_ε^2 are (asymptotic) variances of x and ε, and R_{xz}^2 is the bivariate correlation between $\mathbf{X}$ and $\mathbf{Z}$. It follows that $\sigma_{\hat{\beta}}^2 < \sigma_{\hat{\beta}LS}^2$ only when $F < 0$, that is, when

$$1 - \frac{\sigma_\varepsilon^2}{\alpha^2\sigma_x^2} < R_{xz}^2 < 1. \quad (12.84)$$

Thus, even for a high proportion of missing data on **X**, Kelejian's first-order estimator is not necessarily more efficient than listwise deletion. When σ_ε^2, σ_x^2, and α^2 are held constant in (12.83) the efficiency of σ_β^2 is dependent on R_{xy}^2, higher correlation values leading to higher efficiency of σ_β^2. For very low (or zero) values of R_{xy}^2, however, it is better to simply estimate β from the complete portion of the sample.

   3. $\lambda \to 1$: The same conclusions apply as in (2).

   Strictly speaking Kelejian's (1969) results hold only when one independent regression variable X has missing information. However, it seems plausible that the preceding results can be generalized to the case of two sets of independent variables **X** and **Z** where some data in matrix **X** are missing for more than one variable but **Z** is complete.

   More recently, greater attention has centered on iterative ML methods by which missing data and regression parameters can be estimated simultaneously. Iterative procedures usually begin with initial values for the missing data, from which regression coefficients are computed, which in turn provide new estimates for the missing data. The interactive process is continued until both regression and missing values converge to stable magnitudes. The initial values of the missing data can be guessed, or else computed by zero-order or first-order methods, whichever is thought to be more appropriate. In a numerical simulation study Beale and Little (1975) evaluate various iterative methods and compare these to the more traditional zero-order and first-order procedures for 5, 10, 20, and 40% of the data missing randomly (Type III randomness) for both dependent and independent variables, and R^2 values which range from .089 to .990. Beale and Little evaluate the following procedures:

   1. Listwise deletion (Yates–Tocher)
   2. Buck's (1960) first-order method
   3. An iterative version of Buck's method, developed by the authors and termed as "corrected maximum-likelihood" since it only differs from that of Orchard and Woodbury's (1972) ML procedure (when normality is assumed) by a degree of freedom adjustment
   4. Means, variances, and covariances of the independent variables X are estimated by the corrected ML method (3) for every observation where the dependent variable Y is observed, and these are used to fit missing independent variable values. The OLS parameters are then estimated by OLS for those observations where the dependent variable is present. The effect of this is to give missing X observations "neutral" values, given the known Y values.
   5. Method (4) but with incomplete observations receiving less weight. Let

$$W_i = \begin{cases} \dfrac{S_y^2}{S_{y_i}^2} & \text{if } y_i \text{ is observed} \\[2ex] 0 & \text{otherwise} \end{cases}$$

where $S_{y_i}^2$ and S_y^2 denote the sample conditional variance of Y given the known X values for observation i, and residual variance of Y when all independent variables X are fitted, respectively. The weights W_i are estimated iteratively in a weighted least-squares context.

6. A method combining (3) and (5): Method (3) is used to estimate the covariance matrix for all variables, and method (5) is then applied to find the fitted values and to estimate the weights W_i.

7. The Orchard–Woodbury (1972) ML estimator

Beale and Little conclude that method (3) is generally best, and (4) is poorer than the remaining five. Both methods (2) and (3) are superior to the listwise deletion zero-order OLS, and (6) is generally better than (5). Orchard and Woodbury's ML method is found to be marginally worse (.1%) than (3). The difference between the iterated Buck method (3) and the ML procedure (7), however, is so small that it is probably better to reserve judgment until more evidence is available. See also a recent simulation study by Little (1979).

There has been very little systematic evaluation of the proposed solutions to the missing data problem in regression analysis, and consequently it is difficult to conclude this section with a definite ranking of the methods. Two tentative remarks can be made concerning the estimators. First, based on evidence provided by Haitovsky (1967) and Dagenais (1971, 1972) we can conclude that pairwise deletion performs rather poorly when compared with listwise deletion, which in turn tends to be outperformed by first-order methods in large samples and when a moderate–high proportion of data is missing. Since it is also known that pairwise deletion can result in nonestimable parameters (a non-positive-definite covariance matrix), the procedure should be used with great caution, if at all. Second, although first-order procedures tend to outperform zero-order methods, they in turn are outperformed by iterative estimates, such as the iterative version of Buck's estimator and maximum likelihood methods. Beale and Little's (1975) results indicate, however, that the improvement is not great if the proportion of missing data is small. For a large sample, the computational requirements of iterative estimators may well preclude their use. Therefore, in a large- or medium-sized sample having a small proportion of missing values, the listwise deletion estimator appears to be optimal, especially when its relative ease of use is kept in mind. For a small sample, on the other hand, computational complexity is usually not a problem and iterative procedures can be used more effectively, particularly since they tend to improve efficiency. Table 12.6 provides a classification of the various estimators considered in the literature and discussed in the present section. The table shows which techniques have been evaluated under different conditions, but no evaluation of their performance is indicated.

Conclusions

The literature survey provided here on missing data in regression analysis shows that no single method emerges as uniformly best. Our conclusions are

TABLE 12.6
Conditions under Which Techniques Have been Evaluated

Percentage missing observations	Sample size			
	Small ($n \leq 50$)	Medium ($50 < n \leq 100$)	Large ($n \geq 100$)	
Low 0–10	Yates–Tocher Mean substitution (Dagenais, 1972) Qusave	Yates–Tocher Mean substitution	Yates–Tocher Mean substitution	
Medium 10–25 Large 25	Yates–Tocher Mean substitution Dagenais, 1972 Qusave	Yates–Tocher Mean substitution Dagenais, 1972 Qusave Mean substitution	Yates–Tocher Mean substitution Qusave Mean substitution	Low multicollinearity
Low 0–10 Medium 10–25	Buck Dear Iterative Buck Dear	Buck Dear Iterative Buck Dear	Buck Dear Iterative Buck Dear	Medium multicollinearity
Large 25	Iterative	Iterative Buck Dear	Iterative	
Low 0–10 Medium 10–25	Buck Iterative	Buck Iterative Dear Buck	Buck Dear Iterative Dear Buck	High multicollinearity
Large 25	Iterative	Iterative	Iterative	

therefore in this respect similar to those of Timm (1970), although the author evaluates only three methods—those of Wilks (1932), Dear (1959), and Buck (1959). The principal difficulty encountered in a literature survey of this sort is that most published work studies missing data procedures that vary with respect to the method used, stratification categories (number of variables, sample size, proportion of missing data, degree of multicollinearity, coefficient of multiple determination, etc.), and criteria by which efficiency is measured. Consequently, many authors simply are not comparable in their findings and conclusions. A brief summary of principal results obtained to date concerning regression estimates is nevertheless possible and is presented here. (For the effect of missing data on inference and predictor variables see Rubin, 1976a, 1976b.)

1. The pairwise deletion method, it was seen, can result in a non-positive-definite covariance (correlation) matrix and therefore may lead to biased estimates, even in large samples. Simulation experiments (Dagenais, 1971, 1972;

Haitovsky, 1967) suggest that pairwise deletion is the poorest of the zero-order methods and should therefore be used with great caution, if at all. The Wilks (1932) ML estimator (substitution of column means for missing data) also performs poorly. Work by a number of people (Afifi & Elashoff, 1967, 1969; Beale & Little, 1975; Timm, 1970) seems to suggest that the listwise deletion (and neutral values) estimator is also inferior to the first-order methods. However, we view Beale and Little's numerical simulation results as misleading on this point, since their regression examples exhibit very high multicollinearity among the explanatory variables, which is not always typical of survey data. Evidently, highly intercorrelated independent variables tend to favor first-order estimators. The neutral values or listwise deletion estimators probably are still the simplest solution when the proportion of (randomly) missing data is small, and independent regression variables exhibit low correlation.

2. No first-order methods emerge as uniformly superior. Timm's (1970) work provides the most direct evidence on the relative merits of the Buck (1960) and Dear (1959) estimators, both for the covariance and correlation matrices—the reader is referred to the previous section for Timm's conclusions.

3. When first-order methods are particularly advantageous (high R^2 and multicollinearity amongst independent variables) the results of Beale and Little (1975) clearly indicate the superiority of iterative estimators over that of Buck, when a high proportion of data is missing. Dear's principal components method is, however, not evaluated. The superiority, moreover, appears to be independent of sample size and R^2. However since Timm (1970) finds Dear's procedure to be better than that of Buck (when more than 1% of the data are missing) it is not clear whether the iterative procedures considered by Beale and Little are more efficient (in some sense) than that of Dear, although this seems plausible. However, an iterative version of the principal components method very well may perform better than the iterated Buck estimator, especially if more than a single principal component is retained.[8]

4. Dagenais's (1972) trivariate "Qusave" estimator appears to yield superior mean square errors to the listwise deletion method, and contains a valuable feature in that its performance improves with decreased R^2 values. This is very useful for sample survey data that typically exhibit low R^2 coefficients. It also seems to perform well in small samples and is therefore a valuable addition to the available stock of missing data estimators. For more than two independent regression variables Dagenais (1973) reports good results with his generalized least-squares estimator.

Finally, it may be useful to point out that the problem of missing data in regression analysis so far has only been addressed in terms of OLS regression. Thus no results appear to be known concerning missing data problems in other regression problems such as least squares with errors in the independent vari-

---

[8] A formulation and evaluation of an iterative principal components-factor analysis method is not available in the published literature.

ables (orthogonal and weighted least squares) and minimization of the sum of absolute (or relative) errors.

12.5. OTHER MULTIVARIATE MODELS

The problem of missing data, together with techniques for its solution, has received much attention in the context of classical experimental design and regression models; for this reason separate sections are devoted to both models. In the present section, we group some other important multivariate models—discriminant analysis, simultaneous equations, factor analysis, and contingency tables—that, although in wide use, seem not to have been as widely considered in the context of missing data. Indeed, very little work appears to have been done on missing data problems in such widely employed multivariate sample survey methods as multidimensional scaling (metric, non-metric), hierarchical cluster analysis, or path analysis; these omissions constitute substantial gaps in the literature.

Path analysis however is formally equivalent to simultaneous equations models employed in econometrics, where Sargan and Drettakis (1974), Dagenais (1976), and Dagenais and Dagenais (1977) have considered estimation with missing data. Again, many of the ML estimation procedures described in Section 12.3 are applicable here, since once the covariance (correlation) matrix is estimated by ML (or other) methods in the presence of missing data then multivariate methods (such as factor analysis) can proceed more or less in the usual manner.

Discriminant Analysis

The typical regression problem seeks to infer structural properties of a given sample of individuals from an r-dimensional regression plane. Discriminant analysis, on the other hand, addresses itself to the problem of estimating a multivariate plane whose coefficients can be used to classify individuals with certain characteristics (the variables), into one of K distinct populations. Unlike the more exploratory cluster analysis methodology, the number of populations or groups must be known beforehand. The objective is to isolate those variables, if any, that "discriminate" between individuals in the sample, that is, that provide a criterion for classification. For the general K-group case the estimation of the plane involves latent roots and vectors of certain positive definite matrices, but in the two group case (group A and group B) it is well known that the discriminant plane may be computed by regression methods[9] where the hypothesized discriminating (classificatory) characteristics are the independent variables and the dependent variable is a dichotomous scale, usu-

---

[9] Or, more appropriately, this is done by generalized least squares since individuals in different groups will not usually possess equal residual variance.

ally the 0–1 scale, whose values indicate whether a given individual is in group A or group B. The two-group case can therefore be considered as a particular application of least squares regression, and many missing data procedures discussed in the previous sections are also appropriate here, particularly those concerned with missing data for the independent regression variables.

The first explicit published treatment of missing data on the independent variables in the two-group discriminant analysis model is that of Jackson (1968), who presents results of an empirical study of two types of infant delivery. Almost 50% of the cases had data missing on the independent variables, and Jackson uses the Federspiel *et al.* (1959) iterative process to first estimate the missing values, and then computes the discriminant plane from the whole sample. The iterative process used is similar to other such procedures in regression analysis and consists of the following four steps:

1. Replace missing values by the appropriate variable means, as in the case of zero-order methods.
2. Regress each variable with missing observations on the remaining variables (see Buck's procedure, Section 12.2), obtaining the first stage first-order estimates for both the regression coefficients and the missing values.
3. Replace the mean value estimates in (1) by regression estimates obtained in (2), and recompute the discriminant regression plane to obtain the second stage first-order estimates.
4. Repeat the procedure until the regression coefficients (or the estimated missing values) approach stable numerical values.

Jackson (1968) presents results of a six-step iteration and compares results obtained by the iterative method, the listwise deletion method, and the mean-value replacement zero-order method. She concludes that six iterations are sufficient in her case to achieve stable values, and that the iterative procedure yields more significant regression coefficients and a much higher F-statistic value than the other procedures. She points out that significance testing must be viewed with caution here due to departure from normality. Also it must be kept in mind that the usual significance testing can lead to very misleading conclusions. When missing values are replaced by sample means or regression estimates derived from the same data set there results, as was already noted, an artificial reduction in the sample variance, which can yield more "significant" estimates than otherwise would be the case. For this reason, among others, it is generally better to compare missing data estimators by means of numerical simulation methods rather than real data whose structure is unknown. Real data, such as that used by Jackson, therefore, have a built-in limitation when used to evaluate missing values since there is no way of comparing the estimation results to the complete sample that could have been observed but was not, except by use of statistics that depend on observed sample variance.

Chan and Dunn (1972) conducted a Monte Carlo investigation of missing data techniques developed for regression analysis (see Section 12.3) in an attempt to evaluate the effects of missing data estimators on the expected probability of misclassification, assuming equal costs of misclassification. The authors evaluate the procedures by considering the influences of (a) the number of variables; (b) the Mahalonobis distance measure between two populations; (c) the sample size and percentage of missing data; and (d) various forms of the mean vector. Variables are assumed to be equally correlated and data are missing randomly (Type III.)[10] It appears that there is again no uniformly best technique available, and their applicability tends to vary with factors (a) through (d) (see Chan and Dunn, 1972, for more detail). In a further paper, Chan, Gilman, and Dunn (1976) extend the analysis by considering one variant each of the Buck (1960) and Dear (1959) methods, and also by enlarging the sampling frame to 50 random correlation matrices, so that unlike their previous (1972) study, the independent variable correlations are not restricted to be equal. Three principal results of some importance emerge from the study:

1. In general, sample estimates of the probability of correct classification tend to diverge from true values as the determinant of the correlation matrix decreases (approaches zero); that is, as multicollinearity increases.
2. In all methods considered, there is a tendency for poorer performance in estimating the classification probability as the number of variables increase.
3. The authors' variant of Buck's (1960) method (method D*) appears to be a good choice, unless one finds a near singular correlation matrix. For times when this procedure is too involved, the authors recommend the zero-order method of substituting mean values for the missing data.

Two comments may be made concerning the Chan et al. (1976) findings, which are also equally applicable to the regression problems considered in Section 12.4. First, Dear's principal components method (or the author's variant) did not perform better than the least-squares techniques, even in the case of a near singular correlation matrix. A probable reason for this is that since the structure (and importance) of the dominant principal component also depends on the *pattern* of correlations found among the variables, a high value of the determinant of the correlation matrix is not sufficient to ensure its usefulness unless more than one principal component is used. Second, result (1) may indicate that low determinants of the correlation matrix have opposing effects. High variable correlation (and a higher number of variables) favor more precise first-order estimation of the missing values. High correlation, however, also results in large standard deviations of the regression coefficients, which here apparently tends to countervail the first effect. A better strategy may be to distinguish cases where near singularity is due to high correlations among only a subset of the independent variables, and to omit these from the estimation of missing values as well as from the final discriminant function. Alternatively, multicollinearity can be reduced by a principal components-factor analysis of the independent variables.

---

[10] A precise definition of *randomness* is not provided in the article.

All available literature on the missing data problem in discriminant analysis deals only with (a) the two-group case; and (b) the case where data are missing on the independent variables only. Substituting estimated values results in biased and inconsistent estimators, since classification variables now possess nonzero residual terms. For a consistent regression method in discriminant analysis, see Little (1978). No procedures of dealing with the missing data problem with three or more groups is therefore available, and consequently Jackson's (1968) and Chan and Dunn's (1972) results and conclusions cannot be generalized to more than two groups. When data are missing for the dichotomous dependent variable (i.e., group membership of some individuals is not known in a single sample) one possible ad hoc solution may be as follows. Let $\hat{P}$ denote the proportion of individuals in one of the two groups, obtained from the complete portion of the sample. Group membership can then be assigned randomly (perhaps by using the binomial distribution), and the regression coefficients estimated in the usual way, keeping in mind that the residual error term will most likely be heteroscedastic. Alternatively, another approach is for two or more "classifers" to decide whether each individual belongs to group A or group B. Although the classification probability estimate $\hat{P}$ is in this case generally biased, the direction and magnitude of bias can be computed (see Bryson, 1965). When two independent samples are available, procedures suggested by Elashoff and Elashoff (1974) can be used.

Simultaneous Equations

Simultaneous equations estimators have been recently considered by Sargan and Drettakis (1974), Dagenais (1976), and Dagenais and Dagenais (1977). The methods employed by Sargan and Drettakis take into account all the equations of the system simultaneously and as a result the estimators turn out to be fairly complex and difficult to use. As an alternative we therefore briefly describe the more straightforward procedure developed by Dagenais (1976). Let

$$\mathbf{Y}_i = \mathbf{Y}_i \gamma_i + \mathbf{X}_i \delta_i + \eta_i \tag{12.85}$$

where y_i is an endogenous variable, $\mathbf{Y}_i$ is the matrix of other endogenous variables in the system that appear in the ith equation, $\mathbf{X}_i$ is the matrix of exogenous variables, and γ_i, δ_i, and η_i are regression parameters and residual error terms, respectively, in the ith equation. Dagenais (1976) estimates γ_i and δ_i as follows:

1. Obtain the reduced form version of (12.85) as

$$\mathbf{Y}_k = \mathbf{X}\boldsymbol{\beta}_k + \mathbf{U}_k \tag{12.86}$$

   and estimate the $\boldsymbol{\beta}_k$ using Dagenais's (1973) generalized least-squares method, one equation at a time. This yields $\hat{\mathbf{Y}}_k = \mathbf{X}\hat{\boldsymbol{\beta}}_k$ for the kth reduced form equation.
2. Using $\mathbf{Y}_k$ consistent estimators $\hat{\gamma}_i$ and $\hat{\delta}_i$ are then obtained.

The normal equations are nonlinear and are consequently estimated iteratively. The regression coefficients are jointly, normally distributed, and since consistent estimates of the covariance matrix of $\hat{\gamma}_i$ and $\hat{\delta}_i$ are also provided it is possible to perform significance tests on the parameters. In an unpublished paper, Dagenais and Dagenais (1977) develop a further general approach of dealing with the missing data problem in simultaneous equations, which can be applied to the so-called seemingly unrelated regressions, two-stage least squares, three-stage least squares, linear full-information ML, all models with autocorrelated errors, as well as to nonlinear regression problems that are linear in the variables. Under broad assumptions the Dagenais and Dagenais estimator is also consistent.

Factor Analysis

Most of the techniques used for overcoming missing data problems discussed in the case of regression analysis and maximum likelihood methods can be applied to factor analysis and principal components models as well. We can delete all individuals with missing data, delete observations pairwise, or estimate the missing values before carrying out a factor or a components analysis. Also, iterative methods can be used—mean values, for instance, can be substituted for the missing elements in the data matrix; factor analysis can be carried out and new estimates obtained; and the process can be continued until convergence to stable values is obtained.

One of the first (unpublished) attempts to deal with the missing data problem in factor analysis is that of Christofferson, described briefly in Wold (1966a, pp. 416–417; 1966b, pp. 422–423) where the Yates–Tocher neutral value concept is adapted to the principal components model. The method therefore consists of replacing the missing data by values $\hat{x}_{ij}$ in such a way that they coincide with their principal components representation

$$\hat{x}_{ij} = \sum_{h=1}^{k} a_{ih}z_{hj} \tag{12.87}$$

for $k < r$ significant principal components. In other words, the residual values are set equal to zero for those observations that are missing. It should be kept in mind, however, that the principal components are not independent of scale and location of the variables. Wold (1966a, pp. 416–417) considers a simple Monte Carlo experiment for two cases, when 25 and 50% of the data are missing, and concludes that Christofferson's algorithm is satisfactory. A more extensive evaluation is needed before definite conclusions can be drawn, however.

A similar approach is used by Woodbury, Clelland, and Hickey (1963), and Woodbury and Siler (1966) for the case of factor analysis where, unlike the principal components method, the error structure is considered to be a part of the hypothesis.

$$\mathbf{X} = \mathbf{FA} + \mathbf{E} \tag{12.88}$$

where $\mathbf{E}$ is an $(n \times r)$ error matrix, $\mathbf{F}$ is an $(n \times k)$ matrix of factor scores, and $\mathbf{A}$ the $(k \times r)$ factor loadings matrix. When no data are missing then for any ith individual and jth variable we have

$$x_{ij} = \sum_{h=1}^{k} a_{jh} f_{ih} + e_{ij} \tag{12.89}$$

and factor analysis minimizes $\sum_{i=1}^{n} \sum_{j=1}^{r} e_{ij}^2 = \mathrm{tr}(\mathbf{E}^{\mathrm{T}}\mathbf{E})$, the total error variance where $\mathbf{E}^{\mathrm{T}}\mathbf{E}$ is a diagonal matrix. Minimization is in the least-squares sense. If normality of the e_{ij} is assumed, (12.75) yields maximum likelihood estimates. For when data are missing, Woodbury *et al.* (1963) also employ the Yates–Tocher "neutral values" approach as follows:

1. Select k, the number of significant factors.
2. Fill in the missing data by arbitrary constant values and estimate the loadings a_{jh} and scores f_{ij}, obtaining missing values estimates $\hat{x}_{ij}$.
3. Using the $\hat{x}_{ij}$ in place of the arbitrary constants, reestimate the a_{jh} and f_{ih}.
4. Keep on recycling the missing data estimates through the factor model (12.75) until missing value estimates converge, to any degree of accuracy.

The authors point out that convergence cannot be obtained for all values of k, but covergence is inevitable for k "large enough," that is, there exists a minimal number of factors for which convergence is guaranteed, and which is presumably selected as the final value of k. Thus a certain amount of experimentation is necessary to obtain k, since mathematical conditions under which the iterations converge uniquely do not seem to be well understood at present. As most iterative methods depend heavily on the initial arbitrary values selected, some care must be exercised in this respect. Natural initial guesses of the missing values are the variable sample means of the observed data, particularly when the data are assumed to be normally distributed. Other possible starting points may be zero values, as in the case of the ANOVA and regression models. A more specific algebraic treatment of the problem is provided by Woodbury and Siler (1966), who minimize

$$\psi = \sum_{i=1}^{n} \sum_{j=1}^{r} w_{ij} e_{ij}^2$$

$$= \sum_{i=1}^{n} \sum_{j=1}^{r} w_{ij} (x_{ij} - \sum_{n=1}^{k} a_{jh} f_{ih})^2 \tag{12.90}$$

with respect to a_{jh} and f_{ih} ($h = 1, 2, \ldots, k$), where the w_{ij} are weights that reflect the accuracy of the observations taking values $w_{ij} = 0$ when observations are missing, and positive values for the remaining observations. When no estimates of the w_{ij} are available, we may assign values $w_{ij} = 1$ for the nonmissing data. Then for k significant factors and/or individuals we set $(\partial \psi / \partial f_{ih}) = 0$ for any jth variable that yields

$$\begin{bmatrix} \sum_{i=1}^{n} w_{ij}f_{i1}^2 & \sum_{i=1}^{n} w_{ij}f_{i2}f_{i2} & \cdots & \sum_{i=1}^{n} w_{ij}f_{i1}f_{ik} \\[2mm] \sum_{i=1}^{n} w_{ij}f_{i1}f_{i2} & \sum_{i=1}^{n} w_{ij}f_{i2}^2 & \cdots & \sum_{i=1}^{n} w_{ij}f_{i2}f_{ik} \\[2mm] \vdots & \vdots & & \vdots \\[2mm] \sum_{i=1}^{n} w_{ij}f_{i1}f_{ik} & \sum_{i=1}^{n} w_{ij}f_{i2}f_{ik} & \cdots & \sum_{i=1}^{n} w_{ij}f_{ik}^2 \end{bmatrix} \begin{bmatrix} \hat{a}_{j1} \\[2mm] \hat{a}_{j2} \\[2mm] \vdots \\[2mm] \hat{a}_{jk} \end{bmatrix} = \begin{bmatrix} \sum_{i=1}^{n} w_{ij}x_{ij}f_{i1} \\[2mm] \sum_{i=1}^{n} w_{ij}x_{ij}f_{i2} \\[2mm] \vdots \\[2mm] \sum_{i=1}^{n} w_{ij}x_{ij}f_{ik} \end{bmatrix} \tag{12.91}$$

and $(\partial\psi/\partial f_{ih}) = 0$ for which the ith individual yields

$$\begin{bmatrix} \sum_{j=1}^{r} w_{ij}a_{j1}^2 & \sum_{j=1}^{r} w_{ij}a_{j1}a_{j2} & \cdots & \sum_{j=1}^{r} w_{ij}a_{j1}a_{jk} \\[2mm] \sum_{j=1}^{r} w_{ij}a_{j1}a_{j2} & \sum_{j=1}^{r} w_{ij}a_{j2}^2 & \cdots & \sum_{j=1}^{r} w_{ij}a_{j2}a_{jk} \\[2mm] \vdots & \vdots & & \vdots \\[2mm] \sum_{j=1}^{r} w_{ij}a_{j1}a_{jk} & \sum_{j=1}^{r} w_{ij}a_{j2}a_{jk} & \cdots & \sum_{j=1}^{r} w_{ij}a_{jk}^2 \end{bmatrix} \begin{bmatrix} \hat{f}_{i1} \\[2mm] \hat{f}_{i2} \\[2mm] \vdots \\[2mm] \hat{f}_{ik} \end{bmatrix} = \begin{bmatrix} \sum_{j=1}^{r} w_{ij}x_{ij}a_{j1} \\[2mm] \sum_{j=1}^{r} w_{ij}x_{ij}a_{j2} \\[2mm] \vdots \\[2mm] \sum_{j=1}^{r} w_{ij}x_{ij}a_{jk} \end{bmatrix} \tag{12.92}$$

The two systems (12.91) and (12.92) form the least-squares normal equations for the estimation of the loadings $\hat{a}_{jh}$ and the scores $\hat{f}_{ih}$ ($h = 1, 2, \ldots, k$), which are solved iteratively and which are ML when errors follow a normal distribution. When no data are missing (setting $w_{ij} = 1$), V_{ij} yields the usual factor analysis normal equations. Note that (12.91) and (12.92) have the same form as the usual OLS regression normal equations, but in our case we have two unknown sets of parameters and (12.91) depends on a solution of (12.92), whereas (12.92) in turn depends on a solution of (12.91). Thus solutions for the factor model are iterative even when no data are missing. If factors for the nonmissing data are initially specified to be orthogonal (as is usually the case) then the left-hand side matrix of (12.91) becomes diagonal, which reduces the computational burden.

First-order methods, for example that of Buck (1960), can also be used in factor analysis. The missing data are first estimated by regression least squares and then a factor analysis is performed on the completed data. The advantage here is that error involved in estimating missing values will usually be incorporated into the factor residuals. Pairwise deletion (see Glasser, 1964) is also used at times, but a serious objection to the method is that since the symmetric covariance (correlation) matrix is no longer constrained to be positive definite some eigenroots can turn out negative, thus biasing the factor loadings and scores (see also Rummel, 1970, p. 260). The computational reason for this is that covariances (correlations) are no longer necessarily based on the same set of data when observations are deleted pairwise.

Truncated Contingency Tables

The previous sections were mainly concerned with problems of missing data drawn from continuous populations. Much of social survey data, however, is sampled from discrete populations and is frequently analyzed by means of contingency tables or total frequency counts of presumably joint occurrence of events. The assumption of multivariate normality is then replaced by its discrete analogue, the multinomial distribution, for purposes of maximum likelihood estimation and significance testing. The standard contingency table analysis tends to break down, however, if some of the cell frequencies are missing or cannot be uniquely identified. Incomplete contingency tables, which are usually known as truncated tables, can contain missing frequencies due to two principal reasons.

1. Frequencies can be missing unintentionally, or be improperly identified, because of sampling difficulties or sampling variation. In this case, although certain cell values (frequencies) are not observed in the sample the corresponding population frequencies exist and are defined. When the sample size is increased, the zero frequencies disappear. Also, frequencies may be missing due to truncation.

2. Cell frequencies may be missing due to structural factors such as logically impossible cells. Also it may be desirable at times to impose a priori zero restrictions or other predetermined values. In such cases, the missing cells can be ignored a priori when testing the hypothesis under consideration.

Predetermined values are also termed as structural zeroes, to distinguish them from observed zero values that result solely from sampling variation. In the more recent literature, both types of incomplete contingency tables are considered together, since general iterative methods are now available that can deal with both types of tables. It must be kept in mind, however, that whereas for the latter type, cells are necessarily empty, in the former case, we generally wish to obtain estimates, under the given model, for the missing cell frequencies.

UNINTENTIONALLY MISSING FREQUENCIES

Consider a two-way ($r \times c$) contingency table with $r = 2$ rows and $c = 3$ columns. Let f_{ij} denote frequency in row i and column j, C_i and R_j the column and row totals, respectively, and let $x = f_{11}$ be a missing value. The analysis of Table 12.7 first considered by Watson (1956) (see also Caussinus, 1962) can be carried out as follows. Let p_i and q_j ($i = 1, 2, \ldots, r; j = 1, 2, \ldots, c$) be binomial probabilities and T the total of observed frequencies. The observed cell frequencies f_{ij} constitute a sample from a multinomial distribution with probabilities given by

$$\frac{p_i q_j}{1 - (p_1 q_1)} \qquad \begin{aligned} & i = 1, 2, \ldots, r; \\ & j = 1, 2, \ldots, c, \end{aligned} \qquad (12.93)$$

TABLE 12.7

Variable B	Variable A			
	A_1	A_2	A_3	
B_1	x	f_{12}	f_{13}	R_1
B_3	f_{21}	f_{22}	f_{23}	R_2
	C_1	C_2	C_3	T

on the null hypothesis of no association. Watson (1956) then shows that the ML estimate of the missing frequency is given by

$$x = \frac{R_1 C_1}{T - R_1 - C_1} \tag{12.94}$$

and the χ^2 statistic, with $(r-1)(c-1)-1$ degrees of freedom, is computed in the usual way by adding x to R_1, C_1, and T. Note that the χ^2 statistic receives no contribution from the missing cell $f_{11} = x$ since

$$x = \frac{(R_1 + x)(C_1 + x)}{T + x}. \tag{12.95}$$

Watson's approach therefore is to treat x as a "neutral" value, analogous to the Yates–Tocher ANOVA and analysis procedure. When more than one frequency is missing Watson suggests an iterative estimation procedure. Watson (1956) also provides ML estimates in the case when two (or more) frequencies are "mixed up," that is, when the identity between a subset of the frequencies is lost (see also Craig, 1953, for combining cell frequencies). For certain $(r \times s)$ tables, however, it is possible to find explicit algebraic formulas for the missing values in contingency tables (Kastenbaum, 1958). The effect of misclassification on the χ^2 test is considered by Mote and Anderson (1965).

A PRIORI RESTRICTIONS

Watson's (1956) method is to impute (estimate) the missing cell frequencies and to use these in the usual χ^2 test of significance. When the missing entries correspond to logically impossible row–column combinations, however, it makes no sense to estimate the "missing" contingency table frequencies, and other methods must be employed that use only the observed part of the data. Caussinus (1965), Goodman (1968), Bishop and Fienberg (1969), Mantel (1970), and Fienberg (1972) consider ML estimation in truncated contingency tables under the multiplicative model of quasi-independence, introduced by Goodman (1963, 1964, 1965). Besides extending missing data analysis to more general missing data patterns (for example see Goodman, 1968) quasi-independence can be used to handle the more traditional missing (zero) frequencies considered by Watson (1956).

Consider Table 12.8 a 4×9 table adapted from Harris (1910). Harris analyzed the relationship between the coefficient of radial symmetry and locu-

TABLE 12.8

	A_1	A_2	A_3	A_4	A_5	A_6	A_7	A_8	A_9
B_1	462	—	0	130	—	—	2	—	1
B_2	—	614	138	—	21	14	—	1	—
B_3	—	443	95	—	22	8	—	5	—
B_4	103	—	—	35	—	—	1	—	0

lar composition in his study of selective elimination in Staphylea. Since certain combinations of rows and columns are physically impossible in the context of the study, the contingency table contains "missing" or structural zero values that render the usual χ^2 computations inapplicable (Harris & Treloar, 1927; Harris & Chi Tu, 1929; Harris, Treloar, & Wilder, 1930). As pointed out by Pearson (1930a,b) (see also Goodman, 1968), however, the table can be expressed in an equivalent form, Table 12.9, by rearranging rows and columns resulting in a block-diagonal table. Such tables are also known as separable contingency tables since they can be decomposed into two or more subtables with no row or column in common. A table that cannot be decomposed in this way is said to be connected; for example, the triangular table considered by Bishop and Fienberg (1969), which is formed from the square $(r \times r)$ table in which all the (i, j) cells with $i > r + 1 - j$ are empty, or the $(r \times r)$ table where diagonal entries are zero (Wagner, 1970).

Let p_{ij} be the proportion of cases in the $(r \times c)$ two-way population table that fall in the (i, j) cell. The row and column classifications in a complete contingency table are then independent of

$$p_{ij} = a_i b_j \qquad (i = 1, 2, \ldots, r; \quad j = 1, 2, \ldots, c)$$

where a_i is the proportion of individuals in row i and b_j in column j where $\Sigma a_i = \Sigma b_j = 1$. A parallel definition of independence for incomplete tables has been provided by Goodman (1968), the so-called condition of quasi-independence that dates back to his earlier work on transaction flows and social mobility (Goodman, 1963, 1964, 1965). Let S be a subset of a contingency table, for example a rectangular array or table. For a subset S, the row and column classifications are said to be quasi-independent if the condition holds for all

TABLE 12.9

	A_1	A_4	A_7	A_9	A_2	A_3	A_5	A_6	A_8
B_1	462	130	2	1	—	—	—	—	—
B_2	103	35	1	0	—	—	—	—	—
B_3	—	—	—	—	614	138	21	14	1
B_4	—	—	—	—	443	95	22	8	5

cells (i, j) in the set S. For an incomplete contingency table the test of independence is then replaced by that of quasi-independence, which can be considered as a form of independence conditional on the restriction of the analysis to an incomplete portion S of the contingency table. For the special case of a separable incomplete table the test of quasi-independence is equivalent to testing independence within the (separable) subtables, but for the more general connected incomplete table the usual test of independence breaks down. The ML computations involved in estimating the expected cell frequencies are described by Bishop and Fienberg (1969), Caussinus (1965), and Goodman (1964, 1968), on the assumption that unique ML estimates for the quasi-independent model exist. Fienberg (1970a) provides conditions under which unique ML estimates exist. For a comparison of iterative methods and ML estimates when diagonal cells are missing see Morgan and Titterington (1977).

12.6. SUMMARY

Data missing randomly (in one of the ways discussed previously) often can be treated in some fashion so as to prevent lost information and/or to eliminate sources of bias. The techniques may adjust statistical estimates (correlations, covariances, variances) or make imputations of the missing values. Under certain conditions, the resulting statistical estimates may be unbiased. Which technique is best depends on many factors. Because of the complicated and interacting effects of the various factors influencing the relative success of the competing techniques, no one method for handling the missing data problem can be shown to be uniformly superior. Comparative work continues, particularly with Monte Carlo methods. Some conditional recommendations and guidelines can be put forward.

If data are missing nonrandomly, serious problems usually result. An immediate threat to validity appears; estimates are biased. Moreover, we cannot protect against the problem merely by keeping response rates high. Williams and Mallows demonstrate the danger for the simple problem of estimating change in the unemployment rate at two points in time. A (3×3) table is formed with time 1 crossed with time 2 and each hypothetical case classified as unemployed, employed, or unobserved (missing) at each point in time. In their numerical example *no change* in employment occurs in the population between time 1 and time 2. Time 1 has an 89% response rate and time 2 has a 95% response rate and the nonresponse rates for employed and unemployed are similar. The *estimated change* in the unemployment rate is 14%, even though no change has occurred. These response rates would be welcomed in most surveys and we would likely dismiss the possibility that the missing data could cause bias. Williams and Mallows (1970) conclude that "substantial biases appear with apparently innocuous probability differences and with very low nonresponse rates [p. 344]."

Our preliminary Monte Carlo simulations of nonrandom attrition confirms their finding. We are estimating regression coefficients in a three variable OLS multiple regression model on samples drawn from a population with a known (constructed) structure (equation). Each sample is put through a stochastic filter where the probability of a data point being dropped is some function of the true values on the variables. We vary the equation (the population) and the filter. The resulting estimates from the samples show substantial bias under some conditions even with low rates of nonresponse. It is too early in the research to draw specific conclusions about the factors influencing the magnitude of bias.

The problem of nonrandom attrition remains serious; we believe it to be one of two or three most serious unsolved problems in survey research. The techniques examined in this chapter are generally inappropriate, strictly speaking, unless an assumption of some type of randomness can be made. Yet, the problem is not unapproachable. Imputation and estimation are being done more and more frequently. In recent years there have been conferences and symposia devoted to the topic (Aziz & Scheman, 1978; Madow, 1979). The key seems to be the process producing the nonresponse or missing data. If that mechanism can be known or estimated, then the possibilities for imputations or other adjustments increase. At the present time, the Bayesian approach of Rubin seems in the correct spirit. "What if" games may be played. Estimates or imputations of the missing values may be made based on a model of the underlying nonresponse process. The stability of the results based on reanalysis of the data containing imputed values can be examined under alternative assumptions. If the results stand up, one gains confidence that the degree of bias probably is negligible. If outcomes are unstable, the results can be used to set bounds of possible distortion. This approach would seem most promising when only one or two variables are at issue and when a single process generates the nonresponse. Otherwise, the missing data sensitivity analysis is too costly, for it multiplies several times the number of analyses to be done. It may turn out for some surveys that the most serious source of nonrandom nonresponse can be modeled in this way and that the remaining missing values can be treated as effectively random and can be handled as described in this chapter. Again, though, this depends on an understanding of the structure of the nonrandom process. Work on such fronts continues at a growing rate. See, for example, Barnow, Cain, and Goldberger (1980), Heckman (1980), Olsen (1980), Goldberger (1981), and Berk and Ray (1982). All of these discuss techniques that depend in some way on our ability to model the process producing the missing data.

As things stand now, we are faced with something of a statistical Catch-22. Although this greatly oversimplifies the matter, one may for emphasis say that in the case where bias is least problematic (random nonresponse), we can fix it. For the case where bias is a serious threat (nonrandom nonresponse), the standard methods are not appropriate. We return to the old precept that still holds true: The only real cure for missing data is to not have any.

REFERENCES

Afifi, A. A., and R. M. Elashoff
  1966 Missing observations in multivariate statistics—I. Review of the literature." *Journal of the American Statistical Association* 61: 595–604.
  1967 "Missing observations in multivariate statistics—II. Point estimation in simple linear regression." *Journal of the American Statistical Association* 62: 10–29.
  1969a "Missing observations in multivariate statistics—III. Large sample analysis of simple linear regression." *Journal of the American Statistical Association* 64: 337–358.
  1969b "Missing observations in multivariate statistics—IV. A note on simple linear regression." *Journal of the American Statistical Association* 64: 359–365.
Allen, F. E., and J. Wishart
  1930 "A method of estimating the yields of a missing plot in field experimental work." *Journal of the Agricultural Society* 30: 399–406.
Anderson, R. L.
  1946 "Missing-plot techniques." *Biometrics* 2: 41–47.
Anderson, R. L., and T. A. Bancroft
  1952 *Statistical Theory in Research.* New York: McGraw–Hill.
Anderson, T. W.
  1957 "Maximum likelihood estimates for a multivariate normal distribution when some observations are missing." *Journal of the American Statistical Association* 52: 200–203.
Asano, C.
  1965 "On estimating multinomial probabilities by pooling incomplete samples." *Annals of the Institution of Statistical Mathematics* 17: 1.
Aziz, F., and F. Scheman
  1978 Proceedings of American Statistical Association Session on Survey Imputation and Editing.
Baird, H. R., and C. Y. Kramer
  1960 "Analysis of variance of a balanced incomplete block design with missing observations." *Applied Statistics* 9: 189–198.
Bancroft, T. A.
  1968 *Topics in Intermediate Statistical Methods.* Ames: Iowa State University Press.
Baranchik, A. J.
  1964 Multiple Regression and Estimation of the Mean of a Multivariate Normal Distribution. Stanford: Stanford University Department of Statistical Technical Reports.
Barnow, B. S., G. G. Cain, and A. S. Goldberger
  1980 "Issues in the analysis of selectivity bias." In E. Stromsdorfer and G. Farkas (eds.), *Evaluation Studies Review Annual,* Vol. 5. Beverly Hills: Sage Publications. Pp. 43–59.
Bartholomew, D. J.
  1961 "A method of allowing for 'not-at-home' bias in sample surveys." *Applied Statistics* 10: 52–59.
Bartlett, M. S.
  1937 "Some examples of statistical methods of research in agriculture and applied biology." *Journal of the Royal Statistical Society* (Suppl.) 4: 137–183.
Beale, E. M. L., and R. J. A. Little
  1975 "Missing values in multivariate analysis." *Journal of the Royal Statistical Society* (B) 37: 129–145.
Bennet, C. A., and N. L. Franklin
  1954 *Statistical Analysis in Chemistry and the Chemical Industry.* New York: Wiley.
Berk, R. A., and S. C. Ray
  1982 "Selection biases in sociological data." *Social Science Research* (4.):
Bhargava, R.
  1962 "Multivariate tests of hypotheses with incomplete data." *Applied Mathematics and Statistical Laboratories Technical Report 3.*

Bhoj, D. S.
    1971   "Multivariate tests of hypotheses with missing observations." Unpublished doctoral dissertation. University of Pennsylvania—Philadelphia.
    1972   "Percentage points of the statistics for testing hypotheses on mean vectors of multivariate normal distributions with missing observations." *Journal of Statistical Computation and Simulation.*
Biggers, J. D.
    1959   "The estimation of missing and mixed-up observations in several experimental designs." *Biometrika* 46: 91–105.
Bisco, R. L.
    1970   *Data Bases, Computers and the Social Sciences.* New York: Wiley.
Bishop, Y. M. M., and S. E. Feinberg
    1969   "Incomplete two-dimensional contingency tables." *Biometrics* 25: 119–128.
Blumenthal, S.
    1968   "Multinomial sampling with partially categorized data." *Journal of the American Statistical Association* 63: 542–551.
Boot, J. C. G., W. Feibes, and J. H. C. Lisman
    1967   "Further methods of derivation of quarterly figures from annual data." *Applied Statistics* 16: 65–75.
Box, M. J.
    1970   "Improved parameter estimation." *Technometrics* 12: 219–229.
    1971   "A parameter estimation criterion for multiresponse models applicable when some observations are missing." *Applied Statistics* 20: 1–7.
Box, M. J., N. R. Draper, and W. G. Hunter
    1970   "Missing values in multiresponse nonlinear model fitting." *Technometrics* 12: 613–620.
Brandt, A. E.
    1933   "The analysis of variance in a 2 × 2 table with disproportionate frequencies." *Journal of the American Statistical Association* 28: 164–173.
Brown, M. B.
    1974   "Identification of the sources of significance in two-way contingency tables." *Applied Statistics* 23: 405–413.
Brownlee, V. A.
    1957   "A note on the effects of nonresponse on surveys." *Journal of the American Statistical Association* 52: 29–32.
Bryson, M.
    1965   "Errors of classification in a binomial population." *Journal of the American Statistical Association* 60: 217–224.
Buck, S. F.
    1960   "A method of estimation of missing values in multivariate data suitable for use with an electronic computer." *Journal of the Royal Statistical Society* (B) 22: 302–307.
Caussinus, H.
    1962   "Sur un problème d'analyse de la corrélation de deux charactères qualitatifs." *Comptes Rendues de l'Académie des Sciences* 255: 1688–1690.
    1965   "Contribution à l'analyse statistique des tableaux de corrélation." *Annales de la Faculté des Sciences de l'Université de Toulouse* 29: 77–182.
Chan, L. S., and O. J. Dunn
    1972   "Treatment of missing values in discriminant analysis—I. The sampling experiment." *Journal of the American Statistical Association* 67: 473–477.
Chan, L. S., J. A. Gilman, and O. J. Dunn
    1976   "Alternative approaches to missing values in discriminant analysis." *Journal of the American Statistical Association* 71: 842–844.
Chapman, D. W.
    1976   *A survey of nonresponse imputation procedures.* (Presented at the 1976 Meeting of the American Statistical Association, Boston, Mass.).

Chen, T.
1971   "Mixed-up frequencies and incomplete data in contingency tables." Unpublished research report, Department of Statistics, University of Chicago.
Chipman, J. S.
1964   "On least squares with insufficient observations." *Journal of the American Statistical Association* 59: 1078–1111.
Chow, G. C., and A Lin
1971   "Best linear unbiased interpolation, distribution, and extrapolation of time series by related series." *Review of Economics and Statistics* 53: 372–375.
1976   "Best linear unbiased estimation of missing observations in an economic time series." *Journal of the American Statistical Association* 71: 719–721.
Christoffersson, A.
1965   "A method for component analysis when the data are incomplete." Seminar communication, University Institute of Statistics, Uppsala, Sweden.
Cochran, W. G.
1957   "Analysis of covariance: Its nature and uses to analyze data when some observations are missing." *Biometrics* 13: 261–281.
1963   *Sampling Techniques* (2nd ed.). New York: Wiley.
Cochran, W. G., and G. M. Cox
1957   *Experimental Designs* (2nd ed.). New York: Wiley.
Cohen, A.
1977   "A result on hypothesis testing for a multivariate normal distribution when some observations are missing." *Journal of Multivariate Analysis* 7: 454–460.
Cohen, J.
1968   "Multiple regression as a general data-analytic system." *Psychological Bulletin* 70: 426–443.
1975   *Applied Multiple Regression/Correlation Analysis for the Behavioral Sciences* Hillsdale, N.J.: Lawrence Erlhaum. (Chap. 7).
Coons, I.
1957   "The analysis of covariance as a missing plot technique." *Biometrics* 13: 387–405.
Cornish, E. A.
1940a "The analysis of quasi-factorial designs with incomplete data 1: Incomplete randomized blocks." *Journal of the Australian Institute of Agriculture* 6: 31–39.
1940b "The estimation of missing values in incomplete randomized block experiments." *Annals of Eugenics* 10: 112–118.
1940c "The estimation of missing values in quasi-factorial designs." *Annals of Eugenics* 10: 137–143.
1941a "The analysis of quasi-factorial designs with incomplete data 2: Lattice squares." *Journal of the Australian Institute of Agriculture* 7: 19–26.
1941b "The analysis of quasi-factorial designs with incomplete data 3: Square, triple and cubic lattices." (Unpublished).
1943   "The recovery of inter-block information in quasi-factorial designs with incomplete data 1: Square, triple and cubic lattices." *Bulletin* 158. Australia: Council of Scientific Industrial Research.
1944   "The recovery of inter-block information in quasi-factorial designs with incomplete data 2: Lattice squares." *Bulletin* 175. Australia: Council of Scientific Industrial Research.
Craig, C. C.
1953   "Combination of neighboring cells in contingency tables." *Journal of the American Statistical Association* 48: 104–112.
Dagenais, M. G.
1971   "Further suggestions concerning the utilization of incomplete observations in regression analysis." *Journal of the American Statistical Association* 66: 93–98.
1972   "Asymptotic behaviour and small sample performance: Experiments in regression parameter estimation with incomplete observations." *European Economic Review* 3: 389–398.

1973   "The use of incomplete observations in multiple regression analysis: A generalized least squares approach." *Journal of Econometrics* 1: 317–328.
1976   "Incomplete observations and simultaneous equations models." *Journal of Econometrics* 4: 231–241.

Dagenais, M. G., and D. L. Dagenais
1977   "A general approach for estimating econometric models with incomplete observations." (Unpublished.)

Dear, R. E.
1959   *A Principal Components Missing Data Method for Multiple Regression Models.* SP-86. Santa Monica, Calif.: Systems Development Corporation.

De Lury, D. B.
1946   "The analysis of Latin squares when some observations are missing." *Journal of the American Statistical Association* 41: 370–389.

Dempster, A. P.
1969   *Elements of Continuous Multivariate Analysis.* Reading, Mass: Addison–Wesley.

Dempster, A. P., N. M. Laird, and D. B. Rubin
1977   "Maximum likelihood from incomplete data via the EM algorithm." *Journal of the Royal Statistical Society* (B) 34: 1–38.

Denton, F. T.
1971   "Adjustment on monthly or quarterly series to annual totals: An approach based on quadratic minimization." *Journal of the American Statistical Association* 66: 99–102.

Doran, H. E.
1974   "Prediction of missing observations in the time series of an economic variable." *Journal of the American Statistical Association* 69: 546–554.

Draper, N. R.
1961   "Missing values in response surface designs." *Technometrics* 3: 389–398.

Draper, N. R., and D. M. Stoneman
1964   "Estimating missing values in unreplicated two-level factorial and fractional factorial designs." *Biometrics* 20: 443–458.

Dreze, J., and R. H. Strotz
1964   "Missing data in simultaneous equation estimation." (Unpublished.)

Dykstra, O.
1960   "Rank analysis of incomplete block designs: A method of paired comparisons employing unequal repetitions on pairs." *Biometrics* 16: 176–188.

Eaton, M. L.
1970   "Some problems in covariance estimation." Stanford: Stanford University Department of Statistical (Preliminary Technical Report.)

Edgett, G. L.
1956   "Multiple regression with missing observations among the independent variables." *Journal of the American Statistical Association* 51: 122–131.

Eklund, G.
1954   *Studies of Selection Bias in Applied Statistics.* Uppsala, Sweden: Almqvist and Baktry-cheri.

Elashoff, J. D., and R. M. Elashoff
1974   "Two-sample problem for a dichotomous variable with missing data." *Applied Statistics* 23: 26–34.

Federer, W. T.
1955   *Experimental Design: Theory and Application.* New York: Macmillan. Pp. 124–127 and 133–134.
1963   "Relationship between a three-way classification, disproportionate numbers analysis of variance, and several two-way classification and nested analyses." *Biometrics* 19: 629–637.

Federspiel, C. F., R. J. Monroe, and B. C. Greenberg
  1959 "An investigation of some multiple regression methods for incomplete samples. Institute of Statistical Mimeo Series No. 236. Chapel Hill: University of North Carolina.
Fienberg, S. E.
  1969 "Preliminary graphical analysis and quasi-independence for two-way contingency tables." *Applied Statistics* 18: 153–168.
  1970a "Quasi-independence and maximum-likelihood estimation in incomplete contingency tables." *Journal of the American Statistical Association* 65: 1610–1616.
  1970b "The analysis of multidimensional contingency tables." *Ecology* 51: 419–433.
  1971 "Comments on Hartley, H. O. and Hocking, R. R." *Biometrics* 27: 813–817.
  1972 "The analysis of incomplete multi-way contingency tables." *Biometrics* 28: 177–202.
Fienberg, S. E., and P. W. Holland
  1970 "Methods for eliminating zero counts in contingency tables." Pp. 233–260 in G. P. Patel (ed.), *Random Counts in Models and Structures*. Philadelphia: Pennsylvania State University Press.
Fiering, M. B.
  1962 "On the use of correlation to augment data." *Journal of the American Statistical Association* 57: 20–32.
Finney, D. J.
  1962 "An unusual salvage operation." *Biometrics* 18: 247–450.
Folks, J. L. and D. L. West
  1961 "Note on the missing plot procedure in a randomized block design." *Journal of the American Statistical Association* 56: 933–941.
Ford, B. L.
  1976 *Missing Data Procedures: A Comparative Study*. Washington, D.C.: Statistical Reporting Service, U.S. Department of Agriculture.
Freund, R. J., and H. O. Hartley
  1967 "A procedure of automatic data editing." *Journal of the American Statistical Association* 62: 341–352.
Friedman, M.
  1962 "The interpolation of time series by related series." *Journal of the American Statistical Association* 57: 729–757.
Ginsburgh, V. A.
  1973 "A further note on the derivation of quarterly figures consistent with annual data." *Applied Statistics* 22: 368–374.
Glasser, M.
  1964 "Linear regression analysis with missing observations among the independent variables." *Journal of the American Statistical Association* 59: 834–844.
Glejser, H.
  1966 "Une methode d'evaluation de données mensuelles à partir d'indice trimestriels ou annuels." *Cahiers Economiques de Bruxelles* 19: 45.
Glenn, W. A., and C. Y. Kramer
  1958 "Analysis of variance of a randomized block design with missing observations." *Applied Statistics* 7: 173–185.
Goldberger, A. S.
  1981 "Linear regression after selection." *Journal of Econometrics* (2): 357–366.
Goodman, L. A.
  1963 "Statistical methods for the preliminary analysis of transaction flows." *Econometrica* 31: 197–208.
Goodman, L. A.
  1964 "A short computer program for the analysis of transaction flows." *Behavioral Science* 9: 176–186.

1965 "On the statistical analysis of mobility tables." *American Journal of Sociology* 70: 564–585.

1968 "The analysis of cross-classified data: Independence, quasi-independence, and interactions in contingency tables with or without missing entries." *Journal of the American Statistical Association* 63: 1091–1131.

1969a "How to ransack social mobility tables and other kinds of cross-classification tables." *American Journal of Sociology* 75: 1–40.

1969b "On partitioning χ^2 detecting partial association in three-way contingency tables." *Journal of the Royal Statistical Society* (B) 31: 486–498.

1970 "The multivariate analysis of qualitative data: Interactions among multiple classifications." *Journal of the American Statistical Association* 65: 226–256.

1971 "Partitioning of chi-square, analysis of marginal contingency tables, and estimation of expected frequencies in multidimensional contingency tables." *Journal of the American Statistical Association* 66: 339–344.

Gosslee, D. G., and H. L. Lucas
1965 "Analysis of variance of disproportionate data when interaction is present." *Biometrics* 21: 115–133.

Granger, C. W. J., and M. Hatanaka
1964 *Spectral Analysis of Economic Time Series*. Princeton: Princeton University Press.

Graybill, F. A.
1961 *An Introduction to Linear Statistical Models, Volume I*. New York: McGraw–Hill.

Grizzle, J. E., and O. D. Williams
1972 "Log linear models and tests of independence for contingency tables." *Biometrics* 28: 137–156.

Haberman, S. J.
1971 *Tables Based on Imperfect Observations*. (Unpublished manuscript.)

Haitovsky, Y.
1968 "Missing data in regression analysis." *Journal of the Royal Statistical Society* (B) 30: 67–82.

Harris, J. A., and A. E. Treloar
1927 "On a limitation in the applicability of the contingency coefficient." *Journal of the American Statistical Association* 22: 460–472.

Harris, J. A., and Chi Tu
1929 "A second category of limitations in the applicability of the contingency coefficient." *Journal of the American Statistical Association* 24: 367–375.

Harris, J. A., A. E. Treloar, and M. Wilder
1930 "Professor Pearson's note on our papers on contingency." *Journal of the American Statistical Association* 25: 323–327.

Hartley, H. O.
1956 "A plan for programming analysis of variance for general purpose computers: A universal missing plot formula." *Biometrics* 12: 110–122.

1958 "Maximum likelihood estimation from incomplete data." *Biometrics* 14: 174–194; 562.

Hartley, H. O., and R. R. Hocking
1971 "The analysis of incomplete data." *Biometrics* 28: 783–823.

Hartley, H. O., and J. N. R. Rao
1968 "Classification and estimation in analysis of variance problems." *Interactional Statistical Institute* 36: 141–147.

Healy, M. J. R., and M. Westmacott
1956 "Missing values in experiments analyzed on automatic computers." *Applied Statistics* 5: 203–206.

Heckman, J. J.
1980 "Sample selection bias as a specification error." E. Stromsdorfer and G. Farkas (eds.), *Evaluation Studies Review Annual*, Vol. 5. Beverly Hills: Sage Publications. Pp. 60–74.

Henderson, C. R.
    1953   "Estimation of variance and covariance components." *Biometrics* 9: 226–252.
Hinkelmann, K.
    1968   "Missing values in partial diallel cross experiments." *Biometrics* 24: 903–913.
Hocking, R. R., H. F. Huddleston, and H. H. Hunt
    1974   "A procedure for editing survey data." *Applied Statistics* 23: 121–133.
Hocking, R. R., and H. H. Oxspring
    1971   "Maximum likelihood estimation with incomplete multinomial data." *Journal of the American Statistical Association* 66: 65–70.
Hocking, R. R., and W. B. Smith
    1968   "Estimation of parameters in the multivariate normal distribution with missing observations." *Journal of the American Statistical Association* 63: 159–173.
    1972   "Optimum incomplete multinormal samples." *Technometrics* 14: 299–307.
Hogben, D.
    1959   "Test of difference between treatment and control with multiple replications of control and a missing plot." *Biometrics* 15: 486–487.
Horst, P.
    1965   *Factor Analysis of Data Matrices.* New York: Holt, Rinehart and Winston.
Houseworth, W. J.
    1972   "Hybrid polynomial and periodic regression with and without missing observations." *Biometrics* 28: 1025–1042.
Hughes, E. J.
    1962   "Maximum likelihood estimation of distribution parameters from incomplete data." Unpublished doctoral dissertation, Iowa State University.
Huitson, A.
    1966   *Analysis of Variance.* London: Charles Griffin.
Immer, F. R., H. K. Hayes, and L. Powers
    1934   "Statistical determination of barley varietal adaptation." *Journal of the American Society of Agronomics* 26: 403–419.
Imrey, P. B., and G. G. Koch
    1972   "Linear models analysis of incomplete multivariate categorical data." *Institute of Statistics Mimeo Series* No. 820. Chapel Hill: University of North Carolina.
Jackson, E. C.
    1968   "Missing values in linear multiple discriminant analysis." *Biometrics* 24: 835–844.
Jaech, J. L.
    1966   "An alternate approach to missing value estimation." *American Statistics* 20(5): 27–29.
Jennings, E.
    1967   "Fixed effects analysis of variance by regression analysis." *Multivariate Behavioral Research* 2: 95–108.
John, P. W. M.
    1971   *Statistical Design and Analysis in Experiments.* New York: Macmillan. Pp. 37 and 59.
Johnson, W. E.
    1965   "Multiple regression: Foxed and multivariate data with missing observations." Masters thesis, Texas A & M University.
Jones, R. H.
    1962   "Spectral analysis with regularly missed observations." *Annals of Mathematical Statistics* 33: 455–461.
Kaplan, E. L.
    1958   "Non-parametric estimation from incomplete observations." *Journal of the American Statistical Association* 53: 457–481.
Kastenbaum, M. A.
    1958   "Estimation of relative frequencies of four sperm types in Drosophila melanogaster." *Biometrics* 14: 223–228.

Kelejian, H. H.
   1969 "Missing observations in multivariate regression: Efficiency of a first-order method."
        Journal of the American Statistical Association 64: 1609–1616.
Kelly, J., D. L. Boggs, and K. A. McNeil
   1969 *Multiple Regression Approach.* Carbondale: University of Southern Illinois Press.
Kempthorne, O.
   1952 *The Design and Analysis of Experiments.* New York: Wiley.
Kim, J. O., and J. Curry
   1977 "The treatment of missing data in multivariate analysis." *Sociological Methods and
        Research* 6: 215–240.
Kleinbaum, D. G.
   1969 "A general method for obtaining test criteria for multivariate linear models with more than
        one design matrix and/or incomplete in response variates." *Institute of Statistical Mimeo
        Series* No. 614. University of North Carolina.
Kmenta, J. L.
   1971 *Elements of Econometrics.* New York: Macmillan.
Koch, G. C., P. B. Imrey, and D. W. Reinfurt
   1972 "Linear model analysis of categorical data with incomplete response vectors," *Biomet-
        rics* 28: 663–692.
Kosobud, R.
   1963 "A note on a problem caused by assignment of missing data in sample surveys," *Econo-
        metrica* 31 (No. 3).
Kramer, C. Y., and S. Glass
   1960 "Analysis of variance of a Latin square design with missing observations," *Applied
        Statistics* 9: 43–50.
Krane, S. A.
   1957 "Maximum likelihood estimation from incomplete data for continuous distributions,"
        M.S. Thesis, Iowa State University.
Kruskal, W.
   1961 "The co-ordinate free approach to Gauss-Markov estimation, and its application to miss-
        ing and extra observations," *Proceedings of the 4th Berkeley Symposium on Mathematics
        and Probability* 1: 433–451.
Lin, P. E.
   1971 "Estimation procedures for difference of means with missing data," *Journal of the Ameri-
        can Statistical Association* 66: 634–663.
   1973 "Procedures for testing the difference of means with incomplete data," *Journal of the
        American Statistical Association* 68: 699–703.
Lin, P. E., and L. E. Stivers
   1974 "On difference of means with incomplete data," *Biometrika* 61: 325–334.
Lisman, J. H. C., and J. Sandee
   1964 "Derivation of quarterly figures from annual data," *Applied Statistics* 13: 87–90.
Little, R. J. A.
   1978 "Consistent regression methods for discriminant analysis with incomplete data," *Journal
        of the American Statistical Association* 73: 319–322.
   1979 "Maximum likelihood inference for multiple regression with missing values: A simulation
        study," *Journal of the Royal Statistical Society* (B) 41: 76–87.
Lord, F. M.
   1955a "Equating test scores—A maximum likelihood solution," *Psychometrika* 20: 193–200.
   1955b "Estimation of parameters from incomplete data," *Journal of the American Statistical
        Association* 50: 870–876.
Lynch, C. J.
   1972 "A method for computing regression coefficients utilizing incomplete observations," un-
        published Ph.D. dissertation No. 4535, Graduate School, American University, Washing-
        ton, D.C.

Maddala, G. S.
  1977   *Econometrics*. New York: McGraw-Hill. Pp. 201–207.
Madow, W. G. (Study Director)
  1979   "Symposium on incomplete data: Preliminary proceedings." Washington, D.C.: U.S. Department of Health, Education and Welfare, Social Security Administration, Office of Research and Statistics.
Mantel, N.
  1970   "Incomplete contingency tables." *Biometrics* 26: 291–304.
Marini, M. M., A. R. Olsen, and D. B. Rubin
  1977   "Maximum likelihood estimation on panel studies with missing data." Washington, D.C.: National Institute of Child Health and Human Development.
Matthai, A.
  1951   "Estimation of parameters from incomplete data with application to design of sample surveys." *Sankya* 11: 145–152.
McCallum, B. T.
  1972   "Relative asymptotic bias from errors of omission and measurement." *Econometrica* 40: 757–758.
McDonald, L.
  1971a "On the estimation of missing data in the multivariate linear model." *Biometrics* 27: 535–543.
  1971b "On estimation of parameters from incomplete data." *Biometrics* 27: 535–543.
Mehta, J. S., and J. Gurland
  1969   "Some properties and an application of a statistic arising in testing correlation." *Annals of Mathematical Statistics* 40: 1736–1745.
  1973   "A test for equality of means in the presence of correlation and missing values." *Biometrika* 60: 211–213.
Milliken, G. A., and F. A. Graybill
  1971   "Tests for interaction in the two-way model with missing data." *Biometrics* 27: 1079–1083.
Morgan, B. J. T., and D. M. Titterington
  1977   "A comparison of iterative methods for obtaining maximum-likelihood estimates in contingency tables with a missing diagonal." *Biometrika* 64: 265–269.
Morrison, D. F.
  1967   *Multivariate Statistical Methods*. New York: McGraw–Hill.
  1971   "Expectations and variances of maximum likelihood estimates of the multivariate normal distribution parameters with missing data." *Journal of the American Statistical Association* 66: 602–604.
  1972   "The analysis of a single sample of repeated measurements." *Biometrics* 28: 55–71.
  1973   "Atest for equality of means of correlation variates with missing data on one response." *Biometrika* 60: 101–105.
Morrison, D. F., and D. S. Bhoj
  1973   "Power of the likelihood ratio test on the mean vector of the multivariate normal distribution with missing observations." *Biometrika* 60: 365–368.
Mote, V. L., and R. L. Anderson
  1965   "An investigation of the effect of misclassification on the properties of χ^2-tests in the analysis of categorical data." *Biometrika* 52: 95–109.
Myers, J. L.
  1966   *Fundamentals of Experimental Design*. Boston: Allyn and Bacon.
Neave, H. R.
  1970   "Spectral analysis of a stationary time series using initially scarce data." *Biometrika* 57: 111–122.
Nelder, J. A.
  1954   "A note on missing plot values in connection with query #96." *Biometrics* 10: 400–401.

Nelson, W., and G. H. Hahn
  1972 "Linear estimation of a regression relationship from censored data, part I: Simple methods and their applications." *Technometrics* 14: 247–269.
Nicholson, G. E.
  1957 "Estimation of parameters from incomplete multivariate samples." *Journal of the American Statistical Association* 52: 523–526.
Norton, H. W.
  1955 "A further note in missing data." *Biometrics* 11: 110.
Olsen, R. J.
  1980 "A least squares correction for selectivity bias." *Econometrica* 48(November): 1815–1820.
Orchard, T. A., and M. A. Woodbury
  1972 "A missing information principle: Theory and applications." In *6th Berkeley Symposium of Mathematics and Probability,* Vol. 1. Pp. 697–715.
Ostle, B.
  1963 *Statistics in Research: Basic Concepts and Techniques for Research Workers.* Ames: Iowa State University Press.
Overall, J. E., and D. K. Spiegel
  1969 "Concerning least squares analysis of experimental data." *Psychological Bulletin* 72: 311–322.
Parzen, E.
  1963 "On spectral analysis with missing observations and amplitude modulation." *Sankhya* (A) 25: 383–392.
Pearce, S. C.
  1971 "Black designs and missing data." *Journal of the Royal Statistical Society* (b) 33: 131–136.
Pearson, K.
  1930a "On the theory of contingency, I. Note on Professor J. Arthus Harris' papers on the limitation in the applicability of the contingency coefficient." *Journal of the American Statistical Association* 25: 320–332.
  1930b "Postscript." *Journal of the American Statistical Association* 25: 327.
Preece, D. A.
  1971 "Iterative procedures for missing values in experiments." *Technometrics* 13: 743–753.
  1972 "Non-additivity in two-way classifications with missing values" (Query 327). *Biometrics* 28: 574–577.
Preece, D. A., and Gower
  1974 "An iterative computer procedure for mixed-up values in experiments." *Applied Statistics* 23: 73–74.
Pregibon, D.
  1975 "Typical survey data: Estimation and imputation." *Statistics Canada*/University of Waterloo.
Press, S. J., and A. J. Scott
  1975 "Missing variables in Bayesian regression." In S. Fienberg and A. Zellner (eds.), *Studies in Bayesian Econometrics and Statistics.* Amsterdam: North Holland.
  1976 "Missing values in Bayesian regression, II." *Journal of the American Statistical Association* 71 (354): 366–370.
Quenouille, M. H.
  1953 *The Design and Analysis of Experiments.* London: Charles Griffin.
Rao, C. R.
  1952 *Advanced Statistical Methods in Biometric Research.* New York: Wiley.
  1956 "Analysis of dispersion with incomplete observations on one of the characters." *Journal of the Royal Statistical Society* (B) 18: 259–264.

Ratkowsky, D. A.
  1974 "Maximum likelihood estimation in small incomplete samples from the bivariate normal distribution." *Applied Statistics* 23: 180–184.
Reinfurt, D., and G. G. Koch
  1971 "The analysis of contingency tables with supplemented margins." Unpublished manuscript presented at Spring 1971 Eastern Regional Meetings.
Rubin, D. B.
  1971 "Multivariate data with missing observations—A general approach." Harvard University Department of Statistics Technical Report CP-6.
  1972 "A non-iterative algorithm for least squares estimation of missing values in any analysis of variance design." *Applied Statistics* 21: 136–141.
  1974 "Characterizing the estimation of parameters in incomplete data problems." *Journal of the American Statistical Association* 69: 467–474.
  1976a "Comparing regressions when some predictor values are missing." *Technometrics* 18: 201–205.
  1976b "Inference and missing data." *Biometrika* 63: 581–590.
  1977 "Formalizing subjective notions about the effects of nonresponse in sample surveys." *Journal of the American Statistical Association* 72: 538–543.
  1978 "Bayesian inference for causal effects: The role of randomization." *Annals of Statistics*.
Rummel, R. J.
  1970 *Applied Factor Analysis*. Evanston: Northwestern University Press.
Rundfeldt, H.
  1960 "Notes on the evaluation of nonorthogonal experiments on an electronic computer." *Biometrics* 16: 310.
Sargan, J. D., and E. G. Drettakis
  1974 "Missing data in an autoregressive model." *International Economic Review* 15: 39–58.
Scheffe, H.
  1959 *Analysis of Variance*. New York: Wiley.
Scheinok, P. A.
  1965 "Spectral analysis with randomly missed observations: The binomial case." *Annals of Mathematical Statistics* 36: 971–977.
Schentman, N. C.
  1978 "A note on the Geisser–Greenhouse correction for incomplete data split plot analysis." *Journal of the American Statistical Association* 73: 393–396.
Schuessler, K.
  1971 *Analyzing Social Data: A Statistical Orientation*. Boston: Houghton Mifflin.
Sclove, S. S.
  1972 "On missing value estimation in experimental design models." *American Statistics* 26(2): 25–26.
Searle, S. R.
  1970 "Large sample variances of maximum likelihood estimators of variance components using unbalanced data." *Biometrics* 26: 505–524.
  1971a *Linear Models*. New York: Wiley.
  1971b "Topics on variance component estimation." *Biometrics* 27: 1–76.
Seber, G. A. F.
  1966 "The linear hypothesis: A general theory." *Griffin Monograph No. 19*. New York: Hafner.
  1977 *Linear Regression Analysis*. New York: Wiley.
Shearer, P. R.
  1973 "Missing data on quantitative designs." *Applied Statistics* 22: 135–140.
Shoemaker, D. M.
  1973 *Principles and Procedures of Multiple Matrix Sampling*. Cambridge, Mass.: Ballinger.

Smith, H. F.
    1950 "Error variance of treatment contrasts in an experiment with missing observations: With special reference to incomplete Latin squares." *Indian Journal of Agricultural Statistics* 2: 111–124.
    1957 "Missing plot estimates." *Biometrics* 13: 115–118.

Snedecor, G. W., and G. M. Cox
    1935 "Disproportionate subclass numbers in tables of multiple classification." Research Bulletin 180, Agricultural Experiment Station. Iowa State University.

Snedecor, G. W., G. M. Cox, and W. G. Cochran
    1967 *Statistical Methods*. Ames: Iowa State University Press.

Snedecor, G. W., G. M. Cox, and C. B. Williams
    1952–1953 "Queries 96 and 103." *Biometrics* 8: 384; and 9: 425–427.

Speed, F. M., M. M. Hocking, and Om P. Mackney
    1978 "Methods of analysis of linear models with unbalanced data." *Journal of the American Statistical Association* 73: 105–117.

Steinhorst, R. K., and C. D. Miller
    1969 "Disproportionality of cell frequencies in psychological and educational experiments involving multiple classification." *Educational and Psychological Measurement* 29: 799–811.

Strivastava, J. N.
    1966 "Incomplete multiresponse designs." *Sankhya* (A) 28: 377–388.

Sunter, A. B., C. A. Patrick, and D. A. Binder
    1975 "On the editing of survey data." Presented at the 40th Session of the International Statistics Institute, Warsaw.

Taylor, J.
    1948 "Errors of treatment comparisons when observations are missing." *Nature* 162: 262–263.

Taylor, L. D.
    1964 "A note on the problems of missing observations in cross section." Mimeographed. Cambridge: Department of Economics, Harvard University.

Thomas, H. A., Jr.
    1958 "Correlation techniques for augmenting stream runoff information." Harvard Water Resources Program. (Unpublished report.)

Thompson, H. R.
    1956 "Extensions to missing plot techniques." *Biometrics* 12: 241–244.

Timm, N. H.
    1970 "The estimation of variance–covariance and correlation matrices from incomplete data." *Psychometrika* 35: 417–437.

Tocher, K. D.
    1952 "The design and analysis of block experiments." *Journal of the Royal Statistical Society* 14: 45–100.

Trawinski, I. M., and R. E. Bargmann
    1964 "Maximum likelihood estimation with incomplete multivariate data." *Annals of Mathematical Statistics* 35: 647–657.

Truitt, J. T., and H. F. Smith
    1956 "Adjustment by covariance and consequent tests of significance in split-plot experiments." *Biometrics* 12: 23–39.

Tsao, F.
    1946 "General solution of the analysis of variance and covariance in the case of unequal or disproportionate numbers of observations in the subclasses." *Psychometrika* 11: 107–128.

Wagner, S. S.
    1970 "The maximum-likelihood estimate for contingency tables with zero diagonal." *Journal of the American Statistical Association* 65: 1362–1383.

Walker, H. M., and J. Lev
    1953 *Statistical Inference*. New York: Holt, Rinehart and Winston.

Walsh, J. E.
 1961 "Computer feasible method for handling incomplete data in regression analysis." *Journal of the Association for Computer Machinery* 8: 201–211.
Watson, G. S.
 1956 "Missing and 'mixed-up' frequencies in contingency tables." *Biometrics* 12: 47–50.
Wickens, M. R.
 1972 "A note on the use of proxy variables." *Econometrica* 40: 759–761.
Wilkinson, G. N.
 1957 "The analysis of covariance with incomplete data." *Biometrics* 13: 363–372.
 1958a "Estimation of missing values for the analysis of incomplete data." *Biometrics* 14: 257–286.
 1958b "The analysis of variance and derivation of standard errors for incomplete data." *Biometrics* 14: 360–384.
 1960 "Comparison of missing value procedures." *Australian Journal of Statistics* 2: 53–65.
 1970 "A general recursive procedure for analysis of variance." *Biometrics* 57: 19–46.
Wilks, S. S.
 1932 "Moments and distributions of estimates of population parameters from fragmentary samples." *Annals of Mathematical Statistics* 3: 163–195.
Williams, D. A.
 1966 "Errors of treatment comparisons when observations are missing from a randomized block experiment with additional replication of a control treatment." *Biometrics* 22: 632–633.
Williams, J. D.
 1972 "Two-way fixed effects analysis of variance with disproportionate cell frequencies." *Multivariate Behavioural Research* 7: 67.
Williams, W. II., and C. L. Mallows
 1970 "Systematic biases in panel surveys." *Journal of the American Statistical Association* 65: 1338–1349.
Winer, B. J.
 1962 *Statistical Principles in Experimental Design.* New York: McGraw–Hill. (2nd ed., 1971.)
Wold, H.
 1966a "Estimation of principal components and related models by iterative least squares." In Krishnaiah (ed), *Multivariate Analysis,* Vol. 1. New York: Academic Press.
 1966b "Nonlinear estimation by iterative least squares procedures." *Festschrift Jerzy Neyman.* New York: Wiley.
Woodbury, M. A., R. C. Clelland, and R. J. Hickey
 1963 "Applications of a factor-analytic model in the prediction of biological data." *Behavioural Science* 8: 347–354.
Woodbury, M. A., and V. Hassellblad
 1970 "Maximum likelihood estimates of the variance–covariance matrix from the multivariate normal." Presented at the Share National Meeting, Denver, Colorado.
 1971 "Contribution to the discussion of 'the analysis of incomplete data' by H. O. Hartley and R. R. Hocking." *Biometrics* 27: 808–813.
Woodbury, M. A., and W. Siler
 1966 "Factor analysis with missing data." *Annals of the New York Academy of Sciences* 128: 746–754.
Yates, F.
 1933 "The analysis of replicated experiments when the field results are incomplete." *Empire Journal of Experimental Agriculture* 1: 129–142.
 1934 "The analysis of multiple classifications with unequal numbers in the different classes." *Journal of the American Statistical Association* 29: 51–66.
 1936a "Incomplete Latin squares." Part 2: *Journal of Agricultural Science* 301–315.
 1936b "Incomplete randomized blocks." *Annals of Eugenics* (Part II) 7: 121–140.

Yates, F., and W. G. Cochran
  1938 "The analysis of groups of experiments." *Journal of Agricultural Science* 28: 556–580.
Yates, F., and R. W. Hale
  1939 "The analysis of Latin squares when two or more rows, columns or treatments are missing." *Journal of the Royal Statistical Society* (Suppl.) 6: 67–79.
Yates, F., and R. W. Hale
  1953 *Sampling Methods for Censeses and Surveys* (2nd ed.). London: Charles Griffin.
Zelen, M.
  1953 "The analysis of some incomplete block designs with a missing block." *Biometrics* 9: 263.
Zelen, M.
  1954 "Analysis for some partially balanced incomplete block designs having a missing block." *Biometrics* 10: 273–281.
Zellner, A.
  1966 "On the analysis of first order autoregressive models with incomplete data." *International Economic Review* 7: 72–76.
Zyskind, G.
  1965 "Query 14: Missing values in factorial experiments." *Technometrics* 7: 649–650.

Chapter 13

Applications of the General Linear Model to Survey Data

Richard A. Berk

13.1. INTRODUCTION

The general linear model includes multiple regression, analysis of variance, and analysis of covariance as special cases and has therefore become one of the most popular statistical tools available for analyzing survey data. In the face of this popularity, it is often forgotten that the general linear model is in fact a model. That is, the general linear model is a precise formal statement about a particular set of stochastic processes. A stochastic model, like any model, is only substantively informative if it accurately portrays the empirical world. Although *accuracy* can have many different definitions and operational forms, it is apparent that a poor fit will likely produce misleading conclusions. Moreover, this may occur even if the underlying mathematics are sound; they may simply be the wrong mathematics.

In this chapter, an overview of the general linear model is undertaken, and the correspondence between substantive concerns and statistical concerns provides a unifying theme. Efforts are made to underscore that the application of the general linear model typically involves at least an implicit *theory* of the processes generating the observations at hand. At the same time, however, the treatment is more conceptual than formal with an emphasis on issues of particular relevance to practitioners.[1] This is not to deny the importance of more

[1] For readers with a solid background in calculus and matrix algebra, an excellent technical discussion of the general linear model can be found in Searle (1971), Graybill (1961), Morrison (1976), or any of the more popular econometric texts such as Johnston (1960), Goldberger (1964), or Malinvaud (1970). For readers without these skills, more elementary but nevertheless insightful treatments can be found in Kmenta (1971) and Pindyck and Rubinfeld (1981). Many of these works also provide a brief introduction to the necessary matrix algebra although these chapters are typically either pithy or superficial. An especially useful, though still applied, discussion of matrix algebra can be found in Searle and Hausman (1970) or Green (1978).

HANDBOOK OF SURVEY RESEARCH

mathematical discussions, but to focus on the kinds of issues that surface when survey data are analyzed.[2]

13.2. THE TWO-VARIABLE REGRESSION MODEL

The general linear model can be a very powerful and flexible analytic device; Cohen and Cohen (1975) characterize it as "a general data-analytic system." Also, a thorough understanding of its underlying statistical principles greatly enhances one's grasp of an even greater range of statistical methods including nonlinear least squares, factor analysis, and time-series analysis.

Perhaps the most mathematically sound presentation would begin by presenting the general linear model and then its special cases. However, in part because this approach immediately launches one into a variety of mathematical abstractions, elementary treatments rarely take this path. Rather, at least one of the special cases is initially introduced coupled with some applications, and only after a thorough exegesis is the more general model presented. Such a strategy is approximated here; we begin with bivariate regression.

The usual bivariate regression model rests on an initial, substantive assumption that each observation on some endogenous (dependent) variable is a linear combination of three components: an intercept reflecting the mean of the endogenous variable (among other things); the causal impact of a given exogenous (independent) variable; and a random perturbation. Beyond this opening formulation, however, the properties of each of the three components depend fundamentally on a set of additional considerations *all* of which have substantive implications. There are, for instance, many ways to characterize the random perturbations, and it cannot be overemphasized that one's formal model will differ depending on how these errors are viewed. In this context then, we turn to a substantive problem to illustrate how statistical assumptions have substantive implications.

An Example

Suppose a researcher were interested in the performance of police officers on patrol and in particular, the number of good arrests made per month. A good arrest might be defined as an arrest leading to formal charges by the district attorney, although the researcher could also know that there is far more to police work than facilitating effective prosecutions (Bittner, 1980). Suppose also that the researcher is prepared to assume (far too simply) that the number of good arrests made per month by police officers on patrol is primarily a function of a single causal variable: the amount of training provided by the local

[2] This chapter assumes that the reader has at least a nodding acquaintance with multiple regression and elementary statistical concepts at about the level of Blalock (1972) or Hayes (1973).

police academy. Longer periods of training might provide greater exposure to course material on criminal law, the rudiments of effective investigative work, the rights of offenders that must be upheld, and the proper documentation of events surrounding an arrest. In other words, all other causal influences (e.g., patroling practices, years on the force) each have negligible effects on the number of good arrests; there may be a great many other causal factors, but each by itself makes little difference in the number of good arrests.

In the absence of a better indicator of the amount of training, the researcher settles on the number of weeks of classroom course work provided by the local police academy. With this variable, the researcher is then prepared to assume that the relationship between the number of weeks of classroom training and the number of good arrests per month is linear; the impact of training on arrests is the same across any meaningful range of training. For example, each week of classroom training may lead to 2 more good arrests per month, and this relationship holds whether the additional week refers to the difference between 2 and 3 weeks of classroom training or whether the additional week refers to the difference between 10 and 11 weeks of classroom training.

It should be apparent that the researcher is already making important theoretical assertions. These may rest on extant theory, prior research, intuition, or convention, but they are nevertheless significant statements about causal processes operating in the real world. Much of what follows will rest on these initial assumptions. For example, an alternative view might suggest that the relationship between the number of good arrests per month and the amount of training is more accurately captured in percentage change terms. That is, a 1% increase in the number of weeks of classroom training leads, perhaps, to a 10% increase in the number of good arrests; what matters is relative change, not absolute change. However, a theoretical formulation in percentage change terms implies that one is using the log of the number of good arrests as the endogenous variable and the log of the number of weeks of classroom training as the exogenous variable (Hanushek & Jackson, 1977, p. 98). Clearly, one no longer has a linear relationship between the original variables. In short, even seemingly innocuous alterations in one's initial premises can have enormous effects on the formal statement of a causal relationship.

There are many ways in which the researcher might collect data on the relationship between the number of good arrests per month and the number of weeks of classroom training. In this instance, the researcher decides to focus on a particular urban area with a police force including 150 police officers who go out on patrol. In the absence of official records on the number of good arrests per month broken down by individual police officers, the researcher decides to interview all of the 150 police officers who in principle can make arrests (cf. Rossi, Berk, & Eidson, 1974). From each of these respondents an estimate is obtained of the number of good arrests made over the immediately preceding 30 days. In addition, each respondent is asked about the number of weeks of classroom training experienced while at the police academy, and since the amount of classroom training has varied over the years and since different police officers went to the academy at different times, there is considerable variation in the number of weeks of classroom training.

In thinking through how best to analyze the data, a serious complication immediately arises. Although the researcher is prepared to assume that the neglected causal variables each have small effects by themselves, their impact in the aggregate is less clear. In the given period for which the data were collected, the number of good arrests may be inflated or reduced so that the linear relationship between training and arrests may fail to tell the full story. For example, more good arrests may occur than can be attributed to variability in training. This presents serious *descriptive* problems since the researcher has only specified a precise causal form for the impact of classroom training. There is nothing very clear in the theory about the role of other variables except that their effects taken one at a time are very small.

Faced with such descriptive difficulties, the researcher makes a new theoretical assumption: In the aggregate across all of the 150 police officers, the net effect of the neglected causal variables should be zero. In essence, the cumulative impact of many small (positive and negative) effects cancel each other out.

Additional thought reveals another problem. The researcher is wise enough in the ways of surveys to recognize that there may be many sources of measurement error. Police may occasionally fail to recall arrests, may inadvertently inflate the reported number of good arrests, and so on. Thus once again, explaining good arrests through impact of training alone is descriptively wanting, even if each of the many sources of measurement error has small effects by itself. However, having thought through a procedure for neglected causal variables, the researcher decides to apply a similar strategy here. The effects of measurement error are to be defined much like the effect of neglected causal variables (fundamentally, there are genuine causal variables), and the researcher assumes that the aggregate value of this new kind of error is zero across the 150 police officers.

This is still insufficient. Perhaps police officers with less training are more likely to underreport the number of good arrests. Possibly some fail to consider that if, for instance, four suspects are arrested for a given crime, four good arrests may result (not just one). In contrast, police officers with more training may in their desire to show the importance of their superior training, tend to inflate the number of good arrests reported to the interviewer. Although the *aggregate* impact of the measurement error might still be zero, another empirical dimension of the arrest-generating processes will be neglected. If this could occur from errors in measurement, why not from the impact of other factors? Perhaps individuals with less (more) training are individuals for whom neglected causal variables tend to produce fewer (more) good arrests. (Obvious candidates for such variables include motivation, age, and the assigned beat.) Unfortunately, for the data available and bivariate model proposed there seems no way to address these potential problems. This forces another theoretical assumption: The impact of the measurement error and missing variables (i.e., the "noise") in the sample is uncorrelated with the length of each officer's training experience.

It is important to stress that without an assumption that the impact of the noise is uncorrelated with training, the researcher would have been admitting to a distorted description of the impact of training. If, for example, individuals with less training underreported the number of good arrests, any real, positive, linear relationship between training and arrests would be inflated. Similarly, the relationship would probably be inflated if officers with a greater amount of training were assigned to high crime beats where the prospects for making good arrests were better.

Up to this point, the researcher has only been examining forces affecting the number of good arrests across police officers. What about factors influencing the number of weeks of training? First, the researcher decides to look only at the impact of training, and to take the length of training for each respondent as given. Perhaps other empirical work will consider causes of the number of weeks of training.

In contrast, three types of measurement error (and combinations thereof) must be addressed. In one form, the measurement error is correlated with the real (true) weeks of training. This obviously confounds the impact of the actual weeks of training with the reported number of weeks so that it is not clear which the hypothesized linear relationship reflects. In a second form, the measurement error is uncorrelated with the true training levels, but is consistently underreported or overreported. In this instance, the change in the number of good arrests for each unit change in weeks of training is unaffected, but across the entire range of training, too few or too many good arrests are attributed to the number of weeks of training. Finally, neither of these systematic errors may occur, but errors may occur in some sort of haphazard fashion. Whereas in the aggregate they may even cancel out and be uncorrelated with training, there is still some discrepancy between the real and reported training. This form of measurement error initially seems unimportant. But on further consideration, it appears that the linear relationship will be distorted. Haphazard measurement error in training seems somewhat like the measurement error examined earlier for arrests and can be distinguished from the true variability in the number of weeks of training. yet, both the true variability and the measurement error will be considered simultaneously in the impact of the number of good arrests. This means that the calculated linear relationship will reflect both sources of variance in its description of effects. The likely consequence is that since the measurement error is haphazard and by itself not a genuine cause of good arrests, it should not help explain the number of good arrests. Therefore, the observed linear relationship should be attenuated compared to its real (i.e., error-free) impact.

Although it seems possible that with more information adjustments for the measurement error could be undertaken, no more information is available. Hence the researcher is saddled with another assumption: There is no measurement error of any kind in the reported number of weeks of training.

Just about the time the researcher begins to feel confident with the descriptive nature of the causal model proposed, an entirely new cluster of issues appears. The researcher wants not only to characterize the given data set in terms of the theoretical model but also to generalize from those data. At a minimum, it would be useful to apply findings from the obtained data to a longer period of time than just the one month represented in the data. However, although one could simply assume that the proposed model applies exactly for a range of months, this seems highly unrealistic. Even if the underlying linear relationship between training and good arrests is invariant, as the theory implies (there has been no mention of making the relationship a function of time), making the impact of measurement error and neglected variables invariant seems extremely restrictive. For example, if among the many excluded variables (each with negligible causal effects) are variables that vary over time (e.g., motivation), and if these affect the number of good arrests, it stands to reason that the number of good arrests will also vary over time as a function of these variables; and the same observation holds for the impact of measurement error.

Unfortunately, if one permits the effect of the noise to vary from month to month, significant new problems arise. For many (or most) months, the noise effect will not fulfill the assumptions made earlier. This would apply to the month on which the data were collected. In the aggregate (i.e., across respondents), the impact of the noise might not be zero, for example, and may be correlated with the number of weeks of training. Hence, all of the earlier problems assumed away would reappear.

This suggests an entirely new strategy. Rather than requiring that all of the assumptions about the effect of missing variables and measurement error always fully hold, one might consider that some or all hold "on the average" over time. Although significant violations may occur in any particular month, over a very large number of months the assumptions approximately hold.

Yet this new approach immediately leads to a number of complications. In particular, if in the aggregate the impact of the noise is allowed to vary from month to month, it should also vary for *each respondent* from month to month. Thus, in one month the impact for a given individual may be large and positive whereas in the next it might be small and negative. The upshot is that assumptions about the effect of noise must be considered not just in terms of their aggregate impact on the number of good arrests, but also in terms of their impact on the number of good arrests for given police officers in a large number of monthly "realizations." In other words, since the idea of generalizing across many months leads in principle to the prospect of many different noise effects for each police officer, assumptions about aggregate effects across police officers are insufficient.

Fortunately, the researcher is able to build on earlier insights about the effect of the noise in a single realization. To begin, the researcher is prepared to assume that although for any given police officer the number of good arrests will vary across hypothetical realizations as a function of variation in the noise, on the average across a large number of these "replications" the effect of the noise is zero. That is, on the average, the positive and negative perturbations cancel out. This implies that although in any given realization the number of good arrests will be too high or too low when the impact of training by itself is taken into account, in the long run, there will be no systematic tendency for underestimation or overestimation to occur. That is, if one uses the number of weeks of training for a given police officer to guess the number of good arrests, there will be no systematic tendency over many realizations to predict too many or too few arrests.

If it is proper to assume that the effect of the noise cancels out on the average (in many realizations) for a given police officer, it follows that the same should be true for *all* of the police officers. That is, for each of the entire set of 150 police officers sampled, the number of weeks of training will on the average over the long run neither underestimate nor overestimate the number of good arrests. Clearly, this is a comforting conclusion.

With a bit more thought, it appears that the researcher can do even better. If for each police officer the effect of the noise cancels out on the average over the long run, it should follow that on the average *the impact of the noise will be uncorrelated with the number of weeks of training*. To begin, each police officer is characterized by the same net impact of the noise; the impact is zero for each. Consequently, there is no variability in the average noise effect for each police officer with the result that there can be no association between the average effect of the noise and particular police officers. If there is no association between the average impact of the noise and particular police officers, there can be no association between the impact of the noise and *fixed characteristics* (over time) of the police officers. In this instance, the characteristic of interest is the number of weeks of training. Over time the average effect of the noise for each officer is constant, as is the number of weeks of training for each officer. Therefore, there cannot be any association in the usual sense. What this implies is that on the average, the relationship between training and arrests will not be distorted by the effect of the noise; the average relationship will not be distorted by the perturbations.

What would be the consequences if the number of weeks of training were not fixed over the time period of interest? Would the independence between the impact of the noise and the number of weeks of training still hold? Here, the researcher is not sure, but there does not seem to be any cause for concern. The training experience is far in the past and can now be treated as a fixed attribute for each respondent. That is, although the number of weeks of training varies across police officers, it does not vary by month for the period of interest.

Finally, the researcher turns to the prospect that the size of the impact of the noise on the number of good arrests will vary for different police officers and that these effects will be correlated across officers. In the first instance, some officers may be on average more susceptible to the impact of the noise and this implies that attempts to characterize the linear relationship between weeks of training and arrests will be more difficult for these officers. Since the goal is to examine the impact of training for all officers at once, there is some reason for concern. In essence, all police officers are being treated as if each were equally vulnerable when in fact, this may not be the case. In the absence of any strategy for handling the implications of different sized noise effects across different officers, the researcher makes the following assumption: The variance in the effect of measurement error and missing variables on the number of good arrests are on the average over the long run the same for each police officer.

In the second instance, the possibility of correlated noise effects is also troubling. The researcher is proceeding as if each police officer sampled provides a new piece of information about the impact of training on arrests. But if the impact of missing variables and neglected variables is somewhat the same for at least some of the officers, there is apparently some redundancy in the information being collected. Again, however, the researcher can think of no way to handle this problem and opts for another assumption: The effects of the noise for each police officer are uncorrelated on the average over the long run.

To summarize, the researcher has arrived at the following *substantive* model. The number of good arrests per month for each patrol officer is an invariant linear function of each officer's number of weeks of training plus the impact of noise. The noise is substantive in origin; it results from the small effects of a great many excluded causal variables and from measurement error. At any point in time, the noise makes it difficult to characterize precisely what the real linear relationship is. Yet, the researcher is prepared to assume that over many months the average impact of the noise on the number of good arrests for each police officer is zero, that the effect of the noise for any given officer is independent of the effect of the noise for any other officer, and that variation in effect of the noise is equal across officers. In addition, the causal variable is fixed over the period of interest and free of measurement error.

It cannot be overemphasized that in the transitions from description to estimation an important tradeoff has been made. The assumptions about the impact of the noise now hold only over the long run and for most months, including the month for which data have been collected; that is, the assumptions are violated to some *unknown* degree. Moreover, we will see later how one can estimate the likelihood that serious errors can occur as a result, although these assessments too have meaning only in the long run. It is impossible to determine the amount of distortion present in findings from any given data set (Barnett, 1973).[3]

The Formal Model

Given the theoretical model derived from substantive concerns, and practical constraints, the next issue is whether there exists a mathematical model

[3] An important caveat should be added. Thus far the discussion assumes a classical (relative frequency) approach to inference. A Bayesian perspective can provide estimates of the likely error in a particular data set (Box & Tiao, 1973). However, this requires, among other things, a subjective definition of probability in terms of degrees of certainty.

providing a reasonable *approximation*. In this instance, the bivariate regression model, as a special case of the general linear model, may be useful (not surprisingly). Formally, the bivariate regression model can be represented as:

$$Y_t = \beta_1 + \beta_2 X_t + U_t \qquad (13.1)$$

where Y_t indicates the observations on the dependent or endogenous variable— the number of good arrests across each of the t police officers in our example; X_t represents the observations on the independent of exogenous variable—the number of weeks of training for each of the t police officers. The subscript t for Y_t and X_t ranges from 1 to 150 with T equal to 150. β_1 is the Y intercept, the mean value of the number of good arrest rate across all respondents when the number of weeks of training is zero. As is often the case in applied contexts, the value of β_1 in our example reflects an extrapolation to unrealistic substantive situations (i.e., all police have *some* training). The slope of the linear relationship (i.e., regression line) between Y_t and X_t is β_2 and indicates the average change in Y_t for every unit change in X_t. It is therefore, a measure of the causal impact of training on good arrests. The noise for each of the separate t respondents is U_t, a summary of all the additional forces affecting the number of good arrests for each; U_t is commonly called the error term.

If this formulation is substantively accurate and if one is only interested in a description of the observation on hand, there is little that must be added. One may treat the data as the sole statistical population of interest. All one requires are formulas for each of the coefficients and perhaps some way of gauging the importance of the error term. These in turn require some underlying justification since, in principle, a very wide variety of formulas could be applied.

The most popular justification reflects the notion that the formulas should produce coefficients for the linear relationship that on the average minimize the overall role of the error. For a variety of technical but straightforward reasons, this works out to minimizing the sum of the impacts of the error on each observation on Y_t after each of these "residuals" is first squared. This is the well-known least-squares principle and is fundamental to all forms of the general linear model.[4]

The formulas derived from the least-squares principle have a variety of interesting properties. Perhaps most important, the definitions of what is minimized takes the larger errors into account most heavily; larger errors have a disproportional impact on the calculated coefficients (Berk, Hennessy, & Mc-Cleary, 1976).[5] In our example, the few officers who's arrest rates happen to be heavily influenced by the noise (for the month in which the data were collected) will be overrepresented in the calculated coefficients. Thus, the linear causal relationship will reflect the experiences of these police officers far more than others, a somewhat ironic positive weighting of the officers whose number of

---

[4] See, for example, Hanushek and Jackson (1977, pp. 29–31), for an elementary discussion of these issues and Malinvaud, (1970, chap. 1), for a more advanced consideration.

[5] In part because of this kind of problem, the "robust estimation" tradition has grown. See, for example, Wainer (1976) for an overview.

good arrests is most influenced by things other than the number of weeks of training.

Another byproduct of the least-squares principle is that by *construction* the mean impact of the errors across all observations on the dependent variable will be zero. Similarly, by construction the correlation between the values of the independent variable and the error will be zero (Hanushek & Jackson, 1977, p. 51). Both of these have implications that will be discussed further.

Given the least-squares principle and the derived formulas (which can be found in any of the references listed in footnotes 1 and 2), the values of β_1 and β_2 can be easily calculated. In our example, the value of β_1 may be 1.5 whereas the value of β_2 may be .25. The latter means that for every additional week of training for a given police officer, the number of good arrests increases .25 per month. The former means that officers who have no academy training (an unlikely situation) will still have 1.5 good arrests per month. In addition, one can use Eq. (13.1) to obtain the number of good arrests one would expect from the model for various officers, given a certain amount of training. For example, an officer with 20 weeks' training should have 6.5 good arrests per month [1.5 + (.25 × 20)].

However, for any particular officer the number of good arrests derived from the model will probably not equal the observed number of good arrests. Moreover, this may be true across all officers. These discrepancies are actually the values of U_t (i.e., residuals), and it would be convenient to have some summary measures of how large these tend to be. There are two common descriptive measures: (*a*) the square root of the sum of squared residuals, that sum first being divided by the number of observations (the standard deviation about the regression line); and (*b*) the square of the correlation coefficient between the dependent and independent variable. (With some minor modifications described later, these formulas can also be found in the references listed in footnotes 1 and 2.) The former can be roughly interpreted as the positive square root of the "average" deviation from the regression line or of the "average" disparity between the number of arrests actually observed and the number "predicted" from the model (note, however, it is not actually the mean deviation). The latter can be interpreted as the proportion of variance in the dependent variable that can be attributed to the independent variable. Although the correlation coefficient squared is probably the more popular measure among sociologists, economists seem to prefer the standard deviation of the residuals. This standard deviation comes in the original units of the dependent variable leading to convenient interpretations. The proportion of explained variance depends not only on the size of the impact of X_t on Y_t, but on the variances of the two variables. This means that two different samples that have the exact same causal relationship between X_t and Y_t (the same regression line) could have very different proportions of explained variance depending on the variance of X_t and Y_t (Hanushek & Jackson, 1977, pp. 56–59; Pindyck & Rubinfeld, 1981, pp. 61–64). This also has important implications when different models are compared for their usefulness or when transformations of the data are undertaken. It is not altogether clear why models or transformations producing more explained variance are necessarily better. Perhaps the best overall rule is to report both the standard deviation of the residuals (or, more typically, estimates of it) and the proportion of variance explained as indicators of the amount of error, but to rely far more on theory than on either of these measures for construction of the model. More is said about this later.

Besides the regression coefficient β_2 and the intercept β_1, the bivariate linear regression model can produce several other coefficients for the effect of X_t and Y_t. The square root of the variance explained is the common Pearson correlation coefficient. Unlike the regression coefficient, which is asymmetric in the effect of X_t and Y_t, (except when the standard deviation of X_t equals the standard deviation of Y_t) the correlation coefficient is symmetric; it produces the same results whether X_t is viewed as causally prior or Y_t is viewed as causally prior. Therefore, it is not a measure of causal impact and not especially useful as a descriptive measure in linear regression.

The standardized regression coefficient is the regression coefficient for Y_t regressed on X_t as before, but with both variables transformed into "standard scores." The standardization may be accomplished by first subtracting the mean of each variable from each of the observations on that variable and then dividing this difference by the standard deviation of the variable (Blalock, 1972, p. 100). The standardized regression coefficient may also be calculated directly from the unstandardized ("raw" or "metric") regression coefficient by first dividing the standard deviation of the independent variable by the standard deviation of the dependent variable and then multiplying this quotient by the unstandardized regression coefficient (Pindyck & Rubinfeld, 1981, p. 90). The standardized regression coefficient is interpreted as the average number of standard deviations (Y_t) changes for every standard deviation change in X_t. In the bivariate case or in the multivariate case when the independent variables are uncorrelated with one another, the standardized regression coefficient happens to equal the simple (zero-order) correlation coefficient. This often leads to some confusion in interpretations of the standardized regression coefficient. In most practical situations the two are not equal. The standardized regression coefficient is also identical to the path coefficient, a common measure of "effect" in causal modeling. Finally, the standardized regression coefficient is roughly analogous to factor loadings in factor analysis. These last two parallels are found in the recent work on causal modeling with unobserved variables (e.g., see Aigner & Goldberger, 1977).[6]

In our example, the standardized regression coefficient might equal .60. This would mean that for every standard deviation change in the number of weeks of training, the number of good arrests changes .60 standard deviations.[7] This implies that the correlation coefficient is also .60 and that 36% of the variance in arrests is attributable to training. However, the standardized regres-

---

[6] A useful introduction to these techniques can be found in Burt (1973).

[7] If the analysis is carried out by first standardizing the data, the intercept becomes zero.

sion coefficient even when not equivalent to the correlation, has many of the same interpretive difficulties. As Blalock (1971) argues, in essence, the standardized coefficients can be very misleading when compared across samples with different variances for X_t and Y_t. Perhaps the best application of standardized regression coefficients occurs when one is trying to judge the relative importance of different causal variables *within* a given sample (i.e., in multiple regression) and when the variables do not come in easily interpreted units. Standardizing the data (or coefficients) puts all of the coefficients in standard deviation units, making them more easily compared. In our example, the data come in "common sense" units: the number of good arrests and the number of weeks of training. However, when the data reflected scores on some abstract scale (e.g., instead of weeks of training, some score on a paper and pencil test), the standardized regression coefficient provides a convenient means to transform the regression coefficient into a more easily interpreted value.

A final descriptive measure somewhat less common in bivariate regression is called an elasticity. This coefficient, which has a legitimate equivalent in economic theory (Nicholson, 1972, pp. 99–101), indicates the *percentage* change in Y_t for every *percentage* change in X_t. It may be easily calculated by multiplying the unstandardized regression coefficient by the mean of X_t divided by the mean of Y_t (Pindyck & Rubinfeld, 1981, p. 91). However, these operations imply that the elasticity is evaluated at the means of the two variables and that the value would be rather different if evaluated at other points in their distributions. In other words, an elasticity indicates the percentage change in Y_t for every percentage change in X_t in the immediate neighborhood of the means of the two variables. As such, it has somewhat limited usefulness except in its relation to the theoretical concept of elasticity.[8]

All of the measures discussed so far may have legitimate uses when the data are treated as a population, that is, when all one cares about is describing causal relationships in a particular data set. Typically, however, one asks more of the general linear model. One would like to be able to draw inferences from the data to observations that in fact are not collected. One approach can rely on theoretical arguments—claiming from prior theory, research, or logical extrapolations that the model described is also relevant in other contexts. In our example, the researcher might argue that since there is no reason to believe that the month in which the data were collected is atypical, the model is an accurate representation of the relationship between training and arrests over several years. In addition, the researcher might claim that the model is appropriate for a number of large urban areas, not just the one in which the data are collected. When persuasively argued, this manner of extrapolation is perfectly legitimate and very common.

In contrast, when one employs statistical inference to make statements about unobserved phenomena, the descriptive properties of the general linear model must be extended with a more formal statement of the model's stochas-

---

[8] An important exception is when the model is formulated in terms of the logs of the variables in which case the elasticity is constant (Hanushek & Jackson, 1977, pp. 96–101).

tic properties. In essence, the stochastic formulation assumes that for *each* fixed value on the exogenous variable, there exists a probability distribution on the endogenous variable; for each fixed X_t there are a large number of possible Y_t values with a nonzero probability (and not usually the same probability) of occurring. The particular value or values on Y_t that happen to appear for each X_t in a given data set are therefore a sample of all possible values that could have surfaced. In our example, perhaps three, four, and six good arrests were observed for the three police officers with 15 weeks of training. The stochastic model implies that should another data set for a different month be collected and should once again the officers with 15 weeks of training be examined, the number of arrests might be two, five, and seven. Moreover, if one repeated this process over and over, each time a somewhat different number of arrests would be found for the officers with 15 weeks of training. Note that one is not sampling in the standard survey sense; the model is really closer to a series of independent replications (Kmenta, 1971, pp. 197–202; Malinvaud, 1970, pp. 59–79).[9] Sometimes, such independent replications are called realizations of a particular underlying stochastic process.

Despite the fixed nature of X_t, the stochastic properties of Y_t are such that one would obtain somewhat different estimates of the regression line in a series of realizations. Yet, the model also assumes that there is really only one real regression line that remains invariant. This can be labeled "the population regression line" and defined by a set of fixed population parameters (β_1 and β_2), although superficial analogies to a survey population can be misleading. There is no predetermined sampling frame and the empirical world rather than the researcher produces the sample observations on Y_t. Moreover, in survey sampling, *all* observations in the population are treated as fixed. Stochastic perturbations are introduced only when the researcher draws a probability sample. In the general linear model, the values of Y_t are already stochastic in the population. These differences are too often overlooked in interpretations of statistical inference and a variety of misleading conclusions can result (Berk & Brewer, 1978).[10]

In short, since the least-squares formulas are a function of X_t and Y_t, and since the latter will likely vary from sample (or realization) to sample, the least-squares formulas will produce different values for the slope and intercept from sample to sample. Yet, one wants to estimate the one true and invariant regression line. This leads to a variety of new assumptions as one moves from description to estimation. It is important to remember also that one usually works with a single data set and cannot actually observe the variation in estimated regression lines from sample to sample. This variation and its consequences are therefore estimated as well.

All of the additional assumptions we need have been foreshadowed in our example.

[9] Yet, the mathematics of the two are very similar (Goldberger, 1964, pp. 86–115).

[10] Skeptical readers should compare Kish's statement (1967, pp. 5–6) with Malinvaud's (1970, pp. 59–61).

1. The X_ts Represent a Nonstochastic Variable Whose Values Are Fixed.[11] This first assumption is equivalent to the assertion that the exogenous variable is fully determined by the researcher or some other agent and can be fixed at some predetermined set of values. The general linear model is therefore an approximation of a laboratory experiment in which the kind and level of treatment are fully controlled by the investigator. Like the experimental model, the *statistical* inferences are conditional on the particular values of X_t that have been selected. In our example, the estimated regression line is formally relevant only to the true regression line for the given set of X_t values. In other words, if the range of weeks of training is 10–30, formal statistical inference is not justified for X_ts outside this range or X_ts within the range that were not actually observed. Generalization to unobserved values of the exogenous variable are of course possible, but must rest on theoretical argument or past research. In our case, for instance, one could probably make a good theoretical argument that the sample slope and intercept are reasonable estimates of a population regression line for all possible values of X_t within the full range of the observed X_t values. It might be more difficult to justify generalizations to situations in which the upper or lower bounds were significantly exceeded.

The analogies to experimental designs also imply that formal hypothesis testing actually addresses internal rather than external validity (Campbell & Stanley, 1966); how likely is it that the estimated relationship results from stochastic error (as a function of the U_ts)? In other words, one is trying to assess the importance of an alternative explanation of "chance," that perhaps nonzero values for estimates of β_1 and β_2 are really aberrations in the particular observations obtained.

2. The Error Terms Have an Expected Value of Zero or $E(U_t) = 0$. The expected value of the noise (i.e., over the long run) for any given X_t is zero. That is, the expected impact of the error term for each individual officer is zero. This is equivalent to assuming that the true mean on Y_t for each t falls exactly on the regression line with the mean reflecting the overall impact of the error in a very large number of realizations.

The assumption that $E(U_t) = 0$ is another way of saying that the linear relationship between X_t and Y_t is correct on the average over the long run. Should this be violated for certain police officers, it suggests that either one needs another functional (nonlinear) form to capture the impact of training or that one or more causal variables affecting arrests differentially have been neglected. Both imply that one's model has been misspecified; the former leading to biased[12] estimates of the slope and intercept, the latter leading to biased estimates of the intercept, but not necessarily the slope depending on

---

[11] More formally, one also assumes that X_t has a finite mean and finite and nonzero variance.

[12] An unbiased estimator is one for which the mean of its sampling distribution equals the value of the population parameter. That is, in numerous hypothetical (or stimulated) realizations, the estimates will average to the population value (Kmenta, 1971, pp. 10–15, 155–158).

whether the missing variables are correlated with X_t (Kmenta, 1971, pp. 392–395).[13] These issues are considered in more depth later.

The assumption that $E(U_t) = 0$ implies that the sum of these expected values is also zero. In the aggregate (across the t observations), the expected impact of the error term is zero. Should the expected value not be zero, the regression coefficient remains unbiased, but the intercept is biased. The disparity from the expected value of zero is captured by the estimate of the intercept.

3. The Variance of the Error Term Is Constant or $E(U_t^2) = \sigma^2$. This assumption of homoscedasticity means that the variance of the error term is identical for each X_t (in numerous realizations) over the long run. That is, all observations on Y_t are equally vulnerable to stochastic perturbations that imply that the variance around the regression line is constant. In terms of our example, this means first that variance in the number of good arrests attributable to stochastic forces is equal over the long run for each police officer. Second, it follows that for any given training level (which may reflect several police officers), the variance in number of arrests attributable to stochastic forces is equal over the long run to that associated with any other training level. Finally, over the long run, the variances in arrests around the regression line are therefore constant.

If the assumption of homoscedasticity is violated, estimates of the slope and intercept remain unbiased. However, formally, the estimates are no longer efficient and estimates of the standard errors are biased.[14] This too is considered later.

4. The Expected Correlation between Any U_t and Any Other U_t Is Zero or $E(U_t U_s) = 0$ for $t \neq s$. This assumption means that over the long run, any given U_t is uncorrelated with any other U_t. In our example, the error in arrests for any police officer is uncorrelated with the error in arrests for any other police officer. Correlated errors might result if police officers in adjacent precincts were affected similarly by the random perturbations, although this is but one way in which correlated errors might occur. Indeed, one usually worries most about correlated errors in longitudinal data (e.g., explaining arrests for a single officer over many months rather than across officers in a single month) where the error at time t may be correlated with the error at an earlier time $t - 1$ (or even earlier). Whether the correlations involve errors associated with cross-sectional or longitudinal units, the estimated slope and intercept remain unbiased. However, both are inefficient and the estimated standard errors are bi-

[13] If the missing variables are uncorrelated with X_t, the regression coefficient is unbiased. However, the standard errors and hence confidence intervals and significance tests, are biased regardless.

[14] Definitions of efficiency vary (Kmenta, 1971, pp. 157–161), but in essence, the variance of the sampling distribution of the estimator is larger than it could be. This implies that on the average, one's estimates of population parameters will be farther away from the true values than they may need to be.

ased (among other things). The presence of correlated errors is called serial correlation or autocorrelation (often interchangeably) and we consider it again later.

5. For Each X_t, the Error (and Therefore Y_t) Is Normally Distributed. Actually, in most practical situations this assumption is unnecessary. It affects only the use of statistical tests, and with a reasonably large sample (perhaps 100 or so) it can be usually ignored (Malinvaud, 1970, pp. 84, 93–96, 99–100).[15] One very important exception involves endogenous variables that are truncated. In brief, a truncated endogenous variable is characterized by a restriction on the values that may be observed. Recently it has become common to think about the restriction as a threshold below which (or above which) the real values of the endogenous variable cannot be observed. In place of the real value, one finds the value of the threshold. For example, in our illustration using the number of good arrests per month, it is apparent that whatever the merits of the academy's classroom training, the impact cannot be properly observed among respondents who fail to make any arrests. Imagine for a moment that there are police officers who even after many weeks of training still lack the skills to make good arrests. The worst that such officers can do on our outcome measure is zero arrests in a given month. The problem is that among those with zero arrests, there are individuals who would have scored worse than zero if our measure had allowed for that possibility. Therefore, the lower tail of the distribution is collapsed (i.e., truncated) to a value of zero.

Truncated endogenous variables are common in survey research (e.g., earnings) and can produce seriously biased and inconsistent estimates of the intercept and slope; in this instance, a nonnormal distribution of error cannot be ignored even in large samples. However, the details are well beyond the scope of this chapter, and interested readers are strongly encouraged to pursue the relevant literature. An excellent introduction to truncated endogenous variables can be found in the review piece by Stromsdorfer and Farkus (1980; pp. 32–41). A more thorough discussion can be found in Berk and Ray (1982).

These five assumptions give one the necessary foundation to appropriately apply the general linear model to a wide range of data. However, these assumptions have several important implications that warrant brief discussion.

First, one can easily prove that (assuming proper specifications) if X_t is fixed and $E(U_t) = 0$, X_t and U_t are uncorrelated. This means that one does not have to directly make such an assumption. We see later that when X_t is not fixed, one is not as lucky.

Second, implicit in the idea of a fixed X_t is that measurement error is

---

[15] This requires a bit more elaboration. In order to formally *derive* some of the powerful characteristics of least-squares estimators, one requires the assumption of normality. For example, least-squares estimates can no longer be shown to be maximum likelihood estimates without assumed normality (Kmenta, 1971, p. 248). (For a good introductory discussion of maximum likelihood estimation, see Kmenta, 1971, pp. 174–182.)

absent. Recall that even random measurement error (an expected value of zero and uncorrelated with the true values of X_t) will produce biased estimates.

Third, the general linear model is formally appropriate only when X_t involves nominal or interval measures and when Y_t is interval. Limiting ourselves to the bivariate case, one commonly treats a nominal X_t as a dummy variable in which one category is coded "1" and the other category is coded "0." For example, black police officers might be coded 1 and white police officers might be coded 0. This produces the convenient result that the intercept equals the mean on Y_t for the category coded 0, whereas the regression coefficient equals the *difference* between the mean on Y_t for the category coded 0 and the category coded 1 (Kmenta, 1971, pp. 410–412). In our example, an intercept of 3.0 would indicate that the mean number of good arrests for white officers was 3.0. A regression coefficient of 2.0 would indicate that black officers had a mean of two more good arrests than white officers. This also leads to the result that a *t*-test for the slope is the same as a *t*-test for the difference between the means on Y_t and, formally, one has precisely the same algebraic model as a one-way analysis of variance with two conditions.

Finally, there are other ways of coding nominal exogenous variables that leave the general linear model fundamentally unchanged, but sometimes provide more easily interpreted coefficients (Cohen & Cohen, 1975, pp. 171–211). For example, in the bivariate case, coding one category as +1 and the other category as −1 (called effect coding), produces an intercept equal to the unweighted mean of all groups on Y_t (i.e., the mean of the means with no consideration of the number of cases involved in each mean) and a slope equal to the differences between this overall mean and the mean for the category coded +1. The analogous disparity for the category coded −1 can be easily obtained from some simple arithmetic (Cohen & Cohen, 1975, pp. 190–191).[16] Perhaps the major advantage of effect coding is the link to analysis of variance in which the between group sum of squares reflects the same sorts of comparisons. Still, it has found far more limited applications than the 1–0 coding scheme.[17]

When Y_t is treated as a 1–0 dummy variable, in contrast, the appropriateness of the linear model is suspect. One interprets the regression coefficient as the change in the *probability* of Y_t (for the category coded 1) for each unit change in X_t (Kmenta, 1971, pp. 425–426). For example, if the dependent variable reflects whether an individual has been arrested (coded 1), a regression coefficient indicates the change in the probability of arrest for each unit change in the independent variable. In this form, the general linear model is called the

[16] Multiple Classification Analysis (MCA) is essentially another form of regression with dummy exogenous variables. Its main asset is the immediate provision of measures of effect for *all* categories expressed as deviations from the grand mean. In other words, one does not have to undertake any additional arithmetic to obtain the full range of effects across all categories (Andrews, Morgan, & Sonquist, 1973).

[17] Perhaps the main advantage of 1–0 coding is the ability to easily handle more complicated models including interaction effects and its applications in data possessing both longitudinal and cross-sectional variance (Kmenta, 1971, pp. 508–517).

linear probability model and can be subjected to the following criticisms: (a) one may occasionally obtain estimated probabilities for Y_t outside the 1–0 boundary; (b) by definition, Y_t is heteroscedastic (Pindyck & Rubinfeld, 1981, pp. 275–280).

Partly in response to such difficulties, social scientists have recently begun to employ logit models in which the dependent variable in the dichotomous case is defined as the log of $P_t/1 - P_t$ (where P_t is the probability that $Y_t = 1$). In essence, this places an s shaped logistic curve through the scatter plot that is asymptotic at 0 and 1, and its parameters can be estimated with maximum likelihood procedures whether the exogenous variable (s) is nominal or interval (Pindyck & Rubinfeld, 1981, pp. 287–301). The estimated effect parameters indicate the change in the log of the odds that $Y_t = 1$ for each unit change in the exogenous variable, but with appropriate transformations it is possible to closely approximate interpretations from the linear probability model.[18]

Logit models are not without critics, and in practice these models often provide the same substantive results as the linear probability model. Indeed, if the split on Y_t is no greater than 75–25%, the two models can usually be estimated interchangeably (Goodman, 1976; Knoke, 1975). Moreover, there may be good *theoretical* reasons for preferring the linear probability model under such circumstances (Gillespie, 1977). In short, the logit approach is only likely to be clearly superior to the linear probability model when one of the categories on the dependent variable holds for a very small proportion of the cases.[19]

Finally, we must consider data for X_t and/or Y_t that are measured in an ordinal form. If one is prepared to assume that the underlying metric is in fact interval despite ordinal measures, the general linear model will usually provide few distortions (Labovitz, 1967, 1970). However, there are dissenters (Wilson, 1971), and perhaps the safest strategy is to "degrade" ordinal measures to nominal measures. Alternatively, one may explore some newer techniques that generalize probit procedures (see Footnote 18) to ordinal endogenous variables (McKelvey & Zavoina, 1975).

To summarize, when all of the assumptions we have discussed are met (or closely approximated), one can use the bivariate model with the assurance that estimates of the slope and intercept are unbiased and efficient. Moreover, one can obtain unbiased and efficient estimates of R^2 and the standard deviation around the regression line, although some minor adjustment in the descriptive

---

[18] The logit formulation is one form of log–linear models (Bishop, Fienberg, Holland, 1975, pp. 1–175). Perhaps the main difference is that in logit models, a particular dependent variable is specified, and exogenous variables may be nominal or interval. In addition, the logit model is similar to the probit model except that a different kind of s curve is fit, and the effect coefficients have a somewhat different interpretation (Hanushek & Jackson, 1977, pp. 179–215; Pindyck & Rubinfeld, 1981, pp. 287–288).

[19] This has the convenient consequence of often allowing the researcher to avoid the computationally expensive iterative estimation procedures of many kinds of logit programs. Goodman's ECTA is an exception but is limited to nominal predictors.

calculation formulas must be made (Kmenta, 1971, pp. 224, 365). Finally, standard errors for these and other statistics are routinely available from which confidence intervals may be constructed and/or significance tests undertaken (Kmenta, 1971, pp. 217–245).[20]

Violation of Assumptions

Like any abstraction, the general linear model is only an approximation of reality. Hence, all of its assumptions can be invalid to varying degrees and one's estimates may be seriously distorted. This raises three related questions which are the bread and butter of econometrics research:

1. How does one determine the degree to which particular assumptions have been violated?
2. What are the consequences of these violations?
3. What can be done about it?

In the next few pages we briefly consider such issues as they apply to the bivariate model, although the conclusions provided can be easily generalized to the multivariate case. (There are, however, some assumptions that apply only to the multivariate case and these are considered later.)

1. X_t Is Not Fixed, but Is Stochastic. In our example, X_t was the number of weeks of training experienced by 150 police officers. The amount of training varied across officers but was constant over a several year period. Hence, X_t was a reasonable approximation of a fixed variable. In contrast, consider each officer's beat assignment, perhaps an alternative (or additional) predictor of the number of good arrests. Beat assignments for each officer would probably vary over time in a stochastic manner; over several months one could in theory observe many different beat assignments that for all practical purposes would be beyond the control of the researcher. Similarly, if the exogenous variable was a summary index of police attitudes toward crimes without victims, one might observe rather different index values for the same officer in different months: a distribution of values over which the researcher had no control. Clearly, such independent variables cannot be considered fixed and are probably the rule rather than the exception in most survey research. (We are still assuming perfect measurement.)

Diagnosis of the problem is relatively simple. One should know enough about the nature of X_t and how it was collected to determine whether X_t should be considered fixed or stochastic. Unfortunately, the consequences and solutions are a bit more complicated.

---

[20] Although it is probably of little practical importance, it may be comforting to know that when assumptions 1–4 are met, least-squares estimates are best linear unbiased estimators (i.e., they are "BLUE"). This means that there are no estimators of the slope and intercept that are a linear function of Y_t and unbiased that also have smaller variances (Kmenta, 1971, pp. 209–213).

Probably the most fundamental problem produced by stochastic exogenous variables (measured without error) is that without some new assumptions many of the important assets of the general linear model can no longer be proved. For example, it is no longer necessarily true that $E(X_t U_t) = 0$; and if there is a correlation over the long run, the estimates of the slope and intercept are biased (Kmenta, 1971, pp. 297–304).

Even a brief discussion of some of the ways econometricians reestablish many useful characteristics of least-squares estimators are well beyond the scope of this chapter (e.g., see Goldberger, 1964, pp. 266–287). For example, rather than relying on derivations based on the properties of expected values, one can often rely on what happens to the estimators as the sample size gets very large: asymptotic rather than finite sample properties (Kmenta, 1971, pp. 162–167). Thus, one might assume that over the long run the correlation between X_t and U_t approaches zero as the sample size increases. Therefore, the least-squares estimates become less biased as the sample size becomes large. More generally, this property is sometimes subsumed under the concept of consistency, which usually implies that ultimately the sampling distribution of the estimator collapses on the true value of the population parameter. Analogously, one can speak about asymptotic efficiency. An asymptotically efficient estimator is one for which the variance of the sampling distribution just before it collapses is smaller than the variances of the sampling distributions of some other set of competing estimators (Kmenta, 1971, pp. 162–168). Roughly speaking, the term *asymptotic efficiency* can be used to characterize the efficiency of estimators when large samples are required to approximate unbiasedness.

Fortunately, in most practical situations, a thorough knowledge of such issues is unnecessary. What is critical, however, is that whenever one is required to make assumptions relying on asymptotic properties, one needs a large enough sample so that asymptotic properties are reasonably approximated. One hundred observations are probably sufficient in many situations although the problems are difficult and some expert advice may be worth having.

In the particular instance of a stochastic X_t one has another option. One may "simply" assume that X_t and U_t are independent of one another and then all of the useful properties of least-squares estimators are retained, both the finite sample properties and the asymptotic sample properties. (For this and other options, see Kmenta, 1971, pp. 298–304.) Unfortunately, the independence of X_t and U_t is a theoretical assertion for which there is no directly empirical assessment. Recall that by construction, this will be true for any given estimated model. More generally, this raises the problem of specification error, to which we return later.

The presence of a stochastic X_t also produces some complications for the meaning of statistical inference. Intuitively, it would seem that one has introduced a new source of stochastic error *and* a new population of values to which inferences might be drawn. That is, the observed X_ts can now be considered a realization much like the Y_ts.

The general linear model can handle such difficulties in two related ways. First, one may treat the stochastic X_ts as fixed, *once they are observed*. Then all of the desirable properties of least-squares estimators remain. However, one's generalizations apply only to realizations of Y_t for the particular X_ts actually measured. For example, if the stochastic exogenous variable is police attitudes about the need to enforce the law, one's estimate of the regression line applies only to measures of the attitudes actually observed for the given month. One may, of course, argue from theory or prior research that the findings have a broader meaning, but formal statistical inference is limited to the particular attitudes observed (Kmenta, 1971, p. 300).

Second, one may make two new assumptions: (*a*) the distribution of the exogenous variable is independent of the true regression parameters; and (*b*) the exogenous variable is distributed independently of the errors (U_t). This amounts to saying that whatever values of X_t happened to appear, they estimate the same population regression line in an unbiased manner (Pindyck & Rubinfeld, 1981, p. 134). In other words, if one's data just happen to represent attitudes that tend to be more punitive than the average, the means of the distribution for each Y_t still fall on the same regression line (although farther to the right).

Although one may simply make such assertions, one's hand is greatly strengthened if one can argue on theoretical grounds or from prior research that the relationship between X_t and Y_t is really linear over the probable range of X_t values. This means that an estimated "linear" fit is not actually a segment of some nonlinear relationship. Similarly, it is helpful if one can argue persuasively that had another sample of X_ts appeared, the population regression line would remain unchanged. In other words, there is no reason to believe that what one is treating as a single underlying regression line is in fact more than one; that, for example, the regression line for more punitive attitudes has a different slope and intercept than the regression line for less punitive attitudes. (We see later that should this be expected, one can build multiple regression models to estimate such interaction effects.) Finally, as an empirical matter, these theoretical assertions become more plausible if one's sample of X_ts is selected to be representative of some population of X_t values of interest (e.g., through a simple random sample) and a particular regression line provides a better fit than competitive nonlinear or interaction forms.[21] In other words, at

---

[21] Ideally, the alternative models should be posed before examining the data to avoid capitalizing on Type I and Type II errors. After scanning the residuals, it is always possible to improve the fit in an ad hoc manner, but this is rarely compelling. In addition, there are a variety of approaches to determining which model is "best." As mentioned earlier, some economists seem to prefer minimizing the standard deviation around the regression line. Sociologists seem to prefer maximizing the variance explained. For certain kinds of more advanced models, one can also minimize "forecast errors" (Pindyck & Rubinfeld, 1981, p. 206), "simulation errors" (Pindyck & Rubinfeld, 1981, pp. 360–367), and/or disparities between an observed covariance matrix and an estimated covariance matrix (e.g., Hanushek & Jackson, 1977, pp. 312–321; Joreskog & Sorbom, 1979; Specht & Warren, 1975).

this point the quality of one's sample may become critical (Berk & Brewer, 1978).

2. The Expected Value of U_t Is Not Equal to Zero. As suggested earlier, should one suspect that some of the errors do not have an expected value of zero, it means that one has misspecified the model. Some of the means of Y_t do not in fact fall on the regression line; either some nonlinear form is required or additional exogenous variables must be added. In practice, this is very hard to diagnose since it is hard to tell if any given residual reflects a single random perturbation or a nonzero expected value. Moreover, one is very easily seduced into altering one's model based on random perturbations (capitalizing on Type I error). Perhaps the best advice is to pose several competing models in advance that might capture deviant observations on Y_t and then choose among them (see Footnote 21). Any post hoc alterations should be clearly labeled, significance tests should be discounted where possible (Bielby & Kluegel, 1977),[22] and extensive theoretical justification should be provided.

3. The Variance of the Errors (U_t) Is Not Constant. Heteroscedasticity means that *some* of the observations on the endogenous variable are, over the long run, in numerous realizations, more vulnerable to stochastic perturbations. Hence, although the expected value of these Y_ts is still the regression line, on the average the actual Y_ts will be farther away. For example, perhaps police officers with unusually high amounts of training will experience especially large variability in the number of good arrests over time. With more training, police officers will respond less rigidly in encounters with citizens and thus, whether or not an arrest is made will depend heavily on a host of situational factors. These factors in turn will introduce more stochastic error in the reported number of good arrests.

Heteroscedasticity presents some genuine problems for estimation. First, the good news: Estimates of the slope and intercept are unbiased and consistent. On the average over a large number of replications one's estimates will be approximately correct. (It is not clear, of course, how comforting this is to the typical researcher working with a single data set.) Now the bad news: Least-squares formulas for the slope and intercept produce coefficients whose variances (i.e., for their sampling distribution) are too large; the coefficients are inefficient and asymptotically inefficient. This means that before one even gets to the estimation process with real data, the algebra is guaranteed to produce coefficients that will be on average (in numerous realizations) farther from the population values than necessary. Finally, when one attempts to estimate these inflated variances with data, the variance estimates are biased and inconsistent. That is, the estimation procedures take the inflated variances as true, and then

---

[22] Basically, the problem is that one will on the average obtain five statistically significant coefficients at the .05 level by chance alone in 100 significance tests. Therefore, one has to adjust for such possibilities when many significance tests are applied. For example, a rough safeguard might involve shifting the critical alpha level to .001 rather than .05.

estimates these in a biased manner. The direction of the bias is often hard to anticipate; it may inflate or shrink the resulting standard errors (square roots of the variances). In general, to the degree that larger variances in Y_t are associated with values of X_t that depart significantly from the mean of X_t (larger deviation scores) the bias is negative. That is, the bias will produce estimated standard errors that are too small (Kmenta, 1971, pp. 249–256). This tends to counteract the inflated variances produced by the inefficiency, but in practice it is virtually impossible to know how much compensation has actually occurred. Moreover, if the larger variances for Y_t cluster around the mean of X_t, the impact of the inefficiency is heightened (see Hanushek and Jackson, 1977, p. 154, for an especially instructive demonstration).

Given these complicated interacting processes, one must interpret the impact of heteroscedasticity very carefully. Least-squares formulas produce coefficients whose variances are too large. *Estimates* of these inflated variances may systematically improve matters or make things worse. Yet, when one compares the variances of least-squares estimates to estimated variances after proper adjustments for heteroscedasticity are made (to be discussed briefly next), one typically finds that one's original estimates of the standard errors were too large. That is, one's statistical power was reduced leading to larger confidence intervals and greater difficulty in rejecting the null hypotheses. Thus, the inefficiency and bias typically produces a net *conservative* result.

A discussion of proper adjustments for heteroscedasticity would take us beyond ordinary least squares and hence beyond the scope of this chapter. Basically, appropriate estimation proceeds in three steps: (*a*) a diagnosis of the form and magnitude of the heteroscedasticity; (*b*) adjustments of the data to make Y_t homoscedastic; and (*c*) reestimation of the regression line and the relevant standard errors. The two final steps may be undertaken as separate operations or simultaneously through a technique called generalized least squares.[23]

How can one determine if there are grounds for concern about heteroscedasticity? First, one should think through the substantive processes involved in the production of observations on Y_t and whether some of the Y_ts are likely to be more vulnerable to stochastic error. Second, a scan of the residuals will often reveal a clustering of large positive and negative deviations from the regression line, a signal that perhaps heteroscedasticity exists. If either suggests that the variance of Y_t is not constant, one should immediately consult a good econometrics text in which formal tests for heteroscedasticity can be found.

4. The Correlation between Any U_t and Any Other U_t Is Not Zero or $E(U_tU_2) \neq 0$ for $t \neq s$. In essence this means that errors across observations on

---

[23] Generalized least squares is a technique that formally takes the variance–covariance *matrix* of the errors (U_ts) into account in the estimation process. This matrix drops out in ordinary least squares. A good introductory treatment of generalized least squares can be found in Hanushek and Jackson (1977, pp. 141–178).

Y_t are correlated over the long run. Such correlations may surface in either cross-sectional or longitudinal data and can stem from three sources: (a) a variable or variables excluded from the model which affects a subset of Y_t similarly; (b) the wrong functional form; and (c) a tendency of the errors themselves to move in unison.

In the first case, one might, for example, have neglected beat assignment in the arrest analysis. Hence, officers assigned to beats with more crime might make more good arrests than attributable to their training alone and consequently, evidence positive residuals. In numerous realizations, these positive residuals will tend to covary with one another. Although the degree of correspondence will differ across realizations, it will remain positive on the average.

In the second case, the relationship between training and arrests could be ∪ shaped. Estimating a straight line for a ∪-shaped scatter plot will tend to produce positive residuals for the high and low values of X_t (the extremes of the regression line) and negative residuals for the middle values of X_t. Once again, subsets will tend to covary with one another although in this instance, some of the correspondence will involve residuals below the regression line.

Finally, the stochastic errors may simply tend to move in unison. One cannot think of a few important variables that have been neglected nor is there reason to doubt the linear form. Rather, a host of random perturbations tends to produce a correspondence among the U_t. What this means is that although any given U_t may fall *above or below* the regression line across realizations, it tends to do so in concert with other U_ts. (Recall the example of correlated errors in adjacent beats discussed earlier.)

The causes and consequences of correlated errors can become very complicated and can therefore be subject to a rather lengthy consideration. For our purposes, however, the following points suffice.

First, when correlated errors result from neglected causal variables or from the wrong functional form, one has actually misspecified the model. Hence, estimates of all regression statistics are usually biased and inconsistent. Very serious difficulties are involved. Only when the correlations are inherent in the stochastic errors *alone* is one really considering the consequences of correlated errors per se. The critical difference is that in misspecification, the errors for particular Y_ts will tend to *remain* above or below the regression line in repeated realizations, which in turn leads to the correspondence across those Y_ts. In contrast, when one has the appropriate specification, the error for any particular Y_t is *equally likely to be positive or negative,* but tends to move in unison with the errors in other Y_ts (Pindyck & Rubinfeld, 1981, pp. 152–154). The random perturbations may affect subsets of Y_ts in a similar fashion, but in an *unpredictable direction.* Intuitively, this suggests that the primary casualty is the variance in Y_t since the observations are no longer independent of one another. The implications of such correspondence are considered in more detail shortly.

Second, the correlations among the errors may be positive or negative, although positive correlations are far more common. Fortunately, estimates of the resulting difficulties and useful adjustments are available for both kinds of associations.

Third, the problems caused by correlated errors are also a function of the degree of correspondence among the X_ts. One also has to worry about serial correlation among the values of the exogenous variable(s). Although the mechanisms involved are complicated and in many ways counterintuitive (Malinvaud, 1970, pp. 504–526; Kmenta, 1971, pp. 273–282), especially in cross-sectional data, one can obtain some sense of the role of X_t by remembering that the location of any observation in a scatter plot is a function of both Y_t and X_t. Hence, given that some Y_ts will deviate substantially from the regression line, the *pattern* of these residuals will be a function of X_t; if, for example, Y_ts with large positive residuals happen to have similar values on X_t, the residuals will show a bulge along that section of the regression line. In contrast, if they have rather different values on X_t, the large positive residuals will be spread throughout the scatter plot—perhaps as isolated outliers. Variations in these sorts of patterns, which rest on the relationship between the residuals and X_t, determine the kind and severity of estimation difficulties.

Fourth, much like the difficulties produced by heteroscedasticity, there is good news and bad news. On the positive side, the estimates of the intercept and slope are unbiased. On the negative side, estimates of the R^2, standard error of estimate, and the coefficients' standard errors will be biased and inconsistent, coupled with inefficiency in the standard formulas used for the slope and intercept. As before, the lack of efficiency means that even before one undertakes estimation of the regression line, one is guaranteed to have inflated variances for the slope and intercept. The biases take the inflated variance as the true variances and then produce additional distortions. In practice, the bias usually tends to counteract the impact of inefficiency; the bias is in the direction of producing spuriously powerful significance tests and more narrow confidence intervals than justified. However, this depends on both the serial correlation among the U_ts and the serial correlation among the X_ts. If *both* are either positive or negative, spurious precision results. If they differ in sign, one has a conservative estimate of the role of stochastic error. If *either* correlation is zero, no bias is produced (Malinvaud, 1970, pp. 520–524). In the standard population survey, this is the probable outcome since both the X_ts and the Y_ts are rarely related by geographical or temporal proximity. Hence, one may proceed as usual.

Given these complexities, it is very hard to determine the price one may be paying for serial correlation in a given data set. Perhaps the best advice is to undertake available adjustments whenever correlated residuals are suspected (regardless of what may be going on among the X_ts), and then compare the results to the original least-squares estimates. If they differ and one cannot justify one estimation over another, it is wise to present both sets of results.

Fifth, probably the most common diagnostic procedures focus on the estimated covariance among the U_ts. One popular indicator for longitudinal data routinely available in many statistical packages is the Durbin–Watson statistic.

If its value falls above a certain level, one has a statistically significant *negative* correlation between adjacent U_ts (i.e., adjacent in the scatter plot). If its value falls below a certain level, one has a statistically significant *positive* correlation between adjacent U_ts. Also, there is a middle range for the Durbin–Watson statistic in which no conclusions can be drawn. However, the Durbin–Watson statistic is vulnerable to nontrivial distortions when, for example, missing data exist, and one should consult a solid reference or two before proceeding with adjustments (e.g., Malinvaud, 1970, pp. 505–513; Pindyck & Rubinfeld, 1981, pp. 158–161). Finally, there are a number of ways one can attempt to adjust for the estimation difficulties produced by serial correlation (Pindyck & Rubinfeld, 1981, pp. 154–158; Kmenta, 1971, pp. 282–292). All involve modeling the processes underlying the serial correlation among the U_ts (and implicitly the X_ts) and building this information into one's estimation techniques. Perhaps the most common estimation procedures ultimately utilize some form of generalized least squares (see Footnote 23). In addition, Box–Jenkins (1976) time series techniques can be employed in the modeling of the error processes themselves (Pindyck & Rubinfeld, 1981, pp. 593–605).

Since correlated U_ts surface with some regularity in longitudinal data, perhaps a time-series example should also be briefly considered.[24] Suppose that instead of having data for a given month over 150 police officers, one had data for a given officer over 60 months. One might regress the number of good arrests on a dummy variable capturing whether the police officer was patrolling on foot or in a car (which presumably varies over time). Once again, the bivariate linear model might be appropriate and initially one could proceed as usual. However, there are at least two additional complications that must be seriously addressed whenever working with time-series data.

First, interpretations of statistical inference can become especially tricky (Berk & Brewer, 1978). Basically, it is often unclear what one is trying to make inferences to. This becomes especially problematic if one's data are taken from a particular historical context (e.g., 1970–1977) so that generalizations to other periods are suspect. In order to interpret the obtained observations as a sample or realization, the historical processes generating the data must in some sense be viewed as repeating themselves (Nelson, 1973, p. 26). To the degree that the historical context is unique (as historians would argue almost as a matter of course), the notion of a sampling distribution is at best a convenient fiction (Berk, 1977). Perhaps the best advice is to make sure that before formal statistical inference is applied, careful justifications are provided. In time series data, statistical inference is rarely routine.

[24] Technically, time-series data involve only one observation on Y_t for each point in time (e.g., days, months, weeks). Variation in Y_t occurs only over time. When there is more than one observation for each point in time, one also has potential cross-sectional variation. Such data have been variously characterized as panel data, multiple time-series data, and/or pooled cross-sectional and longitudinal data with such labels depending in part on the research traditions in which the researcher has been schooled. The possibilities and complications such material present are well beyond the scope of this chapter. (See for example, Berk, Hoffman, Maki, Rauma, & Wong, 1979; Hannan & Young, 1977, pp. 52–80; Kmenta, 1971, pp. 508–517.)

Second, besides the regular assumptions required in the bivariate regression model, one must show that the residuals are stationary (Pindyck & Rubinfeld, 1981, pp. 493–508). The property of being stationary for U_t is closely related to the nature of statistical inference mentioned previously, has parallels to error assumptions in cross-sectional data, and involves the stability of the error term over time. In essence, the U_ts must have a joint probability distribution that is invariant with respect to the displacement of time, which for most practical purposes is satisfied when the expected value, variance, and covariance between U_ts are constant over time. This implies that any given segment of the longitudinal data behaves the same as any other segment regardless of what one takes as the starting point. In our example, the monthly U_ts from 1970 to 1973 should have approximately the same mean, variance, and covariance as the monthly U_ts from 1973 to 1976 (within the bounds of sampling error). Fortunately, if one's data do not seem to possess such properties, it is often possible to transform the data to make them stationary (e.g., Box & Jenkins, 1976, pp. 85–114). In any case, before statistical inference is attempted with time series data, the observed U_t *must* be made stationary. Probably the most common kind of nonstationary U_ts surface when the residuals show a gradual increase over a large part of their range.[25]

One final point. Although time series data are rather rare in survey research, they are becoming more common. Hence, it should be stressed that regression approaches to time series are but one of several available techniques. When one's substantive model is uncomplicated (e.g., a single equation with a single exogenous variable), one can capitalize on the flexibility and power of Box–Jenkins extensions directly (Hibbs, 1977). If there is reason to believe that one's time series can be sensibly described as a sum of sine curves, one has the option of spectral analysis (Granger & Hatanaka, 1964; Mayer & Arney, 1974).[26]

5. The Errors U_ts (and Implicitly the Y_ts) Are Not Normally Distributed. We considered this earlier and there are really no new points to add. For most of the samples used in survey research, the sampling distributions of the slope and intercept will closely approximate a normal curve except when the endogenous variable is truncated. Also, recall that with the exception of a truncated endogenous variable, normality only becomes a practical issue when confidence intervals and/or significance tests are employed.

With the brief consideration of normality, our discussion of the bivariate linear model comes to an end. With minor variations, the issues summarized here apply to the multivariate case. However, there are several topics we have necessarily neglected, and at least three warrant some recognition. First, whenever one has measurement error in the exogenous variable, some or all of the regression statistics will be biased and inconsistent (depending on the form of

---

[25] This usually implies that Y_t has a quadratic relationship to X_t.

[26] It is possible to *describe* any time series with sine waves, but this is not necessarily a productive way to characterize the data.

measurement error). Thus, unless one is prepared to attempt adjustments (some of which were alluded to earlier), the important question is how much variation in the observed X_t results from variation in its "true" value and how much results from variation in its measurement error. To the degree that the former is larger than the latter, biases are minimized. Second, in time series data, the use of a lagged endogenous variable as an independent variable presents a host of new difficulties, especially when serial correlation exists (Johnston, 1972, pp. 300–320).[27] For example, if one employs Y_{t-1} to predict Y_t, one's estimates of the slope is at least biased, although not necessarily asymptotically biased. When the model employs a lagged endogenous predictor, one should consult good references. Finally, we have considered each assumption violation in isolation. When more than one occurs simultaneously, serious, and often insurmountable, difficulties may result.

13.3. THE MULTIVARIATE MODEL

With a solid foundation in the bivariate case, the multivariate extension becomes rather straightforward. Indeed, there is little more to add about formal statistical properties; the important issues involve applications and interpretations.

The multivariate model is often represented as follows:

$$Y_t = \beta_1 + \beta_2 X_{t2} + \beta_3 X_{t3} + \cdots + \beta_K X_{tK} + U_t \quad \text{for } t = 1, \ldots, T. \quad (13.2)$$

Thus, the multivariate model portrays Y_t as a linear function of two kinds of effects: systematic or deterministic component, which is the sum of K variables each weighted by a partial regression coefficient, and a stochastic component representing stochastic error. The systematic component may be further disaggregated into a single intercept (as before) and the effects of the independent or exogenous variables. Sometimes the intercept is characterized as the constant since one can view the intercept as a partial regression coefficient whose associated X_{t1} is a vector with every element equal to 1. Hence, every one of the t cases has the same impact on Y_t.

The single new assumption required by the multivariate model reflects the presence of more than one exogenous variable.

No Exact Linear Relationship Exists among Two or More of the Independent Variables. This implies that no single exogenous variable is redundant, that each has the potential to impact Y_t *uniquely*. Consider again our study of good arrests for 150 police officers. To the earlier independent variable of the amount of training, one might add a second and third predictor: the age of each officer

---

[27] An example is predicting the crime rate for the crime rate the year before or the unemployment rate for the unemployment rate the year before. Alternatively, the lag may be more than one year; for instance, predicting the crime rate from the crime rate 3 years earlier.

and each officer's grade point average at the police academy. Hence, one would have three exogenous variables represented by X_{t2}, X_{t3}, and X_{t4} (X_{t1} is the vector of 1s). The assumption of linear independence among the exogenous variables would be violated if a fourth predictor were included that was defined in terms of each officer's year of birth. In this instance, X_{t5} would be perfectly correlated with age and consequently would be redundant. Under such circumstances, the regression coefficients cannot be uniquely determined (i.e., there are an infinite number that fulfill the least-squares criterion), and most common computer programs will return an error message to the effect that the matrix containing the independent variables is "singular." Technically, when any given exogenous variable is a linear function of one or more other exogenous variables, one has "perfect multicollinearity" (Kmenta, 1971, pp. 382–387). This should be carefully distinguished from high multicollinearity and typically occurs through errors in the use of multiple nominal predictors. We return to both of these issues shortly.

Interpreting Measure of Effect

Perhaps the most important feature of the multivariate general linear model is the ability to characterize the impact of any given exogenous variable with all others in the equation held constant. Although this is certainly common knowledge even among inexperienced researchers, there is sometimes genuine confusion about what *held constant* really means.

Consider two predictors of the number of good arrests: the number of weeks of training and the age of each police officer. Focusing on the effect of training with age held constant, imagine that one first regresses arrests on age and then calculates the residuals from this equation (the differences between the observed number of arrests for each officer and the number of arrests solely attributable to age). These residuals represent the variation in arrests that cannot be explained by variation in age, or the original arrest variable purged of the impact of age. Now, one can repeat this exercise but with the training as the dependent variable and, as before, age as the independent variable. Once again, one calculates the residuals: here, the variation in training is not explained by variation in age or training purged of the impact of age.

Having run the two auxiliary regression equations and calculated the residuals for each, one can treat the two sets of residuals as new variables. One represents the number of arrests purged of the effect of age whereas the other represents the number of weeks of training purged of the effect of age (i.e., both have been residualized). As with any pair of variables, one might apply the bivariate model discussed earlier and estimate the regression coefficient for the impact of the purged number of weeks of training on the purged number of arrests. The regression coefficient that results is the partial regression coefficient for the *three* variable model: the effect of training on arrests with age held constant. Similar logic applies to all the coefficients in the multivariate model although in practice one is able to obtain all of the coefficients in a single pass over the data (Pindyck & Rubinfeld, 1981, pp. 96–105).

There are a number of implications for the way the multivariate model controls for overlapping effects among exogenous variables, but perhaps the most important is that causes of Y_t that are shared are lost in the partialling process. Suppose that the regression coefficient for weeks of training is .5 and the regression coefficient for age is −.1. Every additional week of training causes an average of .5 more arrests, holding age constant, and every year of age causes an average of .1 fewer arrests, holding training constant. However, to the degree that these two exogenous variables are correlated with one another, there may be an impact on the number of arrests that cannot be independently attributed to one variable or the other, ceteris paribus.[28] This shared impact is lost since by definition and construction one is only considering unique effects for each predictor. Should one care to estimate the overlapping impact, one must move to more advanced techniques such as path analysis (Duncan, 1975).

Other Multivariate Statistics

All of the measures of effect described earlier for the bivariate model apply to the multivariate case. However, in each instance, the statistics of effect rest on the residualized logic defining *held constant*. Thus, for example, the standardized regression coefficient indicates the number of standard deviations Y_t changes on the average for each standard deviation change in the given X_{tk}, ceteris paribus. Similarly, the partial correlation is the zero-order correlation between a residualized endogenous and exogenous variable (Pindyck & Rubinfeld, 1981, pp. 91–93). As before, there are advantages and disadvantages for each measure of effect (Blalock, 1971; Duncan, 1970). However, there is little new to add to multivariate applications except that the partial correlation is typically the least desirable option. In particular, the partial correlation coefficient often behaves in ways that are inconsistent with the underlying logic of causal modeling (Duncan, 1975, p. 23).

In addition to measures of causal impact, some researchers commonly report how much variance is independently attributable to each exogenous variable. Although there is some debate about how best to define such variance (Darlington, 1968), two measures are often seen. The first is simply the standardized regression coefficient squared and may be justified in part through factor analytic traditions (Creager & Boruch, 1969). Perhaps more important, the use of the squared standardized regression coefficients is convenient since the standardized regression coefficient is also the path coefficient. Hence, one is able to capitalize on concepts from path analysis. The second has been advocated by Darlington (1968) and called such things as the "usefulness" of a

---

[28] This problem disappears if the exogenous variables are uncorrelated and, in this instance, the bivariate regression coefficient equals the partial regression coefficient.

variable and the "unique contribution" of a variable. It is the square of the part (not partial) correlation (McNemar, 1962, pp. 167–168) and is also the square of the zero-order correlation between a given exogenous variable and the endogenous variable when *only* the exogenous variable has been fully residualized. The part correlation squared has a monotonic relationship to the squared standardized regression coefficient (Pugh, 1968) and is never larger in size.

In many practical situations, the debate about the square of the standardized regression coefficient versus the square of the part correlation is beside the point. Both will order the exogenous variables identically in terms of the independent variance explained. That is, the most important variable under one definition will be the most important variable under the other definition; similarly for the second most important variable, and so on.[29] Perhaps the main advantage to the squared standardized regression coefficient is its link to path analysis and factor analysis. If one's research employs such techniques, it is advisable to use the squared standardized regression coefficient. If nothing else, the definitions across techniques remain consistent.

Probably the main advantage of the squared part correlation stems from analogies to the multiple partial coefficient (Blalock, 1972, pp. 458–459), which estimates the unique variance explained by several variables as a group. Consider a model in which one were trying to understand variance in the number of good arrests as a function of two kinds of variables: characteristics of individual police officers (e.g., age, education, race) and characteristics of each officer's beat (e.g., median income, percentage of substandard housing). Through manipulations related to the square of the part correlation, one can determine how much variance in the number of good arrests is uniquely a function of police officers' backgrounds and how much variance is uniquely a function of the assigned beat.[30]

The use of either definition of independent variance also allows one to describe how much explained variance is uniquely attributable to each variable

[29] Importance defined by variance explained uniquely must *not* be confused with *causal* importance. It is common to find variables with large causal effects (large new regression coefficients) and modest unique contributions to explained variance. Indeed, if one is really trying to represent accurately a set of causal relationships, it is not at all clear why one should care a great deal about the variance attributed to each exogenous variable. Perhaps the popularity of variance measures of effect results from the apparent convenience the metric variance provides. Variables with larger contributions are simply more important, and one does not have to worry about the measurement units in which the variables come nor what the larger effect means in the context of one's theory or applications. In fact, for the modeling perspective emphasized here and at least implicit in the mathematics of the general linear model, the convenience of variance measures of effect is illusory. Their substantive meaning is slippery, and if used alone may lead one to ignore exogenous variables that in fact have very large causal effects. More is said about this shortly in the context of stepwise regression.

[30] One can estimate the squared part correlation from the disparity between the R^2 when the variable of interest is included in the equation (along with all other predictors) and the R^2 when that variable is dropped. The amount the R^2 declines is the square of the part correlation. One can also estimate the unique variance explained by a group of variables by subtracting from the R^2 when all of the variables are in the model, the R^2 when the cluster of interest is dropped from the model.

and how much is shared among them.[31] One can fully partition all of the explained variance into unique contributions, contributions that are shared among all possible pairs of predictors, contributions that are shared among all possible triplets of predictors, and so on. However, partitioning the variance is not the only way to decompose the contributions of a set of exogenous variables. One popular alternative involves partitioning differences between the *means* of different groups, such as the difference in the mean income between blacks and whites. Although here too there is some debate about how best to proceed (Althauser & Wigler, 1972), partitioning differences between means can be especially instructive in applied research (Bridges & Berk, 1978). The partitions come in the actual units of the dependent variable, which greatly facilitates one's interpretations in a practical context. One is able to state, for example, that of the $2000 disparity between blacks and whites, $175 is attributable to preexisting differences in education. In contrast, a statement that education accounts for 2% of the variance in income has less immediate meaning to policymakers (and social scientists).

As in the case of the bivariate model, the multivariate model generates at least two measures of goodness of fit. The multiple correlation coefficient squared (the R^2 or coefficient of determination) is the proportion of the variance in Y_t attributable to all of the exogenous variables in the aggregate. It includes not only the sum of unique effects, but all of the overlap contributions as well. As any proportion its range is 0–100%, but it is subject to a number of misinterpretations. As mentioned earlier, it is not at all clear why models that explain more variance are necessarily better, especially since the same causal effects may explain differing amounts of variance (Pindyck & Rubinfeld, 1981, pp. 78–82). Moreover, one may inflate the explained variance by simply adding any assortment of predictors in large numbers. At the very least, one must adjust for the resulting loss in degrees of freedom (Pindyck & Rubinfeld, 1981, pp. 78–79).[32] Finally, R^2s for models using aggregate data (e.g., median income of a community) are typically larger simply because much of the variation resulting from random perturbations cancels out.[33]

This raises a larger question of the role of variance explained in the general linear model. If, as the model assumes, endogenous variables are a function of systematic and stochastic forces, the existence of unexplained variance is to be expected. If the phenomenon of interest is caused by one or two salient variables and a myriad of other factors each with tiny effects, a small R^2 is an

---

[31] The shared variance is not an interaction effect. Interaction effects involve nonlinear causal effects and these will be considered shortly.

[32] Most standard statistical packages report the adjusted R^2 and sometimes also provide the unadjusted R^2. Yet, one cannot always assume that the reported R^2 has in fact been altered to take account of the number of exogenous variables. In short, it is always wise to check.

[33] Actually, there are many important complications involved in working with aggregated data. A good introduction to the consequences of aggregation can be found in Blalock (1964, pp. 95–114). A more thorough consideration can be found in Hannan (1971).

accurate representation of reality. In other words, the amount of explained variance must be interpreted in the context of one's specification (and theory) and cannot be blindly used to determine what a good model should be. In research about individual juvenile delinquents, for example, a theory might suggest that an R^2 of 15% is appropriate. In contrast, an accurate model of turnover in city council seats as a function of economic stagnation (measured by, for example, unemployment rates) may suggest an R^2 of about 30%.

As an alternative to the multiple correlation coefficient squared, some authors recommend the standard error of estimate. The use of this measure for goodness of fit was discussed earlier and there is little to add. If by *goodness of fit* one means how far on the average the observed Y_is depart from the regression line (or regression hyperplane in the multivariate case), the standard error of estimate can be a very informative indicator.

Statistical Inference in the Multivariate Model

All of our earlier discussion of statistical inference for the bivariate case applies here. Standard errors, confidence intervals, and significance tests have the same meaning and are vulnerable to the same kinds of distortions. Moreover, although diagnostic tools and adjustments for assumption violations are typically more complicated, they are by and large the same in principle.

The only really new form of statistical inference for the multivariate case involves the use of F-tests. Since t^2 equals F, the t-test described earlier for individual regression coefficients required no discussion of F. Moreover, in the bivariate case, a t-test that the slope is zero is identical to an F-test for the null hypothesis that R^2 is zero. However, in the multivariate case, the R^2 is now a function of more than one exogenous variable, and tests for particular regression coefficients differ from tests for the R^2. In essence, the usual F-test for an R^2 asserts the null hypothesis that all of the regression coefficients (but not the intercept) are zero. Thus, it is a test for the full set of regression coefficients. If one fails to reject the null hypothesis, it means that one would also almost certainly fail to reject the null hypothesis for each of the particular coefficients. However, one may obtain a statistically significant F and still fail to reject the null hypothesis for each individual regression coefficient (Pindyck & Rubinfeld, 1981, p. 81). Roughly speaking, an F that fails to make the critical level usually suggests that nothing of interest is going on in the model. An F that makes the critical level indicates that the variance explained is not likely to be the result of stochastic error, but it indicates little more.

Probably the most useful application of F-tests involves tests for subsets of coefficients. Consider the example used earlier in which the number of good arrests was regressed on a set of variables characterizing police officers and a set of variables characterizing the officer's beat. One might wish to determine if as a group the beat variables, for instance, make a statistically significant contribution to the variance explained. Basically, an F-test for the null hypothesis that beat variables make no contribution rests on a comparison between the R^2 with all the exogenous variables used as predictors and the R^2 with beat variables excluded. The R^2 decreasing a statistically significant amount when the beat variables are dropped, indicates that the impact of the beat variables can be distinguished from random error (Hanushek & Jackson, 1977, pp. 124–129). Such tests can also be phrased in terms of increases in the error sum of squares.

The Use of Nominal Exogenous Variables

Our earlier discussion of the use of a single dichotomous predictor provided important foundations for the use of more than one nominal variable. Suppose one were interested in determining the impact on the number of good arrests of an officer's ethnic background (e.g., white, black, and Hispanic). The three types of ethnicity might be conceptualized as a single nominal variable, with three categories. (The categories are mutually exclusive and exhaustive.) As a first step, one could construct a 1–0 dummy variable for each of the three categories in which a 1 indicated a given ethnic background and a 0 indicated one of the other two. Then, one might proceed by regressing arrests on the three dummy variables, which actually represent a *single* substantive variable. The regression coefficient for black officers, for example, might then indicate the increment or decrement in the mean number of good arrests achieved by black officers. However, a moment's thought will suggest that one cannot proceed precisely in this fashion. The intercept is supposed to show the mean number of good arrests when all of the predictors equal zero, and in this case since the categories are exhaustive, one exogenous variable will always have a value of 1 (regardless of ethnicity). Indeed, the problem is even more serious. For any set of mutually exclusive and exhaustive categories, any given category is redundant; any given category can be shown to be a linear function of the other categories. Hence, by including all three dummy variables, the model produces perfect multicollinearity. In short, we cannot estimate the model (unless the intercept is deleted).

Fortunately, the solution to perfect multicollinearity is simple in this case. One must delete one dummy variable from the exhaustive and mutually exclusive set. Ideally, the deleted variable should serve as a substantive baseline. Regardless, the raw regression coefficient for any dummy variable indicates the increment or decrement in the mean relative to the mean of the deleted category. For example, if white were the deleted variable, a coefficient for Hispanic of 3.8 would indicate an average of 3.8 more good arrests for hispanic officers compared to white officers. Similarly, if the regression coefficient for black were -1.6, there would be an average of 1.6 fewer good arrests for black officers compared to white officers. Note that in both instances, the regression coefficients take on meaning relative to the same missing category: white officers. (It may also be of interest that the model just described is identical to a

TABLE 13.1
The Number of Good Arrests Regressed on Ethnicity and Community Relations Programs

$$Y_t = \beta_1 + \beta_2 X_{t_2} + \beta_3 X_{t_3} + \beta_4 X_{t_4} + \beta_5 X_{t_5} + U_t$$

Where:

$$X_{t_2} = \text{Black}$$
$$X_{t_3} = \text{Hispanic}$$
$$X_{t_4} = \text{Store front offices}$$
$$X_{t_5} = \text{School visits}$$

Then:

$$\hat{Y}_t \text{ (white, no program)} = \beta_1$$
$$\hat{Y}_t \text{ (black, no program)} = \beta_1 + \beta_2$$
$$\hat{Y}_t \text{ (Hispanic, no program)} = \beta_1 + \beta_3$$
$$\hat{Y}_t \text{ (white, store fronts)} = \beta_1 + \beta_4$$
$$\hat{Y}_t \text{ (white, school visits)} = \beta_1 + \beta_5$$
$$\hat{Y}_t \text{ (black, store fronts)} = \beta_1 + \beta_2 + \beta_4$$
$$\hat{Y}_t \text{ (black, school visits)} = \beta_1 + \beta_2 + \beta_5$$
$$\hat{Y}_t \text{ (Hispanic, store fronts)} = \beta_1 + \beta_3 + \beta_4$$
$$\hat{Y}_t \text{ (Hispanic, school visits)} = \beta_1 + \beta_3 + \beta_5$$

one-way analysis of variance with three groups and can be easily extended to a one-way analysis of variance with any number of groups.)[34]

Suppose now that along with the dummy variable representing the three categories of ethnicity one added a second substantive nominal variable: the kind of police–community relations program provided in the neighborhood patrolled by each police officer. Again, there might be three categories: no program, store front offices, or visits to local schools. As before one would define three dummy variables and to avoid perfect multicollinearity, drop one from the analysis, perhaps no program. Hence, the multivariate model would include four exogenous variables and the deleted categories from *both* substantive variables (ethnicity and police–community relations) would be reflected in the intercept. That is, the intercept would provide the mean number of good arrests for whites patrolling in neighborhoods with no community relations program. Then, the raw regression coefficient for each dummy variable would indicate the difference in the mean number of arrests compared to this baseline (see Table 13.1). For example, if the regression coefficient for school visits was

[34] Notice that one can easily reconstruct the means for all of the categories of patrol. The mean for white officers equals the intercept, perhaps 10.0. The mean for Hispanic officers is then 10.0 plus 3.8 or 13.8. The mean for black officers is 10.0 minus 1.6 or 8.4. This implies that the F-test for the R^2 (actually identical to eta^2 when all nominal variables are used) is the same as the F-test for the between sum of squares. Finally, t-tests for particular regression coefficients are identical to t-tests for differences between means.

−2.5 and the intercept was 15.0, whites patrolling in neighborhoods with school visits would have a mean of 2.5 fewer good arrests compared to whites patrolling in neighborhoods with no police–community relations program (alternatively, the mean for such officers would be 12.5). Suppose that the regression coefficient for Hispanic officers was 2.0. This would indicate that Hispanics patrolling in neighborhoods with no community relations program had a mean of 2 more good arrests than whites patrolling in neighborhoods with no community relations program (alternatively, a mean of 17 good arrests). This makes it possible to characterize the mean number of good arrests for any configuration of the dummy variables. For example, Hispanics patrolling in neighborhoods with school visits would have a mean of .5 fewer arrests (2.0–2.5) compared to whites patrolling in neighborhoods with no community relations program.

In more formal terms, this illustration is an instance of two-way analysis of variance with three groups for each. However, unlike the manner in which traditional analysis of variance usually proceeds, the general linear model does not require that the substantive variables (or factors) be orthogonal (i.e., uncorrelated). When traditional analysis of variance is altered to take account of nonproportional cells (associations among factors), the two approaches are identical.

Given the links between the general linear model and analysis of variance it should not be surprising to learn that one can also specify models to include interaction (i.e., nonlinear) effects as well as main effects. For example, in the simple case of two dummy variables reflecting two separate substantive variables (e.g., male–female and black–white), one could estimate a model with the two dummy variables and an additional variable for an interaction effect, constructed by multiplying the two dummy variables together. (If male were coded 1 and black coded 1, then the interaction variable would show a 1 for all individuals who were both male and black.)[35] Although models with more substantive variables and more dummy variables can become rather complicated, the ability to estimate both main and interaction effects remains. In addition, it is often possible through alternative coding schemes, to simplify not only the construction of interaction variables, but also interpretations of the coefficients and the application of especially relevant significance tests (Cohen & Cohen, 1975, pp. 171–211, 291–301, 324–339).[36]

Analysis of covariance is also a special case of the general linear model. In essence, the new twist is that both nominal and interval exogenous variables are permitted. Suppose the number of good arrests were regressed on whether

[35] In this instance, a nontrivial interaction effect would mean that beyond the effect of race and sex, the coupling of them in a particular configuration also has an impact. For example, men with a given job may receive a higher wage than women, whites on that same job may receive a higher wage than blacks, and if a person happens to be a white male, still another increment exists. That is, the whole is more than the sum of its parts; white males receive higher wages than can be explained by the *sum* of effects from their sex and race. Being a white and a male "potentiate" one another. More is said on this later when nonlinear effects are considered.

[36] For an econometric perspective see Kmenta (1971, pp. 409–419).

the police officer was black or white and each officer's number of weeks of training. The regression coefficient of the number of weeks of training would show the mean change in arrests for every week of training. The regression coefficient for the race of the officer would show the change in the mean number of arrests for black officers (if black was coded 1) compared to white officers. In addition, one could build an interaction variable as the product of the two exogenous variables. (For white officers, the values of the interaction variable would be zeros; for black officers, the values of the interaction variable would be the number of weeks of training.) The regression coefficient for the interaction term would show the difference between the slope for the number of weeks of training for white and black officers (see Table 13.2).

For example, suppose the intercept was 15.0, the regression coefficient for training was .5, the regression coefficient for race of the officer was -1.5, and the regression coefficient for the interaction term was 1.0. Then, black officers would have 1.5 fewer good arrests on the average than white officers. In addition, for white officers each additional week of training produces a mean of .5 additional good arrests. However, the slope for black officers is 1 unit steeper (1.5) for each additional week of training.

Another way of considering the analysis of covariance model in terms of the general linear model is that in the example just presented, one has actually estimated two regression lines at once. The regression line for white officers has an intercept of 15 and a slope of .5. The regression line for black officers has a lower intercept of 13.5 (15.0 $-$ 1.5) and a greater slope of 1.5 (.5 + 1.0). This suggests that at very (and perhaps unrealistically) low levels of training, fewer good arrests are made by black officers. But since for blacks each additional week of training produces a greater number of good arrests, at high levels of training, more good arrests are made by blacks on the average. In

TABLE 13.2
The Number of Good Arrests Regressed on Weeks of
Training and Race

$$Y_t = \beta_1 + \beta_2 X_{t2} + \beta_3 X_{t3} + \beta_4(X_{t2} \cdot X_{t3}) + U_t$$

Where:

$$X_{t2} = \text{black (coded 1)}$$
$$X_{t3} = \text{weeks of training}$$

Then for whites:

$$Y_t = \beta_1 + \beta_2 X_{t3} + U_t$$

For blacks:

$$Y_t = (\beta_1 + \beta_2) + (\beta_3 + \beta_4)X_{t3} + U_t$$

Therefore:

β_2 = the difference in the intercept for blacks and whites
β_4 = the difference in the slope for blacks and whites

short, the dummy variable reveals any difference in intercepts and the interaction (or product) variable reveals any difference in slopes (Kmenta, 1971, pp. 419–425).

Coupled with significance tests for each of the regression coefficients and for sets of coefficients, the simple three variable model just discussed can be readily extended to permit the simultaneous estimation of several regression lines at once (Johnston, 1972, pp. 192–207). However, since many of the interaction variables are built from the products of other variables, one soon finds that very high correlations exist among subsets of exogenous variables (high, but not perfect, multicollinearity). For example, a single dummy variable and a single interval variable will both correlate highly with their product. As we shall see, such correlations present new problems. If these new problems prohibit the estimation of several regression lines simultaneously, one has two options. First, one can estimate the regression lines separately (e.g., estimate a regression line for white officers and then estimate a regression line for black officers).[37] Although this typically costs some degrees of freedom and therefore reduces the power of significance tests for the coefficients in each equation, it may be a small price to pay.[38] However, one often sacrifices the ability to apply significance tests for the difference *between* regression lines (e.g., the slope for white officers versus the slope for black officers), which can be far more serious. Unfortunately, sometimes no other option exists. Second, instead of trying to estimate both different slopes and different intercepts for all possible equations, one may be more selective. Assuming theoretical justification, perhaps one may only care about different intercepts for some equations and different slopes for others. This can sometimes significantly reduce the correlations among subsets of independent variables. Alternatively, if only different intercepts are of interest, no product variables need be constructed, and the correlations one might have otherwise built into the data are eliminated completely. When one has sound theory on which to base such selectivity, one is usually far better off than trying to estimate each regression equation separately.

Inherently Linear and Inherently Nonlinear Functional Forms

In the discussion of the parallels between analysis of variance and analysis of covariance, a new twist in applications of the general linear model was quietly introduced. In the context of analysis of variance, an interaction term was included, derived from the product of two other variables. This product variable captured effects that were more than the sum of components. In the context of analysis of covariance, another kind of interaction variable was constructed as the product of a dummy variable and an interval variable. This

---

[37] In SPSS, for example, this can be easily set up with ''select if'' statements.

[38] One's sample size is typically reduced by more than the number of independent variables.

allowed the consideration of different slopes conditional on whether the dummy variable was a 1 or a 0. Both interaction variables implied that the effects of a given X_{tk} were not invariant; that a unit change in X_{tk} did not necessarily lead to the same amount of change in Y_t. The impact of training, for instance, varied depending on whether the police officer was white or black.

Recall that our definition of the linear model required that the causal effect of any X_{tk} be invariant and therefore, by definition, interaction variables would seem to violate an important premise. They appear to be nonlinear. However, the general linear model makes a critical distinction between inherently linear and inherently nonlinear models; the former can be estimated with ordinary least squares, the latter require more sophisticated techniques (Pindyck & Rubinfeld, 1981, pp. 107–110).

An inherently linear model is a model that, with proper transformation of its variables, can be expressed in a linear form. For example, a parabolic relationship (roughly ∪ shaped) between X_t and Y_t would seem at first glance to present serious problems for ordinary least squares. In other words, the slope for X_t is not constant, but increases as the values of X_t increase. The linear model is unable to estimate such a functional relationship; it cannot produce a regression coefficient to represent a slope that is not constant. However, suppose one defined a new variable Z_t such that $Z_t = X_t^2$. Then, the general linear model will provide an estimate of the linear relationship between Y_t and Z_t. Moreover, with the slope for Y_t regressed on Z_t in hand, one can translate the results back in units of X_t. In other words, the general linear model can be tricked into estimating this nonlinear form. Instead of regressing Y_t on X_t and trying (unsuccessfully) to obtain a nonlinear slope, one regresses Y_t on X_t^2 and obtains a legitimate regression coefficient (in terms of X_t^2).

The estimates produced by regressing Y_t on X_t^2 can be used to derive substantive findings either in terms of X_t^2 or X_t. Suppose the slope of Y_t on X_t^2 equals 4.0 and the intercept equals 5.0. Every unit change in the *square* of X_t results in a four-unit change in Y_t. This also means that if X_t^2 happens to be 9, the expected value of Y_t (the point on the regression line) is 41.0 [(4 × 9) + 5.0]. If X_t equals 2 the value of X_t^2 is 4 and the expected value of Y_t equals 21.0. However, obtaining the slope in terms of X_t is a bit more complicated. The *slope* changes as the value of X_t changes, which means that one must take the first derivative of the product of the regression coefficient and X_t^2 to get an expression for the slope in terms of X_t. In this instance, the derivative is $8.0 X_t$ so that the slope is 8.0 when X_t equals 1.0; 16.0 when X_t equals 2.0; 24.0 when X_t equals 3.0; and so on.

Besides the fact that the general linear model can include many kinds of nonlinear relationships, perhaps the most important point from this example is that it is possible to estimate regression coefficients for variables whose impact on Y_t varies systematically. We have just seen how one can allow the slope for X_t to vary as a function of X_t. One can also allow the slope of X_t to vary as a function of other variables. When the slope of X_t varies with the values of other variables, one's model includes interaction effects; causal implications are conditional on the particular values taken by other variables. These values, in turn, may be nominal categories (as shown earlier), or numbers representing interval and ratio scales. For example, if X_{t_2} is weeks of training and X_{t_3} is age, a new variable, the product of X_{t_2} and X_{t_3}, will capture the interaction of each in their effects on the general number of good arrests.[39]

Nonlinear relationships that can be estimated with the general linear model after proper transformations are very common (see Hanushek and Jackson, 1977, 98–100 for some other examples). Occasionally, there will be nonlinear relationships for which transformations will not produce new variables whose impact can be captured in the general linear model. For example, in order to estimate some kinds of nonlinear models, taking the log of the exogenous and endogenous variables would work except that one or more of the terms has no log equivalent (e.g., Pindyck & Rubinfeld, 1981, p. 108). Hence, the general linear model cannot be properly applied and one must turn to such techniques as nonlinear least squares (Pindyck & Rubinfeld, 1981, pp. 261–269). If possible, such inherently nonlinear variables should be avoided since the available statistical technology is computationally expensive, tricky to interpret, and subject to occasional problems for which no solutions currently exist.[40]

13.4. SOME COMMON PROBLEMS WITH THE MULTIVARIATE MODEL

Most of the significant properties of the general linear model have been briefly considered in the discussion of nonlinear effects. Perhaps the major oversight involves applications in which prediction rather than explanation is the central goal. However, prediction by itself is rarely a critical concern in current survey research, and the additional concepts would have required a lengthy extension of this chapter. Hence, the reader is referred to the relevant sections in Pindyck and Rubinfeld (1981) where an unusually clear introduction to predictive applications can be found.

We have seen that in moving from the bivariate to the multivariate model, the possibilities for creative data analysis have been markedly enhanced. How-

[39] At least two clarifications are perhaps warranted here. First, it is important to understand that the conditional variation in causal effects is systematic, not stochastic. That is, the causal effects change as a function of substantive variables and *only* substantive variables. When the causal effects vary as a function of substantive variables and random perturbations, more advanced estimation procedures are required (Madalla, 1977, pp. 390–404). Second, when working with interval data as opposed to nominal or ratio data, the use of product variables to capture interaction effects has some unfortunate consequences. In essence, although all is well with the regression coefficient for the product variable and its t-test, some or all of the standardized coefficients for the other variables will be distorted, and related t-tests for specific null hypotheses will lose their substantive meaning (Allison, 1977).

[40] For example, in many instances, there are some genuine problems in estimating the standard errors and the variance of the residuals (Draper & Smith, 1966, pp. 282–284).

ever, there seem to be few unmixed blessings in statistics, and multivariate applications highlight several new problems that need to be briefly addressed. We turn to those now.

Multicollinearity

When any exogenous variable is an exact linear combination of one or more other exogenous variables, it is impossible to obtain unique least-squares estimates of the regression parameters. Such perfect multicollinearity was considered earlier and, fortunately, can be easily corrected. Much more problematic are data sets in which one or more exogenous variables are highly correlated with one or more other exogenous variables. Note that far more than bivariate correlations are involved; one may have relatively low zero–order correlations among exogenous variables and still have very high *multiple* correlations. If, for example, one were predicting the number of good arrests from several characteristics of the neighborhoods officers patrol, one would be vulnerable to large bivariate correlations and/or the possibility that any given variable (e.g., median income) would be very nearly a linear combination of the set of other neighborhood variables (e.g., percentage unemployed, percentage blue collar, percentage black, percentage of substandard housing). In either case, high collinearity results.

In essence, high multicollinearity means that the residualizing process of holding things constant allows very little variance in the exogenous variable(s) with which to explain variation in the dependent variable to remain. Since the standard errors for regression coefficients increase as the residualized variance in each of the respective exogenous variables declines, the primary consequence of high multicollinearity is to have reduced statistical power and by implication, far less stable estimates of causal effects. It becomes difficult to distinguish even rather large coefficients from stochastic error. In practical contexts, this also means that rather small substantive alterations in the model being estimated may produce widely differing estimates of causal impact (Pindyck & Rubinfeld, 1981, pp. 87–90; Kmenta, 1971, pp. 380–391).

Unfortunately, the existence of high multicollinearity is hard to diagnose, in part because its effects fall on a continuum and may result from correlations between two or more exogenous variables. If any of the zero-order correlations among pairs of exogenous variables exceed plus or minus .80, there are usually grounds for some concern. Another rule of thumb is that estimates may be highly unstable if the zero-order correlation between any pair of exogenous variables is larger than the zero-order correlation of either with the endogenous variable. Yet another guideline is that if the determinant of the matrix of correlations among exogenous variables is less than .05, multicollinearity may be serious. Alternatively, if substantively large regression coefficients are not statistically significant even with moderately large samples, if removing one or two variables greatly alters the regression coefficients for the remaining predictors and/or if standardized regression coefficients have values in excess of plus or minus 1.0, there may also be reasons to worry. However, probably the very best diagnostics are of very recent origin (Belsley, Kuh, & Welsch, 1980). In brief, these procedures rest on the matrix algebra of singular value decomposition and are especially effective when there are several near dependencies among the regressors. In practice, this means that otherwise overlooked multicollinearity will be properly flagged, and the sources of the problem will be effectively revealed. Although these procedures have yet to be widely applied, they hold enormous promise.

Solutons to high multicollinearity are as hard to come by as accurate diagnostic devices. Dropping collinear variables from the model will reduce the instability, but at the risk of creating specification errors (to be discussed) and hence, biased estimates of causal effect. Combining highly collinear variables into indices or scales, perhaps through principle components (Johnston, 1972, pp. 322–334), will also reduce instability, but unless these new variables have sound *theoretical* justification, one once again risks misspecification.

Another strategy rests on the researcher being able to place linear constraints on the regression coefficients associated with highly collinear variables (e.g., Kmenta, 1971, pp. 430–451). For example, from theory or previous research it might be possible to assume that one of the relevant regression coefficients equals some constant; perhaps previous research indicates that the regression coefficients for the impact of weeks of training on the number of good arrests is .3. This information can be included within the general linear model with the result that the effects of multicollinearity connected to weeks of training will be eliminated. Alternatively, one might be able to specify in advance that one regression coefficient equals another. For example, in predicting a police officer's grade point average at the police adacemy (perhaps to determine who should be admitted), the educational levels of the officer's mother and father can possibly be assumed to each have the exact same impact. Then, constraining these regression coefficients to equal one another will eliminate difficulties produced by collinearity between the two educational variables. Although many statistical packages now provide for linear constraints (e.g., SAS), the trick, of course, is to be able to come up with plausible linear relationships for the regression coefficients of concern. In practice, this may not be easy to do, and more flexible approaches come under the category of mixed estimation (Belsley *et al.*, 1980, pp. 195–204).

Faced with such difficulties, some researchers have recently decided to squarely face the relationship between bias and efficiency with an estimation technique called *ridge regression* (MaCallum, 1970). Ridge regression introduces small amounts of bias while greatly reducing the variances of estimated regression coefficients. Ridge regression has genuine promise, but it is still too early to fairly assess its real merits. In particular, there is still some disagreement about what the optimal amount of bias should be (Fennesey & D'Amico, 1980; Kasarda & Shih, 1977).

Given these problems, it is very difficult to provide useful suggestions for reducing multicollinearity.[41] In practice, many researchers drop collinear variables and simply hope that the resulting biases are not severe. At the very least, however, such decisions should be clearly reported along with speculations about the possible distortions that could result.

Specification Error

Specification error involves a poor fit between the model one is estimating and the empirical phenomenon of interest, that is, when one has the wrong causal model. Specification error is perhaps the most nettlesome problem for the general linear model because it has serious consequences and is almost impossible to diagnose precisely. Since the research enterprise rests heavily on efforts to estimate the parameters of underlying and hence unknown substantive processes, by definition, one has no correct representation to contrast to the equation being estimated. If one knew enough to properly diagnose misspecification, one would not need to undertake the research. Consequently, as a practical matter, the possibility of specification error surfaces when existing theory or prior research suggests that the proposed causal model is inaccurate or that equally plausible competing models have been neglected.

Although misspecification may take many forms (Kmenta, 1971, pp. 392–405), only two of the most common are considered here. The first case is when an important causal variable has been left out of the regression equation. Typically, this produces biased and inconsistent estimates of causal effects and the intercept. The second case is when an irrelevant variable has been included in the regression equation. The regression coefficients, intercept, and standard errors remain unbiased, but the estimates are inefficient. Both types of specification error require some elaboration.

When an important causal variable has been neglected, the direction and size of bias depend on the regression coefficient for the missing variable (if one could have estimated it) and the correlations of the missing variable with other exogenous variables in the equation (if one could have estimated them). By definition, the unknown regression coefficient is not zero since one is assuming that it has important effects on the dependent variable. However, the larger the unknown regression coefficient is likely to be, the more serious the bias. Similarly, the larger the correlations between the missing variable and the included causal variables, the larger the bias (Kmenta, 1971, pp. 392–393). If one can safely assume that the missing exogenous variable is uncorrelated with other causal variables, the estimated regression coefficients are unbiased although the estimate of the intercept is not. In addition, estimates of the standard errors will be biased and will typically lead to unduly weak significance tests coupled with wider confidence intervals (i.e., the standard errors are markedly inflated).

[41] What is clear, however, is that search techniques such as stepwise regression can be very misleading and should *not* be used to eliminate collinear variables (Hanushek & Jackson, 1977, pp. 95–96).

When powerful theory and long research traditions exist and when one's model includes a small number of exogenous variables, it is sometimes possible to provide informed guesses about the size and direction of bias. However, in most practical situations the best that one can do is to speculate about the direction of the bias for particular coefficients. This in part justifies research traditions in which randomized experiments dominate the literature. By randomizing, the expected correlation between a treatment(s) and other exogenous variables is zero, which means that one will obtain unbiased estimates of treatment effects. However, randomizing does not fully solve the problem of neglected causal variables since estimates of the intercept are still biased, as are estimates of the standard errors. The latter point is critical and too often ignored in discussions of randomized experiments. Tests of statistical significance are biased in a conservative direction (i.e., it is harder to reject the null hypothesis).[42]

What happens if variables are included in the model that in fact have no causal impact on the dependent variable; that is, if their population regression coefficients are actually zero? Such null effects are very common in survey research especially when to be on the safe side investigators throw all conceivable predictors into the equation with little theoretical justification. Estimates of the regression coefficients and the intercept will be unbiased. In addition, estimates of the standard errors are unbiased. However, estimates of the regression coefficients and intercept will be inefficient under most circumstances (Kmenta, 1971, pp. 396–399), which means that their sampling distributions have inflated variances. Beside the risk of increased multicollinearity, one has unnecessarily used up one or more degrees of freedom. Hence, one's estimates will be unnecessarily imprecise and on the average farther away from the population values.

The two kinds of specification errors just discussed imply that in practice one walks a fine line between including unnecessary exogenous variables and excluding necessary ones. Out of context, it is not at all clear which kinds of errors will be more severe since a biased estimate of causal effect may still be closer on the average to the population value than an unbiased but inefficient estimate of a causal effect. Even when focused on a particular data set, ignorance about the real nature of the empirical phenomenon makes tradeoffs ambiguous.

Some researchers respond to such difficulties by starting with "kitchen sink" models and eliminating unnecessary variables. Statistically insignificant predictors are dropped and the reduced equation reestimated. This process may then be repeated until all of the regression coefficients are statistically significant or a maximum F-ratio is achieved. Unfortunately, this dramatically capitalizes on Type I and Type II errors, which in turn undermines the very

---

[42] The failure to include important causal variables even if uncorrelated with the treatment leads to a larger error sum of squares (i.e., less explained variance) which in turn inflates the standard errors. More generally, anything that inflates the error sum of squares, such as random measurement error in Y_t, will shift significance tests in a conservative direction.

criterion being used to delete unnecessary variables. Moreover, even with moderate multicollinearity, genuine and important causal variables will typically be dropped. If two predictors are highly related to one another and both are included in the estimated equation, *both* will have relatively large standard errors and hence a markedly reduced likelihood of achieving statistical significance. In other words, they will be dropped not because their regression coefficients are necessarily trivial, but because their standard errors mitigate against statistical significance. In contrast, a variable that may have a far smaller causal impact but that is nearly independent of other predictors, will be retained in the model.

As an alternative strategy some researchers begin with a bare bones model and then try to add variables based on statistical significance. However, the criterion of statistical significance can produce ambiguous results. Often the inclusion of a new variable will make an earlier regression coefficient insignificant, and then it is hard to decide if the new or old variable should be retained. Sometimes, instead of using t-tests for the regression coefficients, investigators will test for the increment to the explained variance when one or more new variables are added. In other words, one retains the initial set of predictors regardless and attempts to find other exogenous variables that increase the R^2. Unfortunately, this presupposes that there is some theoretical justification for deeming the first set more important a priori, and too often such issues are ignored. Then, one may be once again capitalizing on Type I and Type II errors.

Perhaps the best way to proceed involves a clear distinction between two stages in model specification. In the first stage, one should pose several competing causal models and estimate all of them. Then, within the more recent traditions in causal modelings, one should select the model that fits the data best. Besides t-tests for individual coefficients, there are now a range of procedures that consider the model as a whole (see Footnote 21). In essence, one is comparing competing causal explanations based on how well they explain one's observed data. Once this exercise has been completed, a second stage may be undertaken in which the researcher fishes through the data in search of the big one that got away. To the degree that the search can be guided by informal hunches or speculations from the models already estimated, one may reduce the likelihood of capitalizing on Type I and Type II errors. In any case, the meaning of formal statistical inference is now unclear and the best criteria for proclaiming a record catch rest on increments to the explained variance and the size of the new regression coefficients. It cannot be overemphasized that researchers should indicate in the text when they have moved from Stage I to Stage II.

Missing Data

In the vast majority of survey research efforts, not every respondent answers every question. More generally, most empirical social science is vulnerable to missing data and, much like the problems introduced through specification errors, fully satisfactory solutions rarely exist. The kinds of missing data and their consequences involve a large number of complicated questions most of which are well beyond the scope of this chapter. We consider only one rather simple form of missing data and several possible solutions.

First, let us begin by assuming that having missing data occurs solely for exogenous variables. If data are also missing for the endogenous variable, those cases are dropped.[43] Let us also assume that the data are missing at random; that there is no tendency for certain kinds of respondents to have missing data.

Perhaps the easiest solution is to drop all cases for which data are missing on *any* of the exogenous variables. Sometimes, this is operationalized as *listwise deletion* in common statistical packages. If the data are really missing at random, listwise deletion yields unbiased but inefficient estimates of the intercept and slopes. In general, the closer the values of the missing data are to the means of their respective variables and the smaller the sample variance of these missing observations, the smaller the loss in efficiency (Pindyck & Rubinfeld, 1981, pp. 245–249). Of course, one can only speculate about the degree to which either is true. Fortunately, experience suggests that having up to 10% of the data missing do not lead to great losses in efficiency.

As an alternative to dropping all cases when data for any of the exogenous variables are missing, one may try to insert plausible values for the missing observations. In the absence of other information, it is common to insert each variable's mean. In the bivariate case, this is *identical* to listwise deletion; whereas in the multivariate case, it is identical to *pairwise deletion*. In *pairwise deletion*, regression estimates are derived from a matrix of correlations (or variances and covariances) for all variables in which each correlation is based only on the data available for each pair of variables. That is, one allows each variable to operate with a different case base, which usually means that even the smallest pairwise N is larger than the listwise N. Hence, one salvages as much data as possible by retaining cases even if data are missing on some exogenous variables.

Unfortunately, the benefits derived from larger effective samples are often coupled with ill-conditioned data; the patterns of variances and covariances possess internal contradictions. This may cause one's computer either to balk at a request to estimate the regression coefficients, or to produce distorted results. Again, however, one can usually live with missing data rates up to about 10%. If missing data rates are much larger, it is usually wiser to use listwise deletion and pay the price of inefficiency rather than to try to interpret estimates from pairwise deletion procedures. It may also make sense to try to estimate the models using both pairwise and listwise techniques. If the substantive conclusions are approximately the same, one can report either set of esti-

---

[43] If such missing data are relatively infrequent and missing at random, the consequences are usually not serious for cross-sectional data. However, genuine difficulties can occur in time series data and adjustments should be made (Pindyck & Rubinfeld, 1981, pp. 539–548; Madalla, 1977, pp. 201–207).

mates. If the conclusions differ, the listwise estimates are usually more plausible (in part because it is clear what the actual data set is that was used to obtain the estimates).

When the data are not missing at random, the obtained regression coefficients are biased and inconsistent. Moreover, the range of possible solutions typically rest on heroic assumptions, which if violated can actually make matters worse (e.g., Pindyck & Rubinfeld, 1981, pp. 249–252). At the very least, difficult tradeoffs exist between the likely amount of bias and the likely amount of inefficiency. Perhaps the best advice is the most obvious, invest heavily in the data collection stage so that missing data are minimized. (See also Chapter 12.)

Stepwise Regression and Other Fishing Techniques

Stepwise regression is a statistical winnowing technique by which a subset of exogenous variables are selected for a final regression model from a larger group of potential exogenous variables. Although the details of the selection process and the criteria by which variables are deemed worthy can vary widely (Draper & Smith, 1968, pp. 163–195),[44] the basic idea is to add variables to the model in decreasing order of importance until no new variables attain some predetermined level of merit. Typically, the criteria involve a specific increment to the R^2 (e.g., 1%) coupled with a significance test for this increment. Hence, one's final model includes all variables that provide a statistically significant sequential increment to the explained variance and excludes those that do not. For example, the variable that makes the largest initial increment to the R^2 for the number of good arrests may be the number of weeks of training. Then, the technique searches for the variable of the remaining set, which makes the next largest contribution *given* that the first variable is already in the equation, perhaps in this case, the median income in neighborhoods patrolled. This process is then repeated so that the third variable entered contributes the next largest amount of explained variance *given* that the first two variables are already in the equation. At some point either all of the variables are in the model or, more likely, no other variables can meet the inclusion criteria.

There are a large number of serious problems with stepwise regression, most of which have been alluded to in previous sections of this chapter: capitalizing on Type I and Type II errors, the arbitrary exclusion of one or more collinear variables, a lack of justification for using increments to explained variance as a measure of causal importance, and so on. All are likely to produce nontrivial specification errors. In addition, since there are a range of selection devices that often vary across computer installations and statistical packages, different researchers analyzing the same data may well arrive at quite different conclusions. In short, stepwise regression is almost always dangerously mis-

---

[44] Actually, there are several kinds of stepwise procedures and a large number of other closely related fishing techniques. For sheer muscle, "all possible regressions" probably tops the list (Draper & Smith, 1968, pp. 164, 167).

leading, especially if one claims to be interested in the causal meaning of one's model (Einhorn, 1972; Hanushek & Jackson, 1977, pp. 94–96). However, since by chance alone one will almost always find statistically significant effects, the depressing reality is that stepwise regression will probably continue to be popular. At the very least investigators should "'fess up" when their models derive from stepwise procedures and avoid perhaps the most serious error of interpreting the increment to R^2 at each step as a measure of a causal importance.

If users of stepwise regression may be accused of fishing, users of AID may be accused of chumming as well. AID stands for Automatic Interaction Detector (Sonquist, Baker, & Morgan, 1973) and is basically a stepwise analysis of variance in which increasingly higher order interaction effects are added as long as they make significant increments to the explained variance. In addition, since AID requires that predictors be dichotomous variables, it takes predictors with more than two categories and collapses them into all possible dichotomies (with K categories, the number of possible recombinations is $K - 1$ if the categories are ordered) from which the dichotomy is selected making the largest incremental contribution to explained variance. In other words, the search occurs at two levels. To provide some sense of the degree to which AID capitalizes on Type I errors, Berk, Hennessy, and Swan (1977) report an experiment in which with the use of AID, vectors of random numbers were able to account for 14% of the variance in a dependent variable. Clearly, Type I error can lead to serious misspecifications.

AID adds several new difficulties to all of the problems with stepwise regression. Perhaps most important, the selection of a particular collapsed dichotomy (for a given predictor) from all possible combinations of categories allows one to capitalize not only on sampling error, but random measurement error as well. In addition, there is no guarantee that the dichotomy chosen has any substantive meaning.

Are there ever any circumstances when either AID or stepwise regression can be used sensibly? If handled very carefully the answer is yes. After one has posed and tested all of the reasonable a priori models for a given data set, it may be useful to throw out a big net and see what else may be caught. If one's catch is treated very tentatively, it may become the basis for new models to be tested with new data in another study.

13.5. SOME CONCLUDING OBSERVATIONS

After the brief discussion of some popular search techniques and their problems, this chapter ends with a recapitulation of its initial theme. Even with the most sophisticated statistical procedures, there is no substitute for careful thought about the empirical phenomena under scrutiny. Fancy estimators and powerful computers are usually worse than useless without theory, knowledge of previous research, and creative substantive speculations. One cannot subcontract one's social science enterprise to the local computer center.

A second major theme is that there is no such thing as a routine data analysis. The general linear model is vulnerable to a variety of difficulties that are often hard to diagnose and once revealed, often require ambiguous tradeoffs. Time and again one is faced with the proverbial Catch 22 in which if one knew enough to provide a definitive solution to the problem, one would already know enough to make the research unnecessary. Here, there is no substitute for lots of experience and wise colleagues.

Finally, as in any handbook chapter, the content here is closer to a map than a guided tour. Many important issues have been addressed superficially and some topics neglected altogether. There are a large number of excellent references available, and these should be routinely consulted.

REFERENCES

Aigner, D. S., and A. S. Goldberger
  1977 *Latent Variables in Socio-Econometric Models*. New York: North Holland.
Allison, P. D.
  1977 "Testing for interaction in multiple regression." *American Journal of Sociology* 83: 144–153.
Althauser, R. P., and M. Wigler
  1972 "Standardization and component analysis." *Sociological Methods and Research* 1: 97–135.
Andrews, F. M., J. N. Morgan, and J. A. Sonquist
  1973 *Multiple Classification Analysis*. Ann Arbor, Mich.: Institute for Social Science Research.
Barnett, V.
  1973 *Comparative Statistical Inference*. New York: Wiley.
Belsley, D. A., E. Kuh, and R. E. Welsch
  1980 *Regression Diagnostics*. New York: John Wiley
Berk, R. A.
  1977 "Proof? No. Evidence? No. A skeptic's comment on Inverarity's use of statistical inference." *American Sociological Review* 42: 652–656.
Berk, R. A., and M. Brewer
  1978 "Feet of clay in hobnail boots: An assessment of statistical inference in applied research." *Evaluation Quarterly,* forthcoming.
Berk, R. A., M. Hennessy, and R. McCleary
  1976 "Descriptive distortions in covariance based statistics." *Social Science Research* 5: 107–126.
Berk, R. A., M. Hennessy, and J. Swan
  1977 "The vagaries and vulgarities of 'scientific' jury selection." *Evaluation Quarterly* 1: 143–158.
Berk, R. A., D. M. Hoffman, J. E. Maki, D. Rauma, and H. Wong
  1979 "Estimation procedures for pooled cross-sectional and time series data." *Evaluation Quarterly,* 3: 385–410.
Berk, R. A., and S. C. Ray
  1982 "Selection biases in sociological data." *Social Science Research* 11: 352–398.
Bielby, W. T., and J. R. Kluegel
  1977 "Statistical inference and statistical power in applications of the general linear model." Pp. 283–312 in D. R. Heise (ed.) *Sociological Methodology, 1977.* San Francisco: Jossey–Bass.

Bishop, Y. M. M., S. E. Fienberg, and P. W. Holland
    1975 *Discrete Multivariate Analysis*. Cambridge, Mass: MIT Press.
Bittner, E.
    1980 *The Functions of Police in Modern Society*. Cambridge, Mass.: Oelgeschlager, Gunn and Hain.
Blalock, H. M.
    1964 *Causal Inferences in Nonexperimental Research*. Chapel Hill: The University of North Carolina Press.
    1971 "Causal inferences, closed populations, and measures of association." Pp. 139–151 in H. M. Blalock (ed.), *Causal Models in the Social Sciences*. Chicago: Aldine.
    1972 *Social Statistics*. New York: McGraw–Hill.
Box, G. E. P., and G. M. Jenkins
    1976 *Time Series Analysis*. San Francisco: Holden Day.
Box, G. E. P., and G. C. Tiao
    1973 *Bayesian Inference in Statistical Analysis*. Reading, Mass.: Addison–Wesley.
Bridges, W. P., and R. A. Berk
    1977 "Sex, earnings and the nature of work: A job level analysis of male–female income differences." *Social Science Quarterly,* forthcoming.
Burt, R. S.
    1973 "Confirmatory factor-analytic structures and the theory construction process." *Sociological Methods and Research* 2: 131–191.
Campbell, D. T., and J. C. Stanley
    1966 *Experimental and Quasi-Experimental Designs for Research*. Chicago: Rand McNally.
Cohen, J., and P. Cohen
    1975 *Applied Multiple Regression/Correlation Analysis for the Behavioral Sciences*. New York: Halsted Press.
Creager, J. A., and R. F. Boruch
    1969 "Orthogonal analysis of linear composite variance." Pp. 113–114 in *Proceedings, 77th Annual Convention, American Psychological Association*.
Darlington, R. B.
    1968 "Multiple regression in psychological research and practice." *Psychological Bulletin* 69: 161–182.
Draper, N. R., and H. Smith
    1968 *Applied Regression Analysis*. New York: Wiley.
Duncan, O. P.
    1970 "Partials, partitions, and paths." Pp. 38–47 in E. F. Borgatta and G. W. Bohrnstedt (eds.), *Sociological Methodology, 1970*. San Francisco: Jossey–Bass.
    1975 *Introduction to Structural Equation Models*. New York: Academic Press.
Einhorn, H. J.
    1972 "Alchemy in the behavioral sciences." *Public Opinion Quarterly* 36: 367–378.
Fennessey, J., and R. D'Amico
    1980 "Collinearity, ridge regression and investigator judgement." *Sociological Methods and Research* 8: 309–340.
Gillespie, M. W.
    1977 "Log-linear techniques and regression analysis of dummy dependent variables: Further basis for comparison." *Sociological Methods and Research* 6: 103–122.
Goldberger, A. S.
    1964 *Econometric Theory*. New York: Wiley.
Goodman, L. A.
    1976 "The relationship between the modified and more usual multiple regression approach to analysis of dichotomous variables." Pp. 83–110 in D. R. Heise (ed.), *Sociological Methodology, 1976*. San Francisco: Jossey–Bass.
Granger, C. W. J., and M. Hatanaka
    1964 *Spectral Analysis of Economic Time Series*. Princeton: Princeton University Press.

Graybill, F. A.
1961 *An Introduction to Linear Statistical Models.* New York: McGraw–Hill.
Green, P. E.
1978 *Mathematical Tools for Applied Multivariate Analysis.* New York: Academic Press.
Hannan, M. T.
1971 *Aggregation and Dissaggregation in Sociology.* Lexington, Mass.: Heath Lexington.
Hannan, M. T., and A. A. Young
1977 "Estimation in panel models: Results on pooling cross-sections and time series." Pp. 52–83 in D. R. Heise (ed.), *Sociological Methodology, 1977.* San Francisco: Jossey–Bass.
Hanushek, E. A., and J. Jackson
1977 *Statistical Methods for Social Scientists.* New York: Academic Press.
Hayes, W. L.
1973 *Statistics for the Social Sciences.* New York: Holt, Rinehart & Winston.
Hibbs, P. A.
1973 "Problems of statistical estimation and causal inference in time series regression models." Pp. 252–308 in H. L. Costner (ed.), *Sociological Methodology, 1973–74.* San Francisco: Jossey–Bass.
1977 "On analyzing the effects of policy interventions: Box–Jenkins and Box–Tiao versus structural equation models." Pp. 137–179 in D. R. Heise (ed.), *Sociological Methodology, 1977.* San Francisco: Jossey–Bass.
Johnston, J.
1972 *Econometric Methods.* Toronto: McGraw–Hill.
Joreskog, K. G., and D. Sorbom
1979 *Advances in Factor Analysis and Structural Equation Models.* Cambridge, Mass.: Abt Books.
Kasarda, J. D., and W. P. Shih
1977 "Optimal bias in ridge regression approaches to multicollinearity." *Sociological Methods and Research* 5: 461–471.
Kish, L.
1967 *Survey Sampling.* New York: Wiley.
Kmenta, J.
1971 *Elements of Econometrics.* New York: Macmillan.
Knoke, D.
1975 "A comparison of log–linear and regression models for systems of dichotomous variables." *Sociological Methods and Research* 3: 416–434.
Labovitz, S.
1967 "Some observations on measurement and statistics." *Social Forces* 46: 151–160.
1970 "The assignment of numbers to rank order categories." *American Sociological Review* 35: 515–524.
Maddala,
1977 *Econometrics.* New York: McGraw–Hill.
Malinvaud, E.
1970 *Statistical Method of Econometrics.* New York: Elsevier.
Mayer, T. F., and W. R. Arney
1974 "Spectral analysis and the study of social change." Pp. 309–355 in H. L. Costner (ed.), *Sociological Methodology, 1973–74.* San Francisco: Jossey–Bass.
McKelvey, R. D., and W. Zavoina
1975 "A statistical model for the analysis of ordinal level dependent variables." *Journal of Mathematical Sociology* 4: 103–120.
McNemar,
1962 *Psychological Statistics.* New York: Wiley.
Morrison, D. F.
1976 *Multivariate Statistical Methods.* New York: McGraw–Hill.

Nelson, C. R.
  1975   *Applied Time Series Analysis for Managerial Forecasting*. San Francisco: Holden Day.
Nicholson, W.
  1972   *Microeconomic Theory*. Hinsdale, Ill.: Dryden Press.
Pindyck, R. S., and D. L. Rubinfeld
  1981   *Econometric Models and Economic Forecasts* (2nd ed.). New York: McGraw–Hill.
Pugh, R. C.
  1968   "The partitioning of criterion score variance accounted for in multiple correlations."
         American Educational Research Journal 5: 639–646.
Rossie, P. H., R. A. Berk, and B. K. Eidson
  1974   *The Roots of Urban Discontent*. New York: Wiley.
Searle, S. R.
  1971   *Linear Models*. New York: Wiley.
Searle, S. R., and W. H. Hausman
  1970   *Matrix Algebra for Business and Economics*. New York: Wiley.
Simonton, D. K.
  1977   "Cross-sectional time-series experiments: Some suggested statistical analyses." *Psychological Bulletin* 3: 489–502.
Sonquist, J., E. Baker, and J. Morgan
  1973   *Searching for Structure*. Ann Arbor, Mich.: Institute for Social Research.
Specht, D. A., and R. D. Warren
  1975   "Comparing causal models." Pp. 46–82 in D. R. Heise (ed.), *Sociological Methodology, 1976*. San Francisco: Jossey–Bass.
Stromsdorfer, E. W., and G. Farkus
  1980   *Evaluation Studies Review Annual, Volume 5*. Beverly Hills: Sage Publications.
Wainer, H.
  1976   "Robust statistics: A survey and some prescriptions." *Journal of Educational Statistics* 1: 285–312.
Wilson, T. P.
  1971   "Critique of ordinal variables." Pp. 415–431 in H. M. Blalock (ed.), *Causal Models in the Social Sciences*. Chicago: Aldine.

Chapter 14

Analyzing Qualitative Data

D. Garth Taylor

14.1. INTRODUCTION

The title of this chapter is taken from A. E. Maxwell's little book published in 1961. Drawing from the work of statisticians and writing mainly for medical and biological scientists, Maxwell demonstrated many of the statistical results that had some bearing on the questions most commonly asked by the members of his audience as they analyzed qualitative data. The aim of this chapter is similar, with two important qualifications. First, since the audience is made up mostly of social researchers, every effort is made to deal with the problems as well as the opportunities afforded by the analysis of social survey data. The skills and training required for social researchers are shaped by the kinds of substantive questions we put to our data. Therefore some of the questions statisticians have answered are more important, from our point of view, than others. In this chapter the aim is to frame research questions as social researchers would ask them and, if possible, to choose among the available research techniques on the basis of the formulation of the questions that most directly serve our needs. The second qualification is that social researchers have become increasingly skilled at asking and answering their own questions about research methods. Therefore, in this chapter, I pay special attention to the developments in qualitative data analysis that were caused by social scientists' attempts to solve their own problems.

This chapter is not an introduction to qualitative data analysis. The choice of topics is guided by my own experience in learning survey analysis at the National Opinion Research Center and at the University of Chicago. After about 2 years of courses in statistics and qualitative data analysis, I found that there were several topics such as hierarchical modeling and the use of chi-square tests that had been covered quite thoroughly. However, there were other topics, such as the general theory of linear models for qualitative data and the use of particular advanced techniques such as design matrices for causal analysis that had not been covered and for which introductory treatments were not available.

There are two pedagogical aims of this chapter. The first is to discuss, at an advanced level, the key concepts and techniques of qualitative data analysis—an advanced treatment of beginning topics. The second aim is to introduce some advanced topics that are not covered in introductory books or articles. The chapter is written on the assumption that the reader has had some exposure to the ideas involved in qualitative data analysis. In the event that this is not true, there are introductory treatments available for most of the basic methods presented here: See, for example, Fleiss (1973), Payne (1977), or Upton (1978) in addition to the references cited later in this chapter. In addition, I am assuming that the reader is mathematically prepared for an introduction to the general linear model for contingency table analysis. This means that some exposure to matrix algebra and design matrices (or contrast coding) as used in the general linear regression model would be helpful.

This chapter discusses hierarchical modeling, latent structure analysis, log linear modeling, and the regression analysis of percentages in contingency tables. Other authors might have selected different topics. For instance, the discussion of latent structure analysis might have been in a chapter on measurement theory rather than here. On the other hand, I have not covered some topics such as quasi-independence, measures of association, and alternative general models for analysis (e.g., path analysis based on rank–order correlations). Some of these topics were excluded because of lack of space. Others were excluded because they are peripheral to the most interesting developments in the field of qualitative data analysis. What I have tried to do is provide a conceptually integrated approach to the major techniques that are used to analyze survey data and other kinds of qualitative data. The final decision to include or exclude a topic was made on the basis of whether that topic would aid or hinder the overall development of the argument.

Outline of Chapter Topics

Three different types of models are used to analyze qualitative data. First, there are models that focus on fitting the distribution of responses in a contingency table. Hierarchical modeling, analyses of the information in a frequency table, and studies using any of the several proposed indexes of dissimilarity are illustrations of this general approach to qualitative data analysis. These models are discussed in Section 14.2.

The third section of the chapter presents the foundations of latent structure analysis. Latent structure models are usually discussed in the context of measurement theory and factor analysis. The model described in Section 14.3 is in this tradition, but it also has some features that make it particularly helpful for some frequently encountered problems in survey analysis that are not mainly concerned with measurement theory. To illustrate the potential of latent structure analysis for survey problems some detailed examples are discussed.

Finally, Section 14.4 deals with general linear models for estimating proportions or logarithms of cell counts in a contingency table. In the literature on qualitative data analysis the proportion model is known as the Grizzle–Starmer–Koch technique, weighted least-squares for percentages, the Coleman model for effect parameters, and, Davis's model for systems of percentage differences, or, D-systems. The general linear model for logarithms of cell counts is known as log linear modeling, another way of applying the Grizzle–Starmer–Koch model, and, as a general method of logit analysis. The exposition assumes some familiarity with linear algebra and some exposure to the general linear model for regression analysis.

The choice of the percentage difference or the log linear model is often made arbitrarily. In fact, this choice may have important consequences for the interpretation of (and even conclusion as to the significance of) causal connections between variables. The concluding section of this chapter addresses some of the substantive issues involved in the choice between the log linear and the linear percentage difference model as well as some general comments about each of the models discussed in the chapter.

14.2. MODELING THE DISTRIBUTION OF CASES IN A CONTINGENCY TABLE

Hierarchical modeling (Goodman, 1972b, 1972c, 1976) is one of a family of procedures for modeling a set of expected frequencies in a contingency table and then using a chi-square test to compare the expected and observed frequencies to determine whether or not the expected frequencies fit the data. The hierarchical modeling procedure combines elements from two areas of research in theoretical statistics: (a) maximum likelihood procedures for modeling smoothed or adjusted frequencies in a contingency table (Deming, 1938; Deming & Stephan, 1940); and (b) developments in the theory of chi-square significance tests for the sampling designs and modeling techniques most often used in survey analysis (Lancaster, 1969).

This section is not a self-contained introduction to hierarchical modeling. The algorithm used to model the expected frequencies is only specified in nonmathematical terms. On the other hand, there is a fuller discussion of the chi-square tests than is usually found in introductory statements. In particular, we focus on the adjustments that must be made to use chi-square tests effectively with survey data, limitations of chi square as a tool for causal inference, and related problems. The discussion in this section is organized around the different steps in hierarchical modeling.

A Review of the Algorithm for Iterative Proportional Fitting

One of the earliest uses of the Deming–Stephan algorithm for iterative proportional fitting was to improve the accuracy of contingency tables arising from sample surveys. The model for table adjustment was used to supplement the data in the contingency table with better estimates of certain marginal distributions and interrelationships that were available from the U.S. Bureau of the Census. When there is the possibility of improving survey estimates in this way or when one wants to, a priori, set the values of certain parameters—for instance the sex ratio in the sample or the proportion of the sample in particular treatment and control groups (to smooth out the effects of differential attrition in an experimental design)—then the Deming–Stephan algorithm is usually the way to do it. The algorithm incorporates the a priori or external information into the distribution of cases in the contingency table, while leaving the remaining distributions and interrelationships unchanged.

The iterative proportional fitting algorithm has also been used for a quite different purpose: to smooth out the fluctuations in observed cell counts that could be attributed to sampling error in order to gain more accurate estimates of the true rates, proportions, or cell counts in the table. In the National Halothane Study (Bunker, Forest, Mosteller, & Vandam, 1969), for example, many of the principal substantive statements were based on the interpretation of percentages calculated from adjusted contingency tables.

Finally, the algorithm is central to the discussion of log linear modeling. As is explained in Section 14.4 of this chapter, Goodman's method for log linear modeling uses the Deming–Stephan algorithm to estimate a set of expected frequencies. The log linear model is then used to perform a regression analysis of the logarithms of the expected frequencies.

The algorithm for iterative proportional fitting is described in several works that assume no previous exposure to hierarchical modeling (see Davis, 1974; Fienberg, 1977; or Haberman, 1979). More technically advanced treatments of the same material appear in works by Goodman (1970) and Bishop, Fienberg, and Holland (1975). The exact mathematical details, therefore, will not be repeated here. The major features of the algorithm, as used for hierarchical modeling are:

1. The algorithm builds a table of modeled cell counts.
2. The total number of cases in the modeled table is always the same as the total in the observed table.
3. Information is taken from the observed table and added to the modeled table to make the modeled table closer to the observed table in the distribution of cases (this is similar to the early use of the Deming–Stephan algorithm to increase the accuracy of survey tables by adding in information from the Census).
4. At the final stage in hierarchical modeling the modeled table is usually different from the observed table but the difference is not believed to be statistically significant according to a chi-square test.

At this stage the residual differences between the observed and modeled data are interpreted as sampling fluctuations and the modeled data are taken as the more accurate representation of the cross-classification of the variables in the table.

The algorithm builds up the modeled table by selectively adding information from the observed data. The pieces of information that can be added to the modeled data are: the marginal distributions for each variable (called one-variable effects); the collapsed bivariate table for pairs of variables (two-variable interactions or two-way effects); collapsed three-way tables (three variable interactions or three-way effects); and so on up to $(p - 1)$ variable interactions where p is the number of variables in the cross-tabulation. It should be noted that the term *interaction* is used differently when discussing log linear models and hierarchical modeling than when discussing general linear regression models for continuous data. Here, the term *interaction* includes what other authors and other systems for data analysis have called main effects or two-way relationships as well as higher order effects. One should not change conventions of nomenclature without serious consideration and some form of downpayment, but in this case the change is worth the irritation.

When effects are added to a table of modeled frequencies the degrees of freedom for the difference between the observed and modeled data are reduced. The subtleties of hierarchical modeling involve the different ways chi square tests are used to evaluate the significance of particular effects that have been added to or deleted from the modeled data. The goal of hierarchical modeling is to use chi-square tests to determine which effects ought to be included in the iterative proportional fitting algorithm for the modeled data so that the table of modeled frequencies: (*a*) includes all of the important (i.e., significant) effects; and (*b*) excludes all other patterns in the observed data attributable to sampling error. Before discussing the opportunities and limitations arising from the use of chi-square tests for this purpose, we undertake a brief review of the rules for adding or deleting degrees of freedom.

We define a hypothetical four variable cross-classification with a total of 36 cells. Hypothetical variables A and B have three categories each; hypothetical variables C and D have two categories each. The simplest table of modeled frequencies that can be constructed for a table with 36 cells assumes that each cell contains 1/36 of the population. This is noted as model 1 in Table 14.1. Other than the sample size, no information from the observed 36-cell table is used to derive this set of modeled frequencies. Another way to say this is that no effects have been added to the modeled data (other than the sample size, which is always fit in the modeled table). Therefore there are 35 degrees of freedom for the comparison between the observed and modeled frequencies.

If we modify the modeled table so that the marginal totals for the modeled variables A, B, C, and D equal the marginal totals for the observed variables then we reduce the degrees of freedom by 6. When marginal totals for a variable are fit, the degrees of freedom are reduced by one less than the number of categories of that variable.

TABLE 14.1
Some Hierarchical Models for a Hypothetical Four-Way Table[a]

Model number	Effects included in modeled frequencies	Degrees of freedom for difference between modeled and observed frequencies
1	none (equiprobability model)	35
2	$(A)(B)(C)(D)$	29
3	$(AB)(AC)(AD)(BC)(BD)(CD)$	16
4	$(ABC)(D)$	17
5	$(ABC)(AD)$	15
6	$(ABC)(ABD)(CD)$	8
7	$(ABCD)$	0

[a] Hypothetical tables consists of variables A, B, C, and D. A and B have three categories each; C and D are dichotomies.

Usually in survey research the univariate marginal distributions of some or all of the variables in a cross-classification are taken to be a result of factors that do not bear on the substantive interpretations of the results. These factors include the sampling plan, question wording, collapsing of categories, and biological or cultural givens such as the sex or racial distribution of the sample. Thus, the practice is often to fit the marginal distributions before even raising the question of which effects ought to be included in the modeled data. In this sense Model 2 is a baseline for assessing the further contribution to the goodness of fit from models that contain more effects. The substantive interpretation of Model 2 may be further motivated by noting that fitting the marginal distributions is the multivariate extension of the method used to calculate the expected frequencies for the chi-square test for independence in a two-way table.

If there are significant two-way interactions (i.e., bivariate relations) or significant higher order interactions, the expected frequencies under Model 2 will be significantly different from the observed data. If we adjust the modeled data so that one or more collapsed bivariate tables (i.e., a table for the cross-classification of a pair of variables that is found by collapsing the full cross-tabulation over all other variables) in the modeled table is made equal to the corresponding collapsed bivariate table(s) in the observed data, then we are fitting a two-way interaction. The third model in Table 14.1 specifies that all two-way interactions have been fit in the modeled frequencies. The number of degrees of freedom for a two-way effect is equal to the product of the degrees of freedom for the marginal effects of each variable named in the two-way interaction. In the example, the (AB) effect has $(3 - 1) * (3 - 1) = 4$ degrees of freedom. Model 3 shows that when the adjusted data contain all the two-way interactions among variables A, B, C, and D there are 16 degrees of freedom for the discrepancy between the modeled data and the observed data. The total number of degrees of freedom for Model 1 is reduced first by 13 because of the degrees of freedom associated with the two-way interactions and then further reduced by 6 because a model that includes all two-way effects also includes all marginal effects by implication (for reasons explained in the following).

In general, it is possible to use the Deming–Stephan algorithm to fit any order of effect: three-way interactions; four-way interactions; and so on up to one less than the number of variables in the cross-tabulation (fitting the highest order interaction makes the modeled data exactly equal to the observed data—thus there are no degrees of freedom in Model 7). The degrees of freedom of any higher order interaction equals the product of the degrees of freedom for the one-way marginal effects for each variable named in the interaction.

The Deming–Stephan algorithm is such that the lower order effects *implied* by an interaction term are also automatically fit to the expected data when the interaction term is specified to be included in the modeled table. Thus model 5, which fits the (AD) interaction and the (ABC) interaction to the table of expected values, fits several other effects by implication. Fitting the (ABC) effect also fits the (AB), (AC), and (BC) effects as well as the (A), (B), and (C) effects. This is because fitting the (ABC) effect adjusts the expected frequencies so that the table for the three-way (ABC) interaction is the same in the expected and the observed data. Since the collapsed three-way (ABC) table is the same, any table that can be obtained by collapsing the (ABC) table will also be the same in the expected and observed data. In particular, all of the two-way tables and marginal distributions that can be obtained from the three-way (ABC) table will be the same in either set of frequencies. The general rule is that fitting higher order effects has hierarchical implications for some lower order effects. Therefore, the procedure of using the Deming–Stephan algorithm to model tables of expected values is known as hierarchical modeling.

Table 14.1 shows some other models that can be fit to the hypothetical four-variable cross-classification. We will return to some of these models to help clarify the discussion of chi-square statistics. Before leaving the topic of iterative proportional fitting, there is one further comment to be made about the use of baseline models. Model 2 was defined as a baseline model because it automatically fit all the effects that were presumed to be fixed by the design— artifactual, or in other ways of less substantive interest than the higher order effects. It is almost always the case in survey research that some or even most higher order effects are also of peripheral interest and should therefore be included as part of a baseline model. For instance, if the fourth variable in the example—variable D—is a dependent variable and A, B, and C are separate predictors or factors in an experimental design then the observed relation between A, B, and C is usually not of analytic interest. In other words, if the focus of interest is on the two-way and higher order interactions with D, then the appropriate baseline is model 4—$(ABC)(D)$. Further effects are tested to determine whether or not they significantly add to the explanatory power of Model 4. When the analysis is approached this way—when one variable is considered a response variable and all possible interactions among the remaining variables are included in every table of modeled frequencies—then the analysis is equivalent to logit analysis.

Descriptive Measures of the Difference between Observed and Expected Proportions

The Deming–Stephan algorithm is a method for generating expected cell frequencies for a model that assumes a certain causal structure to the observed contingency table. If the observed cell counts do not follow this structure, it is assumed to be due to sampling fluctuations and measurement error. Compared to other ways of modeling expected frequencies, the Deming–Stephan algorithm is especially useful because it is flexible enough to handle a wide range of hypotheses about the structure of the table and because the expected values satisfy the statistical criteria that justify the use of chi-square significance tests. Just as there are different methods for generating expected frequencies, there are many statistics that have been used to measure the dissimilarity between observed and expected cell counts. Chi square is the statistic used for hierarchical modeling because, unlike most other indices of dissimilarity, it can be used to make statistical inferences. Before exploring the pros and cons of chi-square statistics, however, it is useful to look at some of the general properties of indices of dissimilarity.

Several major works in empirical social science have relied on measures of the dissimilarity between observed and expected frequency distributions as the principal tool for analysis. The literature using Gini coefficients is one example of this approach (Duncan & Duncan, 1955). The literature using indices of racial segregation (Lieberson, 1963; Taeuber & Taeuber, 1965) is based on the same idea. The first step in calculating a Gini coefficient or an index of racial segregation is to predict the cell counts in a table of, for instance, race by school attended, under the hypothesis that school attended and racial composition are not correlated. The expected and observed distributions are then compared using one or more measures from a broad family of indices of dissimilarity.

Some measures of dissimilarity are based on the absolute deviation between the observed and expected proportions; most of the others are based on the squared deviation. The index of dissimilarity used by Taeuber and Taeuber (1965) is the average absolute discrepancy between the observed and expected proportions. (See Cortese, Falk, and Cohen, 1976, for an analysis of some of the sampling properties of this index.) It has been used by Hauser, Koffel, Travis, and Dickinson (1975a) as an alternative to chi square for assessing the goodness of fit of a hierarchical model and by Pullam (1975) as a measure of occupational inheritance. This index is particularly useful because of its substantive interpretation as the proportion of the cases that would have to be shifted to produce an even match between the observed and expected distributions. The "S" measure of segregation used by Coleman, Kelly, and Moore (1975) is based on squared deviations rather than absolute deviations. It is interpretable as the amount of variance in the cell counts attributable to racial differences (Zoloth, 1974) and can be shown to be a normed version of the goodness fit chi square under the hypothesis that race and geography are uncorrelated.

Some measures of dissimilarity transform the data before comparing the expected and observed frequency tables. The measure of entropy (Theil, 1970), which has been proposed as a measure of dissimilarity (Theil & Finizza, 1971), transforms the data by taking the proportions in each cell times the logarithm of the proportion and then compares this quantity with the value expected on the basis of the marginal distributions of the table. The resulting relative information statistic (Kullback, 1959) can be shown to be a transformation of the likelihood ratio chi square (Theil, 1970).

In general, any coefficient of association based on a proportional reduction in error (Goodman & Kruskal 1954) can be thought of as a normed index of the discrepancy between the observed frequencies and the expected data under some hypothesis about the way the observed data were generated. Some of these measures are flexible enough to provide additive measures of partial or higher order effects (e.g., Hawkes, 1971; Smith, 1972; Southwood, 1974). Reynolds (1977) reviews most of the literature on ordinal measures of association.

Many descriptive measures of dissimilarity summarize a great deal of information and thus obscure particular patterns in the data that might be of interest. Moreover, they do not possess the properties that will allow for statements of statistical significance. Chi square has the first problem but not the second—it is a summary measure with all the associated drawbacks, but it can be used (when appropriate adjustments are made) for statistical inference with survey data. The remainder of this section is devoted to a discussion of chi-square statistics and their use in hierarchical modeling.

Hierarchical Modeling and Chi-Square Comparisons between Observed and Expected Frequencies

A statement of the rationale for the use of chi square in qualitative data analysis raises a great many ultimate questions about the character of survey data and the statistical properties of cross-classifications. The most advanced treatments of these topics are by Lancaster (1969) and Haberman (1974). This section begins with a discussion of some of these questions since many of the rules of thumb in qualitative data analysis are designed to avoid problems stemming from the use of cell counts as statistical data. With the statistical groundwork in place, we then turn to a discussion of the use of significance tests in hierarchical modeling. The presentation is mainly focused on the complications and contradictions that can arise in the use of this procedure. For an exposition of hierarchical modeling that gives much more attention to the step-by-step details of the procedure the reader should consult Goodman (1971, 1972c) or Davis (1974).

STATISTICAL MODELS UNDERLYING CELL COUNTS

Chi-square tests cannot be used without making assumptions about the processes generating the data. The term *model* is used three different ways in justifying the use of chi-square significance tests. First, the expected frequencies are assumed to arise from some model that predicts the cell counts in the table. The Deming–Stephan algorithm is a procedure for modeling the expected values that incorporates as parameters the marginal effects and interaction effects described previously. Haberman (1979) describes another procedure for modeling the expected frequencies based on a regression model for estimating cell counts. Either procedure may be used for generating the expected frequencies for the chi-square tests and hierarchical modeling steps described here.

The second use of the term *model* is to describe the research design. Chi-square tests may be used when one of the following research designs may be assumed:

1. Each cell count in the table is an independent, Poisson variate and an estimate of the mean of the Poisson distribution generating the observation for that cell. An implication of this model, that motivates the goodness-of-fit chi square, is that the observed cell frequency is also an estimate of the variance of the underlying Poisson distribution. The Poisson model for the frequencies is subject to the constraint of a fixed sample size.

2. The observed contingency table is the realization of a sample from a multinomial distribution, given the sample size.

3. Each row (or column) of the table is an independent multinomial, given the total number of cases in the row (or column).

Practically speaking, designs 1 and 2 assume that the data are independent observations from the same population. This requirement rules out some research designs, such as snowball sampling, that are occasionally used. Design 3 assumes that certain margins in the table are fixed as, for instance, in an experimental design where a fixed number of cases is assigned to each experimental treatment. Again, there is the assumption that observations are independent within each treatment.

In discussions of log linear modeling, the research design is often referred to as the sampling model (e.g., Bishop *et al.*, 1975). This can be confusing because the chi-square formulas assume simple random sampling within the context of one of the three research designs. Most surveys do not use simple random sampling and so the third model that must be considered in using chi square is the sampling procedure. The implications of a multistage, clustered sample design for chi-square statistics are described later in this section.

DERIVATION OF CHI-SQUARE FORMULAS

One way to derive a chi-square formula is to examine the statistical properties of the expected and observed cell counts under each of the research designs just described. Under the Poisson sampling model, the expected value in a cell is a theoretical Poisson mean, and because of the definition of a Poisson distribution, the square root of the expected value is the estimate of the standard error of the estimate of the Poisson mean. In order to test the dissimilarity between the observed data and the frequencies expected under a particular model we construct a normal deviate by subtracting the means (observed minus expected) and dividing by the standard error (the square root of the expected). The square of a normal deviate is a chi-square variate, and thus, if we sum the squares of these normal deviates over all the cells in the table we have the Pearson goodness-of-fit chi square statistic:

$$\chi^2 = \sum_i \left(\frac{O_i - E_i}{\sqrt{E_i}}\right)^2 = \sum_i \frac{(O_i - E_i)^2}{E_i} \tag{14.1}$$

where χ^2 denotes the goodness-of-fit chi square; O_i denotes the observed frequency in cell i, and E_i denotes the expected frequency in cell i. A similar set of calculations can be made under each of the other two research designs and will yield the same chi-square formula.

An alternative derivation of chi square begins with the model generating the expected frequencies (i.e., model in the first sense of the word). The maximum of the likelihood function under the model for the expected frequencies divided by the maximum of the likelihood under a less restrictive model forms the likelihood ratio. The formula for the likelihood ratio for contingency table data is:

$$\text{Likelihood ratio} = \prod_i \left(\frac{E_i}{A_i}\right)^{A_i} \tag{14.2}$$

where E_i denotes the expected frequencies; A_i denotes the observed frequencies or the expected frequencies under a less restrictive model. Chi square is calculated by taking -2 times the logarithm of the likelihood ratio. This is known as the likelihood ratio chi square:

$$L^2 = -2 \sum_i A_i \ln\left(\frac{E_i}{A_i}\right) \tag{14.3}$$

where L^2 denotes the likelihood ratio chi square; ln denotes the natural logarithm; and A_i and E_i are defined as in formula (14.2). One advantage of the likelihood ratio chi square is that the expected cell counts in a more restrictive model (in the sense of the number of degrees of freedom used) can be directly compared with the expected counts in any less restrictive model in testing for the statistical significance of the difference between the two models. With the goodness-of-fit chi square the comparison is always between the expected frequencies and the observed data. Therefore, some authors recommend using the likelihood ratio chi square for sequential tests in hierarchically ordered models.

CHI-SQUARE ADJUSTMENTS FOR COMPLEX SAMPLES

The application of formula (14.1) or formula (14.3) leads to a chi-square statistic that is appropriate for testing hypotheses on data obtained using simple random sampling procedures. In fact, most survey data are collected under multistage, clustered, and/or stratified sampling procedures. These sampling designs are economically more efficient in the sense that they provide the greatest amount of information for the dollar, but one of the costs of a complex design is that the estimate of the variance for a mean or a proportion is too low by a factor known as the design effect (cf Kish, 1965). The impact of the design effect on the chi-square calculation is best understood in terms of formula (14.1). The goodness-of-fit chi square is interpretable as the squared difference between the observed and expected values in a cell divided by the variance of the expected value. The variance of the expected value, however, ought to be increased by some amount to adjust for the effect of the sampling design. Theoretically, this would require that the design effect be calculated for each cell of each table analyzed. In practice this is a costly undertaking. The usual procedure is to calculate a general design effect for the survey and divide each chi square by this factor before drawing conclusions as to significance. Hauser *et al.* (1975a) use a design effect of 1.6 for data from the Current Population Survey. Each chi-square statistic in the series of hierarchical models tested was divided by 1.6 before any inferences were made. Scheuren (1973) reports that the design effect for proportions in his Current Population Survey data is approximately 1.5. After a series of studies using the national surveys from the Survey Research Center at Michigan, Kish (1957) reports that the design effect for most variables is between 1 and 2 although variables that are highly clustered geographically (e.g., factors associated with race) can have much larger design effects. In practice it seems that to minimize the chance of falsely accepting a hypothesis (e.g., Type I error) a safe correction for most survey applications is to use 2.0 as the estimate of the design effect and divide the chi-square statistics by this factor before making inferences.

In an extension of this work, Kish and Frankel (1970) find that under the same sampling procedures the design effects for the linear and log linear regression coefficients considered in Section 14.4 are not likely to be as large as the design effects for the chi-square calculations considered here. If we use 2.0 as the chi-square correction factor, then for the same sample it is necessary to multiply the standard errors for the linear or log linear slopes (effect parameters) by 1.15 before making statistical inferences.

HIERARCHICAL MODELING

The aim of hierarchical modeling is to find the set of modeled cell frequencies that: (*a*) fits the observed data (in the sense that the chi square for dissimilarity between observed and modeled data is not significant); (*b*) does not contain unnecessary effects—effects that are not individually significant according to chi square or some other criterion; and (*c*) does contain all statistically significant effects. It is always possible to increase the goodness of fit of a set of modeled frequencies by adding more information from the observed table. Indeed, fitting the highest order interaction term will make the modeled frequencies exactly the same as the observed frequencies. The goal of hierarchical modeling is to eliminate as many of the interactions as possible and still have a set of modeled data similar to the observed frequencies. Put another way, the aim is to find the most parsimonious set of effects necessary to account statistically for the observed cell counts.

Whether a model fits the data is a question of whether or not the adjusted chi square is too big given the number of effects that were *not* modeled into the expected frequencies. The expected value of chi square under the hypothesis that the observed and modeled frequencies are the same except for sampling fluctuations is equal to the degrees of freedom. When the ratio of chi square to the degrees of freedom is greater than 1.0 there is some indication that the data depart significantly from the model. The magnitude of the ratio that is necessary for a certain level of statistical significance depends on the degrees of freedom and is tabulated in several places. Plackett (1974) and others use the result that the variance of the chi-square distribution is about twice the degrees of freedom to suggest that for reasonably large degrees of freedom (over 7) the quantity:

$$Z = (2 * \chi^2)^{1/2} - [(2 * df) - 1]^{1/2} \qquad (14.4)$$

is distributed approximately as a normal deviate and can be used to assess the significance level for the goodness of fit of a hierarchical model. That is, when Eq. (14.4) is greater than 1.96, the difference between the observed and modeled frequencies is significant at the .05 level.

Whether an individual effect in a hierarchical model is statistically significant or not is a little more difficult to determine. The basic procedure is to: (*a*) calculate the chi square for two models that differ only in the presence of the effect in question; and then (*b*) determine if the difference in chi square for the two models is significant, with the degrees of freedom equal to the degrees of freedom associated with the effect in question. If the difference in chi squares is significant then the effect should be included in the model for generating the expected frequencies. If the "reduction chi square" is not significant then the conclusion is that the effect should not be included in the model. For example, if we determine that Model 5 in Table 14.1 fits the data and we want to test the significance of the (*AD*) term we would proceed as follows:

1. Calculate the chi square for the (*ABC*)(*AD*) model. There are 15 degrees of freedom for this model.
2. Fit the model that is exactly the same as the model in Step 1 except for the absence of the (*AD*) effect. This is Model 4; there are 17 degrees of freedom for this model.
3. Subtract the chi square in Step 1 from the chi square in Step 2. This is the chi square for the significance of the (*AD*) effect, to be tested on 2 degrees of freedom.

This same procedure can be used to test the significance of entire sets of effects. For instance, the significance of the set of all two-way interactions in our hypothetical data can be found by assessing the significance of the difference in chi square between models 2 and 3 on 14 degrees of freedom.

Davis (1974) and Goodman (1971, 1972c) have suggested systematic search procedures for finding the best model (the one that fits the data, contains only significant effects, and does not leave out significant effects). Scheuren (1973) and Hauser *et al.* (1975a) provide several detailed examples of testing models by successively adding and deleting effects. Unfortunately, there is no agreed upon procedure for model selection and different tests can lead to different conclusions regarding the appropriate final model and/or the significance of individual effects. It is to these problems, and other complications with chi-square tests, that we now turn.

COMPLICATIONS WITH CHI SQUARE

The principle threat to the validity of chi-square tests (and the principle cause of ambiguous or confusing results) occurs when a model has produced expected values close to zero. The statistical theory that justifies the use of chi square for statements of significance is only valid for large samples of data. As the sample size becomes smaller and, therefore, as the expected count in each cell becomes smaller, the expected value and the variance of the chi square (for the hypothesis of no difference between modeled and observed cell counts) become larger. This violates the assumption of the significance test and makes the use of the tabulated chi-square tables inappropriate. The expected value of the chi square increases slightly, by a factor of $(df * N)/(N - 1)$, where df is the degrees of freedom and N is the sample size. For survey research applications, this will usually be a trivial adjustment. The variance of the chi-square statistic, however, is much more sensitive to small cells and a small sample size. The details of the problem are explained by Maxwell (1961; see also Cochran, 1954) for the two-way table. In principle, the chi square could be adjusted to take account of the small cells but in practice the exact solution is far too cumbersome to be applied to most three-way and higher order tables.

The practical implication of violating the assumption of large expected values in all cells is that the chi-square tests become unreliable. Because the modeling algorithms adjust the expected frequencies in complicated ways, there are no simple rules of thumb that can be given regarding the type of error that will be made in interpreting the chi square in the face of small expected values. The question naturally arises: When are there too many small expected values? Some theoretical derivations and simulations of the problem have been done, leading to Cochran's (1954) advice: If no more that 20% of the cells have expectations less than 5 then a single expectation near 1 is allowable in computing chi square. Another empirical approach to this problem would be to take the following steps:

1. After fitting a model, examine the expected values and the contribution to the goodness-of-fit chi square for each cell.

2. Using the techniques for fitting structural zeroes [beyond the scope of this chapter, but explained by Haberman (1979) and Goodman (1968)], delete the suspicious cell(s) from the table.
3. Adjust the degrees of freedom and recompute the sequence of chi-square tests (either goodness of fit or likelihood ratio may be used) to determine if the same effects are included in the best fitting model.

If the model arrived at using this technique is different from the original "final" model, then it is likely that the previous result was unduly affected by small expected values that invalidated the chi-square estimates.

When Cochran's rule of thumb suggests that chi-square tests may be inappropriate because of small cells, one of two corrective measures is usually taken. Several authors recommend adding a small constant to each cell in the observed table before beginning the analysis. Gart and Zweifel (1967) show that the numerical adjustment that adds the least bias to the result is to add .5 to each cell at the outset. If this still leaves too many small cells, then one might try collapsing categories of variables that are badly skewed or highly correlated with other variables and therefore produce small frequencies in the table of expected values. The rule of avoiding categories containing less than 20% of the population (e.g., Davis, 1971) almost always avoids the small cell problem. However, Bishop (1971) criticizes this rule on the grounds that it may lose important information about interactions or inconsistencies occurring near the extreme ends of the distribution of responses. In a more forceful vein, one of the readers of the first draft of this chapter argued that the 20% rule would also avoid learning anything sociologically interesting.

Compared to small cells, the other complications with chi square seem completely tractable. Since the goodness-of-fit chi square and the likelihood ratio chi square are calculated using different formulas, they almost never take the same value and sometimes even disagree as to whether a model fits the data or whether a particular effect is significant. Since each chi square is an estimate of the same theoretical value, all we can say is that the tests disagree and there is no basis for choosing one over the other. In the literature on hierarchical modeling there is a preference for the likelihood ratio chi square. The basis for this preference is not that the likelihood ratio is more accurate or less sensitive to small cells. Rather, the preference arises because the goodness-of-fit chi square sometimes yields negative values when individual effects are tested for significance using the steps in hierarchical modeling. These values should be interpreted as zero when they occur. To complicate matters further, a third significance test frequently used in log linear modeling has the form of a t-test: an estimate of a parameter divided by its standard error. If the ratio exceeds some critical value, the effect is believed to be significant. This test does not always agree with the chi-square test for significance of that effect and, once again, neither can be said to be more accurate.

In general, when significance tests of the same set of effects disagree it usually means that the effects are of borderline significance (although small cells may also be complicating the problem). In this event the best procedure is to increase the sample size. In the (usual) event that this is impossible one tries to build an inferential net by: noting whether the sign of the relationship is in the expected direction; replicating the analysis with similar variables from the same data set; studying internal replications that may exist in the same data set—for instance the General Social Survey conducted by the Natonal Opinion Research Center usually repeats the same questions in independent yearly samples; and, finally, studying other data sets that have the same variables to see if the relationship there is of the same magnitude and direction.

The complications with chi square discussed so far have arisen from small expected values and from significance tests that disagree. The third complication is that tests of significance of a particular effect (or set of effects) can give contradictory results depending on the other effects included in the model. For instance, returning to Table 14.1, when the (AD) effect is tested for significance by deleting it from Model 3, the chi square (either one) for the (AD) effect is usually not the same as the chi square obtained by deleting (AD) from other models (for instance Model 5). The disagreement between the chi squares may be large enough that the effect is significant by one test and not by the other. This is usually an indication of borderline significance (although the small cell tests should also be invoked) and the steps outlined in the last paragraph for building a net of inferential evidence should be followed.

A fourth complication with hierarchical modeling is that the best model (defined earlier as the most parsimonious fit of the data, including only significant effects, and including all significant effects) is frequently impossible to define. The reason is that a model may fit the data but exclude significant effects. Model 4 in Table 14.1 may fit the data, however, a comparison between Models 4 and 5 may find that the (AD) effect is significant. In this case, Model 4 is most parsimonious but Model 5 includes more significant effects. This is not usually a problem arising from small cells or borderline significance. Rather, the problem is that the degrees of freedom for the fit of a hierarchical model may include many nonsignificant effects and one or two significant effects. When these are combined into a blanket test, the result is that the average degree of freedom left out of the model is not significant. The solution to this problem is to use some non-chi-square criterion to look at the importance of the effect in question for explaining the patterns in the data. For instance, the index of dissimilarity (Duncan & Duncan, 1955) may find that the observed and expected proportions disagree on average by .10 under the model without the effect in question but only by .03 under the model that includes the effect. In this case, there is evidence that the effect ought to be included even though it makes the final model less parsimonious. This problem with using the index of dissimilarity or some other criterion for the decision of what effects to include in the final model is that the judgments are subjective and therefore the decision rules are hard to state precisely.

The final complicaton with chi square examined in this section is that chi-square tests can lead to the wrong conclusion about the presence of interaction between polytomous variables. To return to the example in Table 14.1, let us assume that variable *A* is religion measured in three categories (Protestant, Catholic, Jew) and variable *B* is attendance at religious services in three categories (daily, weekly, rarely). There are four degrees of freedom for the interaction between religion and attendance. But let us assume that Protestants and Catholics have exactly the same levels of attendance whereas Jews attend less often. A way to focus on the significant patterns in the data, then, is to make each variable a dichotomy with religion coded Jew versus other and attendance coded rarely versus other. The complication with chi square is that the interaction between religion and attendance may be significant in the fourfold table but not in the original ninefold table where each variable was measured in three categories. The reason for this is not small cell sizes (although this will exacerbate the problem) and not exactly the same as the problem of borderline significance (although the problem will occur most often when the interaction in the fourfold table is near borderline significance). The reason is that the interaction in the table is concentrated in one particular degree of freedom (defined by the fourfold table of religion by attendance) whereas the initial chi-square test was based on four degrees of freedom. The problem is that one degree of freedom shows a significant interaction and the other three do not, resulting in an average interaction for the table that is not significant.

Cochran (1954) and Maxwell (1961) suggest ways of collapsing contingency tables to test the significance of individual degrees of freedom that might have been misinterpreted by the blanket chi-square test. Goodman (1969a) applied these "ransacking" procedures to mobility tables. Another method for analyzing individual degrees of freedom is to delete cells from the table using models for fitting structural zeroes (Goodman, 1968; Haberman, 1979). This technique has been used to analyze errors of self-coding of occupation in social surveys (Taylor, 1976). A related method for using the iterative proportional fitting algorithm to focus on individual degrees of freedom has been proposed by Hauser *et al.* (1975a,b) and Duncan (1975).

The advanced techniques for chi-square analysis of individual degrees of freedom are beyond the scope of this chapter. The problems are raised here because they are current areas of new research in qualitative data analysis. The general linear models for qualitative data presented in Section 14.4 are quite flexible in their ability to focus on individual degrees of freedom and therefore do not suffer from some of the complications of chi square.

EXPLAINED VARIANCE?

There are epistemological problems with applying the notion of explained variance to contingency table research. Strictly speaking, every analysis technique described in this chapter attempts to explain, predict, or otherwise account for the cell counts or proportions in a cross-classification. Qualitative data analysis techniques do *not* attempt to predict the scores of individual cases in the survey and so the notion of explained variance, as it is commonly used in regression analysis, is not appropriate.

When there is a reasonable baseline model for a table—that is, when some effects are fixed as part of the research design or are in other ways uninteresting—then it is reasonable to judge the degree of improvement in fitting the observed frequencies that is gained by using a more complex model than the baseline. The statistic, interpretable as the percentage reduction in dissimilarity (using the chi-square dissimilarity measure) is:

$$R^2 = 1 - \frac{L^2 \text{ for the complex model}}{L^2 \text{ for the baseline model}} \qquad (14.5)$$

where R^2 is the percentage improvement and L^2 is the likelihood ratio chi square. It would be preferable to use some symbol other than "R^2" for Eq. (14.5), but this is what has been proposed (Goodman, 1971; Haberman, 1979).

14.3. LATENT STRUCTURE ANALYSIS

This section assumes that the reader has had no introduction to latent structure analysis. The purpose of the section is to convince the reader that it is worthwhile to learn more about the topic. The model that is the basis for the discussion is presented in more complete detail in Goodman (1974a, 1974b). These sources should be consulted for the details of the iterative procedure used to calculate the model parameters and for several interesting applications of the model that go beyond the modest examples presented here.

During most of its history, latent structure analysis has been an esoteric topic in survey analysis with a literature mainly devoted to expository essays and methodological debates (Lazarsfeld, 1951, 1954; Lazarsfeld & Henry, 1968). The recent generation of latent structure models (Goodman, 1974b; Haberman 1979) has solved many of the methodological limitations of previous approaches and promises to be applicable to a wide range of problems in survey analysis.

An Overview of Latent Structure Models

One of the central concepts in survey analysis is the notion of an explanatory variable (Rosenberg, 1968). A relationship between two variables is explained when a third variable is found that, when controlled, causes the partial relationship between the original pair of variables to go to zero. The task of the survey analyst is to find variables that fully or at least partially explain relationships.

Latent structure analysis is an alternative way of explaining the relationships in a table. The model assumes that there is an unmeasured variable that explains (in Rosenberg's sense) the observed relationship in the table. When the latent variable is controlled, the partial relationships and higher order interactions between all of the other variables go to zero. For an explanatory variable to have this effect it must be correlated with each variable in the original table. One group of parameters in the latent structure model estimates the correlations between the latent variable and the observed variables. In order to reproduce the cell counts in the observed table it is also necessary to know the proportion of the sample in each category of the unobserved variable and the sample size. Thus, the second group of parameters in the latent structure model consists of the estimated marginals for the unobserved variable. The third type of parameter is the sample size. (This is always furnished, making the total number of degrees of freedom for modeling one less than the number of cells in the table, just as in hierarchical modeling.)

Once the parameters for the latent class model are estimated, it is possible to generate a set of expected cell counts and test the hypothesis that the specified latent class model explains the data. Either chi-square test (goodness of fit or likelihood ratio) can be used for this comparison. The number of degrees of freedom for this test equals the difference between the number of cells in the table and the number of parameters (including the sample size) in the latent class model.

If the latent class model does not fit the data it means that the observed cross-tabulation could not have resulted from the model as it is specified. That is, the variables could not have been independent given the latent variable, thus violating the assumption used to identify the parameter estimates, thus invalidating the model.

An Algebraic Introduction

Table 14.2 was initially reported by Stouffer and Toby (1951) and used by Goodman (1974b) as an example of latent structure analysis. There are 216 respondents classified with respect to whether they tend toward universalistic (1) or particularistic (2) values when confronted by four different situations of role conflict. The letters A, B, C, and D denote the dichotomous responses when confronted by the four different situations. Before moving to a latent structure model it is instructive to show the formulas for testing the hypothesis that the four variables in Table 14.2 are completely independent of one another. This model is represented by the following equation for the expected proportions:

$$p_{ijkl}^{ABCD} = p_i^A * p_j^B * p_k^C * p_l^D \qquad (14.6)$$

where p_{ijkl}^{ABCD} is the proportion in the ($ijkl$) cell of the cross-classification of variables A, B, C, and D; and $p_i^A p_j^B p_k^C p_l^D$ are the marginal proportions for variables A, B, C, and D. Since each variable is dichotomous, the model in Eq. (14.6) requires four parameters. When the expected cell counts under this model are compared with the observed cell counts in Table 14.2, the result, not surprisingly, is that the model does not fit the data: The different measures of universalism and particularism are, in fact, correlated. The goodness-of-fit chi square for the independence model is 104.12, the likelihood ratio chi square is 81.13, both significant on 11 degrees of freedom.

TABLE 14.2
Cross-Classification of Four Measures of Universalistic versus Particularistic Value Orientations[a]

A	B	C	D 1	D 2
1	1	1	42	23
		2	6	25
1	2	1	6	24
		2	7	38
2	1	1	1	4
		2	1	6
2	2	1	2	9
		2	2	20

[a] From Stouffer S. and J. Toby, 1951, "Role conflict and personality." *American Journal of Sociology* 56: 395–406.

The reason the failure of the independence model is not surprising is that we think of universalism–particularism as a trait possessed by individuals and therefore it is likely that people's scores on different measures of this trait will tend to agree. The correlations among variables A, B, C, and D come about because, in latent structure terminology, there is an unobserved variable that sorts people the same way on each measure. If we could control for this unobserved variable, people's scores on A, B, C, and D would be independent.

The researcher specifies the number of categories in the latent variable. The latent structure model then estimates the proportion of the sample in each category of the latent variable X. This probability is denoted "π_t^x." It is assumed that the latent categories are a mutually exclusive and exhaustive classification of the population. Therefore, the π_t^x sum to one. The marginals on the latent variable are often the most interesting statistics in the analysis since they reflect the classification of the sample into different *types* of people according to their ideology, predispositions, or some other unobserved variable.

If we posit an underlying universalism–particularism variable that accounts for the correlation in Table 14.2, the simplest model assumes that the unobserved variable has two categories. To say that the latent variable, X, accounts for the correlations in Table 14.2 is to say that A, B, C, and D are independent within each category of X. Of course, X is not an observed variable. But if X were an observed variable the model for conditional independence of A, B, C, and D given X implies that the cell probabilities in the full

(*ABCDX*) table could be written as

$$p_{ijklt}^{ABCDX} = \pi_{it}^{\bar{A}X} * \pi_{jt}^{\bar{B}X} * \pi_{kt}^{\bar{C}X} * \pi_{lt}^{\bar{D}X} * \pi_{t}^{X} \qquad (14.7)$$

where p_{ijklt}^{ABCDX} are the cell proportions in the hypothetical (*ABCDX*) table; π_{t}^{X} is the proportion of the population in latent class t; $\pi_{it}^{\bar{A}X}$ is the probability that variable A takes value i given that $X = t$. This is the conditional probability or the conditional marginal for A given X. In this notation the bar indicates a random variable; $\pi_{jt}^{\bar{B}X}$ $\pi_{kt}^{\bar{C}X}$ $\pi_{lt}^{\bar{D}X}$ are the conditional probabilities for B, C, and D. It is assumed that within any latent class the sample is classified into one of the categories of each observed variable. Therefore, for any t the conditional probabilities sum to one.

The conditional probabilities and the latent class marginals are the parameters estimated by the algorithm for latent structure modeling. The details of this procedure are given by Goodman (1974a, 1974b). In the latent structure model we have specified, there are nine independent parameters: the proportion of the sample in latent class 1 (knowing this parameter fixes the proportion in latent class 2 since the latent variable is dichotomous); the probability that $A = 1$ when $X = 1$ (knowing this fixes the probability that $A = 2$ when $X = 1$ since A is dichotomous); the probability that $A = 1$ when $X = 2$; and similar conditional probabilities. The conditional probabilities reflect the correlation between the latent variable and each observed variable. The correlation between the latent variable X and the observed variable A can be thought of as the change in the probability that $A = i$ caused by going from one category to another on X.

The parameters of our two category latent class model for Table 14.2 are shown in Table 14.3. The marginal probabilities for X show 27.9% of the population classified as belonging to the first latent class and therefore 72.1% are in the other. The meaning of these latent classes can be understood by examining the conditional probabilities. The members of latent class 1 have over a .90 probability of answering questions A, B, and C in the universalistic direction (i.e., the probabilities that A, B, and C are 1 when X is 1 are all above .90). It is a little less likely that question D will be answered in a universalistic direction by members of this class but even there the chances are over 75%. So, we can characterize latent class 1 as a relatively small group (27.9% of the sample) that almost always answers in the universalistic direction, whatever the circum-

TABLE 14.3
Estimated Latent Class Parameters for Two-Class
Model for Data in Table 14.2 with Latent Class
Probability $\pi_{1}^{X} = .279$

Latent class	Conditional probabilities			
	π_{1}^{A}	π_{1}^{B}	π_{1}^{C}	π_{1}^{D}
1	.993	.940	.927	.769
2	.714	.330	.354	.132

stance. The other group, the majority of the population, discriminates a great deal between circumstances in its universalistic responses. For question A there is a 71.4% chance that this group will respond in a universalistic direction. On the other hand, it is quite unlikely (.132 probability) that question D will be answered in this direction. We can characterize latent class 2, then, as a large group that discriminates between circumstance in its universalistic responses.

The question arises: Does this model fit the data? The procedure for testing goodness of fit is a little roundabout. We begin by noting that our model has nine parameters, in addition to the sample size, and therefore there are six degrees of freedom for the goodness of fit test. With the marginals on X and the conditional probabilities we use formula (14.7) (and the sample size) to find the expected cell counts in the cross-tabulation of variables $A, B, C,$ and D and unobserved variable X. This is shown in Table 14.4. This table is not the same as other cross-tabulations because X is not an observed variable. Even so, tables such as this are a great help in understanding the latent structure model.

The left half of the table shows the distribution of cases in the first latent category of X. (Note: Table 14.4 shows a whole number of cases in each latent category of X; the actual modeling algorithm does not round the expected frequencies.) Within each category of X the observed variables are independent. The marginals for the observed variables in each category of X equal the conditional probabilities shown in Table 14.3.

Table 14.4 is collapsed over the unobserved variable to generate the expected frequencies under the latent class model. In formal notation, the equation for the expected proportions under any latent class model is:

$$\hat{p}_{ijkl}^{ABCD} = \sum_t \pi_{it}^{\bar{A}X} * \pi_{jt}^{\bar{B}X} * \pi_{kt}^{\bar{C}X} * \pi_{lt}^{\bar{D}X} * \pi_t^X \tag{14.8}$$

TABLE 14.4
Cross-Classification of Universalism–Particularism Measures from Table 14.2 with Hypothetical Two-Category Latent Variable

			D					D	
A	B	C	1	2	A	B	C	1	2
1	1	1	39.92	11.99	1	1	1	1.72	11.29
		2	3.14	.94			2	3.13	20.61
1	2	1	2.55	.77	1	2	1	3.49	22.93
		2	.20	.06			2	6.36	41.85
2	1	1	.28	.08	2	1	1	.69	4.52
		2	.02	.01			2	1.26	8.26
2	2	1	.02	.01	2	2	1	1.40	9.19
		2	.00	.00			2	2.55	16.76

$$\pi_1^x = .279 \qquad\qquad \pi_2^x = .721$$
$$n_1 = 60 \qquad\qquad n_2 = 156$$

TABLE 14.5
Expected Values for Two-Class Latent Structure
Model for Data in Table 14.2

			D	
A	B	C	1	2
1	1	1	41.64	23.28
		2	6.27	21.55
1	2	1	6.04	23.70
		2	6.56	41.91
2	1	1	.97	4.60
		2	1.28	8.27
2	2	1	1.42	9.20
		2	2.55	16.76

where $\hat{p}_{ijkl}^{ABCD}$ is the expected proportion in the $(ijkl)$ cell of the $(ABCD)$ table under a latent class model. The expected frequencies under the two-class latent structure model are shown in Table 14.5. These frequencies are remarkably similar to the observed cell counts. The goodness-of-fit chi square and the likelihood ratio chi square both equal 2.72 (coincidentally) with 6 degrees of freedom. We conclude that the two-class model described earlier fits the data quite well.

Complications and Applications

The major objection to latent structure analysis is that it cannot be rationalized into a series of steps that lead to a relatively unambiguous choice of a final model. The two-class model fits the data in Table 14.2 quite well but there is no guarantee that this is the appropriate way to think of the data or that some other model would not in some sense be better.

There is one mathematical feature of the latent structure model beyond those already considered that makes it an extremely flexible tool and makes the objection even more potent. The latent class marginals and the conditional probabilities can be set to arbitrary values or constrained to equal one another. When there are a priori or theoretical values for certain parameters then these values are substituted at the appropriate place in the modeling algorithm. The result is that fewer parameters are estimated and degrees of freedom are thus saved.

The latent structure analysis of Table 14.2 suggests that one class of people virtually always responds in terms of universalistic criteria. This pattern could be incorporated into the model as an a priori constraint on the conditional probabilities for A, B, C, and D when X equals one: $\pi_{11}^{AX} = \pi_{11}^{BX} = \pi_{11}^{CX} = \pi_{11}^{DX} = 1$. Goodman (1974b) incorporates this restriction into one of his models for the data in Table 14.2. He adds a third latent class for people who always respond according to individualistic criteria (conditional probabilities all equal zero). The resulting model fits the data about as well as the unrestricted two-class model, but there are fewer parameters estimated, suggesting a preference for the three-class model.

This flexibility in allocating degrees of freedom between latent class marginals and conditional probabilities makes it possible to specify a nearly endless number of models for almost any cross-classification. Some of the most interesting developments in latent structure analysis have been the specification and testing of models that, because of their restrictions, incorporate the theoretical properties of Guttman scales (Goodman, 1975) and Likert scales (Clogg, 1979). The example that follows extends to the latent structure model in a different way. The unobserved variables are brought back into a cross-tabulation to be analyzed according to the rules for hierarchical modeling and linear modeling that are outlined in Sections 14.2 and 14.4.

A MIXED MODEL FOR ANALYZING ABORTION OPINION

In this example a three-category latent class model is used to analyze responses to a three-item scale of attitudes toward legalized abortion (Blake, 1971; Ryder & Westoff, 1971). The model is estimated for six different groups in the population: Protestants and Catholics, each at three educational levels. The data for non-Catholics and Catholics who have 12 years of education are shown in Table 14.6.

The latent structure model used to analyze these data assumes there are three latent classes corresponding to three types of people who differ in the way they think about legalized abortion. The formal aspects of the model are similar to Goodman's (1974b) three-class model for the data in Table 14.2. Type 1 consists of people who believe that abortion is a matter of personal choice and should be regulated only by canons of sound medical practice. It is assumed that these people will endorse legalized abortion for any reason asked about in the list of questions. Type 3 consists of people who are, in principal, absolutely opposed to abortion and therefore will oppose it no matter the validity of the reason asked about in the specific question. For Type 1 cases we assume the conditional probability of a proabortion response to any abortion item is 1.0, for Type 3 cases we assume the probability of a proabortion response is 0 no matter the question. In the middle are the Type 2 people, whom we hypothesize evaluate each particular question according to the validity of the circumstance that is offered as a justification for allowing a legal abortion.

There are five parameters to be estimated for this latent class model: the two independent latent class probabilities and the three conditional probabilities of a proabortion response for the Type 2 respondents. It is not necessary to estimate the conditional probabilities of a proabortion response for the Type 1 and Type 3 respondents since these are assumed to be 1.0 and zero under the specification of the model. Since there are five parameters (not including the sample size) to be estimated, there are 2 degrees of freedom for testing the goodness of fit of this model in each of our six sample populations.

TABLE 14.6
Responses to Three-Item Abortion Scale for Catholics and
Non-Catholics Who Have Completed 12 Years of Education[a]

Religion	Abortion			
	Too poor	Defect	Not want any more	
			For	Against
Non-Catholic	For	For	512	34
		Against	10	4
	Against	For	115	339
		Against	8	129
Catholic	For	For	177	18
		Against	1	1
	Against	For	47	175
		Against	4	115

[a] From Pooled 1972–1975 NORC General Social Surveys.
[b] The three questions are: Please tell me whether or not you think it should be possible for a pregnant woman to obtain a legal abortion if . . .
  1. The family is too poor to afford any more children?
  2. If there is a strong chance of a serious defect in the baby?
  3. If she is married and does not want any more children?

The latent class parameters for the high-school-educated Catholics and non-Catholics are shown in Table 14.7. Comparing the distributions in the latent classes, we see that the non-Catholics are more likely to be in latent Class 1 and Catholics are more likely to be in Class 3. The proportion of type 2 respondents is the same for Catholics and non-Catholics—about 49%.

When we look more closely at the conditional probabilities for those in Class 2, we see that they are quite similar for Catholics and non-Catholics. For Type 2 respondents of either religious group, a likely birth defect is an extremely valid reason for allowing an abortion. The conditional probability of a proabortion response to this question is about 90%. The other two reasons are, for the most part, rejected by Type 2 respondents in either religious group. The conditional probability of a proabortion response is near 20–25% if the family is too poor to afford children and near 10% if the family simply does not want any more children.

The overall pattern in Table 14.7 indicates that an equal percentage of high school educated Catholics and non-Catholics are in the Type 2 middle ground (where each reason for an abortion is analyzed on its merits) and that the validity of each reason (the probability of a proabortion response) is about the same for high-school-educated Type 2 people whether they are Catholic or non-Catholic. One major implication of this pattern is that the overall religious

TABLE 14.7
Parameters for Three-Class Latent Structure Model for Abortion Opinion
Data in Table 6.14

	Type of respondent	
	Non-Catholic, high school educated	Catholic, high school educated
Latent class probabilities		
Class 1 (ideologically in favor)	.430	.320
Class 2 (situationally determined)	.494	.493
Class 3 (ideologically opposed)	.076	.186
Conditional probabilities of a proabortion response for class II		
Too poor to afford more	.266	.214
Strong chance of serious defect	.889	.922
Married, not want more children	.110	.094

difference on favorableness toward abortion among high-school-educated people (found by computing the marginals for any item in Table 14.6) is due to the
fact that non-Catholics are more likely to be doctrinaire liberals (proabortion
for any reason) and Catholics are more likely to be doctrinaire conservatives.

A similar analysis was performed on the other four groups of interest—
Catholics and non-Catholics with less than high school or more than high
school education. The proportions of each group in each latent class are shown
in Table 14.8. The conditional probabilities of a proabortion response for the
Type 2 respondents are not shown because in every group these probabilities
are about the same as the ones shown in Table 14.7.

We do find that there is heterogeneity by education and by religion in the
proportion in each latent class. For respondents with less than high school
education, the proportions in each latent class are about the same. The principal finding in Table 14.8 is that as education increases, the effect on abortion
ideology is different for non-Catholics than for Catholics. For non-Catholics,
the effect of increased education is to shift the population out of categories 2

TABLE 14.8
Proportions in Three Latent Classes, by Religion and Education

Religion	Education	Proportion in class			
		1	2	3	N
Non-Catholic	0–11 years	.256	.588	.156	1384
	High school	.430	.494	.076	1155
	College	.586	.348	.066	977
Catholic	0–11 years	.257	.599	.144	458
	High school	.320	.494	.186	538
	College	.363	.445	.192	402

and 3 and into category 1. Increased education causes a higher proportion of ideological liberals for non-Catholics.

For Catholics, increased education causes a 10% increase in ideological liberalism, but it also causes a 5% increase in ideological conservatism. The effect of increased education, in this case, is polarization.

Table 14.8, and more elaborate versions with controls for such variables as age or family size, can be analyzed with hierarchical models or with the linear modeling techniques outlined in Section 14.4. A more complete analysis of the abortion data (Taylor, 1977) traces trends in latent class composition and finds trends in the conditional probabilities of accepting abortion among the Type 2 respondents. The validity of each reason for an abortion, among Type 2 respondents, has generally been increasing, but at a slower rate than the transfer of respondents out of type 2 and type 3 mind sets.

COMPLICATIONS WITH CHI SQUARE, REVISITED

This discussion of complications with chi square builds on the discussion of the same topic in Section 14.2. The strategy for assessing the goodness of fit of a latent class model is the same as the procedure for hierarchical modeling. The latent class model is specified, the cell frequencies are estimated under the hypothesis that the model fits the data, and then the hypothesis is tested using some statistical measure of dissimilarity. The contribution of a particular parameter to a latent class model can be tested by comparing the goodness of fit of two models that differ only in the presence or absence of that parameter.

The implications of sampling design for the chi-square statistics are theoretically the same here as for hierarchical models. Since little work has been done on the sampling properties of latent structure parameters, however, it is impossible to make a recommendation as to the appropriate adjustment.

Similarly, the chi-square goodness-of-fit tests for latent structure models are adversely affected by small expected values. In fact, because of the kinds of models that are usually of interest in latent structure analysis, the need to be wary of chi-square tests is even more pronounced. If a unidimensional scale is well constructed, there are very few cases expected in the "error" cells (i.e., people at the positive end of a "hard" question but at the negative end of an "easy" question). Thus, if the scale is well constructed and the model well specified, the expectations in some cells tend toward zero. This is exactly the circumstance that produces instability in the chi-square estimate. Table 14.9 illustrates this problem with the observed frequencies, the expected values, and some goodness-of-fit measures for the non-Catholic high-school-educated sample. The third cell has a small expectation and contributes almost 90% of the goodness-of-fit chi square. With this cell included in the calculations, either chi square is significant on 2 degrees of freedom. On the other hand, the absolute proportional error, one of the indexes of dissimilarity described earlier, shows that each cell proportion is predicted by the model within .7%.

Just as with hierarchical models, it is usually necessary to expand the decision rules to include some judgmental criteria in assessing goodness of fit.

TABLE 14.9
Observed Frequencies and Expected Frequencies for the Three-Class Latent Structure Model for Non-Catholic High School Educated Respondents

Cell	Observed	Expected	Goodness-[a] of-fit chi square	Likelihood[b] ratio chi square	Absolute[c] proportional error
1	512	512.00	.00	.00	.000
2	34	41.02	1.20	-12.76	.006
3	10	1.86	35.62	33.64	.007
4	4	5.12	.25	-1.97	.001
5	115	120.13	.22	-10.04	.004
6	339	330.85	.20	16.5	.007
7	8	15.01	3.27	-10.07	.006
8	129	129.00	.00	.00	.000

[a] $(O_i - E_i)^2/E_i$
[b] $-2 * O_i^* \ln(O_i/E_i)$
[c] $|(O_i/N) - (E_i/N)|$
where

O_i = Observed frequency in cell i
E_i = Expected frequency in cell i
N = Sample size

The best practice is to calculate absolute and squared deviations and any other indexes of dissimilarity that seem helpful. In addition, one should inspect the cells adding the largest goodness-of-fit chi-square contributions to determine the sensitivity of one's test to small expected values.

14.4. LINEAR MODELS FOR QUALITATIVE DATA

This section assumes that the reader has had some exposure to the general linear regression model (Cohen, 1968; Fennessey, 1968) and especially to the case of the general linear model where observations on the dependent variable are weighted inversely proportional to their variance before performing the regression analysis. The general model is covered in most intermediate statistics books under the topics of heteroscedasticity or generalized least squares. Parts of this section also require familiarity with linear algebra, particularly matrix multiplication and matrix inversion. Given this background, the level of exposition is about the same as in Section 14.2. The basic steps in regression analysis of qualitative data are explained, but a little more quickly than in a purely introductory treatment. The focus then shifts to more advanced problems than are ordinarily covered in introductory chapters.

Just as the theory of the general linear model is the basis for many topics in linear regression and analysis of variance, so generalized linear modeling is the term for the general theory of regression analysis of qualitative data (Grizzle,

Starmer, & Koch, 1969; Nelder, 1974; Nelder & Wedderburn, 1972). Most of the techniques for regression analysis of qualitative data that are known to social researchers—such as log linear models, probit analysis, logit analysis, and weighted regression analysis of proportions—are variations of a general strategy for analyzing qualitative data. That strategy is to perform a weighted regression analysis of some transformation of the cell counts in a contingency table. The log linear model is a weighted regression analysis of the logarithms of the expected cell counts (Goodman, 1972a; Haberman, 1978).

When the log linear model is restricted so as to focus on a single dependent variable, the result is the model for logit analysis (Goodman, 1972b, 1976). Alternatively, logit analysis results from performing a weighted regression analysis of the logarithm of the odds of being in one category rather than another on the dependent variable (Cox, 1970). If one transforms the cell counts by taking the percentage in a particular category of the dependent variable and then performs a weighted regression analysis of this variable, the result is the weighted regression model for proportions (Grizzle *et al.*, 1969) also known as "*D* systems" (Davis, 1976). The final model that is sometimes encountered by social researchers transforms the proportion in a particular category of the dependent variable into the unit normal deviate that generates the proportion as the area under the unit normal curve. The model for the weighted regression analysis of this variable is known as probit analysis (Finncy, 1971).

The use of regression terminology in this section might seem a little surprising. After all, the purpose of this chapter is to explicate techniques that should be used when the level of measurement of the data indicates that regression modeling is inappropriate. The models discussed in this section, however, are not regression models as we normally think of them. Usually regression models are used to analyze and predict the scores of each individual sample member. A scatter diagram for a regression analysis plots the scores of individual people and shows the relation of each score to the regression line. The point was made earlier, in the discussion of explained variance in hierarchical modeling, that qualitative data analysis techniques do not focus on the scores of individuals but on the patterns of cell counts (or proportions or some other transformation of the cell counts) in the contingency table. The same point clarifies the use of regression terminology here. The purpose of regression analysis of qualitative data is to predict the transformed cell counts as a function of scores assigned to categories of the independent variables. The term *generalized linear modeling* is used here because the transformed cell counts must be weighted to correctly perform the regression analysis—just as weights must be used in regression problems requiring the use of *generalized* least squares (e.g., Johnston 1972, pp. 208–243).

This part of the chapter focuses on the two models that are most frequently used for regression analysis of qualitative survey data: weighted regression analysis of proportions and log linear modeling (with its extension to logit analysis). Since each is a variation of the same general strategy for qualitative analysis, the techniques covered in the discussion of one model are usually just as applicable to the other, once appropriate adjustments are made for the differences arising from the use of proportions rather than logarithms of cell counts as the transformation of the dependent variable in the regression. Nevertheless, the models are not completely interchangeable. The final part of this chapter analyzes the situations where the models differ in the substantive conclusions one would draw from using one rather than the other in analyzing a contingency table.

Weighted Regression Analysis of Proportions

The purpose of this technique is to estimate a regression equation that predicts the proportion in a particular category of the dependent variable as a function of the independent variables. Some of the statistical procedures were presented by Goodman (1963) and were later elaborated into a general regression procedure by Grizzle *et al.* (1969). The same model is derived by Coleman (1964). Koch and Reinfurt (1971), Lehnen and Koch (1974), and Higgins and Koch (1977) apply this technique to an array of substantive problems.

One of the distinct advantages of the regression model for proportions, compared to the other methods briefly mentioned at the beginning of this section, is that the regression coefficients from the model analyzing proportions have many of the same properties as the coefficients used in path analysis and other multiequation systems for causal analysis, as the term *causal analysis* is used by Heise (1975). Davis (1975a, 1976) presents a system for path analysis of qualitative variables that is based on the weighted regression model for proportions. We begin by examining some of the details of the regression procedure and then turn to a discussion of the use of this technique for path analysis.

DETAILS OF ESTIMATION

It is best to begin with the simplest situation: a fourfold table. Both variables are scored (0, 1) with the category scored 0 known as the base category and the category scored 1 known as the nonbase category. This is the same coding as is used in dummy variable regression (Draper & Smith, 1966; Suits, 1957). The difference is that the dependent variable as well as the independent variable(s) are given the (0, 1) coding.

From a regression modeling standpoint there are two data points. The regression equation estimates the proportion in the nonbase category of the dependent variable as a function of the independent variable, which is scored (0, 1). When this regression is estimated, the model fits the data perfectly because there are two data points and two parameters in the regression (the intercept and the slope). The parameters are interpreted as follows:

1. The intercept is the proportion in the nonbase category of the dependent variable *among those* in the base category of the independent variable.
2. The unstandardized slope is the difference in proportions.

TABLE 14.10
Cross-Tabulation of Cohort and Party Identification[a]

	Age in		Party identification			
Cohort	1960	1972	Democrat	Independent	Republican	N
Old	54+	66+	.448	.198	.354	1541
Middle	37–53	49–65	.489	.248	.262	1856
Young	21–36	18–48	.409	.380	.211	2108

[a] From pooled 1960, 1962, 1970, and 1972 ICPSR Michigan Election Surveys.

When the slope is added to the intercept the result is the proportion in the nonbase category of the dependent variable among those in the nonbase category of the independent variable. This interpretation is clearer when we use the table in the next example.

The first generalization of the technique is to look at the case of polytomous variables in a two-way table. Table 14.10 shows the cross-tabulation of cohort and party identification, each measured in three categories. With polytomous variables in dummy variable regression the procedure is to create separate (0, 1) dummy variables for each nonbase category of each predictor variable. The procedure is the same here. Dummy variables are created for membership in the middle cohort and for membership in the young cohort. In addition, dummy variables are created for each nonbase category of the dependent variable. The regressions for each dummy dependent variable are then solved simultaneously. The data in Table 14.10 yield the following regression equations:

$$\text{Proportion Independent} = .198 + .050 * \left(\frac{\text{Middle cohort}}{\text{membership}}\right) + .182 * \left(\frac{\text{Young cohort}}{\text{membership}}\right) \qquad (14.9)$$

$$\text{Proportion Republican} = .354 - .092 * \left(\frac{\text{Middle cohort}}{\text{membership}}\right) - .143 * \left(\frac{\text{Young cohort}}{\text{membership}}\right) \qquad (14.10)$$

These regressions also fit the observed data perfectly. There are six observations (six proportions in the nonbase categories of the dependent variable) and there are six parameters estimated in the two equations. The intercept in the first equation is the proportion of independents in the base category of the predictor variable. The first slope in the first equation is the difference between the middle cohort and the base cohort in the proportion of independents. Because the slopes are the same as percentage differences they will sometimes be referred to as Ds, this is also why Davis uses the term D *systems*. When the values of the dummy variables are inserted, the equations predict the proportions on the dependent variable. For instance, to use the second equation to estimate the proportion of Republicans in the young cohort we use the following equation:

$$\text{Proportion Republican} = .354 - .092 * (0) - .143 * (1) = .211.$$

This is exactly the proportion observed in the table.

The standard error for a percentage difference in a two-way table is the square root of the sum of the variances of the two proportions being compared: If $D = p_1 - p_2$ then:

$$s_D = \left(\frac{p_1(1 - p_1)}{n_1} + \frac{p_2(1 - p_2)}{n_2}\right)^{1/2} \qquad (14.11)$$

where s_D denotes the estimated standard error of the percentage difference; and n_1 and n_2 are the sample sizes for the two proportions (i.e., the row totals in Table 14.10). Using this formula, the standard error for the first D in (14.9) is .014, the standard errors for the other slopes are all near this value. One method for determining the significance of a percentage difference is to divide the slope by its standard error, producing a unit normal deviate that can be evaluated using the percentage points of the unit normal integral. Thus all slopes in (14.9) and (14.10) are significant.

The regression model for the two-way table did not require any of the weighting procedures used in generalized linear modeling. When the equation fits the data exactly, there is no need to apply weights to the deviations from the regression line (since there are no deviations). With more than one predictor variable the slopes are partial percentage differences and weights must be used so that percentages measured more accurately (i.e., with a smaller variance) contribute more heavily to the calculation of the coefficients.

The generalized procedure for regression analysis of qualitative data uses the scores on the predictor variables (0 and 1 in this case) to build up a matrix of scores for all of the independent variables. The regression slopes are then solved simultaneously in a matrix multiplication that also incorporates the necessary weights. The generalized procedure is described later in this section as part of the apparatus for log linear modeling, although it could apply here as well.

Goodman (1963) and Davis (1976) use a simpler approach for estimating the partial percentage difference when there is more than one independent variable. To illustrate this approach we examine Table 14.11—the three-way classification of education, cohort membership, and party identification.

In Table 14.11 there are three measures of the cohort difference in party identification when education is controlled. The cohort difference is estimated within each category of education. Thus, among those with 0–11 years of education the middle cohort is 10.3% *less* likely to say they are Republican; among the high school educated the difference is -16.5%; and among the college educated the difference is -11.3%. These are known as conditional percentage differences since they are the difference within (conditional on) categories of education. Under the hypothesis of no interaction, each conditional is an estimate of the cohort difference controlling for education. The best

TABLE 14.11
Cross-Classification of Cohort by Education by Party Identification[a]

		Party identification			
Cohort	Education	Democrat	Independent	Republican	N
Old	0–11 years	.490	.201	.309	1097
	High school	.344	.195	.457	221
	College	.341	.184	.475	223
Middle	0–11 years	.569	.225	.206	925
	High school	.462	.246	.292	.586
	College	.322	.316	.362	345
Young	0–11 years	.485	.361	.154	573
	High school	.425	.389	.186	814
	College	.330	.384	.286	721

[a] For definitions and sources see Table 14.10.

estimate of the cohort difference controlling for education pools the conditional estimates, with weights inversely proportional to the variance of each conditional percentage difference. Thus:

$$D_p = \sum_i w_i D_i \qquad (14.12)$$

where D_p denotes the partial or pooled difference in proportions; D_i denotes the D in the ith conditional table; w_i denotes the weights used for the D in the ith subtable in calculating D_p. The weight w_i for each subtable is:

$$w_i = \frac{1/s_i^2}{\sum_i 1/s_i^2} \qquad (14.13)$$

where s_i^2 denotes the variance of the D in the ith subtable (found using a formula similar to (14.11) but not taking the square root). The standard error for the pooled percentage difference is found using a formula for the variance of a weighted average:

$$S_{D_p} = \sqrt{\sum_i w_i^2 s_i^2} \qquad (14.14)$$

where s_{D_p} denotes the standard error of the pooled D; and w_i and s_i are as defined in the previous equations. The standard error is used in conjunction with the pooled D to construct the usual ratio for significance testing.

The intercept for the regression equation is one of the parameters estimated in the generalized procedure using matrix multiplication. Davis (1976) uses the observed proportion in the combined base category of the table as the intercept for the equation. The combined base category is the category consisting of those in the base group of all the independent variables. Applying Davis's procedure, the following equations are obtained for the proportion Independent and the proportion Republican:

$$\text{Proportion Independent} = .201 + .047 * \binom{\text{Middle cohort}}{\text{membership}} + .180 * \binom{\text{Young cohort}}{\text{membership}}$$
$$+ .021 * \binom{\text{High school}}{\text{education}} + .032 * \binom{\text{College}}{\text{education}} \qquad (14.15)$$

$$\text{Proportion Republican} = .309 - .115 * \binom{\text{Middle cohort}}{\text{membership}} - .185 * \binom{\text{Young cohort}}{\text{membership}}$$
$$+ .069 * \binom{\text{High school}}{\text{education}} + .146 * \binom{\text{College}}{\text{education}} \qquad (14.16)$$

By inserting the values of the dummy variables at the appropriate places, the equations are used to predict the proportions for the dependent variable. For instance, the predicted proportion Republican among college educated members of the young cohort is:

Proportion Republican =
$$.309 - .115 * (0) - .185 * (1) + .069 * (0) + .146 * (1) = .270.$$

This is close to the observed proportion Republican but not exactly the same because there is a slight three-way interaction in Table 14.11 that is smoothed out (i.e., assumed to be insignificant) by the pooling procedure. Another way of saying this is that there are 18 observations (proportions in the nonbase categories of the dependent variable) and 10 parameters estimated in (14.15) and (14.16). There are, thus, eight degrees of freedom for departure between the observed and predicted proportions.

Comparing (14.9) and (14.10) with (14.15) and (14.16) we observe the following results:

1. Controlling education hardly affects the relationship between cohort membership and Independent party identification, the partial effects are nearly the same as the effects calculated from the two-way table.
2. Education suppresses the relationship between cohort membership and Republican party identification, the partial effects are more negative than the two-way relationship.

There are two approaches to assessing the goodness of fit of a regression model for qualitative data. The first is to calculate the expected proportions under the regression model, use these to generate the expected frequencies, and then use a chi-square test for the dissimilarity between the observed and expected frequencies. This is the goodness-of-fit procedure used by Grizzle et al. (1969). It was noted earlier that there are eight degrees of freedom for testing the goodness of fit of the regression specified by (14.15) and (14.16). With this goodness-of-fit procedure we would learn whether it is necessary to add further variables to the regression equation. The added variables would be terms for the interaction of the two independent variables in predicting the proportions in the table. According to the terminology developed in Section 14.2 it is preferable to refer to these as three-way interactions (i.e., two variables interacting to predict the level of a third variable).

The second approach to testing the goodness of fit of the regression model is to directly examine the possibilities of higher order interactions. The regression model will not fit, and higher order interactions are present, when the conditional Ds are significantly different from one another. This violates the assumption of homogeneity that is necessary to justify the equation for the partial percentage difference (14.12). The following chi-square statistic is used to test the hypothesis of no interaction among the conditional Ds:

$$\chi^2 = \sum_i \frac{(D_i - D_p)^2}{s_i^2} \tag{14.17}$$

where χ^2 denotes the chi-square statistic. The number of degrees of freedom for this test is one less than the number of conditional Ds; D_i and D_p are the conditional and pooled Ds, respectively; and s_i^2 is the variance of the conditional D in the ith subtable. By this criterion, there are no significant interactions for the regression slopes in (14.15) and (14.16). When the interaction chi square for one (or more) of the slopes is significant, the regression model is misspecified and some adjustment must be made. The usual procedure in linear regression modeling (and, as we shall see, in log linear modeling) is to add three-way or higher order interaction terms to the model predicting the proportions on the dependent variable. One of the distinct advantages of the regression model for proportions, however, is that when there are no interactions the coefficients can be used in path diagrams and in related multiequation systems for causal analysis. It is possible to continue using the path analysis procedures and still take account of whether interactions may be present in one of two ways. One way to do this is to create a typology for any set of independent variables that interact and use the typology as a predictor variable. Davis (1976) calls this technique *blocking*. If this approach is awkward one can, instead, stratify the sample on one of the interacting variables and estimate the regression equations within each subsample.

When there are more than three variables there are more terms in the regression equation, but the formulas and principles for estimation are exactly the same. With added variables there is an increased risk of encountering some of the complications with the statistical procedure. These are described next. With two or more independent variables, some of the procedures of path analysis can be used to analyze D systems data. These procedures, and an application of them to the analysis of change over time, are the final topics in this exposition of regression models for proportions.

COMPLICATIONS WITH THE STATISTICAL PROCEDURE

As usual, small cell counts are a problem. Under this model a cell that includes zero or 100% of the cases in a row produces a variance for the conditional percentage difference that is undefined. The safest procedure for dealing with this seems to be to add $1/k$ to each cell in the table where k is the number of categories in the dependent variable (Grizzle *et al.*, 1969).

The second complication is the adjustment that should be used to compensate for the sampling procedure when the cases are not drawn according to a simple random sample. The discussion of complications with chi square in Section 14.2 noted that, in principle, a different adjustment factor should be used for every standard error and every chi-square test calculated using this (or any) regression model. In fact, this is impractical (so far) and so the usual procedure is to compute an average adjustment factor to be applied to all calculations, even though this procedure is as hard to justify as the assumption that the data were drawn by simple random sampling. Based on the results cited in Section 14.3 (Kish, 1957; Hauser *et al.*, 1975a; Scheuren, 1973) and on the more advanced work on this topic by Kish and Frankel (1970) the variance of each conditional percentage difference should be multiplied by 1.32 before applying any of the formulas for this model. The adjustment will not affect the estimate of the pooled percentage difference, but it will change the chi-square test for interaction. The standard error of each path should be made larger by a factor of 1.15. The effect of the adjustment is to make it more difficult to obtain a significant slope in the regression equation.

PATH ANALYSIS WITH QUALITATIVE DATA

When there is a unidirectional causal ordering (i.e., no simultaneous effects, no reciprocal causation, no loops) to the entire set of variables in a cross-classification, the D systems model can be used for path analysis. The path model shows the direct and indirect links between the variables in the cross-tabulation. The direct effect between two variables is the percentage difference from the regression equation relating those variables. The size of the indirect effect between two variables can be found by multiplying along all of the forward paths connecting the two variables.

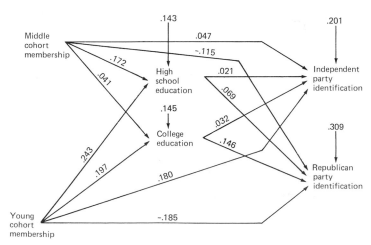

FIGURE 14.1 *D*-Systems path model for the data in Table 14.11.

Figure 14.1 shows the D systems path model for the three variables in Table 14.11. The arrow originating above each variable shows the intercept in the equation predicting that variable as a function of the causally prior variables in the model. Thus, the proportion of Independents is predicted as a function of cohort membership (two dummy variables) and education (also two dummy variables). The equation can be read directly off the graph as (14.15) predicted earlier in this discussion.

$$\begin{array}{c}\text{Proportion}\\\text{Independent}\end{array} = .201 + .047 * \begin{pmatrix}\text{Middle cohort}\\\text{membership}\end{pmatrix} + .180 * \begin{pmatrix}\text{Young cohort}\\\text{membership}\end{pmatrix}$$

$$+ .021 * \begin{pmatrix}\text{High school}\\\text{education}\end{pmatrix} + .032 * \begin{pmatrix}\text{College}\\\text{education}\end{pmatrix}$$

Similarly, the equation for each educational level can be read off the graph. Since education is assumed to be causally prior to party identification, cohort membership is the only predictor of education. The equation for the proportion college educated is:

$$\begin{array}{c}\text{Proportion}\\\text{college educated}\end{array} = .195 + .041 * \begin{pmatrix}\text{Middle cohort}\\\text{membership}\end{pmatrix} + .197 * \begin{pmatrix}\text{Young cohort}\\\text{membership}\end{pmatrix}$$

The indirect effect of young cohort membership on Independent party identification (the amount of the zero order D explained by educational differences) is found by multiplying along the two indirect paths between young cohort membership and Independent party identification (one indirect path via high school education, the other via college education). The indirect effect is $(.243 * .021 + .197 * .032) = .011$. The principal use of path diagrams with qualitative variables is to map out the relationships between the variables and to use this map to calculate the indirect effects.

The complication that arises with the use of path diagrams is that, unlike path diagrams in linear regression analysis (Wright, 1934), the direct, indirect, and spurious effects do not always add up exactly to the zero order relationship. This complication arises because of the weights used in calculating the partial regression coefficients. If the conditional Ds were weighted by the number of cases in each subtable (as they are in linear regression models) or if there were no three-variable or higher interactions then the direct, indirect, and spurious effects would add to the zero-order D. In our example, the direct and indirect effect of young cohort membership on Independent party identification add to .194 whereas the zero-order D is .182.

PATH MODELS FOR ANALYZING CHANGE

The path models considered here take on a particularly interesting dimension when they are used to analyze processes of change in a dependent variable. Davis (1975a,b, 1978) gives several examples of this application. When the variables in a cross-tabulation appear in surveys separated in time, the date of the survey can be used as an additional variable in the contingency table. With surveys done at two different dates time is scored as a dummy variable with 0 for the early date and 1 for the later date. The analysis of change makes the most sense when the time variable is taken as causally prior to every other variable in the table.

Figure 14.2 extends the analysis of party identification to study changes from 1960–1962 to 1970–1972. The paths from time to cohort membership indicate an 11.9% drop in the percentage of the sample in the middle cohort and a 28.6% increase in young cohort membership during the decade considered. The absence of significant direct paths between time and education indicates that the observed changes in educational attainment were completely due to cohort educational differences and cohort replacement (i.e., the indirect effects of time via changes in cohort composition).

The paths between cohort membership, education, and party identification show the relationships between these variables controlling for the time each survey was taken. The relationships between these variables were approximately the same within survey years and so the relationships can be summarized on a path diagram that holds for either survey year. It is very often the case that relationships between variables change over time (i.e., relationships interact with time) and therefore cannot be shown on a path diagram such as the one in Figure 14.2. Taylor (1980) discusses the problem of specifying and testing theories of change in D systems paths.

The direct effects from time to party identification show: (a) a .059 rise in the proportion of Independents that is *not* explained by changes in cohort composition or in levels of educational attainment; and (b) a .023 drop in the proportion of Republicans that is not explained by changes in other variables in the model. The direct effects of time represent the residual change since it is the amount of change left over after the indirect effects of changes in other variables have been accounted for in the model.

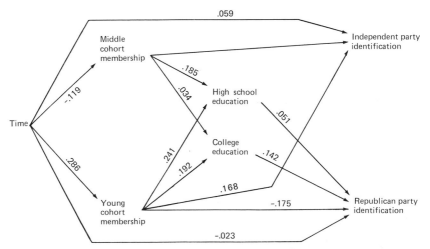

FIGURE 14.2 *D*-Systems path diagram analyzing changes in party identification: 1960–72. Paths not significantly different from zero (.05 level) are deleted from the diagram. The 1960 and 1962 surveys are combined for the first category of "time"; the 1970 and 1972 surveys are combined for the second category.

TABLE 14.12
Analysis of Components of Change in Party Identification

Source of change	Dependent variable	
	Proportion Independent	Proportion Republican
Change in middle cohort		
Direct effect	−.009	.013
Via high school	.000	−.001
Via college	.000	−.001
Change in young cohort		
Direct effect	.052	−.050
Via high school	.000	.004
Via college	.000	.008
Residual change	.059	−.023
Total net change	.102	−.050

The indirect paths from time to party identification trace the changes in the dependent variable that can be attributed to changes in the predictor variables. By multiplying along the indirect paths the sources of change in party identification can be accounted for in detail as shown in Table 14.12.

The indirect sources of change and the direct effects of time add up (approximately, as before) to the total change in the dependent variable. The accounting scheme shown in Table 14.12 can become much more elaborate as additional sources of change are added to the model. Taylor, Sheatsley, and Greeley (1978) consider a model for change in racial tolerance where changes in cohort membership, education, and other liberal attitudes are taken as independent sources of change. Taylor (1978) analyzes a model for trends in support of legalization of marijuana. There, some sources of change push in the prolegalization direction whereas others push the opposite way. The magnitude of the push in either direction is found by calculating the indirect effect of time.

Some additional comments about the D systems model are at the end of this chapter. Of particular importance is the discussion of the circumstances when the choice of a D system model as opposed to a log linear model leads to different conclusions regarding the patterns in the data.

The Log Linear Model

A log linear model is most compactly described as a regression equation predicting the logarithms of the expected cell counts in a contingency table. One important difference between the log linear model and the model for weighted regression analysis of proportions is the use of *expected cell counts* as the dependent variable rather than *observed proportions*. The expected cell counts are estimated by one of two procedures. Haberman (1978) describes an iterative procedure that first estimates the regression coefficients on the basis of the expected cell counts, then updates the expected cell counts on the basis of the most recent set of regression coefficients, and so on until the estimates converge. Goodman (1970, 1971, 1972a) presents an alternative method for arriving at the same regression coefficients. The expected cell counts are estimated using the algorithm for iterative proportional fitting that was described earlier. The logarithms of the expected cell counts are then used in the regression procedure for estimating the parameters of the log linear model.

Both procedures are part of the class of generalized linear models that was described in the introduction of this section. They are both weighted regressions. Haberman's method incorporates the weights explicitly in each cycle of the iteration. Goodman's procedure implicitly incorporates the weights by using the Deming–Stephan algorithm to generate the expected values. The precise details of Haberman's iterative procedure are not given here. The Deming–Stephan algorithm is described, but not completely specified, in Section 14.2. In developing the log linear model here, it is assumed that the expected cell counts are known—either as the result of the Deming–Stephan algorithm or as the final step in the iterative estimation procedure. This section will show how to estimate the coefficients for the regression equation predicting the logarithms of the expected cell counts. A special case arises when the regression equation includes, as predictor variables, all possible interactions among all variables in the contingency table. In this case the regression model is a saturated model and the expected cell counts are the same as the observed cell counts. In this case (only) the log linear model is a regression equation predicting the logarithms of the observed cell counts.

SPECIFYING THE REGRESSION MODEL

The first step in setting up the regression is to assign scores to the categories of each variable. The weighted regression model for proportions is usually illustrated with (0, 1) dummy variable scores assigned to categories of the predictor variables. This coding was also the one used by Cox (1970) and Plackett (1974) in their explanations of the log linear model. Goodman's general exposition (1972a) does not use dummy coding. Rather, with all dichotomous variables (an assumption to be relaxed shortly), Goodman assigns the scores −1 and +1 to the categories of each variable. This procedure is known as *effect coding*.

The effect codes are used to generate the scores for the independent variables in the equation predicting the logarithm of the expected cell counts. The independent variables in the regression are: the grand mean; the one-way effects for each variable in the table; the two-way interactions (the measure of relationship in a two-way table); the three-way interactions; and so on. The calculation and use of the independent variables in log linear analysis is best explained with a concrete example.

Table 14.13 shows the cross-classification of two dichotomous variables—cohort membership and party identification—the data taken from Table 14.10. The table shows the names and scores for each category of each variable. The cells are also named *a, b, c,* and *d* for future reference.

TABLE 14.13
Cross-Classification of Party Identification by Cohort Membership, Based on Table 14.10

	Party identification	
Cohort	Democrats + Republicans	Independent
Old + middle	2631(a)	766(c)
Young	1307(b)	801(d)

The saturated log linear model for this table predicts the logarithm of the expected cell counts as a function of four variables: the grand mean; the one way effects of cohort membership and party identification; and the two-factor interaction of cohort and party, which can also be interpreted as a measure of the correlation between cohort membership and party identification. (As before, the term *interaction* is used differently here than in the discussion of the linear regression model. Here the term refers to two-way and higher order relationships.) The scores for the variable measuring the one way cohort effect are found by assigning each cell in the table the score (either −1 or +1) for the category of cohort membership that is associated with that cell. Thus, cell *a* is assigned a score of −1 because it contains members of the old cohort, cell *d* receives a score of 1 for the one-way cohort effect. A similar procedure is followed to assign the cells scores for the party identification variable. Each cell score for the third variable, the interaction of cohort and party, is found by multiplying the scores for the one-way effects of cohort membership and party identification that are associated with that cell. Cell *a,* which receives a −1 for each one-way effect, receives a 1 for the two-way interaction. The final variable in the equation predicting the log cell counts is the grand mean. In terms of assigning scores to cells this is a special case—each cell receives a score of 1.

Table 14.14 shows the variables that are in the saturated log linear model and the scores for each cell of the fourfold table that are associated with each

TABLE 14.14
Variable Scores in the Saturated Log Linear Model for the Cross-Classification in Table 14.13

	Variable name			
Cell	Grand mean	One-way cohort effect	One-way party effect	Two-way cohort × party interaction
a	1	−1	−1	1
b	1	1	−1	−1
c	1	−1	1	−1
d	1	1	1	1

variable. Each column in Table 14.14 corresponds to an independent variable in the log linear model. The dependent variable—the logarithm of the expected cell count—takes on four values (i.e., there are four cells in the table, each having an expected value under the model). The scores in each row of Table 14.14 show the scores on the independent variables that are associated with each value of the dependent variable. Since there are four observations on the dependent variable and four independent variables, the regression model will fit the data exactly and the expected cell counts are, in this case, the same as the observed cell counts.

The log linear model is based on the following matrix equation for the expected cell counts:

$$\mathbf{X}\boldsymbol{\lambda} = \mathbf{y} \tag{14.18}$$

where $\mathbf{y}$ is the vector of logarithm of expected cell counts; $\mathbf{X}$ is the matrix of scores on the predictor variable, this matrix is the same as the four columns of scores in Table 14.14; $\boldsymbol{\lambda}$ is the vector of regression coefficients that are to be estimated—these measure the effect of each predictor variable on the distribution of logarithms of cell counts in the table of expected frequencies. This equation does not have a term incorporating the weights because the regression model assumes the expected cell counts have been obtained by iteration or by the Deming–Stephan algorithm. Using a procedure in regression modeling, each side of Eq. (14.16) is premultiplied by $[\mathbf{X}^T\mathbf{X}]^{-1}\mathbf{X}^T$ to obtain:

$$\boldsymbol{\lambda} = [\mathbf{X}^T\mathbf{X}]^{-1}\mathbf{X}'_y \tag{14.19}$$

where $\boldsymbol{\lambda}$ is the vector of estimated log linear coefficients; $\mathbf{X}^T$ denotes the transpose of $\mathbf{X}$; $[\mathbf{X}^T\mathbf{X}]^{-1}$ denotes the inverse of $[\mathbf{X}^T\mathbf{X}]$. When all of the variables in the table are dichotomous and scored using effect coding $(-1, 1)$ Eq. (14.19) simplifies. In this case $[\mathbf{X}^T\mathbf{X}]^{-1}$ is equal to an identity matrix multiplied by the reciprocal of the number of cells in the table. The log linear effect for each variable in this special case can be estimated by a formula with the following structure:

$$\lambda_j = f \sum_i c_{ij} y_i \tag{14.20}$$

where λ_i denotes the log linear coefficients; f is the reciprocal of the number of cells in the table; y_i is the logarithm of the expected count in cell i; c_{ij} is the score for cell i used in estimating log linear effect j ($C_{ij} = \pm 1$).

Turning to the analysis of Table 14.13, f equals $\frac{1}{4}$ and the C_{ij} scores for each log linear effect are shown in Table 14.14. Thus, applying (14.19) yields the following estimates for the log linear effects (logarithms of cell counts are rounded to two places):

Grand mean	$= (\frac{1}{4})(7.88 + 7.18 + 6.64 + 6.69)$
One-way effect of cohort membership	$= (\frac{1}{4})(-7.88 + 7.18 - 6.64 + 6.69)$

One-way effect of
   party identification $= (\frac{1}{4})(-7.88 - 7.18 + 6.64 + 6.69)$

Two-way interaction of
   cohort and party $= (\frac{1}{4})(7.88 - 7.18 - 6.64 + 6.69)$

These estimates are interpreted as the slopes in the equation predicting the logarithms of the expected cell counts. The equation for the saturated model for Table 14.13 is:

$$
\begin{aligned}
\text{Logarithm of expected count in cell } i = {} & 7.09 * \begin{pmatrix} \text{cell score} \\ \text{on grand} \\ \text{mean} \end{pmatrix} + .16 * \begin{pmatrix} \text{cell score} \\ \text{on one-way} \\ \text{cohort effect} \end{pmatrix} \\
& -.43 * \begin{pmatrix} \text{cell score} \\ \text{on one-way} \\ \text{party effect} \end{pmatrix} + .19 * \begin{pmatrix} \text{cell score} \\ \text{on two-way} \\ \text{interaction} \end{pmatrix}
\end{aligned}
\tag{14.21}
$$

The cell scores on each predictor variable are given in Table 14.14. Equation (14.21) can be used to estimate the logarithm of the expected cell count in each table. For cell c the logarithm of the expected cell count (abbreviating to two place accuracy) is: $7.09 * (1) - .16 * (-1) - .43 * (1) + .19 * (-1) = 6.64$. The antilogarithm of 6.64 is 766. The equation fits cell c (and every other cell in the table) perfectly. This was to be expected since there are four data points and four predictor variables in (14.21).

The log linear effects in (14.21) have thus far been interpreted as variables that aid in predicting the logarithms of the expected cell counts. This interpretation can be made a little more substantive. The grand mean is the average of the logarithms of the expected values. The one-way effect is close to, but not exactly the same as, a measure of the extent to which the marginal distribution for a variable departs from a 50:50 split. The one-way effects are usually interpreted as measures of marginal skew. The two-way interaction measures the extent to which both variables must be taken account of simultaneously in predicting the logarithms of the expected cell counts. This is a measure of the size of the correlation between the two variables. (Alternatively, the two-way interaction is one-fourth the logarithm of the odds ratio in Table 14.13.)

The usual test for significance in a log linear model is to divide an effect by its standard error. Under the special circumstance when all variables are dichotomous and scored ±1 the standard error for every coefficient is the same and can be estimated as:

$$
s = \frac{[\Sigma_i(1/n_i)]^{1/2}}{f}
\tag{14.22}
$$

where s is the standard error for all coefficients; f is the number of cells in the table; n_i is the expected frequency in cell i. By (14.22) the standard error of each log linear effect is .015. We thus conclude that the correlation between cohort membership and party identification is significant. We also might conclude that the one-way effects are significant although most survey applications take the marginal skews in a table as given for this kind of problem.

In general, the variables will not be dichotomous and/or they will not be effect coded. (I prefer dummy coding for log linear regressions.) In either of these cases the standard error for an effect must be found using a matrix of covariances between the estimated coefficients. Haberman (1979) provides the user's instructions and other documentation for a program for log linear analysis that carries out these computations.

The rest of the discussion of the regression model shows its application to three-way tables, a procedure for handling polytomous variables, the relationship between the regression model presented here and logit analysis, procedures for assessing the goodness of fit of log linear regression models, and, finally, the ubiquitous discussion of complications arising from sampling procedures and small cell counts.

EXTENDING THE REGRESSION MODEL TO THREE-WAY TABLES

Table 14.15 shows the cross-classification of cohort membership, education, and party identification. Each variable is dichotomous with scores of -1 or $+1$ assigned to each category. The cells are labeled a to h for future reference.

The first step in specifying the regression model is to calculate the scores associated with each predictor variable. We begin with a saturated model for Table 14.15 and so the equation has eight independent variables: the grand mean; the one-way effects for each variable (necessitating three predictor variables); the two-way interactions between each pair of variables (three more predictor variables); and one variable for the effect of the three-way interaction. With eight predictors the estimated cell counts are the same as the observed counts and so there are no degrees of freedom for testing the goodness of fit of the regression model.

The scores for the predictor variables are calculated as follows:

1. Each cell receives a score of 1 on the variable that estimates the grand mean.

TABLE 14.15
Cross-Classification of Party Identification by Cohort Membership and Education, Based on Table 14.11

Cohort	Education	Party identification	
		Democrat + Republican (-1)	Independent (1)
Old + Middle (-1)	0–12 years (-1)	2213 (a)	616 (c)
	College (1)	418 (b)	150 (d)
Young (1)	0–11 years (-1)	863 (e)	524 (g)
	College (1)	444 (f)	277 (h)

TABLE 14.16
Scores for Variables in the Log Linear Analysis of Table 14.15

					Independent variables			
		One-way effects			Two-way effects			
	Grand mean (μ)	Cohort (C)	Education (E)	Party (P)	Cohort × Education (CE)	Cohort × Party (CP)	Education × Party (EP)	Three way interaction (CEP)
Cell								
a	1	−1	−1	−1	1	1	1	−1
b	1	−1	1	−1	−1	1	−1	1
c	1	−1	−1	1	1	−1	−1	1
d	1	−1	1	1	−1	−1	1	−1
e	1	1	−1	−1	−1	−1	1	1
f	1	1	1	−1	1	−1	−1	−1
g	1	1	−1	1	−1	1	−1	−1
h	1	1	1	1	1	1	1	1

2. For the one-way effects of a particular variable, each cell is scored +1 or −1 depending on whether it contains cases from the +1 or −1 category of that variable. Thus, cells in the top half of Table 14.14 are scored −1 for the one-way effect of cohort membership and cells in the bottom half of the table are scored +1.

3. The score in each cell for a two-factor interaction is found by multiplying the one way effect scores for the two variables named in the interaction. Thus, the scores in cells a through h for the education by party interaction are {+1 −1 −1 +1 +1 −1 −1 +1}.

4. The score in each cell for the three-way interaction is the product of the one-way effect scores for the three variables named in the interaction.

Table 14.16 shows the predictor variables for the saturated model and the associated cell scores. At the top of each column of scores is the name of each variable and in parentheses an abbreviated name for the same variable. The saturated log linear model for Table 14.15 (corresponding to the matrix expression in equation 14.16) is:

$$y = \mu + \lambda_C * (C) + \lambda_E * (E) + \lambda_P * (P) + \lambda_{CE} * (CE)$$
$$+ \lambda_{CP} * (CP) + \lambda_{EP} * (EP) + \lambda_{CEP} * (CEP)$$

where y denotes the logarithm of the expected frequency in a given cell. The letters in parentheses are the predictor variables, with scores on these variables given in Table 14.16; μ denotes the grand mean. The subscripted lambdas are the slopes in the regression, also called the log linear effects.

When the log linear effects are estimated, using (14.19), the equation for the logarithms of the expected frequencies is (rounding to two-place accuracy):

$$y = 6.24 - .05 * (C) - .55 * (E) - .41 * (P) + .22 * (CE)$$
$$+ .17 * (CP) + .04 * (EP) - .03 * (CEP) \qquad (14.23)$$

Since there are eight independent variables and eight observations the regression model fits the table exactly.

The grand mean and the one-way effects are interpreted the same way here as in the earlier log linear model. The two-way interactions are measures of partial association. The logarithm of the odds ratio relating education and party identification for members of the young cohort can be defined (using a through h for the log cell counts) as $(e - f - g + h)$. Following this notation the λ_{EP} effect is the average of one fourth of the odds ratios relating education and party, one odds ratio for each condition (or category) of cohort membership:

$$\lambda_{EP} = \frac{1}{2} \left(\frac{e - f - g + h}{4} + \frac{a - b - c + d}{4} \right).$$

In the D systems model the partial correlation was found by calculating the weighted average of the conditional percentage differences. With the log linear model, the average of the conditional log odds ratios is interpreted as a partial correlation, controlling for the conditioning variable(s).

The three-way interaction (λ_{CEP}) is a measure of heterogeneity in the conditional odds ratios. Using the previous notation, the three-way interaction is half the difference between the odds ratio in each half of Table 14.15:

$$\lambda_{CEP} = \frac{1}{2} \left(\frac{e - f - g + h}{4} - \frac{a - b - c + d}{4} \right).$$

When all variables are dichotomous, the measure of the three-way interaction is the same no matter which conditional odds ratios are compared.

The standard error for each log linear effect can be found using (14.22) with f equal to $\frac{1}{8}$. [In the general case (14.22) is inappropriate but we are still analyzing a set of dichotomous variables, all with effect coding.] The standard error for each effect is .018 and so we conclude: The cohort difference in party membership controlling for education is significant (the positive value means members of the young cohort are more likely to be Independents); the education effect on party identification controlling for cohort differences in education is barely significant (the positive value means college educated people are more likely to be Independents); the three-way interaction is not significant (the negative value means that the conditional odds ratio relating education and party identification is stronger among members of the older cohorts than in the young cohort); and the partial relationship between cohort membership and education, controlling for party identification, is significant. Finding λ_{CE} significant means that the effect must be included in the equation estimating the logarithms of the expected cell counts, otherwise the expected frequencies will be significantly different from the observed frequencies (significance determined by a chi-square test), thus casting doubts on the applicability of the regression model. But from a causal modeling point of view, it does not make sense to interpret λ_{CE} because the causal order for these variables (discussed in the D systems analysis) specifies that party identification is dependent on cohort membership and education. Therefore, party identification should not be controlled when examining the relationship between cohort membership and education. In log linear modeling, it is usually the case that some effects must be included in the regression equation because they contribute significantly to the goodness of fit of the regression model, but from a substantive point of view there is little interest in interpreting these effects. Logit analysis is a case of the log linear model in which the regression equation for the logarithms of the expected cell counts always includes all possible interactions among all predictor variables as nonsubstantive effects.

LOGIT ANALYSIS

When one variable in the contingency table is assumed to be caused by the other, prior, variables, there are several effects in the saturated model that are not of substantive interest. In general, these effects are the two-way and higher order interactions among the predictor variables. The procedure in logit analysis is to include the nonsubstantive effects in any regression model and refrain from interpreting them even though they are included in the output from the analysis. Thus, with three independent variables A, B, and C and one dependent variable, D, one would automatically include any interactions between A, B, and C in any regression equation. In terms of the log linear parameters, any regression for the logarithms of the expected cell counts would automatically include: $\{\mu\lambda_A\lambda_B\lambda_C\lambda_{AB}\lambda_{AC}\lambda_{BC}\}$.

This is the log linear representation of the previously discussed baseline model for hierarchical modeling when the variables in the table are causally ordered. After fitting the baseline regression model, the remaining log linear effects to be tested are: the one-way effect (marginal skew) for the dependent variable; the two-way interactions (partial correlations) with D; and the higher order interactions involving D. These are exactly the effects that are of substantive interest in the models for logit analysis presented by Goodman (1972b, 1976), Theil (1970), Vanneman and Pampel (1977), and Cox (1970). Page (1977) discusses the log linear model from a similar point of view. He presents it as a regression analysis of the odds ratios on the dependent variable. Some sophisticated extensions of the logit model are presented by McFadden (1974), Duncan (1979), Nerlove and Press (1973), and in a volume published by the National Bureau of Economic Research (1976).

TESTING SIGNIFICANCE

There are three kinds of significance tests that are used in log linear modeling. The first, which was used earlier in this section, is the ratio of a slope [the lambda coefficients in (14.21) and (14.23)] to its standard error.

Formula (14.22) estimates the standard error of each log linear effect when all variables are dichotomous and effect coded $(-1, 1)$. The calculation of the standard error in the general case can become quite complex depending on the number of categories in each variable and the method of scoring the variables in the equation predicting the logarithms of the cell counts (see Haberman, 1978). The standard errors of the lambda effects are also affected when there is a departure from simple random sampling. The discussion in earlier parts of this chapter noted the great need for further theoretical and empirical research on the question of sampling adjustments for qualitative data. At the present time, the recommendation is to multiply the standard error for each log linear effect by 1.15 before calculating the significance test. This will raise one's level of awareness of the need for sampling adjustments and will be the correct adjustment for some typical problems.

The second kind of significance test in log linear analysis is the chi-square test for the goodness of fit of the model. It has been noted several times that the log linear model is a regression model predicting the logarithms of expected cell counts—referred to as y_i in formula (14.21). The antilogarithms of the y_i are the expected cell counts under the regression model. These are compared with the observed cell counts using either chi-square test described in Section 14.2. The chi-square test assesses the goodness of fit of the regression model—a large chi square indicates lack of fit. The number of degrees of freedom for the chi-square test is calculated by subtracting the number of predictor variables in the regression from the number of cells in the table.

The chi square was zero for both log linear models presented in this section because in each case there were as many predictor variables as cells in the table. We noted, however, that λ_{CEP} in the three variable example was not statistically significant because the ratio of the effect to its standard error was quite low. We could delete this effect from the log linear model and assess the goodness of fit of the revised regression. Since there would be seven predictor variables in the revised regression and eight cells in the table there is one degree of freedom for the difference between the observed cell counts and the cell counts expected under the regression model.

In Goodman's approach to log linear modeling (1972a), the expected cell counts for the regression are estimated using the Deming–Stephan algorithm. The regression model is then used to isolate the individual effects that contribute to the pattern of the expected frequencies. When an effect is not incorporated into the Deming–Stephan algorithm, the effect does not appear in the modeled data. A regression model that included this effect in predicting the modeled frequencies would estimate a lambda of zero.

Thus, with Goodman's approach, whether one interprets the chi square as the goodness of fit of a hierarchical model or the goodness of fit of a regression model, the numerical result is the same. There are several published applications of this procedure for testing the goodness of fit of log linear models (Burke & Turk, 1975; Davis, 1974; Guest, 1974; Kasarda & Janowitz, 1974; Knoke, 1974; Knoke, 1976; Knoke & Lane, 1975; Knoke & Long, 1975; Knoke & Isaac, 1976; Mason & House, 1976).

Haberman (1978) presents a different approach to log linear modeling, one that is more consistent with the regression theory as it has been developed in this section. With Haberman's method the expected frequencies are estimated by the regression equation. Since the estimated frequencies are also the dependent variables in the regression it is necessary to use an iterative procedure that estimates the lambdas, then the expected values, and so on until the estimates converge. With this method the chi-square test measures the goodness of fit of the regression. Haberman's method can be used for hierarchical modeling since one can add and delete variables from the regression in an order that tests various hierarchical models. Haberman (1978) gives several examples of this procedure.

A third significance test is sometimes used to test the significance of individual lambdas. The procedure is to estimate two regression equations, the first including the lambda in question the other not. The likelihood ratio chi square for the second model is subtracted from the chi square for the first. The difference in chi square, on one degree of freedom, is the test of significance of the lambda in question. Several complications with this procedure were discussed in Section 14.2. The main objection was that the substantive result (lambda significant or not) might depend on the other variables included in the regression models. It is also possible that the first significance test described here— the ratio of lambda to its standard error—will disagree with the single degree of freedom chi-square test(s). The explanation is that for any significance test the calculated statistics are better estimates of the theoretical parameters as the sample becomes increasingly large. With a sufficiently large sample (probably larger than most surveys) the tests would agree. In most applications, however, the tests are affected differently by the distribution of cases in the table (and probably by the clustering effects) and therefore can lead to different conclusions. In practice, the tests are most likely to disagree when the effect is of borderline significance.

POLYTOMOUS VARIABLES

The D systems model handles a polytomous variable by creating separate dummy variables scored (0, 1) for each nonbase category of the original variable. The same procedure can be used in log linear modeling or, alternatively, other methods of scoring can be used. The general idea is that one creates two or more sets of scores that are used to generate the independent variables in the regression predicting the logarithms of the expected cell counts. If there are c categories in the polytomous variable then one is allowed to create up to $c - 1$ sets of scores for generating variables in the regression.

Most properties of polytomous variables can be illustrated using Table 14.17—the cross-classification of cohort membership and party identification. The categories of each variable are labeled 1 through 3 and the cells are labeled a through i for future reference. Since each variable is measured in three categories, each can contribute two sets of scores in generating the one-way effects and two-way interactions for the regression equation predicting the logarithms of the expected values. Dummy variable coding is one way to generate the scores for the predictor variables. With dummy coding one predictor

TABLE 14.17
Cross-Classification of Cohort Membership and Party
Identification, Each Measured in Three Categories, Based
on Table 14.10

Cohort	Party identification		
	Democrat	Independent	Republican
Old	690 (a)	305 (d)	546 (g)
Middle	908 (b)	461 (e)	487 (h)
Young	862 (c)	801 (f)	445 (i)

variable for the log linear regression is created for each nonbase category of the original polytomous variable. If category 1 is taken as the base category for each variable then the first dummy variable for the cohort polytomy measures whether or not a respondent is a member of the middle cohort. The scores for each cell on this variable are shown in the first column of Table 14.18. This variable is labeled "C1" to indicate that it is the first independent variable arising from the cohort polytomy. The variable "C2" in Table 14.18 scores the cells according to whether or not they contain respondents who are members of the young cohort. The party variables, P1 and P2, classify cells with respect to whether or not they contain Independents (P1) and whether or not they contain Republicans (P2). The variables for the two-way interactions are the four columns on the right side of Table 14.18. The scores for the interaction variables are the products of the scores for the one-way effects. The labels on each of the four columns on the right side show the effects that were multiplied to obtain the scores for the interaction variables. The scores in each column for the interaction variables are all zeroes except for one cell (a different one for each interaction) that receives a 1.

When the predictor variables in the log linear equation are dummy coded there are no simplified procedures for estimating the lambdas or their standard errors. The lambdas must be estimated using the matrix operations in (14.19). The estimates of the standard errors use the diagonal elements of $[\mathbf{X}^T\mathbf{X}]^{-1}$. The detailed procedures are described by Haberman (1978).

There are many other scoring procedures that can be used for polytomous variables instead of dummy coding. The three category analogue of effect coding is to assign scores for the one-way effect that measures the deviation of each category from the overall mean. If the mean of three arbitrary numbers is $(\frac{1}{3}) * (x + y + z)$ then the deviation of x from the mean is $(\frac{1}{3}) * (2x - y - z)$. One procedure in building matrices of category scores is to drop the $\frac{1}{3}$ since it is a scale factor and assign $\{2 -1 -1\}$ as the category scores for the first deviation contrast and $\{-1\ 2\ -1\}$ as the category scores for the second. If we apply this procedure to both variables in Table 14.17 the cell scores in the column for the first cohort contrast in the X matrix are $\{2 -1 -1\ 2 -1 -1\ 2 -1 -1\}$. The cell scores in the C2P2 column are $\{1 -2\ 1 -2\ 4 -2\ 1 -2\ 1\}$. For mean deviated

TABLE 14.18
Dummy Variable Contrasts for Saturated Model Analyzing Table 14.17

	One-way effects				Two-way interactions			
Cell	Middle cohort (C1)	Young cohort (C2)	Independent (P1)	Republican (P2)	Middle × Independent (C1P1)	Middle × Republican (C1P2)	Young × Independent (C2P1)	Young × Republican (C2P2)
a	0	0	0	0	0	0	0	0
b	1	0	0	0	0	0	0	0
c	0	1	0	0	0	0	0	0
d	0	0	1	0	0	0	0	0
e	1	0	1	0	1	0	0	0
f	0	1	1	0	0	0	1	0
g	0	0	0	1	0	0	0	0
h	1	0	0	1	0	1	0	0
i	0	1	0	1	0	0	0	1

effects and polytomous variables the simplified procedures for calculating the lambdas and their standard errors are, once again, not appropriate. Several examples of how to interpret mean deviated contrasts are found in work by Goodman (1972a; 1979), Burke and Turk (1975), and others. The default procedure in Goodman's computer program for log–linear modeling, ECTA, is mean deviated scoring for polytomous variables.

There is not much substantive difference between dummy scoring and mean deviated contrasts as far as the interpretation of the lambdas. The one-way effects measure marginal skews; the two-way interactions measure correlations between the categories of the polytomous variables.

There are other procedures for assigning scores to categories of polytomous variables that make stronger assumptions about the ordinal or interval distances between the categories. For ordinal variables Helmert scores (Bock, 1975) are often used to analyze the intercategory differences. Helmert scores are assigned so that beginning with the second category, each category of a polytomous variable is compared with the average of all previous categories. Thus, if we think of a matrix of scores for predicting the marginals on cohort membership, the Helmert matrix is:

$$\begin{bmatrix} 1 & -1 & -1 \\ 1 & 1 & -1 \\ 1 & 0 & 2 \end{bmatrix}$$

This matrix could be used in (14.19) to estimate the marginals for cohort membership. The first column estimates the grand mean. The second column estimates the lambda for the difference between the middle and the old cohort. The third column estimates the difference between the young cohort and the average of the two older cohorts (as per the earlier discussion of mean deviated scoring). The final empirical example in this section uses these scores to estimate the cohort effects.

When there are numerical distances between the categories of a polytomous variable, then polynomial contrasts (Winer, 1971) can be used. With three categories, the polynomial contrasts show the linear and quadratic effects of a variable. If the cohorts in our example were scored by the average date of birth within each cohort, then polynomial contrasts could be used. If the odds of identifying with the Republican party increased linearly with age then the linear effect of cohort would be highly significant and the lambda for the quadratic effect would not be needed in the regression. (One look at Table 14.10 or calculating odds ratios on Table 14.17 shows, however, that the quadratic effect is significant.)

Duncan and McRae (1978) give several examples of the use of polynomial contrasts for scoring a dependent variable. Yates (1948), Goodman (1971), and Haberman (1974b) show how to use polynomial contrasts to analyze effects of independent variables in a logit regression. The procedures for constructing polynomials when the categories of a variable are not in evenly spaced intervals are explained by Robson (1959). Snell (1964) and Williams and Grizzle (1972) give examples of ways to conceptualize category scores to make use of polynomial contrasts when, at first, these might seem inappropriate.

The coding of party identification in the final empirical example happens to use the scores that would be assigned to the linear and quadratic contrast for a three-category variable. The example does not presume that party identification is an interval variable, rather, the polynomial contrasts can also be interpreted from a different point of view. The matrix of scores for predicting the marginals on party identification is:

$$\begin{bmatrix} 1 & -1 & -1 \\ 1 & 0 & 2 \\ 1 & 1 & -1 \end{bmatrix}.$$

As before, the first column is used to estimate the mean of the logarithms of the marginal frequencies. The second column estimates the lambda for the difference between Republicans and Democrats. The third column estimates the lambda for the difference between Independents and the other categories of party identification.

Since there are two sets of scores for predictors arising from each three category independent variable there are, in all, four one-way effects and four two-way interactions estimated in the saturated model. The cell scores for each predictor variable in the regression model are shown in Table 14.19. Below each column is the label used to describe the effect.

The lambdas are estimated using (14.19). Unlike the previous examples analyzing polytomous variables, there is a simplified procedure for estimating the lambdas and the standard errors. The lambdas are calculated as in (14.20), only in place of f (the reciprocal of the number of cells in the table) the multiplier is the reciprocal of the diagonal element of $[\mathbf{X'X}]$ that corresponds to each lambda. These diagonal elements are shown in the bottom row of Table 14.19. Following this procedure, the equation for the logarithm of the expected count in each in each cell of Table 14.17 is (to two-place decimal accuracy): $y = 6.36 + .10 * (C1) + .08 * (C2) - .25 * (P1) - .09 * (P2) - .10 * (C1P1) + .06 * (C1P2) - .04 * (C2P1) + .09 * (C2P2)$. The one-way effects indicate that there are more middle than old cohort members (C1); there are more young cohort members than the average count of old and middle cohort members (C2); there are fewer Republicans than Democrats (P1); and, there are fewer Independents than the average count of Democrats and Republicans. The two-way effects are interpreted following the same rules as before, the crucial thing is to remember that the effects estimate correlations between methods of scoring categories. A negative C1P1 effect means that, compared to old cohort members, middle cohort members are more likely to be Democrats than Republicans. The C1P2 effect indicates that middle cohort members are more likely than members of the old cohort to be Independents rather than Democrats or Republicans. The small negative C2P1 effect means that young cohort members are a little less

TABLE 14.19

Illustration of Alternative Procedures for Scoring Independent Variables for the Analysis of Table 17.14

Cell	Grand mean	Cohort contrasts (Helmert) Middle–old	Young–(middle + old)	Party contrasts (Polynomial) Republican –Democrat	Independent–(Republican + Democrat)	Two-way interactions			
						C1P1	C1P2	C2P1	C2P2
a	1	−1	−1	−1	−1	1	1	1	1
b	1	1	−1	−1	−1	−1	−1	1	1
c	1	0	2	−1	−1	0	0	−2	−2
d	1	−1	−1	0	2	0	−2	0	−2
e	1	1	−1	0	2	0	2	0	−2
f	1	0	2	0	2	0	0	0	4
g	1	−1	−1	1	−1	−1	1	−1	1
h	1	1	−1	1	−1	−1	−1	−1	1
i	1	0	2	1	−1	0	0	2	−2
Variable label	(μ)	C1	C2	P1	P2	C1P1	C1P2	C2P1	C2P2
Diagonal element of $[\mathbf{X}^T\mathbf{X}]$	9	6	18	6	18	4	12	12	36

likely than the rest to be Republican rather than Democrat. The positive C2P2 effect indicates that young cohort members are more likely than anyone else to be Independents.

The simplified procedures can be used to estimate the lambdas in this example because the columns of the $\mathbf{X}$ matrix used in Eq. (14.17) are orthogonal. When the $\mathbf{X}$ matrix is orthogonal and all the cell scores are ± 1 then Eq. (14.22) can be used to estimate the standard errors. In the present example the scores are not all ± 1 so a slightly more general formula must be used. When the $\mathbf{X}$ matrix is orthogonal, the standard errors are estimated with the following formula:

$$ s_j = \frac{[\Sigma_i(c_{ij}^2/n_i)]^{1/2}}{v_j} \tag{14.24} $$

where s_j denotes the standard error for j; c_{ij} is the score for cell i used in estimating j; n_i is the expected frequency in cell i; v_j is the diagonal element in $[\mathbf{X}'\mathbf{X}]$ corresponding to λ_j.

By this formula the standard errors range between .007 for λ_{C2P2} and .020 for λ_{C1P1}. When tested by forming the ratio of the lambda to its standard error, all effects in the equation are found to be significant.

Using contrast scores for polytomous variables is a way of focusing on the significance of particular patterns in the data. There have not been many other procedures suggested for dealing with polytomous variables in log linear models. Altham (1970a, 1970b) proposes a summary index of association based on pooling certain lambda effects. The dominant trend in the social science literature, however, is to make greater use of the available scoring procedures to find parsimonious, substantively interesting regression models predicting the logarithms of the expected cell counts (Evers & Namboodiri, 1978; Fienberg, 1978).

14.5. CONCLUSION

This chapter discusses four ways of analyzing cell counts in a contingency table. Hierarchical modeling, log linear modeling, and D systems are all ways of disassembling the table, analyzing individual degrees of freedom, and incorporating the significant parts into a model that generates expected cell counts. The modeled data are presumed to be a more accurate reflection of the causal structure of the table since sampling fluctuations have been smoothed out by the modeling procedure. Each method of data analysis uses the same information (the observed cell counts) to achieve the same goal (understanding of the causal connections between variables). It is, therefore, not surprising that each method is affected in roughly the same way by boundary conditions. Small cell counts, causal effects of borderline statistical significance, and departures from simple random sampling create complications in the use of the formulas for estimating effects and testing statistical significance for any of these models.

Latent structure analysis was included in this chapter because it is also a method for analyzing the structure of a cross-classification. In using latent structure analysis, one goal is to smooth sampling fluctuations to arrive at a more reliable table of modeled data. The primary purpose, however, is to simplify the structure of the table by positing a small number of unobserved variables that generate the observed cell counts. With the sample classified into the categories of latent variables it is possible to take the analysis in several directions, some of which are shown in Section 14.3.

In the remaining pages some observations are made about the set of models presented in this chapter. There are several aspects of the statistical analysis of qualitative data that apply with equal force to each model. Some of these procedures are discussed here rather than in one of the previous sections where the impression would be given that the procedures are only appropriate for one type of model.

One purpose of this chapter is to underline the similarities and interconnections among the various approaches to qualitative data analysis. It is not correct, however, to assume that the models are the same and that there are no reasons for preferring one to the other. The differences between the models are considered at the end of this section.

Statistical Similarities between the Models in This Chapter

The point was made at the beginning of Section 14.4 that D systems and log linear models are both members of the family of generalized linear models for qualitative data analysis. The D systems model is a generalized linear model for predicting the proportions in the nonbase category (or categories) of a dependent variable. The D systems model was not presented using matrix equations, scores for categories of predictor variables, or other procedures discussed in the previous section because these methods were not needed to explain the model. There is no reason that alternative scores could not be assigned to the independent variables (instead of 0 and 1) and that a matrix approach could not be used to estimate the coefficients and their standard errors. When this is done there are no simplified procedures for calculating the parameters so computer programs must be used. The FUNCAT procedure in the SAS software package (SAS Institute 1979) can be used to perform a generalized regression analysis of proportions, thus extending greatly the range of models that can be considered using a D systems approach.

Each of the four models has relied on the chi-square test or the ratio of a slope to its standard error as a test for statistical significance. The warnings in the earlier sections about significance tests focus on the problem of the design effect for data arising from multistage, clustered samples. An additional complication with significance tests (either kind, under any model) arises when more than one significance test is to be carried out on a set of data (i.e., always). When more than one comparison is to be made, there is a difference between the alpha level for each comparison (called the nominal alpha level) and the overall alpha level for all of the comparisons. For instance, if three comparisons are made at the .05 level, the overall likelihood of a Type I error is actually equal to: $1 - (.95)^3 = .14$. Therefore, when several comparisons are to be made using survey data and some importance is attached to the overall probability of Type I error, it is better to use a more conservative alpha level for judging the significance of any particular effect (Bock, 1975; Goodman, 1969a). Another way to approach this problem is to recognize that a model can be the appropriate (or true) model for a set of data and yet some of the deleted effects can be individually statistically significant at the nominal alpha level. According to the definition of Type I error, when a model fits the data, about 32% of the "insignificant" slopes will yield a ratio greater than ± 1 when divided by the (adjusted) standard error and about 5% will yield a ratio greater than ± 1.96. A decision made on the basis of this rule of thumb can conflict with the warning issued earlier that a blanket chi-square test used to assess the fit of a model will occasionally miss an important effect. In this situation one turns to the other procedures outlined for establishing a net of inference.

Substantive Differences between the Models in This Chapter

Log linear modeling and D systems are two kinds of generalized linear models for qualitative data. Each can be understood in the general linear modeling framework for estimation and significance testing. Hierarchical modeling, on the other hand, does not estimate slopes and relies on chi-square tests for significance. For reasons stated at the beginning of this section these models usually agree on the set of effects that is necessary and sufficient to describe the data. Even so, this question is sometimes asked: Which method should be used for selecting models? In terms of locating statistically significant effects, the answer is that no method is inherently better, since they usually agree on significance tests except in boundary circumstances where none is superior. On the other hand, as the sample size increases, all three approaches will find most effects to be statistically significant. In this circumstance I believe that generalized linear models (log linear models or D systems) are better tools for data analysis. When linear models are used, both the slopes and standard errors are estimated. Because both parameters are available to describe an effect, it is easy to make the distinction between statistical and substantive significance. With large samples many parameters are statistically significant but too small in magnitude to be substantively interesting. When using hierarchical models the only warning one has of this situation is that certain effects produce a smaller change in chi square than others. It is much more difficult to make precise statements about substantive significance with that kind of information.

Within the family of generalized linear models there are important differences that arise because of differences in scale of measurement of the dependent variable. The log linear model measures main effects and differences on a logistic scale and is analogous to (but not quite the same as) a regression model predicting standardized normal deviates for measuring the area under the normal curve. A predicted normal deviate of 0 corresponds to a predicted proportion of .5. If the predicted normal deviate increases by one unit, the predicted proportion goes up to .84, an increase of 34%. Another unit increase in the predicted normal deviate changes the predicted proportion to .98, a further increase of only 12%. The change in the predicted probability associated with a given coefficient is not a linear function of the coefficient. One advantage that is claimed for the log linear model is that because of the scale of measurement, the predicted proportions can never be outside the bounds of 0 and 1 (just as the area under the normal curve associated with any normal deviate is always between 0 and 100%). With generalized linear models for proportions it is possible to obtain expected values outside the acceptable range.

A further, and very important, consequence of the difference in the scale of measurement is that the two models frequently do not agree on the relative magnitude of a two-way (or higher order) interaction. This can be illustrated by comparing log linear effects and percentage differences in two-way tables. A table with 50% positive among those in the base category of the independent variable and 55% positive among those in the nonbase category has a percentage difference of 5%. The odds ratio (the best measure of association for describing log linear models—cf. Fleiss 1973) in this table is 1.22. This situation is shown as the point labeled "A" in Figure 14.3. If the percentage in each category are changed to 94 and 99.9, respectively, then the difference is still 5%, but the odds ratio becomes 6.32. This is shown as point B in Figure 14.3. In general, the lower line in Figure 14.3 shows the odds ratio corresponding to a D of 5% for several different choices of the marginals on the dependent variable.

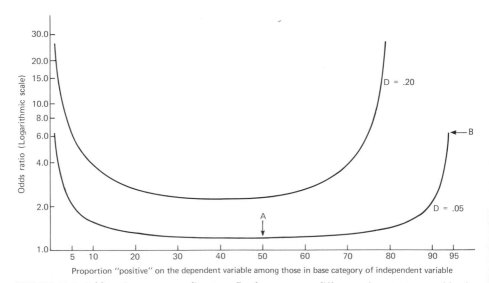

FIGURE 14.3 Odds ratios corresponding to a fixed percentage difference in a two-way table, for different marginal distributions on the dependent variable.

The upper line shows the relationship between the odds ratio and the marginals when the D is 20%.

The flatter area of each curve shows the region where the relative magnitude of the two coefficients is not affected by the marginal distribution of the dependent variable. As the marginals on the dependent variable become skewed the magnitude of the odds ratio, relative to D, becomes greater. Furthermore, the extent of divergence between the two models becomes more extreme and the range in marginal proportions over which the models agree decreases as the effect of the independent variable as measured by the percentage difference becomes stronger.

The difference in scale for the two sets of parameters can result in differing interpretations of the relative magnitude (and even significance) of effects estimated under the log linear and D systems model. The models are most likely to disagree when the dependent variable is skewed. One substantive interpretation of the difference is that the scale for the percentage difference suffers from a ceiling effect. It is impossible for variables to exert a constant additive causal effect as the marginal proportions approach one of the boundaries. Odds ratios (and log linear coefficients based on this measure—see Section 14.4, p. 592) do not suffer from a ceiling effect because a constant multiplicative relationship causes a smaller change in percentages as the marginals become more extreme. Knoke (1975) presents an empirical example of a situation when the models disagree in their substantive conclusions. Goodman (1976) and Mosteller (1968) go into more detail on some of the subtleties of the problem.

The difference in scale of measurement is also the reason that D system parameters can be multiplied to calculate indirect effects in a path model and log linear effects cannot. The diagrams that Goodman reports (1972c, 1973) are not really path diagrams in the sense that the term is usually understood (Wright, 1934). They cannot be multiplied to calculate indirect effects, nor are there simple, general rules for decomposing zero order log linear effects into direct, indirect, and spurious components (Davis & Schooler, 1974).

One reason for this complication with log linear effects is that they are symmetrical measures of interaction. This means that the measure of the relationship between variables in a log linear model is insensitive to causal order (this is not true for the regression model for percentages). This property makes log linear analysis an extremely flexible system for handling sets of variables where the causal order is not clear. On the other hand, it means that there is no way to use instrumental variables to obtain separate measures of one-way causation between variables that affect each other (Brier, 1978; Fienberg, 1977; Goodman, 1977).

WHICH IS BEST

The set of models considered here is better than any other set of procedures for analyzing most kinds of qualitative data. However, within the set, each model has its strengths and weaknesses. As a teacher, I prefer to begin with percentage differences and path models. As a researcher, I find log linear models most attractive (cf. Berkson, 1951) unless the substantive argument requires the calculation of indirect forward effects (as in the D systems models for decomposing indirect sources of change). I also find that some substantive problems are best framed in terms of distribution of cell counts and hierarchical models.

Each model presented here is connected to the rest by statistical theory and by the measurement properties of cell counts as statistical data. Nevertheless, each model has its own set of strengths and flexibilities. The aim of this chapter is to demonstrate some of the basic properties of each model and to show that there is no answer to the question: Which is best?

ACKNOWLEDGMENTS

Several individuals and institutions helped in one way or another in the preparation of this chapter. I thank Arthur L. Stinchcombe, James A. Davis, Otis Dudley Duncan, and the editors of this volume for careful, helpful readings of the first draft. The Department of Sociology at the University of Wisconsin, Madison, and Mimi Devaul in particular provided generous and conscientious help with manuscript preparation. Tom Reif of the National Opinion Research Center worked beyond the call of duty in aiding the preparation of the second draft. Much of the material in this chapter was learned while the author was working on projects funded by the National Science Foundation, the National Opinion Research Center, and the Institute for Research on Poverty at the University of Wisconsin, Madison.

REFERENCES

Altham, P. E.
    1970a   "The measurement of association in a contingency table: Three extension of the cross-ratios and metrics methods." *J. R. Statist. Soc. B 32:* 395–407.
    1970b   "The measurement of association of rows and columns for an $r \times s$ contingency table." *Journal of the Royal Statistical Society B 32:* 63–73.
Berkson, J.
    1951   "Why I prefer logits to probits." *Biometrics* 7: 327–339.
Bishop, Y. M. M.
    1971   "Effects of collapsing multidimensional contingency tables." *Biometrics* 27: 545–562.
Bishop, Y. M. M., S. Fienberg, and P. Holland
    1975 *Discrete Multivariate Analysis: Theory and Practice.* Cambridge: MIT Press.
Blake, Judith
    1971   "Abortion and Public Opinion: The 1960–1970 Decade" *Science* 171: 540–548.
Bock, R. D.
    1975 *Multivariate Statistical Analysis for the Behavioral Sciences.* New York: McGraw–Hill.
Brier, S.
    1978   "The Utility of Systems of Simultaneous Logistic Response Equations." In K. Schuessler (ed.), *Sociological Methodology 1979.* San Francisco: Jossey-Bass.
Bunker, J. P., W. H. Forrest, Jr., F. Mosteller, and L. Vandam, Eds.
    1969   "The National Halothane Study." Bethesda: National Institutes of Health.
Burke, P. J., and A. Turk
    1975   "Factors affecting postarrest dispositions: A model for analysis." *Social Problems* 22: 313–332.

Clogg, C.
1979 "Some latent structure models for the analysis of Likert-type data." *Social Science Research* 8: 287–301.
Cochran, W. G.
1954 "Some methods for strengthening the common χ^2 tests. *Biometrics* 10: 417–451.
Cohen, J.
1968 "Multiple regression as a general data-analytic system." *Psychological Bulletin* 6: 426–443.
Coleman, J. S.
1964 *Introduction to Mathematical Sociology.* New York: Free Press.
Coleman, J. S., S. D. Kelly, and J. A. Moore
1975 "Recent trends in school integration." Washington, D.C.: Urban Institute.
Cortese, C. F., R. F. Falk, and J. K. Cohen
1976 "Further considerations on the methodological analysis of segregation indices." *American Sociological Review* 41: 630–637.
Cox, D. R.
1970 *The Analysis of Binary Data.* London: Methuen.
Davis, J. A.
1971 *Elementary Survey Analysis.* Englewood, N.J.: Prentice–Hall.
1974 Hierarchical models for significance tests in multivariate contingency tables: An exegesis of Goodman's recent papers." In H. Costner (ed.), *Sociological Methodology 1973–74.* San Francisco: Jossey–Bass.
1975a "Communism, conformity, cohorts and categories: American tolerance in 1954 and 1972–73." *American Journal of Sociology* 81: 491–513.
1975b "The log linear analysis of survey replications." In K. Land and S. Spilerman (eds.), *Social Indicator Models.* New York. Russell Sage.
1976 "Analyzing contingency tables with linear flow graphs: D Systems." In D. Heise (ed.), *Sociological Methodology 1976.* San Francisco: Jossey–Bass.
1978 "Studying categorical data over time." *Social Science Research* 7: 151–179.
Davis, J. A., and S. Schooler
1974 "Nonparametric path analysis—The multivariate structure of dichotomous data when using the odds ratio or Yule's Q." *Social Science Research* 3: 267–297.
Deming, W. E.
1938 *Statistical Adjustment of Data.* New York: Wiley.
Deming, W., and F. Stephan
1940 "On a least squares adjustment of a sampled frequency table when the expected marginal totals are known." *Annals of Mathematical Statistics* 11: 427–444.
Draper, N. R., and H. Smith
1966 *Applied Regression Analysis.* New York: Wiley.
Duncan, O. D.
1975 "Partitioning polytomous variables in multiway contingency tables." *Social Science Research* 4: 167–182.
1979 "Constrained parameters in a model for categorical data." *Sociological Methods and Research* 8: 57–68.
Duncan, O. D., and B. Duncan
1955 "A methodological analysis of segregation indexes." *American Sociological Review* 20: 210–217.
Duncan, O. D., and J. McRae, Jr.
1978 "Multiway contingency analysis with a scaled response or factor." In K. Schuessler (ed.), *Sociological Methodology 1979.* San Francisco: Jossey–Bass.
Evers, M., and K. Namboodiri
1978 "On the design matrix strategy in the analysis of categorical data." In K. Schuessler (ed.), *Sociological Methodology 1979.* San Francisco: Jossey–Bass.

Fennessey, J.
   1968 "The general linear model: A new perspective on some familiar topics." *American Journal of Sociology* 74: 1–27.
Fienberg, S.
   1977 *The Analysis of Cross-Classified Categorical Data*. Cambridge: MIT Press.
Finney, D. J.
   1971 *Probit Analysis*. Cambridge, England: Cambridge University Press.
Fleiss, J. L.
   1973 *Statistical Methods for Rates and Proportions*. New York: Wiley.
Gart, J. J., and J. R. Zweifel
   1967 "On the bias of various estimators of the logit and its variance with application to quantal bioassay." *Biometrika* 54: 181–187.
Goodman, L. A.
   1963 "On methods for comparing contingency tables." *Journal of the Royal Statistical Society* 126(Series A): 94–108.
   1968 "The analysis of cross-classified data: Independence, quasi-independence and interactions in contingency tables with or without missing entries." *Journal of the American Statistical Association* 63: 1091–1131.
   1969a "How to ransack mobility tables and other kinds of cross-classification tables." *American Journal of Sociology* 75: 1–40.
   1969b "On the measurement of social mobility: An index of status persistence." *American Sociology Review* 34: 831–850.
   1970 "The multivariate analysis of qualitative data: Interactions among multiple classifications." *Journal of the American Statistical Association* 65: 226–256.
   1971 "The analysis of multidimensional contingency tables: Stepwise procedures and direct estimation methods for building models for multiple classifications." *Technometrics* 13: 33–61.
   1972a "A general model for the analysis of surveys." *American Journal of Sociology* 77: 1035–1086.
   1972b "A modified multiple regression approach to the analysis of dichotomous variables." *American Sociology Review* 37: 28–46.
   1972c "Some multiplicative models for the analysis of cross-classified data." Pp. 649–696 in L. LeCam (ed.), *Proceedings of the Sixth Berkeley Symposium on Mathematical Statistics and Probability*. Vol. 1. Berkeley: University of California Press.
   1973 "Causal analysis of data from panel studies and other kinds of surveys." *American Journal of Sociology* 78: 1135–1191.
   1974a "The analysis of systems of qualitative variables when some of the variables are unabservable. Part I—A modified latent structure approach." *American Journal of Sociology* 79: 1179–1259.
   1974b "Exploratory latent structure analysis using both identifiable and unidentifiable models." *Biometrika* 61: 215–231.
   1975 "A new model for scaling response patterns: An application of the quasi-independence concept." *Journal of American Statistical Association* 70: 755–768.
   1976 "The relationship between the modified and the more usual multiple regression approach to the analysis of dichotomous variables." In D. Heise (ed.), *Sociological Methodology 1976*. San Francisco: Jossey–Bass.
   1977 "Reply to Kritzer: How not to analyze nonrecursive systems pertaining to qualitative variables." *Political Methodology* 4: 23–34.
   1979 "Simple models for the analysis of association in cross-classifications having ordered categories." *Journal of the American Statistical Association* 74: 537–552.
Goodman, L. A., and W. H. Kruskal
   1954 "Measures of associations for cross-classifications." *Journal of the American Statistical Association* 49: 732–764.

Grizzle, J. E., C. F. Starmer, and G. G. Koch
  1969 "Analysis of categorical data by linear models." *Biometrics* 25: 489–504.
Guest, A. M.
  1974 "Class consciousness and American political attitudes." *Social Forces* 52: 496–510.
Haberman, S. J.
  1974a *The Analysis of Frequency Data*. Chicago: University of Chicago Press.
  1974b "Log linear models for frequency tables with ordered classifications." *Biometrics* 39: 589–600.
  1978 *Analysis of Qualitative Data. Vol 1: Introductory Topics*. New York: Academic Press.
  1979 *Analysis of Qualitative Data. Vol. 2: New Developments*. New York: Academic Press.
Hauser, R. M., J. Koffel, H. P. Travis, and P. J. Dickinson
  1975a "Structural changes in occupational mobility among men in the United States." *American Sociological Review* 40: 585–598.
Hauser, R. M., J. Koffel, H. P. Travis, and P. J. Dickinson
  1975b "Temporal change in occupational mobility: Evidence for men in the United States." *American Sociological Review* 40: 279–297.
Hawkes, R.
  1971 "The multivariate analysis of ordinal measures." *American Journal of Sociology* 76: 908–926.
Heise, D. R.
  1975 *Causal Analysis*. New York: Wiley.
Higgins, J., and G. Koch
  1977 "Variable selection and generalized chi-square analysis of categorical data applied to a large cross-sectional occupational health survey." *International Statistical Review* 45: 51–62.
Johnston, J.
  1972 *Econometric Methods* (2nd ed.). New York: McGraw–Hill.
Kasarda, J. D., and M. Janowitz
  1974 "Community attachment in mass society." *American Sociological Review* 39: 328–339.
Kish, L.
  1957 "Confidence intervals for clustered samples." *American Sociological Review* 22: 154–165.
  1965 *Survey Sampling*. New York: Wiley.
Kish, L., and M. R. Frankel
  1970 "Balanced repeated replications for standard errors." *Journal of the American Statistical Association* 65: 1071–1094.
Knoke, D.
  1974 "Religious involvement and political behavior: A log linear analysis of white Americans 1952–1968." *Sociological Quarterly* 15: 51–65.
  1975 "A comparison of log linear and regression models for systems of dichotomous variables." *Sociological Methods and Research* 3: 416–434.
  1976 *Change and Continuity in American Politics: The Social Bases of Political Parties*. Baltimore: Johns Hopkins University Press.
Knoke, D., and L. Isaac
  1976 "Quality of higher education and sociopolitical attitudes." *Social Forces* 54: 524–529.
Knoke, D., and A. Lane
  1975 "Size of place, migration and voting turnout." *Journal of Political and Military Sociology* 3: 127–139.
Knoke, D., and D. E. Long
  1975 "The economic sensitivity of the American farm vote." *Rural Sociology* 40: 7–17.
Koch, G. C., and D. W. Reinfurt
  1971 "The analysis of categorical data from mixed models." *Biometrics* 27: 157–173.

Kullback, S.
    1959 *Information Theory and Statistics.* New York: Wiley.
Lancaster, H. O.
    1969 *The Chi-Squared Distribution.* New York: Wiley.
Lazarsfeld, P.
    1951 "The logical and mathematical foundation of latent structure analysis." In S. Stouffer, L. Guttman, E. Suchman, P. Lazarsfeld, S. Star, and J. Clausen *Studies in Social Psychology in World War II Vol. 4: Measurement and Prediction.* Princeton: Princeton University Press.
    1954 "A conceptual introduction to latent structure analysis." In P. Lazarsfeld (ed.), *Mathematical Thinking in the Social Sciences.* Chicago: Free Press.
Lazarsfeld, P., and N. W. Henry
    1968 *Latent Structure Analysis.* New York: Houghton.
Lehnen, R. G., and G. C. Koch
    1974 "A general linear approach to the analysis of nonmetric data: Applications for political science." *American Journal of Political Science* 2: 283–314.
Lieberson, S.
    1963 *Ethnic Patterns in American Cities.* New York: Free Press.
Mason, W., and J. S. House
    1976 "Reply to Guest." *American Sociological Review* 41: 365–376.
Maxwell, A. E.
    1961 *Analyzing Qualitative Data.* London: Methuen.
McFadden, D.
    1974 "Conditional logit analysis of qualitative choice behavior." In P. Zraembka (ed.), *Frontiers in Econometrics.* New York: Academic Press.
Mood, A. M.
    1950 *Introduction to the Theory of Statistics.* New York: McGraw–Hill.
Mosteller, F.
    1968 "Association and estimation in contingency tables." *Journal of the American Statistical Association* 63: 1–28.
National Bureau of Economic Research
    1976 *Annals of Economic and Social Measurement* 5: 363–561. (Special issue on discrete, qualitative, and limited dependent variables.)
Nelder, J. A.
    1974 "Log linear models for contingency tables: A generalization of classical least squares." *Applied Statistics* 3: 323–329.
Nelder, J. A., and R. W. M. Wedderburn
    1972 "Generalized linear models." *Journal of the Royal Statistical Society* 135(Series A): 370–384.
Nerlove, M., and S. J. Press
    1973 *Univariate and Mulitivariate Log Linear and Logistical Models.* Santa Monica: Rand.
Page, W. F.
    1977 "Interpretation of Goodman's log linear model effects: An odds ratio approach." *Sociological Methods and Research* 5: 419–435.
Payne, C.
    1977 "Log linear models for contingency tables." In C. A. O'Muircheartaigh and C. Payne (eds.), *The Analysis of Survey Data. Vol. 2: Model Fitting.* New York: Wiley.
Plackett, R. L.
    1974 *The Analysis of Categorical Data.* London: Griffin.
Pullum, T. W.
    1975 *Measuring Occupational Inheritance.* (*Progress in Mathematical Social Sciences Series,* Vol. 5.) New York: Elsevier.

Reynolds, H. T.
1977 *The Analysis of Cross-Classification*. New York: Free Press.
Robson, D. S.
1959 "A simple method for constructing orthogonal polynomials when the independent variable is unequally spaced." *Biometrics* 15: 187–191.
Rosenberg, M.
1968 *The Logic of Survey Analysis*. New York: Basic Books.
Ryder, N. B., and C. F. Westoff
1971 "Attitudes toward abortion." In N. B. Ryder and C. F. Westoff, *Reproduction in the United States*. Princeton: Princeton University Press.
SAS Institute
1979 *SAS User's Guide: 1979 Edition*. Raleigh, N.C.: SAS Institute.
Scheuren, F. J.
1973 "Ransacking CPS tabulations: Applications of the log linear model to poverty statistics." *Annals of Economic and Social Measurement* 2: 159–182.
Smith, R. B.
1972 "Neighborhood context and college plans: An ordinal path analysis." *Social Forces* 51: 199–217.
Snell, E. J.
1964 "A scaling procedure for ordered categorical data." *Biometrics* 3: 592–607.
Southwood, K.
1974 "Goodman and Kruskal's Tau–b as a correlation ratio." *Sociological Methods and Research* 3: 82–110.
Stouffer, S., and J. Toby
1951 "Role conflict and personality." *American Journal of Sociology* 56: 395–406.
Suits, D. B.
1957 "Use of dummy variables in regression equations." *Journal of the American Statistical Association* 52: 548–551.
Taeuber, K. E., and A. F. Taeuber
1965 *Negroes in Cities*. Chicago: Aldine.
Taylor, D. G.
1976 "The accuracy of respondent-coded occupation." *Public Opinion Quarterly* 40: 254–255.
1977 "The expansion of abortion rights in American public opinion." Chicago: National Opinion Research Center, University of Chicago.
1978 "Modeling current and future opinion trends: Support for marijuana legalization." *Proceedings of the American Statistical Association, 1978 Social Statistics Section*: 124–129.
1980 "Procedures for evaluating trends in public opinion." *Public Opinion Quarterly* 44: 1 (Spring, 1980) 86–100.
Taylor, D. G., P. Sheatsky, and A. M. Greeley
1978 "Attitudes toward racial integration." *Scientific American* 238: 42–49.
Theil, H.
"On the Estimation of Relationships Involving Qualitative Variables." *American Journal of Sociology* 76: (1, July 1970) 103–154.
Theil, H., and A. J. Finizza
1971 "A note on the measurement of racial integration of schools by means of informational concepts." *Journal of Mathematical Sociology* 1: 187–194.
Upton, G.
1978 "The Analysis of Cross-Tabulated Data." New York: Wiley.
Vanneman, R., and F. Pampel
1977 "The American perception of class and status." *American Sociological Review* 42: 422–437.

Williams, O. D., and J. Grizzle
  1972 "Analysis of contingency tables having ordered response categories." *Journal of the American Statistical Association* 67: 55–63.
Winer, B. J.
  1971 *Statistical Principles in Experimental Design*. (2nd ed.). New York: McGraw–Hill.
Wright, S.
  1934 "The method of path coefficients." *Annals of Mathematical Statistics* 5: 161–215.
Yates, F.
  1948 "The analysis of contingency tables with groupings based on quantitative characters." *Biometrika* 35: 176–181.
Zoloth, B. S.
  1974 "An investigation of alternative measures of school segregation." Institute for Research on Poverty Discussion Paper. Madison, Wisconsin: Institute for Research on Poverty.

Chapter 15

Causal Modeling and Survey Research[1]

Ross M. Stolzenberg and Kenneth C. Land

15.1. INTRODUCTION

The purpose of scientific theory is to understand causation. The purpose of the scientific method is to test scientific theories. But whereas these goals are perfectly clear, and it is hoped, beyond dispute, the sad truth is that the method does not measure up to the demands of theory. The details of why and how scientific method falls short have filled many useful volumes (see, for example, Blalock, 1964; Cohen & Nagel, 1934), but the main outlines of the problem are straightforward: The real world is inherently more complex than our theories about it, and our measurements of real world phenomena are inherently error prone. So when a theory is tested, one must always wonder if phenomena that it neglects have intruded, undetected, to produce the effects that we unsuspectingly attribute to causes identified by the theory. We must be concerned that measurements of theoretical concepts have been so inaccurate that they mislead rather than enlighten. The problem is especially complicated in social research, for although randomized experimental designs can reduce much of the gap between theory and method, experimental tests of social theories are often not possible: In many cases the required randomization and experimental manipulations would be unethical, unlawful, too expensive, too time consuming, or simply impossible to perform. Although ingenious research designs and statistical methods vastly increase the power of nonexperimental research, the

[1] Stolzenberg's work on this chapter was partially supported by grant No. 1 K02 MH 00266-01 from the National Institute of Mental Health, Alcohol, Drug Abuse and Mental Health Administration, U.S. Department of Health, Education and Welfare. Sections 15.1 and 15.3 of this chapter are by Stolzenberg, and Sections 15.2 and 15.4 are by Land.

HANDBOOK OF SURVEY RESEARCH

complexity of the real world is ever present and, in the last analysis, always overwhelming.

Despite the enduring limitations of the scientific method, there is extraordinary consensus that it is better to test theories with a fallible method than to accept them with no empirical tests at all. So one makes simplifying assumptions about the real world and proceeds to build and test theories. Probably the most important of these assumptions concern measurements of phenomena included in theories and the behavior of phenomena excluded from theories. One normally assumes that phenomena under consideration are measured adequately and that no serious damage is done by neglecting factors ignored by the theory. Having made these assumptions, one proceeds to develop a set of empirically verified, interrelated statements about the precise nature of causal linkages among phenomena *under consideration* and *as measured*. The result is not a full-blown theory, but, in the words of Herbert Simon (1953–1957), a *causal model* that is inherently linked to a set of measurement procedures, assumptions about which phenomena are relevant and which can be ignored, and mathematical equations describing the causal effects of measured relevant phenomena on each other. So causal models are serviceable fictions that allow researchers to gain the simplicity that they need to proceed with the task of empirically verified theory building. Although precision is obtained by ignoring parts of the real world, successful simple models can be complicated by adding different measurements of relevant phenomena, and by widening the range of phenomena under consideration. Indeed, the term *causal modeling* has come to mean a strategy of starting with simple models and gradually complicating them until they resemble the real world enough to be considered full-blown theories.

The strategy of causal modeling requires that the researcher make three major decisions: choosing real world phenomena to include in the model, finding empirical measures of these phenomena, and selecting mathematical equations that represent the postulated causal effects of the various phenomena on each other. This chapter deals with the third decision, selection of appropriate mathematical functions. In the following pages, we focus on two key issues: First, we describe several families of mathematical functions that correspond to some common verbal formulations of causal relations. These functions are well suited to models involving interactions among variables as well as models comprising only additive relationships. We also discuss functions that are appropriate when causal effects are curvilinear as well as functions that are appropriate for linear relationships. The second focus of this chapter is the presentation of a consistent set of techniques for measuring causal effects in all kinds of mathematical formulations regardless of whether the relationships involved are linear or nonlinear, additive or nonadditive, one-way or reciprocal. We assume that the reader is familiar with elementary statistics and ordinary least squares linear regression. Some familiarity with elementary calculus and matrix algebra is useful, but not necessary, for following the arguments. Our emphasis is on finding mathematical functions to fit some of the more common verbal formulations of causation, and on describing methods for making causal inferences, *stated in words,* from the parameters of these equations.

The plan of this chapter is as follows: In the next section, we discuss some basic principles of causal inference in nonexperimental contexts which underlie causal modeling. In the third section, we discuss linear, nonlinear, additive, and nonadditive recursive causal models, and we develop a set of techniques for measuring causal effects in all of them. Finally, in the fourth section, we discuss nonrecursive models.

15.2. SOME BASIC PRINCIPLES OF NONEXPERIMENTAL CAUSAL INFERENCE

Under what conditions can nonexperimental (observational) data on covariances (correlations) among a set of variables be used to "make causal inferences" about invariant dependencies among the variables? Thanks to research by many statisticians and social scientists extending over the past 50 years, a precise answer can now be given, and this section explicates the present-day concensus response. The historical route to this answer, has been bumpy, indirect, and sometimes misleading. Therefore, we note the historical origins of the question as well as various key historical contributions to the development of that response.

Mill's Method of Concomitant Variation

To a considerable extent, modern methods of causal modeling and causal inference in nonexperimental research can be considered explications of conditions under which John Stuart Mill's (1875) famous *method of concomitant variation* can be used to corroborate hypotheses of causal connections among variables. Mill's method is: "Whatever phenomenon varies in any manner whenever another phenomenon varies in some particular manner, is either a cause or an effect of that phenomenon, or is connected with it through some fact of causation." In other words, Mill's concomitant variation canon of nonexperimental experimental inquiry essentially asserts that "there can be no positive (or negative) correlation without causation," and that "there can be no causation without correlation."

Stated in this way, the canon clearly needs qualification, and, in fact, it has been the subject of analysis by numerous philosophers of science. For example, Cohen and Nagel (1934, pp. 262–263) argue that the method of concomitant variation cannot be used either for the *discovery* of relevant variables or for *proof* of causation. Merely noting that a phenomenon varies does not lead to a class of circumstances that could have caused the variation. Certainly not *all* the circumstances surrounding the phenomenon, nor even all the varying circumstances, are possible causes. The formulation of hypotheses and judgments of relevance are required before this canon can be employed to unravel causal (i.e., invariant) dependencies. Similarly, the presence of a concomitant variation of a phenomenon and some other factor is not sufficient to *establish* a causal connection. On the contrary, if an invariant connection has been established on the basis of a prior theoretical argument, then correlations can be used as corroborative evidence. In brief, Cohen and Nagel (1934, p. 264) conclude that the primary value of the method of concomitant variation is to help to eliminate irrelevant causes. That is, nothing will be regarded as the cause of a phenomenon if, when the phenomenon varies that thing does not vary, or when the phenomenon does not vary that thing does vary. Thus, *Mill's concomitant variation canon properly can be used only to infer that two phenomena are not causally related if they do not vary concomitantly.*

The Concepts of True and Spurious Correlation

Although Cohen and Nagel's analysis determines what is established by the *absence* of a correlation between two phenomena, it does not clarify what is proved by the *presence* of a correlation. The latter issue has been the subject of analysis by a long line of statisticians and social scientists, including especially Blalock (1962, 1964); Boudon (1965); Duncan (1966, 1975); Kendall and Lazarsfeld (1950); Land (1973); Lazarsfeld (1955); Simon (1952, 1953, 1954, 1968); Yule (1932); and Zeisel (1947).

The early contributions by Yule (1932), Ziesel (1947), Kendall and Lazarsfeld (1950), and Lazarsfeld (1955) developed the distinction between "true" and "spurious" correlation, implying that, although correlation in general may be no proof of causation, true correlation does constitute such evidence. All these treatments deal essentially with correlation among three variables. Within this context, the basic rule of thumb for making causal inferences that emerges is: If the nonzero correlation between variables x and y cannot be made to vanish (i.e., go to zero) by the introduction of one or more theoretically relevant *antecedent* "test factors" z, then the original correlation is true, not spurious (see, for example, Lazarsfeld, 1955, p. 125). Note that the emphasis here is on the requirement that the test factors be antecedent to (i.e., not causally dependent on) both x and y. If z is asserted to *intervene* between x and y, then the destruction of the x–y correlation by controlling for z is said to provide an "interpretation" of their causal relation rather than a proof of spuriousness.

These early discussions of the spurious correlation concept did not produce a routine operational procedure for making causal inferences because of two basic inadequacies. First, the analyses are based almost entirely on the informal analysis of associations in two- and three-way cross-tabulations with no attempt at rigorous statistical inference. Second, although generalizations to more than three variables are indicated, they were not examined in detail. Indeed, in the absence of formal statistical methods of analysis, this leap to situations involving more than three variables is virtually impossible to achieve with reasonable standards of rigor.

Simon's (1952–1957, 1953–1957, and 1954–1957) contributions helped to alleviate these inadequacies by using mid-twentieth-century advances in the theory of identification and statistical estimation of systems of simultaneous structural equations (for an elementary discussion of these advances, see Marschak, 1950; for an advanced treatment, see Koopmans, Rubin, and Leipnik, 1950) to reanalyze the notion of spurious correlation. For this, Simon (1954–1957) first assumes (as in all ordinary correlation analyses) that the relations among the variables under discussion are linear and that the variables are measured from their respective means (so that they can be represented by equations without constant terms). He then examines *causal* or *structural-equation models* of systems of three variables whose behavior is determined by some set of linear mechanisms.

It is well known from linear algebra that if each variable is to be determined by a distinct mechanism, then we need three mechanisms, each represented by an equation, to determine the three variables (see, for example, Nering, 1967, pp. 58–61). The most general case would be that in which each of the variables *directly influences* the other two. That is, in one equation z would appear as the dependent variable, x and y as independent variables; in the second equation x would appear as the dependent variable, y and z as independent; in the third equation, y as dependent variable, x and z as independent. In this case, the equations could be written in standard single-equation regression format as follows:

$$z = a_{12}x + a_{13}y + \varepsilon_1, \tag{15.1}$$

$$x = a_{21}z + a_{23}y + \varepsilon_2, \tag{15.2}$$

$$y = a_{31}z + a_{32}x + \varepsilon_3, \tag{15.3}$$

or, after transposing terms and changing algebraic signs of the corresponding cocfficients, the equations can be put in the form of a system of linear algebraic equations, a form that will be useful subsequently in this section:

$$z + a_{12}x + a_{13}y = \varepsilon_1, \tag{15.1'}$$

$$a_{21}z + x + a_{23}y = \varepsilon_2, \tag{15.2'}$$

$$a_{31}z + a_{32}x + y = \varepsilon_3, \tag{15.3'}$$

where the epsilons are stochastic (random) "disturbance" or "error" terms that measure the net effects of all other variables not explicitly incorporated into the system, and where we normalize the coefficient of the dependent variable in each equation to unity. The matrix of constants (*structural coefficients*)

$$\begin{bmatrix} 1 & a_{12} & a_{13} \\ a_{21} & 1 & a_{23} \\ a_{31} & a_{32} & 1 \end{bmatrix} \tag{15.4}$$

is called the *coefficient matrix* of the system.

Given this representation, Simon articulates the conditions necessary for a direct application of Mill's method of concomitant variation to the problem of causal inference, that is, the conditions under which the presence of correlation between two variables is proof of causation. For this, consider the two-variable system given by equations (15.2′) and (15.3′) with the variable z set equal to zero and the constants and errors relabeled as bs and zetas, respectively:

$$x + b_{12} y = \zeta_1, \tag{15.5}$$

$$b_{21} x + y = \zeta_2. \tag{15.6}$$

Now, to use the language of the spurious correlation literature discussed previously, suppose that whatever process determines the values of the variable x (in a *population* of n observations on x and y, in the present subsection, ignoring issues of sampling variability and statistical inference) occurs independently of the variable y, so that x is *antecedent* to y. In practice, this may occur because the process that determines x *precedes in time* the process that determines y, or it may be due to some *structural constraint* on the system that prevents y from influencing x. Regardless of the source of the assertion that x is antecedent to y, its operational implication is that the coefficient $b_{12} = 0$ in Eq. (15.5) so that the system (15.5)–(15.6) reduces to:

$$x = \zeta_1, \tag{15.7}$$

$$b_{21} x + y = \zeta_2. \tag{15.8}$$

Again, since we have assumed that x is determined by a process that is antecedent to the process that determines y, there may be no reason to believe that the errors in the two equations are dependent. Therefore, we make the additional assumption that ζ_1 and ζ_2 are independent (in the probabilistic or stochastic sense), which means that we assume that the system consisting of x and y is closed to systematic nonrandom effects from other variables. Actually, this assumption is somewhat stronger than necessary for this very simple model, for which we need only the assumption that ζ_1 and ζ_2 are uncorrelated. However, since the stochastic independence assumption is necessary to deduce certain desireable properties in models with more than two equations, and since it is well known in probability theory that stochastic independence implies zero correlation (see, for example, Parzen, 1960, pp. 361–364), we adopt the stronger assumption here.

Notationally, the zero correlation assumption can be written in terms of the population product moment correlation coefficient (rho) of the joint distribution of ζ_1 and ζ_2 as follows:

$$\rho_{\zeta_1 \zeta_2} = \rho(\zeta_1, \zeta_2) = 0. \tag{15.9}$$

Since the product moment correlation coefficient is defined as the ratio of the population covariance of the random variables to their population standard deviations (sigmas):

$$\rho_{\zeta_1\zeta_2} = \frac{\text{cov}(\zeta_1, \zeta_2)}{\sigma_{\zeta_1}\sigma_{\zeta_2}}. \tag{15.10}$$

the constraint (15.9) is equivalent to:

$$\text{cov}(\zeta_1\zeta_2) = 0. \tag{15.11}$$

Finally, since it is well known in probability theory that the covariance of two random variables satisfies the equality (see, for example, Hanushek and Jackson, 1977, p. 331):

$$\text{cov}(\zeta_1\zeta_2) = E(\zeta_1\zeta_2) - E(\zeta_1)E(\zeta_2), \tag{15.12}$$

where $E(\cdot)$ denotes the expected value operator probability theory applied to the variable in parentheses (roughly, the mean value of the indicated variable in a population or sampling distribution), and since we have assumed that we are dealing with variables measured from their means so that $E(\zeta_1) = E(\zeta_2) = 0$, constraints (15.9) and (15.11) are equivalent to

$$E(\zeta_1\zeta_2) = 0. \tag{15.13}$$

Thus, we have three equivalent ways of expressing the assumption that ζ_1 and ζ_2 are uncorrelated—Eqs. (15.9), (15.11), and (15.13).

Given this specification of the model, it is clear that we can rewrite equation (15.8) as

$$y = -b_{21}x + \zeta_2, \tag{15.14}$$

and apply *ordinarily least squares* (OLS) to estimate the coefficient b_{21}, which in population parameter form can be written as:

$$b_{21} = -\left[\frac{\text{cov}(x, y)}{\sigma_x^2}\right] = -\left[\frac{E(xy)}{E(x^2)}\right], \tag{15.15}$$

where $\sigma_x^2 = E(x^2)$ denotes the population variance of x. The applicability of this estimator follows from our specification that x is antecedent to y. We have argued that this implies $b_{12} = 0$ and $E(\zeta_1\zeta_2) = 0$ in the model of (15.5) and (15.6). These two conditions imply that the conditional expectation of ζ_2 given x in (15.14) satisfies the equality

$$E(\zeta_2|X) = 0, \tag{15.16}$$

which is the essential condition necessary to apply OLS in the bivariate case (see, for example, Theil, 1971, pp. 102–106). Now, from the relation

$$b_{21} = -\left[\frac{\text{cov}(x, y)}{\sigma_x^2}\right] = -\left[\frac{\sigma_y}{\sigma_y}\right]\left[\frac{\text{cov}(x, y)}{\sigma_x^2}\right]$$

$$= -\left[\frac{\sigma_y}{\sigma_x}\right]\left[\frac{\text{cov}(x, y)}{\sigma_y\sigma_x}\right] = -\left[\frac{\sigma_y}{\sigma_x}\rho_{xy}, \right], \tag{15.17}$$

it follows immediately that b_{21} will be zero or nonzero as ρ_{xy} is zero or nonzero. Thus, ignoring the issue of sampling variability, we have derived Simon's

(1954, pp. 42–43) specification of the conditions under which Mill's method of concomitant variation can be used to make causal inferences: *Correlation is evidence of causation in the two-variable case if we are willing to make the assumption that one variable is antecedent to the other,* that is, the assumptions that one variable is determined by a process that precedes in time, or is independent of, the other *and* that the error terms are uncorrelated.

Statistical Inferences about Causal Configurations from Data on Covariances (Correlations)

As Simon (1954, p. 42) notes, it is precisely when we are unwilling to defend the assumption of zero correlation among the disturbances that the issue of spurious correlation arises. For, in this instance, we hypothesize that there exists one or more common components of the ζ_1 and ζ_2 terms of Eqs. (15.7) and (15.8). These common variables create a nonzero correlation between the errors, and we proceed to elaborate the two-variable system by bringing them explicitly into the system, as in (15.1′)–(15.3′). However, we are *not* relieved of the necessity of postulating independence of the errors, for at some point we must stop adding variables to the system and argue that the net effects of all other variables left out of the system are not correlated between equations.

Simon (1954) pursued this analysis for the three-variable system of equations (15.1′)–(15.3′), deriving conditions on the patterns of correlations and partial correlations that lead to inferences about which of the possible causal configurations among the variables actually holds up in a given set of data. Blalock (1962, 1964) extended Simon's conditions on zero-order and partial correlations to the four-, five-, and six-variable cases. Boudon (1965) and Duncan (1966, 1975) introduced sociologists to path analysis and argued that the correlational conditions of Simon and Blalock could be equivalently stated in terms of the coefficient matrices [see Eq. (15.4)] of the systems. Morever, Boudon and Duncan argued that, when stated in the form of coefficient matrices, rigorous statistical inference and hypothesis testing is more straightforward than when the conditions are couched in terms of correlations and partial correlations.

To examine these issues more thoroughly, consider again the three-variable system of Eqs. (15.1′)–(15.3′). Suppose that the data are a *sample* of n observations on $x, y,$ and z rather than observations on the entire population, so that sampling considerations and statistical inference become relevant. With a sample of size n, we have $3n$ sample values of $x, y,$ and z which give us $3n$ data equations (3 for each sample point). For statistical estimation, we must regard the $3n$ sample values as fixed numbers given by observation, and the $3n$ error terms, ε_i, together with the six coefficients as variables to be estimated. But then we have $(3n + 6)$ parameters and only $3n$ equations. Thus, in order to have a just-determined system of linear equations so that a unique solution for estimates of the parameters is possible, we need six more equations. We must depend on a priori assumptions for these six equations—by *a priori* we mean that they are not derived from the data on which correlational statistics among x, y, and z are computed. Clearly, these assumptions are empirical.

The a priori assumptions are of the two kinds illustrated in the two-variable system just analyzed. First, assuming that "all other" variables influencing x are *stochastically independent* of "all other" variables influencing y, and so on, we obtain three additional equations:

$$E(\varepsilon_1\varepsilon_2) = 0; \qquad E(\varepsilon_1\varepsilon_3) = 0; \qquad E(\varepsilon_2\varepsilon_3) = 0. \qquad (15.18)$$

Second, we must make some assumptions about *causal ordering* among x, y, and z in the sense of specifying which variables can directly influence, but are not directly influenced by, others. To be concrete, assume, for the present discussion, that z can directly influence, but is not directly influenced by, x and y, and that x can directly influence, but is not directly influenced by y. Then we obtain three additional equations:

$$a_{12} = a_{13} = a_{23} = 0. \qquad (15.19)$$

Thus, our *maintained hypothesis* is the system

$$z = \varepsilon_1 \qquad (15.20)$$

$$a_{21}z + x = \varepsilon_2 \qquad (15.21)$$

$$a_{31}z + a_{32}x + y = \varepsilon_3 \qquad (15.22)$$

together with Eq. (15.18). This yields a system of $3n + 3$ equations expressed in terms of the sample data, from which the $3n + 3$ unknown parameters can be estimated.

Given this maintained hypothesis, we can distinguish several possible *causal configurations* that the data can take depending on which of the coefficients a_{21}, a_{31}, and a_{32} are specified and/or estimated to be zero or nonzero. In fact, since each of these three coefficients can be either zero or nonzero, there are $2^3 = 8$ possible causal configurations that can be distinguished. These are exhibited in Figure 15.1 where we employ the usual path analysis conventions of denoting an asymmetric causal relation between two variables by a straight arrow with its associated parameter (conventions for path diagrams are discussed in Section 15.3). Of these eight possible configurations, the first four are the most interesting. Case 1 sometimes is referred to as the "fully recursive" configuration, because all possible linkages go in one direction to an ultimate dependent variable, and all of these are nonzero. Case 2 is the "two exogenous variable" configuration, because both x and z are determined by processes outside the system under consideration (a more rigorous definition of *exogenous* will be given). Since we have postulated independent errors, and since $a_{21} = 0$ in this configuration, we leave a blank space between variables z and x, as there is no reason to believe that they are not stochastically independent of each other. Case 3 is the "intervening variable" case of the classical spurious correlation literature; it is also known as the "causal chain" model in the path analysis literature (e.g., see Duncan, 1966). In Case 3, the zero-order correlation between z and y vanishes when x is controlled, because x intervenes

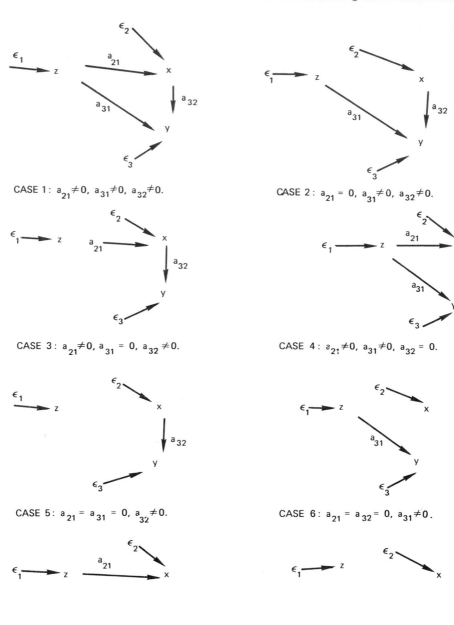

CASE 1: $a_{21} \neq 0$, $a_{31} \neq 0$, $a_{32} \neq 0$.

CASE 2: $a_{21} = 0$, $a_{31} \neq 0$, $a_{32} \neq 0$.

CASE 3: $a_{21} \neq 0$, $a_{31} = 0$, $a_{32} \neq 0$.

CASE 4: $a_{21} \neq 0$, $a_{31} \neq 0$, $a_{32} = 0$.

CASE 5: $a_{21} = a_{31} = 0$, $a_{32} \neq 0$.

CASE 6: $a_{21} = a_{32} = 0$, $a_{31} \neq 0$.

CASE 7: $a_{21} \neq 0$, $a_{31} = a_{32} = 0$.

CASE 8: $a_{21} = a_{31} = a_{32} = 0$.

FIGURE 15.1 Path diagrams for the eight possible causal configurations for the three-variable model of Eqs. (15.20)–(15.22).

between z and y. By contrast, in Case 4, this partial correlation vanishes because z determines both x and y—the classical spurious correlation configuration.

Simon (1954) used constraints on the three-variable system of the form of Eqs. (15.18) and (15.19) to derive the corresponding constraints on the configuration of zero-order and partial correlations among x, y, and z. For example, in Case 1, no constraints whatsoever are placed on the correlations and partial correlations among x, y, and z; all may be nonzero. In Case 2, the only constraint is that $\rho_{zx} = 0$, and this is predicated on the assumption that ε_1 is uncorrelated with ε_2, a condition that is not likely to be satisfied by exogenous variables in nonexperimental research. By contrast, Case 3 requires that $\rho_{zy} = \rho_{zx}\rho_{xy}$ or $\rho_{zy \cdot x} = 0$, and Case 4 implies that $\rho_{xy} = \rho_{xz}\rho_{zy}$ or $\rho_{xy \cdot z} = 0$. As a test of comprehension of the implications of the structural constraints for correlational patterns, the reader should derive the implied constraints of Cases 5–8.

As noted, Blalock (1962, 1964) extended Simon's analysis of correlational constraints to systems of more than three variables, whereas Boudon (1965) and Duncan (1966) argued that a direct analysis of constraints on the coefficient matrix of a system is a more straightforward. Their reasoning was that statistical tests on correlational constraints often are difficult, if not impossible, to construct. Thus, rigorous statistical inference is the exception, rather than the rule, in the so-called Simon–Blalock methods for inferences about causal configurations. By contrast, Boudon and Duncan argued that statistical estimation and hypothesis testing for the coefficient matrix of a recursive model was relatively easy. However, Boudon (1965) developed a kind of *two-stage least-squares* (2SLS) estimator for the coefficients of a less than "fully recursive" or "overidentified" recursive model (the concepts of identification and two-stage least-squares estimation are discussed in Section 15.4), which Goldberger (1970) showed to be statistically less efficient than the OLS estimator in the context of the particular recursive model studied by Boudon.

Land (1973) generalized Goldberger's proof to the general class of recursive models with stochastically independent disturbances and proved several other results as well. Specifically, on the basis of Land's (1973) analysis, the following estimation properties are known about the OLS estimators applied equation by equation to a recursive model with independent disturbances:

1. Within the class of estimators that, conditional on every set of "independent" variables in an equation of the model, are linear and unbiased, the OLS estimators of the structural coefficients have the minimum variances.
2. Conditional on the observed values of the independent variables, and under the assumption that the disturbance of an equation is normally distributed, the OLS estimators of its structural coefficients are equivalent to maximum likelihood estimators and, therefore, are the best asymptotically normal (BAN) (i.e., consistent asymptotically normal and asymptotically efficient) estimators.

3. The OLS estimators applied equation by equation are equivalent to maximum likelihood estimators applied to the model as a whole, provided that there are no cross-equation constraints on the structural coefficients of the model (this last property also is proved in Malinvaud, 1970, pp. 678–680).

These statistical results apply to the structural coefficients of a recursive model with independent disturbances when the variables are measured either in their observed metrics or as deviations from their observed means. If the variables are standardized by dividing each by its observed standard deviation, as is the usual practice in path analysis, then things become a bit more complicated. In this case, if the standard deviations are *given,* then the foregoing results hold without change. If the standard deviations are *estimated* from sample data and the independent variables in the equation are random, then the OLS estimators are (asymptotically) consistent, but no longer asymptotically efficient (in the Cramer–Rao sense). (For a discussion of these and related statistical properties, see Klemmack, Leggete, and Mayer, 1973; and Mayer and Younger, 1974.)

Concerning procedures for testing statistical hypotheses about the structural coefficients of a recursive model with independent disturbances as distinct from their estimation, Land (1973) notes that the foregoing results justify use of one of the standard t- and F-tests for the statistical significance of the estimated coefficients of a single equation of a recursive model, provided that one conditions on the observed values of all of the independent variables in the equation. If the disturbance term of the equation is normally distributed, then these tests are likelihood ratio tests and apply exactly; if not, then the results are only approximate. Land (1973, p. 46) also applied the likelihood ratio principle to derive an asymptotic (large sample) chi-squared likelihood ratio test statistic for testing simultaneously all structural constraints on all equations of a recursive model with independent disturbances, for which McPherson and Huang (1974) found the Hotelling's T^2 small-sample analogue.

Within the context of this rigorous statistical theory of estimation and hypothesis testing for recursive models with independent disturbances, the "straightforward" inference procedures suggested by Boudon (1965) and Duncan (1966, 1975, pp. 46–47) are easily summarized as follows. First, the researcher should specify which elements of the coefficient matrix of the recursive system under consideration are hypothesized (on the basis of theoretical arguments or prior empirical research) to be zero. Second, the analyst should estimate the model with and without the hypothesized constraints and perform an appropriate combination of the t-, F-, χ^2, and T^2 tests. If the tests fail to reject the hypothesized constraints, then the researcher infers (with a known risk of error) their validity in the population from which the sample was drawn and works with the estimated parameters of the constrained model; otherwise, rejecting one or more of the constraints and working with the estimates resulting from the relaxed constraints.

Often it is the case that a researcher does not have a strong set of hypotheses about zero structural coefficients with respect to a given recursive model. This may be due either to the weakness of the theory on which the model is based, or to the paucity of prior research experience in the subject matter under investigation, or both. It is standard practice for the researcher to estimate the "fully recursive" model, apply t- or F-tests to each estimated coefficient, discard the statistically insignificant coefficients, reestimate the constrained model, and recompute the t- or F-tests for the remaining coefficients. Strictly speaking, this use of statistical inference destroys the probability basis on which levels of statistical significance are based in the standard tests and converts the OLS estimator into what has been called a preliminary tests estimator (see Judge, Bock, & Yancey, 1974; Judge & Bock, 1978). The general rule of thumb that emerges from research on preliminary test estimators is that, if the first statistical test is based on level of significance α (say .05), then a smaller α (say .01) should be used for the second test of significance in order to prevent a loss of power of the test. The problem, of course, is that one never knows exactly what the second level of significance should be in order to maintain constant power of the test.

In summary, by using these methods of estimation and hypothesis testing, the researcher can either test a hypothesized causal configuration to determine whether or not it is consistent with the observed pattern of associations among the variables or infer a configuration that is consistent with the data after a preliminary examination of the significance of the estimated coefficients in a fully recursive configuration, although the statistical theory does not apply rigorously to the latter [which, however, does provide a statistical decision making context for Heise's (1968) notion of "theory trimming" in recursive path models]. Note that we have referred to these inferences as *inferences about the causal configuration, conditional on a maintained hypothesis about the causal ordering of the variables*. This is a much more limited notion of "causal inferences" than that often associated with the so-called Simon–Blalock method. The latter is more ambiguous about the possibility of making inferences about the causal ordering of the variables, as well as their precise configuration, from correlational data.

But we have seen that all of the three-variable configurations and the associated constraints on the structural coefficients and correlations previously discussed make sense *only* with the understanding that the underlying causal ordering assumes that variable z may directly influence but is not directly influenced by variables x and y, and variable x may directly influence but is not directly influenced by variable y. This assumed causal ordering is only one of $3! = 6$ possible permutations of the three variables, namely: (z, x, y); (z, y, x); (x, y, z); (x, z, y); (y, x, z); (y, z, x). If any one of these causal orderings is taken as a maintained hypothesis, then one obtains eight possible causal configurations such as those exhibited in Figure 15.1 for the causal ordering (z, x, y). Thus, there is a total of $6 \cdot 8 = 48$ possible causal configurations among the three variables, not all of which yield distinct patterns of correlations and structural coefficient. For instance, the correlational constraint of Case 3 of Figure 15.1, $\rho_{zy} = \rho_{zx}\rho_{xy}$, is consistent with the reverse causal chain $y \rightarrow x \rightarrow z$, with the spurious correlation configuration $y \leftarrow x \rightarrow z$, and, trivially, with the six totally disconnected configurations (one for each causal ordering), of which Case 8 of Figure 15.1 is an example. Which of these nontrivial configurations is inferred as the "true" configuration from correlational data depends on which causal ordering has been incorporated into the maintained hypothesis. It is for this reason that Land (1973, p. 46) and Duncan (1975, p. 47) suggest that *statistical tests of hypotheses about causal configurations within the context of a given causal ordering of variables should be referred to as tests of the overidentifying restriction(s) of the model* (again, the concept of identification is discussed in Section 15.4), a substantially more limited interpretation of the expression *making causal inferences from correlational data* than has sometimes been given by social scientists. In brief, although one can use the methods reviewed here to make rigorous statistical inferences about whether or not a presumed causal configuration is consistent with observed data, one is not thereby relieved of the responsibility of specifying which variables are taken as antecedent to the others. This fact underscores the necessity of developing strong formal social theories that take unambiguous assertions about causal orderings among variables and on the basis of which tests of overidentifying restrictions may be used to make inferences about the causal configuration(s) that are consistent with data on covariations. For, as many authors have noted (e.g., Blalock, 1964, pp. 5–14), the concept of causation is inherently a theoretical concept for which data on covariations can be used as evidence only under very restrictive assumptions about antecedence among variables and closure of the system such as we have illustrated here in our review of Simon's analysis of two- and three-variable systems.

General Notation and Assumptions for Simultaneous Equation Models

Up to this point, almost all of our discussion has concerned the very special two- and three-variable systems, although we have stated some statistical results for more general classes of models. In order for the material in the next two sections to be consistent with that already presented, we need to develop a general notational system for the class of simultaneous equation systems. The notational system and assumptions to be described are conventional, and, for the most part, follows those developed in Land (1973, pp. 22–27). Although the reader can understand the material in the next two sections without having a full understanding of all of the technical statistical properties of this notational system, it is useful to develop an understanding of the main concepts defined here before proceedings.

Consider a *model* which consists of G linear (in parameters) equations in H observable variables and G unobservable disturbances

$$\mathbf{A}\mathbf{x}_n = \mathbf{u}_n \tag{15.23}$$

where n $(n = 1, \ldots, N)$ denotes the nth observation in a sample of size N, $\mathbf{A}$ is a $G \times H$ matrix of parameters to be estimated, $\mathbf{x}_n$ is an H component column vector whose typical element $\mathbf{x}_{hn}$ is the value of the hth variable for the nth observation, and $\mathbf{u}_n$ is a G component column vector whose typical element $\mathbf{u}_{gn}$ is the value of the gth random disturbance or error for the nth observation. When a specific numerical matrix is substituted for $\mathbf{A}$ and a specific probability distribution (with numerically specified parameters) is assumed for the elements of $\mathbf{u}_n$, the resulting instance of the model is called a *structure*.

In the model (15.23), we distinguish between two kinds of variables: (*a*) those that the model determines, called *endogenous*; and (*b*) those that are independently determined outside of the model, called *exogenous*. Corresponding to this distinction, we partition $\mathbf{x}_n$, reordering the variables if necessary, so that the first G components of $\mathbf{x}_n$ are the values of the endogenous variables for the nth observation. We denote the G component column vector of those values by $\mathbf{y}_n$, and the $(H - G)$ component column vector of the values of the exogenous variables for the nth observation by $\mathbf{z}_n$. We define $K = H - G$. We then partition $\mathbf{A}$ correspondingly as $\mathbf{A} = (\mathbf{B}, \mathbf{\Gamma})$ where $\mathbf{B}$ is the $G \times G$ matrix endogenous variables and $\mathbf{\Gamma}$ is the $G \times K$ matrix of structural coefficients of the exogenous variables. Then (15.23) can be rewritten as

$$\mathbf{B}\mathbf{y}_n + \mathbf{\Gamma}\mathbf{z}_n = \mathbf{u}_n, \tag{15.24}$$

where $\mathbf{y}_n$, $\mathbf{z}_n$, $\mathbf{u}_n$ are column vectors of G, K, and G elements, respectively. [Note that in this representation there are no explicit equations for the exogenous variables, as was the case in Eq. (15.20) of the three-variable system (15.20)–(15.22). This is because the researcher is interested only in the processes by which the endogenous variables are affected by the exogenous variables, not in the processes by which the latter are generated.]

Equation (15.24) is a set of linear relations which are assumed to hold for each individual n $(n = 1, \ldots, N)$ in a (random or stratified random) sample of sociological units (e.g., persons, organizations). The model represents a theory explaining the determination of the endogenous variables y_{gn} $(g = 1, \ldots, G)$ in terms of the exogenous variables z_{kn} $(k = 1, \ldots, K)$ and the stochastic disturbances u_{gn} $(g = 1, \ldots, G)$ for the nth observation $(n = 1, \ldots, N)$. It is the function of the theory to specify that some of the coefficients of the $\mathbf{B}$ and $\mathbf{\Gamma}$ matrices in (15.24) are zero. If it did not, then statistical estimation would be impossible since all relations in the model would look alike statistically, and one would not be able to distinguish between them (this point is elaborated in the discussion of the identification problem in Section 15.4.

The form in which the variables are measured will be specified in the context of the following discussions. That is, we shall specify whether we are dealing with the variables in their observed measurement metrics, deviations of the observed variables from arithmetic means, or ratios of the standard deviations of the variables (standard units). If we are dealing with the metric values of the variables, then a constant term in each relation may be incorporated by setting one of the z variables at unity. We also adopt the normalization convention that the diagonal elements of $\mathbf{B}$ are equal to unity, $\beta_{bb} = 1$ ($g = 1, \ldots,$ G), thus identifying the endogenous variable determined by the gth equation as y_g. Finally, when the variables are assumed to be in standard unit form, we sometimes shall denote the elements of the $\mathbf{B}$ and $\boldsymbol{\Gamma}$ matrices by small ps with a first subscript corresponding to the index of the dependent variable of the equation in which p enters and a second subscript corresponding to the index of the variable whose effect is being measured, as is the usual convention in path analysis (e.g., see Duncan, 1966, 1975).

If the model (15.24) is to explain the determination of the endogenous variables in terms of the exogenous variables and disturbances, then we must assume that the rank of $\mathbf{B}$ is $\mathbf{G}$. Therefore, $\mathbf{B}^{-1}$ exists, and the system of equations can be solved uniquely for $\mathbf{y}_n$ in terms of $\mathbf{z}_n$ and $\mathbf{u}_n$:

$$\mathbf{y}_n = -\mathbf{B}^{-1}\boldsymbol{\Gamma}\mathbf{z}_n + \mathbf{B}^{-1}\mathbf{u}_n = \boldsymbol{\Pi}\mathbf{z}_n + \mathbf{v}_n. \tag{15.25}$$

The system of equations 15.25 is called the *reduced form* of the model 15.24, $\boldsymbol{\Gamma} = -\mathbf{B}^{-1}\boldsymbol{\Gamma}$ is a $G \times K$ matrix of reduced form coefficients and $\mathbf{v}_n = \mathbf{B}^{-1}\mathbf{u}_n$ ($n = 1, \ldots, N$) is a column vector of reduced form disturbances.

We specify that the structural disturbances are random variables drawn from a multivariate probability distribution with expected values:

$$E(\mathbf{u}_n) = 0 \qquad (n = 1, \ldots, N). \tag{15.26}$$

In words, each disturbance vector (the set of G disturbances for each observation) has a zero expectation, so $E(u_{gn}) = 0$ for all g and n. The population variance–covariance matrix of the disturbance vector at each observation is specified to be:

$$\boldsymbol{\Sigma} = E(\mathbf{u}_n\mathbf{u}_n') = \begin{bmatrix} \sigma_{11} & \cdots & \sigma_{1G} \\ \vdots & & \vdots \\ \sigma_{G1} & & \sigma_{GG} \end{bmatrix} \tag{15.27}$$

where the prime denotes transposition. In words, the covariance matrix of the disturbances in the different equations is assumed to be the same for all observations. From these assumptions, we thus find that the expectation of the reduced form disturbance vector is $E(\mathbf{v}_n) = \mathbf{B}^{-1}E(\mathbf{u}_n) = 0$, and its variance–covariance matrix at each observation is

$$\boldsymbol{\Omega} = E(\mathbf{u}_n\mathbf{u}_n') = \begin{bmatrix} \omega_{11} & \cdots & \omega_{1G} \\ \vdots & & \vdots \\ \omega_{G1} & & \omega_{GG} \end{bmatrix}$$

$$= E(\mathbf{B}^{-1}\mathbf{u}_n\mathbf{u}_n'\mathbf{B}^{-1'}) = \mathbf{B}^{-1}E(\mathbf{u}_n\mathbf{u}_n')\mathbf{B}^{-1'} = \mathbf{B}^{-1}\boldsymbol{\Sigma}\mathbf{B}^{-1'} \tag{15.28}$$

In this equation, the first and second equalities establish notational definitions, the third equality results from substituting $\mathbf{B}^{-1}\mathbf{u}_n$ for $\mathbf{v}_n$, the fourth from the constancy of **B,** the fifth from applying the definition of Σ. We assume that Σ is positive definite, a necessary condition for which is that all identities have been removed from the model. Then Σ will be nonsingular, and since $\mathbf{B}^{-1}$ also in nonsingular, it follows that Ω is nonsingular, and indeed positive definite.

Note that the general forms of the **B** and Γ matrices are

$$\mathbf{B} = \begin{bmatrix} \beta_{11} & \beta_{12} & \cdots & \beta_{1G} \\ \beta_{21} & \beta_{22} & \cdots & \beta_{2G} \\ \vdots & \vdots & & \vdots \\ \beta_{G1} & \beta_{G2} & & \beta_{GG} \end{bmatrix} \tag{15.29}$$

and

$$\Gamma = \begin{bmatrix} \gamma_{11} & \gamma_{12} & \cdots & \gamma_{1K} \\ \gamma_{21} & \gamma_{22} & \cdots & \gamma_{2K} \\ \vdots & \vdots & & \vdots \\ \gamma_{G1} & \gamma_{G2} & & \gamma_{GK} \end{bmatrix}. \tag{15.30}$$

In recursive systems, however, the matrix **B** takes a special form, so that the equation system (15.24) can be written as follows:

$$y_{1n} \qquad\qquad + \sum_{k=1}^{K} \gamma_{1k}z_{kn} = u_{1n}$$

$$\beta_{31}y_{1n} + \quad y_{2n} \qquad\qquad \sum_{k=1}^{K} \gamma_{2k}z_{kn} = u_{2n}$$

$$\beta_{31}y_{1n} + \beta_{32}y_{2n} + \quad y_{3n} \qquad \sum_{k=1}^{K} \gamma_{3k}z_{kn} = u_{3n}$$

$$\vdots \qquad\qquad\qquad \vdots$$

$$\beta_{G1}y_{1n} + \beta_{G3}y_{2n} + \beta_{G3}y_{3n} + \ldots + y_{gn} + \sum_{k=1}^{K} \gamma_{Gk}z_{kn} = u_{Gn}. \tag{15.31}$$

In brief, the matrix **B** is *triangular* in a recursive system. This amounts to placing zero restrictions on the structural coefficients above the diagonal in **B** and corresponds to the causal ordering assumption that the endogenous variable y_i can directly influence, but is not directly influenced by, y_j, for $j < i$. In addition to the zeros above the diagonal in **B,** other elements of **B** and Γ may be set equal to zero a priori, which corresponds to the theoretical assumption that certain prior variables are assumed a priori to have no direct effect on certain endogenous variables. In the language of the preceding subsection, this corresponds to specifying a priori a particular causal configuration among the variables as well as a causal ordering. Finally, for models that are specified to have independent disturbances as well as being recursive, the Σ matrix is assumed to be *diagonal*.

For future reference, we summarize all of the foregoing specifications together with a few additional requirements in the following two sets of assumptions.

Assumption 1. The following assumptions specify the *general (linear in parameters) class of simultaneous equation models:*

1. $E(\mathbf{u}_n) = \mathbf{0}$ $(n = 1, \ldots, N)$.
2. The $\mathbf{u}_n$ are independently distributed $(n = 1, \ldots, N)$.
3. $E(\mathbf{u}_n\mathbf{u}_n') = \Sigma$, where Σ is positive definite.
4. There are N observations on K exogenous variables, where *exogenous* means that the disturbances of the model are distributed independently of the exogenous variables.
5. The K exogenous variables are linearly independent.
6. All observables are measured without error.
7. The matrix $\mathbf{B}$ has rank G. All of the previous assumptions always are assumed for the model 15.24. In addition, it is often assumed for statistical estimation and hypothesis testing that:
8. The $\mathbf{u}_n$ $(n = 1, \ldots, N)$ have a multivariate normal distribution.

Assumption 2. To obtain the *class of recursive models with independent disturbances,* two additional assumptions are necessary:

1. The matrix $\mathbf{B}$ is triangular.
2. The matrix Σ is diagonal.

For each of the G equations of model (15.24), Assumption 1.1 states that the u_{gn} are random variables with zero expectation. Assumptions 1.2 and 1.3 imply that the disturbances are homoscedastic (that is, the u_{gn} have constant variance σ_{gg}) and are stochastically independent, which implies that $E(u_{gn}u_{gm}) = 0$ for $n \neq m$. The latter requirement is a consequence of requiring random or stratified random sampling. Assumption 1.4 defines what is meant by exogenous in this context. Exact linear relations among the exogenous variables are ruled out by Assumption 1.5. Finally, Assumption 1.6 requires that the measurements of all of the variables are perfectly reliable. [To relax this assumption requires the incorporation of an explicit measurement error structure into model (15.24). Such generalizations will not be treated here, although some references to relevant literature are given at the end of the chapter.] In brief, Assumptions 1.1, 1.2, 1.4, 1.5, and 1.6 are equivalent to those (of the errors-in-equations interpretation) of the standard single equation general linear model (e.g., see Theil, 1971, pp. 102–111). In other words, Assumption 1 requires that each of the G equations of (15.24) satisfies these conventional assumptions.

Turning next to assumptions pertaining to the entire set of equations in the model, Assumption 1.3 says that the covariance matrix of the disturbances in the different equations is the same for all observations, and Assumption 1.7 states that the model can be solved for $\mathbf{y}_n$ in terms of $\mathbf{z}_n$ and $\mathbf{u}_n$. As noted previously, Assumptions 2.1 and 2.2 are necessary to reduce the class of general simultaneous equation models to the class of recursive models with independent disturbances. We have seen in the foregoing subsections that it is within the latter class of models that discussions of causal inferences typically have been couched. By now, the reader should understand that model (15.24) as specified by Assumptions 1 and 2 is a far-reaching generalization of the simple three-variable recursive model specified by Eqs. (15.18)–(15.22). Finally, Assumption 1.8 is that the disturbances at each observation have a G variate normal distribution, which implies that each u_{gn} has a univariate normal distribution. Usually, this assumption is needed only to find maximum likelihood estimators or to derive results that refer to the form of the sampling distribution of estimators. If the researcher prefers to make no explicit assumption about the form of the distribution of disturbances, then the central limit theorem of probability theory can be used to justify the distributional results.

In summary, Assumptions 1 and 2 sufficiently define the two general classes of models that will be discussed in the remainder of this chapter. These assumptions also are sufficient for the derivation of those properties of the estimators and statistical tests for recursive models with independent disturbances that were cited in the preceding subsection as well as for all additional properties to be cited in the following. However, our exposition will not dwell on the proofs of these standard properties; references are readily available for that. Rather, our objectives are to describe some situations that suggest each of several special cases of these classes of models and to develop some techniques for measuring causal effects in each.

15.3. SOME TYPES OF RECURSIVE CAUSAL MODELS AND THEIR REPRESENTATION

Methodological problems involved in recursive models are so much simpler than those involved in recursive models that it makes sense to treat the two types of models separately. This section of this chapter is devoted to recursive models, and the following section discusses nonrecursive models. In the next few pages, we will consider causal structures in which relationships among variables are linear and additive, structures in which relationships are nonlinear but additive, and structures in which relationships among variables are nonadditive or both nonlinear and nonadditive. Although differences in the mathematical properties of these structures require differences in some of the methods used to measure causal linkages between variables, the same general principles can be applied to define causal effects in all three types of structures. To simplify later exegesis, we will discuss those general principles first, and then proceed to the different types of models.

Measuring the Causal Impact of a Variable

If one variable causes another, then variations in the first variable will, on the average, produce variations in the second. The *causal effect* of one variable on another is normally defined as the *extent* to which variations in the first variable produce variations in the second. In general, there are two distinct approaches to operationalizing this definition: one based on rates of change, and the other based on the accuracy with which one can use a causal relationship to predict values of the effect variable from values of the causal variable(s). According to the accuracy-of-predictions view, a strong effect is one that permits very accurate estimates. In contrast, rate-of-change measures of causal effect focus on the average number of units of change in the effect variable associated with a change of one unit in the causal variable. Because there may be considerable deviation about this average, an effect that is strong according to rate-of-change criteria is not necessarily strong according to accuracy-of-predictions criteria. To see this, consider a very simple causal model involving just two variables, X (the cause) and Y (the effect), and consider two distributions of data on X and Y, as shown in Figure 15.2. In panel (a) of Figure 15.2, note that the slope of the line fitted to the data is very steep—a small change in X produces a large change in Y. But, looking at the same panel, notice also that the data points are too widely dispersed to allow accurate predictions of values on Y on the basis of values of X. So although the accuracy-of-prediction criterion suggests a weak relationship between X and Y in panel (a) of Figure 15.2, the rate of change criterion suggests a strong relationship between X and Y. In panel (b) of the figure, notice the opposite case: Y changes very little per unit change of X, but the data points are so compactly arrayed that one could very accurately predict values of Y on the basis of values of X. It is worth noting that answers to important questions have hinged on appropriateness of accuracy-of-prediction measures and rate-of-change measures. For example, the causal effect of a person's years of schooling on earning has been a subject of considerable interest in sociology and in social

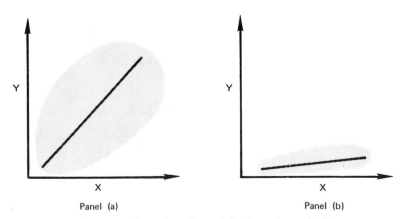

Panel (a)   Panel (b)

FIGURE 15.2 Illustration of two definitions of causal effects.

policy studies. Using rate-of-change measures, Herman Miller (1960) calculated that the effects of schooling on earnings is very large. But when Jencks (Jencks *et al.*, 1972) applied accuracy-of-prediction measures to the data, he found that schooling has only very modest effects on earnings.

Mathematically, rates-of-change measures are based on derivatives (when there is only one causal variable) or partial derivatives (when there is more than one causal variable). The derivative of a dependent variable Y with respect to a variable which causes it X is the rate of change in Y per change with X, expressed as the amount by which Y changes per unit change in X. The *partial* derivative of Y with respect to X is the rate of change in Y per change in X, net of the effects of other variables in the model which cause Y. Pictorially, the derivative is the slope of the graph relating values of Y to values of X. The partial derivative is the slope in the direction of a given variable of the n-dimensional surface relating values of Y to values of n variables that cause Y in the model. As straightforward as rates-of-change may seem, they vary considerably in actual use. The source of this diversity is the choice of scales on which changes in Y and changes in X are measured. For example, changes in X and Y can be measured in the natural units of these variables, or as proportional changes, or in standard deviations of the variables. Further, changes in X can be measured on one type of scale, and change in Y can be measured on a different scale. Table 15.1 lists various combinations of these scales and the commonly used name for the (partial) derivative of Y with respect to X in several of the cases.

Economists tend to use elasticities and rates of return more than sociologists, and sociologists tend to use standardized effects more than economists, but, aside from the obvious connection between investment theory and rates of return, disciplinary differences in these practices seem to be more the result of custom than anything else. Except where motivated by a particular theoretical concern, researchers in both disciplines use the standardized or percentage metric primarily to skirt problems of interpretation when one or both variables are measured according to a scale that has no intuitively obvious meaning, as in

TABLE 15.1
Some Rate-of-Change Measures of Causal Effect of X and Y

Scale for measuring changes in X (independent variable)	Metric for measuring changes in Y (dependent variable)	Common name for derivative of Y with respect to X
Natural	Natural	Unstandardized effect, metric effect, or raw effect
Natural	Proportion	Rate of return of X
Proportion	Proportion	Point elasticity of Y with respect to X
Standardized[a]	Standardized[a]	Standardized effect

[a] That is, normed to zero mean and a unit standard deviation.

the case of many attitude scales used in survey research, or when units of various scales are not directly comparable, as in hours of work and dollars of income.

The relationship between unstandardized effects, standardized effects, point elasticities, and rates of return is straightforward: In the notation of partial derivatives, the rate of change in Y per change in X can be written as $\partial Y/\partial X$, where ∂Y is the change in Y and ∂X is the change in X. (This is a gross simplification of the mathematical concepts, but not a distortion of them.) Thus, the unstandardized effect is $\partial Y/\partial X$. To measure changes in one of these variables in standardized units, we divide it by the variable's standard deviation. Thus, the standardized effect of X on Y is

$$\frac{\partial Y/\sigma Y}{\partial X/\sigma X} = \frac{\partial Y}{\partial X} \cdot \frac{\sigma X}{\sigma Y}.$$

Similarly, to measure change in one of these variables in proportional terms, we divide the change in the variable by the value of the variable. Thus, the elasticity of Y with respect to X is

$$\frac{\partial Y/Y}{\partial X/X} = \frac{\partial Y}{\partial X} \cdot \frac{X}{Y}$$

and the rate of return to X is

$$\frac{\partial Y/Y}{\partial X} = \frac{\partial Y}{\partial X} \cdot \frac{1}{Y}.$$

To give an empirical example, consider the model $Y = 4 + 3X + 2Z + \varepsilon$, where Y, X, and Z are variables and where ε is an error term with a mean of zero. Suppose also that the standard deviation of X is 2 and the standard deviation of Y is 12. The unstandardized effect of X on Y is 3. To get the standardized effect, we multiply 3 by 2 (the standard deviation of X) and divide by 12 (the standard deviation of Y), obtaining a value of .5. To calculate the point elasticity, we must choose values of X and Y. When $X = 7$ and $Y = 4$, the elasticity equals the unstandardized effect multiplied by 7/4, or 3(7/4) = 5.25, indicating that a change of 1% in X will produce a change of 5.25% in Y. Similarly, calculation of the rate of return requires choice of a value of Y. When $Y = 6$, the rate of return is 3(1/6) = .5, indicating a change of 50% in Y per unit change in X. When $Y = 15$, the rate of return = 3(1/15) = .2, indicating a 20% change in Y per unit change in X. Note that the elasticity varies with the values of X and Y in this example, that the rate of return varies with the value of Y, and that the standardized and unstandardized effects are constant over the range of X and Y. Later in this chapter, we discuss models in which the point elasticity or the rate of return is constant and the standardized and unstandardized effects vary with the values of X and/or Y. But now we turn to another type of measure of causal effects, accuracy-of-prediction measures.

The most common accuracy-of-prediction measures of causal effect are based on the notions of variance and correlation. In no particular order, these measures are the standard error of estimate, the coefficient of alienation, the multiple correlation coefficient, and the partial correlation. The standard error of estimate is the standard deviation of the difference between values of Y that are predicted by an estimated model and the values of Y that are actually observed. When the form of the distribution of these errors is specified (e.g., when the distribution is specified to be normal), the standard deviation of the errors gives an accurate and intuitively meaningful summary of how well the model predicts. When the form of the distribution of errors is not specified, the standard error of estimate gives a useful, if vague, notion of how accurately the model predicts values of Y. But when Y is not measured in an intuitively meaningful metric, the standard error of estimate is of limited value, since even if one knows the distribution of errors, one has little sense of how to evaluate the size of these numbers; in such cases, Y is best normed to a standard deviation of one, making the standard error of estimate interpretable in units of standard deviations. When the standard deviation of Y is unity, the standard error of estimate is equivalent to the coefficient of alienation. The coefficient of alienation is the square root of the proportion of variance of Y which is *not* explained by the causal variables in the model. Accordingly, one minus the square of the coefficient of alienation is the squared proportion of variance of Y which *is* explained by causal variables in the model. In recursive models with independent disturbances this value is equivalent to the squared multiple correlation between Y and the variables that cause it in the model.

Note that neither the standard error of estimate, nor the coefficient of alienation, nor the multiple correlation coefficient indicate the contribution of any particular causal variable to the accuracy with which the model predicts values of Y. When a model involves more than one predictor variable, these measures indicate the causal effect of all predictor variables together, but give no information about the relative importance of any one of them. In contrast, the coefficient of partial correlation gives a quantitative measure, albeit a not very useful one, of the extent to which a particular causal variable improves the predictive accuracy of a model, net of the effects of other causal variables in the model. In fact, the partial correlation coefficient has a number of deficiencies when put to this use: First, although the rate-of-change measures described previously can be used to indicate causal effects in *all* kinds of models, the partial correlation can be used only with models that specify linear, additive relationships among variables, or linear, additive relationships among functions of variables. (By *linear, additive relationship among functions of variables,* we mean, for example, a model that specifies a linear additive relationship between Y and the log of X, and Z.) Second, and more important, even when used with linear, additive models, interpreting the partial correlation as a measure of reduction in prediction error requires an assumption that is hard to justify in most applications to causal models: The partial correlation $r_{y,x \cdot z_1, z_2, \ldots, z_K}$ is the square root of the proportionate reduction in unexplained variance of Y that is attributable to x after $z_1, z_2, \ldots, z_K$ have explained all the variance of Y that they can (Blalock, 1972, p. 453). Thus $r_{y,x \cdot z_1, z_2, \ldots, z_K}$ has a meaningful causal interpretation *only* if $z_1, z_2, \ldots, z_K$ are all causally prior to x. But if these variables are prior to x, then other partial correlations would not have meaningful causal interpretations. For example, the partial $r_{y,z_K \cdot x,z_1,\ldots,z_{K-1}}$ has a causal interpretation only if x and $z_1, \ldots, z_{K-1}$ are prior to z_K, but this is not possible if $z_1, \ldots, z_K$ are also prior to x. So if the partial correlation is used to measure the effect of x on y, it cannot be used to measure the effect of z_k on y. Thus, the partial correlation is not very useful as a general purpose measure of causal effect. The reader is directed to Duncan (1970) for a particularly fierce attack on the use of partial correlations in causal models.

It is important to note that under certain circumstances, some of the accuracy-of-prediction measures discussed here are identical to certain rate-of-change measures. For example, when there is only one causal variable and only one dependent variable, and the relationship between these variables is linear, then the square of the standardized effect is equal to the percentage of variance explained by the causal variable. Other correspondences between partial correlations and standardized effects in linear additive models are discussed in most elementary statistics texts (e.g., Blalock, 1972, chap. 19), but although the link between rate-of-change and accuracy-of-prediction measures is an undeniable mathematical fact, it is frequently neither intuitively obvious, nor, once proven, terribly useful in evaluating causal theories.

The conclusion we wish to draw from this discussion is that there is no useful, widely known accuracy-of-prediction measure of the causal effect of one variable on another, net of effects of other variables specified in the model. Accordingly, one is usually best advised to use measures based on partial derivatives (rate-of-change measures) to gauge the net effect of a causal variable.

Linear, Additive Models

Most statistical analysis in sociology treats relationships among variables as linear and additive. By *additive*, we mean that the effect of one variable on a second variable does not vary according to the values of a third variable. By *linear*, we mean that the rate at which changes in one variable are produced by changes in another variable does not itself vary with the values of one or both of the variables. (Mathematically, linearity in the relationship between two variables Y and X means that the partial derivative $\partial Y/\partial X$ equals a constant. Additivity means that, where Z is any other variable, $\partial^2 Y/\partial Z \partial X = 0$.) The great popularity of linear, additive models can be attributed to four factors: First, an enormous range of relationships among variables studied in the social sciences are, in fact, linear and additive—this is an empirical observation, not a rigorously deduced theorem. Second, many of the nonlinear and nonadditive relationships that have been observed do not depart from linearity and additivity so much that great harm is done by treating them as if they were linear and additive—this is a risky procedure to follow without careful evaluation of the assumptions involved, but it quite often turns out to be reasonable. Third, linear, additive relationships pose fewer methodological problems than other types of relationships. In particular, the parameters of linear, additive recursive models usually can be estimated easily and inexpensively with ordinary least-squares regression. Finally, the fourth reason for the popularity of linear, additive models is that their parameters are easy to interpret, especially for persons who are ill at ease with mathematics. The interpretability of parameters can be seen by noting that the general form of a linear, additive equation is

$$Y = a + \sum_{i=1}^{K} b_i X_i + \varepsilon, \tag{15.32}$$

where Y is the dependent variable, a and the b_is are parameters, the X_is are variables that cause Y, and ε is the error term. For any X_i in this equation, the partial derivative $\partial Y/\partial X_i$ is equal to b_i. So the most useful indicator of the net causal effect of each of the X_is, $\partial Y/\partial X_i$, can be calculated with no greater trouble than regressing Y on the X_is. This procedure yields both standardized and unstandardized effects with ease (see Chapter 13 by Berk, on the general linear model for computational details).

When relationships among variables are linear and additive, the common workhorse of causal modeling in social research is *path analysis*. In the next few paragraphs, we discuss some key features of path analysis and then move on to treat some less usual—but not really more difficult—varieties of causal models.

Path analysis is distinguished by its use of a diagram to represent causal relationships. In path diagrams, causation is indicated by a *straight* arrow leading from one variable to another with the corresponding structural coefficient written alongside the arrow. Since the interrelations among exogenous variables are not analyzed, each pair of exogenous variables in a path diagram is connected by a *curved* arrow, indicating a possible correlation among them, but not specifying any causal relationship. As an example of a path analytic representation of a causal model, consider Blau and Duncan's model of the relationships among five variables: father's educational attainment; father's occupational socioeconomic status (SES); his son's educational attainment; the occupational SES of the son's first job; and the occupational SES of the son's present job. Let us assume that the relationship between the father's education and occupation is not of interest, that the father's schooling and occupational SES both act as causes of the son's educational attainment, that the son's occupational attainment on the first job is affected by the father's schooling, the father's occupational SES, and the son's own schooling, and that all of these variables affect the son's present occupational attainment. The path model corresponding to this system is shown in Fig. 15.3. In this figure, ε_1, ε_2, and ε_3 are the residuals; the father's characteristics are the exogenous variables, and the son's characteristics are the endogenous variables.

In all causal models, the effects of one variable on another can be direct or indirect. In the corresponding path diagram, a variable is said to have a *direct*

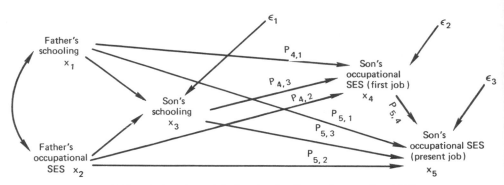

FIGURE 15.3 A path model of son's schooling and occupational SES.

effect on a second variable if a straight arrow runs from the first variable to the second. A variable is said to have an *indirect effect* on a second variable if a chain of direct effects can be traced from the first variable, through one or more other variables, to the second variable. In Figure 15.3, X_1 (father's schooling) has both a direct effect on X_4 (son's occupational SES) and, via X_3 (son's schooling), an indirect effect on X_4.

A causal diagram is a path diagram if it meets the conventions just discussed. There is one equation corresponding to each endogenous variable in a path diagram, and in recursive models with independent disturbances, as we have seen in the preceding section, the equation corresponding to a given endogenous variable is the equation obtained by regressing that variable on all other exogenous and endogenous variables which have direct effects on it. Usually, standardized effects are used to measure causal impact in path analysis, so the parameters of the path model are identical to the standardized regression coefficients of the corresponding regression equations. Thus, the coefficient for the path from one variable to another is the coefficient for the first variable in the regression equation in which the second variable is the dependent variable. Error variables also are assumed to have a mean of zero and standard deviation of one, and the path from an error to an endogenous variable has a coefficient equal to the coefficient of alienation $\sqrt{1 - R^2}$ for the regression equation corresponding to that endogenous variable. (Thus, the path model accounts for all variance in each endogenous variable.) For example, the equations corresponding to Figure 15.3 are as follows.

$$x_3 = p_{3,1}x_1 + p_{3,2}x_2 + p_{3,\varepsilon_1}\varepsilon_1 \tag{15.33}$$

$$x_4 = p_{4,1}x_1 + p_{4,2}x_2 + p_{4,3}x_3 + p_{4,\varepsilon_2}\varepsilon_2 \tag{15.34}$$

$$x_5 = p_{5,1}x_1 + p_{5,2}x_2 + p_{5,3}x_3 + p_{5,4}x_4 + p_{5,\varepsilon_3}\varepsilon_3 \tag{15.35}$$

The coefficients of these equations would be calculated by estimating the parameters of the following regression equations:

$$\hat{x}_3 = \beta_{3,1}x_1 + \beta_{3,2}x_2 \tag{15.36}$$

$$\hat{x}_4 = \beta_{4,1}x_1 + \beta_{4,2}x_2 + \beta_{4,3}x_3 \tag{15.37}$$

$$\hat{x}_5 = \beta_{5,1}x_1 + \beta_{5,2}x_2 + \beta_{5,3}x_3 + \beta_{5,4}x_4 \tag{15.38}$$

Finally, the coefficients of curved arrows in path diagrams are estimated by the zero-order product moment correlations between the two variables connected by the arrow.

One of the great appeals of path diagrams is that they very clearly portray patterns of indirect causation. It may take pages of prose to explain how one variable causes a second variable, how the first and second cause a third, and how all three cause a fourth variable. A path diagram can make such relationships quite clear in a fraction of the space.

Although path diagrams concisely portray the causal linkages that produce indirect effects, they are not very efficient at showing the *total effect* of one variable on another (i.e., the sum of the direct and indirect effects). Nor are path diagrams great aids to intuition when it comes to quantitatively decomposing a total effect into direct and indirect components. To decompose the influence of one variable on another into direct and indirect effects, one can follow either of two equally valid algorithms, one set out in Land (1969) following Duncan (1966) and Wright (1934), and the other set out by Alwin and Hauser (1975), following more the tradition of econometric modeling, but heavily dependent on Duncan, Featherman, and Duncan (1972). The algorithm described by Alwin and Hauser is usually easier to apply and one is less prone to make errors using it than in using the other algorithm, and so we describe it only: The total effect of one variable (the cause) on another can be estimated by regressing the second variable (the one that is caused) on the first variable *and* all other variables that are either causally prior or causally contemporaneous with the first variable. For example, in Figure 15.3, the total effect of x_1 on x_5 is the coefficient for x_1 when x_5 is regressed on x_1 and x_2. In order to divide the total effect of a variable into direct and indirect components, one proceeds in a stepwise fashion, adding to the regression equation the variables at later stages of the model, which cause the variable in question. Thus, in Figure 15.3, one would next regress x_5 on x_1, x_2, and x_3. The coefficient for x_1 in this equation would give the total effect of x_1 on x_5 *minus* the effect of x_1 on x_5, which operates indirectly through x_3. Next, one would regress x_5 on x_1, x_2, x_3, and x_4. The coefficient for x_1 in this equation would be the total effect of x_1 on x_5 *minus* the effect of x_1 on x_5, which is mediated via the direct and indirect effects of x_1 on x_3 and x_4. Table 15.2 summarizes the information given by the various regression equations used in decomposing the effect of x_1 on x_5. Notice that by subtracting the coefficient for x_1 in the second equation in Table 15.2 from the coefficient for x_1 in the first equation, we get the indirect effect of x_1 on x_5, which is mediated through x_3. By subtracting the coefficient for x_1 in the third equation from the coefficient for x_1 in the first equation, we obtain the component of the effect of x_1 on x_5, which is mediated through other variables in the model.

TABLE 15.2
Calculation of Direct and Indirect Effects

Equation	Independent variables in regression	Meaning of coefficient for x_1
1	x_1, x_2	Total effect
2	x_1, x_2, x_3	Total effect minus indirect effect mediated through x_3
3	x_1, x_2, x_3, x_4	Direct effect, that is, total effect minus indirect effect mediated through x_3 and/or x_4

Nonlinear Models

A nonlinear relationship between variables Y and X is one in which the effect of X on Y varies according to the value of X. An example of such a relationship is given in Figure 15.4 relating years of schooling to dollars of income. Recalling that the effect of schooling X on income Y is the rate at which income changes per unit change in school years completed, it is clear that the effect of schooling on income is the slope of the graph shown in Figure 15.4. Looking at that graph, notice that the slope becomes steeper at successively higher levels of schooling, implying that the rate of change in income per unit change in schooling increases as the total amount of schooling increases.

In causal analysis of nonlinear relationships, the researcher must face two problems which are trivial in the case of linear relationships. First, a mathematical representation of the nonlinear relationship must be found, and, second, a precise, concise, and clearly understandable measure of causal effect must be calculated. In this section, we offer some general guidelines for choosing mathematical functions to fit curvilinear relationships, and we show how the rate-of-change measure of causal effect—the partial derivative—neatly adapts to the nonlinear situation.

USES OF THE PARABOLA IN ANALYSIS OF NONLINEAR EFFECTS

Except for the linear additive specification, the parabola is probably the most useful mathematical function in causal modeling of social phenomena. The general functional form of the parabola is $Y = a + b_1X + b_2X^2 + \varepsilon$, but since social science causal models generally involve several independent variables, we can generalize the function to

$$Y = a + b_1X + b_2X^2 + \Sigma c_iZ_i + \varepsilon \qquad (15.39)$$

where a, the bs, and the cs are parameters, where X, Y, and Z_is are variables, and where ε is the error. The usefulness of the parabola grows out of the many shapes it can assume, dependent only on the values of b_1 and b_2. Figure 15.5 shows some of those shapes. Notice the similarity between the parabola shown in the first panel of Figure 15.5 and the curve, fitted by eye, in the schooling–income figure.

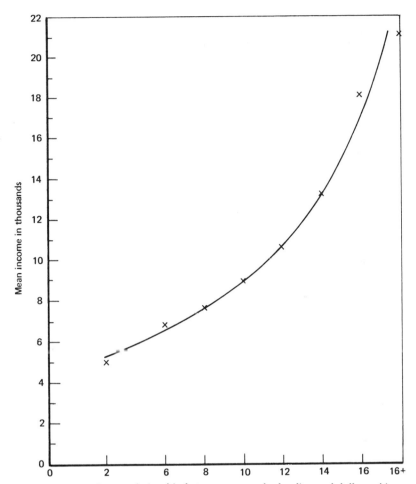

FIGURE 15.4 A nonlinear relationship between years of schooling and dollars of income.

Part of the tremendous appeal of the parabolic function for social science research stems from the fact that its parameters can be estimated with ordinary least-squares regression. Thus, to fit Eq. (15.39), one would merely create a new variable equal to X^2 and then regress Y on X, X^2, and the Z_is. The t-statistic for X^2 would be used to test the null hypothesis that the coefficient for X^2 is zero. If that coefficient is zero, then the relationship between Y and X is either linear or else of a nonparabolic, nonlinear form. But if the coefficient for X^2 is significantly different from zero, then the researcher has evidence that the relationship between Y and X is nonlinear and that this relationship is fitted more accurately by a parabola than by a straight line. *Once one has made this conclusion, the coefficient of X no longer has an interpretation apart from the coefficient of X^2.* As with linear relationships, the effect of X on Y is measured by the partial derivative $\partial Y/\partial X$. In Eq. (15.39), $\partial Y/\partial X$ is equal to $b_1 + 2b_2X$.

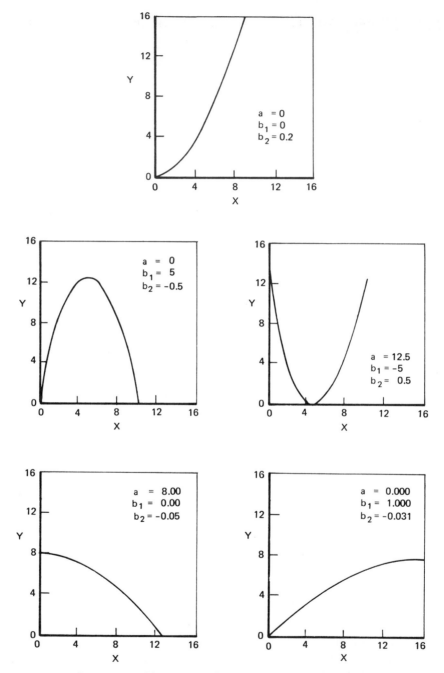

FIGURE 15.5 Shapes assumed by $Y = a + b_1X + b_2X^2$ under varying values of a, b_1, and b_2.

Notice that the *effect of X on Y in the parabolic case is a linear function of X*. Thus, the *effect* of X on Y changes by $2b_2$ units per unit change in X.

For an example of parabolas, we turn to Rees and Shultz's (1970, p. 136) analysis of hourly earnings. Rees and Shultz were interested in finding the effect of workers' age on earnings, but they hypothesized that (*a*) several factors other than age affected earnings; (*b*) earnings increased with age during the first part of a man's career, but decreased with age in the second part of his career; and (*c*) the processes affecting earnings varied from one occupation to another. To allow for occupational differences in the earnings process, Rees and Shultz constructed separate earnings models for incumbents of each occupation they examined. To allow for the effects of variables other than age which they hypothesized to affect earnings, they also included seniority, years of schooling, a measure of job-related experience and training, and distance from the employee's home to his job in the model. To allow for the nonlinear effects of age on earnings, they included age and the square of the age. They did not suspect interactions among any variables, so they used an additive model, and estimated parameters by regressing earnings on age, age squared, and the other variables just mentioned. Applying their model to the earnings of maintenance electricians, they obtained a coefficient for age (in years) of .031 and a coefficient of $-.0032$ for age squared. By applying the formula for the partial derivative we can use these results to find the unstandardized effect of age on earnings at different ages: at an age of X years, the effect of age on earnings is $.031 + 2(-.0032)X$. The effect of age on earnings at various ages is shown in Table 15.3; looking at that table notice how the effect of age on earnings declines and ultimately becomes negative as age increases.

Our discussion of effects in parabolic models has assumed that all variables were measured in their natural, or unstandardized, metrics, and that b_1 and b_2 are unstandardized, or "raw," regression coefficients. However, it is frequently useful (and more often customary) to measure causal effects according to a *standardized* metric. When dealing with a *linear* function, standardized

TABLE 15.3
Results from Rees and Shultz's Parabolic Model of Hourly Earnings

Age (years)	Change in hourly earnings per additional year of age (dollars)
20	.0182
30	.0118
40	.0054
45	.0022
50	−.0010
60	−.0074
70	−.0138

effects are just the standardized regression coefficients of the regression equation and are calculated as an intermediate step in most linear regression algorithms. To find the standardized effect when dealing with a parabolic function, we adjust the numerator and denominator of the partial derivative to measure Y and X in standardized units. Applying the usual arithmetic, we get

$$\frac{\partial Y/\sigma Y}{\partial X/\sigma X} = \frac{\partial Y}{\partial X} \cdot \frac{\sigma X}{\sigma Y}$$

Thus, at a given value of X, the standardized effect of X on Y is obtained by first calculating $\partial Y/\partial X$ from the formula $\partial Y/\partial X = b_1 + 2b_2X$, and then multiplying the result by the ratio of the standard deviation of X divided by the standard deviation of Y. Notice that the standardized effect varies according to the value of X.

In the course of presenting the findings from a parabolic model, the researcher probably will wish to evaluate the standardized effect of X on Y at several different values of X. These values may be chosen for their substantive significance or because they have some intuitive appeal. For example, in the analysis of effects of schooling on earnings, one may wish to calculate the effect of schooling on earnings at 6, 9, and 12 years of school. Or, in another analysis, one may wish to calculate the effect of X on Y at the mean of X, and at one standard deviation above and one standard deviation below the mean.

In conclusion, there are three key points to remember about parabolic functions as devices for capturing nonlinear relationships. First, the parabola is a versatile function which fits a wide variety of curvilinear relationships, and which can be used with the familiar machinery of multiple regression analysis. Second, in the parabolic case, as in the linear case, the effect of a variable X on another variable Y, net of the effects of other variables in the model, is the partial derivative of Y with respect to X, $\partial Y/\partial X$, which is a linear function of X, the coefficient for X, and the coefficient for X^2. Third, the standardized effect of X on Y can be calculated merely by multiplying $\partial Y/\partial X$ by σ_x/σ_y.

USES OF THE LOGARITHMIC FUNCTION IN ANALYSIS OF NONLINEAR EFFECTS

Another common workhorse in analysis of nonlinear effects is the logarithmic function. The general form of the logarithmic function commonly used in additive models is $Y = a + b \ln(x) + \Sigma_{i=1}^{K} c_i Z_i$, where X and the Z_is are variables in the model that cause Y; where a, b, and the c_is are parameters; and where ln is the natural logarithm function. Two examples of the sorts of relationships that can be fitted with the logarithmic function are shown in Figure 15.6. Looking at the solid line in that figure, notice that the logarithmic function can be used when the effect of X and Y is always positive (i.e., increases in X lead to increases in Y), but stronger for low values of X than for high values of X. Looking at the dashed line, notice that the logarithmic function also can be used to fit situations in which the effect of X on Y is negative, but stronger at low values of X than at high values of X. These situations correspond to the notion of decreasing marginal effects of X on Y.

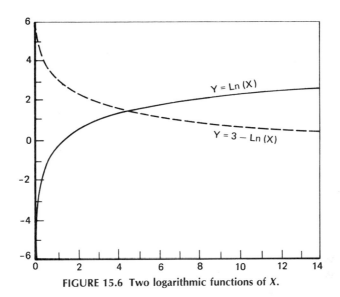

FIGURE 15.6 Two logarithmic functions of X.

One of the great advantages of the logarithmic specification is that it is easy to apply. As long as X assumes only positive values (logarithms are defined only for numbers greater than zero), applying the logarithmic function requires only that one take the log of X and then treat $\ln(X)$ (rather than X) as a variable in ordinary least-squares analysis. The *un*standardized coefficient of $\ln(X)$ can be interpreted as the rate of change in Y per unit change in the *logarithm of X*. The standardized coefficient for $\ln(X)$ can be interpreted as the number of standard deviations of change in Y that occur per standard deviation of change in the *logarithm of X*. But such interpretations are obviously awkward—few variables in real life are measured on logarithmic scales, and so people have little intuitive sense of how big the units of $\ln(X)$ are, even if they are quite familiar with the units of X. Consider, for example, how many *log* years of schooling one must complete in order to obtain a high school diploma. However, the effect of X on Y in a logarithmic specification can be interpreted easily and clearly by turning again to partial derivatives. In the function $Y = a + b \ln(X) + \Sigma c_i Z_i + \varepsilon$ the partial derivative of Y with respect to X, $\partial Y/\partial X$, is b/X. Using this formula, one can easily calculate the unstandardized effect of X on Y at any given value of X. As in the case of the parabola, one can calculate the standardized effect of X on Y at any value of X by first calculating the unstandardized effect at that value and then multiplying it by $\sigma X/\sigma Y$. But, perhaps even more useful is the fact that since $\partial Y/\partial X = b/x$,

$$\frac{\partial Y}{\partial X/X} = \frac{\partial Y}{\partial X} \cdot X = \frac{b}{X} \cdot X = b.$$

Thus, when changes in X are measured as proportions and when changes in Y are measured in the usual metric of Y, the effect of X on Y is precisely equal to the unstandardized regression coefficient for $\ln(X)$.

For an example of the use of the logarithmic specification, we turn to Blau and Schoenherr's (1971, pp. 73–74) analysis of the effects of agency size (i.e., number of employees) on the number of hierarchical levels in agency organization. Blau and Schoenherr regress the number of hierarchical levels on the log of organizational size and measures of automation and the division of labor in the agency. They find a standardized coefficient of .75 for the log of agency size, and coefficients of −.11 and .16 for division of labor and automation, respectively. No doubt because the log of size has little intuitive meaning, they conclude only that size has the "dominant" effect on the number of hierarchical levels (Blau & Schoenherr, 1971, p. 73). However, we can be considerably more precise by calculating the partial derivative of Y (number of levels) with respect to X (size).

The unstandardized coefficient of ln(size) is 4.36. Applying the formula for the partial derivative of Y with respect to X, we find that the unstandardized effect of size (not the logarithm of size!) is 4.36 divided by the size of the organization. Blau and Schoenherr report that the mean of size is 1195 persons; thus, at the mean the unstandardized effect of size on levels is .0036 (= 4.36 ÷ 1195) levels per person. But perhaps the most intuitively appealing measure of the effect of size on number of levels is the change in levels per proportional change in Y. The coefficient of 4.36 for ln(size) indicates a change of .0436 (=4.36/100) levels per change of 1% in organization size, at *any* value of size.[2]

OTHER NONLINEAR SPECIFICATIONS

There is an infinite number of nonlinear mathematical functions, and it is conceivable that each one of them can be of use in causal modeling. However, we will limit our discussion of nonlinear specifications to the parabola and the logarithm, since they are the functions that are most useful most often. We conclude our discussion of nonlinear relationships by noting once again that the partial derivative of Y with respect to X serves as a measure of causal effect in all cases, linear and nonlinear. Thus, the metric effect of X on Y can be calculated for nearly any function that is likely to be of use in causal modeling, and the standardized effect can be easily calculated from the metric effect.

Models That Are Nonadditive and Models That Are Both Nonlinear and Nonadditive

A nonadditive model is one that specifies that the effect of one variable X on another variable Y, varies according to the values of one or more other variables. Thus, for example, when one observes that the effect of educational attainment on occupational achievement is stronger for whites than for blacks,

---

[2] The reader should note that the metric coefficient for $\log_{10}$ (size) was reconstructed from the standardized coefficient for $\log_{10}$ (size) reported by Blau and Schoenherr. I then calculated the coefficient for ln(size) by multiplying the coefficient for $\log_{10}$ (size) by $\log_{10}$ (e), where e is the base of natural logarithms. Note also that a change in size of 100% will not necessarily produce a change in 4.36 levels since the base of the percentage increases as size increases.

one is observing a nonadditive relationship. When one hypothesizes that the effect of a child's IQ on her verbal achievement varies according to her teacher's instructional skills, one is also concerned with a nonadditive relationship. For a final example, when one hypothesizes, as do most students of earnings, that the effect of schooling on earnings varies with an individual's length of labor market experience, one is hypothesizing a nonadditive relationship between schooling and experience in determining earnings.

When dealing with causal models of nonadditive relationships, the key issues are essentially the same as in any other causal modeling situation: One must find a mathematical function that corresponds to theoretical notions of how variables in the model affect the dependent variable, and one must find an accurate, clearly understandable measure of the way in which the effect of one causal variable on the dependent variable varies according to values of one or more other causal variables. Fortunately, we can use the same strategy to measure causal effects in nonadditive models that we used with linear and nonlinear additive models: In nonadditive models, as in other models, the causal effect of a variable X on another variable Y will be measured by the partial derivative of X with respect to Y, $\partial Y/\partial X$, which gives the rate of change in Y per unit change in X. The only complication in the nonadditive case is that $\partial Y/\partial X$ is a function of the other variables in the model that interact with X. Indeed, we *define* nonadditive models as those in which $\partial Y/\partial X$ is a function of one or more other causal variables. Our discussion of causal effects in nonadditive models will be simpler if it is grounded in the context of specific types of verbal formulations and corresponding mathematical functions. So we now turn to brief discussions of four very general types of nonadditive models.

MODELS INVOLVING FACILITATION ("COMPLEMENTARITIES") AND INHIBITION
AMONG SOME, BUT NOT ALL CAUSAL VARIABLES

It is common to talk of facilitation and inhibition in sociology and complementarities in economics—situations in which the effect of a variable X_1 on another variable Y increases or decreases according to values of a third variable X_2. Yet it is often the case that there are variables in the model that are neither hypothesized not observed to facilitate or inhibit the effects of other variables, nor to have their own effects facilitated or inhibited by other variables. In such cases the following function often proves to be both useful and easy to apply:

$$Y + a + b_1X_1 + b_2X_2 + b_3X_1X_2 + \sum_{i=1}^{K} c_iZ_i + \varepsilon \qquad (15.40)$$

where the X_is and the Z_is are causal variables, Y is the dependent variable, and other symbols are parameters. In practice, this is estimated by creating a variable equal to the product of X_1 and X_2 and then regressing Y on it, X_1, X_2 and the Z_is. The null hypothesis that there are not nonadditive effects of X_1 and X_2 on Y (or that these nonadditivities are not captured by the product of X_1 and X_2) is tested with the common t-test of the null hypothesis that $b_3 = 0$. If the coefficient for the product X_1X_2 is significantly different from zero, then the researcher has evidence that the effects of X_1 and X_2 on Y are nonadditive. *Once nonadditivity is established, neither the coefficient for X_1 nor the coefficient for X_2 can be interpreted meaningfully without simultaneously considering the coefficient for the product term.* Notice that this situation is directly analogous to the parabolic nonlinear case—once it is determined that the coefficient for X^2 is nonzero, then the coefficient for X has no meaningful causal interpretation apart from the coefficient for X^2. Similarly, we accomplish this simultaneous consideration by turning once again to partial derivatives. In (15.38) the effect of X_1 on Y is given by $\partial Y/\partial X_1 = b_1 + b_3 X_2$ and the effect of X_2 on Y is given by $\partial Y/\partial X_2 = b_2 + b_3 X_1$. Notice that Z_is do not enter into the formulas for the effects of X_1 and X_2 on Y; this is the mathematical equivalent of saying there is no interaction among any of the Z_is and either X_1 of X_2 in causing Y.

Effects of causal variables can also be expressed in standardized form in the nonadditive case. The procedure is analogous to that developed earlier for the nonlinear case: First, one calculates the metric, or unstandardized, effect of X_1 on Y, and then one multiplies this effect by the ratio of the standard deviation of X_1 divided by the standard deviation of Y. Notice that the standardized effect of X_1, like its unstandardized effect, varies according to the value of X_2.

It is possible to combine various nonadditive and nonlinear models to fit situations in which nonadditivities and nonlinearities are present. Thus, for example, the following function is useful when X_1 and X_2 are believed to interact *and* to have nonlinear effects on Y:

$$Y = a + b_1 X_1 + b_2 X_2 + b_3 X_1 X_2 + b_4 X_1^2 + b_5 X_2^2 + \sum_{i=1}^{k} c_i Z_i. \quad (15.41)$$

In this case, the effect of X_1 on Y varies with the value of X_1 and with the value of X_2. To see this, note that the effect of X_1 on Y, $\partial Y/\partial X_1$, equals $b_1 + 2b_4 X_1 + b_3 X_2$.

It is also possible to allow for situations in which the facilitating effect of one variable on another is nonlinear. To do this, one can add $X_1 X_2^2$ to the specification. Accordingly, in the equation

$$Y = a + b_1 X_1 + b_2 X_2 + b_3 X_1 X_2 + b_4 X_1 X_2^2 + \sum_{i=1}^{k} c_i Z_i, \quad (15.42)$$

the effect of X_1 on Y is $\partial Y/\partial X_1 = b_1 + b_3 X_2 + b_4 X_2^2$. In this specification, the extent to which X_2 influences the effect of X_1 on Y varies nonlinearly over the range of X_2.

In sum, then, the equations discussed in this section provide a flexible set of specifications for considering nonadditivities, or interactions among some, but not necessarily all, causal variables in a model. These specifications are general enough to be appropriate when both nonlinear and nonadditive effects are present, and they can be applied equally well when the nonadditivities themselves are nonlinear. In interpreting these equations, the partial derivative has once again provided a concise, precise measure of the effect of causal variables on the dependent variable, and a parsimonious indicator of the way in which one causal variable affects the effects of another causal variable on the dependent variable. Finally, we have noted that the methods we developed for calculating standardized effects in nonlinear models can be applied directly and easily to these nonadditive models.

THE NONLINEAR–NONADDITIVE MODEL FOR CALCULATING
RATES OF RETURN

There are numerous situations in social and economic life that are usefully conceptualized as investments. For example, "human capital" theory treats time spent in school as an investment; one hears parents speak of the onerous parts of childrearing as investments; the phrase *emotional investment* seems to be commonplace; one makes political investments. Because investment models are so often useful in conceptualizing social phenomena, we now give some attention to the measurement of effects in investment processes.

As always in causal analysis, the first question about investment models concerns the choice of a mathematical function to represent the process. To find such a function, we need go only to the nearest bank and consider the effect of time on money invested there in a savings account: Where R is the interest rate, P is the initial deposit, X is the amount of time during which the money is on deposit, and P' is the amount of money in the account at the end of the deposit period, the effect of X on the deposit is given by the usual interest formula, $P' = P(1 + R)^x$. This formula is the standard model for all investment processes. In passing, note that $1 + R$ is the proportional effect on P per unit of time.

A little algebra can be used to write the interest formula in a more general (and therefore more useful) form: Let $a = \ln P$ and let $b = \ln(1 + R)$. Then, where e is the base of natural logarithms,

$$P' = P(1 + R)^x = e^a e^{bx} = e^{a+bx}. \qquad (15.43)$$

Taking logarithms of both sides, we have $\ln(P') = a + bx$, a function which can be estimated by ordinary linear regression.

In most applications, there are several different investment processes assumed to be operating, and the researcher normally wishes to separate out the effects of each. Accordingly, the logarithmic form of the model can be generalized to $\ln(Y) = a + \sum_{i=1}^{k} b_i X_i$ where the X_i are the amounts of different types of investments, and where Y is a variable (not necessarily dollars) representing the quantity in which the return is "paid." The nonlogarithmic form of the model is $Y = \exp(a + \sum b_i X_i)$.

The metric effect of one of the X_is (say, X_l) on Y is calculated by taking the partial derivative, $\partial Y/\partial X = b_l \exp(a + \sum_i b_i X_i)$. But, clearly this formula is so awkward that it is useless in most circumstances. However, if changes in Y are measured on a proportional basis and changes in causal variables are measured in the natural metric, the logarithmic form of the model allows calculation of partial derivatives with remarkable simplicity. To see this note that the proportional change in Y per unit change in X is

$$\frac{\partial Y / Y}{\partial X_l} = \frac{\partial Y}{\partial X_l} \cdot \frac{1}{Y}.$$

Substituting $b_l \exp(a + \Sigma b_i X_i)$ for $\partial Y / \partial X$ and substituting $\exp(a + \Sigma_{i=1}^k b_i X_i)$ for Y, we get

$$\frac{\partial Y / Y}{\partial X_l} = [b_l \exp(a + \Sigma b_i X_i)] \left[\frac{1}{\exp(a + \Sigma b_i X_i)}\right] = b_l.$$

Furthermore, when b_l is between $-.09$ and $+.09$, b_l is approximately equal to $(\exp b_l) - 1$, so that in practice, the functional form discussed in this section can be used to calculate rates of return with extraordinary ease: when b_l is between $-.09$ and $+.09$, $\exp b_l$ approximately equals $1 + b_l$.

Finally, it should be pointed out that once the rate of return has been calculated, the metric effect can be calculated from it without difficulty, and the standardized effect can be calculated from the metric effect with ease. To see this, note that the rate of return can be written mathematically as $(\partial Y / Y)/\partial X_l$. Thus, at a given value of Y, the metric effect $\partial Y / \partial X$ is equal to the product of Y and the rate of return. Once the rate of return is calculated, the standardized effect can be calculated by multiplying the metric rate by σ_{x_l}/σ_y. But note that in this model, the metric and standardized affects are different at every value of Y, even though the rate of return remains constant.

THE PURELY MULTIPLICATIVE EFFECTS (OR COBB—DOUGLAS) MODEL

The following function occurs with some regularity in sociological research and with great frequency in economic analysis:

$$Y = aX_1^{b_1} X_2^{b_2} \cdots X_k^{b_k}$$

or, in more parsimonious notation

$$Y = a \prod_{i=1}^{k} X_i^{b_i}. \tag{15.44}$$

In economics, this equation is known as the Cobb–Douglas production function. In sociology, it seems to have no established name, though it is often called a multiplicative model. Since there are numerous different other models that are also multiplicative, we will refer to this equation as the Cobb–Douglas function.

One of the appeals of the Cobb–Douglas function is that its parameters can be estimated by ordinary least-squares regression. To see this, take logarithms of both sides of the equation and then apply the laws of logarithms to obtain the following:

$$\ln Y = \ln a + \sum_{i=1}^{k} b_i \ln Xi + \ln \varepsilon. \tag{15.45}$$

So the parameters of the Cobb–Douglas function can be estimated by taking the logarithms of all variables in the model and then regressing the log of Y on the logs of the X_is.

Sociologists and economists tend to apply the Cobb–Douglas function for different reasons. In sociology, the function is usually applied when the researcher expects interactions among *all* the variables in the model. For example, in thinking about performance in school, one might hypothesize that certain characteristics of individuals not only contribute to performance, but also enhance the effects of other characteristics on performance, and that certain other characteristics not only reduce performance, but reduce the effects of other variables on performance. If all causal variables in the model either enhanced or reduced the effects of all the other causal variables, then there would be some basis for using the Cobb–Douglas specification. Mathematically, the interdependence of effects in the Cobb–Douglas function can be seen by calculating the formula for the metric effect of any causal variable on Y:

$$\frac{\partial Y}{\partial X_k} = \left[ab_k \prod_{i=1}^{k-1} X_i^{b_i} \right] X_k^{b_k-1} \tag{15.46}$$

Note that every causal variable in the model appears in the formula for the metric effect of every single other variable in the model. Since the standardized effect is equal to the product of the metric effect with $\sigma X / \sigma Y$, every causal variable in the model also appears in the formula for the standardized effect.

Although the formula for $\partial Y / \partial X_k$ clearly communicates the existence of interactions among variables in the Cobb–Douglas function, it does not seem to communicate any other useful information with any clarity at all. The formula for the partial derivative is too complicated to be enlightening in the Cobb–Douglas specification. However, by measuring causal effects as rates of return rather than as metric and standardized effects, the Cobb–Douglas function yields effect measures that are paragons of simplicity. To see this, recall that the rate of return to X_k is the proportional change in Y per unit change in X_k. Mathematically, then,

$$\text{rate of return} = \frac{\partial Y}{\partial X_k} = \frac{\partial Y}{\partial X_k} \cdot \frac{1}{Y}.$$

So, where R_k is the rate of return to X_k,

$$R_k = \left[(ab_k) \prod_{i=1}^{k-1} X_i^{b_i}(X_k^{b_k-1}) \right] \cdot \frac{1}{Y}. \tag{15.47}$$

But, from the Cobb–Douglas specification, $Y = a\Sigma_{i=1}^{k} X_i^{b_i}$. Substituting for Y,

$$R_k = \left[(ab_k) \prod_{i=1}^{k-2} X_i^{b_i}(X_k^{b_k-1}) \right] \left(a \prod_{i=1}^{k} X_i^{b_i} \right). \tag{15.48}$$

Canceling terms, we get $R_k = b_k/X_k$.

Similarly, when effects are measured as elasticities, then the Cobb–Douglas function offers a blissfully simple formula for the effect of X_k on Y: Recall that the elasticity is the proportional change in Y per proportional change in X. Where E_k is the elasticity of Y with respect to X_k, $E_k = (\partial Y/Y)/(\partial X/X)$. Applying some algebra, $E_k = (\partial Y/\partial X) \cdot (1/Y) \cdot X$, so $E_k = R_k \cdot X$. Substituting b_k/X_k for R_k we get $E_k = (b_k/X_k)X_k = b_k$. In words, when X_k changes by 1%, Y changes by b_k %. So the Cobb–Douglas function offers intuitively appealing, easy to calculate measures of the effects of causal variables on a dependent variable in situations in which all causal variables in the model interact with each other.

THE TREATMENT OF NONADDITIVITIES WHEN ONE OR MORE OF THE INTERACTING CAUSAL VARIABLES IS DISCRETE

The analysis of covariance (ANCOVA) offers a powerful set of statistical techniques for testing hypotheses about interactions among nominal scale variables and other variables. ANCOVA is treated at length in Chapter 13 by Berk, but a few points deserve mention here. The logic behind using ANCOVA in nonadditive models is straightforward: If X_1 and X_2 have nonadditive effects on Y, then the effect of X_2 on Y will vary with the value of X_1. Accordingly, if cases are grouped according to their value on X_1, and if the effect of X_2 on Y is calculated separately in each of these groups, then the interaction of X_1 and X_2 can be observed by noting group differences in the effect of X_2 on Y. Hauser (1971) has used this approach to study the interaction of school characteristics and pupil characteristics in determining educational performance; Duncan (1968) for the interaction of race with socioeconomic characteristics in determining occupational status attainment; and Stolzenberg (1975) to examine the interaction of race, occupation, and educational attainment in determining earnings.

There are at least three major attractions in using ANCOVA to analyze nonadditive effects. First ANCOVA does not require the researcher to specify the functional form of the nonadditive relationship—one need only hypothesize that the effect of one causal variable *differs* according to the values of one or more other causal variables. Second, ANCOVA offers a rich variety of statistical tests of significance. So ANCOVA allows one to test for the existence of interactions without specifying the function that describes them. And, third, because ANCOVA tests for group differences, it is well suited to examinations of interactions of nominal variables with continuous scale variables.

But ANCOVA has some serious drawbacks for the causal models. First, it lacks parsimony, producing a separate measure of the effect of X_2 on Y for every different value of X_1. When there are more than four or five values of X_1, the researcher is often swamped in group-specific effects without a parsimonious method for summarizing the pattern of differences in the effect of X_2 on Y. To avoid such problems, one often combines groups, despite the consequent loss of accuracy. Or, not wishing to lose accuracy, researchers often use a large number of groups but ignore the group-specific effects altogether, focusing their attention entirely on increments in variance explained when interaction effects are allowed. Obviously, neither of these solutions is ideal. A second drawback is that ANCOVA tends to require larger samples than other techniques for dealing with interactions, since fitting an additive model in each of several groups usually requires more data cases than fitting a nonadditive model in one group.

In conclusion, we suggest that the usefulness of ANCOVA can be maximized by using it primarily to test the hypothesis of additivity against the alternative hypothesis of nonadditive effects. If the results of this test suggest nonadditivity, then the researcher's job is to find a mathematical function (and, of course, a theoretical explanation) that parsimoniously explains these nonadditive effects. For an example of this procedure when the interaction involved nominal scale variable and a continuous variable, see Stolzenberg (1973, chap. 4); for an example of this procedure when the interaction involved two continuous variables, see Stolzenberg and Waite (1977).

Decomposition of Effects

When causal models involve more than one equation, and when these equations specify that some variables intervene between other antecedent and consequent variables, standard operating procedure has been to decompose the total effect of the antecedent variable into direct and indirect components. Using the language of path analysis, Alwin and Hauser (1975) say

> the *total effect* of one variable on another is the part of their total association which is neither due to their common causes, to correlation among their causes, nor to unanalyzed (predetermined) correlation (Duncan, 1971). . . . A total effect tells us how much change in a consequent variable is induced by a given shift in an antecedent variable, irrespective of the mechanisms by which the change may occur. . . . *Indirect effects* are those parts of a variable's total effect which are transmitted or mediated by variables specified as intervening between the cause and effect of interest in a model. That is, they tell us how much of a given effect occurs because the manipulation of the antecedent variable of interest leads to changes in other variables which in turn change the consequent variable. The *direct effect* of one variable on another is simply that part of its total effect which is *not* transmitted via intervening variables [pp. 38–39].

We now look at methods for calculating total, direct, and indirect effects in nonlinear, nonadditive multiequation models.

CALCULATION OF THE DIRECT EFFECT

The direct effect of an antecedent variable on a consequent variable is obtained by calculating the antecedent's effect in a way that ignores indirect patterns of causation in the model under consideration. Mathematically, one omits these mediated (indirect) effects by (*a*) ignoring all equations in the model other than the structural equation for the consequent variable, and (*b*) calculating the partial derivative of the consequent variable with respect to the relevant antecedent variable in that equation. For example, consider the model shown in Figure 15.7 and in Eqs. (15.49) and (15.50).

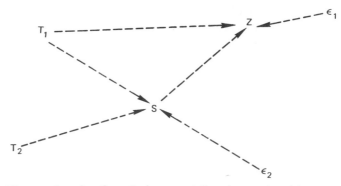

FIGURE 15.7 Diagramatic and mathematical representation of a causal model corresponding to Eqs. (15.49) and (15.50).

$$S = f(T_1, T_2, \varepsilon_1) = a_0 + a_1 T_1 + a_2 \ln T_2 + \varepsilon_1, \tag{15.49}$$

$$Z = g(T_1, T_2, S, \varepsilon_2) = b_0 + b_1 T_1 + b_2 T_2$$
$$+ b_3 S + b_4 T_1 T_2 + \varepsilon_2. \tag{15.50}$$

In this model, the direct effect of T_1 on Z is obtained by ignoring Eq. (15.49) completely and by calculating $\partial Z/\partial T_1$ in (15.50): $\partial Z/\partial T_1 = b_1 + b_4 T_2$.

CALCULATION OF THE TOTAL EFFECT

The procedure for obtaining the total effect of an antecedent variable is only slightly more complicated than the method for calculating its direct effect. A two-step procedure is required to measure the total effect: First, it is necessary to uncover the effects of antecedent variables buried within other variables that intervene between the antecedent and consequent variables in the model. To make these buried effects explicit, one need only substitute the right-hand side of the structural equation for each intervening variable in place of the respective intervening variable in the structural equation for the consequent variable. For example, consider the model shown in Figure 15.7 and in (15.49) and (15.50). To find the total effect on T_1 on Z in this model, $f(T_1, T_2, \varepsilon_1)$ is substituted for S in (15.50) as follows:

$$Z = g[T_1, T_2, f(T_1, T_2, \varepsilon_1), \varepsilon_2]$$
$$= b_0 + b_1 T_1 + b_2 T_2 + b_3 (a_0 + a_1 T_1 + a_2 \ln T_2 + \varepsilon_1)$$
$$+ b_4 T_1 T_2 + \varepsilon_2. \tag{15.51}$$

Multiplying through and collecting terms in equation (15.51) gives:

$$Z = b_0 + b_1 T_1 + b_2 T_2 + b_3 a_0 + b_3 a_1 T_1$$
$$+ b_3 a_2 \ln T_2 + b_3 \varepsilon_1 + b_4 T_1 T_2 + \varepsilon_2$$
$$= b_0 + b_3 a_0 + (b_1 + b_3 a_1) T_1 + b_2 T_2$$
$$+ b_3 a_2 \ln T_2 + b_4 T_1 T_2 + b_3 \varepsilon_1 + \varepsilon_2. \tag{15.52}$$

This substitution procedure transforms the structural equation for the conse-quent variable into the *reduced-form* equation for the consequent variable (see Johnston, 1972, p. 4). Once the reduced-form equation is calculated, the total effect of the antecedent variable is calculated by taking the partial derivative of the consequent variable with respect to the antecedent variable in the reduced-form equation, ignoring all other equations. For example, in the model shown in Figure 15.7, the direct effects of T_1 and T_2 are obtained by differentiating Eq. (15.52) as follows:

$$\frac{\partial Z}{\partial T_1} = b_1 + b_3 a_1 + b_4 T_2 \qquad (15.53)$$

$$\frac{\partial Z}{\partial T_2} = b_2 + \frac{b_3 a_2}{T_2} + b_4 T_1. \qquad (15.54)$$

To recapitulate briefly, the total effect of an antecedent variable on a consequent variable may be obtained by first calculating the reduced-form equation for the consequent variable, and then computing the partial derivative of the consequent variable with respect to the antecedent variable in the re-duced-form equation. In principle, this procedure is identical to the widely used procedure described by Alwin and Hauser (1975) for use with linear additive models.[3] In practice, these procedures differ because Alwin and Hauser take advantage of some convenient mathematical characteristics of linear additive models to avoid the tedium of algebraic substitution to obtain the reduced-form equations and partial derivatives. However the tedium of algebraic substitution can be avoided with nonlinear nonadditive models by application of a funda-mental and elementary theorem of differential calculus, the chain rule for par-tial derivatives (see any elementary calculus text, such as Schwartz, 1967, p. 641). According to the chain rule, if Z is a function of variables $X_1, X_2, \ldots ,$ X_I, and if $X_1, X_2, \ldots , X_I$ are in turn functions of variables $T_1, T_2, \ldots , T_J$, then the partial derivative of Z with respect to some T_j is given by:[4]

$$\frac{\partial Z}{\partial T_j} = \sum_{i=1}^{I} \left(\frac{\partial Z}{\partial X_i} \cdot \frac{\partial X_i}{\partial T_j} \right) \qquad (15.55)$$

To apply the chain rule to the example shown in Figure 15.7 and Eqs. (15.49) and (15.50), it is necessary to rewrite the model so that Z is a function only of the X_is, and so the X_is are functions of only the T_js as follows.

$$X_1 = T_1 \qquad (15.56)$$

$$X_2 = T_2 \qquad (15.57)$$

$$X_3 = S = f(T_1, T_2, \varepsilon_1) = a_0 + a_1 T_1 + a_2 \ln T_2 + \varepsilon_1 \qquad (15.58)$$

---

[3] Alwin and Hauser do not refer to their effect measures as partial derivatives, even though they are identical to partial derivatives in definition, calculation, and interpretation.

[4] Use of the chain rule is subject to certain conditions of differentiability that normally are met in regression analysis.

$$Z = g(X_1, X_2, X_3, \varepsilon_2) = b_0 + b_1 X_1 + b_2 X_2$$
$$+ b_3 X_3 + b_4 X_1 X_2 + \varepsilon_2 \tag{15.59}$$

Equations (15.56) and (15.57) merely clarify notation in subsequent equations, and (15.58) and (15.59) correspond directly to (15.49) and (15.50). According to the rules of calculus, the derivatives are calculated as follows:

$$\frac{\partial X_1}{\partial T_1} = 1, \qquad \frac{\partial X_2}{\partial T_1} = 0, \qquad \frac{\partial X_3}{\partial T_1} = a_1 \qquad \frac{\partial X_3}{\partial T_2} = \frac{a_2}{T_2}$$

$$\frac{\partial Z}{\partial X_1} = b_1 + b_4 X_2, \qquad \frac{\partial Z}{\partial X_2} = b_2 + b_4 X_1 \qquad \frac{\partial Z}{\partial X_3} = b_3$$

Plugging these derivatives into (15.55) gives the total effects of T_1:

$$\frac{\partial Z}{\partial T_1} = \sum_{i=1}^{3} \frac{\partial Z}{\partial X_i} \cdot \frac{\partial X_i}{\partial T_1}$$

$$= (b_1 + b_4 X_2)(1) + (b_2 + b_4 X_1)(0) + b_3(a_1) \tag{15.60}$$

And since $X_2 = T_2$, (15.60) can be rewritten:

$$\frac{\partial Z}{\partial T_1} = b_1 + b_3 a_1 + b_4 X_2, \tag{15.61}$$

which is identical to the expression (15.53) obtained by the tedious two-step process of calculating the reduced-form equation for Z and then computing the partial derivative of Z with respect to T_1 in the reduced-form equation.

CALCULATION OF INDIRECT EFFECT

Once the total and direct effects are calculated, indirect effects may be computed merely by subtraction of the direct effect of an antecedent variable from its total effect. This subtraction procedure is applicable both to linear additive models (see Alwin & Hauser, 1975) and to nonlinear nonadditive models. For example, in the model shown in Figure 15.7 and in (15.49) and (15.50), we saw that the direct effect of T_1 on Z is $b_1 + b_4 T_2$, and that the total effect of T_1 on Z is $b_1 + b_3 a_1 + b_4 T_2$. Subtraction of the direct effect from the total effect yields the indirect effect of T_1 on Z. That is, $(b_1 + b_3 a_1 + b_4 T_2) - (b_1 + b_4 T_2) = b_3 a_1$. However, it is not actually necessary to calculate direct and total effects in order to calculate indirect effects. Some tedious but straightforward algebra will show that the chain rule for partial derivatives expresses the total effect of an antecedent variable as the sum of its direct and indirect effects. That is, where Ts denote antecedent variables, Xs denote intervening variables, and Z denotes the consequent variable, the effect on Z of a given antecedent variable T_j (which is mediated through intervening variable X_i) is given by the product $(\partial Z/\partial X_i)(\partial X_i/\partial T_j)$.

In the case where X_i is just a new name for T_j (as X_1 is merely a new name for T_1 in the example discussed in the previous section), the effect of T_j mediated "through itself" is the direct effect on T_j on Z. Thus, in (15.60), the direct effect of T_1 is

$$\frac{\partial Z}{\partial X_1} \cdot \frac{\partial X_1}{\partial T_1} = (b_1 + b_4 X_2)(1) = b_1 + b_4 X_2;$$

the indirect effect of T_1 on Z mediated through X_2 is

$$\frac{\partial Z}{\partial X_2} \cdot \frac{\partial X_2}{\partial T_2} = (b_2 + b_4 X_1)(0) = 0;$$

and the indirect effect of T_1 on Z mediated through X_3 is

$$\frac{\partial Z}{\partial X_3} \cdot \frac{\partial X_3}{\partial T_1} = b_3 a_1.$$

Note that these values are equivalent to measures of direct and indirect effects obtained first by calculating the direct and total effects and then subtracting direct from total effects to obtain the indirect effects.

Standard Errors and Significance Tests

Sociological literature often gives the impression that computation of standard errors and calculation of significance tests is difficult and complex in nonlinear and nonadditive equations (e.g., see Althauser, 1971; Southwood, 1978). In fact, if parameters of nonlinear nonadditive models are estimated by regression or some other method that provides sampling variances and covariances of parameter estimates, a theorem from mathematical statistics usually makes it trivially simple (though somewhat tedious) to calculate the standard errors of effect measures discussed in this chapter.[5] Once standard errors have been obtained, performance of significance tests is straightforward. The theorem that provides these convenient results states that if $b_1, b_2, \ldots, b_n$ are sample estimates of a model's parameters, if $K_1, K_2, \ldots, K_n$ are constants, if σ_i^2 is the sampling variance of b_i, if $\mathrm{cov}(b_i, b_j)$ is the sampling covariance of b_i and b_j, and if $D = \sum_{i=1}^n K_i b_i$, then sampling variance of D is given by

$$\sigma_D^2 = \sum_{i=1}^n K_i^2 \sigma_i^2 + \sum_{i=1}^n \sum_{j \neq i} K_i K_j \, \mathrm{cov}(b_i, b_j). \tag{15.62}$$

As an example of how to apply (15.62), consider the effect of X_1 on Y in the following interactive model:

$$Y = b_0 + b_1 X_1 + b_2 X_2 + b_3 X_1 X_2 + \varepsilon. \tag{15.63}$$

---

[5] The sampling variance–covariance matrix of regression coefficients normally is computed as an intermediate step in multiple regression programs and a number of widely used regression programs print this matrix (e.g., the BMDP regression program). Equation (15.62) is a trivial extension of Hogg and Craig's (1970, p. 168) work.

The metric effect of X_1 on Y is

$$\partial Y / \partial X_1 = b_1 + b_3 X_2. \tag{15.64}$$

Through application of (15.62), the sampling variance of $\partial Y / \partial X_1$ is

$$\sigma^2_{\partial Y / \partial X_1} = \sigma^2_1 + X^2_2 \sigma^2_3 + 2X_2 \, \text{cov}(b_1, b_3).$$

Note that the sampling variance of $\partial Y / \partial X_1$, like $\partial Y / \partial X_1$ itself, varies with the value of X_1.

As a second example of how to apply (15.62), consider the effect of X_1 on Y in the following nonlinear model:

$$Y = a + b_1 \ln(X_1) + \sum_{i=2}^{I} b_i X_i + \varepsilon. \tag{15.65}$$

The metric effect of X_1 on Y in (15.65) is

$$\frac{\partial Y}{\partial X_1} = \frac{b_1}{X_1} = b_1 \frac{1}{X_1} \tag{15.66}$$

Through application of (15.62), the sampling variance of $\partial Y / \partial X_1$ is $(1/X_1^2)\sigma_1^2$.

We have now discussed a variety of linear, nonlinear additive, and nonadditive, recursive causal models. Table 15.4 summarizes some of the more basic features of these models. In the next few pages, we turn our attention to nonrecursive models.

15.4. SOME USES OF NONRECURSIVE CAUSAL MODELS

Many social science theories lead rather naturally to the specification of stages of *one-way causation* among members of a set of jointly dependent variables (e.g., theories pertaining to life-cycle phenomena) that can be faithfully represented by recursive causal models. But sometimes it is the case that a social science theory specifies intrinsic *simultaneous causal interdependence* among two or more members of a set of endogenous variables (e.g., supply–demand theories in economics). In such cases, interest focuses on the estimation and assessment of reciprocal effect parameters connecting the interdependent variables.

Without attempting to reproduce readily available textbook expositions of statistical methods for nonrecursive models, we briefly sketch some issues raised by such models in this section. First, we use the classical two-equation Keynesian model of national income determination to show how OLS parameter estimators become flawed in the context of nonrecursive models. Second, after citing several recent sociological applications of nonrecursive models, we characterize some circumstances in which such models are likely to arise. Third, in the context of a simple two-equation nonrecursive system, we describe the identification problem. Fourth, we enumerate the main structural

TABLE 15.4
Several Measures of Causal Effect in Several Widely Applicable Mathematical Specifications[a]

Specification	Causal effects of X_1 on Y				
	Metric effect $\dfrac{\partial Y}{\partial X_1}$	Standardized effect $\dfrac{\partial Y/\sigma Y}{\partial X_1/\sigma X_1}$	Effect of proportional change in X_1 $\dfrac{\partial Y}{\partial X_1/X_1}$	Instantaneous rate of return $\dfrac{\partial Y/Y}{\partial X_1}$	Point elasticity $\dfrac{\partial Y/Y}{\partial X_1/X_1}$
1. $\hat{Y} = a + \sum\limits_{i=1}^{I} b_i X_i$	b_1	$b_1 \dfrac{\sigma X_1}{\sigma Y}$	$b_1 X$	$\dfrac{b_1}{Y}$	$\dfrac{b_1 X}{Y}$
2. $\hat{Y} = a + b_1 \ln(X_1) + \sum\limits_{i=2}^{I} b_i X_i$	$\dfrac{b_1}{X_1}$	$\dfrac{b_1}{X_1}\dfrac{\sigma X_1}{\sigma Y}$	b_1	$\dfrac{b_1}{X_1 Y}$	$\dfrac{b_1}{Y}$
3A. $\hat{Y} = a + b_0 X_1 + b_1 X_1^2 + \sum\limits_{i=2}^{I} b_i X_i$	$b_0 + 2b_1 X_1$	$(b_0 + 2b_1 X_2)\dfrac{\sigma X_1}{\sigma Y}$	$b_c X_1 + 2b_1 X_1^2$	$\dfrac{b_0 + 2b_1 X_1}{Y}$	$\dfrac{b_0 X_1 + 2b_1 X_1^2}{Y}$
3B. $\hat{Y} = a + \sum\limits_{j=1}^{J} b_j X_1^j + \sum\limits_{i=2}^{I} c_i X_i$	$\left(\sum\limits_{j=1}^{J} jb_j X_1^{j-1}\right)$	$\left(\sum\limits_{j=1}^{J} jb_j X_1^{j-1}\right)\dfrac{\sigma X_1}{\sigma Y}$	$\sum\limits_{j=1}^{J} jb_j X_1^j$	$\dfrac{1}{Y}\left(\sum\limits_{j=1}^{J} jb_j X_1^{j-1}\right)$	$\dfrac{1}{Y}\left(\sum\limits_{j=1}^{J} jb_j X_1^j\right)$
4. $\hat{Y} = a + \sum\limits_{i=1}^{I} b_i X_i + b_{I+1} X_1 X_2$	$b_1 + b_{I+1} X_2$	$(b_1 + b_{I+1} X_2)\dfrac{\sigma X_1}{\sigma Y}$	$b_1 X_1 + b_{I+1} X_1 X_2$	$\dfrac{b_1}{Y} + b_{I+1}\left(\dfrac{X_2}{Y}\right)$	$\dfrac{b_1 X_1 + b_{I+1} X_1 X_2}{Y}$
5. $\hat{Y} = e^a + \sum\limits_{i=1}^{I} b_i X_i$	$b_1 Y$	$b_1 Y \cdot \dfrac{\sigma X_1}{\sigma X}$	$b_1 X_1 Y$	b_1	$b_1 X_1$
6. $\hat{Y} = a \prod\limits_{i=1}^{I} X_i^{b_i}$	$\dfrac{b_1 Y}{X_1}$	$\dfrac{b_1 Y}{X_1} \cdot \dfrac{\sigma X_1}{\sigma Y}$	$b_1 Y$	$\dfrac{b_1}{X_1}$	b_1

[a] These functions defined only for the domain of $\{X_i\}$ and Y. See text for equivalent formulas for some of these effects. Y is ''dependent''; X_i's are ''independent.''

parameter estimators that have been developed by application of the least-squares and maximum likelihood principles of estimation to nonrecursive models. Fifth, we summarize some known advantages and shortcomings of these estimators. Finally, we return to the topic dealt with in Section 15.2— causal inferences—in the context of nonrecursive models.

Situations That Suggest Nonrecursive Models

Nonrecursive structural equation models have been the mainstay of econometrics for over 40 years; indeed, a substantial part of conventional econometric statistical theory is concerned with generalizations of the least-squares and maximum likelihood estimators for the parameters of the standard single-equation general linear model to nonrecursive simultaneous equation models (see, for example, the expositions in such standard econometrics textbooks as Christ, 1966; Dhrymes, 1974; Goldberger, 1964; Johnston, 1972; Klein, 1962; Kmenta, 1971; Koutsayiannis, 1977; Maddala, 1977; Malinvaud, 1970; Pindyck and Rubinfeld, 1976; Theil, 1971; Wonnacott and Wonnacott, 1970; for applications to social science topics outside economics, see Duncan, 1975; and Hanushek and Jackson, 1977). The necessity of these generalizations arose out of efforts in the 1930s and 1940s to build multiple-equation models of national economies (see, for example, Klein, 1950; Tinbergen, 1939). As soon as these models began to be specified along the lines suggested by Keynes's (1936) general theory, it became apparent that the use of OLS to estimate the parameters of such models produced estimators with undesirable statistical properties. This point can be demonstrated in a few lines.

Consider the simplest possible Keynesian model of national income determination consisting of a consumption function and an income identity, namely

$$C_t = \alpha + \beta Y_t + u_t, \tag{15.67}$$

$$Y_t = C_t + Z_t, \tag{15.68}$$

where C_t = consumption expenditure in year t, Y_t = national income in year t, Z_t = nonconsumption expenditure in year t, and u_t = a stochastic disturbance term in year t. In this two-equation model, Z is assumed to be a set of numbers determined exogenously to the model, for example, by public authorities, independently of C and Y. The latter two variables are endogenous and simultaneously determined by (15.67) and (15.68); C is determined by the simple linear consumption function (of income) of classical Keynesian theory; Y is defined by the national income accounting identity (15.68) that requires consumption and nonconsumption expenditures to sum to national income.

Assume that the disturbance term of (15.67) has the following properties:

$$E(u_t) = 0 \qquad \text{for all } t; \tag{15.69}$$

$$E(u_t u_{t+s}) = \begin{cases} 0 & \text{for } s \neq 0 \quad \text{and for all } t; \\ \sigma^2 & \text{for } s = 0 \quad \text{and for all } t; \end{cases} \tag{15.70} \\ \tag{15.71}$$

Z and u are independent, which will be satisfied if either Z is a set of fixed numbers or if Z is a random variable distributed independently of u.

$$(15.72)$$

Assumptions (15.70) and (15.71) require zero autocorrelation and homoscedasticity of the disturbances. For a valid application of OLS to estimate the α and β parameters of (15.67), there remains only the question of the independence of u and Y. To examine this, we substitute (15.67) in (15.68) to obtain

$$Y_t = \alpha + \beta Y_t + Z_t + u_t \tag{15.73}$$

or, subtracting βY_t from both sides,

$$Y_t - \beta Y_t = \alpha + Z_t + u_t \tag{15.74}$$

dividing each side by $1 - \beta$,

$$Y_t = \frac{\alpha}{1 - \beta} + \frac{1}{1 - \beta} Z_t + \frac{u_t}{1 - \beta}. \tag{15.75}$$

This last equation shows that Y_t is influenced by u_t, and, from it, we obtain the expected value of Y_t:

$$E(Y_t) = \frac{\alpha}{1 - \beta} + \frac{1}{1 - \beta} Z_t \tag{15.76}$$

and the following expression for the expected value of the covariance of u_t and the deviation unit values $Y_t - E(Y_t)$:

$$E\{u_t[Y_t - E(Y_t)]\} = E\left|\frac{u_t u_t}{1 - \beta}\right| = \frac{1}{1 - \beta} E(u_t^2) \neq 0. \tag{15.77}$$

In brief, since this covariance is nonzero, the disturbance term and the explanatory variable in the consumption equation (15.67) are correlated.

To examine the implication of this for the OLS estimator, consider the following form of the least-squares estimator $\hat{\beta}$ of β:

$$\hat{\beta} = \sum_{t=1}^{n} w_t C_t \tag{15.78}$$

where $w_t = Y_t / \sum_{t=1}^{n} y_t^2$ with $y_t = Y_t - \bar{Y}_t$, that is, the deviation unit scores of the explanatory variable Y_t, and the summations are over n sample observations (e.g., see Johnston, 1972, p. 18). It follows directly from the definition of w_t that

$$\sum_{t=1}^{n} w_t = 0 \quad \text{and} \quad \sum_{t=1}^{n} w_t y_t = \sum_{t=1}^{n} w_t Y_t = 1. \tag{15.79}$$

Then we have

$$\hat{\beta} = \Sigma w_t C_t$$

$$= \Sigma w_t(\alpha + \beta Y_t + u_t)$$

$$= \beta + \Sigma w_t u_t, \tag{15.80}$$

where the second equality follows by substituting (15.67) and the third by using (15.79). Thus, we obtain the following expression for the expected value of β:

$$E(\hat{\beta}) = E(\beta + \Sigma w_t u_t)$$

$$= E(\beta) + E(\Sigma w_t u_t)$$

$$= \beta + E\left(\frac{\Sigma y_t u_t}{\Sigma y_i^2}\right) \qquad (15.81)$$

Now, since we have shown in (15.77) that the expected value of the numerator in (15.81) does not vanish, this expression for $E(\hat{\beta})$ does not reduce to β, and, therefore, *the OLS estimator is biased*. This is a bias for any finite sample size, but *the OLS estimator also is inconsistent* (for a proof, see Johnston, 1972, pp. 343–344); that is, a bias persists even for infinitely large samples. Clearly, these are not desirable properties for a statistical estimator to possess. *These characteristics of OLS estimators persist for the class of all nonrecursive simultaneous-equation models* as specified previously in Section 15.2 by (15.24) and Assumption 1, and it is for this reason that other estimators have been derived.

In contrast to the intrinsic importance of nonrecursive models in economics, recursive models (usually with independent disturbances) have been far more frequently applied in sociology and the other social sciences than have nonrecursive models. There are at least three reasons for the predominance of recursive models in sociological analyses. First, processes involving one-way causation among variables have more intuitive appeal and a simpler mathematical representation than those involving two-way, or reciprocal, causation. Second, as we have noted, ordinary least-squares estimators and standard t- and F-tests can be applied equation by equation to recursive models (with independent disturbances) with little modification in their interpretations. By contrast, nonrecursive models require more complicated statistical methods of estimation and hypothesis testing with which noneconomic social scientists generally have not been familiar. Third, and perhaps of greatest importance, recursive models initially were given natural, powerful, and convincing applications in sociological studies of the processes of stratification and status attainment (e.g., see Blau & Duncan, 1967; Hauser, 1971; Duncan *et al.,* 1972; Hauser & Featherman, 1977).

Nevertheless, despite the overwhelming frequency of occurrence of recursive models in sociological analyses, there now exist several published studies using cross-sectional sample survey data in which nonrecursive models have been essential to the faithful representation and analysis of the underlying theoretical hypotheses. Moreover, an examination of the substantive contents of some of these studies yields generalizations about the kinds of situations that suggest nonrecursive rather than recursive formulations.

1. In a major reinterpretation of the process of peer influences on aspirations, Duncan, Haller, and Portes (1968), examined several alternative two-equation models of the effect of a best friend's educational and

occupational aspirations on the formation of ego's aspirations and the reciprocal influence in the opposite direction.

2. In his study of the effects of socioeconomic background on educational performance, Hauser (1971, pp. 78–79) formulated a model of intelligence test performance in which the verbal and quantitative scores were postulated to affect each other.

3. In reformulations of Woelfel and Haller's (1971) model of how the attitudes of significant others affect the educational and occupational aspirations of high school students, Land (1971) and Henry and Hummon (1971) specified and estimated three-equation models that require the joint dependence of significant other's mean occupational and educational expectations for ego, ego's own educational and occupational aspirations, and the individual's academic performance.

4. In their analysis of the relation of occupational experiences to psychological functioning, Kohn and Schooler (1973) estimated a model with two nonrecursive equations in which the substantive complexity of an individual's job both influences and is influenced by intellectual flexibility.

5. In their study of the labor force participation plans and childbearing expectations of young women, Waite and Stolzenberg (1976) formulated a model of the joint dependence of these decisions on each other in order to tease out their relative impacts net of several exogenous variables.

6. In a study of the division of household labor, Berk and Berk (1978) specified and estimated a three-equation model of the proportion of household tasks performed by husbands, wives, and children.

All of these studies have one characteristic in common: In each case, a faithful representation of the theory underlying the process to be modeled requires that the model allow reciprocal, rather than one-way, causation. Moreover, an examination of the substance of these examples suggests that reciprocal causation models are likely to arise in at least the following three situations: (a) in *models of social interaction processes* in which the characteristics of two or more individuals influence each other through direct communication, as in Duncan *et al.* (1968), Woelfel and Haller (1971), Land (1971), and Henry and Hummon (1971); (b) in *models of decision-making processes* in which two or more decisions are to be made each of which is contingent on the other, as in Waite and Stolzenberg (1976) and Berk and Berk (1978); and (c) in *models of interdependent social or psychological processes* in which the dependent variables are conceptualized as causally dependent on each other, as in Hauser (1971) and Kohn and Schooler (1973).

It should be emphasized that reciprocal causation models can be justified on the basis of one or the other of the following arguments. First, a process may be conceptualized as *instantaneously simultaneous* in the sense that a change in the value of any of the jointly dependent variables instantaneously affects the value of one or more of the others which instantaneously feeds back to affect the value of the former, and so forth. This type of formulation seems likely to arise, for example, in models of direct social interaction processes in which attitudes, expectations, and other properties of individuals are simultaneously changing so that recursive stimulus–response causal chains are virtually impossible to separate and therefore impossible to detect and measure. Second, a process may be conceptualized as *ontologically recursive, but effectively nonrecursive* relative to the time intervals of observational data. Many stimulus–response or decision processes are realistically conceptualized as less than completely instantaneous, but aggregation of data over time may not allow the estimation of lagged relationships. For instance, the labor force participation–fertility expectations decision process modeled by Waite and Stolzenberg (1976) may be intrinsically recursive in the sense that experiences affect one or the other variables which, in turn, affects the other after some decision-making time lag, and so forth. However, with data in the form of a cross-section sample survey in which current values of both variables are measured, it is impossible to detect the lagged effects. Therefore, a nonrecursive formulation must be specified relative to the available data.

The latter point also can be illustrated in the context of a supply–demand model, the other major context (besides national income models) in which nonrecursive models have appeared in economics. Wold (1954, 1956, 1959, 1964) argues that an appropriate formulation of supply–demand models necessarily leads to recursive systems, because economic agents usually react to price changes after some finite time lag. Consider, for example, a model in which demand reacts instantaneously to price changes but that has a 1-period (e.g., day, week, month, quarter, year) lag in the supply reaction. Assuming that the market is always cleared and that the supply and demand curves are linear, we have

$$q_t = \alpha_1 + \beta_1 p_t \quad + \varepsilon_{1t} \quad \text{(demand)}, \tag{15.82}$$

$$q_t = \alpha_2 + \beta_2 p_{t-1} + \varepsilon_{2t} \quad \text{(supply)}, \tag{15.83}$$

where the subscript t indicates the time period and the εs are stochastic disturbances. Now, if an analyst is prepared to argue that the disturbances are stochastically independent between equations, then this system can be treated as a recursive model with independent disturbances, as specified by Assumptions 1 and 2 of Section 15.2. If, however, data are not available in intervals corresponding to the lags postulated in the model, then the model has to be reformulated and the new system need not be recursive. For example, suppose that the period of the lag in (15.83) is 1 month but that only quarterly (3-monthly) data are available in the form: $q_{t-1} + q_t + q_{t+2}$; $q_t + q_{t+1} + q_{t+2}$ . . . (total quantity), $(\frac{1}{3})(p_{t-1} + p_t + p_{t+2})$; $(\frac{1}{3})(p_t + p_{t+1} + p_{t+2})$ . . . (average price). It is clear from (15.83) that $q_t + q_{t+1} + q_{t+2}$ is not independent of the price p_t at time t. Therefore, when a supply–demand model is formulated in terms of this type of data, we should not expect it to be recursive.

Identification, Parameter Estimation, and Hypothesis Testing in Nonrecursive Models

A systematic account of the theory of, and computational formulas for, identification, parameter estimation, and hypothesis testing in nonrecursive structural-equation models will *not* be presented here, because standard presentations at various levels of detail and abstraction are readily available in the standard econometric textbooks cited at the beginning of Section 15.4. Rather, our discussion will be limited to a brief statement of some of the mathematical and statistical issues that are raised in models of reciprocal causation.

For this, consider the following two-equation nonrecursive model:

$$y_1 + \beta_{12}y_2 + \gamma_{11}z_1 + \gamma_{12}z_2 + \gamma_{13}z_3 = u_1, \tag{15.84}$$

$$\beta_{21}y_1 + y_2 + \gamma_{21}z_1 + \gamma_{22}z_2 + \gamma_{23}z_3 = u_2, \tag{15.85}$$

where y_1, y_2 are jointly dependent endogenous variables; z_1, z_2, z_3 are exogenous variables; and u_1, u_2 are stochastic disturbance terms. These equations are written in the standard format as specified by (15.24) and Assumption 1 of Section 15.2. Very informally, the *identification problem* for such a system arises from the fact that, without further constraints on the structural coefficients or disturbances of the equations, it is impossible to distinguish them solely on statistical grounds. For instance, if we multiply through (15.84) by β_{12}^{-1}, we obtain an equation that has exactly the same form as (15.85), but with parameters that are labeled differently:

$$(1/\beta_{12})y_1 + (\beta_{12}/\beta_{12})y_2 + (\gamma_{11}/\beta_{12})z_1 + (\gamma_{12}/\beta_{12})z_2 + (\gamma_{13}/\beta_{12})z_3 = u_1. \tag{15.86}$$

But since there can be only one unique equation relating these variables in a complete nonsingular system in which the coefficient of y_2 is normalized to unity, it follows that (15.85) and (15.86) together imply equality of the coefficients of corresponding equations. Moreover, if we estimate each of these equations from a set of sample data, first with y_1 as the dependent variable and then with y_2 as dependent, we will find that this same algebraic relation holds within the limits of computation error, namely, the estimated parameters of (15.84) can be transformed into those of (15.85) by dividing by the estimated β_{12} (provided it is nonzero).

To surmount this nonuniqueness problem, that is, to *identify* uniquely the equations (and their parameters) of a simultaneous equation system, various necessary and sufficient conditions for constraints on the structural coefficients [i.e., on the **B** and **Γ** matrices of (15.24) of Section 15.2] or on the variance–covariance matrix of the distribution of the disturbances [i.e., on the **Σ** matrix of (15.27) of Section 15.2] have been derived. The standard reference for a systematic derivation and statement of these conditions is Fisher (1966).

For recursive models, the constraints of Assumption 2 of Section 15.2, namely, that **B** be triangular and **Γ** diagonal, are all that are needed to prove that all of the equations of a "fully recursive" model are identified (e.g., see Fisher, 1966, pp. 93–99; Land, 1973, pp. 31–32). Any additional constraints on the structural coefficients of a recursive model (for example, that some of them are zero) *overidentify* the equations of the model. This creates the opportunity to use "overidentification tests statistics" to make inferences about causal configurations that are consistent with sample data, as discussed in Section 15.2.

For nonrecursive models with $G \geq 2$ equations, a necessary condition (the order condition) for the identification of an equation is that at least $G - 1$ variables (endogenous or exogenous) be excluded a priori (i.e., have their coefficients set equal to zero) from the equation. The corresponding necessary and sufficient (rank) condition is that it be possible to form at least one nonvanishing determinant of order $G - 1$ from the columns of the coefficient matrices $\mathbf{B}$ and $\boldsymbol{\Gamma}$ corresponding to the variables excluded a priori from that equation. If more than $G - 1$ variables are excluded and the rank of the determinant is correspondingly greater than $G - 1$, then the equation is said to be *overidentified*. For a full discussion of these and related conditions for identification, see Fisher (1966).

Relative to the model given in (15.84) and (15.85), we see that it is necessary to remove at least $G - 1 = 2 - 1 = 1$ variable from each equation in order to achieve identification. Given that the equations have been indentified or overidentified, their structural parameters can be estimated by applying generalized versions of the least-squares and maximum likelihood estimators of the standard single-equation general linear model. These generalized estimators are distinguished by whether they use only the specifying information on the single equation to be estimated or all of the restrictions on all of the equations of the model taken simultaneously. If only the specification of the equation to be estimated is taken into account by an estimator, it is referred to as a *limited-information* or *single-equation* estimator. If the estimator incorporates all of the restrictions on all equations, then it is called a *full-information* or *system* estimator.

As we have seen in our discussion of the model of (15.67) and (15.68) in Section 15.4, the direct application of OLS to estimate the parameters of an equation in a nonrecursive model will in general produce biased and inconsistent estimators, because the usual assumption that the disturbances are distributed independently of the regressors is violated by the internal structure of the model. This deficiency is corrected by the application of the least-squares estimation principle to derive the so-called *two-stage least-squares* (2SLS) estimator (originally developed by Theil, 1953a, 1953b, 1961 and independently by Basmann, 1957) of the parameters of a single identified or overidentified equation of a nonrecursive model. As the name connotes, the 2SLS estimator can be viewed as the application of the least-squares principle in two stages. In the first stage, each endogenous variable is regressed, one at a time, on *all* of the exogenous variables of the model. In the second stage, the equations fitted in the first stage are used to obtain predicted values of the endogenous variables conditional on the observed values of the dependent variables, and these pre-dicted values are used in place of the observed values in a second round of least-squares estimators. Because of the properties of the least-squares estimation method, the predicted values of the endogenous variables will be uncorrelated in the probability limit with the disturbances of the equation. Consequently, since the resulting 2SLS estimator uses only the identifying information pertaining to the specification of the equation to be estimated, 2SLS is a limited information method. However, if all of the equations of a nonrecursive model first are estimated by 2SLS, and if the resulting estimated equations are used in a final generalized least-squares estimation of the parameters of all equations of the model taken simultaneously, then a full-information estimator known as the *three-stage least-squares* (3SLS) estimator (originally developed by Zellner and Theil, 1962) is obtained. Similarly, application of the maximum likelihood principle of estimation to a single equation of a nonrecursive model yields the *limited-information maximum-likelihood* (LIML) estimator (originally developed by Anderson and Rubin, 1949), whereas application of this principle to the system as a whole produces the *full-information maximum-likelihood* (FIML) estimator (originally developed by Koopmans, *et al.,* 1950). For a thorough discussion of the derivations, statistical properties, and computational formulas of these and related estimators as well as the associated overidentification test statistics, Theil (1971) is a particularly good reference.

The existence of several estimators for the structural parameters of nonrecursive causal models requires the researcher to decide which estimator to use. Fortunately, a considerable amount of statistical research has been addressed to the evaluation of the relative performance of these estimators. This research has produced rankings by both asymptotic (large sample) and small sample properties and, for the latter, by the presence or absence of specification errors and/or violations of the assumptions of the class of nonrecursive causal models (see Section 15.2, Assumption 1). The main *asymptotic properties* that have been applied to the estimators are (*a*) *consistency* (i.e., whether or not the expected value of the estimator converges to the population value of the parameter as the sample size gets sufficiently large and the sampling variance of the estimator simultaneously goes to zero) and (*b*) *asymptotic efficiency* (i.e., whether or not an estimator is consistent and has a smaller asymptotic sampling variance than any other consistent estimator). *Small sample properties* that have been examined include (*a*) *bias* (i.e., whether or not the expected value of the sampling distribution of an estimator departs from the population value of the parameter being estimated, an unbiased estimator being one whose bias is zero); (*b*) *minimum variance* (i.e., whether or not the variance of the sampling distribution of an estimator is smaller than the sampling variance of any other— not necessarily unbiased—estimator of the same parameter); (*c*) *minimum mean square error* (i.e., whether or not the sampling variance of an estimator plus the square of its bias is smaller than that of any other estimator—not necessarily possessing any other property); and (*d*) *the proportion of incorrect inferences to which an estimator leads* (i.e., the degree of departure of empirical sampling distributions of t-ratios of an estimator from the corresponding theoretical distributions).

Although the large sample properties of statistical estimators for nonrecursive causal models have been thoroughly analyzed using mathematical methods, the small sample properties have been analyzed primarily by using simulated data in what are known as *Monte Carlo studies*. Partly, this is due to the fact that small sample properties of the estimators typically can be analytically (i.e., mathematically) derived only for very simple and highly constrained models. Furthermore, the study of small sample properties by direct application of the estimators to real world observations is not feasible, because real world data almost surely contain unknown departures from the assumptions under which the estimators were derived. On the other hand, statistical research on small sample properties can be conducted in simulation studies. In such studies, the statistician specifies a model and assigns specific numerical values (the true structural coefficients) to its parameters. The distribution of the disturbances and arrays of numerical values for the exogenous variables also are selected. After obtaining random drawings from the disturbance distribution, the model is solved for the generated values of the endogenous variables. Corresponding to each set of randomly drawn values of the disturbances, a new set of values for the endogenous variables is obtained. These are collected into small samples of a fixed size (usually of 20–100 generated observations of the endogenous variables) that, together with the selected values of the exogenous variables, are used to estimate the structural coefficients by the various estimators.

The statistician obtains empirical sampling distributions of the estimators by repeating such experiments many times. Furthermore, by manipulating the specifications of the models studied and by controlling departures from assumptions, the analyst can study how the estimators behave under various known circumstances. For example, the effects of specification errors (e.g., omission of variables) and violations of assumptions (e.g., multicollinearity, autocorrelation of disturbances, and errors of measurement in observed variables) can be studied either individually or in various combinations.

Almost all of the textbooks referenced at the beginning of this subsection contain summaries of statistical research findings on the foregoing properties of parameter estimators on nonrecursive causal model. Two of the most thorough of these are Johnston (1972, pp. 376–420) and Koutsayiannis (1977, pp. 499–511). Although space does not permit presentation of a detailed review, we summarize the main findings of the Johnston and Koutsayiannis literature surveys in Table 15.5.

Assuming there are no specification errors and/or violations of other assumptions in a nonrecursive causal model, consider first the rankings of the four structural parameter estimators cited previously plus OLS applied directly to the structural equations. This ranking is reported in the upper right cell of Table 15.5. Since OLS is not consistent whereas 2SLS, LIML, 3SLS, and FIML are, OLS clearly ranks last in this case. The other methods are ranked

TABLE 15.5
Rankings of Parameter Estimators for Nonrecursive Causal Models[a]

Specification errors and/or other violations of assumptions	Ranking by	
	Small sample properties	Asymptotic properties
Absent	1. 2SLS 2. FIML, 3SLS 3. LIML 4. OLS	1. FIML 2. 3SLS 3. 2SLS, LIML 4. OLS
Present	1. 2SLS 2. LIML 3. OLS 4. FIML, 3SLS	Uncertain

[a] Summarized from more detailed surveys of literature reported in Johnston (1972, pp. 376–420) and Koutsayiannis (1977, pp. 499–511).

according to relative asymptotic efficiency. In general, the system methods (3SLS and FIML) are the most efficient asymptotically, because they use more information than do the single-equation methods (2SLS and LIML). That is, the system methods use all of the identifying or overidentifying constraints on a model as well as the estimated contemporaneous dependences (covariances) of the disturbance terms of the various equations in the model. In general, 3SLS and FIML have the same asymptotic efficiency. However, in the rare case that the researcher has a priori information on the variances and covariances of the disturbances of a model, this information can be exploited more fully by FIML than by 3SLS. Hence, in this case, FIML is more efficient than 3SLS. Finally, since they use the same amount of information, 2SLS and LIML are of equal asymptotic efficiency.

It should be noted that this ranking of estimators by asymptotic properties holds only if the assumptions under which they are derived are satisfied. Recall that we have assumed that the specification of the model as to variables included, the mathematical form of the equations, and the distribution properties of the disturbances, is correct (no specification error), that there are no errors of measurement in the observed variables, and that there is no serious multicollinearity in the model. If all these assumptions are empirically valid, FIML and 3SLS are the best methods, because they then are the most efficient. However, these full-information methods generally are more sensitive than the others to specification errors, because a specification error anywhere in a model affects all its FIML or 3SLS parameter estimates. Similar uncertainties arise when other assumptions are violated. Thus, when specification errors are present and/or other assumptions are violated, the ranking of the various estimators on the basis of their asymptotic efficiency changes. Furthermore, it has not yet been established what the relative ranking of estimators is when such errors are taken into account. This is noted in the lower right cell of Table 15.5.

Assuming again the absence of specification errors and/or other violations of assumptions, consider next how the estimators rank in terms of the small sample properties cited here. Although simulation studies produce different rankings of the estimators depending on which small sample criterion is applied, 2SLS nearly always is at or near the top. Perhaps most important, it performs best in terms of the proportion of incorrect inferences criterion. Close behind 2SLS are the full-information methods (FIML, 3SLS). Then comes LIML and, finally, OLS. This ranking is recorded in the upper left cell of Table 15.5.

What happens to the small sample ranking when specification errors and/or other violations of assumptions are present? It depends again on which small sample criterion is applied, and on which assumption(s) is (are) violated, but 2SLS holds up relatively well in most cases. LIML is a close second, and OLS moves up to third place. Finally, showing their sensitivity to specification errors and violations of assumptions, the full-information methods (FIML, 3SLS) drop to last place.

In summary, the implication of the rankings exhibited in Table 15.5 is that *the researcher is well-advised to use 2SLS in the initial estimation of a nonrecursive causal model*. This implication is reinforced by the fact that 2SLS estimates involve less complicated computations than do those obtained by LIML, 3SLS, or FIML. *After initial estimation, provided (a) that a model contains overidentifying restrictions that the researcher accepts as empirically valid, (b) that there is substantial contemporaneous correlation among at least some of the disturbance terms in the model; and (c) that the researcher is convinced that other specification errors and assumptions are not grossly violated, it may be prudent to reestimate the model by 3SLS or FIML.* Satisfaction of the first two of these conditions ensures likelihood of some gain in asymptotic efficiency, whereas satisfaction of the last helps to ensure that this gain is not illusory.

It should also be noted that the generally superior performance of 2SLS holds even with respect to the estimation of the coefficients of the reduced form of a nonrecursive causal model [see Eq. (15.25) in Section 15.2]. Since the reduced form solves the structural equations for the endogenous variables as a function solely of the exogenous variables, there are no complications due to simultaneity. Consequently, OLS can be applied directly to each equation of the reduced form. However, because this ignores whatever information is contained in the a priori restrictions on the structural equations, it is generally less efficient than direct estimation of the structural equations by 2SLS followed by algebraic solution for the reduced-form coefficients.

To conclude this discussion of nonrecursive causal models, consider again the topic dealt with at length earlier in the chapter in the context of recursive models—making inferences about causal configurations. Assuming that researchers have obtained estimates for the structural coefficients of a nonrecursive causal model together with the corresponding estimated standard errors, they can proceed to evaluate the causal configurations in much the same way as suggested in Section 15.2 for recursive models. That is, researchers can compute the appropriate t-, F-, or χ^2-tests (e.g., see Theil, 1971, pp. 507–508) and use these *either* to test a hypothesized overidentified causal configuration to determine whether or not it is consistent with the observed pattern of associations among the variables from which the model is estimated *or* to infer a configuration that is consistent with the data after a preliminary examination of the significance of the estimated coefficients. In the latter case, it is necessary that the model be identified; otherwise, its parameters cannot be estimated. As Duncan (1975) notes, this is the theoretical price that must be paid in order "to let the data determine which way the causal arrows run [pp. 86–87]" among the endogenous variables of a nonrecursive model. Furthermore, arbitrary (i.e., theoretically meaningless) identification of a model for this purpose may lead to nonsensical inferences.

Other cautions described earlier for inferences about causal configurations in recursive models also apply to such inferences in nonrecursive models. For instances, the use of preliminary tests of significance to arrive at a final specification alters the true significance levels of subsequent tests. Furthermore, failure to reject one or more overidentifying restrictions constitutes an inference about the causal configuration of the variables *conditional on* a maintained hypothesis about the causal ordering of the variables. In a nonrecursive model, the essence of a maintained hypothesis is the distinction between exogenous and endogenous variables. Tests of overidentifying restrictions generally are irrelevant to this distinction.

15.5. CONCLUSION

This completes our development of topics in causal modeling. As noted in the introduction to the chapter, we have limited the range of topics considered to models in which variables appear as measured. In other words, we have assumed that measurement errors are nonexistent or trivial in data to which the models are to be applied. But, for a variety of reasons that need not be cited here, data from sample surveys often contain substantial amounts of measurement error that cannot be ignored or assumed away. To accommodate such errors in causal models requires the incorporation of explicit measurement models into the causal models. For descriptions of how this can be done, see other chapters in the present volume or in Goldberger and Duncan (1973), Duncan (1975), and Jöreskog and Sörbom (1979). Similarly, we have assumed that all variables in the models are continuous, whereas many variables typically of interest in surveys are discrete. Again, structural models for discrete variables are dealt with in other chapters in the present volume; see also Bishop, Feinberg, and Holland (1975), Fienberg (1977), and Goodman (1978).

REFERENCES

Althauser, R. P.
  1971 "Multicollinearity and non-additive regression models." In H. M. Blalock, Jr., (ed.), *Causal Models in the Social Sciences*. Chicago: AVC.
Alwin, D., and R. Hauser
  1975 "The decomposition of effects in path analysis." *American Sociological Review* 10: 37–47.
Anderson, T. W., and H. Rubin
  1949 "Estimation of the parameters of a single stochastic difference equation in a complete system." *Annals of Mathematical Statistics* 20: 46–63.
Basmann, R. L.
  1957 "A generalized classical method of linear estimation of coefficients in a structural equation." *Econometrica* 25: 77–83.
Berk, R. A., and S. F. Berk
  1978 "A simultaneous equation model for the division of household labor." *Sociological Methods and Research* 6: 431–468.
Bishop, Y. M. M., S. E. Feinberg, and P. W. Holland
  1975 *Discrete Multivariate Analysis: Theory and Practice*. Cambridge, Mass: MIT Press.
Blalock, H. M., Jr.
  1962 "Four-variable causal models and partial correlations." *American Journal of Sociology* 68: 182–194.
  1964 *Causal Inferences in Nonexperimental Research*. Chapel Hill: University of North Carolina Press.
  1972 *Social Statistics*. Second Edition. New York: McGraw–Hill.
Blau, P., and O. D. Duncan
  1967 *The American Occupational Structure*. New York: Wiley.
Blau, P., and R. Schoenherr
  1971 *The Structure of Organizations*. New York: Basic Books.
Boudon, R.
  1965 "A method of linear causal analysis: Dependence analysis." *American Sociological Review* 30: 365–374.
Christ, C. F.
  1966 *Econometric Models and Methods*. New York: Wiley.
Cohen, M. R., and E. Nagel
  1934 *An Introduction to Logic and Scientific Method*. New York: Harcourt, Brace, and World.
Debreu, G.
  1959 *Theory of Value: An Axiomatic Analysis of Economic Equilibrium*. New Haven: Yale University Press.
Dhrymes, P. J.
  1974 *Econometrics: Statistical Foundations and Applications*. New York: Springer–Verlag.
Duncan, O. D.
  1966 "Path analysis: Sociological examples." *American Journal of Sociology* 72(July): 3–16.
  1972 "Partials, partitions, and paths." *Sociological Methodology* 1970: 38–47.
  1975 *Introduction to Structural Equation Models*. New York: Academic Press.
Duncan, O. D., D. L. Featherman, and B. Duncan
  1972 *Socioeconomic Background and Achievement*. New York: Seminar Press.
Duncan, O. D., A. O. Haller, and A. Portes
  1968 "Peer influences on aspirations: A reinterpretation." *American Journal of Sociology* 74(July): 119–137.
Feinberg, S. E.
  1977 *The Analysis of Cross-Classified Categorical Data*. Cambridge, Mass.: MIT Press.

Fisher, F. M.
   1966   *The Identification Problem in Econometrics*. New York: McGraw–Hill.
Fox, J. D.
   1979   "Effect analysis in structural equation models: Extensions and simplied methods of com-
           putation." Mimeographed paper. Toronto, Canada: York University.
Goldberger, A. S.
   1964   *Econometric Theory*. New York: Wiley.
   1970   "On Boudon's method of linear causal analysis." *American Sociological Review* 35(Feb-
           ruary): 97–101.
Goldberger, A. S., and O. D. Duncan, Eds.
   1973   *Structural Equation Models in the Social Sciences*. New York: Seminar Press.
Goodman, L. A.
   1978   *Analyzing Qualitative/Categorical Data*. Cambridge, Mass.: ABT Books.
Hanushek, E. A., and J. E. Jackson
   1977   *Statistical Methods for Social Scientists*. New York: Academic Press.
Hauser, R. M.
   1971   *Socioeconomic Background and Educational Performance*. Washington, D.C.: American
           Sociological Association. (Rose Monograph Series).
Hauser, R. M., and D. L. Featherman
   1977   *The Process of Stratification: Trends and Analyses*. New York: Academic Press.
Heise, D. R.
   1968   "Problems in path analysis and causal inference." *Sociological Methodology* 1969: 38–
           73.
Henry, N. W., and N. P. Hummon
   1971   "An example of estimation procedures in a nonrecursive system." *American Sociological
           Review* 36: 1099–1102.
Hogg, R. J., and A. T. Craig
   1970   *Introduction to Mathematical Statistics* (3rd ed.). New York: Macmillan.
Jencks, C., M. Smith, H. Acland, M. J. Bane, D. Cohen, H. Gintis, B. Heyns, and S. Michelson
   1972   *Inequality: An Assessment of the Effect of Family and Schooling in America*. New York:
           Basic Books.
Johnston, J.
   1972   *Econometric Methods* (2nd Ed.) New York: Macmillian.
Jöreskog, K. G., and D. Sörbom
   1979   *Advances in Factor Analysis and Structural Equation Models*. Cambridge, Mass.: ABT
           Books.
Judge, G. G., and M. E. Bock
   1978   *The Statistical Implications of Pre-Test and Stein-Rule Estimators in Econometrics*. New
           York: North–Holland.
Judge, G. C., M. E. Bock, and T. A. Yancey
   1974   "Post data model evaluation." *The Review of Economics and Statistics* 56: 245–253.
Kendall, P. L., and P. F. Lazarsfeld
   1950   "Problems of survey analysis." Pp. 133–196 in R. K. Merton and P. F. Lazarsfeld (eds.),
           Continuities in Social Research. New York: The Free Press.
Keynes, J. M.
   1936   *The General Theory of Employment, Interest, and Money*. New York: Harcourt, Brace
           and World.
Klein, L. R.
   1950   *Economic Fluctuations in the United States, 1921–1941*. New York: Wiley.
   1962   *An Introduction to Econometrics*. Englewood Cliffs, N.J.: Prentice–Hall.
Klemmack, D. L., T. A. Leggete, and L. S. Mayer
   1973   "Non-random exogenous variables in path analysis." *American Sociological Review* 38:
           778–784.

Kmenta, J.
    1971 *Elements of Econometrics*. New York: Macmillan.
Kohn, M., and C. Schooler
    1973 "Occupational experience and psychological functioning: An assessment of reciprocal
          effects." *American Sociological Review* 38(February): 97–118.
Koopmans, T. C., H. Rubin, and R. B. Leipnik
    1950 "Measuring the equation systems of dynamic economics." Pp. 53–237 in T. C. Koop-
          mans (ed.), *Statistical Interference in Dynamic Economic Models*. New York: Wiley.
Koutsayiannis, A.
    1977 *Theory of Econometrics* (2nd Ed.). New York: Harper and Row.
Land, K. C.
    1969 "Principles of path analysis." *Sociological Methodology* 1969: 3–37.
    1971 "Significant others, the self-reflexive act and the attitude formation process: A reinterpre-
          tation." *American Sociological Review* 36: 1085–1098.
    1973 "Two preliminary models for the analysis of changes in a social indicator indicator of job
          satisfaction." *Proceedings of the Social Statistics Section, American Statistical Associa-
          tion*. Washington, D.C.: American Statistical Association.
Lazarsfeld, P. F.
    1955 "Interpretation of statistical relations as a research operation." Pp. 115–125 in P. F.
          Lazarsfeld and M. Rosenberg (eds.), *The Language of Social Research*. New York: The
          Free Press.
Maddala, G. S.
    1977 *Econometrics*. New York: McGraw–Hill.
Malinvaud, E.
    1970 *Statistical Methods of Econometrics* (2nd rev. ed.). Amsterdam: North–Holland.
Marshak, J.
    1950 "Statistical inference in economics: An overview." In. T. C. Koopmans (ed.), *Statistical
          Inference in Dynamic Economic Models*. New York: Wiley.
Mayer, L. S., and M. S. Younger
    1974 "Procedures for estimating standardized regression coefficients from sample data." *Soci-
          ological Methods and Research* 2: 431–454.
McPherson, J. M., and C. J. Huang
    1974 "Hypothesis testing in path models." *Social Science Research* 3: 127–140.
Mill, J. S.
    1875 *A System of Logic*. London: (2nd ed.) (Two vol., first ed. published in 1843).
Miller, H. P.
    1960 "Annual and lifetime income in relation to education, 1939–59." *American Economic
          Review* 50: 962–986.
Nering, E. D.
    1967 *Linear Algebra and Matrix Theory*. New York: Wiley.
Parzen, E.
    1960 *Modern Probability Theory and Its Applications*. New York: Wiley.
Pindyck, R. S., and L. Rubinfeld
    1976 *Econometric Models and Economic Forecasts*. New York: McGraw–Hill.
Rees, A., and G. Shultz
    1970 *Workers and Wages in an Urban Labor Market*. Chicago: University of Chicago Press.
Schwartz, A.
    1967 *Calculus and Analytic Geometry* (2nd Ed.). New York: Holt, Rinehart and Winston.
Simon, H. A.
    1952 "On the definition of the causal relation." *The Journal of Philosophy* 49: 517–528. Re-
          printed as pp. 50–61 in H. A. Simon, 1957, *Models of Man: Social and Rational*. New
          York: Wiley.
    1953 "Causal ordering and identifiability." Pp. 49–74 in W. C. Hood and T. C. Koopmans

(eds.), *Studies in Econometric Method*. New York: Wiley. Reprinted as pp. 10–36 in H. A. Simon, 1957, *Models of Man: Social and Rational*. New York: Wiley.

1954   "Spurious correlation: A causal interpretation." *Journal of the American Statistical Association* 49: 467–479. Reprinted as pp. 37–49 in H. A. Simon, 1957, *Models of Man: Social and Rational*. New York: Wiley.

1968   "Causation." Pp. 350–355 in D. L. Sills (ed.), *International Encyclopedia of the Social Sciences*. Vol. 2. New York: Macmillan.

Southwood, K.
1978   "Substantive theory and statistical interaction: Five models." *American Journal of Sociology* 83: 1154–1203.

Stolzenberg, R. M.
1973   *Occupational Differences in Wage Discrimination Against Black Men*. Final Report, U.S. Department of Labor Grant 91-26-72-24. Ann Arbor: University of Michigan.

1975   "Education, Occupation, and Wage Differences between White and Black Men." *American Journal of Sociology* 81: 299–323.

Stolzenberg, R. M., and L. J. Waite
1977   "Age, fertility expectations and plans for employment." *American Sociological Review* 42: 769–783.

Theil, H.
1953a   "Estimation and simultaneous correlation in complete equation systems." The Hague: Central Planning Bureau. (mimeographed)

1953b   "Repeated least-squares applied to complete equation systems." The Hague: Central Planning Bureau. (mimeographed).

1961   *Economic Forecasts and Policy* (2nd Ed.). Amsterdam: North–Holland.

1971   *Principles of Econometrics*. New York: Wiley

Tinbergen, J.
1939   *Statistical Testing of Business-Cycle Theories*. Two vol. Geneva: League of Nations.

Waite, L. J., and R. M. Stolzenberg
1976   "Intended childbearing and labor force participation of young women: Insights from nonrecursive models." *American Sociological Review* 41: 235–251.

Woelfel, J., and A. O. Haller
1971   "Significant others, the self-reflexive act and the attitude formation process." *American Sociological Review* 6: 74–87.

Wold, H.
1954   "Causality and econometrics." *Econometrics* 22: 162–177.

1956   "Causal inference from observational data: A review of ends and means." *Journal of the Royal Statistical Society* 119(Series A): 28–50.

1959   "Ends and means in econometric model building." Pp. 355–434 in U. Grenander (ed.), *Probability and Statistics: The Harold Cramer Volume*. New York: Wiley.

1964   *Econometric Model Building: Essays on the Causal Chain Approach*. Amsterdam: North–Holland.

Wonnacott, R. J., and T. H. Wonnacott
1970   *Econometrics*. New York: Wiley.

Wright, S.
1934   "The method of path coefficients." *Annals of Mathematical Statistics* 5: 161–215.

Yule, G. U.
1932   *An Introduction to the Theory of Statistics* (10th ed.). London: Charles Griffin.

Zeisel, H.
1947   *Say it with Figures*. New York: Harper and Brothers.

Zellner, A., and H. Theil
1962   "Three-stage least squares: Simultaneous estimation of simultaneous equations." *Econometrica* 30: 54–78.

Chapter 16

Surveys as Social Indicators: Problems in Monitoring Trends

Elizabeth Martin

16.1. INTRODUCTION

In 1969, Otis Dudley Duncan asserted that "an improved capability and capacity to measure social change is fundamental to progress in the field of social reporting [1969, p. 7]." He suggested several strategies for measuring social change, including trend studies based on extant data (such as public opinion polls), replications of earlier studies to measure past change, and new surveys to provide baseline measurements for future trends. Trends may be estimated by observing the same units in a panel study conducted over time, or by drawing repeated independent samples of the same population. The units sampled may be individuals, households, organizations, events, or records. In all cases, the fundamental principle is a simple one: Change may be monitored by drawing one or more samples of a target population, and repeatedly measuring attitudes, behaviors, and other population characteristics at different points in time. Comparison of the results then allows one to estimate change in the population.

The sine qua non for the accurate assessment of change is comparability of measurement: Measurements must be equivalent to ensure that differences between them are due to the effects of time and not to artifacts produced by differences in the measurement process. We may distinguish between procedural and functional equivalence. Different surveys are procedurally equivalent when they employ identical practices, procedures, and definitions, so that they are exact replicates of one another. Functional equivalence exists when two procedures or sets of procedures yield the same results when applied to the same reality, regardless of whether the procedures are the same or different.

We assume that any particular method is characterized by distinct sources of error and bias. By replicating the procedure, we hope to hold these errors and biases constant in order to estimate change. Unfortunately, the biases and errors associated with a particular procedure may vary among different populations and groups, according to subject matter, and across time. For example, it is known that black people sometimes respond differently to survey questions according to whether the interviewer is black or white. Results presented later suggest that the effect of the interviewer's race depends on the subject matter, may be greater among older than among younger blacks, and may change over time as race relations in American society change. In this case, holding constant the interviewer's race does not hold constant the effect of the interviewer's race. That is, identical procedures may not result in comparable measurements.

The distinction between procedural and functional equivalence suggests two sources of noncomparability in survey estimates of change. The first is the failure to replicate. Precise replication is difficult to achieve because surveys involve many complex, decentralized operations whose effects are unknown, which are difficult to standardize and control, and which may be variable in how they are actually applied. Because the effects of many survey procedures are not well understood, we may not know which procedures are essential to standardize and replicate and which are not because results are unaffected by procedural differences. In addition, survey procedures may be difficult or impossible to replicate if they are undocumented.

A second, more subtle, source of noncomparability is due to change or variation in procedural effects. If the bias associated with a particular method changes over time, then surveys employing that method will not yield comparable results, even if they are otherwise perfect replicates of one another. The problem can be serious, as we shall see, since in some cases true change is confounded with systematic changes in the nature of bias in survey measurement. These conditions suggest that any attempt to monitor change must be guided by two principles. First, the task of replication must be taken seriously, as Duncan advised in 1969. Second, the comparability of the data must be systematically evaluated.

These two principles are well illustrated in the Current Population Survey (CPS), perhaps the most impressive social reporting effort in the United States. The CPS has provided monthly estimates of unemployment and other characteristics of the U.S. population since 1940, when the Sample Survey of Unemployment was first conducted by the Works Progress Administration (see U.S. Bureau of the Census, 1977). Several aspects of this long-term enterprise are noteworthy. First, from its inception, the design and procedures of the survey have been an important concern. Substantial efforts have been devoted to evaluating and controlling the quality and comparability of CPS data. Changes in CPS design and methods have been introduced when careful review and evaluation suggests that old concepts and methods are outmoded, and refinements will improve the quality of the data. One result of the refinements of CPS methods and concepts has been an increase in the efficiency of CPS estimates.

A second result has been modification of the basic concepts of employment and unemployment from time to time. The most recent revisions were recommended by the National Commission on Employment and Unemployment Statistics in 1979, almost 4 decades after unemployment was first measured scientifically.

The history of the Current Population Survey suggests that it is foolish to expect that the problems of devising meaningful social indicators and measuring social change will be solved quickly or easily or on a one-shot basis. It is far more realistic to expect that indicators and methods will undergo continuing revision and refinement as researchers experiment with them and gain experience. Naturally, one is far more likely to discover that methods are unreliable and biased and estimates noncomparable if the data are scrutinized and evaluated carefully than if they are not. The risk of avoiding scrutiny is great however: The producers and potential consumers of social indicators—including the public and government policymakers—may either place undue confidence in the data, or become unduly cynical when their naive faith is undermined by the discovery that the data were fallible after all.

This chapter considers in detail the sources of bias and error in survey measurement, and particularly the sources of noncomparability in estimates of trends. The chapter is concerned with longitudinal studies of change based on independent replications of household surveys; the special problems that arise in panel studies of the same units over time, or in studies of units other than households (such as organizations) are not discussed. Nevertheless, many of the problems considered here arise in any study of change.

16.2. TWO PUZZLES: ASSESSING TRENDS IN CRIMINAL VICTIMIZATION AND CONFIDENCE IN AMERICAN INSTITUTIONS

We begin with an example of an evaluation study of the Cincinnati Team Policing Experiment conducted by the Urban Institute for the Police Foundation (see Clarren & Schwartz, 1976; Schwartz & Clarren, 1977; Tuchfarber & Klecka, 1976). Two household victimization surveys, one conducted by the Urban Institute in March 1973 and one by the Census Bureau for the Law Enforcement Assistance Administration (LEAA) in March 1974, were to be used as before and after measures of victimization in an evaluation of the effectiveness of team policing. Additional data were provided by a telephone survey conducted by the Behavioral Sciences Laboratory while the Census Bureau was completing its fieldwork.

The results were troubling, and the data ultimately proved unusable. For many crime categories, victimization rates in the 1974 census survey were more than double the rates reported in the Urban Institute study conducted a year earlier, a difference too great to be attributed to a real increase in crime. The telephone survey obtained yet a third set of estimates of victimization. Conducted at approximately the same time as the 1974 census survey, the telephone survey nevertheless obtained still higher rates of victimization. Not all crime categories were equally affected by the variability among surveys. Estimates of auto theft, for example, remained relatively constant over all three surveys, whereas assault estimates varied considerably.

The difference between the 1973 and 1974 household surveys is especially troubling because the 1973 Urban Institute survey was explicitly intended to replicate the sampling, interviewing, coding, and other standard procedures used by the Census Bureau to conduct the LEAA victimization surveys. Based on an extensive review of sampling methods, estimation techniques, field procedures, coding, and the like, by the investigators and by survey experts, Clarren and Schwartz (1976) conclude: "No obvious flaws could be detected [p. 128]."

Nevertheless, it is likely that the noncomparability of the estimates resulted from some (perhaps subtle) failure to replicate census procedures in the Urban Institute survey. A possible explanation offered by the investigators for the noncomparability of the estimates is a difference in the quality of supervision and training of the field staff. Interviewers in the 1973 survey received less training and were not supervised as closely as those in the 1974 census survey, perhaps leading to greater interviewer variability and bias in the earlier survey. Perhaps it is unrealistic to expect one survey organization to fully replicate the procedures of another (in advance, no less), especially, as we have noted, when many survey practices and "rules of thumb" may be undocumented. Clarren and Schwartz (1976) also note that the ambiguity of the definitions of some victimization categories may contribute to substantial variation in how interviewers apply them to classify incidents as victimizations. Auto theft is defined less ambiguously than assault, and hence is less variable across surveys. Finally, the Census Bureau obtains a higher response rate than private survey firms, which may contribute to the discrepant findings.

An equally puzzling example concerns the estimation of trends in public confidence in American leaders and institutions, and has been extensively analyzed by Turner and Krauss (1978) and Smith (1978, 1981). Since 1966, Harris polls have regularly measured public confidence in institutions, and beginning in 1973 the same measures have been included in the annual (now biennial) General Social Survey conducted by the National Opinion Research Center (NORC). However, comparison of data obtained by Harris and NORC reveals troubling differences. Although virtually identical measures are used by both survey organizations, NORC and Harris provide divergent estimates of public confidence at (roughly) comparable times. Moreover, inferences about trends in confidence differ depending on whether Harris or NORC data are used. For example, NORC data suggest that public confidence in the Supreme Court was stable between 1973 and 1977, whereas Harris data suggest considerable volatility (Turner & Krauss, 1978).

A number of hypotheses have been offered to account for the disparate findings of the two organizations (see Turner & Krauss 1978; Smith 1981). Different quota selection methods are used by the two organizations, and there are slight variations in the wording of the questions. In addition, the context of the confidence questions varies in two significant ways. First, the composition and sequence of the list of institutions to be evaluated varies from survey to survey. Second, the questions preceding the confidence measures vary among surveys. In particular, the Harris confidence questions are occasionally preceded by a series of alienation questions with a negative flavor that may depress levels of confidence. In one case, substantially higher levels of confidence were obtained in two surveys conducted by Harris and NORC in March 1976 than in a Harris survey, conducted a month later, in which the confidence questions were preceded by questions on political alienation.

The effect of question context was tested in a split-ballot experiment conducted by NORC in which the placement of confidence and alienation questions was varied (Smith 1981). The results are equivocal.[1] When the political alienation questions precede confidence questions, confidence is lower—but only for "major companies," the first item in the list. The different results obtained by NORC and Harris thus remain mysterious.

To some degree, the volatility of confidence in institutions probably reflects real change, since evaluations of confidence might be expected to shift in response to changing events. In addition, "confidence" is a somewhat elusive and ambiguous concept which is not firmly linked to any concrete, specific objects, or criteria for evaluation. Respondents' expressions of confidence may therefore be quite sensitive to subtle cues provided by the wording, order, and context of survey questions. This chapter argues that artifacts of measurement and problems of noncomparability are most likely to arise when measuring vague or nonexistent opinions, when questions employ ambiguous definitions or concepts, or when measuring attitudes that are themselves highly unstable.

The crime and confidence examples illustrate that noncomparable measurements may seriously impair estimation of trends. Moreover, differences between surveys do not have to be glaring in order to produce substantial variation in the obtained results. In the remainder of this chapter, we consider in detail the sources of noncomparability at each stage in the production of survey data. The purpose is to alert the researcher to potential sources of noncomparability, and to provide, where possible, practical solutions for eliminating or estimating artifactual variation.

16.3. SOURCES OF SURVEY NONCOMPARABILITY

Definition of the Target Population

In order to estimate change in a population reliably, the same population must be surveyed at different times. For household surveys, this requires that

---

[1] The experiment is somewhat flawed, since not all of the Harris alienation items were included.

the specification of population units, including households and respondents, and the geographic bounds of the target population, be comparable over time.

Because the distribution and composition of the population change, identical definitions may not specify comparable populations at different times. In such cases, exact replication may be sacrificed for more flexible criteria of comparability. In addition, standardization may be used to separate the effects of changes in the composition of a population from other sources of change.

GEOGRAPHIC BOUNDS OF THE TARGET POPULATION

Comparability may be achieved by replicating boundaries used in a baseline survey, or by attempting to capture a population that is comparable according to other criteria. The target population area for state or national surveys is usually defined in terms of state or coterminous national boundaries. Changes in population distribution make it difficult to specify comparable boundaries for local or community surveys conducted at different times. An example of this problem arose in an investigation of social change in Detroit over a 20-year period. In order to measure change precisely, it was necessary to define an area in 1971 comparable to the area surveyed in baseline studies of the 1950s. Population movement out of the city, change in transportation patterns, and the rapid expansion of the suburbs implied a change in the social boundaries of the Detroit area. Therefore, the investigators "resolved to seek comparability in terms of the concept of a metropolitan population unit—rather than in terms of a fixed geographic area [Duncan 1975, p. 113]" and extended the boundaries of the 1971 study area to include suburban areas of rapid growth. The expanded 1971 sample area captured 86% of the 1970 Detroit SMSA population, or roughly the same fraction of the 1950 Detroit population captured by earlier samples. By this criterion, extending the boundaries in 1971 achieved closer comparability with earlier surveys than fixed boundaries would have provided.[2]

HOUSEHOLDS

Although most censuses and surveys are based on households, survey researchers are often curiously inattentive to the problems of defining a housing unit, determining its occupancy status, and linking the individuals found there to one and only one unit.

Many survey organizations neither define *housing unit* nor specify rules of residency but leave these determinations to the discretion of interviewers. When definitions are provided, they are often vague and require complex judgments by interviewers. Different definitions are employed by different organizations, and by the same organizations at different times. The census definition

---

[2] Residents of the suburban area added in 1971 were highly distinctive. Compared to people living within the boundaries defined by earlier Detroit Area Study surveys, residents of the expanded sample area were far more likely to be white, high-income homeowners who were well satisfied with public schools and visited neighbors frequently. However, because residents of new areas comprised a small fraction of the 1971 sample, differences between estimates based on expanded versus fixed boundaries do not exceed one or two percentage points. In this case, then, expanding the sample boundaries did not materially affect estimates of change.

of a housing unit, for example, has changed with each census since 1940. Most survey organizations base their definitions upon census definitions, but there are often significant differences. Differences in definition may be important when (as is usually the case) survey organizations base the construction of sampling frames, selection probabilities, and the weights used in poststratification on census estimates of housing and population. Survey researchers also frequently assess the representativeness of surveys by comparing census and survey demographic characteristics. This strategy is not valid if the target populations are defined differently.

In this section we discuss in some detail the definitions employed by the census and survey organizations, and how they affect the coverage of the population. Conventional survey definitions may operate to exclude certain groups to varying degrees over time, and thus may bias estimates of change.

Housing Unit. The difficulty of precisely defining *housing unit* is suggested by the detail provided in the U.S. Bureau of the Census (1970a) definition:

> Housing units comprise houses, apartments, groups of rooms, or single rooms which are occupied or intended for occupancy, as separate living quarters. Specifically, there is a housing unit when the occupants live and eat separately from any other persons in the structure and there is either (1) *direct access* to the unit from the outside or through a common hall, or (2) in 1960, a kitchen or cooking equipment for the occupants' exclusive use: in 1970, *complete kitchen facilities* for the occupants' exclusive use [p. 113].

The definition of a housing unit excludes group quarters (or "living arrangements for other than ordinary household life"), defined as "institutions . . . plus other quarters containing six or more persons where five or more are unrelated to the head [U.S. Bureau of the Census 1970a, p. 113]."

The census definition changed with each successive census from 1940 to 1970. (See U.S. Bureau of the Census 1953, 1963, 1970a.) Beginning in 1950, *dwelling unit* was defined explicitly in terms of cooking equipment and a separate entrance; in 1940, enumerators had not been instructed to employ these criteria. Also in 1950, *dwelling unit* was defined to exclude living quarters with five or more lodgers; such units had qualified as dwelling units in 1940. In 1960, the bureau introduced the concept of "housing unit" to replace "dwelling unit." The *housing unit* definition was intended to encompass all private living accommodations that were not covered completely by the dwelling unit concept. The main difference between *housing* units and *dwelling* units was in the treatment of one-room quarters. Compared to 1950, the 1960 definition was more inclusive of one room living quarters with direct access but without separate cooking equipment, and of hotel rooms used as residences (see U.S. Bureau of the Census, 1963, p. LV). The result of the change in definition was an increase in the number of housing units compared to the number of dwelling units for the same population. Finally, in 1970 the definition of *housing unit* was made slightly more restrictive.

   The reason for the changes in definition is the difficulty of unambiguously distinguishing residential from transient quarters. The previous summary suggests that problematic quarters tend to be marginal ones located in hotels and rooming houses, where the distinction between "transient" and "permanent" residents is elusive and probably meaningless.

   Most survey organizations adopt variants of the census definitions of basic survey concepts. Thus, for example, in 1971 the Survey Research Center followed the bureau's change from the dwelling unit concept to the housing unit definition. Definitions used by survey organizations usually depart from census definitions somewhat; for example, SRC excludes all "transient quarters," defined as quarters where five or more units are operated under a single management and more than 50% of the units are intended for transient occupancy (Survey Research Center 1976, p. 40; compare with the 1970 census definition cited previously).

   Vacant housing units are excluded from the census of population and sample surveys. The census in 1970 defined as "vacant" housing units that were under construction (unless floors and external doors were in place), used for nonresidential purposes, "unfit for human habitation," condemned, or scheduled for demolition (U.S. Bureau of the Census 1970a, p. 115). Housing units temporarily vacant or occupied by people with no other usual place of residence were considered occupied.

   The occupancy status of a housing unit may be difficult to determine by these criteria, resulting in errors of classification. Bounpane and Jordon (1978) note that "During the 1970 census, the misclassification of occupied units as vacant was determined to be a serious coverage problem [p. 45]." They suggest procedures to minimize the enumerator's latitude in reporting a unit as vacant. Housing characteristics and distribution affect the ease of applying the rules that define a housing unit and its occupancy status. Evaluations of census coverage indicate that errors resulting from missed or misclassified units are more likely to be in dense, urban areas, or sparsely settled rural areas; for structures which contain multiple units, were built before 1940, or lack plumbing facilities; and for one-person households (U.S. Bureau of the Census 1973b). Housing units (and their occupants) with these characteristics are underenumerated. Other things equal, then, population coverage rates will rise or fall as an inverse function of changes in the proportion of the population residing in such places.

   The 1971 Detroit Area Study again illustrates the difficulty of replication when the definitions used in baseline surveys are vague and inconsistent (Fischer, 1972). *Dwelling unit* was defined identically in the 1950s baseline surveys as a "group of rooms (or it may be only one room) forming separate living quarters and containing cooking facilities"; rooming houses with less than 11 roomers were included as one dwelling unit. All baseline studies excluded "transient hotels," although the definition of *transient hotel* was not specified for any of them. Two baseline surveys instructed interviewers to include permanent apartments in transient hotels, as well as apartments in "apartment hotels" as dwelling units; however, *apartment hotel* was not defined. One might infer that transient and apartment hotels were defined in early Detroit Area Study surveys as in a later Survey Research Center memo: "If 50% or more of the accommodations (rooms, suites) are occupied or intended for occupancy by non-transient guests, the structure contains an *apartment hotel. . . .* If 50% or more of the accommodations (rooms, suites) are occupied or intended for occupancy by transient guests, the structure contains a *hotel for transients . . .* [Survey Research Center 1970]." The former was included in SRC household samples, and the latter was excluded.

In this example, the definition of *eligible dwelling unit* is unclear with respect to apartments in hotels, making precise replication impossible. Interviewers—individually or collectively—may have developed unwritten rules of thumb to decide such cases. To the extent that such rules of thumb varied from survey to survey, estimates of change based on the different surveys may be unreliable and biased. Because of the small number of people affected, the actual effect is likely to be trivial for most statistics, but may be important for phenomena that are highly concentrated among marginal population subgroups (such as people who live in hotels and other "special places").

Respondent Eligibility. Not all people found in occupied housing units are eligible as respondents in household surveys. If the nature of their living arrangements implies that they occupy group quarters, they are usually excluded. Not all surveys exclude group quarters. The National Crime Survey, for example, is a sample of locations rather than households, and includes some "special places," such as correctional institutions, communes, hotels, and motels.

Rules are applied to link individuals to a place of residence, and an individual who does not reside in the housing unit contacted by the interviewer is usually excluded from household surveys. (The census, of course, attempts a complete enumeration.) Residency is defined by the census as the usual place of abode, or where one lives and sleeps, and not in terms of legal or voting residence (U.S. Bureau of the Census, 1970a, p. 93). The assumption is that people have a usual place of residence; when they do not, the rules may be ambiguous. For example, the SRC instructs interviewers that a person staying in a housing unit at time of contact is to be included in the household if he or she has no place of residence at all, but excluded if he or she works or eats there, and sleeps elsewhere (Survey Research Center 1976, p. 93).

Finally, additional criteria may be applied to determine a household resident's eligibility as a respondent. Residents may be ineligible if they are not U.S. citizens or not of voting age. As Glenn (1974) notes, when the voting age was lowered from 21 to 18 years old, most survey organizations changed the age limit accordingly. This source of noncomparability in interperiod comparisons may be rectified easily by excluding respondents who, because of their age, would have been ineligible in earlier surveys.

THE EFFECTS OF SURVEY DEFINITIONS AND ELIGIBILITY CRITERIA ON COVERAGE

The rules that define *housing unit, occupancy status,* and *residency* affect the coverage of the population by the census and surveys. People who are missed or excluded—those who live in group quarters, have no usual place of residence, or occupy places identified as nondwellings or as vacant by conventional definitions—tend to be highly distinctive in their demographic characteristics and behavior. For this reason, the accurate assessment of trends requires that the rules for eligibility—for dwellings and people—be precise and consistent in order to identify comparable populations. Differences in eligibility criteria may result in variability over time or among organizations in the numbers and characteristics of people excluded as ineligible.[3] Even surveys intended to identify cross-sectional samples vary in their criteria for eligibility. This implies, for example, that people who live in marginal dwellings, or whose attachment to a single place of residence is ambiguous or unstable, may be excluded to varying degrees according to the stringency of the rules and their application.

Second, definitions vary in the degree to which they allow interviewers' judgments to influence the inclusion of housing units or respondents in surveys and censuses. When matters are left to interviewer discretion—for example, when interviewers are allowed to apply their own criteria to determine which dwellings are "unfit for human habitation" or who lives in a dwelling—errors and interviewer bias are likely to be introduced. The same criteria for eligibility applied to the same population may not identify comparable groups if (*a*) rules are ambiguous and (*b*) interviewers vary systematically in their application of the rules. (The effects of different practices used to implement survey definitions are considered in the next section.)

Third, even when eligibility criteria are precise and consistent, changing social conditions may result in shifts in the number and characteristics of people who are eligible for inclusion in a survey. For example, during wartime the large numbers of young adult males who reside on army bases or overseas will be excluded from household surveys. In this case, comparable criteria of eligibility may not identify comparable groups among certain birth cohorts in successive surveys conducted during wartime and peacetime. Other changes in the location and nature of living arrangements of the population (e.g., in transiency or mobility) may affect population coverage even in the absence of changes in survey definitions. If a population becomes more mobile or tran-

---

[3] Changes in the rules are not always well documented. For example, Stanley Presser (personal communication) discovered that until 1972 the March Supplement of the CPS included the institutionalized population; after 1972, institutionalized persons—who number about 2 million, or 1% of the total population—were excluded. I have not been able to discover any CPS document that records this change in procedure.

sient, eligibility rules that rely on a stable attachment to a single housing unit may become obsolete. Moreover, it will be difficult to detect trends in lifestyles if definitions and practices employed by most survey organizations exclude people who live in other than ordinary household circumstances.

An insufficient but growing body of evidence concerns the characteristics of people missed in the census and the reasons for their omission. The findings cannot be generalized directly to all household surveys, which generally define the target population more narrowly (excluding, for example, residents of group quarters). Despite differences, it is likely that the bias introduced by undercoverage is similar for the census and surveys, all of which rely on the household as the fundamental population unit. For this reason it is of interest to consider patterns, trends, and sources of census underenumeration.[4]

Coverage by the census has improved very slightly over time. The U.S. population was undercounted by an estimated 3.8% in 1940, 3.3% in 1950, 2.7% in 1960, and 2.5% in 1970 (U.S. Bureau of the Census 1973a). The extent of estimated undercoverage varies among age–race–sex categories and has changed differentially within those categories. Undercount is greatest among blacks and males (an estimated 19% of black males 25–34 years old were missed in 1970). The racial gap narrowed from 1950 to 1970, whereas the gap between males and females widened between 1960 and 1970. Trends in estimated coverage of race–sex categories are presented in Table 16.1.

Small overall improvements in coverage hide opposing trends; from 1960 to 1970, for example, estimated coverage improved markedly among black males age 35–44, for reasons that are not understood. The result is pronounced change in the age pattern of net census error rates and biased estimates of trends, particularly of characteristics associated with age, race, or sex.

Housing units and people who would otherwise be eligible for inclusion in censuses and surveys may be missed for a variety of reasons. Here, however, we consider the possibility that a substantial segment of the population is

---

[4] Several different methods have been used to evaluate the completeness of census population coverage. First, a sample of households may be reinterviewed and their records matched with census records to determine the extent of undercoverage. Second, lists of persons obtained from noncensus sources may be compared with census records for the same persons. Third, coverage may be evaluated by comparing actual census counts with expected counts based on demographic analysis of data from other censuses, and data on births, deaths, and migration. Fourth, aggregated data from administrative records (e.g., birth records, medicare enrollments) may be compared with census counts to determine census coverage. All of these evaluation methods are based on assumptions that may be erroneous, and are further subject to errors due to inadequacies in the data available for evaluation, correlated errors in different sources of data, problems of matching records, and the like. For this reason different coverage evaluation methods generally yield different estimates of coverage, particularly for some age–race–sex categories. The method of demographic analysis, supplemented for older age groups by data on medicare enrollments, was preferred in 1970. The reliability of estimates of net census errors varies among different age–race–sex categories due to differences in the quality of data available for evaluation. In general, the less reliable the basic census data, the less reliable the estimate of error in the data; for example, estimates of net census errors are less reliable for blacks than for whites. (See U.S. Bureau of the Census, 1973a, for a detailed discussion.)

TABLE 16.1
Net Estimated Underenumeration of the
Population by Sex and Race, 1950–1970[a]

	1950	1960	1970
Black males	11.2	9.7	8.9
Black females	8.2	6.6	4.9
White males	2.8	2.4	2.4
White females	2.1	1.6	1.4
Total	3.3	2.7	2.5

[a] From U.S. Bureau of the Census 1973a, Table 3.

excluded by definition—that is, either (a) they reside in places that are not identified as housing units or (b) they do not really reside in any housing unit. In particular, it has been suggested that the severe census undercount of adult black males may occur because these men do not live in households.

Because so little is known about "missing persons," it is difficult to evaluate the extent to which black men are missed because they are unattached to households. However, there is fragmentary evidence that lends some credence to this explanation. First, most black people who are missed in the census do not live in dwellings that were missed. (This is not true of white people; over two-thirds of the whites missed in the census lived in missed dwellings. See Parsons, 1972.) Thus, undercoverage of the black population is not due primarily to the fact that black-occupied housing is underenumerated. This suggests either that the missing blacks do not reside anyplace, or that they are unreported at the places they do reside.

Second, undercoverage of black males is age related: The percentage missing rises when black men are in their teens and falls when they are in their 50s. This age-related pattern of coverage may occur because childhood and old age are times of greater dependency and (one might surmise) more stable attachments to households, where they are more readily found by census takers.

Finally, interviews conducted by the Census Bureau in "casual settings" (e.g., bars, on the streets) indicate that black male urban dwellers missed by the census tend to be lower in education, have fewer family ties, and change residences far more frequently than enumerated men interviewed in the same settings (see Parsons 1972, p. 30). Their having a transient lifestyle implies that these men are less likely to be found attached to households. Parsons (1972) suggests that "Such persons should be considered 'to live' on street corners and in bars, poolrooms, and other 'casual settings' in which censuses are not customarily taken [p. 31]." That their living arrangements are transitory is suggested by the fact that very few of the men identified as uncounted could later be located at addresses given to interviewers. Although suggestive, these results do not yield estimates of the size or extent of underenumeration of the hypothesized "unattached" population.

The hypothesis that black men are missed because they are unattached is partially disputed by evidence offered by Valentine and Valentine (1971). They compared results obtained by an intensive ethnographic study of an inner city community with census interviews conducted at the same households. The study confirms the severe census undercount of adult black males, 61% of whom were unreported to census enumerators for the 25 households studied. Their omission severely distorts estimates of the characteristics of the black inner city households in the study. For example, census data would lead to the inference that 72% of the households were female headed, whereas ethnographic observation indicated that only 12% were headed by women.

Valentine and Valentine find that the reason for the omission is not the transiency of the men, but rather concealment of their presence by female respondents. (Reasons for the failure to report male household members are considered in the following.) None of the men were missed because they lived in missed dwellings or dwellings incorrectly classified as vacant by census enumerators, according to this study.

The Valentines' study is local and small in scale, and the findings may not apply generally. However, the results suggest that the failure of conventional survey definitions to fit the urban population under study was not the main reason why black males were missed in the census enumeration. Nevertheless, the authors note the ambiguity of the concept of "residency" when applied to poor urban black households. They find that many men maintain stable ties to households and behave as household members or heads (by, for example, contributing income) although they do not regularly reside in the household. Valentine and Valentine suggest that for many other men, domestic attachments are so intermittent and tenuous that it would be arbitrary to assign them to any household. The fluidity of the living arrangements would make it difficult to apply conventional criteria, even if the reporting of household members was complete.

The problem of ambiguous household attachments is considered by Montie and Shapiro (1978), who suggest that the single residence rule may be too rigid for many research purposes. They propose that people with multiple residences or loose attachments to any household might be more appropriately classified as *associate residents*. This classification would permit them to be included in two or more households, but tabulated only once for any particular statistic. For example, a college student might be included in the parental household for statistics related to family composition, and included in the college unit for rental data.

THE EFFECT OF CHANGES IN ELIGIBILITY ON SURVEY COMPARABILITY

This section began by stating that reliable estimation of change requires the measurement of comparable target populations at multiple points in time. It is clear, however, that comparability of target populations is not necessarily achieved by the precise replication of survey definitions.

To consider the problem of comparability in more detail, assume that data are collected at two time points ($t = 1$ and $t = 2$) in surveys that employ

TABLE 16.2
Eligibility in Surveys at Time 1 and Time 2

	Eligible at $t = 2$	Ineligible at $t = 2$	
Eligible at $t = 1$	n_{11}	n_{12}	$n_{11} + n_{12}$
Ineligible at $t = 1$	n_{21}	n_{22}	$n_{21} + n_{22}$
	$n_{11} + n_{21}$	$n_{12} + n_{22}$	

identical criteria for eligibility. For example, in order to measure change in the American adult population, one might conduct independent surveys of household residents 18 years old and over in 2 successive decades. Theoretically, then, it would be possible to classify people according to their eligibility in the two surveys, as in Table 16.2.

The two target populations consist of $n_{11} + n_{12}$ people at time 1, and $n_{11} + n_{21}$ people at time 2. First, note that a *constant* bias—however large—does not affect the validity of estimates of change. That is, the size of category n_{22} does not influence the comparability of the two surveys.

This does not mean that category n_{22} can be ignored for the purpose of measuring change. Suppose, for example, one wished to measure trends in assault victimization and had reason to suppose that victimization occurs disproportionately among people who are permanently unattached to households, and who therefore fall in category n_{22}.[5] Victimization might rise or decline among transients, but the change would not be detected in surveys requiring household residency. In this hypothetical example, estimates of change are still valid—provided the investigator carefully limits their generality to the population as defined—but may be meaningless if one were interested in the entire population of potential victims. The fundamental problem here is not one of comparability, but of a target population that is defined inappropriately for the purpose of the study.

The comparability of the two populations depends on the numbers and characteristics of the n_{12} and n_{21} people who were eligible for one survey and not the other. We may differentiate between two sources of variation in the relative numbers and characteristics of the members of n_{12} and n_{21}.

The first is demographic change. Turnover in a population occurs as new members are born, age, and die, or migrate in and out of the population. They carry with them certain traits and experiences that result in systematic changes in the character and composition of a population. For example, younger cohorts have achieved higher levels of education than their predecessors, implying a long-term increase in the overall level of education of the American population as older birth cohorts have been replaced by younger ones. The

---

[5] In fact, there is reason to suspect that victims (and perpetrators) of assault are less likely to be eligible and/or accessible for a household interview than nonvictims. See Martin (1981).

TABLE 16.3
Percentage Agreeing that "Children Born Today Have a Wonderful Future to Look Forward to" among Natives and Inmigrants to Detroit by Year, Race, and Birthdate[a]

Race	Birthdate	1958	1971 Natives	1971 Inmigrants	1971 Total
Black	Before February 1937	89	82	86	82
		(98)	(214)	(21)	(235)
	After February 1937	—	48	59	53
			(75)	(61)	(136)
	Total	89	73	66	71
		(98)	(289)	(82)	(371)
White	Before February 1937	86	55	63	55
		(491)	(848)	(52)	(900)
	After February 1937	—	41	56	44
			(312)	(86)	(398)
	Total	86	51	59	52
		(491)	(1160)	(138)	(1298)

[a] From independent household surveys conducted by the Detroit Area Study, The University of Michigan, in 1958 and 1971. N's are given in parentheses. See Fischer (1974) for analysis.

"entrance" cell in Table 16.2 is cell n_{21}, which includes people who were too young to have been included in survey 1, or had not yet migrated into the population, but were eligible by the time of survey 2. The "exit" cell is cell n_{12}, which includes people who were eligible at the time of survey 1, but had died or migrated away by time 2. Variations in rates of fertility, mortality, and migration imply differences in the numbers and characteristics of those entering and leaving the eligible survey population. For this reason, we expect natural variations in n_{12} and n_{21} over time as the composition of the population changes. Such changes in composition do not impair the comparability of survey estimates, but it is advisable to analyze separately the effects of compositional change on trends.

An example is provided in Table 16.3, which shows that agreement that "Children born today have a wonderful future to look forward to" declined substantially among Detroit area residents from 1958 to 1971. In order to examine the effects of compositional change on the trend, responses are classified by race, date of birth[6], and, in 1971, by length of residence in the Detroit area.

Respondents born after February 1937 were too young to have been interviewed in 1958, but were eligible in 1971. Similarly, people who moved to the Detroit area after 1958 were represented in 1971 but not 1958. Thus, in 1971 native Detroiters born before February 1937 are comparable to 1958 respondents, except that people who lived in Detroit in 1958 but moved away or died

[6] Information on respondent's date of birth is not available for the 1958 baseline survey. To solve this problem, it was assumed that the respondents' ages given in the interview are their ages as of the last day of February 1958. (Interviews were actually conducted during February and March.) On this basis, birthdates were imputed for 1958 respondents. Exact date of birth was obtained in the 1971 DAS survey.

before 1971 are unrepresented in the latter year.[7] To the extent that in migrants or members of the younger cohort are more pessimistic than older, native Detroiters, a decline in optimism is expected even if the attitudes of the older natives did not change.

In 1971 respondents born after February 1937 are more pessimistic than their elders, so part of the decline in optimism from 1958 is due to the younger cohort. Cohort succession is a more important source of change for blacks than for whites. Optimism among blacks fell from 89% in 1958 to 71% in 1971. When the youngest 1971 cohort is excluded, however, the decline is only from 89 to 82%. In contrast, the sharp decline in optimism among whites is not due to cohort replacement: The level of optimism in 1971 is about the same whether the youngest cohort is excluded (55%) or included (52%).

The effects of inmigration are complex. In 1971, inmigrants tended to be more optimistic than native members of the same race and cohort. (Differences are statistically significant only for the youngest 1971 cohort.) However, the in migrants were young and disproportionately black (67% of inmigrants versus 27% of natives were born after 1937; 37% of inmigrants versus 20% of natives were black). Because they were younger, and therefore more pessimistic, black in migrants as a group were less optimistic than native blacks (66 versus 73%). For blacks, then, inmigration contributed very slightly to the decline in optimism. However, the opposite is true for whites. As a whole, white inmigrants were more optimistic than natives (59 versus 51%), so that inmigration slightly inhibited the decline in optimism among whites.

In this example, then, cohort succession is an important source of the decline in optimism for blacks, but not for whites, and inmigration is not very important for either group. Further analyses would be required to explain the dramatic drop in optimism among white natives, and the sharp intercohort differences among blacks.

Returning to Table 16.2, we note that a second source of differences in the characteristics of the members of the n_{12} and n_{21} is change in the living arrangements of the population. Because survey eligibility requires household residency, changes in rates of transiency, institutionalization, residence in group quarters, etc., may result in changes in the number and characteristics of ineligibles. The effect of such changes on the comparability of survey estimates depends on the number of people whose status changes, and the degree to which the social phenomenon of interest is correlated with residency status.

Several solutions to the problem of changing eligibility rates may be suggested. When the nature of aggregate changes in residency status is known, the investigator may compensate by supplementing the sample using revised criteria for eligibility. For example, suppose one wished to replicate during wartime a baseline survey that was originally conducted during peacetime. The increase

[7] Thus, we cannot compare the characteristics of the members of n_{21} and n_{12}. However, the black segment of the Detroit area population increased from 17% in 1958 to 22% in 1971. The change is due both to net in migration among blacks and out migration among whites.

in service in the armed forces during wartime may result in a very substantial drop in the number of young men eligible for the second survey. In order to represent more completely the young adult male population, then, the investigator may wish to supplement the household survey with a special survey of the residents of military bases. The nature of changes in the living arrangements of a population may be unknown; in this case, the numbers and characteristics of ineligibles may change in unknown ways as the result of, for example, an increase or decrease in the rate of transiency among some segments of the population.

In order to estimate the biases that may result, we require better knowledge of changes in Americans' living arrangements and the effects on survey eligibility. The Valentines' study, which compared ethnographic observations with census interviews, offers a promising strategy for further research. This study also has the advantage of providing information about the members of n_{22} as well, who may never turn up in household surveys. However, ethnographic studies are necessarily expensive and small in scale. Another possible strategy is to use national data to construct residential histories in order to investigate the characteristics of the members of n_{12} and n_{21}. For example, in survey 2 one might include retrospective questions in order to classify and analyze the members of n_{11} and n_{21}, as was done in the 1971 Detroit Area Study survey. Alternatively, one might follow a panel of respondents from survey 1 to determine the characteristics of n_{11} and n_{12}. An example of the latter is Fondelier's (1976) analysis of panel attrition in the National Longitudinal Study (NLS).

The problem of changing ineligibility rates in cross-sectional surveys is clearly related to the problem of panel attrition in longitudinal surveys, since both arise in part from the same sources. Panel respondents may be "lost" because they are institutionalized or they join the armed forces, or for a variety of other reasons. Fondelier (1976) shows that different age–sex categories differ in rates and sources of attrition in the NLS, and that in some cases the attrition rate varied substantially between 1967 and 1975. Losses occurring because the respondent was institutionalized are much greater for young men than for young women, mature men, or mature women. Substantial and varying numbers of the panel of young men were lost each year to the armed forces; the proportion increased from .05 in 1967 to .14 in 1969, and dropped to .04 in 1975. The proportion of respondents that the interviewer was simply unable to contact was also greater for young men, and varied considerably over time.

I have argued that target populations are not necessarily comparable even when survey definitions are precise and identical from survey to survey. In addition, survey definitions may be neither precise nor consistent over time. Several suggestions for coping with this situation are offered.

When eligibility criteria vary among baseline surveys, or survey definitions are vague with respect to the inclusion of certain categories of places or people, comparable estimates of change may often nevertheless be obtained by (*a*) using the *most inclusive* eligibility criteria in the replication survey; and (*b*) collecting information on eligibility according to alternative, more restrictive criteria. In this fashion, the investigator may make valid comparisons with baseline surveys with either inclusive or restrictive eligibility requirements by simply including the appropriately defined subset of respondents from the replication survey. In addition, the investigator may examine the effects of different eligibility criteria on estimates of change; this may be useful when the investigator does not know which criteria for eligibility were applied in a baseline survey.

For example, political surveys conducted by Louis Harris often include a "voter screen" that eliminates people who have not voted in previous elections from the survey. Harris voter surveys are thus not strictly comparable to regular Harris cross-sectional surveys that employ no such screen. However, many cross-sectional surveys include the same series of questions on voting behavior in past elections. If so, it is a simple matter to eliminate nonvoting respondents from cross-sectional surveys in order to permit valid comparisons between cross-sectional and voter surveys.

If survey definitions are vague, the investigator may not know whether certain types of people were included in previous baseline surveys or not. (An example is the uncertain treatment of hotel residents in 1950s surveys conducted by the Detroit Area Study.) In such cases, strict comparability cannot be achieved. Again, however, the replication survey may include the category in question, and collect information on eligibility according to more restrictive criteria. Suppose that N_I respondents were selected for the replication survey using inclusive criteria; of these, N_R would also have been eligible by more restrictive criteria. In order to assess the effect of different eligibility criteria on trend estimates, two estimates of change—the first based on baseline and N_I respondents, and the second based on baseline and N_R respondents—should be compared. The investigator can be reasonably confident (assuming other things equal) that "true" change falls within the range defined by the two estimates. One usually hopes, of course, that the two trend estimates are the same. However, different eligibility criteria may result in different estimates of change if the number of uncertain cases ($N_I - N_R$) is large or the phenomenon of interest is concentrated among them.

Sampling and Selection Procedures

Theoretically, the comparability of target populations is determined by the rules of eligibility used in different surveys, and by the numbers and characteristics of the eligible and ineligible segments of the population at different points in time. Even when eligibility criteria remain constant, changes in population characteristics may affect the comparability of target populations.

Empirically, the comparability of survey populations is also influenced by the actual procedures and practices used to implement survey definitions. In particular, procedures used to construct the sampling frame and select respondents may influence the coverage of surveys and their comparability over time.

CONSTRUCTING SAMPLING FRAMES FOR HOUSEHOLD SURVEYS

National household surveys typically involve the selection of population units from sampling frames in multiple stages, involving primary sampling units of counties or groups of counties (which may be stratified), blocks or enumeration districts, housing units, and, finally, individuals. Dwellings are generally selected in clusters that vary in size and homogeneity (depending on the variable under study); larger, more homogeneous clusters result in larger variance in the estimates. The effects of clustering may be held approximately constant by using clusters of equal size in survey replications or by correcting for cluster effects in the estimated variances; see, for example, Kish, 1965.

A good sampling frame represents each element of the defined population by one and only one listing in the frame. Errors in the frame arise when a population unit does not appear in the frame, when it appears in duplicate listings, when multiple units are clustered as one listing, or when elements that are not members of the population appear as listings (Kish, 1965, p. 54). The sources of information used to construct frames (e.g. maps, lists, or directories), the procedures used to update and correct the frame, the age of the frame, and the frequency with which it is updated affect the nature and number of errors present. Information on procedures used to construct and update sampling frames is not readily available from most survey organizations. Nonetheless, in a pilot study evaluating the quality of survey operations, Bailar and Lanphier (1978) conclude that "Overall the problems that occurred in sample design were not usually a result of problems with sampling frames [p. 68]."

The Census Bureau has evaluated errors of coverage resulting from different methods used to construct address lists. (See Bounpane and Jordan, 1978; U.S. Bureau of the Census 1973b for detailed discussions.) In the 1970 census, about 60% of the population was enumerated by mail, with the remaining 40% enumerated by the conventional personal visit by the interviewer. Lists of mailing addresses were compiled by one of two methods. In large urban areas, mailing addresses were purchased from commercial mailing firms and corrected by the post office; in other areas, enumerators prepared address lists by canvassing the area and recording addresses. Estimated coverage in 1970 was more complete in areas covered by commercial mailing lists than in prelisted or conventionally enumerated areas, as can be seen in Table 16.4.

Differential coverage in 1970 was due both to variations in procedures and in the type of land area enumerated. For example, conventional enumeration in 1970 was generally restricted to rural areas, which tend to have lower coverage rates. Column (2) of Table 16.4 shows the transition from 1960 to 1980 in methods of census enumeration. The procedural changes have improved overall coverage from 1960 to 1970, with the gains occurring primarily in large urban areas covered by commercial mailing lists. Table 16.5 documents the small but significant improvement in estimated coverage of central cities which resulted from the procedural change.

TABLE 16.4
Enumeration Method and Estimated Miss Rates of Housing in the Census (before Imputation)[a]

	(1) Estimated miss rates for occupied housing		(2) Estimated percentage of housing units covered by procedure		
Census procedure	1960	1970	1960	1970	1980
Total United States	2.1	1.7	100%	100%	100%
Mailed census forms	—	1.2	0	60	90
Addresses purchased from commercial firms and updated by post office		.9	0	48	60
Addresses prelisted	—	2.6	0	12	30
Non-mail (conventional enumeration)	2.1	2.6	100	40	10

[a] From Bounpane and Jordan 1978, p. 15, Table 4; U.S. Bureau of the Census, 1973b, Table G.

The improvements in coverage resulting from changes in census procedures for listing and enumerating dwellings may affect the comparability of census data over time. The gains in coverage of the residents of central cities may result in apparent shifts in some population characteristics—even in the absence of true change—if more or different types of central city dwellers are included in each successive census.

Pretests for the 1980 census (reported by Bounpane & Jordan 1978) have also investigated the estimated improvements in census coverage resulting from the use of supplemental lists of addresses obtained from drivers' license files, social security files, tribal rolls of American Indians, the Immigration and Naturalization Service list of registered aliens, and other lists. The data suggest that substantial improvements in coverage of hard-to-enumerate groups can result from the use of supplemental sources. In Camden, New Jersey, for example, the estimated improvement in coverage resulting from use of drivers' license files is 2% for the total population, 3.4% for black males aged 17–24 or over 45 years old, and 7.5% for Hispanic men in the same age groups. The

TABLE 16.5
Estimated Miss Rates of Occupied Housing Units, 1960 and 1970[a]

	1960 census	1970 census
Inside SMSA	1.9	1.3
Central city	2.2	1.5
Noncentral city	1.5	1.2
Outside SMSA	2.7	2.6

[a] From U.S. Bureau of the Census, 1973b, Table F.

pretest data indicate that about 7% of the individuals whose drivers' licenses were processed would have been missed by census enumeration.

Several points may be drawn from this evidence. First, sampling frames for household surveys may differ in the extent and nature of undercoverage according to the procedures and sources of information used to construct them. Second, improved methods of constructing sampling frames are likely to result in differential changes in coverage that may bias trend estimates. Such may be the case for estimates of change in the numbers and characteristics of some population subgroups based upon 1960, 1970, and 1980 census data.

LOCATING AND SELECTING RESPONDENTS

Procedures used by interviewers to locate and select respondents affect the rate and character of nonresponse and the composition of the sample. The timing and number of calls to selected households affect the likelihood of finding potential respondents at home; systematic variations in interviewer practices may affect the rate of respondent nonavailability. Methods of selecting a respondent from household members vary in the discretion interviewers are allowed to exercise. Probability selection strictly determines respondent selection by a random device, permitting no interviewer discretion if done properly. Quota methods constrain the interviewer to fill quotas of certain types of respondents (e.g., males versus females) but permit considerable latitude in choosing respondents to meet quotas.

Methods that allow interviewer discretion are potentially more biased (e.g., they overrepresent people who are cooperative and spend much time at home, such as housewives and retired people) and more vulnerable to variability in the extent of bias if systematic change in interviewer practices (e.g., timing and number of visits) occurs. In order to obtain comparable measurements in different surveys, respondents should be selected using the same procedures. However, if the method is one that permits interviewers a great deal of discretion, replication may not ensure comparable results because interviewers' actual practices may vary over time and in different circumstances. Moreover, interviewer practices concerning such factors as timing and number of calls are often not standardized or monitored, making them difficult to replicate.

We first consider examples of the wide variation in selection procedures used by different organizations. Although procedural differences are potential sources of bias, there is little evidence on which to base an evaluation of the effect upon survey comparability. The rate of nonresponse due to nonavailability of respondents varies among surveys—although again evidence is scant—but shows no clearcut trend over time. (But see Steeh, 1981.) The absence of a trend may occur because the increasing nonavailability of respondents has been compensated for by more callbacks by survey organizations.

Examples of selection procedures used by different organizations follow.

The *Survey Research Center* procedure requires the interviewer to list all eligible household residents according to relationship to the head of household.

Election surveys also require U.S. citizenship. The interviewer lists eligible males, oldest to youngest, then eligible females, oldest to youngest. The respondent is selected using a randomized procedure developed by Kish (1949), which is designed to give an approximately equal probability of selection to all adults in households with six or fewer adults. Up to seven calls to the same household to obtain an interview with the designated respondent are routinely employed, and substitutions are prohibited. There are no strict controls exercised over the timing of calls, although interviewers are instructed to "plan to make one call in each of three time periods: 1) days during the week, 2) evenings during the week, and 3) weekends [SRC 1976, p. 29]."

Between 1972 and 1976, the National Opinion Research Center employed quotas to select respondents for the *General Social Survey*. Quotas for four groups (employed and unemployed women, and men over and under 35) were determined by the proportion of each group in that location according to 1970 census tract data. These quotas were imposed to control for the bias introduced by the fact that men, particularly younger men, and employed women tend to spend less time at home than other people. In order to reduce bias due to people not being at home, NORC interviewers were required to interview after 3:00 PM or on weekends or holidays, since housewives tend to be overrepresented in daytime interviews. Interviewers were required to follow a specified travel pattern at the block level, and proceed from one household to another until quotas are filled. No substitutions within households were allowed, and no callbacks were required. In 1975 strict probability selection was introduced for half of the GSS sample, and in 1977 for the entire sample.

The usual selection procedure for polls conducted by *Louis Harris and Associates, Inc.* requires the interviewer to choose one of the adults who live in the housing unit and are at home when the interviewer calls. Interviewers must fill a 50–50 sex quota. If both men and women are present the interviewer may elect to interview either a male or a female respondent, subject to the constraint imposed by the 50–50 sex quota. Either males, or females (but not both) are listed from oldest to youngest, and the respondent is selected randomly. If the designated respondent refuses to be interviewed, the interviewer is instructed to proceed to the next household. No substitutions within households are allowed. The typical Harris survey requires no callbacks, but up to four callbacks are required in government sponsored surveys (Louis Harris, no date).

The effects of using different selection procedures have not been extensively evaluated. However, a NORC split-ballot experiment comparing the results of the NORC block-quota procedure previously described with probability selection of respondents indicates few differences in respondent characteristics or attitudes that may be attributed to the use of different procedures. Stephenson (1979) finds that NORC block quota selection slightly overrepresents larger households and friendly people, and underrepresents men who work full time. On the other hand, block quota selection more adequately represents residents of central cities than does probability selection. Other studies show that different organizations using different procedures obtain samples that are similar but not identical in demographic composition. In comparing NORC and Harris surveys Turner and Krauss (1978) find that they are similar in coverage of persons of different demographic characteristics; Harris surveys include more college educated people, and both Harris and NORC surveys include fewer young and less well-educated people than the census. Presser (1981) compares the sample characteristics of SRC Election Studies, NORC General Social Surveys, and Harris cross-sectional surveys from 1966 through 1976. He finds that, compared to the census, SRC and NORC overrepresent women increasingly over time; blacks are overrepresented in pre-1972 Harris surveys and underrepresented thereafter; SRC, NORC, and (especially) Harris all overrepresent highly educated people; and age distributions for surveys conducted by all three organizations correspond fairly closely to census statistics.

Of course, differences other than respondent selection exist among survey organizations, so the demographic differences cannot be taken as a measure of the effects of the different selection procedures. Indeed, as Presser (1981) concludes, "Given the many factors that could produce different results among the various survey organizations . . . the overall similarity of respondent background characteristics is reassuring [p. 21]."

Selection methods that permit interviewer discretion may be biased because, given the option, interviewers select respondents who are cooperative and readily available. The availability of potential respondents depends in part on the timing and number of calls made by the interviewer. Thus, interviewers' practices concerning the timing and number of calls influence the rate and character of nonresponse due to nonavailability ("not at home," and "respondent absent").[8]

The likelihood that a person will be found at home fluctuates over time (the variations are hourly, daily, seasonal, and yearly) and depends on such characteristics as employment status, sex, and age. Women, unemployed and retired people, people over 65 or in rural areas are most likely to be found at home at almost any time of day (U.S. Bureau of the Census, 1972). Table 16.6 provides data on variations over the course of a day in the probability of finding anyone at home in 1960 and 1971.

In addition, the probability of finding a person at home varies more for some people (e.g., employed men) than others (e.g., housewives). Thus, some hours of the day are more representative of the population of household residents than others. For example, at 9:00 AM the bias due to overrepresentation of housewives is more serious than it is at 6:00 PM. This implies that the time of day an interviewer calls influences the likelihood that anyone will be found at home, and who will be found there. If respondents are selected from the household residents who are actually present when the interviewer calls, the effect of the timing of interviewer calls on rates of nonresponse and the characteristics

---

[8] Nonavailability also occurs when respondents are available but cannot be interviewed due to illness, language barrier, or the like. Respondent absence may also represent a passive form of refusal.

TABLE 16.6
Proportion of U.S. Households in Which at Least One Person over
14 Years Old Was at Home at the Interviewer's First Call[a]

Time of day	1960 census	November 1971 Current Population Survey
8:00 AM–2:59 PM	.69	.57
3:00–4:59 PM	.71	.69
5:00–6:59 PM	.78	.74
7:00–7:59 PM	.80	.71
8:00–8:59 PM	.76	.78

[a] From U.S. Bureau of the Census, 1972, Table A.

of respondents may be quite substantial. Thus, distribution of interviewer calls across time of day is hypothesized as one determinant of the representativeness of a sample. The extent to which the timing of calls varies among surveys or over time is not known. Most survey organizations instruct interviewers to vary the timing of their visits, although as Hawkins (1977) notes, interviewer call procedures are usually not standardized or monitored. Moreover, the timing of interviewer calls may vary systematically; Hawkins finds a trend toward earlier calls to black households than to white households in Detroit Area Study surveys, and attributes it to interviewers' fear of crime in black neighborhoods. If he is correct, it implies that changes or differences in crime rates may systematically affect the timing of calls.

The coverage of sample surveys is also affected by seasonal and long-term changes in the availability of potential respondents at home. Nonavailability is greater during vacation months; Marquis (1977) notes the .6% seasonal difference in CPS response rates, which, though small, apparently results in a significant bias in estimates of labor force status. Table 16.6 indicates a long-term decline in availability, which may be due to there being more working wives, more multicar families, and a smaller number of persons per housing unit (U.S. Bureau of the Census, 1972).

The decline in the availability of people in their homes makes it surprising that there is no change in rates of respondent nonavailability, although there is substantial variability among surveys (Marquis 1977). Marquis presents data which suggest nonresponse rates exclusive of refusals ranging between 2–12%, with variation apparently resulting in part from differences in criteria for respondent eligibility. He suggests that the absence of a trend "may reflect successful efforts made by these organizations to overcome availability problems; for example, by increasing the number of calls made per completed interview [p. 12]." (Steeh [1981] finds that nonavailability in SRC surveys increased in metropolitan areas in the 1970s.)

The number as well as the timing of calls to households affects the magnitude and distribution of nonresponse. Callbacks are more effective as means to locate respondents who are not at home than to convert refusals (Kish 1965, p. 537). Therefore, both the total amount of nonresponse, and the proportion due to nonavailability, are expected to decline as the number of calls increases. This implies that the number of calls affects the nature of the bias due to nonresponse, a conclusion supported by evidence presented by Hawkins (1977), who finds that the number of calls influences to a varying degree the demographic characteristics of the sample, the coefficients and standard errors of parameter estimates, and intercorrelations among variables.

Two other studies demonstrate the changing characteristics of respondents obtained in successive waves of interviewing. In a mail survey investigating college dropouts, Eckland (1965) eventually obtained a 94% response rate with up to three mailouts, and (if necessary) follow-ups by telephone and certified letter. The proportion of respondents who had dropped out of college increased dramatically in later waves of interviewing. Only 19% of those who responded to the first mailed questionnaire were college dropouts, compared to 65% of those who did not respond until they had received three mailings, a telephone call, and a certified letter.[9] Wish, Robins, Helzer, Hesselbrock, and Davis (1978) also went to great effort to secure a high response rate (94%) in a study of Vietnam veterans. They find that veterans who were interviewed only after several callbacks were more likely to be unemployed, divorced, addicted to heroin, or transient than veterans who were interviewed early. Veterans who were more accessible to interviewers thus differ systematically from veterans who were difficult to locate.

These studies suggest that differences in callback procedures may dramatically affect the comparability of survey results. The problem is more serious because the effect of the number of calls is not limited to simple effects upon the distribution of variables, but may—as in Hawkins's study—affect interrelations among them as well.

It is not necessarily true that more callbacks always produce samples that are more representative. Wilcox (1977) argues that the biasing effects of nonavailability counteract to some extent the biasing effects of refusals. Day and Wilcox (1971) conducted a simulation experiment suggesting that total bias due to nonresponse first declines and then increases as data from additional calls are added. Thus, the number of calls optimal for the reduction of nonresponse bias may be less than the maximum. If Wilcox is correct, that is, if biases due to nonavailability versus refusals "cancel," one might propose that the optimal number of calls would produce a balance between the two types of nonresponse. We defer consideration of this possibility, and of the possible effects of nonresponse on estimation of trends, until we consider refusals, the second source of nonresponse bias.

RESPONDENT SELF-SELECTION: THE PROBLEM OF REFUSALS

Regardless of how they are selected, designated respondents always have the option of refusing. They may refuse to be interviewed at all, or they may

---

[9] Eckland's (1965) findings may result from the fact that college dropouts are less accessible, and hence respond later. In addition, it is likely that respondents who have something positive to report (e.g., college completion) respond more quickly than those who do not.

agree to an interview but refuse to provide accurate information in response to particular questions. Refusal to answer specific items may take the form of intentionally falsifying or withholding information as well as overtly refusing to respond. (Of course, it is easier to detect overt than covert refusals.) In either case, missing and erroneous data reduce the reliability of the results, and to the extent that omissions and errors are correlated with survey or respondent characteristics, introduce bias.

It seems reasonable to suppose that motivation to participate in a survey and report accurately and completely is influenced by the perceived costs of reporting. Motivation to participate is low, and therefore refusals and underreporting are high, when respondents are afraid of being victimized by crime, are concerned about legal or other consequences of accurate reporting, or are embarrassed or threatened by the information sought by interviewers. Moreover, all of these factors are subject to variations over time and among groups which affect the comparability of measurements.

Refusal Rates and Fear of Crime. Evidence suggests systematic changes in the rate of respondent refusals that, according to some, were sparked by rising crime of the 1960s. Such changes have potentially serious consequences for estimates of trends. Hawkins (1977), House and Wolf (1978), and Steeh (1981), find a monotonic increase in refusal rates in national surveys conducted by the Survey Research Center between 1956 and 1979, with the increase particularly marked in large urban centers, especially central cities. Refusal rates increased by an average of .75 to 1% per year in surveys conducted since 1970 by the Los Angeles Metropolitan Area Survey (cited by Marquis 1977, p. 14). House and Wolf find that the strongest predictor of the refusal rate obtained in a PSU is the crime rate, with variations in total crime rates accounting for over one-half of the variance in refusal rates over time and among urban and nonurban places. Their results support the argument that rising crime led to an increasing suspicion of strangers—including interviewers—that made people reluctant to grant interviews.

If refusal to participate in surveys results from generalized mistrust or fear of crime, trends in indicators of mistrust underestimate true change. In the most extreme case, shifts in attitudes will not be registered as changes in indicators of mistrust, but will show up as changes in refusal rates. In fact, national survey data indicate only slight increases in mistrust over time (Fischer, 1976, p. 61) and no substantial urban–nonurban differences in mistrust (House & Wolf, 1978). The inference that time and size of place of residence do not affect mistrust may be faulty, however. House and Wolf (1978) conclude that "surveys suffer from potentially serious biases due to nonresponse. . . . The lack of survey evidence for differences across places of residence in general attitudes regarding trust in people may be due to the fact that the least trusting people have refused. . . [p. 104].''[10] Mistrust is related to

---

[10] A second possible example of the effect of change in refusal rates is provided by Farley, Hatchett, and Schuman (1979), who find an increase in alienation among blacks in Detroit from

other forms of nonresponse as well. A 1971 survey of Detroit finds that mistrustful respondents are more likely than others to refuse to give a phone number to the interviewer (Fischer, 1974).

An increase in fear of crime is underestimated to the extent that fearful respondents refuse to participate. In addition, estimates of trends in variables correlated with fear of crime may also be biased. Stinchcombe, Adams, Heimer, Scheppele, Smith, and Taylor (1980) find that fear of crime is associated with race, sex, size of place of residence, racial prejudice, whether the person lives alone, and victimization by crime in the previous year. Refusal rates are high among ethnic whites with little education and low income, who reside in central cities, probably due to fear and suspicion of strangers. (See Dunkelberg & Day, 1973; Hawkins, 1977; O'Neil, 1979; and Wilcox, 1977.) O'Neil suggests that people who are reluctant to participate in surveys are less likely to participate in social activities generally. People with these various characteristics may therefore be underrepresented. In addition, a differential increase in fear (and hence refusals) among particular demographic groups implies a differential increase in the underrepresentation of such groups in surveys. Available evidence indicates that over time women became more fearful relative to men (Stinchcombe et al., 1980) and urban dwellers became more fearful relative to nonurban dwellers (House & Wolf, 1978), implying (other things equal) a relative decline in the representation of these groups in sample surveys.

Perceived Costs of Accurate Reporting. Information reported by respondents may be potentially damaging or embarrassing to them, and may be withheld or refused for these reasons. Fear of the consequences of reporting may be exacerbated among respondents who do not believe interviewers' assurances of the confidentiality of their answers.

Information varies in its sensitivity. Fear of legal or other repercussions may account for high rates of refusal to report income and the underreporting of criminal victimization by acquaintances and family members (Penick & Owens, 1976, p. 119).

Valentine and Valentine (1971) attribute the severe undercount of black men residing in urban households to respondents' fears of the consequences of accurate reporting. Many poor urban black households derive income from a variety of sources—including conventional employment, public assistance, and extralegal activities—that may be jeopardized by disclosure to authorities. Most forms of public assistance require that no significant wage earner reside in the household, so that respondents may be very reluctant to report the presence of such a person to anyone in an official capacity, including census takers.

1968 to 1971, and a subsequent decline in 1976. Unfortunately, the conclusion that alienation declined between the latter 2 years is somewhat suspect due to an increase in the rate of refusals among blacks of nearly 10% from 1971 to 1976. The authors note the possibility that "the drop [in alienation] is accounted for by the refusal of the most alienated blacks in Detroit to take part in the more recent survey [p. 442]," although there is little empirical evidence to support or refute this hypothesis.

Valentine and Valentine also express extreme skepticism about the quality of the income data provided by such respondents. Similarly, the income or presence of illegal residents of public housing may not be accurately reported (Parsons, 1972, p. 27).

Fear of the consequences of reporting sensitive information is exacerbated by the low rate of public confidence in the confidentiality of survey data. A national survey sponsored by the National Academy of Sciences (NAS, 1979) indicates that only 5% of the respondents believed that census records are completely confidential; 80% did not believe that census records are confidential, or did not believe that confidentiality could be maintained if other government agencies "really tried" to obtain census records. An experimental study indicates that interviewers' promises of confidentiality varying in the fact and duration of protection have small but consistent effects on refusal rates, which varied by 1%.[11]

Organizational auspices may affect beliefs about confidentiality and willingness to participate in a survey.[12] The Bureau of Census secures higher response rates than the University of Michigan's Survey Research Center (NAS, 1979), undoubtedly due in part to the perceived legal requirement to participate. The difference in refusal rates is greatest in large cities and among people over 65 years of age. However, blacks and Hispanics in Camden, New Jersey, who knew that a pretest survey was conducted by the U.S. Census Bureau were slightly less likely to cooperate than those who were unaware of the census auspices (Moore & Rothwell, 1978). Valentine and Valentine (1971) also note the mistrust of the official census auspices on the part of many inner city residents who believed that any information they provided would be available to other agencies and would be used against them.

Respondent willingness to report accurately is affected by less tangible costs as well, such as the social desirability of the event or attitude. Health events and incidents of criminal victimization that are sources of threat or embarrassment to respondents may be underreported. Respondents reporting on the reasons for their hospitalization overreport some diagnoses and severely underreport others, such as mental disorders (U.S. Department of Health, Education, and Welfare, 1977a, p. 10). Penick and Owens (1976) speculate that embarrassment may be the reason for underreporting assault by an offender who is known to the victim (p. 73). Events that reflect positively on the respondent, on the other hand, tend to be overreported. Postelection surveys gener-

[11] The effect is quite small. It is possible that people who did not believe in survey confidentiality to begin with also mistrusted interviewers' assurances, implying that the attempt to manipulate confidentiality experimentally may not have been effective for cynical respondents.

[12] The geographic location of the survey organization may also influence respondents' willingness to participate. Groves and Kahn (1979) find a curvilinear relation between distance and rates of refusal in a telephone survey conducted by the Survey Research Center. Response rates were highest in areas both near and far from Ann Arbor. They suggest that among Michigan residents, knowledge of and respect for the university may enhance cooperation, whereas very distant residents may be impressed with a long distance phone call from Michigan.

ally find the number of people claiming that they voted for the winner to be greater than the number of people who actually did vote for the winner. Overreporting desirable events may reflect respondents' tendency to distort answers in a positive direction, or it may occur because respondents who have something positive to report are more likely to participate in the survey. Examples of the latter are a mail survey on hunting, which obtained a quicker response from successful hunters than from unsuccessful ones (Mosteller, 1968, p. 119), and Eckland's (1965) study of college dropouts, discussed earlier.

Changes in incentives to report may result from legal changes concerning, for example, reporting income or eligibility requirements for public assistance, from changing beliefs about the confidentiality of survey results, and from cultural changes that affect the social desirability of particular events. Declining public confidence in survey confidentiality and increasing concern with privacy are adduced as reasons for the decline in response rates (e.g., see NAS, 1979). As with fear of crime, it is difficult to estimate accurately trends in public concerns about confidentiality using survey data if disbelief in confidentiality leads people to refuse to participate.

SUMMARY: TRENDS IN THE MAGNITUDE AND CHARACTER OF NONRESPONSE

Hawkins (1977) concludes that "Over the last 20 years nonresponse rates have increased for most survey research organizations from average rates of around 15% to current rates averaging 30% or more [p. 10]." The change is due in large part to an increase in refusals, which increased relative to other sources of nonresponse, such as nonavailability.[13] Brooks and Bailar (1978) also find that refusals accounted for an increasing proportion of noninterviews in the Current Population Survey from 1970 to 1976. Thus, the magnitude and character of nonresponse changed over time. In addition, there is substantial variability among surveys in amount and correlates of nonresponse.

Because refusal and nonavailability are correlated with (different) demographic traits and other characteristics, variations in either the magnitude or the pattern of nonresponse may affect the comparability of survey findings. Estimation of trends should be based on surveys that are affected in similar ways by nonresponse bias. One strategy for achieving this may be to attempt to "replicate" rates and patterns of nonresponse of baseline surveys, as was done in the 1971 Detroit Area Study. In order to ensure comparability with the 1950s baseline surveys in which response rates varied between 82 and 87%, a response rate of 80% was set as a target and achieved. In addition, a roughly comparable pattern of nonresponse was obtained: Refusals account for 51%, 69%, and 70% of total nonresponse in the 1954 and 1959 baseline and the 1971 replication surveys, respectively. If it is valid to assume that the correlates of nonresponse remain constant, these results imply a roughly constant bias due to nonresponse in baseline and replication surveys. However, the latter as-

---

[13] House (1978) is skeptical of Marquis's (1977) cautious assertion that there are no clear-cut trends in nonresponse. House finds a clear increase in refusals and in overall nonresponse rates and notes that Marquis compares surveys in which both subject matter and respondent rules vary.

sumption is uncertain: It is quite possible that the reasons for refusals change substantially over time, implying change in the correlates as well as the magnitude of this source of nonresponse.

Interviewing

The social interaction between interviewer and respondent is the least standardized and probably the most variable aspect of data collection. Moreover, there is increasing recognition of the influence of respondent–interviewer interaction on the quality of data, whether the interview pertains to objective facts (such as health events or victimization by crime) or subjective attitudes and beliefs.

The degree to which interviewers may influence survey statistics is demonstrated experimentally by Bailey, Moore, and Bailar (1978). Interpenetrated random assignments of interviewers were used to estimate precisely the influence of interviewers on the quality of National Crime Survey (NCS) data. The authors find that variability among interviewers is high, especially in some cities and for some categories of victimization. It is possible that interviewers vary in how they apply some NCS definitions and concepts to classify incidents. The investigators find no evidence of any simple relationship between interviewer variability and the socioeconomic characteristics of respondents, although variability may be greater when the races of interviewer and respondent differ.

These results suggest that error and bias due to interviewing may potentially influence the comparability of survey data over time and place. In this section, we will consider how variations in style and method of interviewing, interviewer training and experience, and the composition of interviewing staffs, may influence the comparability of survey statistics. In addition, we will consider how the interview itself orders and structures topics, questions, and response alternatives in ways that may produce variability among surveys.

STYLE OF INTERVIEWING

Survey practitioners once viewed interviewer–respondent rapport as the key to a good interview, and interviewers were trained to try to achieve it. Rapport is difficult to standardize, and in addition the evidence indicates that a personalistic style of interviewing may motivate ingratiating behavior and socially acceptable responses, or may reduce respondents' motivation to take the task seriously (DHEW, 1977b). One aspect of a personal interviewing style is the interviewer's use of positive feedback to encourage respondents. However, interviewers traditionally use feedback in a way that may impair rather than improve the quality of the data: The evidence suggests that interviewers give positive feedback indiscriminately for both adequate and inadequate responses, and they are most likely to make positive statements after the respondent refuses to answer—presumably to alleviate ' ·· tension that such a refusal creates (Marquis & Cannell, 1969). The quality of data is improved by feedback

that is contingent upon respondent performance. More complete health information is obtained if respondents receive positive feedback when they report
such information (DHEW, 1977b).

A second factor related to quality of reporting is the amount of verbal
activity during the interview. The more the interviewer talks, the more the
respondent talks, and the result is better, more complete information from the
respondent (DHEW, 1977b). The quality of health reporting is influenced by
interviewer motivation; interviewers with positive attitudes toward the survey
obtain more complete information from respondents. Positive attitudes may be
communicated to respondents in such subtle ways as the interviewer's voice
inflection, which according to one experiment has a substantial effect on the
number of health incidents reported (Barath & Cannell, 1976). [This finding
must be considered tentative, however, since Blair (1977–78) was unable to
replicate it in a field setting.]

There have been long-term changes in interviewing practices that influence
the quality of survey results. The most notable is a general trend away from a
personalistic interviewing style, with its emphasis on rapport with respondents,
and a greater emphasis on the desirability of interviewer impersonality. The
effects of the change are uncertain, although one comparison of personal
interviewing (with noncontingent positive feedback) and impersonal interviewing (with no feedback) found no differences in quality of reporting health information (DHEW, 1977b). It is likely, however, that there have been changes in
the quality of reporting. The results of investigations such as those reported
previously are used to revise interviewer training and practices to improve the
accuracy of reporting in, for example, the Health Interview Survey. If they are
effective, improvements in interviewing methods would be expected to lead to,
for example, increased reporting of health incidents, even in the absence of a
real trend. To the extent that the trend away from a personal interviewing style
emphasizing rapport with respondents, and other changes in interviewing
methods, have resulted in changes in interviewers' motivation, verbal activity,
or effective use of positive feedback, the comparability of surveys conducted
over time will be affected.

INTERVIEWER TRAINING AND EXPERIENCE

Traditional wisdom is that trained and experienced interviewers obtain
data of higher quality, and to a large extent this appears to be true. In an
experimental evaluation of the performance of Current Population Survey interviewers in mock interviews, Rustemeyer (1977) compared new interviewers
who had completed classroom training but had no field experience, trained
interviewers who had completed two to three interviewing assignments, and
trained interviewers with more than 3 months' field experience. As one would
expect, overall interviewer accuracy increases with experience. The rate of
labor force classification errors was 10.3% for new interviewers, 8.7% for end-
of-training interviewers, and 3.2% for interviewers with several months' experience. Because different survey organizations vary in the extent of training,

supervision, and experience of the interviewing staff (Bailar & Lanphier, 1978), Rustemeyer's finding implies that the quality of the information collected may vary considerably from one organization to another. The quality and experience of the interviewing staff may vary from place to place as well. Bailey *et al.* (1978) cite the difficulty of recruiting good interviewers in crime-prone cities and suggest that the quality of interviewing and enumeration may be lower in such areas, resulting in higher interviewer variability in victimization estimates.

It is disturbing to find that experience does not reduce the likelihood that some of the most serious types of interviewer errors will occur. We have noted that comparability across time requires precise replication of survey procedures, including the phrasing of questions, the use of probes, and (if possible) question sequence and order. As we will see in the section on interview effects (pp. 712–722), variations in the way questions are asked may substantially affect the answers given. Therefore, it is troublesome to learn that an analysis of tape recorded interviews actually conducted by Survey Research Center professionals shows that 36% of the questions were not asked as written, and 20% were altered sufficiently to destroy comparability (Cannell, Lawson, & Hausser, 1975); 19% of the probes were directive, introducing the likelihood of response bias. Rustemeyer (1977) finds that in mock interviews CPS interviewers— regardless of experience—asked only about 60% of the questions exactly as they were worded. That SRC and CPS professionals so frequently deviated from the format and wording of survey questions is more disturbing because these two interviewing staffs have very good reputations. Other survey field staffs probably have even higher error rates.

In some ways, experienced CPS interviewers were more careless than inexperienced interviewers—they were more likely to alter the scope of questions, to change the sequence of questions, and to probe directively. Perhaps the reason that experience does not always enhance interviewer performance is that these errors are extremely difficult to detect. Rustemeyer (1977) estimates that only 19% of all interviewer errors found in her study could have been detected in an office review. Therefore, there can be little feedback provided to interviewers concerning these "invisible" errors, and little incentive for interviewers to improve performance. These findings imply that office edits and reviews are not sufficient to ensure low interviewer error rates. That an experienced interviewer's error rate is modestly (although significantly) correlated with her or his noninterview rate ($r = .25$; see Rustemeyer, 1977) may provide a rough guide to help field supervisors identify error-prone interviewers. In general, however, Rustemeyer's study suggests that it is almost impossible to detect and control many serious interviewer errors without systematic, direct observation of the interviewer's performance. Cannell *et al.* (1975) have devised a method for evaluating interviewer performance from tape recordings of household interviews. It would be desirable if survey organizations routinely tested interviewers and reported error rates. Such data would provide useful feedback to the interviewers, and it could be used to improve interviewer training and questionnaire construction and to evaluate overall interviewing quality for different survey organizations. Information on interviewer error rates (both aggregated and question specific) would be extremely valuable to investigators who want to know how much confidence to place in survey data and estimates of trends based on them.

INTERVIEWER CHARACTERISTICS

Interviewer characteristics, such as race, sex, and age, have variable effects on response rates and the content of responses obtained in interviews. The effect of interviewer's race on responses is well documented (e.g., see Schuman & Converse, 1971). Schuman (1974) concludes that two types of items are susceptible to race of interviewer effects: items dealing with antiwhite sentiments, and nonracial political items that tap symbolic allegiance to the polity. On racial items, blacks are less likely to express antiwhite sentiments to white interviewers than to black interviewers. Sudman and Bradburn (1974, p. 137) conclude that the race of the interviewer affects responses only for questions pertaining to race. Other interviewer characteristics, such as sex, age, whether the interviewer is a college student, and social class may also affect responses, depending on the question topic.

The demographic composition of field staffs is variable among survey organizations and changes over time. Bailar and Lanphier (1978) find in their pilot study of surveys that most interviewers are female and work part time; some organizations rely almost exclusively on college students. The most important change in the composition of field staffs has been the dramatic increase in reliance upon black interviewers since the mid-1960s. Early surveys relied exclusively on white interviewers to interview both white and black respondents, whereas most survey organizations currently make some attempt to match race of interviewer and race of respondent. Other substantial changes in the composition of field staffs have occurred. For example, the SRC field staff has grown older and more predominantly female over time, reflecting a declining reliance on graduate student interviewers. From 1950 to 1977 the proportion of males declined from .31 to .03, and the proportion under 34 declined from .23 in 1958 to .13 in 1977 (John Scott, personal communication).

These changes may be associated with changes in aggregate rates of interviewer errors. Rustemeyer (1977) finds that among experienced CPS interviewers, age (but not education) is positively correlated with error rate. If this result holds generally, it means that (other things equal) error rates are higher for older interviewing staffs than for younger ones.

Changes in the composition of interviewing staffs may seriously affect the comparability of survey results over time. Because interviewer characteristics influence responses, shifts in field staff composition may result in artifactual changes in attitudes. The 1971 Detroit Area Study illustrates the effects of and a possible solution to the problem of change in racial composition of interviewing staffs.

Early DAS surveys in which white interviewers interviewed black respondents were replicated in 1971 using both black and white interviewers. In order to assess and control for the effects of changes in field staff over time, sample blocks estimated to be at least 15% black were randomly assigned to black or white interviewers. The results of the experimental manipulation of race of interviewer indicate that the effects upon some items are substantial. An example of a nonracial, nonpolitical item that is subject to a complex race of interviewer effect is analyzed by Fischer (1974). Black respondents in 1971 were more likely to agree with a Srole measure of anomia when the interviewer was white than when she was black.[14] Table 16.7 shows the level of agreement with the item among three birth cohorts of black respondents in 4 years, with 1971 data presented separately for black and white interviewers.

The effect of interviewer's race depends on the respondent's age. Young black respondents do not respond differently to black and white interviewers, but older black respondents are far more likely to agree with white interviewers than with black interviewers. (In 1971, the three-way interaction between respondent's age, interviewer's race, and response is statistically significant at the .05 level.) This result may be due to changing patterns of black–white relations, with younger blacks less deferential to whites than older blacks. The evidence is consistent with Glenn's (1974, p. I–27) speculation that the race of interviewer effect has declined over time as race relations have changed. However, it should be noted that evidence presented by Schuman and Converse (1971) and Hatchett and Schuman (1975–76) suggests no effect of respondent's age on the race of interviewer effect.

The data in Table 16.7 imply that the inferences one draws about the magnitude of the increase in anomia among blacks, about patterns of cohort change, and about the relationship between age and anomia in 1971 depend on whether comparisons are based on results obtained by black or white interviewers. Comparison of baseline results with 1971 results obtained by white interviewers indicates a substantial increase in anomia in all cohorts; age and anomia are not strongly related in 1971. Assessment of trends using 1971 data obtained by black interviewers reveals a much smaller overall increase in anomia, with anomia actually declining in the oldest cohort; in 1971 age and anomia are negatively related. The former comparison, which holds constant interviewer's race by excluding data obtained by black interviewers, is the more appropriate basis for inferring trends. Substantive conclusions about patterns of change would have been seriously in error had the analysis included noncomparable data obtained in 1971 by black interviewers. This particular example illustrates the result of confounding the effects of time and cohort with the effects of interviewer's race. Schuman (1974) speculates that the same source of noncomparability may impair SRC analyses of trends: "it is my guess that

---

[14] For three of five Srole anomia measures, blacks were more likely to agree with interviewers of their own race, which casts some doubt on an interpretation of agreement as deference to white interviewers. Only the difference reported here was statistically significant, however.

TABLE 16.7
Percentage Agreeing that "It's Hardly Fair to Bring Children into the World the Way Things Look for the Future" among Detroit Blacks in 4 Years[a]

Birthdate	Age in February 1956	Age in February 1971	Survey year			1971	
			1956	1958	1959	White interviewer	Black interviewer
March 1935–February 1950	<21	21–35	—	—	—	56 (61)	49 (87)
March 1921–February 1935	21–34	36–49	19 (57)	27 (39)	33 (15)	50 (42)	36 (75)
March 1906–February 1921	35–49	50–64	30 (44)	28 (35)	29 (17)	56 (39)	31 (49)
Before March 1906	50+	65+	44 (32)	28 (21)	46 (13)	67 (12)	11 (18)
Total			29 (133)	27 (95)	36 (45)	55 (154)	38 (229)

[a] From independent household surveys conducted by the Detroit Area Study, The University of Michigan in 1956, 1958, 1959, and 1971. N's are given in parentheses. Data are analyzed by Fischer (1974).

the very sharp rise in black political alienation reported in trend analysis based on [1972] and earlier election studies . . . is in part (though not by any means entirely) an artifact of changing interviewer composition [p. 7].''

The solution to noncomparable field staffs in the 1950s and 1971 was to hold constant the effects of interviewer's race by excluding black respondents who were interviewed by black interviewers in 1971 (but only if responses were affected by interviewer's race). The validity of this simple strategy rests on the assumption that the race of interviewer effect remained constant from the 1950s to 1971. As we have noted, it is likely that blacks have changed in the way they respond to white interviewers, perhaps by becoming less deferential. To the extent that this is true, the validity of comparisons over time is reduced in a way that would be difficult to assess, since true attitude change is confounded with change in the biasing effect of interviewer's race. If the race of interviewer effect interacts with time, then, as Schuman (1974) notes, ''nothing short of repeated experimental manipulations will allow us to avoid errors in conclusions about attitude change [p. 7].'' In addition, the solution offered here to control for the effects of changes in race of interviewers ignores the possible effects of changes in the sex and age composition of interviewing staffs.

INTERVIEW EFFECTS

Survey questions require respondents to make inferences, formulate judgments and preferences, and to supply information and facts about themselves. The way a question is asked—the wording, order, and context of the question, the response alternatives offered—and the interviewer's treatment of uncertain, vague, or ambivalent answers can affect responses and thus are potential sources of noncomparability among surveys.

Imputing Meaning to the Question. In order to formulate a response, the respondent must impute meaning to the question. Survey questions vary considerably in the extent to which they constrain respondents' interpretations of them. For example, when asked *As far as the people running the scientific community are concerned, would you say you have a great deal of confidence, only some confidence, or hardly any confidence at all in them?*, the respondent must decide to whom the question refers and what it means to have ''confidence'' in these people. Smith (1981) finds that respondents in the General Social Survey vary considerably in the meanings they attribute to this and other survey questions. For example, when respondents were asked what particular people or group they had in mind when asked about ''the people running the scientific community,'' over a third said they had no referent in mind; others mentioned particular fields in science, such as space, medicine, atomic energy, and electricity. The frame of reference thus may be quite variable, or entirely inappropriate, as for the 2% of respondents who thought that *scientific community* meant their own local community. The respondent's frame of reference was associated with differences in expressed evaluations. For example, confidence in ''the people running the scientific community'' was greater among respondents who had no referent in mind, or who thought of the space program, than among respondents with other referents in mind (Smith, 1981).

Respondents also varied in how they interpreted *confidence*. Smith (1981) finds that respondents offered four broad interpretations of what it means to have confidence in leaders: Leaders can be trusted; leaders are competent; leaders act in the common good; or leaders are carrying out policies that the respondent personally favors. The four interpretations of *confidence* were relatively distinct, since only 12% of respondents offered multiple or overlapping definitions. In this case, however, Smith (1981) finds few differences in confidence evaluations according to a respondent's definition of *confidence*.

Accurate and consistent reporting is facilitated when survey questions are specifically defined, have concrete referents, and do not require complex or ambiguous inferences on the part of the respondent. When a survey question is ambiguous, the meaning imputed to it may vary a great deal among respondents and may be sensitive to changes in measurement procedures. This is true of objective events as well as subjective phenomena, such as confidence. For example, respondents in a crime survey may be asked to infer whether a "threat" was made, "force" was used or "attempted," and what the "intent" of the other party was. The ambiguity of these inferences makes it difficult to judge whether a person has been victimized or not, allowing great latitude for the classification of incidents by interviewers and respondents. Clarren and Schwartz (1976) assert that "the upper bound for the number of 'crimes' that could be elicited is limited only by the persistence of the interviewers and the patience of the respondent [p. 129]." They recommend that crimes be defined in terms of specific behaviors or incidents that are not subject to varying interpretations by interviewers or respondents. Auto theft is defined more specifically than assault, which may be why estimates of victimization by auto theft appear to be less affected by the conditions of measurement and more highly and consistently correlated with UCR estimates than assault estimates.[15] It is noteworthy that in both the Cincinnati surveys of victimization (Clarren & Schwartz, 1976) and the interviewer variance study (Bailey *et al.*, 1978), the estimates of victimization by some forms of assault were more vulnerable to the effects of procedural differences than were estimates of auto theft. Interviewers as well as respondents have different views of crime, which may contribute to the variability in estimates of crimes such as assault. Bailey *et al.* (1978) speculate that "perhaps the variability among interviewers reflects the manner in which they view assaultive violence involving acquaintances or relatives and friends [p. 21]."

The meaning that respondents impute to a question is obviously influenced by the wording of the question, and rather subtle changes in wording can dramatically alter response distributions. For example, Schuman and Presser (1977) report that in 1974, 72% of Americans supported freedom of speech

---

[15] Even in the case of auto theft, it may be difficult to distinguish joy-riding from auto theft, since the difference rests on the intent of the thief.

when asked *Do you think the United States should forbid public speeches against democracy?* but that only 56% did so when the word *allow* replaced *forbid* in the question. Moreover, the effect of question wording was greater for respondents low in schooling than for those who had been to college. Although civil libertarian sentiments were positively related to education for both wordings, one would draw different conclusions about the strength of the relationship depending on the wording of the question.

Schuman and Presser (1977) find that, in this particular case, the effect of the two alternative question wordings remained remarkably invariant from 1940 to 1974, despite a substantial shift in responses to both forms of the question. However, the invariance of wording effects may not always hold: The meaning imputed to a particular question may change even if the wording does not. An example is provided by Fischer (1974). Comparable measurements of five items devised as a scale of anomia were obtained in the 1950s and in 1971. Interpretations of two items concerning optimism about the future of children evidently changed, because the two items became more associated with each other, and less associated with other measures of anomia. The changing pattern of associations possibly reflected the growing awareness of the problems of overpopulation, so that items referring to children tapped attitudes in this domain as well as feelings of anomia. In this case, change in the meaning of individual items influenced the measurement properties of the scale. Because the pattern of associations changed, the items were not combined as a scale but were analyzed separately.

This example suggests that questions are likely to change in meaning as words or phrases lose or acquire symbolic significance. For example, questions that refer to *colored people* or *welfare* do not mean the same thing in the 1970s as they did in the 1950s.

Changes in question meaning and frame of reference may also reflect true population change. Beverly Duncan (personal communication) notes that a question about "why most women work" would probably elicit different responses depending on whether the respondent had in mind young, single women or older, married women—*to find a husband* would be a plausible response in the former case, but not in the latter. Since the composition of the female labor force has in fact changed, a change in frame of reference is not artifactual but real. Similarly, Hyman (1972, p. 249) notes that changing American stereotypes of Jews may reflect the rise and decline of Jewish immigration, and changes in the nativeness and geographical and occupational distribution of Jews in the United States.

Question meaning may also vary in different cultural contexts. Subcultural variations in perceptions of crime, for example, may result in differential rates of reporting. Rossi, Waite, Bose, and Berk (1974) find a high level of consensus among Baltimore residents about the relative seriousness of different crimes. However, they find that poorly educated black males disagree most with other subgroups, particularly concerning crimes of violence when victims and offender are known to each other. For example, "beating up an acquaintance" is regarded less seriously by poorly educated black males than by others in the sample. If serious crimes are more likely to be reported to interviewers, differences in the meaning and evaluation of assault may result in a tendency for some blacks to underreport minor and attempted assaults (Penick & Owens, 1976, p. 142).

It seems advisable in a study of change to include probes and follow-up questions to explore respondents' varying interpretations of survey questions. It is probably desirable to investigate more fully and in depth changes in the meanings of the social objects in survey questions—after all, the changing meanings of *colored people* or *welfare* are not artifactual, but reflect real cultural change. At the same time, it seems desirable to attempt to develop questions that are relatively invariant in meaning over time and place. An example of an attempt that may prove fruitful is provided by Biderman (1975). He notes that criminal assaults are difficult to measure because they are defined by "elusive, complex, nonobjective and variant criteria [p. 2]." In an exploratory study, he attempts to overcome the problems of definition by screening respondents who were currently experiencing pain or were handicapped because of an injury; such people were asked if the injury was due to acts of others and whether "negligent, reckless, or hostile" acts were involved (Biderman, 1975). Presumably, respondents are better able to report current, objective events (injuries) than to report crime events, which may be poorly recalled, subject to complex, varying definitions and interpretations, or may be unreported because respondents are reticent about the circumstances leading to the "crime." Biderman (1975) notes that "events which might not come to a subject's mind when his task is recalling 'crimes' thereby become available for exploration by detailed interviewing. . . . The technique also allows consideration of victimizing events that fall in large and shadowy gray areas between the criminal and noncriminal [p. 2]." Although the results of Biderman's study are not definitive, the attempt to measure events in terms of their current and immediate consequences for respondents seems a promising approach, for the measurement of crime and other social phenomena.

Searching for Relevant Information. On the basis of the meaning imputed to the question, the respondent searches for relevant facts in order to formulate a response. For example, a respondent asked *Why do you think most women work?* may think about particular working women he or she knows, general impressions based on portrayals of working women in the mass media, statistics on working women, stereotypes of women as a group, someone else's opinion of female workers, or other information. Clearly, the facts that respondents call to mind—whether they are substantial or sparse, integrated or incoherent, relevant or irrelevant—will influence their answers to the question.

The likelihood that particular sentiments, opinions, or events are recalled and judged relevant by the respondent may be influenced by the phrasing of a survey question, the response alternatives offered or implied, and the topics that precede a particular item. Question wording, form, and context may direct and influence respondents' search for relevant facts by supplying information or criteria of relevance, or by sensitizing or desensitizing respondents to facts or feelings already at their disposal. An obvious illustration of the constraint that the question places upon the search for alternative responses is that respondents are unlikely to give responses other than those explicitly offered as part of the question, even when the proffered categories exclude obvious response options. (See Schuman and Presser 1979b, p. 707, for an example.)[16]

Open versus Closed Questions. The differences in responses elicited by comparable open versus closed questions may arise from differences in the search process evoked by different types of questions. Schuman and Presser (1979b) conducted a careful comparison of open versus closed versions of a question about respondent's preferred characteristics in a job. Their investigation is unusual in that the categories for the closed version of the question were not created on an a priori basis, but were constructed using responses to an open version of the question. The closed and open versions of the question were then compared in a split-ballot experiment in national studies conducted in 1977 and 1978. Despite the attempt to frame closed alternatives that correspond closely to the spontaneous answers given by respondents, the closed and open versions elicited substantially different responses. For example, results in Table 16.8 show that *work that gives a feeling of accomplishment* was far more likely to be mentioned in the closed than in the open form.

Schuman and Presser argue that this difference may occur because interviewers asking the open form failed to probe vague mentions of *satisfaction* or *liking the job* sufficiently, and that many of these responses, if probed, would have fallen into the "accomplishment" category. In fact, in Table 16.8 the percentage of responses to the open question falling in categories 3 and 4 sums to 30%, which is almost identical to the percentage of respondents who chose category 3 in response to the closed question.

Other differences in the response distribution for the two forms of the question may occur because the question as it is phrased directs respondents to think about positive attributes of jobs (e.g., high pay, creative work), and not about negative attributes that by their absence make a job more desirable (e.g., being free from interference, no chance of being fired). These latter characteristics may not come to mind readily, given the way the question is asked, unless they are explicitly offered as possible responses, as they are in the closed version of the question. This hypothesis is consistent with the finding that positive attributes are mentioned with approximately equal frequency for both versions of the question (67% for the open versus 64% for the closed), whereas nonnegative attributes are more likely to be mentioned in the closed (32%) then in the open (15%) question.

---

[16] A major exception is the response *don't know*. A substantial proportion of respondents—up to 63% in an example offered by Schuman and Presser (1979b)—volunteer that they do not know even when it is not offered as an explicit alternative. Even in this case, however, many (about 20%) more respondents give *don't know* as a response when it is offered as an option than when it is not.

TABLE 16.8

Response Distributions for an Open versus Closed Version of a Question on Work Values[a]

This next question is on the subject of work. People look for different things in a job. What [which one of the following five things] would you most prefer in a job?

	Closed	Open
Presence of positive attributes		
1. WORK THAT PAYS WELL	13%	17%
2. WORK THAT IS PLEASANT AND WHERE OTHER PEOPLE ARE NICE TO WORK WITH	20	14
3. WORK THAT GIVES A FEELING OF ACCOMPLISHMENT	31	14
4. Satisfaction–liking the job (nonspecific answers)	[b]	16
5. Other positive attributes: opportunity for advancement; good physical working conditions; benefits	[b]	6
Absence of negative attributes		
6. WORK WHERE THERE IS NOT TOO MUCH SUPERVISION AND YOU MAKE MOST DECISIONS YOURSELF	12	5
7. WORK THAT IS STEADY WITH LITTLE CHANCE OF BEING LAID OFF	20	8
8. Short hours and lots of free time	[b]	2
Residual responses (including *don't know*, other; not ascertained, and mention of a specific job)	4	18
Total	100%	100%
N	1194	1153

[a] From Schuman and Presser (1979b, Table 4). Reprinted by permission.
[b] Categories 4, 5, and 8 were not included in the closed question.

Schuman and Presser's (1979b) analysis of open versus closed questions has important implications for the measurement of change. Generally, we assume that comparability over time requires the replication of the exact wording of questions and response alternatives in surveys conducted at different points in time. Their findings suggest that precise replication will not ensure comparable findings if closed alternatives that captured respondents' frame of reference at an earlier time do not represent respondents' views at a later point. Change may not be detected if respondents are led to adopt an outdated and inappropriate frame of reference implied by a question and its response alternatives. Unfortunately, respondents are all too willing to accommodate researchers' a priori notions of what responses are probable, interesting, or legitimate.

One might conclude that change can only be detected by asking questions that do not impose a particular set of response alternatives on respondents. However, as we see later, the classification of open-ended material creates its own problems. Schuman and Presser (1979b) also note the disadvantages of open questions which arise from "vagueness of expression by respondents, frequent failures to probe adequately by interviewers, and occasional misunderstandings by coders [p. 704]." In the particular example just cited, they conclude that "while open questions seem essential for obtaining the frame of reference of respondents and for wording alternatives appropriately, once this is done we are unable to find any compelling reason to keep the open form [p. 704].'' This advice appears sound, but leaves unanswered the question of how one may properly replicate a question—open or closed—if respondents' frames of reference change over time.

Contextual Effects. Prior topics and questions in a survey can influence answers to subsequent questions. Earlier questions can call to mind a general frame of reference or particular experiences that remain salient when later questions are asked. For example, the number of victimization incidents reported by respondents in the National Crime Survey is influenced by prior questions. A split-ballot experiment shows that when NCS victimization questions were preceded by a lengthy series of questions on attitudes toward crime, significantly more incidents were reported (Cowan, Murphy, & Wiener, 1978; Gibson, Shapiro, Murphy, & Stanko, 1978). The additional questions evidently stimulated respondents' memories, leading them to recall more incidents of crime. (It is also possible that asking the attitude questions prior to the factual questions led respondents to adopt looser, more liberal criteria for judging what sorts of incidents should be reported.) The effect on reporting was selective: Only less serious crimes showed an increase, and serious crimes were somewhat less likely to be reported to interviewers when preceded by the attitude supplement (Cowan *et al.*, 1978).

A second type of context effect can occur if respondents try to answer survey questions consistently. Giving a response to a question represents a verbal commitment that can constrain answers to later questions. An especially dramatic example is analyzed by Schuman and Presser (1981). Respondents who were asked, *Do you think the United States should let Communist newspaper reporters from other countries come in here and send back to their papers the news as they see it?* were much more likely to agree if they had first answered a question about allowing American reporters into Communist countries. The interpretation is that respondents are more favorable to American reporters than to Communist ones, but also feel bound by their belief in fair play to give the same rights to American and Communist reporters. For this reason, the answer to whichever question is asked first constrains an answer to the second question.

Although the examples of context effects given here are readily interpretable, many others are not. (See Schuman and Presser, 1981, for a more complete discussion of types and examples of context effects.) Unfortunately, it is not always possible to predict when context effects will be found, or to explain why they occur. The potential bias due to the context created by preceding questions is especially problematic in a study of trends. Unless a questionnaire is replicated in its entirety (which is rarely done), one cannot rule out the chance that estimates of change are contaminated by contextual bias.

It is still not possible to say definitively whether, and how, an investigator can replicate the context in which a question appeared without including all of the questions that preceded it in an original baseline study. What might seem to be a plausible, though partial, solution to the problem—separating items that might contaminate each other by interspersing questions on unrelated topics—may not help. Context and order effects apparently can occur even when items are widely separated in a questionnaire (for examples, see Schuman & Presser, 1981, p. 39; Schuman, Kalton, & Ludwig, 1983).

Split-ballot experiments can be conducted to test hypotheses about suspected context effects (see e.g., Smith, 1979). However, split-ballot experimentation can leave one uncertain about the magnitude and direction of change, as in the case of the American/Communist reporters items. The split-ballot experiment conducted by Schuman and Presser (1981) in 1980 replicated a 1948 experiment. Although an order effect was found in both experiments, the effect changed over time. This meant that the two contexts, even when held constant, lead to different conclusions about change. When the Communist reporters item is asked first, there is an increase of 18% between 1948 and 1980 in tolerance of Communist reporters. When the American reporters item is asked first, there is essentially no change (Schuman & Presser, 1981, pp. 28–29). An interpretation of trends in these items must take into account the changing effect of the context in which they are asked. It is appropriate to interpret the change in the artifact as one aspect of the trend, rather than to treat it as a separate "methodological" finding with no substantive import (see Schuman, 1982).

Formulating a Judgment. Finally, the respondent must integrate the information in order to formulate a response—whether a statement of belief, attitude, preference, or intention. Obviously, respondents vary greatly in the amount and quality of information they bring to bear in formulating an answer to a survey question (see Converse, 1970). In addition, they vary both in the extent to which they have already formed opinions and in their ability to form meaningful responses "on the spot" when questioned by the interviewer. How people answer questions in surveys is closely related to how they form judgments in general. The latter topic is the subject of extensive research in psychology. This evidence is not reviewed here, although it is useful to illustrate how some of the findings may contribute to an understanding of the sources of response error and invalidity, especially as they affect estimates of change.

Implicitly, we often assume that when respondents are asked a question, they refer to their own thoughts and feelings to arrive at a statement of personal preference, belief, or motive. However, introspection may be quite limited, and respondents may use entirely different strategies to formulate responses. For example, psychological evidence suggests that subjects have little insight into the causes of their judgments or behavior; when asked why they acted as they did, they resort to implicit causal theories that may be quite inaccurate (Nisbett & Bellows, 1977; Nisbett & Wilson, 1977). Slovic and Lichtenstein (1971) review evidence suggesting that subjects tend to overestimate the complexity of their own judgments. Subjects generally believe that they have considered more factors than they have, and "apparently are quite unaware of the extent to which their judgments can be predicted by only a few cues [p. 684]." The more complex the question, and the more information a person has to integrate to formulate an answer, the more likely a respondent is to ignore relevant information in formulating a response, and the greater the error that characterizes the final judgment. (See Slovic & Lichtenstein, 1971.) This suggests that data from survey questions that require complex inferences or judgments may be more unreliable and less valid than data from questions requiring simpler judgments.

Even when respondents' reports are valid, they may not be stable over time. Tversky and Kahneman (1974) argue that subjective inferences are based on various heuristics, such as availability. "A person is said to employ the availability heuristic whenever he estimates frequency or probability by the ease with which instances or associations can be brought to mind. . . . For example, one may assess the divorce rate in a given community by recalling divorces among one's acquaintances [Tversky & Kahneman, 1973, p. 208]." The ease of retrieval is influenced by such factors as the recency and saliency of past occurrences as well as their actual frequency. (For evidence on the extreme recency bias that affects recall of past events, see Biderman and Lynch, 1981.) In addition, the evidence suggests that people do not consider the reliability of information when drawing inferences; subjects draw about the same inferences from a sample of 10 events as from a sample of 1000 (Tversky & Kahneman, 1974).

Together, these experimental findings imply that subjective inferences may be quite sensitive to the availability of relevant instances, both at the individual and aggregate levels. Well-publicized instances of human kindness or cruelty, for example, may result in shifts in collective judgments about whether or not "most people" can be trusted. In fact, experimental evidence demonstrates that subjects who overhear a radio newscast portraying a single altruistic act subsequently view people in general more positively and are more likely to help a stranger than subjects exposed to newscasts involving acts of human malice, harmful or beneficial acts of nature, or subjects not exposed to any newscast. Even though it involved the actions of a single individual, the newscast influenced subjects' inferences about social norms and human nature (Hornstein, LaKind, Frankel, & Manne, 1975).[17]

The fact that the induced shift in views of human nature had behavioral consequences suggests that the change was real, although it might have been quite short lived. Indeed, Smith (1981) and Turner and Krauss (1978) find rapid and substantial shifts in public confidence in institutions. Such changes may reflect media coverage of changing events and people. It is also possible that the complexity of the judgment required to assess confidence in a group or institution contributes to the unreliability of measurements over time.

This section has touched on just a few of the psychological and other factors that may influence the validity of respondents' answers to survey ques-

---

[17] Other experimental evidence that "hearing is believing" is provided by Hasher, Goldstein, and Toppino (1977), who find that subjects' assessments of the truth of plausible statements are influenced by the number of occasions they hear the assertion made. The effect of frequency of occurrence on believability held regardless of the actual truth or falsity of the statement.

tions. The need for a comprehensive theory of response formulation is indicated by two related problems characterizing the literature on survey measurement artifacts. The first is that empirical results are often difficult to explain, given the present level of knowledge. Artifactual differences do not materialize when or in the form expected; when they do occur, they are complex and resist ad hoc, intuitive explanations. (See Duncan & Schuman, 1976, for an intricate example.) A related problem is that in many cases traditional assumptions about the nature and meaning of survey responses, and the errors characterizing them, may be faulty, or do not hold generally.

For example, it has been assumed that variations in question wording, order, and context may affect univariate response distributions, but not associations among items. Schuman and Presser (1977) refer to this as the assumption of "form-resistant correlations." However, in some cases variations in wording and order affect both associations among items and univariate distributions. Thus, it cannot be assumed that substantive conclusions about the causes and effects of a phenomenon are unaffected by the design of questions and questionnaires.

A second assumption that may not hold generally is that people who are uneducated or uninformed are more affected by variations in format than educated, knowledgeable respondents. Turner (1981) finds that the effect of context on occupational prestige ratings is most pronounced for the highly educated. Presser and Schuman (1980) find that neither education nor information influences the effect on responses of including or excluding a middle alternative. Rather, respondents who feel strongly about the issue are less affected by the presence of a middle position than those who do not. These findings are consistent with Hyman's interpretation of differences between two split-ballot experiments conducted in 1944 and 1948 preelection polls (Mosteller, Hyman, McCarthy, Marks, & Truman, 1949, p. 170). He argues that when candidate preferences are unstable (as in the 1948 presidential election) the order in which candidates are listed will influence poll results. When voter preferences are firm (as in 1944), variation in the order of presentation has no effect on the results.

A third possibly false assumption is that encouraging respondents with vague or uncertain opinions to respond to survey questions will necessarily increase random error and hence reduce intercorrelations among items. In one case, Schuman and Presser (1979a) hypothesize that the respondents affected by whether or not a "no opinion" response is explicitly offered (a group they label "floaters") are people with general attitude dispositions but no opinions on the specific issue asked about. When encouraged to, floaters express *no opinion*, but otherwise base responses on the general disposition (a trusting or distrusting attitude). Thus floaters may provide more consistent (i.e., more or less trusting) answers to rather disparate items than people with firmer and more specific opinions, so that their inclusion increases intercorrelations among items. In another case, however, Schuman and Presser's results are more consistent with the traditional assumption that filtering selects respondents with the most interconnected attitudes and therefore increases correlations.

Artifactual variations in the size of the "middle" or no opinion categories apparently do not influence substantive conclusions about trends. Offering a middle alternative in a forced-choice attitude item typically increases the percentage of respondents choosing that alternative by about 10–15% (Presser & Schuman, 1980). Offering *don't know* or *no opinion* as explicit alternatives leads to a modal increase in that category of about 20–25% (Schuman & Presser, 1979a). Nevertheless, the relative proportions in substantive categories tend to be unaffected by the presence or absence of an explicit no opinion category (Schuman & Presser, 1979a) or a middle position on a forced-choice attitude item (Presser & Schuman, 1980). In both cases, simply excluding *no opinion* or the middle alternative achieves comparability. These results are encouraging for the estimation of trends, and suggest that no opinion and other residual categories can be routinely excluded when plotting trend lines.[18] These results indicate that filtering out respondents who hold no opinion does not affect the distribution of substantive response but can affect interrelations among items. This implies that surveys that vary in the use of filter questions may provide comparable data for some purposes (e.g., monitoring trends) and not others (e.g., measuring changes in correlations among items).

The proportion choosing *don't know* is sensitive not only to response alternatives and cues provided in the question, but to interviewing instructions to probe noncommittal responses. An analysis of responses given before and after follow-up probes shows that probing uncertain respondents does not increase random error, but in some cases significantly alters univariate response distributions and associations between items (Martin, 1980).[19] It is possible, therefore, that survey results may not be comparable when the instructions given to interviewers concerning probing vary from one survey to the next. In fact, organizational differences in survey questions, and in the extent to which "no opinion" responses are discouraged, result in systematic differences between survey organizations in the size of the "no opinion" category (Converse, 1976–77; Smith, 1978). Harris polls typically elicit more "no opinions" than Gallup polls, for example. Such differences in organizational practices may reduce the comparability of results obtained by different survey organizations.

Finally, the structure of the interview may influence responses in another way that might easily be ignored by investigators. Frequently, a long series of questions is made contingent on the response to an earlier question: For example, if the respondent reports a health problem or an incident of victimization, a series of detailed questions about the incident may follow. This may create an incentive—for interviewers and respondents alike—not to report the incidents in order to shorten the interview. For example, Gibson et al. (1978) report that when a special supplement of questions about recent acute conditions was

---

[18] Of course, the trend in "no opinion" may itself be of interest. If so, the investigator should be certain that different surveys are comparable in their treatment of noncommittal and ambiguous responses.

[19] However, it should be noted that the effects of probing found by Martin (1980) were neither pervasive nor large, so that it made little actual difference whether responses to probes were included or excluded from that particular analysis.

added to the Health Interview Survey, reports of such conditions dropped by 20%, then returned to previous levels when the supplement was dropped from the interview. Similarly, when a supplement of some 60 questions to be asked of discouraged workers (who are not in the labor force but want or intend to look for work) was added to the Current Population Survey, there were substantial and atypical changes in labor force classification: The number of classified as discouraged workers dropped. This occurred even though labor force classification was determined early in the interview and interviewers were instructed not to change it.

The findings reported by Gibson *et al.* (1978) strongly suggest that an investigator who wishes to monitor trends should not inadvertently change the amount of time associated with accurate reporting. If the structure of the interview is changed so that reporting a particular condition becomes much cheaper or more costly in time, the investigator may observe an entirely artifactual increase or decrease in such conditions.

METHOD OF DATA COLLECTION: TELEPHONE VERSUS PERSONAL INTERVIEWS

Differences in the method of data collection may affect population coverage, respondents' willingness to be interviewed, and the content of the responses. Therefore, differences in method of data collection may affect the comparability of surveys over time. This potential source of noncomparability is important, because many survey organizations increasingly conduct interviews by telephone rather than in person. Groves and Kahn (1979) found some differences in coverage in their comparison of telephone and personal interviews. In 1970, 13% of U.S. households did not have telephones, rendering them inaccessible for a telephone survey. Households without phones tend disproportionately to be rural, single adult households in rental dwellings, occupied by low-income blacks; thus, people with these characteristics are underrepresented in telephone surveys. On the other hand, some types of dwellings and respondents are more accessible by telephone than in person. For example, residents of multiunit structures are better represented in telephone surveys than in personal interview surveys. Respondents in their telephone survey tended to be younger than respondents in the personal interview survey.

Differences in the method of data collection affect the nature and context of the interaction between respondent and interviewer, and may influence response content. The most obvious difference between telephone and personal interviews is that on the telephone the respondent and interviewer cannot see each other. This implies that visual aids (such as show cards) that can be provided to respondents in face-to-face interviews cannot be used in telephone interviews. Groves (1979) finds different distributions on "feeling thermometer" scales by telephone and in person. Telephone respondents tend to give answers divisible by 10, whereas respondents in personal interviews tend to give points on the scale that are labeled on the show card.

The fact that the respondent cannot see the interviewer implies that interviewer characteristics—including race, age, and social status—are less certain, although the interviewer's voice may provide some clues. The respondent's lack of knowledge about the interviewer's personal traits may account for the greater unease in telephone interviews. Telephone surveys have higher rates of breakoffs and missing data than personal surveys (Groves & Kahn, 1979). Telephone respondents are more likely to report unease about discussing sensitive topics (such as financial matters and political opinions), and to say they would prefer some other mode of interviewing, than respondents interviewed in person.

In the absence of clearcut cues about the interviewer's identity, telephone respondents may be more prone to give "safe" answers which would not offend anybody. This possibility is suggested by Groves and Kahn's (1979) finding that telephone respondents are more likely to advocate open housing for blacks than are personal interview respondents. They also find that blacks are more likely to report themselves as conservative and whites to call themselves liberal on the telephone than in person.

One might infer that respondents are more likely to give socially desirable answers when interviewed by telephone. However, other evidence does not support this conclusion. Colombotos (1965) finds no significant difference in the number of socially desirable answers given in personal and telephone interviews in a survey of physicians. In some cases, respondents appear more likely to report sensitive information on the telephone than in person. Bushery, Cowan, and Murphy (1978) find that telephone interviews elicit significantly more reports of aggravated assaults by nonstrangers than the standard National Crime Survey procedure,[20] but only for whites and females; blacks and males are more likely to report such incidents in personal interviews.[21] Although the authors do not interpret this finding, one might speculate that the privacy afforded by the telephone encourages respondents (especially females) to report violent incidents involving friends and relatives that might be risky to discuss openly within possible earshot of other household members.[22] Similarly, Hochstim (1967) finds that women are more likely to report that they drink alcohol when interviewed by telephone than in person.

[20] Bushery et al. (1978) and Turner (1977) compare results obtained from a control group interviewed according to the standard National Crime Survey procedure (which employs both telephone and personal interviewing) with two experimental groups in which face-to-face and telephone interviews, respectively, are maximized. In the control group, 78% of the interviews were in person and 22% by phone; comparable figures are 96% and 4%, respectively, for the "maximum personal visit" group, and 20% and 80% for the "maximum telephone" group. Interviews were permitted by other than the method assigned for the group if respondents could not or would not be interviewed by that method.

[21] The authors do not explain the perplexing result that all groups report this crime more frequently in the two experimental groups than in the control group, which employed both personal and telephone interviews. Therefore, these reported results should be interpreted with caution.

[22] Dodge and Lentzner (1978) note that "many [victims of domestic violence], particularly those who continue to live under the threat of attack, are too embarrassed or frightened to talk about the problem in their own home [p. 12]."

In other cases, evidence suggests that reporting is less complete and accurate by telephone. Groves and Kahn (1979) find that telephone respondents name fewer important problems facing the country than respondents in personal interviews. Turner (1977) and Bushery et al. (1978) conclude that generally lower rates of victimization are reported by telephone than in person, particularly for males and for some crimes. However, only one of 13 major crime categories (personal theft) shows a statistically significant difference by interviewing method. Bushery et al. (1978) argue that the "effectiveness of telephone interviewing depends in large part on the information required from the respondent [p. 19]." If the interview requires detailed information, as the National Crime Survey does, telephone interviews may obtain less adequate or complete information.

Even when levels of reporting do not differ according to interviewing method, information obtained by telephone may be subject to higher rates of error. Larsen's (1952) validation of respondent reports using external checks indicates that more valid data were obtained in person than by telephone. Bailar and Woltman (1978) find no effect of interviewing method on mean levels of reporting in the Current Medicare Survey, but find higher variances in the telephone survey.

Some of the results reported above suggest that discomfort on the telephone may be greater for some people (such as men and blacks) than others. If so, the interviewing method may have different effects depending on the respondent's characteristics. Groves and Kahn (1979) find some evidence consistent with this possibility, although they note that their effort to identify subgroups that exhibit differential method effects was largely unsuccessful. In general, low-income respondents exhibited larger differences than higher income groups, but differences were small. An exception was the tendency to report fewer problems facing the country by telephone, which occurred disproportionately among high-income, young respondents. Groves (1979) finds that racial comparisons are sometimes affected by mode of interviewing (as discussed), and Bushery et al. (1978) report similar findings. They find that in the telephone group, blacks and whites report crimes of violence at the same rates. In the control group (standard NCS procedure) blacks report crimes of violence at a rate 38% higher than the rate for whites, with the difference in rates increasing to 77% in the personal interview group. The differences were not statistically significant, however.

In the absence of more complete data, it is difficult at this point to draw firm conclusions about the effect of interviewing method upon the results obtained in surveys. It seems likely, as Groves and Kahn conclude, that different types of questions are affected in different ways by interviewing method. It also seems likely that subgroups respond differently to different interviewing methods, although evidence to date suggests that any differential effects are not very great. Nevertheless, caution should be exercised when comparing results from surveys that differ in interviewing method.

Coding and Classification Procedures

Information supplied by the respondent is classified by the interviewer, coder, or analyst. Comparability over time generally requires replication of classification and coding procedures. The most difficult procedures to standardize and replicate are those used to code responses to open-ended questions which do not require respondents to choose among fixed alternatives. Even when formal codes are developed, the ambiguity and variety of the material usually require that additional conventions be adopted to facilitate consistent coding. If they are unwritten and informal, coding conventions are almost impossible to replicate. Moreover, it is impossible to assess from the written codes the extent to which informal rules governed the coding process. Unwritten rules are especially likely to prevail when coding staffs are small. Bailar and Lanphier (1978) note that many survey organizations have only a few coders; one coder may code all responses to one question, "This reduces or avoids variability among coders, but many increase coder biases quite markedly [p. 84]."

An example illustrates the sensitivity of the results to small variations in coding procedures. The 1971 Detroit Area Study replicated a number of open-ended questions from the 1950s. Because of investigators' concerns about the comparability of coding operations in the 1950s and 1971, the original interviews (which fortunately had been preserved) were recoded in 1971 using original codes. Schuman's (1974) summary of the findings indicates that concerns about the comparability of coding were justified. One item showed an apparent increase from 1953 to 1971 in the immediacy with which mothers claim they would respond to a crying child. Recoding the original 1953 interviews revealed that the difference was due largely to differences in the use of the 1953 codes by 1953 and 1971 coders. What appeared to be a striking change in childrearing practice was an artifact of coding procedures. Using data from the same study, Duncan and Evers (1975) find that 25% of 1956 responses to an open-ended question concerned with attitudes toward women's work were coded inconsistently by 1956 and 1971 coders. They attribute the inconsistencies to a lack of fit between responses and code categories.

Several lessons may be drawn from these examples. First, original coding rules should be carefully documented and retained (including any modifications or rules of thumb developed to handle ambiguous cases) if the survey is to be the baseline for a future replication. The difficulty of faithfully replicating coding procedures leads Schuman (1974) and Schuman and Presser (1979b) to recommend that open-ended material be preserved intact for future recoding in studies of change. Second, when the comparability of classification or coding procedures is in doubt, they should be calibrated by applying the different procedures to the same raw data. In the example given here, this implied a comparison between 1953 and 1971 coders' use of 1953 codes to classify the original 1953 responses. Calibration enables the investigator to determine whether a difference between surveys is due to true change or to differences in classification procedures.

In general, replication requires that classification rules be fully documented, standardized, and calibrated so that measurements are comparable over time and place. These principles are well-illustrated by the occupational coding procedures followed in the 1972 replication of the 1962 Occupational Changes in a Generation study (Hauser & Featherman, 1977). In both years, occupational coding was based on explicit, standardized, detailed listings of job titles (*Alphabetical Index of Industries and Occupations,* U.S. Bureau of the Census, 1971a) and detailed descriptions for job titles (*Dictionary of Occupational Titles,* U.S. Department of Labor, 1977). These documents are applied to code occupation and industry in an explicit series of steps. The standardized conventions for coding occupation to a large extent eliminate ad hoc and subjective judgments that may introduce bias. However, Hauser and Featherman (1977) note that "While most surveys collect similar detail about employment, few study directors specify procedures for the classification and storage of their data which parallel those of the Bureau of the Census [p. 55]." This unfortunate failure to follow standardized census conventions reduces the quality and cross-survey comparability of occupational data.[23]

Reliable classification requires not only a standardized classification scheme, but that adequate and complete information be available to classify. Proper classification is enhanced when interviewers know enough about survey concepts and distinctions to elicit complete and detailed information. Thus, Hauser and Featherman find that interviewers who are familiar with occupational classification rules obtain better and more complete information from respondents.

The years of testing and development invested in census classification of occupation (and related measures of occupational prestige, developed by O. D. Duncan, 1961; Siegel, 1971; and others) have been rewarded by robust measures that evidence suggests are valid over time and place. Hauser and Featherman (1977, p. 52) summarize empirical results that show that rankings of the prestige of occupational titles vary neither as a result of different instructions to coders nor as a function of their socioeconomic characteristics.[24]

---

[23] Standardized instruments to measure variables in addition to occupation have been developed and researched by a number of survey organizations. Publications such as *Basic Background Items for U.S. Household Surveys* (Social Science Research Council, 1975), *Measures of Political Attitudes* (Robinson, Rusk, & Head, 1968), *Measures of Occupational Attitudes and Occupational Characteristics* (Robinson, Athanasiou and Head, 1969), and *Measures of Social Psychological Attitudes* (Robinson & Shaver, 1973) provide useful summaries of many survey instruments and their properties. In addition, published and unpublished reports by the U.S. Census Bureau investigate the properties of measurement instruments. Bibliographies of articles concerned with particular problems in survey methodology are produced by the Survey Methodology Information System, Statistical Research Division, U.S. Bureau of the Census, Washington, D.C. 20233. See also U.S. Bureau of the Census (1974).

[24] But see Turner's (1981) results cited on page 721.

One might surmise from the examples given that behavioral data (such as occupation) are more reliably classified than subjective measures (such as attitudes toward womens' work or childrearing). However, behavioral measures are also vulnerable to bias in classification. An example is the classification in the National Crime Survey of multiple victimizations as discrete incidents or as a series. Interviewers are instructed to classify a group of similar incidents as a series victimization according to the following criteria:

1. The incidents must be very similar in detail.
2. There must be at least three incidents in a series. . . .
3. The respondent must not be able to recall dates and other details of the individual incidents well enough to report them separately . . . reporting incidents as a series is not to be used for your convenience but only if necessary, and as a last resort [Penick & Owens 1976, p. 175].

Respondents are asked to estimate for each series the number of incidents involved and to provide details only for the most recent incident in each series. An evaluation by the National Academy of Sciences (Penick & Owens, 1976) is critical of this procedure, in part because of its vulnerability to classification errors. Depending on the interviewer's persistence and the respondent's ability to recall details, repetitive incidents may be disaggregated into discrete incidents, or discrete incidents may be classed as a series. Interviewers vary in the proportion of events they classify as series, with the proportion generally declining over time as the interviewing staff became more experienced (Penick & Owens, 1976, p. 89).

Bias in the classification of incidents as discrete versus series is important, because the latter are excluded from official estimates of personal victimization.[25] Thus, an increase in the proportion of victimizations classified as discrete would (other things equal) lead to an apparent increase in victimization. Such systematic variation in classification over time and place biases estimates of trends and differences.

This example illustrates two problems. First, the distinction between series and discrete incidents is ambiguous, if not meaningless. In part because of its ambiguity, the distinction is not understood in the same way by all interviewers, leading to systematic variations in classification. Although it would be possible to assess intercoder reliability in classifying discrete versus series incidents, it is difficult or impossible to evaluate consistency among interviewers. One might suggest that interviewers should be instructed to obtain information that is as complete and detailed as is feasible, but not required to classify

[25] Penick and Owens are critical of the exclusion of series victimization from official estimates, arguing that estimated rates of assault would be increased by about 70% if series events were included (1976, p. 134). Series victimizations are also more likely to be violent, although it is possible that respondents remember and report the most violent rather than the most recent incident in a series (1976, p. 121). Penick and Owens argue that exclusion of series incidents underestimates the rate of assault victimization, especially among acquaintances and family members, and especially assaults involving violence.

the information according to abstract or difficult schemes. The latter operation should be carried out under centralized control, in conditions that permit assessment of the reliability and consistency of classification. However, it may be useful to provide interviewers with training in coding schemes and concepts, so that they will obtain information that can be classified.

16.4. CONCLUSIONS AND RECOMMENDATIONS

The evidence presented here shows how essential and how difficult it is to heed Duncan's admonition to "take replication seriously." Clearly, the failure to replicate may result in serious distortions of trend estimates, yet careful replication is not sufficient to ensure that estimates of change are valid. One might reach the pessimistic conclusion that the obstacles that stand in the way of precise replication and comparable measurement are insurmountable. First, replication is difficult or impossible when survey definitions and procedures are not explicit, documented, or subject to control. Second, the effects of many survey operations on survey results are not known, and if known, are not well understood. Even when a source of bias—for example, the race of the interviewer, question wording or context—has been identified, we frequently do not know why or when it is operative. Under some conditions the effects are large, and under others, nonexistent. This suggests that factors that are still unknown condition the effect of survey procedures on survey data. Third, biases change over time and are intricately related to and confounded with the reality we attempt to measure. This implies that true change is confounded with systematic changes in the sources of bias in survey measurement. For example, the effect of the interviewer's race on responses is probably influenced by, and responds to changes in, relations between the races. We have a paradox then: In order to measure changing racial attitudes adequately, we must know how black–white relations and the race of interviewer effect have changed. But since we cannot develop adequate theories in the absence of good data, this seems to leave us in a hopeless quandary.

The quandary is only hopeless, however, if we assume that substantive theory and techniques of measurement can be developed independently. The two endeavors should proceed in a coordinated fashion. Improvements in our understanding of substantive phenomena should be applied to refine measurement concepts and procedures, and/or to estimate biases of existing survey instruments. Once we understand the sources of survey artifacts, we can more adequately estimate and correct for the biases they introduce in measurements of change.

In addition, errors and biases of measurement can provide important clues about the nature of the phenomena we study. Instead of treating them as nuisance factors, measurement artifacts should be regarded as pieces of evidence that can inform social theory. Indeed, when we begin to understand them, survey artifacts may themselves be treated as social indicators. House and Wolf (1978), for example, present evidence that refusal rates are indicators of societal mistrust. Experimental evaluations of the race of interviewer effect, to take another example, represent a unique source of information about how black people actually present themselves to a white versus a black person in one particular social situation—the survey interview. Unlike most surveys, actual rather than self-reported behavior is studied. Unlike most experiments, cross-sectional rather than haphazard samples of blacks are selected. Replication of these experiments over time could provide a valuable measure of change in relations between the races. (See Schuman, 1982, on this point.)

Some practical guidelines for studies of social change, and some recommendations for research that can shed light on sources and magnitude of errors in survey measurements of trends, are offered next in the context of Duncan's recommended strategies for monitoring trends.

Constructing a New Baseline for Future Measurements of Change

Baseline data should be collected in such a fashion that the survey can be replicated in the future. The possibility of future replication is enhanced when the investigator adheres to the following guidelines:

EMPLOY EXPLICIT, STANDARDIZED SURVEY DEFINITIONS AND PROCEDURES

Ideally, survey concepts, measures, definitions, and rules should be sufficiently detailed, concrete, complete, and unambiguous so that they are not susceptible to varying interpretations that may change over time, place, or situation. Complex procedures should be broken down into a series of simple explicit instructions or rules in order to reduce variability in how procedures are applied. Standardization requires centralized monitoring or control to ensure that explicit procedures are actually followed and consistently applied. Differences in the use and interpretation of the rules point to ambiguities, and suggest that more clearcut, explicit criteria are required.

A new baseline is most appropriate when the investigator wishes to learn about phenomena that have not been investigated in previous studies, or when novel approaches to old problems are to be implemented. This usually means that new measurement instruments or techniques are to be developed. Thorough pretesting should precede final data collection to standardize and refine the new measures. It is highly desirable to calibrate new and old instruments by including both in the same survey. As O. D. Duncan (1969) notes, this strategy permits the investigator to splice future series based on the new instrument or procedure to previous series employing the old technique.

The investigator should innovate quite selectively. The utility of a survey for comparative purposes is greatly reduced when nonstandard measures are employed. Before developing new measures, the investigator should assess the suitability of existing instruments (e.g., standard census definitions, questions, and classification procedures for occupation and income). Measures and procedures that have been standardized, refined, and tested in previous surveys are likely to provide data of higher quality, and facilitate comparisons with other surveys.

It is desirable to collect detailed, exact information which can later be categorized in a variety of ways. Information on exact date of birth, for example, permits precise cohort matches with past and future surveys, regardless of how age is categorized in those surveys. Similarly, detailed information on income will permit investigators decades hence to recategorize income according to categories more appropriate at that time.

DOCUMENT ALL SURVEY PROCEDURES

The need for complete and detailed documentation cannot be overemphasized. In particular, the investigator should:

1. Preserve the survey instrument itself.

2. Preserve detailed descriptions of survey definitions, as they are actually applied, including the definitions of *household, housing unit, residency, vacancy,* and the like, and the criteria for respondent eligibility.

3. Keep a record of the design of the sample, including the sources and methods used to construct the sampling frame, and the explicit steps used to select blocks or segments (if appropriate), households, and respondents.

4. Keep a copy of an interviewers' manual[26] that instructs interviewers how to interpret and implement survey rules; how much and what kind of information should be obtained for particular questions; whether noncommittal answers should be probed or accepted; what sort of opening to use; when and how many times to call back; and so on. The manual should be updated as unanticipated problems are resolved and changes are made.

5. Record coding and classification procedures, including any revisions and supplementary instructions; if possible, open-ended material should be preserved for future recoding.

6. Keep a procedural history of the survey describing who did what, when, and how. How and by whom were interviewers recruited, selected, trained, and supervised? How were they paid? What sorts of quality control were exercised? How were codes developed and what procedures were followed in coding? What were the checks on coding reliability? How were the data processed and cleaned? What problems came up, and how were they resolved? A detailed procedural history can prove invaluable when the survey is replicated.

7. Record error rates, calculated according to standard definitions. Rates of coverage, eligibility, and nonresponse (separated into its components: refusals, not-at-home, or respondent absent, etc.) should be reported. Report the number of households selected in the sample, the number visited or called by interviewers, and the outcomes of the visits. The reliability of coding and classification operations should be evaluated and reported.

[26] Interviewers' manuals developed by the Survey Research Center (1976) and the Current Population Survey (U.S. Bureau of Census, 1971b) are excellent models.

Data on survey operations would prove useful in future attempts to replicate the survey and/or to evaluate the extent and effects of changes in survey
practices. For example:

1. Record information on the characteristics of nonrespondents. As
House notes, such data would facilitate analyses of correlates and trends in
response such as those conducted by Steeh (1981), House (1978), and Hawkins
(1977).

2. Record information on the circumstances of interview and noninterview situations, including timing and number of calls made by the interviewer,
duration, date and time of day of the interview, the presence of others, the
identity and characteristics of the interviewer, and so forth. Analysis of such
data can be applied to improve and standardize interviewer practice as well as
to evaluate the extent and effects of systematic bias in such practices.

3. Record more precise locational data, including characteristics of the
dwelling, and neighborhood in which respondents (and nonrespondents) reside.
If blocks are identified by census tract or enumeration district, the investigator
can employ additional sources of data on the characteristics of tracts. Such
information would permit analysis of the locational determinants of nonresponse, and would permit useful substantive analyses as well.

4. Survey the interviewers.[27] Information on the characteristics, attitudes,
experience, training, and practices of the interviewers would provide a baseline
for assessing future changes in interviewing staff and techniques. In addition, it
would be useful to determine interviewers' knowledge and interpretation of
survey concepts, definitions, and procedures, and their views of organizational
practices. If asked, interviewers can prove quite informative about the problems and ambiguities that arise in conducting a survey.

1. Make experimental evaluations of procedural effects, such as split-
ballot experiments based on randomized assignments of different forms of the
interview schedule to respondents. Other factors (e.g., race of interviewer,
telephone versus personal interviewing) may be randomly varied to assess the
effect of procedural variations. Split-ballot experiments are useful but crude
devices; they permit investigation of only a few (usually two) variations in
question order and context. Similarly, experiments based on interpenetrated
random assignments of interviewers—such as that conducted by Bailey *et al.*
(1978)—provide estimates of the magnitude but not the sources of interviewer
bias. In addition, large-scale survey experiments often rely on rather crude
randomization techniques, and cannot always ensure that interviewers are unaware of the aims of the experiment. It would seem useful and economical to
conduct controlled small-scale experiments to formulate, refine, and pretest
hypotheses about procedural effects. Other topics, such as the psychological

---

[27] Suggested by Mark Schulman of Louis Harris and Associates, Inc.

processes that account for the puzzling wording and context effects reported earlier, and shifts in the respondent's frame of reference, might fruitfully be explored in depth in small-scale studies. Refinements in measurement techniques could then be introduced and tested in a controlled fashion in large-scale sample surveys.

2. Do follow-up and reinterview surveys that investigate the effects of residential mobility and transiency, and other lifestyle characteristics, on respondent accessibility. Reinterview surveys would provide useful data on patterns of change and stability in attitudes.

3. Do exploratory participant-observation studies, such as the investigation of census underenumeration conducted by Valentine and Valentine (1971). These researchers compared results obtained by an intensive participant-observation study of one neighborhood with census interviews conducted at the same households. The comparison of methods was double-blind; that is, neither census interviewers nor ethnographers were aware of the work of the other group until after the study was completed. Although the sample is small and cannot be assumed to represent the larger population, the study yields a wealth of hypotheses and insights that could be subjected to further test.

It is important to note that the richness of the study derives from the rigorous application of different methods of observation to the same group. It seems reasonable to suppose that the more diverse the methods of observation, the less likely they are to be subject to the same sources of error and bias. This suggests that through controlled experimental comparison of different methods of observation, we may gain important insights into the errors and biases characterizing each method, including survey methods. If such comparative studies were carefully replicated over time, we would have a better understanding of changes in survey biases. Ultimately, the results would contribute substantive knowledge as well as more precise estimates of measurement errors in surveys.

Replicating Baseline Surveys

An excellent example of a replication study of social change is the 1971 Detroit Area Study omnibus replication of baseline surveys conducted during the 1950s. The design of the study, its results, and the general strategy of replication are described elsewhere (see e.g., O. D. Duncan, 1969, 1975; Duncan, Schuman, & Duncan, 1973). Several general guidelines may be offered here:

RECONSTRUCT BASELINE SURVEY PROCEDURES AND ASSESS THE REPLICABILITY OF THE BASELINE SURVEY

In order to be replicated, original survey materials must be available and original survey procedures must be documented explicitly. Often the investigator can reconstruct the original procedures by careful detective work—digging through old files and talking to the original investigators, staff, and study directors. Knowledge of the general procedures used by the organization that conducted the survey, and procedural changes made over time, is quite helpful. It is through this process of detective work that an investigator can begin to reconstruct how a survey was actually conducted and assess the quality of the data and the replicability of the survey.

It is wise to invest considerable time in the task of selecting a baseline survey and reconstructing the methods used, for the success of the project hinges on the investigator's ability to demonstrate that measurements over time are comparable. This does not mean that one should never replicate an old survey unless the documentation is absolutely complete and in order. Unfortunately this ideal is rarely met, even for recent surveys. The older the survey— and therefore the greater its historical value—the less likely the documentation is to be complete.

REPLICATE BASELINE SURVEY PROCEDURES FAITHFULLY AND/OR EVALUATE THE EFFECTS OF PROCEDURAL VARIATIONS CAREFULLY

This advice does not mean that replication should be carried out in a mechanical fashion. Depending on the phenomenon of interest, it will be more essential to replicate some survey procedures than others. An investigator studying trends in black racial attitudes must pay particular attention to possible bias due to changes in the racial composition of the interviewing staff, and the possible underrepresentation of blacks in early national surveys (see Glenn, 1974). If trends in female labor force participation and attitudes toward work are to be analyzed, then the biasing effects of certain types of quota samples should be considered. Different social phenomena are more or less vulnerable to different sources of error and bias; familiarity with the literature on artifacts of measurement may help the investigator identify the problem areas for the particular topic of interest. In addition, ingenuity on the part of the investigator is called for when original survey rules and procedures are outdated or not fully specified, inconsistencies are apparent, the investigator suspects that the same survey definitions will not produce comparable results at different points in time, or different methods were employed in different baseline surveys.

In some cases, it will be possible to employ multiple rules or procedures in the replicated survey in order to evaluate the effects of variations in definitions on trend estimates (see pp. 693–694). Sometimes it will be advisable to revise or expand survey definitions to capture a comparable target population, as discussed on pages 682–683. Of course, the investigator should be quite explicit when such changes are made. In other cases, it is advisable to evaluate experimentally the effects of procedural variations. If the difference in method influences the survey results, then the noncomparable data should be excluded from the analysis of change. (An example is the evaluation of and correction for the effect of changes in the racial composition of the interviewing staff on DAS estimates of trends in black attitudes, reported on pages 710–712.)

It may not be possible to exclude noncomparable data if the investigator does not know exactly what procedure was followed in the original survey. But if a careful analysis of original survey materials suggests that there are only a few ways that an ambiguous procedure could have been implemented, then the alternative interpretations of the baseline procedure can be tested experimentally. Of course, there is no basis for deciding that one or the other interpretation truly replicates the past, but it can be argued that together they establish a range within which the comparable estimate must fall. (In this case, the investigator attempts to set a confidence limit based on variations in procedures rather than sampling fluctuations.)

Analysis of Trends Based on Secondary Sources of Data

The data archives of this and other countries hold a wealth of historical data based on public opinion polls, censuses, and surveys. These sources of data offer several advantages for the analysis of trends. The historical value is often unique, and archived data often represent the only means to analyze quantitatively changes in mass attitudes, opinions, and behavior during particular historical periods. Second, the number of timepoints that can be constructed in a time series is often large, and the number of topics that can potentially be studied is vast. Obviously, the time and expense of conducting a survey are eliminated.

However, the potential value of archived data for the study of trends has not been fully exploited, in part because the vast amount of data makes it difficult to cull through surveys in search of repeated items that may be used to construct time series. More serious, historical data may be of lower quality and are often insufficiently documented so that it is difficult or impossible to establish the comparability of sampling and survey procedures used by different organizations or at different times.

For a discussion of these and other problems and benefits of secondary analysis, the reader is referred to Hyman (1972) and Glenn (1974). Those authors also provide examples of trend studies based on secondary analysis. Several general guidelines may be helpful.

SEARCH THE ARCHIVE FOR APPROPRIATE TREND STUDIES

The initial selection of surveys for inclusion in an analysis of change might be based on several criteria:

1. The surveys should include comparable and appropriate measures of the phenomenon of interest, and independent variables important to the investigator's analysis.
2. They should span a sufficient period of time to produce interesting results.
3. The target populations should be, or should be able to be made, comparable; or the investigator should believe, and have a reasonable hope of showing, that the noncomparability does not affect estimates of change.

Listings of trend items included in surveys archived by The Roper Center, the Inter-University Consortium for Political and Social Research, and the

Louis Harris Data Center are available, so that time series may readily be constructed.[28]

As with a replication survey, the secondary analyst should become familiar with survey conventions and instruments used by the organization that collected the data. Discontinuities in organizational practice over time should be carefully recorded so that their effects on the time series can be noted and, if possible, corrected. Once again, discussions with the staffs of the original survey organization and the archiving facility may help piece together the information needed to assess survey comparability over time.

The researcher should be cautious when constructing a time series based on surveys conducted by different organizations. Survey procedures and conventions—both documented and undocumented—vary, so the same or similar questions may not produce comparable results in surveys conducted by different organizations. (See pages 680–681 for a discussion of the varying estimates of confidence in institutions produced by NORC and Harris. Turner and Krauss [1978] and Smith [1978, 1979] discuss the sources and extent of "house effects.")

Survey comparability may be evaluated as suggested earlier. Usually, however, experimental evaluations of procedural variation are not possible with secondary analysis. In lieu of experimentation, the investigator may evaluate the results using other sources of data.

Biases and changes in sample composition may be assessed by comparing data from several sources. Turner and Krauss (1978) and Presser (1981) demonstrate small but systematic differences between survey organizations in the educational and racial composition of the samples. Presser finds shifts over time in the racial composition of Harris polls. These sources of noncomparability are eliminated by introducing the biased variable (e.g., race) as a control variable in the analysis of change.

If possible, the investigator should consider whether alternative time series, based on the same or similar indicators of the phenomenon of interest

[28] *A Continuing Guide to the American National Election Surveys of the Center for Political Studies, 1952–1974,* prepared by the Center for Political Studies, may be obtained from ICPSR. The General Social Survey is an annual (now biennial) survey conducted by NORC that replicates questions culled from earlier polls and surveys. The General Social Surveys, available from the Roper Center, are an excellent and easily accessible source of data on trends. *A Compendium of Trends on General Social Survey Questions* (Smith & Rich, 1979) is available from NORC. The Roper Public Opinion Research Center, in cooperation with the Social Science Research Council, has produced *Survey Data for Trend Analysis: An Index to Repeated Questions in U.S. National Surveys held by the Roper Public Opinion Research Center* (Southwick, 1974). Trend questions archived by the Louis Harris Data Center are published in a *Sourcebook of Harris National Surveys: Repeated Questions 1963–1976* (Martin *et al.*, 1981).

collected by the same or another organization, show similar patterns of change. If so, the investigator may be more confident that the measured fluctuations are real and not produced by random variations or variations in survey techniques.

ACKNOWLEDGMENT

I am grateful to Philip Converse, Beverly Duncan, Otis Dudley Duncan, Mark Evers, Stephen Fienberg, William Kruskal, Frank Munger, Robert Parke, Stanley Presser, Albert Reiss, Jr., Howard Schuman, Eleanor Sheldon, Tom Smith, Charles Turner, and James Wright for helpful comments on an earlier draft. Any errors are the responsibility of the author.

REFERENCES

Bailar, B. A., and M. Lanphier
 1978 *Development of Survey Methods to Assess Survey Practices*. Washington, D.C.: American Statistical Association.
Bailar, B. A., and H. Woltman
 1978 "Evaluation and improvement of data quality." (Unpublished U.S. Bureau of the Census manuscript.)
Bailey, L., T. Moore, and B. A. Bailar
 1978 "An interviewer variance study for the eight impact cities of the National Crime Survey cities sample." *Journal of the American Statistical Association* 73: 16 23.
Barath, A., and C. F. Cannell
 1976 "Effect of interviewer's voice intonation." *Public Opinion Quarterly* 40: 370–373.
Biderman, A. D.
 1975 *A Social Indicator of Interpersonal Harm*. Discretionary Grant Final Technical Report for LEAA Grant No. 74-55-99-6003. Washington, D.C.: Bureau of Social Science Research.
Biderman, A. D., and J. P. Lynch
 1981 "Recency bias in data on self-reported victimization." *Proceedings of the American Statistical Association (Social Statistics Section)* 1981: 31–40.
Blair, E.
 1977–78 "More on the effects of interviewer's voice intonation." *Public Opinion Quarterly* 41: 544–548.
Bounpane, P., and C. Jordan
 1978 "Plans for coverage improvement in the 1980 census." Paper presented at the annual meeting of the American Statistical Association, San Diego, California, August.
Brooks, C. A., and B. A. Bailar
 1978 *An Error Profile: Employment as Measured by the Current Population Survey*. Statistical Policy Working Paper 3. Washington, D.C.: U.S. Department of Commerce.
Bushery, J. M., C. D. Cowan, and L. R. Murphy
 1978 "Experiments in telephone-personal visit surveys." *Proceedings of the American Statistical Association (Survey Research Methods Section)* 1978, 564–7.
Cannell, C. F., S. A. Lawson, and D. L. Hausser
 1975 *A Technique for Evaluating Interviewer Performance*. Ann Arbor: Survey Research Center of the Institute for Social Research, The University of Michigan.
Center for Political Studies
 1976 *A Continuity Guide to the American National Election Surveys of the Center for Political Studies, 1952–1974*. Ann Arbor: Center for Political Surveys and Inter-university Consortium for Political and Social Research, Institute for Social Research, The University of Michigan.

Clarren, S., and A. Schwartz
  1976   "Measuring a program's impact: A cautionary note." In W. Skogan (ed.), *Sample Surveys of the Victims of Crime*. Cambridge, Mass.: Ballinger.
Colombotos, J.
  1965   "The effects of personal vs. telephone interviews on socially acceptable responses." *Public Opinion Quarterly* 29: 457–458.
Converse, J. M.
  1976–77 "Predicting no opinion in the polls." *Public Opinion Quarterly* 40: 515–530.
Converse, P. E.
  1970   "Attitudes and non-attitudes: Continuation of a dialogue." In E. Tufte (ed.), *The Quantitative Analysis of Social Problems*. Reading, Mass.: Addison-Wesley.
Cowan, C. D., L. R. Murphy, and J. Wiener
  1978   "Effects of supplemental questions on victimization estimates from the National Crime Survey." *Proceedings of the American Statistical Association* (*Survey Research Methods Section*) 1978: 277–282.
Day, R., and J. Wilcox
  1971   "A simulation analysis of nonresponse error in survey sampling." Combined Proceedings Spring and Fall Conferences, American Marketing Association. Pp. 478–483.
Dodge, R., and H. Lentzner
  1978   "Patterns of personal series incidents in the National Crime Survey." Paper presented at the annual meeting of the American Statistical Association, San Diego, California, 1978.
Duncan, B., and M. Evers
  1975   "Measuring change in attitudes toward women's work." In K. Land and S. Spilerman (eds.), *Social Indicator Models*. New York: Russell Sage.
Duncan, O. D.
  1961   "A socioeconomic index for all occupations." Pp. 109–138 in A. J. Reiss, Jr. (ed.), *Occupations and Social Status*. New York: Free Press.
  1969   *Toward Social Reporting: Next Steps*. New York: Russell Sage.
  1975   "Measuring social change via replication of surveys." In K. Land and S. Spilerman (eds.), *Social Indicator Models*. New York: Russell Sage.
Duncan, O. D., and H. Schuman
  1976   "An experiment on order and wording of attitude questions." Unpublished paper.
Duncan, O. D., H. Schuman, and B. Duncan
  1973   *Social Change in a Metropolitan Community*. New York: Russell Sage.
Dunkelberg, W., and G. Day
  1973   "Nonresponse bias and callbacks in sample surveys." *Journal of Marketing Research* 10: 160–168.
Eckland, B. K.
  1965   "Effects of prodding to increase mail-back returns." *Journal of Applied Psychology* 49: 165–169.
Farley, R., S. Hatchett, and H. Schuman
  1979   "A note on changes in black racial attitudes in Detroit: 1968–1976." *Social Indicators Research* 6: 439–443.
Fischer, E. M.
  1972   "Sampling report for the 1971 Detroit Area Study." Unpublished DAS report #7163.
  1974   "Change in anomie in Detroit from the 1950s to 1971." Unpublished doctoral dissertation. Ann Arbor: The University of Michigan.
  1976   *Altruism and rationality: A conceptual scheme with implications for social change*. Paper prepared for the Advisory and Planning Committee on Social Indicators of the Social Science Research Council.
Fondelier, S. E.
  1976   "Keeping track of respondents in longitudinal surveys." (Unpublished U.S. Bureau of the Census manuscript #78-107, presented at the American Medical Association/Census Conference, October.)

Gibson, C. O., G. M. Shapiro, L. R. Murphy, and G. J. Stanko
  1978 "Interaction of survey questions as it relates to interviewer–respondent bias." *Proceedings of the American Statistical Association* (*Survey Research Methods Section*) 1978: 251–256.
Glenn, N.
  1974 "Trend studies with available survey data: Opportunities and pitfalls." In J. C. Southwick (ed.) *Survey Data for Trend Analysis: An Index to Repeated Questions in U.S. National Surveys held by the Roper Public Opinion Research Center.* Williamstown, Mass.: The Roper Public Opinion Research Center, with the cooperation of the Social Science Research Council.
Groves, R. M.
  1979 "Actors and questions in telephone and personal interview surveys." *Public Opinion Quarterly* 43: 190–205.
Groves, R. M., and R. Kahn
  1979 *Surveys by Telephone: A National Comparison with Personal Interviews* . New York: Academic Press.
Hasher, L., D. Goldstein, and T. Toppino
  1977 "Frequency and the conference of referential validity." *Journal of Verbal Learning and Verbal Behavior* 16: 107–112.
Hatchett, S., and H. Schuman
  1975–76 "White respondents and race-of-interviewer effects." *Public Opinion Quarterly* 39: 523–528.
Hauser, R. M., and D. L. Featherman
  1977 *The Process of Stratification: Trends and Analysis.* New York: Academic Press.
Hawkins, D. F.
  1977 *Nonresponse in Detroit Area Study Surveys: A Ten-year Analysis* Working Papers in Methodology No. 8. Chapel Hill, N.C.: Institute for Research in Social Science.
Hochstim, J. R.
  1967 "A critical comparison of three strategies of collecting data from households." *Journal of the American Statistical Association* 62: 976–989.
Hornstein, H. A., E. LaKind, G. Frankel, and S. Manne
  1975 "Effects of knowledge about remote social events on prosocial behavior, social conception, and mood." *Journal of Personality and Social Psychology* 32: 1038–1046.
House, J. S.
  1978 "Trends in response rates and their implications for survey validity." Paper presented at the Southern Association for Public Opinion Research, Chapel Hill, N.C., March.
House, J. S., and S. Wolf
  1978 "Effects of urban residence on interpersonal trust and helping behavior." *Journal of Personality and Social Psychology* 36: 1029–1043.
Hyman, H. H.
  1972 *Secondary Analysis of Sample Surveys: Principles, Procedures, and Potentialities.* New York: Wiley.
Kish, L.
  1949 "A procedure for objective respondent selection within the household." *Journal of the American Statistical Association* 44: 38–387.
  1965 *Survey Sampling.* New York: Wiley.
Larsen, O. N.
  1952 "The comparative validity of telephone and face-to-face interviews in the measurement of message diffusion from leaflets." *American Sociological Review* 17: 471–476.
Louis Harris and Associates, Inc.
  (no date) "About interviewing." (Unpublished document.)
Marquis, K. H.
  1977 "Survey response rates: Some trends, causes, and correlates." Paper presented at the Biennial Conference on Health Survey Research Methods, Williamsburg, Virginia, May.

1978   "Inferring health interview response bias from imperfect record checks." Rand Paper #P-6159, September.
Marquis, K. H., and C. F. Cannell
1969   *A Study of Interviewer–Respondent Interaction in the Urban Employment Survey.* Ann Arbor: Survey Research Center.
Martin, E.
1980   "The effects of item contiguity and probing on measures of anomia." *Social Psychology Quarterly* 43: 116–120.
Martin, E.
1981   "A twist on the Heisenberg principle: Or, how crime affects its measurement." *Social Indicators Research* 9: 197–223.
Martin, E., D. McDuffee, and S. Presser (eds.)
1981   *Sourcebook of Harris National Surveys: Repeated Questions 1963–1976.* IRSS Technical Papers 6. Chapel Hill: Institute for Research in Social Science, University of North Carolina.
Montie, I. C., and G. M. Shapiro
1978   "Residence rules for household surveys. Paper No. 1—Multiple residences." (U.S. Bureau of the Census memorandum #78-126, March 15.)
Moore, J., and N. Rothwell
1978   "Evaluation of the effectiveness of the Public Information Campaign for the 1976 Census of Camden, New Jersey." (Unpublished U.S. Bureau of the Census manuscript, April 26.)
Mosteller, F.
1968   "Nonsampling Errors." Pp. 113–131 in *The International Encyclopedia of the Social Sciences.* Vol. 5 New York: Crowell Collier and Macmillan.
Mosteller, F., H. Hyman, P. McCarthy, E. S. Marks, and D. B. Truman
1949   *The Pre-Election Polls of 1948: Report to the Committee on Analysis of Pre-election Polls and Forecasts.* New York: Social Science Research Council.
National Academy of Sciences
1979   *Privacy and Confidentiality as Factors in Survey Response.* Washington, D.C.: National Academy of Sciences.
National Commission on Employment and Unemployment Statistics
1979   *Counting the Labor Force.* Washington, D.C.: Government Printing Office.
Nisbett, R. E., and N. Bellows
1977   "Verbal reports about causal influences on social judgments: Private access versus public theories." *Journal of Personality and Social Psychology* 35: 613–624.
Nisbett, R. E., and T. D. Wilson
1977   "Telling more than we can know: Verbal reports on mental processes." *Psychological Review* 84: 231–259.
O'Neil, M. J.
1979   "Estimating the nonresponse bias due to refusals in telephone surveys." *Public Opinion Quarterly* 43: 218–232.
Parsons, C.
1972   *America's Uncounted People: Report of the Advisory Committee on Problems of Census Enumeration.* Washington, D.C.: National Academy of Sciences.
Penick, B. K. E., and M. Owens, (eds.)
1976   *Surveying Crime.* Washington, D.C.: National Academy of Sciences.
Presser, S.
1981   "The Harris Data Center, Harris national surveys, and trend analysis." In E. Martin *et al.* (eds.), *Sourcebook of Harris National Surveys: Repeated Questions 1963–1976.* IRSS Technical Papers 6. Chapel Hill: Institute for Research in Social Science, University of North Carolina.
Presser, S., and H. Schuman
1980   "The measurement of a middle position in attitude surveys." *Public Opinion Quarterly* 44: 70–85.

Robinson, J. P., R. Athanasiou, and K. B. Head
  1969 *Measures of Occupational Attitudes and Occupational Characteristics*. Ann Arbor: Institute for Social Research, The University of Michigan.
Robinson, J. P., J. G. Rusk, and K. B. Head
  1968 *Measures of Political Attitudes*. Ann Arbor: Institute for Social Research, The University of Michigan.
Robinson, J. P., and P. R. Shaver
  1973 *Measures of Social Psychological Attitudes*. Rev. ed. Ann Arbor: Institute for Social Research, The University of Michigan.
Rossi, P., E. Waite, C. Bose, and R. Berk
  1974 "The seriousness of crimes: Normative structure and individual differences." *American Sociological Review* 39: 224–237.

Rustemeyer, A.
  1977 "Measuring interviewer performance in mock interviews." *Proceedings of the American Statistical Association, (Social Statistics Section)* 1977: 341–346.

Schuman, H.
  1974 "Old wine in new bottles: Some sources of response error in the use of attitude surveys to study social change." Paper prepared for the Research Seminar Group in Quantitative Social Science at the University of Surrey, England.

Schuman, H.
  1982 "Artifacts are in the mind of the beholder." *American Sociologist* 17: 21–28.

Schuman, H., and J. Converse
  1971 "The effects of black and white interviewers on black responses in 1968." *Public Opinion Quarterly* 35: 44–68.

Schuman, H., G. Kalton, and J. Ludwig
  1983 "Context and continguity in survey questionnaires." *Public Opinion Quarterly* 47: 112–115.

Schuman, H., and S. Presser
  1977 "Question wording as an independent variable in survey analysis." *Sociological Methods and Research* 6: 151–170.
  1979a "The assessment of 'no opinion' in attitude surveys." In K. F. Schuessler (ed.), *Sociological Methodology 1979*. San Francisco: Jossey–Bass.
  1979b "The open and closed question." *American Sociological Review* 44: 692–712.

Schuman, H., and S. Presser
  1981 *Questions and Answers in Attitude Surveys: Experiments on Question Form, Wording, and Context*. New York: Academic Press.

Schwartz, A., and S. Clarren
  1977 *The Cincinnati Team Policing Experiment: A Summary Report*. Washington, D.C.: The Urban Institute and Police Foundation.

Siegel, P. M.
  1971 "Prestige in the American occupational structure." Unpublished doctoral dissertation, The University of Chicago.

Slovic, P., and S. Lichtenstein
  1971 "Comparison of Bayesian and regression approaches to the study of information processing in judgment." *Organizational Behavior and Human Performance* 6: 649–744.

Smith, T. W.
  1978 "In search of house effects: A comparison of responses to various questions by different survey organizations." *Public Opinion Quarterly* 42: 443–463.

Smith, T. W.
  1979 "Happiness: Time trends, seasonal variations, intersurvey differences, and other mysteries." *Social Psychology Quarterly* 42: 18–30.
  1981 "Can we have confidence in confidence? Revisited." In D. Johnston (ed.), *Measurement of Subjective Phenomena*. Washington, D.C.: Government Printing Office.

Smith, T. W., with G. J. Rich
   1979   *A Compendium of Trends on General Social Survey Questions.* GSS Technical Report
           No. 15. Chicago: National Opinion Research Center, University of Chicago, August.
Social Science Research Council
   1975   *Basic Background Items for U.S. Household Surveys.* New York: Social Science Re-
           search Council.
Southwick, J. C., (ed.)
   1974   *Survey Data for Trend Analysis: An Index to Repeated Questions in U.S. National
           Surveys Held by the Roper Public Opinion Research Center.* The Roper Public Opinion
           Research Center, in cooperation with the Social Science Research Council.
Steeh, C. G.
   1981   "Trends in nonresponse rats, 1952–1979." *Public Opinion Quarterly* 45: 40–57.
Stephenson, C. B.
   1979   "Probability sampling with quotas: An experiment." *Public Opinion Quarterly* 43: 477–
           496.
Stinchcombe, A., R. Adams, C. Heimer, K. Scheppele, T. W. Smith, and D. G. Taylor.
   1980   *Crime and Punishment—Changing Attitudes in America.* San Francisco: Jossey-Bass.
Sudman, S., and N. Bradburn
   1974   *Response Effects in Surveys: A Review and Synthesis.* Chicago: Aldine.
Survey Research Center
   1966   *Interviewer's Manual.* Ann Arbor: Institute for Survey Research.
   1970   "Building listing instructions." Ann Arbor (June memorandum.)
   1976   *Interviewer's Manual* (rev. ed.). Ann Arbor: Institute for Social Research.
Tuchfarber, A., and W. Klecka
   1976   *Random Digit Dialing: Lowering the Cost of Victimization Surveys.* Washington, D.C.:
           Police Foundation.
Turner, A. G.
   1977   "An experiment to compare three interview procedures in the National Crime Survey."
           (Unpublished U.S. Bureau of the Census manuscript #70.)
Turner, C. F.
   1981   "Surveys of subjective phenomena: A working paper." In D. Johnston (ed.), *Measure-
           ment of Subjective Phenomena.* Washington, D.C.: Government Printing Office.
Turner, C. F., and E. Krauss
   1978   "Fallible indicators of the subjective state of the nation." *American Psychologist* 33: 456–
           470.
Tversky, A., and D. Kahneman
   1973   Availability: A heuristic for judging frequency and probability." *Cognitive Psychology*
           5:207–232.
   1974   "Judgment under uncertainty: Heuristics and biases." *Sciences* 185: 1124–1131.
U.S. Bureau of the Census
   1953   *Census of Housing: 1950. Vol. 1: General Characteristics.* Washington, D.C.: Govern-
           ment Printing Office. (chap. 1, U.S. Summary).
   1963   *Census of Housing: 1960. Vol. 1: States and Small Areas.* Washington, D.C.: Govern-
           ment Printing Office. (United States Summary. Final Report HC(1)-1.)
   1970a *1970 Census Users' Guide.* Part 1. Washington, D.C.: Government Printing Office.
   1970b "Victim recall pretest (Washington, D.C.) household survey of victims of crime." (Un-
           published memorandum 70-237, June 10.)
   1971a Census of Population: 1970 *Alphabetical Index of Industries and Occupations.* Washing-
           ton, D.C.: Government Printing Office.
   1971b *Current Population Survey: Interviewers Reference Manual.* Washington, D.C.: Govern-
           ment Printing Office.
   1972   *Who's Home When,* by D. Weber and R. C. Burt (Working Paper No. 37). Washington,
           D.C.: Government Printing Office.
   1973a *Estimates of Coverage of Population by Sex, Race, and Age: Demographic Analysis,* by

J. S. Siegel. Census of Population and Housing: 1970. Evaluation and Research Program PHC (E)-4. Washington, D.C.: Government Printing Office.

1973b *The Coverage of Housing in the 1970 Census.* Census of Population and Housing: 1970. Evaluation and Research Program PHC (E)-5. Washington, D.C.: Government Printing Office.

1974 *Indexes to Survey Methodology Literature.* Technical Paper No. 34. Washington, D.C.: Government Printing Office.

1977 *The Current Population Survey: Design and Methodology.* Technical Paper 40. Washington, D.C.: Government Printing Office.

U.S. Department of Health, Education, and Welfare

1977a *A Summary of Studies of Interviewing Methodology.* By C. F. Cannell, K. H. Marquis, and A. Laurent. Vital and Health Statistics Series 2, Data Evaluation and Methods Research, No. 69. Washington, D.C.: Government Printing Office.

1977b *Experiments in Interviewing Techniques: Field Experiments in Health Reporting, 1971–1977.* NCHSR Research Report Series. Hyattsville, Maryland: National Center for Health Services Research.

U.S. Department of Labor

1977 *Dictionary of Occupational Titles* (4th ed.) Washington, D.C.: Government Printing Office.

Valentine, C. A., and B. L. Valentine

1971 "Missing Men: A Comparative Methodological Study of Undernumeration and Related Problems." (Unpublished manuscript.)

Wilcox, J. B.

1977 "The interaction of refusal and not-at-home sources of nonresponse bias." *Journal of Marketing Research* 14: 592–597.

Wish, E. D., L. N. Robins, J. E. Helzer, M. Hesselbrock, and D. H. Davis

1978 "Monday morning quarterbacking on limiting call-backs: Evidence from a panel study of veterans." Paper presented at the annual meeting of the American Association for Public Opinion Research, Roanoke, Virginia, June.

Index

A

Ability to win contracts, 126–127
Abortion opinion, 570–572
Additive conjoint measurement, 267
Additivity, 636–639
Ad hoc surveys, 14
Admissible transformation, 241, 245
Aggregation, 406
AID, *see* Automatic Interaction Detector
Aided recall, 309
Alienation items, 718–719
Allocation, 38–39
    optimal, 41–43, 44
Analysis of covariance (ANCOVA), 430–432,
    451, 530–532, 652–653
Analysis of variance (ANOVA), 50, 419, 422,
    434, 451, 529–530, 532
ANCOVA, *see* Analysis of covariance
Anomie, 316, 710, 714
Anonymity, 297–298
ANOVA, *see* Analysis of variance
Apartment hotel, 685
Area probability sampling, 6, 7
Asymptotic efficiency, 514, 667, 669
Asymptotic properties, 667
Attitudes, 204
    scaling, 231, 246–281
    strength of, 204
Attrition, 417, 426, 437, 480, 693
Automated monitoring, 385, 386
Automatic Interaction Detector (AID), 17, 542
Autonomy, 141

B

Balanced repeated replication (BRR), 64–65
Baseline surveys, 733–735
Batch processing, 396–397
Bayesian theory of inference, 23, 29, 459
Behavior, prediction of, 217
Best asymptotically normal (BAN) estimators,
    623–624
Bias, 27–28, 71, 74, 135, 150, 157, 183,
    198–199, 349, 537–538, 667, 693, 698, 732,
    736
    question order, 198
    response, 15, 315
    yea-saying, 316, 317
Binary operation, 238
Binary relation, 236–238
Bipolar adjectival scales, *see* Semantic differential
Bivariate regression model, 459–461, 496–522
Block-triangular patterns, *see* Monotonic patterns
Blocking, 581
BMDP system files, 403, 407, 409
Boolean logic, 405
Bounded recall, 309–310
Box–Jenkins time series techniques, 520–521
Breakoffs, 220, 221
BRR, *see* Balanced repeated replication
Bureau of Applied Social Research, 6, 7
Bureau of the Census, 6, 7, 8, 146, 170–171

C

Callbacks, 698, 700, 701
Cardinality, 241

Cartesian product, 236
Casual settings, 688–689
Category scales, 266
CATI, *see* Computer-assisted telephone interview
Causal analysis, 576, 581
Causal effect
  accuracy-of-prediction measures, 632, 634–636
  defined, 632
  rate-of-change measures, 632–634
Causal inference, 615–631
Causal modeling, 613–675
  nonrecursive, 658–671
  reciprocal, 663
  recursive, 631–658, 662
Census Bureau, *see* Bureau of the Census
Censuses, 2–3, 146
  use of, 218–219
Central limit theorem, 28, 30
Centralization, 141–143
Certified mail, 368
Chain rule, 655
Channels of communication, 140
Chain of command, 132, 141–142
Chi square test, 273, 549, 551, 554, 555–564, 565, 573–574
  derivation of, 556–557
  goodness-of-fit, 92, 93, 108, 112–114, 557–558, 561
  likelihood ratio, 557, 561, 624
  problems with, 560–563, 573–574
Classical inference theory, 23, 25, 28, 29
Classical measurement theory, 76, 231
Classical operationism, 233
Classification errors, 727–729
Closed questions, 206–208
Cluster sampling, 6, 37, 47–62, 383, 695
  theory, 48–55
Cluster size, 60–62
Clustering, *see* Cluster sampling
Cobb–Douglas function, 650–652
Codebook documentation, 410, 411, 413
Coding, 380, 392, 726–727, 731
Coefficient of alienation, 635
Coefficient matrix, 617
Coefficient of reproducibility, 259
Cognitive congruity, 265
Cognitive mapping, 268–269
Cohort succession, 690–692
Collaborative research, 155–156
Combined ratio method, 58
Common factor, 90
Comparability of results, 677–741
Complete linear model analysis, 425
Compression of time, *see* Telescoping

Computer-assisted telephone interviewing (CATI), 9, 15, 391–392
Computers, 8, 9, 17, 132, 379–414
  cost, 391, 410
Conceptual data model, 398–402, 403, 404
Concomitant variation, 615–616, 618, 620
Concurrent validity, 97–98
Confidence in American institutions, 680–681
Confidence interval, 28
Confidence limits, 30, 31
Confidentiality, 703–705
Conformity, 161
Congeneric measures, 92–96, 102, 104
Congruence relation, 240
Consistency, 303–304, 667
Construct validity, 100–105
Consumer-marketing research, 3, 5, 8
Consumer preferences, 3
Content analysis, 195
Content validity, 98–100
Contextual effects, 406
Contingency table, 549–564
  accuracy of, 550
  truncated, 476–479
Contract bids, 126–127
Convergent validity, 105
Cooperation rates, 24, 157, 173, 183–184
Correlation, 620–626
  concepts of, 616–620
  spurious, 616, 620, 621–623
Cost control, 354–355
Covariance, *see* Correlation
CPS, *see* Current Population Survey
Credibility scale, 154–158
Credible interval, 29
Credible limits, 30, 31
Crime
  fear of, 702–703
  rate, 336
  reporting of, 713, 718
Criterion-related validity, 97–99
Crossley Polls, 5
Cultural context, 714–715
Cumulative scaling, *see* Guttman scaling
Current Population Survey (CPS), 146–147, 184, 296, 558, 678–679, 718

D

D-Systems, *see* Weighted regression analysis for proportions
Data analysis, 17, 547–612
Data-base management costs, 229
Data Base Management Systems (DBMS), 402–403, 409

Data base organization, 398–404
Data capture, 387–392
Data cleaning, 392–397
Data collection, 329–358, 732
  costs, 330–331
  method selection, 333–338
Data distribution, 406
Data exchange, 409
Data, missing, *see* Missing data
Data model, *see* Conceptual data model
Data retrieval, 404–408
  software, 407–408
Data transcription, 388–389
DBMS, *see* Data Base Management Systems
Debriefing, 226
Decision making, 6, 663, 664
DEFF, *see* Design effect
Degrees of freedom, 551–553
Delegation of tasks, 136
Deletion of data, 450–457
Demand characteristics, 291
Deming–Stephan algorithm, 550–554, 556, 586, 594
Demographic change, 690–694
Demographic variables, 151, 204
Departmentalization, 137
Design (cost) efficiency, 35, 43
Design effect, 35–36
  and intraclass correlation, 51–52
Design requirements, 143
Detroit Area Study (DAS), 147, 684, 685, 709–710, 733
Direct entry terminal devices, 390–391
Directories, *see* Lists
Disaster recovery, 410
Discriminant analysis, 469–472
Discriminant validity, 105–106
Disproportionality of data, 420–434
Dissimilarity, 554–555, 562, 573
Distribution of work, 128–129
Division of labor, 136–137
Double-barreled questions, 216
Documentation, 397–398, 409–411, 413, 731
Double negatives, 217
Drivers' license files, 696–697
Dummy variable regression, 576–577, 595–598
Durbin–Watson statistic, 519–520
Dwelling unit, 683–685

E

Econometric modeling, 9, 660
Economies of scale, 132–133, 372, 373
Editing, 387, 389, 390
  interactive, 396–397

Effects
  calculation of, 653–657
  coding, 511, 586
  direct, 653–654
  indirect, 656–657
  total, 654–656
Effective sample size, 35–36
Elasticity, 506, 652
Electronic computers, *see* Computers
Element, defined, 23
Eligibility criteria, 685–694
Embarrassment, 305
Empirical validity, 97–99
Employment statistics, 146
Equal appearing intervals, 248, 251
Equivalence relation, 237
EPSEM, 40, 46
Error
  communication, 291
  deliberate, 291
  detection, 393–395
  memory, 291–292
  resolution, 395–397
  term, 508, 509
Estimated primary unit size, 61
Estimator, 25, 27
  biased, 27
Exception reporting, 385
Exchange theory, 361
Expectations, 204
Expected frequencies method, 421–422
Experimenter effects, 149–150, 162–163
Explained variance, 563–564
Extrapolation, 506

F

F-tests, 527–528
Facilitation, 647–649
Factor analysis, 89–96, 107, 232, 255, 269–281, 473–475, 525
  confirmatory, 91–92
  exploratory, 89–90
Factor loadings, 274–279
Factor scale, construction of, 279–280
False premise questions, 216
Fatigue effect, 304
Favorableness, degree of, 248–250
Federal government, 11, 126, 143
Feedback to interviewers, 351, 352, 708
Field editing, 352
Field experiments, 195
Field monitoring, 384–386
Field staff, 135–136, *see also* Interviewers
FIML, *see* Full-information maximum-likelihood

Finite population correction factor, 31
First-order methods, 457–466, 474
Fitting constants method, 422, 423–424
Five-point scales, 209
Floaters, 721
Focus groups, *see* Group discussion
Follow-up mailings, 361, 366–367, 384
Forecasting, accuracy of, 3
Form letters, 367–368
Frame of reference, 712, 714, 718
Full-information maximum-likelihood (FIML),
    667–670
Function, 238
Functional equivalence, 677–678
Funding, 32, 34, 126, 143, 330
    federal, 8, 16, 126–128

G
Gallup Poll, 5, 14, 147, 722
General linear model, 496–546
General Social Security, 698
Generalizability of results, 152, 154, 158
Generalized least squares, *see* Heteroscedasticity
Goodness of fit, 526, 527, 554, 580–581 *see also*
    Chi square test
Gramian matrices, 270–271
Grant proposals, 126–127
Grizzle–Starmer–Koch techniques, 549
Group discussion, 334
Group quarters, 685
Growth, 130–133
Guttman scaling, 256–260, 261, 303, 570

H
Harris polls, *see* Louis Harris and Associates, Inc.
Heteromethod block, 106
Heteroscedasticity, 457, 516, 517, 574
Heterotrait–monomethod triangles, 106
Hierarchical analysis, 425
Hierarchical modeling, 549–564, 594, 603
    goal of, 558–559
Hierarchy, 399, 401, 402, 405
    management, *see* Chain of command
High School and Beyond survey, 389, 401, 403,
    404
Homomorphism, 238–239, 240
Homoscedasticity, 509
Hot-deck procedure, 395, 396, 457
Household
    defined, 151, 682–685
    without telephones, 24, 176, 383, 723
Housing unit, 682–684
Human ecology, 3

I
Image, 238
Immediacy of events, 718
Impersonality, 295
Income, 152
Independent verification, 393
Individual difference models, 269
INDSCAL, 269
Inductive method, 343
Inference theories, 23
Ingratiating behavior, 706
Inhibition, 647–649
In-house surveys, 14
Instructions, standardized, 197
Instrument design, 379–382
Intention to act, 217
Interest of respondent, 203–204
Interitem correlations, 261
Interval measures, 247
Interview
    costs, 354–355
    degree of impersonality, 295
    effects, 292–293
    face-to-face, 148, 199, 294–296, 335, 336–338,
        723–725
    falsified, 353
    interactive, 336
    length of, 201–202, 332
    monitoring, 353–354
    objectives, 329–330
    observation, 353–354, 708
    practice, 347–348
    schedule, 299
    simultaneous, 337, 373–374
    techniques, 4
    telephone, 148, 199, 294–296, 335–336, 353,
        382–383, 391, 723–725
    termination of, 220–223
    validation, 352–353
Interviewer
    accuracy, 707–708, 727–729
    attrition, 332
    college students as, 311
    debriefing of, 226
    discretion, 697, 699
    expectations, 313, 314, 350, 351–352
    experience, 311, 312, 340–341, 707, 728
    fears of, 344
    instructions to, 197, 391
    manual, 346, 348–350, 357
    performance during interviews, 313–314,
        707–708
    race of, 312–313, 314, 678, 709, 730

reading errors, 314
recruitment, 126, 138–139, 141, 332–333,
    338–340, 357, 708
role of, 343–345
selection criteria, 340–342, 357
sex of, 312–313
skills, 344–350, 357
specifications, *see* Interviewer, manual
speech behavior of, 314, 707
status, 311–312
style, 706–707
supervision, 311, 315, 331, 333, 341, 350–357
training, 311, 312, 313, 315, 330, 331,
    332–333, 342–350, 707
variability, 207, 310–314
Intraclass correlation, 51–52
Invalidity, 91
Investment models, 649–650
Isomorphism, 238–239
Item analysis, 254–255
Item construction, 99
Item development, 332
Item uniqueness, 90
Item writing, 4
Iterative proportional fitting, 550–554, 563

J

Jackknife repeated replication (JRR), 64
JRR, *see* Jackknife repeated replication
Judgment formulation, 719–725
Judgment sample, 165

K

Keynesian model of national income, 658, 660
Keypunching, 388
Kinsey Report, 7–8
Knowledge, 203
Known group technique, 98

L

Laboratory model, 3
Latent class analysis, 247
Latent distance model, 260, 262
Latent structure analysis, 260, 261–263, 564–574,
    602
Latent variable, 269–270
Law of comparative judgment, 249, 250
Least-squares regression, 396, 419, 422–426,
    445–446, 470, 503, 507
Life histories, 401
Likelihood function, 30
Likelihood ratio test, 434

Likert scale, 252–255, 266, 570
advantages of, 255
criticism of, 255
Limited-information maximum-likelihood (LIML)
    estimator, 667–670
LIML, *see* Limited-information maximum-
    likelihood estimator
Line drawing, 267
Linear probability model, 511–512
Linearity, 636–639
Linkage, 399, 406
Lists, 170–176, 192, 368–369, 695–697
blanks on, 172–173
duplications on, 173–175
ineligible units on, 172–173
multiple, 174–175
of items, 210
omissions from, 175–176
types of, 170–172
Listwise deletion, 450, 462, 463, 466, 468, 470,
    540
Literary Digest, 3, 5
Loaded questions, 214–216
Log linear effects, 591, 604, 605
Log linear models, 17, 549, 550, 556, 561, 575,
    585–601, 603
Logarithmic function, 644–646
Logical representation, 398
Logit analysis, 512, 549, 575, 593
Louis Harris and Associates, Inc., 14, 680, 694,
    698

M

Magnitude scaling, 266–267
Mail surveys, 9, 148, 157, 183, 198, 359–373,
    375
Management
hierarchy, *see* Chain of command
through participation, 142
principles of, 141–143
problems, 123–144
structure, 138, 140–141
MANOVA, *see* Multivariate analysis of variance
Mapping, 233–234, 238
cognitive, 268–269
homomorphic, 234
isomorphic, 234
perceptual, 268–269
Marlowe–Crowne Social Desirability Scale, 316,
    318
Mass media, 13
Maximum likelihood (ML) estimates, 92, 102,
    435, 436, 448–449, 623

Maximum-likelihood factor analysis, 269, 273–274, 549
Meaningful parametrization, 244–245
Meaningfulness, 243–245
Measurability, 242
Measurable samples, 32
Measure of equivalence, 79, 85–89
  internal consistency methods, 86–89
  split-half, methods, 85
Measure of size (MOS), 61–62
Measure of stability, *see* Test–retest reliability
Measurement, 69–121
  defined, 70, 232
  levels of, 232
  theory, 231, 232, 233, 235, 236–246
Measurement error, 16–17
  defined, 70
  types of, 499
Memory errors, 290–292, 308–310
  effect of time on, 310, 718–719
Minimum marginal reproducibility (MMR), 259
Minimum mean square error, 667
Minimum variance, 667
Misclassification, 471
Missing data, 415–494, 539–541
  definitions of, 416–417
  disproportionality in, 420–434
  randomness of, 416–417, 442–446
  retrieval, 354–357
  in specific patterns, 436–442
  strategies for, 418–420
Missing persons, *see* Underunemeration
ML, *see* Maximum likelihood
MMR, *see* Minimum marginal reproducibility
Monotonic patterns, 436–437, 441, 449
Monte Carlo methods, 446, 470, 480, 668
Monthly Labor Force Survey, 7
Morale, *see* Staff, morale
Morphism, 238
MOS, *see* Measure of size
Multicollinearity, 523, 528, 529, 535–537, 539
Multiple choice, *see* Closed questions
Multiple correlation coefficient, 635
Multiplicative model, *see* Cobb–Douglas function
Multistage area sample, 33
Multistage selection, 36
Multitrait–multimethod matrix, 105–108
Multivariate analysis, 18
Multivariate analysis of variance (MANOVA), 420, 434
Multivariate contingency tests, 394
Multivariate log linear models, 9
Multivariate regression model, 522–542
  problems with, 534–542

N
N-dimensional scale, 240
National Opinion Research Center (NORC), 6, 7, 8, 680, 698–699
Need for social approval, 317
Negative information, reporting of, 294
Network, 399–401
Network sampling, 179
Neutral values, 427, 429–430, 433, 473, 474
No-opinion responses, 211, 307, 721, 722
Nonadditive models, 646–653
Noncomparability sources, 678–679
Noncoverage, 24
Nonlinear models, 640–646
Nonlinear relationships, 532–534
Nonmetric multidimensional scaling, 268
Nonprogrammed speech of interviewer, 314
Nonresponse, 24
Nonsampling errors, *see* Response effects
Nonscale types, 259
Nonverbal behavior, 337, 354
NORC, *see* National Opinion Research Center
Norms, internalized, 135
Numeric estimation, 267

O
Observation, 195
Occupancy status, 682–689
OCR, *see* Optical character readers
Office of Public Opinion Research, 5–6
Office of Radio Research, 6, 7
OLS, *see* Ordinary least squares
OMR, *see* Optical mark readers
On-line terminal, 390
One-dimensional scale, 240
One-to-one linking, 399
Open questions, 206–208, 224, 299–302, 318, 369, 392
Operationism, 233
Opinion, dimensions of, 203–205
Optical character readers (OCR), 389
Optical mark readers (OMR), 389
Ordered pair, 236
Ordering, 238
Ordinal measures, 247
Ordinary least squares (OLS), 427, 449, 619, 625, 650, 660–662, 668
Orthogonal rotations, 274–279
OSIRIS, 8
Overlapping alternatives, 217

P
Pacing, 345–346
Paired comparisons, 248–249, 251

Pairwise deletion, 450, 452–455, 461, 466, 467–468, 475, 540
Parabolic function, 640–644
Parallel measures, 77
Parameter estimation in nonrecursive models, 665–671
Parent record, 399
Partial correlation coefficient, 635–636
Partial data, 426
Path analysis, 469, 524, 525, 576, 581, 582–585, 623, 637, 653
Path coefficient, 505
Pearson correlation coefficient, 505
Percentage model, 549
Periodicity, 169–170
Personal interviews, *see* Interview, face-to-face
Personalized letters, 367–368, 384, 386
Physical representation, 398
Pilot tests, *see* Pretests
Planning, 130
Pluralistic ignorance, 204
Political orientation, 160–161
Political polls, 3, 5, 7, 147
Polynomial conjoint measurement, 267
Polytomous variables, 590, 595, 598
Population, 151–153
  availability, 32–34
  defined, 23
  mean, 25
  overdefinition of, 152
  parameters, 25, 27
  regression line, 507
  screening, 152, 179
  special, 148, 157, 179
  variance, 25
Poststratification, 44–45, 184
Poverty, definition of, 152
Power, 161
PPS sampling, *see* Probability proportional to size
Precolumning, 228
Predictive validity, 97
Preelection surveys, 3, 5, 7
Preferences, 3
  ranking, 263–264
Preliminary test estimators, 625
Preordering, 238
Prestige, 125–127
Pretesting, 181, 198, 225–227, 254, 331–332
  successive, 227–228
Primary sampling areas, 184
Principal components model, 272–273, 442–444, 457, 473
Privacy, 294, 335, 375, 724
Probability level, 29

Probability proportional to size (PPS), 61–62
Probability sample, 3, 21–23, 164, 179, 182
Probability of selection, 56–62
Probes, 715, 717
Probit analysis, 575
Procedural equivalence, 678–679
Product–moment correlation coefficient, 618–619
Product testing, 3
Progress reports, 355–356
Project management, 133–143
  skills, 137–141
  successful, 138
Proportionate stratified sampling, 40–41, 44
Proportions, 31
Proxy reports, 718
Public opinion polls, 6
Purchase behavior, prediction of, 217

Q
Qualitative data analysis, 547–612
Quality control, 352–357
Quasi-ordering, 238
Question, 205–225, 297–308, 318, 716–718
  administration methods, 293–298, 318
  bank, 380–382
  closed, 207–208, 209–302, 318, 716–718
  content, 313, 380, 715
  context, 681, 714–715
  demographic, 218
  double-barreled, 216
  false premise, 216
  format, 248
  imputed meaning of, 712–715
  length, 304, 306, 318
  loaded, 214–216
  open, 206–208, 224, 299–302, 318, 369, 392, 716–718
  order, 219–220, 300–304, 318, 370
  pacing of, 345–346
  precoded, 301
  sensitive, 220–222, 294, 296–298, 313, 336, 374
  threatening, 8, 297, 299, 301
  throwaway, 220–221
  wording, 197, 212–217, 248, 293, 296, 301, 306–308, 315, 318, 681, 713–714
  vague, 216, 713
Questionnaire
  construction, 195–230, 362–367, 376
  construction errors, 216–217
  content, 202–205
  cover pages of, 362–366
  data-base considerations, 228–229, 330–331
  development, 334

dimensions of, 203–205
format, 223–225
group administration of, 334, 375
illustrations, 363, 365
introduction to, 219
length of, 222–223, 418
mail, 359–373, 375
mode of administration, 198–199
pretesting, 181, 198
purposes of, 200–202
self-administered, 198, 199, 294, 306, 335,
    376, *see also* Questionnaire, mail
standardized, 196–198
Total Design Method, 360–368
tryout, 339
Quotas, 4, 21, 147, 183, 226, 312, 681, 697

R
Racism, 162–163
Random digit dialing (RRD), 9, 15, 148,
    177–178, 192, 333, 335, 382–383
Random numbers, 164–166, 192
Random number table, 24, 165
Random response technique, 297, 298
Ranking, 242
    preference, 263–264
Rapport effect, 304
Rate of return, 649–650, 651
RDD, *see* Random digit dialing
Readiness to act, 204
Reading errors, 314
Real-values function, 238
Recall, *see* Memory errors
Recency of events, 718, 720
Recruitment, 126, 138–139, 141, 332–333
Redundancy effect, 303
Reflexivity, 237
RFP, *see* Requests for proposals
Refusal to be interviewed, 291, 355, 701–706,
    730, *see also* Cooperation rates
Regression analysis, 418, 435, 457, *see also*
    Generalized linear model
    with incomplete observations, 449–469
Reinforcement, 304–306
Relational system, 239–240
    defined, 239
    empirical, 239
    numerical, 239
Reliability, 73–89, 231, 329–330
    defined, 73, 91
    estimation of, 83–85, 88
    test–retest, 79–85
    types of, 79–89
RELIABILITY (SPSS), 255

Repeated sampling, 30
Replication of results, 156, 183, 383, 507, 678,
    726, 730–735
Report writing, 411–412
Requests for proposals (RFP), 126–127
Residency, 689
    rules, 682–685
Respondents, 203–205, 220–223, 315–318
    age of, 710
    availability, 330, 333, 699–701
    characteristics of, 203–205, 318
    cooperation of, 220–223, 699
    education of, 218, 369, 699
    eligibility, 685–694, 731
    interest of, 203–204
    knowledge of, 203
    nonverbal behavior of, 337, 354
    occupation of, 218
    race of, 313
    selection, 697–702
    social status of, 313
Response biases, 15, 315–318
Response categories, 208–212
Response codes, 380, 382, 386–387
Response consequences, 719–725
Response depth, 300
Response distortion, 297–298, 702
Response effects, 289–328
    interviewer, 310–315
    respondent, 315–318
    task variables, 293–310
Response formulation, 719–725
Response rates, 5, 9, 198, 335, 375
    to mail questionnaires, 360
Response set, 315–316
Ridge regression, 536
Role playing, 347–348
Rules of correspondence, 70

S
Saliency, 204, 302, 303, 718, 720
Sample
    censored, 415
    defined, 24, 150
    design, 24, 32–34, 149–150
    estimators, 25
    judgment, 165
    mean, 25
    quality of, 146–148
    size, 149, 157, 180–182, 331, 441, 560, 562,
        565, 603, 653
    space, 24
    surveys, 1–20

type of, 199–200
variance, 25
Sampling, 382–383
applied, 145–194
area probability, 6, 7
clustered, *see* Cluster sampling
distribution, 25–27, 30
error, 421, 695
interval, 167–169, 173
from lists, 170–176, *see also* Telephone
directories
network, 179
nonrandom, 21
probability, 4
repeated, 30
small-scale, 153–163
stratified, *see* Stratification
systematic, 166–170
theory, 21–67
of time periods, 170
SAS, *see* Statistical Analysis System
Scale
absolute, 241, 243
anomie, 316
cardinal, 242
category, 266
difference, 241–243
Guttman, 256–260, 261, 303, 570
interval, 241, 242–243, 244
Likert, 252–255
nominal, 241
one-dimensional, 240
ordinal, 241, 242
ratio, 241–243
reliability, 254
taxonomy of, 241
Thurstone, 248–251
types, 241–243
Scale-index construction, 397–398
Scaling methods, 232, 246–281
Scalogram analysis, *see* Guttman scaling
Scientific Information Retrieval (SIR), 402, 407
Screening, 152, 179, 334
Secondary analysis, 12, 157, 735
Self-administered questionnaire, *see*
Questionnaire, self-administered
Self-disclosure, 295
Self-esteem, 159–160
Self-weighting, *see* Proportionate stratified
sampling
Semantic differential, 264–265
Semantic effects, 712–714
Sensitive questions, 220–222, 294, 296–298, 313,
336, 374

Separate ratio estimator, 58
Sets, 236–239
Show card, *see* Visual cues
Significance testing, 272–273, 470, 593–595, 602,
658
Simon–Blalock method of inference, 625
Simple random samples (SRS), 24, 32, 35,
163–170, 556
defined, 164
Simultaneous equations, 472–473, 626–631
Single-equation estimator, 666
Single-item measures, 16, 247–248
SIR, *see* Scientific Information Retrieval
Skip patterns, 225, 347, 370, 384, 391, 392
Smallest space analysis, 268
Small sample properties, 667–668
Social class differences, *see* Socioeconomic status
Social desirability, 72, 298, 316–318, 374,
704–705, 724
Social distance, 316
Social position, 159–160
Social rank, 158–159
Social rewards, 361
Socioeconomic status, 312, 317
Sociometric data, 400–401
Source data entry, 388, 389–392
Spearman–Brown prophecy formula, 78, 85,
86
Specialization, 136–137, 139–140
Specific factor, 90
Specification error, 537–539
Split-half reliability, 254
SPSS, 8, 255, 403, 407, 409
SRC, *see* Survey Research Center
SRS, *see* Simple random samples
Staff
expansion, 136
field, 135–136
levels, 134–143
morale, 129
quality, 128–130
recruitment, 126, 138–139, 141
senior management, 141–143
senior professional, 137–141
supervision, 135
technical, 136–137
training, 135
utilization of, 139, 141
Standard deviation, 30
Standard error, 29, 30, 657
Standard error of estimation, 33, 527, 635
Standard error of the sample mean, 30
Standard Industrial Classification (SIC) Codes,
171

Standardized regression coefficient, 505–506, 524, 525
Statistical Analysis System (SAS), 407–408, 409, 602
Statistical inference, 22–32
Statistical packages, 8
Status inconsistency, 158–159
Stepwise regression, 17, 541–542
Straightforward fetch, 405
Stratification, 36, 37–47, 98–99, 159, 170, 175
  costs of, 190
  optimum, 186–189
  reasons for, 182
  and unequal size cluster sampling, 57–60
  uses of, 182–191
Stratum weight, 38
Straw polls, 3
Subjective time, 310
Subpopulations, see Stratification
Subsampling, replicated, 62–64
Subsets, 405–406
Successive intervals, 248, 251
Summated rating scales, see Likert scales
Supervision, 135, 311, 315, 331, 336
  of telephone interviews, 336
Supply–demand model, 664
Survey costs, 9, 15–16, 35–36, 43 44, 47, 330
Survey data analysis, see Data analysis
Survey population, 24
Survey Research Center, University of Michigan, 7, 8, 147, 697
Survey research organizations
  employment, 8, 9
  goals of, 125–133
  growth of, 130–133
  income, 13, 14
  management of, 123–144
  optimal size of, 130–133
  reputation of, 126
  sectors, 10–15
  staff levels in, 134–143
Survey-specific materials, 342–343, 348–350
Survey technology, 131–132, 143
Survival, 127–130
Suspicion of strangers, 702–703
Symmetry, 237
System estimator, 666

T

T-test, 527
Table of random numbers, 24
Target population, 24, 681–683
Task definition, 293

Task schedule, 330
Task variation, 221
TDM, see Total Design Method
Technological changes, see Survey technology
Telephone directories, 148, 176, 177–178, 368–369
Telephone interviewing, 9, 177–178, 179
  cost of, 295
Telescoping, 291, 308–310
Test–retest reliability, 79–85
Text-scanning, 392
Threatening questions, 8, 297, 299, 301
Three-stage least square (3SLS), 667, 668–670
Throwaway question, 220–221
Thurstone scales, 248–252
  criticism of, 251–252
Time series data, 519–520
Tocher procedure, see Analysis of covariance
Total Design Method (TDM), 360–368
  costs, 370–373
Tracking software, 385–386
Transcriptive data entry, 388
Transient hotel, 685
Transient quarters, 684
Transivity, 237–238
Trends, monitoring of, 677–741
Triangulation, 105
True scores, 84–85
  non-Platonic, 70–73
  Platonic, 70–73, 74
Truncated sample, see Sample, censored
Trust, 361, 702–703
Tucker–Lewis coefficient, 93–95
Two-stage least squares (2SLS), 623, 666, 668–670
Two-variable regression model, see Bivariate regression model

U

Ultimate clusters, 50, 53, 57, 58
Unadjusted main effects method, 424–425
Undercount, see Underenumeration
Underenumeration, 687–689, 696–697, 733
Underreporting, 297, 298, 301, 308
Unfolding analysis, 263–264
Unidimensionality, 256–257
Uniformity, 329–330, 334
Unit of analysis, 151
Units of measure
  convertible, 271
  diverse (nonconvertible), 271–272
Unlisted telephones, 178, 369
Unobserved variables, 108–114

Unweighted means method, 421
User-written programs, 408
Utility, 243
  cardinal, 244
  function, 240, 241
  scale, 240, 241
  theory, 268

V

Validity, 97–114, 231
  concurrent, 97–98
  construct, 100–105
  content, 98–100
  convergent, 105
  criterion-related, 97–99
  defined, 97
  discriminant, 105
  empirical, 73–74, 97–99
  predictive, 97
  theoretical, 73–74, 91, 101
Variance estimation, 50
Varimax procedure, 277–278
Vertical mobility, 158–159
Victimization, 679–680, 713, 718
Visual cues, 296, 332, 336, 337, 723
Vocabulary, 212–214
Volume of work, 128–129

Von Neumann–Morgenstern system of utility, 243, 244
Voting behavior, 5, 6, 7, 694, 721

W

Waksberg sampling algorithm, 383, 392
War Against Poverty, 8
Weighted least-squares, 549
Weighted means approach, 422
Weighted regression analysis for proportions (D-Systems), 549, 575–585, 592, 595, 602, 603, 605
Weighted squares of means, *see* Weighted means approach
Weighting, 37, 38, 45–47, 255, 396
Willingness to respond, 196, 704
Within-strata homogeneity, 41
Word-processing systems, 380–382, 384, 386, 411–412
Wording, *see* Question, wording
Work incentives, 135

Y

Yates method, 426–430, 451
Youden squares designs, 428

Z

Zero-order methods, 450–457, 470

QUANTITATIVE STUDIES IN SOCIAL RELATIONS
(Continued from page ii)

Neil Fligstein, **GOING NORTH:** *Migration of Blacks and Whites from the South, 1900–1950*

Howard Schuman and Stanley Presser, **QUESTIONS AND ANSWERS IN ATTITUDE SURVEYS:** *Experiments on Question Form, Wording, and Context*

Michael E. Sobel, **LIFESTYLE AND SOCIAL STRUCTURE:** *Concepts, Definitions, Analyses*

William Spangar Peirce, **BUREAUCRATIC FAILURE AND PUBLIC EXPENDITURE**

Bruce Jacobs, **THE POLITICAL ECONOMY OF ORGANIZATIONAL CHANGE:** *Urban Institutional Response to the War on Poverty*

Ronald C. Kessler and David F. Greenberg, **LINEAR PANEL ANALYSIS:** *Models of Quantitative Change*

Ivar Berg (Ed.), **SOCIOLOGICAL PERSPECTIVES ON LABOR MARKETS**

James Alan Fox (Ed.), **METHODS IN QUANTITATIVE CRIMINOLOGY**

James Alan Fox (Ed.), **MODELS IN QUANTITATIVE CRIMINOLOGY**

Philip K. Robins, Robert G. Spiegelman, Samuel Weiner, and Joseph G. Bell **(Eds.), A GUARANTEED ANNUAL INCOME:** *Evidence from a Social Experiment*

Zev Klein and Yohanan Eshel, **INTEGRATING JERUSALEM SCHOOLS**

Juan E. Mezzich and Herbert Solomon, **TAXONOMY AND BEHAVIORAL SCIENCE**

Walter Williams, **GOVERNMENT BY AGENCY:** *Lessons from the Social Program Grants-in-Aid Experience*

Peter H. Rossi, Richard A. Berk, and Kenneth J. Lenihan, **MONEY, WORK, AND CRIME:** *Experimental Evidence*

Robert M. Groves and Robert L. Kahn, **SURVEYS BY TELEPHONE:** *A National Comparison with Personal Interviews*

N. Krishnan Namboodiri (Ed.), **SURVEY SAMPLING AND MEASUREMENT**

Beverly Duncan and Otis Dudley Duncan, **SEX TYPING AND SOCIAL ROLES:** *A Research Report*

Donald J. Treiman, **OCCUPATIONAL PRESTIGE IN COMPARATIVE PERSPECTIVE**

Samuel Leinhardt (Ed.), **SOCIAL NETWORKS:** *A Developing Paradigm*

Richard A. Berk, Harold Brackman, and Selma Lesser, **A MEASURE OF JUSTICE:** *An Empirical Study of Changes in the California Penal Code, 1955–1971*

Richard F. Curtis and Elton F. Jackson, **INEQUALITY IN AMERICAN COMMUNITIES**

QUANTITATIVE STUDIES IN SOCIAL RELATIONS

Eric Hanushek and John Jackson, STATISTICAL METHODS FOR SOCIAL SCIENTISTS

Edward O. Laumann and Franz U. Pappi, NETWORKS OF COLLECTIVE ACTION: A Perspective on Community Influence Systems

Walter Williams and Richard F. Elmore, SOCIAL PROGRAM IMPLEMENTATION

Roland J. Liebert, DISINTEGRATION AND POLITICAL ACTION: The Changing Functions of City Governments in America

James D. Wright, THE DISSENT OF THE GOVERNED: Alienation and Democracy in America

Seymour Sudman, APPLIED SAMPLING

Michael D. Ornstein, ENTRY INTO THE AMERICAN LABOR FORCE

Carl A. Bennett and Arthur A. Lumsdaine (Eds.), EVALUATION AND EXPERIMENT: Some Critical Issues in Assessing Social Programs

H. M. Blalock, A. Aganbegian, F. M. Borodkin, Raymond Boudon, and Vittorio Capecchi (Eds.), QUANTITATIVE SOCIOLOGY: International Perspectives on Mathematical and Statistical Modeling

N. J. Demerath, III, Otto Larsen, and Karl F. Schuessler (Eds.), SOCIAL POLICY AND SOCIOLOGY

Henry W. Riecken and Robert F. Boruch (Eds.), SOCIAL EXPERIMENTATION: A Method for Planning and Evaluating Social Intervention

Arthur S. Goldberger and Otis Dudley Duncan (Eds.), STRUCTURAL EQUATION MODELS IN THE SOCIAL SCIENCES

Robert B. Tapp, RELIGION AMONG THE UNITARIAN UNIVERSALISTS: Converts in the Stepfathers' House

Kent S. Miller and Ralph Mason Dreger (Eds.), COMPARATIVE STUDIES OF BLACKS AND WHITES IN THE UNITED STATES

Douglas T. Hall and Benjamin Schneider, ORGANIZATIONAL CLIMATES AND CAREERS: The Work Lives of Priests

Robert L. Crain and Carol S. Weisman, DISCRIMINATION, PERSONALITY, AND ACHIEVEMENT: A Survey of Northern Blacks

Roger N. Shepard, A. Kimball Romney, and Sara Beth Nerlove (Eds.), MULTIDIMENSIONAL SCALING: Theory and Applications in the Behavioral Sciences, Volume I — Theory; Volume II — Applications

Peter H. Rossi and Walter Williams (Eds.), EVALUATING SOCIAL PROGRAMS: Theory, Practice, and Politics